CRYSTAL PALACE

THE COMPLETE RECORD
1905-2011

CRYSTAL PALACE

THE COMPLETE RECORD 1905-2011

IAN KING

First published in Great Britian in 2011 by The Derby Books Publishing Company Limited, 3 The Parker Centre, Derby, DE21 4SZ. (ISBN 978-1-85983-809-9)

Reprinted in paperback 2012. ISBN 978-1-78091-221-9

Printed and bound by Copytech (UK) Limited, Peterborough.

Contents

Introduction

It has been over 20 years since DB Publishing (formerly Breedon Books) produced a Complete Record of Crystal Palace FC, and in that time a lot has occurred in the history of the club, probably its most tumultuous period, while the opportunity has been taken to update with various corrections the previous edition. Although it is my name on the cover, I am truly indebted to a number of people involved with this publication.

The written text has been provided by Revd Nigel Sands, former Crystal Palace FC Chaplain and historian and author in his own right of a number of books and articles about the football club, whose use of the English language in such publications I could never aspire to. I was expecting our joint names to appear on the cover, but he has expressed the wish for his name not to be included, and I humbly accept this.

I have to mention the unstinting help I have received from the following supporters whose diligence and expertise in collating material and details of all aspects of the club over the years has meant many hours spent in the Local Studies Libraries of Croydon and Bromley. This has led to cross-checking of such material with the many and various books and annuals produced concerning football.

Therefore, I give sincere thanks to Tony Bowden, David Keats, Terry Morley and Alan Russell (who also provided the 'Did You Know').

With regard to the pictorial content I have to thank Peter Hurn for utilising his vast archive on the club and dedicated photographers Hy Money and Neil Everitt, whose pictures continue to astound me.

The spread of the internet and the increased availability of archive material over the past 10 years or so, coupled to today's near saturation point of football statistics etc, through the various media has meant there has been a lot more detail to check, cross reference and update.

Best efforts, therefore, have been made with regard to the accuracy contained within this book but, especially with regard to older material from the days when matters relating to football and this club were not so widely covered in the press, where there has been a conflict of information a measured decision has had to be made - an example is three varying reports of the same match! In the days of numberless shirts and players possibly appearing out of position a reporter could easily, if not familiar with the club, had difficulty identifying players, consequently some player's appearances and goals have had their figures adjusted. The same can be applied to player's biographical details, where a clash of detail has been found, while with regard to attendance figures, prior to 1925 these were rounded up or estimated by the press and can still these days provide variance. Anybody who takes pleasure in looking up figures and statistics will know that they can be a frustration as well as rewarding.

Concerning the Records part of the book, there are a few details that have continued to elude, and these include some World War One line-ups when three matches were played in a short space of time and only scorers noted.

Substitutes first appeared in the 1965–66 season when one only was allowed with shirt number 12, a second was introduced from 1986–87 and most clubs opted for a number 14 shirt, then a third one was allowed from 1995–96 and in this volume the number 13 has been used. The book has utilised the number 1–14 system in the team line-ups, but with the introduction of squad numbers in the mid-1990s, together with team formations and players becoming more flexible, it has proved difficult at times to illustrate by a number a player in a certain position. A first player substituted is in bold, the second underscored and the third in italics although 'double' substitutions does add an extra dimension to obtaining accuracy!

I trust that readers will enjoy this updated and enlarged edition and I will gladly appreciate receiving anything that you might consider incorrect or not included.

The History of Crystal Palace FC

Palace Pioneers

Although it is disappointing to have to admit it, the fact is that, when compared with many of the northern footballing giants with whom Crystal Palace regularly rub shoulders, the pedigree of the club does lack something of the lustre of those counterparts. And, what is more, many of the club's southern rivals were formed before Palace in the 19th century. For example, Arsenal, Spurs, Southampton, Fulham, Brentford and the Bristol clubs were founded in that era, even if not all of them played in the Football League until the 1900s. Even Palace's historic local rivals Millwall were in existence 20 years before Crystal Palace FC was formed, while the primary adversaries to modern-day fans, Brighton, began in 1901.

Yet, curiously, it can certainly be argued that the present-day Crystal Palace FC owes its origins, at least in part, to several of the northern and Midlands giants. It was when, for example, Aston Villa (founded in 1874), Sheffield (United 1889) (or Wednesday 1867), Manchester (City 1887) (or United 1878), Everton (1878) or Newcastle (1881) came to The Crystal Palace to take part in the FA Cup Final, which was staged at the majestic Palace ground from 1895–1914, and brought thousands of provincial fans with them to mingle with football enthusiasts from London and the South, that the enormous attraction of football became apparent to several visionaries from the Crystal Palace company. Eventually it became clear if a club was to be established there, it would secure sufficient regular fans to become a profitable venture.

So it was then, that in 1904 the FA was approached on the matter of forming a football club, but, perhaps understandably for such a conservative group, that body announced that it was unwilling to approve such a move from the Crystal Palace company itself. However, 12 months later a proposal to form a club bearing the Crystal Palace name but pioneered by local businessmen and other entrepreneurs from the adjacent South London suburbs was sanctioned. It must be noted too that distinguished officials at The Crystal Palace were enthusiastic about the latter plan, and general manager Mr J.H. Cozens, along with his predecessor Mr Gillman, were fully supportive of the founding of the new club.

Further help from illustrious football folk was also clearly evident. Mr Cozens was inspired to approach perhaps the greatest club in the land at that time, Aston Villa, about the venture, and Villa's chairman, Mr William McGregor, known to all serious students of football history as 'the father of the Football League', provided his extremely influential and distinctive patronage. Writing in *The Football Star* in December 1904, Mr McGregor went on record as saying the following: 'The highwater mark of prosperity in the metropolis has not [yet] been reached, and I believe that a really good team at the Crystal Palace would be a tremendous draw.' With that sort of endorsement from such a footballing giant, not even the FA could stand in the way of the club's foundation. But Mr McGregor's influence upon the as yet unborn Crystal Palace FC was not limited to merely backing its foundation; he also advocated the appointment of a young assistant secretary at Villa Park, one Edmund Goodman, to be appointed to the task of constituting the new outfit and its playing team.

The procurement of Mr Goodman was both stunningly effective and hugely fruitful: without doubt, as we shall see, it was probably the most successful 'transfer' in the entire history of the Palace club. Mr Goodman's own football career had been full of promise, but he had had the misfortune to experience an awful knee injury which was so dreadful that he was forced to submit to major surgery and lost his leg at the tender age of only 19. He overcame this terrible setback, however, and after two years, during which he was inevitably preoccupied in the setting-up and administration of the new Palace club (for example, it was he who secured the services of the talented first manager of the club, John Robson, who had formerly been in charge of Middlesbrough and led the Teessiders to promotion from Division Two, together with the appointment of the club's excellent first chairman, Mr Sydney Bourne), he became Palace's combined secretary and manager for the 1907–08 season and held both positions in tandem until 1925.

Sydney Bourne – Chairman from 1905 until his death in 1930.

In later years Mr Goodman revealed how he came to acquire the appealing, persuasive and charismatic Sydney Bourne for the club, and the revelation itself is an enormous tribute to Mr Goodman's sagacity. It appears that Mr Goodman devoted close and prolonged scrutiny to The Crystal Palace company records that related to the FA Cup Finals hosted at the Palace, and that he there discovered that Mr Bourne always purchased several or more tickets for the great occasion. When Mr Goodman approached Mr Bourne and told him of the plans for the new club, he found him to be so extremely enthusiastic that Mr Bourne was soon prompted to join the club's board of directors and was elected as chairman at their first-ever official meeting.

It should be acknowledged at this point that 'our' Crystal Palace was not, in fact, the first club to play under that name! It was during the heyday of the amateur football clubs like The Wanderers and The Old Etonians that the initial Crystal Palace club was formed from the staff at the great building, and thus, when the inaugural FA Cup was contested in 1871–72, it was among the founder entrants. While it was, to some extent at least, a knock-out competition, it was not organised in the manner with which we are familiar today, so that, with the benefit of a drawn game against The Wanderers, which allowed both sides to progress, Crystal Palace reached the semi-final before losing to The Royal Engineers. That Palace club went on to take part in the subsequent four competitions but thereafter disappeared despite having provided four international representitives in the England versus Scotland fixtures between 1870 and 1876. It is perfectly conceivable, therefore, that when 'our' Crystal Palace club came to play its early-season fixtures in 1905–06 at The Crystal Palace ground there were present among the spectators at least some of those who had watched, or even played for, the earlier club of the same name.

In 1905 the new Crystal Palace club applied for membership of the Football League but were rejected, and, for reasons that remain obscure, were then refused (by one vote) admission to the Southern League First Division, so that it was necessary to begin playing as a member of the Second Division, which was largely made up of reserve teams of established First Division clubs or much more humble outfits. Probably due to the fact that the Palace were denied First Division status, Mr Goodman requested and obtained admission to the United League which, although mainly a midweek competition, at least provided fixtures against other Southern League clubs' first XIs. In fact, Crystal Palace's first fixture under any auspicies was in the United League on Friday 1 September 1905, away at New Brompton (who later became Gillingham), which was won 3–0.

Southern League Prelude

Most of the players who were signed for Crystal Palace during the midsummer months of 1905 were men with whom manager John Robson was familiar. For example, the skipper was a Geordie from Newcastle United, Ted Birnie. However, there was to be a nasty shock for the new club, its backers and its followers, when just 24 hours after the 3–0 United League success Palace went down 3–4 at home to Southampton Reserves in their first Southern League game.

But Mr Robson and his men soon remedied matters and were subsequently unbeaten in the Southern League throughout the remainder of the campaign. Our best victories were achieved over Fulham Reserves, the Division Two champions, who were humbled 5–0 and, in the following home game, Grays United were thrashed 9–1. In the FA Cup similar early-season successes were earned against Clapham (7–0) and The Grenadier Guards (3–0), and then when Chelsea had the temerity to send a weakened team to Crystal Palace they were trounced 7–1 in a third-round qualifying tie. Ultimately, Palace took Football League side Blackpool to a second replay in the first round proper before bowing out of the competition to a single goal at Villa Park.

Towards the end of the season Palace took the Southern League Division Two title by beating closest rivals Leyton, in East London. By this time the club had a local boy as their star player – George Woodger – who played as a goalscoring inside- or centre-forward, and his refined skills earned him the odd nickname of 'Lady'.

George Birnie, having moved to Chelsea in the close season, was replaced as captain by Wilfred Innerd for 1906–07, but the club toiled upon its First Division debut, finishing next to bottom. However, in the FA Cup Palace were exemplary. The first round took the club to

1905–06. Back row, left to right: Mr J. Robson (manager), Mr T.C. Walters, Mr A. Daniels (directors), J. Thompson, W. Oliver, A. Grant, R. Ross, H. Astley, M. Edwards, Mr A. St P. Cufflin, Mr S. Bourne (directors), Mr E.F. Goodman (secretary), Mr A. Birch (trainer). Second row: G. Thompson, R. Hewitson, A. Needham, W.M. Watkins, E.L. Birnie, W.A. Innerd, G. Walker, R.J. Roberts. Front row: R. Harker, C.W. Wallace.

Newcastle, where they beat probably the best team in the country at that time with a Horace Astley goal scored a few minutes before half-time. Fulham, the Southern League champions, were similarly beaten in a Palace replay after a goalless game at Craven Cottage, and then Brentford were despatched in round three. In the quarter-final Palace's opponent was mighty Everton, who were held at The Palace but then subjected Palace to a three-goal blitz in the opening half hour at Goodison Park. Nevertheless, the Glaziers (Palace's apt and original nickname) added to these FA Cup triumphs in the following two seasons, especially in 1908–09 when the Cup holders themselves, the powerful Wolves no less, were beaten in a first-round replay at The Crystal Palace. The scores were level after 90 minutes and barely moments remained of extra-time with Palace leading 3–2. The crowd, inevitably, were in ferment. Then Archie Needham scored an individualist goal of the highest calibre to settle the contest. It was such a wonderful strike that veteran fans of the club could still recall it (and describe it in detail, with gusto and emotion) some 60 or 70 years afterwards!

With Mr Goodman now serving as manager as well as secretary, the new boss was faced with a crucial decision as the 1907–08 season approached because Palace's capable goalkeeper in the first two seasons, Rob Hewitson, moved to Oldham. But what a replacement Mr Goodman provided! Josh Johnson was a 6ft, handsome, scholarly fellow, and he became first-choice goalkeeper immediately and remained so until World War One hostilities temporarily ended the Southern League competition. He made an extraordinary 295 appearances for Palace, easily the club's highest appearance total from the club's Southern League days.

Other new players for 1907–08 were Welsh international winger Bill Davies and wing-half John Brearley from Tottenham. The versatile Wilfred Innerd largely figured at right-half, but a grand club servant who came back to the fore during 1907–08 was Harry Collyer, a dependable but cultured full-back, who later played for the Southern League in a representative fixture.

Although Palace began poorly, they rose to fourth place in 1907–08 with George Woodger topping the scoring chart with 13 goals; although a late-season signing, Jimmy Bauchop from Norwich, notched six in the closing eight games, including a debut strike to help Palace overcome Millwall on 21 March.

For 1908–09 Mr Goodman signed the twinkling, diminutive and experienced winger George Garratt, who became a great favourite among the supporters. He spent five years with the Glaziers, made 185 League and Cup appearances and was called upon for several representative fixtures. Palace began the season well, but they faltered after Christmas and finished down in 16th place. The highlight of the season was the goalscoring exploits of Colin McGibbon, who joined the club from New Brompton and hit 13 goals from just 17 appearances, including a hat-trick on his debut in an early-season 4–0 victory over Brighton.

Wilfred Innerd returned to his north-eastern roots in the 1909 close season, but George Woodger assumed the mantle of club captain and led Palace to seventh place in the Southern League. Playing now mainly at inside-forward, Woodger himself netted eight League goals, but Palace's principle scorers were centre-forward J.W. 'Ginger' Williams with 20 strikes and another newcomer, George Payne from Tottenham, with 25. Williams became an enormous Palace favourite and went on to gain Welsh international honours in Glaziers colours. Other key newcomers for the 1909–10 campaign were wing-half Bob Spottiswood from Croydon Common, big centre-half Jimmy Hughes, who was to represent the Southern League, and Harry Hanger, a wing-half of great refinement who succeeded Woodger as captain when the latter left Palace in October 1910. Left-back Joe Bulcock came from Exeter City and, as well as gaining Southern League honours, played for an FA touring side in South Africa. All these men provided excellent service to the club and assisted Palace to impressive finishing positions in the five seasons before the outbreak of World War One. The club's lowest final placing in the Southern League was seventh (twice) and they were also runners-up in 1913–14 when only goal average denied Palace the title.

Knowledgeable Palace fans of the period, and many others besides, realised that George Woodger would soon be leaving the club in order to move to a bigger outfit. George himself knew that he was a player of sufficient calibre to represent England, but he also knew that it would be neccessary for him to play for a more senior club than Palace in order to do so. He joined Oldham Athletic, then among the stronger sides in the Football League's First Division and, curiously, made his Latics debut at one of Palace's closest neighbours, Woolwich Arsenal!

Woodger was succeeded at centre-forward for Palace by Charlie Woodhouse, who immediately became the club's top scorer in 1910–11 with 15 goals in his 33 Southern League outings, before he died suddenly in late 1911. Also appearing for the club from 1910–11 was Charlie Hewitt, a speedy, forceful inside-right from West Bromwich Albion, so that probably Palace's best side so far was able to finish in fourth position behind Swindon, Northampton and Brighton.

Crystal Palace 1911–12.

Postcard of the players and officials taken on the steps of The Crystal Palace, 1912–13.

Ted Smith took over the mantle of Palace centre-forward from Charlie Woodhouse and immediately justified his move to the club from Hull City by hitting a hat-trick in both his first two games. This 1911–12 season brought Ted 19 League and Cup strikes and his Palace career produced 124 goals in total, meaning that only Peter Simpson has scored more.

Palace finished 1911–12 seventh in the Southern League and fifth in 1912–13. Modern readers will blanche (and modern footballers quail) at the fact that Palace had played four League games in an eight-day period over Christmas 1911, including three matches in four days and then, over Easter 1912, turned out four times in five days! Palace's victory over Brentford in the last game of 1911 was the Bees' second defeat of the term at The Crystal Palace, as the Glaziers had beaten them 4–0 in a first-round FA Cup replay in mid-January after a scoreless draw at Griffin Park. The prize was a home tie against Sunderland from the First Division of the Football League. The Wearsiders held Palace 0–0 on a bone-hard, icy pitch, then crept through in extra-time of the replay with a goal contrived by the great Charlie Buchan.

During 1912–13 Palace were occasionally favoured by the appearance of the distinguished England amateur international half-back, the Revd Kenneth Hunt, who had played against Palace for the Wolves in the great FA Cup tie back in 1909 and been lavish in his praise of his team's conquerors afterwards. The great Southern League highlight of the season was the 8–0 thrashing of Southampton at home in November, although only a modest (estimated) crowd of some 8,000 actually saw the fog-shrouded rout. In the last quarter of an hour, Saints were complaining about the light and requesting an abandonment!

Later in the term Palace had a creditable FA Cup run which took us to the then third round and a meeting with Aston Villa at Villa Park in front of a 42,000 plus attendance – the largest crowd to watch a Palace match before World War One. Former Palace starlet,

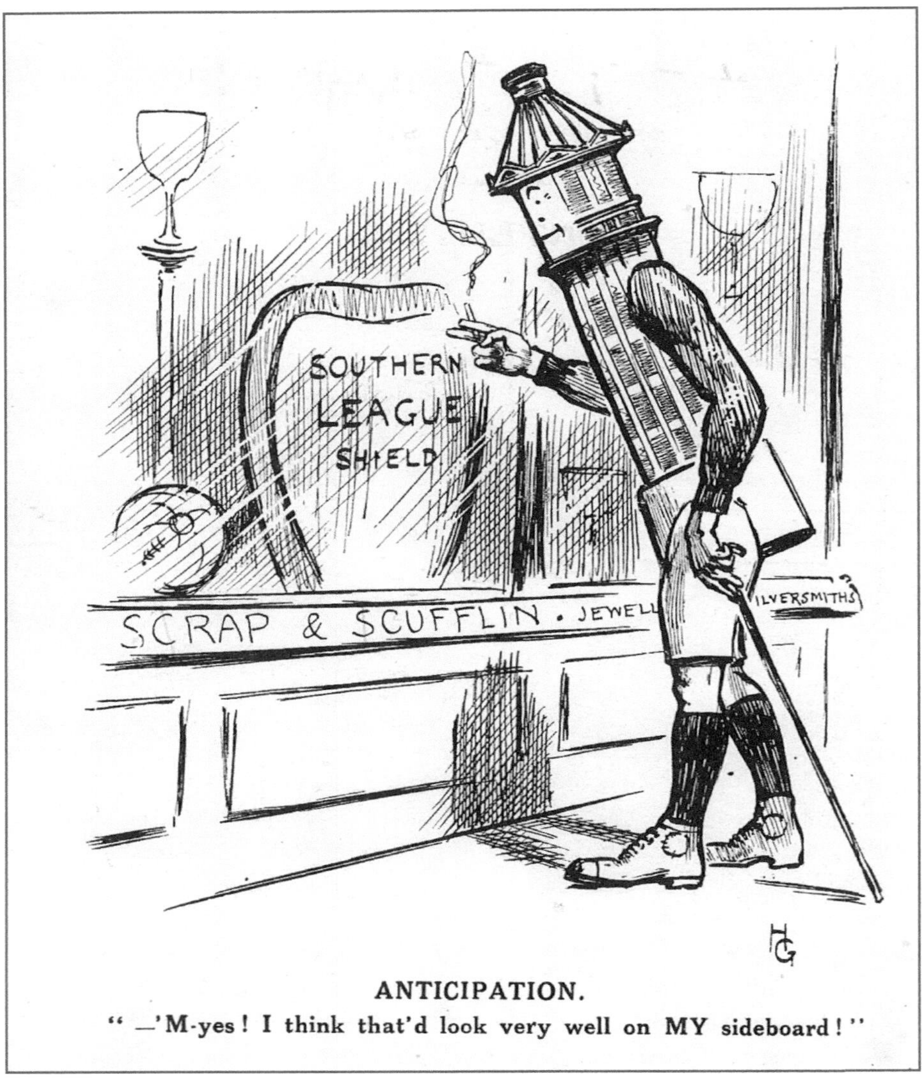

ANTICIPATION.

" —'M-yes! I think that'd look very well on MY sideboard!"

Topical cartoon from 1913 of the club's aspirations.

winger Charlie Wallace, ensured that there would be no giant-killing that day and he ultimately assisted Villa to win the FA Cup at the Palace ground in front of a record crowd in English football of over 120,000.

The 1913–14 campaign was Palace's best in the Southern League. Full-back Horace Colclough, formerly of Crewe, took over at left-back when Joe Bulcock was hurt in only the second game and developed superbly, so much so that he earned Palace's first full England cap later that term. The Glaziers might have won the Southern League title, but in their final game they could only gain a draw at Gillingham, while closest rivals Swindon earned a point at Cardiff, their better goal average meaning that they took the honour.

Crystal Palace v Reading on 15 November 1913.

The Great War took a a heavy toll on Crystal Palace FC even in its early years. Not only were the club not allowed to complete their 1914–15 home fixtures at their headquarters (because the Palace and its grounds had been requisitioned by the Admiralty at short notice in February 1915) and were forced to play the last seven 'home' games elsewhere, but their attendances (and therefore income) had also dwindled alarmingly. Captain Harry Hanger left for the Front in December and wingers Ben Bateman and John Whibley went to serve their country too. An indication of the strictures the club endured during this period may be found in the fact that, having gained a praiseworthy 2–2 draw at Football League club Birmingham in the FA Cup first round, it was deemed prudent to cede the replay venue and return to St Andrew's a week later, where a much larger attendance was ensured than could be expected at The Palace. The Glaziers played well enough to take the Blues to extra-time, but they found the additional period just too much and lost the clash 3–0.

World War One

There will, inevitably, be those among the readers of this section of Palace's history who have read somewhere or carry a distant memory of hearing that Palace fared extremely well during the period of hostilities. While this is true enough, it certainly is not applicable to the 1914–18 war! Playing with borrowed players (as did most of the clubs who competed through those difficult years) and on a borrowed ground, Palace found World War One an extremely demanding time.

The Glaziers spent the war seasons between 1915 and 1918 at Herne Hill. It was not that the other South London clubs had not offered to help Palace in their dilemma after The Crystal Palace had been requisitioned; they had, generally, been willing to enable Palace to fulfil their remaining programme of the 1914–15 home matches on their grounds, and would, presumably, have been pleased to come to some sort of accommodation with the club for the future, but Palace's directors considered that it would be better for the club to play somewhere within the club's acknowledged catchment area and took the decision to make Herne Hill athletic and cycling arena, the home of the distinguished local amateur side West Norwood, Palace's headquarters for the forseeable future.

Quite properly, the Southern League and the FA Cup were suspended for the duration of the hostilities, but Palace joined the other London and, sometimes, provincial clubs in the London Combination, though inevitably, as the war progressed, there were times when Palace's sides included not one pre-war Palace player and there would occur the

Crystal Palace 1914–15.

intermittent farcical game. The club's most dreadful experience of these came at West Ham in April 1918, when a Palace side lost 11–0, but twice Palace conceded eight goals and seven on another two occasions. On the plus side, Palace beat Reading 10–1 in March 1916.

Palace's best finishing position during the Herne Hill years occurred in the second half of 1915–16 when they completed a supplementary competition in sixth place – but the war news at Crystal Palace FC was increasingly dismal: club captain Harry Hanger had been killed, as had erstwhile Palace stars Ginger Williams and Joe Bulcock.

There was, however, some better news when it was announced that Palace were to have their own headquarters once more, at The Nest, opposite Selhurst railway station. The Nest had been Croydon Common's ground since 1908 but The Robins had ceased to operate after the conclusion of 1915–16. Untenanted for two years, Palace leased the ground in time to play the 1918–19 season there, the final wartime campaign.

That 1918–19 London Combination season saw the arrival of two new, key, defenders at Crystal Palace. Jack Little, a former quality full-back with Croydon Common, played a few games in the side and went on to make 242 Southern League and Football League appearances for Palace, mainly in Division Two of the Football League. Jack Alderson, from Crook in County Durham, took over from Josh Johnson as Palace's goalkeeper and, in May 1923, became the first of only two Palace 'keepers to earn a full England international cap. With this pair regularly in the side and home games taking place at The Nest, Palace's attendances rose to encouraging levels in 1919–20 and the team finished the first post-war season third in the Southern League First Division, just two points adrift of Portsmouth and Watford.

Palace Progress

Despite previous antagonism to the notion of extending to three or four divisions, the Football League warmly embraced the concept in the immediate post-war years and in

May 1920 it accepted all the Southern League First Division outfits – Crystal Palace among them – to comprise a new Third Division for 1920–21 (though there were a couple of jugglings of a pair of clubs) and the Glaziers made their entry a hugely successful one!

Admittedly there was absolutely no early sign that this might be so. The new season opened on 28 August 1920 with Palace travelling to South Wales to meet Merthyr Town, losing 2–1. The midweek home game against Plymouth was goalless, but then Palace secured a splendid run of six consecutive victories.

However, any aspirations harboured during the autumn of 1920 were shrouded by two potentially calamitous events. In early November a midweek home game against a rugged Southend side brought an end-of-match pitch invasion by Palace fans who were angered by the Shrimpers' rough tactics and a 3–2 defeat. The FA reacted strongly; The Nest was closed for two weeks and Palace's home game against Exeter was relocated to Southampton! Palace won that match 2–1, and with intentional sarcasm the band played *Home Sweet Home* when the club returned to The Nest against Swansea. Unfortunately, Palace's Northern Ireland international wing-half, the cultured Robert McCracken, suffered a broken leg in that game and Palace lost 1–0, so there was little indication before Christmas of what was to follow, though First Division Manchester City were humbled 2–0 in the first round of the FA Cup in January.

In fact, it was a magnificent climax to the season that brought triumph to The Palace. They had an undefeated run of 16 games, including eight victories in a row before Easter to bring the club to the verge of success. Palace's Easter opponents included closest rivals Southampton, but Palace came from behind in both the Easter games to force draws, and ultimately a 5–1 rout of Northampton in Palace's last home game, followed by a point from the return, left them supreme.

1920–21 – A different slant on the usual team picture.

Mention should be made of several of the key players in Palace's 1921 promotion. Skipper Ted Smith led the side in the first half of the season, while top scorer was the prolific Scotsman, ever-present John Conner, who bagged 29 goals, but it was the defensive triumvirate of goalkeeper Jack Alderson and full-backs Jack Little and Ernie Rhodes, none of whom missed a match, who were the principal reason for Palace's success. They developed an understanding that was quite astonishing and helped to provide the defence which was statistically Palace's best for over 50 years. J.T Jones, a Welsh international half-back, deputised ably for Robert McCracken after the latter's injury, but the most fascinating figure in the Palace side was Phil Bates at centre-half. Phil had experienced an appalling injury to his right arm during his war service which had become withered and lifeless. This season the injury was little handicap and, in those days of attacking, inventive centre-halves, Phil provided a superb, prompting, aggressive axis to the side.

Following long overdue enhancements to The Nest, Palace opened their Second Division career with a hugely attractive fixture against Nottingham Forest, who included England goalkeeper Sam Hardy and drew another near ground record attendance of some 20,000 fans. Palace demonstrated probably their best form of the entire campaign and despatched the powerful visitors 4–1.

Unquestionably, one of Palace's greatest-ever FA Cup victories occurred during this season. An old first-round tie took the Glaziers back to Goodison Park, Everton, where Palace had already lost two Cup matches without so much as scoring a goal, but won on this occasion in absolutely unrestrained fashion 6–0, against one of the best outfits in the country. The contemporary sporting press lauded the club, and it was certainly a magnificent victory – one perhaps without parallel in Palace's history. Yet Palace contrived to lose to Millwall in a replay in the following round.

A particularly noteable Palace debut took place towards the end of March 1922, when a diminutive Albert Harry lined up in his original position of centre-forward against Bury at The Nest and netted a brace of goals – one a header – in a 4–1 win.

An amazingly complicated transfer between Palace and Coventry gained a blaze of publicity in the 1922 close-season, when three players left the club for the Midlands and three came to join Palace, including Charles Cross, who took over from 'Dusty' Rhodes at left-back early in 1922–23 and went on to make 237 senior appearances for the club, and inside-left Billy Morgan, about whom more will be heard shortly. Nevertheless, Crystal Palace had little to enthuse over that season, in which they finished in 16th place, though goalkeeper Jack Alderson earned himself considerable kudos by performing well in goal for England when he played for his country against France in Paris, where Engalnd won 4–1 and Jack was only beaten in the dying seconds.

The 1923–24 season saw Palace perform fitfully in League matches to finish in 15th place, but the Glaziers had a noteable FA Cup run in which, for the third time in four seasons, they beat top-flight opponents, this time putting two First Division teams to the sword. The first-round opponents were Tottenham, at The Nest, but Palace relished the heavy conditions and skipper Billy Morgan scored once in each half to bring about another famous victory. Paired with Notts County in round two, the clubs played three 0–0 draws before Palace finally despatched The Magpies, winning 2–1 at Villa Park, but then Swindon from Division Three South beat Palace at The Nest in round three.

Crystal Palace v Barnsley, 3 May 1924 – the last League game at The Nest.

Palace had been in negotiation for the purchase of the land which was eventually to become Selhurst Park since 1919. It had formerly been a brickfield. Selhurst Park was designed by Archibald Leitch, probably the foremost creator of football stadia at that time, and built by Messrs Humphreys of Knightsbridge to a contract rated at some £30,000. Regrettably, though, an industrial dispute delayed work in the main stand so that parts of it were incomplete when the ground was formally opened prior to Palace's first match of 1924–25, against The Wednesday on 30 August 1924.

The Wednesday were a pedigree club of renown at that time and their side that day included six present or future internationals. The occasion attracted a crowd of some 25,000, but most were disappointed by the outcome for a goal conceded just four minutes after the start was sufficient to defeat Palace.

1924–25 – A cartoon of the most prominent players at the club.

Palace overcame this setback, and by 1 November they were in fifth place, though surely the best performance of the entire campaign was the reverse fixture against The Wednesday two days after Christmas when Palace won a match played in a downpour and on the heaviest possible pitch with a well-taken goal notched just before half-time.

From that point on, however, Palace were a side in decline. They only won two more games, slid alarmingly down the table and lost their last three matches, including the final all-important one that had to be won to ensure the club's survival in Division Two, against Oldham, and Palace's increasingly likely relegation became a certainty.

During the autumn and early winter a former guardsman, Jimmy Hamilton, had added steel to the Palace defence, and the team's progress at that time had much to do with him. But he sustained an eye injury early in the New Year and Palace were almost a lost cause without him.

With the 1925–26 season just three weeks old, Palace had lost all five of their Third Division fixtures, had goal aggregates of 5–16 and seemed in dire peril. What the team lacked was a proven goalscorer, but Edmund Goodman knew precisely where one was to be found. The player in question was strong, harrying Percy Cherrett, who soon turned Palace's fortunes around. He finished the campaign with

A cartoon depicting the four FA Cup games with Notts County, 1924.

26 goals from 35 League appearances and had formed a thrilling, effective partnership with Cecil Blakemore, the pair of them blossoming, greatly to Palace's advantage, from the first-class service provided for them by wingers Albert Harry and the newly arrived, red-haired outside-left George Clarke.

Two games at Selhurst Park in which Cherrett starred are of note. He scored in the amazing, highest-scoring draw ever to be played in a first-class Palace game (5–5) when Plymouth were the visitors in November 1925, and it was Cherrett again who put Palace in the driving seat and on the way to a 2–1 victory over Chelsea in a January FA Cup tie which established a ground record attendance of some 41,000 fans that lasted all but 40 years. Another, less appealing, record was established three weeks later when Palace were involved in a match with more than 10 goals when they travelled to First Division Manchester City. Regrettably, while Palace scored four goals against City, they conceded no fewer than 11!

Cherrett was actually the last major signing made by Edmund Goodman for that distinguished gentleman stood down from the post of manager at Crystal Palace in November 1925. He was succeeded by Mr Alex Maley, who was a Scot and instigated a strategem of signing Scottish players.

An event of unique significance at Selhurst Park took place on St David's Day, 1 March 1926, when Palace hosted the England vs Wales full international, and the visitors won 3–1 to the pleasure of large parts of the Monday afternoon crowd of 23,000.

Given the dreadful start that Palace had made to the 1925–26 season, it was clearly imperative that a much-improved opening was established for 1926–27, so imagine how Palace fans felt when their team were in arrears after only 30 seconds of the first match of the season, against Queen's Park Rangers at Selhurst Park. Palace managed to come from behind to win that game but, even though they lost just one in the first eight fixtures, that still left the club two points and five places adrift of the leaders at the end of September. Thus, Palace's final placing of sixth was probably appropriate, but emerging into the footballing spotlight was another man who was to become a major player in the Glaziers' activities between the wars – Billy Turner.

Billy did not score a vast number of goals himself, his forte was creating them for others, and there was no doubt that right-winger Albert Harry clearly benefitted from having Billy at inside-right beside him or at right-half behind him. Billy soon gained the epithet 'Rubber' from Palace fans, and certainly his buoyancy and flexibility were invaluable features in those days when most players were one-position-only men. In fact, the only positions Billy did not fill for Palace were those of goalkeeper, centre-forward and centre-half, but he gave all he could for the club in over 300 first-team games.

Palace made another poor start to the 1927–28 season and, following two 6–1 reverses and then a London Challenge Cup defeat by old amateur rivals Leyton, it was inevitable that manager Alex Maley would resign. Under Edmund Goodman's temporary charge there was a modest improvement, but then new boss Fred Mavin arrived from Exeter City and inspired his charges to a much better second half to the campaign, highlighted by a run of six consecutive victories in March and early April, so that a fifth-placed finish was a credit to all concerned.

Manager Mavin spent an active 1928 close season in the transfer market on behalf of his new club. From Exeter he bought the captain of his remade Palace side, full-back Stan

Charlton, and, to play alongside him, Tom Crilly arrived from Derby. These two developed into an invaluable pairing and it is indicative that, while they were together at Selhurst Park, the Palace were able to make two genuine attempts at promotion.

Lewis Griffiths, a little Welshman from Torquay, had a clear proclivity for goalscoring, as demonstrated by his 18 goals from 27 League appearances in 1928–29, while Hubert Butler came from Chorley and established himself at inside-left that season.

Back in 1925 the offside law had been changed so that only two defenders were required to be between the goalline and the receiving attacker, rather than three as previously, and while this created many more opportunities for goalscoring, it did inevitably take defenders some time to adjust. Just so at Crystal Palace, by 1928 the club was scoring plenty of goals but conceding too many. The worst example being an 8–1 defeat at Northampton in October when player-coach Walter Betteridge made his only appearance for the club at the age of 40! But an answer was at hand in the person of 'Jimmy' Wilde.

Jimmy made his Palace debut in a demanding FA Cup tie against Kettering Town, who were not only champions of the Southern League Eastern section but also possessed a goalscoring centre-forward of some renown, one Peter Simpson. Palace won the game 2–0, Jimmy earned his centre-half spot and Palace went on a 17 match unbeaten run in Division Three South which the club has never improved upon within a single season.

After the Easter games Palace were within a point of top place amid intense competition, but by the last day of the season, with Palace at home to Brighton, the Glaziers would take the title and gain promotion if they could gain a point upon Charlton, who were away at Walsall. A crowd of 22,146 poured into Selhurst Park but Palace could only acheive a narrow victory courtesy of a Stan Charlton penalty. Rumours began to circulate that Charlton had been held at Walsall, but then their praiseworthy 2–0 victory was announced and Palace fans had to accept the fact that their club was remaining in the Third Division South.

For the first time since the war, Palace made some commendable progress in the FA Cup. The victory over Kettering was followed by others over Bristol Rovers, Luton and Millwall so that in round five Palace travelled up to leading top-flight club and finalists in 1928 Huddersfield Town and were beaten 5–2. Several of the Kettering side that had played against Palace in the first round signed for the Glaziers towards the end of that season; others, including Peter Simpson, arrived in the summer.

Peter Simpson must register as one of the best signings made by Crystal Palace FC. He soon made his mark as a sensational goalscoring centre-forward who could change the outcome of a match in a moment. His debut epitomised his Palace career and remains unique at the club, for no one else has hit a Football League hat-trick upon their senior debut for the club. Palace were behind to visiting Norwich in an early-season encounter until Peter equalised, put Palace in front with a header and then pressured the 'keeper into conceding a third. He topped Palace's goalscorers for his first five seasons at the club, had a career total of 165 senior goals for Palace and long after his retirement remained a respected and sought-after figure at his newsagent/tobacconist's shop in West Croydon.

Yet, despite having Peter Simpson, Palace could not gain promotion in 1929–30, and they lost, embarrassingly heavily (8–1), at Leeds in a third-round Cup tie. An intriguing

Palace 1931. Back row, left to right: Jones (trainer), Charlesworth, Parry, Lloyd, Crilly, Turnbull, Lane, Fishlock, Butler, Cartwright (assistant trainer). Second row: Rivers, Jewett, Wilcockson, Callender, Wilde, Dunn, Charlton, Greener, Barrie, Nicholas. Third row: Simpson, Mr E.F. Goodman (secretary), Mr F. Gates, Mr R.S. Flew (directors), Mr L.T. Bellatti (chairman), Mr M. Derisley, Mr H. Watson-Humphries (directors), Mr J. Tresadern (manager), Clarke. Front row: Turner, Harry, Manders.

figure playing at outside-left for us in that Cup debacle and in 12 Division Three South games was Laurie Fishlock, Surrey's opening, left-handed batsman for over 20 years.

While Palace's forward line in 1930–31 was the club's best for fully 30 years – notching 107 League goals, Peter Simpson claiming 46 of them – the Third Division South also contained the club with the best defence in the Football League, Notts County. The games between the pair both ended even, 1–1 at The Palace and 2–2 at Meadow Lane. Thus, although Palace finished with four straight wins, culminating in a 5–0 spree against Torquay, which assured the club of second place, Palace remained a Third Division club.

During 1930–31 Palace's original chairman, Sydney Bourne, died in September, and then in October manager Fred Mavin resigned and was replaced by former England international wing-half Jack Tresadern, who came from Northampton Town.

In the FA Cup Taunton Town and Newark Town were both dismissed 6–0 at Selhurst Park, then Reading were knocked out after a second replay at Stamford Bridge, but Everton handed out a 6–0 beating of their own in round four to precisely avenge Palace's 1922 victory at their headquarters.

Palace's Lacklustre Decade

The remaining inter-war years of the 1930s were comparitively lacklustre for Crystal Palace FC. They had a thoroughly praiseworthy home record in 1931–32 which could have provided a launchpad for another challenge for promotion, but Palace were much less impressive on their travels – so much so that non-League Bath City beat the Glaziers at Twerton Park in a second-round FA Cup tie.

Of far greater significance, however, was the appalling death at Selhurst Park in the summer of 1932 of Palace's superb goalkeeper Billy Callender, who committed suicide. The blow was felt by Billy's teammates for months afterwards, but at least Ronnie Dunn had the temperament as well as the aptitude to take over Billy's position in the side. Ronnie missed just one game in Palace's 1932–33 season (and that was through illness) and was the first-choice goalkeeper for four seasons.

Palace finished fifth in Division Three South in 1932–33, but this was a rather colourless season with little of significance in it; although, at the end of it secretary Edmund Goodman retired after 28 years with the club in that capacity. Manager Jack Tresadern added the secretary's duties to his own but then somewhat recklessly stated that 1933–34 was 'going to be Palace's year'. Regrettably, however, although Palace opened the campaign with three victories, the Palace of 1933–34 were no more than an average Third Division South side and ended the campaign in 12th place in the table despite the arrival of striker Albert Dawes from Northampton in December 1933. Palace did reach round four of the FA Cup with victories over Norwich, Stockport and Aldershot to earn a visit to Highbury, but Arsenal trounced Palace 7–0. The Glaziers did, however, have the compensation of sharing the proceeds of the 56,177 gate – until the 1990 Cup Final the biggest crowd ever to watch a Palace game.

By 1934–35 Palace's usual line up was inevitably and substantially different from that in the earlier years of the decade. Ronnie Dunn in goal had full-backs Ted Owens and Oswald Parry in front of him. Ted joined Palace in the summer of 1934 from Preston and was resilient and hardy and certainly one of Jack Tresadern's best signings for the club. Tall, fair-haired Parry was a Welshman who played exactly 150 senior games for the club between 1931 and 1936, when he moved on to Ipswich Town. Jimmy Wilde was still Palace's pivot and was joined in the middle line for 1934–35 by the durable and steadfast Nick Collins, who kept his place in Palace sides for over a decade. Billy Turner replaced the lamed Alf Haynes at right-half before Christmas but Albert Harry's long tenure of the right wing had reached an end and he was replaced by Scotsman Jimmy Carson. Frank Manders was at inside-right alongside Peter Simpson for whom this would be the final season with Palace. Albert Dawes played at inside-left and outside him was local boy Bob Bigg.

Pre-season, summer 1935 – Palace players including Jimmy Wilde, Bob Bigg and Albert Dawes get in some heading practice.

Jack Tresadern broke a leg during a preseason training session in 1934–35, but Palace's discomfort continued throughout the campaign, which included a 3–0 defeat at then non-League Yeovil in the FA Cup and heavy League losses at Reading and Torquay. Palace finished fifth in the table before Jack Tresadern left the club to manage Tottenham and Peter Simpson was transferred to West Ham. But Peter was to meet up with Palace once more, as we shall soon see.

Palace's new manager was Tom Bromilow, an ex-England wing-half and former manager of Burnley. He claimed to regard his move to Selhurst Park as his 'golden opportunity' – though he proved unable to grasp it straight away.

The Glaziers fared reasonably well in 1935–36 and finished in sixth position without ever seriously troubling the leading clubs in the section, and that campaign is really only of significance for some interesting new signings, the disgraceful 'Pools War' and the passing of two Palace chairmen.

Frank Manders left Palace for Second Division Norwich City in October and Mr Bromilow invested the substantial transfer fee in Bob Birtley, a versatile player from Coventry, and Jack Blackman, a strong, hustling centre-forward from Queen's Park Rangers. Both not only scored on their Palace debuts but also provided worthwhile inputs to the club right up to World War Two.

In December non-League Margate put Palace out of the FA Cup, and in response to that humiliation Mr Bromilow made his best signing for the club when he brought Fred Dawes from Northampton Town to Palace in February 1936. If the war had not interrupted Fred's career it is likely that he would have led Palace's all-time appearances chart, but he became the only man at Selhurst Park to play 100 games on both sides of the hostilities.

The 'Pools War' erupted after increasing ill will between the Football League and the Pools giants over the latter's use of the former's fixtures, and early in 1936 it came to a head. The League withdrew its fixtures for 29 February at short notice and replaced them with other matches. This went on for three Saturdays but by then the antipathy towards the Pools companies had largely disappeared and attendances all over the country had been adversely affected.

At the end of the season Albert Dawes had netted 39 League and Cup goals from 43 appearances that merited his inclusion in an England squad during that campaign.

In October 1935 Mr Louis Bellatti, Palace's chairman in succession to Sydney Bourne, died suddenly – but only six weeks later *his* successor, Mr R.S. Flew, succumbed as well. Carey Burnett took on the role – presumably with some misgivings!

The second half of 1936 was highly charged at Crystal Palace FC. Matters began with the resignation of Mr Bromilow at the end of June, accompanied by director Mr C.H. Temple. Mr R.S. Moyes, also a director, became club manager and provided one piece of top class service to Palace by signing Scottish international centre-half George Walker from Notts County. George was a splendid defender and rarely missed a match; indeed, his absence in the second half of 1938–39 could be argued to have been the reason why Palace missed out on promotion that season.

Palace disappointed badly in the 1936–37 campaign. Not only were they nowhere near the leading places in Division Three South, but Southend knocked them out of the FA Cup in a first-round replay. Mr Moyes resigned, then so did the chairman. Albert Dawes was transferred to Luton, but then it was announced that Mr Temple was to rejoin the directorate and that Mr Bromilow would take up the management of the club again from the New Year. Under his guidance Palace managed to finish 14th – the club's poorest showing since they joined the Football League; although it could have been much, much worse.

The signing of Les Lievesley, a strong, forceful wing-half from Torquay, right at the end of 1936–37, was a major reason for Palace's improved showing in the following campaign, and with George Walker and Nick Collins, Les formed a magnificent half-back line that is still spoken of with veneration. The return of Albert Dawes from Luton in mid-February 1938 was another factor in Palace's improvement, and by early April the club stood just three points behind the leading outfit, Millwall; however, a mixed run-in saw Palace finish the season in seventh place, and, for an ambitious club that was not nearly good enough.

It must be acknowledged, however, that but for a considerable misfortune with injuries, Palace might have squeezed the top clubs more closely. This misfortune was highlighted when Palace met Liverpool in the FA Cup third round but had to do so with reserve full-backs. Palace only lost out in an Anfield replay to two contentious goals in a 3–1 defeat.

Ten days later Palace were re-acquainted with Peter Simpson, now of Reading. At half-time at Elm Park Palace were in command and in the lead; enter Peter, who scored twice in the second half to lead Reading's revival and send Palace back to South London beaten 3–2.

1937–38 – Players and officials in the first season that the club wore stripes – unconfirmed but said to be red and blue. Back row, left to right: R. Greener, S. Booth, H. Fielding, D. Jordan, A. Robson, H. Pritchard, F. Dawes, E. Owens, J. Blackman, G. Irwin. Second row: C. Quayle, L. Lievesley, G. Daniels, G. Walker, V. Blore, A. Chesters, W. Wilde, R. Shanks, R. Bigg, J. Turton. Third row: G. Stanbury, T.G. Bromilow, C.E. Truett Esq, C.H. Temple Esq, E.T. Truett Esq, R. Cornell Esq, R.H.E. Blaxill Esq, F.E. Burrell, Dr T.E.M Wardill. Front row: E. Waldron, H. Davis, F. Beresford, R. Birtley, N. Collins, J. Horton.

Crystal Palace v Bristol Rovers, 2 September 1939, the day before World War Two was declared and the Football League suspended.

In the 1938–39 season Tom Bromilow took Palace closer to gaining promotion to the Second Division than any of his counterparts between 1929 and 1964. He made a couple of signings, those of wingers Eric Steele from Millwall and of Albert Wilson from Mansfield, to bolster the team's menace from those positions, while a youthful Bert Robson improved so much that he became the club's main striker from mid-December and netted 11 League goals from his 20 appearances. That season, however, was to prove the one campaign of triumph for Newport County. On 8 October Palace lost 2–0 at Somerton Park, so it became imperative that the Glaziers should beat them in the Selhurst Park return on 11 February. Although Albert Wilson put Palace ahead as the hour approached, County levelled when fate intervened and the ball stuck in some mud from a free-kick and their outside-right was able to scramble it into the net. Palace's hopes of catching the men from Monmouth were virtually extinguished, and in the final analysis the club finished as runners-up to County, with a three-point margin separating the sides.

Mr Bromilow left Palace in the summer of 1939 to manage Leicester City. George Irwin, a well-suited and knowledgeable former Palace goalkeeper, took over and it fell to him to steer the club through the difficult years of World War Two.

World War Two

As soon as the war was declared, the Football League's 1939–40 season was abandoned and, throughout the hostilities, the clubs were divided into several regional leagues and divisions. Competitions ran for various lengths of time, from a few weeks to many months, and at times they even ran concurrently.

As in World War One, the 'guest' system was encouraged and several top-class stars appeared in Palace sides, including, for example, at different times, Bernard Joy and Sam Bartram. Also appearing in this way were goalkeeper Dick Graham and centre-forward Freddie Kurz who were signed by Palace and became valued performers for the club during and after the war years.

Palace achieved three wartime successes: they topped the (rather modest) division of the 1939–40 South Regional League, which ran until 8 June and included a 10–0 demolition of hapless Brighton, then, in 1940–41, won an interesting competition which ran for over nine months when each club arranged as many or as few fixtures as they chose! The competition was decided purely on goal average, and Palace's triumph owed much to the prowess of Bert Robson, who hit 36 goals in 40 Palace appearances, and erstwhile favourite Albert Dawes, whose 23 games brought him 27 goals. Palace's final wartime honour was gained by winning the (again modest) 20-match southern section of the 1945 Third Division South.

Many curious things occurred during wartime football, but perhaps two bizarre examples will suffice: on 9 November 1940 300 fans waited outside Selhurst Park for the 'all-clear' to sound so that a match against Watford could go ahead – but it never did and so the gates remained locked all afternoon. On 19 October that year Clapton Orient arrived at Selhurst Park with a depleted team and Palace allowed Fred Gregory to 'guest' for them. When Orient were awarded a penalty the Palace fans urged Orient to allow Fred to take the kick, for they knew well the power of Fred's kicking. Orient did as bidden, Fred lashed home the award – but Palace won anyway!

As the war drew towards an end, the FA permitted a full FA Cup competition for 1945–46 and, for the only time in its entire history, the ties were played over home and away legs. Palace played two exciting but scoreless matches against Queen's Park Rangers before large crowds, but then they lost a midweek replay at Fulham to a goal conceded after just a few minutes' play.

Palace In Decline

No club in Division Three South opened the post-war footballing era with higher aspirations than Crystal Palace, but the fact is that, for 1946–47 and well beyond, Palace were among the poorer outfits in the section. The first couple of matches told the whole story: at Mansfield on the opening day of the season Palace lost 3–1, then at a blustery Elm Park they lost the midweek clash with Reading by the astonishing margin of 10–2!

Palace laboured on and eventually finished 18th in a 22-club division. Top scorer was Billy Bark (who later changed his surname to Naylor), who netted nine times for Palace before he was transferred to Brentford in early February. In view of the poor showing, it was inevitable that Palace would have a new manager for the 1947–48 campaign, and Jack Butler was appointed. He was a former Arsenal and England centre-half whose managerial and coaching careers were impressive. But it made little difference at Selhurst Park! In 1947–48 Palace were always, but only, a mid-table side and finished 13th. In 1948–49 Palace were dreadful, finished bottom of the table and Jack Butler resigned, for there had been few glimmers to lighten the gloom, in fact perhaps the only one had been an amazing 5–0 victory at Watford on 14 February 1948.

Palace returned to Arsenal in the wake of Butler's departure and clinched the appointment of Ronnie Rooke as player-manager. Rooke had played for Palace in the mid-1930s and been a prolific scorer in the reserve side, but he was never able to produce such form in the first team. Then, at Fulham and Arsenal, he became prodigious! His appointment at Palace accorded with the then forward thinking among lower-division clubs: Hull City and then Notts County had signed stars of the day in Raich Carter and Tommy Lawton and become successful outfits. Rooke, it was hoped, would lead Palace the same way.

In fact, in his first season at Selhurst Park Rooke did well for Palace, though when the club was pitted against Lawton's County, Palace were beaten by the odd goal in three before a near 30,000 crowd, who relished an exciting encounter. Nevertheless, Rooke lifted Palace to a much-improved seventh-place finish (the club's best in the post-war Third Division South) and concluded the season as top goalscorer with 21 League goals. Another, less savoury, event was the derby at Millwall in early October when Rooke was dismissed during a 3–2 Palace victory. Making his debut that day at The Den was left-back Jack Edwards, who became an esteemed idol of the fans of the day and later became Palace captain. The media caught the new enthusiasm at Selhurst Park and dubbed the club 'The Rooke Regiment', and there were some big crowds to see the team play, at home and away.

That was the peak of Rooke's achievements at the Palace, however. In the summer of 1950, with the encouragement of a new and naïve board of directors it must be said, he spent nearly £30,000 on new players – a prodigious outlay. The enormous costs proved to be of little, indeed no, avail: Palace lost five of the opening six matches of 1950–51, deployed no fewer than 17 players in the process, and it was all too clear that Palace were facing a troubled future.

By mid-November Palace were adrift at the foot of the division and had been knocked out of the Cup in the first round by Millwall. The directors decided that Rooke should go – his resignation was sought and accepted – but the carnage wrought could not so easily be resolved.

For reasons which are obscure Rooke was replaced by two men, veteran Fred Dawes, whose playing career had been ended some 12 months earlier by a head injury, and Charlie Slade, a highly thought-of coach and chief scout. But the task they took on was beyond redemption. Palace were clearly destined to finish bottom of the table again, but they did so having scored just 33 goals in the 46 League matches, Palace's lowest-ever total.

There was, therefore, a feeling of apprehension at Selhurst Park as 1951–52 opened. The managers had reduced the inflated playing staff and made a couple of signings of their own in wing-half George McGeachie and forward Les Devonshire, but Palace were quickly in deep trouble again and in mid-October yet another change at the helm was deemed necessary. The board returned again to Arsenal, where they persuaded England international right-back Laurie Scott to take over the club, and he made his debut for Palace on 20 October 1951 when Ipswich were the visitors. A large crowd came to witness the game and most were encouraged by the emphatic 3–1 victory. Scorer of two of the Palace goals was a striking phenomenon named Cam Burgess. He had been recommended to Palace by Les Devonshire and collected 21 League goals in 22 appearances that season.

Matters steadied somewhat under Scott, but while re-election was at least avoided, Palace only finished in 19th place. However, 1952–53 was a much better season. Scott signed experienced forwards Bob Thomas and Les Fell from Fulham and Charlton respectively, plus wing-half 'Archie' Andrews from Portsmouth and versatile Bill Simpson from Aston Villa. Palace began poorly, then improved and Cam Burgess hit a terrific run of form,

Ronnie Downs, Les Devonshire and Geoff Chilvers in 1953.

netting 12 goals in six late autumn fixtures. Another unrewarding period in December and the New Year was epitomised by the club's FA Cup second-round defeat at non-League Finchley. Amazingly, with Palace losing 3–1, the fog-shrouded original fixture was abandoned, but Palace were quite unable to take any advantage of that reprieve and were beaten by the same scoreline when the match was restaged.

The shadow of a third application for re-election began to hover over Selhurst Park but, thankfully, in the final six weeks of the season Bill Simpson and Bob Thomas started to really thrive on crosses provided by Les Fell and Les Devonshire, while Roy Bailey returned from National Service to reclaim the goalkeeper's position and add some much needed defensive security. Palace climbed slowly away from the troubled regions of the table and by the end of the campaign would have taken on anybody, even beating the divisional champions, Bristol Rovers, in the final game to finish 13th in the table.

Despite Cam Burgess's departure to York City, Palace started 1953–54 in fine form, losing only twice in the opening dozen games, but thereafter the rather more familiar Palace form applied, so that the club slid down the table to finish 22nd, thus avoiding the re-election places by a whisker, and were beaten by Great Yarmouth in the FA Cup. Palace's first floodlighting system was installed during the early autumn, after which Chelsea came to Selhurst Park for the inaugural friendly (1–1), followed by top-flight Cardiff (2–2), and Palace achieved some praiseworthy results in such games.

At the end of September 1954 Laurie Scott was dismissed. Palace's poor opening to 1954–55 included a 7–1 drubbing at Watford, and the Glaziers won just a single game in

A 1955–56 team. Back row, left to right: Don Moss, Len Choules, Roy Bailey, Jack Saunders, Alf Noakes, Jim Sanders. Front row: Ron Brett, Jim Belcher, Mike Deakin, George Cooper, Peter Berry.

their first 11 engagements. After a hiatus of two weeks Cyril Spiers was appointed and the former Villa, Spurs and Wolves goalkeeper, who had served Cardiff and, briefly, Norwich, well as manager, became Palace's secretary-manager. Spiers's talent lay in finding and developing young players – a total change of strategy at Palace, where, for decades, the club had brought in most of their players from other clubs.

There was an expectation of the new policy yielding immediate progress but Palace finished the term just four points and three places away from the re-election positions. Mr Spiers' youngsters had, however, shown that, on occasions, they were capable of surprising other more established players at stronger clubs in the section, beating Brighton, Queen's Park Rangers and Coventry at Selhurst Park and drawing at highly placed Southampton to demonstrate the potential value of the new approach. That said, few Palace fans will ever forget the utter despair after losing at home to Northern League Bishop Auckland in the FA Cup (4–2), the third consecutive exit at the hands of non-League opponents and an outcome which spelt *finis* to a number of Palace players' careers.

The youth policy was extended into 1955–56 but, although the fans' favourites could play attractively and effectively at times, and were quite outstanding in an early-season midweek 3–0 victory at Queen's Park Rangers, for example, while flame-haired Jimmy Murray netted both Palace goals on his debut when Walsall were the visitors at the end of September, neverthless, the club still finished next to bottom and so it was necessary to seek re-election once more.

The average age of the Palace side for 1956–57 was probably among the lowest in the club's history and at least the young players raised the team to a 20th-placed finish, but among the splendid stars of the future assembled by Mr Spiers and now playing regularly in the Palace side were wing-half Terry Long and forward Johnny Byrne. The highlight of the season for most Palace fans was the 3–2 extra-time defeat of Brentford in a pulsating second-round FA Cup tie in which another youthful star, Barry Pierce, netted a hat-trick. It was the final game of the season which drew the biggest crowd to Selhurst Park for a League game because the visitors were Torquay and, if they could beat Palace, they would gain promotion to Division Two. A fine game ended 1–1.

The 1957–58 season was utterly crucial for every club in the regional Third Divisions, following a series of initiatives dating back to the early years of the decade proposing the establishment of national Third and Fourth Divisions, as it had finally been decided to introduce the new arrangement at the end of 1957–58. Despite entertaining hopes that the club would finish in the upper half of the regional table in May 1958, and thus join the

Third Division fraternity, the by now all-too-recognisable story was played out. Although Palace produced occasional praiseworthy performances, Palace were never able to string together a run of victories and, as the end of the term approached, matters looked ominous.

Mr Spiers signed experienced men, winger Tony Collins from Watford and Johnny McNichol from Chelsea, who netted on his debut against Port Vale on 13 March to secure a Palace win and hit seven goals in the last 12 games, but in the end two draws over Easter against Colchester, then two defeats in four days by Queen's Park Rangers, consigned Palace to 14th place. Mr Spiers accepted the situation and left Selhurst Park a few days after the season had ended.

From Humble Beginnings

As founder members of the national Fourth Division, any progress that Palace might, eventually, make would have to be from those humble origins. Engaged as Palace's boss for the first attempts to escape from the new League basement was George Smith, who asserted upon his appointment that, should he not take the club to promotion within two seasons, he would resign. It was quickly clear that he would not be successful in his initial attempt!

Palace opened the new era with a fine 6–2 victory over Crewe at Selhurst Park when both Mike Deakin and Johnny Byrne netted hat-tricks, but Palace never seriously appeared able to displace the strongest teams and concluded the season six points behind Shrewsbury Town who had claimed the fourth promotion place.

In fact, Palace's strongest showing that season was in the knockout competitions. In the FA Cup, victories over Ashford and Shrewsbury earned a third-round tie at Second Division Sheffield United, which was lost 2–0, while in the Southern Floodlit Cup, Palace earned a gripping Final at home to Arsenal which drew a near 33,000 crowd, but was lost 2–1.

Goalkeeper Vic Rouse, signed by Cyril Spiers from Millwall, was selected to play for Wales against Northern Ireland in Belfast, thus becoming the first international player from the Fourth Division. Wales were beaten 4–1, but Palace's 23-year-old had a splendid game and earned a lot of admiring press coverage.

Manager George Smith could make no progress in 1959–60 either. The one eminent feature of that season was Palace's 9–0 rout of Barrow at Selhurst Park in October in which Roy Summersby netted four goals. The club gained some praise for an animated and courageous display at Second Division Scunthorpe in a third-round FA Cup tie which was lost 1–0, but as spring arrived and April 1960 began with a home defeat by Workington, it was very evident that the season was not going to be one that anybody at Crystal Palace would enthuse over. True to his promise, George Smith left the club before the end of the season.

Palace immediately appointed assistant manager Arthur Rowe as Smith's successor. The close-season signings were those of experienced winger Ron Heckman and George Petchey, a wing-half from Queen's Park Rangers, but in October, and with several forwards injured, Mr Rowe also secured striker Dennis Uphill from Watford.

Palace fans were quickly enthralled by Mr Rowe's tactical style of 'push and run' which he had used previously and with great success at Tottenham, but also by the early-season results which included a 9–2 victory over Accrington Stanley on the opening afternoon and four wins in the ensuing six matches.

Under Rowe's adroit leadership, Palace were always among the division's top sides, but Peterborough, who had done the double over Palace early in the campaign, were an even stronger outfit than the Glaziers and probably deserved to take the title. However, Palace's run-in of four consecutive victories ensured that they gained the runners'-up position and a promotion for the first time in 40 years. The season was actually also one in which new club records were established: 110 League goals were scored to beat the previous record established 30 years previously by Peter Simpson and his colleagues, while Johnny Byrne's 30 League goals was the club's best since the war and Roy Summerby's 25 was also ahead of Mike Deakin's previous record of 23. The early-season home match against Peterborough drew a new Fourth Division record crowd of over 36,000 but that was surpassed when Palace hosted Millwall on Good Friday when 37,774 watched The Lions win 2–0.

The 1960–61 season was also the first season of the Football League Cup, but Palace went out at the first hurdle at Darlington in October. Former manager Laurie Scott came back to Selhurst Park with amateurs Hitchin Town in the first round of the FA Cup, but Palace won 6–2 before going out to Watford after two gripping matches when the only goal to separate the sides was scored in injury time in the replay at Vicarage Road.

Arthur Rowe made four summer signings for Palace ahead of 1961–62, but the one which was masterly was that of England international striker/winger Ronnie Allen from

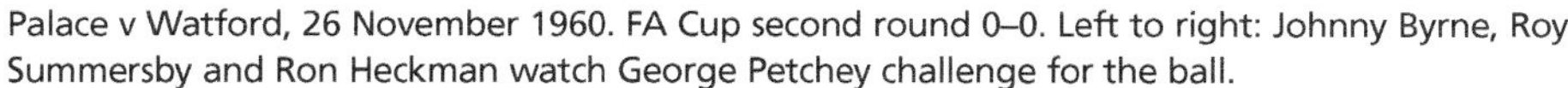

Palace v Watford, 26 November 1960. FA Cup second round 0–0. Left to right: Johnny Byrne, Roy Summersby and Ron Heckman watch George Petchey challenge for the ball.

West Bromwich Albion. Thus, continuing to play his favoured 'push and run' tactics, Palace opened the new campaign with an engagement at Torquay and those fans who travelled to the West Country for the fixture were well satisfied with the outcome, a 2–1 success for Palace, and also at the manner in which Ronnie Allen and Johnny Byrne immediately blended. It came as no surprise to any Palace fan when Byrne was selected for England against Northern Ireland at Wembley in November and so secured Palace's first full England cap since Jack Alderson in 1923.

In early March 1962 and with Palace in 10th place, Johnny Byrne inevitably left Selhurst Park to play for West Ham at the record fee of £60,000 plus the return to Selhurst Park of Ron Brett. Palace never looked the same without Byrne, however; indeed, between March and September 1962 Palace went 20 League games without a win. Palace finished 1961–62 in 15th place, which was disappointing after the results gained in the first half of the campaign. The club's best showing of all was in the FA Cup, third-round tie at Aston Villa, where Palace looked to be in their element and seemed to have brought the highly placed top-flight club back to Selhurst Park with a thrilling 3–3 draw. But in the 90th minute Palace conceded another goal when a curious cross from Villa's outside-left swung towards goal, eluded Vic Rouse's attempts to catch it and finished in the top corner of the net.

A night of huge importance at Palace occured on 18 April 1962 when the kings of European football, Real Madrid, came to Selhurst Park for the official opening of the new floodlighting system. It had been a dreadful day for weather, but Palace fans flocked to see the clash, which ended in a 4–3 victory for the visitors.

The summer months of 1962 were not in the least positive for Palace. Arthur Rowe was never a strong man and was struck down by illness; then the death of Ron Brett in a car crash, just after the season had begun, hit the club and players alike. It became necessary for Rowe to resign and he was replaced by his assistant, Palace's former goalkeeper Dick Graham. Dick made Palace play a more direct style straight away and signed two strikers, clever Dickie Dowsett and powerful Cliff Holton.

There was an immediate change to Palace's fortunes. The club's forwards became a real threat and, with the help of several big victories, Palace climbed the table to safety and an eventual finish in a praiseworthy 11th place.

Dick Graham made just one signing in the summer of 1963, that of hard-working little winger or midfielder Bobby Kellard, but, as the season progressed, he added full-back John Sewell from Charlton, then Brian Whitehouse from West Bromwich Albion.

Despite a modest start (including a 5–1 loss at Coventry on opening day), Palace improved, although they lost John Sewell to injury in the match at Millwall (1–0) on 22 February which kept him out for the rest of the season, reached the top of the table by Easter and gained promotion with a 2–2 draw at Wrexham on 22 April. Palace could (or perhaps should) have taken the title – all that was required was a home draw against Oldham three days later to secure it in the last match of the season, but a second-half aberration enabled the Latics' gnome-like winger to grab an 11-minute hat-trick, so Palace lost 3–1 and Coventry snatched the Championship honours.

Palace ever-presents in that promotion season were Bill Glazier and full-back Bert Howe, while centre-half Brian Wood missed just one game. Thus it is no surprise that, in contrast to 1960–61, this 1963–64 triumph was led by a resolute defence, in which Don Townsend (37 appearances), the emerging Alan Stephenson (26), Terry Long (27) and George Petchey (24) all also played invaluable roles. Nevertheless, it is goals that win games, and the club's top goalscorers were Cliff Holton and Peter Burridge with 20 strikes apiece, while Brian Whitehouse bagged six more in Palace's final nine games.

Palace began their first season in the upper half of the Football League for 39 years with a home game against Derby. Dick Graham put his faith in his promotion-winning men of the previous season, but the Rams administered a footballing lesson and won 3–2. Six changes for the midweek trip to Swindon (0–2) included the debut of John Jackson in goal, and in mid-October, to the chagrin of most Palace supporters, Bill Glazier was sold to Coventry for the then highest fee for a goalkeeper of £35,000.

Palace lost their opening three games, but then won seven of the next eight fixtures, plus their League Cup tie at Tranmere, for the club's first victory in that competition in five attempts. Southampton were beaten in the next round but Palace then lost a Selhurst Park replay to eventual finalists, top-flight Leicester City.

Dick Graham kept Palace's high work-rate of the previous season and a half, but he also slowly adapted his tactics to embrace a larger measure of finesse through the additions to the squad of Keith Smith from Peterborough and David Burnside from Southampton. Smith gained immortal Palace fame as the scorer of the club's fastest-ever goal, after just six seconds in the return match at Derby (3–3), while Burnside netted twice on his Boxing Day debut for the club against Portsmouth (4–2).

Palace provided several matches for the emerging, talented young wing-half or midfield star of the future David Payne, and they finished the 1964–65 season in seventh place in Division Two – a most praiseworthy performance, but it is the FA Cup progress which most fans recall when reminiscing about that campaign. Palace beat Bury 5–1 with only 10 men, having lost Brian Wood with a broken leg, then won at Southampton with a brace from Peter Burridge. Palace then overcame top-flight Nottingham Forest in style (3–1) on a snow-flecked Selhurst Park pitch, before a new record attendance of 41,667, to reach the quarter-finals for the first time since 1907 to bring mighty Leeds to Crystal Palace's headquarters. Another ground record record was set up of 45,384, but Leeds powered to a 3–0 win in a muscular clash.

The 1965–66 campaign was to provide Dick Graham's last few months as Palace manager. He upset many of the club's supporters when he transfer-listed Cliff Holton and the big striker moved back to Watford. Graham's image was further marred when his chosen replacement for Holton, former England international striker Derek Kevan, proved a huge disappointment. But, in Dick's final game in charge, a 1 January fixture at Bristol City (1–1), he gave a debut to 17-year-old Steve Kember, who was to have a lengthy association with Palace as a player and as a manager which was enormously valuable.

Dick Graham was dismissed on 3 January 1966. This followed a highly publicised falling out with the Palace players at Euston Station as the group assembled prior to a match at Carlisle, after which Alan Stephenson was sent home. Nevertheless, Dick had made a hugely positive contribution to Palace and left knowing that he had done very well at Selhurst Park.

Arthur Rowe took temporary charge but in April it was announced that Bert Head was to become the new manager. He had earned a name for himself in charge of Swindon, but Palace secured his services from Bury.

Palace had finished 1965–66 in 11th place: Bert Head had improved on that in 1966–67 when the club concluded Second Division matters in seventh position. Two new men, Tom White and Bobby Woodruff, each netted twice on their debuts in their first match, against Carlisle (4–2), and the latter went on to have an impressive Palace career. He was famous in football at the time for his amazing long throw-ins, but he was also an excellent header of the ball and a sublime passer. He could also find the opposition net too, as his 18 League goals that season testify. Bert Head also signed central-defender John McCormick and forward Cliff Jackson, both of whom were to become invaluable, key members of Palace's 1968–69 promotion side. But Bert's most popular signing was that which brought about the return of Johnny Byrne, but, regrettably, Johnny was not able to offer much to Palace this time and some 13 months later he moved across London to Fulham, having played 259 senior games in two spells for Palace, scoring 101 goals.

Palace began the 1967–68 season without any major summer signings and, apart from losing a Football League Cup tie at Barrow, continued to move forward, so that, following Palace's single-goal victory over Queen's Park Rangers on 30 September, the club topped the Second Division table for the first time ever. Scorer of the all-important Palace goal had been the perhaps unlikely figure of Terry Long, who, it may be remembered, had made his Palace debut back in September 1955. Terry was an ideal footballer and Palace awarded him a thoroughly deserved testimonial in October 1966. With 480 senior Palace games to his name, Terry stands only below Jim Cannon in the club's all-time appearances chart.

A signing which was to provide an invaluable component of Palace's 1968–69 season was made in December 1967 when Mr Head paid Queen's Park Rangers £11,000 for winger Mark Lazarus, but Alan Stephenson moved to West Ham in order to secure the top-flight competition which he craved. Palace coped well enough without him and the club finished 1967–68 in 11th place.

Mr Head assembled his men for the 1968–69 season as thoughtfully as a chess master manoeuvres his pieces. To the players already with the club he quickly added winger Colin Taylor, of the fearsome shot, and then tall, muscular Mel Blyth, who was soon moulded into a magnificent central-defender. His partnership with John McCormick became a feature of that season and of those that followed in Division One. After the season got underway, Mr Head signed up hardy defender Roger Hoy from Spurs and full-back John Loughlan and winger Tony Taylor from Greenock Morton, although the latter became a marvellous midfield dynamo for Palace later in his career.

While Palace's earliest form declared their objective, the 1968–69 season fell into two distinct parts, and there were at least six clubs earnestly engaged in the promotion race – Palace among them. But any loss of form, misfortune with injury or a poor performance could mean a slip of two or three places in the table.

Then, at the end of January 1969, a four-week interruption was caused to the fixture list by bleak, winter weather – but when Palace recommenced business they hit a dazzling run. They did not lose a single match, from the resumption, at home to Hull (2–0) on 22

February, until early the following season and Palace won 10 of the 16 outstanding 1968–69 fixtures!

Fans of the period always look back to one particular match which indicated that Palace were on their way to promotion: it was at table-topping, champions-elect Derby on Wednesday 5 March, where Palace won with a goal from Bobby Woodruff. Three days later another awesome display disposed of Birmingham at St Andrew's, as Steve Kember's strike grabbed both points for Palace.

With just two games left, there was only Charlton who could deny Palace the runners'-up place, provided they won and Palace lost both the remaining games. There were 36,126 fans at Selhurst Park for the final home game, against Fulham. Palace made certain that there was no upset and won 3–2, although Fulham had led 2–0 at one stage and coach George Petchey had had to have a few apposite words with the players during the interval. In any case, Charlton lost at home anyway!

The scenes were quite amazing. Readers should remember that this was the first-ever time on which Palace had gained entry to the top flight, and that five years previously the club had been playing in Division Three; 10 years and the club had been Fourth Division also-rans.

One thing remains to be said about the 1968–69 season. While the team were forging their relentless way to glory, there began to arise, along the Park Road side of Selhurst Park, the girders that would form the skeleton of the Arthur Wait stand. It was an act of supreme belief by the club chairman and a statement of his confidence in the players' ability to claim a spot among the game's elite clubs.

Palace's See-saw Seventies

Frankly, it was probably inevitable that Palace's initial four years in the top flight would prove largely to be a struggle for survival.

It did not begin that way, however, because Palace's opening-day fixture was at home to Manchester United, then, as now, the most glamorous club in the country. A new record crowd of 48,610 witnessed a fine Palace performance in which goals from Mel Blyth and Gerry Queen twice had Palace ahead, with the Red Devils coming from behind both times to earn a 2–2 draw. Gerry Queen was a stylish striker from Kilmarnock and probably Bert Head's best signing during this spell among football's aristocrats. Queen was leading scorer in 1969–70 with 11 League and Cup goals. Palace's last game of 1969 saw the ground record broken again: this time the visitors were Chelsea and 49,498 paid to watch them demolish Palace 5–1, Gerry Queen again Palace's scorer.

Ultimately, Palace's survival at the end of the season was assured because neither Sunderland nor Sheffield Wednesday could gain the three points they needed from their two outstanding games after Palace's own programme had been completed.

For 1970–71, Mr Head added several players with proven top-flight experience to the squad, most notably forwards Alan Birchenall and Bobby Tambling (the latter had spent three weeks on loan with Palace between December 1969 and January 1970) from Chelsea and full-back Peter Wall from Liverpool.

Palace began the season well, winning four of their first eight games and then beating Manchester United at Old Trafford with a Bobby Tambling drive. However, Palace's best

Crystal Palace v Chelsea, 2 January 1971. FA Cup third round, 2–2. Steve Kember, Gerry Queen and Tony Taylor acknowledge Alan Birchenall's (No.10) goal.

performance of 1970–71 was not in Division One at all, where they lost the final game 6–0 at Southampton, but in the League Cup. Victories over Rochdale and Lincoln paired Palace with Arsenal, but the club's success seemed to be running out when an exciting game at Selhurst Park finished goalless so that most of the pundits and North London fans regarded the replay as little more than a necessary procedure for Arsenal, but Palace won 2–0 at Highbury to record Arsenal's only home defeat in their double season, and then went on to draw the League match there the following Saturday.

Skipper John Sewell left at the end of the 1970–71 season, having helped to lead the club into Division Two in 1964 and captained Palace throughout 1968–69. He put in 70 top-flight appearances between 1969 and 1971 and will always be remembered at Palace.

Palace made a dreadful start to 1971–72, losing seven of the first nine matches, and thereby being firmly anchored at the bottom of the table. Bert Head took radical, remedial action: within a week in mid-September he had raised some funds by selling Alan Birchenall to Leicester and Steve Kember to Chelsea, so that he could secure Bobby Kellard's return to Palace, John Craven from Blackpool, with a couple of younger players and more to come.

Most Palace folk regarded Kellard as the mainspring of Palace's revival, and he soon became club captain. In October Celtic forwards Willie Wallace and John Hughes arrived.

Wallace, never missed a game in 1971–72 after joining Palace, but Hughes was less fortunate. He inspired a glorious Palace victory over Sheffield United on 4 December (5–1) in which he netted twice and terrorised the Blades' defence, but he then suffered a bad injury and was never the same force again.

Palace scrapped their way to survival with a four-point margin eventually separating them from the relegated pair, Nottingham Forest and Huddersfield.

The 1972–73 season started with a boardroom change, Ray Bloye taking over as club chairman and Arthur Wait becoming life president. On the playing side, Terry Long became assistant manager to Bert Head.

Peter Wall's broken leg against his former club Liverpool, in only the third game, proved to be a portent of difficulties ahead. By mid-October Palace were bottom of the table again with just two wins from the first 13 games, but on 4 November they moved up a place after beating Everton. That game was Don Rogers's Palace debut after his transfer from Swindon, and he scored the goal which separated the sides. Rogers quickened Palace for a while and the next victory was a 5–0 rout of Manchester United in which Rogers himself netted a brace. However, Palace never improved sufficiently to climb away from the relegation struggle. Malcolm Allison was appointed manager, with Bert Head becoming general manager, in a final attempt to remedy the perilous situation, and for his first match in charge, at home to Chelsea, young defender Jim Cannon came into the starting line up. Jim scored on his debut, and Palace won 2–0, but the club then gained only one point from the next six games! The defeat to a very late Norwich goal in the last of those matches consigned Palace to relegation along with West Bromwich Albion.

Having been relegated from the First Division, Palace did not remain long in Division Two, as they went immediately down to Division Three.

Palace's opening match of 1973–74 was disastrous and set the tone for the season, losing 4–1 at home to Notts County. Worse followed. Palace actually went the first 15 matches without a win and were knocked out of the Football League Cup by Fourth Division Stockport in the club's worst-ever beginning to a season. Clearly, the issue was the all-too-familiar one of survival.

Despite an FA Cup defeat by Wrexham at Selhurst Park, things did improve somewhat as the campaign progressed. This was partly due to the signing in October 1973 of Peter Taylor, a left-footed right-winger of pace, trickery and an explosive shot. He was clearly a player of real ability and became Malcolm Allison's on-field inspiration for the team. That said, Palace's only result of real merit was a 3–0 victory over Sunderland on 9 March, but, in this first season of three-up, three-down, a draw at lowly Cardiff in the re-arranged last match kept the Bluebirds in Division Two but consigned Palace to a second consecutive relegation, finishing 20th and going down with Preston and Swindon.

Palace were scarcely an inspired force in Division Three in 1974–75, however, arriving from Queen's Park Rangers in an exchange deal which took Don Rogers to Loftus Road, were Terry Venables and central-defender Ian Evans. Venables' playing career with Palace was modest but he initially became a hugely successful coach then manager with the club, while Evans became club captain and led Palace back to Division Two before injury ruined his playing career.

In October 1974 Palace hosted an England Under-23 encounter with Czechoslovakia in which Peter Taylor starred, scoring one goal and making another, but in the League Palace could only manage to finish in fifth place. The last game of the term was a re-arranged one at Tranmere (2–0) where the little band of Palace fans witnessed the debut of 16-year-old left-back Kenny Sansom, who would have a distinguished career with several clubs and with England.

The 1975–76 season was an extraordinary one. Palace set a sizzling pace in the League from August to January, beginning the campaign with a new club record of five straight victories, establishing a table-topping lead of seven points at one stage and remaining unbeaten away from home until 20 December. The club's foremost scorer at this point was David Kemp, but Palace fell away badly and finished the season in fifth place.

In the FA Cup, however, Palace excelled, setting a new club record in becoming only the fifth Third Division club to reach the semi-finals. The club's progress included magnificent victories at Leeds and Sunderland, while a fifth-round 3–2 triumph at Chelsea showed Peter Taylor at his inspirational best. The semi-final was against Southampton at Stamford Bridge, but Palace were beaten 2–0 in an uncompromising, leaden game in which the players completely failed to do themselves justice.

Palace's League and Cup progress, however, led to Peter Taylor and Ian Evans making their full international bows for England and Wales respectively; in fact, the pair played in opposing sides on 24 March 1976 when the countries met at Wrexham.

Malcolm Allison left the club in mid-May and Terry Venables took over as Palace manager on 1 June 1976, leading Palace to an immediate promotion, but the extraordinary

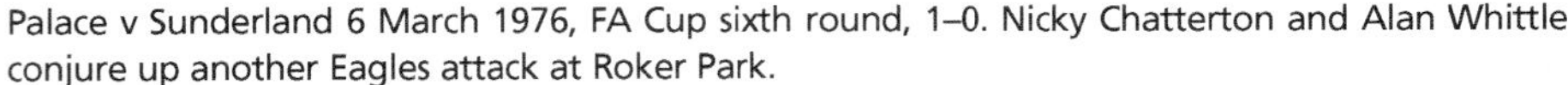

Palace v Sunderland 6 March 1976, FA Cup sixth round, 1–0. Nicky Chatterton and Alan Whittle conjure up another Eagles attack at Roker Park.

feature of that success was that Palace only reached the promotion places *after* their last match of the season. Meanwhile, in the FA Cup Palace had two memorable matches. The first-round second replay victory over Brighton, on a foul evening at Stamford Bridge, witnessed the origins of the rivalry that today exists between the clubs, while, in round three, Third Division Palace silenced Liverpool's Kop as their illustrious hosts were held to a 0–0 draw before going out in the Selhurst Park replay, which finished 2–3.

In the League it was not until Jeff Bourne joined Palace from Derby in early March that the club really became a team that looked capable of gaining promotion, but then, in the final 13 games Palace lost only once and drew just three times. Jeff himself netted nine goals in that sequence, including the last one in the club's amazing 4–2 victory at Wrexham in the final match of the season. That win put Palace above Wrexham for the first time, though they had one game left to play so could have snatched third place and gained promotion if they won. In fact they lost and Palace went up behind Brighton and Mansfield.

There was one more triumph for the Palace that season: the club's juniors won the FA Youth Cup for the first time, beating Everton 1–0 in a two-legged Final.

Probably the most significant feature of Palace's 1977–78 season was that it saw the senior debuts of Peter Nicholas, Billy Gilbert and vital goalscorer in both the 1977 and 1978 FA Youth Cup Finals, Terry Fenwick, but the importance of the signing of exuberant goalkeeper John Burridge from Aston Villa just ahead of the transfer deadline in March should not be minimised.

However, Palace's season was thrown into disarray by the injury sustained by skipper and central-defender Ian Evans in a disgraceful tackle by George Best of Fulham on 1 October. So horrendous was the break of his right leg that Ian was unable to play for virtually two years and never played for his country or the senior Palace side again.

Despite the absence of their captain, Palace nevertheless finished the campaign in ninth place, but by the end of the campaign the side regularly included six members who were products of the youth scheme and the juniors retained the Youth Cup, beating Aston Villa in a one-off Final at Highbury.

Skippered now by Jim Cannon, Palace made 1978–79 another promotion campaign; indeed, a Championship-winning one!

Palace were always up among the leaders in Division Two, but it was a League Cup tie, which, indirectly, brought about a significant acquisition which turned the season completely in Palace's favour. In round three of that competition Palace were paired in early October with top-flight Aston Villa. A Nick Chatterton penalty at Villa Park brought about a replay which itself produced an extra-time 0–0 draw. The second replay, at Coventry's Highfield Road, played without the injured Jim Cannon, went Villa's way, but the earnings from the three games were sufficient to fund the £40,000 transfer fee that Leicester wanted for Steve Kember. Back at his original home, Kember was a vastly experienced asset among the Palace youngsters, even despite the cruel loss of striker Mike Elwiss, and the forfeiting of the club's place in the table. Palace continued to have the look of a promotion side, because, when the goals became more difficult to obtain the defence became virtually unbreachable, conceding just eight goals in the entire second half of the season.

All the promotion candidates had a tense run-in but, despite their relative lack of experience, Palace lived with the stress better than most and, with a game in hand because of a postponement, the issue became ever more clear. Palace needed a single point from their final fixture, against Burnley, to gain promotion – win, and they would go up as champions.

Such was the interest generated by the climactic match on the eve of the Cup Final that the Selhurst Park gates were locked a full hour before kick-off, although hundreds of fans found other, unofficial, means of entry into the ground, so that inevitably a record crowd of 51,482 was registered. And Palace did not disappoint them! With little under a quarter of an hour to go, Ian Walsh headed Palace in front, then Dave Swindlehurst doubled the lead just before the final whistle – and many of the huge crowd massed upon the pitch to accolade their favourites.

Particular heroes of the season were ever presents John Burridge and Kenny Sansom; central-defenders Jim Cannon and Billy Gilbert, who each missed a single game; and top scorer Dave Swindlehurst with 14 goals from his 40 appearances; however, all 18 players whom Terry Venables deployed during that season were superstars as far as Palace fans were concerned.

Palace Plunge

The next few years developed into an harrowing period for everyone at Palace, although they seemed to begin in positive fashion. During the summer of 1979, there arrived at Selhurst Park, each for record fees, former England captain Gerry Francis and then England B striker Mike Flanagan. By the end of September Palace were top of Division One following a magnificent 4–1 victory over Ipswich. Parts of the media dubbed Palace 'The team of the 80s', but, following a November home victory against Arsenal (1–0) and a 1–1 draw at Old Trafford, Palace's hopes began to dwindle.

Ultimately, Palace finished in 13th place in Division One, but the closing 10 games of 1979–80 had provided only one win, and 1980 saw the departure of Dave Swindlehurst in the spring to Derby, and Ian Evans in the autumn to Barnsley, while in August the transfer of Kenny Sansom to Arsenal in exchange for Clive Allen was quite breathtaking.

Two events crystallised 1980–81 for Palace fans. At Coventry on 6 September a perfectly legitimate 'goal' from Clive Allen failed to count because none of the officials saw the ball enter the net or rebound from the stanchion therein, so Palace ended up losing a game they had actually won, and then, in early-mid-October, rumours abounded of increasing rancour between manager Terry Venables and the Palace board. This culminated in the boss's departure for Queen's Park Rangers on 14 October.

With only two victories in 27 games from early November, Palace were certainties for relegation long before it became statistically sure a full month before the season ended, but by then Palace had come under new ownership, for Ron Noades and his small, go-ahead association took over the club on 26 January 1981. There followed frenetic activity: Dario Gradi became the club's fourth manager of that season, while players moved out and others came in at an astonishing rate as the new administration sought to pay off the debts it had inherited from the former board.

The 1981–82 season was always destined to be a difficult one for Crystal Palace, even in the second tier of domestic football. But, as events turned out, it actually became more traumatic than difficult. Palace found goalscoring a real problem that season – top scorer was October signing Kevin Mabbutt with eight goals from his 31 appearances – so it is not surprising that Palace were merely in mid-table by mid-November when Dario Gradi was dismissed as manager, with youth-team coach Steve Kember replacing him. In Steve's first match in charge, Palace won a demanding Football League Cup tie at First Division Sunderland with a goal netted by Jim Cannon just before the hour.

The highlight of that season was Palace's FA Cup run to the quarter-finals, where the opposition was Queen's Park Rangers on their artificial pitch at Loftus Road. Clive Allen, then of Rangers, netted the single goal three minutes before the end, and then he could have sparked a riot by taunting the Palace fans in his celebration.

Many fans hoped that Steve Kember would have the opportunity of leading Palace in 1982–83, but the club appointed Alan Mullery to the position instead. Regrettably, Alan's two years at Palace proved to be grievously unsatisfactory. The club were in the bottom half of the table from the end of October but, by the time of the last match, at home to Burnley, Palace could even have been relegated. However, in front of a crowd of nearly 23,000 (some three times the average), Palace won with an Ian Edwards' goal just after the hour and relief swept across Selhurst Park.

If Mullery's first season in charge was poor, then the 1983–84 campaign was worse. Palace spent most of the season on the fringes of the relegation battle, and it was not until the last-but-one home game that the club's security was guaranteed. Vince Hilaire played 40 League games for Palace, but he left in the summer to play in South Africa and then for Luton Town, and only the goalkeeper, Scottish international George Wood (Mullery's best signing for Palace), played in every game. After the dreadful season had ended, no one who followed Palace matters was at all surprised that Mullery was dismissed.

Coppell – Calm and in Control

After Palace's extraordinary three-day dalliance with Dave Bassett, Steve Coppell took charge on 4 June 1984 and, with former club captain Ian Evans as his assistant, ushered in an era of dedicated commitment to the club based upon firm leadership principles, but he informed his new employers soon after his arrival that promotion could not be achieved overnight and that patience would be a prerequisite of any progress.

Initially at least, Coppell possessed an uncanny ability to recognise footballing potential, even when it was in a raw state, and in the autumn of 1984 he signed striker Andy Gray from non-League Dulwich Hamlet. Gray made 21 appearances for Palace that season, and Coppell followed up that signing by later recruiting central-defender Ken O'Doherty and the versatile Tony Finnigan, both of whom developed into useful Palace performers in the League side.

Coppell and Palace found the 1984–85 season a steep learning experience, and the club's survival hinged upon two late April victories that were, to some extent at least, rather unexpected ones. The defence had been strengthened by the arrival of veteran, giant centre-half Micky Droy, while midfield dynamo Kevin Taylor proved a considerable asset.

Crystal Palace v Middlesbrough, 4 May 1985.

Promotion hopefuls Portsmouth were beaten in sodden conditions at Selhurst Park 2–1, then promotion favourites Blackburn fell at Ewood Park to an Alan Irvine far-post header from a Micky Droy flick-on after a rare Palace corner. Those two successes virtually secured the club's continued Second Division status, though Palace finished the season in 15th place.

Micky Droy was amenable to re-signing for the 1985–86 season, and with the addition of Steve Ketteridge Palace gained further steel for the midfield, but Steve Coppell signed another player from non-League ranks who subsequently became familiar to all football followers during his Palace, Arsenal and England career – Ian Wright.

Coppell himself was now firmly established in the fans' affections, and when Palace were drawn to meet his former club, Manchester United, over two legs in the League Cup second round, most of the fans were delighted for him. Palace inevitably lost both games, but many pundits were surprised by the narrowness of the margin both times, with each game finishing 1–0. However, that illustrious Cup tie was not the matter of lasting significance that season, rather it was the announcement by Charlton that they would be leaving The Valley and coming to share Selhurst Park as Palace's tenants in a unique ground-sharing agreement!

Palace fared much better in Division Two in the 1985–86 campaign, finishing in fifth place. Andy Gray topped the goalscoring charts with 10 League goals, while Ian Wright and Phil Barber hit nine apiece. Manager Coppell summed up Palace's improvement by saying that it was 'good, but not good enough'.

Hopes were high for the 1986–87 season, particularly after a 3–2 opening-day victory at Barnsley with a makeshift team, but Palace flattered to deceive and, even with the arrival of striker Mark Bright and central-defender Gary O'Reilly, the sixth-place finish was not sufficient to allow the club a place in the newly introduced Play-offs. As so often happens, Palace's goalscoring had simply not been frequent enough, particularly away from home. Strikers Ian Wright and Mark Bright notched eight goals each and so did Kevin Taylor, but Palace failed to score at all in over half the away games.

During the 1987–88 campaign the tally of goals was much more impressive: it rose to 86, mainly due to Mark Bright netting 24 times and Ian Wright 20. Features of that season were the arrivals of battling wide midfielder Neil Redfearn from Doncaster, and Geoff Thomas from Crewe for the start of the campaign and, during it, the replacements of goalkeeper George Wood by Perry Suckling, of Paul Brush by David Burke at left-back and of Andy Gray by Alan Pardew in midfield. A place in the Play-offs might have been possible after a 2–0 victory over Manchester City in the last game of the season, but it was snatched away by Blackburn on account of Rovers' emphatic and praiseworthy 4–1 win at Millwall.

A long-standing defender retired from Crystal Palace at the end of the term, Jim Cannon's magnificent career coming to an end after 571 League appearances for the club. Not only were Palace his only club, but it must also remain doubtful whether any subsequent club player will ever surpass Jim's wonderful career total.

For the 1988–89 season it was necessary for Steve Coppell to find a replacement for Jim Cannon, and he did so in Welsh international Jeff Hopkins, who signed from Fulham. Another valuable defender was John Pemberton, who had arrived from Crewe in time to make a couple of substitute appearances at the end of the previous season, while the signing of winger Eddie McGoldrick from Northampton proved popular and effective in January 1989.

Palace v Brighton, 27 March 1989.

However, the season was not without its setbacks in regard to personnel. Neil Redfearn's self-esteem had been offended when he was substituted in a couple of games in the autumn, and, after smouldering for several weeks, the matter was only concluded when he left the club for Watford in mid-November. Alex Dyer, Palace's nemesis at Hull 18 months earlier, was brought in to take over Redfearn's role, but Alex was unfortunate with injuries and Redfearn's ultimate successor turned out to be Eddie McGoldrick.

A further setback became evident when Geoff Thomas had to leave the action during the 30 December victory at Oldham, and the following month the skipper was admitted to hospital for an internal operation: it was clear that he would be out for the remainder of the season.

Despite Palace's goalscoring prowess now being acknowledged throughout football, but particularly in Division Two, and, of course, attempts being made to counter it, the efforts of Mark Bright and Ian Wright were sufficient to take Palace to third place in the table in 1988–89. Bright, in fact, played in every fixture and his 20 strikes, allied to Wright's 24, were the key factor in the club's success.

That said, Palace's eventual promotion was not secured until 3 June 1989 and was only made possible by a thrilling final third of the season. Following early-March defeats at Oxford (1–0) and at home to Bournemouth (3–2), Palace lay in 12th place – but only once Sunderland were beaten with a Mark Bright penalty on 18 March, did Palace slowly but inexorably climb the table.

The most memorable game during this sequence was the Easter Monday home match against Brighton (2–1). It made Football League history because, in bizarre fashion, referee Kelvin Morton bestowed no fewer than five penalties! Palace, already a goal to the good from Ian Wright, netted from the first award, while the Seagulls' reply inevitably came from their own spot-kick.

Ultimately, after winning three and drawing two of the last five games, Palace finished third and so entered the Play-offs, plus, they did so as the in-form side. The dismissal of Swindon in the semi-final was secured at Selhurst Park, where Mark Bright quickly nullified Town's single strike at the County Ground, and Ian Wright volleyed another eight minutes before half-time.

The Play-off Final – played over two legs for the last time – was against Blackburn. Although a 3–1 defeat at Ewood Park looked as if it might be a deficit too great to overturn, Palace had the majority of a near 30,000 crowd behind them and netted in each half, before scoring again in extra-time. Tumultuous delight broke out everywhere at Selhurst Park as the Palace fans once more celebrated the club's return to the top flight.

Coppell and Company Lead Palace to New Hights

Steve Coppell made early plans for Palace's top-flight season of 1989–90 by re-signing midfielder Andy Gray, but the feature of the League season was surely the 9–0 defeat at Liverpool on 12 September, in the fallout from which Palace purchased the nation's first £1 million goalkeeper, Nigel Martyn, along with defender Andy Thorn. The latter's Palace debut was at Manchester United on 9 December where Palace won 2–1. Andy himself netted the following Saturday when Palace were 'away' to Charlton (2–1) at Selhurst Park.

Palace's reinforced side slowly rose to First Division safety and finished in a creditable 15th place, even in the absence of Ian Wright with a twice-broken leg, but of course 1989–90 was the season in which Palace took part in the FA Cup Final. Revenge was taken upon Liverpool, who were defeated 4–3 after extra-time at Villa Park, Alan Pardew heading the winning goal early in the second period of extra-time in front of the ranks of excited and by now ecstatic Palace fans.

At Wembley, against Manchester United, Palace were again engaged in an extra-time thriller; though matters ended even at 3–3 Palace had led the Old Trafford giants twice, and substitute Ian Wright netted a glorious equaliser three minutes after coming on. The replay was different, however, being dour, tense and even. Until, that was, United scored the only goal on the hour after the referee had previously conferred a Palace free-kick when the marks on the turf clearly showed that Geoff Thomas had been fouled *inside* the penalty area!

The 1990–91 season produced Palace's best term ever. They finished third in the First Division and won a Wembley Cup Final! Adding his vast experience to Palace's defence was John Humphrey, while giant central-defender Eric Young was a Welsh international who stifled opposing strikers in fearsome fashion.

Highlights of Palace's superb League season were the single-goal victories over Liverpool on 30 December and at Nottingham Forest on 2 February, then the 2–1 success at Leeds on 23 March. As the season ended Ian Wright scored a glorious, artistic hat-trick at Wimbledon, and then Manchester United left Selhurst Park on the wrong end of a 3–0 scoreline.

Zenith Data Systems Cup-winners 1991.

But, of course, 1990–91 was also the season in which Palace won a Wembley Cup Final. The cup in question was the Zenith Data Systems Cup, played on a single-game, knock-out basis and, having gone so close to winning the FA Cup the previous May, there was probably little chance of Everton denying Palace that year; indeed, the match finished 4–1. Geoff Thomas opened Palace's account, Ian Wright again netted two Wembley goals and then John Salako rounded matters off with a header.

Stardom was beckoning for the two youngest members among the Palace Cup-winning side, John Salako and Richard Shaw, while Simon Osborn and Gareth Southgate made senior debuts towards the end of the momentous season.

Welsh Under-21 defender Chris Coleman joined Palace for the 1991–92 season, but the term marked the end of the Palace career of Ian Wright, who chose to join Arsenal in September, just two days after netting his last Palace goal at Oldham, having scored a Palace career total of 117 in all competitions. Marco Gabbiadini joined the club as Wright's replacement, but he left little more than four months later for a reduced fee.

Highlights of the 1991–92 season were undoubtedly Palace's 'double' over Liverpool, 2–1 at Anfield on 2 November then 1–0 at Selhurst Park on 14 March, while the Palace juniors reached the FA Youth Cup Final, where their opponents were Manchester United, the games finishing in 3–1 and 3–2 reverses for the Palace youths.

There was huge media coverage of the formation of the FA's Premier League in the summer of 1992; although, sadly, Palace's first involvement in it was to be the least possible because, despite opening 1992–93 with a fabulous 3–3 draw with cash-rich Blackburn Rovers, the term ultimately brought huge frustration for every Palace person and Steve Coppell's resignation as Palace manager.

Mark Bright was offered the transfer he had craved for a long time when Sheffield Wednesday tempted Palace with the diminutive Paul Williams plus cash in early September. However, eager, young Chris Armstrong, a former Millwall striker, at least partly replaced Palace's former goalscoring ace by hitting 15 League goals in the season.

Yet it was not long before experienced Palace fans realised that continued Premier League existence would be the most the club could hope for at the end of the season. Palace were not scoring enough goals, were missing penalty awards with disdain and were yielding goals to the opposition far too easily.

The only comfort was to be found in the League Cup. Liverpool boss Graeme Souness ranted and raged after Palace's 1–1 draw at Anfield in the competition, though his reaction after his costly troops lost the replay just prior to Christmas is not known! Chelsea were beaten in round five, but Arsenal beat Palace comfortably in both legs of the semi-final to put even those efforts into perspective.

In the finale, Palace needed a draw at Arsenal for Premier League continuance, but once Ian Wright had converted an early chance for the Gunners, the outlook was dire. Without looking entirely comfortable, Arsenal netted again 10 minutes from the end and once more right at the finish. There was no escape for Palace now as Oldham Athletic had won their last three games. Some of the team left the arena in tears, many fans departed Highbury saddened as well, and a few days later Steve Coppell decided that he should go too.

Alan Smith In Charge

Tall, voguish Alan Smith was the indisputable choice to take on the management of Crystal Palace FC in the summer of 1993. He had been Steve Coppell's assistant throughout Palace's top-flight seasons and he swiftly established the club's target for the 1993–94 campaign as an immediate return to the Premier League.

That aim was accomplished, by the final reckoning in majestic style, but it was not easily achieved. For example, Geoff Thomas and Eddie McGoldrick left Selhurst Park for Wolves and Arsenal respectively, and relegation implied that there was no money available to fund the purchase of replacements.

But Alan Smith's emphasis upon a more elegant style of play appealed to many fans, even though, to begin with, that response was dampened, for Palace could only draw 0–0 with visiting Tranmere on the opening day and then lost 2–0 at Bristol City. The club's riposte was immediate and stunningly effective, as they won the next five fixtures to go top of the table by mid-September. Palace were never out of the top four places in the remainder of the term and were never off the summit itself after Christmas.

However, Palace did need one extra spark to ensure a successful outcome to the season, and Alan Smith supplied it in the loan transfer of Paul Stewart, Liverpool's England international striker-midfielder at the end of February. Stewart was out of his class at the lower levels so that an ever-widening margin grew between Palace and their nearest rivals.

This progress was made despite the loss for the rest of the season of central-defender and experienced skipper Andy Thorn, from early in November with cartilage and hamstring problems. Gareth Southgate assumed the captaincy, Chris Coleman partnered Eric Young for the remainder of the campaign and Dean Gordon slotted in perfectly at left-back, so that Palace's defence was, statistically, the best in the division by far. Chris Armstrong proved himself highly capable at Second Division level too; he netted 23 League goals from his 43 appearances while Gareth Southgate included some glorious efforts in his tally of nine.

Crystal Palace v Middlesbrough, 1 May 1994.

By Easter it was apparent to everyone that Palace were promotion-bound, and a single-goal win at Luton on 16 April, netted by Chris Coleman in the opening minute, followed by a draw the next day between the club's two closest rivals, Millwall and Nottingham Forest, ensured that promotion was achieved. Naturally, the club's objective now was the title itself: another single-goal victory over dour, defensive, visiting Barnsley, meant that Palace had the chance to settle matters on Sunday 1 May when they met Middlesbrough at Ayresome Park in front of a nationwide TV audience. An efficient, organised display led to a 3–2 success and the title belonged to Palace!

The season finished on Sunday 8 May with Watford visiting Selhurst Park on the last day of the Holmesdale terracing. Before a packed capacity crowd the team was presented with the Dvision One trophy. However, the Hornets played bravely, sensibly and well, netting twice in the second half without reply. Nonetheless, Palace had achieved the stated aim of an immediate return to the top flight and had done so in fine style – as champions.

Although mitigated to some degree by two most praiseworthy Cup runs and a fabulous League victory over Arsenal at Highbury, Palace's 1994–95 season was a disappointing one because it ended in relegation, and the opening match of the term, against Liverpool at Selhurst Park (which was three-sided now, because of the redevelopment of the Holmesdale Road end), was perhaps a precursor of this because Palace lost 6–1, among the heaviest defeats borne by the club at any of their grounds.

Nevertheless, the Highbury victory on 1 October – Palace's first and only one there in the League – was immensely pleasing. John Salako, playing as a striker, was Arsenal's nemesis, netting both goals in Palace's 2–1 success.

During the second half of the season, Alan Smith bought Northern Ireland striker Iain Dowie and Eire midfielder Ray Houghton to Palace, and these two men certainly lifted the performances of the side. But even before the arrival of this pair, Palace had battled their way to a League Cup semi-final against Liverpool and only lost that two-legged duel by the finest margin on each occasion.

Then, despite Palace's lowly League placing, they viewed the FA Cup semi-final against Manchester United at Villa Park on 9 April with an augmented side and a quiet confidence. If anything Palace's fans were a little disappointed that their display had only earned a 2–2 draw and a replay the following Wednesday evening. However, Nigel Martyn had broken an index finger in the first game and would miss the replay, and several of the matches in the crucial run-in to the season.

Palace went down 2–0 in the replay but still had hopes of earning Premiership survival in their remaining eight League games. However, they were only able to win two of them, which meant that a victory at either Leeds or Newcastle in the final pair of matches was a necessity. Sadly, that proved beyond Palace and at the end of the season – the only one in which *four* teams have been relegated from the most senior English division – they went down along with Norwich, Leicester and Ipswich, while the club's relegation unavoidably led to the departure of manager Alan Smith.

Palace are Wembley Winners Again

The feature of the Crystal Palace story for the period between 1995 and 1997 is that those years brought the club two Wembley appearances – and, of course, Palace won one of them!

The new boss for the 1995–96 season was Ray Lewington, with Steve Coppell appointed as technical director, but these men had to draw on all of their vast experience to cope with and to stem the departures of the talented players in the wake of relegation.

With full-back Marc Edworthy arriving from Plymouth, then club-record signing Andy Roberts, a midfielder, coming from Millwall for £2.5 million and Scottish Under-21 star David Hopkin joining from Chelsea, it was very much a team in transition in the early part of the season.

Equally, the new Holmesdale Road stand was approaching completion. It had cost the club some £6 million, was available to the fans for the second home game of 1995–96 on 26 August when Charlton (1–1) were the visitors and was officially opened by chairman Ron Noades and Steve Coppell before the game.

The departures continued, however, and although Dougie Freedman arrived from Barnet in September 1995, it was only occasionally that Palace's constantly changing side played with any flair or conviction. Thus, in February 1996 another change in the managerial sturcture was announced, with Dave Bassett installed.

Dave's impact was not quite immediate, but within a month Palace had soared up the table and established themselves among the leading clubs, while the run-in proved irresistable entertainment for the club's fans, culminating in the drama and excitement of the Play-offs after a League finish of third place, a position Palace had occupied since mid-March.

The semi-final opponents were Charlton. Palace won 2–1 at The Valley despite conceding a first-minute goal, and then Ray Houghton netted in only the fourth minute of the second leg to put Palace through to the Wembley Final.

Pitted against Leicester on Bank Holiday Monday, 27 May 1996, this match went to extra-time for the third time in Palace's four visits to the famous stadium. Andy Roberts had put Palace in front in the first half, and Leicester had equalised with a second-half penalty. All but two seconds of the additional half hour had been played when heartbreak and disbelief struck the Palace players and fans, as former Palace reserve striker Steve Claridge volleyed the ball past Nigel Martyn, off his shin and via a deflection, to keep Palace anchored in the second tier of English football.

The major summer departure from Selhurst Park in 1996 was that of Nigel Martyn, the club's England goalkeeper, who moved to Leeds for a £2.5 million fee. Curiously, after the quietest close season many fans had ever known at the club, the next two moves were the arrivals of two goalkeepers, Carlo Nash from Clitheroe and Chris Day from Spurs. Then, just before the season got underway, Australian skipper Kevin Muscat signed for the club from South Melbourne.

After the early-season matches Palace were almost always in the top six places during the 1996–97 campaign. The highlight was unquestionably the 6–1 demolition of Reading at Elm Park on Carlo Nash's debut and, augmented by striker Neil Shipperley from Southampton, plus the return of Dean Gordon after a long lay-off necessitated by an Achilles tendon injury, Palace were among the more dependable promotion hopefuls, particularly once powerful defender Andy Linighan had arrived from Arsenal at the end of January.

Leeds United v Crystal Palace, 23 August 1997.

But, at this point, Palace fans were amazed and angered to learn of manager Dave Bassett's move to Nottingham Forest, although most were mollified by the announcement that Steve Coppell would return to the Palace helm, and he steadily guided the club to a sixth-place finish.

In the Play-offs for the second season running, Palace's semi-final pitted them against Wolves. At 1–0 with two minutes left in the Selhurst Park first leg, some fans had already left for home, but Dougie Freedman doubled Palace's lead, then Wolves responded before Freedman lobbed the 'keeper from 12 yards! Despite the unrestrained malevolence faced at Molineux the team coped well and, although Wolves won 2–1 on the night, Palace were on their way to Wembley once more.

This time, the final opponents were Sheffield United, who had done the double over Palace earlier in the season. Chances were few and, in the intense heat, set-pieces began to look the most dangerous openings. Then, in the 88th minute came the all-important moment. A glorious strike from some 22 yards from David Hopkin curled beyond the goalkeeper's reach and into the net to win the encounter for Palace.

Takeover and Administration

Palace's summer 1997 celebrations were marred for many fans by the continuous hearsay that David Hopkin, scorer of the promotion-winning goal that had defeated Sheffield United at Wembley in May, was eager to leave Selhurst Park. Finally, he did so and joined Leeds for a £3.5 million fee.

But there was exhilarating news to come: Palace were making an audacious attempt to secure the services of Attilio Lombardo. Eventually it was announced that the Serie A star was leaving Juventus to play for Palace! More mundane was the signing of goalkeeper Kevin Miller from Watford and of the unknown Icelandic central-defender Herman Hreidarsson.

Early in the season Palace fans heard of a new director named Mark Goldberg, whose plans for himself and for the club were ambitious in the extreme, and of whom much more will be heard. As the season progressed a reasonable Premier League start deteriorated and in January to March 1998 Palace lost no fewer than eight consecutive matches, meaning that they started sinking quickly towards the bottom of the table. It was after a 6–2 reverse at Chelsea that Steve Coppell stood down as manager, to be succeeded by...Attilio Lombardo! This was bizarre to say the least because, supreme footballing maestro though he undoubtedly was, Attilio could not speak English!

Palace were soon destined for relegation, although they had, at last, won at home when Derby were beaten 3–1 on 18 April; although, statistically, Palace's fate was sealed in a televised 3–0 defeat against Manchester United on 27 April, after which Ron Noades himself assumed the mantle of Palace manager.

Despite the goal scored by late substitute and debutant Clinton Morrison with his first touch, securing victory over visiting Sheffield Wednesday, and a double on 10 May in the final Premier League game, there was considerable chagrin for Palace fans. The club finished adrift of Everton in 17th place by a seven-point margin and had deployed an almost unbelievable total of 36 players in the 38 League matches. Eleven of them had been foreign and of them just two (Lombardo and Hreidarsson) had played in even half of the games.

It need only be added that Mark Goldberg's takeover of the club took place on 5 June 1998, and that outgoing chairman Ron Noades had become the second-longest serving chairman at the club behind only Sydney Bourne.

Mark Goldberg immediately appointed Terry Venables as head coach, and Terry himself swiftly purchased full-back Dean Austin from Spurs, but the new term began with a unique piece of Palace history, when they were engaged in a two-legged European Cup tie in the Intertoto Cup against Samsunspor of Turkey, although Palace unfortunately lost both games 2–0. However, this reverse was quickly forgotten because it was announced that Palace were in the process of securing the captain of China, 29-year-old defender-midfielder Fan Zhiyi, while his younger teammate Sun Jihai was also arriving for a trial. Both men became valued, if occasionally eccentric, members if the Palace team.

Inevitably, the season was extraordinary. Results varied enormously, players signed or left at a bewildering pace, some of the latter by their own choice and some because the deteriorating financial situation demanded it. Nevertheless, so dire was the position that in November 1998 a cull of personnel was necessary, and Terry Venables left the club along with his costly entourage.

Steve Coppell took over as manager (again!), but in March the club formally entered administration, several more players left, those remaining were advised of swingeing pay cuts and 46 members of Palace's administrative staff were made redundant. Yet there was considerable relief on the playing side, for a splendid six-week period of results either side of the entry into administration ensured that the club's status was not threatened. Most memorable of these was the single-goal victory gained at Norwich when over 2,000 Palace fans travelled to Carrow Road to cheer their team, which included four debutants and seven teenagers! Dean Austin netted the vital goal in the first quarter of an hour.

One last memory of that term deserves mention. The final game was at Queen's Park Rangers, for whom Palace central-defender Andy Linighan was appearing on loan. Andy came across the pitch at the end of the game to demonstrate his affinity with the Palace fans and his continuing commitment to the club.

The period in which Crystal Palace FC endured in the peculiar shadows of administration lasted throughout the entire 1999–2000 season, and its effects continued to be felt throughout the club at every level.

Palace chairman Mark Goldberg resigned during the first week of the new campaign and slowly disappeared from the club. He was replaced by the well-known and much-liked Peter Morley.

A poor opening to the season saw Palace bottom of Division One in mid-September, the lowest standing for precisely 15 years and a clear sign of the damage the club had suffered in its recent past. However, manager Steve Coppell had become a shrewd wielder of the loan-transfer market, as well as an exceptional stimulator of his players, and he used both characteristics in stunning fashion to ensure that the club retained its status at the end of the season. Thus, with regard to loan transfers, experienced former Wimbledon defender Terry Phelan spent the winter months at Palace, while Ashley Cole, then of Arsenal and later Chelsea and England, was with the club for the final three months and scored one wonderful goal in his 14 games. Mikael Forssell, an 18-year-old Finnish international striker, came from Chelsea, played 13 games and netted three priceless goals.

Two experienced defenders were key features of Palace's eventual survival in Division One: Dean Austin, who became captain after Simon Rodger was injured, and Player of the Year Andy Linighan. Both missed only one game all season. Meanwhile, rising midfield star Hayden Mullins usually looked a class above his First Division opponents, while among his vital League goals was a glorious volley at Walsall that many fans rated as Palace's best strike of the season.

Off the park there was a sublime attempt made by a group of Palace fans to raise funds, to help, if necessary, to buy Palace out of administration. Calling themselves 'The Crystal Palace Supporters' Trust', and firmly headed by Steve Coppell, this marvellous initiative was the product of Richard House, Paul Newman, Jim Piddock and Ray Bateup.

At last, in the 16th month of administration, a bidder to the club emerged in the person of Simon Jordan, and on 5 July 2000 it was announced that Jordan would head a new company called 'Crystal Palace 2000' and buy the club out of the murky shadows of administration.

The New Era

Among several summer 2000 signings at Crystal Palace was that of young striker Mikael Forssell, on loan from Chelsea for the whole season, and playing alongside Clinton Morrison the pair netted a total of 34 League and Cup goals for Palace.

Important as that signing was, it was not the major news of the close season at Palace: with 11 days before the opening of the new 2000–01 season, Steve Coppell renounced his managerial position at the club and, as in 1993, he was replaced by Alan Smith. Alan made sundry aquisitions for the club but, without doubt, his most significant one was to bring about the return to Selhurst Park of Dougie Freedman in October. As the season progressed it became profusely clear that it was rescued from calamity by this move.

The amazing fact, however, is that, despite Dougie being ineligible from appearing for Palace in the League Cup competition, the club secured impressive victories over Premiership opponents to earn a third semi-final under this auspicies. Palace's last-four opponents were Liverpool and in the first leg at Selhurst Park Palace produced the best performence of Smith's second managerial tenure with the club. Liverpool, five times winners of the League Cup and expecting to be so again, paid a heavy price for some poor finishing by Michael Owen and Emile Heskey, while Palace themselves netted two outstanding goals through Andrejs Rubins and Clinton Morrison and, although Liverpool quickly reduced their arrears, they were unable to score again and left Selhurst Park embarrassed and angry.

However, Palace's season tapered away after this uplifting success: they were knocked out of the FA Cup, routed at Anfield, then slid down the divisional table, even after the return of another former Palace favourite, David Hopkin. A dreadful performance in the final home game, a 2–0 defeat by Wolves, brought about the dismissal of Alan Smith, with Steve Kember made responsible for securing victories at both the two, difficult, remaining matches, at Portsmouth and Stockport.

The first was accomplished in brilliant style (4–2), but at Edgeley Park Palace left matters unbearably late. It was in the 87th minute that Dougie Freedman thrashed home a rising drive from 10 yards following a typical neat, controlled, incisive run – and Palace retained Division One status at the end of their new chairman's first season.

While many Palace fans would probably have been pleased by the appointment of Steve Kember as the club's manager for the 2001–02 season after his brilliant leadership of the quest for survival at the end of the previous term, it was Steve Bruce, the former Huddersfield and Sheffield United boss, who was installed.

It must be admitted, too, that Bruce's tenure was a successful one because, although he was only in charge at Selhurst Park until early November, the results achieved under him were enough to settle the club within the leading two or three in the division, those results including a run of seven consecutive wins. But then there came a thoroughly disgraceful episode, when Bruce sought to resign his position in order to take up the post at Palace's divisional rivals Birmingham City. Chairman Simon Jordan declined to allow this, stating categorically that Bruce must abide by his contract. After a period of stalemate Palace appointed the former Birmingham manager, vastly experienced Trevor Francis, who was accorded an appreciative 'welcome back' when Palace travelled to St Andrew's in mid-December.

Palace actually secured their best win of the entire season, given the calibre of the opposition, when champions-elect Manchester City were beaten 2–1 at Selhurst Park in Francis' second match in control. In general, however, the second half of the season was disappointing for Palace fans. Many readers will recall the return of Steve Bruce to Selhurst Park on Easter Monday 1 April 2002 and the disparaging reception he received as Palace and Birmingham battled out a 0–0 draw, Bruce fleeing to the dressing room at the final whistle to avoid any further indignity.

Portsmouth v Crystal Palace, 2 May 2001.

Palace finished the 2001–02 campaign in 10th place, while Bruce's Birmingham gained promotion via the Play-offs after finishing fifth.

Trevor Francis secured defender Danny Butterfield from Grimsby, while striker Andy Johnson came from Birmingham in the 2002 close season as part of the deal which took Clinton Morrison to St Andrew's. Midfielder Shaun Derry and central-defender Darren Powell had skippered Portsmouth and Brentford respectively.

A fabulous feature of the early part of the following season was a magnificent sequence of goalscoring by Andy Johnson, whose 10 strikes in five games – Palace's best post-war effort, eclipsing even Cam Burgess' feat of 50 years previously – and then nine goals in nine games by former Arsenal winger-midfielder Tommy Black. As the term progressed, however, it was Black's ex-Highbury teammate Julian Gray, on Palace's left wing, who began to take the plaudits. Nowhere was this better witnessed than in Palace's fourth-round FA Cup tie against Liverpool. The Reds had drawn 0–0 at Selhurst Park to take the tie to Anfield, where Gray unleashed a 55th-minute volley past Jerzy Dudek, right in front of the Kop! Then, in the 79th minute, he climaxed a wonderful left-side run with a cross that so bewildered big Swiss defender Stephane Henchoz, that he could do no more than deflect the ball into his own net. In round five it was also Gray who equalised Leeds' opening goal with a spectacular volley that ripped into the Whitehorse Lane goal past the bemused and helpless Leeds and England goalkeeper, Paul Robinson.

Sadly, as in 2001–02, the second half of the Palace's 2002–03 League campaign offered little for the loyal supporters to enthuse about, and Palace could finish no higher than 14th in Division One. It was not until late March 2003 after the turn of the year that Palace won a home game, so it was no surprise when the chairman's composure gave way just before

Easter. Trevor Francis left the club and Steve Kember led Palace through the remaining few matches of the term.

It is difficult to think of more than half a dozen men who contributed more to the club as a player than Steve Kember but, even allowing for the amazing escape from relegation that he fashioned for Palace at the close of 2000–01, Steve's talents were not particularly suited to management. This was, regrettably, all too apparent in the first half of 2003–04 after Steve had been appointed as Palace boss during May 2003.

Palace certainly started the term in fine style. A 3–2 win at Burnley in intense heat was followed by a muted 1–0 midweek success over Watford, then a 3–1 win at Wimbledon took Steve's Palace to the top of the table, but the same season fell away from that point and Kember was dismissed in early November following a dreadful 5–0 defeat at Wigan which left the club in 20th place. Under the temporary charge of Kit Symons, Palace achieved a mixed bag of League results and Simon Jordan appointed former striker Iain Dowie a day or two before Christmas.

Iain's first match as Palace manager was a home defeat by Millwall on Boxing Day, but Dowie soon transformed the term from a tussle to avoid relegation into a surge for promotion via the Play-offs. Stunning home and away successes were recorded, morale became high and Palace became clearly the best side in the division.

The transformation came about mainly because of Julian Gray's availability after an unfruitful bid to earn himself a Premier League contract; Dowie's preference for experienced left-back Danny Granville; and the loan signing of Fulham's central-defender Mark Hudson.

Crystal Palace's Play-off semi-final opponents were third-placed Sunderland. Palace had beaten the Wearsiders 3–0 three weeks previously, so accordingly they played a most cautious first half, before netting from the penalty spot soon after the break. Palace levelled quickly, then went ahead. A goal apiece in the closing minutes enabled Palace to take a narrow lead into the second leg at the Stadium of Light, but the home side scored twice without reply – until, that is, Darren Powell crashed in a late aggregate-levelling header! Extra-time was unable to separate the sides, but Palace proved the more reliable in the deciding penalty shoot-out and Michael Hughes sent them through to the Final in Cardiff.

London rivals West Ham were managed by Palace's former star Alan Pardew, but Palace were quite unyielding and settled matters with an easy touch from Neil Shipperley after the Hammers' goalkeeper, Stephen Bywater, had been unable to hold a fierce drive from Andy Johnson.

The club and its fans were euphoric throughout the summer of 2004 ahead of another top-flight adventure, but most of manager Dowie's close-season signings were unknown to fans of the club. Best among them was Fitz Hall, a central-defender from Southampton, and goalkeeper Gabor Kiraly from Hertha Berlin, who, in his droopy tracksuit bottoms, became an adept – if occasionally capricious – Premier League custodian.

Palace's top player of the season was undoubtedly Andy Johnson, who was the club's leading scorer with a tally of 21 League goals. But Palace always found the 2004–05 Premier League campaign tough going, though they sometimes surprised even the best sides – for example, Palace came close to beating Arsenal at Selhurst Park. But, apart from another victory over Liverpool (1–0) at Selhurst Park near the end of April, the club faced the last game, at Charlton on Sunday 15 May, needing to win to have some chance of survival. Palace came from behind to lead through Dougie Freedman and an Andy Johnson penalty, only for a late defensive lapse to present Charlton with an equaliser. Thus, West Bromwich Albion survived and Palace went back down to the Championship with Norwich and Southampton.

Play-off Palace

Plotting an immediate return to the Premiership, manager Iain Dowie used the cash he received from Tottenham for the precocious talents of Wayne Routledge to fund the arrivals of winger Jobi McAnuff from Cardiff, central-defender Darren Ward from Millwall and striker Jon Macken from Manchester City, but Palace were slow starters in the 2005–06 season, gaining a single point from the opening three games.

Celebrating the club's centenary throughout this term, Palace improved sufficiently to gain fifth place by mid-October following consecutive victories at home to Sheffield Wednesday (2–0) and then at Queen's Park Rangers (3–1) and Coventry (4–1). Palace were subsequently seldom out of the running for a place among the Play-off contenders, though the club proved unable to match the pace set by the leading pair, Reading and Sheffield United.

Consistency was always a problem area for Palace. To the woe of the fans Palace lost at home to bitter rivals Brighton (1–0), but nevertheless they managed a by-now expected Selhurst Park victory over European champions Liverpool (2–1) in the League Cup. Palace led through a Dougie Freedman header and, though Liverpool were quickly on terms through Steven Gerrard, Palace won the tie with a goal netted by German star Marco Reich just after the hour.

Despite winning only one of the last five League games, Palace concluded the 2005–06 season in sixth place and thus met Watford in the Play-off semi-final. However, the Hornets netted three second-half goals without a reply to make the second leg at their headquarters a formality, before going on to gain promotion at the Millennium Stadium.

Summer 2006 was marred at The Palace by the early close-season departure, 'by mutual consent', of manager Iain Dowie, who allegedly wished to be closer to his home in the North West. Many fans rued Dowie's going, but when it emerged, little more than a week later, that he was to become the boss at Charlton, the Palace chairman Simon Jordan was furious and set in motion a claim for damages against his former manager.

Although linked with Graeme Souness, Palace soon appointed former player, and 1970s fans' favourite, Peter Taylor to the managerial vacancy. Peter arrived to boundless goodwill from Palace fans and with a burgeoning reputation gained from his spells in charge at Southend, Hull and the England Under-21s.

Missing from the players available to him, however, were Andy Johnson, who joined Everton for £8.5 million, Fitz Hall and Player of the Year Emmerson Boyce, who both linked up with Wigan, but Taylor moved to secure his former central-defender at Hull, Leon Cort. Also signed were forward James Scowcroft from Coventry and midfielders Mark Kennedy from Wolves and Carl Fletcher from West Ham. Fletcher was immediately made club captain.

Taylor's Palace began the season well. Three consecutive victories at Ipswich (2–1), then at Selhurst Park over Southend (3–1) and Leeds (1–0), actually put Palace top of the table, but they then faltered, dropped to midtable, lost at home to League Two side Notts County 2–1 in the League Cup and then found themselves floundering in the lower reaches, on the fringe of the relegation places by November.

An interesting signing occured late on 31 August 2006, when Palace secured burly, strong Shefki Kuqi, a Finnish striker from Blackburn. Dubbed 'The Flying Finn' on account of his acrobatic goalscoring celebrations, Shefki only netted seven times in 35 League appearances that season and rarely looked like a quality player in Palace colours.

In some quarters supporter satisfaction with Palace's performances and League position fell to a low ebb, but chairman Simon Jordan publicly backed Peter Taylor and the playing staff. Matters slowly improved and Palace edged away from trouble into the more tranquil mid-table areas of the Championship, but the team never looked capable of improving upon that and finished in a disappointing 12th place.

Palace began the 2007–08 season with a fine 4–1 victory at Southampton, but a run of nine games for just one victory saw the club slump to 19th place by early October and brought about the departure of Peter Taylor. Replacing him as the Palace manager was the greatly experienced Neil Warnock.

Warnock watched his new charges slip even further down the table, to next-to-bottom place, but against Watford on 29 October 2007 he introduced the youngest-ever Palace debutant in John Bostock (aged 15 years and 287 days) and the club's season turned for the better at that point. Palace climbed the table to fifth place before a last-minute goal brought defeat at Leicester on 28 January 2008, but the Eagles finished the campaign in fifth place following a 5–0 thrashing of visiting Burnley on the last day of the season.

The Play-off opponents were Bristol City, but the West Country men stunned the Palace faithful by gaining a 2–1 victory at Selhurst Park in the first leg and, although they drew level on aggregate at Ashton Gate, Palace ultimately went down 4–2 over the two games.

In contrast, the 2008–09 season was considerably less lustrous, despite the arrival of Bristol City midfielder Nick Carle and Charlton's central-defender Paddy McCarthy.

Perhaps driven by The Eagles' customary early exit from the League Cup, striker Craig Beattie was signed on loan from West Bromwich Albion and returned a praiseworthy five goals for the club before he was recalled to The Hawthorns. Also enjoying his most productive spell in Palace colours at that stage was Finnish striker Shefki Kuqi. Thus, by the turn of the year Palace were well placed but, with Ben Watson transferred to Premier League club Wigan and Paddy McCarthy injured, the team's performances and results began to fade.

A top-half position was temporarily restored with a fine 3–1 victory in a rearranged fixture at Plymouth in mid-February, but it took five more games before Palace could record another goal, let alone a victory (over visiting Play-off contenders Preston, who were managed by former Palace winger Alan Irvine), and by this time (7 March) it was apparent that any prospects Palace may have entertained had largely drained away. The fixture list then required Palace to fulfil three tough, consecutive away fixtures within seven days: perhaps inevitably Palace were only able to take points from one of them, but manager Neil Warnock admitted that already his thoughts and plans were geared towards the prospects for the following 2009–10 season.

Thus, unusually, Palace were not involved in either a relegation battle or a chase for promotion as the 2008–09 campaign drew to an end, but the fans enjoyed the emergence of youthful prospects, particularly full-backs Lee Hills and Nathaniel Clyne and wingers Victor

Moses, Sean Scannell and Keiron Cadogan, who netted a splendid goal on his senior debut against Coventry in early April.

Under this duo, Palace secured crucial home victories over fellow relegation candidates Preston and Middlesbrough, the over promotion hopefuls Cardiff City.

However, 2009–10 proved to be a far-from-positive season for Crystal Palace FC, and there was an infamous portent of the difficulties the club would face when, playing their first away game, at Bristol City, a perfectly sound goal by Freddie Sears (on loan from West Ham) was disallowed – because the referee had failed to notice the fact that the ball had entered the Robins' net! A little later in the term The Eagles lost 4–0 at home to Scunthorpe, then a praiseworthy run of 12 matches for only one defeat (at Leicester) shuddered to a halt when Doncaster Rovers won 3–0 at Selhurst Park in early December.

Financially, too, the club endured some bleak moments. Among the worst of these was in December 2009 when the HMRC placed a winding-up order on the club for tax owed to them. Some funds were raised by the sale of defender Jose Fonte to Southampton for £1.2 million, but at the end of January 2010 the club was plunged into administration by hedge fund Agilo (to whom many millions of pounds were owed by Crystal Palace FC), with Brendan Guilfoyle of the P and A Partnership appointed as administrator and the now-mandatory 10-point deduction applied to the club's playing record. Simon Jordan himself departed soon after the club's status was demeaned, again, by administration.

The highlight of the club's playing season was a fourth-round FA Cup victory on 2 February 2010 over Premiership Wolves at Selhurst Park when Danny Butterfield registered a stunning six-minute hat-trick. Palace almost gained another top-flight scalp in round five when, but for another dreadful refereeing abberation, Aston Villa would have been knocked out at Selhurst Park. Instead, they salvaged a late equaliser and won the replay 3–1.

In the Championship, following the 1–1 draw at Doncaster at the end of February, Neil Warnock left the club to manage Queen's Park Rangers. Experienced manager Paul Hart was appointed, assisted by former Palace favourites Dougie Freedman and John Pemberton, to steer the club through the remainder of the season and to survival in the Championship. This was ultimately secured by virtue of a 2–2 draw in the final, televised, match of the season, at Sheffield Wednesday on Sunday 2 May 2010.

However, there was a further cliff-hanger for the fans as the legalities and monetary matters surrounding the club's ownership and that of Selhurst Park were tackled. At the end of May some 29 non-playing members of the club staff were made redundant, and the administrator threatened to begin the process of liquidating the club if the purchase of Selhurst Park was not agreed by 1 June. As the news of this circulated, some fans gathered at the ground to protest (peaceably, if occasionally volubly), and on 1 June itself rather more supporters (estimated at about 250 in number) demonstrated, again peacefully, outside the City headquarters of Lloyds Bank, where a crucial meeting was being held between the bank and the consortium. It came as no surprise that it was at least an hour after the publicised deadline of 3pm that it was at last announced that a deal had been struck whereby Crystal Palace 2010 would purchase Selhurst Park.

George Burley, a hugely experienced manager, was appointed to take charge of the Palace (again assisted by Dougie Freedman) as soon as the club had been lifted out of administration

Crystal Palace v Sheffield Wednesday, 2 May 2010.

by the new consortium, headed by co-chairmen Steve Parish and Martin Long, but comprising only four members. Mr Burley's tenure as the Palace boss lasted little more than six months, however, for he was dismissed immediately after a 3–0 humiliation on New Year's Day at Millwall.

Palace secured the services of veteran former Holland midfielder Edgar Davids on a pay-as-you-play basis early in the 2010–11 term, but Edgar made little impression, and Palace were immersed in the relegation struggle as the year drew to its close.

Chris Hughton, Steve Coppell himself and (then) Bournemouth boss Eddie Howe were all linked with Palace's managerial vacancy, but late on Tuesday 11 January 2011 former favourite Dougie Freedman stepped up from his position as assistant manager, accepted the vacant post and signed a two-and-a-half-year contract.

In mid-January 2011 it was reported that the club was considering a move to the Crystal Palace Sports Ground Centre, but of more immediate interest was the appointment, at Dougie Freedman's request, of vastly experienced manager Lennie Lawrence as Palace's assistant manager.

Under this duo, Palace secured crucial home victories over fellow relegation candidates Preston and Middlesbrough, then over promotion hopefuls Cardiff City and mid-table Barnsley, but relegation-threatened Scunthorpe closed to within three points of The Eagles by winning a mid-April clash at Selhurst Park.

Palace responded well by drawing at Doncaster on Good Friday and then dismissed Play-off aspirants, powerful Leeds United on Easter Monday before the club's biggest attendance of the season. This success ensured Palace's Championship survival in all but a purely statistical sense, but, requiring a single point for complete assurance, a praiseworthy draw was secured at Hull on the penultimate Saturday of the season. Meanwhile, Scunthorpe lost and Sheffield United's home draw meant that they would both be joining Preston in the relegation places in the Championship's final table.

Thus, Palace finished 2010–11 in 20th place, six points ahead of the demoted trio though with a vastly superior goal difference, although, unusually, not involved in the promotion or relegation issues in any way.

Crystal Palace FC Grounds

The Crystal Palace (1905–15)

The Crystal Palace itself had been originally built to house the 1851 Great Exhibition, but Prince Albert's brainchild had to leave its Hyde Park location and architect Joseph Paxton eventually settled upon a new site upon one of the highest points in South London; on the ridge which runs from Sydenham Hill along to Upper Norwood.

The extended building was opened by Queen Victoria on 10 June 1854 and was a privately-run concern until 1920 when it was 'purchased for the nation', but on 30 November 1936 the entire property burned down in a spectacular fire. The water towers at each end of the structure survived, but these were demolished during World War Two to prevent enemy bombers using them as navigational aids.

Served by two railway stations (the higher level one has long since closed), the Palace was one of London's greatest attractions and became the centre for all kinds of sporting activities. It was due to these sporting events, including spectacular FA Cup Finals and England international matches, which were hosted at the Crystal Palace Exhibition Ground from 1895, that 10 years later a club was formed to play at the enormously prestigious venue. In fact, it must be doubtful whether there has ever been a British club that has played at such a stunningly impressive home

Postcard of the aerial view of the Crystal Palace grounds with the main (or Exhibition) ground to the left and part of the North (or Cycle Track) ground to the right.

ground before modern super-stadia, with Glasgow outfit Queens Park, who play at Hampden Park usually in front of three-figure crowds, the only possible challengers.

Crystal Palace FC played at the Crystal Palace from their 1905 foundation until early 1915. It was a successful stage for the club as they were elected to the Southern League, which was followed by progression into Division One in 1906, and Palace finished their final full season at the ground (1913–14) as Southern League runners-up on goal average, having twice previously reached fourth place. They also gained several fine FA Cup successes over Football League opponents while based at the Crystal Palace Exhibition Ground.

Palace's first match at their initial home was their opening Southern League fixture, a 4–3 defeat by Southampton Reserves on 2 September 1905, while their last game at the ground as the home team was a 4–1 victory over Reading on 6 February 1915; however, Palace did play three friendly matches at the ground as the visitors against The Corinthians, after the amateurs had adopted it as their home in the 1920s. In the late 1960s Palace visited the Crystal Palace Sports Centre, which had been built over part of the old structure. The club took part in the inaugural fixture at the Centre on 19 August 1964 against West Ham and played further pre-season games there in 1965, 1968, 1969 and 1970.

Crystal Palace FC had to leave the Crystal Palace in February 1915 after the Admiralty had requisitioned it to serve as a recruitment and training centre for Royal Navy volunteers. The remaining home fixtures for 1914–15 were completed at Herne Hill.

Herne Hill (1915–18)

Banished from their original home in February 1915, Crystal Palace FC sought urgently to find what they initially thought would be a temporary accomodation. The club was offered the opportunity to fulfil their seven outstanding home fixtures of the 1914–15 season by several other Southern League clubs, but they chose instead to move to a rather less well-known ground at Herne Hill. It was the base of the distinguished amateur club West Norwood and had been the venue for the 1911 Amateur Cup Final in which Bromley beat Bishop Auckland with a goal netted by inside-right R.W. Dilley. Palace's first opponents there were Southampton on Wednesday 3 March 1915, who won the match 2–1.

The Herne Hill ground had been built in 1891 as a cycle-racing track, or velodrome, and it remains as such to this day. There is a small grandstand (at the time of writing it is still there), and in the centre of the racing circuit was the football pitch. The combined effect of World War One, the ground's distance from the majority of the club's supporters and the absence of most of Palace's players, who were now engaged in the Services or in other war work, all combined to suppress Palace's attendances at Herne Hill (although Spurs managed to draw an estimated 10,000 gate in

Herne Hill.

April 1916 and Arsenal some 7,000 in October the following year). The club's low attendances were despite the fact that the Football and Southern League clubs in the metropolis had formed a London Combination for the duration of the hostilities.

One curious and little-known feature of wartime football applied while Palace were at Herne Hill: it was decided in December 1915 that fixtures staged between mid-November and mid-January should be restricted to 80 minutes' duration and that the referee could dispense with the half-time interval.

Taken overall, Palace fared creditably enough in the three full wartime seasons in which they played at Herne Hill. In 1915–16 they finished ninth among the 12 competing clubs in the main competition and sixth in a shorter, supplementary one. In the augmented London Combination of 1916–17 Palace were eight, and they improved upon that by one place in 1917–18.

The Nest (1918–24)

The best news that Crystal Palace FC received during the first four years of World War One was that there was a new home awaiting them – The Nest at Selhurst. The club moved there in the summer of 1918, and for six seasons it served the club admirably and proved advantageous in several respects.

The Nest was located on the site of the present-day railway carrige depot opposite Selhurst Station. It had been erected on land that was the property of the Church Commissioners in *c.*1900. It became the home of the local side Croydon Common in 1908 and, since Croydon's strip consisted of red shirts and white shorts and they carried the nickname of 'The Robins', it was no surprise that their ground became known, quite

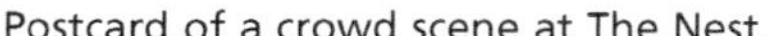
Postcard of a crowd scene at The Nest.

mockingly, as 'The Nest'. Croydon Common died as a club in 1916 and The Nest remained unused until Crystal Palace took out a sub-lease from the London, Brighton and South Coast Railway (who leased the land from the Church Commissioners) and fulfilled the final World War One season of 1918–19 at their new home.

Palace's first home fixture at The Nest was the 31 August 1918 charity match in aid of local hospitals, which was played against Millwall. The Mayor of Croydon, Alderman Howard Houlder, welcomed the teams and kicked-off. Millwall opened the scoring but Palace replied strongly and won 4–1.

There was an unusual feature relating to Palace's time at The Nest: it was insisted upon by the owners that no games be played on the ground on Good Friday or Christmas Day (on both of which days, at that time, there was a full fixture list). Southern League and Football League pairings appeared to take this requirement into account, although in 1923 and 1924 the restriction had either lapsed or was relaxed in the club's favour, because Palace played (and lost) Division Two home games at The Nest on Good Friday in both those years.

When Palace took over The Nest the venue was described as 'a small ground with a 200-seater stand on one side and mounds of earth to stand upon at the other side, with a ditch at the back touching the railway line.' There were no terraces or bars to prevent crushing, and there was only one means of entry or exit, which was opposite the railway station entrance; although extra turnstiles were put in during the 1919 close season. Railings were erected around the playing pitch during 1920–21 (possibly after the incursion of an angry crowd during a game against Southend), and after Palace had taken the Division Three title 'considerable' further improvements were made. Still, a number of Second Division outfits objected to the level of accommodation and facilities at The Nest, and these would not have been improved upon in any way by a fire in the (so-called) grandstand during a London Challenge Cup match against Charlton (2–1) on Monday 31 October 1921, or by the smoke generated by the nearby railway shunting engines!

Nevertheless, and unlike Herne Hill, The Nest proved to be a happy and successful home for Crystal Palace FC. Initially, the move to Selhurst certainly enlarged both the area and the numbers of supporters because, no doubt, some, perhaps many, former Croydon Common adherents changed their loyalty to their new local team, and with Selhurst so easily reached from Croydon and the towns of northern Surrey, the club's attendances at The Nest and, later, Selhurst Park were well in advance of clubs with better or more successful sides for several subsequent decades.

Equally, Palace made substantial progress while based at The Nest. The club gained entry to the Football League while they were based there and then gained promotion to Division Two, while the tight, modest little ground was the perfect place to launch giant-killing feats against prestigious clubs in Cup competitions. Indeed, Palace fans, both new and those of nearly 20 years' standing, saw top-flight Tottenham and Manchester City humbled at The Nest and saw the club reach the Final of four consecutive London Challenge Cup competitions, winning it in 1921.

The final game played by Palace at The Nest was the Division Two fixture against Barnsley which was won 3–1 on Saturday 3 May 1924.

Aerial view of Selhurst Road showing former ground of The Nest.
(by permission of Croydon Local Studies Library)

Selhurst Park (1924 to date)

Somewhat astonishingly, perhaps, Selhurst Park used to be a brickfield! There were, in fact, two great chimney stacks on the site of today's playing pitch. Palace purchased the field for some £2,750 during 1922 and the stadium was built by Messrs Humphreys of Knightsbridge to the specifications of Mr Archibald Leitch, who was probably the top designer of football grounds at that time. Regrettably, however, the work on the stand was delayed by a strike and was therefore incomplete, with some seats and other fittings missing, when the new ground was formally opened before the club's initial fixture of 1924–25 when The Wednesday from Sheffield were the visitors on 30 August 1924.

Selhurst Park was opened by the Lord Mayor of London, Sir Louis Newton, who was joined by Palace's chairman, Mr Sydney Bourne, and president, Mr F.J. Nettlefold, the latter having provided some £24,000 towards the expense of building the ground (and remitting that whole enormous debt some 10 years later).

There could scarcely have been more illustrious opponents for this important occasion than The Wednesday, whose side boasted many present or future international stars and, in one sense, it was no suprise that the visitors won the game with a goal netted by their inside-right Joe Marsden after only four minutes' play.

It was regrettable that the Wednesday defeat should be a precursor to relegation, although it should be acknowledged that such an outcome appeared most unlikely midway through the season. But by the time of Palace's final match of the 1924–25 season, against Oldham Athletic at Selhurst Park, it was necessary for the home side to win, as failure to do so would require the club to forfeit their Second Division status. It proved beyond Palace's capabilities. Thus, the club's first term at Selhurst Park ended in bitter disappointment for everyone connected with Crystal Palace FC. The club's programme editor of the day declared that 'it would be a calamity' if the club was relegated, and there are few who would say that he had overstated the matter for it took Palace a full 39 years to bring Second Division football back to Selhurst Park.

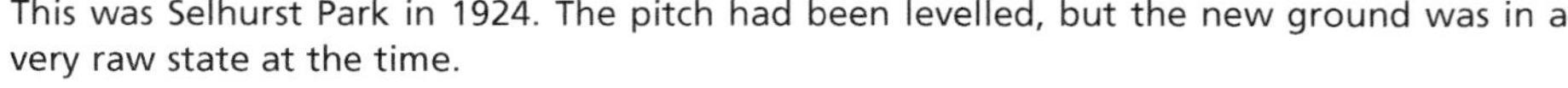

This was Selhurst Park in 1924. The pitch had been levelled, but the new ground was in a very raw state at the time.

Aerial view of Selhurst Park soon after its opening in 1924.
(by permission of Croydon Local Studies Library

The FA had promised Crystal Palace that the club would be awarded a full English international to stage after Selhurst Park was opened, and the pledge was honoured on St David's Day, 1 March 1926, when the ground hosted the England versus Wales (1–3) match in the home international tournament. To this day, that fixture remains the most distinguished one ever to have been played at Selhurst Park. Palace have also hosted two England Under-23 games, however, in October 1974 and November 1975, as well as a European Youth Championship quarter-final in 1983; several amateur international games, including two matches in the 1948 Olympic Games; Amateur Cup Finals and semi-finals, plus the 1951 replay; the 1957 annual contest between the regional Third Divisions; and the 1987 Third Division Play-off replay. During the war, forces representative fixtures, where the teams frequently included current international and other illustrious players, were played at Selhurst Park, while the Palace club themselves have hosted prestigious friendly games at the ground on occasions, the most significant of which was when Real Madrid provided the opposition on 18 April 1962.

Apart from minor repairs and the most modest of improvements, that fabric of Selhurst Park remained unaltered for nearly 30 years following its opening, but in the summer of 1953 the first floodlighting system was set up, with four bunches of 12 lamps each erected along the top of the main stand and four more perched at the top of poles erected for the purpose along the open enclosure opposite (where the Arthur Wait Stand is currently situated), with electricity cables looped and hanging between them. These initial lights were opened by club chairman David Harris before an inaugural friendly fixture against First Division Chelsea (2–2) on Monday 28 September 1953.

During the close season of 1961, after Palace had gained promotion to Division Three, a new, much better floodlighting system was put in at Selhurst Park with the greater number of lamps now erected on four pylons, one in each corner of the ground. Two friendly matches against top-class Continental opposition, which greatly appealed to the fans, were arranged to proclaim the new advance. Accordingly, Bratislava of Czechoslovakia were Palace's guests on Wednesday 31 January 1962 (3–2) and then, on Wednesday 18 April 1962, the club was host to the illustrious Real Madrid, who triumphed 4–3.

Naturally, Palace's lighting arrangements at Selhurst Park have been improved and updated over the years. For example, the pylons at the Whitehorse Lane end of the ground were repositioned during the summer of 1980 in order to accomodate the Sainsburys development.

In terms of facilities for supporters, Selhurst Park was in no way improved until Palace gained top-flight status in 1969 when the Arthur Wait Stand was erected. Mr Wait was the chairman of the club at that time and was thoroughly conversant with the building trade. He arranged the contract for the building of the stand and helped in its construction; the stand was given his name upon his death in 1981.

In 1979 the main stand was altered to become an all-seater stand, with the tiers of seats extended forward over what had formerly been the (covered) enclosure, while the Arthur Wait Stand became all-seating in the summer of 1990.

During the early and mid-1980s a major scheme was undertaken which involved the development of the Whitehorse Lane end terracing and banking to incorporate the Sainsburys superstore, the club offices and other facilities, and several shops. Then, in the

1990 close season, extensive modernisation took place to the main stand to incorporate new dining areas, dressing rooms and administrative and reception suites.

For many thousands of Palace fans the most significant development at Selhurst Park was the 1994–95 erection of the new Holmesdale Road all-seater stand. Double tiered and with a capacity of 8,500, it cost the club nearly £6 million but was financed by long-term season ticket sales plus grants and loans from banks and the Football Trust. It was opened for the use of supporters for the second home match of the 1995–96 season on Saturday 26 August 1995, when Charlton Athletic were the visitors, and was officially opened before the game by chairman Ron Noades and manager Steve Coppell in a traditional ribbon-cutting ceremony.

Selhurst Park became the first Football League ground to be the subject of a ground-sharing agreement of anything other than a temporary or emergency nature in September 1985 when Charlton Athletic moved their headquarters across from The Valley. The first match between the two clubs on their shared ground was actually a Palace 'home' game on Saturday 11 January 1986. Palace won 2–1 but Charlton were promoted to Division One at the end of the season. The arrangement with Charlton remained until 1991. It became, ultimately, amicable enough, but it was immediately replaced by a similar arrangement with Wimbledon! The Dons tenanted Selhurst Park until 2004 when they moved away from South London altogether and changed their name accordingly, so that today they are known as Milton Keynes Dons.

Attendances at Selhurst Park have inevitably varied with the relative success of the Palace team, though it has been matches of special interest to supporters which have drawn the record crowds. The longest-standing ground record at Selhurst Park was the 41,586 who came to watch visiting Chelsea beaten in an FA Cup fourth-round tie on 30 January 1926 – an attendance that was not bettered for over 39 years!

Then, two ground record attendances were beaten within three weeks of each other. Nottingham Forest's fifth-round FA Cup visit to the newly promoted Palace headquarters on 20 February 1965 pulled in 41,667 fans, and then the delayed sixth-round tie against Leeds on Wednesday 10 March 1965 attracted no fewer than 45,384 on a bitterly cold evening.

Manchester United were Palace's first-ever top-flight opponents when they came to Selhurst Park on Saturday 9 August 1969 and established another record crowd of 48,610, only for the clash against neighbouring Chelsea on 27 December 1969 to pass that figure by drawing 49,498 London soccer fans. But it was the final, decisive Second Division game at Selhurst Park against Burnley on 11 May 1979 which eclipsed all previous statistics, for the official attendance was set at 51,482, but anyone who was present that night will confirm that hundreds, perhaps thousands, made their entry by unofficial means!

In view of the adoption of all-seater stadia and greatly reduced capacities everywhere, it is quite certain that the Burnley crowd quoted above will never be exceeded at Selhurst Park, but it also remains unusual in that the highest-ever attendance at Palace's ground was established, not for a later-round Cup tie or First Division/Premier League clash, or even a local derby, but in a game from a lower tier in League football.

Matches to Remember

MEMORABLE MATCH 1

12 January 1907

NEWCASTLE UNITED 0 CRYSTAL PALACE 1

FA Cup round one (old)

The contrast in pedigree between these two sides could hardly have been greater. Palace were still in their infancy; Newcastle were renowned among the great clubs in the land and had dominated the sport over the previous half-decade. They were favourites to win this clash by a huge margin.

Of course, Palace had to cope with plenty of Newcastle pressure but, just as half-time drew near, that which had been beyond belief actually occurred! Horace Astley avoided the full-backs who tried to close him down, then sped onto a precision pass from George 'Lady' Woodger and crashed the ball past the astonished goalkeeper, the great Scottish international Jimmy Lawrence, to put Palace ahead. Newcastle gave all they had to redress the situation, but without success, and even though our manager finished with only 10 men, Palace held out to the end. A little girl called Lucy was inspired to write the following words as part of her poem concerning this tremendous victory:

Mark my words my friends, I'll bet,
That the Palace will win the 'Tin Pot' yet.

Newcastle United: Lawrence, McCombie, McCracken, Gardener, Veitch, McWilliam, Rutherford, Howie, Speedie, Orr, Gosnell.
Palace: Hewitson, Needham, Edwards, Innerd, Ryan, Forster, Wallace, Harker, Astley, Woodger, Roberts.

MEMORABLE MATCH 2

21 January 1909

CRYSTAL PALACE 4 WOLVES 2 (AET)

FA Cup round one (old) replay

Palace had astonished everyone in football by gaining a 2–2 draw at Molineux, but most of the pundits expected the mighty Wolves to win the replay; indeed, the visitors went ahead in the very first minute to endorse that opinion. Palace were quickly on terms, however, when amateur Billy Lawrence found the target. Despite an injury incurred by Ted Collins, Palace's jaunty right-winger George Garratt put his team ahead midway through the second half, only for Wolves to level with eight minutes remaining.

Palace framed another goal as the first period of extra-time was drawing to a close, when the ever-reliable John Bauchop netted, but it was as the game approached its end that Archie Needham scored one of the best goals ever scored by Palace. He took possession within the centre-circle and in the Palace half, surged forward through the cloying mud, powering past the tiring defenders, then crashed the ball into the Wolves goal before collapsing in the Wolves penalty area. It was a goal of such supreme quality that Palace fans who saw it still talked about it in glowing terms some 60 or 70 years later!

Palace: Johnson, Collins, Collyer, Innerd, Ryan, Brearley, Garratt, W. Lawrence, Bauchop, Woodger, Needham.
Wolves: Lunn, Jones, Collins, Shelton, Revd K. Hunt, Bishop, Harrison, Blunt, Hedley, Radford, Pedley.

MEMORABLE MATCH 3

7 January 1922

EVERTON 0 CRYSTAL PALACE 6

FA Cup round one (old)

Even though Palace were now a Second Division club, the prospect of an old first-round FA Cup tie at Everton was a daunting one, as Everton were a top-class and in-form side. But Palace did not just win – they did so in rampageous fashion! To state that the result was a shock is to hugely cheapen it. It was fabulous and there are Palace fans who consider it to be the club's best Cup result ever.

It appears that Palace were rarely pushed back and had two additional efforts disallowed while another hit the crossbar. Jack Alderson entered Palace's legendary history by peeling and eating an orange during the proceedings!

John Whibley put Palace in front with a headed goal from Ben Bateman's fourth-minute corner, and Bert Menlove added to the lead midway through the first half so that an unlikely victory began to appear possible. Naturally, Everton rallied somewhat but without any success whatever, and it was left to Palace to net four more goals in the last 20 minutes of the game! John Conner scored from a Whibley cross, then Menlove headed another. Alan Wood and John Conner completed the rout either side of a missed Everton penalty.

The *Athletic News* said that the outcome was a 'sensation'. No one from South London who was at Goodison Park that day would disagree with that!

Everton: Fern, Macdonald, Livingstone, Brown, Fleetwood, Peacock, Chedgzoy, Fazackerley, Irvine, Wall, Harrison.
Palace: Alderson, Little, Rhodes, McCracken, Jones, Feebery, Bateman, Conner, Menlove, Wood, Whibley.

MEMORABLE MATCH 4

2 April 1923

NOTTS COUNTY 0 CRYSTAL PALACE 4

Football League Division Two

Palace were a poor side throughout 1922–23 and everyone at the club must have viewed the Good Friday and Easter Monday fixtures against the champions-elect Notts County with more than a little trepidation. Just so: County won comfortably at The Nest (1–0) and the Meadow Lane return looked ominous.

Palace were glad enough to reach the interval without conceding a goal and with dignity and confidence a little restored. But, during an amazing eight minutes in the second half Palace netted three times and went on to notch up a glorious 4–0 victory!

Billy Morgan hammered home the first with a low drive, George Whitworth crashed in the second and left-winger Bill Hand lobbed the goalkeeper for the third. The outside-left completed the scoring when he converted Ben Bateman's immaculate cross, but the fact that this 5ft 6in fellow did so with a header conveys to us just how comprehensive this victory was.

Notts County: Streets, Cope, Ashurst, Kemp, Dinsdale, Flint, Price, Hill, Cook, Cooper, Platts.
Palace: Alderson, Little, Cross, McCracken, Millard, Dreyer, Bateman, Blakemore, Whitworth, Morgan, Hand.

MEMORABLE MATCH 5

12 January 1924

CRYSTAL PALACE 2 TOTTENHAM HOTSPUR 0

FA Cup first round (old)

It has been recorded elsewhere in this volume that Crystal Palace's tight, cramped headquarters from 1918–24, The Nest, was the ideal place to record FA Cup giant-killings, and this is probably the most prestigious one.

Straight from the start, Palace refused Spurs any time at all to settle and many observers considered that a feature of the game was the way in which the great 'Fanny' Walden was subdued by Palace's Bobby Greener.

Palace gained the lead on around the half-hour mark when Robert McCracken sent little Albert Harry away. After beating Arthur Grimsdell the tiny winger swept the ball back from the byline, a couple of feet above the turf, and Billy Morgan flashed a spectacular header past the goalkeeper. Ten minutes into the second half the skipper netted his and Palace's second goal during a frantic scramble in the Tottenham goalmouth, and from that point on the issue was never in doubt.

The Nest had its problems, certainly, but it had its advantages too!

Palace: Alderson, Little, Cross, McCracken, Cracknell, Greener, Harry, Whitworth, Hoddinott, Morgan, Hand.
Tottenham Hotspur: Maddison, Carr, Forster, Smith, Lowe, Grimsdell, Walden, Thompson, Lindsay, Elkes, Handley.

MEMORABLE MATCH 6

30 January 1926

CRYSTAL PALACE 2 CHELSEA 1

FA Cup fourth round

From an FA Cup success at The Nest to another at Selhurst Park, one that set up an early ground record attendance that remained unchallenged for almost 40 years.

The game was full of drama, excitement and tension and was played at a scorching pace. George Clarke was unlucky not to score early on when his shot hit a Chelsea post. Stung, if repreived, Chelsea then brought the best out of Billy Callender several times, but Palace were never second best in the game.

Palace went ahead shortly after the half-hour mark with a swift counter-attack following a Chelsea corner. Cecil Blackmore initiated the move, feeding burly Percy Cherrett, who had made a devastating upfield surge, and the big man thrashed the ball home. Chelsea held the initiative immediately after the interval, but in the 52nd minute Alf Hawkins doubled Palace's lead after Chelsea's defence had been opened up with a four-man move involving Robert McCracken, George Clarke and Albert Harry as well as the scorer himself.

Chelsea replied with 10 minutes left but Palace held on comfortably enough to register another glorious FA Cup victory.

Palace: Callender, Little, Cross, McCracken, Coyle, Greener, Harry, Blakemore, Cherrett, Hawkins, Clarke.
Chelsea: McKenna, Smith, Barrett, Priestly, Rodger, Ferguson, Crawford, Thain, Turnbull, Wilding, McNeil.

MEMORABLE MATCH 7

11 February 1950

CRYSTAL PALACE 6 BRIGHTON 0

Football League Division Three South

The appointment of Ronnie Rooke as Palace's player-manager in the summer of 1949 brought about an immediate, if short-lived, improvement in the club's fortunes. Rooke himself led Palace to seventh place in the Third Division South and hit 21 League goals.

Among Palace's best displays in the 1949–50 season was a 6–0 victory over Brighton in early February, whan Ronnie set Palace on the way with an early, powerful shot following a pass from Ted Harding. Just after the half-hour mark Freddie Kurz, Rooke's goalscoring foil, banged the ball home for the second after Ray Howells' effort had been deflected.

After the interval Rooke netted in glorious fashion: he took a cross from the right, pivotted and then lobbed the ball over the advanced goalkeeper. Ray Howells himself sped clear and finished neatly, Charlie Chase beat 'keeper Baldwin with a volley and then Rooke completed his hat-trick, converting a Howells cross.

Sadly, however, matters fell apart for Rooke and Palace the following season and the club parted company with him at the end of November.

Palace: Graham, Harding, Murphy, Chase, Watson, Ross, Blackshaw, Mulheron, Kurz, Rooke, Howells.
Brighton: Baldwin, Tennant, Vitty, Whent, Wilkins, J. Brennan, Reed, McNichol, Lancelotte, Kavanagh, Davies.

MEMORABLE MATCH 8

1 May 1953

CRYSTAL PALACE 1 BRISTOL ROVERS 0

Football League Division Three South

Another mini-revival in Palace's fortunes took place in the last third of the 1952–53 season. A further application for re-election had seemed likely but matters improved, and did so to such a degree that by the end of the term Palace were a match for most teams in the division.

However, the most serious examination was posed by the club's final opponents of the season, champions of the southern section Bristol Rovers, who came to Selhurst Park to play an early evening game on the eve of the FA Cup Final. The weather was foul, the pitch dreadful.

The decisive moment came midway through the first half when 'Archie' Andrews hoisted the already saturated ball into the visitors' goalmouth, where Bob Thomas found the net with an adroit header, and although Rovers pressed strongly after the interval Palace held on for a worthy victory.

Palace: Bailey, George, Choules, Rainford, Briggs, Andrews, Fell, Hancox, Besagni, R. Thomas, Downs.

Bristol Rovers: Anderson, Bamford, Fox, Pitt, Warren, Sampson, Petherbridge, Bush, Lambden, Roost, Watling.

MEMORABLE MATCH 9

12 December 1956

CRYSTAL PALACE 3 BRENTFORD 2 (AET)

FA Cup second-round replay

Palace were a humble outfit in the mid-1950s, but the club's fans were encouraged by a first-round victory over Walthamstow Avenue in the 1956–57 FA Cup competition and by the 1–1 draw that followed at Brentford.

The Selhurst Park replay was highlighted by a hat-trick from Barry Pierce, Palace's first in the FA Cup for over a quarter of a century. Although the Bees went ahead early, Palace replied midway through the first half when Pierce headed past Gerry Cakebread from Peter Berry's cross, only for Brentford to forge in front again just before the break. Nevertheless, there was still time for Palace to level again when a glorious move on the right flank culminated in a cross from which Pierce beat Cakebread at the second attempt from close range.

After a goalless second half the game went to extra-time and, after Brentford had largely dominated the first half of those proceedings, Bernard Harrison sped away along the right touchline then crossed for the unmarked Pierce to net the winner with a strong downwards header.

Palace: Potter, Edwards, McDonald, Long, Choules, Noakes, Harrison, Belcher, Berry, Pierce, Deakin.

Brentford: Cakebread, Tickeridge, Dargie, Peplow, Bragg, Coote, Parsons, Morgan, Francis, Towers, Newcombe.

MEMORABLE MATCH 10

23 August 1958

CRYSTAL PALACE 6 CREWE A 2

Football League Division Four

This fixture was Palace's first in Division Four and occurred on the opening day of the 1958–59 season. Crewe were making their first appearance at Selhurst Park.

The match was only two minutes old when Crewe opened the scoring; although, thankfully, Palace proved to be the stronger side and ultimately cruised to a 6–2 win. Palace's hero that afternoon was centre-forward Mike Deakin. Mike had been laid low by a nasty cartilage injury and in this, his comeback game, he bagged a first-half hat-trick. Emulating him, 19-year-old Johnny Byrne also provided Palace fans with a hat-trick of his own.

However, while Palace cleared this first hurdle easily enough, they rarely looked capable of taking any of the promotion places from the League basement and ultimately finished seventh.

Palace: Rouse, Edwards, Noakes, Truett, Choules, Long, Harrison, McNichol, Deakin, Byrne, Collins.
Crewe Alexandra: Lowery, McDonnell, Millar, Campbell, Barnes, Ward, McNamara, Llewellyn, Pearson, Finney, Daley.

MEMORABLE MATCH 11

10 October 1959

CRYSTAL PALACE 9 BARROW 0

Football League Division Four

It seems extremely unlikely that any of the 9,500 Palace enthusiasts who were at Selhurst Park for the visit of Barrow could have had any idea that they would see the club's biggest victory in all competitions. After all, Palace were lying 10th in the Division Four table!

The game itself became a wonderful success for one of Palace's often underrated stars, Roy Summersby, who contributed four of the goals. But the opening strike was netted by outside-left Ray Colfar, who had joined Palace in 1958 from manager George Smith's former club, Sutton United. Ray crashed home a long pass from Dave Sexton from some 20 yards midway through the first half, and by half-time Palace were four goals ahead. Johnny Gavin netted direct from a corner, then Summersby struck twice.

Ray Colfar netted again early in the second half, then Roy Summersby hit two in quick succession, the second from the penalty spot. Johnny Byrne turned a pass from Colfar past the poor goalkeeper then banged a low drive past him with a minute to go.

However, enormous victories like this do not mean that a side will gain promotion; Palace finished the season eighth in Division Four.

Palace: Rouse, Long, Noakes, Truett, Evans, McNichol, Gavin, Summersby, Sexton, Byrne, Colfar.
Barrow: Heys, Lindores, Cahill, O'Connor, Robinson, McNab, Kerry, Murdoch, Robertson, Bannan, Kemp.

MEMORABLE MATCH 12

20 August 1960

CRYSTAL PALACE 9 ACCRINGTON STANLEY 2

Football League Division Four

Under new manager Arthur Rowe, whose renown was famed among all London football fans, Palace fans had renewed optimism for the 1960–61 season.

This game represents Accrington's only appearance at Selhurst Park and it must be doubtful if they will be keen ever to make another. Palace were leading 3–1 after only eight minutes, and by half-time the scoreline was 5–2. The second half was a debacle for the visitors, with Palace reaching a total of nine goals for the second time in under a year.

Johnny Byrne claimed four goals for himself, including the quickest one of the new season, which came after only 50 seconds. Powerful Alan Woan also scored a hat-trick and Ron Heckman, a blond, fast-raiding left-winger who had joined from Millwall, hit a brace upon his Palace debut.

Palace: Rouse, Long, Noakes, Petchey, Evans, McNichol, Gavin, Woan, Byrne, Summersby, Heckman.
Accrington Stanley: McInnes, Forrester, Smith, Tighe, Harrower, Sneddon, Bennett, Swindells, Hudson, Logue, Devine.

MEMORABLE MATCH 13

18 April 1962

CRYSTAL PALACE 3 REAL MADRID 4

Friendly

Although this game was indeed a friendly encounter, it was also a momentous, hugely impressive Palace event, and it almost certainly was the biggest single club match to have taken place at Selhurst Park in terms of the relative monetary worth of the luminaries who took part in it. And modern-day fans should realise that Real Madrid were not just the reigning champions of Europe – they had been so for five years, and that is a record beyond comparison even today!

Palace's board had discussed which club should be invited to mark the official opening of the club's new, much improved floodlights. The English clubs who were approached all wanted enormous guarantees on top of such costs as would be incurred, so, under the far-sighted chairmanship of Arthur Wait, the board felt that they should invite the topmost club in Europe. No one knows quite how Mr Wait persuaded Real, but they came! Palace put up their prices and made a profit on the evening despite the foul weather.

It was breathtaking for Palace fans to see the legendary stars and perhaps there was no surprise that Real cruised to a two-goal lead in eight minutes. Ron Heckman reduced the deficit, Puskas crashed in a thunderbolt, then Sanchez made it 4–1.

After the break Andy Smillie prodded home a pass from Roy Summersby and Terry Long hammered in a 25-yarder. It was 3–4 and the *Señors* were worried! But that was how it finished, so Real's pride remained undented.

Several changes were made to the teams in the second half, and these are shown in brackets.

Palace: Rouse (Glazier), McNichol, Little, Long, Wood, Petchey, Brett, Summersby, Byrne, Smillie, Heckman (Lewis).
Real Madrid: Araquistain (Vicente), Casao, Miera, Sanchez (Ruiz), Santa Maria (Marquitos), Pachin, Tejada, Del Sol (Pepillo), Di Stefano, Puskas, Gento.

MEMORABLE MATCH 14

20 February 1965

CRYSTAL PALACE 3 NOTTINGHAM FOREST 1

FA Cup fifth round

This performance by Palace represented the club's best showing under manager Dick Graham, and even though Palace were certainly the underdogs, even the neutrals acknowledged the possibility of an upset. And an upset there most certainly was!

Played on a cold, late winter's afternoon and on a heavy, snow-flecked pitch, Palace showed no respect whatsoever for Forest's undoubted class, and it only reflected the balance of play when David Burnside had Palace ahead from Bobby Kellard's cross in the 41st minute.

Forest showed their calibre with an equaliser, but Palace restored their advantage with a majestic, left-footed volley from Peter Burridge. With five minutes to go, all doubts about the outcome were stifled when Cliff Holton netted from close range.

Palace: Jackson, Howe, Long, Holsgrove, Stephenson, Burridge, Whitehouse, Horobin, Holton, Burnside, Kellard.
Nottingham Forest: Grummitt, Hindley, Mochan, Newton, McKinlay, Whitefoot, Moore, Addison, Wignall, Barnwell, Hinton.

MEMORABLE MATCH 15

19 April 1969

CRYSTAL PALACE 3 FULHAM 2

Football League Division Two

Because of the matters that would be decided by the result of this match, it will always be regarded as one of the most historic games in which Palace ever took part for, barring a disaster, Palace would gain promotion to the First Division for the first time.

But Fulham, already fated to be relegated, were much the better side in the first half and were full value for their two-goal lead. During the interval, Palace coach George Petchey delivered a few choice words to his charges and it so revitalised them that the deficit was overcome with time to spare.

Palace's first response was netted within 50 seconds of the start of the second half. Fulham 'keeper Jack McClelland could not hold a Tony Taylor drive and the ball ran to Steve Kember, who simply touched it home. Cliff Jackson might have put Palace level straight away, but in the 59th minute Mark Lazarus put the home side on terms from 20 yards following an incisive opening created by Colin Taylor and Cliff Jackson. As fans of the period will recall, upon scoring Mark would set off on a highly individualistic goal celebration. This occasion was no different – except perhaps that John Jackson was not expecting to receive an embrace from his excited colleague!

Almost immediately Palace were in front, Cliff Jackson taking the chance made for him by Colin Taylor and Roger Hoy, arrowing his shot into the top corner then lifting his arm in his distinctive champions' salute.

Palace were up! Now members of the elite League for the first time, the players, fans and officials celebrated the fact in jubilant style.

Palace: J. Jackson, Sewell, Loughlan, Payne, McCormick, Hoy, Lazarus, Kember, C. Jackson, T. Taylor, C. Taylor.
Fulham: McClelland, Moreline, Callaghan, Horne, Roberts, Byrne, Jones, Lloyd, Large, Dear, Conway.

MEMORABLE MATCH 16

9 August 1969

CRYSTAL PALACE 2 MANCHESTER UNITED 2

Football League Division One

This match was Palace's entry into the First Division and drew a record attendance to Selhurst Park of 48,610. In hot, humid and sunny conditions, the game fell some way short of being a classic; although it is doubtful if any Palace fans went home disappointed.

Manager Bert Head included two of his summer signings, stylish striker Gerry Queen and muscular defender Roger Hynd, although when Palace edged in front the goalscorer was Mel Blyth. Most of the fans were astonished that United appeared not to realise the danger when Roger Hoy shaped to take the throw-in from which Mel delivered the header that looped over Jimmy Rimmer and under the crossbar.

Bobby Charlton levelled for the visitors but Palace were in front again by half-time, Gerry Queen endearing himself to all Palace fans as bedlam erupted. Willie Morgan made it 2–2, but the Palace players and supporters had had a great day, and it was apparent that no club could expect an easy time when they came to Selhurst Park.

Palace: J. Jackson, Sewell, Loughlan, Hoy, McCormick, Hynd, Lazarus (T. Taylor 86), Kember, C. Jackson, Queen, Blyth.
Manchester United: Rimmer, Dunne (Givens), Burns, Crerand, Foulkes, Sadler, Morgan, Kidd, Charlton, Law, Best.

MEMORABLE MATCH 17

10 October 1970

MANCHESTER UNITED 0 CRYSTAL PALACE 1

Football League Division One

No match at Old Trafford is anything but extremely demanding, but this was especially so because it was the occasion of Bobby Charlton's 500th League appearance for United – and he needed just one more strike to pass the United record of 198 League and Cup goals set by Jack Rowley.

Once Palace had checked United's early frenzied pressure, however, they began to assert themselves too. Of course, Charlton delivered a pair of his thunderbolts towards the Palace goal, but these were turned aside by the alert defenders and John Jackson was untroubled by them. Thus, by half-time it was clear that Palace could provide the shock of the day, because United's midfield was in thrall to Steve Kember and David Payne, Mel Blyth and John McCormick were on top of their game in the middle of the defence and Alan Birchenall, Bobby Tambling and Gerry Queen were posing threats of their own.

The *coup de grace* came just after the hour. Peter Wall overlapped down the Palace left and his pass inside to Bobby Tambling was hit sweetly from the edge of the penalty area to record a strike that was worthy of Charlton himself and gave Jimmy Rimmer no hope at all. There were very few Palace fans at Old Trafford that afternoon, but United certainly knew they were present after that!

Manchester United: Rimmer, Watson, Burns, Fitzpatrick, James, Sadler, Morgan, Gowling, Charlton, Kidd, Best.
Palace: Jackson, Sewell, Wall, Payne, McCormick, Blyth, Taylor, Kember, Queen, Birchenall, Tambling.

MEMORABLE MATCH 18

9 November 1970

ARSENAL 0 CRYSTAL PALACE 2

Football League Cup fourth-round replay

Palace were under a great deal of pressure throughout this Highbury replay, but when Jim Scott's shot was mishandled by Bob Wilson after some 15 minutes, Gerry Queen was on hand to slip the ball into the Gunners' net!

However, Sewell was injured shortly afterwards and had to be replaced by John Loughlan, so it seemed unlikely that Palace could hold their lead – but they did more than that, scoring a second time to increase the margin.

With Arsenal's big crowd roaring them on, their strapping Welsh defender John Roberts allowed his frustration to surface and he pulled down Gerry Queen in the penalty area. Bobby Tambling slammed the award home and ensured Palace's most significant shock result during their spell in the top flight between 1969 and 1973.

Arsenal: Wilson, Rice, McNab, Kelly, McLintock, Roberts, Armstrong, Storey, Radford, Kennedy, Graham.
Palace: Jackson, Sewell (Loughlan), Wall, Payne, McCormick, Hoadley, Taylor, Scott, Queen, Birchenall, Tambling.

MEMORABLE MATCH 19

16 December 1972

CRYSTAL PALACE 5 MANCHESTER UNITED 0

Football League Division One

Perhaps surprisingly, United were experiencing a poor season and were only two places and two points better off than Palace whose manager, Bert Head, had augmented his squad by importing four players, with another set for his club debut in this game, Alan Whittle.

Just seconds after John Jackson had denied Ian Moore, right-back and Palace captain Paddy Mulligan began United's downfall. He raced on to a Don Rogers pass on the right flank, then cut in towards goal and steered the ball past Alex Stepney.

Three minutes before the break, Mulligan increased the lead. Don Rogers supplied the perfect pass and the Eire star lashed the ball home from 12 yards. A minute after half-time Palace were three ahead. Alan Whittle sent Don Rogers clear in the penalty area and he rounded Stepney himself one way while pushing the ball the other side of the poor 'keeper, then drove it into the empty Holmesdale Road goal.

With four minutes left Alan Whittle netted the debut goal he and the fans wanted, and then, to cries of 'We want five', Don Rogers seared through the visiting defence again, rounded Stepney once more and duly obliged.

Palace: Jackson, Mulligan, Taylor, Philip, Bell, Blyth, Hughes, Payne, Whittle, Cooke, Rogers.
Manchester United: Stepney, O'Neil, Dunne (Law 14), Young, Sadler, Buchan, Morgan, MacDougal, Kidd, Davies, Moore.

MEMORABLE MATCH 20

14 February 1976

CHELSEA 2 CRYSTAL PALACE 3

FA Cup fifth round

Palace had never beaten Chelsea at Stamford Bridge before, but the packed stadium provided the perfect setting for Malcolm Allison's Palace side and Peter Taylor to excel.

After half an hour, Palace struck twice in three minutes to set the tie alight. Taylor beat two Blues defenders but his shot hit the crossbar, only for Nick Chatterton to net from close range, then Taylor himself sent a left-footed shot beyond Peter Bonetti.

It was in the third quarter of the match that Chelsea responded, twice, and the advantage now appeared to lie with the home side, but then Bill Garner fouled Alan Whittle some 20 yards from the Chelsea goal, seemingly unaware of Palace's potency from such awards. Just so – big Dave Swindlehurst dummied an attempt but left the ball for Peter Taylor to sweetly, gracefully but lethally chip it over the forward-positioned Bonetti and into the roof of the net for a stunning winning goal.

Chelsea: Bonetti, Locke, Harris, Cooke, Droy (Hay), Wicks, Britton, R. Wilkins, Maybank, Swain, Garner.
Palace: Hammond, Wall, Cannon, Jeffries, Jump, Evans, Chatterton, M. Hinshelwood, Whittle, Swindlehurst, Taylor.

MEMORABLE MATCH 21

11 May 1979

CRYSTAL PALACE 2 BURNLEY 0

Football League Division Two

Palace approached the last week of the 1978–79 season in fourth place in the Division Two table, but with a game in hand of the clubs above them. With a victory at Leyton Orient on the final Saturday of the term, that outstanding fixture assumed huge significance. If Palace won it, they would be promoted as champions; a draw would see promotion, but a defeat would throw the whole season's work away.

Played on the Friday evening before the FA Cup Final, Palace's opponents were Burnley. Promotion fever so gripped South London that 51,482 fans gained official entry, with hundreds more finding other ways of ingress.

The Clarets proved no mean opponents. For 77 minutes they kept Palace at bay, after which they began to pose problems themselves. But with 12 minutes to go little Vince Hilaire sent over a consummate cross for Ian Walsh to leap and head the ball into the top corner of the net. So great had been the tension that it was inevitable that this would lead to a pitch invasion by Palace fans, but order was restored and it began to look as if this narrow victory would suffice. Then, with two minutes remaining Dave Swindlehurst drove home a right-footed shot, and the celebrations at the end were ecstatic.

Palace: Burridge, P. Hinshelwood, Sansom, Kember, Cannon, Gilbert, Nicholas, Murphy, Swindlehurst, Walsh, Hilaire.
Burnley: Stevenson, Scott, Brennan, Noble, Thomson, Rodaway, Hall, Ingram, Morley, Kindon, James.

MEMORABLE MATCH 22

29 September 1979

CRYSTAL PALACE 4 IPSWICH TOWN 1

Football League Division One

Augmented by the major signings of Gerry Francis and Mike Flanagan, Palace's first season back in the First Division had begun in greatly encouraging fashion and now, with Ipswich Town as the visitors, Palace were lying second in the table. The weather and the occasion were glorious, but by the finish the Suffolk club was painfully aware that a new force had arrived in the top flight for 1979–80.

Palace's first half was quite outstanding. Dave Swindlehurst converted a Vince Hilaire cross in the 17th minute, then Paul Hinshelwood nodded a Gerry Francis free-kick home as the half hour approached. Swindelhurst was felled by Russell Osman, the penalty was converted by Gerry Francis, at the second attempt, and the game was already over.

However, this match is recalled by Palace fans mostly for Jim Cannon's goal in the second half. Vince Hilaire sent Mike Flanangan free on the left while Cannon powered 80 yards down the middle. Flanagan saw him, sent over a cross and the skipper did the rest. It was a magnificent goal which brought everyone to their feet, and it was this strike which took Palace to the top of the entire Football League.

Ipswich's consolation goal was netted by Eric Gates as half-time approached.

Palace: Burridge, P. Hinshelwood, Sansom, Nicholas, Cannon, Gilbert, Murphy, Francis, Swindlehurst, Flanagan, Hilaire.
Ipswich Town : Cooper, Burley, Mills (Osbourne 46), Thijssen, Osman, Butcher, Wark, Muhren, Mariner, Gates, McCall.

MEMORABLE MATCH 23

3 June 1989

CRYSTAL PALACE 3 BLACKBURN ROVERS 0 (AET)

Football League Division Two Play-off second leg

Palace's task for this fixture was plain: score three times to win the Play-off on aggregate and thus gain promotion to the First Division once more. Ultimately, this was achieved in imperious fashion, though Blackburn's clearest chance of capsizing Palace arrived in only the 10th minute when Ian Miller fired just over the crossbar from the edge of the penalty area.

From that moment, there was only one winner. In the 16th minute, Alan Pardew's left-side cross found Ian Wright close to Rovers's goal. Gennoe kept out Ian's first effort, but the Palace striker slipped the second one into the net.

Early in the second half little Eddie McGoldrick was unbalanced by Mark Atkins and Dave Madden coolly slotted the penalty home. The aggregate scores were now level for Blackburn had won their home leg 3–1, and as the second half drew to its close Rovers began to press forward, requiring one glorious save by Perry Suckling.

In extra-time both teams went close without success, but Palace knew that as things stood they were in command because of their goal at Ewood Park. Then, after 118 minutes Ian Wright was unchallenged to head home a cross from McGoldrick and there was a tumult at Selhurst Park.

Palace: Suckling, Pemberton, Burke, Madden, Hopkins, O'Reilly, McGoldrick, Pardew, Bright, Wright, Barber.
Blackburn Rovers: Gennoe, Atkins, Sulley, Reid, Hendry, Mail, Gayle (Ainscow 104), Millar, Miller (Curry 57), Garner, Sellars.

MEMORABLE MATCH 24

8 April 1990

CRYSTAL PALACE 4 LIVERPOOL 3 (AET)

FA Cup semi-final

Palace's prospects for this illustrious fixture were poor; at least, they were to anyone who did not have affinities in SE25! Liverpool were the Cup holders, clear leaders of the First Division and champions-elect, and had already done the League 'double' over Palace, including a 9–0 Anfield annihilation.

In the dour first half at Villa Park, during which Ian Rush put the Reds ahead, there was little to suggest that the match would not result in a Liverpool victory. But in the remaining 75 minutes Palace destroyed their opponents, beginning just 16 seconds after the restart. John Pemberton's 60-yard run and cross saw efforts from Phil Barber and John Salako blocked before Mark Bright volleyed an unstoppable shot into the top corner.

In the 69th minute Gary O'Reilly was on target for Palace following an Andy Gray free-kick, only for Liverpool to net twice in 90 seconds with 10 minutes to go. But with just two minutes of normal time left, Andy Gray took the tie into extra-time.

The climax came early in the second half of extra-time, when Alan Pardew headed home after Andy Thorn had flicked-on an Andy Gray corner right in front of the Palace fans, who could scarcely believe what they had seen and celebrated in style.

Palace: Martyn, Pemberton, Shaw, Gray, O'Reilly, Thorn, Barber, Thomas, Bright, Salako, Pardew.
Liverpool: Grobbelaar, Hysen, Burrows, Gillespie (Venison 45), Whelan, Hansen, Beardsley, Houghton, Rush (Staunton 29), Barnes, McMahon.

MEMORABLE MATCH 25

12 May 1990

CRYSTAL PALACE 3 MANCHESTER UNITED 3 (AET)

FA Cup Final

Engaged in an FA Cup Final for the first time, Palace began well and, a little after a quarter of an hour, took the lead when Gary O'Reilly's header from Phil Barber's free-kick found the net in front of the Palace fans. Ten minutes before half-time, United were level via a deflection off John Pemberton's shin.

This Cup Final developed into one of the best, and Palace certainly contributed in full to that. Mark Hughes had put United ahead soon after the hour, but then Ian Wright came on and within three minutes of his arrival had put Palace level. He danced past Mike Phelan, ghosted past Pallister and then shot low into the net. Then Palace made it 3–2, but the game had gone into extra-time just two minutes before. The strike was a flying Ian Wright header from a Phil Barber cross. Mark Hughes scored again for United to set up the replay five days later.

The replay was edgy and strained. United won it with a goal on the hour, but Palace should have been awarded a penalty before that, and despite the media's attention of Palace's apparently over-zealous approach, little mention was made of the turned-down spot-kick.

Palace: Martyn, Pemberton, Shaw, Gray (Madden 117), O'Reilly, Thorn, Barber (Wright 69), Thomas, Bright, Salako, Pardew.
Manchester United: Leighton, Phelan, Ince, Martin (Blackmore 88), Bruce, Pallister (Robins 93), Robson, Webb, McClair, Hughes, Wallace.

MEMORABLE MATCH 26

7 April 1991

CRYSTAL PALACE 4 EVERTON 1 (AET)

Zenith Data Systems Cup Final

Having been controversially denied the FA Cup the previous May, Palace and a full entourage of fans returned to Wembley to contest the Zenith Data Systems Cup with Everton. No one so much as suggested any sort of parity between the two competitions but, nevertheless, Palace supporters were delighted with the success.

The first half was goalless but with a pervading air of tension. Precisely halfway through the second period Palace went in front, with skipper Geoff Thomas slicing the Toffees' defence open and netting with a bold diving header. Everton were on terms almost immediately through Robert Warzycha, but with no further scoring extra-time was required.

Four minutes prior to the interval Ian Wright controlled a huge clearance from Nigel Martyn, before beating Neville Southall with a right-footed drive. In the final session, Palace netted twice more: John Salako headed past Southall and Ian Wright slipped the ball beyond the now dispirited 'keeper. At last the Palace fans had something to celebrate at Wembley – and they certainly made the most of it!

Palace: Martyn, Humphrey, Shaw, Gray (McGoldrick 54), Young (Thompson 116), Thorn, Salako, Thomas, Bright, Wright, Pardew.
Everton: Southall, McDonald, Hinchcliffe, Keown (Ratcliffe 80), Watson, Milligan, Warzycha, McCall, Newell (Nevin 70), Cottee, Sheedy.

MEMORABLE MATCH 27

2 November 1991

LIVERPOOL 1 CRYSTAL PALACE 2

Football League Division One

Probably as a result of their 9–0 Anfield drubbing, Palace and their fans have found particular delight in defeating Liverpool, and this victory represented the pinnacle of the 1991–92 season for many.

The match began in pouring rain, and just before half-time big Glenn Hysen put his side ahead following a left-side corner. But, playing now towards the Kop, Palace made the second half their own and the Reds' defence was breached twice. Soon after the restart Marco Gabbiadini swept the ball past Grobbelaar to level the scores, following a right-side move which involved four Palace players and finished with Gareth Southgate sending over a low cross.

After equalising, Palace folk had little doubt that their team would go on to win. They did so, despite losing two well-seasoned men to injuries and the fruitless attempts of the Reds' fans to lift their disconcerted team. The goal came in the 72nd minute, when Eric Young flicked-on a corner from the right and Geoff Thomas nodded into the net.

There was no doubt that this was one of Palace's finest successes – and for those who had witnessed the 9–0 debacle of two seasons before, it was a highly memorable and blissful occasion.

Liverpool: Grobbelaar, Jones, Burrows, Hysen, Molby (Rosenthal 78), Tanner, Saunders, Houghton, Rush, Ablett, McMahon.
Palace: Martyn, Southgate, Sinnott, Gray (Pardew 55), Young, Humphrey, Mortimer (Rodger 54), Thomas, Bright, Gabbiadini, McGoldrick.

MEMORABLE MATCH 28

1 October 1994

ARSENAL 1 CRYSTAL PALACE 2

FA Premiership

Palace's distinguished and impressive victory at Highbury was their first-ever League success there, and surely embodied the peak of the club's achievements while Alan Smith was manager. Agreed, Arsenal were not a team at the top of their form at the time, but they had won the European Cup-Winners' Cup and were managed by a former player of both clubs, George Graham, whose teams were always hard to overcome.

Palace's main man on this overcast and damp afternoon was John Salako. He not only netted both of Palace's goals, but this was also the third anniversary of the awful cruciate ligament injury he had suffered in a top-flight game against Leeds. Salako was playing as a striker alongside Chris Armstrong, and the lissom, shimmering pair made Arsenal's big defenders, Tony Adams and Andy Linighan, appear heavy and cumbersome. Both strikes were pleasing affairs: the opener was set up by little midfielder Bobby Bowry after 19 minutes after he won a tackle that enabled him to release Armstrong. The speedy frontman outpaced Linighan, then shot past David Seaman, hitting the far post. The rebound, however, was put in by Salako. Just prior to the interval, Gareth Southgate found Armstrong with space on the right, and his low centre was converted appreciatively and attractively.

Ian Wright then headed a goal for Arsenal but the day belonged to Palace, with the occasion especially cherished by those faithful Palace fans who had seen all too many beatings at the stately North London ground.

Arsenal: Seaman, Dixon, Linighan, Adams, Winterburn, Selley, Davis (Campbell 45), Schwarz, Merson, Wright, Smith.
Palace: Martyn, Patterson, Coleman, Shaw, Gordon, Southgate, Newman, Bowry, Salako, Armstrong, Ndah.

MEMORABLE MATCH 29

9 April 1995

CRYSTAL PALACE 2 MANCHESTER UNITED 2 (AET)

FA Cup semi-final

Although Palace were doomed to relegation at the end of the season, the team provided a beguiling performance in their third appearance in the FA Cup semi-finals.

The match was a contest of talent and dedication, and Palace fans were downhearted that the prize for such a fine display was merely a replay. Before the break Palace were much the better side: Schmeichel had been much busier than Nigel Martyn, but not even he could intercept a cross to the far post from Chris Armstrong, where John Salako nodded it back and Iain Dowie headed into the net.

United managed an equaliser with a deflected free-kick, and the game was into extra-time before Chris Armstrong eased the ball over Schmeichel from some 15 yards, but United replied swiftly and a replay was required the following Wednesday.

What was not clear until the morning after the game was that Nigel Martyn had fractured his index finger in the left hand and would not be available for that replay, although no blame should be apportioned to Rhys Wilmot, his deputy, for the 2–0 defeat in that uninspiring contest.

Palace: Martyn, Patterson, Coleman (Gordon), Southgate, Shaw, Young, Dowie, Houghton, Armstrong, Pitcher, Salako.
Manchester United: Schmeichel, G. Neville, Irwin, Keane, Sharpe, Pallister, Beckham (Butt), Ince, McClair, Hughes, Giggs.

MEMORABLE MATCH 30

27 May 1996

CRYSTAL PALACE 1 LEICESTER CITY 2 (AET)

Football League Division One Play-off Final

It was reckoned that Palace had some 34,000 fans at Wembley for this game, while, for the third time in four visits to the national stadium (at that time), the game went into extra-time.

Palace grabbed an early, 13th-minute lead when Andy Roberts took a return pass from Ray Houghton and fired a right-footed thunderbolt into the bottom left-hand corner of the Leicester net. Palace might have extended their lead but, just before the hour, Nigel Martyn tipped an Emile Heskey effort over the bar, only to be given no chance with Garry Parker's 76th-minute penalty.

Leicester now had the advantage, but Palace fought their way back to a moral equality and, despite the extra half-hour, a penalty shoot-out seemed to be the only conclusion. Clearly Leicester's manager, Martin O'Neill, thought so, because in the last minute of the game he brought on his enormous Australian goalkeeper, the 6ft 7in Zeljko Kalac. But there were to be no more penalties, because in the dying seconds of the match Leicester's one-time Palace reserve striker, Steve Claridge, sent a volley past Nigel Martyn off his shin with a minor deflection.

Palace: Martyn, Edworthy, Brown, Roberts, Quinn, Hopkin (Veart), Pitcher, Houghton, Freedman (Dyer), Ndah, Tuttle (Rodger).
Leicester City: Poole (Kalac), Grayson, Whitlow, Watts, Walsh (Hill), Izzet, Lennon, Taylor (Robins), Claridge, Parker, Heskey.

MEMORABLE MATCH 31

26 May 1997

CRYSTAL PALACE 1 SHEFFIELD UNITED 0

Football League Division One Play-off Final

As well as the inescapable pressure generated by this and every Play-off Final, the players in this one also had to battle the great heat and high humidity, the temperature inside the ground reliably reported as exceeding 90 degrees Farenheit at its peak.

Palace had the upper hand during the first half's proceedings but the second period was a much more even contest. Chances were few; both sides were at their most threatening from set-pieces. It was with some 10 minutes remaining that something unusual, possibly unique, happened. The ranks of Palace fans began to clap, sing, chant and cheer in unison, to compelling effect. Perhaps 20 different Palace fans have since claimed to have been the creative originators of this, though of course it did not necessarily spring from only one source. Although not commented on by the media, its effect upon the players was uplifting, and perhaps match-winning.

The game was into its penultimate minute, and Palace had a corner on the right. Andy Roberts played a short ball for Simon Rodger to send over an in-swinger which Carl Tiler headed away from goal. It fell to David Hopkin, unmarked and just to the left of the 'D'. He controlled it, measured the distance and then unleashed such a strike as was fit to settle any showpiece. The ball curved round and over United's defenders, then dipped into the top right-hand corner of the net, bringing every Palace fan to his or her feet, punching the air with joy and relief in an amazing eruption of sound.

Palace: Nash, Edworthy, Gordon, Roberts, Tuttle, Linighan, Hopkin, Muscat, Shipperley, Dyer, Rodger.
Sheffield United: Tracey, Holdsworth, Tiler, Nilsen, Spackman (Walker 90), White, Hutchinson (Sandford 45), Ward, Whitehouse, Fjortoft, Katchouro (Taylor 25).

MEMORABLE MATCH 32

10 January 2001

CRYSTAL PALACE 2 LIVERPOOL 1

Football League Cup semi-final first leg

Palace drew a capacity crowd to Selhurst Park for the home leg of their tie against the five-times winners of the competition, who were favourites to do so again. However, as so often happens when Palace meet the Reds, it was the Palace fans who went home delighted by an inspiring victory.

Liverpool matched Palace's early pace and set up chances for Michael Owen and Emile Heskey which both England men spurned, and from that point the match was in Palace's favour. The goals came after the break when, initially, Palace were indebted to Latvian international goalkeeper Alex Kolinko, but with 56 minutes played the home side's other Latvian star, winger Andrejs Rubins, crashed a left-footed drive high into the Liverpool net from the edge of the penalty area. Some 20 minutes later, after intense Palace pressure, Clinton Morrison hammered a right-footed shot beyond Westerveldt and into the top corner.

Liverpool rescued themselves from utter humiliation by responding quickly through Vladimir Smicer, but Palace's victory was most thoroughly deserved and probably did not fully demonstrate their superiority on the night.

Palace: Kolinko, Mullins, Austin, Zhiyi, Harrison, Smith, Thomson, Rodger, Rubins, Forssell, Morrison.
Liverpool: Westerveldt, Babbel, Henchoz, Hyypia, Carragher, Barmby (Hamann 80), Biscan, Gerrard, Murphy (Smicer 64), Owen (Litmanen 64), Heskey.

MEMORABLE MATCH 33

5 February 2003

LIVERPOOL 0 CRYSTAL PALACE 2

FA Cup fourth-round replay

Palace and Liverpool had drawn 0–0 at Selhurst Park, so Division One Palace travelled to Anfield for the replay knowing that the pundits saw this as a home banker. Palace had an unlikely hero at Anfield, however, in the form of goalkeeper Cedric Berthelin, who had only made two previous starts for the club!

Berthelin had a splendid first half, saving wonderfully from Bruno Cheyrou and several more times from Michael Owen, then, early in the second half from Emile

Heskey. Moments later Palace were ahead. The goal was inspired by a magnificent right-side break by Danny Butterfield and his cross was crashed past Dudek by Julian Gray. The hordes on the Kop could scarcely believe what they were seeing happen in front of them as the Reds began reeling. Palace were then reduced to 10 men when the referee dismissed Dougie Freedman, who had reacted to Sami Hyypia's protracted kicking, which was blithely ignored by the official. It seemed that Liverpool might now be able to grasp victory.

In the 79th minute, however, the tie was settled: Julian Gray made a wonderful left-side run, then crossed, only for the bemused Swiss international defender Stephane Henchoz to deflect it into his own net off his right calf.

Liverpool: Dudek, Carragher, Riise, Hamann, Henchoz, Hyypia, Murphy (Baros), Diouf, Heskey, Owen, Cheyrou.
Palace: Berthelin, Butterfield, Granville (Freedman), Symons, Popovic, Powell, Mullins, Derry, Adebola (Akinbiyi), Johnson (Thomson), Gray.

MEMORABLE MATCH 34

14 May 2004

CRYSTAL PALACE 3 SUNDERLAND 2

Football League Division One Play-off semi-final first leg

Palace's Play-off semi-final was a titanic illustration of just how gripping these end-of-season contests can be.

The first leg took place in the shadow of the big victory Palace had gained over Sunderland just three weeks earlier. The visitors were content to just keep the home side at bay, hoping to pinch something through their proven strikers, Marcus Stewart and Kevin Kyle.

Sunderland became more adventurous after the break and Marcus Stewart put them in front from a 49th-minute penalty, but only two minutes later Palace were level through a clever, looping back-header from Neil Shipperley. Then, a little after the hour, the home side went ahead. Michael Hughes played a free-kick square for Danny Butterfield to fire at the target, the ball deflected off Gary Breen and entered the net just inside the right-hand post.

With six minutes left Kevin Kyle despatched a loose ball in the Palace penalty area, but two minutes later Andy Johnson proved the match winner. He had netted 27 times in the League programme, but this one was crucial. Clear on the left, he cut inside along the edge of the penalty area and then unleashed a right-footed drive that beat Mart Poom at the far post. The score stood at 3–2 and there was still the second leg to come!

Palace: Vaesen, Butterfield, Granville, Leigertwood, Popovic, Riihilahti, Routledge, Gray, Johnson, Shipperley (Powell), Hughes (Derry).
Sunderland: Poom, Williams (Bjorklund), McCartney, Robinson, Breen, Babb, McAteer (Thornton), Whitley, Kyle, Stewart (Smith), Oster.

MEMORABLE MATCH 35

17 May 2004

SUNDERLAND 2 CRYSTAL PALACE 1 (AET)

Football League Division One Play-off semi-final second leg

Palace had the better of the opening stages and certainly looked the stronger side in the first half, but with two minutes left Kevin Kyle chested down a cross from Jason McAteer and slammed the ball through Nico Vaesen's legs. Two minutes into added time at the end of the first half Marcus Stewart nodded another McAteer cross past the Palace 'keeper. Sunderland were now ahead on aggregate.

Julian Gray was dismissed late on, but then the contest turned again! With the tie into added time after 90 minutes, Darren Powell headed Palace level from a Shaun Derry corner to put the game into extra-time.

The extra 30 minutes was not able to separate the sides, so the contest went to penalties. Locked at four conversions apiece, Nico Vaesen saved Jeff Whitley's kick and the stage was set for Michael Hughes to step up, crack the ball home and send Palace through to the Millennium Stadium showpiece.

Sunderland: Poom, McCarthy, Bjorklund (Williams), McAteer, Breen, Babb, Oster, Whitley, Kyle, Stewart (Smith), Thornton (Robinson).
Palace: Vaesen, Butterfield (Freedman), Granville (Powell), Leigertwood, Popovic, Riihilahti (Derry), Routledge, Gray, Johnson, Shipperley, Hughes.

MEMORABLE MATCH 36

29 May 2004

CRYSTAL PALACE 1 WEST HAM UNITED 0

Football League Division One Play-off Final

Palace were full of self-assurance when they met West Ham for the 2004 Play-off Final at the Millennium Stadium, Cardiff. Not only had the manager, Iain Dowie, played for both clubs, but the Hammers' boss was also Palace's former Villa Park hero, Alan Pardew.

No one could have asked for more from this Palace side, who refused to yield anything to their opponents, denied them space or possession and spurned any submission even to tiredness in the heat, as they persued their unrelenting quest for supremacy.

Ultimately, this hugely important match for both clubs – for as well as the prestige of appearing again in the Premiership, it was calculated by the game's mandarins to offer a financial prize of £25–30 million – was settled by a simple tap-in from barely five yards out by Palace's skipper Neil Shipperley. Added zest was provided because this was the goal behind which the Palace fans were ranked, and they showed their delight in exuberant fashion. The chance had been made by Andy Johnson's fierce low drive, which the Hammers' 'keeper, Stephen Bywater, had been unable to hold.

Few observers, be they fans of either club or neutrals, would deny that Palace had been the better team on the day and deserved their success.

Palace: Vaesen, Butterfield (Powell), Granville, Leigertwood, Popovic, Riihilahti, Routledge, Derry, Johnson, Shipperley, Hughes.
West Ham United: Bywater, Repka, Lomas, Mullins, Melville, Dailly, Carrick, Connolly (Hutchison), Harewood (Reo-Coker), Zamora (Deane), Etherington.

MEMORABLE MATCH 37

23 April 2005

CRYSTAL PALACE 1 LIVERPOOL 0

FA Premiership

Palace's penultimate home match of the 2004–05 season was against Liverpool. The prospects of top-flight survival were becoming increasingly bleak at this time, but the Reds still cherished hopes of a sufficiently high finish to qualify for the Champions League in the season ahead.

A spirited Palace showing turned the form book upside down, however, and provided a thrilling, if narrow, victory for the fans to savour, while at the same time denting Liverpool's aspirations. The goal that won the game came in the 34th minute and followed a long, looping cross from Danny Granville. The visitors' big defenders repulsed it, but the clearance only went as far as Wayne Routledge, who volleyed the ball goalwards again. Andy Johnson connected with it with his head from some 12 yards out, and deflected it away from Jerzy Dudek so that it flew into the left-hand corner of the Whitehorse Lane goal. Palace retained the initiative for the remainder of the first half, and Andy Johnson might have added to the lead but he placed his shot inches wide of the near post.

The second half was fiercely contested, with Palace fans cheering their side through to victory – and most observers agreed that it was a fully deserved one.

Palace: Kiraly, Granville, Popovic, Routledge, Johnson, Leigertwood, Riihilahti, Hughes, Soares (Watson 90), Hall, Sorondo.
Liverpool: Dudek, Finnan, Hyypia, Baros (Potter 37), Gerrard, Pellegrino (Riise 54), Le Tallec, Morientes, Traore (Cisse 69), Carragher, Welsh.

MEMORABLE MATCH 38

7 April 2008

STOKE CITY 1 CRYSTAL PALACE 2

Championship

Palace's trip to promotion-bound Stoke City was re-arranged for live television coverage and provided spellbinding entertainment as Palace gave what was probably their best performance of the entire season. Stoke had won at Selhurst Park in October but Palace's two first-half goals at the Britannia Stadium had the Potters reeling.

Mamady Sidibe's header bounced along the Palace goalline off an unguarded post in the ninth minute, but no Stoke player was on hand to convert the rebound, and midway through the first half it was their defence which was open to criticism. On-loan Scott Sinclair danced past Danny Pugh on Palace's right flank, and picked out Tom Soares with his cross. Soares rose unmarked and planted a precise header past former Palace goalkeeper Carlo Nash to secure his fourth goal of the season. Just before the interval Palace went further ahead. Stoke repelled a Palace free-kick but only as far as José Fonte who volleyed home ferociously from some 20 yards.

Stoke brought on their top scorer Ricardo Fuller early in the second half and this inspired something of a seige upon the Palace goal. However, Stoke's only reward was a volleyed strike from David Whelan following an 85th-minute corner.

Stoke City: Nash, Griffin, Cort, Riggott, Pugh, Cresswell, Delap, Whelan, Pearson (Bothroyd 76), Sidibe (Fuller 56), Ameobi.
Palace: Speroni, Lawrence, Fonte, Hudson, Hill, Soares (Scannell 89), Derry, Watson, Moses (Reid 56), Sinclair (Fletcher 89), Morrison.

MEMORABLE MATCH 39

14 February 2010

CRYSTAL PALACE 2 ASTON VILLA 2

FA Cup fifth round

Palace, rooted in the Championship relegation dogfight due to their administration plight, were drawn against the club with the meanest defensive record in the Football League, League Cup finalists Aston Villa. But twice Palace rocked Villa by seizing the lead in emphatic fashion and made a mockery of Villa's League and Cup aspirations.

The goal which set the tie alight was netted for Palace midway through the first half in front of the massed Holmesdale Stand by Johnny Ertl, who headed past Brad Friedel from a left-side corner delivered by Darren Ambrose. Some 11 minutes later Villa equalised, again with a headed goal from a set piece, James Collins converting a Stewart Downing free-kick.

Palace's second was the goal of the round and perhaps of the season's competition. Palace were awarded a free-kick, almost straight but 36 yards out. Man of the Match Darren Ambrose's ability in these situations was well known to Palace fans but not, clearly, to the Villa defence! Darren struck the ball with such power that it was still rising when, despite Friedel getting a hand to it, it crashed into the top left-hand corner of Villa's goal.

Villa's equaliser came from a corner under the main stand that the officials should never have awarded – a decision which sent Palace boss Neil Warnock understandably incandescent with rage. Villa's Stiliyan Petrov stooped to send a low header speeding past Julian Speroni's right hand and into the bottom left-hand corner of the net.

Palace fans could barely believe it, but a moral victory is better than nothing, and this was certainly one of those!

Palace: Speroni, Clyne, Butterfield, Ertl, Davis, Hill, Ambrose, Derry, Danns, Carle, Lee (Andrew 90).
Aston Villa: Friedel, L. Young, Dunne, Collins, Warnock, A. Young, Milner, Delph (Delfounso 75), Petrov, Downing, Heskey (Carew 46).

MEMORABLE MATCH 40

27 February 2010

DONCASTER ROVERS 1 CRYSTAL PALACE 1

Football League Championship

Palace, having been deducted 10 points as a result of the club entering another period of administration, found themselves engaged in the relegation dog-fight at the foot of the Championship, and three consecutive home defeats had done nothing to ease their plight. Indeed, when Palace travelled to Doncaster's Keepmoat Stadium at the end of February 2010 they were in the third relegation place, with a tough League programme ahead of them in the countdown to the last analysis.

Thus, the band of loyal travelling supporters knew that it was crucial that Palace gained at least some reward from this difficult fixture against a team that had beaten them 3–0 at Selhurst Park earlier in the season. Matters appeared bleak as Doncaster dominated the opening half and deserved their lead, gained for them by a well-struck shot by James Coppinger.

Nevertheless, manager Neil Warnock, whose last match in charge of the club this was, inspired his side to a second-half rally which climaxed in a neat far-post leveller from close range from Keiran Djilali following a penetrating run in the old inside-left channel, followed by an inch-perfect cross from Darren Ambrose. The resulting point was invaluable, since it took the Palace out of the relegation places, and the most loyal Palace fans and the departing manager applauded each other after the final whistle in mutual regard.

Palace: Speroni, Clyne, Davis (Hills 6 [Ertl 46]), Lawrence, Hill, Carle, Derry, Djilali (Andrew 90), Ambrose, Butterfield, Lee.
Doncaster Rovers: Sullivan, O'Connor, Ward, Hird, Chambers, Wilson (Sheil 90), Oster (Mutch 83), Coppinger, Roberts, Hayter (G. Thomas 76), Sharp.

MEMORABLE MATCH 41

2 May 2010

SHEFFIELD WEDNESDAY 2 CRYSTAL PALACE 2

Football League Championship

This match was a crucial fixture for both clubs, because upon its outcome depended the continuance of one of them in the Championship and the relegation of the other to League One. Largely because of Palace being in administration (with its attendant docking of 10 points, plus of course the departure of manager Neil Warnock and star player Victor Moses) there was a distinct possibility that Palace could return to the lower level.

Palace fans travelled in commendable numbers (nearly 6,000) to South Yorkshire for the showdown and were delighted with the compact, uncompromising manner which hteir side displayed. This attitude and tactic enabled The Eagles to control most of the contest, with Paddy McCarthy outstanding at the heart of the Palace defence and skipper Shaun Derry utterly resolute throughout.

Palace might have conceded two penalties before the scoring opened, but midway through the first half Alan Lee powered home a thunderous header from a right side corner delivered by Palace Man of the Match Darren Ambrose. Wednesday levelled just before the interval through Leon Clarke, then brought on former Palace starlet Tom Soares as a substitute.

With Wednesday attacking the goal in front of their packed Kop, Palace came under intense pressure, but moments after the hour Sean Scannell worked his way to the deadball line, then picked out Darren Ambrose with an accurate cutback, and Palace's top scorer netted with a crisp, low drive.

Wednesday's last attempt to revive their fortunes came with a quarter of an hour to go when they brought on former Arsenal man Francis Jeffers, and in the time that remained Palace were forced deeper and deeper, although it was Palace's fans' chants which could be heard accross the huge arena.

There were just three minutes remaining when Wednesday levelled the score through Darren Purse from close range, but Wednesday had to win the game to survive and, despite their goalkeeper Lee Grant twice joining his teammates in the Palace box, the final whistle signalled another brave and successful escape from a future among the shadows.

Sheffield Wednesday: Grant, Nolan (Jeffers 74), Purse, Beevers, Spurr, Johnson, O'Connor (Esaias 66), Potter, Varney, Tudgay, Clarke (Soares 45).
Palace: Speroni, Butterfield, Lawrence, McCarthy, Hill, Scannell (Davies 89), Ertl, Derry, Ambrose, Andrew (N'Diaye), Lee (John 83).

MEMORABLE MATCH 42

Easter Monday 25 April 2011

CRYSTAL PALACE 1 LEEDS UNITED 0

Football League Championship

Under Dougie Freedman's management, plus, no doubt, the astute guidance of veteran boss Lennie Lawrence, Palace had slowly inched away from the Championship's relegation places: this was virtually entirely due to the Eagles' home form, but that progress had been stalled mid-April when visiting Scunthorpe had won at Selhurst Park. Thus, with just three games of the season remaining, this match was crucial to the Palace. It was important to Leeds, too, but their hopes of a second consecutive promotion had faded with defeats in their previous three matches away from Elland Road.

Therefore, Palace could not have been pitted against more dangerous opponents, but the sunlit Bank Holiday occasion, which drew a season's best attendance at Selhurst Park, featured a welcome early goal, for Neil Danns put the Palace ahead just eighty seconds into the contest, shooting firmly past Kasper Schmeichel into the Whitehorse Lane goal from the edge of the penalty area for his ninth goal of the season.

Thus inspired, Palace were the better side throughout the first half, but Leeds made two substitutions immediately after the interval in an attempt to enhance their performance, and the second period developed into a battle royale. However, Palace were always resolute and largely in command, so that a final Leeds flurry was simply not sufficient to affect the scoreline, even though Neil Danns was dismissed just before the final whistle.

Palace: Speroni, Clyne, McCarthy, Gardner, Moxey, Easter (Vaughan 72), Wright, Dikgacoi (Agustien 77), Danns, Iversen (Davis 80), Zaha.
Leeds United: Schmeichel, Connolly (Kilkenny 46), Naylor, O'Brien, Lichaj, Livermore (Watt 46), Howson, Johnson, Gradel, Snodgrass, Paynter (Somma 72).

The Crystal Palace Programme from 1921

Interwar Strictures

It must surely have been interesting for modern-day readers of the history of Crystal Palace FC to learn that the changes in fortune which the club and its followers endure in the present era were equally a part of life at the club in previous generations too. Certainly, the interwar period was a saga of ups and downs, joys, sorrows and frustrations just as is the present time.

Equally, the Palace match-day programmes of those days varied markedly. At times they were very poor; at other times it was probably among the better productions, certainly when compared to others in the Third Division South.

Palace's programme cost two pence in 1921, and that price did not vary at all during the period. At times the club was obviously aware of financial restrictions and produced a cheap article, even when a Division Two club. But, equally, by using sports photography, cartoons, clever sketches or caricatures, it increasingly attempted to produce something that appealed to its followers and offered a degree of value for money, even if an extended number of pages implied a greater cost, which, in turn, could only be met by increasing the number of advertisements.

Usually in this interwar period, the Palace programme was very much an organ that was produced from within the club, even if it was printed elsewhere. But the best of the club's interwar programmes was the 1921–22 edition which had an 'outside' publisher – the advertising agency T.W. Morris of High Holborn – and editor, who could be reached at the same address. Less than half the programme featured publicity for other businesses, and most of them were local ones, while its 20 pages (including the somewhat stiff, buff-coloured cover) provided comment of previous matches, general football matters, clever cartoons (which were not necessarily intended to be funny), coverage of the visitors, a gallery of Palace players, the up-to-date tables of all the divisions plus that of the London Combination in which the reserve team competed, the full fixture list and results to date for both the sides, and a half-time scoreboard! Forthcoming matches featured prominently on the front cover while the special trains' timetables were promoted on the back cover of the early-season editions. A full programme was also produced for reserve games.

After Palace had moved to Selhurst Park in 1924 various improvements were made to the programme. Aerial sketches of the stadium were depicted on the cover (which was either red or blue for most of the period), and action photos were introduced, on the cover and occasionally elsewhere. The Supporters' Club was accorded a page in the 1936–39 editions, presumably in a further attempt to widen the programme's appeal.

Of course, the contents of the editorial pages were not impartial, although that should not be construed as a criticism of them! However, at times they were reflective, and when

A Palace programme from 1936–37.

commenting upon away matches it should be remembered that it was well-nigh impossible for ordinary supporters to travel in those days, and the comment would be what would be expected today in the coach or car or on the train when returning home from an away fixture.

As far as can be determined, no Palace manager in the interwar years wrote his own column or page in the programme, while the identity of the editor is a matter of conjecture. He was obviously particularly close to the directors and managers of the period, and was afforded privileged opportunities to meet with players and officials and to be present at away games. He had clearly been a part of the Palace scene from the beginning and was informed about 19th-century football. It might be thought that he could have been Mr Edmund Goodman, secretary-manager until 1925 and secretary alone until 1933, but the editorial style does not vary after Mr Goodman left the club and all links he had with Palace were severed in 1933, so the matter remains an intriguing mystery.

Wartime Privations

Initially, Palace produced a single, turn-over sheet for the 1939–40 and 1940–41 seasons based on the former reserve-team format, but after that the programme, along with many others no doubt, was little more than a team sheet. For the 1943–44 season it was just a little larger, so manager George Irwin offered some brief comments under the heading 'Club Gossip'.

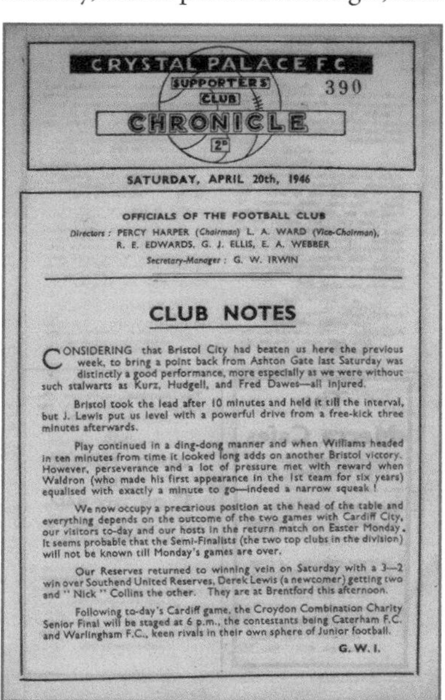

CRYSTAL PALACE F.C.
SUPPORTERS CLUB
CHRONICLE
2D
390

SATURDAY, APRIL 20th, 1946

OFFICIALS OF THE FOOTBALL CLUB

Directors: PERCY HARPER (*Chairman*) L. A. WARD (*Vice-Chairman*), R. E. EDWARDS, G. J. ELLIS, E. A. WEBBER

Secretary-Manager: G. W. IRWIN

CLUB NOTES

CONSIDERING that Bristol City had beaten us here the previous week, to bring a point back from Ashton Gate last Saturday was distinctly a good performance, more especially as we were without such stalwarts as Kurz, Hudgell, and Fred Dawes—all injured.

Bristol took the lead after 10 minutes and held it till the interval, but J. Lewis put us level with a powerful drive from a free-kick three minutes afterwards.

Play continued in a ding-dong manner and when Williams headed in ten minutes from time it looked long adds on another Bristol victory. However, perseverance and a lot of pressure met with reward when Waldron (who made his first appearance in the 1st team for six years) equalised with exactly a minute to go—indeed a narrow squeak!

We now occupy a precarious position at the head of the table and everything depends on the outcome of the two games with Cardiff City, our visitors to-day and our hosts in the return match on Easter Monday. It seems probable that the Semi-Finalists (the two top clubs in the division) will not be known till Monday's games are over.

Our Reserves returned to winning vein on Saturday with a 3—2 win over Southend United Reserves, Derek Lewis (a newcomer) getting two and "Nick" Collins the other. They are at Brentford this afternoon.

Following to-day's Cardiff game, the Croydon Combination Charity Senior Final will be staged at 6 p.m., the contestants being Caterham F.C. and Warlingham F.C., keen rivals in their own sphere of Junior football.

G. W. I.

This continued until the New Year of 1945 – but the additional space that was then permitted was simply devoted to an advertisement for the next day's *Sunday Chronicle*.

The Supporters' Club Shows the Way

It was, however, for the 1945–46 season that the Palace Supporters' Club really proved its worth. Under the editorship of Mr L.W. Davis, an excellent eight-page journal was produced for

A simple wartime programme from 1945–46.

almost all the home games, complete with manager's notes, player profiles, a topical cartoon, lucky programme number and a half-time scoreboard, while that old favourite the 'Penny On The Ball' competition was reintroduced, to the delight of many of the younger followers of the club.

What a tribute those programmes represent to the Palace fans of that time.

The Post-war Years

Following the cessation of hostilities the programme returned to the club's hands for the 1946–47 season, and a 10-page programme in black and white was produced and sold for 3d. However, many items, including paper, were in short supply after the war and the programme was unable to match its pre-war standard for a number of seasons. The emphasis was on contact with the supporters; for example, there was a page for letters and two more dedicated for fans to 'Choose the Team', while around a dozen programmes were marked each game for those lucky patrons to come and have tea with players and officials after the game. The cover featured a picture of captain Fred Dawes making a high kick, with an out-of-focus Holmesdale end in the background. It was printed by Andress Printers of Waddon in New Road, Croydon, who would be associated with the programme production for the next 25 years.

A slightly smaller programme in measurement followed for the 1947–48 campaign. It was the same price but a better quality production, with details of A team and Junior results and a page dedicated to Supporters' Club Notes, together with a player feature in most issues. The cover remained a picture of Fred Dawes, but this time kicking with his other foot over a drawn outline of a football pitch designed by a person named Townsend. A similar sized production followed for the next three seasons, with some changes in content, and in 1948–49 the cover showed a less distinct footballer. The club had returned to the colours of claret and light blue from white shirts and black shorts, while the pages were increased to 14, mainly for advertising. The price remained at 3d. Then, in 1949-50, the same cover was produced in mixed colours for the first time, the footballer on the front now being in club colours. With the page number increased to 16, brief notes on the opposition were now included, along with reports concerning the reserve team. The price remained the same at 3d, although one issue had a cover price of 6d (for the home game against Notts County, who included Tommy Lawton in their team). A further two pages were added in the 1950–51 season with a feature on Palace players returning, while the changes at boardroom level were shown with vice-chairman Arthur Wait using the back cover to promote his building business. Despite the club struggling on the pitch, the programme had now become a far superior production than many of its contemporaries.

This did not last, and for the next two seasons the page numbers dropped back to 10, mainly at the expense of advertising, while the cover was changed completely to feature a diagonal drawing of a goalkeeper about to catch a football (which contained the price, still 3d). Across the same diagonal the right side remained in white, while the other segment, containing the club name, and the goalkeeper were printed in alternative issues in a shade of either red or blue, a style that would not have looked out of place 20 years earlier. There was another retrograde step in 1953–54, as although the programme size increased slightly, page numbers dropped back again, this time to eight. For League issues the programme was produced on light blue paper and the print was in a claret colour, but with nearly half the programme given over to advertising, reading content was kept to the bare necessities.

The programme for the 1954–55 season was similar in size and content, being eight pages, but utilised plain paper and black print, and confusingly most of them advertised forthcoming matches on the cover. During the season the club began playing friendly

A 1961 Palace programme.

games under the recently installed floodlights. For these fixtures a four-page programme was generally issued but the cover cleverly used the double 'O's in 'floodlight' and 'football' to show a pair of floodlights highlighting a drawing of a football pitch.

For the next two seasons the design of the programme remained the same and a better quality paper was utilised, while the cover contained a large black-and-white monogram of the club crest at the time that took up a third of the cover. The chairman's and directors' details also appeared on the front, along with an advert for a local television and radio shop. Helpfully, each programme carried the date and the number of the programme.

Into the Sixties

In 1957–58 the programme size changed to one that some other clubs had adopted and became pocket-sized, consisting of 16 pages (the teams were listed in the centre pages) of print and an outer cover of stiffer paper, and this size would remain for the next 11 seasons. For that season the cover was changed to cerise, and the priced changed to 4d. There was certainly more content and information in these programmes, and for the 1959–60 season the cover was changed to show a drawing of goalmouth action with two players in Palace colours. This was retained up to the 1961–62 season, during which time the price rose to 6d. For the 1962–63 season the outer cover changed to plain white with a black-and-white illustration of the club's crest of the two Crystal Palace towers and glass central nave with 'Crystal Palace FC' written in a scroll. The final season for this pocket-sized programme was 1967–68, and in keeping with a more modern outlook the crest was dropped and the cover consisted of a bold club name, underneath which was a claret 'C' and 'P' in a square design with a blue football in the middle of the 'C'.

During the 1960s the Football League produced their own magazine *Football League Review*, which was included as a free insert in a growing number of clubs' programmes. In the 1968–69 season Palace joined this band and increased the programme size. The page numbers went up to 20, but the plain white cover was retained with the original club crest and scroll. The club invited fans to design a programme cover for the coming season, which would be the first ever in Division One, and the winning design, by Terry Golding, has become possibly the most iconic

A 1964 Palace programme.

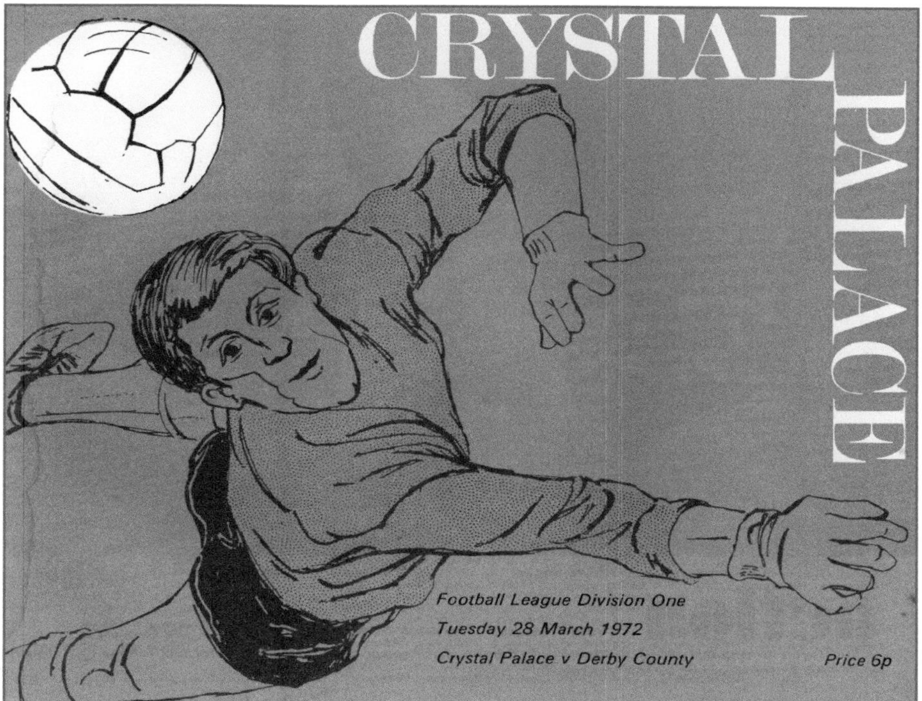

CRYSTAL
PALACE
Football League Division One
Tuesday 28 March 1972
Crystal Palace v Derby County
Price 6p

The oblong programme from the 1971–72 season.

in the club's post-war history, simply utilising the club's shirt colours of claret with a thin light blue stripe headed by the club crest on a white background. Again the pages numbered 20, while the team line ups were moved to the back page.

Top Flight Programmes

The club's four years in the top flight would see a new programme size each season, and in 1970–71 an innovative upright 'inner pocket' size was chosen with a reversion to a plain white cover as used in the mid-1960s. For this slimmer design the number of pages increased to 26, but the inclusion of the *Football League Review* made it difficult for the programme sellers, while it was the last to be printed by Andress Printing of Waddon New Road, Croydon.

A complete change followed in 1971–72 as the club's first oblong programme was introduced, featuring a turquoise-blue cover consisting of an outline drawing of a goalkeeper attempting to save a white ball. Monetary decimalisation in February 1971 meant that the price was now 6p and page numbers went back to 14 as some regular articles fell by the wayside. The 'Ajax'-style shirt that had been worn in the 1971–72 season was replicated in the cover design for 1972–73 and again a size change took place, this time to a more upright style that incorporated the new circular club badge together with an action picture from a previous Palace game, the first time this had appeared on the cover, in a large circle. The 18-page content was printed by Ward & Woolverton Ltd. The price rose to 7p, and for the last time, it is thought, the *Football League Review* was included.

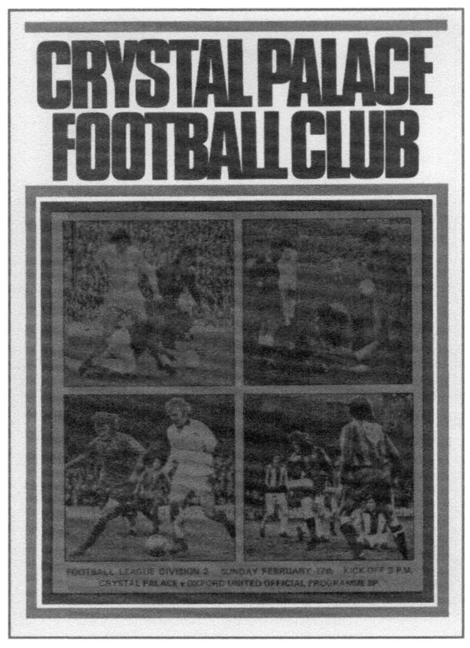

A Palace programme from the 1973–74 season.

Following the arrival of Malcolm Allison as manager in March 1973, everything at the club changed. The programme for the coming season reflected these changes with the new club colours being incorporated in the 24-page programme which, during the fuel and energy crisis that winter, was halved in content for three or four home games in January and February 1974 while a more standard size was adopted for this and the next four seasons. In the 1977–78 season the same size was kept but changed into an oblong format with a colour photograph on the cover. The number of pages dropped back to 16, although now incorporating regular articles by club historian Revd Nigel Sands, and the previous four years had seen the price rise to 15p. There was a 33 per cent price hike to 20p for the 1978–79 production, which utilised a better quality paper for an A5 size programme with 20 pages that would be the standard for the next three years as football programmes generally turned to more polished productions, and awards made by various bodies appeared on the scene.

There was a slight increase in the measurements of the programme for 1981–82 but with a retrograde step, for the cover appeared with a montage of cartoon-style drawings of some of the players, while a prominant 'Palace' appeared over the top of them. Although content was still primarily black and white, a few internal pages were printed on different coloured paper and again the price continued to rise, this time to 35p. The 1982–83 season brought another oblong publication similar in size and

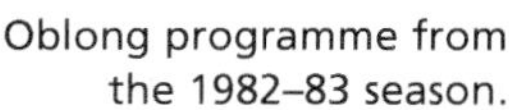

Oblong programme from the 1982–83 season.

production to the previous year, but it was becoming evident that editorial responsibility was now being handled outside the club.

In the 1983–84 season the programme reverted to the standard dimensions, and this size has been used for the programme ever since. The outside influence was even more prominent as, although the number of pages had increased from 20 to 28, the extra ones were given to a more general football supplement in the middle and the price rose another 10p to 50p. Matters were slightly better a year later with the supplement feature being discontinued.

The Programme Returns to Palace

A complete change took place in the summer of 1985 as responsibility for the programme returned to the hands of the club, with Pete King being put in charge, assisted by a youthful Terry Byfield, who had joined the club the previous January, and the Revd Nigel Sands making up the production team. Later, the mantle fell upon the broad shoulders of the club's communications manager Terry Byfield, now supported by four colleagues responsible for its content and graphic design.

By the mid-1990s the programme had become a full-colour publication up to 48 pages in length as the historical and statistical content expanded and other additional features were included, such as for a couple of seasons there was a pull-out picture of a player in the centre while reproduced programmes from earlier important matches were included on an irregular basis. For the club's centenary season of 2005–06, each programme carried a centre section of eight pages charting the club's progress over 100 years, together with profiles of important people in the club's history. This could be removed and kept separately to form a 'mini history' on its own.

Thus in the past 15 years or so computer-aided techniques have taken over, with production improving markedly. The matchday programme now contains 80 pages for £3 and is more magazine-like in its composition and paper quality, while a laminated outer cover had recently been included. There is naturally an element of advertising and some club corporate material, but many pages are given over to the visitors and also historical elements together with articles on current football matters and statistics, coupled with the magnificent action pictures taken by club photographer Neil Everitt. This has meant that the Palace programme has consistently been to the forefront of awards from the Football League and other periodicals produced by football programme dealers and clubs.

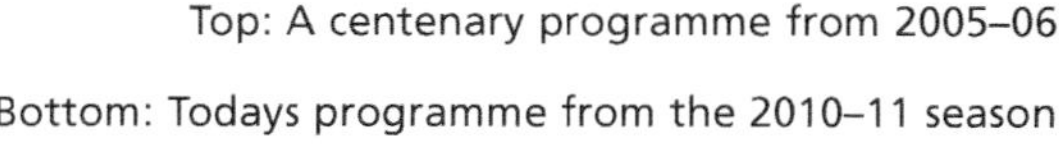
Top: A centenary programme from 2005–06.

Bottom: Todays programme from the 2010–11 season.

The Crystal Palace Chaplaincy

In 2004 Tempus Publishing (no longer in existance) brought out a book entitled *The Men Who Made Crystal Palace Football Club.* The publisher considered that the book should properly include a chapter about Palace's (then) honorary chaplain, Revd Nigel Sands, who had written most of that book and, of course, has contributed to this one. Since Crystal Palace was among the earliest football clubs to experience the benefits of a chaplain's service, it is considered by the publisher of this *Complete Record* that it is only right that a brief chapter should be provided about that work.

Football chaplains were once a rarity in the Football League, but the last 20 or 30 years have seen a major advance, to the extent that today well over half the Premier and Football League clubs now profit from their involvement.

Revd Sands served Crystal Palace in that capacity between 1974 and 2007 and was instrumental in the early advance of football chaplaincy, being involved in the appointment of several of his colleagues. Some readers may think unusual the idea of the close association of a clergyman with a major football club, but Nigel has pointed out several times that about 20 per cent of all Premier and Football League clubs were either founded by a parson (examples being Barnsley and Swindon Town) or owe their origins to a church or Sunday School (for example Queen's Park Rangers, Southampton and Aston Villa), so a clergyman's presence is actually perfectly natural. At the first national conference of the football chaplains, Palace's (then) manager, Steve Coppell, spoke appreciatively of the chaplain's involvement at his own club, and across professional football today there are plenty of folk who enthusiastically endorse and share Steve's view.

The role of chaplain is a supportive, rather than supporting, one. The injured or out-of-form player; the bereaved club official or supporter; the bitterly disappointed former youth-team player; the promising midfielder who faces a career-threatening operation; the lonely new signing who is living away from home, family and friends – these are all examples of those connected with a big football club who have been glad of a chaplain. Also, there are numerous Christian footballers, administrators, stewards, directors, referees (and assistants) as well as supporters, who are glad to have the presence of a minister at their place of work or recreation, and to use him as a focus for and demonstration of their own Christian allegiance.

By and large the chaplains do not actively seek publicity for themselves or their office, although, for example, the local media are often glad to have a measured response to the issue of fixtures that are re-arranged to take place on Good Friday as well as on all sorts of other football matters.

The football chaplains are men whose increasing involvement in our national sport can only be for its benefit and that of those engaged in any way in it. Palace's former chaplain was one of those who helped to establish this work in football, so that every football follower owes him and his colleagues a debt of gratitude.

Revd Sands passed on his chaplaincy involvement at Crystal Palace FC in 2007 to Revd Chris Roe, who was the minister at Folly's End Church in central Croydon at the time of his appointment but since the summer of 2008 has been the minister of Croydon Jubilee Church in Selsdon.

Crystal Palace Songs

It is known that in early 1946 the hugely active Crystal Palace Supporters' Club produced its own *Crystal Palace March* for the football club. Present-day fans should be aware that this was still, of course, the era during which many football clubs had their own marching bands. The club and its fans were intensely proud of their band, which would provide a measure of entertainment for the supporters before a game as well as during the half-time interval.

The *Crystal Palace March* was composed for the supporters' club by Mr Jack Morgan, who was musical director at the Empire Theatre in Croydon, was recorded by the London Military Band and subsequently adopted by the football club's directors. A version of this stirring tune, together with the vocal refrain, was also written for the piano, and it would be wonderful if a copy or two had survived to the present day; although this is, alas, not the case.

Palace fans from the 1950s and 1960s will recall with pleasure, and be pleased to confirm, that, in the days when fans were permitted to stand wherever they chose on the Selhurst Park terraces, the supporters' favourite record played over the loudspeaker system prior to kick-off was *Glad all Over* by the Dave Clark Five. The original recording was released in the UK in November 1963, and the song reached number two in the UK singles chart in January 1964. Palace's own recording of the song, after the fabulous 1990 FA Cup semi-final victory over Liverpool, was produced by Tony Hillier and arranged by Barry Upton, and the players performed the song on radio and television as the Cup Final itself approached. They may also recall how the younger generation of fans would position themselves around the perimeter in order to emphasise the beat with their fists on the advertising hoardings!

A quarter of a century later a Palace devotee from that period, Mr John Henty (who still features prominently at Selhurst Park on match days), became the Eagles' DJ and re-introduced the song, which took a hold on the 1980s supporters and became, and remains, the club's theme song. Palace took the field to it at Selhurst Park in the promotion campaign of 1988–89 and throughout the FA Cup run to Wembley as a top-flight club the following season. The Palace players themselves recorded their own version of the song as the club's Cup Final record, along with *Where Eagles Fly*, in April 1990 and, by virtue of the club's supporters singing it, in victory and defeat (though never better, surely, or with more enthusiasm, than at Wembley after the 1997 Play-off Final success), it remains the song with which Crystal Palace FC is associated at every ground in the country.

Probably Palace's next favourite song was recorded by the then playing staff for Christmas 1972. It was entitled *Claret and Blue* and the lyrics were produced for the benefit of all the club's fans in the match-day programme for the game against Manchester United on 16 December 1972. The reverse side of the disc was a song rendered by the players and their wives or girlfriends called *Why Can't We All Get Together*, but it must be acknowledged that it was scarcely a memorable item!

The club's run to the FA Cup semi-final in 1976 generated *Power to the Palace*, again sung by the then players. It is still sometimes offered to the fans at Selhurst Park prior to modern-day matches. Stage and TV comedian Ronnie Corbett heeded the injunction in the lyrics to 'bring a pal to see [the Palace] play', by bringing along his fellow star and comedy partner Ronnie Barker.

Meanwhile, the ebullient Palace manager Terry Venables and several of his friends recorded *Bye Bye Blackbird*, and since the 1990 FA Cup Final a whole plethora of Palace songs have been produced by various groups of supporters (for example, the Eastern Eagles – heralding from East Anglia rather than the Orient – offered *We All Follow the Palace* and *We Are The Eagles*) or individual fans like 'Lady Helen of Selhurst', who proclaimed to music that she was 'in love with Harry Bassett'. In 1997 Cherry Red Records compiled an anthology of 17 Palace songs on a CD for the interest and enjoyment of the club's supporters.

Palace's Greatest Teams

Introduction

In a previous Palace volume relating to 'great' players, a discussion was initiated as to what constitutes 'greatness'. The discussion was well received at the time, so that now the area is opened up further – partly with the help of comments contributed in reponse to the earlier debate. Certainly, this chapter requires some boundaries to be established for the discussion of 'great' Palace teams.

In one sense it would be perfectly possible to argue that Palace's top-flight sides of the 1980s, 90s and 2000s must comprise the club's greatest teams. but there is only one of those included here. Why? Because the adjective 'great' or 'greatest' in the chapter title is not construed to mean 'great' or 'greatest' in comparison to other Palace teams, but rather with reference to other clubs against which a particular side was pitted week in, week out, in matches in the division in which it played, and finished some way ahead of the normal aspirations of the supporters of the time.

Thus, it happens that the selection of Palace teams offered in this chapter includes the highest goalscoring side in the club's history – that of 1960–61, which bagged 110 League strikes in 46 matches – but also to be found here is another Palace team that secured only 50 League goals – the side which finished the 1990–91 campaign in third place in the top flight. Both were exceptional triumphs: extraordinary, glorious, wonderful and, to some degree at least, beyond what anyone anticipated before those seasons began.

Palace's best in the Southern League: 1913–14

Palace's Southern League First Division experiences since 1906 had been perfectly acceptable: two fourth-place finishes had been in 20-club divisions, along with two more in seventh, then in 1912–13 Palace finished fifth. Accordingly, hopes were high up at the old Crystal Palace that the club might make a really encouraging show in 1913–14.

The opening half of the season certainly demonstrated that such progress was feasible for, without ever showing a ruthless streak, except perhaps in a 5–1 defeat of a poor Reading side in mid-November, Palace had lost only three times in the first half of the season – and Palace avenged one of those defeats in early February when they secured their first-ever Southern League victory at Swindon's County Ground to go ahead of the Railwaymen on goal average at the top of the table. Palace lost just twice more: at greatly improved Reading and home to West Ham, but, as Easter approached we were still ahead of the Wiltshire club as divisional leaders.

The key to the season's eventual outcome can be seen in retrospect as being the matches that were played on Saturday 4 April: Palace beat Coventry 3–1 but Swindon trounced Portsmouth 5–0, so slipping ahead of Palace on goal average.

That was how it remained until the final day of the season, 25 April, when Palace were at Gillingham and Swindon at Cardiff. Ever-reliable goalscorer Ted Smith hit a

Back row, left to right: B. Bateman, J. Rogers, A. Waghorn, W. Beckerleg, J. Johnson, F. Wood, J. Bulcock, F. Smith (assistant trainer). Second row: A. Leake (trainer), W. Middleton, W. York, A. Michael, E. O'Conor, E. Rhodes, J. Walters, S. Stretton. Seated: Mr Goodman (secretary-manager), R. Spottiswood, E. Smith, J. Hughes, H. Hanger, H. Colclough, H. Collyer, J. Whibley. Front row: W.C. Davies, J. Williams, P. Keene, C. Hewitt.

Palace leveller at Gillingham: Swindon drew 0–0 and thus took the title by the slender margin of one tenth of a goal.

Palace's fine work was built upon the division's best defence, in which goalkeeper 'Josh' Johnson and the full-backs, Harry Collyer and Horace Colclough, were quite outstanding. Colclough in fact gained Palace's first full England international cap when he played for England against Wales at Cardiff on 16 March, while the half-back line, comprising Bob Spottiswood, Jimmy Hughes and captain Harry Hanger, was legendary. Meanwhile, centre-forward Ted Smith was the only ever-present player of the term and continued his superb run of goalscoring, netting 26 times in the 38-game programme.

Palace take a title on their Football League debut: 1920–21

Palace's Third Division Championship of 1920–21 was inevitably greeted with huge delight by the fans, but it must be regarded as doubtful whether they were particularly optimistic about the team's chances after they learned that Palace had lost their opening-day fixture against Merthyr Town. And had they known that the club would have to contend with three potentially major setbacks during the season, then, surely, few would have expected their favourites to romp home by a five-point margin the following spring.

But that is exactly what happened. In early November and with Palace well placed in the table, a fracas broke out at the end of a home defeat by Southend who had contested Palace's sophistication with some dubious physical tactics. Palace fans found this hard to take and engulfed Southend's worst offender. Inevitably, The Nest was closed by the FA and Palace had to play the home game at the end of the month down in Southampton.

Back row, left to right: Joe Nixon, Albert Harry, F. King, Jack Alderson, Arthur Swift (assistant trainer), George Irwin, Jimmy Allen, Bill Hand, Harry Dreyer. Middle row: W. Jones (trainer), Robert McCracken, 'Tom' Jones, Andrew Kennedy, Albert Feebery, Mr Edmund Goodman (manager), Albert Wells, Ernie Rhodes, J. Collier, Jack Little, A. Greig (assistant trainer). Front row: Ben Bateman, Tom Storey, John Conner, Ted Smith, Alf Wood, Bert Menlove, John Cartwright, John Whibley.

However, Palace manager Edmund Goodman refused to allow his men to become ruffled or to lose their focus. Palace won the match in question, but then, in the following home game, against Swansea, another major (and lasting) setback occured when Northern Ireland international wing-half Robert McCracken fell with a badly broken ankle. McCracken had been a key component of an excellent defence, but Mr Goodman was a shrewd manager as well as an inspirational one and deployed Welsh international half-back J.T. Jones as McCracken's deputy.

And then another, possibly key, absentee became veteran centre-forward and captain Ted Smith, who fell ill and whose need for a operation prevented him from playing after 1 January. However, the prolific John Conner simply upped his own scoring rate and, after Palace had put top-flight Manchester City out of the FA Cup, the team took the Third Division by storm.

Following defeat at Grimsby in early February, Palace put together a run of 16 unbeaten games, including eight consecutive wins prior to Easter, which took the club to the brink of success. Closest rivals for the title were Southampton and two drawn games ensued, at The Dell and The Nest. Ultimately, a 5–1 rout of Northampton in the last home game, followed by a point at The Cobblers' headquarters, ensured the Championship.

Perhaps Palace's greatest on-field contribution to the success was the little inside or centre-forward John Conner, who notched no fewer than 29 League goals that season, including nine in the last five games. But Jack Alderson was a fabulous goalkeeper, while Jack Little and Ernie Rhodes were experienced full-backs who had developed a marvellous accord, and the wingers, Ben Bateman and John Whibley, possessed pace, trickery and the ability to deliver accurate crosses.

Thus, given the potential setbacks, the Palace 1920–21 success was a hugely hard-fought but deserved one. The pity was that it would be 40 years before another promotion could be secured.

Palace's near miss 1928–29

Palace came closest to returning to the Second Division in the 1928–29 season, but with only one promotion place awarded to the regional Third Divisions, coming second counted for nothing. Nevertheless, Palace took Charlton to the final match before conceding the title on goal average alone.

In truth, Palace had not made impressive attempts at a return to the higher sphere in the three seasons that had elapsed since their 1925 drop into Division Three. Playing now at their Selhurst Park headquarters, Palace had finished the 1926–27 campaign in sixth place and the following term in fifth. Managed now by Fred Mavin, however, several useful new players had been secured during the close season, including full-backs Stan Charlton and Tom Crilly plus forwards Lewis Griffiths and Hubert Butler, while 'Jimmy' Wilde dominated at centre-half from November onwards.

In fact, it was not until the tall, slim, elegant Wilde joined Palace that the team began to look like anything approaching one of the stronger Third Division outfits. But after helping Palace to an FA Cup first-round victory over Kettering Town, Jimmy became a key figure in the side which set up a 17-match unbeaten run in the League (never bettered by a Palace side in a single season) and by the Saturday after Easter Palace were within a point of top place. By the final matches on Saturday 4 May 1929 Palace were level on points but second on goal average to Charlton, with everything hingeing on the clubs' final fixtures.

Back row, left to right: S. Charlton, M. Salt, W. Betteridge, J. Gill, L. Goodman (assistant secretary), M. Moyle, T. Wetherby, H. Butler, W. James. Second row: J. Jones (trainer), W. Routledge, L. Smith, R. Greener, W. Callender, S. Dean, J. Hamilton, H. Thoms, C. Fletcher, J. Cartwright (assistant trainer). Third row: H. Hopkins, T. Crilly, L. Griffiths, H. Havelock E.F. Goodman (secretary), F. Mavin (manager), T. Walsh, A. Davis, P. Mulcahy, G. Clarke. Front row: A. Harry, J. Scott, W. Turner, T. Conaty.

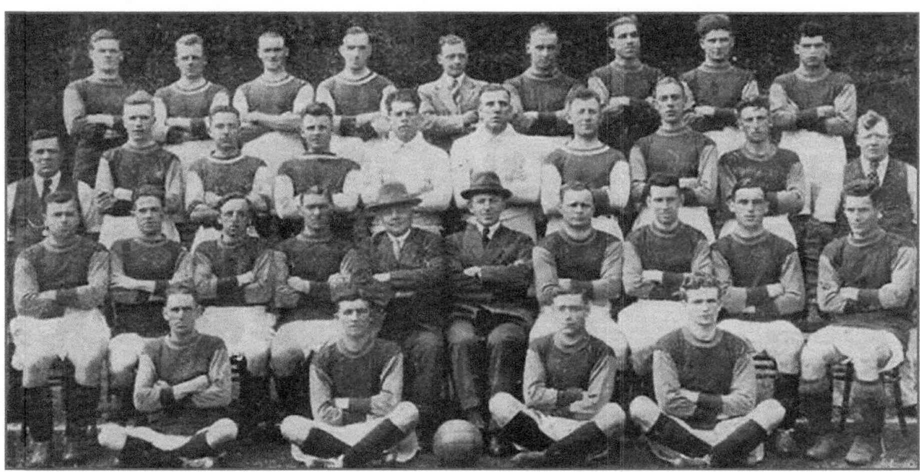

Palace's match was at home to Brighton, Charlton were at Walsall. Palace won their game with a 17th-minute Stan Charlton penalty, but Charlton also won at Fellows Park and so took the title and the promotion place that went with it. Despite netting 81 League goals – with Harry Havelock (20), Lewis Griffiths (18) and Hubert Butler (10) the top goalscorers – Palace were still rooted in the Third Division.

Another promotion at last 1960–61

As previously noted, there was to be 40 years between Palace's 1921 promotion and the next one, but when it did eventually arrive it came with such panache and style, allied to fabulous finishing, that Palace fans were purring with pleasure virtually throughout the entire season.

It all hinged upon the appointment of former Spurs boss Arthur Rowe as manager in April 1960. Mr Rowe made two vital close-season additions to his squad and, with another signing made early in the campaign, Palace became superior to every other club but one in Division Four. Using the gloriously attractive 'push and run' play which had been a feature of Mr Rowe's earlier successes at White Hart Lane, and with the summer additions of powerful wing-half George Petchey from Queen's Park Rangers and goalscoring left-winger Ron Heckman from Millwall, Palace began the new season both emphatically and effectively. Then, in October, Mr Rowe bought burly, tough centre-forward Dennis Uphill from Watford, principally to counter the heavy treatment being meted out to Johnny Byrne and Roy Summersby by some unscrupulous defenders, although Dennis was also a neat footballer and should not be thought of merely as a battering-ram centre-forward.

Palace's first match was the precursor to the goal-fest that was 1960–61, when they beat Accrington Stanley 9–2, with Byrne netting four times and Heckman securing a brace on

Back row, left to right: Brolly (trainer), Petchey, Byrne, Truett, Barnett, Evans, Rouse, Choules, Kerrins, Lunnis, Long, Mr A. Rowe (manager). Front row: Uphill, Summersby, Noakes, McNichol, Easton, Colfar, Gavin, Heckman.

his club debut. The only real setback occurred in mid-September when Palace met new Football League members, direct, no-nonsense Peterborough United, twice in five days and lost both times, meaning that Palace handed over top place in the division to them.

Palace responded effectively, however, especially at home, where Southport, Mansfield, Barrow and Bradford Park Avenue were all despatched by emphatic margins, while three consecutive away victories in December, at York, Accrington and Exeter, established the club as divisional leaders once again. It was in March that Palace began to falter and the lead was eroded, then lost. Four consecutive defeats enabled Peterborough to overtake Palace again so that even with six victories in the final seven games Palace were unable to catch their rivals.

Ultimately, Palace hit 110 League goals (still the club record, albeit from 46 matches), and Johnny Byrne's 30 remains unbeaten at Selhurst Park while Roy Summersby's 25 strikes also beat the club's previous post-war record of 23.

Perhaps Mr Rowe was fortunate in one respect – he inherited a club captain, the intelligent, experienced Johnny McNichol, who began 1960–61 as a wing-half but concluded it at right-back and played in every game. Vic Rouse in goal was another ever-present and the Welsh international was quite superb. George Petchey and Terry Long ran the midfield, with central-defensive duties shared by bulwarks Gwyn Evans and Len Choules. wingers Johnny Gavin and Ron Heckman, both Arthur Rowe protégés, were marvellously effective on the flanks and scored 22 goals between them.

For large parts of the season it was clear that the Palace side was the best one in the division, but under Mr Rowe it was never one that simply ground out a sequence of results – it accomplished promotion to Division Three with footballing skills that at times were utterly sublime.

Another Palace promotion 1963–64

Just three years on from the success recorded above, Palace won promotion again. But the manner in which they did so was startlingly different.

Dick Graham, the club's former goalkeeper and assistant manager, had replaced Arthur Rowe as Palace's manager in midwinter 1962–63 when the great man fell ill. Graham had then transformed the Palace team, and by the dawn of the following season there was a steely confidence at Selhurst Park that the side would now prove to everyone what an effective team they could be. And so it proved.

Dick Graham's preferred mode of play was rumbustious, exciting and hard-working. It relied upon physical and mental discipline, and Graham was among the first managers in the League to use dual centre-halves, with Brian Wood and Alan Stephenson paired in this way from midway through the season. He also pioneered the squad system, drafting players into and out of the side to promote or counter a particular tactic.

The start to the 1963–64 season could not have been more emphatic, as Palace lost 5–1 to Coventry! A draw at Reading was then followed by a 3–1 home win over Mansfield, and this pair of results and scorelines typified the way the season progressed. At Selhurst Park Palace were unbeatable until the last three weeks of the campaign, while the defence was seldom breached at home or away. Thus, on their travels the team became hard to beat, rarely conceding a goal, but drawing more games than they won.

Back row, left to right: A. Howe, C. Holton, D. Townsend, B. Wood, W. Glazier, J. Jackson, A. Stephenson, G. Petchey, T. Long, R. Little. Middle row: T. Brolly (trainer), S. Imlach, M. Griffiths, R. Allen, P. Burridge, D. Dowsett, W. Fuller, S. Forster, E. Werge, W. Birch. Front row: C. Catlett (groundsman), Mrs M. Hutchings (canteen manageress), Mr D. Graham (manager), Mr V. Ercolani (director), Mr J.R.H. Dunster JP (director), Mr R. Shrager (director), Mr A. Rowe (assistant manager), Miss M.E. Montague (secretary).

Although Palace were never out of the top four places after October, it was not until March that they rose to the pinnacle itself after a single-goal victory over Queen's Park Rangers. But the pace in the finale never slackened. Palace's closest rivals were Coventry, but Bournemouth and Watford were always at their heels, so that it was only by securing a point from the penultimate game, at Wrexham on 22 April, that Palace gained promotion. However, the title itself was still undecided and could go to either Palace or Coventry.

Needing just a point from the final match, Palace lost at home to Oldham while Coventry scraped out a 1–0 victory over Colchester and thus took the title on goal average. Palace still went up of course, and celebrated the fact, but everyone at Selhurst Park felt the anti-climax deeply.

Much of the credit for this promotion, gained by such an exciting, virile Palace team, must be given to Dick Graham. Single-minded and authoritarian, tough and hard, Graham would brook no disagreements with his plans and objectives. He drove his men and drew from them commitment that was unwavering. All of his players were experienced, seasoned professionals – yet each of them gave more than possibly they realised they had to give. Peter Burridge and Cliff Holton scored 20 Third Division goals apiece, augmented by Ronnie Allen and Brian Whitehouse who both netted seven times though from many fewer appearances and from creative positions rather than striking ones. The defence was magnificent – and the best bar one in the entire division – while George Petchey and Terry Long proved themselves to be consummate professionals. They had gained a promotion in 1960–61 in one way and now they had done so again in quite a different manner.

Palace's best team yet 1968–69

Bert Head was once described as 'the best manager in the business' by an authority on such matters. Few Palace fans of the late 1960s would disagree! And certainly the Palace team that he built for the 1968–69 season was the best side to don the shirt up to that date.

Left to right, extreme top: Steve Kember. Top: Brian Snowdon, Mark Lazarus. Second row: Colin Taylor, John Loughlan, John Jackson, Tony Taylor, John Sewell. Bottom: Cliff Jackson, Roger Hoy, Mel Blyth, John McCormick, David Payne.

Appointed as Palace boss in April 1966, Mr Head inherited the peerless goalkeeper John Jackson, able veteran John Sewell, the immaculate Steve Kember and his fellow midfielder David Payne, all of whom played key roles in the 1968–69 success. But Mr Head also began to bring together the men he believed he needed to a forge promotion-winning side. He brought in goalscoring inside-forward Bobby Woodruff, winger/striker Cliff Jackson, craggy centre-half John McCormick and powerful winger Mark Lazarus. In the summer of 1968 the manager added Colin 'Cannonball' Taylor, a raiding winger from Walsall who packed an explosive shot, along with midfielder Mel Blyth from Scunthorpe, whom Mr Head made into an ideal foil for John McCormick. Three autumn signings completed Mr Head's assembly: defender Roger Hoy arrived from Tottenham, while left-back John Loughlan and midfielder Tony Taylor, both from Morton, finalised the most successful squad Crystal Palace FC had ever known...although that was not immediately apparent.

Captained by John Sewell at right-back, Palace began the 1968–69 campaign with three consecutive victories, only for two away defeats to temper any over-confidence among the fans. That said, Palace were never far away from the leading clubs in Division Two, but, even well into the second half of the season, they were seldom among the top two.

Then bad weather ripped a full month of matches out of the club's fixture list, but, upon the resumption, Palace were a team inspired and inexorably hunted down the leading outfits. In the 16 remaining fixtures, Palace were undefeated and won 10 games, including prestigious victories at Derby (the champions-elect) and at Birmingham (one of Palace's closest challengers), though it was not until the weekend before Easter that Palace eventually slipped into second place at Middlesbrough's expense after a 2–1 win at Carlisle. A huge, 43,381 crowd came to Selhurst Park on Good Friday morning when Palace and Boro fought out an untidy, uncompromising goalless draw, but the following afternoon Portsmouth were beaten 3–1 before a rather smaller attendance.

Palace now had to negotiate two apparently tricky, northern away games, but with dogged defending they wrestled a point from each. However, after the game at Deepdale, the results from the other Second Division games made it clear that Palace's promotion had been all but grasped. Yet, needing now only a point, by half-time in the final home match on Saturday 19 April 1969 Palace were trailing Fulham by two goals. Thankfully, an interval address from coach George Petchey inspired an emphatic revival. Goals after less than a minute, then a little less than a couple of minutes after a quarter of an hour, from Steve Kember, Mark Lazarus and Cliff Jackson, ensured the victory that confirmed Palace's promotion to the top flight for the first time. Jubilation and a carnival atmosphere prevailed everywhere as the team, the fans and the board celebrated the fact.

Palace take another title 1978–79

Palace manager Terry Venables had already led The Eagles to promotion from Division Three in 1976–77. That success had been gained largely with experienced players but, with captain Ian Evans badly injured and many of the others simply too old, Venables wrought a minor revolution at Selhurst Park.

Back row, left to right: Nick Chatterton, Dave Swindlehurst, John Burridge, David Fry, Ian Walsh, Jim Cannon. Middle row: Dave Horn (trainer), Ernie Walley (coach), Allan Harris (coach), Terry Fenwick, Paul Hinshelwood, Billy Gilbert, George Graham, Charlie Simpson (physio), Terry Venables (manager). Front row: Vince Hilaire, Terry Boyle, Mike Elwiss, Martin Hinshelwood, Ian Evans, Peter Nicholas, Jerry Murphy, Ken Sansom, Barry Silkman.

Retaining only the brilliant Kenny Sansom; his full-back partner Paul Hinshelwood; defender Jim Cannon, now playing at centre-half and the club skipper; and brave centre-forward David Swindlehurst, Venables made two astute purchases in the build-up to the 1978–79 season. He had paid £40,000 to Aston Villa in March for the irrepressible, extrovert goalkeeper John Burridge – who at 26 years old was the oldest member of that 1978–79 promotion squad – and then during the close season paid £200,000 to Preston for their stylish, goalscoring captain Mike Elwiss. For the rest, Venables simply promoted members of Palace's highly successful FA Youth Cup-winning sides of 1977 and 1978, and then in October 1978 he brought Steve Kember back to Palace from Leicester for £40,000. What judgement that transfer showed! Palace benefitted hugely from Kember's experience and talent and he then became the only Palace man to star in two promotion seasons to the First Division.

The key to Palace's triumph lay firmly with the defence. John Burridge kept a fabulous 21 clean sheets, and the defence as a whole only conceded 24 goals in the entire season! That established a club record by a considerable distance that has barely been approached in the ensuing years.

Palace's ultimate success in 1978–79 is seen to be even more creditable when it is pointed out that that particular Second Division was extremely competitive. After the initial stages of the season there were four firm favourites for the title: Palace, Brighton, Stoke and Sunderland (indeed, just two points separated them in the final table), with West Ham as outsiders. But there were few poor sides in the division. For example, Burnley, whom Palace beat in the final climactic game, finished 13th, yet they had beaten Palace at Turf Moor and played well enough to have taken at least a point from Selhurst Park. And, if Palace had lost to The Clarets that night, they would have missed out on promotion altogether.

Put simply then, Terry Venables's young team had emulated their predecessors of 10 years earlier and returned Palace to the top flight – but they had done better, for they had achieved that landmark as champions.

Palace's 'best moment in football' 1988–89

The early-to-mid-1980s had been a difficult period for Crystal Palace FC and its fans, but, under Steve Coppell (appointed 1984) matters began to improve so that, had the present-day Play-off arrangements pertained then, Palace would have taken part in them in 1986, 1987 and 1988!

That said, although the 1988–89 season ended in glorious fashion for everyone at Selhurst Park, it began in a dreadful, stuttering manner. And it continued that way until at least the New Year, so that Palace fans – and probably Palace's manager too – certainly entertained fears that the campaign was not likely to see a change in status any more than the previous one had.

As the year changed, two particular developments occurred which brought contrasting emotions. Firstly, Palace fans had been delighted at a splendid 3–2 Friday night victory at Oldham on 30 December, but that pleasure was marred by the news that club skipper Geoff Thomas had sustained an internal injury which proved so difficult to diagnose that Geoff was unable to play for the club again for the rest of the season. Secondly, Steve Coppell made one last attempt to build a promotion-winning side for 1988–89 by signing tough little right-winger Eddie McGoldrick from Northampton Town for £200,000, in January 1989.

Palace did spend one week in the Play-off places in February following a 2–1 victory at Ipswich, despite the referee mistaking Jeff Hopkins for John Pemberton, and sending the Welsh international pivot off in error, but it was only in early April, after another fine away win, at Leeds 2–1, that Palace entered the top six with serious intent. Quite suddenly, the Palace side gelled into a most effective unit: the victory at Leeds was the first match of an excellent run of 11 games for only one defeat (at Swindon on 25 April), but including no fewer than eight victories which made Palace not only the in-form side of the division, but also ensured that the team finished the original programme of matches in third place.

Involved in the Play-offs for the first time, Palace lost both the first legs in the semi-final and Final at Swindon (1–0) and Blackburn (1–3) respectively. But the power and goalscoring prowess at Selhurst Park was formidable and enabled Palace to emerge victorious on aggregate against both opponents. Among Steve Coppell's many talents lay a gift for summing up any situation in a few words: after Palace's promotion had been secured in front of a 30,000 full house at Selhurst Park, Coppell claimed that this was his 'best moment in football', and there was no doubt that he spoke for every Palace fan.

Simply Palace's best-ever side 1990–91

Among all of the fine Palace teams featured in this chapter, there must be the best one of all, and surely there can be little debate about which one that is. It must be the one which finished 1990–91 in third place in the top flight, and won a Wembley Cup Final as well.

Agreed, during the 1990–91 season Palace never achieved top place in the senior division as they had done for a week on 29 September 1979 following a 4–1 victory over visiting Ipswich, but the team was never out of the top five First Division places from August to December, took over third place after beating Manchester City 2–0 at Maine Road on 22 December and retained that position for the remaining 20 games of the 38-match programme. That, surely, represents the better accomplishment – and, up to the time of writing at least, it represents Palace's greatest-ever achievement.

Equally, wonderfully exhilarating as the 1979 victory over Ipswich was, the 1990–91 run included marvellous individual match successes too. Liverpool were beaten in a televised match with a Mark Bright goal on 30 December; Nottingham Forest were undone by a late Eric Young header on 2 February at the City Ground; Leeds were defeated at Elland Road on 23 March when Ian Wright and John Salako scored; and Manchester United were despatched 3–0 at Selhurst Park in the final game of the season. While, for the purists, Ian Wight's dazzling second half, 18-minute hat-trick at Plough Lane, in Wimbledon's last match there, was unforgettable.

But Palace also won a major Cup that season too. No one pretended that the Zenith Data Systems Cup had any parity with the FA Cup, but the 4–1 extra-time victory over Everton on Sunday 7 April 1991 brought huge satisfaction to the club and its followers.

Palace's most impressive Championship yet! 1993–94

Palace's 1993–94 Championship was achieved in imperious style under the guidance of new manager Alan Smith and, in comparison with the 1978–79 Championship, this one was vastly superior.

Initially, some supporters may have possessed doubts about the quality of the 1993–94 team: two former Premiership stars departed from Selhurst Park for clubs which they considered bigger and better equipped than Palace. Alan Smith then announced that his

Back row, left to right: Chris Coleman, David Whyte, John Humphrey, Eric Young, Gareth Southgate, Richard Shaw, Chris Armstrong, Bruce Dyer, Nigel Martyn. Front row: John Salako, Andy Woodman, Damian Matthew, Dean Gordon, Simon Rodger.

team would be adopting a more sophisticated approach than the fans had witnessed for many years. Smith called the new style 'pass and move', and the Palace side of 1993–94 certainly demonstrated far greater levels of refinement than had been seen for a long time.

Some other Palace fans' only doubts about the prospects for 1993–94 concerned one particular obstacle that Alan Smith faced: to follow Steve Coppell, who had managed the club for nine years, was a daunting task. But Smith's infectious enthusiasm and utterly positive attitude totally overcame this arduous task, together with many other difficulties, so that, apart from the perhaps inevitable lapse at the opening of the season, the division was taken by storm. Palace were top of the table by mid-September, were never out of the top-four places all season and finished as champions with a huge seven-point margin over the second-placed club, Nottingham Forest.

Palace were not entirely robust, however, for their away form might have left them potentially vulnerable to other ambitious challengers. But this matter was brilliantly resolved by Alan Smith in mid-January, following two defeats in eight days at Wolves, when he signed Liverpool and England international striker or midfielder Paul Stewart on loan. Stewart was out of his class at Division One level and his signing proved brilliantly effective because Palace immediately went on a nine-match unbeaten run, before bringing the season near to its end with six consecutive victories, including a 3–2 success at Middlesbrough in the penultimate match on Sunday 1 May.

The season finished with a degree of anti-climax, it is true. In front of a capacity crowd at Selhurst Park of 28,749, Palace lost to Watford 2–0 on the day when the Holmesdale terrace was used for the last time before being closed for redevelopment. But the (then) 106-year-old trophy and the players' medals were presented by the League's president Mr Gordon McKeag, and, regardless of the outcome of the match, Palace marched triumphantly back to the top flight, having achieved the most significant margin of all the Championship sides, and having put all the divisional challengers to distant flight.

New administration achieves another promotion 2003–04

New Palace owner Simon Jordan had bought the club out of administration in July 2000, but it was some time before it settled down or was able to make a serious attempt to bring Premier League football back to Selhurst Park. But under Steve Kember, the Palace fans' choice as manager, the club appeared to be poised to make that challenge for, initially at least, everything went wonderfully well and the team appeared to be completely capable. By 23 August Palace were top of the Football League and from top to bottom the club's sights were set upon another promotion. That arrived, but by no means in the manner in which the chairman, the fans or even, one suspects, the players anticipated that it would.

The fact was that autumn 2003 was a period most at the club would rather forget: Palace won just one League game between mid-August and mid-November, plummetted down the table and were barely out of the relegation places when the chairman's patience snapped. Assistant manager Kit Symons, in temporary control, fared better but just before Christmas Mr Jordan appointed former Northern Ireland international and Palace favourite Iain Dowie as boss.

The response was virtually instantaneous. Slowly Palace climbed the table, and by the end of February 2004 they had reached ninth place; by the end of April, seventh. Then a crucial victory over Walsall in the last home game took the team into sixth place, a Play-off place secured by a late West Ham goal at Wigan eight days later.

In retrospect, several factors were in the chairman and Iain Dowie's favour. With three points for a win, Palace's victories under the new appointee carried greater emphasis, while Julian Gray's December return from a fruitless search for a Premiership contract greatly enhanced the attacking options. But most important of all, Palace striker Andy Johnson hit a tremendous vein of goalscoring form, as from just before Dowie's arrival he notched 14 goals in 10 games. After a gap, he added five more in the final four games.

The Play-off semi-final with Sunderland was exhausting and draining – and that was just for the onlookers! Palace won 3–2 in the first leg at Selhurst Park, but the Black Cats had the Eagles by the throat at the Stadium of Light, scoring twice, only for Palace substitute Darren Powell to send his team back level on aggregate with a header in stoppage time to force extra-time. In fact, the contest went all the way to penalties, with Palace winning 5–4, the decisive kick coming from Michael Hughes.

The game at the Millennium Stadium against West Ham was taut and tension-filled. Ultimately it was settled by a simple tap-in by skipper Neil Shipperley after the Hammers' 'keeper failed to hold a low drive from Andy Johnson.

It was not Palace's greatest-ever promotion, or even their best-ever team, but the chairman and his colleagues, as well as the players and fans, celebrated what was the club's most unlikely resurgence and which had ended in another Palace triumph.

Palace's Finest Players 1905–Present

ALDERSON, Jack

Born: 28 November 1891, Crook, Co. Durham
Died: 17 February 1972, Sunderland
Apps: 205
Goals: 0

Jack Alderson was one of the marvellous goalkeepers who have served Crystal Palace, but he was the first of them to gain full England international honours while a player at the club.

Alderson came from Crook in County Durham and had played for the local amateur side as a junior before joining Newcastle at the age of 17. When World War One broke out he served in the army, and it was while he was stationed at Woolwich that he was noticed by Palace's secretary-manager Mr Edmund Goodman. He played a few of the wartime fixtures for Palace at The Nest and then signed for the club as soon as he left the forces.

Alderson's first-class debut for Palace was the opening match of the 1919–20 season, when Palace hosted a Southern League clash against Northampton on 30 August 1919, which finished 2–2. He then played in every League and FA Cup game that season, helped Palace to a praiseworthy third-place finish and established himself in the affections of all the Palace patrons of the period. Statistically speaking, 1920–21 was his best season with the club, for he was an ever present in the 42-match programme in the newly-formed Football League Third Division and conceded only 34 goals – easily the best by a Palace goalkeeper for over half a century! His splendid record helped the club to gain promotion to the Second Division, although the club did not find life in that higher tier at all easy; indeed, the fact that Palace remained there for four seasons was not a little due to Alderson's presence between the posts. He earned applause and admiration at many grounds for his brave and spectacular displays and clearly improved with time because, in his final season with Palace, 1923–24, he became a wonderful and renowned penalty-saver, to enormous acclaim!

There is little doubt that, had Jack Alderson been with a more glamorous club, or a more successful one, he would have gained many more international caps than the single one he gained when playing for England against France in Paris on 10 May 1923, where England triumphed 4–1 and he was only beaten in the last 90 seconds when the game was well won.

Alderson's Palace career ended regrettably, in a dispute over bonuses, in May 1924. He played for a season with Pontypridd before Sheffield United secured his registration. He played 122 League games for the Blades and then joined Exeter in May 1929 but was forced into retirement by injury after appearing in 36 League matches for the Grecians, including both their fixtures against Palace in the 1928–29 season.

ALLEN, Ronnie

Born: 15 January 1929, Fenton, Staffordshire
Died: 9 June 2001
Apps: 109
Goals: 37

Among the football fans who refer to this volume there will be those who recall England teams of the 1950s which, depending on the curious predilections of the selectors, sometimes included a dark-haired, skilful, nimble little winger or centre-forward named Ronnie Allen. Some may be surprised to discover his name here and wonder how this adroit footballer came to spend his twilight years of his illustrious career with a humble club like Crystal Palace, a long way from his native Black Country.

Allen joined Palace in the summer of 1961 when manager Arthur Rowe sought additional quality resources following the club's promotion to the Third Division. Allen may have been approaching the end of an illustrious career – at club level this was spent at Port Vale and West Bromwich Albion – but this was a wise move by Mr Rowe which proved highly beneficial to Palace and popular among the fans.

Ronnie Allen immediately struck up an exciting and productive partnership with Johnny Byrne which delighted Palace supporters and confounded opponents. But it was later in his Palace career that Allen was seen at his vintage best, as he played the passes and supplied the crosses from which Cliff Holton, Dickie Dowsett and then Peter Burridge scored the goals, which first of all kept the club in the Third Division and then took them into Division Two at the end of the 1963–64 campaign. Allen was actually Palace's captain for that promotion seaon, although injuries restricted his contribution as the campaign drew towards its climax, and he then completed precisely a century of League appearances for the club before moving back to the Black Country to take up a coaching position with Wolves.

Before he did so, however, he performed delightfully in Division Two: any Palace fan who saw it will be thrilled to be reminded of a hat-trick of the greatest sophistication which graced one of his last games for the club, a midweek fixture against visiting Charlton on 30 September

1964. The first was a 25-yard curler from a free-kick routine which never left the turf as it zipped round the wall. The second, just after the hour, was a thumping cross-shot following a corner, and the final goal was a silky penalty in injury time, stroked rather than struck past the hapless goalkeeper. A near 30,000 crowd gave Allen a standing ovation at the final whistle to show their appreciation.

AMBROSE, Darren

Born: 29 February 1984, Harlow
Apps: 79+3
Goals: 27

England Youth, Under-20 and Under-21 international midfielder, 27-year-old, 6ft and 11st, Darren Ambrose joined Palace on 1 July 2009 on a free transfer from local rivals Charlton Athletic, having previously played for Ipswich and Newcastle. He soon became a firm favourite with the fans at Selhurst Park.

Darren is a diligent and enterprising midfielder, but he is absolutely supreme at the Palace in the important matter of free-kicks. Darren's devastating power and accuracy in this is feared by all opposition defences, and hugely admired by his colleagues and fans at Selhurst Park. Probably the best among his astonishing top-scoring tally of 20 goals in 2009–10 (15 in League matches) was his stunning 35-yard stike in Palace's FA Cup fifth-round tie against Aston Villa which, but for a dreadful abberation by the officials, would have taken the club through to the sixth round. Nevertheless, the ball was still rising as it swerved past Villa's goalkeeper, veteran United States international Brad Friedel.

However, injuries, the closest possible marking by opponents due to his reputation and, frankly, Palace's highly indifferent away form, all combined to minimise Darren's effectiveness in 2010–11, but even so his 28 League appearances and seven goals for the club that season were impressive in their own right and compared creditably with those he had secured at his previous clubs.

BATEMAN, Ben

Born: 20 November 1892, Shepherds Bush
Died: 24 March 1961
Apps: 180
Goals: 10

Ben Bateman was a London boy – and in the early days of the club, right up to the end of the 1920s, that was unusual. But during that period, in which most of Palace's players came from the north or the Midlands, Bateman was a popular and welcome exception to the rule.

Prior to World War One, Bateman served Palace excellently while remaining an amateur, and in 1913–14 he earned amateur international honours while touring Scandinavia with the England Amateur XI. But the schoolmaster was

already an established Southern League player by that time. At 5ft 10in tall and 13 stone, Bateman was big for a winger, but he made 29 appearances in the 38-match programme, was a first-choice for manager Edmund Goodman and netted a couple of valuable goals. By choice his position was outside-right, though later in his career he would occasionally switch wings, and his place as a regular if unpaid member of Palace's 1913–14 side tells us much about him because that was the season in which Palace only conceded the Southern League Championship to Swindon on goal average.

Bateman made nine appearances at the start of the 1914–15 season, but he was among the first to respond to the call to serve in the forces, and upon his return he simply resumed his duty as Palace's first-choice outside-right, making 37 League appearances in the 1919–20 campaign and netting another two useful goals. However, it was during Palace's excellent drive to promotion from the newly formed Third Division that Bateman's fine turn of speed and immaculate crosses were seen at their best for the club. Innumerable times he laid on precision centres from which initially Ted Smith, then John Conner, the regular centre-forwards at that time, were able to score.

Palace's first-ever season in the higher division was 1921–22 and must rank as Ben Bateman's best for the club. Not only did he prove himself to be the master of many accredited and experienced Division Two full-backs, but he was in his usual position of outside-right for Palace's glorious FA Cup victory over Everton, a 6–0 win at Goodison Park on 7 January 1922. During that frolic, Bateman laid on Palace's first goal for John Whibley after only four minutes, hit the bar himself and then made Palace's fourth goal, netted by Bert Menlove in the second half.

BLYTH, Mel

Born: 28 July 1944, Norwich
Apps: 250+4
Goals: 12

Precious few Palace fans could possibly have so much as heard of Mel Blyth when manager Bert Head secured his transfer from Scunthorpe in July 1968, but he became one of those figures that bestrode the Palace scene of the late 1960s to the mid-1970s like a colossus. A tall, strong, fair-haired Adonis, Blyth was signed as an old-style left-half but developed into a magnificent back-four man, where his 6ft-plus stature and hearty 12 stone frame made him a natural central-defender and fearsome opponent.

Blyth immediately became a prominent and regular member of Palace's 1968–69 promotion side from the old Second Division, and then, in the club's first-ever match at the highest level, gained a permanent niche in all Palace record books by scoring the club's first goal with a controlled, dipping header, which put Palace in the lead and on the way to a

creditable 2–2 draw against illustrious visitors, Manchester United. Blyth scored a cracking goal the following Saturday as well, a searing 25-yarder at Goodison Park against Everton, but the Toffees came back to win with the help of a debatable penalty.

When Palace inevitably came under pressure in the top flight Blyth became a permanent fixture in the defensive line up and, alongside John McCormick, made up the twin pillars around which so much of the action centred. Over Palace's first four First Division seasons, 1969–73, only John Jackson played more times than Mel Blyth, and his appearance record of 151 games at that level speaks volumes about a stalwart, dependable defender who could be relied upon at all times.

After Palace dropped out of the First Division a long spell of injury reduced Blyth's appearances. After the start of the 1974–75 season he moved to Southampton for a £60,000 fee. He became Saints' Player of the Year in 1975 and then won an FA Cup-winners' medal with them in 1976.

But Mel was to appear again, briefly, for Palace. In the winter of 1977–78, then manager Terry Venables brought him back to Selhurst Park on loan after Ian Evans' leg had been broken. His extra half-dozen games for Palace at that time took him into the elite company of men who have played over 250 senior matches for the club since its formation in 1905.

BRIGHT, Mark

Born: 6 June 1962, Stoke on Trent
Apps: 282+4
Goals: 113

Mark Bright was Palace's supreme goalscorer and sophisticated striker throughout the most successful years the club has ever known, and most Palace fans of that period have their own unforgettable memories of his exploits in Palace colours.

Mark was recruited by manager Steve Coppell from Leicester City, where he was languishing in the reserve side. Initially on loan in November 1986, it was his goals, along with those of Ian Wright, which took Palace back to the old First Division in 1989. Those strikes helped to make the duo Palace's top goalscorers in the Leagues' higher divisions, as well as one of the most prolific striking partnerships in the country at that time.

In fact, 'Brighty' earned the Golden Boot for the highest scorer in the division in 1987–88 when he notched 24 goals. The following term, the 1988–89 promotion season, in which he played in every match, took him past his half-century of League goals for the club, while his 12 goals in the top flight in the 1989–90 campaign were an important and sometimes spectacular feature of the club's showing. Palace fans will never forget that it was Mark's crashing drive at the start of the second half that began the club's recovery against Liverpool in the FA Cup semi-final and ultimately helped to take Palace to Wembley.

As Palace impressed in the First Division in 1990–91, Mark's prowess gained further national recognition when he scored the decisive goal against Liverpool in a televised League match at Selhurst Park on 30 December. He proved his predatory skills at the highest level of the domestic game with a sequence of seven goals in just 10 games during midwinter as Palace pursued Arsenal and Liverpool at the top of the table, ultimately finishing in third place, easily the best final placing the club has ever attained.

Even after Ian Wright left Selhurst Park, 'Brighty' continued his sparkling form, and many of the club's fans from that period would agree that the 1991–92 season was actually Bright's best of all. Not only did he captain the side for a few games in the early winter, but he also netted a remarkable 17 top-flight goals – Palace's best-ever at that level – and was the only player to make full appearances in every competition in which the club was engaged.

Bright joined Sheffield Wednesday early in the inaugural Premier League season of 1992–93, but he remains a firm favourite among everyone at Crystal Palace and is a welcome visitor whenever he returns.

BURRIDGE, John

Born: 3 December 1951, Workington, Cumbria
Apps: 102
Goals: 0

Simply in terms of statistics, when compared with many of the men who feature in this chapter, John Burridge would seem to lack stature, but, in terms of goalkeeping ability, most Palace fans would probably agree that John Burridge has only John Jackson and Nigel Martyn ahead of him in the post-war era.

Photo © HY Money

Burridge's astonishing football career, which spanned over a quarter of a century, began at Workington in 1968–69, where he was a contemporary of a former Palace star, Brian Wood. But Palace fans of the late 1970s will never forget this amiable, extrovert gymnast, joker and goalkeeper supreme, who was an ever-present member of the club's 1978–79 promotion side and starred in what is, statistically speaking, Palace's best-ever defence. His fabulous record that term of 21 clean sheets is the highest ever recorded by any goalkeeper at the club; his concession of only 24 League goals all season is Palace's best by a distance and seems unlikely ever to come under challenge; and in the second half of the 42-match programme 'Budgie' had let in just eight goals in what is an amazing record of defensive brilliance.

But, impressive as all these figures undoubtedly are, they only reveal part of John Burridge's contribution to Palace. His imposing presence exuded confidence, which spread to his teammates and supporters alike; he used his voice to great advantage in a way few goalkeepers did, to help, direct and encourage his colleagues; and he simply refused to allow any opponent to even consider that he might just have a chance of beating him – with the result that few of them ever did.

Palace fans immediately took Burridge to their hearts after his arrival from Aston Villa, and would throng the terraces of Selhurst Park long before kick-off to witness his extraordinary pre-match warm-up sessions, in which he entertained and amused fans before returning to the dressing room as mud-stained as if he had played a full game.

It was a mark of the esteem in which he was held at Palace, both as a goalkeeper and as a showman, that whenever he returned to the ground with his later clubs, he was invariably accorded a warm welcome, both from Palace fans and from his former playing colleagues.

BURRIDGE, Peter

Born: 30 December 1933, Harlow, Essex
Apps: 124
Goals: 49

There has never been a more shrewd football manager than Mr Arthur Rowe, and it was to this silver-haired genius that Crystal Palace and their fans were indebted

for the arrival at Selhurst Park in the summer of 1962 of former Millwall captain Peter Burridge.

Naturally left-footed, but possessing a venomous shot in both feet, plus the ability to head the ball with power and accuracy, it was surprising that Palace had no rivals from bigger clubs when Mr Rowe prised Burridge away from The Den. Peter immediately demonstrated his worth as he was Palace's leading goalscorer in the 1962–63 season with 14 goals, including a hat-trick in the Easter Monday 5–0 rout of Wrexham.

Burridge then managed to net 20 strikes in Palace's 1963–64 promotion season and thereby finished as joint top scorer with Cliff Holton. It should be kept in mind, however, and with no dishonour at all to 'Big Cliff', that the latter was Palace's penalty taker, while all of Peter Burridge's goals came from open play.

The strike for Crystal Palace for which all fans of that period will forever remember him was the one which Peter himself later described as the best of his career. Palace were enjoying a fine, if long overdue, FA Cup run in the winter of 1964–65 and faced a fifth-round tie against sophisticated Nottingham Forest from the top flight. Palace had taken the lead but were pulled back to 1–1 just after the interval. Come the 64th minute of the game and Cliff Holton swung over a cross from the left for Peter to volley, left-footed and from some 25 yards out, and it crashed into the top corner of the net to an explosion of sound from the packed Palace crowd.

Towards the end of his time with Palace, Burridge began to develop a midfield role in the craftier confines of the Second Division, but it is for his goalscoring exploits that Crystal Palace fans chiefly remember him – and no wonder.

BYRNE, Johnny

Born: 13 May 1939, West Horsley, Surrey
Died: 27 October 1999, Cape Town, South Africa
Apps: 259
Goals: 101

It was to Vincent Blore, a goalkeeper with Crystal Palace for a couple of seasons in the mid-1930s, that the club owed the fact that the supreme skills of Johnny Byrne were developed on Palace's behalf and to such advantage. Stylish and skilful, the youthful prodigy signed for Palace on the day after his 17th birthday and progressed to become one of the greatest players ever to grace the club.

Byrne was given the prototype nickname 'Budgie' on account of his ceaseless chatter on the pitch. He was certainly the prime reason for Palace's success in climbing out of the Fourth Division in 1960–61, and his 30 League goals that season remains Palace's post-war scoring record for a single season. His silky talent, deft touches and ball-playing skills, nurtured and refined by the great Arthur Rowe, were tailor-made for the 'push-and-run' style advocated by the manager, and drew huge admiration from the fans who thronged to see him play. Of course, it was inevitable that such a player would become a target for the bigger clubs, but he was still with Palace when he gained his first full England international cap against Northern Ireland at Wembley on 22 November 1961 – Palace's first such honour in 38 years.

When Byrne moved to West Ham for £60,000 plus the return of poor Ron Brett in March 1962, the fee was the biggest between British clubs at that time, and his career flourished amid the glamour and publicity of the First Division. However, to the delight at everyone at Crystal Palace, Byrne returned to Selhurst Park in the spring of 1967 and he was given an emotional reception by the fans at the friendly against Leicester City, played on the evening after he had re-signed. 'Well hello, Johnny, welcome home Johnny,' the Palace faithful sang, to the tune of the theme song of *Hello Dolly*, 'it's so good to have you back where you belong'. Byrne hit the side's 36th-minute goal to add to the home crowd's pleasure that evening, but unfortunately his return to Palace was not successful overall and, little more than a year later, he moved on to struggling Fulham, for whom he appeared at Selhurst Park in Palace's final home game of their 1968–69 promotion season.

Johnny Byrne's aggregate total of 259 Palace games keeps him well to the fore in the club's all-time appearances chart, while his 90 League goals have rarely been exceeded. It should be remembered, however, that Byrne had several spells out on the wing or at inside-forward/midfield, and so goalscoring was not always his prime responsibility. Quite simply, at his peak, Johnny Byrne was one of the most gifted footballers that Crystal Palace FC has ever known. Thus, it was a great pleasure for fans of the club when he was invited back to Palace as a guest on a couple of occasions in the 1990s, when he was given a rapturous reception by the supporters as an indication of the permanence of his reputation at Selhurst Park.

It was, therefore, with much sadness as well as shock that the club learned of his sudden and untimely death in South Africa in the autumn of 1999, and Palace published a moving obituary and reminiscence in his honour in the club's programme in mid-November that year.

CALLENDER, Billy

Born: 5 January 1903, Prudhoe
Died: 26 July 1932, Selhurst Park
Apps: 225
Goals: 0

Billy Callender, Palace's first-choice goalkeeper from 1926 to 1932, was considered by some of his contemporaries to have had sufficient skill and character to follow his illustrious predecessor, Jack Alderson, not just as the Crystal Palace custodian but also into the full England international side itself.

Callender joined the Palace staff in October 1923 as a 20-year-old from his local club, Prudhoe Castle in Northumberland, and saved a penalty against West Ham reserves in his first match for his new club. He took undisputed possession of the goalkeeper's jersey in the Palace dressing room in January 1926 and earned himself a place in a Football League representative side later that year. Callender was only ever missing from Palace line ups from that time as a result of injury or illness, although his playing record demonstrates that he was prone to neither, and it was while Palace had Billy Callender in goal that the club came closest to returning to the Second Division in the 1928–29 season, finishing runners-up to Charlton, level on points but with a slightly inferior goal average.

Callender was awarded a benefit match on Wednesday 15 April 1931 against the Combined Universities, but a knock he received in the League match the previous Saturday prevented him from playing – so he appeared as a linesman instead! That was typical behaviour from Billy Callender, and his popularity at Selhurst Park as a result knew no bounds.

Sadly, however, the story of Billy Callender ended not in triumph in an England team, but in tragedy. His beloved fiancée was striken with polio, and over a two-year period her health slowly deteriorated. Billy refused to allow this to affect his performances in goal, however, and he never played better than in his last pair of League games at the end of the 1931–32 season. A fortnight later Billy's fiancée died. With no football to relieve his loss, Billy took her death very hard and on Tuesday 26 July 1932, the day after the players had reported back for training for the new season, he was found dead in one of the dressing rooms, having hanged himself.

Those who knew Billy Callender were still speaking of him with great affection and high regard some 60 years later. That in itself is a full measure of the standing and ability of the Palace goalkeeper who, but for one of life's tragedies, might have reached the highest honours in the game.

CANNON, Jim

Born: 2 October 1953, Glasgow
Apps: 656+4
Goals: 35

Palace's strong, tough central-defender or left-back throughout most of the 1970s and 1980s, Jim Cannon is one of those rarities in the modern game – he is a one-club footballer. As such, he typifies those few men who are entirely content to devote their whole careers to the club which gave them their first opportunity. It is the judgement of many Palace fans that Jim's contribution to Crystal Palace FC stands head and shoulders above that of all the rest.

Cannon joined Palace from Glasgow Amateurs as an apprentice in February 1970 and turned professional on 3 May 1971. Almost everyone connected with the club knows the story of how he made his senior debut in the London derby against Chelsea at Selhurst Park on 31 March two years later. 'I'll never forget it,' he recalled some years later. 'We desperately needed the points, it was a packed house and the pressure was on the club. But we managed it and I capped a fantastic day by scoring a goal!' Eleven minutes into the second half, Chelsea were desperately seeking an equaliser, but Don Rogers curved a ball to the far post where Jim soared high above all challengers to head it downwards for a fine goal, ensuring that Palace gained the victory they deserved.

In 1975–76 Jim Cannon was appearing regularly for Palace's Third Division side

at left-back, and this was the season when the club made its first really impressive impact in the FA Cup by reaching the semi-final for the first time; although, regrettably, the club failed to do themselves justice against Southampton.

With the departure of Derek Jeffries, Jim Cannon took over at the centre of the back four alongside Ian Evans, and this partnership was a key factor in the club's promotion in the 1976–77 season when both men made full appearances. Naturally, Palace's plans for the Second Division focussed around the two defensive bulwarks, but it is now part of the folklore of Crystal Palace that Ian's leg was badly broken in the match against Fulham on 1 October and he was never able to play for the first team again.

A new central-defensive partnership was forged between Cannon and Billy Gilbert which became highly effective, but it was also necessary to appoint a new team captain and in mid-December 1977 the role fell to Jim Cannon. He remained captain for the rest of his career, and he must be among the longest-serving captains in the game, as 10 and a half years is a long time for a player to remain as skipper of a single club.

In the 1978–79 season Palace's defence was absolutely superb. It had Jim Cannon at its heart and, statistically at least, it remains the club's best ever. Only 16 goals were conceded in the first half of the season and a mere eight in the final 22 matches. They kept a clean sheet in exactly half of the fixtures, and this stunning record is the biggest single reason why Palace won the Second Division Championship, making Cannon the first man to captain Palace into the top flight as champions.

An analysis of Cannon's career also shows him to be the scorer of many crucial goals, although probably the one for which he will be longest remembered was his spectacular final strike in the 4–1 victory over Ipswich on 29 September 1979, a win that took Palace to the top of the entire Football League for the first and only time. Jim received a first testimonial in the 1980–81 season, but he then proceeded to capture every appearance record at the club and in 1988 became the only post-war player to have been awarded a second testimonial when Tottenham provided the opposition.

Taken overall, Jim Cannon's career with Palace represents an amazing catalogue of magnificent service. He was the first man to have been Palace Player of the Year on three occasions and he has earned the undying admiration and gratitude of all Palace fans.

CLARKE, George

Born: 24 July 1900, Bolsover
Died: 11 February 1977, Mansfield
Apps: 299
Goals: 106

After John Whibley left Crystal Palace in 1923, the outside-left position became

something of a problem for manager Edmund Goodman. He filled it, however, some two years later, with a stroke of absolute genius, when he obtained the signature of auburn-haired George Clarke from Aston Villa. Most Palace historians, and fans of that period, would agree that, had Mr Goodman been able to do this even a month before the end of the 1924–25 season rather than a few weeks after the close of it, then Palace would never have been relegated from the Second Division.

George immediately became a fixture in the Palace side, and he remained so for seven seasons. He was a magnificent winger who was probably way out of his class in the Third Division: he was a ball player with craft and artistry, but he was also fast, clever and possessed a lethal shot – skills that have etched his name for all time into the Palace records. Only centre-forwards or strikers have ever improved upon the 99 League goals he scored for the club, while, of course, no winger has ever approached it. George also holds the goalscoring record for a single season from the flank with a fabulous 22 League goals in the 1927–28 campaign.

Clarke's best performance of all time for Palace was probably his truly excellent hat-trick scored in dreadful conditions when Palace rallied from 3–1 down at half-time against Southend on 13 November 1926 to win 5–3. George subsequently notched up two further hat-tricks for the club: both came at Selhurst Park, against Bournemouth in February 1928 and against Exeter in December 1931. Such scoring feats are indicative of Clarke's prowess, for no other Palace winger has bettered this record and only one, Bob Bigg, had equalled it.

However, Clarke's primary contribution to Palace was as a provider of opportunities from which the club's centre-forwards could score their goals. Big Percy Cherett fed off Clarke's passes and crosses for two seasons, but it was Peter Simpson who benefitted most from the work of the talented, flame-haired left-winger, so that it is no coincidence that Peter scored more goals in each of the three campaigns in which George Clarke was his teammate than in any of the succeeding seasons.

George Clarke – a prince among Palace wingers.

CLYNE, Nathaniel

Born: 5 April 1991, Stockwell
Apps: 102+4
Goals: 1

Palace's superb current right-back is 20-year-old Nathaniel Clyne, and Eagles fans have quickly come to recognise that the youngster is something of a Palace prodigy. Nathaniel is a graduate of the Palace Academy and a former England Youth international. He made his senior debut in Palace colours as a 17-year-old when The Eagles hosted Barnsley in October 2008, and he netted his first goal for the club at Reading in a mid-week victory in December 2009.

But there can be no doubt that Nathaniel's best season to date was 2010–11, in which he not only started every Palace game in the League and both Cups, but was also never once substituted! Add to that the fact that he made his 100th appearance for the club when Palace played Ipswich in April 2011 and deservedly won the club's Player of the Year award at the end of the term.

Discerning older fans see clear similarities between Nathaniel and another Palace full-back of a previous era – Kenny Sansom no less. Clyne's tenacity, pace and ball-winning skills are all reminiscent of Sansom at his best in a Palace shirt. Clyne also posseses the equable temperament and attractive unassuming modesty which helped to make Sansom such a powerful magnet for the attentions of the biggest clubs: they will assuredly do so for Clyne, and Palace will follow his career with studied interest.

COLEMAN, Chris

Born: 10 June 1970, Swansea
Apps: 177+13
Goals: 16

Chris Coleman was already a Welsh Under-21 international defender when he signed for Palace in the summer of 1991, but he was unable to break into the club's top-flight side in that capacity, and manager Steve Coppell deployed him largely as a stand-in, reluctant but highly effective, striker in his first two terms in Palace colours.

Coleman netted for Wales on his full debut for the Principality to earn them a draw against Austria in Vienna in April 1992, and was finally able to demonstrate

the primary reason for his acquisition when the new Palace manager, Alan Smith, used him in defence from the opening of 1993–94, first at left-back, then as a pivot alongside his Welsh international colleague Eric Young. It was with the latter formation that Palace stormed to the top of the table in the autumn and mid-winter, then, to the delight of the fans, took the Championship in style the following May, with Coleman having made full appearances in that attractive and successful side. Accordingly, he was the popular winner of the supporters' vote for Player of the Year.

Coleman also scored some spectacular goals during Palace's quest for an immediate return to the top flight, and these unquestionably enhanced his claims to such distinction. In September his powerful header at West Bromwich Albion put Palace back on level terms and en route to a comprehensive victory; in January, on his 100th Palace appearance, he levelled matters against visiting Leicester, while a first-minute strike with his left foot won the three points at Luton in the penultimate away game in mid-April, and this was the goal that ensured Palace's promotion back to the Premiership.

Coleman became a regular member of the full Welsh international side while Palace were in the top flight in 1994–95. He gained 11 caps while a Palace player and then passed his 150th League appearance for the club in October 1995. But, to the disappointment of the fans, Chris chose to leave Selhurst Park and moved to Blackburn Rovers a couple of weeks before Christmas.

Nevertheless, Coleman made a big impact at Crystal Palace and deserves inclusion in this gallery both for the extent of his Palace career and also the content of it.

COLLYER, Harry

Born: c.1885, Bromley, Kent
Apps: 281
Goals: 1

Harry Collyer was a tough, sturdy, strong, muscular full-back with a giant-sized heart, who played for Palace throughout 10 season prior to World War One. As far as we know, Crystal Palace was his only senior club.

Collyer was a local boy who hailed from nearby Bromley. He joined the club in September 1906, just as it was embarking upon only its second season, and made his Southern League debut on Boxing Day at Watford's Cassio Road ground. From that point he progressed with his club, becoming a respected defender and gaining several personal honours during his career.

He was a rugged little full-back who sported a distinctive 'Pentonville' style

haircut which would have certainly been the height of fashion among many of the supporters 100 years later! He began initially at left-back, but it was on the right that he really excelled and became a recognised quality player. Once he had settled in at number two for the Palace first team it became quite impossible for anyone to shift him, and he appeared there regularly for the club until World War One brought about an end to fully competitive football and threw everyone's lives into confusion.

The best demonstration of Collyer's playing quality came in the 1909–10 season when he appeared in the English international trial match. It was not surprising that he was unable to displace the famous and immensely popular England captain, Bob Crompton of Blackburn Rovers, from the national side, but the fact that a comparison was even made indicates the sheer calibre of player that Harry Collyer was.

In the 1912–13 season, Collyer was awarded representative honours and played for the Southern League in all three inter-League fixtures against the Football League and the League of Ireland. Several distinguished clubs from the Football League sought to lure Collyer away from Palace, all without success, and he became the first Palace player to be awarded a benefit by the club – the Southern League encounter with Coventry City at the Crystal Palace on 12 October 1912. Some 9,000 fans turned up for it to see Palace win 3–0.

When Harry Collyer joined Crystal Palace FC the club had not even played a First Division match in the Southern League. When World War One broke out, eight years later, Harry was still there, the longest-serving member of the playing staff, having helped the side to rise within an ace of the Southern League Championship and becoming an extablished and respected club in the process.

DAVIES, Bill

Born: November 1883, Forden, nr Welshpool, Monmouthshire
Died: 1960
Apps: 207
Goals: 24

Winger Bill Davies had two successful spells with Palace prior to World War One, either side of a couple of seasons at West Bromwich Albion, who were an aspiring Second Division League club at that time. Altogether, Davies played nearly 200

Southern League fixtures for the club, featuring on either wing, although, certainly with the Palace, he was used more often on the left flank during his career.

Davies is certain of a unique place in the Palace annals because he was the first player from the club to gain international honours, when he was selected for Wales's 2–1 loss to Scotland at Dundee on 7 March 1908. Later that year, after being prominent in Palace's astonishingly successful 1907–08 Southern League season, he was signed by West Bromwich Albion, but after two terms at The Hawthorns he returned to Palace where, once again, he played consistently well as the club really began to make a steadily improving impact upon the Southern League.

Like several of his colleagues, Davies' best season with Palace was the 1913–14 campaign, when the club was only denied the Southern League Championship on goal average, but he had also starred in the 1907–08 season, his first with the club when they finished in a hugely impressive fourth place in the Southern League at the end of what was only Palace's third term in existence. Bill Davies is the only outfield player to have appeared in both those superb seasons for the club.

Davies was more of a goal-maker than a goalscorer, yet he once netted six Southern League goals in a season for Palace, and he hit some useful FA Cup strikes too. He was on target in the 4–2 defeat of Coventry in his first senior Cup tie for the club, scored again in the victory over Football League club Bury and once more in the praiseworthy 2–2 draw gained at another Football League outfit, Birmingham, just before the war.

Bill Davies's versatility was an extremely valuable part of Palace's attacks in the early years of the club. Only three players made more Southern League appearances for the club than Bill – and he gained a second international honour as a Palace player (the fourth of his career) too.

DAWES, Albert

Born: 23 April 1907, Frimley Green, Surrey
Died: 23 June 1973, Goring-by-Sea, Sussex
Apps: 156
Goals: 92

Albert Dawes signed for Crystal Palace FC from Northampton Town on the Wednesday before Christmas 1933 and incidentally thereby began an association of members of the Dawes family with Crystal Palace which lasted until the Autumn of 1951.

In two spells with Palace before the war (interrupted only by 15 months with Luton Town whom he helped to win the Third Division South in 1937), he became Palace's third-highest goalscorer in the Football League at that time behind Peter Simpson and George Clarke. His total of 91 League goals has been improved on, but it should be noted that, whenever it has been, the men concerned always had substantially longer Palace careers than Dawes.

He was, without question, a brilliant marksman. His powerful shooting, sometimes from long range, was spectacular and effective, and it should be remembered that Dawes played in the days when the leather ball grew heavier and heavier in wet conditions, soaking up any moisture and eventually weighing several pounds. It was some player indeed who could unleash a powerful drive with a ball that was more akin to a cannonball than a football.

There are several reasons why Albert Dawes would earn himself a niche in any Palace hall of fame. On 1 September 1934 he hit five goals against Cardiff City, and only Peter Simpson had bettered that in a single match for the club. In the 1935–36 season Dawes came within a single goal of topping the entire list of Football League marksmen with 38 strikes. It is a tally that is almost beyond comprehension today. That same season, Dawes was honoured by the FA when he was selected for the England squad for the international against Scotland at Wembley on 4 April. What an honour for a Third Division player! Unfortunately for Dawes, he was made 12th man and, with no substitutes allowed in those days, he spent the entire match idle on the players' bench.

During the seasons of World War Two, as his career drew to a close, Albert Dawes became a magnificent utility player for Palace, turning out in any position: as a full-back one week, a winger or striker the next, and then as centre-half the next. In fact, in the 1943–44 season Dawes played in every outfield position at least once, and he scored goals that set the fans' interest alight from all of them!

DAWES, Fred

Born: 2 May 1911, Frimley Green, Surrey
Died: 12 August 1989, Shirley, Surrey
Apps: 237
Goals: 2

Fred Dawes was born at Frimley Green in the heart of Surrey, but his first Football League club was Northampton, from whom he moved to Crystal Palace in February 1936. Fred was a full-back and made his Palace debut at Clapton Orient, appearing in the 13 remaining matches of that season and teaming up again with his brother Albert, who had come to Selhurst Park from the Cobblers in 1933.

Fred was appointed as club captain for the 1936–37 season and made full appearances for the Palace side that term, only to be badly hampered by injuries in the following campaign. His best season with the club was undoubtedly 1938–39 when he was an ever-present member of the team that was beaten for promotion by Newport County and a margin of three points. Fred netter his brace of League goals for Palace in that season too, and one of them, at Exeter, was a 40-yarder!

After World War Two, Fred Dawes put in another 110 League appearances for Palace and thus became the only player at the club to make a century of appearances on either side of the war. He was awarded

a richly deserved benefit towards the end of the first post-war season, although Palace lost their Third Division South match against Bournemouth 1–0 on 22 March 1947. Dawes continued playing until October 1949, when his career was brought to an abrupt end by a dreadful head injury incurred at Bournemouth. George Irwin, the former Palace goalkeeper and manager in 1946–47, summed Fred up admirably well: 'Fred is a good, honest, clean player and a credit to the Palace side.' Those who watched Dawes play will fully endorse those sentiments.

But the association of Fred Dawes with Crystal Palace lasted somewhat longer. He became Ronnie Rooke's assistant manager, then was appointed as joint-manager with Charlie Slade in November 1950. The club was in a dreadful state: Palace faced re-election at the end of the club's worst-ever season, 1950–51, and with a swollen overdraft there was no possibility of signing any new players. Inevitably, the first two months of 1951–52 promised little or no improvement, and the board of directors decided that Dawes and his colleague would have to be dismissed. It was regarded at the time as a shabby way to treat a grand and loyal club servant, and there is no reason to change that opinion today.

One is simply left with the reflection that Fred Dawes gained an excellent reputation with Crystal Palace, even though the teams he played in, particularly after the war, were in all honesty usually poor quality. Had he been with one of the stronger or more successful clubs at that time, then his name would now be held in respect by a far wider clientele than the relatively small number of supporters who were privileged to see him play his heart out for Crystal Palace.

DERRY, Shaun

Born: 6 December 1977, Nottingham
Apps: 199+27
Goals: 3

Shaun Derry is a tough-tackling, hardworking, sweet-passing midfielder who joined Palace from Portsmouth, where he had been club captain, for a £400,000 fee at the start of the 2002–03 season. His experience proved invaluable to the club, while his sheer versatility has been most useful on occasions when he has been called upon to provide cover in the back four, and fans of the early years of this millennium will recall that he filled in at left-back and played down the left flank in the successful Cardiff Play-off Final of 2004.

Derry is a focussed, committed footballer who never shirks his responsibilities and produces an occasional goal for the team. The opening

matches of the 2003–04 season saw him wearing the captain's armband, and throughout that term he was always a valued member of the squad which took Palace to the Play-offs and to the Millennium Stadium, where his performance contributed in no small way to the outcome and the club's promotion.

Derry spent a couple of mid-season months on loan at Nottingham Forest in the 2004–05 season before Leeds paid Palace £250,000 to secure his services. However, after Neil Warnock became Palace manager in October 2007 he quickly brought Shaun back to Selhurst Park to once again anchor the midfield. Neil greatly admired Shaun's tenacious approach to his responsibilities, and it is happily recalled by the club's supporters how the side clawed its way up the Championship table to reach the Play-offs again.

Thus, it was a popular move at all levels at Palace when the boss appointed Shaun Derry as captain at the start of the 2008–09 season.

Indeed, Shaun was always greatly admired by Neil Warnock, so that, upon the expiry of Shaun's contract at Selhurst Park, he moved accross London to re-join his former manager at Queen's Park Rangers on 21 June 2010.

DUNN, Ronnie

Born: 24 November 1908, Southall, Middlesex
Died: 1994
Apps: 175
Goals: 0

Goalkeeper Ronnie Dunn first attracted the interest of the Crystal Palace management when he appeared in goal for the British Army in a thrilling 5–4 clash with their French counterparts at Selhurst Park on 23 February 1929, and again when the Belgian Army provided the opposition

12 months later. After Dunn left the forces he signed, initially as an amateur but then as a professional, for Palace to become the regular understudy to Billy Callender in the 1931–32 season. In fact, Dunn made his debut in an excellent Palace 3–0 victory at Brighton on 9 September 1931, where his fearless display and accurate clearances were a feature of the success.

Of course, it was to Ronnie Dunn that there fell the unenviable task of taking over as Palace's first-choice goalkeeper for the 1932–33 season after Callender's tragic suicide, but the young man proved emotionally and physically equipped to do so. He missed just one match that season, because of a dose of 'flu, and he was widely regarded as having a fine future.

Regrettably, that promise was only partly fulfilled. Dunn remained at Selhurst Park for a further four seasons and was the first-choice 'keeper until 1936–37. During this period Palace only once finished outside the top six clubs in the division, but the old Third Division South was a tough school, with no margin allowed whatever for mistakes, loss of form or sheer misfortune, because only the top club was promoted – all the rest were as good as nowhere.

Thus, along with several of his contemporaries at Palace, Ronnie Dunn was only really appreciated by the club's fans and not on the bigger stages that his prowess undoubtedly deserved. However, Palace supporters from the 1930s most certainly do recall Ronnie Dunn with no little esteem. For most of his career with the club he was producing form that was not far short of Alderson or Callender – and that is some company to be in.

EDWARDS, Jack

Born: 6 July 1929, Risca, Monmouthshire
Apps: 239
Goals: 0

Jack Edwards was Palace's strong, sturdy, stocky, teak-tough full-back throughout much of the 1950s, and he became a great favourite among the Selhurst Park faithful.

Edwards's opportunity to break into the limelight came when skipper Fred Dawes was so badly injured that he could not play again. Thus, Edwards' debut on 8 October 1949, within just a few weeks of his joining the club from Lovells Athletic, was as demanding as any Palace debut could be – it was at Millwall. But, along with his teammates, the 20-year-old had a tremendous game. He also played his part in one of Palace's best-ever performances in the old Third Division South, helping the club to gain a splendid 3–2 victory and earning himself an accolade from Palace manager Ronnie Rooke, who said that Jack 'came through [his debut] with flying colours'.

Fearless and aggressive, Edwards became one of Palace's youngest captains up to that time, when he took over as skipper in 1956, his determination and enthusiasm admirably suiting him for the role. He served under no fewer than six different Palace managers during his time at Selhurst Park and never appeared to be flurried; his cool, unruffled play was a

hallmark of his game, along with some immensely powerful clearances.

Jack Edwards became an invaluable asset to Crystal Palace when the team was managed by Cyril Spiers, who appointed Jack as his skipper and used him as the on-field mentor and guide for the youthful players the manager installed around him. Of course, those were difficult times for the club and its captain, but it was while Jack was skipper that such Palace stars of the 1960–61 promotion team as Vic Rouse and Johnny Byrne had their initiation, while Terry Long and Len Choules started to come to maturity alongside him.

Edwards shared a benefit match at Palace with goalkeeper Roy Bailey in October 1955. He was transferred to Rochdale in 1959 and had two seasons at Spotland (where he once helped to greatly embarrass a visiting Palace side to the tune of 4–0). Subsequently, he had a successful career in management, scouting and coaching for various clubs, the highlight of which was guiding Exeter City to promotion from the Fourth Division in 1964.

EVANS, Ian

Born: 30 January 1952, Egham, Surrey
Apps: 163
Goals: 16

Ian Evans made two distinctive contributions to the progress of Crystal Palace FC but, while reference is made to the second of these towards the end of this piece, he appears in this chapter solely because of his effective and influential playing career.

Evans first joined Palace as a tall, rangy Welsh international Under-23 central-defender in the early autumn of 1974, and he was immediately plunged into Palace's League side by manager Malcolm Allison. Ian quickly made a name for himself with the fans in his favourite number-six shirt: he performed with some distinction at Division Three level and scored some spectacular headed goals; indeed, on 30 August 1975 he carved a unique niche in the Palace record books by becoming the first defender to net a competitive hat-trick, and since Palace fans had been denied a hat-trick of any kind for all but nine years, it was not only highly memorable but also most welcome!

Photo © HY Money

Later in that 1975–76 season, and under Ian's captaincy, Palace reached the FA Cup semi-final for the first time and as a Third Division outfit, while Ian also gained his first full international honour for the Principality. His best term for Palace was undoubtedly 1976–77 when he skippered the side to promotion to the Second Division, playing in every match and, alongside Jim Cannon, setting a new defensive record for the club by conceding only 40 League goals in 46 matches, which was then an unparalleled feat since the war and which has only been improved upon by Palace Championship-winning sides of 1921 and 1979.

It was also during the 1976–77 season that Ian's international career really blossomed: he became the regular central-defender for Wales and was part of their most successful side for many years. Probably their finest achievement during Ian's time with them was their single-goal victory over England at Wembley on 31 May 1977, Wales' first victory over England since 1955 and their first in England for over 40 years.

However, the precarious nature of a footballer's life was never demonstrated more cruelly than with Ian Evans, for on 1 October 1977, Ian was involved in a tackle with George Best, then of Fulham, that saw Ian stretchered off from the Selhurst Park pitch with a double fracture of his right leg, and he was out of action for two full years. In a curious way, Ian's enormous courage and determination in overcoming that fearsome injury, which many pundits feared would become a permanent disablement, won him the hearts of all Palace followers. This, allied to the respect and admiration he had already gained as captain of the 1977 promotion team and as a member of the full Welsh international side, established an empathy between him and the fans which made him part of the folklore of Crystal Palace FC.

In fact, it took a revolutionary medical technique for Ian to be able to play again, but only for Palace's reserve side, because the first team was, at that time, more than holding its own in the top flight. So, Ian moved north to join Barnsley and there began a lengthy association with Mick McCarthy which continued almost to the present day.

After completing another century of appearances for the Tykes and assisting them to promotion in 1981, Ian's link with Crystal Palace was re-established in June 1984 when he joined Steve Coppell as assistant manager at Selhurst Park and helped to fashion the team that restored top-flight status in 1989. However, by the time of Palace's promotion Ian had taken over as manager at Swansea City.

FREEDMAN, Dougie

Born: 21 January 1974, Glasgow
Apps: 241+127
Goals: 108

Scottish international striker Dougie Freedman had proved an exceptional goalscorer with Barnet in little more than a season when Palace initially secured him in the club's first-ever transfer deal with the Bees.

Genuinely two-footed, nimble, neat and inventive, Dougie's splendid tally of 20 goals from his 42 appearances in his first season in Division One was an invaluable contribution to Palace's progress in 1995–96, and two of his exploits that season were exceptional. When Wolves were the visiting side, Freedman hit a hat-trick to enable Palace to secure a 3–2 victory, and he was accorded a raptuous reception at the end by the fans who stood

to applaud the matchwinner when he left the field. Another brilliant hat-trick was the stunning quick-fire treble which sunk Grimsby 5–0 in March 1996. This extraordinary, 11-minute effort was then Palace's fastest hat-trick of all time, as well as Palace's 100th in League and Cup matches since the club joined the Football League back in 1920.

However, Freedman's most important goals in his first spell at Selhurst Park were the two late strikes he netted as a substitute – a vicious volley and a clever lob in the 88th and 90th minutes respectively, which ensured the defeat of Wolves in the 1997 Play-off semi-final first-leg match at Selhurst Park, and, ultimately, Palace's progress to the victorious Wembley Final.

When Dougie Freedman left Palace for Wolves in October 1997, he had accumulated just enough Palace games to enter the club's roll of 'centurions', but he received an ecstatic response from the fans upon his re-signing for the club in October 2000 in a £650,000 deal from Nottingham

Forest. Dougie quickly repaid the enthusiasm and faith of the fans by netting four goals in four games upon his return, leaving many surprised that he was subsequently deployed most often as a substitute striker. Most Palace fans will contend that it was his double at Portsmouth in the penultimate game of the 2000–01 season, allied to his late, brilliant winner at Stockport in the final match, were invaluable contributions to the Palace cause in his second spell. They were certainly quite sufficient to ensure his inclusion in this gallery in their own right, but add to them the facts that Dougie assisted the club to the Play-offs in both 2003–04 and 2005–06, and that his goal at Charlton in Palace's final Premiership game of 2004–05 could (some would say 'should') have helped the club to survive at that level. More information about Dougie to be found in the Managers section of the book.

GILBERT, Billy

Born: 10 November 1959, Lewisham
Apps: 271+2
Goals: 4

Billy Gilbert was Palace's tough-tackling, no-nonsense central-defender and occasional full-back from 1977 to 1984 and was a vital member of the Second Division Championship side of 1978–79.

Gilbert first came to the attention of Palace devotees when the junior side proceeded to the Final of the 1977 FA Youth Cup and then beat Everton over two legs, but he came into the League side in October of that year as deputy for injured skipper Ian Evans and had taken undisputed possession of Palace's number-six shirt by the end of the 1977–78 season.

After gaining another Youth Cup-winners' medal in 1978, Gilbert became a dominant central-defender alongside Jim

Photo © HY Money

Cannon and was an integral feature of the side which took Palace back into the old First Division with the best defensive record in the club's history. Billy also gained the first of his 11 England Under-21 caps that season. He missed only one game during the 1978–79 triumph which held the capital's football pundits in thrall and brought admiration and delight to all Palace fans at the maturity of the performance of Terry Venables' young team and its sophisticated displays.

Billy was a tower of strength in Palace's two years in the top flight, between 1979–81. His debut at that level was made at at rather less that 20 years of age, and he was only out of the side a couple of times through illness in 1979–80 as Palace powered their way to the top of the League with attractive and hugely effective performances.

Overall, Billy was absent for only five out of 84 games at the highest level, and then his sturdy and dependable displays helped to keep the club from further embarrassment after Palace had returned to the Second Division. When he opted to leave the club for Portsmouth in the 1984 close season, every fan was sorry to see him go because, while circumstances at the club had deteriorated badly during the interim, Gilbert had continued to serve Palace most loyally and had been voted Player of the Year for his final season at Selhurst Park.

HANGER, Harry

Born: 1886, Kettering
Died: Killed in Action 23 March 1918, Flanders, Belgium
Apps: 178
Goals: 8

Harry Hanger was tall, good looking and wavy-haired. Had he been born in the USA he could surely have become a film star. As it was, he became a professional footballer, and after appearing in the Football League with Bradford City he joined Crystal Palace in the summer of 1909, where his stylish performances at wing-half became an attractive feature of the side until the outbreak of World War One.

Hanger's control of the ball was renowned. 'No player [...] has shown greater ability to retain possession of the ball [...] his passes are invariably accurate and reach a forward so that the latter can make rapid headway,' eulogized a Palace scribe back in 1913, while a contemporary photograph has captured the player in graceful airborne action. These attributes combined to make Hanger the obvious successor to George Woodger as club captain when the latter was transferred to Oldham in the autumn of 1910.

It was while Harry Hanger was skipper that Palace had their best season in the Southern League, coming within a whisker of winning the Championship in 1914, when the race with Swindon for the title went all the way to the final games.

Neat, precise, clever, controlled, Hanger had it all, and he was a fine and respected club captain. He was also always ready to conjure the occasional crucial goal for the club's cause; although, curiously, he usually did this when Palace were playing away from home. While not prolific in these matters, it does appear, from the accounts of the period, that he was particularly accurate with headers from set-pieces and highly likely to get on the score sheet when games were drawing towards their end.

Honoured by the Southern League, Hanger was awarded a benefit by Palace in 1914–15. Sadly, it is highly unlikely that the match ever took place, because the designated fixture against Croydon Common could not be played on its originally scheduled date, and by that time Harry was already away in France in the forces. He was killed in action during the conflict.

HARRY, Albert

Born: 8 March 1897, Surbiton, Surrey
Died: 3 January 1966, Shrewsbury
Apps: 440
Goals: 55

Every footballing epoch has produced a player at Palace who has become idolized by the fans. For example, in the 1930s and 40s it was Fred Dawes, in the 1970s and 80s it was Jim Cannon, while in the 1920s and 30s it was a diminutive, bow-legged winger by the name of Albert Harry.

Albert Harry was was a man of character who always gave 100 per cent effort on behalf of his team and club, and who was endowed with skills that drew admiration from the press, his teammates and opposition alike, and particularly from Palace fans of the period.

Harry signed for Palace after manager Edmund Goodman had seen him play for the amateur side Kingstonian in a Surrey Charity Shield Final at The Nest early in the summer of 1921. He had learned his football in the army and was a menacing, attacking centre-forward. After joining Palace, Harry appeared in eight of the last nine matches of the 1921–22 season and scored two goals in the last eight minutes to help Palace defeat Bury on his debut at The Nest on 25 March.

Manager Goodman soon became aware that Harry's modest stature (he stood only 5ft 6in tall) was something of a handicap when playing down the middle in Second Division football and successfully moved him to the outside-right position. Albert was understandably somewhat diffident about this at first, but he soon settled down and made his first Palace appearance on the right wing when he came into the side on 30 September 1922 at Leicester.

Albert Harry's great merit was that once he had been given the ball he was a speedy and direct raider. He had a powerful shot in both feet, and his ball control was excellent. By the next term, 1923–24, the outside-right position was his own – and he held on to it for another full decade!

The player with whom Albert Harry is often mentioned is Peter Simpson, the prolific goalscorer from the first half of the 1930s. Those who were lucky enough to see these two players in the same team for four and a half seasons are certainly among the most privileged Palace supporters. They blended together from the first, and there can be no doubt that Harry's forceful play on the right wing was one of the prime reasons why Simpson was able to crack in so many goals.

Albert Harry himself scored 53 League goals for Palace and two more in the FA Cup; how many he laid on for other forwards we can only guess. He put in 410 League appearances for the club and that figure stood as a club record for over 30 years until it was overtaken by by Terry Long in the late 1960s. Albert finally left Palace at the end of the 1933–34 season, and Crystal Palace was the only Football League club for which he played.

There have always been heroes at Crystal Palace, but those fans who saw Albert Harry play were fortunate indeed.

HILAIRE, Vince

Born: 10 October 1959, Forest Hill, London
Apps: 276+17
Goals: 36

Vince Hilaire was a supremely talented winger who came to the fore in Palace's great FA Youth Cup-winning side of 1977 and then matured in the Second Division the following season, while helping the club to retain the Youth Cup at the same time.

Quicksilver, darting and with wonderful balance and control, Hilaire was at his best at Selhurst Park in the 1978–79 and 1979–80 seasons. Still a teenager throughout the first of those campaigns, he was usually deployed wide on the left flank, from where his teasing, mercurial runs frequently left defenders floundering, and then, later in the season, when most opponents were using tight, defensive formations, his magic often provided the key to unlock the most determined of them. He also provided six useful goals to augment Palace's low scoring Championship quest.

In the top flight, Hilaire was subjected to a lot of dubious physical challenges that would not be tolerated today, but he was an ever present throughout the 1979–80 season and scored five League goals for the club. He was awarded nine England Under-21 caps, fully deserving his selection and scoring on his debut against Bulgaria in November 1979.

Hilaire's style, however, was best suited to a bright, attacking side, and consequently, when Palace's fortunes began to fade and managers at Selhurst Park came and went, each of them required something different from him. Hilaire became something of an enigma to Palace fans, who would marvel one week at his sinuous skills and near-perfect control, but then despair at his virtual anonymity the next.

Photo © HY Money

Nevertheless, Vince Hilaire remained loyal to Palace for three more seasons in the Second Division, and even if the club was usually at best an inconsistent side, he was always a potential matchwinner. One extraordinary game against visiting Middlesbrough provided just the opportunity for Hilaire to reveal his precocious skills to full advantage. A miserable February afternoon had drawn a crowd of considerably fewer than 5,000, and even those diehards' aspirations took a knock when the referee chose to dismiss Billy Gilbert and Kevin Mabbutt together for innocuous offences. But Palace pushed Vince up front on his own and knocked long balls up to him, knowing that, on the treacherous surface, the Boro defenders would always struggle to contain him. Sure enough, one of them eventually fouled Hilaire in the penalty area, Peter Nicholas knocked home the spot-kick and Palace won by that single goal.

There are players who have appeared in Palace colours more often than Vince Hilaire, though not many, and none of them has exceeded his popularity.

HINSHELWOOD, Paul

Born: 14 August 1956, Bristol
Apps: 314+5
Goals: 28

Some Palace fans regarded Paul Hinshelwood as ungainly, uncommunicative and lacking in poise or artistry. Certainly, he was cruelly nicknamed by them. But that attitude fails to appreciate the sheer hard work that he put in to ensure his continued place in the Palace team, the opinions of the five managers for whom he featured and it was certainly not representative of the majority of Palace folk.

Photo © HY Money

It was upon the recommendation of Mr Arthur Rowe that both Paul and Martin Hinshelwood were invited to Selhurst Park for trials, and Paul went on to wear Palace colours with distinction.

Paul began as a striker, but in November 1976 he undertook a new role as a full-back and his partnership with Kenny Sansom was a feature of Palace's rise from the Third Division to the First in the late 1970s. The defensive unit of which Paul was a part created new club records in both promotion seasons of 1976–77 and 1978–79, and it was only a torn cartilage in October 1978 that prevented Hinshelwood from making full appearances in the Second Division Championship season.

It was in his adopted position of right-back that Paul Hinshelwood gained two England Under-21 caps, and he is one of very few players who have appeared for the club in 10 post-war seasons. His 319 games played for Palace keeps him high in the club's all-time appearances chart.

Perhaps the best measure of his ability and commitment to the Palace cause (and the complete answer to his detractors) was that, although he was never a player who sought publicity or acclaim, he was voted Player of the Year for two consecutive seasons, both of which were spent in the old First Division in 1979–80 and 1980–81.

HOLTON, Cliff

Born: 29 April 1929, Oxford
Died: 30 May 1996, Spain
Apps: 112
Goals: 49

Cliff Holton was manager Dick Graham's solution to Palace's perilous situation as mid-winter 1962–63 set in. Holton had had a supremely successful career with Arsenal, Watford and Northampton. He was a regular goalscorer and had a magnificent physique, while Palace fans were all too aware of his commanding presence and fearsome shot from previous encounters against the clubs for whom he had appeared.

Holton made his Palace debut on Boxing Day 1962, teaming up for the first time with another new signing, Dickie Dowsett, and Ronnie Allen, helping Palace romp to a thrilling, uplifting 3–0 win on a

freezing surface. A few weeks later he scored the first of three hat-tricks he secured for the club, when Palace beat his former club Watford 4–1 at Vicarage Road. Such was his performance that the Hornets fans rose at the end to applaud their former star from the pitch.

Cliff Holton's contribution to Palace would have been deserving of praise and appreciation even if it had stopped at the end of that season, with Palace safely in midtable. Twelve months later, however, and courtesy of 20 strikes from the big man himself, Palace were back in Division Two after an absence of 39 years. Furthermore, Holton headed the list of scorers for Palace that season in the Second Division in 1964–65 with 11 goals, and that was despite him spending several games at centre-half.

Many of Cliff's goals were spectacular ones, the sort that inspire teammates and supporters alike. Take his second goal against Millwall, for example, early in the promotion season of 1963–64: the clash was as passionate and intense as any meeting between the old rivals. Ronnie Allen spent half an hour off the pitch with concussion, and during that time 10-man Palace lost their rhythm and style in the face of the Lions onslaught, as well as, eventually, their early lead. With a quarter of an hour to go, Palace restored their advantage after being awarded a free-kick some 25 yards out from goal. Holton strode up, measured the range and then crashed the ball into the top corner of the net.

Modern-day readers will not be surprised to learn that when Holton was transferred back to Watford in early May 1965, the supporters of that time were greatly displeased, and the move was certainly one of the few mistakes that Dick Graham made during his time as manager. But, today, Cliff Holton is recalled at Selhurst Park with enormous pleasure by those who were privileged to see him play and he was, without any question, one of the most inspiring men ever to appear in Palace colours.

HOPKIN, David

Born: 21 August 1970, Greenock
Apps: 113+13
Goals: 33

Flame-haired David Hopkin joined Crystal Palace from Chelsea for a fee of £850,000 at the end of June 1995 and made an indelible contribution to Palace's advance over the ensuing two seasons, becoming a powerful and extremely effective performer for the club.

Terse and uncommunicative off the field, Hopkin was fluent and intensely positive out on the pitch. He was a strong runner and powerful in the tackle, possessed a prodigious long throw-in and had a flair for scoring spectacular and important goals to help reinforce Palace's challenge for promotion to the top flight – and then to bring it about!

Several examples of his goalscoring prowess will come flooding back to Palace-based readers: his 86th-minute winner against a resilient if defensive Tranmere on a bitterly cold evening in March 1996 provided Palace with two extra points as they forged towards the top of the table, then, early the following term, Palace handed out a 3–1 thrashing to a star-laden Manchester City whom the pundits fancied for outright promotion. David Hopkin was absolutely outstanding in this game, crowned his performance with two fine goals and lifted everyone's hopes for Palace's prospects in the months ahead.

In fact, the climax of Hopkins's two spells at Palace came in the late spring-early summer of 1997. Palace had entered the end-of-season Play-offs and, having beaten Wolves at Selhurst Park, needed only a composed performance in the second leg at Molineux. Wolves had reduced Palace's overall lead and were on their way to Wembley before David Hopkin swung the night Palace's way, beating two defenders and then shooting past the goalkeeper from the edge of the penalty area.

It was at Wembley that Hopkin produced the moment for which every Palace fan will always remember him. With the game scoreless, Hopkin curled the ball in from 22 yards following a corner in the penultimate minute.

HUGHES, Jimmy

Born: December 1885, Bootle
Apps: 209
Goals: 15

Big Jimmy Hughes was Palace's creative bulwark at centre-half from 1909 – when he joined from Liverpool, for whom he had appeared in the Football League – until 1920, and only World War One prevented him from amassing a huge total of appearances for the club. Even with four seasons lost to the war, Hughes played in 200 Southern League games for Palace – so many, in fact, that he has only relatively recently been ousted from Palace's top 40 players in terms of appearances, while only Josh Johnson and Harry Collyer played more matches for the club in the Southern League.

Jimmy Hughes began his Palace career at wing-half but was absolutely terrific in the middle of the defence: it is certainly no coincidence that Palace's best Southern League seasons occurred when he was in that position, including the 1913–14 campaign when Palace were denied the Championship itself solely on goal average by Swindon Town. The issue was only finally determined at the last matches of the programme.

Hughes was totally dominant in the air and a tough tackler on the ground, but perhaps the best feature of his game was the stream of stylish, sweeping passes he delivered to his wingers after he had won the ball. Consequently, it came as no surprise at all when he was chosen to represent the Southern League.

He scarcely missed a match for the club once he had come into the side at the beginning of October 1909. His was a winning debut in a hard London derby at the old and intense rivals Leyton, and he scored with a crashing 20-yard drive early in the second half of his first senior match at the Crystal Palace to ensure a handsome 3–0 victory over Plymouth.

Palace awarded Jimmy Hughes a benefit to be taken in the 1913–14 season along with Harry Hanger and Bob Spottiswood. Unfortunately, the designated local derby with Croydon Common had to be deferred until Palace were playing at Herne Hill and it is unclear what, if any, arrangements were made on the players' behalf.

Hughes continued playing for Palace after the war, but he was hurt in a London Challenge Cup tie early in the 1919–20 campaign and was forced to retire from the game shortly afterwards.

JACKSON, John

Born: 5 September 1942, Hammersmith
Apps: 388
Goals: 0

John Jackson signed for Palace on 8 March 1962 and made his club debut as Bill Glazier's deputy at Swindon in the second match of the 1964–65 season, but Coventry swooped for Glazier's signature in mid-October and, although manager Dick Graham purchased Tony Millington to replace him, by the end of the term it was 'Jacko' who was the undisputed first choice between the posts.

In the next four Second Division seasons John Jackson was a model of consistency, putting in total League appearances of 38, 38, 42 and 42 respectively, and he was one of only three ever-present players in the team that took Palace into the First Division in the 1968–69 season for the first time.

At the highest level Jackson really came into his own. He played 138 consecutive League matches there before he missed his first game, through illness. No other Palace player ever attained one season's maximum appearances in the club's first three seasons – but Jackson did, all three times! It was as well that he did, because, as any fan of the period will confirm, it was his superb displays that salvaged precious points for Palace, against the odds. Points which, at the end of the season, made all the difference between survival and relegation.

Ultimately, of course, not even John Jackson could keep Palace in the First Division. He had played in all but four of the top-flight fixtures, and there were many fans around the country who acknowledged that he had the misfortune to be a great goalkeeper in an age of great goalkeepers: Gordon Banks, Peter Shilton and Ray Clemence to name but three. In a different generation, or, perhaps, at a more fashionable club, John Jackson would have gained many more honours than his single appearance for the Football League.

Jackson was a surprise omission at the start of 1973–74 but he came back after two matches, only to be dropped again. It was now obvious to everyone that the goalkeeping hero of the finest days the club had known would not be long in leaving – and on 16 October 1973 he moved over to Orient for a £30,000 fee.

But Jackson has been back to Palace several times in recent years for player reunions and the like, and it is evident to all who are there that his popularity remains forever undimmed at Selhurst Park.

JOHNSON, Andrew

Born: 10 February 1981, Bedford
Apps: 154+6
Goals: 84

Andy Johnson appeared on the Palace scene rather like a shooting star. For four seasons he brought the club a blaze of publicity with some prodigious scoring feats, but then he left Palace, leaving fans with only memories of his brilliance.

Johnson arrived at Selhurst Park at the beginning of the 2002–03 season as the 'makeweight' in a deal which had taken Clinton Morrison to Birmingham City. Johnson stood only 5ft 7in and sported a fashionably shaven head. He was strong, brave and sturdily built, and was speedy, tenacious and a fabulous finisher. Accordingly, it did not take the Palace fans long to realise which club had got the better deal!

Johnson's scoring record with the Blues had been some way short of of prolific, so he was probably as delighted as the Palace fans with his 14 goals in his initial season at Selhurst Park, which included a glorious, club-record breaking burst of 10 strikes in five games in October and November 2002. Among them was his first Palace hat-trick, against Steve Coppell's Brighton, which certainly endeared him to the fans. In the 2003–04 season he notched 28 goals, easily the club's highest in the higher division,

helping Palace to the Play-offs and, ultimately, back to the Premiership.

In the Premier League season of 2004–05 Johnson's reputation soared. With 21 goals, he was the League's highest scoring Englishman. However, over half of those goals came from the penalty spot – though not always for fouls upon himself – and Andy became the target for accusations that he would stumble or fall over too easily when challenged by opposition defenders in the box. Nevertheless, in the second half of the 2004–05 campaign Johnson gained a full England cap as a Palace player to add to his lustre and credentials.

By the following season he was a much sought-after striker, but he chose to stay with Palace and his 15 League goals from a reduced number of appearances simply added to his appeal as, once again, Palace reached the Play-offs. But then early in the 2006 close season Johnson moved to Everton, with Palace receiving an £8.5 million fee – not bad business on a transfer makeweight!

JOHNSON, Joshua

Born: 1884, Tibshelf, Derbyshire
Apps: 295
Goals: 0

Joshua Johnson (nicknamed 'Joe' or 'Josh' by the Palace fans of the day) was the club's splendid goalkeeper from early December 1907 until World War One brought a temporary end to competitive football in 1915. He was also a committed Christian; he was a lay preacher, and for religious reasons would never play on Christmas Day or Good Friday.

Johnson made his Palace debut at Bristol Rovers on 7 December 1907 and the occasion was totally forgettable. The River Frome had burst its banks after torrential rain and the Rovers' ground was completely waterlogged. Today, the game would have been postponed. Nevertheless, a weakened Palace side fought valiantly to stay in contention and the new goalkeeper was quite magnificent, keeping his team in the match despite intense and continuous pressure. He produced a string of brilliant saves, kept out a penalty and in the end Palace only lost 2–1 to a very late goal.

Johnson played in every remaining Southern League match in that 1907–08 season and in the three FA Cup ties: in fact, he was only ever displaced by injury (or personal choice, for reasons explained above) during the next seven seasons. By the time the war brought an end to Joe's Palace career, he had played 276 Southern League games for the club, the highest figure achieved by any Palace player in the pre-war era. There is also a context to be taken into account here too, however; not only were the maximum possible appearances per season lower than we are familiar with today, but goalkeepers were subject to much more physical attention than would be tolerated today. However, Johnson was 6ft tall and weighed in at 13 stone, so he was ideally equipped for his onerous responsibilities on the pitch.

His prowess was quickly recognised and when the first representitive match was staged between the Southern and Football Leagues at Stamford Bridge on 11 April 1910 (2–2) it was Palace's man between the posts for the former.

The days of Palace in the Southern League may appear to be remote to followers of the club today, but even at this distance in time and culture, fans can clearly recognise in Joe Johnson a player who made a sterling contribution to the Palace cause in the early and formative years of the club.

KEMBER, Steve

Born: 8 December 1948, Croydon, Surrey
Apps: 286+5
Goals: 38

Steve Kember is a Croydon lad, and as such he has always been a great favourite at his local football club. He signed for Crystal Palace as an apprentice in 1963, and on his 17th birthday in 1965 as a full professional.

In Kember's first spell with Palace he quickly matured under manager Dick

Graham, and he became a key member of Bert Head's sides in the late 1960s when his talented midfield displays were one of the most attractive hallmarks of Palace's performances. Steve was an ever-present member of the promotion side of the 1968–69 season and netted several vital goals in the process. When playing at the highest level he shone as brightly as any of the illustrious players who opposed him and gained his first England Under-23 cap in October 1970.

Kember succeeded John Sewell as Palace's captain after the latter's departure, but in September 1971 he was transferred to Chelsea for a fee quoted as £170,000 when Mr Head sought funds in order to drastically reshape his squad for top-flight survival. An impressive four years at Stamford Bridge was followed by a move to Leicester and Steve greatly enjoyed his time at Filbert Street.

In the autumn of 1978 following a spell with Vancouver Whitecaps, Kember returned to Selhurst Park when Terry Venables paid £40,000 to add Steve's experience to the precocious skills of a young team that was seeking to put Palace back into the First Division. Steve missed just one of the remaining games and his influence was an important feature of Palace's glorious Second Division Championship.

He remained with the Palace until the following March when he crossed the Atlantic to play for Vancouver again, but he joined the Palace for a third time in the summer of 1981 as youth coach, but he was appointed as manager in mid-November with the brief to keep Palace in Division Two – a charge in which he was successful.

When Alan Smith became Palace's boss in 1993, Palace fans were delighted when he added Steve to his coaching staff. The outcome, another Palace Championship at the end of the 1993–94 season, provided Kember with the amazing record of having been involved with no fewer than three of Palace's promotions to the top flight – one that he extended to four in 1997 – and in both of the club's post-war Championships.

Understandably, many modern-day Palace fans will consider that Steve Kember's most valuable contribution to the club was made in the spring of 2001 when he led Palace to the narrowest possible escape from the drop into the lower divisions by winning the final two tricky away fixtures. But any discussions as to which of Steve's achievements for the club has been the most significant is to miss the point: with a record such as his there can be few men who have made a greater impact for Crystal Palace.

LOMBARDO, Attilio

Born: 6 January 1966, St Maria La Fossa, Italy
Apps: 45+3
Goals: 10

Attilio Lombardo's Palace career span and statistics are not particularly impressive in terms of years, appearances or goals, but every Palace fan of the late 1990s will wholeheartedly agree that the Italian international midfielder made a substantial impression upon and for the club after he joined Palace from Juventus for £1.58 million in August 1997.

It was a terrific morale-booster for Palace and the supporters when the audacious signing of the 31-year-old winger was announced. He had become a household name among the home-based football fans through Channel Four's live Sunday afternoon coverage of Italy's Serie A, *Football Italia*, and he made an immediate impact for Palace in the Premiership, helping to inspire the club to victories in the opening two away games.

Yet, if ever a man looked a parody of a footballer it was Attilio! He was prematurely bald, bandy-legged, had an awkward gait and an almost gnome-like stance. But, in terms of sophistication and vision, it seems unlikely that Palace have ever offered so much in a single player. Perhaps, inevitably, he found the sheer pace and intensity of the First Division too much at times in 1998–99, but, during a difficult time for the club and its players, it was always apparent that he gave his best for the team.

And that 'best' so endeared him to the supporters that they would sing 'Just one Lombardo' to the tune of *El Sole Mio*, which was used in a popular television advert at the time!

LONG, Terry

Born: 17 November 1934, Tylers Green, Beaconsfield, Bucks
Apps: 470+10
Goals: 18

Terry Long joined Crystal Palace in May 1955 and did not leave the club until the autumn of 1973, over 18 years later. Thus, only Bobby Greener, Johnny McNichol and Steve Kember have served the club for longer than him.

Originally, Long was a wing-half who captured the eye of manager Cyril Spiers, and, after one season of settling into the demands of League football, he put together a run of 214 consecutive League appearances (234 including major Cup competitions) which was a club record at the time and has only once been exceeded, by the superb John Jackson.

Long made a major contribution to the club's promotion season of 1960–61 and remained as a cornerstone of the defence as the side was remodelled in the Third Division. Terry himself and George Petchey of the 1961 side were members of the 1963–64 squad which put Palace back into the Second Division after an absence of 39 years.

He was a wonderful club man. He simply had no desire to play for anyone

else, and certainly no one at Selhurst Park wanted him to do so. His loyal service to Palace was rewarded with a testimonial in October 1966 and a crowd of over 17,000 came along to support and thank him.

Although Long was a steady and capable defender, he could and did play upfield as an inside-forward. He did not often score goals, but no one who saw it will ever forget the one he hit from 25 yards in the floodlit friendly against Real Madrid! Another memorable strike was the last goal he netted for Palace, on 30 September 1967, when, in front of a then record crowd for a League fixture of 38,006, he struck the only goal of the game against Queen's Park Rangers and put Palace on top of the old Second Division for the first time in the club's history.

Terry Long was still making League appearances (even if not scoring goals) for Palace in the 1968–69 season, when the club again achieved promotion, this time to the elite of the First Division, but, to his disappointment and that of all his admirers, he was never able to turn out for the club in the top flight.

Nevertheless, he remained a respected and integral part of the Palace scene, and his subsequent appointment as assistant manager to Bert Head in 1972 was a thoroughly deserved reward for this most likeable of men. And it was typical of him that he should agree to come to Selhurst Park in October 1984 to give recognition to Jim Cannon, who is the only player to have appeared in more Palace games than Long himself.

McCORMICK, John

Born: 18 July 1936, Glasgow
Apps: 225
Goals: 7

Strong, tall central-defender John McCormick had had a distinguished career in Scotland, where he had been on the verge of international honours, but, amazingly, it was as a makeweight that he came south to play for Crystal Palace.

Centre-forward Tom White was manager Bert Head's primary target when he made one of his many forays north of the border to conduct transfer business, but he came back with both White and

McCormick. The tough, craggy defender, who became such a staunch and resolute pillar of the Palace rearguard and helped to guide the club to top-flight status and relative security there, cost Crystal Palace just £1,500.

Not only did he make full appearances for the Palace promotion side of 1968–69, but he also absolutely relished the challenge of the old First Division. With Mel Blyth alongside him and John Jackson in goal, John McCormick was part of the triumvirate who did most to keep the club in that section for four years. McCormick made international strikers appear anonymous, he constantly inspired his colleagues, his headed clearances saved Palace in scores of tight situations and his red hair stood out like a beacon. It was only after he had given up playing that Palace at last fell out of the top flight, so it was entirely proper that in September 1974 the club awarded him a richly deserved testimonial for his magnificent services.

Speaking about John McCormick many years later, Bert Head confided that he regarded his signing of him as the best one he had ever made for Crystal Palace, and it is impossible, even after a great deal of consideration, to argue this point.

McCRACKEN, Robert

Born: 25 June 1900, Dromore, Co. Down
Apps: 190
Goals: 2

A belief that exists in some quarters of football suggests that it is always useful to have an Irishman in any would-be successful team: certainly it is a belief which has found frequent credibility at Crystal Palace FC and one which proved true in the case of the club's first Championship-winning side.

The Irishman in question in 1920–21 was Robert McCracken, known to all his admirers at Palace, and at home in Ireland, as 'Roy'. He joined Palace from Belfast Distillery in the summer of 1920 in a transfer that caused much media attention. Until he had the misfortune to break a leg in December, Roy was Palace's first-choice right-half in the promotion-seeking, and ultimately Championship-winning, team that season.

Although the break was a nasty one, McCracken came back successfully at the beginning of the 1921–22 season when Palace made their debut in the Second Division, and he played more games in that division than anyone else at the club during its four-year tenure between 1921–25. Such consistency was of enormous value to Palace as they sought to establish themselves in the higher division, and it should be understood that the club's ultimate relegation in 1925 was certainly not due to the frailties of the side's overworked defenders.

McCracken's intelligent, mature, skilful performances earned him a deserved reputation as a neat and clever footballer, and he came to be respected by press and public alike as one of Palace's most reliable performers during the six years he was on the staff. He won four full international caps for Northern Ireland, is one of only four Palace men ever to have gained full recognition for the Province and was the first Third Division player to be selected for a full international, when Northern Ireland met England at Sunderland's former ground Roker Park on 23 October 1920. It was, however, McCracken's third cap, against Wales in Belfast some 18 months later, that produced a real curiosity, for he lined up against his fellow half-back at Palace, J.T. Jones. Perhaps it was as well that honours remained even in that game, with a scoreline of 1–1.

McCracken was the younger brother of Newcastle and Northern Ireland defender Billy McCracken, who so manipulated the offside law of the period that it was ultimately altered in 1925. Robert is less well known than his famous brother – except at Palace, of course, where he graced the best teams in the first 60 years of the club's existence, and is still recognised as being among the most cultured players ever to have appeared in Palace's colours.

McGOLDRICK, Eddie

Born: 30 April 1965, Islington, London
Apps: 178+11
Goals: 16

Dapper, little Eddie McGoldrick was a twinkling winger who joined Palace from Northampton in January 1989 and was the final component in Steve Coppell's assembling of a promotion-winning squad for that season. McGoldrick went on to become a huge favourite with Palace supporters, even if many of them were surprised when he won the Player of the Year award for 1991–92.

Eddie McGoldrick's teasing runs to the byline and supply of crosses were an integral and attractive feature of Steve Coppell's Palace teams. While he was at Selhurst Park they were a major reason for the club's success, via the Play-offs in the spring of 1989, together with its growing top-flight maturity in the early 1990s.

He was seldom a great goalscorer, but when he did deliver it was usually in vital circumstances. He netted at Blackburn in the Play-off Final to provide Palace with an invaluable away goal, plus hope and incentive for the second leg at Selhurst Park. He put the team on the way to the area final of the Zenith Data Systems Cup with an early strike against Luton Town in

the semi-final in February 1991, while his strikes in 1991–92 helped Palace to earn points at Norwich and Luton, win at Tottenham and should have been sufficient to dismiss eventual finalists Nottingham Forest from the League Cup in a fifth-round tie at Selhurst Park.

However, McGoldrick's skill was not limited to wing play, for he could also perform as an immaculate sweeper behind the back four, and Palace deployed him there most effectively in the latter part of his career with the club, although many fans would have preferred to see him used in a more adventurous role.

Partly, no doubt, because of his adaptability, Eddie was called-up for international recognition with Eire, but he chose to leave Palace in the summer of 1993, after the club's relegation from the Premier League, in which he netted a commendable eight goals to finish the season as Palace's second-highest goalscorer of the term.

McNICHOL, Johnny

Born: 20 August 1925, Kilmarnock
Died: 17 March 2007, Brighton, Sussex
Apps: 205
Goals: 15

Johnny McNichol came to Selhurst Park in March 1958 as manager Cyril Spiers's last attempt to prevent Palace from becoming founder members of the new, national Fourth Division which was to come into being the following August, comprised of the clubs which finished in the lower halves of the regional Third Divisions at the end of the 1957–58 season. McNichol was immediately appointed as captain, a position he held for nearly five years, and he scored the only goal of the game upon his debut to defeat visiting Port Vale, but even his seven goals from the remaining 12 fixtures could not keep Palace out of the new basement division.

McNichol was an old-fashioned inside-foward (the position in which he had won a League Championship medal with Chelsea in 1955), but he gradually moved, via wing-half, to full-back, and it was from there that he skippered Palace's first promotion side for 40 years, leading the club out of Division Four in 1960–61.

He had another couple of seasons as a player, extending his club record of consecutive League appearances from his debut to 153, which remained unbeaten until Nigel Martyn passed it early in the 1993–94 season, but was forced to retire after a particularly nasty fractured cheekbone and broken jaw early in 1962–63. Johnny McNichol turned to the commercial side of the game and began to build another successful career there. It was he who set up the first weekly pools and bingo competitions at Palace, and it is from those humble beginnings that the massively successful marketing operations at the club have grown.

By the time he moved back to Brighton (for whom he had played for four seasons in Division Three South, and nearer to his Sussex home), he had spent over 20 years at Selhurst Park and made an invaluable contribution to Palace's progress both on and off the field.

MARTYN, Nigel

Born: 11 August 1966, Bethel, near St Austell, Cornwall
Apps: 349
Goals: 0

Cornishmen are rare in Football or Premier League teams, but Nigel Martyn was Palace's superb goalkeeper throughout the first six seasons of the 1990s and carried the nickname 'Blaze', with which he was dubbed by his teammates after his first-ever club, St Blazey in the Western League.

Martyn came to prominence at Bristol Rovers, but he became the country's first £1 million goalkeeper when he joined

Crystal Palace in November 1989 when manager Steve Coppell sought to strengthen the team's defensive capabilities. Strong and powerful at 6ft 2in, but possessing an ideal temperament as well as considerable 'presence', Martyn soon impressed the Palace fans with his performances in the top flight. He played well in the 2–1 victory at Manchester United in the month after he joined the club and then made two stunning saves the following week to ensure another 'away' win, when the Palace beat Charlton at Selhurst Park during their groundshare period. A further vital save was the one he made in the final minute of the hard-fought FA Cup fifth-round tie against lowly Rochdale, which protected Palace's narrow lead and prevented the embarrassment of a hazardous Spotland replay.

Martyn became a member of Palace's best-ever defence at top-flight level in 1990–91 and, after earning a series of England B caps, he was awarded his first full international honour in Moscow on 29 April 1992 when he came on as a late substitute for England against the Confederation of Independent States. It was also during that 1991–92 season that he moved into the top 10 appearances of Palace goalkeepers, moving ahead of such greats as Billy Callender and John Burridge, and by that time he had kept more clean sheets in Division One than anybody except the magnificent John Jackson.

Folowing Palace's 1993 relegation, Martyn was an ever-present member of the Championship side in the new Division One in 1993–94 which brought about an immediate return to the Premier League.

Despite the absence necessitated by the injury to Nigel's hand in the 1995 FA Cup semi-final, by the early weeks of 1996 he had passed his 250th League appearance mark for Palace, and he then moved into the leading five players in the club's entire history when he remained unbeaten during the visit of Sheffield United on 10 February 1996.

But Palace's unfortunate defeat by Leicester in the 1996 Wembley Play-off Final was to cost the club its brilliant goalkeeper. Having played 349 games in the major competitions for the club, he moved to Leeds for £2.5 million, thus becoming Britain's costliest goalkeeper for the second time. Palace fans inevitably rued his depature, but they recognised that such a quality goalkeeper wanted to be playing regularly in the top flight and supporters wished him well for the future.

MORRISON, Clinton

Born: 14 May 1979, Tooting, London
Apps: 265+51
Goals: 113

Clinton Morrison was Palace's lively striker who marked his debut as an 18-year-old by scoring the only goal of Palace's last match of the 1997–98 season, against Sheffield Wednesday, after joining the action as a late substitute. Full of confidence in his ability, Morrison proved to be a regular goalscorer for Palace in Division One, and there were times when he hinted at the possibility that he could become prolific in these matters. While he was still a teenager, he netted 12 League goals in 1998–99 and established himself as an immediate choice in any Palace line up.

In the 1999–2000 season Morrison was again Palace's leading goalscorer with 13 strikes, but these were secured despite a protracted layoff brought about by a dislocated shoulder, then, during 2000–01 he once more topped the club's scoring chart with 14 in the League, although that was the term in which he notched several League Cup goals against Premiership opponents. He had already been on target in the 3–0 demolition of Leicester at Filbert Street, and then struck a glorious winner which beat Sunderland at Selhurst Park before Christmas. He also crowned Palace's best performance of the entire season with a rising drive into the top corner of the Holmesdale Road netting to put the League Cup semi-final first leg beyond Liverpool, and it was exploits like these which brought about Morrison's call-up for Eire (for whom he qualified through a Galway-born grandmother), and he netted on his full international debut in mid-August 2001.

After an excellent 2001–02 season in which he netted 22 League goals, many of them coming in pairs and with half scored before the term had even reached one third of its course, so that he looked to be on course for a huge haul, he astonished most Palace fans by signing for newly romoted Birmingham a week before the opening of

the new season, only to return to Palace some three years later after a rather disappointing time at St Andrew's.

Morrison's second spell at Palace was rather more to his liking than his time in the Midlands, and he moved into the select group of Palace strikers who have scored over 100 League goals for the club. He also helped Palace into the Championship Play-offs in 2005–06 and 2007–08, but was never quite the same sharpshooting leader of the attack that he had previously been, so that he left the club again in the summer of 2008 to join Championship rivals Coventry City.

MURPHY, Jerry

Born: 23 September 1959, Stepney, London
Apps: 253+16
Goals: 25

Jerry Murphy was an outstandingly talented young footballer who came to the attention of Palace fans when playing on the left side of midfield in the highly acclaimed and hugely successful Palace junior side which won the FA Youth Cup in 1977 and 1978 under the management of John Cartwright. The following two years saw Murphy at his best for the club. With his silken left foot, he was a vital member of the Palace side which won the Second Division Championship in 1979 and then, initially at least, took the top flight by storm.

Murphy had vision, culture and refinement. He possessed a temperament which sometimes made him appear aloof from the proceedings around him, so that he seemed much more mature than his years when his career was at its peak. Some of his occasional goals were real gems, while, even if his clever lob midway through the second half of Palace's match at Stoke's former Victoria Ground in the 1978–79 season was perhaps not quite Jerry's absolute best, it certainly became a piece of Palace folklore as, just before he scored, the bench had brandished aloft his number to indicate his substitution – and then hurriedly lowered it during the celebrations!

Murphy earned three full international caps for Eire (qualifying on

Photo © HY Money

account of his father's nationality), but once Palace began to lose their way, his laconic, if delicate and sometimes moody, style became, on occasions at least, something of a luxury which the the struggling side could ill afford. That said, his final term with the club was the first season of Steve Coppell's management career, and no one doubted Murphy's commitment to the cause then. In fact, all Palace fans were disappointed when, having become a free agent in the summer of 1985, he chose to move across town to play for Chelsea.

NICHOLAS, Peter

Born: 10 November 1959, Newport, Monmouthshire
Apps: 199
Goals: 16

Peter Nicholas was a magnificent, driving defensive midfield player, whose wholehearted commitment to the club endeared him to every Palace fan who watched him perform.

Nicholas was in the Palace junior side which won, and then retained, the FA Youth Cup in 1977 and 1978, and he then became a regular member of the Second Division Championship side of 1978–79, as well as of the team which did so well in the early part of the 1979–80 campaign in the top flight.

Arsenal were pleased to pay a bargain £500,000 for Peter in March 1981, after Palace's First Division return had gone sour and the club badly needed the cash, but he came back to Selhurst Park on loan in October 1983 when his tenacious and skilful experience was a key reason for Palace's Second Division survival in a most difficult season. Palace secured his full registration during the close season but Nicholas was anxious to be on the move again in the winter of 1984–85 and,

Photo © HY Money

to the regret of all Palace followers, he signed for First Division Luton Town for £165,000.

Peter Nicholas was seldom a goalscorer for Palace, although he never had a blank season. He netted four times – while still a teenager – during the 1978–79 promotion season, and it was Peter who beat Manchester United at Selhurst Park on 1 November during the awful 1980–81 season. His floated shot-cum-cross from the byline in front of the Arthur Wait stand sailed over Gary Bailey to present Ernie Walley with his third but final victory as Palace manager. After his return to Selhurst Park, Nicholas took responsiblity for penalties. The best remembered one of these is the first, which he converted for the club on 4 February 1984 to defeat Middlesbrough at Selhurst Park: this was the climax of a Palace riposte after the beleaguered team had seen two players sent off together in terribly bizarre circumstances.

Nicholas is one of the players that the Palace fans have always held in great affection as well as respect.

PARDEW, Alan

Born: 18 July 1961, Wimbledon, London
Apps: 148+20
Goals: 12

Although Alan Pardew is probably best known to younger fans as the manager of Newcastle and the former boss of Charlton and West Ham (who Palace beat in the 2004 Play-off Final in Cardiff), he was also one of a number of excellent signings made for Crystal Palace from the ranks of non-League football. The versatile midfielder made such tremendous progress with the club that he missed only one match of the extended 1988–89 promotion campaign, for which his drive, energy and cultured right foot proved an invaluable component, and then was absent for only two more games the following term upon Palace's return to the top division.

During the 1989–90 season, Alan Pardew was Palace's joint third top scorer with six priceless goals, while it was he who notched Palace's extra-time winner against Liverpool in the FA Cup semi-final at Villa

Park to secure the club's first-ever FA Cup Final appearance, along with everlasting fame and glory among the supporters who dubbed him 'Super Al' – the nickname by which he will always be remembered at Selhurst Park.

Another supremely important and morale-boosting strike by Pardew was the one which secured victory at big-spending Tottenham in March of the same year, some five weeks prior to the semi-final. This one demonstrated both vision and technical skill when he spotted Spurs 'keeper Erik Thorstvedt off his line and, from just inside the penalty area, Alan headed a poor clearance back over him and into the unguarded net for three priceless points to help ensure Palace's top-flight survival.

Pardew reached his 100th League game for the club when Arsenal came to Selhurst Park on Easter Saturday 14 April 1990 (1–1). He could always be relied upon to give 100 per cent to the Palace cause, and it was in recognition of his services to the club that he was allowed to move to Charlton on a free transfer in November 1991.

PAYNE, David

Born: 25 April 1947, Thornton Heath, Surrey
Apps: 315+3
Goals: 12

David Payne had supported Palace from the Whitehorse Lane terraces as a boy and he joined the club as an apprentice on 1 January 1964. He signed as a full professional later that year and made his senior, then Football League debuts in quick succession during the closing months of it as a 17-year-old.

The former was in a testing League Cup tie at the home of the holders, Leicester City of the First Division. Palace deployed a formation that was typical of then manager Dick Graham – tightly defensive, yet resilient and disciplined. So effective was it that John Jackson was scarcely troubled in the Palace goal and, despite an injury to Alan Stephenson in those pre-substitute days, Palace and David Payne held on comfortably enough for a thoroughly deserved and highly praiseworthy 0–0 draw at Filbert Street.

Dick Graham only released his protégé upon the Second Division scene slowly – his first game was at Preston in early December – but he became a regular midfield member of the League team in the following term, 1965–66, and in three seasons he rarely missed a match, although a mid-term injury at Millwall restricted his appearances in the club's 1968–69 promotion season. However, Payne was fit for the final eight games of that triumph and was immediately restored to the side as Palace clawed their way remorselessly to the runners'-up position. Fans of that period remember his contribution to that magnificent achievement with pleasure

and admiration – seemingly tireless, Payne's ceaseless, energetic displays, his tough tackling and midfield vision alongside Steve Kember, were all vital components in that success.

He was not a big man but, like several Palace midfielders and defenders of that period, he excelled under intense and almost continuous pressure in the top flight. As the situation demanded, Payne would play almost anywhere – he actually wore eight different numbered shirts for Palace in those four seasons in the First Divison between 1969 and 1973 – and rarely, if ever, even in such illustrious company, was he outshone. In fact, it was in that elite division that his unflagging workrate, intelligent and selfless running and accurate distribution proved him to be a footballer of high calibre.

England manager Sir Alf Ramsey included Payne as a substitute for the Under-23 side against Wales in Swansea on 1 November 1967, but Palace folk from that era will always contend that he was worthy of further and higher honours.

David eventually left Selhurst Park for Orient in 1973, joining several other former Palace stalwarts at Brisbane Road when Malcolm Allison was reshaping the Selhurst Park side, but his departure was regretted by Palace fans who had always held the likeable young man in immense respect and affection.

Delightfully, however, over recent years David Payne has reappeared in public at Selhurst Park, and his efforts in establishing a former Palace players' association have been greatly appreciated by his contemporary colleagues and supporters of all generations.

PETCHEY, George

Born: 24 June 1931, Whitechapel, London
Apps: 153
Goals: 12

George Petchey was a driving, inspirational wing-half and certainly one of the best in that position in the old Third Division South, but he joined Fourth Division Crystal Palace in the summer of 1960 to play under Mr Arthur Rowe.

Petchey proved a terrific signing, among the best that Arthur Rowe made for the club, for he helped Palace to secure promotion from the League basement in his first season at Selhurst Park, during which he made full appearances. He continued as a first-team regular under Dick Graham to become one of only two men to appear in both the 1961 and 1964 promotion sides. His strong, assertive displays were a feature of Palace's progress back to the Second Division, but his playing career was brought to a premature end by a troublesome eye complaint and his final match for the club was the delayed sixth-round FA Cup defeat (3–0) against mighty Leeds United on 10 March 1965.

After Dick Graham left Palace in January the following year, Petchey assisted Arthur Rowe and then Bert Head in the role of team coach, helping to mould the

side that earned top-flight status in 1969. Eventually, though, after 11 years with Palace, George left Selhurst Park to become manager of Leyton Orient, and a feature of his time at Brisbane Road was his regular purchasing of Palace players, such as Phil Hoadley, Gerry Queen and John Jackson, to help to keep his new club in the Second Division.

His efforts for Palace, both as a player and in support of the managers, were acknowledged by the club when they awarded Petchey a testimonial in November 1967, when an International XI assembled to provide the opposition. Palace won 6–3 on a gala night, the side's last three goals coming in the final five minutes, to the delight of over 10,000 fans who had come along to enjoy it and show their appreciation of this greatly admired player.

QUEEN, Gerry

Born: 15 January 1945, Glasgow
Apps: 119+8
Goals: 30

Palace fans of the early 1970s remember Gerry Queen. He was a brave, exciting and intelligent goalscorer who joined the club in July 1969 when manager Bert Head was seeking additional and experienced striking power for the First Division battle which lay ahead. Queen was probably Mr Head's most effective signing for Palace over the four years the club spent in the top flight, and he certainly topped the long line of successful transfers negotiated by the manager which brought talented footballers from north of the border.

Queen made an immediate impact at Palace by scoring upon his debut in the 2–2 draw with Manchester United on the opening day of the 1969–70 season. He went on to become Palace's top scorer that season. On his day he was as good a centre-

forward as any in the country, and he would almost certainly have won a string of Scottish international caps had he been with a more fashionable or successful club. He possessed considerable skill, had grace and power and was strong in the air, yet he was also willing to battle against the odds right to the final whistle.

The value of Gerry Queen to Crystal Palace can perhaps best be measured by the fact that he was easily the club's top scorer in the First Division between 1969 and 1973 with 24 goals, while his 18 strikes between 1969 and 1971 represented a quarter of the club's tally over those two seasons. Meanwhile, several of his goals were crucial, point-saving or point-winning ones and, because of that, were morale bosters for his manager, teammates and the fans.

A fine Gerry Queen goal came at Anfield, where Palace had lost badly in the earlier 1969–70 season and most Scousers were expecting a repeat performance from the Reds. But Palace were made of sterner stuff in the 1970–71 season and took the match to their opponents. Palace were unlucky to be in arrears, but with a quarter of an hour to go, he rose in front of the Kop to head a left-side cross from Tony Taylor towards the goal, and Ray Clemence could do no more than palm it into the back of the net.

RODGER, Simon

Born: 3 October 1971, Shoreham-by-Sea, Sussex
Apps: 286+42
Goals: 12

Simon Rodger was a fair-haired, industrious and tenacious midfielder for Crystal Palace right through the 1990s and beyond. His career was cruelly hit by a number of injuries, but he was always a great favourite with the fans, who quickly nicknamed him 'Jolly' and greatly appreciated his whole-hearted displays as well as his ability, which enabled him to play on the left or in the centre of midfield. He sometimes appeared at left-back, and he would deliver dangerous, in-swinging crosses from free-kicks or corners on the right. Rodger made his debut in a demanding top-flight encounter at Sheffield Wednesday in October 1991 and was involved with Palace for 11 consecutive seasons.

Quiet and reserved off the pitch, his eager, pacy and hardworking contribution to the Palace cause was initially linked with that of his fellow 'Bisto-Kid', Simon Osborn. While the 1993–94 season provided nothing but frustrations for his colleague, the season developed into a huge success for Simon Rodger and was probably the best of his long Palace career. He played a major role in the First Division Championship win, while everyone who saw his last-minute goal which beat defiant Southend in a nighttime game at Selhurst Park over Christmas will remember the exhilaration that it produced.

A cruel and debilitating back injury, sustained after just four Premier League fixtures in 1994–95, not only deprived Palace of Rodger's presence for the rest of the season, but also kept him out of the team for a year. Upon his return he played a full part in ensuring his and the club's presence in two consecutive Wembley Play-off Finals in 1996 and 1997. There are fans who contend that his 29 Premiership appearances in Palace's traumatic 1997–98 season actually represented the best indicator of his loyalty and commitment to the club.

One great advocate of Rodger's singular importance to the cause was the club's long-serving and hugely respected manager, Steve Coppell. Steve was always a great admirer of the player and appointed him as skipper of the side. It was largely with him as captain that Palace put on such a performance of dogged resistance throughout the dreadful, worsening adversity of the 1999–2000 campaign, when the club was in the legal state of administration from beginning to end.

Palace finished that awful season comfortably in mid-table, despite losing player after player to rival clubs at cut-price fees just to stay afloat. For that season's efforts, many Palace folk consider that Simon Rodger could claim a place among any group of Palace giants; certainly, he is one of those players whom the fans knew would never let their club down.

ROGERS, Don

Born: 25 October 1945, Paulton
Apps: 76+2
Goals: 30

At his peak, Don Rogers was a superb goalscoring winger. His former club boss, Bert Head, paid a Palace record fee to bring Don to Selhurst Park in the late autumn of 1972. Palace badly needed a goalscorer to help remedy an awful start to the season, but Rogers immediately obliged with the only strike of his debut match against Everton.

Don's talent was a cultivated and lethal left foot, phenomenal acceleration, even on a slippery surface, and top-class control. His shooting was accurate and sometimes explosive. Palace's younger fans idolised him and it did initially appear that Bert Head's protegé would rescue Palace from a dire situation. Certainly, several distinguished clubs, and their defenders, were terrorised by Rogers, none more so than Manchester United when Palace routed them 5–0 a week before Christmas, with Don twice on target.

However, Rogers's reputation made him a heavily marked man: Palace failed to survive and were relegated. Then, along with many other Palace players, Don lost his touch and the club floundered badly after relegation. Under Malcolm Allison, Rogers played a less aggressive role and at times became almost anonymous. Indeed,

Palace's players and fans became greatly disappointed with his performances, and it was a relief to everyone when he moved to Queen's Park Rangers in September 1974.

ROUSE, Vic

Born: 16 March 1936, Swansea
Apps: 257
Goals: 0

It is a clear indication of the quality of Vic Rouse's goalkeeping that he succeeded the great Roy Bailey between the Palace posts and then went on to set a club record of 238 Football League appearances, a tally which has only ever been exceeded at Palace by the invincible John Jackson and England international Nigel Martyn. It then took another goalkeeper who was destined for stardom in the top flight, Bill Glazier, to oust him.

Rouse's debut for Palace was interesting, for he made it in the same game as Johnny Byrne, and since it was a

0–0 draw (against Swindon at Selhurst Park in October 1956) it could perhaps be argued that Vic had the better start of the pair! Of course, both went on to gain full international recognition, but Rouse goes down in football's annals as the first international player to be chosen from the ranks of the old Fourth Division (for Wales against Northern Ireland in Belfast in April 1959). Palace fans ought to be aware that this was no freak selection: Rouse had impressed many with his splendid run of quality performances. During the game he made some stunning saves and certainly prevented the Principality from an annihilation.

Vic Rouse subsequently made full appearances in Palace's promotion season of 1960–61, thus helping the club to make progress for the first time in 40 years. A feature of his game was the accurate and powerful throw he developed, which could reach the halfway line, by which he frequently set up fast and effective Palace counter-attacks, usually via one of the wingers, notably Johnny Gavin or Ron Heckman, who were always alert to the possibility.

Understandably, Rouse was a great favourite with the fans of his day, so it was an enormous pleasure when he returned to Selhurst Park in May 1982 in charge of the Metropolitan Police side, and he has also attended several of the player reunions which have been organised over recent years.

SALAKO, John

Born: 11 February 1969, Lagos, Nigeria
Apps: 222+51
Goals: 34

John Salako was a product of the club's junior ranks. He was a pacy winger who also had a eye for goal, but after Palace's return to the top flight in 1989, he demonstrated a most praiseworthy capacity for filling other roles. For example, he performed splendidly as a mobile left wing-back in the latter stages of the 1989–90 season, notably in the FA Cup semi-final against Liverpool and in the Wembley Finals, and he was Palace's stand-in goalkeeper against Wimbledon on a torrid evening in August 1991.

Salako's career record demonstrates that it took him some while to establish himself as a first-team regular, but having done so in the autumn of 1990 he proceeded to win the Barclays Young Eagle of the Month award for the region twice in four months, having impressed no less a respected observer than Bill Nicholson of Tottenham and England.

One of Salako's best games for Palace at that stage of his career was the FA Cup third-round first replay at Nottingham Forest in January 1991, when he provided the cross from which Ian Wright volleyed the opener and then scored a magnificent, last-gasp equaliser which revealed

considerable vision and no little technique, catching the Forest goalkeeper off his line with a dipping, curling shot from some 45 yards. Equally, his brace against Manchester United in the last match of the 1990–91 season (coincidentally, also his 150th Palace appearance) demonstrated that he was on the verge of international recognition.

The exciting promise that he had revealed was rewarded with a place on the England tour of Australasia in June 1991, where he again showed his capacity to excite the crowd and bemuse the opposition, playing in all four matches. But Salako's progress was then cruelly cut short on 1 October 1991 when, early in the night game against Leeds United, he fell badly after putting in a header at the Holmesdale Road end. Obviously in acute pain, he was stretchered to the dressing room, and an exploratory operation the following afternoon revealed the severance of both crucial ligaments behind his left knee.

He was able to play a dozen or so games in the autumn of 1992, but the new technique used in rebuilding his joint required further refinement, and it was not until days before the second anniversary of the injury that he was properly able to begin the restoration process. However, on 2 October 1993, in his first full appearance, Salako struck a stunning hat-trick against Stoke City on a waterlogged pitch at Selhurst Park to bring the Palace crowd to a fever pitch of excitement and delight as Palace romped to an impressive 4–1 win.

SANSOM, Kenny

Born: 26 September 1958, Camberwell, London
Apps: 197
Goals: 4

Those who saw Kenny Sansom play for Crystal Palace will confirm that he was probably the most polished and certainly the best left-back to have played for the club, and his distinguished career with Palace, as well as with Arsenal, Newcastle, Queen's Park Rangers and Coventry, all

Photo © HY Money

demonstrate the sheer quality of his play, while his 86 full international caps simply prove the point beyond any debate.

Sansom made his debut for Palace as a 16-year-old and is the third youngest player ever to have appeared in the first team. Within two years, he had become the captain of the England Youth team, had skippered the Palace juniors to an FA Youth Cup triumph in 1977 and become an ever-present member of the Palace senior side that won promotion from the old Third Division that same year. Indeed, he only missed one game in the three seasons from 1976 to 1979 and altogether had a run of 156 League games with only that one omission.

In the higher sphere Sansom simply excelled, and he helped Palace to gain the Championship of the old Second Division with the club's best-ever defensive record, and then to reach the summit of the entire Football League in September 1979. He was also the only Palace player to make full appearances in both the promotion seasons in the late 1970s.

By now, he was a prized Palace asset and was eagerly sought by the bigger clubs. Fresh-faced and perky, Sansom was ideally built for a full-back: he was strong and sturdy, with a low centre of gravity and possessed remarkable stamina and resilience. His tackling was precise, and he was seldom beaten in any tussle for the ball. His positional sense was almost perfect and, although much less overlapping was required of 1970s and 1980s defenders than is demanded today, Kenny Sansom's pace was blistering when he used it.

Never was this better demonstrated than in an old Second Division game at Tottenham just before Christmas 1977. Playing now for Spurs – and in direct opposition to Kenny – was England winger and former Palace star Peter Taylor. Permanently retained in the memory is the sight of Sansom beating Taylor for speed down the flank and wresting the ball from him – several times! And Sansom had not even reached his peak at that time.

Ultimately, Sansom won nine full England caps while he was with Palace, plus another eight for the Under-21s and two for England B. He was the club's Player of the Year in both 1977 and 1979, while only Jim Cannon and Julian Speroni have won that coveted award more times than Kenny Sansom (although Kenny remains the youngest Palace man ever to have done so).

It took a record fee to take him to Arsenal in an exchange deal in the close season of 1980, when both he and Clive Allen were valued at £1 million. Palace fans were desperately sorry to see Kenny leave Selhurst Park, recognising that quality such as he possessed is irreplaceable at any price.

SEWELL, John

Born: 7 July 1936, Brockley, London
Apps: 255+3
Goals: 9

John Sewell has a gloriously unique place in any gallery of Palace heroes because he was the popular and talented captain of the team which took the club into the top flight for the first time in Palace's history, in 1969.

Sewell's career in the upper echelons of the League appeared to have ended when he moved from Charlton to Palace in October 1963 after eight years at The Valley. He soon made a niche for himself in the Palace defence and scored his first goal for the club three weeks after his debut, during the 8–2 defeat of Harwich and Parkstone in the FA Cup. He made 18 consecutive appearances for the club in that Third Division season and captained the side on occasions, but he then received a nasty injury at Millwall on 22 February and Palace had to claw their way into the Second Division without his able assistance.

He had made a few First Division appearances for Charlton, but undoubtedly the climax of his career came when he captained Palace to promotion to the top flight at the end of the 1968–69 season. He then maintained his high level of performance by helping to keep Palace in the senior division for the two remaining seasons in which he stayed with the club.

There can be no doubt that Sewell's efforts in assisting Palace to retain that hard-won place in the First Division were magnificent. Often playing with or against men who were 10 years his junior, the immaculate full-back (who dressed as smartly off the pitch as he performed on it) always looked fresh and resilient, and his presence was a boost to the confidence of every Palace side. He made 70 top-flight appearances for the club, and during that time the defence was usually under considerable pressure; most of the matches were tense affairs and the demands upon the captain were inevitably therefore much greater. His 70 appearances were only bettered over that period by the evergreen John McCormick, goalkeeper John Jackson and the much younger Mel Blyth, which speaks volumes for the fitness, charisma and sheer determination of the man.

Sewell's bright character was always apparent, but it was also demonstrated by the two pairs of top-flight goals he scored for Palace – scored, it should be noted, at a time when Palace goals were at a premium. He hit one against Liverpool in a 3–1 defeat and another to secure a point at Manchester United in 1969–70, while in the 1970–71 campaign he stunned Leeds United with a late equaliser and at Ipswich his penalty set Palace on the way to an invaluable 2–1 win.

After Palace's 1970–71 season had ended, the club marked John Sewell's time at the club with a testimonial against FC Bruges from the Belgian League. John had played 258 senior games for the club, and nearly 9,000 fans came along to demonstrate their appreciation. Some of today's rather older, greyer and more rotund fans were delighted when Sewell came back to Selhurst Park for a reunion with his 1969 promotion-winning colleagues in March 2001.

SIMPSON, Peter

Born: 13 November 1904, Leith, nr Edinburgh
Died: 14 March 1974, Croydon
Apps: 195
Goals: 165

Peter Simpson, tall, fashionably good-looking and Crystal Palace's greatest-ever goalscorer, must rank as one of the best signings in the entire history of the club. He first came to the attentions of Crystal Palace supporters when the club were drawn to play Kettering Town in the first round of the FA Cup on 24 November 1928. Jimmy Wilde, making his Palace debut that afternoon at centre-half, had an excellent game and prevented Simpson

from scoring, but the manager at the time, Fred Mavin, immediately recognised that the visitors' number nine was a man who could do great things for Crystal Palace.

Mavin actually signed several of the Kettering players, and some of them appeared in Palace sides later in the season, but Simpson was not signed until the following summer. But having once arrived at Selhurst Park, his impact was almost immediate! He came into the League side for the fifth match of the 1929–30 campaign on 14 September for the home game with Norwich City. He scored the equaliser with a crisp, low drive, and headed the second early in the second half. He then so pressurized the Norwich goalkeeper that he conceded a third goal, which Palace naturally enough credited to Simpson, to sew up the match.

Peter Simpson had become prominent with St Bernard's in the Scottish League Division Two, but Kettering urged him to leave his homeland and assist them in the Southern League. They won the Eastern Region title in 1927–28 and 1928–29 and, although St Bernard's had placed what we today call a 'selling-on fee' should he subsequently join a Football League club, Simpson's eminent place in Palace history ensures that even if the club had had to pay a dozen such fees, it would still have been money well spent.

Peter Simpson has a lasting legacy at Palace as a famed goalscorer. He most certainly was that, but he was also very much more. His distributive skills were prodigious: he fed Albert Harry and George Clarke on Palace's flanks with rare ability, and they returned the compliment with a stream of centres and crosses. Simpson read the game brilliantly, while his high-scoring feats tell of a man who could always find that split-second of time, the extra half-yard of space or ounce of energy to beat an opponent.

By March 1930, with a mere 26 games plus an FA Cup appearance for Palace to his name, and an average of exactly one goal per match, Simpson had attracted the attentions of several big clubs, but he stayed at Selhurst Park and set a new scoring record of 36 League strikes (in his first season and from just 34 games), topped the divisional scorers chart for that campaign and was only improved upon by two men in the entire Football League. In 1930–31 Simpson was absolutely magnificent. He rattled up no fewer than 46 League goals (inevitably an all-time club record which would appear to be invincible), including six in succession in the 7–2 defeat of Exeter on 4 October. He proceeded to top Palace's list of goalscorers for each of his first five seasons and between September 1929 and April 1935 he played 180 League and 15 FA Cup games, netting a fabulous tally of 153 and 12 goals respectively, to establish a goals total which no one at Palace has ever approached, either before or since.

The Peter Simpson era at Selhurst Park ended with a knee injury in 1934–35. He lost some of his sparkle after this and was transferred to West Ham in the close season. After two years at Upton Park he joined Reading, and he came up against his old club on 22 January 1938. Palace led at half-time, but Simpson had a superb second half, netted twice and sent Palace home defeated 3–2.

Palace staged a benefit for Simpson on 31 October 1934 against the ever-popular Corinthians but it was wretched misfortune that the weather was so grim that only a little more than 1,000 fans turned out to see Palace win 3–2.

After he retired he took over a newsagent and tobacconist's shop in West Croydon. He died at the age of 69 in March 1974, but at Crystal Palace FC Peter Simpson remains immortal.

SMITH, Edwin 'Ted'

Born: 1884, Birmingham
Apps: 192
Goals: 124

Ted Smith was a marvellous goalscorer for Crystal Palace on both sides of World War One, and if that awful event had not reduced the impact of his career with the club then it is almost certain that he would have netted so many strikes that even Peter Simpson would not have been able to emulate him.

Smith was a Birmingham lad, but he joined Palace from Hull City in December 1911. His debut was at West Ham on 30 December, where Palace won 6–1 and the new centre-forward hit a hat-trick. He then repeated the feat a week later in his next game, when Bristol Rovers came to the Crystal Palace. And Smith simply carried on from there. He topped the club's list of goalscorers for the four pre-war seasons he was with Palace, and again in 1919–20, so that during that period his record was the equal (at least) of any player in the game.

He was burly and strong, weighed in at 12 stone and stood some 5ft 9in tall. As a header of the ball he was phenomenal, scoring many with his head, while he also possessed an extremely powerful shot – and modern-day fans should realise that in those days the leather ball collected any moisture on the pitch and could end up weighing several pounds!

Smith's efforts for the club were fully recognised by everyone at Crystal Palace and he was awarded a benefit in 1920–21. It was the (new) Third Division match against Gillingham on 5 March, and some 12,000 fans were at the game. Palace won 4–1, and the band played *For He's a Jolly Good Fellow* before the start.

After World War One Ted became the captain of the side. It is rare for an out-and-out striker to skipper any side and only an exceptional player could do so. But he captained the side throughout the first half of the Third Division Championship season of 1920–21 before injury prevented him from playing, and subsequently in the opening matches in the Second Division.

Ted Smith was certainly 'a jolly good fellow' – and that is a sentiment with which everyone at Crystal Palace FC agreed!

SOUTHGATE, Gareth

Born: 3 September 1970, Watford, Herts
Apps: 186+5
Goals: 22

Gareth Southgate matured to stardom under the guidance of his mentor Alan Smith when the latter was in charge of Palace's youth and then reserve teams. There was always an evident and strong bond between the pair, and it was obvious from an early stage to judicious Palace fans that Gareth was a future skipper in the making. Sure enough, just after he had completed his first 100 senior appearances for Palace, Southgate captained the League side for the first time at Barnsley in a 3–1 win on 20 November 1993, although he had previously taken the armband for two Anglo-Italian Cup ties earlier that season.

Extremely versatile and admired as well as respected by Palace fans, Gareth Southgate played at full-back, in central defence and in the middle or on the right of midfield. But wherever he performed he exuded confidence, authority and class. It was also in 1993–94 that he began to score some valuable, often spectacular goals, to usefully augment Palace's charge to the top of Division One. His nine League strikes that term made him Palace's second-highest scorer behind Chris Armstrong.

Palace fans of the early to mid-1990s will recall several of his goals with delight, and some are unforgettable: the early-season strikes against Portsmouth at Selhurst Park and West Bromwich Albion at The Hawthorns were fabulous efforts which helped to turn victories into morale-boosting triumphs, to the tune of 5–1 and 4–1 respectively.

Southgate's final goal of the 1993–94 season turned the away fixture, at Middlesbrough, in Palace's favour and thereby helped to assure the club of the divisional title: he had headed a Simon Rodger free-kick with grace and style and Palace went on to win 3–2. Thus, Gareth fully earned the honour of holding aloft the Championship trophy when the celebrations took place at Selhurst Park before the last match of the season a week later. He also carries the distinction of being the youngest Palace skipper to lead the club to promotion, let alone to a Championship.

With Palace now back in the Premier League, Southgate became the only player to appear in every League game – indeed, in every fixture of that 1994–95 season – and came close to leading the club to a Wembley Final because Palace were the only club to appear in the last four of both the major Cup competitions. Palace lost the two-legged League Cup semi-final against Liverpool by the narrowest of margins, while the FA Cup semi-final opponents were Manchester United at Villa Park. Gareth's team matched the Red Devils throughout and might have won on points, only for United to snatch the replay in a game marred by a disgraceful foul on Palace's young captain.

But, despite the run-in to the season, Palace were relegated from the top flight at the end of the term, and when Alan Smith left Selhurst Park, most Palace fans realised that Gareth Southgate would also soon be on his way. Nevertheless, he will always hold an honoured place in the club's story and in the hearts of Palace fans everywhere.

SPERONI, Julian

Born: 18 May 1979, Buenos Aires, Argentina
Apps: 216+1
Goals: 0

Julian Speroni has become a firm favourite among the fans as a stylish, spectacular goalkeeper who is occasionally quite outstanding.

The Argentinian Under-20 and Under-21 international joined The Eagles from Dundee for £500,000 in the summer of 2004 after Palace had gained promotion to the Premiership via the Championship Play-offs.

Iain Dowie initially made Speroni his first-choice goalkeeper, but, after one or two erratic displays, replaced him with Hungarian international stopper Gabor Kiraly, for whom Speroni deputised at times during the ensuing two seasons.

Speroni, however, again became the Palace first-choice 'keeper for the 2007–08 campaign and played in every game as they reached fifth place in the Championship table, and he then appeared in both the Play-off matches against Bristol City, so that most Palace fans emphatically approved his selection as the club's Player of the Season.

Speroni was again quite exceptional throughout the 2008–09 season, appearing in all but one of Palace's Championship fixtures and, on occasions, proving quite superb between the posts. But, perhaps, he kept his best performance of the season until the final game, when third-placed Sheffield United were the visitors, hoping to gain a victory to put added pressure on second-placed Birmingham. The prime reason why they were disappointed was the inspired display by Julian Speroni, which was exemplified by two jaw-dropping saves to ensure another clean sheet and force The Blades to extend their season.

Speroni's contribution to the Palace in the ensuing period is demonstrated by the fact that he was the club's Player of the Year at the end of each of the three seasons up to 2010, has aggregated almost 200 League appearances for The Eagles and is sometimes spectacularly impressive when keeping rampant opponents at bay on our behalf.

SPOTTISWOOD, Bob

Born: 20 January 1884, Carlisle
Apps: 189
Goals: 2

Bob Spottiswood was a strong and pacy defensive right-half who played for his home-town club, Carlisle United, before Croydon Common brought him south to

play for them in the summer of 1908. However, after just one season with the Robins, he joined Crystal Palace – and what an excellent signing that was!

Spottiswood quickly became a huge favourite with the club's pre-war fans, who loved his fiercely determined performances. He missed few games in a Palace career which spanned six seasons and was only brought to an end by World War One. His appearance record was exemplary; his first season, in which he missed just one game and helped Palace to finish seventh in the Southern League, established a pattern for his time with the club. A bad knee injury virtually wiped out the 1910–11 season for him, although he did play a couple of games as a stand-in centre-forward during an injury crisis at the club and scored a goal in the process! Bob came to his peak in the seasons before the war: in 1912–13 Palace finished fifth and the defensive record was not bettered by any club in the division, while 1913–14 was quite outstanding, as Palace came cruelly close to winning the Southern League Championship, only being denied on goal average by Swindon Town.

The 1914–15 season was traumatic at Crystal Palace, as the club had to leave its headquarters and players left to join the services, but Bob Spottiswood was an absolute mainstay and, along with full-back Horace Colclough, became a real pillar for the club at a most difficult time.

Bob's abilities were recognised by the Southern League authorities, who selected him for one of their inter-League games during the 1912–13 season, and he was awarded a benefit by the club in 1914–15, along with his half-back colleagues Jimmy Hughes and Harry Hanger. Unfortunately, Palace had been forced to move to Herne Hill by the time of the chosen fixture, against Bob's old club Croydon Common, and it is not known what arrangements were made on the players' behalf.

STEPHENSON, Alan

Born: 26 September 1944, Cheshunt, Herts
Apps: 185
Goals: 13

Alan Stephenson was a tall, stylish, slimly built but strong centre-half, who played for Palace with grace and power in the tough footballing days of the mid-1960s. Stephenson was dominating in the air and a solid and reliable tackler, so that he was a perfect defender for a team marshalled by manager Dick Graham, and he made a major contribution to Palace's progress, deservedly becoming the club captain and also earning England Under-23 honours.

Alan Stephenson actually began at Palace as an amateur, travelling across London upon hearing that trials were being held at Selhurst Park. He made his debut at the age of 17, against Bradford Park Avenue at Selhurst Park on 24 March 1962, and helped his team keep a clean sheet for the first time in 18 matches and three and a half months! His next outing, the following September, saw him net his

first Palace goal when, despite a facial injury, he put the club 2–1 ahead against visiting Brighton. Unfortunately, however, these were difficult times at Selhurst Park and Albion were able to pull it back to 2–2.

In the 1963–64 season Alan forced his way into the Third Division promotion team, playing alongside Brian Wood in an early dual central-defender's role. From then on, missing only an occasional game through injury for four years in the Second Division, he developed into a distinguished centre-half, who defended most capably and led his team with authority while also scoring useful goals, usually from aerial set pieces. His best efforts in this latter respect were probably the pair he netted in the first half on 27 December 1965 to put Palace well on course to a victory over Ipswich at Selhurst Park.

Stephenson himself always believed that his best game of all for the club was the fifth-round FA Cup tie against Nottingham Forest the previous February, when the team beat the top-flight sophisticates 3–1.

Inevitably, and quite properly, Alan Stephenson went on to play in the First Division himself. He joined West Ham in March 1968, although it took a club record fee of around £80,000 before Palace would allow him to leave Selhurst Park.

Most agreeably, Alan is among the most regular of the former players who return to Selhurst Park for players' reunions, when these are organised on behalf of the club.

SUMMERSBY, Roy

Born: 19 March 1935, Lambeth, London
Apps: 190
Goals: 60

Roy Summersby was a tough, stocky inside-forward who joined Palace from neighbouring Millwall when the club was struggling to make an impact upon the Fourth Division leadership in its initial season.

Fast, adroit and clever, Roy was a typical inside man of his day: strong, industrious and an accurate passer of the ball. But he

was better than many, certainly at the level in which Palace were playing at the time of his purchase. He had a most successful career at Selhurst Park, providing the ideal foil to the mercurial Johnny Byrne and helping to make the club a respected side in Division Three, before leaving to join his former Palace manager George Smith at Portsmouth.

While Summersby's goalscoring feats for Palace were eclipsed by Johnny Byrne's, the present-day fans should understand that there were occasions when quite the reverse occurred! For example, Roy hit a hat-trick to rout Mansfield 4–1, who were managed by Raich Carter on 1 October 1960 at Selhurst Park, with Johnny Byrne unable to get on the scoresheet, while at the climax of the season, with Byrne now heavily shackled by opposing defences, Summersby had a marvellous finale, netting five times in the last four matches to ensure promotion and a glorious conclusion.

If it is records that count, however, then Roy has two great claims. First, he is one of the select few Palace players who have made over 100 consecutive appearances immediately following his debut, and his run of 123 games has only ever been beaten by Johnny McNichol and Nigel Martyn.

Then there is his goalscoring tally. His 25 League goals in 1960–61 put him as runner-up to Johnny Byrne in that promotion season, but he remains only behind Byrne's figure of 30 and Andy Johnson's 28 in 2003–04 for the highest number of goals in a post-war League season of up to 46 games. Roy's 59 League goals for the club is still an impressive figure, even today, while many of those who have scored more times than him had considerably longer Palace careers.

Photo © HY Money

SWINDLEHURST, Dave

Born: 6 January 1956, Edgware, Middlesex
Apps: 260+16
Goals: 81

Dave Swindlehurst was Palace's big, strong goalscorer as the club forced its way back to the First Division limelight from the obscurity of Division Three between 1974 and 1979.

Brave, and accurate in the air, Swindlehurst consistently proved his abilities to find the net at all levels, but perhaps the single goal for which he will always be remembered by Palace fans of that era would be the one he scored at Elland Road in January 1976, when Third Division Palace dismissed the mighty Yorkshire outfit on the way to the club's first FA Cup semi-final. It was Dave's gloriously directed header, from a Peter Taylor free-kick, that arrowed its way into the top corner of Leeds' net to settle the fourth-round tie.

Equally memorable, although arguably more important, was Swindlehurst's 88th-minute low, right-footed volley against Burnley, in front of Selhurst Park's biggest-ever crowd of 51,482 on 11 May 1979, which clinched the old Second Division Championship and took Palace back to the top flight.

Dave was Palace's leading goalscorer for four seasons in the mid-to-late 1970s, and his 14 strikes in that Championship season of 1978–79 was his most significant contribution, representing as it did well over a quarter of the club's total of 51. His more modest total of 10 in 1976–77, when the club gained promotion from the Third Division, was also extremely valuable. Not only did his goals include the one which opened the scoring in the all-important final match of the season against fellow contenders Wrexham, but he had struck the winner against the Welshmen at Selhurst Park eight days earlier, thus providing vital goals at crucial times that would, ultimately, earn the points which put Palace in front of Wrexham in the final table and enabled the club to take the third promotion place.

For a long while Swindlehurst was second only to Johnny Byrne among Palace's post-war goalscorers; although, of course, all but a handful of 'Budgie's' goals were scored in the lower divisions.

In spite of his imposing physique, and like many big strikers, Dave was a sensitive fellow and pre-match tension was a real problem for him in his earlier days, but he overcame that worry successfully and went on to make an indelible contribution to Palace's return to the big-time before moving to Derby County in a £400,000 deal in February 1980.

TAYLOR, Peter

Born: 3 January 1953, Rochford, Essex
Apps: 142
Goals: 39

Peter Taylor was a speedy, stocky goalscoring winger who was brought to Palace by Malcolm Allison. He was

Photo © HY Money

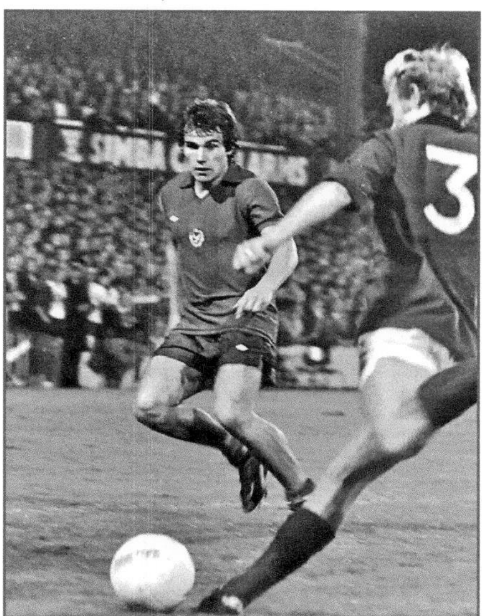

certainly Malcolm's best signing for the club, repaying his transfer fee several times over, and those Palace fans who saw him play carry permanent memories of him marauding down the right flank, then cutting inside and delivering a rasping left-footed drive or tantalising cross.

Usually wearing the number-11 shirt despite operating largely on the right, Taylor had great pace and neat control. His shooting was accurate and his use of dead-ball situations was intelligent and effective. While he was with Palace he gained four England Under-23 caps (two of them in matches staged at Selhurst Park) and scored in every game. He also won four full England caps while with the club and netted on his first two appearances for the national side.

Taylor came very much to the attention of the country's football followers with spectacular displays for Palace during the fabulous run to the FA Cup semi-final in 1976, where he was the on-field inspiration as the side gained some magnificent victories. Despite being only a Third Division club, Palace won at Leeds, Chelsea and Sunderland. Against Leeds and Sunderland Taylor created the opportunities from which Dave Swindlehurst and Alan Whittle respectively scored the single goals which separated the sides. At Chelsea in the fifth round, he scored two exquisite goals of his own to win the match, while his strikes in the much less publicised earlier rounds had helped Palace dismiss Millwall (in a replay) and Scarborough.

It was soon evident that Peter Taylor would move to a bigger club, and in September 1976 he joined Tottenham for £200,000. While his career there never completely fulfilled its earlier promise, a measure of his popularity and standing at Crystal Palace may be gained from the splendid reception he recieved from the fans when he returned to Selhurst Park a full 17 years later as the manager of Southend for a Christmas holiday match in December 1993.

Taylor was appointed as Palace manager in June 2006, and, while his time with the club could not be in any way regarded as successful, those Palace folk who watched him play in the early 1970s will always retain great admiration and affection for him.

TAYLOR, Tony

Born: 6 September 1946, Glasgow
Apps: 217+5
Goals: 11

Bert Head brought many fine footballers to Crystal Palace from north of the border, but none was of greater value to the club than tough little Tony Taylor. His hardworking, selfless style rarely caught the attention of the media, but Palace patrons of the late 1960s and early 1970s thoroughly appreciated his worth.

After joining the club in the autumn of 1968, Taylor played in every remaining

match of that wonderfully successful season. He immediately established a productive, intuitive midfield partnership with Steve Kember, which was a key reason for the club's 1969 promotion to the top flight, and he netted two goals in the process: the first, early in the second half to put Palace on the way to a 4–2 win over visiting Aston Villa in mid-December, and the other a neat downward header just before the half hour in a 3–1 home victory against Cardiff in March.

Palace owed much to Taylor's midfield contribution in the First Division, but he also played in a variety of other positions, from attacking winger on his debut to left-back. In fact, he became known as Tony 'play me anywhere as long as you play me' Taylor! It may be the longest sobriquet in the club's annals, but it perfectly sums up this splendid servant of the club.

It is no surprise that Taylor put in more First Division appearances for Palace than anyone except John Jackson and Mel Blyth between 1969 and 1973, but many Palace fans believe that they saw him at his best at left-back. This came about after he had initially filled in at number three for the stunning 2–1 Anglo-Italian Cup victory against Italian champions Inter Milan at their San Siro headquarters on 4 June 1971. Certainly, Taylor played extremely well in that position after Peter Wall was injured for most of the 1972–73 season, and in the first half of the following campaign, and it was from that position that he captained the Palace side.

A football man through and through, Tony Taylor took up coaching after his playing days were over and graduated to become the chief coach of the Canadian national side for three years in the late 1980s.

THOMAS, Geoff

Born: 5 August 1964, Manchester
Apps: 244+5
Goals: 35

Geoff Thomas was Palace's inspirational, attacking midfield supremo and occasional central-defender who became club captain 12 months after he had joined the club from Crewe Alexandra in May 1987 and went on to skipper the Palace side through the most successful years the club has ever experienced.

Fair-haired and with a distinctive, upright stance, his powerful running and cultured style soon made him a firm favourite with the Palace fans, who voted him Player of the Year in his first season. Injury reduced his availability in the 1988–89 season, but he captained the side throughout the following term upon their return to the top flight, and he scored crucial goals against Portsmouth and at Cambridge in the fabulous run to the 1990 FA Cup Final, where his performances impressed many neutral observers.

The first match of the 1990 Cup Final between Palace and Manchester United was acknowledged as among the best in the long history of the competition and, of course, Geoff Thomas has the distinction of being the first skipper to captain a Palace side on such an occasion. But his dream, and that of many fans, probably rested upon an appalling decision in the replay which concerned an incident that had involved Geoff himself. Half-time was approaching when a foul was committed on him some five yards inside the penalty area, yet the referee awarded the free-kick outside the area by some distance. As Geoff himself reflected afterwards, 'It was clear as day what had happened. It's decisions like this that turn a Cup Final.'

He continued to progress in the top flight throughout the 1990–91 season when, in company with Andy Gray, the midfield continually outplayed high-ranking opponents and helped Palace secure some wonderful results.

Thus it was that Palace reached the top three places before Christmas, and Thomas himself was honoured with an England B cap in an international in Algeria. Perhaps partly because of Palace's victory and Thomas's opening goal in the defeat of Everton at Wembley in the Zenith Data Systems Cup Final in April 1991, he was awarded his first full international cap when England travelled to Turkey on May Day 1991.

With all these achievements it was almost inevitable that Thomas should gain his second Player of the Year award that term, while the fact that he earned it in Palace's best season ever is a clear demonstration of his immense value and contribution to the club.

THORN, Andy

Born: 12 November 1966, Carshalton, Surrey
Apps: 168
Goals: 7

Andy Thorn was a proven top-flight centre-half and possessor of a coveted FA Cup-winners' medal when Palace manager Steve Coppell brought the 6ft-tall defender back to South London after a brief spell on Tyneside at the end of November 1989. The fee of £650,000 appeared to be a considerable one, but it proved to be a billiant signing, for Thorn immediately shored up Palace's hitherto rather porous defence to help ensure First Division survival in the 1989–90 season, while his experience assisted in the club's run to their first-ever appearance in an FA Cup Final. Then, teamed up alongside his former Wimbledon colleague Eric Young, he proceeded to secure the club's best-ever defensive record at top-flight level along with its highest finishing position of third in that top division.

In fact, the brilliant portent of his impact at Crystal Palace was to be seen on his debut, which took place at Old Trafford. Palace, previously without an away win that season, came from behind to beat Manchester United, and then Andy netted with a far-post header from a set-piece in the following match in only the fourth minute against Charlton 'away' at Selhurst Park (during the groundshare between the clubs) to set Palace on course to another success.

Tough, unrelenting, obdurate and a fearsome opponent, Thorn won five England Under-21 caps in his early years in the game. Upon joining Palace, he proved more than capable of subduing the nation's best strikers week after week, serving as skipper, first in the absence of

Geoff Thomas and then in his own right, and he earned the respect, then admiration and gratitude of all Palace supporters as a wholehearted footballer of the old breed, always giving his best whatever the circumstances.

It was, therefore, no surprise that Thorn won the club's Player of the Year award in 1993, but a troublesome knee injury incurred later that year proved difficult to treat. By the time he was fit for action again, there was no place for him in Palace's Premiership defence and he returned to his first club Wimbledon in mid-October 1994.

TURNER, Billy

Born: 16 November 1901, Tipton, Staffs
Died: 1989, Worcester
Apps: 302
Goals: 37

Billy Turner signed for Crystal Palace from Bromsgrove Rovers in the summer of 1925 as a skilled, but tough little inside-forward. He came into the Palace side at the start of the following term and, injuries or illness apart, was a fixture there for the next 11 seasons, accumulating so many appearances that he still remains near to the top 10 in the club's all-time charts.

Turner was not a great goalscorer in his own right, but everyone who saw him play for Crystal Palace agrees that he helped to make hundreds of goals for the club. There was no doubt that right-winger Albert Harry played very much better with Turner there beside him and, under his neat and shrewd direction, Palace's forwards could become really quite devastating.

Billy Turner became known to Palace fans as 'Rubber', and his resilience and adaptability were certainly an unusual feature of the game in those pre-war days; later in his Palace career he played in the wing-half positions, out on either wing and then, towards the end, even as full-back. The fact is that in an age when players were never encouraged or expected to be particularly adaptable, the only positions that he did not fill for Crystal Palace at one time or another were those of goalkeeper, centre-forward and centre-half.

Add this to the fact that Turner was one of those players whose consistency improved as his career progressed. But it was not just long service which endeared him to Palace fans – or, indeed, which brings about his inclusion within this chapter. Billy Turner was an enthusiastic player, full of pep and fight, with the 'never-say-die' attitude that supporters of a club long to see. He was never a showman or at all flamboyant – he simply won the hearts of the Palace fans with his wholehearted and full-blooded displays.

Perhaps the most fitting tribute to Billy Turner came from the last Palace manager under whom he played, Mr Jack Tresadern. The boss was asked one day by a pressman which position he considered to be Billy Turner's best. To which Tresadern replied 'Everywhere. He's 100 per cent wherever you play him!'

WALSH, Ian

Born: 4 September 1958, St Davids, Pembrokeshire
Apps: 133
Goals: 27

Ian was a bright, young striker who, after helping the Palace Juniors win the FA Youth Cup in 1977, forced his way into the League side and became a lay member of the 1979 Second Division Championship line ups, scoring eight invaluable goals to become Palace's second top scorer behind Dave Swindlehurst.

Among Ian's several crucial strikes that season were Palace's single goal that accounted for Wrexham at Selhurst Park in early March, his wicked, angled drive with less than two minutes remaining which gave Palace both points at Bristol Rovers on Easter Saturday, and of course the first one, an arrow-like header into the top corner with 14 minutes to go in the decisive victory over Burnley which clinched the title in the final game of the season.

With the Eagles in the top flight, Ian became a regular choice for the full Welsh international squad, and he is one of three Palace players to have gained 14 full caps for their country while at the club.

WHIBLEY, John

Born: 1892, Sittingbourne, Kent
Apps: 150
Goals: 27

John Whibley was a Crystal Palace star in a previous era: he contributed significantly to the club's progress in the early 1920s.

Whibley was a quiet young man from Sittingbourne. Tall and willowy, he was a winger of quality and promise sufficient for manager Edmund Goodman to deploy him as deputy for Welsh international Bill Davies before World War One, and when fully competitive football resumed after the hostilities Mr Goodman made him an automatic choice at outside-left, and that was where he played for four seasons. Thus, his effectiveness can be measured by the fact that he retained his place on the Palace flank while aiding the club's progress from Southern League also-rans to Third Division champions, and then to a position of relative dignity in Division Two.

Even as a youngster before the war, Whibley had scored on his occasional senior outings, for while his slight build made him a tantalising opponent, he also possessed scorching pace and neat control together with the ability to cut inside an opponent and shoot powerfully – and thereby be relied upon for several useful goals each season.

Immediately upon the resumption of the Southern League after the war, he netted in the first game of the season and scored eight times from the flank that term, then added five more in the 1920–21 promotion season which followed. But actually, it is two of his goals in 1921–22 for which Palace fans of that period will

always remember him and which are worthy of mention. Palace began their Second Division career with a plum home tie against the favourites and eventual champions Nottingham Forest, and Whibley had much to do with Forest's downfall. He forced the early corner from which Palace opened the scoring, and, with Palace comfortably in control at 3–1 he dribbled through the visitors' defence from the half-way line, drew England international goalkeeper Sam Hardy and then lashed a magnificent fourth goal to ensure an emphatic victory.

Rather fewer Palace fans were able to see Whibley's other notable strike that season, but its significance can still be measured today, nearly 90 years later, because it was the opening goal in the amazing 6–0 rout of Everton at Goodison Park in an FA Cup first-round tie in January 1922. He headed in Ben Bateman's fourth-minute corner. He also provided the cross from which John Conner put Palace three ahead midway through the second half.

Altogether, he netted 27 League and Cup goals for Palace from his 150 senior appearances. Crystal Palace was his only club, and when he left a the end of the 1922–23 season he returned to his home town to play for Sittingbourne.

WHITWORTH, George

Born: 14 July 1896, Wellingborough, Northants
Apps: 118
Goals: 50

George Whitworth was a brave, strong centre-forward from Wellingborough. Discerning Palace fans had recognised his quality when he guested for the club during the special arrangements regarding these matters during World War One, for he had done so effectively – and then, he had scored against Palace for Northampton Town, on at least two occasions in the two seasons in which the teams met following the end of the war.

Palace manager Edmund Goodman had inevitably also taken note of Whitworth's ability, so that when Palace needed a proven striker at short notice after Bert Menlove moved to Sheffield United in March 1922, he acted decisively and without prevarication or delay.

Whitworth made his Football League debut for Palace up at Bury, where he equalised for the team before half-time, hit the bar soon after the break and then set up Ben Bateman for the winner. Some debut! Whitworth then notched 17 goals from his 36 Second Division appearances in 1922–23 when he became the first Palace centre-forward to benefit from Albert Harry's efforts on the right wing. Frankly, Palace's problem was that if George himself did not score, hardly anyone else would either! The next highest scorer was Billy Morgan with just seven.

Thus it was only after Frank Hoddinott joined the club in 1923 that the Palace fans (sadly, all too briefly), saw Whitworth at his supreme best. Now playing at inside-right, he was again top scorer with 16 goals, but he also combined so effectively with Hoddinott that Palace had a comfortable Second Division season. Again Whitworth headed the club's goalscoring chart for 1924–25, when, but for an eye injury which kept him out for six games from the late winter until early spring, he might have kept Palace in Division Two. As it was he scored a late winner to defeat Chelsea on 1 April in the second game after his return, but that was to prove Palace's last victory at that level for over 39 years and, before the term ended in relegation, George had been signed by Sheffield Wednesday.

However, his 48 goals for Palace in the higher divisions, scored generally when the club was far from being a great or confident side, were easily the best tally achieved in the period between 1921 and 1925 and have only rarely been improved upon subsequently.

WILDE, 'Jimmy'

Born: 24 September 1904, Lyndhurst, Hampshire
Died: 18 June 1976
Apps: 293
Goals: 6

'Jimmy' (his real names were William Charles) Wilde was a Palace first-team regular for eight full seasons from 1928 and was club captain for six of them.

Tall, slim and elegant, but totally dominant at centre-half, Wilde joined Palace in October 1928 and for his debut he was plunged into the testing FA Cup first-round tie against the Southern League (Eastern Section) champions, Kettering Town. The visitors' centre-forward was renowned in non-League football as a prolific goalscorer, so Palace fans of the time might justifiably have been a little anxious as to the wisdom of pitting an unproven defender against such a man. But Wilde played Peter Simpson in immaculate style, Palace won 2–0 and Jimmy earmarked that central-defensive spot for his own. Having won the Cup tie, Palace then embarked upon a 17-match unbeaten run in the League – never improved upon at the club within a single season – and rose from mid-table to become possible, then likely, champions!

Regrettably, Wilde and his colleagues were just shaded out of the title – and, of course, the single promotion place that went with it – by local rivals Charlton on goal average alone, in the most exciting finish to a Third Division South season in the history of the club. But it is perfectly possible to argue that, had Jimmy Wilde become available just one or two matches earlier, the club would have crowned his first season at Selhurst Park with success.

Following his first term at Palace, Wilde continued to make a pleasing and

positive impact upon the Third Division South scene. He was quickly recognised as one of the most accomplished half-backs in the section, and his displays won him the approval of the fans on many grounds besides Selhurst Park. He usually appeared at centre-half, but when necessary he could and did provide constructive driving displays in both the wing-half berths.

Interestingly (and perhaps surprisingly to modern-day readers), after Wilde ceased to be a first-team player he elected to remain with the club, playing in the reserves for two seasons. This was to prove of considerable value to Palace because there was a young lad there who benefitted greatly from the nurturing that an experienced campaigner like Jimmy Wilde could provide, before breaking into the first-team himself – and then being transferred to a top-flight club for a record fee, for the young man's name was Arthur Hudgell.

Jimmy Wilde was one of the great unsung heroes of Crystal Palace between the wars: hopefully this chapter is the perfect place to remedy that!

WOOD, George

Born: 26 September 1952, Douglas, South Lanarkshire
Apps: 221
Goals: 0

Scottish international goalkeeper George Wood joined Palace and proved to be one of manager Alan Mullery's best signings. He had a deserved reputation as a top-class custodian and quickly demonstrated his class and skill to Palace patrons.

Wood was ever present for nearly three seasons and became only the second post-war goalkeeper at the club to put together a run of 100 consecutive League games (inevitably, John Jackson was the first),

while his 100 appearances straight from his debut were Palace's first for over a quarter of a century. In fact, during Wood's four and a half seasons at Selhurst Park, he missed only three senior games and those absences were forced upon him by the urgent need for surgery.

George Wood was not simply a fine goalkeeper, an imposing figure between the posts and a most loyal club man, he was also exceptionally brave. Following a nasty knee injury against Shrewsbury in November 1984, when he was carried from the pitch with his leg cut to the bone, he played again, with massive strapping and padding, just four days later, and in all the ensuing games, in considerable pain and in spite of the injury.

His best seasons with Palace were his two last complete ones, when, now under Steve Coppell, the club improved substantially and finished fifth then sixth in the old Second Division. However, probably his finest single game was in the second leg of a wonderful League Cup second-round tie with Manchester United at Old Trafford in October 1985, when he matched the high standards of his counterpart, Gary Bailey; made several saves of the highest calibre, particularly when United were rampant immediately after the interval; was unquestionably the best Palace player on the night and thoroughly deserved the accolades offered by Steve Coppell and the fans afterwards.

A top-class goalkeeper is expected to be both courageous and consistent. George Wood, the gentle Scotsman in the Palace goal, provided both qualities in full measure while he was with the club. Evidence of his popularity was clearly to be seen 'below stairs' when he returned to Selhurst Park with Cardiff City for a League Cup match in August 2000.

WOODGER, George

Born: 3 September 1883, Croydon
Died: 6 March 1961, Croydon
Apps: 177
Goals: 47

George Woodger, an inside or centre-forward of the highest quality, played for Palace in the club's earliest years and soon became the first Crystal Palace superstar. He was a local boy from Croydon and made his Palace debut on 1 November 1905 at Swindon in a United League game, where he helped the club to a 6–1 win and netted two goals.

It soon became apparent that Woodger was a prodigy: he quickly became a permanent feature of Palace's Southern League line ups, and his poise and delicate ball-playing skills so endeared him to the supporters that they dubbed him 'Lady'.

Fans of the club must all be thankful that Palace had Woodger with the club for much of the 1905–06 season and throughout the ensuing four Southern League campaigns. He contributed eight goals from his 12 appearances in the first season and continued to progress as a valuable goalscorer and footballing artist the following term, appearing in most League games of an arduous campaign and in all eight FA Cup ties where spectacular victories took the infant Palace club to the quarter-finals.

His best season with the club was undoubtedly 1907–08 when he was top scorer with 13 Southern League strikes, missed only three games and assisted Palace to a glorious fourth-place finish.

Such was Woodger's talent that he was called-up for the full England squad for the international against Scotland in Glasgow (1–1) but, perhaps understandably if certainly frustratingly, he remained the unused reserve (in the days before substitutes).

Woodger became Palace's captain for the 1909–10 season in succession to Wilfred Innerd, but by now his responsibility was more that of supplying ace strikers George Payne and 'Ginger' Williams than of scoring goals himself. So successful was this tactic that Palace netted no fewer than 69 goals in the 42 matches, and only a disappointing run of results in the closing few games prevented the club from finishing at least in the top three places.

By now Woodger was a well-known and much-appreciated performer. He was also, quite rightly, an ambitious star, and it became clear to him and to the fans that the only way in which he would gain the international recognition that he craved – and so obviously deserved – would be for him to join a club in the more prestigious Football League. After weeks of speculation, he eventually moved to newly promoted Oldham and, intriguingly, made his Latics debut at nearby Woolwich Arsenal in a 0–0 draw. There is no means of knowing whether any of his former fans travelled over to watch him, but certainly everyone at Palace was delighted for him when he at last gained his coveted England recognition against Ireland at Derby in a 2–1 win the following February.

WOODRUFF, Bobby

Born: 9 November 1940, Highworth, Wiltshire
Apps: 136+3
Goals: 48

Bobby Woodruff rejoined his former Swindon Town boss Bert Head when he moved to Selhurst Park in June 1966, and that wily manager's shrewdness was again demonstrated when Bobby became a prominent member of Palace sides in the late 1960s. His chart of appearances shows that he made full appearances for two seasons after coming to the club, while only a broken collarbone prevented him from making an even more impressive

contribution towards the club's promotion to the top flight in 1968–69.

Woodruff had an excellent goalscoring record with Palace and his 18 League goals in both 1966–67 and 1967–68 were not approached in the top divisions by a Palace player for two decades. In fact, Bobby was a two-edged weapon for the club. Firstly, he was a magnificent header of the ball and graceful too, and secondly he also possessed that all-important talent for a striker of being in the right place to snap up any half chance that came his way in the six-yard box. This was never better demonstrated than in the late winter to early spring of 1969, when Palace really began to assert themselves in the old Second Division promotion race and Bobby hit five goals in six games to put his team right on the shoulders of the front runners. His winner at League leaders Derby on 5 March was what kindled the hopes and beliefs that Palace could claim success by the end of the season – and, in fact, the club went right through the rest of the programme unbeaten.

Equally, Woodruff possessed a prodigious long throw-in; it was the League prototype for the ploy and Palace exploited it most successfully, for Bobby could reach the penalty spot without any difficulty. The fact was that the tactic was novel and by the time most defenders and even coaches had come to terms with it, Palace had usually taken full advantage!

WRIGHT, Ian

Born: 3 November 1963, Woolwich, London
Apps: 253+24
Goals: 117

Mercurial striker Ian Wright joined Crystal Palace in the summer of 1985 and quickly made his mark as a highly effective 'super sub' in his initial season to finish as the club's second-highest scorer of the campaign with Phil Barber on nine goals apiece.

When Mark Bright arrived on the Palace scene the following year, the duo soon established a marvellously effective striking partnership and it was largely their goals which took Palace to the promotion Play-offs and a return to the top flight in 1989.

A twice-cracked shin bone reduced Wright's opening impact upon his bow in the old First Division, although he completely proved his worth among the distinguished company and was called-up for England B duty in December 1989

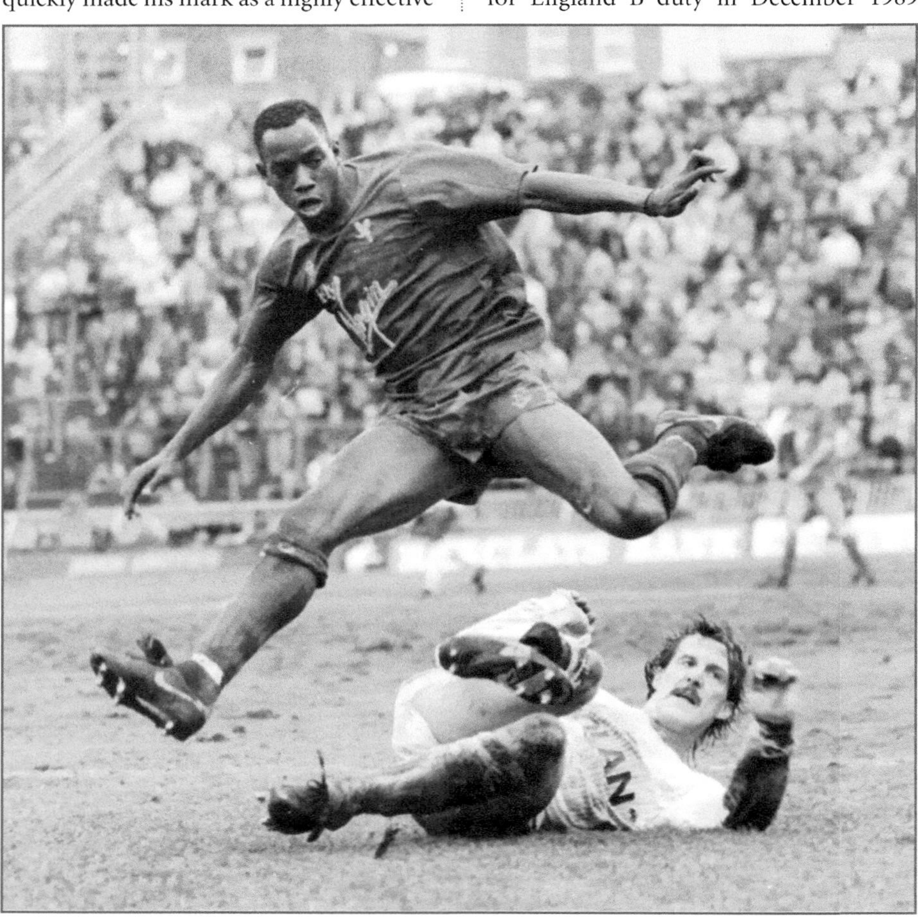

before the injuries were sustained. Equally, no one, friend or foe alike, will ever forget his dramatic appearance, again as a 'super sub', in the FA Cup Final of 1990. Palace had led but were 2–1 down when Steve Coppell made his perfectly judged substitution, bringing Ian on to replace Phil Barber in the 69th minute. Within three minutes Palace were level. And it was a goal worthy of the finest the grand old stadium had ever witnessed! The lissom, eager Palace striker skipped clear of the lunging Mike Phelan, turned inside Gary Pallister – the defender who at £2.3 million had cost more than the entire Palace team – leaving the poor, embarrassed fellow on the seat of his pants, and then delivered a low shot past Scottish international goalkeeper Jim Leighton to make the score 2–2.

Wright scored again too, but sadly it was not until early in extra-time. Young John Salako sent over a long, testing cross, and Ian saw its possibilities early and launched himself to volley the ball into United's net while several feet off the ground. What a Cup winner that would have been! However, United had time to regroup, showed one more moment of high-quality finishing and made it 3–3. In the replay, even Ian's arrival, again as substitute, could not remedy a 1–0 defecit.

The 1990–91 season was another eventful one for Ian Wright and Palace. It became the club's most successful season ever, while 'Wrighty' himself gained full England international honours, completed his century of Palace goals and scored twice as Palace beat Everton to win the Zenith Data Systems Cup Final at Wembley. His virtuoso hat-trick, scored at Wimbledon, demonstrated in magnificent style that, when he was on form, there was no more dangerous or exciting player than him in the entire Football or Premier League.

YOUNG, Eric

Born: 25 March 1960, Singapore
Apps: 204
Goals: 17

Eric Young was Palace's superb 6ft 3in central-defender who joined the club from Wimbledon in the summer of 1990 for a fee of some £850,000. At the time he joined, manager Steve Coppell averred that, besides an accomplished central-defender, he was obtaining a most useful goalscorer. Some critics voiced disquiet at the size of the fee Young commanded, but the manager's judgement proved

completely accurate on both counts, while some of Eric's strikes were highly significant and often spectacular affairs. He was always a terror to opponents in their own penalty areas, while the sight of him bearing down upon them in readiness for a Palace corner or free-kick was a massively daunting one. Thus, besides his goal upon his Palace debut, perhaps his best remembered effort was the strike he secured at the Holmesdale Road end of Selhurst Park to beat Liverpool in March 1992 and at the same time secure the double over them. He also scored a brilliant late winner at Nottingham Forest to provide a victory which infuriated Forest's then chairman and restored the club's dignity after an FA Cup replay defeat at the City Ground earlier that same week. Another glorious headed goal was Palace's second at Tottenham on the second Saturday of the inaugural Premier League season of 1992–93.

As a defender, Young was magnificent and, wearing the headband that made him instantly recognisable, he was soon nicknamed 'Ninja' by Palace's admiring fans after the similarly attired turtles that featured in a popular cartoon at that time. Thus, it was with Eric at centre-half that Palace won the Zenith Data Systems Cup at Wembley in April 1991 and achieved the club's best-ever final placing of third in the top flight of the League that same season.

Unusually, Eric Young's international career with Wales burgeoned late, but once he had been selected he became a regular and key member of the Principality's side that so narrowly missed out on qualification for the 1994 World Cup finals, although it was in June 1993 that he established a new club record at Palace by winning his 15th appointment for his country.

ZHIYI, Fan

Born: 22 January 1970, Shanghai, China
Apps: 101+1
Goals: 6

Fan Zhiyi arrived at Selhurst Park with his compatriot Sun Jihai amid a blaze of publicity in September 1998 because the duo were the first Chinese nationals to sign for a British League club. Sun only stayed at Palace for the remainder of the 1998–99 season but Fan progressed marvellously in the team during a turbulent time for the club, and his contribution to Palace gained increasing appreciation from the supporters as the months passed.

Despite being the captain of the Chinese national side and the Asian Footballer of the Year in 1999, Zhiyi took time to adjust to the Football League, but his mobility, adaptability, athleticism and enthusiastic tenacity blended to make him an invaluable asset to any Palace manager, as well as a great favourite with all the club's fans. Such popularity was partly because he was also the scorer of the occasional, usually spectacular and often long range, goal which turns a game and salvages points. Perhaps his best remembered strike was the 30-yard skimmer just before half-time that beat promotion-bound Bradford City at Selhurst Park at the end of March 1999.

For his first season, Zhiyi was usually deployed in a defensive midfield position, but his last two full terms saw him in commanding form at the centre of Palace's back line. Discerning supporters recognised that Palace's Division One survival in 1999–2000 was owed to no small degree to Fan's partnership with Andy Linighan, where Fan was dominating and composed in a defence, which at times came under a lot of pressure, and sometimes quite dazzling when venturing forward in support of the attack.

Another reason for Zhiyi's popularity at Palace lay in the evident fact that he was so obviously pleased to be playing for the club and proud to be wearing the red and blue. His endeavours on Palace's behalf were seen to be fully committed as well as passionate, and every football follower empathizes with a player who wears his heart upon his sleeve. Fan Zhiyi was as much a Palace man as any supporter who may have been born in the Holmesdale Road!

Managers

John Robson (1905–07)

Born: May 1860, Durham
Died: January 1922, Manchester
Manager: Middlesbrough, Crystal Palace, Croydon Common, Brighton and Hove Albion, Manchester United.

Palace's initial manager was Mr John Robson, who came to the club from Middlesbrough. His reputation had been established at Ayresome Park, where he had taken Boro to promotion to the top flight of the Football League in 1902, and he immediately signed several players from the North East for Crystal Palace who proved to be most useful aquisitions.

Of course, it was with Mr Robson at the helm that Palace won the Southern League's Second Division title at the first attempt in 1905–06. And even if the team did find the senior section hard going in 1906–07, it was Robson who steered the club through a fabulous FA Cup run that season to the last eight, including the legendary victory over the then Football League champions Newcastle United at their headquarters, where they had not previously lost a match for over a year.

It has always been a widely held opinion that that astonishing victory must still, and probably always will, rank as Palace's finest of all time. Given the relative status of the two clubs in January 1907 it is difficult to argue otherwise – and remember that it was gained while Mr Robson was the manager.

Edmund Goodman (1907–25)

Born: October 1873, Birmingham
Manager: Crystal Palace.

As Palace fans know well, Mr Edmund Goodman was virtually THE founding father of Crystal Palace FC. Not only did he serve for 28 years as club secretary – inevitably longer than has ever been accorded to any other senior club officer – but he was also the club's manager for 18 of them. The story of how he came to Palace in the first place is also well known, but there is no doubt that all Palace followers of all time owe Aston Villa and their then chairman Mr William McGregor ('the founder of the Football League') an enormous debt of gratitude for encouraging the club to appoint the young man in the first place.

To begin with, of course Mr Goodman was completely immersed in the tough, grinding responsibilities of establishing the new club and selecting and appointing Palace's admirable first manager together with the initial chairman, Mr Sydney Bourne. It must surely rank as THE transfer bargain of all time.

Mr Goodman took on the duties of team management from 1907, and he held the job until 1925. Straight away Palace

rose to fourth place in the Southern League table for 1907–08 and were quickly established as one of that League's leading performers. Palace never won the Championship, but in 1913–14 they only ceded it to Swindon Town on goal average and then, after World War One, were admitted to the newly-formed Third Division of the Football League and immediately won promotion to Division Two.

Not only did Mr Goodman retain Palace's elevated status for four seasons, but he also led the club to several hugely impressive FA Cup triumphs, of which the victory over FA Cup holder Wolves, in a 1908 Crystal Palace replay, and the 6–0 rout of prestigious Everton at their own ground were probably the greatest of them all.

Lastly, after Mr Goodman had assisted in bringing the club to Selhurst Park, it was virtually his Palace team which beat Chelsea in an FA Cup fourth-round tie which set a ground record attendance which lasted all but 40 years.

After handing over his managerial responsibilities in 1925, Mr Goodman continued to serve Palace as secretary for another eight years. He then bought a greengrocer's business in Anerley and, while always having a kind and gentle word for enquiring pressmen who subsequently approached him, allowed the veil of time to enable him to pass from the public scene.

Alex Maley (1925–27)

Manager: Clyde, Clydebank, Hibernian, Crystal Palace, Clydebank.

The surname Maley was a well known one to football fans on both sides of the border in the early years after World War One because there were several footballing brothers who carried it. Alex was not the best known of them, although he was prominent enough in Edinburgh, where he was the boss of Hibernian prior to coming to Selhurst Park to manage Palace in November 1925.

Inevitably, Mr Maley introduced a series of players from Scotland to the club, of which the most useful was full-back Bobby Orr who joined in 1926–27 and made 70 League appearances during the ensuing two seasons.

Mr Maley's Palace side of 1926–27 was more dependable than those of the then recent past: not only did Palace win their opening games of the season for the first time in five years, but they finished in sixth place, which was a considerable improvement upon the previous term.

Regrettably, however, Palace's start to the following season was way below what was expected. The team suffered two 6–1 defeats in the Third Division South and then Leyton put Palace out of the London Challenge Cup in early October. Mr Maley resigned after that game and returned north of the border.

Fred Mavin (1927–30)

Born: 1884, Newcastle
Died: May 1957, Bradford
Player: New Brompton, Fulham, Bradford Park Avenue, Reading.
Manager: Exeter City, Crystal Palace, Gillingham.

Fred Mavin was an experienced manager with a long career as a player behind him when he arrived at Selhurst Park late in 1927, and he immediately galvanised the team to achieve a fifth-place finish in Division Three South in that 1927–28 season.

Having spent an industrious summer in the transfer market, Mr Mavin and his charges faced the 1928–29 season with some confidence and a largely remodelled side. He brought Stan Charlton, a full-back, from his previous club and immediately installed him as skipper, pairing him with Tom Crilly, who had been secured from Derby County. During the period these two men were together at Selhurst Park, Palace made two earnest if ultimately unsuccessful charges upon the one promotion place allowed to the regional Third Divisions.

Mr Mavin also made other telling signings. Dapper little Welsh goalscorer Lewis Griffiths came from Torquay and scored in his first game; Hubert Butler, another goalscorer, arrived from Chorley; and then, in the autumn, Mavin further strengthened the defence with centre-half 'Jimmy' Wilde. So it was that Palace's 1928–29 side was the best one to represent the club between the relegation back to the Third Division South in 1925 and the start of World War Two and – plenty of fans would insist – for a long time thereafter as well! Mr Mavin's Palace side came so close to gaining promotion. There was an attendance of over 22,000 at Selhurst Park for the last match of the season, who only learned at the conclusion that the 1–0 win over Brighton (earned by a Stan Charlton penalty) was not sufficient to stop neighbouring Charlton from taking the top place, on goal average alone.

Mr Mavin made another hugely significant signing for Palace during the following summer, when he induced Peter Simpson to join several of his former Kettering Town colleagues at Selhurst Park. Peter's career at Palace was a marvellous one, but it was to Fred Mavin that the fans owed his presence and goals.

It was with huge regret that Palace agreed to Mr Mavin leaving the club, because of his wife's ill-health, in October 1930, and it was largely his team that again finished as Third Division South runners-up in 1930–31.

Jack Tresadern (1930–35)

Born: September 1890, Leytonstone
Died: December 1959, Tonbridge
Player: West Ham United, Burnley, Northampton Town, England.
Manager: Northampton Town, Crystal Palace, Tottenham Hotspur, Plymouth Argyle.

Jack Tresadern came to Palace in October 1930 from Northampton Town, where he had been in charge for five years. He had played in the first Wembley Cup Final for West Ham and had gained full England international honours as a wing-half.

There can be little doubt that Mr Tresadern's best aquisition for Palace was that of striker Albert Dawes, who joined from Northampton in December 1933; although not even the great man's 16 League goals from his 22 games could redeem another vapid season. Another valuable signing he made was of full-back Ted Owens from Preston in the summer of 1934.

It has to be acknowledged, however, that under Mr Tresadern's management Palace were never able to make a genuine title attempt, even if they were among the stronger sides in the division. When the calibre of players available to him is remembered, that omission is a serious one and certainly many folk who were associated with the club were disconcerted, though far from despondent, when Mr Tresadern moved across London to manage Tottenham in July 1935.

Tom Bromilow (1935–36 and 1937–39)

Born: October 1894, Liverpool
Died: March 1959, Nuneaton
Player: Liverpool, England.
Manager: Burnley, Crystal Palace, Leicester City, Newport County.

Tom Bromilow had earned a fine reputation with England and Liverpool as a player and then coached in Amsterdam and managed Burnley before he moved to Selhurst Park in July 1935.

Like many men before and since, however, Tom found the harsh challenges of managing at Third Division level very much more demanding than playing for a leading club or for an international side. Nevertheless, it was Mr Bromilow who took Palace closer to returning to the

Second Division than any of his predecessors since 1928–29 and any successors until 1963–64. It was in 1938–39 that Mr Bromilow's team at Selhurst Park pushed Newport County all the way to a thrilling climax in the old Third Division South, so that Palace finished as runners-up to the men from Monmouthshire with just a three-point margin separating the two clubs.

There is no doubt that Tom Bromilow was one of Palace's better managers, even though the times in which he was in charge were tough ones. Not only did he come closer to restoring Palace's Second Division status than any other manager in a period of 35 years, but he also made several extremely clever signings for the club as well as developing a talented crop of youngsters.

Among the acquisitions Mr Bromilow secured were Albert Wilson, a marauding, goalscoring outside-left from Mansfield; powerful wing-half Les Lievesley from Torquay; and, supreme even among such colleagues, left-back Fred Dawes from Northampton who became club captain and was the only player to appear more than 100 times both before and after World War Two.

Palace supporters of the late 1930s and the 1940s remember with affection those youthful footballers whom Bromilow helped to groom into accomplished players: Arthur Hudgell would probably be the pick of this bunch because he became the Third Division's most expensive defender when he moved to Sunderland during the first post-war season, but there were also Nick Collins, Jack Lewis and Tommy Reece (all wing-halves), as well as Bert Robson and little Ernie Waldron who, at his best restricted even Albert Dawes to a role in the reserves.

The frustrating fact is that World War Two greatly reduced the value of all these stars to Crystal Palace FC, but in the summer of 1939 Bromilow left Selhurst Park to take over at Leicester City. He left having done a fine job for Palace and on cordial terms with everybody at the club.

R.S. Moyes (1936)

Born: West Norwood
Manager: Crystal Palace

Bewilderment was the overwhelming response to the appointment of club director Mr R.S. Moyes as successor to Tom Bromilow, but his tenure was to be the shortest of all the club's managers, saving the curious three-day flirtation with Dave Bassett in the summer of 1984 (though it has never been acknowledged that Dave was the club's manager during that brief time).

Mr Moyes brought about one superb venture for Palace when he secured Scottish international centre-half George Walker from Notts County, and the absence of their skipper in the second half of 1938–39 continues to be regarded as the primary reason why Palace missed out on promotion that term.

Poor Mr Moyes's difficulties started even prior to the 1936–37 season, when ace

striker Albert Dawes broke his jaw in a practice game, but nevertheless Palace were dismissed from the FA Cup in the first round by Southend.

Mr Moyes resigned his position in early December 1936, probably with some relief, over some of the dealings relating to a pair of transfers and, a week or so later, the chairman also resigned. During the furore Albert Dawes was allowed to move to Luton Town but then a measure of sanity prevailed at Selhurst Park when Tom Bromilow was restored with effect from 1 January 1937.

George Irwin (1939–47)

Born: January 1891, Smethwick, Birmingham
Player: Crystal Palace, Reading.
Manager: Crystal Palace, Darlington.

George Irwin was the popular choice for the Palace manager to succeed Tom Bromilow. He was the first former Palace player to lead the club, and he did so throughout the years of World War Two, plus the immediate post-war season.

As the team's former trainer, Mr Irwin was not merely well-known by the players and supporters at Selhurst Park but was regarded with deference by them. He was affable and amusing but had a streak of iron in his personality that enabled him to quicken both himself and his players when the situation demanded.

No one would doubt for a moment that the war years required a great deal from everyone in every aspect of life, but it was fortunate for Crystal Palace FC that its prospects lay in such adept hands and with such a balanced personality.

Mr Irwin accomplished much for Crystal Palace during that demanding era in which titles were won and the club's reputation enhanced. The regret must be that those successes came about when the

Football League was in abeyance, so that Palace did not advance from them, and George Irwin chose to leave the club after a greatly disappointing first post-war season.

Jack Butler (1947–49)*

Born: August 1894, Colombo, Ceylon
Died: January 1961
Player: Arsenal, Torquay United, England.
Manager: Torquay United, Crystal Palace, Colchester United.

Jack Butler, formerly a distinguished player with Arsenal and an England international, came to Selhurst Park to manage Crystal Palace for the last three matches of the extended, but disappointing, 1946–47 season. He arrived with an impressive coaching and managerial pedigree, having coached the Belgian national side, the Denmark FA and Leicester City, and had been in charge at Torquay United.

Mr Butler's tenure of the manager's chair at Palace came at an extremely

difficult time. The club was in the doldrums and there was little or no money available to strengthen the playing squad, so that his two seasons at Selhurst Park were thoroughly depressing ones for everyone connected with the club. In 1947–48 Palace were never more than a midtable outfit and, always finding goals hard to come by, finished in 13th place. The 1948–49 season was, however, nothing short of disastrous. Mr Butler put out no fewer than 33 different players but could never field a settled side. Palace were always in the lower reaches of the Third Division South, hit rock bottom after Christmas and were never able to get off it, thus having to apply for re-election for the first time in the club's history.

Jack Butler himself was bitterly disappointed by it all and insisted that his letter of resignation be accepted. He later returned to coaching in Belgium, then had a spell as manager of Colchester United.

*This entry is reproduced with grateful acknowledgements to Des Beamish, who had close, personal connections with Mr Butler.

Ronnie Rooke (1949–50)

Born: December 1911, Guildford, Surrey
Died: July 1985
Player: Guildford City, Woking, Crystal Palace, Fulham, Arsenal, England (wartime), Crystal Palace.
Manager: Crystal Palace, Bedford Town.

The association of Ronnie Rooke – he of the distinctive craggy features, the Latin nose, fulminating shot and hip-swivelling tread, who became a celebrated top-flight sharpshooter – is regrettably one of baffling and sour discontent at Crystal Palace FC and among its fans.

In the Palace reserve sides of the mid-1930s Mr Rooke was quite phenomenal with 160 goals to his credit in just three and a half seasons, but he was never able to replicate even a flicker of such form in the first team. Would that he could have done!

Ronnie Rooke moved to Fulham in October 1936, where he played with great

success and even gained a wartime international cap. In 1946 Arsenal sought his services and he rewarded them by assisting them to the League title as the country's top goalscorer with 33 goals.

Rooke then returned to Selhurst Park as player-manager in the summer of 1949 and Palace rose from last place in Division Three South in 1948–49 to seventh in 1949–50. The manager notched up 21 League goals himself, and some big crowds came along to Selhurst Park to watch and support 'The Rooke Regiment', as the side was temporarily nicknamed by the press.

But, with the encouragement and assent of the board of directors, it must be said, Rooke then proceeded to sign a veritable torrent of highly priced veterans to play for the club. The outcome was awful: the playing record at the outset of the 1950–51 season was terrible, the club finances were straitened, so that Rooke himself was relieved of his post at the end of November.

Thus, as far as Crystal Palace FC is concerned, Ronnie Rooke was the total conundrum. His proven goalscoring talent paid small dividend for the club and his managerial stay, short as it was, was nothing short of catastrophic.

Fred Dawes (1950–51 joint manager)

Born: May 1911, Frimley Green, Surrey
Died: August 1989, Croydon
Player: Northampton Town, Crystal Palace.
Manager: Crystal Palace (joint manager).

Fred Dawes had become a great idol during his long and illustrious playing career with Palace and had been assistant manager to Ronnie Rooke, so that everyone at Selhurst Park knew that the club had been placed in a strong and loyal pair of hands at an especially disquieting

time when Fred was appointed to manage alongside Charlie Slade.

However, anyone with any footballing sagicity perfectly understood that the circumstances that Fred and his colleague had taken on were appallingly difficult ones: Palace were bottom of the League with a paltry nine points from 18 matches and had already been dismissed from the FA Cup in the first round, having plunged 4–1 at home to Millwall for the seventh defeat on the bounce.

Regrettably, there was to be no gallant, lion-hearted revival – such a thing was quite impossible. Palace inevitably faced re-election for the second time at the end of their most dreadful season ever. Once again the club had put out no fewer than 33 different players, but that season the team scored not only the lowest total of goals in its history, but also the worst ever recorded in the annals of the Third Division South. With an inflated overdraft there was no possibility of bringing in new men: rather it was a case of seeking to redeem some modest return from the enormous outlay of the summer of 1950.

The 1951–52 season offered little or no encouragement and the directors agreed that Mr Dawes and his associate must leave. It was a poor, cheap ending to the Palace career of as fine and loyal a servant as the club would ever know. It was unworthy of Fred and of the men who brought it about.

Charlie Slade (1950–51 joint manager)

Born: January 1891, Bristol
Died: April 1971, Doncaster
Player: Aston Villa, Huddersfield Town, Middlesbrough, Darlington.
Manager: Crystal Palace (joint manager).

Charlie Slade had been a well-known football player with several northern clubs between the wars but was probably hardly more than a name to most Crystal Palace supporters when he was appointed as joint-manager with Fred Dawes in November 1950, although he had been working as the club's chief scout at the time of that appointment.

There can be no doubt that Slade's greatest boost to the fortunes of Crystal Palace was his awareness of Chester striker Cam Burgess, whom he and Fred Dawes acquired, partly upon the advocacy of another former Chester player, Les Devonshire, in September 1951. Cam certainly added greatly to Palace's potency in front of goal and went on to become the club's most effective striker for some while, though the irony is that, by the time he had established his reputation at the club, the managers who had signed him for Palace had been removed from their charge. Slade, in fact, reverted to his role as chief scout and was with Palace until the summer of 1955.

Laurie Scott (1951–54)

Born: April 1917, Sheffield
Died: August 1999, Yorkshire
Player: Bradford City, Arsenal, Crystal Palace, England.
Manager: Crystal Palace.

Although, like his predecessors Jack Butler and Ronnie Rooke, Laurie Scott had played with great excellence for Arsenal, his

period in charge of Palace failed in every way to further the club's hopes and potential for future advancement.

Scott came to Crystal Palace with 17 full England caps and a 1948 League Championship medal to be Palace's player-manager, and he helped his new charges to gain a bright 3–1 win over Ipswich Town on his debut for the club. But, the joy lasted for only a short while. Palace were despatched from the FA Cup in the first round by Great Yarmouth some five weeks after his arrival and ended the 1951–52 Third Division South season in 19th place – exactly the position they had been in when Scott joined the club in October 1951.

Injury precluded Laurie Scott from offering much to Palace's cause on the pitch during 1952–53, but he oversaw the debacle at Finchley where the team lost to the amateurs in the FA Cup, and another fragile start the following season saw him dismissed from his office at the end of September.

Cyril Spiers (1954–58)

Born: April 1902, Witton, Birmingham
Died: May 1967
Player: Aston Villa, Tottenham Hotspur, Wolverhampton Wanderers.
Manager: Cardiff City, Norwich City, Cardiff City, Crystal Palace, Exeter City.

Cyril Spiers became Palace's secretary-manager on 13 October 1954. His own footballing career had been as a highly thought of goalkeeper, but, upon turning to management, he learnt his profession under Frank Buckley at Wolves, then served at Cardiff and Norwich. However, upon joining Crystal Palace, he simply extended the lengthening list of famous names who had been quite unable to bring any success to Selhurst Park.

Any critic must acknowledge that Spiers's assignment at Palace was huge. He

took over a group of players who were largely past their prime and a club which had settled among the lesser Third Division South outfits. But Spiers's forté lay in finding and grooming his own young players, and he made changes in their favour. This was a complete reversal of policy at the club, for, like many clubs, Palace had simply bought new players from other outfits up to that point. Thus, under Spiers's tutelage, goalkeeper Vic Rouse came to the fore, spirited Johnny Byrne was developed initially under him, while Mike Deakin, another of Spiers's products, established a club post-war scoring record with 23 League goals in 1958–59 in the Fourth Division.

Mr Spiers's first season saw Palace end up in 20th place but, in his first full campaign in charge, the club had to seek re-election. In 1956–57 Palace again ended the season in 20th place, but 1957–58 provided the challenge of finishing in the upper half of the regional division or helping to form a new, national Fourth Division. Spiers was unable to reach this target, for Palace finished 14th in the final Third Division South table.

George Smith (1958–60)

Born: April 1915, Bromley, Kent
Died: October 1983, Bodmin, Cornwall
Player: Charlton Athletic, Brentford, Queen's Park Rangers, Ipswich Town.
Manager: Crystal Palace, Portsmouth.

George Smith arrived at Crystal Palace to take on the role of manager in the summer of 1958. His was the task of raising Palace out of the slough of the newly contrived national Fourth Division. Mr Smith was a seasoned stickler for regimentation and order, whose ultimatum to the Palace directors upon his appointment was that, should he fail to gain promotion for the club within two years, he would resign.

Certainly, in 1958–59 Palace gained some much-needed credentials by reaching the Final of the Southern Floodlit Cup, losing 2–1 against Arsenal at Selhurst Park. But, although it was in this season and under Mr Smith's management that Palace gained their record victory over Barrow with a 9–0 win, the team never seriously looked as if the longed-for promotion might materialise throughout the two years George had allowed himself. True to his word, he departed in April 1960.

Arthur Rowe (1960–62, 1966)

Born: September 1906, Tottenham, London
Died: November 1993, Wallington, Surrey
Player: Tottenham Hotspur, England.
Manager: Tottenham Hotspur, Crystal Palace, Orient, Walsall, Colchester.

Arthur Rowe was already a luminary in the capital's footballing world when he first came to Crystal Palace in November 1958 to act as assistant to George Smith. His acclaimed and widely acknowledged playing career at Tottenham had been followed after the war by an awesome period as Tottenham's manager during which, in consecutive seasons, he gained promotion, then the League title, with a breathtaking style of play which was soon dubbed 'push and run'.

In April 1960 when he followed Smith as manager at Selhurst Park, Palace were a labouring club in the League's basement division and carrying a worrying deficit at

the bank. Palace were undoubtedly menaced by the possibility of extinction. But Arthur Rowe adjusted the club – who had no dearth of accomplished players on their books at that time, with Johnny Byrne dominant among them – to his attested style and, with the addition of several adroit new signings, led his club to instant promotion with sharp, attractive football which achieved Palace's post-war goalscoring record and drew some enormous attendances to Selhurst Park, including the 37,774 Fourth Division record crowd when Palace played Millwall on 31 March 1961.

The aforementioned Johnny Byrne flourished under Mr Rowe's guidance: he gained international selection, and then the interest of West Ham, who paid an English record transfer fee of £60,000 to obtain the talented star.

Mr Rowe seldom enjoyed good health, and he had to give up his position at Selhurst Park during the midwinter months of the 1962–63 season, even though he came back to aid Dick Graham in the push for promotion to Division Two in the spring of 1964, and then took full control again in 1966 after Dick had left the club. He went back to less-demanding responsibilities under Bert Head as Palace forged their way to the top flight for the first time.

Understandably, Palace fans of the 1960s always held Arthur Rowe in high regard, and club folk everywhere were sorry to learn of his passing in November 1993.

Dick Graham (1962–66)

Born: May 1922, Corby, Northants
Player: Crystal Palace.
Manager: Crystal Palace, Orient, Walsall, Colchester.

When popular goalkeeper Dick Graham's playing career with Palace came to an end he turned to coaching, and, after a spell at West Bromwich Albion in that capacity, he rejoined the club as assistant manager to Arthur Rowe in 1961.

Mr Graham was elevated to full control at Selhurst Park in November 1962 after the great man had been forced to reliquish his post. His initial job was to fend off the mounting threat of relegation back to Division Four. As soon as possible, he made two shrewd signings, those of proven strikers Dickie Dowsett and Cliff Holton, and altered the team's style of play to a much more direct and vigorous one. Palace rallied straight away, did really well in the late winter and spring, climbed the table and at the end of the season ended in a praiseworthy 11th place.

In the 1963–64 season Graham's Palace side was always among the leading clubs, assuming top spot during the vital run-in to the season and appearing to everyone to be probable title winners. But Palace were thwarted in that objective by 15 minutes aberration in the last game, so that a 1–0 lead over Oldham turned into a 3–1 deficit and eventual defeat.

Another successful season followed in 1964–65. Palace reached the FA Cup last eight and concluded Second Division matters in seventh place, but, perhaps surprisingly to some, Mr Graham's team selections were becoming more and more quixotic, and his choice to transfer list the enormously favoured Cliff Holton bordered upon heresy among many supporters. Then, as the 1965–66 season progressed, it became more and more clear that there were differences of opinions between the boss and some of his men. The denoument could not long be delayed and so it was that, in early January 1966, Dick Graham made his exit from the club and brought a conclusion to his colossal input to Palace.

Regrettably, for Mr Graham himself though, because he did personify a measure of confrontation to the accepted manner of reasoning, there would be a minimal chance of him being invited to consider a position at a major club, but there was no doubt that he possessed a genius for working with the smaller outfits. And while Palace were the first to gain from it, he did later have effective periods in charge of other, similar clubs.

Bert Head (1966–73)

Born: June 1916, Midsomer Norton
Died: February 2002
Player: Torquay United, Bury.
Manager: Swindon Town, Bury, Crystal Palace.

Bert Head had been a long-serving defender with Torquay and as such had been known to Palace fans since before World War Two. After playing for Bury, then serving The Shakers as assistant manager, he became the boss at Swindon

Town. However, it was from Bury that he joined the Palace as manager on 14 April 1966 and began a hugely successful partnership with the man who became his close friend as well as his chairman, Mr Arthur Wait.

In his first two seasons with the Palace he led the club to seventh, then 11th place finishes in Division Two, but then in 1968–69 he took Palace into the First Division for the first time. This was done with the inspiring and emotional climax of a wonderful run of 16 matches without loss in the spring of 1969 (the best run in a single season at the Palace since World War Two and only once bettered by the club) to earn a standing for the Palace which even the most avid fans would have considered to be quite beyond the club only a year or so earlier.

However, Bert's task was then even more difficult – he had led Palace into Division One, now he had to ensure that the club retained that elevated status. Although most football pundits would regard the latter task as being the more difficult one, Bert showed that he had the talent to fulfil it. Partly with the use of clever handling of the transfer market, Bert built and rebuilt the team so that, on three occasions, possible demotion was fended off. Then, in March 1973, with another close-run conclusion looming, the new owners of the club brought in Malcolm Allison and Bert was appointed general manager. He departed quite quickly and without fuss, joined Bath City, and led them to a Southern League promotion in 1975.

Bert Head's exploits for the Palace must forever remain without parallel here and are always recalled with the greatest pleasure. He led the club to the top flight for the first time, he retained that status, in the most difficult of circumstances, for nearly four seasons, and he was, without doubt, one of the most attractive personalities ever to be part of Crystal Palace FC.

Malcolm Allison (1973–76, 1980–81)

Born: September 1927, Dartford, Kent
Died: October 2010
Player: Charlton Athletic, West Ham United.
Manager: Bath City, Toronto City, Plymouth Argyle, Manchester City, Crystal Palace, Galatasaray, Plymouth Argyle, Manchester City, Crystal Palace, Sporting Club Portugal, Middlesbrough, Kuwait, Vittoria Setubal, SC Farense, Bristol Rovers.

Malcolm Allison is probably the most complicated and open-to-debate personality ever to have been part of Crystal Palace FC. He had turned out for Charlton and West Ham, then been in charge at Bath City and Plymouth, but he came to the fore when he linked up with Joe Mercer at Manchester City and helped to take that club to prestige and renown in both home-based and European competitions.

Mr Allison appeared with his customary swashbuckling demeanour on the afternoon of 31 March 1973 for Palace's home match against Chelsea and inspired the team to achieve its first and only success over rivals from the capital in 32 top-flight matches between 1969 and 1973! However, he could not stop Palace from dropping out of the leading section, and they lost all but two of the next seven games under his charge. Then Palace had the most awful opening to the 1973–74 season when he rebuilt almost the entire team in a useless endeavour to halt the descent. The alterations he made included a number of highly contentious ones, chief among which was to supplant John Jackson with Paul Hammond as goalkeeper, and some fans never absolved him for that. Relegated for the second season in succession, Allison's huge persona frequently proved a trial in Division Three, because it raised the ambitions and longings of the fans far too early and certainly inspired every other club to play their best game of the season against Palace.

Mr Allison's best season at the club was 1975–76, when at last the club started to deserve some of the praise he heaped upon the side and in the FA Cup he led the team to glorious successes at Leeds, Chelsea and Sunderland to gain a first-ever position in the semi-finals. But Malcolm found it difficult to bear the defeat by

Photo © HY Money

Southampton, and when Palace then managed to discard the chance of promotion to Division Two that had seemed so likely, he was quite unable to cope. He left Palace in May 1976 – only to come back for a couple of midwinter months in 1980–81 when Palace were again in dire trouble in Division One, but he was removed from office upon the takeover of the club by the Ron Noades consortium in January 1981.

Terry Venables (1976–80, 1998–99)

Born: January 1943, Dagenham, Essex
Player: Chelsea, Tottenham Hotspur, Queen's Park Rangers, Crystal Palace, England.
Manager: Crystal Palace, Queen's Park Rangers, Barcelona, Tottenham Hotspur, England, Australia, Crystal Palace, Middlesbrough (joint), Leeds United.

Terry Venables holds a singular and elevated place in the history of Crystal Palace FC because he was the first man to take the club to two promotions and to the distinction of gaining promotion to the First Division as champions of Division Two in the 1978–79 season. And yet, Venables was soon considered by many Palace fans at the time, and still that is the case today, with very much less than total admiration, so that even now many followers of the club believe that they and the club have been badly let down by him.

This distaste is in such disparity to the way in which Mr Venables was eulogized at the peak of his first period with the club that the question must be posed as to why this should be so. It is a baffling, teasing conundrum, but few folk would disagree with the suggestion that Terry has been a total puzzle to Palace fans during both his managerial periods, or that, on both occasions when he left the club, he did so with Palace in a particularly difficult situation from which it would take a long time to recover.

Photo © HY Money

In the 1976–77 season, Venables's initial term in football management, he led the club to immediate promotion from the old Third Division in supremely dramatic circumstances, and then, two years later and with a completely altered, marvellously gifted young side, enhanced by the return of the by now hugely accomplished Steve Kember, won the old Second Division Championship with an unrestrained 2–0 victory over Burnley before Selhurst Park's highest-ever attendance of 51,482.

Palace's advance under Terry Venables continued, but only for a little while. Having surprised the top flight and actually headed the entire Football League at the end of September 1979, Palace became a languishing club by the end of that season and it soon became clear in 1980–81 that, while the slump was continuing, Terry Venables was either powerless or disinclined to check it. He then departed for Queen's Park Rangers, leaving Palace in dismay at the bottom of the First Division table.

Because of this background, Venables's installation as Palace boss by new chairman Mark Goldberg in the summer of 1998 was emphatically not welcomed by many people, although it should be acknowledged that he received an ecstatic welcome at the first game of the 1998–99 season. Sadly, though for some reasons beyond his control, Venables was not able to bring even the least prosperity to the club.

He then went on to sell some of the fans' favourite players, including several who might have reckoned to lead an effort to restore top-flight ranking straight away, and these men were only superceded by lightweights of men of lesser ability. It was, therefore, no surprise that Palace rarely even appeared in the upper half of the First Division table, and some of the team's displays on other grounds were little short of abysmal.

The conclusion came in mid-January 1999. Terry Venables was forced to step aside in a sequence of moves to reduce the expense of running the club, leaving those supporters who had been worried about his re-appointment now emphatically disenchanted by him and having no pleasure whatsoever in seeing their earlier anxieties about his return brought to pass in the most emphatic style.

Ernie Walley (1980)

Born: April 1933, Caernarvon
Player: Tottenham Hotspur, Middlesbrough.
Manager: Crystal Palace.

Because Ernie Walley had been Palace's youth and reserve-team coach, many of the first team of 1980 had grown to adulthood under his leadership and instruction. It was not surprising therefore that he was easily their clear preference to take over the post of club manager vacated by Terry Venables.

Mr Walley was a hard, strong man, a former professional footballer himself, and quickly won over the doubters among the Palace fans by steering the side to two home victories within four days, which at the very least raised morale at the stricken club. Then his Palace side gained a draw at Norwich and another home success, this time over Manchester United on 1 November.

Sadly, Ernie Walley was not able to maintain such advancement, but by that time there were several senior members of the team who were eyeing a move to Loftus Road in the wake of their former boss, and Ernie's task had become beyond him. At the end of November, following a 3–2 defeat at Selhurst Park by Manchester City, the Palace board announced that it would reinstate Malcolm Allison to join Ernie at the helm. Soon, inevitably, Walley was acting as Allison's number two, and he was pleased to help his club in that capacity under Dario Gradi as well.

Photo © HY Money

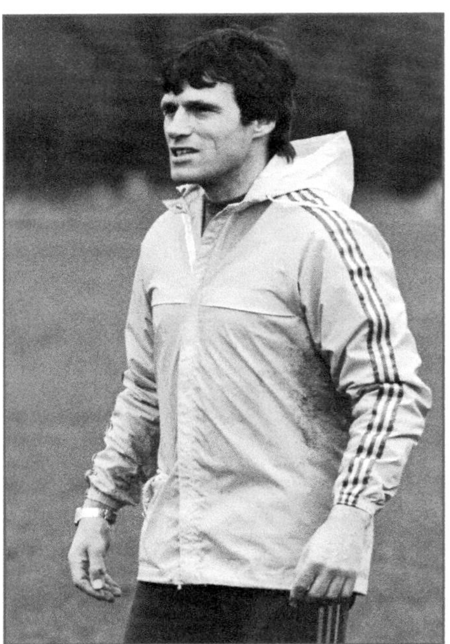

Dario Gradi (1981)

Born: 1943, Milan, Italy
Player: England (amateur).
Manager: Wimbledon, Crystal Palace, Crewe Alexandra.

No sooner had the legal procedures surrounding the takeover of Crystal Palace FC on 26 January 1981 been completed in favour of Ron Noades and his consortium, than Dario Gradi, the erstwhile Wimbledon supremo, was established as the new Palace manager, becoming the fourth boss during the months of November and December 1980 and January 1981. Turbulent times indeed!

Of course, Dario Gradi carried the best wishes of all Palace supporters as he set about his difficult task, but he lacked one vital ingredient during his tenure – good luck. Leading players continued to depart, either because they wished to do so or in order to generate cash to aid the club's hugely under-funded condition. Palace lost their first seven games under the new board and its manager, while an assembly of new players were quite unable to arrest the decline and Palace were consigned to relegation long before the conclusion of the campaign.

The beginning of 1981–82 offered little solace, and with Palace flagging in 15th place in the old Second Division, Dario Gradi resigned in mid-November.

Steve Kember (1981–82, 2001, 2003)

Born: December 1948, Croydon
Player: Crystal Palace, Chelsea, Leicester City, Crystal Palace, Vancouver Whitecaps.
Manager: Crystal Palace.

It was Palace's youth-team coach Steve Kember who was chosen to fill the vacancy created by Dario Gradi's departure in November 1981, and this was an appointment that received the backing of all Palace folk for Kember had always been a hugely popular figure at Selhurst Park. He was, after all, the only man to appear

regularly in both the 1968–69 and 1978–79 teams that won promotion to the old First Division.

Kember's first fixture in charge of the club was an extremely tough one – a League Cup tie against Sunderland at Roker Park. However, he revealed his credentials by leading the team to a 1–0 victory, and his early results in Division Two were heartening too. But his initial spell as Palace boss will be best recalled for the run he inspired to the FA Cup quarter-finals in the spring of 1982. Wins over Enfield, Bolton and Orient gave Palace a place in the sixth-round draw which pitted the team against Queen's Park Rangers at Loftus Road. Kember's side were brutally unfortunate to go down to a single, very late, goal netted for Rangers by a former Palace player, Clive Allen.

Palace fans believed that it would have been unfair to expect more of the side than Steve Kember was able to generate in the Second Division of 1981–82, in which the club barely avoided another relegation and finished in 15th place. Thus, all were dismayed when Kember was ousted in the close season and replaced by Alan Mullery.

Kember's second period in charge at Crystal Palace was shorter, but very much more influential. In April 2001 Palace were slipping towards apparently inevitable relegation, and after an appalling display against Wolves in the last home game Steve was awarded the task of averting disaster. Palace had two games left, both away, and had to win them both to have any hope of retaining their status. At Portsmouth he oversaw a brilliant 4–2 victory, then Palace won with an 87th-minute strike at Stockport.

Steve Kember was again put in temporary charge towards the end of the 2002–03 season, and then given full responsibility during the summer of 2003. To the immense pleasure of the fans he began in wonderful style: Palace won their first three First Division games and topped the table, but they foundered after that and, when Palace were trounced 5–0 at Wigan in early November, Steve's departure became inevitable.

Alan Mullery (1982–84)

Born: November 1941, Notting Hill, London
Player: Fulham, Tottenham Hotspur, England.
Manager: Brighton and Hove Albion, Charlton Athletic, Crystal Palace, Queen's Park Rangers, Brighton and Hove Albion, Barnet.

Alan Mullery had been an exhilarating midfielder with Fulham, Tottenham and England, been presented with the MBE and chosen as Footballer of the Year in 1975. His later time in management had been similarly striking.

He joined Crystal Palace in June 1982, but his selection as manager was a highly controversial one because the fans

remembered that he had been a violent adversary towards the club, especially in his time on the south coast, when there had been a number of passionate quarrels between Alan and Palace's managers and supporters.

Neither did it help matters that his two years with Palace were bitter, painful and quite fruitless. The fact was that Mullery's formerly effective ploy of signing experienced and well-known players from other clubs on free transfers or for small fees simply did not produce any team spirit or even the beginnings of a successful side. For a large number of the fans of the period the lasting memory of his time in charge remains the team's hugely embarrassing exit from the League Cup at Peterborough via a penalty shoot-out, after Palace had allowed a 3–0 lead from the first leg at Selhurst Park be nullified.

Thus, having finished the 1982–83 campaign in 15th position and then the folowing season even further down the Second Division table, no one who followed Palace at that time was in the least disappointed when Mullery was discarded, in stark contrast to his previously eminent career as a player and in management.

Steve Coppell (1984–93, 1995–96, 1997–98, 1999–2000)

Born: July 1955, Liverpool
Player: Tranmere Rovers, Manchester United, England.
Manager: Crystal Palace, Manchester City, Brentford, Brighton and Hove Albion, Reading, Bristol City.

Steve Coppell is easily Palace's longest-serving post-war manager and has proved to be the most successful in the whole 100-plus years of the club's history.

When he first took over as Palace manager the club was in a bad way, but by clever manouvering in the transfer market, plus a mutually trusting relationship with chairman Ron Noades, Coppell assembled a team that was able to fend off the worries concerning relegation and then demonstrate commendable calibre by ending the season with the club's best run of results of the entire campaign. Then, quite soon after his arrival, he disclosed a skill that he would use much to Palace's benefit in the future. He was able to recognize true footballing talent even when it is still in a raw state, and his gathering of men from the lower divisions, or from reserve or even non-League football, before developing them into useful players, was a most beneficial aspect of his management years at Palace. The first such was Andy Gray, and he was followed in the summer of 1985 by Ian Wright.

Under Steve Coppell's guidance the Palace team and the club in general matured, so that with a style of play that became progressivly more pleasing to watch – and which, almost always, included the use of wingers – Palace were only just denied promotion or a place in the Play-offs for three consecutive years. But, by the 1988–89 season, Coppell's selected pair of strikers, Ian Wright and Mark Bright, were netting so often that they set up new club records for the upper divisions of the League, and as a result Palace were strong enough over the season to conclude matters in third place. That impetus never slowed during the Play-offs, despite defeats in the away legs, while the team's sheer potency at Selhurst Park was breathtaking to watch.

However, Palace fans were aware from earlier sour experiences that keeping a First Division position is even harder than securing it in the first place. Coppell masterminded Palace's way to survival in 1989–90 with a laudable 15th-place finish,

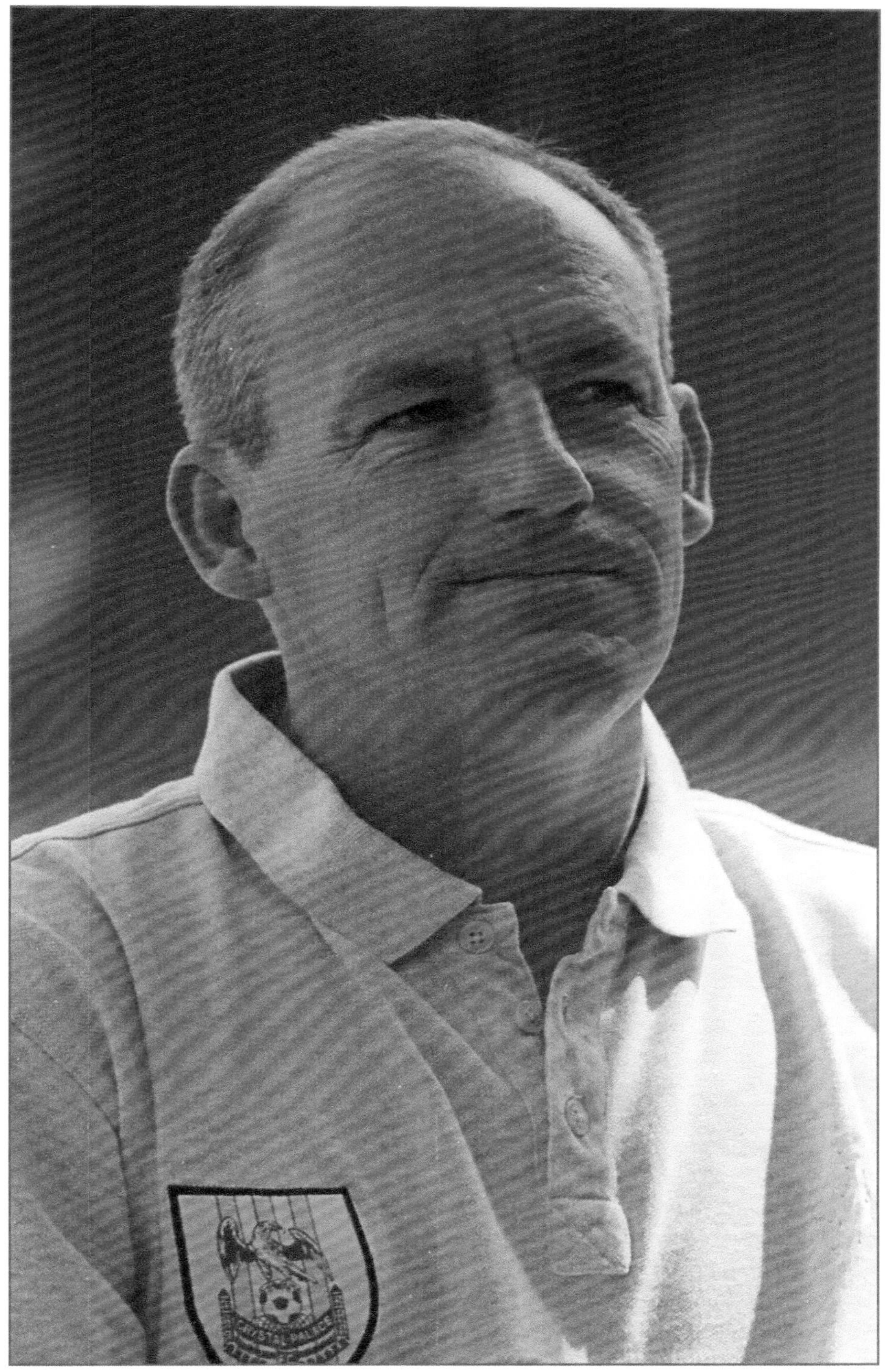

and he also took the club to a glorious revenge win over Liverpool in the FA Cup semi-final at Villa Park, an achievement which is looked upon by some Palace fans as the best one-off victory that they have ever witnessed.

Steve Coppell balanced that attainment the following season, when with the assistance of two excellent signings, those of defenders John Humphrey and Eric Young, he built the best Palace side to play in the Football League. The team concluded the 1990–91 season in third place in the old First Division and, before a large contingent of Palace fans, won a Wembley Cup Final by beating Everton in the Zenith Data Systems Cup.

That which subsequently came about under Steve Coppell was certainly sad, but it does need to be seen in relation to previous times, for this was the season in which Palace did the 'double' over Liverpool and the youth team reached the FA Youth Cup Final. Equally, Ian Wright *chose* to leave the club in September 1991 for Arsenal, while injuries and loss of form to and by senior players certainly created expensive absences from the side.

The fact is that Palace were uniquely unfortunate to be relegated at the end of the 1992–93 season, because not only would the club have survived under the old system of two points for a win, but only one other outfit has ever been relegated from the senior section with the same tally of 49 points. Even so, Coppell chose to resign at the end of May 1993 to the distress of everyone at the club.

Two years later he was back at Selhurst Park, however, with the imprecise title of 'director of football', but in February 1997 he again took full responsibility and retained Palace's momentum in an historic drive for promotion which he brought to a winning conclusion in the very last minute of a gripping Wembley Play-off Final, gained by a legendary strike from skipper David Hopkin. Steve Coppell thereby became the only manager of Crystal Palace to have led the club into the top flight on two occasions.

He stayed in charge for the first seven months of the 1997–98 season, which were distinguished by several glorious away wins in the Premier League, but this season was darkened by the plans for a boardroom takeover in which the chairman-elect repeatedly announced that he would be appointing Terry Venables when he assumed control. Naturally enough, Coppell believed his own position and authority to have been usurped and he moved aside in mid-March with typical graciousness and decorum.

Steve had one more spell at Palace to fulfil, however. The corrosive situation at the club, with whole series' of senior Palace players being sold merely as an expediency to keep a string of creditors at arms length, was quite deranged. Thus, made to depend ever increasingly upon lads from the youth team, Coppell galvanised them to such an extent that he gained some of the team's best results of the season in the spring of 1999 and brought about a 14th-place finish, which is quite remarkable for a club in the depths of legal administration.

Matters worsened in 1999–2000. The chairman at last had to depart and the financial crisis bit ever deeper, but Coppell upeheld both morale and the League standing by clever use of the loan transfer system and his superb inspirational talent. The midsummer 2000 takeover of the club by new chairman Simon Jordan brought welcome relief to Steve, but with only 11 days left before the 2000–01 season opened, he chose to resign. Palace fans have always rued the day, and many find it difficult, still, to accept that his link with the club had been forever severed. Nevertheless, and come what may, all at the club are grateful to him as the most successful manager the club has ever known.

Alan Smith (1993–95, 2000–01)

Manager: Crystal Palace, Wycombe Wanderers.

Palace turned to tall, suave Alan Smith to lead the club in the wake of their 1993 demotion. Alan had been with the club since November 1983, when he had taken charge of the youth team, and he was number two to Steve Coppell when Palace had reached the 1990 FA Cup Final, won the Zenith Data Systems Cup and finished third in the old First Division.

Assuming responsibility for a relegated side is never an easy option for any manager but, in the end in majestic style, Smith took Palace to an immediate return to the Premier League as the undoubted and celebrated champions of the First Division, by playing an appealing brand of his pass-and-move football. Smith also demonstrated an adroit mastery of the transfer market, and certainly his best signing for the club was that of Liverpool's Paul Stewart on loan in January 1994.

Alan Smith's 1994–95 season in control saw him lead Palace to two major Cup semi-finals, with superb victories over Premiership sides en route, even if, ultimately, the team were beaten by Manchester United in an FA Cup semi-final replay and by Liverpool over the two-legged semi-final of the League Cup.

In the League itself Palace were relegated on the final day of the season following a defeat at Newcastle. That Smith would depart at this stage was assured, but he was held in such high regard by the fans that his return to Palace management in August 2000 was received with acclaim.

Curiously, Smith's second spell at the club followed a similar sequence to the first. In the League Cup there were some magnificent victories leading to the highlight of his tenure, the game at home to Liverpool in the first leg of the League Cup semi-final. The Reds were fortunate to escape with just a 2–1 defeat that night after missing several good chances of their own.

Following a defeat to Liverpool in the Anfield return and a 2–0 defeat to Wolves in the final home game, the chairman dismissed Alan Smith and his staff, leaving the supporters with only the League Cup nights to remember with relish from his Selhurst Park return.

Dave Bassett (1996–97)

Born: September 1944, Hendon
Player: Wimbledon, England (amateur).
Manager: Wimbledon, Watford, Sheffield United, Crystal Palace, Nottingham Forest, Barnsley, Leicester City.

Dave Bassett, he of the saucy, bracing persona, was made Palace's manager in early February 1996 with the straightforward brief to turn the flagging side into genuine promotion competitors.

Bassett's instant impression was to make Palace into a team that jumped 13 places up the table within a month, fixing itself among the group of topmost outfits and winning five straight Selhurst Park matches with a 15–3 aggregate. Actually, Palace's advance under him was absolutely inexorable. The home match successes were pushed on to six, Bassett himself was quite properly named First Division Manager of the Month for March 1996 and the end of the normal campaign proved fascinating entertainment for the fans, although it ended in defeat with a fluke Leicester goal which put The Filberts into the Premiership at Palace's expense.

Nine months later, however, and with Palace again in the Play-off places, once more looking like genuine promotion contenders, Palace folk everywhere were astounded to learn that Dave Bassett had moved to Nottingham Forest. Chairman Ron Noades declared himself to be 'left reeling' by this defection, while some fans were manifestly incensed. Palace moved swiftly, however, and on the following day Steve Coppell returned to the Palace helm.

Attilio Lombardo (1998)

Born: January 1966, St Maria la Fossa, Italy
Player: Sampdoria, Juventus, Crystal Palace, Lazio, Italy.
Manager: Crystal Palace.

Two days after Palace had endured a disheartening 6–2 midweek Premiership beating at Chelsea on 11 March 1998, Attilio Lombardo took the place of Steve Coppell as Palace manager, but the selection of the great Italian international was most extraordinary because, even accepting his tremendous skill as a player, he was totally lacking in managerial experience and was not able to speak more than a word or two of English!

The appointment invited (and certainly received!) mockery from the media, but Attilio inspired an impressive 2–1 win at Newcastle and he also led Palace to their long overdue first home Premiership victory, over Derby in mid-April. Nevertheless, Lombardo was more than happy to surrender the post at the end of that month after they had been statistically relegated following a home defeat by Manchester United.

Steve Bruce (2001)

Born: 31 December 1960, Durham
Player: Gillingham, Norwich City, Manchester United, Birmingham City, Sheffield United.

Manager: Sheffield United, Huddersfield Town, Wigan Athletic, Crystal Palace, Birmingham City, Wigan Athletic, Sunderland.

Although many Palace fans would have preferred the naming of Steve Kember as the club's new manager for 2001–02 after the way in which he had engineered the club's First Division existence when many pundits had deemed such a thing quite impossible, it was the former Norwich City and Manchester United captain and central-defender Steve Bruce whom chairman Simon Jordan put into that position on the last day of May.

As a player at his clubs Bruce's career had been exemplary, but as a manager he had gained no credentials, while his fidelity to his employers had appeared at times to be in doubt. And thus it was that, in mid-October, with Palace contentedly within the Play-off places and playing some attractive football as well, there arose one of the less elevated episodes in the club's history, when Steve Bruce tried to resign his charge at Palace in order to take up an identical position at Birmingham City. To begin with, Simon Jordan refused to accept Bruce's resignation and much ill-will was uttered on both sides, but, after a measure of dignity had been found, Steve was allowed to depart. But Palace fans were hurt and angry, so that when he returned to Selhurst Park with his new club on Easter Monday he received a torrent of abuse throughout the proceedings and sprinted from the dug-out at the final whistle in order to minimise the abasement.

Trevor Francis (2001–03)

Born: April 1954, Plymouth
Player: Birmingham City, Nottingham Forest, Manchester City, Glasgow Rangers, Queen's Park Rangers, Sheffield Wednesday, England.
Manager: Queen's Park Rangers, Sheffield Wednesday, Birmingham City, Crystal Palace.

Trevor Francis was Palace's second manager for 2001–02 after the defection of Steve Bruce. He was appointed on 30 November and was a familiar name to all Palace fans because, not only had Francis enjoyed a supremely successful playing career in which he had been the game's first £1 million player and gained 52 full international caps, but he was also a hugely experienced manager and a popular football pundit on TV.

Much of what remained of that season was devoted to signing those players whom Francis considered wouldmeld into a team that could gain promotion. His first acquisition was former Manchester City, Fulham and Portsmouth centre-half, Welsh international Kit Symons, and Palace ended the term 10th in the table. Francis's first year at Palace was dubbed 'a revolution' in some quarters because over 20 players either joined or left the club during that period.

A lethargic opening to 2002–03 was given needed momentum in the autumn by a run of nine undefeated League games, and Palace fans started to think that here might be a side which could fulfil their hopes for promotion. However, in the final analysis this proved to be beyond Francis's ability, and all that the fans had to look back on under him was the FA Cup fourth-round defeat of Liverpool. Trevor Francis left Palace on 18 April with the club going nowhere, static in midtable.

Kit Symons (2003)

Born: March 1971, Basingstoke, Hampshire
Player: Portsmouth, Manchester City, Fulham, Crystal Palace, Wales.
Manager: Crystal Palace.

Kit Symons became Palace's sixth manager in just over three years when the chairman appointed him as Steve Kember's temporary successor in November 2003. At 32 years old Symons was the club's youngest manager since Steve Coppell, and he was the first player-manager since Laurie Scott. Even so, and with all his 36 appearances for Wales and over 400 League appearances, his managerial assignment was a tough one.

His efforts at Palace were commendable, his eight League matches in charge bringing three wins and three draws, and his time in charge culminated

in a splendid 3–0 success at Reading (managed by Steve Coppell no less), but a couple of poor performances were sufficient to provoke the club chairman to seek a more experienced manager.

Iain Dowie (2003–06)

Born: January 1965, Hatfield
Player: Luton Town, Fulham (loan), West Ham United, Southampton, Crystal Palace, West Ham United, Queen's Park Rangers, Northern Ireland.
Manager: Oldham Athletic, Crystal Palace, Charlton Athletic, Coventry, Queen's Park Rangers, Hull City, Newcastle United.

Iain Dowie was appointed Palace manager in December 2003 and, although his period in charge opened with a home defeat by Millwall on Boxing

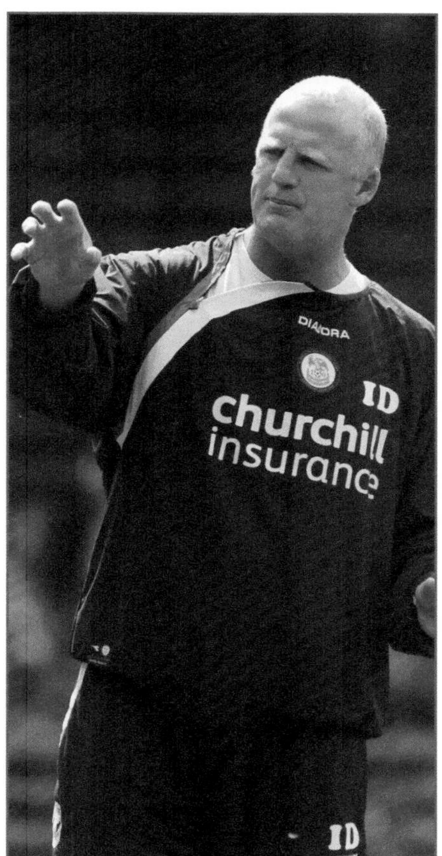

Day, he so revolutionised the club that Palace were once more an outfit full of hope long before the 2003–04 campaign had run its course.

The complete change which Iain Dowie brought about at Palace was not quite instantaneous, but it was both deep and complete – so much so that Palace powered their way to a Play-off place after beating the champions-elect Norwich City 1–0, West Ham 1–0 and Sunderland 3–0. Meeting the Mackems again, Palace won the first leg 3–2 and and then reached the Final by winning an agonizing penalty shoot-out at the Stadium of Light. Against West Ham at the Millennium Stadium, Palace were the better side in every respect and deserved their slender but definitive 1–0 victory to bring another return to the top division and ensure the club's 100th season would be spent among the game's elite.

In the Premiership, Dowie's leadership skills were inevitably hugely tested. But, with dignity and occasional inspiration, he guided the club to within a few minutes of top-flight survival as well as to some memorable victories like the 3–0 denoument of Tottenham and the 1–0 success over Liverpool. Understandably, Dowie was greatly disappointed by Palace's ultimate surrender of their Premiership status. The team had come back from a goal behind to lead 2–1 at The Valley in the last game of the season, but a late error gifted Charlton an equaliser which led to Palace's demise.

Although Dowie himself was eager to gain Palace an immediate return to the top flight, he was not able to do more than take the club to another Play-off, which was lost to Watford. Dowie and the fans were miserable through the early part of the summer of 2006 but matters deteriorated further when Iain left Selhurst Park, saying that he wanted to be nearer to his family in the North West. Mayhem erupted when he then moved in as Charlton boss. After things had settled down, Palace fans remained grateful to Iain Dowie for his achievements at Selhurst Park, but disgruntled at the manner of his departure.

Peter Taylor (2006–07)

Born: January 1953, Rochford, Essex
Player: Southend United, Crystal Palace, Tottenham Hotspur, Orient, Oldham Athletic (loan), Maidstone United, Exeter City, England.
Manager: Southend United, Gillingham, Leicester City, Brighton and Hove Albion, Hull City, England Under-21, Crystal Palace, Wycombe Wanderers, Bradford City.

Most Palace fans were delighted when Peter Taylor was appointed as manager in June 2006. Fans of the mid-1970s had thrilled to his devastating free-kicks and craft on the right wing. Many had accorded him a fine welcome when he brought his Southend United side to Selhurst Park in December 1993. But, regrettably, Taylor's time as Palace manager was almost always rather too much for him so that the overwhelming reaction of most fans to his early autumn departure in 2007 was one of relief.

Upon his appointment Taylor added penetration to the front line by securing proven striker Jamie Scowcroft from Ipswich, and he strengthened the defence by paying former club Hull City over £1 million for powerful defender Leon Cort. Midfielder Mark Kennedy arrived on a free transfer from Wolves.

Despite winning the opening pair of matches under Taylor (at Ipswich 2–1 and at home to Southend 3–1), Palace spent much of the 2006–07 season as a labouring club in midtable, and although the manager added big striker Shefki Kuqi, the team finished the campaign in a disappointing 12th place and had been knocked out of both Cup competitions in front of their own fans.

Matters did not improve at the start of 2007–08; indeed, while Taylor was in control Palace were firmly in the relegation places, so that it appeared to many discerning fans that Taylor's strengths lay in managing smaller clubs, often at lower levels rather than bigger outfits with aspirations for improvement in status, such as Crystal Palace.

Neil Warnock (2007–10)

Born: December 1948, Sheffield
Player: Chesterfield, Rotherham United, Hartlepool United, Scunthorpe United, Aldershot, Barnsley, York City, Crewe Alexandra.
Manager: Scarborough, Notts County, Huddersfield Town, Oldham Athletic, Bury, Sheffield United, Crystal Palace, Queen's Park Rangers.

Neil Warnock was appointed as Crystal Palace manager to follow Peter Taylor. When he arrived in October 2007 Palace were in a dire situation: just above the relegation places in the Championship table, with low morale and depressingly low gates. But, in little more than six months Warnock had transformed the side into favourites to win promotion via the Play-offs and thus raised morale sky high. Attendances also picked up, with nearly 23,000 coming to Selhurst Park for the Play-off semi-final against Bristol City on 17 May.

Warnock is an abrasive, no-nonsense manager. As he had been as a player, he simply expends everything he has for the cause in hand and expects those around him to do the same. He is renowned for vociferous confrontations with opposition managers and match officials, yet, while in the calm, clear light of day one may reason that such outbursts are unprofessional, still, equally, in the volatile, high-octane atmosphere of a League football match, Warnock's behaviour is seen to be perfectly understandable.

Like all Palace fans, Warnock was disappointed to lose out to Bristol City in the 2008 Championship semi-finals of the Play-offs.

But Warnock's woes continued in 2009–10. He was seldom able to lift his charges and the club suffered 4–0 and 3–0 home defeats, by Scunthorpe (one of Neil's former clubs!) and Doncaster. When the chairman Simon Jordan departed and the club was placed in administration (with its mandatory 10-point deduction) it became clear that the

manager would soon be leaving too. However, before he left Neil inspired Palace to a first-rate FA Cup replay victory over Premiership Wolves and, just before he vacated his position, a 1–1 draw at Doncaster.

The speed and manner of Neil's departure from Selhurst Park probably reflected the strength of his relations with former chairman Simon Jordan, for Mr Warnock never related positively with Palace administrator Brendan Guilfoyle.

Paul Hart (2010)

Born: 4 May 1953
Player: Stockport County, Blackpool, Leeds United, Nottingham Forest, Sheffield Wednesday, Birmingham City, Notts County.
Manager: Chesterfield, Nottingham Forest, Barnsley, Rushden & Diamonds, Portsmouth, Queen's Park Rangers, Crystal Palace, Swindon Town.

Paul Hart took over at Crystal Palace as manager in early March 2010 after the departure of Neil Warnock to Queen's Park Rangers. Paul is vastly experienced in the game, both as a former player and as a manager, having previously had charge of Portsmouth and Queen's Park Rangers earlier in the 2009–10 season, and prior to that at Chesterfield, Nottingham Forest and Barnsley.

Paul's appointment at Selhurst Park was greeted with an invaluable single-goal victory over Sheffield United on 6 March, but The Eagles laboured after that success, and Paul's second Palace victory was not achieved until the penultimate day of that month when they won a re-arranged match at Watford 3–1.

Palace fans relished the appointment of former favourites at the club, Dougie Freedman and John Pemberton, as assistants to Mr Hart, and everyone at

Selhurst Park was delighted when the temporary management team eventually led the side to Championship survival in the most testing of circumstances.

George Burley (2010–11)

Born: 3 June 1956
Player: Ipswich Town, Sunderland, Gillingham, Motherwell, Ayr United, Falkirk, Colchester United.
Manager: Ayr United, Colchester United, Ipswich Town, Derby County, Heart of Midlothian, Southampton, Scotland, Crystal Palace.

George Burley was appointed as Palace manager in June 2010, after the take-over of the club by the consortium headed by co-chairmen Steve Parish and Martin Long. Mr Burley had a distinguished place in British football management: he had previously been in charge of Ipswich Town, Derby County, Heart of Midlothian, Southampton and the Scottish international side.

However, despite winning his first match as the Palace manager, George's leadership at Selhurst Park proved to be ineffectual, so much so that The Eagles won just six of their 24 League games under him. It ws also evident that Mr Burley was quite unable to motivate or enthuse his players for the Palace cause.

Mr Burley was relieved of his responsibilites at the Palace immediately after their lacklustre 3–0 defeat at Millwall on New Year's Day 2011, which had extended an unbroken, winless run since late November and seen the club anchored, next to bottom in the Championship relegation zone.

Dougie Freedman (2011–)

Born: 25 May 1974
Player: Barnet, Crystal Palace, Wolverhampton Wanderers, Nottingham Forest, Leeds United, Southend United.
Manager: Crystal Palace.

Dougie Freedman had accumulated a considerably sized following among Palace fans during his two spells as a player at Selhurst Park so that his appointments as assistant manager to Paul Hart and then to George Burley before becoming Palace's manager in his own right in early January 2011 were all hugely welcomed by Palace afficionados everywhere.

Dougie knew at the outset that the monetary resources available to him were modest and that the situation he faced as the Palace boss was a daunting one, with the club ensconced in the relegation zone and a potentially bleak future looming for it. However, his first major move was to secure the services of vastly experienced manager of many clubs, Lennie Lawrence, as his assistant, and the duo led the club with dignity through the turbulent second half of 2010–11 to a thoroughly praiseworthy finishing position of 20th in the Championship table, and with a six-point margin separating Palace from the relegation places.

This was recognised by everyone connected with Crystal Palace as being a most commendable achievement, given the plight of the club when Dougie took on the management. In fact, allied to his crucial goal at Stockport when Palace were in similar straits in 2001, Dougie must now rank as Palace's leading escapologist of all time!

League Seasons

1905-06

Southern League Division Two

Manager: John Robson

Did you know that?

There are at least three previous clubs called Crystal Palace, the earliest dating as far back as 1861, and including the differently named Crystal Palace Rovers of 1883. The first known fixture of the first Crystal Palace club was a 1–0 defeat to Forest FC in a friendly on 15 March 1861. The 1870s incarnation of Palace featured in the FA Cup when it was founded in 1871, going as far as the semi-finals the following season.

Match No.	Date		Venue	Opponents	Result		Scorers	Attendance
1	Sep	2	H	Southampton Res.	L	3–4	Roberts, Needham, Thompson	3,000
2		16	A	Swindon Town Res.	W	2–1	Birnie, Harker	
3		18	A	West Ham United Res.	D	0-0		
4		23	H	Leyton	D	0-0		5,000
5	Oct	14	H	Fulham Res.	W	5-0	Wallace, Watkins 2, Needham 2	1,500
6		21	A	Southern United	W	1-0	Watkins	
7	Nov	4	H	Grays United	W	9-1	Birnie, Harker 2, Watkins 2, Needham 2, Astley, Roberts	
8		25	A	Watford Res.	W	3-1	Roberts 2, Ross	
9	Dec	13	H	Reading Res.	W	3-0	Harker, Roberts, Watkins	3,000
10		23	H+	Swindon Town Res.	W	3-0	Astley, Ross 2	
11		26	H	Portsmouth Res.	W	1-0	Needham	2,000
12	Jan	6	A	Wycombe Wanderers	W	4-1	Thompson, Needham, Wallace 2	
13		20	H	St Leonards United	W	3-1	Woodger 2, Thompson	3,000
14		27	A	Grays United	W	3-0	Walker 2, Needham	
15	Feb	10	H+	West Ham United Res.	W	3-1	Woodger 2, Needham	2,000
16		21	A	St Leonards United	W	3-0	Needham 2, Wallace	
17		28	H+	Southern United	W	4-0	Needham 2, Woodger, own-goal	
18	Mar	3	H	Watford Res.	W	4-0	Roberts, Needham 2, Woodger	2,000
19		10	A	Southampton Res.	W	2-0	Thompson, Needham	
20		24	A	Reading Res.	W	1-0	Needham	
21	Apr	7	A	Leyton	W	2-1	Wallace, Needham	3,000
22		13	A	Portsmouth Res.	D	1-1	Watkins	8,000
23		14	H	Wycombe Wanderers	W	4-0	Woodger 2, Moody, Needham	
24		17	A	Fulham Res.	D	2-2	Needham, Harker	5,000

Final League Position: 1st in Southern League Division Two — Appearances

+ Thought to have been played on the North (Cycle Track) Ground — 1 own-goal — Goals

FA Cup

Match No.	Date		Venue	Opponents	Result		Scorers	Attendance
1Q	Oct	7	H	Clapham	W	7-0	Watkins 3 (2 pens), Innerd, Astley, Roberts, Harker	1,500
2Q		28	A	Second Grenadier Guards	W	3-0	Harker, Wallace, Astley	1,200
3Q	Nov	18	H	Chelsea	W	7-1	Watkins 3, Innerd 2, Harker, Needham	3,000
4Q	Dec	9	H	Luton Town	W	1-0	Harker	5,000
1	Jan	13	A	Blackpool	D	1-1	Harker	2,500
R		17	H	Blackpool	D	1-1*	Birnie	4,000
2R		22	N+	Blackpool	L	0-1		5,000

+ Played at Villa Park. * After extra-time — Appearances

Goals

Hewitson	Walker	Edwards M.	Innerd	Birnie	Astley	Thompson G.	Harker	Watkins	Needham	Roberts	Wallace	Ross	Grant	Palmer	Wilson	Woodger	Mills	Bryden	Cubberley	Henwood	Moody	Dick
1	2	3	4	5	6	7	8	9	10	11												
1	2	3	4	5	6	7	8	9	10	11												
1	2	3	4	5	6		8	9	10	11	7											
1	2	3	4	5	6		8		9	11	7	10										
1	2		4	5	6		8	9	10	11	7		3									
1	2	3	4	5	6		8	9	10	11	7											
1	2			5	6		8	9	10	11	7		3	4								
1	2			5	6		8	9	4	11	7	10	3									
1	2	3	4	5	6		8	9	10	11	7											
1	2		4	5	6	7	8	9		11		10	3									
1	2	3		5	6		8		10	11	7				4	9						
1	2		4	5	6	7		9	10	11	8		3									
1	2	3				7				11	9	8	6		4	10	5					
1	2		6	5				9	8	11	7		3		4	10						
1	6	3	4	5					8	11	7		2			10		9				
1	2	3	4	5		7			10	11	8		6			9						
1	2	3		5		7		8	10	11	4		6			9						
1	2	3		5				8	10	11	7		6		4	9						
1	2	3		5		7	8		10	11	4		6			9						
1	2	3		5			8		10	11	7		6			9			4			
1	2	3	6	5			8		10	11	7				4	9						
1	2		4	5	6		8	9		11	7		3			10						
1	2		4			7			10	11			3		5	8				6	9	
1	2		6	3		7	8	9	10	11					4							5
24	24	15	16	22	13	10	16	15	21	24	19	4	15	1	7	12	1	1	1	1	1	1
	2			2	2	4	5	7	20	6	5	3				8					1	

Hewitson	Walker	Edwards M.	Innerd	Birnie	Astley	Thompson G.	Harker	Watkins	Needham	Roberts	Wallace	Ross	Grant
1	2	3	4	5	6		8	9	10	11	7		
1	2	3	4	5	6		8	9		11	7	10	
1	2		4	5	6		8	9	10	11	7		3
1	2	3	4	5	6		8	9	10	11	7		
1	2	3	4	5	6		8	9	10	11	7		
1	2	3	4	5	6		8	9	10	11	7		
1	2	3	4	5		7	8		10	11	9		6
7	7	6	7	7	6	1	7	6	6	7	7	1	2
			3	1	2		5	6	1	1	1		

1906-07

Southern League Division One

Manager: John Robson

Did you know that?

George Woodger (nicknamed 'Lady' by the fans) was the first local player to join Palace. The Croydon-born inside-forward signed in 1905 after playing local amateur football, and stayed for five seasons before moving onto Oldham Athletic and then Tottenham, winning one England cap in the process while at Oldham.

Match No.	Date		Venue	Opponents	Result		Scorers	Attendance
1	Sep	1	H	Northampton Town	W	3-0	Woodger 2, Harker	7,000
2		8	A	Queen's Park Rangers	L	0-1		7,900
3		15	H	Fulham	L	0-3		8,000
4		19	H	Reading	W	4-1	Harker, Woodger, Roberts, Hodgkinson	4,000
5		22	A	Southampton	D	1-1	Edwards (pen)	4,500
6		29	H	West Ham United	D	1-1	Wallace	10,000
7	Oct	6	A	Tottenham Hotspur	L	0-3		18,000
8		13	H	Swindon Town	W	3-2	Wallace 3	7,000
9		20	A	Norwich City	L	2-4	Edwards (pen), Wallace	9,000
10		27	H	Luton Town	L	0-1		8,000
11	Nov	3	A	Bristol Rovers	D	1-1	Wallace	5,000
12		10	A	Brentford	L	0-2		6,000
13		17	H	Millwall	W	3-0	Roberts, Wallace, Innerd	6,000
14		24	A	Leyton	W	4-0	Astley 2, Wallace, Harker	
15	Dec	1	H	Portsmouth	W	1-0	Woodger	7,500
16		15	H	Plymouth Argyle	L	0-2		6,000
17		22	A	Brighton & Hove Albion	L	1-2	Wallace	5,000
18		26	A	Watford	L	0-2		3,000
19		29	A	Northampton Town	L	1-2	Roberts	3,000
20	Jan	5	H	Queen's Park Rangers	W	5-1	Astley 4, Harker	6,000
21		19	A	Fulham	L	1-2	Astley	15,000
22		26	H	Southampton	D	1-1	Roberts	6,500
23	Feb	9	H	Tottenham Hotspur	L	0-1		8,000
24		16	A	Swindon Town	L	1-2	Astley	5,000
25	Mar	2	A	Luton Town	L	1-2	Astley	8,000
26		16	H	Brentford	L	0-3		7,000
27		23	A	Millwall	L	0-2		10,000
28		25	A	West Ham United	D	1-1	Harker	3,000
29		29	A	Reading	D	1-1	Weston	10,000
30		30	H	Leyton	W	1-0	Woodger	7,000
31	Apr	1	H	Watford	L	1-3	Roberts (pen)	10,000
32		6	A	Portsmouth	L	0-6		7,000
33		13	H	New Brompton	L	1-3	Edwards (pen)	5,500
34		17	H	Bristol Rovers	D	3-3	Astley, Roberts, Woodger	2,000
35		20	A	Plymouth Argyle	D	0-0		
36		24	H	Norwich City	L	0-1		2,000
37		27	H	Brighton & Hove Albion	D	2-2	Harker, Edwards (pen)	4,000
38		29	A	New Brompton	L	2-4	Harker, Roberts	3,000

Final League Position: 19th in Southern League Division One

Appearances
Goals

FA Cup

Match No.	Date		Venue	Opponents	Result		Scorers	Attendance
4Q	Dec	8	N+	Rotherham County	W	4-0	Roberts 2, Harker, own-goal	1,500
1	Jan	12	A	Newcastle United	W	1-0	Astley	28,000
2	Feb	2	A	Fulham	D	0-0		28,000
R		6	H	Fulham	W	1-0	Woodger	20,000
3		23	H	Brentford	D	1-1	Harker	31,123
R		27	A	Brentford	W	1-0	Roberts	21,478
4	Mar	9	H	Everton	D	1-1	Astley	35,000
R		13	A	Everton	L	0-4		34,340

+ Played at Stamford Bridge

Appearances

1 own-goal

Goals

Hewitson	Edwards M.	Wills	Innerd	Ryan	Forster	Wallace	Harker	Woodger	Needham	Roberts	Astley	Menzies	Hodgkinson	Wilson	Ransom	Ledger	Weston	Collyer	Littlewort	Sans	Edwards J.	Jackson	Swann	Hunter	Lawrence
1	2	3	4	5	6	7	8	9	10	11															
1	3	2	4		6	7	8	9	10	11	5														
1	3		4	5	6	7	8	9	10	11		2													
1	3		4	5	6	7	8	9		11		2	10												
1	3		4	5	6	7	8	9	10	11		2													
1	3	2	4	5	6	7	8	9	10	11															
1	3	2	4	5	6		8	9	7	11			10												
1	3	2	6	5		7	8	9	10	11	4														
1	3	2	6	5		7	8	9	10	11	4														
1	3	2	6	5		7	8	9	10	11	4														
1	3	2	6	5		7	8	10		11	9			4											
1	3	2	5			7	8	10		11	9			6	4										
1	3	2	5		6	7	8	10		11						4	9								
1	3	2	5		6	7	8	10		11	9					4									
1	3	2	5		6	7	8	10		11	9					4									
1		3	5	6		7	8	10		11	9	2				4									
1	3	2	5		4	7	8	10		11	9					6									
1			5		6	7	8	10	2	11	9					4		3							
1	3	2	4	5	6	7	8	10	9	11															
1	3		4	5	6	7	8	10	2	11	9														
1	3		4		6	7	8		2	11	9		10						5						
1	3		5		6	7	8		2	11						4	9			10					
1	3		4	5	6	7	8	10	2	11	9														
1	3		4	5	6	7	8	10	2	11	9														
1		3	5		6			10	2	11	9		8			4	7								
1	3		4	5	6	7		10	2	11	9		8												
1	3	2	4	5		7	8	9	10							6				11					
1			9	5	6	11	10	8	2							4		3			7				
1			4	5	6	7	8	10	3	11							9					2			
1			4		6	7	8	10	3	11							9	2				5			
1			4	5		7	8	10	2	11						6	9					3			
1	3		4		6	7	8	10	2	11												5	9		
1	3			5	4	7	8	10	2	11												6	9		
1	2		4	5	6	7		10		11	9											3	8		
1	3		4	5	6	7	10			11	9											2	8		
1	3		4	5	6	7	8	10	2	11													9		
	3		4	5	6	7	8	10	2	11													9	1	
	3		4	5	6		8		7	11								2					9	1	10
36	31	17	37	26	30	35	35	34	28	36	19	4	5	2	1	11	6	4	1	2	1	7	7	2	1
	4		1			9	7	6		7	10		1				1								

Hewitson	Edwards M.	Wills	Innerd	Ryan	Forster	Wallace	Harker	Woodger	Needham	Roberts	Astley	Menzies	Hodgkinson	Wilson	Ransom	Ledger	Weston	Collyer	Littlewort	Sans	Edwards J.	Jackson	Swann	Hunter	Lawrence
1	3	2	5		6		8	10	7	11	9					4									
1	3		4	5	6	7	8	10	2	11	9														
1	3		5		6	7	8	10	2	11	9					4									
1	3		4	5	6	7	8	10	2	11	9														
1	3		4	5	6	7	8	10	2	11	9														
1	3		4	5	6	7	8	10	2	11	9														
1	3		4	5	6	7	8	10	2	11	9														
1	3		4	5	6	7	8	10	2	11	9														
8	8	1	8	6	8	7	8	8	8	8	8					2									
							2	1		3	2														

1907-08

Southern League Division One

Manager: Edmund Goodman

Did you know that?

Welshman Bill Davies holds the honour of being the first-ever capped player at Crystal Palace when the outside-left, or right, represented his country in March 1908 against Scotland.

Match No.	Date		Venue	Opponents	Result		Scorers	Attendance
1	Sep	4	H	Northampton Town	L	0-2		5,000
2		7	A	Southampton	W	3-2	Davies, Woodger, Edwards (pen)	5,000
3		14	H	Plymouth Argyle	L	0-4		8,000
4		21	A	West Ham United	L	0-1		8,000
5		28	H	Queen's Park Rangers	L	2-3	Roberts 2	8,000
6	Oct	5	A	Tottenham Hotspur	W	2-1	Innerd, Needham	17,000
7		7	A	Northampton Town	D	1-1	Innerd	
8		12	H	Swindon Town	W	4-1	Woodger 3, Owens	8,000
9		19	H	New Brompton	D	3-3	Owens, Davies, Woodger	8,000
10		26	A	Luton Town	L	0-4		6,000
11	Nov	2	H	Brighton & Hove Albion	W	2-1	Owens, Innerd	10,000
12		9	A	Portsmouth	W	1-0	Swann	8,000
13		16	H	Bradford Park Avenue	D	1-1	Roberts (pen)	11,000
14		23	A	Millwall	L	0-1		5,000
15		30	H	Brentford	W	2-1	Roberts, Woodger	7,000
16	Dec	7	A	Bristol Rovers	L	1-2	Roberts	7,000
17		14	H	Leyton	W	3-0	Swann 2, Owens	6,000
18		21	A	Reading	L	1-2	Brearley	5,000
19		25	A	Norwich City	W	1-0	Brearley	13,500
20		28	H	Watford	W	3-1	Roberts (pen), Woodger 2	7,000
21	Jan	4	H	Southampton	W	1-0	Roberts (pen)	8,000
22		18	H	West Ham United	L	1-3	Woodger	10,000
23		25	A	Queen's Park Rangers	W	2-1	Smith, Swann	8,000
24	Feb	8	A	Swindon Town	D	0-0		7,000
25		12	H	Tottenham Hotspur	L	0-2		8,000
26		15	A	New Brompton	D	2-2	Smith, Woodger	2,000
27		29	A	Brighton & Hove Albion	W	1-0	Owens	4,000
28	Mar	4	H	Luton Town	W	4-2	Needham, Owens 2, Davies	4,000
29		7	H	Portsmouth	D	2-2	Woodger, Ryan	10,000
30		14	A	Bradford Park Avenue	W	1-0	Owens	8,000
31		21	H	Millwall	W	2-0	Needham, Bauchop	13,500
32		28	A	Brentford	D	1-1	Bauchop	9,000
33	Apr	4	H	Bristol Rovers	D	1-1	Woodger	10,000
34		8	A	Plymouth Argyle	D	1-1	Bauchop	7,000
35		11	A	Leyton	D	0-0		5,000
36		18	H	Reading	W	2-0	Bauchop, Woodger	10,000
37		20	H	Norwich City	W	2-1	Needham, Bauchop	14,000
38		25	A	Watford	L	1-4	Bauchop	3,000

Final League Position: 4th in Southern League Division One

Appearances
Goals

FA Cup

1	Jan	11	A	Coventry City	W	4-2	Roberts, Woodger 2, Davies	9,992
2	Feb	1	A	Plymouth Argyle	W	3-2	Roberts, Smith, Swann	17,830
3		22	A	Grimsby Town	L	0-1		8,828

Appearances
Goals

Hall	Needham	Edwards M.	Innerd	Owens	Brearley	Davies	Swann	Smith G.	Woodger	Roberts	Forster	Walker	Baker	Balding	Ryan	Collyer	Johnson	Wilson	Lewis	Bauchop	Higgins
1	2	3	4	5	6	7	8	9	10	11											
1	2	3			6	7	9	8	10	11	4	5									
1	2	3	8		6		8	7	10		4	5	11								
	2	3	4	9	5	7	8		10	11		6		1							
1	2	3	4	9	5		8		10	7		6	11								
1	8	2	6	9	4		10		7	11		3			5						
1			4	9		7	8		10	11	6	3			5	2					
1			4	9	6	11	8		10	7		3			5	2					
1		3	4	9	6	11	8		10	7		2			5						
1		3	4	9	6	11	8		10	7		2			5						
1	7		4	9	6	11	8		10		5	3				2					
			4	9	6	11	8		10	7		3		1	5	2					
			4	9	6	11	8		10	7		3		1	5	2					
	2		4	9	6	11	8		10	7		3		1	5						
		3	4	9	6	11	8		10	7		2		1	5						
	2	3	4	9	6	11	8		10	7					5		1				
	2		4	9	6	11	8		10	7		3			5		1				
	2		4		6	10	8			7	9	3	11		5		1				
	2		4		9	11	8		10	7	6	3			5		1				
	3		4		9	11	8		10	7	5	2					1	6			
	2		4		9	11	8		10	7	6	3			5		1				
	2	3	9		6	11	8	7	10		4				5		1				
			6		5	11	8	9	10	7	4	3				2	1				
	7		4		5	11	8		10		6	3				2	1		9		
	7		4	9			8		10		6	3	11		5	2	1				
	3		9		6	11	8	7	10		4				5	2	1				
	11			9	6		8	7	10		4	3			5	2	1				
	7			9	6	11	8		10		4	3			5	2	1				
	11			9	6		8	7	10		4	3			5	2	1				
	11		6	9		7	8		10		4	3			5	2	1				
	11		6			7	8		10		4	3			5	2	1			9	
	11		4			7	8		10			3			5	2	1		6	9	
	11		4	5			8	7	10			3				2	1		6	9	
	11		4		6	7	8		10			3			5	2	1			9	
	11		4			7	8		10		6	3			5	2	1			9	
	11		4	8	6	7			10			3			5	2	1			9	
	11		4		10	7	8				6	3			5	2	1			9	
	11		4		6	7	8					3			5	2	1			9	10
10	30	11	34	22	31	31	37	9	35	20	20	34	4	5	28	21	23	1	3	8	1
	4	1	3	8	2	3	4	2	13	7					1					6	

Hall	Needham	Edwards M.	Innerd	Owens	Brearley	Davies	Swann	Smith G.	Woodger	Roberts	Forster	Walker	Baker	Balding	Ryan	Collyer	Johnson	Wilson	Lewis	Bauchop	Higgins
	2		9		6	11	8		10	7	4	3			5		1				
			4		5	11	8	9	10	7	6	3				2	1				
			9		6	11	8	7	10		4	3			5	2	1				
	1		3		3	3	3	2	3	2	3	3			2	2	3				
						1	1	1	2	2											

1908-09

Southern League Division One

Manager: Edmund Goodman

Did you know that?

James Bauchop became the first-ever Palace player to be sent off, when he was dismissed during a September match against Croydon Common in the London Challenge Cup.

Match No.	Date		Venue	Opponents	Result		Scorers	Attendance
1	Sep	1	A	Coventry City	D	1-1	Bauchop	5,000
2		5	H	Leyton	W	5-1	Bauchop 2, Swann, Woodger	10,000
3		12	A	West Ham United	W	1-0	Woodger	10,000
4		16	H	Southampton	L	2-3	Swann, Bauchop	
5		19	H	Brighton & Hove Albion	W	4-0	McGibbon 3, Bauchop	10,000
6		26	A	Plymouth Argyle	D	0-0		8,000
7		30	H	Norwich City	W	4-0	Woodger, Haywood, McGibbon, Lawrence	5,000
8	Oct	3	A	Brentford	W	3-1	Haywood, Barker, McGibbon	6,000
9		5	A	Southampton	D	4-4	McGibbon 3, Lawrence	5,000
10		10	H	Luton Town	W	2-0	McGibbon, Woodger	10,000
11		15	A	Norwich City	L	0-2		5,000
12		17	A	Swindon Town	L	0-4		7,000
13		21	H	Queen's Park Rangers	W	3-0	Garratt, Lawrence 2	6,000
14		24	H	Portsmouth	W	3-2	Bauchop 3	9,500
15		31	A	Exeter City	D	1-1	McGibbon	7,000
16	Nov	7	H	Northampton Town	L	2-3	Swann 2	12,000
17		14	A	New Brompton	L	1-2	McGibbon	4,000
18		21	H	Millwall	W	2-1	Swann, Bauchop	10,000
19		28	A	Southend United	L	0-1		6,000
20	Dec	12	A	Bristol Rovers	D	2-2	Ryan, Bauchop	6,000
21		19	H	Watford	W	3-1	McGibbon 2, Swann	8,000
22		26	A	Reading	D	2-2	Woodger 2	11,000
23	Jan	2	A	Leyton	L	0-2		4,000
24		9	H	West Ham United	D	2-2	Bauchop, Woodger	6,000
25		23	A	Brighton & Hove Albion	L	0-3		5,000
26		30	H	Plymouth Argyle	L	0-1		6,000
27	Feb	13	A	Luton Town	L	1-4	Bauchop	5,000
28		20	H	Swindon Town	D	1-1	Swann	7,000
29		27	A	Portsmouth	D	1-1	Bauchop	5,000
30	Mar	6	H	Exeter City	D	0-0		1,500
31		13	A	Northampton Town	L	0-1		7,000
32		17	H	Southend United	L	1-3	Brearley	
33		20	H	New Brompton	L	1-2	Bauchop	4,000
34		27	A	Millwall	L	1-2	Swann	5,000
35		31	H	Brentford	W	3-1	Woodger 2, Bauchop	2,000
36	Apr	3	A	Queen's Park Rangers	D	1-1	Swann	5,000
37		10	H+	Coventry City	L	0-1		5,000
38		12	H	Reading	D	0-0		5,000
39		17	H	Bristol Rovers	W	4-1	Lee 2, Swann, Bauchop	4,000
40		24	A	Watford	L	1-5	Bauchop	4,000

Final League Position: 16th in Southern League Division One — Appearances

+ Thought to have been played on the North (Cycle Track) ground — Goals

FA Cup

1	Jan	16	A	Wolverhampton Wanderers	D	2-2	Bauchop 2	18,653
R		21	H	Wolverhampton Wanderers	W	4-2*	Lawrence, Garratt, Bauchop, Needham	12,300
2	Feb	6	H	Burnley	D	0-0		17,076
R		10	A	Burnley	L	0-9		12,000

* After extra-time — Appearances

Goals

Johnson	Collyer	Walker	Innerd	Ryan	Brearley	Garratt	Swann	Bauchop	Woodger	Roberts	Collins E.	Thorpe	Kyle	Haywood	McGibbon	Barker	Lawrence	Needham	Lewis	Higgins	Hullock	Balding	Lee	Wilson
1	2	3	4	5	6	7	8	9	10	11														
1	2	3	4	5	6	7	8	9	10	11														
1		3		5	6	7	8	9	11		2	4	10											
1		3		5	6	7	8	9	11		2	4	10											
1		2	4	5	6	7		10	11		3			8	9									
1		3	4	5	6				11		2			8	9	7	10							
1			4	5	6				11		2			8	9	7	10	3						
1			4	5	6				11		2			8	9	7	10	3						
1			4	5	6				11		2			8	9	7	10	3						
1			4	5	6	7			11		2			8	9		10	3						
1		3	4	5	6			9	11		2			8			10		7					
1		3	4	5	6			10	11		2		8		9			7						
1			4	5	6	7		10	11		2				9		8	3						
1			4	5	6	7		10	11		2				9		8	3						
1	2		4	5	6	7	8	10	11						9			3						
1	2		4	5	6	7	8	10	11						9			3						
1	3			5	6	7	8	10	11		2	4			9									
1	3			5	6	7	8	10	11		2	4			9									
1	3		4	5	6	7	8	10	11		2				9									
1	3		4	5	6	7	8	9	11		2						10							
1	3		4	5	6	7	8	10	11		2				9									
1	3		4		6	7	8	11	10		2				9				5					
1			4	5	6	7	8	11	10		3				9					2				
1	3		4	5	6	7		9	10		2						8	11						
	3				6			9	10			2				7	8	11	4		5	1		
1	3		4	5	6	7		9	10			2					8	11						
	2				6	7		9	11			4					8	3	5			1	10	
1	2			5	6	7	8	9	11			3		10					4					
1	2				5	7	8	9	11			6						3	4				10	
1	2				5	7	8	9	11			6						3	4				10	
1	2			5		7	8	9	11			6					10	3	4					
1	2			5	10	7		9	11			6					8	3	4					
1	2		4		5	7	8	9	11			3									6		10	
1	2				5	7	8	9			3	6					10	11	4					
1	2				5	7	8	9	10		3	6						11	4					
1	2		6		5	7	8	9	10		3							11	4					
1	2		6		5	7	8	9	10		3							11	4					
1	2				5	11	8	9						10		7		3			4			6
1	2			5	11	7	8	9				6						3			4		10	
1	2				5	7	8	9	11			6						3			4		10	
38	27	8	24	28	39	33	25	35	37	2	24	17	3	9	17	6	16	24	13	1	5	2	6	1
				1	1	1	11	17	9					2	13	1	4						2	

1	3		4	5	6	7		9	10		2						8	11	
1	3		4	5	6	7		9	10		2						8	11	
1	3		4	5	6	7		9	11								10	2	8
1	3		4	5	6	7		9	10		2						8	11	
4	4		4	4	4	4		4	4		3						4	4	1
						1		3									1	1	

1909-10

Southern League Division One

Manager: Edmund Goodman

Did you know that?

In an age before floodlights, Palace's Thursday afternoon January game in the London Challenge Cup against Croydon Common was abandoned due to darkness at the Crystal Palace, with the Glaziers losing 2–1. Palace went on to win the re-scheduled game only a few weeks later.

Match No.	Date		Venue	Opponents	Result		Scorers	Attendance
1	Sep	1	H	Brentford	W	1-0	Payne	4,500
2		4	A	Coventry City	D	1-1	Collyer (pen)	8,000
3		8	H	Bristol Rovers	W	3-1	Hanger, Payne, Woodger	
4		11	H	Watford	D	1-1	Payne	8,000
5		13	A	Brentford	L	0-1		3,000
6		18	A	Reading	D	1-1	Williams	4,000
7		25	H	Southend United	W	6-0	Williams 5, Payne	10,000
8	Oct	2	A	Leyton	W	1-0	Payne	14,000
9		9	H	Plymouth Argyle	W	3-0	Payne, Woodger, Hughes	10,000
10		13	H	Norwich City	W	4-0	Payne 3, Williams	5,000
11		16	A	Southampton	W	3-0	Payne 3	15,000
12		23	H	Croydon Common	W	2-0	Williams, Griffin	15,000
13		25	A	Norwich City	L	0-1		12,000
14		30	A	Millwall	W	2-0	Williams, Payne	8,000
15	Nov	6	H	New Brompton	W	6-2	Payne 4, Williams 2	12,000
16		13	A	Northampton Town	L	0-1		10,000
17		17	A	Portsmouth	L	0-2		8,000
18		20	H	Queen's Park Rangers	L	0-1		12,000
19		27	A	Luton Town	W	4-2	Young 2, Williams, Payne	4,000
20	Dec	4	H	Swindon Town	W	2-0	Payne 2	6,000
21		11	H	Exeter City	W	3-0	Hughes, Williams 2	6,000
22		18	A	Brighton & Hove Albion	W	2-1	Payne, Williams	7,000
23	Jan	1	A	Bristol Rovers	D	1-1	Spottiswood	
24		8	H	Coventry City	L	1-2	Payne (pen)	
25		22	A	Watford	L	0-3		3,000
26		29	H	Reading	D	1-1	Woodger	4,000
27	Feb	12	H	Leyton	L	1-2	Woodger	
28		19	A	Plymouth Argyle	L	0-2		5,000
29		23	A	Southend United	L	0-3		1,700
30		26	H	Southampton	W	2-0	Woodger 2	
31	Mar	5	A	Croydon Common	W	1-0	Young	10,000
32		9	H	Portsmouth	W	4-2	Young 2, Garratt, Woodger	2,000
33		12	H	Millwall	W	4-1	Young, Williams 2, Woodger	4,000
34		19	A	New Brompton	L	1-3	Young	5,000
35		25	A	West Ham United	L	1-3	Williams	15,000
36		26	H	Northampton Town	W	1-0	Williams	10,000
37		28	H	West Ham United	L	2-4	Payne 2	20,000
38	Apr	2	A	Queen's Park Rangers	W	2-1	Gibson, Payne	10,000
39		9	H	Luton Town	L	1-3	Williams	
40		16	A	Swindon Town	L	1-2	Griffin	
41		23	A	Exeter City	L	0-2		
42		30	H	Brighton & Hove Albion	D	0-0		10,000

Final League Position: 7th in Southern League Division One

Appearances

Goals

FA Cup

1	Jan	15	H	Swindon Town	L	1-3	Payne	14,000

Appearances

Goals

Johnson	Collyer	Bulcock	Spottiswood	Clark	Hanger	Garratt	Payne	Williams	Woodger	Griffin	Hughes	Hullock	Young	Moult	Forgan	Myers	Wood N.	Bradley	Gibson	Collins E
1	2	3	4	5	6	7	8	9	10	11										
1	2	3	4	5	6	7	8	9	10	11										
1	2	3	4	5	6	7	8	9	10	11										
1	2	3	4	5	6	7	8	9	10	11										
1	2	3	4	5	6	7	8	9	10	11										
1	2	3	4	5	6	7	8	9	10	11										
1	2	3	4	5	6	7	10	9	8	11										
1	2	3		5		7	10	9	8	11	4	6								
1	2	3	4	5		7	10	9	8	11	6									
1	2	3	4	5		7	10	9	8	11	6									
1	2	3	4	5		7	10	9	8	11	6									
1	2	3	4	5		7	10	9	8	11	6									
1	2	3	4	5		7	10	9	8	11	6									
1	2	3	4	5		7	10	9	8	11	6									
1	2	3	4	5		7	10	9	8	11	6									
1	2	3	4	5		7	10	9	8	11	6									
1	2	3	4	5		7	10	9		11	6		8							
1	2	3	4	5		7	10	9	8	11	6									
1	2	3	4	5		7	10	9		11	6		8							
1	2	3	4	5		7	10	9	8	11	6									
1	2	3	4	5		7	10	9	8	11	6									
1	2	3	4	5		7	10	9	8	11	6									
1	2	3	4	5		7	10	9	8	11	6									
1	3		4	5	6	7	10	9	8	11	2									
	2	3	4	5		7	10	9	11		6		8	1						
1	2	3	4	5		7	10	9	11		6		8							
1		3	4	5	6	7	10	9	8	11	2									
1		3	4	5	6	7	10	9	8	11	2									
1	2	3	4		6	7		8	10		5				9	11				
1	2	3	4		6	7		8	10	11	5		9							
1	2	3	4		6	7		8	10	11	5		9							
1	2	3	4		6	7		8	10		5		9			11				
1	2	3	4		6	7	11	8	10			5	9							
1	2	3	4		6	7	11	8	10		5		9							
1	2	3	4	5	6	7		8	10				9				11			
1	2		4	5	6	7		8	10	11			9					3		
1	2		4	5	6		10	8		11	9							3	7	
1	2	3	4		6		10	9		11	5		8						7	
1	2	3	4		6	7	10	9	11		5		8							
1		3	4		6	7		9	8	11	5		10							2
1	2	3	4		6	7		9	8	11	5		10							
1	2	3	4		6	7	10	9	8	11	5									
41	39	39	41	31	24	40	34	42	38	34	32	2	15	1	1	2	1	2	2	1
	1		1		1	1	25	20	8	2	2		7						1	

Johnson	Collyer	Bulcock	Spottiswood	Clark	Hanger	Garratt	Payne	Williams	Woodger	Griffin	Hughes	Hullock	Young	Moult	Forgan	Myers	Wood N.	Bradley	Gibson	Collins E
	2	3	4	5		7	10	9	8	11	6			1						
	1	1	1	1		1	1	1	1	1	1			1						
							1													

1910-11

Southern League Division One

Manager: Edmund Goodman

Did you know that?

Derbyshire-born goalkeeper Joshua Johnson, played the most number of games for the club in the Southern League – 274 in total.

Match No.	Date		Venue	Opponents	Result		Scorers	Attendance
1	Sep	3	A	Swindon Town	D	0-0		7,000
2		10	H	Bristol Rovers	W	1-0	Hanger	8,500
3		14	A	Exeter City	W	4-3	Payne 3, Davies	3,000
4		17	H	Norwich City	L	0-3		6,000
5		24	A	Brentford	L	1-2	Payne	
6	Oct	1	H	Leyton	W	5-4	Woodhouse, Hughes 2 (2.pens), Lawrence, Davies	
7		5	H	Portsmouth	L	0-1		4,000
8		8	A	Watford	D	1-1	Hanger	4,000
9		15	H	Plymouth Argyle	W	6-1	Williams 2, Woodhouse 2, Garratt, Hewitt	
10		22	A	Southampton	W	3-0	Hughes 2 (2 pens), Hanger	
11		29	H	Southend United	D	0-0		6,000
12	Nov	5	A	Coventry City	W	2-0	Williams, Woodhouse	7,000
13		12	H	New Brompton	W	3-2	Collins, Hewitt, Woodhouse	8,000
14		19	A	Millwall	W	1-0	Williams	18,000
15		26	H	Queen's Park Rangers	W	2-1	Garratt, Hewitt	9,000
16	Dec	3	A	West Ham United	D	1-1	Woodhouse	8,000
17		10	H	Luton Town	W	3-1	Spottiswood, Woodhouse, Hughes	
18		17	A	Portsmouth	D	0-0		7,500
19		24	H	Northampton Town	D	0-0		
20		26	A	Brighton & Hove Albion	L	0-2		12,000
21		27	H	Brighton & Hove Albion	D	1-1	Hewitt	
22		31	H	Swindon Town	L	2-5	Woodhouse, Williams	12,000
23	Jan	7	A	Bristol Rovers	D	3-3	Hanger, Woodhouse, Hewitt	
24		21	A	Norwich City	W	1-0	Hewitt	4,000
25		28	H	Brentford	D	1-1	Payne	8,000
26	Feb	4	A	Leyton	W	1-0	Woodhouse	5,000
27		11	H	Watford	W	1-0	Williams	6,000
28		18	A	Plymouth Argyle	L	1-5	Davies	7,000
29		25	H	Southampton	D	2-2	Hewitt, Woodhouse	6,000
30	Mar	4	A	Southend United	D	0-0		
31		11	H	Coventry City	W	2-0	Woodhouse, Hewitt	5,000
32		18	A	New Brompton	L	0-2		
33		25	H	Millwall	W	1-0	Woodhouse	6,000
34	Apr	1	A	Queen's Park Rangers	D	0-0		9,000
35		8	H	West Ham United	W	4-1	Williams, Woodhouse, Bulcock, Garratt	8,000
36		15	A	Luton Town	D	1-1	Williams	
37		17	H	Exeter City	W	1-0	Woodhouse	13,000
38		18	A	Northampton Town	L	0-5		4,000

Final League Position: 4th in Southern League Division One

Appearances
Goals

FA Cup

1	Jan	14	H	Everton	L	0-4		35,000

Appearances
Goals

Johnson	Collyer	Bulcock	Spottiswood	Hughes	Hanger	Garratt	Woodger	Williams	Lawrence	Davies	Payne	Hatton	Myers	Thompson H.	Woodhouse	Hewitt	Collins J.	Humphreys	Mitchell	Goodhind	Glover
1	2	3	4	5	6	7	8	9	10	11											
1	2	3	4	5	6	7	8	9	10	11											
1	2	3	4	5	6	7	8	9		11	10										
1	2	3	4	5	6	7	8	9		11	10										
1	2	3	4		6		8	9		7	10	5	11								
	1	2		4	5	6	7		8	10	11				3	9					
1	2	3	4	5	6	7		8	10				11		9						
1		3	4	5	6	7		8	10				11	2	9						
1	2	3		5	6	7		10		11		4			9	8					
1	2	3		5	6	7		10		11		4			9	8					
1	2	3		5		7		10		11		4			9	8	6				
1	2	3		5		7		10		11		4			9	8	6				
1	2	3		5		7		9		11		4			10	8	6				
1	2	3		5		7		9		11		4			10	8	6				
1	2	3		5		7		9		11		4			10	8	6				
1	2	3		5		7		9		11		4			10	8	6				
1	2	3	9	5		7						4	11		10	8	6				
1	2	3		5		7			8			4	11		10	9	6				
1	2	3		5		7		9		11		4			10	8	6				
1	2	3		5		7		9		11		4			10	8	6				
1	2	3			5	7				11	10	4			9	8	6				
1	2	3			5	7		9		11		4			10	8	6				
1	2		9		5	7						4	11	3	10	8	6				
1	2	3			6	7					10	5	11		9	8		4			
1	2	3		5	6	7					10	4	11		9	8					
	2	3		5		7		9		11		4			10	8	6		1		
1	2	3		5		7		9		11		4			10	8	6				
1	2	3		5	6	7		9		11		4			10	8					
1	2			5	6	7				11	10	4		3	9	8					
1	2				6	7				11	10	4			9	8	5			3	
1	2	3		5	6	7				11	10				9	8	4				
1	2	3		5	6					7	10		11		9	8	4				
	2	3		5	6	7				11	10				9	8	4				1
1	2	3		5	6	7		10		11					9	8	4				
1	2	3		5	6	7		9		11					10	8	4				
1	2	3		5	6	7		9		11					10	8	4				
1	2	3		5	6	7		9		11					10	8	4				
1	2	3		5	6	7		9		11					10	8	4				
36	37	34	10	32	26	36	5	27	6	31	11	23	9	4	33	30	24	1	1	1	1
		1	1	5	4	3		8	1	3	5				15	8	1				

Johnson	Collyer	Bulcock	Spottiswood	Hughes	Hanger	Garratt	Woodger	Williams	Lawrence	Davies	Payne	Hatton	Myers	Thompson H.	Woodhouse	Hewitt	Collins J.	Humphreys	Mitchell	Goodhind	Glover
1	2	3			6	7		9	8	11		4			10		5				
1	1	1			1	1		1	1	1		1			1		1				

1911-12

Southern League Division One

Manager: Edmund Goodman

Did you know that?

The Kent Senior Shield Final between Palace and New Brompton (later Gillingham) on 27 November was the first-ever Cup Final that Palace participated in. Palace went on to win 3–1 thanks to a hat-trick from Charlie Woodhouse.

Match No.	Date		Venue	Opponents	Result		Scorers	Attendance
1	Sep	2	H	West Ham United	W	1-0	Williams	14,000
2		9	A	Bristol Rovers	D	0-0		10,000
3		16	H	Swindon Town	D	2-2	Harker, Hewitt	8,000
4		23	A	Northampton Town	D	1-1	Hewitt	9,000
5		30	H	Brighton & Hove Albion	D	1-1	Williams	10,000
6	Oct	7	A	Stoke City	D	1-1	Williams	14,000
7		14	H	Coventry City	W	3-0	Woodhouse 2, Hughes (pen)	10,000
8		21	A	Leyton	W	3-1	Williams, Woodhouse, Davies	3,000
9		28	H	Norwich City	W	6-0	Williams 2, Woodhouse 2, Hewitt 2	5,000
10	Nov	4	A	Luton Town	W	1-0	Woodhouse (pen)	5,000
11		11	A	Southampton	W	4-2	Hewitt, Davies, Williams 2	
12		25	A	Reading	L	0-2		4,000
13	Dec	9	A	New Brompton	D	1-1	Harker	5,000
14		16	H	Exeter City	W	5-0	Williams, Harker, Davies 2, Hewitt	8,000
15		23	A	Brentford	L	0-1		5,000
16		25	A	Queen's Park Rangers	L	2-3	Williams 2	22,000
17		26	H	Queen's Park Rangers	W	3-0	Williams 2, Davies	3,000
18		30	A	West Ham United	W	6-1	Smith 3, Harker 3	3,000
19	Jan	6	H	Bristol Rovers	W	4-1	Harker, Smith 3	5,000
20		20	A	Swindon Town	L	1-2	Smith	6,000
21		27	H	Northampton Town	L	1-2	Smith	10,000
22	Feb	10	H	Stoke City	L	1-2	Smith	10,000
23		17	A	Coventry City	L	2-3	Myers, Smith	5,000
24		24	H	Leyton	D	1-1	Smith	
25		28	H	Plymouth Argyle	L	0-1		
26	Mar	2	A	Norwich City	D	1-1	Bourne	6,000
27		9	H	Luton Town	W	3-1	Smith 2, Williams	10,000
28		16	H	Southampton	W	3-1	Smith 2, Bourne	5,000
29		20	A	Watford	L	0-2		2,000
30		23	A	Plymouth Argyle	L	1-3	Bourne	
31		30	H	Reading	D	1-1	Williams	5,000
32	Apr	5	A	Millwall	L	1-2	Bourne	20,000
33		6	H	Watford	W	2-0	Smith, Hewitt	5,000
34		8	H	Millwall	W	3-0	Davies, Hewitt 2	14,000
35		9	A	Brighton & Hove Albion	L	1-4	Smith	3,000
36		13	H	New Brompton	D	1-1	Smith	6,000
37		20	A	Exeter City	D	1-1	Hewitt	3,000
38		27	H	Brentford	W	2-0	Smith, Garratt	4,000

Final League Position: 7th in Southern League Division One

Appearances
Goals

FA Cup

1	Jan	13	A	Brentford	D	0-0		19,000
R		17	H	Brentford	W	4-0	Smith, Hewitt, Hanger, Harker	9,000
2	Feb	3	H	Sunderland	D	0-0		20,000
R		7	A	Sunderland	L	0-1*		38,000

* After extra-time

Appearances
Goals

Johnson	Collyer	Bulcock	Collins J.	Hughes	Hanger	Garratt	Hewitt	Williams	Woodhouse	Davies	Harker	Myers	Hatton	Beach	Spottiswood	Smith E.	O'Conor	Lawrence	Williamson	Bourne	Boyd	Page
1	2	3	4	5	6	7	8	9	10	11												
1	2	3	4	5	6	7	8	9	10	11												
1	2	3	4	5	6	7	8		10		9	11										
1	2		4	5	6	7	8	9	10			11	3									
	2		4	5	6	7	8	9	10			11	3	1								
1	2	3	4	5	6	7	10	9		11	8											
1	2	3		5	6	7	8	10	9	11					4							
1	2	3		5	6	7	8	10	9	11					4							
1	2	3		5	6	7	8	10	9	11					4							
1	2	3		5	6	7	8	10	9	11					4							
1	2	3		5	6	7	8	10	9	11					4							
1	2	3		5	6	7		10	9	11	8				4							
1	2	3		5	6	7		10		11	8		9		4							
1	2	3		5	6	7	8	9		11	10		4									
1		3		5	6	7	8	9		11	10		2		4							
1	2	3		5	6	7	8	9		11	10				4							
1	2	3		5	6	7	8	9		11	10				4							
1	2	3		5	6	7	8			11	10				4	9						
1		3		5	6	7	8			11	10		2		4	9						
1	2	3		5	6	7	8			11	10				4	9						
1		3		5	6	7	8			11	10		2		4	9						
1	2	3			6		8	10		7		11	5		4	9						
1	2				6	7		10			8	11	5		4	9	3					
1	2			5	6	7	8					11			4	9	3	10				
1	2	3			6	7	8	10				11	5		4	9						
1	2	3			6						8	11	5		4	9			7	10		
1	2				6			8		7		11	5		4	9	3			10		
1	2				6			8		7		11	5		4	9	3			10		
1	2	3			6		8	10		7		11	5		4	9						
1	2	3			6	7		8		11			5		4	9				10		
1	2	3		5	6	7		8		11					4	9				10		
	2	3		5	6	7		8		11					4	9				10	1	
1	2			5		7	8	10		11			6		4	9	3					
1	2			5	6		8	10		11			4		7	9	3					
1	2	3			6		8	10		7			4			9	5			11		
	2			5		7	8			11	10		6	1		9	3					4
	2	3		5	4	7	8	10		11			6	1		9						
1	2	3		5	6	7	8	10		11					4	9						
34	35	29	6	29	36	31	29	30	11	31	15	11	20	3	28	21	8	1	1	7	1	1
				1		1	10	15	6	6	7	1				19				4		

Johnson	Collyer	Bulcock	Collins J.	Hughes	Hanger	Garratt	Hewitt	Williams	Woodhouse	Davies	Harker	Myers	Hatton	Beach	Spottiswood	Smith E.	O'Conor	Lawrence	Williamson	Bourne	Boyd	Page
1	2	3		5	6	7	8			11	10				4	9						
1	2	3		5	6	7	8			11	10				4	9						
1	2	3		5	6	7	8	10		11					4	9						
1	2	3			6		8	10		7		11	5		4	9						
4	4	4		3	4	3	4	2		4	2	1	1		4	4						
					1		1				1					1						

1912-13

Southern League Division One

Manager: Edmund Goodman

Did you know that?

Formed in 1897, Palace's very first rivals were Croydon Common, also of the Southern League. The Robins' fourth ground was the Nest, and they played here from September 1908 until they went bust in March 1917 when they were wound up. Several Palace players also turned out for Croydon Common, including Bob Hewitson, Jack Little, Charles Ryan and Cyril Smith.

Match No.	Date		Venue	Opponents	Result		Scorers	Attendance
1	Sep	4	H	Brentford	W	3-1	Smith, Garratt, Hewitt	6,000
2		7	A	Swindon Town	L	0-1		7,000
3		14	H	Portsmouth	W	2-0	Davies, Smith	8,000
4		18	A	Brentford	L	1-2	Bulcock	4,200
5		21	A	Exeter City	D	1-1	Smith	4,000
6		28	H	West Ham United	D	1-1	Smith	15,000
7	Oct	5	A	Brighton & Hove Albion	W	2-1	Hewitt, Smith (pen)	7,000
8		12	H	Coventry City*	W	3-0	Smith, Hewitt, Davies	9,000
9		19	A	Watford	D	1-1	Williams	4,000
10		26	H	Merthyr Town	W	2-1	York, Hewitt	5,000
11	Nov	2	H	Stoke City	W	1-0	Smith	6,000
12		9	A	Plymouth Argyle	D	0-0		10,000
13		16	H	Southampton	W	8-0	Hewitt 4, Williams 3, York	8,000
14		23	A	Reading	L	0-2		10,000
15		30	H	Norwich City	W	1-0	Smith	6,000
16	Dec	7	A	Gillingham	W	2-1	Smith, Hanger	5,000
17		14	H	Northampton Town	D	2-2	Smith 2 (1 pen)	7,000
18		21	A	Queen's Park Rangers	L	0-2		10,000
19		25	A	Millwall	W	1-0	Hewitt	15,500
20		26	H	Millwall	W	2-0	Smith (pen), Williams	8,000
21		28	H	Swindon Town	W	1-0	Smith	12,000
22	Jan	4	A	Portsmouth	L	0-2		12,000
23		18	H	Exeter City	L	0-1		8,000
24		25	A	West Ham United	D	1-1	Hewitt	14,000
25	Feb	8	H	Brighton & Hove Albion	D	1-1	Smith	13,500
26		15	A	Coventry City	W	2-1	Smith, York	5,000
27	Mar	1	A	Merthyr Town	D	1-1	Hanger	8,000
28		8	A	Stoke City	D	0-0		9,000
29		15	H	Plymouth Argyle	W	1-0	Smith (pen)	10,000
30		21	A	Bristol Rovers	D	2-2	Smith 2	9,000
31		22	A	Southampton	L	0-1		8,000
32		24	H	Bristol Rovers	W	3-0	York, Williams 2	20,000
33		29	H	Reading	W	4-2	Williams, Smith 3	10,000
34	Apr	5	A	Norwich City	D	2-2	Smith, Williams	5,000
35		12	H	Gillingham	L	0-1		8,000
36		19	A	Northampton Town	L	1-2	Smith (pen)	6,000
37		23	H	Watford	W	2-1	Hewitt, Smith	4,000
38		26	H	Queen's Park Rangers +	L	1-2	Smith	6,000

Final League Position: 5th in Southern League Division One — Appearances

* H. Collyer Benefit Match, + J. Johnson Benefit Match — Goals

FA Cup

1	Jan	11	H	Glossop	W	2-0	Smith, Williams	8,000
2	Feb	1	H	Bury	W	2-0	Smith, Davies	13,000
3		22	A	Aston Villa	L	0-5		42,000

Appearances

Goals

Johnson	Collyer	Bulcock	Spottiswood	Hughes	Hanger	Garatt	Hewitt	Smith E.	Williams	Davies	York	Mortimer	Collins J.	Lloyd	Keene	Rev. K. Hunt	O'Conor	Colclough	Bourne	Beach	Whibley	Williamson
1	2	3	4	5	6	7	8	9	10	11												
1	2	3	4	5	6	7	8	9	10	11												
1	2	3	4	5		7	8	9	10	11	6											
1	2	3	4	5		7	8		10	11	6	9										
1	2	3		5		7	8	9		11	6		4	10								
1	2	3	4	5	6	7	8	9						10	11							
1	2	3	4		5	7	8	9	10	11	6											
1	2	3	4	5	6	7	8	9	10	11												
1	2	3	4	5	6	7	8		10	11	9											
1	2	3	4	5		7	8	9		11	10					6						
1	2		4		6	7	8	9		11	10					5	3					
1	2		4	5	6		8		9	11	10			7				3				
1	2	3	4	5	6	7	8		9	11	10											
1	2	3		5	6	7	8		9	11	10					4						
1	2	3	4	5		7	8	9	10	11						6						
1	2	3	4	5	6	7	8	9	10	11												
1	2	3	4		6	7	8	9	10	11						5						
1	2	3		5	6	7		9	8	11	10		4									
1	2	3		5	6	7	8	10	9	11	4											
1	2	3	7	5	6		8	10	9	11	4											
1	2	3		5	6		8	10	9	7	4								11			
1	2	3		5	6		8	10	9	7	4								11			
1	2	3	4	5	6	7	8	9	10	11												
1	2		4	5	6	7	8	9	10	11							3					
1	2	3		5	6	7	8	9		11	10					4						
1	2	3	4	5	6	7	8	9		11	10											
1	3		4	5	6	7	8	9		11	10							2				
1	2		4		5	7	8	9		11	10		6					3				
1	2	3	4		5	7	8	9		11	10		6									
	2	3	4		5	7		9	8	11	10		6							1		
1	2		4		5	7		9	8	11	10		6					3				
1		3	4		6	7		9	8	11	10					5		2				
1	2	3	4		5	7		9	8	11	10		6									
1	3		4		5	7		9	8	11	10		6					2				
1		3	4		5	7		9	8	11	10		6					2				
1		3	4		5	7	8	9	10		6							2			11	
1		3	4	5		7	8	9	10		6							2			11	
1	2	3	4	5	6		8	9	10												11	7
37	34	31	31	26	32	33	31	33	29	34	28	1	9	3	1	7	2	9	2	1	3	1
		1			2	1	11	25	9	2	4											

1	2	3	4	5	6	7	8	9	10	11
1	2	3	4	5	6	7	8	9	10	11
1	2	3	4	5	6	7	8	9	10	11
3	3	3	3	3	3	3	3	3	3	3
								2	1	1

1913-14

Southern League Division One

Manager: Edmund Goodman

Did you know that?

The first known photograph of Palace playing in a different kit to their claret and blue was from the London Challenge Cup Final replay of December 1912 at White Hart Lane. Clad in an all-white strip, they defeated West Ham 1–0 thanks to a goal from Welsh forward Ginger Williams.

Match No.	Date		Venue	Opponents	Result		Scorers	Attendance
1	Sep	4	A	Northampton Town	D	1-1	Williams	5,000
2		6	H	Portsmouth	W	3-1	Hewitt, Smith 2 (1 pen)	5,000
3		13	A	Millwall	D	0-0		28,000
4		17	H	Northampton Town	W	3-0	Smith 2, Williams	5,000
5		20	H	Exeter City	D	0-0		20,000
6		27	A	Cardiff City	W	2-1	Williams, Bateman	15,000
7	Oct	4	H	Swindon Town	L	0-1		16,000
8		11	A	Bristol Rovers	W	1-0	Smith	8,000
9		18	H	Merthyr Town	W	3-1	Smith, Williams, Hewitt	8,000
10		25	A	West Ham United	W	2-1	Williams, Smith	18,000
11	Nov	1	H	Plymouth Argyle	D	2-2	Whibley, Smith	14,000
12		8	A	Southampton	D	2-2	Smith 2 (1 pen)	9,000
13		15	H	Reading	W	5-1	Davies, Smith 2, Keene, Hewitt	12,000
14		22	A	Queen's Park Rangers	L	0-3		10,000
15		29	A	Coventry City	L	0-2		20,000
16	Dec	6	H	Watford	W	3-0	Bright 2, Smith	6,000
17		20	H	Gillingham	W	1-0	Smith	6,000
18		25	A	Southend United	D	3-3	Davies, Bright, Hughes	5,000
19		26	H	Southend United	D	0-0		15,000
20		27	A	Portsmouth	D	1-1	Smith	16,000
21	Jan	3	H	Millwall	W	3-0	Hewitt, Smith 2	12,000
22		17	A	Exeter City	D	1-1	Bright	6,000
23		24	H	Cardiff City	W	4-0	Bright, Smith 2, Davies	
24	Feb	7	A	Swindon Town	W	2-0	Bateman, Bright	3,000
25		14	H	Bristol Rovers	W	5-3	Smith 2, Bright 2, Davies	8,000
26		21	A	Merthyr Town	W	1-0	Smith (pen)	
27		28	H	West Ham United	L	1-2	Smith	15,000
28	Mar	7	A	Plymouth Argyle	D	0-0		10,802
29		14	H	Southampton	D	0-0		
30		21	A	Reading	L	1-2	Davies	7,500
31		28	H	Queen's Park Rangers	W	2-1	Bright, Smith	
32	Apr	2	A	Norwich City	D	0-0		5,000
33		4	H	Coventry City	W	3-1	Whibley, Smith, Hughes	
34		10	A	Brighton & Hove Albion	D	0-0		12,000
35		11	A	Watford	D	1-1	Hughes	5,000
36		13	H	Brighton & Hove Albion	D	0-0		25,000
37		18	H	Norwich City	W	3-0	Hughes, Hewitt 2	9,000
38		25	A	Gillingham	D	1-1	Smith	8,000

Final League Position: 2nd in Southern League Division One

Appearances
Goals

FA Cup

1	Jan	10	H	Norwich City	W	2-1	Hewitt, Smith	8,888
2		31	A	West Ham United	L	0-2		18,000

Appearances
Goals

Johnson	Collyer	Bulcock	Spottiswood	Hughes	Hanger	Davies	Hewitt	Smith E.	Williams	Keene	Colclough	Whitley	Bateman	Wood F.	Rev. K. Hunt	York	Rhodes	Lawrence	Bright	Middleton	Collins J.
1	2	3	4	5	6	7	8	9	10	11											
1		3	4	5	6	7	8	9	10	11	2										
1	2		4	5	6	7	8	9	10		3	11									
1	2		4	5	6	7	8	9	10		3	11									
1	2		4	5	6	11	8	9	10		3		7								
	2		4	5	6	11	8	9	10		3		7	1							
1	2		4	5	6	11	8	9	10		3		7								
1		3	4	5	6		8	9	10		2	11	7								
1	2			5	6		8	9	10		3	11	7		4						
1	2		4	5	6		8	9	10		3	11	7								
1	2		4				8	9	10		3	11	7		5	6					
1			4	5	6	7	8	9		11	3						2	10			
1				5	6	7	8	9	10	11	3				4		2				
1			4	5			8	9	10	11	3		7		6		2				
	2	3	4	5	6	7	8	9	10	11				1							
1	2			5	6	11	8	9			3		7		4				10		
1	2		4	5		11	8	9			3		7		6				10		
1	2		4	5	6	11	8	9			3		7						10		
1	2		4	5	6	11	8	9			3		7						10		
1	2		4	5	6	11	8	9			3		7						10		
1	2			5	6	11	8	9			3		7			4			10		
1	2			5	6	11	8	9			3		7			4			10		
1			4	5		11	8	9			3		7			6	2		10		
1	2		4	5	6	11	8	9			3		7						10		
1	2		4		6	11	8	9			3		7			5			10		
1	2		4	5	6	11	8	9			3		7						10		
1	2		4		6	11	8	9			3		7		5				10		
1	2		4		6	11		9			3		7			5				8	10
1	2				6	11	8	9			3		7		5	4					10
1	2		4		6	11		9			3		7			5				8	10
1	2		4	5	6	11		9			3		7						10		8
1	2		4	5	6	11		9			3		7						10		8
1	2		4	5	6	11		9			3	7	8						10		
	2		4	5	6	11	8	9			3		7	1					10		
1	2		4	5	6	11	8	9					7				3		10		
1	2		4	5	6	11	8	9			3		7						10		
1	2		4	5	6	11	8	9				7				10	3				
1	2		4	5	6	11	8	9			3	7				10					
35	32	4	32	32	34	33	33	38	14	6	34	9	29	3	8	10	6	1	18	2	5
				4		5	6	26	5	1		2	2						9		

Johnson	Collyer	Bulcock	Spottiswood	Hughes	Hanger	Davies	Hewitt	Smith E.	Williams	Keene	Colclough	Whitley	Bateman	Wood F.	Rev. K. Hunt	York	Rhodes	Lawrence	Bright	Middleton	Collins J.
1	2			5	6	11	8	9			3		7			4			10		
1	2		4	5	6	11	8	9			3		7						10		
2	2		1	2	2	2	2	2			2		2			1			2		
							1	1													

1914-15

Southern League Division One

Manager: Edmund Goodman

Did you know that?

Palace were forced to move home in February 1915. After 10 years playing on the two grounds of the Crystal Palace, the outbreak of World War One saw the Admiralty requisition the park for the use of training troops. Forced to move at short notice, the club selected the nearby Herne Hill Stadium as a temporary replacement.

Match No.	Date		Venue	Opponents	Result		Scorers	Attendance
1	Sep	5	A	Bristol Rovers	D	1-1	Collins	4,000
2		10	A	Norwich City	L	1-2	Hewitt	2,000
3		12	H	Brighton & Hove Albion	L	0-2		2,900
4		19	A	Croydon Common	D	1-1	York	8,500
5		26	H	Cardiff City	L	0-2		6,000
6	Oct	3	A	Reading	L	0-3		4,000
7		10	H	Exeter City	D	0-0		4,000
8		17	A	Southampton	W	3-2	Smith 2, York (pen)	
9		24	H	Luton Town	L	2-3	Smith, Whibley	
10		31	A	Northampton Town	L	1-2	Hewitt	7,000
11	Nov	7	H	Portsmouth	W	1-0	Smith	
12		14	A	Watford	L	0-1		4,000
13		21	H	Swindon Town	W	3-1	Smith, Keene 2	6,000
14		28	A	Plymouth Argyle	W	4-1	Smith 3 (1 pen), Middleton	3,000
15	Dec	5	H	Southend United	D	1-1	Middleton	3,000
16		12	A	West Ham United	W	2-1	Middleton, Smith	5,000
17		19	H	Queen's Park Rangers	D	2-2	Hewitt, Smith	3,000
18		25	A	Millwall	D	0-0		20,000
19		26	H	Millwall	L	0-1		9,000
20		28	H	Norwich City	W	2-1	Middleton, Hughes	1,000
21	Jan	2	H	Bristol Rovers	W	1-0	Smith	3,000
22		30	A	Cardiff City	L	0-5		8,000
23	Feb	6	H	Reading	W	4-1	Hooper, Smith 2, Feebery	4,000
24		13	A	Exeter City	D	1-1	Davies	2,000
25		27	A	Luton Town	W	2-1	Smith 2	5,000
26	Mar	3	H+	Southampton	L	1-2	Smith	1,500
27		6	H+	Northampton Town	D	1-1	Lane	3,000
28		10	H+	Croydon Common	L	1-5	Smith (pen)	
29		13	A	Portsmouth	L	0-1		6,000
30		20	H+	Watford	L	0-1		
31		27	A	Swindon Town	L	2-5	Hughes, Smith	
32	Apr	2	A	Gillingham	L	0-3		
33		3	H+	Plymouth Argyle	W	2-1	Middleton, Davies	2,000
34		5	H+	Gillingham	W	1-0	Lane	
35		10	A	Southend United	W	3-2	Lane, Hewitt, Smith	3,000
36		17	H+	West Ham United	W	2-1	Lane 2	3,000
37		24	A	Queen's Park Rangers	L	2-3	Hooper, Smith	4,000
38	May	1	A	Brighton & Hove Albion	L	0-1		2,000

Final League Position: 15th in Southern League Division One — Appearances

+ Played at Herne Hill — Goals

FA Cup

1	Jan	9	A	Birmingham City	D	2-2	Davies, Middleton	18,000
R		16	A+	Birmingham City	L	0-3*		17,000

+ Played at St Andrew's at Crystal Palace request * After extra-time — Appearances

Goals

Johnson	Collyer	Colclough	Spottiswood	Hughes	Hanger	Bateman	Hewitt	Collins J.	Hooper	Davies	York	Smith E.	Whibley	Shaw	Michael	Feebery	Bradley	Middleton	Keene	Lane	Bowler	Sanders
1	2	3	4	5	6	7	8	9	10	11												
1	2	3	4	5	6	7	8		10	11	9											
1	2	3	4	5	6	7	8				10	9	11									
1	2	3	4	5	6	7			8	11	10	9										
	2	3	4	5	6	7	8	9		11	10			1								
	2	3		5	6	7	8			11			10	1	4	9						
	2	3	4	5	6	7	8				10	9	11	1								
		3	4	5	6		8			11	10	9	7	1			2					
1		3	4		6		8			11	10	9	7			5	2					
1	2	3	4	5	6		8			7	10	9	11									
1	2	3	4	5	6		8			7	10	9	11									
1	2	3	4	5	6		8					9	7					10	11			
1	2	3	4	5	6	7	8					9						10	11			
1	2	3	4	5	6		8			7		9						10	11			
1	2	3	4	5	6	7	8					9						10	11			
1	2	3	4	5	6		8			7		9						10	11			
1	2	3	4	5			8			7		9				6		10	11			
1	2	3	4	5			8			7		9				6		10	11			
1	2	3	4	5			8			7	11	9				6		10				
1	2	3	4	5			8			7	11	9				6		10				
1	2	3	4						8	11	5	9				6		10		7		
1		3	4				8	6		7	2	9				5		10	11			
1		3	4						8	11	5	9				6		10		7	2	
1	2	3						4	8	11	5	9				6		10		7		
1	2	3	4	5					8	11		9				6		10		7		
1	2	3	4	5					10	11		9				6				7		8
1	2	3	4	5			8		10	11		9				6				7		
1	2	3	4						10	11	5	9				6		8		7		
1	2	3	4	5			8		10	11		9				6				7		
1	2	3	4	5			8	10	11	7		9				6						
1	2	3	4	5					8	11		9				6		10		7		
1	2	3	4	5			8			11		9				6		10		7		
	2	3	4	5			8			11		9		1		6		10		7		
	2	3	4	5			8		10	11		9		1		6				7		
1	2	3	4	5			8		10	11		9				6				7		
1	2	3	4	5			8		10	11						6		9		7		
1	2	3	4	5					10	11		9				6		8		7		
1	2	3	4	5					10	11	8					6		9		7		

32	34	38	36	32	16	9	28	5	18	33	17	32	8	6	1	24	2	21	8	16	1	1
				2			4	1	2	2	2	20	1			1		5	2	5		

1	2	3	4				8			7	5	9				6		10	11			
1		3	4				8				5	9	7			6		10	11		2	
2	1	2	2				2			1	2	2	1			2		2	2		1	
										1								1				

1915-16

London Combination

Manager: Edmund Goodman

Did you know that?

Local amateur forward Sidney Sanders, who played for Palace during the World War One years, holds the first record for the number of goals scored by a Palace player in one game. He bagged himself six as Palace recorded a 10–1 victory over Reading at Herne Hill on 4 March.

Match No.	Date		Venue	Opponents	Result		Scorers	Attendance
1	Sep	4	A	Croydon Common	L	1-2	Lawrence	3,000
2		11	H	Arsenal	W	3-1	Whitworth 2, Lawrence	3,500
3		18	A	Brentford	L	0-1		2,500
4		25	H	West Ham United	W	2-0	Whitworth 2	2,500
5	Oct	2	A	Tottenham Hotspur	W	4-2	Sanders 2, York, Poulton	1,800
6		9	H	Chelsea	L	1-5	Rogers	4,200
7		16	H	Queen's Park Rangers	W	1-0	Marsh	1,800
8		23	A	Fulham	L	0-5		5,000
9		30	H	Clapton Orient	L	1-2	own-goal (Dunn)	1,200
10	Nov	6	A	Watford	L	1-7	Green	2,000
11		13	H	Croydon Common	W	4-2	Sanders, Fordham, Lockton, Keene	600
12		20	A	Arsenal	D	2-2	Lockton, Sanders	5,000
13		27	H	Brentford	W	1-0	Hughes	400
14	Dec	4	A	West Ham United	L	1-3	Fordham	3,000
15		11	H	Tottenham Hotspur	W	4-2	Lockton 3, Fordham	400
16		18	A	Chelsea	L	1-6	Sanders	
17		25	H	Millwall	L	0-1		
18		27	A	Millwall	L	1-4	Lockton	
19	Jan	1	A	Queen's Park Rangers	L	1-5	Rogers	1,000
20		8	H	Fulham	D	2-2	Keene, Sanders	800
21		15	A	Clapton Orient	W	3-2	Sanders 3	
22		22	H	Watford	D	1-1	Dobson	

Final League Position: 9th in London Combination (Principal Comp.) Appearances

1 own-goal Goals

Supplementary Tournament

Match No.	Date		Venue	Opponents	Result		Scorers	Attendance
1	Feb	5	H	Millwall	L	1-5	Sanders	2,600
2		12	A	Chelsea	W	1-0	Keene	10,000
3		19	H	Watford	W	1-0	Gilboy	500
4	Mar	4	H	Reading	W	10-1	Sanders 6, Gilboy 2, Keene, Marsh	
5		11	A	Clapton Orient	W	5-1	Sanders, Lockton 2, Martin, Keene	
6		18	H	Chelsea	W	4-2	Lockton 3, Gilboy	5,000
7		25	A	Watford	L	0-4		
8	Apr	1	H	Brentford	W	6-3	Booth 2, Martin, Keene 3	
9		8	A	Reading	D	1-1	Sanders	
10		15	H	Clapton Orient	W	2-1	own-goal (Redward), Sanders	
11		21	A	Tottenham Hotspur	L	1-3	Hughes	10,000
12		22	H	Tottenham Hotspur	W	4-0	Keene 2, Gilboy, Marsh	10,000
13		29	A	Millwall	D	2-2	Nicol, Cracknell	7,000
14	May	6	A	Brentford	L	3-6	Shields, Keene, Lawrence	1,200

Final League Position: 6th in London Combination (Supplementary Comp.) Appearances

1 own-goal Goals

Bennett	Collyer	Colclough	Spottiswood	York	Smart	Gilboy	Sanders	Lawrence	Marsh	James	Fisher	Hughes	Whitworth	Dawson	Booth	Martin	Poulton	Rogers J.	Hart	Jones A.	Gren	Fordham	Lockton	Keene	Bowring	Johnson	Thompson	Shilds T.	Feebery	Dobson	Keeble	Griffiths	Page	Davies	Rogers E.	Siggs	Jamieson	Smith	Millett	Brown	Nicol S.	Elrick	Cracknell	Drummond	Hill	Swales		
1	2	3	4	5	6	7	8	9	10	11																																					
1		3		6		7	8	10	4		2	5	9	11																																	
1		3				7	8	10			2	5		11	4	6	9																														
1		3				7	8	10	11		2	5	9		4	6																																
1		3		6		7	8	10			2	5			4		9	11																														
1		3		6		7	8	10	4		2	5	9					11																														
1	3		4	6		7	8	10	9	11	2	5																																				
1	3		4			7		11	6		2	5	9				8		10																												
1		3	4	6		7	8	10	11		2	5					9																															
	2	1		3		7	8	6	4	11		5								9	10																										
1		3		4		7	8		6		2	5										9	10	11																								
1		3		9	6	7	8		11		2	5											10		4																						
		3			6	7	8				2	5											10	11	4	1	9																				
1		3		4		7	8		6		2	5										9	10	11																								
1		3			6	7	8		4		2	5										9	10	11																								
	2				4	7	11		9			5											10			1		3	6	8																	
1					4	7	8				2	5											10								3	6	9	11													
						7																	10																									
						7	8		6			2										10	11	4	1						3		5		9													
			4			7	8					5										10	11		1		3			6					2	9											
1	3					7	8		10			5						9						11							6	4				2											
1		3				7	8					5											10	11	4			2		9	6																
16	6	14	5	10	6	22	20	10	15	3	14	20	4	2	3	2	4	3	1	1	1	3	11	8	4	4	1	3	1	2	5	2	2	1	1	2	1										
				1			9	2	1			1	4				1	1			1	3	6	2						1					1												

Bennett	Collyer	Colclough	Spottiswood	York	Smart	Gilboy	Sanders	Lawrence	Marsh	James	Fisher	Hughes	Whitworth	Dawson	Booth	Martin	Poulton	Rogers J.	Hart	Jones A.	Gren	Fordham	Lockton	Keene	Bowring	Johnson	Thompson	Shilds T.	Feebery	Dobson	Keeble	Griffiths	Page	Davies	Rogers E.	Siggs	Jamieson	Smith	Millett	Brown	Nicol S.	Elrick	Cracknell	Drummond	Hill	Swales		
		3				7	8		6			5						9						10		4	1						2		11															
		3				7	8					5											10	11		1		2			6	4						9											
		3				7	8		4			5											10	11		1		2			6								9										
		3				7	8		9			5											10	11		1		2			6	4																
		3					8		7			5				9							10	11		1		2			6	4																
		3				7	8					5											10	11		1		2			6	4										9								
		3				7	8		4			5				10				11						1		2			6											9								
		3			6	7	8					5			9	10								11		1		2			4																	
		3				7	8	9				5												11		1		2			6	4										10							
		3			4	7	8	10	9			5												11		1		2			6																	
		3					8					5			9													2			6										11	1	4	7	10			
		3			4	7	8		9			5			10								11		1		2			6																	
		3			2		8		4															11		1					6	5										9		10	7					
							8	9	5			3												11		1		2			6													10	7		4		
		13			4	10	14	3	9			13			3	3		1		1			6	11	1	13		12			14	6	1					1	1	2	3	1	3	3	1	1		
						5	10	1	2			1			2	2								5	9				1														1		1					

1916-17

London Combination

Manager: Edmund Goodman

Did you know that?

Lt Donald Simpson Bell, who was killed in action in July 1916 during World War One and posthumously awarded the Victoria Cross, played for Palace reserves during 1907–08.

Match No.	Date		Venue	Opponents	Result		Scorers	Attendance
1	Sep	2	H	Brentford	W	4-0	W. Johnson 4	650
2		9	A	Chelsea	L	1-4	Lockton	9,000
3		16	H	Arsenal	W	1-0	Hughes	3,000
4		23	A	Luton Town	L	1-3	W. Johnson	
5		30	H	Reading	W	5-3	Lawrence 2, Gilboy, Shields, Hughes	1,500
6	Oct	7	A	Millwall	L	2-3	Keene, Fox	5,000
7		14	H	Watford	L	0-1		1,000
8		21	A	Clapton Orient	D	2-2	R. Shields 2	3,000
9		28	H	Fulham	W	1-0	Driver	1,500
10	Nov	4	A	Queen's Park Rangers	L	0-1		1,500
11		11	H	West Ham United	L	1-8	Beech	2,000
12		18	A	Tottenham Hotspur	L	1-3	R. Shields	1,500
13		25	A	Brentford	L	1-3	own-goal (Rhodes)	
14	Dec	2	H	Chelsea	D	1-1	R. Shields	1,000
15		9	A	Arsenal	W	2-1	Peach, Elkington	4,000
		16	H	Luton Town	Not Played			
16		23	A	Portsmouth	D	2-2	Burton, Keene	
17		25	H	Southampton	D	2-2	R. Shields, Keene	
18		26	A	Southampton	D	2-2	Gilboy, Keene	5,000
19		30	H	Millwall	D	1-1	Dunk	1,000
20	Jan	6	A	Watford	D	2-2	R. Shields 2	800
21		13	H	Clapton Orient	W	3-0	Sanders, Hughes, R. Shields	
22		20	A	Fulham	L	3-4	Sanders, Hughes, Whalley	
23		27	H	Queen's Park Rangers	W	4-0	Sanders 2, Beech 2	1,500
24	Feb	3	A	West Ham United	L	0-1		3,000
25		10	H	Tottenham Hotspur	L	0-1		2,000
26		17	H	Clapton Orient	W	3-0	R. Shields, Fenwick, Beech	
27		24	A	Tottenham Hotspur	L	1-4	Ritchie	5,000
28	Mar	3	H	West Ham United	W	3-1	Beech 2, Keene	5,000
29		10	A	Queen's Park Rangers	L	2-3	McGinn, R. Shields	
30		17	H	Arsenal	W	1-0	Dunk	2,500
31		24	H	Southampton	W	4-2	Lockton 2, R. Shields, Keene	2,000
32		31	A	Clapton Orient	W	4-1	Lockton 2, Ritchie, Lancaster	
33	Apr	6	A	Portsmouth	W	2-1	York, Booth	4,000
34		7	H	Tottenham Hotspur	L	0-3		5,000
35		9	H	Portsmouth	L	2-3	Hewitt 2	
36		14	A	West Ham United	L	1-2	Lancaster	7,000
37		21	H	Queen's Park Rangers	W	3-0	Hill, Keene, R. Shields	
38		28	A	Arsenal	L	0-4		4,500
	May	5	A	Southampton	Not Played			

Final League Position: 8th in London Combination

		Appearances
	1 own-goal	Goals

Johnson J.	Shields T.	Colclough	Griffiths	Hughes	Keeble	Fox	Sanders	Johnson W.	Lockton	Keene	Yenson	Gilboy	Shields R.	Lawrence	Robson	Spottiswood	Langford	Mackintosh	Niblo	Marsh	Driver	Jameson	Beech	Whalley	Leese	Albrighton	Bollington	Bradshaw	Jackson	McGill	Bailey	Bartlett	Dunk	Quinn	Dodd	Elkington	Bennett	Hawkins	McCullum	Burton	Smart	Elerick	Ritchie	Elrick	Rogers E.	Pearson	Alderson	Green C.	Gilbert	Norman	Nicol S.	Alborough	Mayo	Curtis	Hunt Rev. K.	Fenwick	Hill	Champion	Bateman	Green	Maskey	Berrington	Philpott	Lancaster	Gates	Newell	Swales	York	Booth	Luckie	Nicholas	Baptist	Hewitt	Suttie	Cracknell
1	2	3	4	5	6	7	8	9	10	11																																																																	
1	2	3		5	6		8		10	11	4	7	9																																																															
1	2	3		5	6	7	8			11	4		9	10																																																												
1	2	3	4	5	10	7	8	9		11	6																																																													
1	2	3		5	6		8			11	4	7	9	10																																																											
1		3		5	6	7				11		8	9	10	2	4																																																									
1		3		5	11						6	7	9	10	2	4	8																																																								
1	2	3		5	6		8				4	7	9					10	11																																																							
1	2	3		5	6					11			9					10		4	7	9																																																				
1	3				6	7				11	5		9		2		4		10				8																																																			
1		3		5	6	7	8						9		2		4						10	11																																																		
	2		4			7							9												1	3	5	6	8	10	11																																												
1	2			5	6	7					4		9						11										8			3	10																																										
1	2			5	3	8				11		7	9							4										10				6																																									
1				5	3		8			11	4								10	6			9												2	7																																							
	2			5	3					11			9						10															6			1	4	7	8																																					
1	2			5	3					11		7	8																			6									4	9	10																																
	2			5	3					11		7	9																			6											10	1	4	8																														
				5	3		8		9	11	2																4						7												6		1	10																												
	2			5						11			9						10							3	4																				1		6	7	8																									
	2			5	3		8			11			9																																	1	10				4	6	7																						
	2			5	3		8			11			9							7				10			4					6												1																															
	2			5			8			11			10						7				9				4								3									1											6																				
	3			5	6		8			11		7	10							4			9												2									1																															
	2			5			8			11			9						7								4								3											1								6	10																			
	2			5						11			8										10				4								3									1											6	9	7																		
	2			5	4					11			8																						3								10	1											6	9		7																	
	2			5	6					11			8										9				4			10					3											1												7																
	2			5	6	7				11			8										9				4			10					3																								1															
	2			5	4				10	11			8										9										7		3																									1	6													
				5	3				10	11			9														4								2					6									8							7							1												
	2			5	6				10	11			9														4								3							8	1																					7											
				5																																				6			1																					7	2	3	4	8	9	10	11					
	2			5	6				10	11			4										9												3																					7															1	8		
																																																																					8		
				5	6				10	11			9																						2					4		8	1																					7										3	
	8			5	3				10	11			9														4								2								1													7																		6
				5	3				10	11			9																				7		2								1													8										4								6
15	28	10	3	35	31	10	14	2	10	31	10	9	32	4	4	2	3	2	8	5	1	1	10	2	1	2	12	1	2	4	1	4	4	2	15	1	1	1	1	1	4	1	5	11	2	1	5	2	1	1	2	1	1	1	4	3	5	1	1	1	1	1	1	3	1	1	2	1	1	1	1	1	2	1	2
				4		1	4	5	5	7		2	13	2							1		7							1			2			1				1			2													1	1								2				1	1				2		

1917-18

London Combination

Manager: Edmund Goodman

Did you know that?

Forward Ted Smith, who was at Palace for 10 seasons, holds Palace's record for the most number of goals scored in the Southern League, 113. Ted also scored in over 60 per cent of the games he played.

Match No.	Date		Venue	Opponents	Result		Scorers	Attendance
1	Sep	1	H	Tottenham Hotspur	L	2-4	Whitworth, Sanders	2,000
2		8	A	Fulham	L	1-7	Hill	4,500
3		15	H	Chelsea	L	0-3		3,500
4		22	A	Queen's Park Rangers	L	1-4	Keene	
5		29	H	Brentford	W	4-0	Keene 2, York, Slade	
6	Oct	6	A	Clapton Orient	W	3-2	Sanders, Gilboy, Whitworth	2,000
7		13	H	Arsenal	W	2-0	Sanders, Lowe	7,000
8		20	A	Millwall	L	1-2	Gilboy	
9		27	A	Tottenham Hotspur	L	0-1		5,000
10	Nov	3	H	Fulham	W	2-1	Slade, York	1,200
11		10	A	Chelsea	W	1-0	Slade	5,000
12		17	H	Queen's Park Rangers	W	4-1	Slade, Hughes, Hill, Keene	
13		24	A	Brentford	L	0-3		3,000
14	Dec	1	H	Clapton Orient	W	3-1	Gibbs, Hughes, York	
15		8	A	Arsenal	W	2-0	Slade, Smart	3,500
16		15	H	Millwall	L	1-5	Martin	
17		22	H	Tottenham Hotspur	L	2-3	York, Smart	4,000
18		25	A	West Ham United	L	1-2	Slade	7,000
19		26	H	West Ham United	W	4-0	Gibbs, Smart, Slade, Cracknell	5,000
20		29	A	Fulham	D	1-1	Piggott	3,000
21	Jan	5	H	Chelsea	D	0-0		6,000
22		12	A	Queen's Park Rangers	L	1-2	Cartwright	
23		19	H	Brentford	L	3-4	Wiggins, Keene, Martin	
24		26	A	Clapton Orient	D	0-0		1,500
25	Feb	2	H	Arsenal	L	1-4	Slade	3,500
26		9	H	West Ham United	D	1-1	Keene	4,000
27		16	A	Tottenham Hotspur	L	0-8		7,000
28		23	H	Fulham	W	5-2	Jameson 2, Hughes, Slade, Cartwright	3,000
29	Mar	2	A	Chelsea	L	0-2		7,000
30		9	H	Queen's Park Rangers	L	0-2		
31		16	A	Brentford	W	2-0	Jameson, York	
32		23	H	Clapton Orient	W	3-1	Gibbs 2, Slade	
33		29	A	Millwall	W	3-1	Dunk 2, Jameson	
34		30	A	Arsenal	L	0-3		800
35	Apr	1	H	Millwall	L	0-2		
36		6	A	West Ham United	L	0-11		4,000

Final League Position: 7th in London Combination

Appearances
Goals

War Fund Matches

No.	Date		Venue	Opponents	Result		Scorers	Attendance
1	Apr	13	A	Queen's Park Rangers	L	1-2	Armstrong	1,500
2		20	H	Queen's Park Rangers	W	3-1	Lancaster, Whitworth, Dunk	
3		27	H	Clapton Orient	W	2-0	Dunk, Jameson	
4	May	4	A	Clapton Orient	W	2-0	Cartwright, Lancaster	

Appearances
Goals

McKee	Dodd	Bulcock	Luckie	Hughes	Keeble	Bateman	Sanders	Whitworth	Mullaney	Keene	Spottiswood	Martin	Hill	Moule	Hudspeth	Nichol	Cracknell	Chesser	Smith	Smart	Broad	Walker	York	Slade	Watts	Bollington	Bradley	Gilboy	Lowe	Harvey	Pertland	Norman	Little	Isley	Gates	Cartwright	Lancaster	Gwilliam	Rollaston	Griffiths	Fox	Goldie	Piggott	Tanner	Gibbs	Arnold	Baker	Crisp	Wiggins	Rae	Fergus	Busby	Blain	Jameson	Mowbray	Beston	Evans	Cushway	Thompson	Nicholl C.	Dunk	Pearson	Rogers J.	Emmeson	Stansfield	Armstrong	Harris	Scott	Buttesby	Stephenson
1	2	3	4	5	6	7	8	9	10	11																																																													
1	2			5	3	7		9		11	4	6	8	10																																																							
1	2				4	7		9		11			8		3	5	6	10																																																				
1	2			5	3	9				11			8					10	4	6	7																																																		
	2			5	4					11			7		3		6			10		1	8	9																																														
	2			5	3	7	8	9									6									1	4	10	11																																										
	2			5	4	7	8	9								3		6					1	10						11																																								
	3			5	2		10			7							6			4								11		1	8	9																																					
				5	2		8			11						6									9				7		1		10	3	4																																			
				5						11					3	4				6			10	9				8		1					2	7																																	
				5	3		10								2	6	4			8		1	9													7	11																																
				5	2	7				11												1	4	9												10																																	
				5	2					11														9						1								3	4	6	7	8	10																												
				5						11					3		6						9							1						7				4			8	2	10																								
				5	4					11					3		6			10		1	8	9				7																		2																										
	2			5	6	7	8			11		9																		10		1																3		4																								
	2			5	3		7					11					6			8		1	9																							10		4																						
																								9																																																
																		6			8				9																						10																								
	3				4		10								2					8		1		9		6									5	7							11																												
	2			5	6	7	8								3		10					1	9													11										4																								
	2			5		7										3		6			8		1	10	9												11										4																								
	2				3					11		9															1	5						10		4									8					6	7																				
	2				4	7				11		10														1	5								9									8	3				6																					
	3					7	8			11							6						9		5								4																		1	2	10																	
	2									11														9		6								4												3					7	1		10	5	8																
						7				11														9		4													2		5													10		8	1	3	6													
	2			5										3		6					1	10	8													11										4		7					9																	
				5	3					7			11		2								8	10																		4							6			1				9																	
	2			5		7																			8		6								4										10							1				9				3	11											
				5	2										3		6					1	10												11										4		7					9						8										
				5		7				11					3		4							8																		6					10					1	2			9																	
																																																								9							8									
	2				4					11					3							1														7									10		5																			6	8	9						
	2														3																																			1																					
	2				4					11					3																					8									6					7	1		10	5	9																	
4	22	1	1	23	23	15	11	5	1	22	1	5	5	1	17	4	16	2	1	10	1	12	13	17	3	8	1	6	1	6	1	3	1	7	2	10	1	2	1	5	1	1	6	6	5	1	7	2	5	7	2	4	2	9	1	1	1	1	1	1	1	1	1	1						
				3			3	2		6		2	2				1			3			5	10				2	1							2							1		4				1					4							2									

McKee	Dodd	Bulcock	Luckie	Hughes	Keeble	Bateman	Sanders	Whitworth	Mullaney	Keene	Spottiswood	Martin	Hill	Moule	Hudspeth	Nichol	Cracknell	Chesser	Smith	Smart	Broad	Walker	York	Slade	Watts	Bollington	Bradley	Gilboy	Lowe	Harvey	Pertland	Norman	Little	Isley	Gates	Cartwright	Lancaster	Gwilliam	Rollaston	Griffiths	Fox	Goldie	Piggott	Tanner	Gibbs	Arnold	Baker	Crisp	Wiggins	Rae	Fergus	Busby	Blain	Jameson	Mowbray	Beston	Evans	Cushway	Thompson	Nicholl C.	Dunk	Pearson	Rogers J.	Emmeson	Stansfield	Armstrong	Harris	Scott	Buttesby	Stephenson
	5				6					11																									4									8	3						1											2			7	9	10			
				5				9								3					6		1	2													11	7											4																	10							8		
	3				6											2							1				5								4		11																			9								10							8	7	
				5				9								3							1											4	2	11	7										6																						8		10
	2			2	2			2		1					3					1		3	1			1									3	1	3	2						1	1			2			1				1						2	1			1	1	1	3	1	1
								1																															1	2																		1								2					1				

1918-19

London Combination

Manager: Edmund Goodman

Did you know that?

After moving in, Palace's first game at the Nest was a friendly against Millwall in August 1918, which they won 4–1. Palace had twice been offered the use of the Den as their new home by Millwall – once before moving to Herne Hill, and then again before settling on Croydon Common's former ground, The Nest.

Match No.	Date		Venue	Opponents	Result		Scorers	Attendance
1	Sep	7	A	Clapton Orient	W	2-1	Howarth 2	2,000
2		14	H	Queen's Park Rangers	W	4-2	Keene 3, Turner	2,000
3		21	A	Millwall	W	2-0	Whitworth 2	3,000
4		28	H	Fulham	W	1-0	Beech	5,000
5	Oct	5	A	Brentford	W	3-2	Keene, Dunk 2	3,000
6		12	H	West Ham United	D	0-0		4,000
7		19	A	Tottenham Hotspur	L	0-2		10,000
8		26	H	Arsenal	W	2-1	Keene, Dunk	5,000
9	Nov	2	H	Clapton Orient	W	6-1	Bird 2, Keene, Beech, Whitworth 2	
10		9	A	Queen's Park Rangers	L	2-3	Whitworth, Bates	
11		16	H	Millwall	D	2-2	Beech, Castle	4,000
12		23	A	Fulham	L	1-5	Beech	6,000
13		30	H	Brentford	L	0-4		6,000
14	Dec	7	A	West Ham United	L	0-2		10,000
15		14	H	Tottenham Hotspur	W	6-3	Whitworth 5, Cartwright	2,500
16		21	A	Arsenal	D	3-3	Stephenson, Cartwright, Lockton	9,000
17		25	A	Chelsea	W	2-0	Stephenson, Whitworth	10,000
18		26	H	Chelsea	D	0-0		12,000
19		28	A	Clapton Orient	W	4-0	Lockton, Whitworth 2, Cartwright	7,000
20	Jan	4	H	Queen's Park Rangers	L	0-2		6,000
21		11	A	Millwall	L	1-2	York	9,000
22		18	H	Fulham	L	1-4	Beech	6,000
23		25	A	Brentford	L	1-6	Bateman	
24	Feb	1	H	West Ham United	W	3-0	Smith 3	4,000
25		8	A	Tottenham Hotspur	L	2-4	Beech, Whitworth	14,000
26		15	H	Chelsea	W	1-0	Humphries	15,000
27		22	H	Clapton Orient	W	4-1	Humphries, Whitworth 2, Smith	5,000
28	Mar	1	A	Queen's Park Rangers	L	2-3	Humphries, own-goal (Draper)	9,000
29		8	H	Millwall	L	1-4	Humphries	10,000
30		15	A	Fulham	D	1-1	Smith	15,000
31		22	H	Brentford	L	2-3	Bateman, Kimpton	10,000
32		29	A	West Ham United	W	3-1	Smith, Whitworth 2	10,000
33	Apr	5	H	Tottenham Hotspur	D	2-2	Edmonds, Smith	10,000
34		12	A	Chelsea	L	0-3		12,000
35		18	H+	Arsenal	L	0-3		20,000
36		21	A	Arsenal	L	2-3	Smith 2	10,000

Final League Position: 7th in London Combination — Appearances

+ Played at The Den — 1 own-goal — Goals

London Victory Cup

	Date		Venue	Opponents	Result		Scorers	Attendance
	Feb	17	H	Brentford	W	1-0	Stephenson	
	Apr	19	N+	Chelsea	L	0-4		22,000

+ Played at Highbury — Appearances

Goals

Rae	McDonald	Males	Isley	Lewis	Whitelum	Turner	Howarth	Whitworth	Beech	Keene	Blackwell	Tanner	Blain	Bates	Jameson	Keeble	Castle	Sanders	Dunk	Aiken	Turner Pte	Stevens	Callendine	Whitehouse	Dunn	York	Richardson	Fenwick	Bird	Boxley	Broad	Stansfield	Theobald	Langley	Wilson	Jones	Fergus	Walford	Walker	Hudspeth	Gates	Lancaster	Stephenson	Lockton	Cartwright	Bollington	Bateman	Hudson	Bennett	Little	Humphries	Winspear	Cripps	Alderson	Weston	Shields T.	Hughes	Booth	Smith E.	Sifto	Cracknell	White	Gregory	Bartlett	Bee	Kimpton	Edmonds	Fisher	Gilboy	Lamb				
1	2	3	4	5	6	7	8	9	10	11																																																															
	2		4	10		7			9	11	1	3	5	6	8																																																												
	2		4					9	10	11	1	3		5		6	7	8																																																							
	2		4		6				9	11	1			5	8	3			7	10																																																						
	2		4		6		9		10	11				5	8	3			7		1																																																					
	2		4		6				9	11	1			5	8	3			7			10																																																				
	2		7				9		10	11	1			5	8	3								4	6																																																	
1	2		4						10	11				9		6			7						3	5	8																																														
1	2		4					9	10	11				5					7							3		6	8																																												
	2		4					9	10	11				5		3			8							6				1	7																																										
	2		4						9		1	3		5		6	8															7	10	11																																							
	2				6				10	11	1			5		3	9												8		7				4																																						
1	2				6		9		10	11		3		5																8		7					4																																					
	2			8			9		7		1			5			10											4			11						3	6																																			
								9						5												6											2		1	3	4	7	8	10	11																												
								9						5												6		4									2		1	3		7	8	10	11																												
								9						5												6		4									2		1	3		7	8	10	11																												
								9						5		6																				2		1	3			8	10	11	4	7																										
								9						5												6												1	3		7	8	10	11	4		2																									
										11				5	8											6					7									3				10		4			1	2	8																							
									8	11				10		3			9							5					7															4		2	1			6																					
			4						9						10	3		8								5					7																	2	1			6	11																				
								9	8																	6					7													10		4	11								1	2	3	5																
								8							5		3			11																											6	7	2			10			1				4	9															
								9	8					5		3			11																												7	2			10			1				4		6													
														5					11																					3							7	2			10			1				4	9		6	8											
								8							5																																7	2			10			1				4	9			11	3	6									
																																															7	2			10			1				4	9	6		11	3	5	8								
														5		3			11																												7	2			10			1				4		6		8				9							
														5																																	7	3		2	10			1				4	9	6		11				8							
																																															7	3		2				1			5	4	9	6		11				8	10						
								9																																							7							1			5	4	8	6		11		3			10	2					
														5																																	7							1				4	9	6				3		6	10	2	11				
																																															7	3		2				1			5	4	9	11				6		8	10						
			4																																												7	3		2	10			1			5		9	6		11				8							
														5																																	7	3							1				4	9	6		11				8	10	2					
4	14	1	13	3	6	2	5	14	18	14	8	4	1	28	7	15	4	2	11	1	1	1	1	1	1	11	1	4	3	1	8	1	1	1	1	1	5	1	5	7	1	4	5	7	5	6	15	14	3	5	9	2	1	14	1	1	5	12	11	10	1	9	2	5	1	6	6	3	1					
						1	2	18	6	6				1			1		3							1			2														2	2	3		2				4								9								1	1								

Rae	McDonald	Males	Isley	Lewis	Whitelum	Turner	Howarth	Whitworth	Beech	Keene	Blackwell	Tanner	Blain	Bates	Jameson	Keeble	Castle	Sanders	Dunk	Aiken	Turner Pte	Stevens	Callendine	Whitehouse	Dunn	York	Richardson	Fenwick	Bird	Boxley	Broad	Stansfield	Theobald	Langley	Wilson	Jones	Fergus	Walford	Walker	Hudspeth	Gates	Lancaster	Stephenson	Lockton	Cartwright	Bollington	Bateman	Hudson	Bennett	Little	Humphries	Winspear	Cripps	Alderson	Weston	Shields T.	Hughes	Booth	Smith E.	Sifto	Cracknell	White	Gregory	Bartlett	Bee	Kimpton	Edmonds	Fisher	Gilboy	Lamb				
								8						5					11																				1	3			10				7	2												4	9	6															
																																															7	3				10			1			5	4	8	6						9		2		11				
								1						1					1																				1	1			1				2	2				1			1			1	2	2	2						1		1		1				
																																												1																																

1919-20

Southern League Division One

Manager: Edmund Goodman

Did you know that?

As well as holding the distinction of being a man of the cloth, the Revd Kenneth Hunt, who featured for Palace over a period of several seasons, was an England international and British Olympic athlete who won a gold medal. He later wrote a book on how to play association football, and won an FA Cup medal with Wolves.

Match No.	Date		Venue	Opponents	Result		Scorers	Attendance
1	Aug	30	H	Northampton Town	D	2-2	Middleton, Whibley	
2	Sep	3	A	Portsmouth	D	0-0		
3		6	A	Watford	L	1-4	Whibley	
4		10	H	Portsmouth	W	2-1	Middleton, E. Smith	
5		13	A	Southend United	D	1-1	E. Smith	
6		20	H	Norwich City	W	3-1	Conner 2, E. Smith	
7		27	A	Brentford	D	0-0		
8	Oct	4	H	Merthyr Town	D	1-1	E. Smith	
9		11	A	Plymouth Argyle	D	0-0		
10		15	H	Swindon Town	L	1-2	Wood	4,000
11		18	H	Bristol Rovers	W	5-1	E. Smith 4, Whibley	
12		25	A	Reading	D	0-0		
13	Nov	1	H	Southampton	W	3-0	Conner 2, Wood	
14		8	A	Luton Town	W	4-1	Barber, E. Smith, Conner, Bateman	
15		15	H	Gillingham	W	4-1	E. Smith 2, Conner, Whibley	
16		22	A	Swansea Town	W	1-0	Conner	
17	Dec	6	A	Cardiff City	L	1-2	Hughes (pen)	
18		13	H	Queen's Park Rangers	W	1-0	Conner	
19		20	A	Swindon Town	D	2-2	Whibley, E. Smith	
20		25	A	Brighton & Hove Albion	W	3-2	Whibley, E. Smith 2	
21		26	H	Brighton & Hove Albion	W	4-0	Barber 2, Conner, E. Smith	15,000
22		27	H	Millwall	W	1-0	Cracknell	17,000
23	Jan	3	A	Northampton Town	W	1-0	E. Smith	
24		17	H	Watford	W	2-1	Barber 2	15,000
25		24	H	Southend United	D	0-0		15,000
26		31	A	Norwich City	L	0-2		
27	Feb	7	H	Brentford	D	1-1	Barber	12,000
28		14	A	Merthyr Town	W	1-0	Conner	
29		28	A	Bristol Rovers	L	0-1		
30	Mar	3	H	Plymouth Argyle	W	1-0	Barber	6,000
31		6	H	Reading	W	2-1	E. Smith, Conner	10,000
32		13	A	Southampton	L	1-5	Conner	
33		17	H	Exeter City	W	1-0	Conner	5,000
34		20	H	Luton Town	W	4-1	Green 2, Whibley, Menlove	
35		27	A	Gillingham	W	4-2	Menlove 3, Conner	
36	Apr	2	A	Newport County	L	0-1		
37		3	H	Swansea Town	W	2-1	Green, Conner	
38		5	H	Newport County	W	3-0	Conner 2, Bates	15,000
39		10	A	Exeter City	L	1-2	E. Smith	
40		17	H	Cardiff City	D	1-1	Menlove	
41		24	A	Queen's Park Rangers	W	3-2	Bateman, E. Smith, Whibley	
42	May	1	A	Millwall	D	1-1	Conner	22,000

Final League Position: 3rd in Southern League Division One

Appearances

Goals

FA Cup

Match No.	Date		Venue	Opponents	Result		Scorers	Attendance
1	Jan	10	A	Newcastle United	L	0-2		15,000

Appearances

Goals

Alderson	Little	Grainger	Feebery	Hughes	Cracknell	Bateman	Smith C.	Conner	Middleton	Whitley	Rhodes	Wiggins	Bates	Smith E.	Wood A.	Isley	Barber	Menlove	Revd K. Hunt	Green
1	2	3	4	5	6	7	8	9	10	11										
1	2		4	5	6		8	9	10	11	3	7								
1	2		4		6	7	8	9	10	11	3		5							
1	2		4		6	7		8	10	11	3		5	9						
1	2		4	5	6	7		8	10	11	3			9						
1	2		4	5	6	7		8	10	11	3			9						
1	2		4	5	6	7	8		10		3			9	11					
1	2		6	5		7		8	10	11	3			9		4				
1	2		6	5	8	7				11	3			9	10	4				
1	2		6	5		7			10	11	3		4	9	8					
1	2		6	5	4	7	10			11	3			9	8					
1	2		6	5	4	7		8		11	3			9	10					
1	2		6	5	4	7		8		11	3			9	10					
1	2		6	5	4	7		8		11	3			9			10			
1	2		6		4	7		8		11	3		5	9			10			
1	2		6		4	7		8		11	3		5	9			10			
1	2		6	5	4	7		8		11	3			9			10			
1	2		6	5	4	7		8		11	3			9			10			
1	2		6		4	7		8		11	3		5	9			10			
1	2		6		4	7		8		11	3		5	9			10			
1	2		6		4	7		8		11	3		5	9			10			
1	2		6	5	4	7		8		11	3			9			10			
1	2		6	5		7		8		11	3			9		4	10			
1	2		6	5	4	7		8		11	3			9			10			
1	2		6		4	7		8		11	3		5				10	9		
1	2		6		4	7		8		11	3		5	9			10			
1	2		6		4		7	8			3			9	11		10		5	
1	2		6		4	7		8			3		5	9	11		10			
1	2		6		4			8		7	3		5	9	11		10			
1	2		6		4					11	3		5	9			10	7		8
1	2		6		4	7		8			3		5	9	11					10
1	2		6		4	7		9			3		5		11		8			10
1	2		6				7	8			3		5		11	4		9		10
1	2		6			7		8		11	3		5				4	9		10
1	2		6			7		8		11	3		5			4		9		10
1	2		6		4	7		8		11	3		5					9		10
1	2		6			7		8		11	3		5			4		9		10
1	2		6		4	7		8			3		5		11			9		10
1	2		6		4	7		8		11	3		5	9				10		
1	2		6		4	7		8		11	3		5	10				9		
1	2		6			7		8		11	3		5	10		4		9		
1	2		6			7		8		11	3		5	10		4		9		
42	42	1	42	17	33	37	7	37	9	35	41	1	25	31	13	8	19	12	1	9
				1	1	2		18	2	8			1	19	2		7	5		3

Alderson	Little	Grainger	Feebery	Hughes	Cracknell	Bateman	Smith C.	Conner	Middleton	Whitley	Rhodes	Wiggins	Bates	Smith E.	Wood A.	Isley	Barber	Menlove	Revd K. Hunt	Green
1	2		6		4	7		8		11	3		5	9			10			
1	1		1		1	1		1		1	1		1	1			1			

1920-21

Division Three

Manager: Edmund Goodman

Did you know that?

Palace finally made it to the Football League, when the Southern League Division One became Division Three in the Football League, consisting of all the clubs that had participated in the Southern League the previous season. Palace had originally applied to join the Football League back in 1905 but were refused entry.

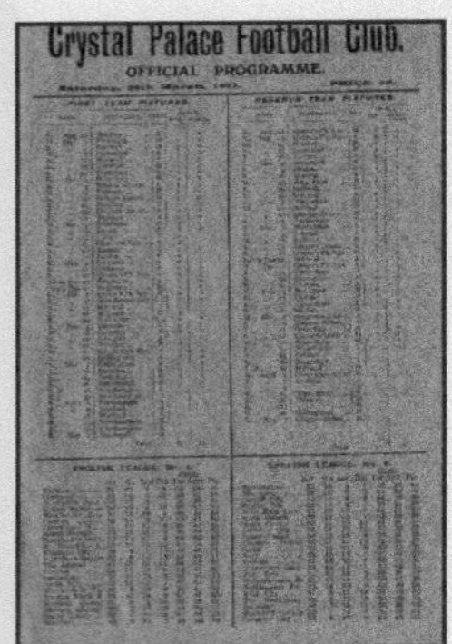
Crystal Palace Football Club.
OFFICIAL PROGRAMME.

Match No.	Date		Venue	Opponents	Result		Scorers	Attendance
1	Aug	28	A	Merthyr Town	L	1-2	Milligan	15,000
2	Sep	1	H	Plymouth Argyle	D	0-0		9,500
3		4	H	Merthyr Town	W	3-0	Conner 2, Whibley	12,500
4		8	A	Plymouth Argyle	W	1-0	Storey	12,000
5		11	A	Norwich City	W	1-0	Whibley	11,000
6		18	H	Norwich City	W	1-0	Conner	14,000
7		25	A	Brentford	W	4-0	Smith 2, Whibley, Menlove	13,000
8	Oct	2	H	Brentford	W	4-2	Whibley, Conner, Feebery, Smith	15,000
9		9	A	Bristol Rovers	L	1-2	Conner	20,000
10		16	H	Bristol Rovers	W	3-0	Smith 2, Conner	16,000
11		23	A	Reading	L	0-1		10,000
12		30	H	Reading	W	2-0	Smith, Menlove	18,000
13	Nov	3	H	Southend United	L	2-3	Conner, own-goal (Capper)	9,000
14		6	A	Luton Town	D	2-2	Conner, Whibley	10,000
15		13	H	Luton Town	W	2-1	Conner, Feebery	12,000
16		20	A	Exeter City	D	1-1	Conner	12,000
17		27	H+	Exeter City	W	2-1	Storey, Smith	12,000
18	Dec	4	A	Swansea Town	D	0-0		20,000
19		11	H	Swansea Town	L	0-1		9,000
20		18	A	Queen's Park Rangers	L	0-3		18,000
21		25	A	Brighton & Hove Albion	W	2-0	Conner 2	14,000
22		27	H	Brighton & Hove Albion	W	3-2	Feebery, Smith 2	22,000
23	Jan	1	H	Queen's Park Rangers	D	0-0		15,000
24		15	A	Millwall	W	1-0	Conner	20,000
25		22	H	Millwall	W	3-2	Wood, Menlove 2	18,000
26	Feb	5	A	Grimsby Town	L	0-1		
27		9	H	Grimsby Town	W	2-0	Menlove, Wood	6,000
28		12	A	Newport County	W	1-0	Conner	15,000
29		19	H	Newport County	W	2-0	Conner 2	16,000
30		26	A	Gillingham	W	1-0	Conner	
31	Mar	5	H	Gillingham	W	4-1	Jones 2, Conner, Wood (pen)	12,000
32		12	A	Swindon Town	W	3-1	Jones, Feebery, Conner	12,000
33		19	H	Swindon Town	W	1-0	Wood	20,000
34		26	H	Portsmouth	W	3-0	Conner, Wood, Bates	18,000
35		28	A	Southampton	D	1-1	Bates	20,000
36		29	H	Southampton	D	1-1	Wood	20,000
37	Apr	2	A	Portsmouth	D	0-0		18,353
38		9	H	Watford	D	2-2	Conner 2	16,000
39		16	A	Watford	D	1-1	Conner	8,000
40		23	H	Northampton Town	W	5-1	Storey 2, Conner 2, Jones	20,000
41		30	A	Northampton Town	D	2-2	Conner 2	8,000
42	May	7	A	Southend United	W	2-0	Conner 2	

Final League Position: 1st in Division Three + Played at The Dell, Southampton after The Nest was closed due to crowd trouble

1 own-goal

Appearances

Goals

FA Cup

1	Jan	8	H	Manchester City	W	2-0	Bateman, Menlove	18,500
2		29	H	Hull City	L	0-2		21,000

Appearances

Goals

Alderson	Little	Rhodes	McCracken	Jones	Feebery	Bateman	Conner	Smith	Milligan	Whibley	Bates	Menlove	Storey	Collier	Wood	Swift	Hand	Kennedy
1	2	3	4	5	6	7	8	9	10	11								
1	2	3	4	5	6	7	8	9	10	11								
1	2	3	4		6	7	8	9		11	5	10						
1	2	3	4		6		8	9		11	5	10	7					
1	2	3	4		6		8	9		11	5	10	7					
1	2	3	4		6		8	9		11	5	10	7					
1	2	3	4		6		8	9		11	5	10	7					
1	2	3	4		6		8	9		11	5	10	7					
1	2	3	4		6		8	9		11	5	10	7					
1	2	3	4		6		8	9		11	5	10	7					
1	2	3		4	6		8	9		11	5	10	7					
1	2	3	4		6		8	9		11	5	10	7					
1	2	3	4		6		8	9		11	5	10	7					
1	2	3	4			7	9			11	5	10	8	6				
1	2	3	4		6	7	9			11	5	10	8					
1	2	3	4		6	7	9			11	5	10	8					
1	2	3	4		6	7	10	9		11	5		8					
1	2	3	4		6	7	10	9		11	5		8					
1	2	3	4		6	7	10	9			5		8		11			
1	2	3		4	6	11	8	9			5	10	7					
1	2	3		4	6	7	10				5		8		11	9		
1	2	3		4	6	7	9	10			5		8		11			
1	2	3		4	6	7	9	10			5		8		11			
1	2	3		4	6	7	8			11	5	10			9			
1	2	3		4	6	7	8			11	5	10			9			
1	2	3		4	6	7	8				5	10			9		11	
1	2	3		4	6	7	8				5	10			9		11	
1	2	3			6	7	9			11	5				10		8	4
1	2	3		4	6	7	9			11	5		8		10			
1	2	3		4	6	7	9			11	5		8		10			
1	2	3		4	6	7	9			11	5		8		10			
1	2	3		4	6	7	9			11	5		8		10			
1	2	3		4	6	7	9			11	5		8		10			
1	2	3		4	6	7	9			11	5		8		10			
1	2	3		4	6	7	9			11	5		8		10			
1	2	3		4	6	7	9				5	10	8		11			
1	2	3		4	6	7	9				5		8		10		11	
1	2	3		4	6	7	8				5	9			10		11	
1	2	3		4	6	7	9			11	5		8				10	
1	2	3		4	6	7	9			11	5		8				10	
1	2	3		4	6	7	9			11	5		8				10	
1	2	3		4	6	7	9			11	5		8				10	
42	42	42	18	25	41	32	42	19	2	32	40	21	33	1	19	1	9	1
				4	4		29	9	1	5	2	5	4		6			

Alderson	Little	Rhodes	McCracken	Jones	Feebery	Bateman	Conner	Smith	Milligan	Whibley	Bates	Menlove	Storey	Collier	Wood	Swift	Hand	Kennedy
1	2	3		4	6	7	8			11	5	9			10			
1	2	3		4	6	7	8				5	9			10			11
2	2	2		2	2	2	2			1	2	2			2			1
						1						1						

League Table

	P	W	D	L	F	A	Pts
Crystal Palace	42	24	11	7	70	34	59
Southampton	42	19	16	7	64	28	54
Queen's Park Rangers	42	22	9	11	61	32	53
Swindon Town	42	21	10	11	73	49	52
Swansea Town	42	18	15	9	56	45	51
Watford	42	20	8	14	59	44	48
Millwall	42	18	11	13	42	30	47
Merthyr Town	42	15	15	12	60	49	45
Luton Town	42	16	12	14	61	56	44
Bristol Rovers	42	18	7	17	68	57	43
Plymouth Argyle	42	11	21	10	35	34	43
Portsmouth	42	12	15	15	46	48	39
Grimsby Town	42	15	9	18	49	59	39
Northampton Town	42	15	8	19	59	75	38
Newport County	42	14	9	19	43	64	37
Norwich City	42	10	16	16	44	53	36
Southend United	42	14	8	20	44	61	36
Brighton & Hove Albion	42	14	8	20	42	61	36
Exeter City	42	10	15	17	39	54	35
Reading	42	12	7	23	42	59	31
Brentford	42	9	12	21	42	67	30
Gillingham	42	8	12	22	34	74	28

1921-22

Division Two

Manager: Edmund Goodman

Did you know that?

Palace defender Robert McCracken became the first Division Three player to win an international cap when he represented Ireland against England in October 1920.

Match No.	Date		Venue	Opponents	Result		Scorers	Attendance
1	Aug	27	H	Nottingham Forest	W	4-1	Jones, Conner, Smith, Whitbley	20,000
2		29	A	Barnsley	L	1-3	Bateman	12,000
3	Sep	3	A	Nottingham Forest	L	1-2	Wood	18,000
4		7	H	Barnsley	L	0-1		
5		10	H	Rotherham County	W	2-0	Menlove, Wood	12,000
6		17	A	Rotherham County	D	1-1	Smith	
7		24	H	The Wednesday	D	2-2	Conner 2	14,000
8	Oct	1	A	The Wednesday	L	0-1		18,000
9		8	H	Fulham	W	2-0	Conner, Menlove	20,000
10		15	A	Fulham	D	1-1	Conner	32,000
11		22	H	Blackpool	W	1-0	Hand	15,000
12		29	A	Blackpool	W	3-1	Dreyer, Whibley, Hand	
13	Nov	5	H	Clapton Orient	W	1-0	Hand	18,000
14		12	A	Clapton Orient	D	0-0		19,000
15		19	A	Wolverhampton Wanderers	W	1-0	Feebery (pen)	14,000
16	Dec	3	A	Stoke	L	1-5	own-goal (McGrory)	
17		7	H	Wolverhampton Wanderers	D	1-1	Menlove	8,000
18		10	H	Stoke	L	0-2		14,000
19		17	A	Leeds United	D	0-0		12,000
20		24	H	Leeds United	L	1-2	Whibley	10,000
21		26	H	Notts County	W	1-0	Conner	
22		27	A	Notts County	L	2-3	Conner, Whibley	
23		31	A	Hull	L	0-1		
24	Jan	14	H	Hull	L	0-2		
25		21	H	Bristol City	D	1-1	Menlove	7,000
26	Feb	4	H	South Shields	L	1-2	Menlove	
27		8	A	Bristol City	W	2-1	Menlove 2	10,000
28		11	A	South Shields	D	1-1	Waite	12,000
29		18	H	Port Vale	D	0-0		
30		25	A	Port Vale	L	0-3		
31	Mar	4	H	West Ham United	L	1-2	Cartwright	
32		11	A	West Ham United	L	0-2		22,000
33		18	A	Bury	W	2-1	Whitworth, Storey	8,000
34		25	H	Bury	W	4-1	Wood, Whibley, Harry 2	10,000
35	Apr	1	A	Leicester City	L	0-2		12,000
36		8	H	Leicester City	W	1-0	McCracken	10,000
37		15	A	Derby County	L	0-2		12,000
38		17	H	Bradford Park Avenue	D	1-1	Cartwright	10,000
39		18	A	Bradford Park Avenue	D	0-0		
40		22	H	Derby County	W	3-1	Conner, Jones, Cartwright	7,000
41		29	A	Coventry City	D	1-1	Cartwright	
42	May	6	H	Coventry City	D	1-1	Whitworth	10,000

Final League Position: 14th in Division Two

Appearances

1 own-goal — Goals

FA Cup

Match No.	Date		Venue	Opponents	Result		Scorers	Attendance
1	Jan	7	A	Everton	W	6-0	Whibley, Menlove 2, Conner 2, Wood	41,167
2		28	H	Millwall	D	0-0		25,000
R	Feb	1	A	Millwall	L	0-2		35,000

Appearances

Goals

Alderson	Little	Rhodes	McCracken	Jones	Feebery	Bateman	Conner	Smith	Menlove	Whibley	Dreyer	Cartwright	Hand	Wood	Kennedy	Storey	Wells	Waite	Allen	Nixon	Forword	Irwin	Whitworth	Harry	Greener
1	2	3	4	5	6	7	8	9	10	11															
1	2	3	4	5		7	8	9	10		6	11													
1	2	3	4	5		7		9			6	11	8	10											
1		3	4	5		7		9			6	11	8	10	2										
1		3	4	5		7			9		6	11		10	2	8									
1		3	4	5		7		8	9		6	11		10	2										
1	2	3	4	5		7	8		9		6	11		10											
1	2	3	4	5		7	9		10		6	11				8									
1	2	3	4	5	6	7	9		10	11						8									
1	2	3	4	5		7	9		10	11	6		8												
1	2	3		5		7	9		10	11	6		8				4								
1	2	3	4	5		7	8		9	11	6		10												
1	2	3	4	5		7	8		9	11	6		10												
1	2	3	4	5	6	7			9	11	8		10												
1	2	3	4	5	6	7			9		8	11	10												
1	2	3	4	5	6	7	9			11	8		10												
1	2	3		5	6				9	11	4		10			7		8							
1	2	3	4		5	7			9	11	6		10					8							
1	2	3	4	5	6	7			9				11	10				8							
1		3	4	5	6	7		9		11				10				8	2						
1		3	4	5	6	7	8		9	11				10					2						
1		3	4		6	7	8		9	11				10					2	5					
1	2	3	4	5	6	7	8		9	11				10											
1	2	3	4		6	7	8		9	11	5			10											
1	2			5		7	8		9	11	6			10			4		3						
1	2	3	4			7			9		6		11			8				5	10				
1	2	3	4	5					10	11	6		7			8		9							
	2	3	4	5		7			10	11	6					8		9				1			
	2		4	5		7	9		10	11	6					8			3			1			
	2	3	4	5		7			10	11	6					8		9				1			
	2	3		5	6	7			9	11	4	10				8						1			
	2	3	5		6					11	4	10	8			7		9				1			
	2	3		5	6	7				11	4			10		8						1	9		
	2	3	4	5	6	7				11				10		8						1		9	
	2	3			6	7				11				10		8	4			5		1		9	
	2	3	4	5	6	7				11						8						1	9	10	
	2	3	4	5		7				11	6					8						1	9	10	
	2	3	4	5		7				11	6	10										1	9	8	
	2	3	4	5						11		10				7						1	9	8	6
	2	3	4	5			9				6	10	11			7		8				1			
	2	3	4	5	6	7						10	11			8						1		9	
	2	3		5	6	7						10	11				4					1	9	8	
27	36	40	35	36	21	37	17	6	27	29	29	15	18	15	3	19	4	9	5	3	1	15	6	8	1
			1	2	1	1	8	2	7	5	1	4	3	3		1		1					2	2	

Alderson	Little	Rhodes	McCracken	Jones	Feebery	Bateman	Conner	Smith	Menlove	Whibley	Dreyer	Cartwright	Hand	Wood
1	2	3	4	5	6	7	8		9	11				10
1	2	3	4	5		7	8		9		6	11		10
1	2	3	4	5		7	8		9		6	11	10	
3	3	3	3	3	1	3	3		3	1	2	2	1	2
							2		2	1				1

League Table

	P	W	D	L	F	A	Pts
Nottingham Forest	42	22	12	8	51	30	56
Stoke	42	18	16	8	60	44	52
Barnsley	42	22	8	12	67	52	52
West Ham United	42	20	8	14	52	39	48
Hull City	42	19	10	13	51	41	48
South Shields	42	17	12	13	43	38	46
Fulham	42	18	9	15	57	38	45
Leeds United	42	16	13	13	48	38	45
Leicester City	42	14	17	11	39	34	45
The Wednesday	42	15	14	13	47	50	44
Bury	42	15	10	17	54	55	40
Derby County	42	15	9	18	60	64	39
Notts County	42	12	15	15	47	51	39
Crystal Palace	42	13	13	16	45	51	39
Clapton Orient	42	15	9	18	43	50	39
Rotherham County	42	14	11	17	32	43	39
Wolverhampton W	42	13	11	18	44	49	37
Port Vale	42	14	8	20	43	57	36
Blackpool	42	15	5	22	44	57	35
Coventry City	42	12	10	20	51	60	34
Bradford Park Avenue	42	12	9	21	46	62	33
Bristol City	42	12	9	21	37	58	33

1922-23

Division Two

Manager: Edmund Goodman

Did you know that?

Goalkeeper Jack Alderson won his only England cap in May 1923 and stood between the posts as England beat France 4–1 in Paris.

Match No.	Date		Venue	Opponents	Result		Scorers	Attendance
1	Aug	26	A	Manchester United	L	1-2	Whitworth	30,000
2		30	H	Coventry City	D	0-0		8,000
3	Sep	2	H	Manchester United	L	2-3	Waite, Whitworth	12,000
4		7	A	Coventry City	L	1-2	Morgan	14,000
5		9	H	Fulham	D	0-0		12,000
6		16	A	Fulham	L	1-2	Feebery (pen)	26,000
7		23	H	Leicester City	L	0-1		10,000
8		30	A	Leicester City	L	0-3		16,000
9	Oct	7	H	Hull City	D	1-1	Waite	10,000
10		14	A	Hull City	D	1-1	Nixon	10,000
11		21	A	Bury	L	1-2	Whitworth	10,000
12		28	H	Bury	D	1-1	Feebery	12,000
13	Nov	4	A	The Wednesday	L	1-3	Rhodes (pen)	17,000
14		6	A	Rotherham United	L	1-4	Johnson	7,000
15		11	H	The Wednesday	W	2-0	Bateman, Whitworth (pen)	10,000
16		18	H	Barnsley	W	2-0	Whitworth, Johnson	12,000
17		25	A	Barnsley	W	2-1	Hand, Whibley	11,000
18	Dec	2	A	Blackpool	L	0-4		10,000
19		9	H	Blackpool	D	1-1	Dreyer	10,000
20		16	A	Port Vale	L	0-2		4,000
21		23	H	Port Vale	W	2-0	Millard, Douglas	9,000
22		25	A	Derby County	L	0-6		17,000
23		26	H	Derby County	D	2-2	Morgan 2	10,000
24		30	A	Bradford City	D	1-1	Harry	12,000
25	Jan	6	H	Bradford City	W	2-0	Whitworth 2 (1 pen)	12,000
26		20	A	Southampton	W	2-0	Whitworth, Whibley	13,000
27		27	H	Southampton	W	1-0	Whibley	9,000
28	Feb	10	H	Rotherham United	W	4-0	Millard, Whibley, Morgan, Harry	6,000
29		17	A	Clapton Orient	L	1-3	Whitworth	22,000
30		24	H	Clapton Orient	W	2-0	Whitworth, Morgan	15,000
31	Mar	3	A	Stockport County	D	2-2	Whitworth 2	5,000
32		10	H	Stockport County	W	3-0	Johnson 2, Whibley	10,000
33		17	H	Leeds United	W	1-0	Whitworth (pen)	15,000
34		24	A	Leeds United	L	1-4	Johnson	8,000
35		30	H	Notts County	L	0-1		9,000
36		31	H	West Ham United	L	1-5	Blakemore	10,000
37	Apr	2	A	Notts County	W	4-0	Morgan, Whitworth, Hand 2	20,000
38		7	A	West Ham United	D	1-1	Bateman	25,000
39		14	H	South Shields	D	1-1	Blakemore	9,000
40		21	A	South Shields	L	0-2		4,000
41		28	H	Wolverhampton Wanderers	W	5-0	Whitworth 3, Blakemore, Morgan	4,000
42	May	5	A	Wolverhampton Wanderers	L	0-1		7,000

Final League Position: 16th in Division Two

Appearances
Goals

FA Cup

Match No.	Date		Venue	Opponents	Result		Scorers	Attendance
1	Jan	13	A	Queen's Park Rangers	L	0-1		18,030

Appearances
Goals

Alderson	Little	Rhodes	McCracken	Millard	Feebery	Bateman	Ward	Whitworth	Morgan	Whibley	Waite	Dreyer	Allen	Greener	Forward	Harry	Cross	Cartwright	Nixon	Conner	Hand	Johnson	Blakemore	Douglas	Wells	Irwin
1	2	3	4	5	6	7	8	9	10	11																
1	2	3	4	5	6	7	8	9	10	11																
1	2	3	4	5	6	7		9	10	11	8															
1	2	3	4		5			9	10	7	8	6						11								
1	2		4		5	7	8	9	10	11			3	6												
1	2		4		5	7	8	9	10	11			3	6												
1	2		4		5	7		8		11	9		3	6	10											
1	2				5			9	10	11	8	4	3	6		7										
1			4	5	6			9		11	8		3			7	2	10								
1	2		4					8		11				6		7	3	10	5	9						
1	2		4		6			8		11				10		7	3		5	9						
1	2		4		9			8		11	10			6		7	3		5							
1		3	4			7				11				6	10	9	2		5		8					
1		3	4							11				6	10	9	2		5		7	8				
1	3		6			7		9		11				4			2		5		10	8				
1	2		4			7		9		11				6			3		5		8	10				
1	2		4			7		9		11		5		6			3				8	10				
1	2		4			7		9		11		5		6			3				8	10				
1	2		4					8		11		5		6		9	3				7	10				
1	2		4						11	8	10	5		6		7	3						9			
1	2		4	5						11		6				7	3					8	9	10		
1	2		4					8	11			5		6		7	3						9	10		
1	2		4						10	11		6				7	3					8	9		5	
1	2		4	5					10			6				7	3				11	8	9			
1	2		4	5				9	10			6				7	3				11	8				
1	2		4	5				9	10	11		6				7	3					8				
1	2		4	5				9	10	11		6				7	3					8				
	2		4	5				9	10	11		6				7	3					8				1
	2		4	5				9	10	11		6				7	3					8				1
1	2		4	5				9	10	11		6				7	3					8				
1	2		4	5				9	10	11		6				7	3					8				
1	2		4	5				9	10	11		6				7	3					8				
1	2		4	5				9	10	11		6				7	3					8				
1	2	3	4	5		7		9	10				6					11				8				
1	2		4	5				9	10			6				7	3				11	8				
1	2		4	5				9	10			6				7	3				11		8			
1	2		4	5		7		9	10			6					3				11		8			
1	2		4	5		7		9	10			6					3				11		8			
1	2		4	5		7		9	10			6					3				11		8			
1	2		4	5		7		9	10			6					3				11		8			
1	2		4	5		7		9	10					6			3				11		8			
1	2			5		7		9	10			6		4			3				11		8			
40	39	7	40	24	11	18	4	36	29	30	7	26	5	19	3	24	33	4	7	2	17	20	12	2	1	2
		1		2	2	2		17	7	5	2	1				2			1		3	5	3	1		

Alderson	Little	Rhodes	McCracken	Millard	Feebery	Bateman	Ward	Whitworth	Morgan	Whibley	Waite	Dreyer	Allen	Greener	Forward	Harry	Cross	Cartwright	Nixon	Conner	Hand	Johnson	Blakemore	Douglas	Wells	Irwin
1	2		4	5				9	10			6				7	3				11	8				
1	1		1	1				1	1			1				1	1				1	1				

League Table

	P	W	D	L	F	A	Pts
Notts County	42	23	7	12	46	34	53
West Ham United	42	20	11	11	63	38	51
Leicester City	42	21	9	12	65	44	51
Manchester United	42	17	14	11	51	36	48
Blackpool	42	18	11	13	60	43	47
Bury	42	18	11	13	55	46	47
Leeds United	42	18	11	13	43	36	47
The Wednesday	42	17	12	13	54	47	46
Barnsley	42	17	11	14	62	51	45
Fulham	42	16	12	14	43	32	44
Southampton	42	14	14	14	40	40	42
Hull City	42	14	14	14	43	45	42
South Shields	42	15	10	17	35	44	40
Derby County	42	14	11	17	46	50	39
Bradford City	42	12	13	17	41	45	37
Crystal Palace	42	13	11	18	54	62	37
Port Vale	42	14	9	19	39	51	37
Coventry City	42	15	7	20	46	63	37
Clapton Orient	42	12	12	18	40	50	36
Stockport County	42	14	8	20	43	58	36
Rotherham County	42	13	9	20	44	63	35
Wolverhampton W	42	9	9	24	42	77	27

1923-24

Division Two

Manager: Edmund Goodman

Did you know that?

Palace's last game at The Nest, their third home and one time residence of Croydon Common FC, resulted in a 3–1 win over Barnsley. After Palace left, it was used by local amateur Selhurst football clubs and also for cricket and bird keeping, before the railway company eventually redeveloped the land to become part of the modern-day rail depot.

CRYSTAL PALACE FOOTBALL CLUB

OFFICIAL PROGRAMME

No. 30 FEBRUARY 16th, 1924 Price 2d.

Dress Suitings
Black Coatings
Stripe Trouserings
Grey Suitings
Brown Suitings

S. W. POORE

High-Class Tailor

57, GEORGE St., CROYDON.

Match No.	Date		Venue	Opponents	Result		Scorers	Attendance
1	Aug	25	H	Port Vale	L	1-2	Hoddinott	12,000
2		27	A	Leeds United	L	0-3		10,000
3	Sep	1	A	Port Vale	W	4-3	Millard, Bateman, Johnson, Whitworth	14,000
4		5	H	Leeds United	D	1-1	Whitworth	8,000
5		8	H	Fulham	D	1-1	Whitworth (pen)	12,000
6		15	A	Fulham	L	0-1		10,000
7		22	H	Blackpool	W	3-1	Millard, Whitworth, Blakemore	
8		29	A	Blackpool	L	0-2		12,000
9	Oct	6	H	Nelson	D	1-1	Blakemore	10,000
10		13	A	Nelson	L	2-4	Morgan, Whitworth	
11		20	H	Bradford City	W	3-0	Whitworth, Hand, Bateman	12,000
12		27	A	Bradford City	W	1-0	Hoddinott	13,000
13	Nov	3	H	Hull City	D	0-0		10,000
14		10	A	Hull City	D	2-2	Morgan 2	10,000
15		17	A	Stoke	D	1-1	Morgan	5,000
16		24	H	Stoke	W	5-1	Hoddinott 3, Morgan, Hand	
17	Dec	1	A	Derby County	L	0-5		11,237
18		8	H	Derby County	L	0-1		8,000
19		15	H	The Wednesday	W	3-0	Whitworth 3	10,000
20		22	A	The Wednesday	L	0-6		10,000
21		25	A	Bristol City	D	0-0		10,000
22		26	H	Bristol City	W	1-0	Hoddinott	10,000
23		29	A	Coventry City	D	0-0		15,000
24	Jan	5	H	Coventry City	W	3-1	Whitworth, Hoddinott, Morgan	15,000
25		19	H	Leicester City	W	4-3	Whitworth 2, Hoddinott, Morgan	10,000
26		26	A	Leicester City	L	0-1		
27	Feb	9	A	Clapton Orient	L	0-1		
28		16	H	Stockport County	D	1-1	Hoddinott	10,000
29	Mar	1	H	Oldham Athletic	L	2-3	Hoddinott 2 (1 pen)	8,000
30		8	A	Oldham Athletic	L	0-1		9,915
31		10	A	Stockport County	D	2-2	Hand, Harry	
32		15	A	South Shields	L	0-2		8,000
33		22	H	South Shields	W	1-0	Blakemore	8,000
34		29	A	Bury	D	1-1	Hand	15,000
35	Apr	5	H	Bury	W	1-0	Whitworth	12,000
36		12	A	Manchester United	L	1-5	Hand	8,000
37		18	H	Southampton	D	0-0		8,000
38		19	H	Manchester United	D	1-1	Whitworth (pen)	6,000
39		21	A	Southampton	L	0-1		10,000
40		22	H	Clapton Orient	W	2-1	Blakemore, Whitworth	6,000
41		26	A	Barnsley	L	2-5	Harry, Whitworth (pen)	4,000
42	May	3	H	Barnsley	W	3-1	Hoddinott 2, Blakemore	

Final League Position: 15th in Division Two

Appearances
Goals

FA Cup

1	Jan	12	H	Tottenham Hotspur	W	2-0	Morgan 2	17,000
2	Feb	2	H	Notts County	D	0-0		19,500
R		6	A	Notts County	D	0-0*		20,600
2R		11	N+	Notts County	D	0-0*		11,370
3R		18	N+	Notts County	W	2-1	Hoddinott, Hand	6,000
3		23	H	Swindon Town	L	1-2	Whitworth	20,000

+ Played at Villa Park, Birmingham. * After extra-time

Appearances
Goals

Alderson	Little	Cross	McCracken	Millard	Feebery	Bateman	Whitworth	Hoddinott	Morgan	Osbourne	Nixon	Harry	Allen	Johnson	McKenna	Blakemore	Greener	Hand	Cracknell	Hamilton	Nicholson	Callender	Forward
1	2	3	4	5	6	7	8	9	10	11													
1	2	3	4		6		8	9	10	11	5	7											
1	2		4	5	6	7	8	9	11				3	10									
1	2		4	5	6	7	8	9	11					10	3								
1	2	3	4	5	6	7	8	9	11					10									
1	2	3	4	5	6	7	8	9	11					10									
1	2	3	4	5	6	7	8		10			11				9							
1		3	4	5	6	7	8		10			11			2	9							
1	2	3	4	5			8		10			7				9	6	11					
1	2	3	4	5	6		8		10			7				9		11					
1	2	3	4		6	7	8	9	10									11	5				
1	2	3	4		6		8	9	10									11	5	7			
1	2	3	4		6		8	9	10			7						11	5				
1	2	3	4		6		8	9	10			7						11	5				
1	2	3	4		6		8	9	10			7						11	5				
1	2	3	4		6		8	9	10			7						11	5				
1	2	3	4		6		8	9	10			7						11	5				
1	2	3	4		6	7	8	9	10									11	5				
1	2	3	4		6		8	9	10			11							5		7		
1	2	3	4	8	6			9	10			11							5		7		
1	2	3					8	9	10			7	4				6	11	5				
1	2	3					8	9	10			7	4				6	11	5				
1	2	3					8	9	10			7	4				6	11		5			
1	2	3	4				8	9	10			7					6	11	5				
1	2	3	4				8	9	10			7					6	11	5				
1	2	3	4				8	9	10			7					6	11	5				
1	2						8	9	10		3	7	4				6	11	5				
1	2	3	4				8	9	10	11		7	6						5				
1	2	3	4				8	9				7		10			6	11		5			
1	2	3	4					9	10	11		8					6	7		5			
1	2	3	4					9	10	11	6	7						8		5			
1	2	3	4			7	8	9	10								6	11	5				
	2	3	4					9	10			7				8	6	11	5			1	
1	2	3	4				9		10			7				11	6	8		5			
1	2	3	4				9			11		7				10	6	8		5			
1	2	3					9		8			7				10	6	11	4	5			
1		2	4				8	9	10		3	7					6	11	5				
1		2	4				8	9	10		3	7					6	11	5				
1	2	3	4				9		10			7				8	6		5				11
1		2	4				8				3	7		10		9	6			5			11
1		2	4				8		11		3	7		10		9	6		5				
1		2	4				8	9	11		3	7				10	6		5				
41	36	39	37	10	19	10	38	32	39	6	8	33	6	7	2	12	21	27	25	9	2	1	2
				2		2	16	13	7			2		1		5		5					

Alderson	Little	Cross	McCracken	Millard	Feebery	Bateman	Whitworth	Hoddinott	Morgan	Osbourne	Nixon	Harry	Allen	Johnson	McKenna	Blakemore	Greener	Hand	Cracknell	Hamilton	Nicholson	Callender	Forward
1	2	3	4				8	9	10			7					6	11	5				
1	2	3	4				8	9	10			7					6	11	5				
1	2	3	4				8	9	10			7					6	11	5				
1	2	3	4				8	9	10			7					6	11	5				
1	2		4					9	10		3	7		8				11	6	5			
1	2		4				8	9	10		3	7					6	11	5				
6	6	4	6				5	6	6		2	6		1			5	6	6	1			
							1	1	2									1					

League Table

	P	W	D	L	F	A	Pts
Leeds United	42	21	12	9	61	35	54
Bury	42	21	9	12	63	35	51
Derby County	42	21	9	12	75	42	51
Blackpool	42	18	13	11	72	47	49
Southampton	42	17	14	11	52	31	48
Stoke	42	14	18	10	44	42	46
Oldham Athletic	42	14	17	11	45	52	45
The Wednesday	42	16	12	14	54	51	44
South Shields	42	17	10	15	49	50	44
Clapton Orient	42	14	15	13	40	36	43
Barnsley	42	16	11	15	57	61	43
Leicester City	42	17	8	17	64	54	42
Stockport County	42	13	16	13	44	52	42
Manchester United	42	13	14	15	52	44	40
Crystal Palace	42	13	13	16	53	65	39
Port Vale	42	13	12	17	50	66	38
Hull City	42	10	17	15	46	51	37
Bradford City	42	11	15	16	35	48	37
Coventry City	42	11	13	18	52	68	35
Fulham	42	10	14	18	45	56	34
Nelson	42	10	13	19	40	74	33
Bristol City	42	7	15	20	32	65	29

1924-25

Division Two

Manager: Edmund Goodman

Did you know that?

Selhurst Park, which finally opened in August when Palace took on Sheffield Wednesday, took its name from a former gated estate housing retired military, which existed around the current site of the ground in the 1850s.

Match No.	Date	Venue	Opponents	Result		Scorers	Attendance
1	Aug 30	H	The Wednesday	L	0-1		25,000
2	Sep 1	A	Coventry City	W	4-1	Hamilton, Whitworth, Blakemore 2	16,000
3	6	A	Clapton Orient	L	0-3		
4	13	H	Hull City	W	1-0	Blakemore	15,000
5	20	H	Southampton	W	3-1	Whitworth 2, Blakemore	15,000
6	27	A	Chelsea	D	2-2	Harry, Whitworth	40,000
7	Oct 1	H	Coventry City	D	0-0		8,000
8	4	H	Stockport County	W	3-0	Hoddinott, Blakemore 2	
9	6	A	Oldham Athletic	W	2-0	Blakemore, Osbourne	7,661
10	11	A	Manchester United	L	0-1		27,750
11	18	H	Leicester City	L	0-2		20,000
12	25	A	Blackpool	W	1-0	Whitworth	12,000
13	Nov 1	H	Derby County	W	2-0	Blakemore, Osbourne	10,000
14	8	A	South Shields	D	1-1	Whitworth	
15	15	H	Bradford City	W	4-1	Whitworth 3 (1 pen), Blakemore	12,000
16	22	A	Port Vale	L	0-3		8,000
17	29	H	Middlesbrough	D	2-2	Hoddinott, Whitworth	12,000
18	Dec 6	A	Barnsley	L	0-3		7,000
19	13	H	Wolverhampton Wanderers	W	2-1	Hoddinott, Hand	12,000
20	20	A	Fulham	L	1-3	Whitworth	18,000
21	25	A	Portsmouth	D	0-0		14,836
22	26	H	Portsmouth	L	1-2	Harry	24,229
23	27	A	The Wednesday	W	1-0	Whitworth	10,000
24	Jan 3	H	Clapton Orient	L	0-1		18,000
25	17	A	Hull City	L	0-5		12,000
26	24	A	Southampton	L	0-2		9,000
27	Feb 7	A	Stockport County	L	0-1		9,000
28	14	H	Manchester United	W	2-1	Hoddinott 2	11,250
29	28	H	Blackpool	L	1-2	Osbourne	15,000
30	Mar 7	A	Derby County	L	0-3		15,381
31	12	A	Leicester City	L	1-3	Groves	
32	14	H	South Shields	D	0-0		10,000
33	21	A	Bradford City	D	0-0		15,000
34	28	H	Port Vale	D	0-0		10,000
35	Apr 1	H	Chelsea	W	1-0	Whitworth	12,000
36	4	A	Middlesbrough	D	0-0		18,000
37	10	H	Stoke	L	0-1		15,000
38	11	H	Barnsley	L	0-1		12,000
39	13	A	Stoke	D	1-1	Blakemore	
40	18	A	Wolverhampton Wanderers	L	1-3	Groves	20,000
41	25	H	Fulham	L	1-2	Blakemore	10,000
42	May 2	H	Oldham Athletic	L	0-1		17,500

Final League Position: 21st in Division Two

Appearances
Goals

FA Cup

Match No.	Date	Venue	Opponents	Result		Scorers	Attendance
1	Jan 10	H	South Shields	W	2-1	Blakemore, Whitworth	22,000
2	31	A	Hull City	L	2-3	Hoddinott, Groves	20,085

Appearances
Goals

Harper	Little	Cross	McCracken	Cracknell	Greener	Harry	Whitworth	Hoddinott	Morgan	Hand	Hamilton	Blakemore	Groves	Jones	Osbourne	Nixon	Strang	Blake	McKenna	Hedley	Johnson	Middlemiss	Pettit	Callender
1	2	3	4	5	6	7	8	9	10	11														
1	2	3	4		6	7	8	9		11	5	10												
1	2	3	4		6	7	8	9		11	5	10												
1	2	3	4		6	7	8	9		11	5	10												
1	2	3	4		6	7	9				5	10	8	11										
1	2	3	4		6	7	9				5	10	8	11										
1	2	3	4		6	7	9			11	5	10	8											
1	2	3		4	6	7	9	8			5	10			11									
1	2	3		4	6	7	9	8			5	10			11									
1	2			4	6	7	9	8			5	10			11	3								
1	2		4	3	6	7	9	8			5	10			11									
1	2	3		4	6	7	9	8				10			11		5							
1	2	3		4	6	7	9	8			5	10			11									
1	2	3		4	6	7	9	8			5	10			11									
1	2	3	4	5	6	7	9	8				10			11									
1	2			4	6	7	9	8				10			11		5	3						
1	2			4	6	7	9	8		10	5				11	3								
1	2		4	6		7		9		8	5	10			11	3								
1	2	3			6	7	9	8		10	5				11		4							
1	2	3			6	7	9	8		10	5				11		4							
1	2	3		4	6	7	9	8		10					11	5								
1	2	3		4	6	7	9	8		10	5				11									
1	2	3		4	6	7	9	8		10	5				11									
1	2	3		4	6		9	8		10	5				11				7					
1	2			4	6	7	9	8		11	5	10								3				
1	2	3	4	5	6	7	9	8		11		10												
1	2	3	4		6	7	9		11		5		8								10			
1		3	4		6	7		9	11	10	5		8					2						
1		3	4		6	7		9			5	10	8		11			2						
1		3	4		6	7		9				10			11		5	2			8			
1		3	4		6	7		9				10	8		11		5	2						
1		3			6	7		10		11	4	9	8				5	2						
1		3	4		6	7		8		10	5	9			11			2						
1		3	4		6	7	9	8	11			10					5	2						
1		3	4	6		7	9	8		11		10					5	2						
1		3	4		6	7	9	11		8		10					5	2						
1		3	4		6	7	9			8		10			11		5	2						
1		3	4		6	7	9		10	8		11					5	2						
1		3				7			10			9	8	11		5		2				4	6	
1		3	4		6	7		11	10			9	8			5		2						
1		3	4			7			10			9	8	11		6	5	2						
		3	4			7		9				10	8		11	6	5	2						1
41	27	36	25	19	37	41	31	34	8	22	25	32	12	4	23	8	14	16	1	1	2	1	1	1
						2	13	5		1	1	11	2		3									

Harper	Little	Cross	McCracken	Cracknell	Greener	Harry	Whitworth	Hoddinott	Morgan	Hand	Hamilton	Blakemore	Groves
1	2	3		4	6	7	9	8		11	5	10	
1	2	3	4		6	7		9	11		5	10	8
2	2	2	1	1	2	2	1	2	1	1	2	2	1
							1	1				1	1

League Table

	P	W	D	L	F	A	Pts
Leicester City	42	24	11	7	90	32	59
Manchester United	42	23	11	8	57	23	57
Derby County	42	22	11	9	71	36	55
Portsmouth	42	15	18	9	58	50	48
Chelsea	42	16	15	11	51	37	47
Wolverhampton W	42	20	6	16	55	51	46
Southampton	42	13	18	11	40	36	44
Port Vale	42	17	8	17	48	56	42
South Shields	42	12	17	13	42	38	41
Hull City	42	15	11	16	50	49	41
Clapton Orient	42	14	12	16	42	42	40
Fulham	42	15	10	17	41	56	40
Middlesbrough	42	10	19	13	36	44	39
The Wednesday	42	15	8	19	50	56	38
Barnsley	42	13	12	17	46	59	38
Bradford City	42	13	12	17	37	50	38
Blackpool	42	14	9	19	65	61	37
Oldham Athletic	42	13	11	18	35	51	37
Stockport County	42	13	11	18	37	57	37
Stoke	42	12	11	19	34	46	35
Crystal Palace	42	12	10	20	38	54	34
Coventry City	42	11	9	22	45	84	31

1925-26

Division Three South

Manager: Edmund Goodman until 24 November 1925, then Alex Maley.

Did you know that?

Edmund Goodman who had been manager at Palace since April 1907, finally stepped down in November of this season after 749 League games in charge, although he continued as club secretary.

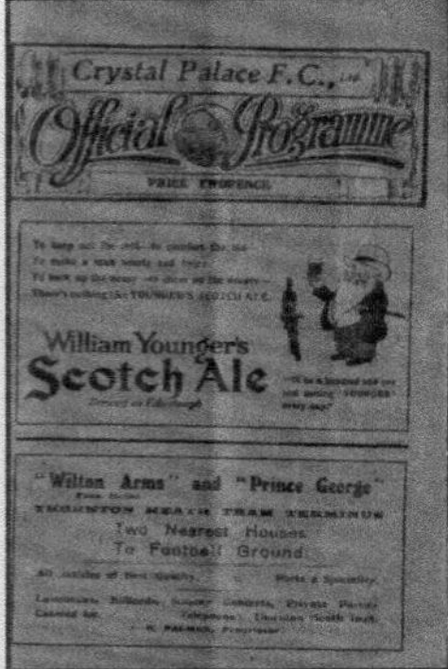

Match No.	Date		Venue	Opponents	Result		Scorers	Attendance
1	Aug	29	H	Millwall	L	1-2	Blakemore	23,617
2	Sep	2	A	Plymouth Argyle	L	2-6	Blakemore 2	12,934
3		5	A	Northampton Town	L	0-4		9,005
4		12	H	Aberdare Athletic	L	0-1		12,471
5		19	A	Brighton & Hove Albion	L	2-3	Hand 2	11,738
6		23	H	Bristol City	W	5-2	Cherrett 2, Blakemore 3	8,078
7		26	H	Watford	W	4-0	Hand, Cherrett 3	14,065
8	Oct	3	H	Brentford	W	2-0	Cherrett, Clarke	15,724
9		7	A	Bristol City	L	0-1		6,144
10		10	H	Bristol Rovers	L	0-2		14,272
11		17	A	Swindon Town	L	1-3	Cherrett	7,564
12		24	H	Exeter City	W	3-2	Harry, Blakemore (pen), Clarke	11,332
13		31	A	Luton Town	L	2-3	Turner, Blakemore (pen)	7,980
14	Nov	7	H	Queen's Park Rangers	W	1-0	Cherrett	11,829
15		14	A	Charlton Athletic	D	1-1	Harry	11,465
16		21	H	Gillingham	L	0-2		11,879
17		28	H	Plymouth Argyle	D	5-5	Hoddinott 2, Cherrett, Hawkins 2	12,300
18	Dec	19	H	Bournemouth	W	3-1	Harry, Cherrett, Clarke	10,682
19		25	A	Norwich City	L	3-4	Cherrett, Blakemore 2 (1 pen)	8,166
20		26	H	Norwich City	W	2-0	Cherrett, Clarke	20,208
21		28	A	Reading	L	1-2	Cherrett	12,452
22	Jan	2	A	Millwall	L	0-1		18,126
23		16	H	Northampton Town	W	1-0	Blakemore	7,113
24		25	A	Merthyr Town	L	0-4		2,755
25	Feb	6	A	Watford	L	0-3		6,693
26		10	H	Newport County	W	4-2	Blakemore (pen), Cherrett 2, Hawkins	4,228
27		13	A	Brentford	L	2-3	Coyle, Hawkins	10,140
28		27	H	Swindon Town	W	1-0	Coyle (pen)	11,534
29	Mar	6	A	Exeter City	W	1-0	Cherrett	5,996
30		10	H	Brighton & Hove Albion	W	2-1	Cherrett, Clarke	5,871
31		13	H	Luton Town	W	3-0	Greener, Cherrett 2	12,306
32		20	A	Queen's Park Rangers	W	3-1	Blakemore, Harry, Clarke	8,389
33		24	A	Bristol Rovers	L	1-3	Cherrett	2,417
34		27	H	Charlton Athletic	W	4-1	Cherrett, Hawkins 2, Clarke	11,179
35	Apr	2	H	Southend United	W	3-0	Hamilton, Blakemore, Cherrett	17,260
36		3	A	Gillingham	D	1-1	Clarke	7,371
37		5	A	Southend United	L	1-5	Cherrett	10,908
38		10	H	Merthyr Town	W	3-0	Cherrett, Blakemore 2	11,411
39		17	A	Newport County	W	3-2	Blakemore 3	4,477
40		19	A	Aberdare Athletic	L	0-2		2,839
41		24	H	Reading	W	3-0	Cherrett 2, Clarke	20,758
42	May	1	A	Bournemouth	L	1-6	Hawkins	6,051

Final League Position: 13th in Division Three South

Appearances
Goals

FA Cup

3	Jan	9	A	Northampton Town	D	3-3	Cherrett 2, Blakemore	14,467
R		13	H	Northampton Town	W	2-1	Cherrett 2	15,000
4		30	H	Chelsea	W	2-1	Cherrett, Hawkins	*41,586
5	Feb	20	A	Manchester City	L	4-11	Cherrett 2, Clarke, McCracken	51,630

*Record attendance

Appearances
Goals

Harper	Blake	Cross	McCracken	Strang	Greener	Harry	Turner	Blakemore	Keenan	Clarke	Callender	Nixon	Little	Cracknell	SmithL	Pettit	Hamilton	Groves	Hand	Cherrett	Hawkins	Hoddinott	Hampton	Coyle	Hunt	Moore	Osbourne	Hedley
1	2	3	4	5	6	7	8	9	10	11																		
	2	3		5	4	7	8	9	10	11	1	6																
1		3				7	8	9	10	11			2	4	5	6												
1	2	3			6	7		9	10	11				4			5	8										
1	2	3		5	6	7		10		11							4		8	9								
1	2	3		5	6	7		10		11							4		8	9								
1	2	3		5	6	7		10		11							4		8	9								
1	2	3		5	6	7		10		11							4		8	9								
1	2	3	4	5	6	7		10		11									8	9								
1	2	3	4	5	6	7		10		11									8	9								
1	2	3		5	6			10		11							4	8	7	9								
1	2	3	4	5	6	7		10		11									8	9								
1	2	3	4		6	7	8	10		11							5			9								
1	2	3	4		6	7	8	10		11							5			9								
1	2	3			6	7	8	10		11				5			4			9								
1	2	3	4		6	7	8	5		11										9	10							
1	2	3	4		6	7		5		11										9	10	8						
		3	4		6	7		10		11			2							9		8	1	5				
		3	4		6	7		10		11			2							9		8	1	5				
		3	4		6	7		10		11			2							9		8	1	5				
		3			6	7		10		11			2							9		8		5	1	4		
		3	4		6	7		10		11			2							9		8		5	1			
		3	4		6	7		8			1		2								10	9		5			11	
		3	4		6	7		10		11	1		2							9		8		5				
		3	4		6	7				11	1		2							9	10	8		5				
		3	4		6	7		8		11	1		2							9	10			5				
			4		6	7		8		11	1	3	2							9	10			5				
		3	4		6	7	8			11	1		2							9	10			5				
		3			6	7		8		11	1		2				4			9	10			5				
		3			6	7		8		11	1		2				4			9	10			5				
		3			6	7		8		11	1		2				4			9	10			5				
		3			6	7		8		11	1		2				4			9	10			5				
		3			6	7		8		11	1		2				4			9	10			5				
		3			6	7		8		11	1		2				4			9	10			5				
		3			6	7		8		11	1		2				4			9	10			5				
		3			6	7	8			11	1		2				4			9	10			5				
		3	4		6	7	8			11	1						5			9		10		2				
		2			6	7	8	10		11	1						4			9				5				3
		2			6	7		8		11	1						4				10	9		5				3
		2			6	7		8		11	1						4				10	9		5				3
	2	3			6	7		8		11	1						4			9	10			5				
	2	3	4		6			8		11	1						5			9	10	7						
16	18	41	20	10	41	40	11	38	4	41	21	2	20	3	1	1	23	2	8	35	19	13	3	24	2	1	1	3
					1	4	1	19		9							1		3	26	7	2		2				

Harper	Blake	Cross	McCracken	Strang	Greener	Harry	Turner	Blakemore	Keenan	Clarke	Callender	Nixon	Little	Cracknell	SmithL	Pettit	Hamilton	Groves	Hand	Cherrett	Hawkins	Hoddinott	Hampton	Coyle	Hunt	Moore	Osbourne	Hedley
		3	4		6	7		10		11			2							9		8		5	1			
		3	4		6	7		10		11	1		2							9		8		5				
		3	4		6	7		8		11	1		2							9	10			5				
		3	4		6	7		8		11	1		2							9	10			5				
		4	4		4	4		4		4	3		4							4	2	2		4	1			
			1					1		1										7	1							

League Table

	P	W	D	L	F	A	Pts
Reading	42	23	11	8	77	52	57
Plymouth Argyle	42	24	8	10	107	67	56
Millwall	42	21	11	10	73	39	53
Bristol City	42	21	9	12	72	51	51
Brighton & Hove Albion	42	19	9	14	84	73	47
Swindon Town	42	20	6	16	69	64	46
Luton Town	42	18	7	17	80	75	43
Bournemouth	42	17	9	16	75	91	43
Aberdare Athletic	42	17	8	17	74	66	42
Gillingham	42	17	8	17	53	49	42
Southend United	42	19	4	19	78	73	42
Northampton Town	42	17	7	18	82	80	41
Crystal Palace	42	19	3	20	75	79	41
Merthyr Town	42	14	11	17	69	75	39
Watford	42	15	9	18	73	89	39
Norwich City	42	15	9	18	58	73	39
Newport County	42	14	10	18	64	74	38
Brentford	42	16	6	20	69	94	38
Bristol Rovers	42	15	6	21	66	69	36
Exeter City	42	15	5	22	72	70	35
Charlton Athletic	42	11	13	18	48	68	35
Queen's Park Rangers	42	6	9	27	37	84	21

1926-27

Division Three South

Manager: Alex Maley

Did you know that?

In the middle season of three with Scotsman Alex Maley as manager, Palace managed to record scores exactly the same for their highest win and biggest defeat of the season. Recording a 7–1 victory against Norwich at home in October, they then went down to a 7–1 defeat away to Plymouth in February.

Match No.	Date		Venue	Opponents	Result		Scorers	Attendance
1	Aug	28	H	Queen's Park Rangers	W	2-1	Blakemore, Cherrett	18,261
2	Sep	1	A	Brighton & Hove Albion	D	1-1	Hilley	7,209
3		4	A	Charlton Athletic	W	2-1	Clarke 2	13,499
4		8	H	Watford	L	0-1		12,350
5		11	H	Bristol City	W	4-2	Blakemore 3 (1 pen), Clarke	16,902
6		15	A	Watford	W	2-1	Cherrett 2	7,000
7		18	A	Bournemouth	D	1-1	Cherrett	7,504
8		25	H	Plymouth Argyle	D	1-1	Blakemore	20,497
9	Oct	2	A	Newport County	L	1-2	Flood	6,985
10		9	H	Aberdare Athletic	D	0-0		13,003
11		16	H	Brentford	W	4-3	Flood, Cherrett, Blakemore, Clarke	14,860
12		23	A	Northampton Town	D	1-1	Blakemore	5,676
13		30	H	Norwich City	W	7-1	Flood, Turner, Cherrett 4, Clarke	12,184
14	Nov	6	A	Luton Town	L	0-1		7,343
15		13	H	Southend United	W	5-3	Cherrett 2, Clarke 3	4,101
16	Dec	4	A	Swindon Town	L	1-6	Cherrett	6,190
17		18	A	Millwall	L	0-1		15,445
18		25	A	Coventry City	L	1-3	Cherrett	12,507
19		27	H	Coventry City	L	1-2	Blakemore	18,220
20	Jan	1	H	Brighton & Hove Albion	W	2-0	Blakemore, Clarke	14,346
21		15	A	Queen's Park Rangers	W	2-0	Grant, Cherrett	11,506
22		22	H	Charlton Athletic	W	2-1	Cherrett, own-goal (Smith)	7,606
23		29	A	Bristol City	L	4-5	Turner, Cherrett 2, Grant	11,938
24	Feb	5	H	Bournemouth	D	2-2	Grant, Cherrett	11,474
25		9	H	Exeter City	W	1-0	Cherrett	4,454
26		12	A	Plymouth Argyle	L	1-7	Hawkins	11,781
27		19	H	Newport County	W	6-2	Orr, Grant, Cherrett 2, Blakemore 2	10,328
28		26	A	Aberdare Athletic	W	3-2	Greener, Smith, Harry	745
29	Mar	5	A	Brentford	L	0-3		8,205
30		12	H	Northampton Town	W	3-0	Greener, Hilley, Grant	11,460
31		16	H	Bristol Rovers	W	7-4	Turner 2, Cherrett 2, Blakemore, Clarke 2	5,327
32		19	A	Norwich City	W	1-0	Orr	7,087
33		26	H	Luton Town	D	1-1	Cherrett	9,264
34	Apr	2	A	Southend United	L	1-3	Cherrett	6,270
35		9	H	Merthyr Town	D	1-1	Cherrett	5,968
36		15	A	Gillingham	L	1-2	Blakemore	7,584
37		16	A	Exeter City	L	1-3	Turner	6,182
38		18	H	Gillingham	D	2-2	Cherrett, Blakemore	10,386
39		23	H	Swindon Town	W	5-0	Cherrett 2, Blakemore 2, Clarke	10,670
40		30	A	Bristol Rovers	L	1-4	Clarke	5,905
41	May	2	A	Merthyr Town	W	2-1	Cherrett 2	1,435
42		7	H	Millwall	L	1-6	Cherrett	12,896

Final League Position: 6th in Division Three South

Appearances
Goals

FA Cup

Match No.	Date		Venue	Opponents	Result		Scorers	Attendance
1	Nov	27	H	Norwich City	D	0-0		15,000
R	Dec	2	A	Norwich City	L	0-1		9,821

Appearances
Goals

Callender	Cross	Orr	Hamilton	Coyle	Greener	Harry	Blakemore	Cherrett	Hilley	Clarke	Smith L.	Flood	Hopkins	Gallagher	Turner	Tonner S.	Grant	Nixon	Hawkins	Morgan R.	Barnes V.
1	2	3	4	5	6	7	8	9	10	11											
1	2	3	4	5	6	7	8	9	10	11											
1	2	3	4	5	6	7	8	9	10	11											
1	2	3	4	5	6	7	8	9	10	11											
1	2	3	4		6		10	9		11	5	7	8								
1	2	3	4		6		10	9		11	5	7	8								
1	2	3	4		6		10	9		11	5	7	8								
1	2	3	4		6	7	10	9		11	5	8									
1	2	3	4		6	7	10	9		11	5	8									
1	2	3			6	7		9	10	11	5	8		4							
1	2	3			6		10	9		11	5	7		4	8						
1	2	3			6		10	9		11	5	7		4	8						
1	2	3			6		10	9		11	5	7		4	8						
1	2	3			6		10	9		11	5	7		4	8						
1		3	5				10	9	6	11		7		4	8	2					
1	3						10	9	6	11	5	7		4	8	2					
1	2					7	9		6	11	5		3	4	8		10				
1	2					7	10	9	6	11	5		3	4	8						
1						7	10	9	6	11	5		2	4	8			3			
1		3				7	10	9	6	11	5		2	4			8				
1	2	3			4	7	10	9	6	11	5						8				
1	2	3			4		10	9	6	11	5	7					8				
1	2	3						9	6	11	5	7		4	8		10				
1	2	3	4				10	9	6	11	5	7					8				
1	2	3	4				10	9	6	11	5	7					8				
1	2	3				7	8	9	6	11	5			4					10		
1	2	3			4	7	10	9	6	11	5						8				
1	2	3			4	7	10	9	6	11	5						8				
1	2	3		5	4		10	9	6	11					8		7				
1	2	3			4		10	9	6	11	5				8		7				
1	2	3			4		10	9	6	11	5				8		7				
1	3	9			6				10	11	5		2	4	8		7				
1	2	3					10	9	6	11	5			4	8		7				
1	2	3					10	9	6	11	5	7		4			8				
1	2	3					10	9	6	11	5			4	8					7	
1	2	3	5				10	9	6	11		7		4			8				
1	2	3	5				10	9	6	11		7		4	8						
1	2	3			5		10	9	6	11		7		4	8						
1	2	3			5		10	9	6	11				4	7		8				
1		3			5		10	9	6	7			2	4	8						11
1	2	3	5		6		10	9	8	11				4	7						
1	2	3	5		6		8	9	10	11				4	7						
42	38	38	16	5	27	15	39	40	33	42	29	20	9	24	22	2	17	1	1	1	1
		2			2	1	16	32	2	13	1	3			5		5		1		

Callender	Cross	Orr	Hamilton	Coyle	Greener	Harry	Blakemore	Cherrett	Hilley	Clarke	Smith L.	Flood	Hopkins	Gallagher	Turner	Tonner S.	Grant	Nixon	Hawkins	Morgan R.	Barnes V.
1	2	3	5				10	9	6	11		7		4	8						
1	3		5				10	9	6	11		7		4	8	2					
2	2	1	2				2	2	2	2		2		2	2	1					

League Table

	P	W	D	L	F	A	Pts
Bristol City	42	27	8	7	104	54	62
Plymouth Argyle	42	25	10	7	95	61	60
Millwall	42	23	10	9	89	51	56
Brighton & Hove Albion	42	21	11	10	79	50	53
Swindon Town	42	21	9	12	100	85	51
Crystal Palace	42	18	9	15	84	81	45
Bournemouth	42	18	8	16	78	66	44
Luton Town	42	15	14	13	68	66	44
Newport County	42	19	6	17	57	71	44
Bristol Rovers	42	16	9	17	78	80	41
Brentford	42	13	14	15	70	61	40
Exeter City	42	15	10	17	76	73	40
Charlton Athletic	42	16	8	18	60	61	40
Queen's Park Rangers	42	15	9	18	65	71	39
Coventry City	42	15	7	20	71	86	37
Norwich City	42	12	11	19	59	71	35
Merthyr Town	42	13	9	20	63	80	35
Northampton Town	42	15	5	22	59	87	35
Southend United	42	14	6	22	64	77	34
Gillingham	42	11	10	21	54	72	32
Watford	42	12	8	22	57	87	32
Aberdare Athletic	42	9	7	26	62	101	25

1927-28

Division Three South

Manager: Alex Maley until 12 October 1927, then Fred Mavin from 21 November 1927.

Did you know that?

A new attendance record was set for Palace on 30 January 1926 at Selhurst Park, when 41,586 packed in for the FA Cup fourth-round tie against Chelsea. Palace romped home to a 4–1 victory and record gate receipts of £2,554.

Match No.	Date		Venue	Opponents	Result		Scorers	Attendance
1	Aug	27	A	Norwich City	L	1-4	Hallam	13,140
2		29	H	Exeter City	W	2-0	Hallam, Clarke	11,329
3	Sep	3	H	Northampton Town	W	1-0	Hilley	13,771
4		7	A	Exeter City	D	2-2	Williamson, Hilley	5,906
5		10	A	Southend United	L	1-6	Clarke	6,808
6		17	H	Brighton & Hove Albion	D	1-1	Hamilton	13,557
7		24	A	Bournemouth	D	2-2	Flood, Turner	5,933
8	Oct	1	H	Brentford	L	0-2		11,552
9		8	A	Luton Town	L	1-6	Clarke (pen)	8,844
10		15	H	Millwall	L	0-4		18,930
11		22	H	Queen's Park Rangers	D	1-1	Clarke	7,115
12		29	A	Watford	L	1-2	Turner	7,346
13	Nov	5	H	Charlton Athletic	W	5-0	Turner, Havelock 2, Clarke 2	16,694
14		12	A	Swindon Town	D	3-3	Flood, Hopkins, Turner	7,608
15		19	H	Newport County	W	2-0	Clarke 2	8,863
16	Dec	3	H	Gillingham	D	2-2	Harry, Hopkins	4,299
17		17	H	Merthyr Town	W	2-0	Harry, Barnes	6,809
18		24	A	Plymouth Argyle	L	1-5	Harry	11,515
19		27	A	Torquay United	W	2-0	Tonner, Brown	3,353
20		31	H	Norwich City	W	2-1	Clarke, Hopkins	7,446
21	Jan	7	A	Northampton Town	D	1-1	Greener	9,860
22		14	A	Walsall	D	1-1	Hopkins (pen)	4,279
23		21	H	Southend United	W	4-1	Tonner 2, Brown, Clarke	10,606
24		28	A	Brighton & Hove Albion	L	2-4	Hopkins, Clarke	4,494
25	Feb	4	H	Bournemouth	W	6-1	Clarke 3, Hopkins, Tonner 2	10,862
26		11	A	Brentford	L	1-2	Turner	7,580
27		13	A	Coventry City	D	2-2	Hopkins, Tonner	2,059
28		18	H	Luton Town	W	3-2	Tonner 2, Salt	13,370
29		25	A	Millwall	D	1-1	Clarke	27,736
30	Mar	3	A	Queen's Park Rangers	L	0-2		16,468
31		10	H	Watford	W	2-1	Hopkins, Tonner	9,851
32		14	H	Torquay United	W	3-2	Hopkins, Clarke, Turner	4,842
33		17	A	Charlton Athletic	W	4-0	Hopkins 2, Clarke, Harry	11,083
34		24	H	Swindon Town	W	1-0	Harry	8,373
35	Apr	6	H	Bristol Rovers	W	3-2	Clarke 2, Mulcahy	16,126
36		7	H	Walsall	W	5-1	Hopkins, Clarke 2, Harry, Mulcahy	12,530
37		9	A	Bristol Rovers	D	1-1	Harry	6,275
38		14	A	Gillingham	L	1-3	Mulcahy	3,623
39		21	H	Coventry City	W	1-0	Mulcahy	5,908
40		26	A	Newport County	W	3-0	Clarke, Hopkins, Harry	2,554
41		28	A	Merthyr Town	D	2-2	Mulcahy, Turner	2,169
42	May	5	H	Plymouth Argyle	L	0-2		12,218

Final League Position: 5th in Division Three South

Appearances
Goals

FA Cup

1	Nov	26	A	Dartford	W	3-1	Hopkins 2, Smith	6,227
2	Dec	10	A	Swindon Town	D	0-0		16,360
R		14	H	Swindon Town	L	1-2	Hopkins	8,500

Appearances
Goals

Callender	Orr	Cross	Gallagher	Hamilton	Hilley	Rood	Williamson	Tonner J.	Hallam	Clarke	Greener	Turner	Kelly	Hopkins	Grant	Holmes	Smith	Hunt	Harry	Barnes	James	Havelock	Brown	Ivey	Salt	Mulcahy
1	2	3	4	5	6	7	8	9	10	11																
1	2	3	4	5	6	7	8	9	10	11																
1	2	3	4	5	10	7	9			11	6	8														
	2	3	4	5	6	7	9	10		11		8	1													
		3	4	5	6	7		10		11		8	1	2	9											
	2		4	5	6	7		10		11		8	1		9	3										
	2		4	5	6	7	9	10		11		8	1			3										
	2		4	5	6	7		10		11		8	1		9	3										
	2			5		7	9	10		11	6	8	1			3	4									
	2			5				9		11	6	8				3	4	1	7	10						
1	2		4	5	6			10		11		8				3			7		9					
1	2		4	5	6					11		8			10	3			7		9					
1	2			4		7				11	6	8		10		3	5					9				
		2	4			8				11	6	10	1	9		3	5		7							
		2		4		7				11	6	8	1	10		3	5					9				
		2		4		8				11	6	10	1	9		3	5		7							
		2		4							6	8	1	9		3	5		7	11			10			
		2		4				8			6		1	9		3	5		7	11			10			
		2		4				8		11	6		1	9		3			7				10	5		
		2		4				8		11	6		1	9		3	5		7				10			
		2		4				8		11	6		1	9		3	5		7				10			
		2		4				8		11	6		1	9		3	5		7				10			
	3	2		4				8		11	6		1	9					7				10		5	
	3	2		4				8		11	6		1	9					7				10		5	
	3	2		4				10		11	6	8	1	9					7						5	
	3	2		4				10		11	6	8	1	9					7						5	
	3	2		4		8		10		11	6		1	9					7						5	
1	3	2		4				10		11	6			9					7						5	8
1	3	2		4				10		11	6	8		9					7						5	
1	3	2						10		11	6	8		9			4		7						5	
1	3	2		4				10		11	6	8		9					7						5	
1	3	2		4						11	6	8		9					7						5	10
1	3	2		4						11	6	8		9					7						5	10
1	3	2		4						11	6	8		9					7						5	10
1	3	2		4						11	6	8		9					7						5	10
1	3	2		4						11	6	8		9					7						5	10
	3	2		4						11	6	8	1	9					7						5	10
	3	2		4						11	6	8	1	9					7						5	10
1	3	2		4						11	6	8		9					7						5	10
1	3	2		4						11	6	8		9					7						5	10
1	3	2		4						11	6	8		9					7						5	10
1	3	2		4						11	6	8		9					7						5	10
19	32	34	11	40	10	14	6	24	2	40	33	31	22	31	4	17	12	1	31	3	2	2	8	1	20	12
				1	2	2	1	9	2	22	1	7		13					8	1		2	2		1	5

Callender	Orr	Cross	Gallagher	Hamilton	Hilley	Rood	Williamson	Tonner J.	Hallam	Clarke	Greener	Turner	Kelly	Hopkins	Grant	Holmes	Smith	Hunt	Harry	Barnes	James	Havelock	Brown	Ivey	Salt	Mulcahy
		2		4		7				11	6	8	1	10		3	5					9				
1		2		4		8				11	6	10		9		3	5			7						
1		2		4		8				11	6	10		9		3	5			7						
2		3		3		3				3	3	3	1	3		3	3			2		1				
														3			1									

League Table

	P	W	D	L	F	A	Pts
Millwall	42	30	5	7	127	50	65
Northampton Town	42	23	9	10	102	64	55
Plymouth Argyle	42	23	7	12	85	54	53
Brighton & Hove Albion	42	19	10	13	81	69	48
Crystal Palace	42	18	12	12	79	72	48
Swindon Town	42	19	9	14	90	69	47
Southend United	42	20	6	16	80	64	46
Exeter City	42	17	12	13	70	60	46
Newport County	42	18	9	15	81	84	45
Queen's Park Rangers	42	17	9	16	72	71	43
Charlton Athletic	42	15	13	14	60	70	43
Brentford	42	16	8	18	76	74	40
Luton Town	42	16	7	19	94	87	39
Bournemouth	42	13	12	17	72	79	38
Watford	42	14	10	18	68	78	38
Gillingham	42	13	11	18	62	81	37
Norwich City	42	10	16	16	66	70	36
Walsall	42	12	9	21	75	101	33
Bristol Rovers	42	14	4	24	67	93	32
Coventry City	42	11	9	22	67	96	31
Merthyr Town	42	9	13	20	53	91	31
Torquay United	42	8	14	20	53	103	30

1928-29

Division Three South

Manager: Fred Mavin

Did you know that?

Missing promotion only by a whisker, Palace's second-place finish in Division Three South saw the club complete a still record 17-game unbeaten run in one season between November and March.

Crystal Palace F.C., Ltd.
Official Programme

No. 32. March 9th, 1929. Price: 2d.

CAN WE GAIN PROMOTION?

Match No.	Date		Venue	Opponents	Result		Scorers	Attendance
1	Aug	25	H	Watford	W	3-0	Harry, Gill, Davis	19,466
2	Sep	1	A	Walsall	L	1-3	Walsh	7,243
3		5	H	Fulham	W	2-1	Moyle, Griffiths	15,005
4		8	H	Newport County	D	1-1	Davis	14,796
5		10	A	Fulham	D	2-2	Griffiths 2	11,239
6		15	A	Norwich City	W	1-0	Harry	9,892
7		22	A	Swindon Town	L	2-3	Charlton (pen), Gill	7,999
8		29	H	Torquay United	W	2-0	Havelock 2	14,091
9	Oct	6	A	Gillingham	W	1-0	Harry	5,923
10		13	H	Plymouth Argyle	L	1-4	Gill	17,980
11		20	H	Charlton Athletic	L	0-2		12,551
12		27	A	Northampton Town	L	1-8	James	7,299
13	Nov	3	H	Coventry City	L	0-3		12,470
14		10	A	Luton Town	L	3-5	Havelock 3	9,606
15		17	H	Brentford	W	1-0	Harry	11,323
16	Dec	1	H	Merthyr Town	W	2-0	Butler 2	9,100
17		15	H	Exeter City	W	1-0	Griffiths	6,041
18		22	A	Brighton & Hove Albion	W	5-1	Havelock 2, Butler 3	3,899
19		25	A	Bristol Rovers	D	1-1	Griffiths	12,106
20		26	H	Bristol Rovers	W	5-2	Harry, Havelock, Butler 2, Clarke	9,083
21		29	A	Watford	D	3-3	Havelock 2, Clarke	9,693
22	Jan	5	H	Walsall	D	1-1	own-goal (O'Brien)	9,057
23		19	A	Newport County	W	3-1	Havelock, Griffiths, Clarke	3,399
24	Feb	2	H	Swindon Town	W	6-1	Charlton (pen), Thomas, Havelock, Griffths 2, Clarke	10,364
25		9	A	Torquay United	W	2-1	Havelock, Clarke	4,178
26		23	A	Plymouth Argyle	D	1-1	Hamilton	9,213
27	Mar	2	A	Charlton Athletic	W	3-1	Griffiths, Butler, Clarke	26,364
28		6	H	Norwich City	W	2-1	Havelock 2	9,171
29		9	H	Northampton Town	W	1-0	Butler	25,072
30		16	A	Coventry City	W	3-1	Charlton (pen), Clarke, Griffiths	12,289
31		23	H	Luton Town	W	3-0	Harry, Havelock 2	22,981
32		29	H	Queen's Park Rangers	L	1-4	Havelock	33,160
33		30	A	Brentford	W	4-2	Harry, Griffiths 2, Butler	13,314
34	Apr	1	A	Queen's Park Rangers	D	1-1	Griffiths	19,341
35		6	H	Bournemouth	L	1-3	Griffiths	20,792
36		10	A	Southend United	L	0-3		3,084
37		13	A	Merthyr Town	D	2-2	Harry, Griffiths	2,750
38		20	H	Southend United	W	3-2	Havelock, Charlesworth, Dunsire	16,327
39		24	A	Bournemouth	L	0-2		5,005
40		27	A	Exeter City	W	2-1	Charlesworth, Griffiths	5,743
41	May	1	H	Gillingham	W	3-0	Havelock, Griffiths 2	15,679
42		4	H	Brighton & Hove Albion	W	1-0	Charlton (pen)	22,146

Final League Position: 2nd in Division Three South

Appearances

1 own-goal — Goals

FA Cup

Round	Date		Venue	Opponents	Result		Scorers	Attendance
1	Nov	24	H	Kettering Town	W	2-0	Butler, Clarke	13,000
2	Dec	8	H	Bristol Rovers	W	3-1	Harry, Charlton, Havelock	13,500
3	Jan	12	A	Luton Town	D	0-0		14,200
R		16	H	Luton Town	W	7-0	Havelock 3, Wilde, Griffiths, Butler, Hamilton	17,000
4		26	A	Millwall	D	0-0		40,460
R		30	H	Millwall	W	5-3	Butler 3, Griffiths, Harry	26,405
5	Feb	16	A	Huddersfield Town	L	2-5	Griffiths, Charlton (pen)	19,000

Appearances

Goals

Callender	Crilly	Charlton	Moyle	Thoms	Greener	Harry	Gill	Walsh	Davis	Clarke	Smith	Salt	Griffiths	Fletcher	Turner	Mulcahy	Conaty	Havelock	Wetherby	James	Butler	Betteridge	Hamilton	Wilde	Charlesworth	Dunsire	Imrie
1	2	3	4	5	6	7	8	9	10	11																	
1	2	3	4		6	7	8	9	10	11	5																
1	2	3	4		6	7	8		10	11		5	9														
1	2	3	4		6	7	8		10			5	9	11													
1	2	3				7	8			11		5	9		10	4	6										
1	2	3				7	8	9				5		11	10	4	6										
1	2	3				7	8			11		5			10	4	6	9									
1		3			6	7	8		10	11		5				4		9	2								
1	2	3			6	7	8					5		11	10	4		9									
1	2	3			6	7	8					5		11	10	4		9									
1		3	4	5		7		9				6		11	8	10			2								
1		3		5		7				11		6				4		8		9	10	2					
1	2	3			6	7				11		5		10	8					9			4				
1		3		5	6	7		9		11	2							8			10		4				
1	2	3		5	6	7		9		11	4							8			10						
1	2	3			6	7		9		11								8			10		4	5			
1	2	3			6	7							9	11				8			10		4	5			
1		3			6	7				11			9					8	2		10		4	5			
1		3			6	7				11			9					8	2		10		4	5			
1		3			6	7				11			9					8	2		10		4	5			
1		3			6	7				11			9					8	2		10		4	5			
1		3			6	7				11			9					8	2		10		4	5			
1		3			6	7				11			9					8	2		10		4	5			
1		3		5		7				11		6	9					8	2		10		4				
1		3				7				11		6	9					8	2		10		4	5			
1		3			6	7		9		11								8	2		10		4	5			
1		3			6	7				11			9					8	2		10		4	5			
1		3			6	7				11			9					8	2		10		4	5			
1	3				6	7				11			9					8	2		10		4	5			
1		3			6	7				11			9					8	2		10		4	5			
1		3			6	7				11			9					8	2		10		4	5			
1		3			6	7				11			9					8	2		10		4	5			
1		3				7						6	9					8	2		10		4	5	11		
1		3				7						6	9					8	2		10		4	5	11		
1		3				7						6	9					8	2		10		4	5	11		
1		3				7						6	9			2		8					4	5	11	10	
1		3			6	7							9			2		8					4	5	11	10	
	2	3			6	7				11		4						8						5	9	10	1
1		3			6	7				11		4	10			2		8						5	9		
1	2	3			6					11		4	9					8			10			5	7		
1	2	3			6	7				11		4	9					8			10			5			
1	2	3			6	7				11		4	9					8			10			5			
41	18	41	5	6	31	41	10	8	5	31	3	22	27	7	7	11	3	34	20	2	26	1	24	26	8	3	1
		4	1	1		8	3	1	2	7			18					20		1	10		1		2	1	

Callender	Crilly	Charlton	Moyle	Thoms	Greener	Harry	Gill	Walsh	Davis	Clarke	Smith	Salt	Griffiths	Fletcher	Turner	Mulcahy	Conaty	Havelock	Wetherby	James	Butler	Betteridge	Hamilton	Wilde	Charlesworth	Dunsire	Imrie
1	2	3			6	7		9		11								8			10		4	5			
1	2	3			6	7				11			9					8			10		4	5			
1		3			6	7				11			9					8	2		10		4	5			
1		3			6	7				11			9					8	2		10		4	5			
1		3				7				11		6	9					8	2		10		4	5			
1		3		5		7				11		6	9					8	2		10		4				
1		3			6	7				11			9					8	2		10		4	5			
7	2	7		1	5	7		1		7		2	6					7	5		7		7	6			
		2				2				1			3					4			5		1	1			

League Table

	P	W	D	L	F	A	Pts
Charlton Athletic	42	23	8	11	86	60	54
Crystal Palace	42	23	8	11	81	67	54
Northampton Town	42	20	12	10	96	57	52
Plymouth Argyle	42	20	12	10	83	51	52
Fulham	42	21	10	11	101	71	52
Queen's Park Rangers	42	19	14	9	82	61	52
Luton Town	42	19	11	12	89	73	49
Watford	42	19	10	13	79	74	48
Bournemouth	42	19	9	14	84	77	47
Swindon Town	42	15	13	14	75	72	43
Coventry City	42	14	14	14	62	57	42
Southend United	42	15	11	16	80	75	41
Brentford	42	14	10	18	56	60	38
Walsall	42	13	12	17	73	79	38
Brighton & Hove Albion	42	16	6	20	58	76	38
Newport County	42	13	9	20	69	86	35
Norwich City	42	14	6	22	69	81	34
Torquay United	42	14	6	22	66	84	34
Bristol Rovers	42	13	7	22	60	79	33
Merthyr Town	42	11	8	23	55	103	30
Exeter City	42	9	11	22	67	88	29
Gillingham	42	10	9	23	43	83	29

1929-30

Division Three South

Manager: Fred Mavin

Did you know that?

Palace's renowned goalscorer Peter Simpson bagged himself a hat-trick against Norwich in his first Football League start and on his Palace debut, a 3–2 victory on 14 September that earned rave reviews from the local press.

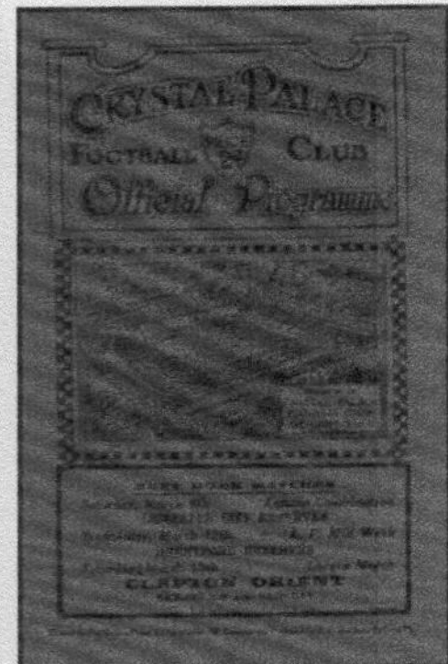

Match No.	Date	Venue	Opponents	Result		Scorers	Attendance
1	Aug 31	H	Queen's Park Rangers	D	1-1	Havelock	20,268
2	Sep 2	A	Southend United	L	2-3	Wilde, Griffiths	6,954
3	7	A	Fulham	W	2-1	Griffiths, own-goal (Barrett)	23,273
4	11	H	Southend United	L	1-2	Havelock	13,279
5	14	H	Norwich City	W	3-2	Simpson 3	14,067
6	18	A	Bournemouth	L	1-2	Simpson	6,635
7	21	A	Swindon Town	L	1-3	Simpson	6,606
8	25	H	Newport County	W	1-0	Simpson	9,445
9	28	A	Gillingham	D	1-1	Simpson	6,818
10	Oct 5	H	Northampton Town	L	1-3	Turner	17,562
11	12	A	Exeter City	L	1-6	Simpson	6,158
12	19	H	Brighton & Hove Albion	D	2-2	Fishlock, Charlton (pen)	13,882
13	26	A	Bristol Rovers	W	3-2	Simpson, Wilde, Havelock	6,498
14	Nov 2	H	Brentford	W	2-1	Duthie 2	16,939
15	9	A	Clapton Orient	L	1-2	Simpson	14,114
16	16	H	Coventry City	W	4-3	Charlton (pen), Clarke, Havelock, Duthie	2,862
17	23	A	Watford	D	1-1	Havelock	5,646
18	30	H	Swindon Town	W	1-0	Simpson	11,128
19	Dec 7	A	Torquay United	D	2-2	Havelock 2	3,400
20	14	H	Merthyr Town	W	6-1	Wilde, Simpson 3, Havelock 2	10,625
21	21	A	Plymouth Argyle	L	1-6	Simpson	15,728
22	25	A	Walsall	D	0-0		5,612
23	26	H	Walsall	W	5-1	Harry 2, Simpson 2, Butler	19,940
24	28	A	Queen's Park Rangers	L	1-4	Butler	12,709
25	Jan 4	H	Fulham	W	4-3	Havelock, Simpson 2, Fishlock	17,732
26	18	A	Norwich City	D	2-2	Turner, Simpson	10,348
27	Feb 1	H	Gillingham	W	5-1	Turner, Simpson 3, Harry	8,783
28	8	A	Northampton Town	L	0-2		8,480
29	15	H	Exeter City	D	1-1	Simpson	11,966
30	22	A	Brighton & Hove Albion	W	2-1	Simpson 2	11,530
31	Mar 1	H	Bristol Rovers	W	3-0	Butler 2, Turner	13,078
32	8	A	Brentford	L	0-2		19,555
33	15	H	Clapton Orient	W	3-0	Havelock 2, Harry	14,649
34	22	A	Coventry City	L	0-1		10,360
35	29	H	Watford	D	1-1	Turner	12,310
36	Apr 5	A	Newport County	D	0-0		3,324
37	12	H	Torquay United	W	4-2	Charlesworth 3, Clarke	9,555
38	18	A	Luton Town	D	2-2	Simpson 2	9,135
39	19	A	Merthyr Town	L	2-5	Simpson 2	842
40	21	H	Luton Town	W	4-1	Simpson 3 (1 pen), Clarke	15,167
41	26	H	Plymouth Argyle	W	3-0	Clarke, Simpson 2	18,649
42	May 3	H	Bournemouth	D	1-1	Simpson	10,678

Final League Position: 9th in Division Three South — Appearances

1 own-goal — Goals

FA Cup

3	Jan 11	A	Leeds United	L	1-8	Simpson	31,418

Appearances

Goals

Callender	Wetherby	Charlton	Hamilton	Wilde	Greener	Harry	Havelock	Griffiths	Butler	Clarke	Turner	Duthie	Simpson	Fishlock	Charlesworth	Rivers	Dunsire	Cilly	Swan	Imrie	Jamieson	Barrie
1	2	3	4	5	6	7	8	9	10	11												
1	2	3	4	5	6	7	8	9	10	11												
1	2	3	4	5	6	7	8	9		11	10											
1	2	3	4	5	6	7	8	9		11	10											
1	2	3	4	5		7	8		10	11		6	9									
1	2	3	4	5		7	8	6		11			9	10								
1	2	3	4	5		7		10			8	6	9	11								
1	2	3	4	5		7	8		10			6	9	11								
1	2	3	4	5		7			10		8	6	9	11								
1	2	3	4	5		7				10	8	6	9	11								
1	2	3	4	5					10		8	6	9	11	7							
1	2	3	4	5		7		10				6	9	11		8						
1	2	3	4	5		7	8			11		10	9			6						
1	2	3	4	5		7		10		11		8	9			6						
1	2	3	4	5		7			10	11		8	9			6						
1	2	3	4	5		7	8			11		10	9			6						
1	2	3	4	5		7	8			11		10	9			6						
1	2	3	4	5		7	8			11		10	9			6						
1	2	3	4	5		7	8			11			9			6	10					
1	2	3	4	5		7	8			11			9			6	10					
1	2	3	4	5	6	7	8		10	11			9									
1	2		4	5	6	7	8		10				9	11				3				
1	2		4	5	6	7			10		8		9	11				3				
1	2		4	5	6	7			10		8		9	11				3				
1	2	3		5			8		10		7		9	11		6			4			
		3		5		7				11	8		9			6		2	4	1	10	
		3		5		7				11	8		9			6		2	4	1	10	
				5		7				11	8		9			6		3	4	1	10	2
		3		5		7				11	8		9			6		2	4	1	10	
	2			5	6	7			10	11	8		9					3	4	1		
	2		4	5	6	7		9	10	11	8							3		1		
	2		4	5	6	7	9		10	11	8							3		1		
	2		4	5	6	7	9		10	11	8							3		1		
	2		4	5	6	7			10	11	8		9					3		1		
	2		4	5	6	7			10		8		9	11				3		1		
	2		4		6	7			10	11	8		9					3		1		5
	2		4		6	7			10	11	8				9			3		1		5
	2		4	5	6	7			10	11	8		9					3		1		
	2		4	5	6	7			10	11	8		9					3		1		
	2		4		6	7				11	8		9		10			3		1		5
	2				6	7				11	8		9		10	4		3		1		5
	2				6	7				11	8		9		10	4		3		1		5
25	38	25	34	37	21	40	18	9	22	32	26	13	34	12	5	16	2	20	6	17	4	6
		2		3		4	12	2	4	4	5	3	36	2	3							

Callender	Wetherby	Charlton	Hamilton	Wilde	Greener	Harry	Havelock	Griffiths	Butler	Clarke	Turner	Duthie	Simpson	Fishlock	Charlesworth	Rivers	Dunsire	Cilly	Swan	Imrie	Jamieson	Barrie
1	2	3	4	5			8		10		7		9	11		6						
1	1	1	1	1			1		1		1		1	1		1						
													1									

League Table

	P	W	D	L	F	A	Pts
Plymouth Argyle	42	30	8	4	98	38	68
Brentford	42	28	5	9	94	44	61
Queen's Park Rangers	42	21	9	12	80	68	51
Northampton Town	42	21	8	13	82	58	50
Brighton & Hove Albion	42	21	8	13	87	63	50
Coventry City	42	19	9	14	88	73	47
Fulham	42	18	11	13	87	83	47
Norwich City	42	18	10	14	88	77	46
Crystal Palace	42	17	12	13	81	74	46
Bournemouth	42	15	13	14	72	61	43
Southend United	42	15	13	14	69	59	43
Clapton Orient	42	14	13	15	55	62	41
Luton Town	42	14	12	16	64	78	40
Swindon Town	42	13	12	17	73	83	38
Watford	42	15	8	19	60	73	38
Exeter City	42	12	11	19	67	73	35
Walsall	42	13	8	21	71	78	34
Newport County	42	12	10	20	74	85	34
Torquay United	42	10	11	21	64	94	31
Bristol Rovers	42	11	8	23	67	93	30
Gillingham	42	11	8	23	51	80	30
Merthyr Town	42	6	9	27	60	135	21

1930-31

Division Three South

Manager: Fred Mavin until 18 October 1930, then Jack Tresadern from 27 October 1930.

Did you know that?

Palace's first chairman Sydney Bourne, passed away in September, aged 77. Bourne was a writer and actor in his younger days and played amateur football and cricket in the late 1800s and was also a member at Surrey Cricket Club for over 50 years.

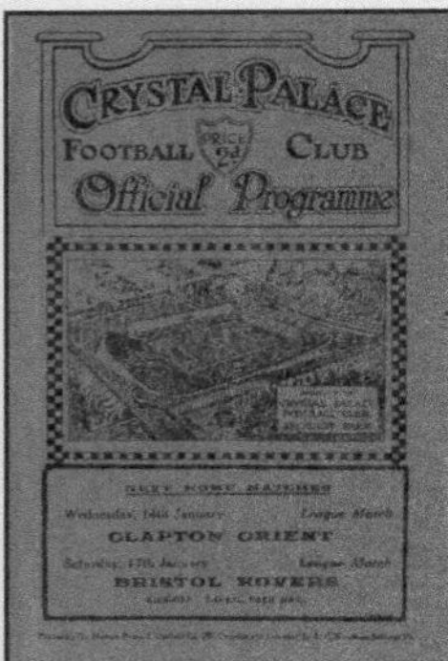

Match No.	Date	Venue	Opponents	Result		Scorers	Attendance
1	Aug 30	A	Southend United	W	4-2	Havelock, Butler 2, Simpson	7,413
2	Sep 3	A	Torquay United	L	1-3	Frost	6,163
3	6	H	Luton Town	W	5-1	Clarke, Frost, Simpson 3	15,237
4	8	A	Northampton Town	D	0-0		10,040
5	13	A	Bristol Rovers	L	1-2	Simpson	5,799
6	17	H	Northampton Town	D	0-0		11,253
7	20	H	Newport County	W	7-1	Simpson 3, Butler, Havelock, Harry, Clarke	12,625
8	27	A	Gillingham	L	2-6	Clarke, Simpson	7,123
9	Oct 4	H	Exeter City	W	7-2	Simpson 6, Butler	12,805
10	11	A	Brighton & Hove Albion	D	1-1	Clarke	9,730
11	18	H	Fulham	W	5-2	Harry 2, Clarke 2, Simpson	21,110
12	25	A	Coventry City	W	5-3	Simpson 3, Havelock, Clarke	11,460
13	Nov 1	H	Walsall	W	6-3	Simpson, Rivers, Havelock 2, Clarke, Butler	13,668
14	8	A	Queen's Park Rangers	L	0-4		12,040
15	15	H	Norwich City	W	2-1	Butler 2	10,415
16	22	A	Thames	W	2-0	Simpson 2	3,117
17	Dec 6	A	Notts County	D	2-2	Simpson 2	11,935
18	17	H	Watford	W	6-1	Simpson 4, Clarke 2	5,127
19	20	A	Bournemouth	D	0-0		5,077
20	25	A	Brentford	L	2-8	Crilly (pen), Clarke	11,770
21	26	H	Brentford	W	5-1	Clarke 2, Simpson, Wilde, Harry	15,853
22	27	H	Southend	W	3-1	Butler, Simpson, Clarke	16,466
23	Jan 3	A	Luton Town	W	2-1	Simpson, Clarke	6,051
24	17	H	Bristol Rovers	L	0-2		14,849
25	26	A	Newport County	L	1-2	Simpson	1,967
26	31	H	Gillingham	W	5-0	Simpson 3, Harry, Lane	15,042
27	Feb 7	A	Exeter City	L	3-4	Simpson 2, Clarke	5,756
28	14	H	Brighton & Hove Albion	L	0-1		16,986
29	21	A	Fulham	L	0-2		15,433
30	28	H	Coventry City	W	1-0	Lane	10,546
31	Mar 7	A	Walsall	L	1-2	Simpson	3,384
32	14	H	Queen's Park Rangers	W	4-0	Clarke 2, Turner, Harry	14,366
33	21	A	Norwich City	L	1-2	Simpson	7,756
34	28	H	Thames	W	2-1	Simpson, Butler	12,071
35	Apr 3	H	Swindon Town	W	3-1	Turner, Simpson 2	12,283
36	4	A	Clapton Orient	L	2-3	Clarke, Butler	7,414
37	6	A	Swindon Town	D	4-4	Turner, Simpson 3	4,842
38	11	H	Notts County	D	1-1	Harry	19,638
39	18	A	Watford	W	2-0	Harry, Butler	5,377
40	20	H	Clapton Orient	W	3-1	Lane 2, Butler	6,567
41	25	H	Bournemouth	W	1-0	Clarke	7,754
42	May 2	H	Torquay United	W	5-0	Simpson, Butler 2, Clarke, Harry	12,172

Final League Position: 2nd in Division Three South

Appearances

Goals

FA Cup

Round	Date	Venue	Opponents	Result		Scorers	Attendance
1	Nov 29	H	Taunton Town	W	6-0	Clarke, Simpson 3, Greener, Butler	13,038
2	Dec 13	H	Newark Town	W	6-0	Butler, Simpson 4, Clarke	15,300
3	Jan 10	H	Reading	D	1-1	Butler	22,800
R	14	A	Reading	D	1-1*	Clarke	15,873
2R	19	N+	Reading	W	2-0	Clarke, Simpson	19,737
4	24	H	Everton	L	0-6		38,000

+ Played at Stamford Bridge, Chelsea. * After extra-time

Appearances

Goals

Imrie	Wetherby	Charlton	Frost	Barrie	Greener	Harry	Havelock	Simpson	Butler	Clarke	Hamilton	Crilly	Watson	Callender	Wilde	Rivers	Lloyd	Legg	Turner	Brennan	Fishlock	Lane	Charlesworth	Nicholas	Wilcockson
1	2	3	4	5	6	7	8	9	10	11															
1	2	3	4	5	6	7	8	9	10	11															
1	2	3	4	5	6	7	8	9	10	11															
1	2	3		5	6	7	8	9	10	11	4														
1	2	3		5	6	7	8	9	10	11	4														
1		3	4	5	6	7		9	10	11		2	8												
1		3		5	6	7	8	9	10	11	4	2													
1		3		5	6	7	8	9	10	11	4	2													
		3			6	7	8	9	10	11		2		1	5	4									
		3			6	7		9	10	11		2		1	5	4	8								
		3			6	7	8	9	10	11		2		1	5	4									
		3			6	7	8	9	10	11		2		1	5	4									
	2				6	7	8	9	10	11		3		1	5	4									
					6	7	8	9	10	11		3		1	5	4		2							
	2				6	7		9	10	11		3		1	5	4			8						
				3	6	7	8	9	10	11		2		1	5	4									
				3	6	7		9	10	11		2		1	5	4			8						
				3	6	7		9	10	11		2		1	5	4			8						
				3	6	7		9	10	11		2		1	5	4			8						
				3	6	7		9	10	11		2		1	5	4				8					
		3			6	7		9	10	11		2		1	5	4			8						
		3			6	7		9	10	11		2		1	5	4			8						
		3			6	7		9	10	11		2		1	5	4			8						
		3			6	7		9	10			2		1	5	4			8		11				
1		3				7		9			6	2	8		5	4				10	11				
1		3			6	7		9	10			2			5	4						8	11		
1				3	6	7		9	10	11		2			5	4						8			
1		3			6	7		9	10	11		2			5	4						8			
1		3			6	7		9	10	11		2			5				4			8			
1		3		5		7		9	10	11		2			6	4						8			
1		3		5		7		9	10	11		2				4			6			8			
1		3			6	7		9		11	4	2			5				10			8			
1		3			6	7		9		11	4	2			5				10			8			
		3			6	7		9	10	11	4	2		1	5				8						
		3			6	7		9	10	11	4	2		1	5				8						
		3			6	7		9	10	11		2		1		4			8					5	
		3		2				9	10	11				1		4	6		7			8		5	
		3			6	7		9	10	11		2		1					4			8		5	
		3			6	7		9	10	11		2		1					4			8		5	
		3			6	7		9	10	11		2		1					4			8		5	
		3			6	7		9	10	11		2		1					4			8		5	
		3			6	7		9	10	11		2		1					4			8		5	
17	7	33	4	17	38	41	13	42	39	39	9	36	2	25	26	24	2	1	21	2	2	14	1	7	
			2			9	5	46	14	21		1			1	1			3			4			

Imrie	Wetherby	Charlton	Frost	Barrie	Greener	Harry	Havelock	Simpson	Butler	Clarke	Hamilton	Crilly	Watson	Callender	Wilde	Rivers	Lloyd	Legg	Turner	Brennan	Fishlock	Lane	Charlesworth	Nicholas	Wilcockson
				3	6	7		9	10	11		2		1	5	4			8						
				3	6	7		9	10	11		2		1	5	4			8						
		3			6	7		9	10	11		2		1	5	4			8						
		3			6	7		9	10	11		2		1	5	4			8						
		3			6	7		9	10	11		2		1	5	4			8						
1		3				7		9	10	11		2			5	4			8						6
1		4		2	5	6		6	6	6		6		5	6	6			6						1
					1			8	3	4															

League Table

	P	W	D	L	F	A	Pts
Notts County	42	24	11	7	97	46	59
Crystal Palace	42	22	7	13	107	71	51
Brentford	42	22	6	14	90	64	50
Brighton & Hove Albion	42	17	15	10	68	53	49
Southend United	42	22	5	15	76	60	49
Northampton Town	42	18	12	12	77	59	48
Luton Town	42	19	8	15	76	51	46
Queen's Park Rangers	42	20	3	19	82	75	43
Fulham	42	18	7	17	77	75	43
Bournemouth	42	15	13	14	72	73	43
Torquay United	42	17	9	16	80	84	43
Swindon Town	42	18	6	18	89	94	42
Exeter City	42	17	8	17	84	90	42
Coventry City	42	16	9	17	75	65	41
Bristol Rovers	42	16	8	18	75	92	40
Gillingham	42	14	10	18	61	76	38
Walsall	42	14	9	19	78	95	37
Watford	42	14	7	21	72	75	35
Clapton Orient	42	14	7	21	63	91	35
Thames	42	13	8	21	54	93	34
Newport County	42	11	6	25	69	111	28
Norwich City	42	10	8	24	47	76	28

1931-32

Division Three South

Manager: Jack Tresadern

Did you know that?

The previous season (his second of League football), Peter Simpson hit a quite magnificent 54 goals in 48 games in all competitions, still a club record and likely never to be bettered. This season he scored four hat-tricks and recorded his 100th goal in a Palace shirt, as they remained unbeaten at home all season.

Match No.	Date		Venue	Opponents	Result		Scorers	Attendance
1	Aug	29	H	Torquay United	W	7-0	Simpson 4, Lane, Butler, Clarke	18,479
2		31	A	Clapton Orient	W	3-1	Simpson 3	7,344
3	Sep	5	A	Bristol Rovers	L	1-6	Clarke	12,979
4		9	A	Brighton & Hove Albion	W	3-0	Simpson, Lane, Turner	11,175
5		12	H	Queen's Park Rangers	D	1-1	Clarke	11,000
6		16	H	Brighton & Hove Albion	W	2-0	Charlesworth, Clarke	12,071
7		19	A	Bournemouth	L	1-4	Lane	9,638
8		26	H	Coventry City	D	2-2	Clarke 2	16,259
9	Oct	3	H	Watford	W	2-1	Lane, Simpson	20,953
10		10	A	Mansfield Town	D	1-1	Clarke	10,849
11		17	A	Gillingham	D	0-0		4,856
12		24	H	Luton Town	D	1-1	Clarke	15,327
13		31	A	Cardiff City	W	3-1	Simpson 2, Butler	6,757
14	Nov	7	H	Northampton Town	W	4-0	Simpson 3, Harry	16,119
15		14	A	Reading	L	0-3		9,114
16		21	H	Southend United	W	3-2	Clarke (pen), Butler, Simpson	29,335
17	Dec	5	H	Thames	W	2-1	Simpson, Charlton (pen)	14,106
18		19	H	Exeter City	W	3-0	Clarke 3	8,905
19		25	H	Swindon Town	D	0-0		17,713
20		26	A	Swindon Town	L	2-3	Cropper, Clarke	9,905
21	Jan	2	A	Torquay United	L	1-3	own-goal (Fowler)	2,703
22		9	H	Mansfield Town	W	2-1	Clarke, Charlesworth	10,817
23		16	H	Bristol Rovers	W	5-0	Harry, Greener, Clarke, Charlesworth, Wilcockson	10,691
24		18	A	Fulham	L	0-4		8,446
25		28	A	Queen's Park Rangers	D	2-2	Harry 2	8,369
26		30	H	Bournemouth	D	1-1	May	12,493
27	Feb	6	A	Coventry City	L	0-8		11,459
28		17	A	Watford	W	2-1	Simpson, Murphy	4,854
29		27	H	Gillingham	W	1-0	Turner	11,596
30	Mar	5	A	Luton Town	L	0-3		6,105
31		12	H	Cardiff City	W	5-0	Clarke, Turner, Simpson 3	13,206
32		19	A	Northampton Town	L	0-5		6,685
33		25	H	Norwich City	W	3-1	May 2, Simpson	18,974
34		26	H	Reading	D	1-1	Murphy	15,987
35		28	A	Norwich City	L	2-3	Simpson, Lane	16,412
36	Apr	2	A	Southend United	L	0-1		8,745
37		9	H	Fulham	W	2-0	Simpson, Clarke	21,326
38		13	A	Brentford	D	1-1	Clarke	5,816
39		16	A	Thames	W	3-1	May, Harry, Lane	1,348
40		23	H	Brentford	W	1-0	Clarke	12,138
41		30	A	Exeter City	W	1-0	Turner	5,538
42	May	7	H	Clapton Orient	D	0-0		10,286

Final League Position: 4th in Division Three South — Appearances

1 own-goal — Goals

FA Cup

1	Nov	28	A	Reading	W	1-0	Clarke	14,135
2	Dec	12	A	Bath City	L	1-2	Simpson	6,400

Appearances

Goals

Callender	Crilly	Charlton	Turner	Nicholas	Greener	Harry	Lane	Simpson	Butler	Clarke	Barrie	Wilde	Dunn	Parry	Rivers	Charlesworth	Wilcockson	Manders	Jewett	Lloyd	Murphy	Fishlock	Cropper	May	Clifford
1	2	3	4	5	6	7	8	9	10	11															
1		3	4		6	7	8	9	10	11	2	5													
1		3	4	5	6	7	8	9	10	11	2														
			4		6	7	8	9	10	11	2	5	1	3											
			8		6	7			10	11	2	5	1	3	4	9	10								
			8		6	7			10	11	2	5	1	3	4	9									
			4		6	7	8		10	11	2	5	1	3		9									
		3	8		6	7			10	11	2		1	5				9	4						
	2	3	4		6	7	8	9	10	11			1	5											
1		3	4		6	7	8	9	10	11		5		2											
1		3	4		6	7	8	9	10	11		5		2											
1		3	4		6	7	8	9	10	11		5		2											
1		3	4	5		7	8	9	10	11				2						6					
1		3	4	5		7	8	9	10	11				2						6					
1		3	4	5		7	8	9	10	11				2						6					
1		3	4			7		9	10	11	2	5								6	8				
1	2	3	4			7		9	10			5								6	8	11			
1	2	3	4		6	7			10	11		5									8		9		
1	2	3	4		6	7		9		11		5									10			8	
1	2	3	6			7	8		10	11				5	4								9		
1	2		4		6	7	8		10	11	3			5									9		
1	2		4		6	7			10	11	3			5		9					8				
1	2		4		6	7				11	3	5				9	10						8		
1	2		4		6	7				11	3	5				9	10						8		
	2		10		6	7		9		11		5	1	3						4				8	
	2	3	4			7		9	10	11		5	1							6				8	
	2	3	4		6	7	10	9				5	1									11		8	
			10		6	7		9		11	3	5	1	2						4	8				
			10		6	7		9		11	3	5	1	2						4	8				
			8		6	7		9		11	3	5	1	2			10			4					
			8		6	7		9		11	3	5	1	2						4				10	
			8			7		9		11	3	5	1	2	6					4				10	
1		3	8			7		9				5		2	4		6				11		10		
1		3	10	5		7								2	4	9					8	11			6
1		3		5		7	8	9		11		4		2										10	6
1		3		5		7	8	9		11		4		2	6									10	
1	3			5		7	8	9		11		4		2	6									10	
1	3		10	5		7	8	9		11		4		2	6										
1	3			5		7	8	9		11		4		2	6									10	
1	3		8	5		7		9		11		4		2	6									10	
1	3		8	5		7		9		11		4		2	6									10	
1	3		8	5		7		9		11		4		2	6									10	
28	19	22	38	14	24	42	20	31	21	38	17	31	14	31	13	7	5	1	1	12	8	4	3	16	2
		1	4		1	5	6	23	3	19						3	1				2		1	4	

Callender	Crilly	Charlton	Turner	Nicholas	Greener	Harry	Lane	Simpson	Butler	Clarke	Barrie	Wilde	Dunn	Parry	Rivers	Charlesworth	Wilcockson	Manders	Jewett	Lloyd	Murphy	Fishlock	Cropper	May	Clifford
1	2	3	4			7		9	10	11		5							6	8					
1	2	3	4			7		9	10	11		5							6	8					
2	2	2	2			2		2	2	2		2							2	2					
								1		1															

League Table

	P	W	D	L	F	A	Pts
Fulham	42	24	9	9	111	62	57
Reading	42	23	9	10	97	67	55
Southend United	42	21	11	10	77	53	53
Crystal Palace	42	20	11	11	74	63	51
Brentford	42	19	10	13	68	52	48
Luton Town	42	20	7	15	95	70	47
Exeter City	42	20	7	15	77	62	47
Brighton & Hove Albion	42	17	12	13	73	58	46
Cardiff City	42	19	8	15	87	73	46
Norwich City	42	17	12	13	76	67	46
Watford	42	19	8	15	81	79	46
Coventry City	42	18	8	16	108	97	44
Queen's Park Rangers	42	15	12	15	79	73	42
Northampton Town	42	16	7	19	69	69	39
Bournemouth	42	13	12	17	70	78	38
Clapton Orient	42	12	11	19	77	90	35
Swindon Town	42	14	6	22	70	84	34
Bristol Rovers	42	13	8	21	65	92	34
Torquay United	42	12	9	21	72	106	33
Mansfield Town	42	11	10	21	75	108	32
Gillingham	42	10	8	24	40	82	28
Thames	42	7	9	26	53	109	23

1932-33

Division Three South

Manager: Jack Tresadern

Did you know that?

After 28 years' service and having played a major part in the creation of Palace back in 1905, Edmund Goodman stepped down from his post as club secretary and retired from football, going on to run a grocery store in the Anerley area where he lived. He later moved to Kent after World War Two, before moving back to Anerley, and continued watching Palace when he could until his death in 1960.

Match No.	Date		Venue	Opponents	Result		Scorers	Attendance
1	Aug	27	A	Bristol Rovers	W	3-2	Simpson 2, Roberts	13,588
2		31	H	Brighton & Hove Albion	W	5-0	Doncaster, May, Roberts 2, Simpson	13,704
3	Sep	3	H	Aldershot	W	3-0	Roberts, May, Doncaster	12,167
4		7	A	Brighton & Hove Albion	W	2-1	Simpson, Roberts	9,302
5		10	A	Queen's Park Rangers	L	1-2	Simpson	15,955
6		17	H	Southend United	W	4-1	Manders 2, Doncaster, May	19,419
7		24	A	Exeter City	D	1-1	May	8,734
8	Oct	1	A	Gillingham	L	0-2		9,827
9		8	H	Watford	L	0-3		12,095
10		15	A	Cardiff City	D	1-1	Doncaster	7,144
11		22	H	Torquay United	W	2-1	Roberts, Rivers	10,031
12		29	A	Brentford	L	0-2		17,827
13	Nov	5	H	Coventry City	L	1-3	Simpson	12,203
14		12	A	Bristol City	D	3-3	Simpson, May 2	7,804
15		19	H	Northampton Town	W	2-0	Roberts, Harry	6,463
16	Dec	3	H	Swindon Town	W	4-3	Goddard, Turner (pen), Wilde, Harry	8,936
17		10	A	Bournemouth	L	2-3	May, Walters	2,862
18		17	H	Newport County	D	0-0		8,644
19		24	A	Luton Town	D	1-1	Berry	7,042
20		26	H	Reading	D	1-1	Manders	10,400
21		27	A	Reading	W	3-2	Harry, Roberts, Berry	21,180
22		31	H	Bristol Rovers	W	2-0	Manders, Roberts	10,636
23	Jan	7	A	Aldershot	L	1-3	Roberts	7,979
24		14	A	Clapton Orient	L	1-4	Manders	3,130
25		21	H	Queen's Park Rangers	L	0-1		8,157
26	Feb	1	A	Southend United	W	2-1	Berry, Manders	3,008
27		4	H	Exeter City	D	2-2	Walters, Roberts	10,361
28		11	H	Gillingham	W	5-1	Berry, Harry, own-goal (Lester), Roberts, Manders	8,280
29		18	A	Watford	L	0-1		5,425
30		25	H	Cardiff City	W	4-1	Simpson 3, Harry	5,805
31	Mar	4	A	Torquay United	L	1-2	Walters	3,467
32		11	H	Brentford	W	2-1	Roberts, Manders	20,261
33		18	A	Coventry City	L	2-6	Goddard (pen), Manders	14,610
34		25	H	Bristol City	D	2-2	Clarke, Goddard	9,641
35	Apr	1	A	Northampton Town	L	0-1		4,799
36		8	H	Clapton Orient	W	2-1	Manders, Goddard	8,394
37		14	H	Norwich City	W	4-0	Turner, Goddard, Clarke 2	18,265
38		15	A	Swindon Town	L	0-1		4,642
39		17	A	Norwich City	L	0-3		20,540
40		22	H	Bournemouth	W	3-0	Simpson 2, Clarke	7,825
41		29	A	Newport County	W	3-1	Turner 2, Walters	5,168
42	May	6	H	Luton Town	W	3-0	Harry, Simpson 2	6,554

Final League Position: 5th in Division Three South

Appearances

1 own-goal

Goals

FA Cup

Round	Date		Venue	Opponents	Result		Scorers	Attendance
1	Nov	26	H	Brighton & Hove Albion	L	1-2	Simpson	14,870

Appearances

Goals

Dunn	McGregor	Parry	Wilde	Nicholas	Rivers	Harry	May	Simpson	Roberts	Doncaster	Crilly	Turner	Manders	Hopkins	Clarke	Clifford	Goddard	Berry	Barrie	Walters	Turnbull	Nash	Brown	Smith T.	Goodcliffe
1	2	3	4	5	6	7	8	9	10	11															
1	2	3	4	5	6	7	8	9	10	11															
1	2	3	4	5	6	7	8	9	10	11															
1	2	3	4	5	6	7	8	9	10	11															
1		3	4	5	6	7	8	9	10	11	2														
1		3	4	5	6	7	8		10	11		2	9												
1		3	4	5	6	7	8		10	11		2	9												
1		3	4	5	6	7	8		10	11		2	9												
1		3	4	5	6	8		9	10			2		7	11										
1		3	4		6	7		9	10	11		2	8			5									
1		3	5		6			9	10	11		2	8	7		4									
1		3	5		6			9	10	11		2		7		4	8								
1		3	5		6			9	10	11		2		7		4	8								
1		3	5		6	7	8	9	10			2				4		11							
1		3	4		6	7	8	9	10			2						11	5						
1		3	4	5		7	8	9		11		2				6	10								
1			4			7	10	9			3	2				6		11	5	8					
1			4			7	10	9		11	3	2				6			5	8					
1		2	4		6	7			8		3		9					11	5	10					
1			4		6	7			8		3	2	9					11	5	10					
1			4		6	7			8		3	2	9					11	5	10					
1			4		6	7			8			2	9					11	5	10	3				
1			4		6	7			8		3	2	9					11	5	10					
1		3	4	5		7			8			2	9			6	10	11							
			4		6	7			8	10	3		9					11	5		2	1			
1					6	7			8		3	2	9					11	5	10			4		
1					6	7			8		3	2	9					11	5	10			4		
1						7			8		3	2	9					11	5	10			4	6	
1					6	7			8		3	2						11	5	10			4		9
1						7		10	8		3	2	9					11	5				4	6	
1						7			8		3	2	9					11	5	10			4	6	
1		3				7			8			2	9		11		10		5				4	6	
1		3			4	7			8			2	9		11		10		5					6	
1		3				7			8		2	4	9		11		10		5					6	
1		3				7					2	8	9		11		10		5				4	6	
1		3				7					2	8	9		11		10		5				4	6	
1		3			6	7					2	8	9		11		10		5				4		
1		3				7					2	8	9		11		10		5				4	6	
1		3				7		10			2	8	9		11	6			5				4		
1		3			6	7		9			2	8			11		10		5				4		
1		3			6	7		9			2	8			11				5	10			4		
1		3	6			7		9			2	8						11	5	10			4		
41	4	29	26	11	28	39	13	20	31	15	23	35	25	4	11	10	12	17	26	14	2	1	15	9	1
			1		1	6	7	14	13	4		4	10		4		5	4		4					

Dunn	McGregor	Parry	Wilde	Nicholas	Rivers	Harry	May	Simpson	Roberts	Doncaster	Crilly	Turner	Manders	Hopkins	Clarke	Clifford	Goddard	Berry	Barrie	Walters	Turnbull	Nash	Brown	Smith T.	Goodcliffe
1		3	4		6	7	8	9	10			2			11				5						
1		1	1		1	1	1	1	1			1			1				1						
								1																	

League Table

	P	W	D	L	F	A	Pts
Brentford	42	26	10	6	90	49	62
Exeter City	42	24	10	8	88	48	58
Norwich City	42	22	13	7	88	55	57
Reading	42	19	13	10	103	71	51
Crystal Palace	42	19	8	15	78	64	46
Coventry City	42	19	6	17	106	77	44
Gillingham	42	18	8	16	72	61	44
Northampton Town	42	18	8	16	76	66	44
Bristol Rovers	42	15	14	13	61	56	44
Torquay United	42	16	12	14	72	67	44
Watford	42	16	12	14	66	63	44
Brighton & Hove Albion	42	17	8	17	66	65	42
Southend United	42	15	11	16	65	82	41
Luton Town	42	13	13	16	78	78	39
Bristol City	42	12	13	17	83	90	37
Queen's Park Rangers	42	13	11	18	72	87	37
Aldershot	42	13	10	19	61	72	36
Bournemouth	42	12	12	18	60	81	36
Cardiff City	42	12	7	23	69	99	31
Clapton Orient	42	8	13	21	59	93	29
Newport County	42	11	7	24	61	105	29
Swindon Town	42	9	11	22	60	105	29

1933-34

Division Three South

Manager: Jack Tresadern

Did you know that?

Forward Ronnie Rooke scored an amazing 160 Goalsin just over three years for Palace's reserves and averaged a goal every other game during his first-team career at Selhurst Park. He later returned to the club in 1949 as player-manager.

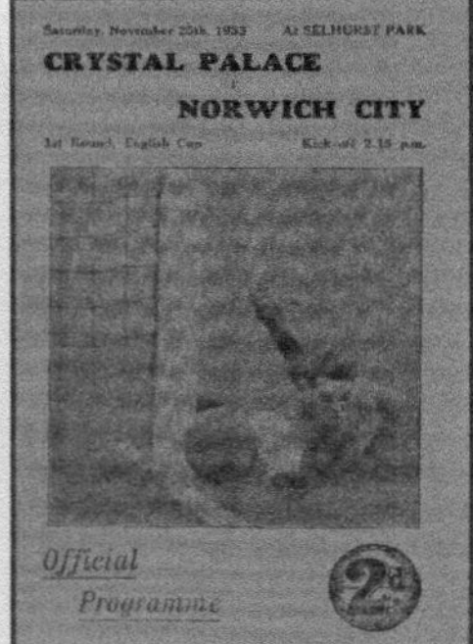

Match No.	Date	Venue	Opponents	Result		Scorers	Attendance
1	Aug 26	A	Southend United	W	4-0	Simpson 2, Earle, Norris	10,285
2	30	A	Bristol Rovers	W	1-0	Simpson	17,657
3	Sep 2	H	Coventry City	W	2-1	Norris, Simpson	17,888
4	6	H	Bristol Rovers	L	1-2	Norris	15,843
5	9	A	Reading	D	0-0		11,172
6	13	H	Luton Town	D	2-2	Simpson, Roberts	9,457
7	16	H	Watford	W	4-3	Turner, Simpson, Earle 2	14,542
8	23	A	Charlton Athletic	L	2-4	Roberts 2	10,532
9	30	H	Bournemouth	W	4-1	Norris, Simpson 2, Roberts	13,502
10	Oct 7	A	Cardiff	L	0-4		9,022
11	14	H	Exeter City	D	0-0		10,698
12	21	A	Bristol City	D	2-2	Turner, Simpson	8,919
13	28	H	Clapton Orient	W	3-2	Manders, Simpson, Hayward	11,693
14	Nov 4	A	Swindon Town	L	2-3	Turner, Manders	8,908
15	11	H	Brighton & Hove Albion	W	2-1	Simpson 2 (1 pen)	10,562
16	18	A	Aldershot	W	4-0	Simpson 4	4,297
17	Dec 2	A	Northampton Town	L	2-4	Roberts, Simpson	5,034
18	16	A	Queen's Park Rangers	L	1-2	Simpson	12,849
19	23	H	Newport County	D	1-1	Simpson	10,755
20	25	H	Norwich City	L	0-1		22,126
21	26	A	Norwich City	L	0-2		16,386
22	30	H	Southend United	D	1-1	Edwards	8,383
23	Jan 6	A	Coventry City	L	1-5	Simpson	17,065
24	20	H	Reading	D	0-0		12,416
25	31	A	Watford	L	1-3	Dawes	2,391
26	Feb 3	H	Charlton Athletic	W	1-0	Manders	9,324
27	10	A	Bournemouth	D	1-1	Dawes	4,852
28	17	H	Cardiff City	W	3-2	Rooke, Turner, Dawes	6,290
29	24	A	Exeter City	W	2-1	Rooke, Dawes	5,948
30	Mar 3	H	Bristol City	L	0-1		10,947
31	10	A	Clapton Orient	L	0-2		11,907
32	17	H	Swindon Town	D	0-0		8,327
33	24	A	Brighton & Hove Albion	L	1-4	Turner	5,356
34	30	H	Gillingham	W	3-2	Dawes 2, Crompton	12,836
35	31	H	Aldershot	W	4-1	Dawes 3, Manders	9,362
36	Apr 2	A	Gillingham	W	5-0	Dawes 2, Manders, Crompton, Goddard	9,089
37	7	A	Luton Town	L	1-2	Turner	6,841
38	14	H	Northampton Town	L	1-2	Dawes	7,984
39	21	A	Torquay United	L	1-2	Goddard	3,052
40	25	H	Torquay United	W	4-1	Goddard, Haynes, Dawes, Crompton	3,683
41	28	H	Queen's Park Rangers	W	4-1	Dawes 3, Crompton	7,777
42	May 5	A	Newport County	L	0-1		3,930

Final League Position: 12th in Division Three South

Appearances
Goals

FA Cup

1	Nov 25	H	Norwich City	W	3-0	Roberts, Manders, Turner	22,905
2	Dec 9	A	Stockport County	W	2-1	Simpson, Manders	17,400
3	Jan 13	H	Aldershot	W	1-0	Manders	23,628
4	27	A	Arsenal	L	0-7		56,177

Appearances
Goals

Dunn	Hayward	Parry	Brown	Barrie	Wilde	Turner	Norris	Simpson	Roberts	Earle	Parker	Nicholas	Howe	Finn	Harry	Thompson	Manders	ClarkeW	SmithWS	May	Edwards	Rossiter	Haynes	Dawes A.	Rooke	Robertson	Ward	Crompton	Goddard
1	2	3	4	5	6	7	8	9	10	11																			
1	2	3	4		6	7	8	9	10		11	5																	
1	2	3	4		6	7	8	9	10			5	11																
1	2	3	4		6	7	8	9				5	11	10															
1	2	3		5	6	4	8	9		11					7	10													
1	2	3		5	6	4	8	9	10	11					7														
1	2	3	4	5	6	7	8	9		11							10												
1	2	3	4	5	6		8	9	10	11					7														
1	2	3	4	6			8	9	10	11				5	7														
1	2	3	4	5			8	9	10	11				6	7														
1	2	3	4	5			8	9	10		11			6	7														
1	2	3	4	5	6	7		9	10								8	11											
1	2	3	4		5	7		10									9	11	6	8									
1	2	3			5	7		10	8								9	11	6		4								
1		3	6		5	7		9	10								8	11			4	2							
1		3			6	7		9	10								8	11			4	2	5						
1		3				7		9	10								8	11	6		4	2	5						
1		3			4	7		9	10								8	11	6			2	5						
1	2	3			5	7		9	8									11	6		4			10					
1		3			5	7				4		2						11	6	8				10	9				
1	2				5	7		9		6		3				11	8				4			10					
1				5	6	7						3					8	11			4	2		10	9				
	2			5	6	11		9	10			3					8	7			4					1			
1	2	3			5	10		9		11							8	7			4						6		
1		3			5	10		9							7			11			4	2		8			6		
		3			5	4		10						6	7		8					2		9		1		11	
		3			5	4		9						6	7		8					2		10		1		11	
		3			5	8								6	7							2	4	10	9	1		11	
1		3			4	8								6	7							2	5	10	9			11	
1		3			4	8								6	7							2	5	10	9			11	
1		3	4		6	8									7		9					2	5	10				11	
1		3	4		6	8									7		9					2	5	10				11	
1		3			6	4									7		8					2	5	10	9			11	
1	2	3			5	7											8		6				4	10				11	9
1		3			5	7											8					2	4	10			6	11	9
1		3			5	7											8					2	4	10			6	11	9
1		3			5	7											8					2	4	10			6	11	9
1		3			5	7											8					2	4	10			6	11	9
1		3			5	7											8					2	4	10			6	11	9
1		3			5	8												7			6	2	4	10				11	9
1		3			5	8												7			6	2	4	10				11	9
1		3			5	8												7			6	2	4	10				11	9
38	19	39	14	11	38	38	11	25	16	10	2	7	2	9	15	2	23	16	7	2	13	22	18	22	6	4	7	17	9
	1					6	4	20	5	3							5				1		1	16	2			4	3

Dunn	Hayward	Parry	Brown	Barrie	Wilde	Turner	Norris	Simpson	Roberts	Earle	Parker	Nicholas	Howe	Finn	Harry	Thompson	Manders	ClarkeW	SmithWS	May	Edwards	Rossiter	Haynes	Dawes A.	Rooke	Robertson	Ward	Crompton	Goddard
1		3			5	7		9	10								8	11	6		4	2							
1		3			4	7		9	10								8	11	6			2	5						
1	2	3			5	10		9		11							8	7					4				6		
1		3			5	10	4	9							7		8	11				2					6		
4	1	4			4	4	1	4	2	1					1		4	4	2		1	3	2				2		
						1		1	1								3												

League Table

	P	W	D	L	F	A	Pts
Norwich City	42	25	11	6	88	49	61
Coventry City	42	21	12	9	100	54	54
Reading	42	21	12	9	82	50	54
Queen's Park Rangers	42	24	6	12	70	51	54
Charlton Athletic	42	22	8	12	83	56	52
Luton Town	42	21	10	11	83	61	52
Bristol Rovers	42	20	11	11	77	47	51
Swindon Town	42	17	11	14	64	68	45
Exeter City	42	16	11	15	68	57	43
Brighton & Hove Albion	42	15	13	14	68	60	43
Clapton Orient	42	16	10	16	75	69	42
Crystal Palace	42	16	9	17	71	67	41
Northampton Town	42	14	12	16	71	78	40
Aldershot	42	13	12	17	52	71	38
Watford	42	15	7	20	71	63	37
Southend United	42	12	10	20	51	74	34
Gillingham	42	11	11	20	75	96	33
Newport County	42	8	17	17	49	70	33
Bristol City	42	10	13	19	58	85	33
Torquay United	42	13	7	22	53	93	33
Bournemouth	42	9	9	24	60	102	27
Cardiff City	42	9	6	27	57	105	24

1934-35

Division Three South

Manager: Jack Tresadern

Did you know that?

Peter Simpson holds the record for the most hat-tricks scored by a Palace player, 19 in total, including one on his debut in a victory against Norwich on 14 September 1929.

Match No.	Date		Venue	Opponents	Result		Scorers	Attendance
1	Aug	25	A	Aldershot	D	2-2	Bigg, Dawes	6,091
2		30	A	Queen's Park Rangers	D	3-3	Carson, Bigg, Dawes	9,415
3	Sep	1	H	Cardiff City	W	6-1	Dawes 5, Bigg	17,641
4		5	H	Queen's Park Rangers	L	2-3	Simpson 2	15,843
5		8	A	Brighton & Hove Albion	L	0-3		10,560
6		15	H	Luton Town	W	2-1	Simpson, Dawes	13,416
7		22	A	Southend United	W	4-1	Manders 2, Crompton, Carson	7,032
8		29	H	Bristol Rovers	W	2-0	Simpson 2	15,556
9	Oct	6	A	Charlton Athletic	D	2-2	Dawes, Simpson	21,157
10		13	H	Coventry City	W	3-1	Dawes, Crompton, Carson	20,943
11		20	A	Clapton Orient	L	0-2		12,105
12		27	H	Gillingham	W	2-0	Dawes 2	12,942
13	Nov	3	A	Bristol City	W	1-0	Bigg	11,289
14		10	H	Millwall	D	1-1	Dawes	10,736
15		17	A	Bournemouth	D	1-1	Simpson	4,828
16	Dec	1	A	Newport County	W	3-2	Manders, Carson 2	4,317
17		15	A	Reading	L	1-6	Carson	8,756
18		22	H	Northampton Town	W	2-0	Collins, Bigg	9,318
19		25	A	Torquay United	L	1-7	Dawes	2,893
20		26	H	Torquay United	D	2-2	Simpson, Manders	19,025
21		29	H	Aldershot	W	3-0	Rooke, Collins, Manders	9,972
22	Jan	5	A	Cardiff City	L	0-2		9,648
23		12	H	Watford	D	0-0		11,288
24		19	H	Brighton & Hove Albion	W	3-0	Carson, Manders, Simpson	11,189
25		26	A	Exeter City	W	6-0	Manders 2, Carson 3, Bigg	3,718
26		30	A	Luton Town	D	2-2	Simpson, Bigg	3,410
27	Feb	2	H	Southend United	W	1-0	Simpson	13,313
28		9	A	Bristol Rovers	L	3-5	Carson, Bigg, Simpson	7,028
29		16	H	Charlton Athletic	L	1-2	Simpson	27,110
30		23	A	Coventry City	D	1-1	Carson	15,041
31	Mar	2	H	Clapton Orient	W	1-0	Bigg	13,214
32		9	A	Gillingham	L	0-2		2,712
33		16	H	Bristol City	W	3-1	Rooke 2, Manders	10,357
34		23	A	Millwall	L	2-3	Dawes, Rooke	9,630
35		30	H	Bournemouth	W	1-0	Dawes	8,029
36	Apr	6	A	Watford	L	0-2		6,588
37		13	H	Newport County	W	6-0	Bigg 3, Manders 2, Purdon	8,323
38		19	H	Swindon Town	W	7-0	Dawes 2, Manders 2, Purdon, Bigg 2	13,506
39		20	H	Exeter City	L	0-1		9,382
40		22	A	Swindon Town	D	1-1	Simpson	5,660
41		27	H	Reading	W	3-1	Bigg, Collins, Manders	8,969
42	May	4	A	Northampton Town	L	2-3	Bigg, Dawes	4,629

Final League Position: 5th in Division Three South

Appearances

Goals

FA Cup

1	Nov	24	A	Yeovil & Petters United	L	0-3		10,000

Appearances

Dunn	Purdon	Owens	Haynes	Wilde	Smith W.S.	Carson	Handley	Simpson	Dawes A.	Bigg	Heineman	Turner	Collins	Parry	Manders	Crompton	Rossiter	Brown T.B.	Tizard	Barnes	Reed	Rooke	Waldron
1	2	3	4	5	6	7	8	9	10	11													
1	2	3	4	5	6	7	8	9	10	11													
1	3	2	4	5	6	7	8	9	10	11													
1	3	2	4	5		7	8	9	10	11	6												
1	3	2	4	5		7		9		11	6	8	10										
1		2	4	5		7	8	9	10	11	6			3									
1		2	4	5		7		9	10		6			3	8	11							
1		2	4	5		7		9	10		6			3	8	11							
1		2	4	5		7		9	10		6			3	8	11							
1		2	4	5		7		9	10		6			3	8	11							
1		2	4	5		7		9	10		6				8	11	3						
1		2		5	6	7		9	10	11	4			3	8								
1		2		5		7		9	10	11	6	4			8			3					
1		2	4	5		7		9	10	11	6			3	8								
1		2	4	5		7		9	10	11	6			3	8								
		2	4	5		7		8	10	11			6		9			3	1				
		2	4	5		7			10	11			6		9			3	1	8			
		2	8	5		7			10	11		4	6	3	9				1				
		2	8	5		7			10	11		4	6		9		3		1				
1				5	6	7		9	10			4		2	8	11		3					
1		2		5								7	6	3	8	11					4	9	10
1		2		5								7	6	3	8	11					4	9	10
1		2		5		7		9	10			4	6	3	8	11							
1		2		5		7		9	10	11	6	4		3	8								
1		2		5		7		9	10	11	6	4		3	8								
1		2		5		7		9		11	6	4	10	3	8								
1		2		5		7		9	10	11	6	4		3	8								
1		2		5		7		9		11	6	4	10	3	8								
1		2		5		7		9		11	6	4	10	3	8								
1		2		5		7		9		11	6	4	10	3	8								
1		2		5		7				11	6	4	10	3	8							9	
1		2		5		7		9		11	6	4	10	3	8								
1		2		5		7			10	11	6	4		3	8							9	
1		2		5		7			10	11	6	4		3	8							9	
1		2		5		7			10	11	6	4		3	8							9	
1	7	2		5	6				9	11		4	10	3	8								
1	7	2		5	6			9		11		4	10	3	8								
1	7	2		5	6				9	11		4	10	3	8								
1		2		5		7				11	6	4	10	3	8							9	
1	7	2	5	4	6			9	10	11				3	8								
1	7	2	5	4	6				9	11		3	10		8								
1	7	2	5	4	6				9	11		3	10		8								
38	11	41	20	42	11	34	5	28	31	33	25	26	20	30	36	9	2	4	4	1	2	7	2
	2					12		14	19	16			3		14	2						4	

Dunn	Purdon	Owens	Haynes	Wilde	Smith W.S.	Carson	Handley	Simpson	Dawes A.	Bigg	Heineman	Turner	Collins	Parry	Manders	Crompton	Rossiter	Brown T.B.	Tizard	Barnes	Reed	Rooke	Waldron
1		2	4	5		7		9	10		6			3	8	11							
1		1	1	1		1		1	1		1			1	1	1							

League Table

	P	W	D	L	F	A	Pts
Charlton Athletic	42	27	7	8	103	52	61
Reading	42	21	11	10	89	65	53
Coventry City	42	21	9	12	86	50	51
Luton Town	42	19	12	11	92	60	50
Crystal Palace	42	19	10	13	86	64	48
Watford	42	19	9	14	76	49	47
Northampton Town	42	19	8	15	65	67	46
Bristol Rovers	42	17	10	15	73	77	44
Brighton & Hove Albion	42	17	9	16	69	62	43
Torquay United	42	18	6	18	81	75	42
Exeter City	42	16	9	17	70	75	41
Millwall	42	17	7	18	57	62	41
Queen's Park Rangers	42	16	9	17	63	72	41
Cl apton Orient	42	15	10	17	65	65	40
Bristol City	42	15	9	18	52	68	39
Swindon Town	42	13	12	17	67	78	38
Bournemouth	42	15	7	20	54	71	37
Aldershot	42	13	10	19	50	75	36
Cardiff City	42	13	9	20	62	82	35
Gillingham	42	11	13	18	55	75	35
Southend United	42	11	9	22	65	78	31
Newport County	42	10	5	27	54	112	25

1935-36

Division Three South

Manager: Tom Bromilow

Did you know that?

Fred and Albert Dawes were the first brothers to play together at Palace. Their first game in the same team was on 26 February 1936 against Clapton (later Leyton) Orient.

Match No.	Date		Venue	Opponents	Result		Scorers	Attendance
1	Aug	31	H	Cardiff City	W	3-2	Bigg 3	16,694
2	Sep	4	A	Southend United	L	1-7	Turner	7,580
3		7	A	Gillingham	W	2-0	A. Dawes 2	8,914
4		11	H	Southend United	W	3-0	Carson, A. Dawes, Manders	11,954
5		14	H	Bournemouth	W	2-0	A. Dawes 2	15,651
6		16	A	Northampton Town	L	1-3	Goodcliffe	6,319
7		21	A	Luton Town	L	0-6		13,206
8		23	H	Northampton Town	W	6-1	A. Dawes 4, Bigg, Carson	5,134
9		28	H	Notts County	D	0-0		16,153
10	Oct	5	A	Bristol Rovers	W	4-2	A. Dawes 2, Carson 2	10,568
11		12	H	Clapton Orient	D	2-2	A. Dawes, Waldron	16,619
12		19	H	Aldershot	W	2-1	A. Dawes, Manders	11,741
13		26	A	Torquay United	L	2-3	A. Dawes, Carson	4,440
14	Nov	2	H	Millwall	W	5-0	Birtley, A. Dawes 3, Blackman	19,239
15		9	A	Coventry City	L	1-8	Birtley	20,818
16		16	H	Watford	L	1-2	A. Dawes	9,376
17		23	A	Queen's Park Rangers	L	0-3		13,414
18	Dec	7	A	Exeter City	L	0-1		3,337
19		18	H	Newport County	W	6-0	Bigg 2, Blackman 3, A. Dawes	2,165
20		25	A	Swindon Town	W	2-0	Blackman, Bigg	5,450
21		26	H	Swindon Town	W	5-1	Blackman 3, Smith, A. Dawes	15,867
22		28	A	Cardiff City	D	1-1	Bigg	7,411
23	Jan	4	H	Gillingham	D	1-1	Blackman	11,726
24		15	H	Brighton & Hove Albion	W	4-0	A. Dawes 3, Blackman	3,030
25		18	A	Bournemouth	W	5-2	A. Dawes 2 (1 pen), Blackman, Birtley, Wood	6,926
26		29	H	Luton Town	W	5-1	A. Dawes 2 (1 pen), Birtley 2, Blackman	6,804
27	Feb	1	A	Notts County	L	1-3	A. Dawes	8,385
28		8	H	Bristol Rovers	W	5-3	Wood, A. Dawes 2, Blackman, Bigg	11,050
29		22	A	Aldershot	W	3-1	Birtley, Wood, Bigg	3,807
30		26	A	Clapton Orient	L	0-1		5,699
31		29	H	Coventry City	W	3-1	A. Dawes, Blackman 2	14,638
32	Mar	7	A	Newport County	W	5-2	Blackman, Birtley, A. Dawes 3	3,232
33		14	H	Torquay United	W	1-0	Wood	15,324
34		21	A	Watford	L	2-3	Blackman, Bigg	10,432
35		28	H	Queen's Park Rangers	L	0-2		22,389
36	Apr	4	A	Brighton & Hove Albion	L	1-2	Waldron	5,879
37		10	H	Reading	W	2-0	Blackman, A. Dawes	23,025
38		11	H	Exeter City	D	2-2	Blackman, A. Dawes (pen)	10,059
39		13	A	Reading	W	1-0	Waldron	18,716
40		18	A	Millwall	L	0-4		14,498
41		25	H	Bristol City	W	6-1	Bigg, Waldron 2, Edwards, A. Dawes 2 (1 pen)	6,244
42		29	A	Bristol City	L	0-2		5,099

Final League Position: 6th in Division Three South

Appearances
Goals

FA Cup

1	Nov	30	A	Bristol City	W	1-0	A. Dawes	13,997
2	Dec	14	A	Margate	L	1-3	Blackman	6,081

Appearances
Goals

Read	Smith Wilf	Waterfield	Haynes	Wilde	Smith W.S.	Turner	Manders	Rooke	Dawes A.	Bigg	Comrie	Owens	Parry	Carson	Goddard	Goodcliffe	Waldron	Dunn	Rumbold	Purdon	Thorpe	Birtley	Blackman	Booth	Collins	Levene	Hanson	Wood	Turton	Dawes F.	Edwards
1	2	3	4	5	6	7	8	9	10	11																					
1	3		4	5	6	7	9		10	11	8	2																			
1			2	5	6	4	9		10	11			3	7	8																
1			2	5	6	4	9		10	11			3	7	8																
1			2	5	6	4	9		10	11			3	7	8																
1			2	5	6	4	8		10	11			3	7		9															
1			2	5	6	4	8		9	11			3	7			10														
				5	6	4	8		9	11		2		7			10	1	3												
			2	5	6	4	8		9	11				7			10	1	3												
			4	5	6		8		9	11		2		7			10	1	3												
			4	5	6		8		9	11		2		7			10	1	3												
				5	6	2	8		9	11			3	7			10	1		4											
				5	6	4			9	11	8			7			10	1	3		2										
				5	6	4			10	11		2					8	1			3	7	9								
				5	6	4		9	10	11		2					8	1			3	7									
		3			6				10	11		9		7			8	1		5	2	4									
				5		4			10	11			3	7				1				8	9	2	6						
				5		4			10				3				8	1				7	9	2		6	11				
				5		4			10	11			3	7				1				8	9	2		6					
				5	6	4			10	11			3	7				1				8	9	2							
				5	8	4			10	11			3	7				1					9	2	6						
				5	8	4			10	11			3	7				1					9	2	6						
				5	8	4			10	11			3	7				1					9	2	6						
				5		4			10	11		2						1				8	9	3	6			7			
				5		4			10	11		2						1				8	9	3	6			7			
				5		4			10	11		2						1				8	9	3	6			7			
				5		4			10	11		2						1				8	9	3	6			7			
				5					10	11		2						1				8	9	3	6	4		7			
				5		4			10	11								1				8	9	3	6			7	2		
1				5		4			10	11												8	9		6			7	2	3	
1				5					10	11												8	9		6			7	2	3	4
1				5					10	11												8	9		6			7	2	3	4
1				5					10	11												8	9		6			7	2	3	4
1				5				7	10	11												8	9		6				2	3	4
1				5				7	10	11												8	9		6				2	3	4
1				5						11		2					8			4		7	9		10	6				3	
1				5					10	11		2					8					7	9		6					3	4
1				5					10	11		2					8					7	9		6	4				3	
				5					10	11		2					8	1				7	9		6					3	4
				5					10	11		2					8	1				7	9		6					3	4
				5					10	11		2					8	1				7	9		6					3	4
				5					10	11		2					8	1				7	9		6					3	4
16	2	2	10	41	20	26	12	4	41	41	2	19	13	18	3	1	18	26	5	3	4	26	27	13	23	5	1	10	7	13	10
					1	1	2		38	12				5		1	5					7	19					4			1

Read	Smith Wilf	Waterfield	Haynes	Wilde	Smith W.S.	Turner	Manders	Rooke	Dawes A.	Bigg	Comrie	Owens	Parry	Carson	Goddard	Goodcliffe	Waldron	Dunn	Rumbold	Purdon	Thorpe	Birtley	Blackman	Booth	Collins	Levene	Hanson	Wood	Turton	Dawes F.	Edwards
				5	6	4			10	11			3				8	1				7	9	2							
				5		4			10	11			3	7				1				8	9	2		6					
				2	1	2			2	2			2	1			1	2				2	2	2		1					
									1														1								

League Table

	P	W	D	L	F	A	Pts
Coventry City	42	24	9	9	102	45	57
Luton Town	42	22	12	8	81	45	56
Reading	42	26	2	14	87	62	54
Queen's Park Rangers	42	22	9	11	84	53	53
Watford	42	20	9	13	80	54	49
Crystal Palace	42	22	5	15	96	74	49
Brighton & Hove Albion	42	18	8	16	70	63	44
Bournemouth	42	16	11	15	60	56	43
Notts County	42	15	12	15	60	57	42
Torquay United	42	16	9	17	62	62	41
Aldershot	42	14	12	16	53	61	40
Millwall	42	14	12	16	58	71	40
Bristol City	42	15	10	17	48	59	40
Clapton Orient	42	16	6	20	55	61	38
Northampton Town	42	15	8	19	62	90	38
Gillingham	42	14	9	19	66	77	37
Bristol Rovers	42	14	9	19	69	95	37
Southend United	42	13	10	19	61	62	36
Swindon Town	42	14	8	20	64	73	36
Cardiff City	42	13	10	19	60	73	36
Newport County	42	11	9	22	60	111	31
Exeter City	42	8	11	23	59	93	27

1936-37

Division Three South

Manager: R.S. Moyes from July to 8 December 1936,
Tom Bromilow from 1 January 1937.

Did you know that?

Former Palace outside-left/forward Laurie Fishlock, who had left the club four years previously, also played cricket professionally for Surrey and made his England test debut in July of this year against India in Manchester.

Match No.	Date		Venue	Opponents	Result		Scorers	Attendance
1	Aug	29	A	Clapton Orient	D	1-1	Quayle	12,647
2	Sep	2	H	Notts County	L	1-2	Quayle	11,740
3		5	H	Walsall	W	3-1	Blackman, Waldron, Bigg	9,936
4		7	A	Notts County	W	1-0	Waldron	7,042
5		12	A	Luton Town	L	2-5	Birtley, Blackman	14,187
6		19	H	Cardiff City	D	2-2	Birtley, McMenemy	18,348
7		23	H	Queen's Park Rangers	D	0-0		9,467
8		26	A	Gillingham	L	0-2		6,441
9	Oct	3	A	Exeter City	L	2-3	Birtley, Bigg	6,080
10		10	H	Reading	W	3-1	Blackman, McMenemy, Bigg	15,981
11		17	H	Newport County	W	6-1	Birtley 2, A. Dawes, Collins, Palethorpe 2	14,882
12		24	A	Southend United	L	1-2	Palethorpe	10,281
13		31	H	Watford	W	2-0	A. Dawes, Birtley	7,707
14	Nov	7	A	Brighton & Hove Albion	L	0-1		7,768
15		14	H	Bournemouth	D	2-2	Waldron 2	14,108
16		21	A	Northampton Town	L	0-2		14,163
17	Dec	5	A	Millwall	L	0-3		19,063
18		19	A	Aldershot	D	2-2	Liddle, McMenemy	3,278
19		25	A	Bristol City	L	0-1		13,346
20		26	H	Clapton Orient	L	2-3	Coulston, Bigg	15,120
21		28	H	Bristol City	W	1-0	Blackman	4,195
22	Jan	2	A	Walsall	L	0-1		6,145
23		9	H	Luton Town	L	0-4		15,211
24		16	H	Swindon Town	W	2-0	Blackman, Bigg	7,648
25		20	H	Bristol Rovers	W	3-0	Bigg, Blackman 2	3,769
26		23	A	Cardiff City	D	1-1	Bigg	9,415
27		30	H	Gillingham	D	1-1	Bigg	6,506
28	Feb	6	H	Exeter City	W	8-0	Birtley (pen), Blackman 2, Watson 2, Bigg 3	10,019
29		13	A	Reading	D	1-1	Watson	9,783
30		20	A	Newport County	D	1-1	Waldron (pen)	8,319
31		27	H	Southend United	D	1-1	Palethorpe	8,830
32	Mar	6	A	Watford	L	1-3	Waldron	7,671
33		13	H	Brighton & Hove Albion	W	2-0	Palethorpe 2 (1 pen)	16,255
34		20	A	Bournemouth	L	1-3	Blackman	5,047
35		26	H	Torquay United	D	0-0		15,370
36		27	H	Northampton Town	D	2-2	Palethorpe (pen), Waldron	9,523
37		29	A	Torquay United	L	0-3		3,861
38	Apr	3	A	Bristol Rovers	L	0-1		6,282
39		14	H	Millwall	W	1-0	Gillespie	6,781
40		17	A	Swindon Town	L	0-4		6,306
41		24	H	Aldershot	W	3-0	Blackman, Palethorpe, Birtley	6,816
42	May	1	A	Queen's Park Rangers	W	3-1	Fielding, Blackman, Gillespie	6,142

Final League Position: 14th in Division Three South

Appearances
Goals

FA Cup

1	Nov	28	H	Southend United	D	1-1	Birtley	15,932
R	Dec	2	A	Southend United	L	0-2		9,000

Appearances
Goals

Knox	Owens	Dawes F.	Telling	Walker	Collins	Birtley	Quayle	Blackman	Watson	Bigg	McMenemy	Coulston	Waldron	Dunn	Levene	Wilde	Dawes A.	Rooke	Liddle	Palethorpe	Blore	Robson	Beresford	Stanbury	Reeve	Gillespie	Fielding	Lievesley
1	2	3	4	5	6	7	8	9	10	11																		
1	2	3		5	6		8	9		11	4	7	10															
	2	3		5	6		8	9		11	4	7	10	1														
	2	3	4	5			8	9		11		7	10	1	6													
	2	3			6	7	8	9		11	4			1		5	10											
	2	3		5	6	7		9		11	4		8	1			10											
1	2	3		5	6			9		11	4	7	8				10											
	2	3		5	6		8			11	4	7	10	1				9										
	2	3		5		8		9		11	4		10	1	6				7									
	2	3		5	6	8		9		11	4			1			10		7									
	2	3		5	6	8				11	4			1			10		7	9								
	2	3		5	6	8				11	4			1			10		7	9								
	2	3		5	6	8				11	4	7					10			9	1							
	2	3		5	6	8				11	4	7					10			9	1							
	2	3		5	6	7				11	4		8				10			9	1							
	2	3		5	6	7				11	4		8	1			10			9								
	2	3	4	5		8		7	11				10		6					9	1							
	2	3		5	11						4				6		10		7	9	1	8						
	2	3		5		8				11	4		10		6				7	9	1							
	2	3		5		4		9		11	10	7			6						1		8					
	2	3		5	10	4		9		11		7			6						1	8						
	2	3		5		8				11	4	7	10		6					9				1				
	2	3		5		8		9	10	11	4	7			6						1							
	2	3		5		7		9		11	4				6					10	1		8					
	2	3		5		8		9		11	4	7			6					10	1							
	2	3		5	6	8		9	7	11					4					10	1							
	2	3		5	6	8		9	7	11					4					10	1							
	2	3		5	6	4		9	7	11			8							10	1							
	2	3		5	6	4		9	7	11			8							10	1							
	2	3		5	6			9	7	11			8		4					10	1							
	2	3		5	6			9	7				8		4					10	1				11			
	2	3		5	6	4		9	7				11							10	1					8		
	2	3		5	6			9	7						4					10	1					8	11	
	2	3		5	6			9							4				7	10	1					8	11	
	2	3		5	6	4		9	7				8							10	1						11	
	2	3		5	6	4							10						7	9	1					8	11	
	2	3		5		7		9			6					4				10	1	8					11	
	2	3		5				9			6					4			7	10	1		8				11	
	2	3		5	6						4		10						7	9	1					8	11	
	2	3		5	6						4		10						7	9	1					8	11	
	2	3		5	6	4		9											7	10	1					8	11	
	2	3		5	4			9											7	10	1					8	11	6
3	42	42	3	41	31	28	6	29	12	28	25	12	21	10	17	3	11	1	13	29	28	3	3	1	1	8	10	1
					1	8	2	12	3	11	3	1	7				2		1	8						2	1	

Knox	Owens	Dawes F.	Telling	Walker	Collins	Birtley	Quayle	Blackman	Watson	Bigg	McMenemy	Coulston	Waldron	Dunn	Levene	Wilde	Dawes A.	Rooke	Liddle	Palethorpe	Blore	Robson	Beresford	Stanbury	Reeve	Gillespie	Fielding	Lievesley
	2	3		5	6	8				11	4						10		7	9	1							
	2	3		5	6	8		7		11	4						10			9	1							
	2	2		2	2	2		1		2	2						2		1	2	2							
						1																						

League Table

	P	W	D	L	F	A	Pts
Luton Town	42	27	4	11	103	53	58
Notts County	42	23	10	9	74	52	56
Brighton & Hove Albion	42	24	5	13	74	43	53
Watford	42	19	11	12	85	60	49
Reading	42	19	11	12	76	60	49
Bournemouth	42	20	9	13	65	59	49
Northampton Town	42	20	6	16	85	68	46
Millwall	42	18	10	14	64	54	46
Queen's Park Rangers	42	18	9	15	73	52	45
Southend United	42	17	11	14	78	67	45
Gillingham	42	18	8	16	52	66	44
Clapton Orient	42	14	15	13	52	52	43
Swindon Town	42	14	11	17	75	73	39
Crystal Palace	42	13	12	17	62	61	38
Bristol Rovers	42	16	4	22	71	80	36
Bristol City	42	15	6	21	58	70	36
Walsall	42	13	10	19	63	85	36
Cardiff City	42	14	7	21	54	87	35
Newport County	42	12	10	20	67	98	34
Torquay United	42	11	10	21	57	80	32
Exeter City	42	10	12	20	59	88	32
Aldershot	42	7	9	26	50	89	23

1937-38

Division Three South

Manager: Tom Bromilow

Did you know that?

Ex-Palace manager and club secretary Edmund Goodman had two sons, the eldest of which, Leslie, played for Palace's reserves during the 1930s.

Match No.	Date		Venue	Opponents	Result		Scorers	Attendance
1	Aug	28	H	Aldershot	D	1-1	Walker	17,123
2	Sep	1	A	Swindon Town	L	0-4		8,776
3		4	A	Millwall	D	2-2	Blackman, Gillespie	25,894
4		8	H	Swindon Town	L	0-1		8,879
5		11	H	Reading	W	3-1	Waldron 3	12,677
6		15	H	Watford	W	4-1	Collins, Waldron 2, Quayle	6,391
7		18	A	Bournemouth	L	0-1		8,520
8		25	A	Notts County	W	1-0	Blackman	18,164
9	Oct	2	H	Newport County	W	3-0	Blackman 2, Waldron	15,362
10		9	A	Bristol City	D	0-0		13,262
11		16	H	Brighton & Hove Albion	W	3-2	Waldron 2, Blackman	19,121
12		23	A	Queen's Park Rangers	L	0-1		12,982
13		30	H	Southend United	W	2-1	Waldron, Palethorpe	15,324
14	Nov	6	A	Clapton Orient	W	2-0	Pritchard 2	11,125
15		13	H	Torquay United	W	4-1	Palethorpe 2, Waldron, Pritchard	13,718
16		20	A	Mansfield Town	L	0-2		8,207
17	Dec	18	A	Cardiff City	L	2-4	Blackman 2	18,374
18		27	A	Exeter City	D	2-2	Waldron, Blackman	12,263
19		28	H	Exeter City	D	2-2	Robson, Pritchard	6,450
20	Jan	1	A	Aldershot	L	0-1		5,400
21		15	H	Millwall	D	0-0		22,355
22		19	H	Bristol Rovers	W	3-2	Gregory (pen), Horton, Pritchard	5,492
23		22	A	Reading	L	2-3	Waldron, Robson	11,016
24		29	H	Bournemouth	L	0-1		10,485
25	Feb	3	A	Northampton Town	D	1-1	Gillespie	3,672
26		5	H	Notts County	W	3-1	Davis, Smith, Waldron	16,244
27		12	A	Newport County	D	0-0		7,933
28		19	H	Bristol City	D	1-1	Smith	16,129
29		26	A	Brighton & Hove Albion	L	1-2	Gregory (pen)	9,707
30	Mar	5	H	Queen's Park Rangers	W	4-0	Blackman 2, A. Dawes, Pritchard	25,522
31		12	A	Southend United	D	2-2	Blackman, Smith	6,300
32		16	H	Walsall	W	3-1	Blackman 2, Lievesley	5,242
33		19	H	Clapton Orient	W	1-0	Blackman	15,395
34		26	A	Torquay United	D	0-0		3,358
35	Apr	2	H	Mansfield Town	W	4-0	Collins, Davis, Smith 2	13,105
36		9	A	Bristol Rovers	L	0-1		5,316
37		15	H	Gillingham	W	3-0	A. Dawes, Blackman 2	15,390
38		16	H	Northampton Town	L	0-1		14,057
39		18	A	Gillingham	W	4-2	Davis 2, Dawes 2	6,602
40		23	A	Walsall	D	1-1	Horton	3,975
41		30	H	Cardiff City	W	1-0	Smith	9,018
42	May	7	A	Watford	W	2-1	Horton, Waldron	13,713

Final League Position: 7th in Division Three South

Appearances
Goals

FA Cup

1	Nov	27	H	Kettering Town	D	2-2	Gillespie, Davis	9,778
R	Dec	2	A	Kettering Town	W	4-0	Pritchard 2, Blackman, Waldron	7,514
2		11	A	Accrington Stanley	W	1-0	Owens	5,400
3	Jan	8	H	Liverpool	D	0-0		33,000
R		12	A	Liverpool	L	1-3*	Waldron	35,918

*After extra-time

Appearances
Goals

Bore	Owens	Dawes F.	Daniels	Walker	Lievesley	Davis	Fielding	Jordan	Palethorpe	Pritchard	Birtley	Waldron	Chesters	Booth	Collins	Gillespie	Blackman	Turton	Quayle	Horton	Robson	Gregory F.	Shanks	Smith T.	Dawes A.
1	2	3	4	5	6	7	8	9	10	11															
1	2	3		5	6	7	8	9		11	4	10													
	2			5	6		11		10	7			1	3	4	8	9								
	2			5	6		11		10	7			1	3	4	8	9								
		3		5	6					7	8	10	1		4			2	9	11					
		3		5	6					7	8	10	1		4			2	9	11					
	2	3		5	4					7	8	10	1		6				9	11					
	2	3		5	4					7		10	1		6	8	9			11					
	2	3		5	4					7		10	1		6	8	9			11					
	2	3		5	4					7		10	1		6	8	9			11					
	2	3		5	4					7		8	1		6		9			11	10				
	2	3		5	4					7		10	1		6		9		8	11					
	2	3		5	4		11		9	7		10	1		6						8				
	2	3		5	4		11		9	7	6	10	1								8				
	2	3		5	4	7			9	11	6	10	1								8				
		3		5	4	7	8		9	11	6		1					2			10				
		3		5	4	7				11		10	1		6	8	9					2			
				5	4					7		10	1	3	6		9			11	8	2			
				5	4					7		10	1	3	6		9			11	8	2			
				5	4	8				7	10		1		6		9	2		11		3			
					4				9	7		10	1	3	6	8				11		2	5		
					4					7		10	1	3	6		9			11	8	2	5		
				5	4					7		10	1	3	6		9			11	8	2			
				5	4	7			9	11		10	1	3	6						8	2			
				5	4	7				11		10	1	3	6	8		2				9			
				5	4	7				11		10	1	3	6		9					2		8	
				5	4	7				11		10	1	3	6		9					2		8	
				5	4	7				11			1	3	6		9					2		8	10
	2			5	4		11			7			1		6		9					3		8	10
1	2			5	4		11			7					6		9					3		8	10
1	2			5	4	7	11								6		9					3		8	10
1	2			5	4	7	11						1		6		9					3		8	10
	2			5	4	7	11						1		6		9					3		8	10
	2			5	4								1		6		9			11	7	3		8	10
	2			5	4	7							1		6		9			11		3		8	10
	2			5	4	7							1		6		9			11		3		8	10
	2			5	4								1		6		9			11	7	3		8	10
	2			5	4								1		6		9			11	7	3		8	10
	2			5	4	7							1		6		9			11		3		8	10
	2			5	4	7			9				1		6					11		3		8	10
	2			5	4						6		1				9			11	10	3		8	7
	2			5	4							10	1		6		9			11		3		8	7
5	27	15	1	40	42	18	12	2	10	30	9	23	37	12	36	8	29	5	4	23	14	26	2	17	15
				1	1	4			3	6		14			2	2	16		1	3	2	2		6	4

Bore	Owens	Dawes F.	Daniels	Walker	Lievesley	Davis	Fielding	Jordan	Palethorpe	Pritchard	Birtley	Waldron	Chesters	Booth	Collins	Gillespie	Blackman	Turton	Quayle	Horton	Robson	Gregory F.	Shanks	Smith T.	Dawes A.
	2	3		5	4	7			9	11		10	1		6	8									
	2	3		5	4	7				11		10	1		6	8	9								
	2	3		5	4	7				11		10	1		6	8	9								
				5	4				9	7		10	1	3	6	8		2		11					
				5	4				9	7		10	1	3	6	8		2		11					
	3	3		5	5	3			3	5		5	5	2	5	5	2	2		2					
	1					1				2		2				1	1								

League Table

	P	W	D	L	F	A	Pts
Millwall	42	23	10	9	83	37	56
Bristol City	42	21	13	8	68	40	55
Queen's Park Rangers	42	22	9	11	80	47	53
Watford	42	21	11	10	73	43	53
Brighton & Hove Albion	42	21	9	12	64	44	51
Reading	42	20	11	11	71	63	51
Crystal Palace	42	18	12	12	67	47	48
Swindon Town	42	17	10	15	49	49	44
Northampton Town	42	17	9	16	51	57	43
Cardiff City	42	15	12	15	67	54	42
Notts County	42	16	9	17	50	50	41
Southend United	42	15	10	17	70	68	40
Bournemouth	42	14	12	16	56	57	40
Mansfield Town	42	15	9	18	62	67	39
Bristol Rovers	42	13	13	16	46	61	39
Newport County	42	11	16	15	43	52	38
Exeter City	42	13	12	17	57	70	38
Aldershot	42	15	5	22	39	59	35
Clapton Orient	42	13	7	22	42	61	33
Torquay United	42	9	12	21	38	73	30
Walsall	42	11	7	24	52	88	29
Gillingham	42	10	6	26	36	77	26

1938-39

Division Three South

Manager: Tom Bromilow

Did you know that?

During the 1920s and 1930s, Palace's first team regularly competed pre-season in the *Evening News* cricket cup tournament against other Football League sides from London.

Match No.	Date		Venue	Opponents	Result		Scorers	Attendance
1	Aug	27	A	Bournemouth	D	1-1	Blackman	9,075
2		31	A	Notts County	W	1-0	Lievesley	10,434
3	Sep	3	H	Watford	W	2-0	Blackman 2	18,910
4		7	H	Northampton Town	W	2-0	Horton, A. Dawes	14,570
5		10	A	Port Vale	L	0-2		10,478
6		17	H	Swindon Town	D	1-1	Horton	20,100
7		24	A	Torquay United	W	2-1	Gregory 2	3,988
8	Oct	1	H	Clapton Orient	W	4-2	Gregory 3, Horton	19,182
9		8	A	Newport County	L	0-2		10,631
10		15	A	Walsall	D	1-1	A. Dawes	7,726
11		22	H	Brighton & Hove Albion	W	1-0	Horton	18,999
12		29	A	Queen's Park Rangers	W	2-1	Smith, A. Dawes	17,440
13	Nov	5	H	Southend United	W	4-3	Smith, Lievesley, Blackman, Steele	17,685
14		12	A	Exeter City	D	4-4	Steele, A. Dawes 2, F. Dawes 1	5,523
15		19	H	Cardiff City	W	2-0	A. Dawes 2	17,898
16	Dec	3	H	Reading	D	0-0		15,565
17		17	H	Mansfield Town	W	6-2	A. Dawes, Robson 3, Gregory (pen), Smith	10,224
18		24	H	Bournemouth	W	3-0	Robson, Bigg 2	4,403
19		26	H	Aldershot	W	3-0	Steele, Robson, A. Dawes	5,417
20		27	A	Aldershot	L	1-2	A. Dawes	7,003
21		31	A	Watford	L	1-4	Robson	9,853
22	Jan	14	H	Port Vale	W	1-0	Wilson	13,773
23		18	A	Ipswich Town	L	1-2	A. Dawes	5,352
24		21	A	Swindon Town	D	2-2	Smith, Robson	11,825
25		28	H	Torquay United	L	1-3	Blackman	14,342
26	Feb	4	A	Clapton Orient	L	0-4		8,890
27		11	H	Newport County	D	1-1	Wilson	29,155
28		18	H	Walsall	W	4-0	Steele 2, Gregory, A. Dawes	13,906
29		25	A	Brighton & Hove Albion	D	0-0		7,146
30	Mar	4	H	Queen's Park Rangers	L	0-1		13,328
31		11	A	Southend United	L	1-3	Steele	6,244
32		18	H	Exeter City	W	3-2	Wilson 2, Waldron	9,152
33		25	A	Cardiff City	W	1-0	Smith	11,910
34	Apr	1	H	Ipswich Town	W	3-0	Robson, Wilson, Smith	13,764
35		7	H	Bristol City	W	3-2	Robson, Smith, Waldron	21,913
36		8	A	Reading	L	1-3	Collins	10,131
37		10	A	Bristol City	D	1-1	F. Dawes (pen)	11,055
38		15	H	Bristol Rovers	D	0-0		11,714
39		17	A	Bristol Rovers	W	2-1	Smith, Robson	4,610
40		22	A	Mansfield Town	D	0-0		3,016
41		29	H	Notts County	W	5-1	Wilson, Robson, Steele 2, Waldron	6,841
42	May	6	A	Northampton Town	D	0-0		4,056

Final League Position: 2nd in Division Three South

Appearances
Goals

FA Cup

1	Nov	26	H	Queen's Park Rangers	D	1-1	Blackman	33,276
R		28	A	Queen's Park Rangers	L	0-3		16,400

Appearances
Goals

Chesters	Owens	Dawes F.	Lievesley	Walker	Collins	Davis	Smith T.	Blackman	Dawes A.	Horton	Gregory	Waldron	Steele	Birtley	Gillespie	Bigg	Robson	Reece	Wilson	Daniels	Shanks	Toothill	Jordan	Lewis
1	2	3	4	5	6	7	8	9	10	11														
1	2	3	4	5	6	7	8	9	10	11														
1	2	3	4	5	6	7	8	9	10	11														
1	2	3	4	5	6	7	8	9	10	11														
1	2	3	4	5	6	7	8	9	10	11														
1	2	3	4	5	6	7	8	9	10	11														
1	2	3	4	5	6		8		7	11	9	10												
1	2	3	4	5	6	7	8		10	11	9													
1	2	3	4	5	6	7	8			11	9	10												
1	2	3	4	5	6		8		10	11	9		7											
1	2	3		5	6		8		10	11	9		7	4										
1	2	3	4	5	6		8	9	10	11			7											
1	2	3	4	5	6		8	9	10	11			7											
1	2	3	4	5	6			9	10	11			7		8									
1	2	3	4	5	6			9	10				7		8	11								
1		3	4	5	6		8	9	10		2		7			11								
1		3	4	5	6		8		9		2		7			11	10							
1		3	4	5	6		8		9		2		7			11	10							
1		3	4	5	6		8		9		2		7			11	10							
1		3	4	5	6		8		9		2		7			11	10							
1	2	3	4	5			8		9				7			11	10	6						
1	2	3	4		6		8		9				7				10		11	5				
1	2	3			6		8		9				7	4			10		11	5				
1	2	3	4		6		7	9	8								10		11	5				
1	2	3	4		6		7	9	8								10		11	5				
1	2	3	4		6		8				9	10					7		11	5				
1	2	3	4		6		8		10		9		7						11		5			
1	2	3	4		6		8		10		9		7						11		5			
1	2	3	4		6		8		10		9		7						11		5			
1	2	3	4		6		8		10		9		7						11		5			
1	2	3			6		8	9					7		10				11	4	5			
1	2	3	4				8		9			10	7					6	11		5			
	2	3	4				8			11		10	7				9	6			5	1		
1	2	3			6		8					10	7				9	4	11		5			
1	2	3	6				8					10	7				9	4	11		5			
1	2	3			6		8					10	7				9	4	11		5			
1	2	3	4		6		8						7		10		9		11		5			
1	2	3					8					10	7				9		11		5		4	6
1	2	3					8						7		10		9	6	11		5		4	
1	2	3					8					10	7				9	6	11		5		4	
1		3					8				2	10	7				9	6	11		5		4	
1		3					8				2	10	7				9	6	11		5		4	
41	35	42	32	21	33	8	40	14	29	15	17	12	30	2	5	7	20	10	20	6	16	1	5	1
		2	2		1		8	5	12	4	7	3	8			2	11		6					

Chesters	Owens	Dawes F.	Lievesley	Walker	Collins	Davis	Smith T.	Blackman	Dawes A.	Horton	Gregory	Waldron	Steele	Birtley	Gillespie	Bigg
1	2	3	4	5	6		8	9	10				7			11
1	2	3	4	5	6		8	9	10	11			7			
2	2	2	2	2	2		2	2	2	1			2			1
								1								

League Table

	P	W	D	L	F	A	Pts
Newport County	42	22	11	9	58	45	55
Crystal Palace	42	20	12	10	71	52	52
Brighton & Hove Albion	42	19	11	12	68	49	49
Watford	42	17	12	13	62	51	46
Reading	42	16	14	12	69	59	46
Queen's Park Rangers	42	15	14	13	68	49	44
Ipswich Town	42	16	12	14	62	52	44
Bristol City	42	16	12	14	61	63	44
Swindon Town	42	18	8	16	72	77	44
Aldershot	42	16	12	14	53	66	44
Notts County	42	17	9	16	59	54	43
Southend United	42	16	9	17	61	64	41
Cardiff City	42	15	11	16	61	65	41
Exeter City	42	13	14	15	65	82	40
Bournemouth	42	13	13	16	52	58	39
Mansfield Town	42	12	15	15	44	62	39
Northampton Town	42	15	8	19	51	58	38
Port Vale	42	14	9	19	52	58	37
Torquay United	42	14	9	19	54	70	37
Clapton Orient	42	11	13	18	53	55	35
Walsall	42	11	11	20	68	69	33
Bristol Rovers	42	10	13	19	55	61	33

1939-40

League South 'A' and 'D' Divisions

Manager: George Irwin

Did you know that?

Initially the 1939–40 season opened as usual, but after only three games when World War Two broke out, there was a suspension of the Football League. In late October the first of the Wartime Regional Leagues started, with Palace alongside most of the other sides from London, plus Norwich and Southend in the new London South A League.

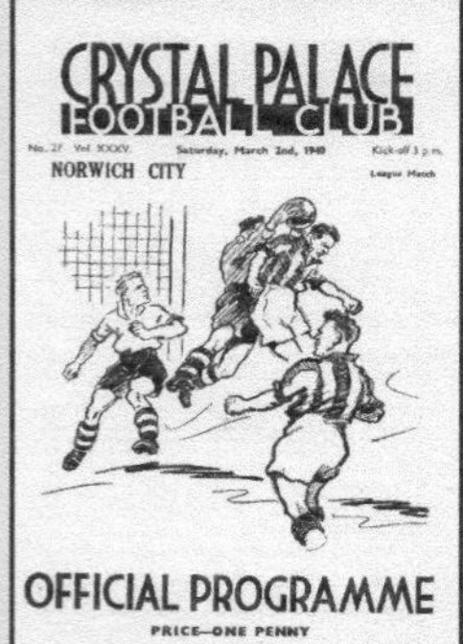

Match No.	Date		Venue	Opponents	Result		Scorers	Attendance
1	Aug	26	A	Mansfield Town	W	5-4	Steele, Robson, Waldron 3	7,658
2		30	A	Reading	L	0-5		9,277
3	Sep	2	H	Bristol Rovers	W	3-0	Waldron 2, Smith	7,033
Final League Position: 7th in Division Three South								Appearances
								Goals
League South 'A' Division								
4	Oct	21	A	West Ham United	W	6-2	Bark, Blackman 3, Robson, Gregory (pen)	6,700
5		28	H	Watford	D	3-3	Bark, Wilson, Blackman	3,000
6	Nov	4	A	Arsenal	L	0-5		7,306
7		11	H	Charlton Athletic	L	3-4	Gregory (pen), Bark 2	6,725
8		18	A	Clapton Orient	L	3-5	Blackman 2, Robson	3,000
9		25	H	Southend United	W	4-2	Gregory 3 (2 pen), Blackman	3,724
10	Dec	2	H	Norwich City	W	1-0	Smith	5,400
11		9	A	Tottenham Hotspur	W	3-1	Smith 3	4,265
12		16	H	Millwall	W	4-1	Smith, Robson 2, own-goal (E. Smith)	5,600
13		25	A	Watford	L	1-5	Blackman	3,000
14		26	H	Arsenal	L	0-3		10,400
15		30	A	Charlton Athletic	L	4-5	Wilson, Robson, Blackman, Gregory (pen)	1,910
16	Jan	6	H	Clapton Orient	D	1-1	Smith	3,600
17		13	A	Southend United	L	1-3	Smith	2,000
18		17	H	West Ham United	L	0-3		896
19	Feb	28	H	Tottenham Hotspur	D	1-1	Smith	1,700
20	Apr	13	A	Norwich City	L	2-5	Robson, Gregory (pen)	4,000
21	May	25	A	Millwall	L	2-7	Gregory (pen), Blackman	4,332
Final League Position: 7th in League South 'A' Division								Appearances
							1 own-goal	Goals
League South 'D' Division								
22	Feb	10	A	Brighton & Hove Albion	W	3-1	Smith, Robson, Bark	1,739
23		17	H	Reading	W	4-1	Gregory, Smith, Robson, Bark	1,139
24		24	A	Queen's Park Rangers	W	5-2	Gillespie 2, Smith 2, Wilson	6,500
25	Mar	2	H	Norwich City	W	2-0	Gillespie, Robson	4,600
26		9	A	Watford	L	2-5	A. Dawes, Bark	4,611
27		16	H	Aldershot	L	3-4	Gregory 2 (1 pen), Robson	4,948
28		22	A	Clapton Orient	W	1-0	Wilson	5,000
29		23	H	Southend United	W	5-2	Robson 4, Bark	6,742
30		25	H	Clapton Orient	W	7-1	Wilson 2, Bark 2, Robson, Smith, Gregory	7,892
31		30	A	Bournmouth	W	3-2	Robson 2, Blackman	5,000
32	Apr	6	H	Brighton & Hove Albion	W	10-0	Bark 3 (1 pen), Robson 3, Gregory, Blackman, Smith, Wilson	7,529
33	May	8	A	Reading	W	4-2	Robson 2, A. Dawes, Wilson	
34		13	A	Queen's Park Rangers	D	2—2	Smith, Robson	3,954
35		18	H	Bournmouth	W	6-0	A. Dawes 3, Smith 2, Blackman	3,442
36		29	H	Watford	W	2-1	A. Dawes, Wilson	3,335
37	Jun	1	A	Aldershot	L	2-3	Owens, A. Dawes	1,300
38		5	A	Southend United	L	0-3		500
39		8	A	Norwich City	W	3-1	Robson 2, A. Dawes	1,000
Final League Position: 1st in League South 'D' Division								Appearances
								Goals
Football League War Cup								
1	Apr	20	H	Tottenham Hotspur	W	4-1	Wilson 2, Robson, Bark	15,423
		27	A	Tottenham Hotspur	L	1-2	Robson	12,376
2	May	4	A	Arsenal	L	1-3	Robson	15,423
		11	H	Arsenal	L	0-2		21,406
								Appearances
								Goals

Chesters	Owens	Dawes F	Lievesley	Shanks	Collins	Steele	Smith	Robson	Waldron	Wilson	Reece	Tootill	James	Gregory F	Millbank	Hudgell	Bark	Blackman	Gillespie	Gregory M	Bigg	Dawes A	Lewis J	Milligan	Joy B	Taylor H
1	2	3	4	5	6	7	8	9	10	11																
1	2	3	4	5		7	8	9	10	11	6															
	2	3	4	5		7	8	9	10	11	6	1														
2	3	3	3	3	1	3	3	3	3	3	2	1														
						1	1	1	5																	

Chesters	Owens	Dawes F	Lievesley	Shanks	Collins	Steele	Smith	Robson	Waldron	Wilson	Reece	Tootill	James	Gregory F	Millbank	Hudgell	Bark	Blackman	Gillespie	Gregory M	Bigg	Dawes A	Lewis J	Milligan	Joy B	Taylor H
		3			4		8	7		11		1		2	5	6	10	9								
		3			4		8	7		11		1		2	5	6	10	9								
		3			4		8	7				1	11	2	5	6	10	9								
	2				4		8	7		11		1		3	5	6	10	9								
	2				4			8		11		1		3	5	6	10	9	7							
	4				6			8		11		1		2	5	3	10	9	7							
	4				6		8			11		1		2	5	3	10	9	7							
	4				6		8	9		11		1		2	5	3	10		7							
	4				6		8	9		11		1		2	5	3	10		7							
1	4	3		5	6		8						11	2			10	9	7							
	4				6		8	9		11		1		2	5	3	10		7							
		3			4		8	10		11		1		2	5	6		9	7							
		3			4		8	9		11		1		2	5	6	10		7							
		3			4		8	9		11		1		2	5	6	10		7							
					6		8	9		7		1	11	2	5	3	10			4						
1	4				6		10	9		7				2	5	3		8			11					
	4				6		8	9		11		1		2	5	3	10	7								
	4				6		8	9				1		2	5	3		7	11			10				
2	11	7		1	18		16	16		15		16	3	18	17	17	15	12	11	1	1	1				
							8	6		2				8			4	10								

Chesters	Owens	Dawes F	Lievesley	Shanks	Collins	Steele	Smith	Robson	Waldron	Wilson	Reece	Tootill	James	Gregory F	Millbank	Hudgell	Bark	Blackman	Gillespie	Gregory M	Bigg	Dawes A	Lewis J	Milligan	Joy B	Taylor H
1	4				6		8	9		11				2	5	3	10		7							
	4				6		8	9		11		1		2	5	3	10		7							
1	4				6		8	9		11				2	5	3	10		7							
1	4				6		8	9		11				2	5	3	10		7							
								9		11		1		2	5	3	10		7			8	4	6		
	4				6		8	9		11		1		2	5	3	10	7								
	4				6		8	9		11		1		2	5	3		7				10				
	4						8	9		11		1		2	5	3	10	7				6				
	4				6		8	9		11		1		2	5	3	10	7								
	4				6		8	9		11		1		2		3	10	7					5			
	4				6		8	9		11		1		2	5	3	10	7								
	4				6		8	9		11		1		2	5	3			7			10				
	4				6		8	9				1		2	5	3		7	11			10				
	4				6		8	9		11		1		2	5	3		7				10				
	4				6		8	9		11		1		2		3		7				10			5	
	7				6		8					1		2		3		9	11	4		10				5
	2	3			6		8	7				1				5		9	11	4		10				
	2	3			11		8	9				1				6		7		4		10				5
3	17	2			16		17	17		14		15		16	13	18	10	12	9	3		10	2	1	1	2
	1						9	19		7				5			9	3	3			8				

Chesters	Owens	Dawes F	Lievesley	Shanks	Collins	Steele	Smith	Robson	Waldron	Wilson	Reece	Tootill	James	Gregory F	Millbank	Hudgell	Bark	Blackman	Gillespie	Gregory M	Bigg	Dawes A	Lewis J	Milligan	Joy B	Taylor H
	4				6		8	9		11		1		2	5	3	10	7								
	4				6		8	9		11		1		2	5	3	10	7								
	4				6		8	9		11		1		2	5	3	10	7								
	4				6		8	9		11		1		2	5	3		7				10				
	4				4		4	4		4		4		4	4	4	3	4				1				
								3		2							1								

1940-41

South Regional League

Manager: George Irwin

Did you know that?

Having claimed the League South D Division title the previous year, Palace won another regional League, finishing first in the South Regional League. Despite many players being absent during the war years, they managed the feat by using only 23 players.

Match No.	Date		Venue	Opponents	Result		Scorers	Attendance
1	Aug	31	H	Chelsea	W	6-3	Robson, A. Dawes, Blackman, M. Gregory, A. Wilson 2	1,157
2	Sep	7	H	Brighton & Hove Albion	W	5-2	Robson, Blackman, A. Dawes, A. Wilson 2	1,508
3		14	A	Millwall	L	0-1*		600
4		21	H	Norwich City	W	7-1	A. Dawes 2, Blackman 3, Robson 2	1,040
5		28	H	Millwall	W	2-1	A. Dawes 2 (1 pen)	1,600
6	Oct	5	A	Norwich City	L	1-3	Waite	1,200
7		12	A	Watford	W	2-1	Robson 2	1,000
8		19	H	Clapton Orient	W	6-2	Blackman, A. Dawes 2, Robson 3	1,500
9		26	A	Southampton	W	4-1	A. Dawes 3, Waite	1,000
10	Nov	2	A	Bournmouth	L	2-3	Blackman, A. Dawes	2,000
11		16	A	Clapton Orient	W	4-2	A. Wilson, Robson 2, Blackman	200
12		23	H	Southend United	L	1-2#	Blackman	1,097
13		30	A	Arsenal	D	2-2	F. Gregory (pen), Robson	761
14	Dec	7	H	Bournmouth	W	6-0	A. Dawes 4, Gillespie, Robson	1,121
15		14	A	Chelsea	W	2-1	Blackman, A. Dawes	940
16		21	H	Arsenal	D	3-3	Robson, Bark, Gillespie	4,000
17		25	H	Charlton Athletic	L	0-2		4,015
18		28	A	Brighton & Hove Albion	W	5-1	Robson 2, Gillespie, A. Dawes 2	1,000
19	Mar	8	H	Millwall	W	5-3	Hudgell 2 (2 pens), Blackman, Robson, M. Gregory	5,000
20		15	A	Brentford	W	3-2	Bark, Smith 2	4,000
21		22	H	Brentford	W	5-0	Hudgell (pen), Bark, Robson 2, A. Wilson	2,638
22		29	H	Fulham	D	1-1	Robson	3,000
23	May	10	A	Tottenham Hotspur	D	1-1	Robson	3,000
24		17	H	Southend United	W	7-0	Gillespie 2, Collins, Blackman, Smith, Robson 2	2,519
25		24	A	Aldershot	W	3-0	Hudgell 2 (2 pens), A. Wilson	2,000
26	June	2	H	Reading	L	1-3	A. Dawes	5,500
27		7	A	Millwall	L	2-3	Smith, Robson	2,000

Final League Position: 1st in South Regional League (decided on goal average)

Appearances

* Abandoned after 30 minutes, # Abandoned after 65 minutes but counted towards final table

Goals

London War Cup

Match No.	Date		Venue	Opponents	Result		Scorers	Attendance
28	Jan	4	A	Brentford	D	2-2	A. Dawes 2	1,000
29		11	H	Brentford	D	2-2	A. Dawes, Robson	2,841
30		25	H	Fulham	W	5-2	A. Dawes 3 (2 pens), Robson, Smith	2,000
31	Feb	1	A	Aldershot	D	3-3	Smith, Blackman, Robson	2,000
32		8	H	Chelsea	D	3-3	Blackman, Robson, A. Dawes	3,703
33	Mar	1	A	Fulham	W	4-1	Robson 4	2,500
34	Apr	5	A	Chelsea	W	3-1	A. Wilson 2, Robson	2,491
35		12	H	Queen's Park Rangers	L	1-2	Blackman	4,353
36		14	H	Aldershot	W	1-0	Robson	4,300
37		19	A	Queen's Park Rangers	L	1-2	Robson	2,300
SF	May	31	A	Reading	L	1-4	Blackman	7,000

Appearances

Goals

Football League War Cup

Match No.	Date		Venue	Opponents	Result		Scorers	Attendance
1	Feb	15	H	Queen's Park Rangers	L	0-1		3,700
		22	A	Queen's Park Rangers	L	2-3	Robson, Smith	3,500

Appearances

Goals

Tootill	Hudgell	Dawes FW	Gregory M	Millbank	Collins	Blackman	Dawes A	Robson	Bark	Wilson A	Taylor	Gillespie	Waite	Halliday	Eastman D	Ridley T	Gregory F	Smith T	Revill	Lievesley	Wilson R	Jackson J
1	2	3	4	5	6	7	8	9	10	11												
1	2	3	4		6	7	10	9		11	5	8										
1	2	3	4		6	7	10	9		11	5		8									
1	2	3	4	5	6	7	10	9				11	8									
1	2	3	4	5	6	7	10	9				11	8									
1	2		4		11	7		9			5	10	8	6	3							
1	2	3	4	5	6	7	10	9				11	8									
1	2	3	4	5	6	7	10	9				11	8									
1	2	3	4	5	6	7	10	9				11	8									
1	2	3	4		6	7	10	9			5		8			11						
1	2	3	4	5	6	8	10	9		7						11						
1	2	3	4		6	7	10	9			5	11	8									
1	6	3	4	5			10	9		11			8				2	7				
1	2	3	4		6	7	10	9			5	11						8				
1		3	4	5	6	7	10	9		11					2			8				
1		3	4	5	6		7	9	10			11					2	8				
1		3	2		6	4	7	9	10	11	5							8				
1		3	2	5	6	4	10	9				11	7					8				
1	2	3	4	5	6	10		9		11								8	7			
1	2	3	4	5	6	7		9	10			11						8				
1	2	3	4	5	6	7		9	10	11								8				
1	2	3	4	5	6			9	10			11						8	7			
1		3	5		4	10		9				11		6				8		2	7	
1		3	2	5	4	10		9		11		7		6				8				
1	3		4	5	6	10		9		11		7						8		2		
1	6	3	4	5	10	7	8	9				11								2		
1	2	3	5		6	4		9	10	11		7						8				
27	21	25	27	18	26	24	18	27	7	12	7	18	11	3	2	2	2	14	2	3	1	
	5		2		1	12	20	24	3	7		5	2				1	4				

Tootill	Hudgell	Dawes FW	Gregory M	Millbank	Collins	Blackman	Dawes A	Robson	Bark	Wilson A	Taylor	Gillespie	Waite	Halliday	Eastman D	Ridley T	Gregory F	Smith T	Revill	Lievesley	Wilson R	Jackson J
1		3	2	5	6	4	10	9				7				11		8				
1		3	2	5	6	4	10	9		11			7					8				
1	2	3	5		4	7	10	9				11		6				8				
1	2	3	5		4	7	10	9				11		6				8				
1	2	3	4	5	6	7	10	9		11								8				
	2	3	4	5	6	10		9		11								8			7	1
1	2	3	4	5	6	10		9		11								8	7			
1	2	3	4	5	6	10		9		11		7						8				
1	2	3	4	5	6	10		9				11	8						7			
1	2	3	5		6	10		9		11		7						8		4		
1	2	3	4	5	6	7		9	10	11								8				
10	9	11	11	8	11	11	5	11	1	7		6	2	2		1		10	2	1	1	1
						4	7	11		2								2				

Tootill	Hudgell	Dawes FW	Gregory M	Millbank	Collins	Blackman	Dawes A	Robson	Bark	Wilson A	Taylor	Gillespie	Waite	Halliday	Eastman D	Ridley T	Gregory F	Smith T	Revill	Lievesley	Wilson R	Jackson J
1	2	3	4	5	6	7		9		11		10						8				
1	2	3	4	5	6	10		9		11		7						8				
2	2	2	2	2	2	2		2		2		2						2				
								1										1				

1941-42

London League

Manager: George Irwin

Did you know that?

Palace and all other London clubs, plus some others in the South, rebuffed the FA's Regional War League plans for this season and instead formed their own 'London League' and 'London War Cup'. The FA threatened expulsion, but in the end all the clubs returned to the FA fold for the following season.

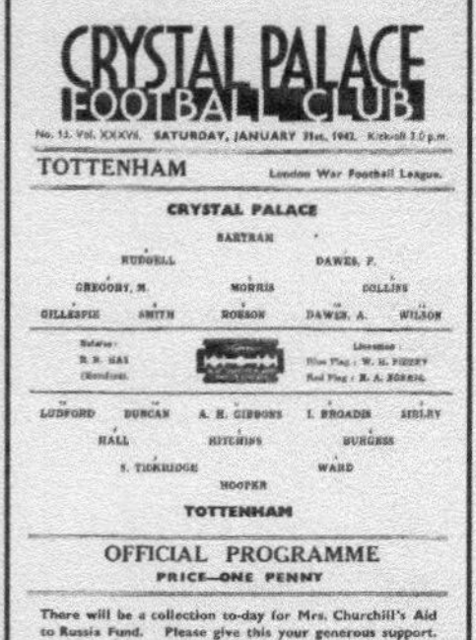

Match No.	Date		Venue	Opponents	Result		Scorers	Attendance
1	Aug	30	H	Millwall	W	2-0	Robson, Gillespie	4,767
2	Sep	6	A	Arsenal	L	2-7	Hawkes, Robson	6,207
3		13	H	Queen's Park Rangers	W	2-1	Robson, A. Dawes	4,500
4		20	A	Reading	L	2-6	Robson, Blackman	4,000
5		27	A	Brighton & Hove Albion	D	2-2	Hudgell (pen), Robson	4,000
6	Oct	4	A	Brentford	W	2-1	Blackman, Smith	4,700
7		11	H	Clapton Orient	W	2-0	Wilson, A. Dawes	3,400
8		18	H	Fulham	W	3-1	Bark, Robson 2	5,000
9		25	A	Tottenham Hotspur	D	1-1	Robson	4,807
10	Nov	1	H	Portsmouth	W	3-1	Collins, Robson 2	5,493
11		8	A	Chelsea	L	0-1		3,000
12		15	H	Charlton Athletic	W	4-0	Gillespie 2, Robson 2	5,300
13		22	A	West Ham United	W	5-0	Bark 2, Blackman, Gillespie, Robson	5,000
14		29	H	Watford	W	6-1	Gillespie, Blackman, A. Dawes, Wilson, Bark 2	4,800
15	Dec	6	A	Aldershot	W	2-1	Collins, Robson	2,000
16		13	A	Millwall	L	0-1		5,100
17		25	A	Queen's Park Rangers	W	3-1	Smith 3	8,500
18		27	H	Reading	D	1-1	Robson	6,550
19	Jan	3	H	Brighton & Hove Albion	W	10-1	Robson 4, Gillespie 2, A. Dawes 2 (1 pen), Smith 2	4,771
20		10	H	Brentford	W	2-0	A. Dawes (pen), Bark	6,000
21		17	A	Clapton Orient	L	0-4		2,000
22		31	H	Tottenham Hotspur	D	2-2	A. Dawes (pen), Henley	5,300
23	Feb	7	A	Portsmouth	L	1-3	Wilson	4,515
24		14	H	Chelsea	W	3-2	Robson, M. Gregory, A. Dawes	5,583
25		21	A	Charlton Athletic	L	1-3	Bark	2,760
26		28	H	West Ham United	D	1-1	Robson	7,790
27	Mar	7	A	Watford	L	1-2	Bark	1,030
28		14	H	Aldershot	L	1-2	Bark	5,700
29	May	9	H	Arsenal	D	3-3	A. Dawes 2 (1 pen), Geldard	10,024
30		23	A	Fulham	L	3-4	J. Smith, Collins, G. Lewis	3,000

Final League Position: 6th in London League — Appearances / Goals

London War Cup

Match No.	Date		Venue	Opponents	Result		Scorers	Attendance
31	Mar	21	A	Chelsea	D	3-3	Bark, Robson, A. Dawes (pen)	4,412
32		28	H	Portsmouth	L	0-2		7,329
33	Apr	4	H	Chelsea	L	0-3		5,900
34		6	A	Portsmouth	L	1-2	A. Dawes	11,671
35		11	A	Fulham	L	1-4	own-goal (Hiles)	6,000
36		18	H	Fulham	L	3-4	McPhee 2, A. Dawes (pen)	5,378

Crystal Palace finished 4th in the London War Cup Qualifying Group 4 and thus did not qualify for the semi-finals. Appearances

1 own-goal — Goals

Tootill	Hudgell	Dawes FW	Gregory M	Millbank	Collins	Gillespie	Smith T	Robson	Bark	Wilson	Blackman	Hawkes	Dawes AG	Fuller	Raynor	Lester	Morris	Gregory FC	Young	Reece	Hobbins	Sibley	Chivers	Scaife	Moffitt	Bartram	Henley	Boulton	Hooper	Oakes John	Geldard	Duncan	Catlin	Lewis J	Hitchins	Lewis G	Smith J	Tweedy	Mather	Mulligan	Weale	Forder	McPhee	Halford
1	2	3	4	5	6	7	8	9	10	11																																		
1	2	3	5		6	7	8	9		11	4	10																																
1	2	3	4	5	6			9	10	11	7		8																															
1	2	3	4		6	7		9		11	10	8		5																														
1	2	3	4	5	6	8		9	10	11					7																													
1	2	3	4	5	6	7	8		10	11	9																																	
1	2	3	4	5	6	7			10	11	9		8																															
1	2	3	4	5	6	7	8	9	10	11																																		
1		3	4	5	6	10	8	9		11	7					2																												
1	2	3	4	5	6		8	9	10	11			7																															
1	2	3	4	5	6		8	9	10	11	7																																	
1	2	3	4		6	7	8	9		11			10				5																											
1	2		4		6	8		9	10	11	7		3				5																											
1	3				6	8		9	10	11	7		4				5	2																										
	3				6	10	8	9		11	7						5		2	4	1																							
1	2	3			6	8		9		11	10						5			4		7																						
1	2	3		5	6	11	8	9			7		10				4																											
1	3			5	6	10	8	9		11	7		6				4																											
1	3				6	7	8	9		11			10				5						4	2																				
1	3		4		6		8	9	10	11			7				5							2																				
1	2	3			6	7	8	9		11			10				5								4																			
	2	3	4		6	11	8	9					7				5									1	10																	
1	2	3			6	7	8	9		11			10				5										4																	
1	2	3	4		6			9	10	11	7		8				5																											
	2	3	4		6	7	8	9	10	11							5											1																
	2	3	4		6		8	9	10	11			7				5									1																		
1	2	3			6		8	9	10		7		11				5										4																	
1	2	3	4		6	7	8	9	10				11				5																											
	2	3	4		6			9		11			10																1	5	7	8												
1	3				6	7		9		11																							2	4	5	10	8							
25	29	23	20	11	30	22	20	28	16	26	15	2	18	1	1	1	17	1	1	2	1	1	1	2	1	2	3	1	1	1	1	1	1	1	1	1	1							
	1		1		3	7	6	21	9	3	4	1	10														1				1					1	1							

Tootill	Hudgell	Dawes FW	Gregory M	Millbank	Collins	Gillespie	Smith T	Robson	Bark	Wilson	Blackman	Hawkes	Dawes AG	Fuller	Raynor	Lester	Morris	Gregory FC	Young	Reece	Hobbins	Sibley	Chivers	Scaife	Moffitt	Bartram	Henley	Boulton	Hooper	Oakes John	Geldard	Duncan	Catlin	Lewis J	Hitchins	Lewis G	Smith J	Tweedy	Mather	Mulligan	Weale	Forder	McPhee	Halford
	2	3			6	7	8	9	10	11			4				5																					1						
	2	3	4		6		8	9	10	11			7				5				1																							
	2	3			6	7		9					10				5				1																		4	8	11			
1	2	3	4		6	11		8			7		10				5																									9		
1	2	3	4		6	11					7		10				5								8																	9		
1	2	3	4		6				10	7			8				5																										9	11
3	6	6	4		6	4	2	4	3	3	2		6				6				2				1													1	1	1	1	2	1	1
								1	1				3																														2	

1942-43

Football League - South

Manager: George Irwin

Did you know that?

Now aged 38, Peter Simpson was still playing football, albeit for the RAF at outside-left while stationed in Malta during the war.

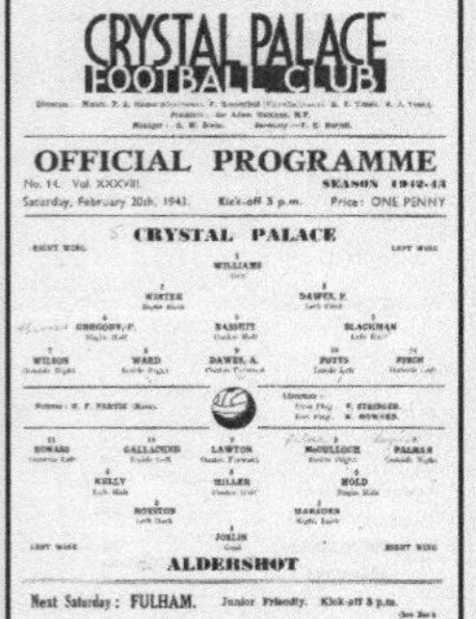

Match No.	Date		Venue	Opponents	Result		Scorers	Attendance
1	Aug	29	A	Tottenham Hotspur	W	3-1	Wilson, Robson 2	5,623
2	Sep	5	H	Clapton Orient	W	5-3	M. Gregory, Smith, Robson 2, Gillespie	4,431
3		12	A	West Ham United	D	2-2	Wilson, Lowes	7,000
4		19	H	Queen's Park Rangers	L	0-1		5,600
5		26	A	Brighton & Hove Albion	W	8-1	A. Dawes 2, Smith, Wilson, Bark 2, Robson, own-goal (Ford)	1,350
6	Oct	3	A	Charlton Athletic	D	4-4	Bark, A. Dawes (pen), Robson 2	4,396
7		10	H	Fulham	L	2-4	Dawes 2 (1 pen)	4,608
8		17	A	Portsmouth	L	1-2	Bark	6,374
9		24	A	Chelsea	L	1-4	Robson	7,824
10		31	H	Arsenal	L	1-7	Bark	12,900
11	Nov	7	A	Watford	L	3-5	A. Dawes (pen), Ware, Wilson	1,970
12		14	A	Aldershot	L	2-3	Bastin, Smith	4,000
13		21	H	Southampton	W	2-1	Bark, Robson	3,368
14		28	H	Tottenham Hotspur	D	0-0		4,893
15	Dec	5	A	Clapton Orient	W	2-1	A. Dawes, Bastin	2,800
16		12	H	West Ham United	D	0-0		5,127
17		19	A	Queen's Park Rangers	L	0-3		3,900
18		25	A	Millwall	L	1-2	Gillespie	4,000
19		26	H	Millwall	D	2-2	Bark, A. Dawes	6,350
20	Jan	2	H	Brighton & Hove Albion	L	1-4	Lowes	2,667
21		9	H	Charlton Athletic	L	0-2		2,850
22		16	A	Fulham	W	2-1	Wright, Smith	3,824
23		23	H	Portsmouth	L	1-2	Wright	4,365
24		30	H	Chelsea	L	0-2		4,172
25	Feb	6	A	Arsenal	L	0-9		7,926
26		13	H	Watford	L	0-2		2,750
27		20	H	Aldershot	W	5-2	A. Dawes 2, Ward 2, Potts	2,500
28		27	A	Southampton	L	1-5	Blackman	8,000

Final League Position: 15th in Football League – South — Appearances

1 own-goal — Goals

Football League Cup – South

Match No.	Date		Venue	Opponents	Result		Scorers	Attendance
29	Mar	6	A	Luton Town	D	0-0		3,000
30		13	H	Portsmouth	L	0-1		4,763
31		20	A	Charlton Athletic	L	0-1		3,836
32		27	H	Luton Town	W	4-0	Wilson, Smith 3	3,000
33	Apr	3	A	Portsmouth	D	3-3	Smith 3	9,137
34		10	H	Charlton Athletic	L	0-4		6,394

Cryslal Palace played in Group 4 of the Qualifying Competition but did not qualify for the semi-finals — Appearances

Goals

Hudgell	Dawes FW	Gregory M	Lewis J	Morris	Dawes AG	Smith TJ	Robson	Bark	Wilson	Batey	Lewis G	Poland	Reece	Gillespie	Brown	Bassett	Young	Ware	Ford	Blackman	Harding	Lowes AR	Millbank	Joslin	Scaife	Bastin	Tootill	Johnson	Henley	Wright	Waller	Bratley	Ward	Allen	Briscoe	Finch	Smith C	Spencer	Gregory F	Porritt	Callend	Williams C	Delaney	Williams CE	Potts	Girling	Davie	Driver
2	3	4	5	6	7	8	9	10	11																																							
3		4	5		2	8	9		11		10		6	7																																			
2	3	4		5		8	9		11			1	6	7							10																										
3			5		2	8	9	10	11			1	4	7																																			
6	3				8	7	9	10	11			1	4		2	5																																	
	3				8	7	9	10	11			1	6		4		2	5																															
	3			6	4	8	9			5				10					1																				2									
	3		6		2	7	9	10	11		8				5				1	4																												
	3				11		9	10						6					5	1	7	2	8																										
	3				4	7	9	10	11		8	1	6				2						5																									
					6	7		10	11									9	1		2		5																									
				5		7	9	10	11				6							4	2			1	3	8																					
		3		4		8	9	10	11				6			5				7	2						1																				
	3			6	4	7	9	10	11						5					2					8	1																				
	3				2	8	9		11				6	7						4						10	1																				
	3				2	7	9							11		5				4								1	6	8																		
	3				4	8	9		11					7			2			6						10	1																				
	3				4	8	9		11			1		7		5				6	2																			10							
	3				2	7	9	10				1	6	11		5						4				8																					
						7	10					1		11		5	2			4		9			3			6																8					
	3				8				11		10			7		5				4		9					1	6														2						
	3				2	10	7					1		11		5				6		8							9	4																		
	3				2	10	7		11											6		8					1			9	5		4																
						10			11					8		5				4				1						9	6	2					7												
	3	2				10	8		11							5				4				1				6		9							7												
		4			8	10								11		5											1			9	6	2	7										3					
	3				9				7							5				6														10			11		4						1	8			
2	3				10	8															6			5				1												7	4									11	9	
6	20	6	4	6	22	25	22	12	20	1	4	9	11	14	4	12	4	3	4	16	6	7	3	3	2	5	9	4	1	5	4	2	3			1	3	2	1	1	1	1	1	1	1	1	1	
		1			10	4	9	7	4					2				1		1		2				2				2			2												1			

Hudgell	Dawes FW	Gregory M	Lewis J	Morris	Dawes AG	Smith TJ	Robson	Bark	Wilson	Batey	Lewis G	Poland	Reece	Gillespie	Brown	Bassett	Young	Ware	Ford	Blackman	Harding	Lowes AR	Millbank	Joslin	Scaife	Bastin	Tootill	Johnson	Henley	Wright	Waller	Bratley	Ward	Allen	Briscoe	Finch	Smith C	Spencer	Gregory F	Porritt	Callend	Williams C	Delaney	Williams CE	Potts	Girling	Davie	Driver
3			4		10		9		11					7						6												2							5							1				
	3		4		9				11		10			7		5																									6	2									8
	3		4		2	8			11											9									6						7	10		5							1				
	3		6		10	8			7							5	2			9							1									11		4										
	3		6		2	8			11		10									9							1							5	7			4										
					4	8	7		11								2			9							1		6				10	5													
1	4		5		6	4	2		6		2			2		2	2			5							3		2		1		1	2	2	2		5	1					2				1
						6			1																																								

Hobbins played number 1 in Match 1; M. Turner played number 1 in Match 2; Collins played number 6 in Match 4; Hawkes played number 7 in Match 7; Mennie played number 11 in Match 7; Lowe played number 4 in Match 9; Fletcher played number 3 in Match 11; Fenton played number 4 in Match 11; J. Smith played number 8 in Match 11; Barnes played number 5 in Match 15; Milton played number 10 in Match 16; Farmer played number 5 in Match 17; Buckley played number 3 in Match 24; Winter played number 2 in Match 27; Potts played number 8 in Match 27 and scored once; C.J. Walker played number 8 in Match 29; Walker played number 1 in Match 31; Kirk played number 3 in Match 34.

1943-44

Football League - South

Manager: George Irwin

Did you know that?

Palace forward Albert Dawes missed only four games this season. Although his brother Fred was largely absent due to duties in the civil defence police, Albert filled in for the Glaziers in almost every position, and wore every outfield shirt apart from number seven during the campaign.

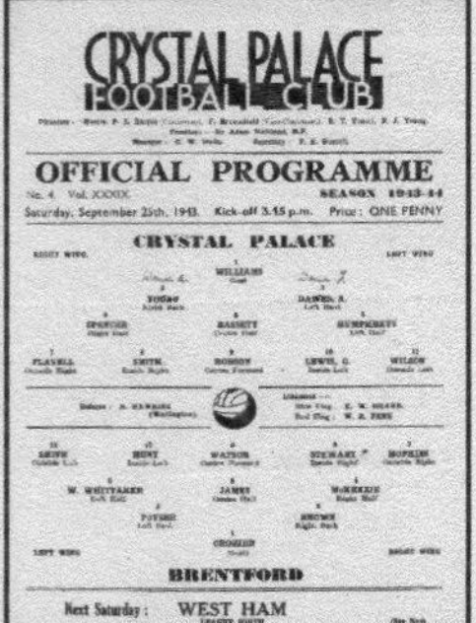

Match No.	Date		Venue	Opponents	Result		Scorers	Attendance
1	Aug	28	A	Tottenham Hotspur	D	1-1	Wilson	8,139
2	Sep	4	H	Clapton Orient	W	5-2	Smith 2, Bryant 2, A Dawes	4,653
3		11	A	Luton Town	W	2-1	Redfern, Wilson	4,000
4		18	H	Reading	L	1-5	Wilson	7,500
5		25	H	Brentford	D	1-1	Wilson	5,131
6	Oct	2	H	West Ham United	L	1-6	Spencer	7,040
7		9	A	Fulham	W	5-4	A. Dawes 2 (1 pen), Wilson, Ward, Somerfield	8,000
8		16	H	Portsmouth	L	2-3	A. Dawes 2 (1 pen)	7,065
9		23	A	Chelsea	L	1-2	A. Dawes	8,373
10		30	H	Arsenal	D	1-1	Briscoe	14,000
11	Nov	6	A	Watford	W	4-2	Wilson, Ferrier 2, Biggs	3,783
12		13	H	Aldershot	W	4-1	Robson 2, Ferrier 2	5,121
13		20	A	Southampton	D	2-2	Smith, Robson	7,000
14		17	H	Tottenham Hotspur	W	3-0	Ferrier, Wilson 2	6,138
15	Dec	4	A	Clapton Orient	W	6-1	Robson, Cuthbertson, Girling, Smith 2, Ferrier	1,200
16		11	H	Luton Town	W	5-0	Ferrier 2, A. Dawes 2, Girling	2,767
17		18	A	Millwall	L	1-5	Girling	2,055
18		25	A	Brighton & Hove Albion	W	3-1	Ferrier 2, Smith	6,800
19		27	H	Brighton & Hove Albion	W	6-2	Ferrier 3, Smith, Robson, Allen	3,500
20	Jan	1	A	Reading	W	3-0	G. Lewis, Wilson, Ferrier	5,000
21		8	H	Watford	W	1-0	Ferrier	5,000
22		22	A	West Ham United	L	0-3		9,500
23		29	H	Fulham	W	6-2	Ferrier 2, A. Dawes, Smith, Wilson, J. Robinson	7,000
24	Feb	5	A	Portsmouth	L	0-1		8,309
25		12	H	Chelsea	W	1-0	Allen	10,692
26	Apr	8	A	Arsenal	L	2-5	Smith, Robson	11,563
27		10	A	Brentford	L	0-2		7,500
28		22	H	Millwall	W	2-0	Robson, A. Dawes	5,270
29		29	A	Aldershot	W	6-0	Wilson, Robson, Ferrrier 2, A. Dawes, Smith	5,000
30	May	6	H	Southampton	D	0-0		5,000

Final League Position: 5th in Football League – South

Appearances

Goals

Football League Cup – South

Match No.	Date		Venue	Opponents	Result		Scorers	Attendance
31	Feb	19	A	Brentford	W	4-3	Girling, Ferrier 2, J. Lewis	4,110
32		26	H	Brighton & Hove Albion	L	2-3	Wilson 2	6,000
33	Mar	4	H	Charlton Athletic	W	5-1	Smith, Wilson, A. Dawes 2, Robson	6,000
34		11	H	Brentford	L	1-2	Wilson	8,659
35		18	A	Brighton & Hove Albion	W	4-2	A. Dawes 2, Robson, Spencer	3,500
36		25	A	Charlton Athletic	D	0-0		19,722

Crystal Palace finished 2nd in Group 'A' of the Qualifying Competition and did not qualify for the semi-finals

Appearances

Goals

Williams	McAra	Dawes FW	Dawes A	Spencer	Russell	Redfern	Smith T	Bryant	Gallagher	Wilson A	Wilson CF	Blackman	Young	Ravell	Bassett	Humphreys	Robson	Lewis G	Mountford	Tootill	Tennant	Millbank	Brophy	Ward	Page	Cabrelli	Ferrier	Girling	Cuthbertson	Allen K	Robinson P	Pond	Robinson J	Nunn	Lewis J	Tunney	Bray	Embleton	Lambert	Franko	Gilbert	Grogan	Brown A	Somerfield	Briscoe	Biggs	Mittitt	Compton L
1	2	3	4	5	6	7	8	9	10	11																																					
1	2	3	6	4		7	8	9	10	11	5																																				
1			3	5		8		9		11		6																											2	7	10	4						
1		3	6	5			8	9		11		4	2	7																														10					
1		3	2	4			8			11				7	5	6	9	10																													
1			3	4			8		10	11				7	5	6	9		2																												
		3	10			7				11									2	1	4	5	6	8																				9				
		3	10	5		7				11						9		2		4			8																								
		3	10				8			7								2	1			4		5	6	9	11																			
		3	8	4						11						10		2	1					5	6	9																		7			
		3	8	5						11						7		2	1						6	9																			10	4	
		3	10	4			8			11						7		2	1					5	6	9																				
			10	5			8			11			3				7		2	1	4						9																				
				5			8			11			2				4	10		1						6	9																					3
			3	4			8										5	7		2	1						6	9	11	10																		
		3	10	4			8					6				5	7		2	1							9	11																			
			3	4			8			10						7		2	1		5				6	9	11																			
			3	4			8			10						5	7		2	1						6	9	11																			
			3	4			8					10				5	7		2	1						6	9			11																	
			6	4			8			11			3			5	7	10	2	1								9																				
			10				8					4	3			5	7		2	1						6	9	11																			
			11	5			8						3				7		2	1						6	9		10																		
			4	5			10			11			3				7		2	1						6	9						8														
			3	4			8			11					5		7		2	1						6	9	10																			
							8						3		5		7	10	2	1						4	9			11		6															
			5				8			11		6					7		2	1							10				4			9		3											
			10				8			11		6					7		2	1											4			9	5	3											
			6	5			8			11			3				7	10	2	1							9										4										
			10	5			8			11		6	3				7		2	1							9									4											
			9				8			11		6	3				7	10	2	1																5	4											
6	2	11	28	23	1	5	25	4	3	24	1	9	11	3	4	8	24	6	24	23	3	2	2	2	3	14	20	7	2	2	2	1	1	2	2	4	1		1	1	1	1	1	1	1	1	1	1
			11	1		1	10	2		11							8	1						1			19	3	1	2			1											1	1	1		
				5			8						3				7	10	2	1						6	9	11								4													
				4			8			11			3		5		7	10	2	1						6	9																					
			9				8			11			3		5		7	10	2	1						6						4																		
			6	5			8			11			3				7	10	2	1							9				4																		
			4	5						11			3				7	10	2	1						6	9												8											
			10	5			8			11			3				7		2	1						6	9																					
			4	5			5			5			6		2		6	5	6	6						5	5	1			2				1			1											
			4	1			1			4							2									2	1							1														

J. Brown played number 1 in Match 8; Henley played number 6 in Match 8; Malpass played number 6 in Match 13; Thompson played number 7 in Match 14; Lieut. Collins played number 4 in Match 22; M. Gregory played number 4 in Match 36.

1944-45

Football League - South

Manager: George Irwin

Did you know that?

Palace used a record number of players this season – 66 in total as World War Two finally came to an end.

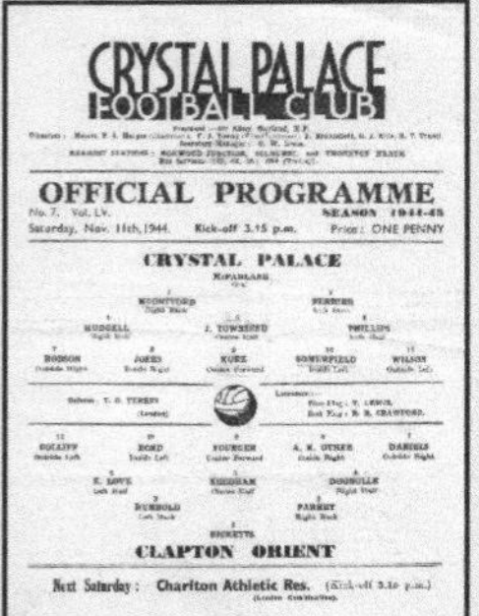

Match No.	Date		Venue	Opponents	Result		Scorers	Attendance
1	Aug	26	H	Queen's Park Rangers	W	7-4	Driver, Kurz 3, Wilson 2, Somerfield	7,000
2	Sep	2	A	Watford	W	4-2	Kurz, Driver 2, own-goal (R. Williams)	7,500
3		9	H	Brighton & Hove Albion	W	5-2	Blackman 3, Wilson, Robson	6,000
4		16	A	Chelsea	L	2-8	A. Dawes (pen), Robson	20,000
5		23	A	Fulham	L	2-6	Wilson, Spencer	8,000
6		30	H	Luton Town	D	1-1	Robson	7,000
7	Oct	7	H	Tottenham Hotspur	L	1-3	A. Dawes	10,000
8		4	A	Reading	L	1-4	Kurz	6,000
9		21	A	Aldershot	W	4-0	Somerfield 4	4,000
10		28	H	Arsenal	W	4-3	Mountford (pen), Somerfield, Parlane, Kurz	14,369
11	Nov	4	A	Millwall	W	2-1	Somerfield, Conner	6,000
12		11	H	Clapton Orient	W	6-1	Kurz 3, Wilson, Mountford (pen), Somerfield	4,950
13		18	A	Brentford	W	2-1	Wilson, Stock	11,100
14		25	H	West Ham United	W	3-0	Jones, Somerfield, Kurz	11,600
15		2	A	Queen's Park Rangers	D	0-0		8,661
16	Dec	9	H	Watford	L	2-3	Somerfield, Wilson	5,897
17		16	A	Brighton & Hove Albion	W	3-0	Somerfield 2, Cheetham	3,500
18		23	H	Portsmouth	W	1-0	A. Dawes (pen)	7,160
19		26	A	Portsmouth	L	1-9	Blackman	13,063
20		30	H	Chelsea	D	3-3	Somerfield, F. Dawes, Kurz	10,106
21	Jan	6	H	Fulham	L	0-2		6,000
22		20	A	Tottenham Hotspur	L	1-3	own-goal (Adams)	11,015
23		27	H	Reading	W	4-1	Jones 2, Somerfield, Kurz	2,000
24	Mar	17	H	Aldershot	W	3-1	A. Dawes 2, Wilson	4,419
25		24	A	Arsenal	L	0-1		9,619
26		31	H	Millwall	W	2-1	G. Lewis, Wilson	9,272
27	Apr	2	A	Luton Town	D	3-3	Blackman, A. Dawes, Betts	
28		14	A	Clapton Orient	D	1-1	Stevens	2,500
29		21	H	Brentford	W	6-1	Kurz 2, Ferrier 3, Betts	6,492
30		28	A	West Ham United	L	0-5		6,257

Final League Position: 6th in Football League – South

Appearances

2 own-goals

Goals

Football League Cup – South

Match No.	Date		Venue	Opponents	Result		Scorers	Attendance
31	Feb	3	A	Southampton	L	1-4	Cheetham	10,000
32		10	H	Charlton Athletic	L	0-2		7,000
33		17	H	Chelsea	D	1-1	Cheetham	12,000
34		24	H	Southampton	D	3-3	Robson, Kurz, Stevens	9,000
35	Mar	3	A	Charlton Athletic	L	0-1		10,000
36		10	A	Chelsea	L	0-2		20,690

Crystal Palace finished 5th in Group 4 of Qualifying Competition and did not qualify for the semi-finals

Appearances

Goals

Tootill	Mountford	Dawes F	Dawes A	Millbank	Phillips	Driver	Somerfield	Kurz	Lowes	Wilson	Lievesley	Reece	Robson	Blackman	Lewis G	Ferrier	Spencer	Briscoe	Townsend	Hudgell	Parlane	McFarlane	Harding	Moore	Jones	Challis	Cheetham	Lewis J	Betts	Gillespie	Stephens	Stevens	Bradshaw	Ferrier R	McCormick	Clarkson	Barrett	Tickeridge	Conner	Stock	Brown H	Morrad	Young	Scarr	Stanley	Blair	Horn	
1	2	3	4	5	6	7	8	9	10	11																																						
1	2	3		5	6	7	8	9	10	11	4																																					
1	2	3	8							11	5	6	7	9	10																																	
1	2	3	10				8					6	7	9	11																																	
	2			5	6		8		10	11			9			3	4	7																														
1	2	3	6							11	4		10					7	5																													
1	2		8				9			11	4		10	6			5	7		3																												
1	2		7					9	10	11			6				5			3	8																											
	2						10			11			7	9		3	5			6	8	1		4																								
1	2						10	9		11						3	5	7		6	8			4																								
	3		8				10											7	5	6		1	2	4															9									
	2				6		10	9		11			7			3			5	4		1			8																							
	2		7		6					11					10	3	5			4		1			8															9								
	2				6		10	9								3	5			4	8	1			11	7																						
	2				6		10	9		11						3	5			4		1			8	7																						
					6		10	9		11						3	5			4		1	2		8	7																						
	2				6		10	7						11		3	5			4		1			8		9																					
	2		4				8			11						3	5			6					7		9														1	10						
			2							11				6			5			3					4	7															1							
1	2	7			6		8	9		11					10	3	5			4																												
	2		7				8	9		11				4		3	5			6		1																				10						
	2				6		10	9		11						3				4	8	1			7			5																				
	2				6		10	7		11						3	5			4		1			8		9																					
	2		9							7					8		5			6		1						4	11		3																	
	2		9		6			7		11					10	3	5			4		1																										
1	2		4				10	9		11			7		8	3	5			6																												
1	2		10											9			5			6									11		3												4	7	8			
1		11	4					9								3				6			2									8	7													5	10	
1			4					8							10	3				6			2					5	11	7				9														
1			10					9								3				6			2					4	11						7	8										5		
14	25	7	18	3	13	2	19	18	4	22	4	2	9	8	8	19	19	5	3	24	5	13	5	3	10	4	3	4	4	1	2	1	1	1	1	1			1	1	2	2	1	1	1	2	1	
	2	1	6			3	14	14		9			3	5	1		1				1				3		1		2			1		3					1	1								
	2									11			7	6	10		5			3		1			8		9	4																				
	2	7			6		10			11						3											9	4		8							5											
	2		8									4		7			5			6		1					9					10						3										
	2							9		11			7							6		1			8			5			3	10																
	2						10	9								3	5			6								4				8																
	2						10			11			7			3	5			6		1			8		9	4																				
	6	1	1		1		3	2		4		1	3	2	1	3	4			5		4			3		4	5		1	1	3					1	1										
								1					1														2					1																

Burke played number 4 in Matches 3 and 4; Stewart played number 5 in Match 4; Cruikshank played number 1 in Match 5; Redfern played number 8 in Match 6; Foreman played number 9 in Match 6; Wales played number 4 in Match 8; Buchanan played number 11 in Match 11; Storey played number 8 in Match 19; Cheddingham played number 9 in Match 19; Ramplin played number 10 in Match 19; Jackman played number 10 in Match 24; Hurrell played number 8 in Match 25; E. Gregory played number 1 in Match 32; Paton played number 11 in Match 33; Muir played number 4 in Match 34; Taylor played number 1 in Match 35; Ward played number 7 in Match 35; Burley played number 11 in Match 35.

1945-46

Division Three South (South Region)

Manager: George Irwin

Did you know that?

Not recognised in official football records, many clubs scored a high number of goals per game during the World War One and Two years, due to the varying quality of guest players used. Palace scored 10 goals once, in March 1916 against Reading. This was followed by 10 goals against Brighton (twice) in April 1940 and September 1941, then 10 versus Swindon Town in November 1945.

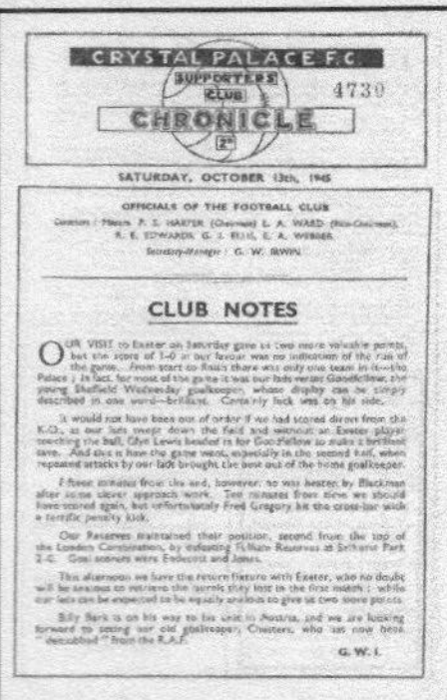

CRYSTAL PALACE F.C. SUPPORTERS CLUB CHRONICLE 2d 4730

SATURDAY, OCTOBER 13th, 1945

OFFICIALS OF THE FOOTBALL CLUB

Directors: Messrs. P. S. HARPER (Chairman) L. A. WARD (Vice-Chairman), R. E. EDWARDS, G. J. ELLIS, E. A. WEBBER.

Secretary-Manager: G. W. IRWIN

CLUB NOTES

OUR VISIT to Exeter on Saturday gave us two more valuable points, but the score of 1-0 in our favour was no indication of the run of the game. From start to finish there was only one team in it—the Palace; in fact, for most of the game it was our lads versus Goodfellow, the young Sheffield Wednesday goalkeeper, whose display can be simply described in one word—brilliant. Certainly luck was on his side.

It would not have been out of order if we had scored direct from the K.O., as our lads swept down the field and without an Exeter player touching the ball, Glyn Lewis headed in for Goodfellow to make a brilliant save. And this is how the game went, especially in the second half, when repeated attacks by our lads brought the best out of the home goalkeeper.

Fifteen minutes from the end, however, he was beaten by Blackman after some clever approach work. Ten minutes from time we should have scored again, but unfortunately Fred Gregory hit the cross-bar with a terrific penalty kick.

Our Reserves maintained their position, second from the top of the London Combination, by defeating Fulham Reserves at Selhurst Park 2-0. Goal scorers were Endecott and Jones.

This afternoon we have the return fixture with Exeter, who no doubt will be anxious to retrieve the points they lost in the first match; while our lads can be expected to be equally anxious to give us two more points.

Billy Bark is on his way to his unit in Austria, and we are looking forward to seeing our old goalkeeper, Chesters, who has now been "demobbed" from the R.A.F.

G. W. I.

Match No.	Date		Venue	Opponents	Result		Scorers	Attendance
1	Aug	25	H	Aldershot	D	0-0		
2	Sep	1	A	Aldershot	W	5-2	Kurz, Wilson, Surtees, A. Dawes 2	
3		5	H	Reading	D	2-2	Kurz 2	
4		8	A	Bristol City	W	2-1	F. Dawes, Wilson	
5		12	H	Cardiff City	W	3-0	Addinall 2, A. Dawes (pen)	
6		15	H	Bristol City	L	0-1		
7		19	A	Reading	W	4-3	Addinall 2, Fagan, Wilson	
8		22	A	Brighton & Hove Albion	L	3-7	Kurz, Stevens 2	
9		29	H	Brighton & Hove Albion	W	5-1	Bark 2, Kurz, Robson, Ferrier	
10	Oct	6	A	Exeter City	W	1-0	Blackman	
11		13	H	Exeter City	W	2-1	Kurz, Blackman	
12	Nov	3	A	Swindon Town	W	3-1	Kurz, Robson 2	
13		10	H	Swindon Town	W	10-1	Blackman 3, Kurz 3, Robson 2, Stamps, Wilson	
14	Dec	1	A	Bristol Rovers	D	1-1	Kurz	
15		15	A	Torquay United	W	2-1	Kurz, Blackman	
16		19	H	Bristol Rovers	W	1-0	Kurz	
17		22	H	Torquay United	W	5-0	Kurz 2 (1 pen), Stamps, G. Lewis 2	
18		25	H	Bournemouth	W	4-1	Kurz 3, Stamp	
19		26	A	Bournemouth	L	1-2	Kurz (pen)	
20		29	A	Cardiff City	L	1-6	Kurz	

Final League Position: 1st in Division Three South (South Region)

Appearances
Goals

Match No.	Date		Venue	Opponents	Result		Scorers	Attendance
21	Jan	12	A	Brighton & Hove Albion	D	2-2	Smith, G. Lewis	
22		19	H	Brighton & Hove Albion	W	6-1	Kurz 2, G. Lewis 2, Reece 2	
23	Feb	2	H	Aldershot	W	6-0	Lievesley 3, Reece 2, G. Lewis	
24		9	H	Reading	D	3-3	Lievesley, Kurz, Reece	
25		16	A	Reading	W	2-0	G. Lewis, Reece	
26		23	H	Bournemouth	W	2-1	Smith, Kurz	
27	Mar	2	A	Bournemouth	L	0-4		
28		9	H	Norwich City	L	2-3	Lievesley, Kurz	
29		16	A	Norwich City	L	1-6	Kurz	
30		23	H	Exeter City	W	3-0	Hudgell, Kurz 2 (1 pen)	
31		30	A	Exeter City	W	3-2	Kurz 2, Reece	
32		3	A	Aldershot	W	3-0	Kurz, Bark, Reece	
33	Apr	6	H	Bristol City	L	1-2	Kurz	
34		13	A	Bristol City	D	2-2	J. Lewis, Waldron	
35		20	H	Cardiff City	D	1-1	Girling	
36		22	A	Cardiff City	L	0-3		

Final League Position: 4th in League Cup Qualifying Competition

Appearances
Goals

FA Cup

Round	Date		Venue	Opponents	Result		Scorers	Attendance
3	Jan	5	A	Queen's Park Rangers	D	0-0		
		9	H	Queen's Park Rangers	D	0-0*		
R		16	N+	Queen's Park Rangers	L	0-1		

+ Played at Craven Cottage, Fulham. * After extra-time.

Appearances
Goals

Ford	Dawes F	Hudgell	Reece	Hindle	Lewis J	Wilson	Jackman	Kurz	Male	Allen	Matthewson	Dawes A	Surtees	Fagan	Stevens	Harding	Humpreys	Blackman	Addinall	Bark	Forder	Gregory F	Millbank	Robson	Lewis G	Stamps	Graham	Morris	Collins	Bassett	Lievesley	Chilvers	Smith	Eastman	Gillespie	Girling	Burrell	Waldron	Hughes	Winter	McFarlane	Corbett	Woodward	Ferrier	Stewart	Henley		
1	2	3	4	5	6	7	8	9	10	11																																						
1	2	3	4		6	11		9	10		5	7	8																																			
	3	6	4			11		9			5	7		8	10																								1	2								
1	11	3	4		6	7			10			8				2	5	9																														
	3	6	4		10	11						7		8		2	5		9																						1							
1	3	2	4		6	11			8			7					5			10																						9						
1	3		4			11		7				6		8					9		2		5																				10					
1	2	3	4		6	11		9	8			7			10								5																									
1	3	6			4	11		8									5			10		2		7																				9				
1	3	6			4	11		8									5	9				2		7	10																							
1	3	6			4	11		8									5	9				2		7	10																							
1	3	6			4	11		9								2	5	7						8	10																							
1	3	6			4	11		8									5	9				2		7		10																						
	3	6			4	11		9									5					2		8	10		1						7															
	3	6			4	11		9									5	7				2			10		1						8															
	3	6			4	11		9									5	7				2				10	1						8															
	3				6			9									5	4				2			11	10	1	7					8															
	3	6			4			9									5	7				2		8		10	1									11												
	3	6			4			9									5	7				2		8	11	10	1																					
	2	3			4	11		9									5								10		1	7	6				8															
11	20	18	8	1	18	17	1	17	5	1	2	7	1	3	2	3	15	10	2	2	1	10	2	8	8	5	7	2	1				5			1			1	1	1	1	1	1				
	1					4		20				3	1	1	2			6	4	2				5	2	3																		1				
	3	6			4			9										7				2		8	11		1			5			10															
	3	6	10		4			8														2			11		1	7		5	9																	
	3	6	10		4			8														2			11		1			5	9		7															
	3	6	10		4	11		8														2					1			5	9		7															
	3	6	10		4			8														2			11		1			5	9		7															
	3	6	10		4	11		8														2					1			5	9		9															
	3	2	8		6			9																	11		1			5		4	7				10											
	3	6	10		4			8														2			11		1			5	9		7															
	3	6	10		4	11		7												10		2	5				1				9																	
	3	6	4		5	11		9												10		2					1						7				8											
	3	6	10		4	7		9										11				2					1			5			8															
		6	8		4	7		9												10	3	2					1			5						11												
		6	8		4	7		9				3								10		2					1			5						11												
			6		4															10							1			5	3		7	2		11		8							9			
		6			4	7																					1			5	3			2		11	10	9								8		
		3	6		4	7												9		8							1			5				2		11	10											
	11	15	14		16	9		13				1						3		6	1	12	1	1	6		16	1		14	9	1	10	3		5	4	2							1			
		1	8		1			12												1					5						5		2			1		1								1		
	3	6	8		4	11		9														2			10		1			5					7													
	3	6			4	11		9										7				2			10		1			5			8															
	3	6			4	7		9														2		8	11		1			5			10															
	3	3	1		3	3		3										1				3		1	3		3			3			2		1													

1946-47

Division Three South

Manager: George Irwin

Did you know that?

Former Palace goalkeeper George Irwin became the first ex-player to take over the managerial reigns at the club, when he took over at the beginning of the 1939–40 season. Steering the team through World War Two, he stepped down at the end of this season.

Match No.	Date		Venue	Opponents	Result		Scorers	Attendance
1	Aug	31	A	Mansfield Town	L	1-3	Girling	9,508
2	Sep	4	A	Reading	L	2-10	Reece, Waldron	8,241
3		7	H	Bristol Rovers	W	2-1	Kurz, Corbett	18,141
4		11	H	Brighton & Hove Albion	W	1-0	Robson	11,983
5		14	A	Southend United	L	0-2		9,288
6		18	H	Reading	W	2-1	Burrell 2	9,617
7		21	H	Queen's Park Rangers	D	0-0		27,517
8		26	A	Norwich City	W	3-2	Naylor 2, Burrell	12,264
9		28	A	Leyton Orient	W	1-0	Naylor	11,802
10	Oct	5	H	Ipswich Town	D	1-1	Hudgell (pen)	20,873
11		12	A	Watford	L	0-1		9,904
12		19	A	Exeter City	L	1-2	Girling	9,928
13		26	H	Port Vale	L	1-2	J. Lewis	14,492
14	Nov	2	A	Bristol City	L	0-3		26,418
15		9	H	Swindon Town	W	4-1	Reece, Kurz 2, Naylor	15,741
16		16	A	Bournemouth	L	0-4		13,383
17		23	H	Cardiff City	L	1-2	Naylor	25,296
18	Dec	7	H	Notts County	W	2-1	Kurz, Girling	12,461
19		21	H	Aldershot	D	0-0		6,696
20		25	H	Torquay United	W	6-1	Naylor 2, Girling 2, Russell, own-goal (Head)	11,786
21		26	A	Torquay United	L	1-2	G. Lewis	7,584
22		28	H	Mansfield Town	D	1-1	Naylor	15,347
23	Jan	4	A	Bristol Rovers	L	1-2	Robson	13,341
24		18	H	Southend United	L	0-3		18,968
25		25	A	Queen's Park Rangers	W	2-1	Mycock, Girling	13,022
26	Feb	1	H	Leyton Orient	W	2-0	Naylor, Russell	8,326
27		8	A	Ipswich Town	D	1-1	Robson	9,168
28		15	H	Watford	W	2-0	Mycock, Robson	10,779
29		22	H	Exeter City	W	1-0	Mycock	7,097
30	Mar	15	A	Swindon Town	L	0-1		13,711
31		22	H	Bournemouth	L	0-1		11,825
32		29	A	Cardiff City	D	0-0		24,214
33	Apr	4	H	Walsall	D	1-1	Jones	2,906
34		5	H	Norwich City	L	0-1		13,315
35		7	A	Walsall	D	3-3	Reece, Russell, Robson	13,315
36		12	A	Notts County	D	0-0		14,890
37		19	H	Northampton Town	D	2-2	Millbank, Russell	10,920
38		26	A	Aldershot	W	2-0	Reece, Kurz	4,125
39	May	3	A	Brighton & Hove Albion	L	0-1		6,957
40		17	A	Northampton Town	L	0-1		5,690
41		24	H	Bristol City	D	0-0		11,634
42		26	A	Port Vale	L	2-4	Russell, Robson	10,414

Final League Position: 18th in Division Three South — Appearances

1 own-goal — Goals

FA Cup

Round	Date		Venue	Opponents	Result		Scorers	Attendance
3	Jan	11	A	Newcastle United	L	2-6	Naylor 2	43,183

Appearances

Goals

Graham	Eastman	Dawes	Lewis J.	Bassett	Hudgell	Coates	Lewis G.	Kurz	Burrell	Girling	Felton	Waldron	Reece	Lucas	Webb	Mycock	Corbett	Robson	Bark/Naylor	Guthrie	Russell	Millbank	Harding	Howells	Jones	Hann	Deakin
1	2	3	4	5	6	7	8	9	10	11																	
1		3	4	5	6			7	10	11	2	9	8														
		2	5		3	7		9		11			6	1	4	8	10										
		2	5		3	7		9		11			6	1	4	8		10									
		2	5		3	7		9		11			6	1	4	8		10									
1		3	4	5	2		7	9	10	11			6						8								
1		3	4	5	2		7	9	10	11			6						8								
1		3	4	5	2			9	10	11		7	6						8								
1		3	4	5	2			9	10	11		7	6						8								
1		3	4	5	2		7		10	11			6					9	8								
1		3	4	5	2		8	7	10	11			6					9									
1		3	4	5	2			9	10	11		8	6					7									
1		3	4	5	2		8	9	10	11			6					7									
1		3	4	5	2		10	9		11			8					7		6							
1		3	4	5	2		7	9		11			8						10	6							
1		3	4	5	2		7	9		11			8						10	6							
1		3	4	5	2		7	9		11								8	10	6							
1		3	4	5	6		7	9		11									10	2	8						
1		3	4	5	2		7	9		11			6						10		8						
1		3	4	5	2		7	9		11			6						10		8						
1		3	4	5	2		7	9		11			6						10		8						
1		3	4	5	2		7	9		11			6					8	10								
1		3	4	5	6			9		11								7	10		8	2					
		3	4	5	2		7	8		11			6	1				9	10								
1		3	4	5	2		7			11			6			8		9	10								
1		3	4	5						11			6			7		9	10		8		2				
1		3	4	5			11						6			7		9	10		8		2				
1		3	4	5			11		10				6			7		9			8		2				
1		3	4	5			11	10					6			7		9			8		2				
1		3	4	5			10						6			7		9			8		2	11			
1		3	4	5				10	11				6			7		9			8		2				
1		3	4					10	11				6			7		9			8	5	2				
1		3	4					10	11				6					9			8	5	2		7		
1		3	4					10	11				6			7		9			8	5	2				
1		3	4				11	9					6			7		10			8	5	2				
1		3	4				11	10					9			7					8	5	2			6	
1		3	4				11	10					6			7		9			8	5	2				
1		3	4				11	10					6			7		9			8	5					2
1		3	4				11	10					6			7		9			8	5					2
1		3	4				11	7					6			10		9			8	5					2
1		3	4				10	8					6			7		9				5	2	11			
1		3	4					10					6			7		9			8	5	2	11			
38	1	42	42	28	25	4	28	36	15	26	1	4	38	4	3	20	1	28	18	5	21	12	14	3	1	1	3
			1		1		1	5	3	6		1	4			3	1	6	9		5	1			1		
1		3	4	5	2		7	8		11			6					9	10								
1		1	1	1	1		1	1		1			1					1	1								
																			2								

League Table

	P	W	D	L	F	A	Pts
Cardiff City	42	30	6	6	93	30	66
Queen's Park Rangers	42	23	11	8	74	40	57
Bristol City	42	20	11	11	94	56	51
Swindon Town	42	19	11	12	84	73	49
Walsall	42	17	12	13	74	59	46
Ipswich Town	42	16	14	12	61	53	46
Bournemouth	42	18	8	16	72	54	44
Southend United	42	17	10	15	71	60	44
Reading	42	16	11	15	83	74	43
Port Vale	42	17	9	16	68	63	43
Torquay United	42	15	12	15	52	61	42
Notts County	42	15	10	17	63	63	40
Northampton Town	42	15	10	17	72	75	40
Bristol Rovers	42	16	8	18	59	69	40
Exeter City	42	15	9	18	60	69	39
Watford	42	17	5	20	61	76	39
Brighton & Hove Albion	42	13	12	17	54	72	38
Crystal Palace	42	13	11	18	49	62	37
Leyton Orient	42	12	8	22	54	75	32
Aldershot	42	10	12	20	48	78	32
Norwich City	42	10	8	24	64	100	28
Mansfield Town	42	9	10	23	48	96	28

1947-48

Division Three South

Manager: Jack Butler

Did you know that?

Since the club was founded in 1905, Palace have contributed to their own downfall by chipping in with over 50 own-goals. Thankfully, over 80 have gone in the other way round, though.

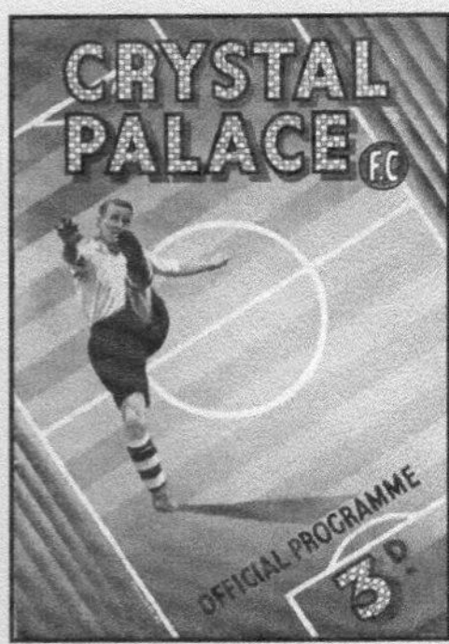

Match No.	Date		Venue	Opponents	Result		Scorers	Attendance
1	Aug	23	A	Leyton Orient	D	1-1	Kurz	18,243
2		27	H	Aldershot	W	1-0	Russell	11,205
3		30	H	Torquay United	W	2-1	Mycock, Burrell	14,490
4	Sep	3	A	Aldershot	L	0-2		5,209
5		6	A	Swindon Town	D	0-0		17,619
6		8	A	Bristol Rovers	D	1-1	Kurz	12,430
7		13	H	Port Vale	W	2-0	Reece, Mycock	15,063
8		17	H	Bristol Rovers	D	0-0		12,172
9		20	A	Queen's Park Rangers	L	0-1		25,199
10		27	H	Watford	L	1-2	Robson	16,764
11	Oct	4	A	Brighton & Hove Albion	D	1-1	Robson	10,240
12		11	A	Exeter City	L	0-2		7,992
13		18	H	Newport County	W	2-1	Kurz, Robson	16,353
14		25	A	Southend United	L	1-2	Kurz	10,560
15	Nov	1	H	Notts County	D	1-1	own-goal (Howe)	16,019
16		8	A	Swansea Town	L	0-2		19,584
17		15	H	Bournemouth	W	2-0	Kurz 2	14,244
18		22	A	Ipswich Town	L	0-3		12,387
19	Dec	6	A	Walsall	D	1-1	Somerfield	10,669
20		20	H	Leyton Orient	W	2-0	G. Lewis, Clough	9,994
21		25	H	Northampton Town	W	1-0	Mycock	15,095
22		27	A	Northampton Town	L	1-3	Mycock	9,631
23	Jan	3	A	Torquay United	D	3-3	Clough, Somerfield, Howells	6,016
24		17	H	Swindon Town	D	1-1	Clough	11,881
25		24	H	Walsall	L	2-3	Clough, Somerfield	11,705
26		31	A	Port Vale	L	1-4	Kurz	13,419
27	Feb	14	A	Watford	W	5-0	Clough 2, Gaillard, G.Lewis, Kurz	14,767
28		28	H	Exeter City	L	1-2	Kurz	15,627
29	Mar	6	A	Newport County	L	1-3	Burrell	8,732
30		13	H	Southend United	D	0-0		14,458
31		15	H	Queen's Park Rangers	L	0-1		22,086
32		20	A	Notts County	L	0-1		30,558
33		26	A	Norwich City	L	1-3	Mycock	24,802
34		27	H	Swansea Town	W	4-0	Kurz 3, Clough	16,036
35		29	H	Norwich City	W	2-0	Kurz 2	20,724
36	Apr	3	A	Bournemouth	D	0-0		16,597
37		5	H	Bristol City	W	4-0	Kurz 2, G. Lewis, Clough	13,405
38		10	H	Ipswich Town	W	2-1	J. Lewis, Kurz	18,151
39		12	H	Brighton & Hove Albion	D	0-0		16,463
40		17	A	Bristol City	L	0-2		12,560
41		21	A	Reading	D	0-0		8,582
42		24	H	Reading	W	2-1	Mycock, Kurz	11,735

Final League Position: 13th in Division Three South — Appearances

1 own-goal — Goals

FA Cup

Round	Date		Venue	Opponents	Result		Scorers	Attendance
1	Nov	29	H	Port Vale	W	2-1	Farrington, Clough	16,000
2	Dec	13	A	Bristol City	W	1-0*	Robson	22,327
3	Jan	10	H	Chester	L	0-1		22,000

* After extra-time — Appearances

Goals

Graham	Harding	Dawes F.	Lewis J.	Bassett	Reece	Robson	Mycock	Kurz	Russell	Lewis G.	Burrell	Millbank	Stubbs	Clough	Deakin	Somerfield	Howells	Buckley	Gaillard	Farrington
1	2	3	4	5	6	7	8	9	10	11										
1	2	3	4	5	6	7	8	9	10	11										
1	2	3	4	5	6		7	9	8	11	10									
1	2	3	4	5	6		7	9	8	11	10									
1	2	3	4	5	10	9	7	8		11		6								
1	2	3	4	5	10	9	7	8		11		6								
1	2	3	4	5	10	9	7	8		11		6								
1	2	3	5		6	9	8		10	11			4	7						
1	2		4	5	10	9	8			11		6		7	3					
1	2		4	5	6	9	8		10	11		3		7						
1	2		4	5	6	9	8		10	11				7	3					
1	2		4	5	6	9	8		10	11				7	3					
1	2	3		5	6	9		8	10	7		4		11						
1	2	3		5	6	9	10	8		7		4		11						
1	2	3	4		6			9	8	11		5		7		10				
1	2	3	4		6		7	9			8	5				10	11			
1	2	3	4		6		7	9		8		5		11		10				
1	2	3			6		7	9	8			5	4	11		10				
1	2	3	4			9	7	10				5				8	11	6		
1	2	3			6	9	7	10		8		5		11				4		
1	2	3			6	9	7	10		8		5		11				4		
1	2	3			6	9	7			8		5		11		10		4		
1	2	3	4		6	10				8		5		7		9	11			
1	2	3	4		6	10	7			8		5		11		9				
1	2	3	4		6		7	10		8		5		11		9				
1		3	4	2	6	10	7	9				5		11				8		
1	2	3	4				8	9		10		5		7				6	11	
1	2	3	4				8	9		10		5		7				6	11	
1	2	3	4				8	9	10		11	5		7				6		
1	2	3	4				8	9		10		5		7				6	11	
1	2	3	4				8	9		10		5		7				6	11	
1	2	3	4		10	8	7	9				5		11				6		
1	2	3	4		10		7	9	8			5		11				6		
1	2	3	4	5			7	9	8	10				11				6		
1	2	3	4	5			7	9	8	10				11				6		
1	2	3	4	5			7		8	10				11		9		6		
1	2	3	4	5			7	9	8	10				11				6		
1	2	3	4	5			7	9	8	10				11				6		
1	2	3	4	5			7	9	8					11				6		10
1	2	3	4	5	10		7	9	8					11				6		
1	2	3	4	5			7	9	8					11				6		10
1	2	3	4	5			7	9	8	10				11				6		
42	41	38	36	23	28	20	39	33	22	32	4	26	2	33	3	10	3	21	4	2
			1		1	3	6	18	1	3	2			8		3	1		1	

Graham	Harding	Dawes F.	Lewis J.	Bassett	Reece	Robson	Mycock	Kurz	Russell	Lewis G.	Burrell	Millbank	Stubbs	Clough	Deakin	Somerfield	Howells	Buckley	Gaillard	Farrington
1	2	3			6		7	9				5		11		10		4		8
1	2	3			6	9	7	10		8		5		11				4		
1	2	3	4		6	10	7			8		5		11		9				
3	3	3	1		3	2	3	2		2		3		3		2		2		1
						1								1						1

League Table

	P	W	D	L	F	A	Pts
Queen's Park Rangers	42	26	9	7	74	37	61
Bournemouth	42	24	9	9	76	35	57
Walsall	42	21	9	12	70	40	51
Ipswich Town	42	23	3	16	67	61	49
Swansea Town	42	18	12	12	70	52	48
Notts County	42	19	8	15	68	59	46
Bristol City	42	18	7	17	77	65	43
Port Vale	42	16	11	15	63	54	43
Southend United	42	15	13	14	51	58	43
Reading	42	15	11	16	56	58	41
Exeter City	42	15	11	16	55	63	41
Newport County	42	14	13	15	61	73	41
Crystal Palace	42	13	13	16	49	49	39
Northampton Town	42	14	11	17	58	72	39
Watford	42	14	10	18	57	79	38
Swindon Town	42	10	16	16	41	46	36
Leyton Orient	42	13	10	19	51	73	36
Torquay United	42	11	13	18	63	62	35
Aldershot	42	10	15	17	45	67	35
Bristol Rovers	42	13	8	21	71	75	34
Norwich City	42	13	8	21	61	76	34
Brighton & Hove Albion	42	11	12	19	43	73	34

1948-49

Division Three South

Manager: Jack Butler

Did you know that?

Having not worn it since the late 1930s, Palace returned to their original claret-and-blue shirts/white shorts combination for this season's kit.

Match No.	Date		Venue	Opponents	Result		Scorers	Attendance
1	Aug	21	A	Reading	L	1-5	Kurz	17,712
2		25	H	Swansea Town	D	1-1	Broughton	13,464
3		28	H	Millwall	D	1-1	Davidson	30,556
4	Sep	2	A	Swansea Town	L	0-3		14,277
5		4	H	Watford	W	3-1	Broughton, Clough, Beresford	16,003
6		8	H	Bristol Rovers	W	1-0	Kurz	10,827
7		11	A	Bournemouth	L	0-2		17,517
8		13	A	Bristol Rovers	L	0-1		14,509
9		18	H	Ipswich Town	D	1-1	Chase	18,982
10		25	A	Notts County	L	1-5	Kurz	24,061
11	Oct	2	H	Walsall	L	1-3	Kurz	16,300
12		9	A	Aldershot	L	0-3		8,109
13		16	H	Brighton & Hove Albion	L	0-2		15,170
14		23	A	Bristol City	L	0-2		14,913
15		30	H	Swindon Town	D	1-1	Broughton	12,290
16	Nov	6	A	Norwich City	L	0-3		23,890
17		13	H	Exeter City	D	1-1	Thomas	13,350
18		20	A	Southend United	W	1-0	Clough	10,357
19	Dec	4	A	Leyton Orient	D	1-1	Kurz	12,336
20		25	A	Newport County	L	0-5		15,115
21		27	H	Newport County	L	0-1		10,951
22	Jan	1	A	Millwall	L	0-1		19,484
23		8	H	Reading	L	0-1		10,842
24		15	A	Watford	L	0-2		7,410
25		22	H	Bournemouth	W	2-1	Thomas, Broughton	13,862
26		29	H	Northampton Town	D	2-2	Kurz, Lewis	13,972
27	Feb	5	A	Ipswich Town	L	2-3	Thoma 2	10,226
28		12	H	Port Vale	D	1-1	Kurz	12,409
29		19	H	Notts County	L	1-5	Thomas	30,925
30		26	A	Walsall	L	1-3	Davidson	10,913
31	Mar	5	H	Aldershot	W	2-1	Clough 2	9,856
32		12	A	Brighton & Hove Albion	D	1-1	Thomas	15,413
33		19	H	Bristol City	W	4-0	Lewis, Chilvers, McCormick, own-goal (Roberts)	11,840
34		26	A	Swindon Town	L	0-1		11,678
35	Apr	2	H	Norwich City	D	1-1	Kurz	16,501
36		9	A	Exeter City	L	1-3	Kurz	7,625
37		16	H	Southend United	W	2-1	Gaillard 2	14,168
38		18	H	Torquay United	L	0-1		12,140
39		19	A	Torquay United	L	0-2		7,552
40		23	A	Northampton Town	L	2-3	Kurz, McCormick	7,717
41		30	H	Leyton Orient	W	2-1	Kurz 2	7,869
42	May	7	A	Port Vale	D	0-0		7,821

Final League Position: 22nd in Division Three South — Appearances

1 own-goal — Goals

FA Cup

Match No.	Date		Venue	Opponents	Result		Scorers	Attendance
1	Nov	27	H	Bristol City	L	0-1*		16,700

* After extra-time — Appearances

Goals

Graham	Harding	Dawes	Lewis J.	Bassett	Buckley	Broughton	Beresford	Kurz	Freeman	Clough	George	Davidson	Chase	Mullen	Stubbs	Farington	Briggs	Chilvers	Taylor	Sille	Howells	Thomas J.	Mulheron	Bumstead	Wyatt	Ross	McCormick	Gaillard	Murphy	Bostock	Saward	Rainford
1	2	3	4	5	6	7	8	9	10	11																						
1	2	3	4	5	6	7	8	9	10	11																						
1	2		4	5	6	7		9		11	3	10	8																				
1	2		4	5	6	7		9		11	3		8	10																			
1	2		4	5	6	7	10	9		11	3		8																				
1	2		4	5	6	7		9		11	3	10	8																				
1	2		4	5	6	7	10	9		11	3		8																				
1			4	5	6	7		9		11	3		8		2	10																	
1	2		4		6	7	10	9		11	3		8				5																
1	2		4		6	7		9		11	3	10	8				5																
1	2			5	6			9		7	3		8					4	10	11												
1	2				6	7		9			3	10	8				5	4		11												
1	2	3	4		6	7		10		11			8				5				9												
1	2	3	4	5	6		8	9		7		10								11												
1	2	3	5		6	11		8		7		10		4								9										
1	2	3	5		6	11				7		10		4							9		8									
1	2	3		5	6	7				11		10		4								9	8									
1	2	3		5	6	7	8			11				4							9		10									
1	2	3	4		6	7		8		11			5								9		10									
1	2	3	4		6	7		9						5	11							10	8									
	2	3	4		6	7		9							11			5					10	8	1								
	2	3	5		6	7		9				10		11								8	1		4							
	2	3	5		6	7		9		11				10				4				8	1								
	2		4	5	6	7		9		11				10								8	1	3							
	2	3	4	5	6	7		10		11											9	8	1								
	2	3	4	5	6	7		10		11				8							9		1								
	2			5	6	7		10		11			8					4			9		1	3							
	2	3		5		7		10		11			4								9		1		6	8					
	2	3	4			7		9		11			5								10		1		6	8					
		3		5						7	2	11	4				6			9	10	1			8					
		3		5		11		9		7	2		4					6				10		1			8					
		3	4					9		7	2		5					6				10		1			8	11				
			4					9		7	2		5					6				10		1	3		8	11				
			4			10				7	2		5					6				9		1	3		8	11				
			4			10		9		7	2		5					6						1	3		8	11				
			4			10		9		7	2		5					6						1	3		8	11				
1	2		4			10		9		7			5					6							3		8	11				
1	2		4			10		9		7			5					6								8	11	3			
1						10		9			2	8	5					6									11	3	7	4	
1						10		9			2		5					6								8	11	3	7	4	
1			4			8		9			2					5	6				10							11	3	7		
1						10		9			2					5	6					4					11	3	7		8
26	30	20	31	19	27	37	7	37	2	34	21	11	27	11	1	1	7	17	1	3	4	15	12	16	7	3	12	11	5	4	2	1
			2			4	1	12		4		2	1					1				6					2	2				

Graham	Harding	Dawes	Lewis J.	Bassett	Buckley	Broughton	Beresford	Kurz	Freeman	Clough	George	Davidson	Chase	Mullen	Stubbs	Farington	Briggs	Chilvers	Taylor	Sille	Howells	Thomas J.	Mulheron	Bumstead	Wyatt	Ross	McCormick	Gaillard	Murphy	Bostock	Saward	Rainford
1	2	3	4		6	7				11			5	8							9		10									
1	1	1	1		1	1				1			1	1							1		1									

League Table

	P	W	D	L	F	A	Pts
Swansea Town	42	27	8	7	87	34	62
Reading	42	25	5	12	77	50	55
Bournemouth	42	22	8	12	69	48	52
Swindon Town	42	18	15	9	64	56	51
Bristol Rovers	42	19	10	13	61	51	48
Brighton & Hove Albion	42	15	18	9	55	55	48
Ipswich Town	42	18	9	15	78	77	45
Millwall	42	17	11	14	63	64	45
Torquay United	42	17	11	14	65	70	45
Norwich City	42	16	12	14	67	49	44
Notts County	42	19	5	18	102	68	43
Exeter City	42	15	10	17	63	76	40
Port Vale	42	14	11	17	51	54	39
Walsall	42	15	8	19	56	64	38
Newport County	42	14	9	19	68	92	37
Bristol City	42	11	14	17	44	62	36
Watford	42	10	15	17	41	54	35
Southend United	42	9	16	17	41	46	34
Leyton Orient	42	11	12	19	58	80	34
Northampton Town	42	12	9	21	51	62	33
Aldershot	42	11	11	20	48	59	33
Crystal Palace	42	8	11	23	38	76	27

1949-50

Division Three South

Manager: Ronnie Rooke

Did you know that?

Keeping with a theme, Palace went from one ex-Arsenal player to another when manager Jack Butler was replaced by Palace's ex-forward Ronnie Rooke, who returned to the club in a player-manager capacity and scored 21 goals.

Match No.	Date		Venue	Opponents	Result		Scorers	Attendance
1	Aug	20	A	Exeter City	L	1-2	Hanlon	12,180
2		24	H	Leyton Orient	D	1-1	Rooke	17,764
3		27	H	Ipswich Town	W	2-0	Rooke 2	19,173
4	Sep	1	A	Leyton Orient	D	2-2	Rooke, Blackshaw	14,868
5		3	A	Port Vale	L	0-2		13,788
6		7	H	Walsall	W	2-0	Hanlon, Thomas	12,264
7		10	H	Notts County	L	1-2	Lewis	26,847
8		17	A	Southend United	D	0-0		13,797
9		24	H	Bristol Rovers	W	1-0	Rooke	15,466
10	Oct	1	A	Bournemouth	L	0-2		16,738
11		8	A	Millwall	W	3-2	Rooke, Mulheron, own-goal (McMillen)	30,043
12		15	H	Swindon Town	D	2-2	Thomas 2	15,954
13		22	A	Torquay United	L	0-1		7,018
14		29	H	Aldershot	W	2-1	Hanlon, Rooke	13,299
15	Nov	5	A	Notts F	L	0-2		18,471
16		12	H	Northampton Town	L	0-4		12,486
17		19	A	Norwich City	L	0-2		23,558
18	Dec	3	A	Bristol City	L	0-2		15,304
19		17	H	Exeter City	W	5-3	Kurz 2, Mulheron, Blackshaw, Howells	7,416
20		24	A	Ipswich Town	D	4-4	Watson. Rooke 2, Howells	9,460
21		26	H	Watford	W	2-0	Rooke, Blackshaw	15,065
22		27	A	Watford	D	0-0		16,985
23		31	H	Port Vale	L	0-1		12,609
24	Jan	7	A	Brighton & Hove Albion	D	0-0		13,289
25		14	A	Notts County	W	1-0	Kurz	31,381
26		21	H	Southend United	W	2-1	Kurz, Howells	13,509
27		28	H	Newport County	W	1-0	Kurz	9,875
28	Feb	4	A	Bristol Rovers	D	0-0		17,259
29		11	H	Brighton & Hove Albion	W	6-0	Rooke 3, Kurz, Chase, Howells	13,973
30		18	H	Bournemouth	W	1-0	Rooke	22,322
31		25	H	Millwall	W	1-0	Blackshaw	30,432
32	Mar	4	A	Swindon Town	L	2-4	Kurz 2	15,217
33		11	H	Torquay United	L	1-3	Rooke (pen)	20,533
34		18	A	Aldershot	D	0-0		8,034
35		25	H	Notts F	D	1-1	Rooke (pen)	17,480
36	Apr	1	A	Northampton Town	D	2-2	Rooke 2	10,277
37		7	H	Reading	D	1-1	Rooke	22,644
38		8	H	Norwich City	W	2-0	Rooke, Thomas	18,067
39		10	A	Reading	W	2-1	Blackshaw, Kelly	12,730
40		15	A	Newport County	D	2-2	Kurz, Rooke	11,459
41		22	H	Bristol City	D	1-1	Kurz	17,263
42	May	6	A	Walsall	L	1-3	Hanlon	5,379

Final League Position: 7th in Division Three South — Appearances

1 own-goal — Goals

FA Cup

1	Nov	26	H	Newport County	L	0-3		13,000

Appearances

Goals

Graham	George	Dawes	Lewis	Watson	Chivers	Hanlon	Kurz	Rocke	Mulheron	Gaillard	Blackshaw	Chase	Broughton	ThomasJ	Surtees	Ross	Cleland	Edwards	Sherwood	Howells	Delaney	Murphy	Harding	Bailey	Kelly	Bumstead	Penn	Buckley
1	2	3	4	5	6	7	8	9	10	11																		
1	2	3	4	5	6		8	9	10	11	7																	
1	2	3	4		6	11	10	9	8		7	5																
1	2	3	4	5	6	11	8	9			7	10																
1	2	3	4	5	6	11					8	10	7	9														
1	2	3	4	5	6	11		8		10				9	7													
1	2	3	4	5	6	11		8						9	7	10												
1	2	3	4	5	6	11	8	9		10					7													
1	2	3	4	5	6	11	8	9		10							7											
1	2	3	4	5	6	11		9	8					10			7											
1	2		4	5	6	11		9	8				7	10				3										
1	2		4	5	6	11		9	8				7	10				3										
1	2			5	6	11		9	8				7	10				3	4									
1	2		4	5		11		9	8				7	10		6		3										
1	2		4	5		11			8				7	10		6		3		9								
1	2			5	6	11			8				7	10				3	4	9								
1	2			5	6	11		9	8			4	7	10				3										
1				5				9	8		7	4		10		6		3		11	2							
1				5			10	9	8		7	4				6				11	2	3						
1				5			10	9	8		7	4				6				11	2	3						
1				5			10	9	8		7	4				6		2		11		3						
1				5			10	9	8		7	4				6		2		11		3						
1				5			10	9	8		7	4				6		2		11		3						
1				5			10	9	8		7	4				6				11		3	2					
1				5			10	9			7	4		8		6				11		3	2					
1				5			10	9			7	4		8		6				11		3	2					
1				5			9	10	8		7					6				11		3	2					4
1				5			9	10	8		7	4				6				11		3	2					
1				5			9	10	8		7	4				6				11		3	2					
1				5			9	10	8		7	4				6				11		3	2					
1				5			9	10	8		7	4			11	6						3	2					
1				5			9	10	8		7	4			11	6						3	2					
				5		11	9	10			7	4				6						3	2	1	8			
				5			9	10		11	7	4				6						3	2		8	1		
				5				9	8		7	4				6						3	2		10	1	11	
				5		11		10	7			4		9								3	2		8	1		6
1				5		11		10			7	4		9								3	2		8			6
1				5		11		10			7	4		9								3	2		8			6
1				5		11		10			9	4	7									3	2		8			6
1				5		11	9	10			7	4										3	2		8			6
1	3			5		11	9	10			7	4											2		8			6
1	3			5		11	9	10			7	4											2		8			6
38	19	10	14	41	15	24	25	39	26	6	28	28	9	17	5	21	2	11	2	15	3	22	19	1	10	3	1	8
			1	1		4	10	21	2		5	1		4						4					1			

Graham	George	Dawes	Lewis	Watson	Chivers	Hanlon	Kurz	Rocke	Mulheron	Gaillard	Blackshaw	Chase	Broughton	ThomasJ	Surtees	Ross	Cleland	Edwards	Sherwood	Howells	Delaney	Murphy	Harding	Bailey	Kelly	Bumstead	Penn	Buckley
1	2			5	6	11		9	8			4	7	10				3										
1	1			1	1	1		1	1			1	1	1				1										

League Table

	P	W	D	L	F	A	Pts
Notts County	42	25	8	9	95	50	58
Northampton Town	42	20	11	11	72	50	51
Southend United	42	19	13	10	66	48	51
Nottingham Forest	42	20	9	13	67	39	49
Torquay United	42	19	10	13	66	63	48
Watford	42	16	13	13	45	35	45
Crystal Palace	42	15	14	13	55	54	44
Brighton & Hove Albion	42	16	12	14	57	69	44
Bristol Rovers	42	19	5	18	51	51	43
Reading	42	17	8	17	70	64	42
Norwich City	42	16	10	16	65	63	42
Bournemouth	42	16	10	16	57	56	42
Port Vale	42	15	11	16	47	42	41
Swindon Town	42	15	11	16	59	62	41
Bristol City	42	15	10	17	60	61	40
Exeter City	42	14	11	17	63	75	39
Ipswich Town	42	12	11	19	57	86	35
Leyton Orient	42	12	11	19	53	85	35
Walsall	42	9	16	17	61	62	34
Aldershot	42	13	8	21	48	60	34
Newport County	42	13	8	21	67	98	34
Millwall	42	14	4	24	55	63	32

1950-51

Division Three South

Manager: Ronnie Rooke until 29 November 1950, then Fred Dawes/Charlie Slade.

Did you know that?

It was all change behind the scenes as a consortium of local businessmen including Arthur Wait took over ownership of the club and tried a first with the joint appointment of Fred Dawes and Charlie Slade as managers.

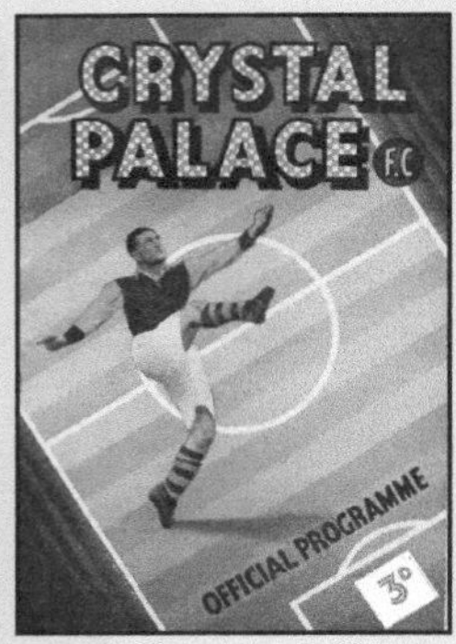

Match No.	Date		Venue	Opponents	Result		Scorers	Attendance
1	Aug	19	H	Aldershot	L	0-2		24,968
2		23	A	Torquay United	L	1-4	Stevens	11,776
3		26	A	Swindon Town	L	0-2		13,699
4		30	H	Torquay United	W	2-1	Whittaker, Rooke (pen)	11,212
5	Sept	2	H	Colchester United	L	1-3	Thomas	22,544
6		6	A	Bristol City	L	0-2		13,422
7		9	A	Bristol Rovers	D	1-1	Hanlon	16,804
8		13	H	Bristol City	W	1-0	Stevens	12,937
9		16	A	Millwall	L	0-1		29,874
10		23	H	Brighton & Hove Albion	L	0-2		17,800
11		30	A	Newport County	W	4-2	Rooke 2, Kelly, Jones	10,114
12	Oct	7	H	Gillingham	W	4-3	Jones 2, Rooke 2 (1 pen)	18,896
13		14	A	Bournemouth	L	0-5		14,187
14		21	H	Exeter City	L	0-1		16,133
15		28	A	Southend United	L	2-5	Stevens, Thomas	10,387
16	Nov	4	H	Reading	L	0-3		12,479
17		11	A	Plymouth Argyle	L	0-4		18,414
18		18	H	Ipswich Town	L	1-3	Kelly	12,146
19	Dec	2	H	Walsall	W	1-0	Herbert	12,083
20		9	A	Watford	L	0-1		7,987
21		23	H	Swindon Town	W	2-0	Kelly 2	7,267
22		25	H	Northampton Town	D	0-0		11,001
23		26	A	Northampton Town	L	0-2		12,607
24		30	A	Colchester United	L	0-1		8,587
25	Jan	6	A	Nottingham Forest	L	0-1		12,923
26		13	H	Bristol Rovers	W	1-0	Kurz	10,632
27		20	H	Millwall	D	1-1	Kurz	22,392
28		27	H	Nottingham Forest	L	1-6	Kurz	17,179
29	Feb	3	A	Brighton & Hove Albion	L	0-1		6,790
30		10	A	Leyton Orient	L	0-2		11,793
31		17	H	Newport County	D	1-1	Rundle	9,990
32		24	A	Gillingham	D	0-0		11,478
33	Mar	3	H	Bournemouth	L	0-1		13,323
34		10	A	Exeter City	W	2-1	Broughton, Herbert	6,534
35		17	H	Southend United	L	0-2		12,898
36		24	A	Reading	D	1-1	Saward	16,720
37		26	H	Port Vale	L	0-2		11,320
38		31	H	Plymouth Argyle	L	0-1		10,411
39	Apr	7	A	Ipswich Town	D	1-1	Thomas	11,032
40		14	H	Leyton Orient	D	1-1	Evans (pen)	10,390
41		18	H	Norwich City	L	0-5		14,782
42		21	A	Walsall	D	0-0		7,838
43		26	A	Port Vale	D	2-2	Marsden 2	7,069
44		28	H	Watford	D	1-1	Marsden	5,258
45	May	2	A	Aldershot	L	0-3		4,279
46		5	A	Norwich City	L	1-3	Thomas	15,693

Final League Position: 24th in Division Three South

Appearances
Goals

FA Cup

1	Nov	29	H	Millwall	L	1-4	Kelly	14,817

Appearances
Goals

Graham	Harding	Murphy	Smith	Watson	Whittaker	Stevens	Kelly	Rundle	Jones	Hanlon	Blackshaw	Kurz	Thomas J.	George	Rooke	Bumstead	Ross	Briggs	McDonald	Chilvers	Buckley	Broughton	Herbert	Saward	Cushlow	Marsden	Bailey	Hughes	Evans	Edwards	Hancox	Rainford
1	2	3	4	5	6	7	8	9	10	11																						
1	2	3	4	5	6	8			10	11	7	9																				
1	2	3	4	5	6	8			10	11	7		9																			
1	2		4	5	6	7	8			11		9		3	10																	
1	2		4	5	6	7	8			11			9	3	10																	
	2		4	5	6		10		8	11	7		9	3		1																
	2		4	5	6		10		8	11	7		9	3		1																
	2				6	7	10		8	11			9	3		1	4	5														
		2			6	7	10		8	11			9	3		1	4	5														
		2		9	6	11	10		8			7		3		1	4	5														
		2			6	11	10		8			7		3	9	1	4	5														
		2			6	11	10		8			7		3	9	1	4	5														
1					6	11	10		8			7		2	9		4	5	3													
1		4			6	11	10		8			7		2	9				3	5												
1		4				11			9	10		7	8	2					3	5	6											
1	2	4			5	11	7	9	8	10				3							6											
1	2			4	5	7	8	9		11			10	3							6											
1	2			4	5	11	8	9	10										3		6	7										
	2			5			8	10		11				3		1				6	4	7	9									
	2			5			8	10		11				3		1				6	4	7	9									
	2			5			8	10		11				3		1				6	4	7	9									
	2			5			8	10		11				3		1				6	4	7	9									
	2			5			8	10		11		9		3		1				6	4	7										
	2			5			8	10		11			9	3		1				6		7		4								
	2			5			8		10	11			9	3		1				6		7		4								
	2			5	4		8	10		11		9		3		1				6		7										
	2			5	4		8		10	11		9		3		1				6		7										
	2			5	4		8	10		11		9		3		1				6		7										
	2				4	7		10		11		9				1			3	6					5	8						
	2				4	11	8	10				7				1			3	6					5	9						
	2				4	7	8	10		11									3	6					5	9	1					
	2				4	7	8	10		11									3	6					5	9	1					
	2				4		8	10		11		7							3	6			9		5			1				
	2				4			10		11									3	6		7	9	8	5			1				
	2				4			10		11				3						6			9	8	5			1	7			
	2				4			8		11									3	6			9	10	5			1	7			
	2				4		7			11		8								6				10	5			1	9	3		
	2				4		8			11										6		7		10	5			1	9	3		
	2				4		8	10		11			9							6		7			5			1		3		
	2				4			10		11			9							6		7			5			1	8	3		
	2				4					11			9							6		7			5	10		1	8	3		
	2				8					11						1	4			6	9	7			5	10				3		
					4					11				2		1	8			6		10			5	9				3	7	
										11				2		1	8			6	4	10			5	9				3	7	
										11				2		1				6	4	10			5	9			7	3		8
	2									11		9	10			1			3	6	4	8			5				7	3		
11	36	10	7	20	35	20	32	22	17	39	4	17	14	28	6	24	9	6	12	30	13	21	8	7	18	9	2	9	8	9	2	1
					1	3	4	1	3	1		3	4		5							1	2	1		3			1			

Graham	Harding	Murphy	Smith	Watson	Whittaker	Stevens	Kelly	Rundle	Jones	Hanlon	Blackshaw	Kurz	Thomas J.	George	Rooke	Bumstead	Ross	Briggs	McDonald	Chilvers	Buckley	Broughton	Herbert	Saward	Cushlow	Marsden	Bailey	Hughes	Evans	Edwards	Hancox	Rainford
	2			5	4	11	8	9	10							1			3		6	7										
	1			1	1	1	1	1	1							1			1		1	1										
							1																									

League Table

	P	W	D	L	F	A	Pts
Nottingham Forest	46	30	10	6	110	40	70
Norwich City	46	25	14	7	82	45	64
Reading	46	21	15	10	88	53	57
Plymouth Argyle	46	24	9	13	85	55	57
Millwall	46	23	10	13	80	57	56
Bristol Rovers	46	20	15	11	64	42	55
Southend United	46	21	10	15	92	69	52
Ipswich Town	46	23	6	17	69	58	52
Bournemouth	46	22	7	17	65	57	51
Bristol City	46	20	11	15	64	59	51
Newport County	46	19	9	18	77	70	47
Port Vale	46	16	13	17	60	65	45
Brighton & Hove Albion	46	13	17	16	71	79	43
Exeter City	46	18	6	22	62	85	42
Walsall	46	15	10	21	52	62	40
Colchester United	46	14	12	20	63	76	40
Swindon Town	46	18	4	24	55	67	40
Aldershot	46	15	10	21	56	88	40
Leyton Orient	46	15	8	23	53	75	38
Torquay United	46	14	9	23	64	81	37
Northampton Town	46	10	16	20	55	67	36
Gillingham	46	13	9	24	69	101	35
Watford	46	9	11	26	54	88	29
Crystal Palace	46	8	11	27	33	84	27

1951-52

Division Three South

Manager: Fred Dawes/Charlie Slade until 11 October, then Laurie Scott.

Did you know that?

Winger Les Devonshire, who signed in August and stayed with Palace for the next four seasons, is the father of West Ham and England winger Alan Devonshire.

Match No.	Date	Venue	Opponents	Result		Scorers	Attendance
1	Aug 18	H	Exeter City	W	2-1	Marsden, Hanlon	15,464
2	22	A	Plymouth Argyle	L	0-5		15,252
3	25	A	Colchester United	W	2-1	Price, Devonshire	10,135
4	29	H	Plymouth Argyle	L	0-1		14,167
5	Sep 1	A	Millwall	L	1-3	McGeachie (pen)	22,436
6	3	A	Bristol Rovers	L	0-4		14,467
7	8	H	Swindon Town	L	0-1		14,264
8	12	H	Bristol Rovers	L	0-1		10,289
9	15	A	Leyton Orient	W	4-0	Burgess 3, Evans	12,461
10	22	H	Walsall	W	2-1	Burgess, Rundle	16,901
11	29	A	Shrewsbury Town	L	1-2	Burgess	12,493
12	Oct 6	H	Gillingham	L	0-2		20,380
13	13	A	Torquay United	W	5-1	Burgess 2, Evans 2, Devonshire	7,085
14	20	H	Ipswich Town	W	3-1	Burgess 2, Price	21,220
15	27	A	Bristol City	L	0-2		18,857
16	Nov 3	H	Port Vale	W	3-1	Broughton, Evans 2	16,401
17	10	A	Northampton Town	L	2-5	Burgess 2	14,845
18	17	H	Reading	L	1-2	Burgess	14,679
19	Dec 1	H	Southend United	W	1-0	Burgess	16,037
20	8	A	Bournemouth	W	2-1	Burgess 2	7,153
21	22	H	Colchester United	D	2-2	Burgess 2	11,618
22	25	H	Brighton & Hove Albion	L	1-2	Burgess	15,439
23	26	A	Brighton & Hove Albion	L	3-4	Marsden, Price, Evans	24,228
24	29	H	Millwall	D	1-1	Marsden	20,834
25	Jan 5	A	Swindon Town	W	2-0	Price, Evans	10,663
26	12	H	Aldershot	L	0-2		12,981
27	19	H	Leyton Orient	W	2-1	Marsden, Price	14,266
28	26	A	Walsall	L	0-3		4,666
29	Feb 2	A	Norwich City	L	0-1		18,277
30	9	H	Shrewsbury Town	D	1-1	Burgess	13,514
31	16	A	Gillingham	D	4-4	Thomas, Burgess, Evans, McGeachie (pen)	11,991
32	23	H	Norwich City	W	2-0	Thomas, Burgess	19,491
33	Mar 1	H	Torquay United	D	1-1	Bennett	15,178
34	8	A	Ipswich Town	D	1-1	McGeachie	10,352
35	15	H	Bristol City	W	2-1	Bennett, Thomas	13,285
36	22	A	Port Vale	L	0-2		11,686
37	26	A	Exeter City	W	1-0	Evans	4,242
38	Apr 5	A	Reading	L	1-3	Bennett	11,561
39	11	A	Watford	L	0-2		10,273
40	12	H	Newport County	D	1-1	McGeachie (pen)	14,933
41	14	H	Watford	W	2-0	McGeachie (pen), Evans	12,143
42	19	A	Southend United	L	0-4		7,728
43	24	A	Newport County	L	0-1		6,942
44	26	H	Bournemouth	D	2-2	Hancox 2	10,765
45	30	A	Aldershot	L	0-3		5,617
46	May 3	H	Northampton Town	D	3-3	Marsden 2, Rainford	7,214

Final League Position: 19th in Division Three South

Appearances
Goals

FA Cup

Match No.	Date	Venue	Opponents	Result		Scorers	Attendance
1	Nov 24	H	Gillingham	L	0-1		21,868

Appearances
Goals

Bumstead	Harding	McDonald	Price	Cushlow	McGeachie	Devonshire	Broughton	Marsden	Rainford	Hanlon	Hughes	Briggs	Hancox	Rundle	Evans	Thomas J.	Edwards	Burgess	Anderson	Scott	Chilvers	Bennett R.	Nelson	George
1	2	3	4	5	6	7	8	9	10	11														
1	2	3	4	5	6	7	8	9	10	11														
	2	3	4		6	7	8	9		11	1	5	10											
1	2	3	4		6	7	8	9		11		5		10										
1	2	3	4		6	7	8	9		11		5		10										
1	2	3	4		6	11	8	9				5			7	10								
1		3	4		6	7	8			11		5		10	9		2							
1		3	4		6	11	7	8				5			9		2	10						
1		3	4		6	11	7					5		8	9		2	10						
1		3	4		6	11	7					5		8	9		2	10						
1		3	4		6		7			11		5		8	9		2	10						
		3	4		6	7	11				1	5		8	9		2	10						
		3	4		6	11	7					5		8	9		2	10	1					
		3	4		6	11	7		8			5			9			10	1	2				
		3	6		4	11	7		8			5			9			10	1	2				
		3	6		4	11	7		8			5			9			10	1	2				
		3	6		4	11	7		8			5			9			10	1	2				
		3	6		4		7		8	11		5			9			10	1	2				
		3			4	7			8	11		5			9			10	1	2	6			
		3			4	7			8	11		5			9			10	1	2	6			
		3			4	7			8	11		5			9			10	1	2	6			
		3			4	7			8	11		5			9			10	1	2	6			
			10		4			9	8	11		5			7		3		1	2	6			
			10		4			9	8	11		5			7		3		1		6			2
			10		4			9	8	11		5			7		3		1		6			2
			10		4			9	8	11		5			7		3		1		6			2
			10		4			9	8	11		5			7		3		1	2	6			
			10		4			9	8	11		5			7		3		1	2	6			
		3			4			9	8			5			7			10	1	2	6	11		
		3			4			9	8			5			7			10	1	2	6	11		
		3			4				8			5			7	9		10	1	2	6	11		
		3			4				8			5			7	9	2	10	1		6	11		
		3			4				8		1	5			7	9	2	10			6	11		
		3			4				8		1	5		10	7	9	2				6	11		
		3			4				8		1	5		10	7	9	2				6	11		
		3			4				8		1	5		10	7	9	2				6	11		
		3			4		7		8	11	1	5		10	9		2				6			
		3		5	4		7		8		1			10	9		2				6	11		
		3		5	4		7		8		1			10	9		2				6	11		
		3		5	4				8						9		2	10	1	7	6	11		
		3		5	4				8						9		2	10	1	7		11	6	
		3		5	4		10							8	9		2		1	7		11	6	
		3		5	4		7		8					10	9				1	2		11	6	
		3		5	4			9	8	11			10		7				1	2			6	
		3		5	4			9	8	11			10		7		2		1				6	
		3			4		7	9	8			5	10				2		1			11	6	
10	6	40	24	10	46	20	24	18	34	21	9	36	4	16	40	7	26	22	27	20	22	15	6	3
			5		5	2	1	6	1	1			2	1	10	3		21				3		

Bumstead	Harding	McDonald	Price	Cushlow	McGeachie	Devonshire	Broughton	Marsden	Rainford	Hanlon	Hughes	Briggs	Hancox	Rundle	Evans	Thomas J.	Edwards	Burgess	Anderson	Scott	Chilvers	Bennett R.	Nelson	George
1			10		4		7			11		5		8	9		3			2	6			
1			1		1		1			1		1		1	1		1			1	1			

League Table

	P	W	D	L	F	A	Pts
Plymouth Argyle	46	29	8	9	107	53	66
Reading	46	29	3	14	112	60	61
Norwich City	46	26	9	11	89	50	61
Millwall	46	23	12	11	74	53	58
Brighton & Hove Albion	46	24	10	12	87	63	58
Newport County	46	21	12	13	77	76	54
Bristol Rovers	46	20	12	14	89	53	52
Northampton Town	46	22	5	19	93	74	49
Southend United	46	19	10	17	75	66	48
Colchester United	46	17	12	17	56	77	46
Torquay United	46	17	10	19	86	98	44
Aldershot	46	18	8	20	78	89	44
Port Vale	46	14	15	17	50	66	43
Bournemouth	46	16	10	20	69	75	42
Bristol City	46	15	12	19	58	69	42
Swindon Town	46	14	14	18	51	68	42
Ipswich Town	46	16	9	21	63	74	41
Leyton Orient	46	16	9	21	55	68	41
Crystal Palace	46	15	9	22	61	80	39
Shrewsbury Town	46	13	10	23	62	86	36
Watford	46	13	10	23	57	81	36
Gillingham	46	11	13	22	71	81	35
Exeter City	46	13	9	24	65	86	35
Walsall	46	13	5	28	55	94	31

1952-53

Division Three South

Manager: Laurie Scott

Did you know that?

The decade of the 1950s is not the most fondly remembered for Palace. Apart from having to be re-elected to the Football League after finishing near the bottom of Division Three South, there were two FA Cup defeats to non-League opposition in the early stages. An away defeat at Finchley this season in the second round was trumped by a poorer first-round exit the following year at the hands of Great Yarmouth.

Match No.	Date	Venue	Opponents	Result		Scorers	Attendance
1	Aug 23	A	Brighton & Hove Albion	L	1-4	Marsden	23,905
2	27	H	Gillingham	D	0-1		15,754
3	30	H	Newport County	W	2-1	Simpson, Bennett	14,642
4	Sep 3	A	Gillingham	L	0-1		13,023
5	6	A	Millwall	D	0-0		25,932
6	10	H	Reading	L	0-3		11,546
7	13	A	Bristol City	L	0-5		17,163
8	17	A	Reading	L	1-4	Devonshire	9,988
9	20	H	Torquay United	D	2-2	Devonshire, Marsden	12,557
10	24	H	Norwich City	D	1-1	Thomas	7,544
11	27	A	Northampton Town	L	1-5	Bennett	12,805
12	Oct 1	A	Ipswich Town	L	0-2		5,763
13	4	H	Leyton Orient	D	2-2	Fell, Grimshaw	17,040
14	11	H	Walsall	W	4-1	Burgess 3, Fell	13,685
15	18	A	Shrewsbury Town	D	1-1	Fell	8,221
16	25	H	Queen's Park Rangers	W	4-2	Burgess 3, Rainford	19,181
17	Nov 1	A	Swindon Town	W	6-3	Burgess 3, Rainford 3	9,106
18	8	H	Aldershot	W	3-0	Burgess, Thomas 2	17,979
19	29	A	Coventry City	L	2-4	Burgess 2	11,628
20	Dec 13	A	Bristol Rovers	L	0-2		20,042
21	20	H	Brighton & Hove Albion	W	2-1	Simpson 2	10,081
22	26	A	Watford	L	0-2		12,422
23	Jan 3	A	Newport County	L	2-3	Burgess, George (pen)	8,062
24	10	H	Bournemouth	W	1-0	Rainford	12,394
25	17	H	Millwall	L	0-1		24,830
26	24	H	Bristol City	L	1-3	George (pen)	12,296
27	31	A	Bournemouth	L	2-4	Thomas, Burgess	7,724
28	Feb 7	A	Torquay United	D	1-1	Hancox	6,077
29	14	H	Northampton Town	W	4-3	Burgess 3, Thomas	6,409
30	21	A	Leyton Orient	D	0-0		12,240
31	28	A	Walsall	W	4-2	Burgess 2, Devonshire, Thomas	5,931
32	Mar 7	H	Shrewsbury Town	L	1-2	Thomas	13,300
33	14	A	Queen's Park Rangers	D	1-1	Rainford	12,972
34	19	A	Colchester United	L	0-3		3,382
35	21	H	Swindon Town	W	3-0	Simpson 3	10,462
36	28	A	Aldershot	W	1-0	Thomas	5,673
37	Apr 3	A	Southend United	D	2-2	Simpson 2	10,341
38	4	H	Colchester United	W	3-1	Thomas, Rainford, Briggs	12,373
39	6	H	Southend United	D	0-0		12,845
40	11	A	Norwich City	L	1-5	Simpson	16,270
41	15	H	Exeter City	W	2-0	Simpson 2	4,916
42	18	H	Coventry City	D	2-2	Grimshaw, Downs	13,192
43	22	H	Ipswich Town	D	1-1	Devonshire	10,135
44	25	A	Exeter City	L	0-2		7,357
45	29	H	Watford	W	1-0	Grimshaw	6,675
46	May 1	H	Bristol Rovers	W	1-0	Thomas	5,712

Final League Position: 13th in Division Three South

Appearances
Goals

FA Cup

Match No.	Date	Venue	Opponents	Result		Scorers	Attendance
1	Nov 22	H	Reading	D	1-1	Rainford	24,340
R	26	A	Reading	W	3-1	Fell 2, Rainford	8,167
2	Dec 10	A	Finchley	L	1-3	Thomas	4,500

Appearances
Goals

Anderson	Scott	Edwards	Price	Briggs	Chilvers	Broughton	Rainford	Marsden	Simpson	BennettR	MacDonald D.	McDonald H.	Burgess	Evans	Nelson	Hancox	Devonshire	Andrews	Thomas R.	Hanlon	George	Grimshaw	Fell	Higgins	Bailey	Harding	Downs	Choules	Besagni
1	2	3	4	5	6	7	8	9	10	11																			
	2		4	5	6	7	8		9	11	1	3	10																
	2		4	5	6		8		9	11	1	3	10	7															
	2			5	6			9		11	1	3	10	7	4	8													
	2			5	6		8	9		11	1	3	10	7	4														
	2			5	6	9	8			11	1	3	10		4		7												
1	2			5		9						3	10		4		7	6	8	11									
1		2		5		9						3			4	8	7	6	10	11									
1		2	4	5	6		8	9		11		3					7		10										
1		2	4	5	6		8	9		11		3					7		10										
1		3	4	5	6		8	9		11							7		10		2								
		3	4	5	6		8	9		11	1						7		10		2								
		3	4	5	6						1		10				11		9		2	8	7						
			4	5	6						1	3	10				11		9		2	8	7						
			4	5	6						1	3	10				11		9		2	8	7						
				5	6		8				1	3	10				11		9		2	4	7						
				5	6		8				1	3	10				11		9		2	4	7						
				5	6		8				1	3	10				11		9		2	4	7						
				5	6		8				1	3	10				11		9		2	4	7						
	2			5	6		8		9		1	3					11		10			4	7						
				5	6				9		1	3	10				11		8		2	4	7						
				5	6		10		9		1	3					11		8		2	4	7						
				5	6		8		9		1	3	10				11				2	4	7						
				5	6		8		9		1	3	10		4		11				2		7						
				5	6				9		1	3	10				11		8		2	4	7						
				5	6					11	1	3		9		8	10				2	4	7						
					6					11	1	3	10			8			9		2	4	7	5					
1					6							3	10			8	11		9		2	4	7	5					
1					6							3	10			8	11		9		2	4	7	5					
1					6							3	10			8	11		9		2	4	7	5					
1												3	10			8	11	6	9		2	4	7	5					
1												3	10			8	11	6	9		2	4	7	5					
							8					3	10				11	6	9		2	4	7	5	1				
							8						10				11	6	9		3	4	7	5	1	2			
				5					9							8		6	10		3	4	7		1	2	11		
				5					9							8		6	10		3	4	7		1	2	11		
				5					9							8		6	10		3	4	7		1	2	11		
				5			9					3				8		6	10		2	4	7		1		11		
		3		5			8		9									6	10			4	7		1	2	11		
		3		5			8		9								11	6	10		2	4			1		7		
		3		5			8		9									6	10		2	4	7		1		11		
		3		5			8		9								11	6	10		2	4			1		7		
				5			8		9								11	6	10		2	4			1		7	3	
							8		9								11	6	10		2	4		5	1		7	3	
				5			8										11	6	10		2	4			1		7	3	9
				5			4									8		6	10		2		7		1		11	3	9
11	8	11	10	37	28	5	28	7	18	12	21	30	25	4	6	14	33	18	37	2	34	32	29	9	14	5	12	4	2
				1			7	2	11	2			19			1	4		10		2	3	3				1		

Anderson	Scott	Edwards	Price	Briggs	Chilvers	Broughton	Rainford	Marsden	Simpson	BennettR	MacDonald D.	McDonald H.	Burgess	Evans	Nelson	Hancox	Devonshire	Andrews	Thomas R.	Hanlon	George	Grimshaw	Fell
				5	6		8				1	3	10				11		9		2	4	7
				5	6		8				1	3	10				11		9		2	4	7
	2			5	6		8				1	3	10				11		9			4	7
	1			3	3		3				3	3	3				3		3		2	3	3
							2												1				2

League Table

	P	W	D	L	F	A	Pts
Bristol Rovers	46	26	12	8	92	46	64
Millwall	46	24	14	8	82	44	62
Northampton Town	46	26	10	10	109	70	62
Norwich City	46	25	10	11	99	55	60
Bristol City	46	22	15	9	95	61	59
Coventry City	46	19	12	15	77	62	50
Brighton & Hove Albion	46	19	12	15	81	75	50
Southend United	46	18	13	15	69	74	49
Bournemouth	46	19	9	18	74	69	47
Watford	46	15	17	14	62	63	47
Reading	46	19	8	19	69	64	46
Torquay United	46	18	9	19	87	88	45
Crystal Palace	46	15	13	18	66	82	43
Leyton Orient	46	16	10	20	68	73	42
Newport County	46	16	10	20	70	82	42
Ipswich Town	46	13	15	18	60	69	41
Exeter City	46	13	14	19	61	71	40
Swindon Town	46	14	12	20	64	79	40
Aldershot	46	12	15	19	61	77	39
Queen's Park Rangers	46	12	15	19	61	82	39
Gillingham	46	12	15	19	55	74	39
Colchester United	46	12	14	20	59	76	38
Shrewsbury Town	46	12	12	22	68	91	36
Walsall	46	7	10	29	56	118	24

1953-54

Division Three South

Manager: Laurie Scott

Did you know that?

During the summer, floodlights were installed for the first time at Selhurst Park.

Match No.	Date		Venue	Opponents	Result		Scorers	Attendance
1	Aug	20	H	Northampton Town	D	2-2	Thomas, Foulds	13,935
2		22	H	Southampton	W	4-3	Thomas 2, Randall, Foulds	17,790
3		24	A	Shrewsbury Town	D	1-1	Thomas	11,845
4		29	A	Colchester United	L	1-4	Andrews	6,811
5	Sep	2	H	Shrewsbury Town	W	3-2	Randall 2, Thomas	11,877
6		5	A	Millwall	D	2-2	Fell, Thomas	21,997
7		7	A	Newport County	W	3-1	Foulds, Devonshire, Randall	6,913
8		12	H	Bristol City	L	1-2	Randall	18,723
9		16	H	Newport County	W	3-0	Randall 2, Thomas	8,730
10		19	A	Aldershot	W	2-1	Randall, Fell	8,308
11		21	A	Queen's Park Rangers	D	1-1	Willard	7,485
12		26	H	Swindon Town	W	3-2	Fell, Randall, Briggs	18,766
13		30	H	Queen's Park Rangers	L	0-3		9,409
14	Oct	3	A	Walsall	L	0-1		11,020
15		10	H	Bournemouth	W	3-1	Thomas 2, Downs	15,756
16		17	A	Coventry City	D	0-0		13,554
17		24	H	Gillingham	L	1-2	Choules	18,856
18		31	A	Northampton Town	L	0-6		12,450
19	Nov	7	H	Torquay United	W	4-1	Foulds, Thomas 2, Andrews	10,195
20		14	A	Watford	L	1-4	Andrews	14,547
21		28	A	Southend United	W	2-1	Randall, Thomas	7,748
22	Dec	5	H	Reading	W	1-0	Hanlon	12,085
23		19	A	Southampton	L	1-3	Willard	12,221
24		25	H	Norwich City	W	1-0	Thomas (pen)	11,742
25		26	A	Norwich City	L	1-2	Bennett	21,293
26	Jan	2	H	Colchester United	L	0-1		7,154
27		9	A	Exeter City	L	0-7		7,382
28		16	H	Millwall	L	2-3	Bennett, Willard	16,320
29		23	A	Bristol City	L	0-4		17,552
30		30	H	Exeter City	D	0-0		5,595
31	Feb	6	H	Aldershot	D	0-0		8,375
32		13	A	Swindon Town	D	1-1	Thomas	8,907
33		20	H	Walsall	W	1-0	Tilston	10,370
34		27	A	Bournemouth	L	0-2		8,740
35	Mar	6	H	Coventry City	W	3-1	Thomas 2, Tilston	10,519
36		13	A	Brighton & Hove Albion	L	0-3		19,312
37		20	H	Southend United	W	4-2	Tilston 2, Thomas 2	9,371
38		27	A	Torquay United	L	0-1		5,662
39	Apr	3	H	Watford	D	1-1	Simpson	9,553
40		8	A	Leyton Orient	L	0-2		5,346
41		10	A	Reading	L	1-4	Devonshire	7,467
42		16	A	Ipswich Town	L	0-2		18,290
43		17	H	Leyton Orient	D	2-2	Morton, Thomas	12,516
44		19	H	Ipswich Town	D	1-1	Simpson	15,660
45		24	A	Gillingham	L	2-3	Morton, Thomas	8,729
46		28	H	Brighton & Hove Albion	D	1-1	Morton	12,515

Final League Position: 22nd in Division Three South

Appearances

Goals

FA Cup

1	Nov	21	A	Great Yarmouth	L	0-1		8,944

Appearances

Goals

Bailey	George	McDonald H.	Willard	Briggs	Andrews	Fell	Thomas R.	Randall	Foulds	Downs	Devonshire	Higgins	Hanlon	Bennett K.	Woods	Moss	Choules	Simpson	Edwards	Chivers	Berry	Tilston	Potter	Morton
1	2	3	4	5	6	7	8	9	10	11														
1	2	3	4	5	6	7	8	9	10	11														
1	2	3	4	5	6		8	9	10	7	11													
1	2	3	4		6	7	8	9	10	11		5												
1	2	3	4		6	7	8	9	10	11		5												
1	2	3	4	5	6	7	8	9	10		11													
1	2	3	4	5	6	7	8	9	10		11													
1	2	3	4	5	6	7	8	9	10		11													
1	2	3	4	5	6	7	8	9	10		11													
1	2	3	4	5	6	7	8	9	10				11											
1	2	3	4	5	6	7	8	9	10				11											
1	2	3		5	6	7	8	9	10				11		4									
1	2	3		5	6	7	8	9					11	10	4									
1	2	3	4	5	6	7	8	9					11	10										
1		3	4	5		7	8	9		11				10		6	2							
1		3	4	5		7	8		10	11						6	2	9						
1	2	3	4	5		7	8		10	11						6	9							
1	2	3	4	5		7	8		10	11						6	9							
1			4	5	8	7	9		10		11						2		3	6				
1			4	5	9	7	8		10		11						2		3	6				
1		3	4	5			10	9		7			11	8			2			6				
1		3	4	5			8	9		7			11	10			2			6				
1		3	4	5		7	10	9					11	8			2			6				
1			4	5		7	10	9					11	8			2	6	3					
1			4	5	9	7	10						11	8			2		3	6				
1			4	5	9	7	8						11			10	2	6	3					
1			4	5	9	7	10						11	8			2	6	3					
1	2	3	8	5		7	9						11	10		4		6						
1		3	8	5	9						10		11			4		6	2		7			
1		3	4	5		7	9				10		11	8			2	6						
1		3	4	5		7	9						11	8			2	6				10		
1		3	4	5		7	9						11	8			2	6				10		
1		3	9	5			8						11		4		2	6			7	10		
1		3	9	5			8						11		4		2	6			7	10		
1		3	9	5		7	8						11		4		2	6				10		
1		3	9	5		7	8						11		4		2	6				10		
1		3	9	5			8						11		4		2	6			7	10		
1		3		5			8				10		11		4		2	6			7	9		
1		3		5			8						11	10	4		2	6			7	9		
		3		5			8						11	10	4		2	6			7	9	1	
1	2	3			9	7	8				10		11		4		5	6						
1		3		5	6	7	8				10		11		4				2					9
1		3		5	6	7	8				11				4				2			10		9
1		3		5	6	7	8						11		4			10	2					9
1				5	6	7	8						11	10	4		2		3					9
1				5	6	7	8						11	10	4		2		3					9
45	18	38	35	43	26	36	45	19	17	11	13	2	30	17	16	7	27	19	12	6	7	11	1	5
			3	1	3	3	20	10	4	1	2		1	2			1	2				4		3

Bailey	George	McDonald H.	Willard	Briggs	Andrews	Fell	Thomas R.	Randall	Foulds	Downs	Devonshire	Higgins	Hanlon	Bennett K.	Woods	Moss	Choules	Simpson	Edwards	Chivers	Berry	Tilston	Potter	Morton
1			4	5	6	7	8	9	10		11						2		3					
1			1	1	1	1	1	1	1		1						1		1					

League Table

	P	W	D	L	F	A	Pts
Ipswich Town	46	27	10	9	82	51	64
Brighton & Hove Albion	46	26	9	11	86	61	61
Bristol City	46	25	6	15	88	66	56
Watford	46	21	10	15	85	69	52
Northampton Town	46	20	11	15	82	55	51
Southampton	46	22	7	17	76	63	51
Norwich City	46	20	11	15	73	66	51
Reading	46	20	9	17	86	73	49
Exeter City	46	20	8	18	68	58	48
Gillingham	46	19	10	17	61	66	48
Leyton Orient	46	18	11	17	79	73	47
Millwall	46	19	9	18	74	77	47
Torquay United	46	17	12	17	81	88	46
Coventry City	46	18	9	19	61	56	45
Newport County	46	19	6	21	61	81	44
Southend United	46	18	7	21	69	71	43
Aldershot	46	17	9	20	74	86	43
Queen's Park Rangers	46	16	10	20	60	68	42
Bournemouth	46	16	8	22	67	70	40
Swindon Town	46	15	10	21	67	70	40
Shrewsbury Town	46	14	12	20	65	76	40
Crystal Palace	46	14	12	20	60	86	40
Colchester United	46	10	10	26	50	78	30
Walsall	46	9	8	29	40	87	26

1954-55

Division Three South

Manager: Laurie Scott until October 1954, then Cyril Spiers from approx. 13th October.

Did you know that?

Palace goalkeeper Roy Bailey was the father of Manchester United and England 'keeper Gary Bailey.

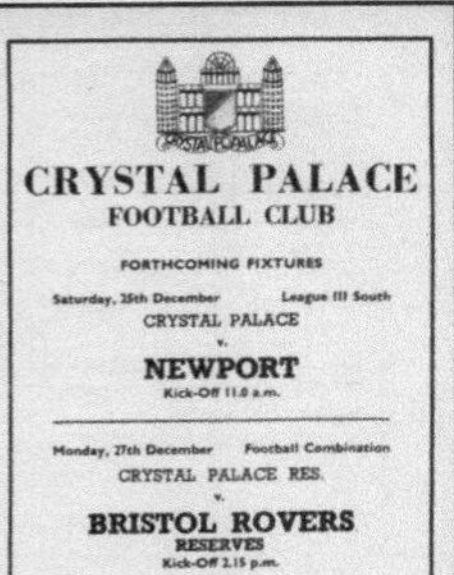

Match No.	Date		Venue	Opponents	Result		Scorers	Attendance
1	Aug	21	A	Exeter City	L	0-2		12,465
2		26	A	Northampton Town	D	1-1	Grieve	11,735
3		28	H	Colchester United	D	0-0		14,348
4	Sep	1	H	Northampton Town	W	3-1	H. McDonald, Thomas, Addinall	11,626
5		4	A	Norwich City	L	0-2		14,542
6		7	A	Watford	L	1-7	Devonshire	11,861
7		11	H	Southend United	D	2-2	Willard 2	11,526
8		15	H	Watford	D	1-1	Addinall	9,549
9		18	A	Aldershot	L	0-3		7,002
10		22	A	Bournemouth	L	1-4	Andrews (pen)	10,486
11		25	H	Swindon Town	D	0-0		11,540
12		29	H	Bournemouth	W	2-1	Grieve, Belcher	6,165
13	Oct	2	A	Leyton Orient	L	1-2	Devonshire	16,422
14		9	H	Reading	D	1-1	Belcher	14,305
15		16	A	Shrewsbury Town	D	1-1	Andrews	7,322
16		23	H	Walsall	W	3-1	Hearn, Belcher, own-goal (Russon)	11,416
17		30	A	Millwall	L	2-5	Hanlon, Briggs (pen)	19,427
18	Nov	6	H	Torquay United	D	1-1	Devonshire	11,673
19		13	A	Brighton & Hove Albion	L	0-1		16,440
20		27	A	Coventry City	L	1-4	Berry	14,839
21	Dec	4	H	Southampton	L	1-2	Briggs (pen)	9,875
22		18	H	Exeter City	D	1-1	Devonshire	7,010
23		25	H	Newport County	W	2-1	Deakin 2	8,934
24		27	A	Newport County	W	1-0	Rutter	13,025
25	Jan	1	A	Colchester United	L	0-2		5,806
26		8	H	Gillingham	L	0-2		8,379
27		22	A	Southend United	L	2-3	Andrews 2 (1 pen)	5,100
28		29	A	Gillingham	L	1-2	Belcher	11,338
29	Feb	5	H	Aldershot	W	3-2	Grieve, Belcher 2	8,076
30		12	A	Swindon Town	D	0-0		4,959
31		19	H	Leyton Orient	D	1-1	Randall	12,789
32		26	A	Reading	L	0-5		5,389
33	Mar	5	H	Shrewsbury Town	D	2-2	Deakin, Tilston	7,348
34		12	A	Walsall	W	4-1	Berry, Belcher 2, Cooper	10,773
35		19	H	Millwall	D	1-1	Andrews (pen)	13,708
36		26	A	Torquay United	D	2-2	Belcher, Berry	4,373
37	Apr	2	H	Brighton & Hove Albion	W	1-0	Berry	11,869
38		8	H	Queen's Park Rangers	W	2-1	Deakin, Belcher	17,238
39		9	A	Brentford	L	0-3		12,013
40		11	A	Queen's Park Rangers	L	0-1		8,974
41		16	H	Coventry City	W	1-0	Cooper	9,464
42		19	A	Bristol City	L	0-3		27,657
43		23	A	Southampton	D	2-2	Andrews, Belcher	8,788
44		27	H	Brentford	D	1-1	Berry	8,170
45		30	H	Bristol City	L	1-2	Tilston	14,425
46	May	4	H	Norwich City	W	2-0	Andrews (pen), Belcher	7,379

Final League Position: 20th in Division Three South

Appearances

1 own-goal

Goals

FA Cup

No.	Date		Venue	Opponents	Result		Scorers	Attendance
1	Nov	20	A	Swindon Town	W	2-0	Hanlon, Randall	11,359
2	Dec	11	H	Bishop Auckland	L	2-4	Choules, Thomas	20,155

Appearances

Goals

Bailey	Choules	McDonald H.	Woods	Briggs	Simpson	Grieve	Thomas	Addinall	Tilston	Devonshire	Moss	Belcher	Andrews	Edwards	Saunders	Willard	Hearn	Hanlon	Gumming	Berry	Greenwood A.	Greenwood R.	MacDonald D.	Deakin	Randall	Taylor	Rutter	Cooper	McDonald G.	Hyatt	Felton
1	2	3	4	5	6	7	8	9	10	11																					
1	2	3	6	5		7	8	9	10	11	4																				
1	2	3		5		7	8	9	10	11		4	6																		
1	2	3		5		7	8	9	10	11	4		6																		
1		3		5		7	8	9	10	11	4		6	2																	
1		3		5		7	8	9	10	11			6	2	4																
1	2			5		7		9					6	3	4	8	10	11													
1	2	3		5		7		9					6		4	8	10	11													
1	2	3		5		7		9					6		4	8	10		11												
1	2	3				7		9				8	6		5	4	10		11												
1	2	3		5		7	8	9		10			6			4		11													
1	2	3		5		11	9			10		8	6			4				7											
1	2	3		5		11	9			10		8	6			4				7											
1	2	3		5		11	9			10		8	6			4				7											
1	2	3		5			9			10		8	6			4		11		7											
1	2	3		5						10		9	6			4	8	11		7											
1		3		5				9				8	6			4	10	11		7	2										
	6			5			8		9	10		4						11		7	2	3	1								
	2			5					10			4	6				8	11		7		3	1	9							
	8	6		5			10					4		2				11		7		3	1	9							
		6		5			10		8			4		2				11		7		3	1		9						
1	8	3		5					9	11		4	6	2										10		7					
1	8								9	11		4	6	2	5							3		10		7					
1									9	11		4	6	2	5					7		3		10			8				
1									9	11		4	6	2	5					7		3		10			8				
1						7						4	6	2	5		10		11			3		9			8				
1						7			10		4	8	6	2	5				11			3		9							
1						7			10		4	8	6	2	5				11			3		9							
1						7			10		4	8	6	2	5				11			3		9							
1						7			10		4	8	6	2	5				11			3		9							
1						7			10		4	8	6	2	5				11			3			9						
1						7			10		4	8	6	2	5				11			3			9						
1									10		4	8	6	2	5				11	7		3		9							
1		3							9		4	8	6	2	5				11	7								10			
1									9		4	8	6	2	5				11	7		3						10			
1									9		4	8	6	2	5				11	7		3						10			
1											4	8	6	2	5				11	7		3		9				10			
1											4	8	6	2	5				11	7		3		9				10			
1											4	8	6	2	5				11	7		3		9				10			
1	4											8	6	2	5				11	7		3		9				10			
	9								10		4	8	6	2	5					7			1					11	3		
						7			10			4	6	2	5				11	8		3	1							9	
	4								10			8	6	2	5				11	7		3	1								9
	4								10			8	6	2	5				11	7		3	1	9							
	4								10			8	6	2	5				11	7		3	1	9							
1	4								10			8	6	2	5				11	7		3		9							
37	25	20	2	21	1	22	14	12	29	17	17	37	41	30	29	11	8	10	22	26	2	26	9	19	3	2	3	8	1	1	1
		1		2		3	1	2	2	4		12	7			2	1	1		5				4	1		1	2			

Bailey	Choules	McDonald H.	Woods	Briggs	Simpson	Grieve	Thomas	Addinall	Tilston	Devonshire	Moss	Belcher	Andrews	Edwards	Saunders	Willard	Hearn	Hanlon	Gumming	Berry	Greenwood A.	Greenwood R.	MacDonald D.	Deakin	Randall	Taylor	Rutter	Cooper	McDonald G.	Hyatt	Felton
	8	6		5			10					4		2				11		7		3	1		9						
	8	6		5			10		9			4		2				11		7		3	1								
	2	2		2			2		1			2		2				2		2		2	2		1						
	1						1											1							1						

League Table

	P	W	D	L	F	A	Pts
Bristol City	46	30	10	6	101	47	70
Leyton Orient	46	26	9	11	89	47	61
Southampton	46	24	11	11	75	51	59
Gillingham	46	20	15	11	77	66	55
Millwall	46	20	11	15	72	68	51
Brighton & Hove Albion	46	20	10	16	76	63	50
Watford	46	18	14	14	71	62	50
Torquay United	46	18	12	16	82	82	48
Coventry City	46	18	11	17	67	59	47
Southend United	46	17	12	17	83	80	46
Brentford	46	16	14	16	82	82	46
Norwich City	46	18	10	18	60	60	46
Northampton Town	46	19	8	19	73	81	46
Aldershot	46	16	13	17	75	71	45
Queen's Park Rangers	46	15	14	17	69	75	44
Shrewsbury Town	46	16	10	20	70	78	42
Bournemouth	46	12	18	16	57	65	42
Reading	46	13	15	18	65	73	41
Newport County	46	11	16	19	60	73	38
Crystal Palace	46	11	16	19	52	80	38
Swindon Town	46	11	15	20	46	64	37
Exeter City	46	11	15	20	47	73	37
Walsall	46	10	14	22	75	86	34

1955-56

Division Three South

Manager: Cyril Spiers

Did you know that?

Palace again had to be re-elected to the Football League (for the last time) as they finished next to bottom of Division Three South.

Match No.	Date		Venue	Opponents	Result		Scorers	Attendance
1	Aug	20	H	Northampton Town	L	2-3	Deakin, Tilston	13,841
2		24	A	Torquay United	D	1-1	Tilston	9,267
3		27	A	Aldershot	D	1-1	Belcher	7,203
4		31	H	Torquay United	W	3-0	Tilston, Berry, Moss (pen)	11,245
5	Sep	3	A	Millwall	D	1-1	Belcher	16,497
6		5	A	Queen's Park Rangers	W	3-0	Tilston, Brett 2	9,083
7		10	H	Brighton & Hove Albion	L	1-2	Tilston	20,284
8		14	H	Queen's Park Rangers	D	1-1	Belcher	10,543
9		17	A	Southampton	L	1-3	Andrews	11,530
10		22	A	Newport County	W	1-0	Andrews	6,601
11		24	H	Shrewsbury Town	L	0-1		13,899
12		28	H	Walsall	W	2-0	Murray 2	7,298
13	Oct	1	A	Ipswich Town	D	3-3	Berry, Belcher, Deakin	15,332
14		8	H	Watford	L	1-2	Belcher	13,993
15		15	A	Brentford	L	0-3		13,636
16		22	H	Coventry City	W	3-0	Cooper 3	7,734
17		29	A	Southend United	L	3-4	Deakin 3	12,107
18	Nov	5	H	Exeter City	L	0-1		12,631
19		12	A	Leyton Orient	L	0-8		13,547
20		26	A	Norwich City	L	1-3	Moss	14,556
21	Dec	3	H	Bournemouth	L	1-3	Murray	9,047
22		17	A	Northampton Town	D	1-1	Gunning	9,302
23		24	H	Aldershot	W	1-0	Gunning	6,526
24		26	A	Swindon Town	D	0-0		9,082
25		27	H	Swindon Town	L	0-2		10,710
26		31	H	Millwall	D	2-2	Deakin, Tilston	12,248
27	Jan	7	H	Colchester United	D	1-1	Tilston	6,488
28		14	A	Brighton & Hove Albion	L	0-5		13,602
29		21	H	Southampton	L	0-2		8,848
30		28	A	Gillingham	D	1-1	Pierce	4,281
31	Feb	11	H	Ipswich Town	W	1-0	Deakin	5,739
32		18	A	Watford	W	2-0	Pierce, own-goal (Bateman)	4,865
33		25	H	Brentford	L	0-2		10,054
34	Mar	3	A	Coventry City	W	3-1	Gunning, Pierce, own-goal (Kirk)	17,082
35		10	H	Southend United	L	1-2	own-goal (Williamson)	13,093
36		17	A	Exeter City	L	1-6	Deakin	6,826
37		24	H	Leyton Orient	L	1-2	Gunning (pen)	19,165
38		30	H	Reading	L	2-3	Moyse, Choules	13,463
39		31	A	Colchester United	W	4-2	Murray 2, Noakes, Berry	7,397
40	Apr	2	A	Reading	L	0-1		9,886
41		7	H	Norwich City	W	2-0	Berry, Cooper	9,446
42		14	A	Bournemouth	L	0-1		5,981
43		21	H	Gillingham	L	1-3	Berry	10,495
44		26	A	Walsall	L	0-4		6,277
45		28	H	Newport County	W	1-0	Belcher	7,635
46		30	A	Shrewsbury Town	L	0-2		9,663

Final League Position: 23rd in Division Three South | Appearances
3 own-goals | Goals

FA Cup

1	Nov	19	H	Southampton	D	0-0		16,864
R		23	A	Southampton	L	0-2		11,883

Appearances
Goals

Bailey	Edwards	Greenwood	Moss	Saunders	Andrews	Berry	Belcher	Deakin	Tilston	Gunning	Brett	Choules	Noakes	Cooper	Murray	Long	Sanders	Morgan	Potter	Pierce	Felton	Moyse	Fry	Harrison
1	2	3	4	5	6	7	8	9	10	11														
1	2	3	4	5	6	7	8	9	10	11														
1	2	3	4	5	6	7	8	9	10	11														
1	2	3	4	5	6	7	8	9	10	11														
1	2	3	4	5	6	7	8	9	10		11													
1	2	3	4		6	7	8	9	10		11	5												
1	2	3	4		6	7	8	9	10		11	5												
1	2	3	4	5	6	7	8	9	10		11													
1	2	3	4	5	6	7	8	9	10				11											
1	2	3	4		6	7	8	11	9			5		10										
1	2	3	4		6	7	8	11	9			5		10										
1	2	3	6			7	8	9		11		5			10	4								
1	2	3	6			7	8	9		11		5			10	4								
1	2	3	6			7	8	9		11		5			10	4								
1	3		6	5		11	8				7	2	4	9	10									
1			4	5		11	8	9			7	2	3	10			6							
1			4	5		11	8	9			7	2	3	10			6							
1			4	5		11	8	9			7	2	3	10			6							
1			4	5		11	8	9				2	3	10			6	7						
	2		4	5					9		7	3	10	11	8		6		1					
	2		4	5		11	8	9			7	3			10		6		1					
		3	4	5	6	7		9		11		2		8					1	10				
		3	4	5	6	7		9	8	11		2							1	10				
		3	4	5	6	7		9	8	11			2						1	10				
		3	4	5	6	7		9		11	8		2						1	10				
		3	4	5	6	7		9	8	11			2						1	10				
		3	4	5	6			9	8	11	7	2							1	10				
		3	4		6			9	10	11	7	2			8				1		5			
	2	3	4	5	6	7		9		11				8					1	10				
	2	3	4	5		7		9		11			6	8					1	10				
	2	3		5		7	4	9		11				8		6			1	10				
	2	3		5		7	4	9		11				8		6			1	10				
	2	3		5		7	4	9		11				8		6			1	10				
	2	3		5		7	4			11				8		6			1	10		9		
	2	3		5		7	4	9		11				8		6			1	10				
	2	3		5		7	4	9		11				8		6			1	10				
	2	3					4	7		11		5		8		6			1	10		9		
	2	3					4	7		11		5		8		6			1	10		9		
	2	3				9	4			11		5	6	10	8								1	7
	2	3				9	4	7		11		5	6	10	8								1	
	2	3				9	4			11		5	6	10	8								1	7
	2	3				9	4			11		5	6	10	8								1	7
	2	3				9	4	7		11		5	6	10	8								1	
	2	3	6			9	4	7	10			5			8					11			1	
	2			5		9	4			11		3	7		8	6			1	10				
	2			5		9	4			11		3	7		8	6			1	10				
19	35	37	31	30	19	41	36	38	18	31	13	28	18	24	15	13	6	1	21	19	1	3	6	3
			2		2	5	6	8	7	4	2	1	1	4	5					3		1		

Bailey	Edwards	Greenwood	Moss	Saunders	Andrews	Berry	Belcher	Deakin	Tilston	Gunning	Brett	Choules	Noakes	Cooper	Murray	Long	Sanders	Morgan	Potter	Pierce	Felton	Moyse	Fry	Harrison
	3		4	5		7	8			11	9	2	6	10					1					
	3		4	5		7	8	9		11		2	6	10					1					
	2		2	2		2	2	1		2	1	2	2	2					2					

League Table

	P	W	D	L	F	A	Pts
Leyton Orient	46	29	8	9	106	49	66
Brighton & Hove Albion	46	29	7	10	112	50	65
Ipswich Town	46	25	14	7	106	60	64
Southend United	46	21	11	14	88	80	53
Torquay United	46	20	12	14	86	63	52
Brentford	46	19	14	13	69	66	52
Norwich City	46	19	13	14	86	82	51
Coventry City	46	20	9	17	73	60	49
Bournemouth	46	19	10	17	63	51	48
Gillingham	46	19	10	17	69	71	48
Northampton Town	46	20	7	19	67	71	47
Colchester United	46	18	11	17	76	81	47
Shrewsbury Town	46	17	12	17	69	66	46
Southampton	46	18	8	20	91	81	44
Aldershot	46	12	16	18	70	90	40
Exeter City	46	15	10	21	58	77	40
Reading	46	15	9	22	70	79	39
Queen's Park Rangers	46	14	11	21	64	86	39
Newport County	46	15	9	22	58	79	39
Walsall	46	15	8	23	68	84	38
Watford	46	13	11	22	52	85	37
Millwall	46	15	6	25	83	100	36
Crystal Palace	46	12	10	24	54	83	34
Swindon Town	46	8	14	24	34	78	30

1956-57

Division Three South

Manager: Cyril Spiers

Did you know that?

Palace's 2–0 FA Cup win against Walthamstow Avenue was the club's first-ever game recorded by the TV cameras, when it was shown as recorded highlights on BBC1's football coverage. The footage still exists to this day.

Match No.	Date		Venue	Opponents	Result		Scorers	Attendance
1	Aug	18	A	Norwich City	L	0-1		16,057
2		22	H	Colchester United	L	2-4	Whitear, Murray	9,980
3		25	H	Coventry City	D	1-1	Proudler (pen)	9,657
4		27	A	Colchester United	D	3-3	Harrison, Deakin, Berry	6,979
5	Sep	1	A	Southampton	L	0-3		14,118
6		5	H	Reading	D	1-1	Long	10,575
7		8	H	Exeter City	D	0-0		11,801
8		12	A	Reading	W	2-1	Deakin 2	11,209
9		15	H	Millwall	D	2-2	Harrison, Deakin	16,112
10		19	H	Newport County	W	2-1	Berry, Cooper	14,132
11		22	A	Southend United	D	1-1	Cooper	10,504
12		27	A	Newport County	D	2-2	Cooper, own-goal (Thomas)	8,108
13		29	H	Northampton Town	D	1-1	Berry	13,904
14	Oct	6	A	Gillingham	L	1-4	Cooper	8,567
15		13	H	Swindon Town	D	0-0		13,459
16		20	A	Brentford	D	1-1	Pierce	11,345
17		27	H	Aldershot	W	2-1	Deakin 2	11,846
18	Nov	3	A	Watford	W	4-1	Murray 2, Belcher, Pierce	8,785
19		10	H	Shrewsbury Town	L	0-1		13,700
20		24	H	Ipswich Town	L	1-3	Harrison	10,431
21	Dec	1	A	Bournemouth	D	2-2	Berry, own-goal (Hughes)	9,584
22		15	H	Norwich City	W	4-1	Berry, Noakes, Pierce, own-goal (Englefield)	8,371
23		25	H	Queen's Park Rangers	W	2-1	Belcher, Pierce	9,988
24		26	A	Queen's Park Rangers	L	2-4	Berry, Pierce	5,307
25		29	H	Southampton	L	1-2	Belcher	15,769
26	Jan	12	A	Exeter City	L	1-2	Harrison	5,015
27		19	A	Millwall	L	0-3		16,192
28		26	H	Plymouth Argyle	W	2-1	Berry 2	10,656
29	Feb	2	H	Southend United	W	2-0	Deakin, Pierce	9,545
30		9	A	Northampton Town	L	0-1		8,651
31		16	H	Gillingham	L	1-2	Belcher (pen)	11,410
32		23	A	Swindon Town	L	1-3	Pierce	6,499
33	Mar	2	H	Brentford	L	0-2		11,679
34		9	A	Torquay United	L	0-3		5,110
35		11	A	Plymouth Argyle	W	1-0	Deakin	13,374
36		16	H	Watford	D	0-0		8,830
37		23	A	Shrewsbury Town	D	1-1	Murray	6,674
38		30	H	Walsall	W	3-0	Murray 2, Deakin	9,338
39	Apr	1	A	Coventry City	D	3-3	Deakin 2, Byrne	5,626
40		6	A	Ipswich Town	L	2-4	Murray, Deakin	12,559
41		13	H	Bournemouth	D	1-1	Pierce	8,571
42		19	H	Brighton & Hove Albion	D	2-2	Pierce, Deakin	15,514
43		20	A	Aldershot	L	1-2	Deakin	4,685
44		22	A	Brighton & Hove Albion	D	1-1	Deakin	11,382
45		27	A	Walsall	W	2-1	Deakin, Murray	9,748
46	May	1	H	Torquay United	D	1-1	Pierce	22,627

Final League Position: 20th in Division Three South

Appearances

3 own-goals

Goals

FA Cup

Round	Date		Venue	Opponents	Result		Scorers	Attendance
1	Nov	17	H	Walthamstow Avenue	W	2-0	Murray, Cooper	17,760
2	Dec	8	A	Brentford	D	1-1	Pierce	16,750
R		12	H	Brentford	W	3-2*	Pierce 3	23,137
3	Jan	5	A	Millwall	L	0-2		26,790

* After extra-time

Appearances

Goals

Potter	Choules	Greenwood	Belcher	Proudler	Long	Harrison	Whitear	Berry	Murray	Deakin	Edwards	Moss	Morris	Gunning	Cotton	Noakes	Pierce	Cooper	Rouse	McDonald G	Byrne	Moyse	Sanders
1	2	3	4	5	6	7	8	9	10	11													
1	2		4	5		7	8	9	10		3	6	11										
1	5	3	4	6		7	10	8		9	2			11									
1	5	3	4	6		7		8		9	2			11	10								
1	5	3	4	6		7		8		9	2			11	10								
1	5		4		6	7		8			2			11	10	3	9						
1	5		4		6	7		8			2			11	10	3	9						
1	5		4		6	7		8		9	2		11			3	10						
1	5		4		6	7		8		9	2		11			3	10						
1	5		4		6	7		8		9	2		11			3		10					
1	5		4		6	7		8		9	2		11			3		10					
1	5		4		6	7		8		9	2		11			3		10					
1	2	3	4		6	7		8		9	2		11					10					
1	5	3	4	9	6	7		8			2		11					10					
	5		4		6	11		7			2						8	10	1	3	9		
	5				4			7		9	2						8	10	1	3		11	6
	5		8		4	11		7		9	2					3		10	1				6
	5		4		8	11		7	9		2						10		1	3			6
	5		4		8	11		7	9		2						10		1	3			6
	5				4	11		7	8	9	2							10	1	3			6
1	5		8		4	7		9	10	11	2									3			6
1	5		8		4	7		9		11	2					6	10			3			
1	5		8		4	7		9		11	2					6	10			3			
1	5		8		4	7		9		11	2					6	10			3			
1	5		8		4	7		9		11	2					6	10			3			
1	5		8		4	7		9		11	2					6	10			3			
1	5		4		6	11		7			2					3	10	8			9		
	5		4		6	7		8		9	2			11			10		1	3			
	5		4		6	7		8		9	2			11		3	10		1				
	5		4		6	7		8		9	2			11		3	10		1				
	5		4		6	7		8	11	9	2					3	10		1				
	5		4		6	7	11	8		9	2					3	10		1				
	5		4		6	11	8	7		9	2					3	10		1				
	5	3			4	7		9	8		2			11				10	1				6
	5	3			4	7			8	9	2					10			1		11		6
	5	3			4	7			8	9	2					10			1		11		6
	5			6	4	7			8	9	2					3	10		1		11		
	5			6	4	7			8	9	2					3	10		1		11		
	5			6	4	7			8	9	2					3	10		1		11		
	5			6	4	7			8	9	2					3	10		1		11		
	5			6	4	7			8	9	2					3	10		1		11		
	5			6	4	7			8	9	2					3	10		1		11		
	5			6	4	7			8	9	2					3	10		1		11		
	5			6	4			7	8	9	2					3	10		1		11		
	5			6	4			7	8	9	2					3	10		1		11		
	5			6	4			7	8	9	2					3	10		1		11		
21	46	9	31	16	42	42	5	37	20	37	45	1	8	9	4	31	30	11	25	12	14	1	9
			4	1	1	4	1	8	8	16						1	10	4			1		

Potter	Choules	Greenwood	Belcher	Proudler	Long	Harrison	Whitear	Berry	Murray	Deakin	Edwards	Moss	Morris	Gunning	Cotton	Noakes	Pierce	Cooper	Rouse	McDonald G	Byrne	Moyse	Sanders
	5		8		4	11		7	9		2							10	1	3			6
1	5		8		4	7		9		11	2					6	10			3			
1	5		8		4	7		9		11	2					6	10			3			
1	5		8		4	7		9		11	2					6	10			3			
3	4		4		4	4		4	1	3	4					3	3	1	1	4			1
									1								4	1					

League Table

	P	W	D	L	F	A	Pts
Ipswich Town	46	25	9	12	101	54	59
Torquay United	46	24	11	11	89	64	59
Colchester United	46	22	14	10	84	56	58
Southampton	46	22	10	14	76	52	54
Bournemouth	46	19	14	13	88	62	52
Brighton & Hove Albion	46	19	14	13	86	65	52
Southend United	46	18	12	16	73	65	48
Brentford	46	16	16	14	78	76	48
Shrewsbury Town	46	15	18	13	72	79	48
Queen's Park Rangers	46	18	11	17	61	60	47
Watford	46	18	10	18	72	75	46
Newport County	46	16	13	17	65	62	45
Reading	46	18	9	19	80	81	45
Northampton Town	46	18	9	19	66	73	45
Walsall	46	16	12	18	80	74	44
Coventry City	46	16	12	18	74	84	44
Millwall	46	16	12	18	64	84	44
Plymouth Argyle	46	16	11	19	68	73	43
Aldershot	46	15	12	19	79	92	42
Crystal Palace	46	11	18	17	62	75	40
Exeter City	46	12	13	21	61	79	37
Gillingham	46	12	13	21	54	85	37
Swindon Town	46	15	6	25	66	96	36
Norwich City	46	8	15	23	61	94	31

1957-58

Division Three South

Manager: Cyril Spiers

Did you know that?

Bristol-born Bert Brown was amazingly still playing local League football in his home town well into his 70s, only a decade ago.

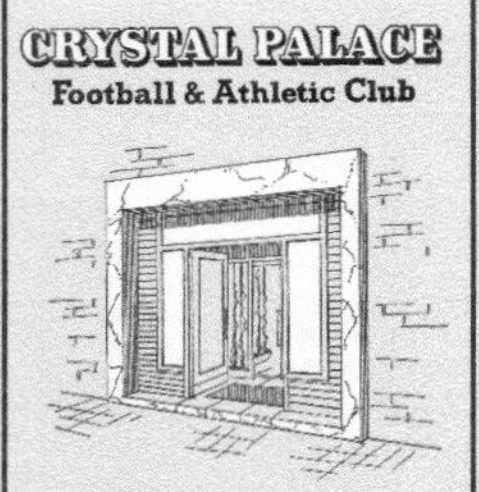

Match No.	Date		Venue	Opponents	Result		Scorers	Attendance
1	Aug	24	A	Norwich City	L	2-3	Deakin, Byrne	21,571
2		28	H	Millwall	L	0-1		22,681
3		31	H	Bournemouth	W	3-0	Byrne, Cooper 2	13,752
4	Sep	2	A	Millwall	L	0-3		20,159
5		7	A	Walsall	L	1-2	Cooper	11,768
6		11	H	Gillingham	W	3-0	Byrne, Cooper, Harrison	7,343
7		14	H	Coventry City	W	2-0	Cooper, Berry	11,543
8		18	A	Gillingham	L	0-3		6,324
9		21	A	Shrewsbury Town	D	0-0		7,607
10		25	A	Torquay United	D	1-1	Deakin	4,665
11		28	H	Reading	D	2-2	Berry, Cooper	12,577
12	Oct	2	H	Torquay United	D	1-1	Cooper	6,498
13		5	A	Northampton Town	W	2-1	Cooper 2	7,594
14		12	H	Swindon Town	W	4-1	Cooper 2, Byrne, Berry	14,953
15		19	A	Aldershot	L	1-4	Proudler (pen)	6,214
16		26	H	Plymouth Argyle	W	3-0	Deakin, Pierce, Cooper	14,532
17	Nov	2	A	Port Vale	L	0-4		13,602
18		9	H	Newport County	D	2-2	Cooper (pen), Deakin	11,082
19		23	H	Brighton & Hove Albion	L	2-4	Cooper, Harrison	15,757
20		30	A	Southend United	D	1-1	Long	10,706
21	Dec	14	A	Exeter City	W	1-0	Harrison	5,493
22		21	H	Norwich City	L	0-3		11,478
23		25	A	Brentford	W	3-0	Harrison, Berry 2	12,394
24		26	H	Brentford	W	2-1	Harrison, Pierce	16,797
25		28	A	Bournemouth	L	1-3	Byrne	13,073
26	Jan	11	H	Walsall	W	4-1	Collins 3, Pierce	10,587
27		18	A	Coventry City	D	2-2	Pierce, Harrison	8,211
28		25	A	Southampton	L	1-2	Cooper	13,046
29	Feb	1	H	Shrewsbury Town	W	3-0	Long, Berry, Pierce	11,739
30		8	A	Reading	D	2-2	Cooper, Collins	11,062
31		15	H	Northampton Town	L	1-3	Long	16,245
32		22	A	Swindon Town	D	0-0		10,316
33	Mar	1	H	Aldershot	D	1-1	Cooper	12,569
34		8	A	Plymouth Argyle	L	0-1		18,719
35		15	H	Port Vale	W	1-0	McNichol	13,577
36		22	A	Brighton & Hove Albion	L	2-3	Harrison, Pierce	19,611
37		25	A	Watford	L	1-2	McNichol	4,304
38		29	H	Exeter City	W	2-0	McNichol, Collins	10,601
39	Apr	4	H	Colchester United	D	1-1	Byrne	17,787
40		5	A	Newport County	D	0-0		4,118
41		7	A	Colchester United	D	1-1	Berry	9,528
42		12	H	Southend United	W	2-0	Pierce, McNichol	12,843
43		16	H	Queen's Park Rangers	L	2-3	Brett, Long	18,712
44		19	A	Queen's Park Rangers	L	2-4	Brett, Byrne	11,868
45		23	H	Watford	W	4-2	McNichol 2, Berry 2	10,139
46		26	H	Southampton	L	1-4	McNichol	10,480

Final League Position: 14th in Division Three South

Appearances
Goals

FA Cup

1	Nov	16	A	Margate	W	3-2	Deakin 3	8,200
2	Dec	7	H	Southampton	W	1-0	Berry	14,794
3	Jan	4	H	Ipswich Town	L	0-1		21,940

Appearances
Goals

Rouse	Edwards	Noakes	Long	Choules	Proudler	Berry	Belcher	Deakin	Pierce	Byrne	Truett	Cooper	Farrell	Harrison	Brown	Greenwood	Murray	Muxworthy	Sanders	Potter	Hopgood	Collins	Redmond	Brett	McNichol
1	2	3	4	5	6	7	8	9	10	11															
1	2	3	4	5	6	7	8	9	10	11															
1	2	3	4	5	6	7		9		11	8	10													
1	2	3	4	5	6	7				11	8	10	9												
1	2	3	4	5	6	7		9		8		10		11											
1	2	3	4	5		7	8			9		10		11	6										
1	2	3	4	5		7	8			9		10		11	6										
1	2	3	4	5		7	8			9		10		11	6										
1	2		4			7	6		10		5		9			3	8	11							
1	2		4			7	8	9			5					3	10	11	6						
1	2		4			7	6	9		10	5	8		11		3									
1	2		4		5	7	6	9		10		8		11		3									
1	2		4		5		6	9	10	7		8		11		3									
1	2		4		5	7			10	9	6	8		11		3									
1	2		4		5	7			10	9		8		11		3			6						
1	2		4	5			6	9	10	7		8		11		3									
	2		4	5			6	9	10	7		8		11		3				1					
	2		4	5			6	9	10	7		8		11		3					1				
	2		4	5			6	9	10			8		7		3					1	11			
1	2		4	5			8					10	9	7		3			6			11			
1	2		4	5		9	8					10		7		3			6			11			
1	2	3	4	5		9	8					10		7					6			11			
1	2		4	5		9	8		10	11				7		3			6						
1	2		4	5		9	8		10	11				7		3			6						
1			2	5		9	8		10	11	4			7		3			6						
1			4	5		8			10				9	7		3			6			11	2		
1			4	5		8			10			9		7		3			6			11	2		
1	2		4	5		8			10			9		7		3			6			11			
1	2		4	5		8			10			9		7		3			6			11			
1	2		4	5		8			10			9		7		3			6			11			
1	2		4	5		8			10			9		7		3			6			11			
1		2	4	5		8			10			9		7		3			6			11			
1		2	4	5		8			10			9		7		3			6			11			
1		2	4	5		9			10					7		3			6			11		8	
1		2	4	5		9			10					7		3			6			11			8
1		2	4	5		9			10					7		3			6			11			8
1		2	4	5		9			10					7		3			6			11			8
1	2		4	5		8				9						3			6			11		7	10
1		2	4	5		8				9						3			6			11		7	10
1		2	4	5		8				9						3			6			11		7	10
1		2	4	5		9	8			11						3			6					7	10
1		2	4	5		9			10	11						3			6					7	8
1		2	4	5		9			10	11						3			6					7	8
1		2	4	5		9			10	11						3			6					7	8
1		2	4	5		9	8			11				7		3			6						10
		2	4	5		9	8			11				7		3			6		1				10
42	29	23	46	39	9	40	23	12	28	28	7	25	4	33	3	37	2	2	29	1	3	19	2	8	12
			4		1	9		4	7	7		17		7								5		2	7

Rouse	Edwards	Noakes	Long	Choules	Proudler	Berry	Belcher	Deakin	Pierce	Byrne	Truett	Cooper	Farrell	Harrison	Brown	Greenwood	Murray	Muxworthy	Sanders	Potter	Hopgood	Collins	Redmond	Brett	McNichol
	2		6	5			4	9	10		11	8		7		3					1				
1	2		8	5		9	4		10					7		3			6			11			
1			4	5		9			10	11		8		7		3			6				2		
2	2		3	3		2	2	1	3	1	1	2		3		3			2		1	1	1		
						1		3																	

League Table

	P	W	D	L	F	A	Pts
Brighton & Hove Albion	46	24	12	10	88	64	60
Brentford	46	24	10	12	82	56	58
Plymouth Argyle	46	25	8	13	67	48	58
Swindon Town	46	21	15	10	79	50	57
Reading	46	21	13	12	79	51	55
Southampton	46	22	10	14	112	72	54
Southend United	46	21	12	13	90	58	54
Norwich City	46	19	15	12	75	70	53
Bournemouth	46	21	9	16	81	74	51
Queen's Park Rangers	46	18	14	14	64	65	50
Newport County	46	17	14	15	73	67	48
Colchester United	46	17	13	16	77	79	47
Northampton Town	46	19	6	21	87	79	44
Crystal Palace	46	15	13	18	70	72	43
Port Vale	46	16	10	20	67	58	42
Watford	46	13	16	17	59	77	42
Shrewsbury Town	46	15	10	21	49	71	40
Aldershot	46	12	16	18	59	89	40
Coventry City	46	13	13	20	61	81	39
Walsall	46	14	9	23	61	75	37
Torquay United	46	11	13	22	49	74	35
Gillingham	46	13	9	24	52	81	35
Millwall	46	11	9	26	63	91	31
Exeter City	46	11	9	26	57	99	31

1958-59

Division Four

Manager: George Smith

Did you know that?

Goalkeeper Vic Rouse was the first Fourth Division player to win an international cap. While with Palace he lined up for Wales against Northern Ireland in April 1959, although he was on the losing end of a 4–1 result.

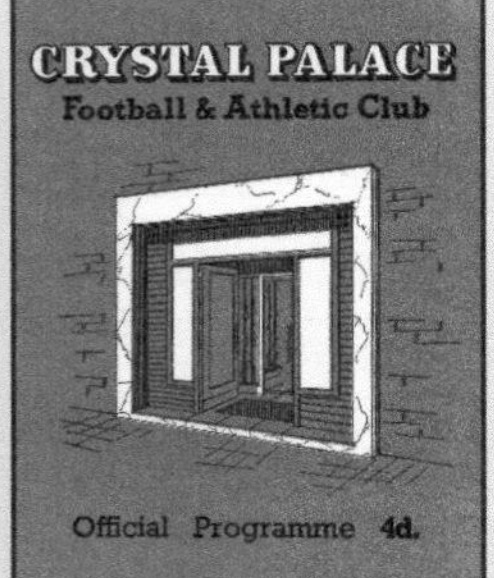

Match No.	Date		Venue	Opponents	Result		Scorers	Attendance
1	Aug	23	H	Crewe Alexandra	W	6-2	Deakin 3, Byrne 3	13,551
2		27	H	Chester	D	3-3	Byrne 2, Deakin	18,170
3		30	A	Northampton Town	L	0-3		11,288
4	Sep	3	A	Chester	L	2-3	Deakin 2	7,993
5		6	H	Workington Town	D	1-1	Byrne 2, Deakin	13,352
6		9	A	Watford	D	2-2	Deakin 2	10,327
7		13	A	York City	D	1-1	Collins	8,368
8		17	H	Watford	W	3-0	Collins, Truett, Harrison	16,034
9		20	H	Bradford Park Avenue	W	2-0	Deakin, Collins	14,134
10		22	A	Hartlepools United	L	1-4	Deakin	8,368
11		27	A	Port Vale	W	3-2	Long, Truett 2	13,952
12	Oct	1	H	Hartlepools United	L	1-2	Deakin	16,596
13		4	A	Millwall	L	1-2	Deakin	20,446
14		8	H	Southport	W	1-0	Collins	13,780
15		11	H	Gateshead	W	3-1	Brett 2, Pierce	13,643
16		18	A	Oldham Athletic	L	0-3		6,884
17		25	H	Barrow	D	2-2	Pierce (pen), Long	14,046
18	Nov	1	A	Carlisle United	D	3-3	Pierce, Deakin, Noakes	7,384
19		8	H	Gillingham	W	4-1	Collins 2, Brett 2	13,640
20		22	H	Coventry City	D	1-1	McNichol	12,319
21		29	A	Shrewsbury Town	L	1-2	Byrne	4,135
22	Dec	13	A	Walsall	W	2-0	Summersby, Byrne	5,361
23		20	A	Crewe Alexandra	L	1-4	Summersby	4,586
24		26	A	Aldershot	W	2-1	Deakin 2	6,080
25		27	H	Aldershot	W	4-1	Byrne 2, Collins, Priestley	19,344
26	Jan	1	A	Southport	W	2-0	Byrne, Summersby	2,280
27		3	H	Northampton Town	D	1-1	Priestley	17,462
28		24	H	Darlington	W	4-1	Byrne, Long, Noakes, Summersby	12,909
29		31	H	York City	D	0-0		16,175
30	Feb	7	A	Bradford Park Avenue	L	0-5		6,276
31		14	H	Port Vale	D	1-1	McNichol	13,305
32		21	H	Millwall	W	4-0	Noakes (pen), Deakin, Byrne, Collins	18,365
33		28	A	Gateshead	W	3-1	Long, Deakin, Summersby	3,614
34	Mar	7	H	Oldham Athletic	W	4-0	Deakin 2, Collins, Noakes	13,735
35		14	A	Barrow	L	0-1		2,862
36		16	A	Workington Town	W	4-0	Deakin 2, Summersby 2	4,096
37		21	H	Carlisle United	L	0-2		15,319
38		27	H	Torquay United	W	3-1	Noakes 2, Byrne	18,971
39		28	A	Gillingham	D	1-1	Byrne	8,714
40		30	A	Torquay United	W	2-0	Byrne, Brett	5,318
41	Apr	4	H	Exeter City	D	1-1	McNichol	20,977
42		11	A	Coventry City	L	0-2		12,503
43		15	A	Exeter City	L	1-3	Brett 2, Pierce	8,556
44		18	H	Shrewsbury Town	W	4-3	Deakin, McNichol, Byrne, Brett	9,027
45		25	A	Darlington	W	4-1	Brett, Deakin, Colfar, Summersby	2,643
46		29	H	Walsall	L	1-3	Summersby	8,848

Final League Position: 7th in Division Four

Appearances
Goals

FA Cup

1	Nov	15	A	Ashford	W	1-0	Collins	6,500
2	Dec	6	H	Shrewsbury Town	D	2-2	Deakin 2	16,207
R		11	A	Shrewsbury Town	D	2-2*	Byrne 2	5,428
2R		15	N+	Shrewsbury Town	W	4-1	Collins, Byrne, Deakin 2	8,062
3	Jan	10	A	Sheffield United	L	0-2		22,179

+Played at Molineux, Wolverhampton. * After extra-time

Appearances
Goals

Rouse	Edwards	Noakes	Truett	Choules	Long	Harrison	McNichol	Deakin	Byrne	Collins	Greenwood	Hopgood	Skingley	Brett	Farrell	Pierce	Nastri	Proudler	Cooper	Priestley	Summersby	Colfar	Sanders	Howe	Barnett	Evans	
1	2	3	4	5	6	7	8	9	10	11																	
1	2		4	5	6	7	8	9	10	11	3																
1	2	3	4	5	6	7	8	9	10	11																	
1	2	3	4	5	6	7	8	9	10	11																	
1	2	3	4	5	6	7	8	9	10	11																	
1		2	4	5	6	7	8	9	10	11	3																
1	2	3	4	5	6	7	8	9	10	11																	
1	2	3	4	5	6	7	8	9	10	11																	
1	2	3	4	5	6	7	8	9	10	11																	
1	2	3	4	5	6	7	8	9	10	11																	
		3	4	5	6	7	8	9	10	11		1	2														
		3	4	5	6	7	8	9	10	11		1	2														
		3	4	5	6	7	8	9	10	11		1	2														
		3	4	5	6	7	8	9	10	11		1	2														
		3		5	6		4		8	11		1	2	7	9	10											
		3		5	6		4		8	11		1	2	9		10	7										
		3		5	6		4		8	11		1	2	9		10	7										
		3		5	6		4	9	8	11		1	2	7		10											
		3			6		4	9	8	11		1	2	7		10		5									
		3		5	6		4		8	11		1	2			9			10	7							
1		3		5	6		4		8	11			2	9		10				7							
1	2	3		5	6		4	9	10	11										7	8						
1	2	3		5	6		4	9	10	11										7	8						
1	2	3		5	6		4	9	10	11										7	8						
1	2	3		5	6		4	9	10	11										7	8						
1	2	3		5	6		4	9	10	11										7	8						
1	2	3		5	6		4	9	10	11										7	8						
1		2		5	6		4		10					9						7	8	11	3				
1		3		5	6		4		10					9						7	8	11		2			
1		3		5	6		4							9		10				7	8	11		2			
1		3			6		4	9	10	11										7	8		5	2			
1		3		5	6		4	9	10	11										7	8			2			
1		3		5	6		4	9	10	11										7	8			2			
1		3		5	6		4	9	10	11										7	8			2			
1		3		5	6		4	9	10	11										7	8			2			
1		3		5	6		4	9	10	11										7	8			2			
1		3		5	6		4	9	10	11										7	8			2			
1		3		5	6		4	9	10	11										7	8			2			
1		3		5	6		4	9	10	11										7	8	`		2			
1		3		5	6		4		10					7							8	11		2	9		
1		3		5	6		4		10					7							8	11		2	9		
1		3		5	6		4		10											7	8	11		2	9		
1		3		2	6		4	9	10					7							8	11				5	
1		3		2	6		4	9	10					7							8	11				5	
1		3		2	6		4	9	10					7							8	11				5	
1		3		2	6		4		10					7							8	11			9	5	
36	15	45	14	44	46	14	46	34	45	36	2	10	11	15	1	8	2	1	1	21	25	10	2	14	4	4	2
		6	3		4	1	4	23	17	9				8		3				2	9	1					

Rouse	Edwards	Noakes	Truett	Choules	Long	Harrison	McNichol	Deakin	Byrne	Collins	Greenwood	Hopgood	Skingley	Brett	Farrell	Pierce	Nastri	Proudler	Cooper	Priestley	Summersby	Colfar	Sanders	Howe	Barnett	Evans
		3		5	6	7	4		8	11		1	2	9		10										
1	2	3		5	6		4	9	10	11				7						8						
1	2	3		5	6		4	9	10	11				7						8						
1	2	3		5	6		4	9	10	11				7						8						
1		2		5	6		4	9	8	11						10				7						3
4	3	5		5	5	1	5	4	5	5		1	1	4		2				4						1
								4	3	2																

League Table

	P	W	D	L	F	A	Pts
Port Vale	46	26	12	8	110	58	64
Coventry City	46	24	12	10	84	47	60
York City	46	21	18	7	73	52	60
Shrewsbury Town	46	24	10	12	101	63	58
Exeter City	46	23	11	12	87	61	57
Walsall	46	21	10	15	95	64	52
Crystal Palace	46	20	12	14	90	71	52
Northampton Town	46	21	9	16	85	78	51
Millwall	46	20	10	16	76	69	50
Carlisle United	46	19	12	15	62	65	50
Gillingham	46	20	9	17	82	77	49
Torquay United	46	16	12	18	78	77	44
Chester	46	16	12	18	72	84	44
Bradford Park Avenue	46	18	7	21	75	77	43
Watford	46	16	10	20	81	79	42
Darlington	46	13	16	17	66	68	42
Workington	46	12	17	17	63	78	41
Crewe Alexandra	46	15	10	21	70	82	40
Hartlepools United	46	15	10	21	74	88	40
Gateshead	46	16	8	22	56	85	40
Oldham Athletic	46	16	4	26	59	84	36
Aldershot	46	14	7	25	63	97	35
Barrow	46	9	10	27	51	104	28
Southport	46	7	12	27	41	86	26

1959-60

Division Four

Manager: George Smith until 12 April 1960; Arthur Rowe from 15 April 1960

Did you know that?

Palace's record club win is the 9–0 scoreline at home to Barrow in a Division Four match on 10 October 1959, although they did also score 10 twice, once during the World War One years, and then again during World War Two when players changed clubs virtually every week.

Match No.	Date		Venue	Opponents	Result		Scorers	Attendance
1	Aug	22	A	Carlisle United	D	2-2	Deakin, Noakes (pen)	7,011
2		24	A	Oldham Athletic	L	0-1		5,224
3		29	H	Notts County	D	1-1	Byrne	16,466
4	Sep	2	H	Oldham Athletic	W	3-2	Summersby, Gavin, Roche	16,405
5		5	A	Walsall	L	0-3		11,593
6		7	A	Stockport County	W	1-0	Noakes	11,882
7		12	H	Hartlepools United	W	5-2	Byrne 2, Sexton, Noakes 2	14,722
8		16	H	Stockport County	W	3-1	Gavin, Sexton, Byrne	18,534
9		19	A	Crewe Alexandra	D	1-1	Roche	7,786
10		23	H	Watford	W	8-1	Byrne 2, Colfar 2, Roche 2, Gavin, Noakes	21,938
11		26	H	Chester	L	3-4	Colfar, Byrne, Summersby	18,312
12		29	A	Watford	L	2-4	Summersby, Sexton	14,881
13	Oct	3	A	Southport	L	1-3	Byrne	4,210
14		7	A	Bradford Park Avenue	L	1-3	Summersby	3,220
15		10	H	Barrow	W	9-0	Summersby 4 (1 pen), Byrne 2, Colfar 2, Gavin	9,566
16		17	A	Aldershot	L	0-1		6,751
17		24	H	Darlington	W	2-0	Sexton, Summersby	14,936
18		28	H	Millwall	L	1-2	Easton	28,929
19		31	A	Gateshead	W	2-0	Rees, Byrne	3,901
20	Nov	7	H	Rochdale	W	4-0	Woan, Byrne, Sexton, Summersby	14,906
21		21	H	Doncaster Rovers	W	4-0	Sexton 2, Roche, Woan	15,263
22		28	A	Northampton Town	W	2-0	Byrne, Roche	8,121
23	Dec	12	A	Millwall	L	0-1		17,147
24		19	H	Carlisle United	W	2-1	Summersby (pen), Roche	9,045
25		28	H	Gillingham	D	3-3	McNichol, Summersby, Byrne	18,248
26	Jan	2	A	Notts County	L	1-7	Woan	15,804
27		16	H	Walsall	L	1-2	Woan	14,925
28		23	A	Hartlepools United	W	1-0	Woan	3,981
29		30	H	Torquay United	D	1-1	Woan	15,764
30	Feb	6	H	Crewe Alexandra	W	4-0	Woan, Roche, Sexton 2	13,567
31		13	A	Chester	W	1-0	Sexton	5,132
32		20	H	Southport	D	2-2	Sexton, Byrne	13,612
33		25	A	Workington Town	D	1-1	Woan	3,687
34		27	A	Barrow	W	1-0	Roche	5,949
35	Mar	5	H	Aldershot	D	1-1	McNichol	16,575
36		12	A	Darlington	D	1-1	McNichol	4,834
37		19	H	Gateshead	D	2-2	Summersby (pen), Byrne	13,868
38		26	A	Rochdale	L	0-4		2,562
39	Apr	2	H	Workington Town	L	0-1		12,214
40		9	A	Doncaster Rovers	W	2-1	Summersby, Roche	6,105
41		15	H	Exeter City	W	1-0	Roche	15,831
42		16	H	Northampton Town	L	0-1		15,943
43		18	A	Exeter City	D	2-2	Gavin 2	6,591
44		23	A	Torquay United	L	1-2	Gavin	7,293
45		27	H	Bradford Park Avenue	W	1-0	Summersby	9,920
46	May	4	A	Gillingham	D	0-0		5,077

Final League Position: 8th in Division Four

Appearances
Goals

FA Cup

Round	Date		Venue	Opponents	Result		Scorers	Attendance
1	Nov	14	H	Chelmsford City	W	5-1	Byrne 3, Woan, Sexton	17,249
2	Dec	5	A	Margate	D	0-0		8,203
R		9	H	Margate	W	3-0	Roche 2, Woan	28,753
3	Jan	9	A	Scunthorpe United	L	0-1		12,561

Appearances
Goals

Rouse	Long	Noakes	McNichol	Choules	Summersby	Gavin	Sexton	Deakin	Byrne	Colfar	Roche	Howe	Evans	Truett	Barnett	Priestley	Rees	Easton	Woan	Pyke	Hopgood	Lunnis
1	2	3	4	5	6	7	8	9	10	11												
1	2	3	4	5	6	7	8	9	10	11												
1	2	3	4	5	6	7	8	9	10	11												
1	2	3	4	5	6	7	8		10	11	9											
1	2	3	4	5	6	7	8		10	11	9											
1	2	3	4	5	6	7	8		10	11	9											
1	2	3	4	5	6	7	8		10	11	9											
1	2	3	4	5	6	7	8		10	11	9											
1	2		4	5	6	7	8		10	11	9	3										
1	2	3	4	5	6	7	8		10	11	9											
1	2	3	4	5	6	7	8		10	11	9											
1	2		4		6	7	8		10	11	9	3	5									
1	2	3	6		8	7	9		10	11			5	4								
1	2	3	6		8	7	9		10	11			5	4								
1	2	3	6		8	7	9		10	11			5	4								
1	2	3	6		8	7			10	11			5	4	9							
1	2	3	6	5	4		8		10		9					7	11					
1	2	3	6	5	4		8				9					7	11	10				
1	2	3	6	5	4		9		10		7						11		8			
1	2	3	6	5	4		9		10		7						11		8			
1	2	3	6	5	4		9		10		7						11		8			
1	2	3	6		4		8		10	11	7		5					9				
1	2		6	5	4	7			10	11	9	3							8			
1	2		6		4				10	11	7	3	5		9				8			
1	2		6	5	4				10	11	7	3			9				8			
1	2		6	5	4				10	11	9	3				7			8			
1	2		6	5	4				10		9	3				7	11		8			
1	2	3	6		4		9		10		7		5				11		8			
1	2	3	6		4		9		10		7		5				11		8			
1	2	3	6		4		9				7		5	8			11		10			
1	2	3	6		4		9		10		7		5				11		8			
1	2	3	6		4		9		10	11	7		5						8			
1	2	3	6		4	7	9		10				5				11		8			
1	2		3		4	7			10		9		5	6			11		8			
1	2		3		4	7			10		9		5	6			11		8			
1	2		6		4	7			10		9	3	5				11		8			
1	2	3	6		4	7			10	11	9		5						8			
1	2	3	6		4	7			10	11	8		5						9			
1	2	3	6		4				11		7		5	8				10	9			
1	2	3	6		4				11		7		5	8		10			9			
1	2	3	6		4				11		7		5	8		10			9			
1	2	3	6		4				11				5	8		10	7		9			
1	2	3	6		8	7			10		9		5				11			4		
1	2	3	6		8	7			10		9		5				11			4		
	4	3	6		8	7				11	9		5						10		1	2
1	4	3	6		8	7				11			5					9	10			2
45	46	36	46	20	46	27	27	3	42	26	36	8	26	11	3	7	17	4	25	2	1	2
		5	3		15	7	11	1	16	5	11						1	1	8			

Rouse	Long	Noakes	McNichol	Choules	Summersby	Gavin	Sexton	Deakin	Byrne	Colfar	Roche	Howe	Evans	Truett	Barnett	Priestley	Rees	Easton	Woan	Pyke	Hopgood	Lunnis
1	2	3	6	5	4		9		10		7						11		8			
1	2	3	6	5	4				10	11	9					7		8				
1	2		6	5	4				10	11	9	3				7			8			
1	2		6	5	4				10	11	9	3				7			8			
4	4	2	4	4	4		1		4	3	4	2				3	1	1	3			
							1		3		2								2			

League Table

	P	W	D	L	F	A	Pts
Walsall	46	28	9	9	102	60	65
Notts County	46	26	8	12	107	69	60
Torquay United	46	26	8	12	84	58	60
Watford	46	24	9	13	92	67	57
Millwall	46	18	17	11	84	61	53
Northampton Town	46	22	9	15	85	63	53
Gillingham	46	21	10	15	74	69	52
Crystal Palace	46	19	12	15	84	64	50
Exeter City	46	19	11	16	80	70	49
Stockport County	46	19	11	16	58	54	49
Bradford Park Avenue	46	17	15	14	70	68	49
Rochdale	46	18	10	18	65	60	46
Aldershot	46	18	9	19	77	74	45
Crewe Alexandra	46	18	9	19	79	88	45
Darlington	46	17	9	20	63	73	43
Workington	46	14	14	18	68	60	42
Doncaster Rovers	46	16	10	20	69	76	42
Barrow	46	15	11	20	77	87	41
Carlisle United	46	15	11	20	51	66	41
Chester	46	14	12	20	59	77	40
Southport	46	10	14	22	48	92	34
Gateshead	46	12	9	25	58	86	33
Oldham Athletic	46	8	12	26	41	83	28
Hartlepools United	46	10	7	29	59	109	27

1960-61

Division Four

Manager: Arthur Rowe

Did you know that?

Fourth Division Palace set a new club goalscoring record. Winning promotion to Division Three by finishing second, the Glaziers bagged themselves 110 goals on the way to going up, still the most they have scored in one season.

Match No.	Date		Venue	Opponents	Result		Scorers	Attendance
1	Aug	20	H	Accrington Stanley	W	9-2	Byrne 4, Woan 3, Heckman 2	15,653
2		24	H	Darlington	W	3-2	Woan, Byrne, Summersby	21,784
3		27	A	Doncaster Rovers	W	5-1	Woan 2, Byrne 2, Gavin	6,511
4		31	A	Darlington	W	1-0	Byrne	5,607
5	Sep	3	H	Hartlepools United	D	2-2	McNichol, Woan	19,099
6		7	H	Peterborough United	L	0-2		*36,478
7		10	A	Wrexham	W	2-1	Byrne, Gavin	10,609
8		12	A	Peterborough United	L	1-4	Heckman	21,171
9		17	H	Carlisle United	D	1-1	Summersby	15,867
10		20	A	Southport	D	3-3	Gavin, Byrne, Lunnis	5,434
11		24	A	Rochdale	D	2-2	Petchey, Summersby	4,819
12		28	H	Southport	W	5-0	Byrne 4, Noakes	15,969
13	Oct	1	H	Mansfield Town	W	4-1	Summersby 3, Woan	15,018
14		3	A	Stockport County	L	2-5	Woan 2	10,729
15		8	H	Barrow	W	4-2	Woan, Uphill 2, Petchey	13,845
16		15	A	Gillingham	W	2-1	Summersby 2	10,999
17		22	H	Bradford Park Avenue	W	4-1	Heckman, Byrne, Gavin, Petchey	14,946
18		29	A	Northampton Town	W	2-1	Uphill, Byrne	13,943
19	Nov	12	A	Oldham Athletic	L	3-4	Heckman 2, Byrne	18,435
20		19	H	Workington Town	W	4-2	Summersby 2, Heckman, Uphill	17,006
21	Dec	3	H	Crewe Alexandra	D	0-0		11,161
22		10	A	York City	W	2-0	Petchey, Heckman	6,538
23		17	A	Accrington Stanley	W	3-2	Byrne, Summersby, Heckman	3,385
24		26	A	Exeter City	W	3-2	Gavin, Byrne, Summersby	7,551
25		27	H	Exeter City	D	0-0		28,551
26		31	H	Doncaster Rovers	W	5-1	Uphill 2, Byrne, Summersby, Gavin	17,911
27	Jan	7	A	Chester	L	0-3		4,243
28		14	A	Hartlepools United	W	4-2	Heckman, Summersby, Byrne, Woan	4,430
29		21	H	Wrexham	W	3-2	Woan, Byrne 2	15,353
30		28	H	Chester	W	5-1	Byrne 3, Summersby 2	14,150
31	Feb	4	A	Carlisle United	L	0-2		4,464
32		11	H	Rochdale	W	4-1	Gavin 2, Heckman, own-goal (Bushby)	17,655
33		18	A	Mansfield Town	W	2-1	Summersby, Petchey	5,874
34		25	A	Barrow	W	3-0	Byrne, Heckman, Summersby	3,724
35	Mar	4	H	Gillingham	W	2-0	Byrne, Summersby	22,559
36		11	A	Bradford Park Avenue	L	1-3	Petchey	17,017
37		18	H	Northampton Town	L	2-3	Summersby, Heckman	20,688
38		25	A	Aldershot	L	1-2	Petchey	11,389
39		31	H	Millwall	L	0-2		*37,774
40	Apr	1	H	Oldham Athletic	W	2-1	Byrne 2	13,964
41		3	A	Millwall	W	2-0	Heckman, Barnett	15,748
42		8	A	Workington Town	L	0-1		3,776
43		19	H	Aldershot	W	2-1	Barnett, Summersby	19,983
44		22	A	Crewe Alexandra	W	2-1	Summersby, own-goal (Jones)	6,163
45		26	H	Stockport County	W	2-1	Summersby 2	15,822
46		29	H	York City	W	1-0	Summersby	17,885

Final League Position: 2nd in Division Four — Appearances

* Fourth Division attendance record (broken twice) — 2 own-goals — Goals

FA Cup

No.	Date		Venue	Opponents	Result		Scorers	Attendance
1	Nov	5	H	Hitchin Town	W	6-2	Uphill 2, Byrne, Gavin 2, Heckman	21,118
2		26	H	Watford	D	0-0		33,699
R		29	A	Watford	L	0-1		28,500

Appearances

Goals

League Cup

No.	Date		Venue	Opponents	Result		Scorers	Attendance
1	Oct	12	A	Darlington	L	0-2		9,940

Appearances

Goals

Rouse	Long	Noakes	Petchey	Evans	McNichol	Gavin	Woan	Byrne	Summersby	Heckman	Kerrins	Lunnis	Jones	Easton	Colfar	Choules	Uphill	Truett	Barnett	Lewis	Swannell
1	2	3	4	5	6	7	8	9	10	11											
1	2	3	4	5	6	7	8	9	10		11										
1	5	3	4		6	7	8	9	10	11		2									
1	5	3	4		6	7	8	9	10	11		2									
1	5	3	4		6	7	8	9	10	11			2								
1	5	3	4		6	7	8	9	10	11		2									
1	5	3	4		6	7		9	10	11		2		8							
1	5	3	4		6	7		9	10	11		2		8							
1	5	3	4		6	7		9	10	11		2		8							
1	5	3	4		6	7		9	8	11		2			10						
1	5		4		6	7		9	8	11		2	3		10						
1	4	2	6		3	7	10	9	8	11						5					
1	4	2	6		3	7	10	9	8	11						5					
1	4		6		3	7	10	9	8	11		2				5					
1	4		6	5	3	7	10		8	11		2					9				
1	4	3	6	5	2	7	10		8	11							9				
1	4	3	6	5	2	7		10	8	11							9				
1	4		6	5	2	7		10	8	11			3				9				
1	4		6	5	2	7		10	8	11			3				9				
1	4	3	6	5	2	7		10	8	11							9				
1	4	3	6	5	2	7		10	8	11							9				
1	4	3	6	5	2	7		10	8	11							9				
1	4	3	6	5	2	7		10	8	11							9				
1	4	3	6	5	2	7		10	8	11							9				
1	4	3	6	5	2	7		10	8	11							9				
1	4	3	6	5	2	7		10	8	11							9				
1	4	3	6	5	2	7	10	9	8	11											
1	4	3	6	5	2	7	10	9	8	11											
1	4	3	6	5	2	7	10	9	8	11											
1	4	3	6	5	2	7	10	9	8	11											
1	4	3	6	5	2	7	10	9	8	11											
1	4	3	6	5	2	7		8	10	11							9				
1	4	3	6	5	2	7		10	8	11							9				
1	4	3	6	5	2	7		10	8	11							9				
1	4	3	6	5	2	7		10	8	11							9				
1		3	6	5	2	7		10	8		11						9	4			
1	4	3	6	5	2	7		10	8	11							9				
1	4	3	6		2	7		10	8	11						5	9				
1	4	3	6		2	7		9	8						11	5		10			
1	4		6		2			10	8			3			11	5	9		7		
1	4	3	6		2			10	8	11						5	9		7		
1	4	3	6		2				8	10					11	5	9		7		
1	4	3	6		2			10	8	11						5	9		7		
1		3	6		2				8	10	11					5	9	4	7		
1	4	3	6		2			9	8	10	11					5			7		
1		3	6		2			9	8	10	11					5			7	4	
46	43	40	46	25	46	39	16	42	46	42	5	11	4	3	5	12	24	3	7	1	
		1	7		1	8	13	30	25	14		1					6		2		

Rouse	Long	Noakes	Petchey	Evans	McNichol	Gavin	Woan	Byrne	Summersby	Heckman	Kerrins	Lunnis	Jones	Easton	Colfar	Choules	Uphill	Truett	Barnett	Lewis	Swannell
1	4		6	5	2	7		10	8	11			3				9				
1	4	3	6	5	2	9		10	8	11							9				
1	4	3	6	5	2		7	10	8	11							9				
3	3	2	3	3	3	2	1	3	3	3			1				3				
						2		1		1							2				

Rouse	Long	Noakes	Petchey	Evans	McNichol	Gavin	Woan	Byrne	Summersby	Heckman	Kerrins	Lunnis	Jones	Easton	Colfar	Choules	Uphill	Truett	Barnett	Lewis	Swannell
	4		6	5	3		10		8	7	11	2							9		1
	1		1	1	1		1		1	1	1	1							1		1

League Table

	P	W	D	L	F	A	Pts
Peterborough United	46	28	10	8	134	65	66
Crystal Palace	46	29	6	11	110	69	64
Northampton Town	46	25	10	11	90	62	60
Bradford Park Avenue	46	26	8	12	84	74	60
York City	46	21	9	16	80	60	51
Millwall	46	21	8	17	97	86	50
Darlington	46	18	13	15	78	70	49
Workington	46	21	7	18	74	76	49
Crewe Alexandra	46	20	9	17	61	67	49
Aldershot	46	18	9	19	79	69	45
Doncaster Rovers	46	19	7	20	76	78	45
Oldham Athletic	46	19	7	20	79	88	45
Stockport County	46	18	9	19	57	66	45
Southport	46	19	6	21	69	67	44
Gillingham	46	15	13	18	64	66	43
Wrexham	46	17	8	21	62	56	42
Rochdale	46	17	8	21	60	66	42
Accrington Stanley	46	16	8	22	74	88	40
Carlisle United	46	13	13	20	61	79	39
Mansfield Town	46	16	6	24	71	78	38
Exeter City	46	14	10	22	66	94	38
Barrow	46	13	11	22	52	79	37
Hartlepools United	46	12	8	26	71	103	32
Chester	46	11	9	26	61	104	31

1961-62

Division Three

Manager: Arthur Rowe

Did you know that?

The £65,000 Palace received in March for Johnny Byrne when he was transferred to West Ham, then a British transfer record fee.

Match No.	Date		Venue	Opponents	Result		Scorers	Attendance
1	Aug	19	A	Torquay United	W	2-1	Summersby, Byrne	10,319
2		23	H	Notts County	W	4-1	Werge, Summersby, Smillie 2	28,567
3		26	H	Swindon Town	W	3-1	Allen 2 (2 pens), Byrne	24,184
4		31	A	Notts County	D	0-0		11,633
5	Sep	2	A	Halifax Town	D	1-1	Allen	9,583
6		6	H	Northampton Town	L	1-4	Little	25,535
7		9	H	Queen's Park Rangers	D	2-2	Smillie, Allen	27,179
8		16	A	Barnsley	W	3-0	Uphill, Allen, Byrne	6,699
9		20	H	Lincoln City	L	1-3	Smillie	19,601
10		23	H	Portsmouth	L	1-2	Heckman	24,586
11		27	A	Lincoln City	L	2-3	Byrne, Smillie	8,793
12		30	H	Southend United	D	2-2	Byrne, Lewis	15,388
13	Oct	3	A	Watford	L	2-3	Smillie, Heckman	14,228
14		7	A	Shrewsbury Town	W	5-1	Byrne 2, Allen 2, Uphill	7,909
15		11	H	Watford	D	1-1	Lewis	23,390
16		14	H	Peterborough United	W	5-2	Allen 2, Byrne 2, Uphill	28,886
17		17	A	Northampton Town	D	1-1	Heckman	13,827
18		20	A	Reading	L	1-2	Heckman	14,432
19		28	H	Newport County	W	2-0	Summersby, Smillie	17,885
20	Nov	11	H	Grimsby Town	W	4-1	Smillie 3, Heckman	13,661
21		17	A	Coventry City	W	2-0	Allen (pen), Uphill	13,757
22	Dec	2	A	Port Vale	W	1-0	Smillie	9,761
23		9	H	Bristol City	L	2-3	Allen, Uphill	17,365
24		16	H	Torquay United	W	7-2	Uphill 2, Heckman 2, Byrne, Smillie, own-goal	13,884
25		23	A	Swindon Town	L	0-5		7,707
26		26	A	Hull City	W	4-2	Petchey, Byrne, Heckman, own-goal	7,559
27	Jan	13	H	Halifax Town	W	4-3	Uphill, Heckman, Byrne, own-goal	17,696
28		20	A	Queen's Park Rangers	L	0-1		18,003
29		27	H	Brentford	D	2-2	Lewis, Uphill	19,323
30	Feb	3	H	Barnsley	L	1-3	Summersby	14,095
31		10	A	Portsmouth	L	1-2	Byrne	22,541
32		17	A	Southend United	D	2-2	Heckman, Allen	8,733
33		24	H	Shrewsbury Town	W	2-1	Smillie, Allen	12,493
34	Mar	3	A	Peterborough United	L	1-4	Byrne	12,095
35		7	A	Bradford Park Avenue	L	0-2		3,606
36		10	H	Reading	L	3-4	Summersby 2, Truett	12,507
37		17	A	Newport County	L	1-2	Truett	2,276
38		21	H	Hull City	L	1-2	Summersby	7,041
39		24	H	Bradford Park Avenue	D	0-0		8,527
40		30	A	Grimsby Town	D	0-0		12,535
41	Apr	7	H	Coventry City	D	2-2	Smillie, Brett	8,438
42		13	A	Brentford	L	2-4	Summersby, Uphill	9,926
43		20	A	Bournemouth	L	0-1		13,499
44		21	H	Port Vale	D	0-0		10,519
45		23	H	Bournemouth	D	0-0		11,319
46		28	A	Bristol City	D	2-2	Smillie 2	7,199

Final League Position: 15th in Division Three

Appearances

3 own-goals — Goals

FA Cup

1	Nov	4	H	Portsmouth	W	3-0	Byrne, Heckman 2	30,464
2		25	A	Bridgewater Town	W	3-0	Smillie, Heckman, Long	6,045
3	Jan	6	A	Aston Villa	L	3-4	Byrne 2, Uphill	39,011

Appearances

Goals

League Cup

1	Sep	13	A	Queen's Park Rangers	L	2-5	Smillie 2	10,561

Appearances

Goals

Rouse	McNichol	Little	Long	Choules	Petchey	Werge	Summersby	Byrne	Smillie	Allen	Noakes	Lunnis	Uphill	Heckman	Lewis	Evans	Cartwright	Wood	Glazier	Easton	Truett	Brett	Stone	Stephenson
1	2	3	4	5	6	7	8	9	10	11														
1	2	3	4	5	6	7	8	9	10	11														
1	2	3	4	5	6	7	8	9	10	11														
1		3	4	5	6	7	8	9	10	11	2													
1		3	4	5	6	7	8	9	10	11		2												
1		3	4	5	6	7	8	9	10	11	2													
1		3	4	5	6			8	10	7		2	9	11										
1		3	4	5	6			8	10	7		2	9	11										
1		3	4	5	6		8		10	7		2	9	11										
1		3	4	5	6			8	7			2	9	11	10									
1		3	4	5	6			8	10			2	9	11	7									
1		3	4	5	6		8	9	10			2		11	7									
1		3	4	5	6		8	9	10			2		11	7									
1		3	2		6		4	8		9			10	11	7	5								
1		3	2		6		4	8		9			10	11	7	5								
1		3	2		6		4	8		10			9	11	7	5								
1		3	2		6		4	8		10			9	11	7	5								
1		3	2		6		4	8		10			9	11	7	5								
1	3		2		6		4	8	10				9	11	7	5								
1	3		2		6		4	8	10	7			9	11		5								
1	3		2		6		4	8	10	7			9	11		5								
1	3		2		6		4		10	7			9	11		5	8							
1	3		2		6		4	8	10	7			9	11		5								
1	3		2		6		4	8	10	7			9	11		5								
1	3		2		6		4	8	10	7				11			9	5						
1	3		2		6		4	8	10	7			9	11				5						
	3		2		6		4	8		7			9	11	10			5	1					
	3		2		6		4	8		7			9	11	10			5	1					
	3		2		6		4	8		7			9	11	10			5	1					
	3		2		6	11	4	8					9		7		10	5	1					
		3	2		6	7	4	9	10						8			5	1	11				
		3	2		6	7	4	8	10	9				11				5	1					
	3		2		6	7	4	8	10	9				11		5			1					
	3		2		6	7	8	9	10					11	4	5			1					
	3		4		6	7	8		10			2		11		5			1		9			
	3		4		6		8		10			2		11		5			1		7	9		
	3		4				8			9		2		11				5	1		7	10	6	
1	2	3	4				6		10	8				11			7	5				9		
1	2	3	4				8		10				9				7	6				11		5
1	2	3	4				8		10				9	11		5		6				7		
1	2	3	4			6	8		10				9	11				5				7		
1	2	3	4			6	8		10				9	11				5				7		
	2	3	4		6		8		10				9	11				5	1			7		
	2	3	4		6	7	8		10				9		11			5	1					
1	2	3			6	7	4		10					11	8		9	5						
1	2	3	4		6	7	8		10					11			9	5						
33	29	29	45	13	40	17	42	32	36	28	2	11	27	36	18	16	7	18	13	1	3	8	1	1
		1			1	1	8	14	16	13			10	10	3						2	1		

Rouse	McNichol	Little	Long	Choules	Petchey	Werge	Summersby	Byrne	Smillie	Allen	Noakes	Lunnis	Uphill	Heckman	Lewis	Evans	Cartwright	Wood	Glazier	Easton	Truett	Brett	Stone	Stephenson
1	3		2		6	7	4	8	10				9	11		5								
1	3		2		6		4	8	10	7			9	11		5								
1	3		2		6		4	8		7			9	11			10	5						
3	3		3		3	1	3	3	2	2			3	3		2	1	1						
			1					3	1				1	3										

Rouse	McNichol	Little	Long	Choules	Petchey	Werge	Summersby	Byrne	Smillie	Allen	Noakes	Lunnis	Uphill	Heckman	Lewis	Evans	Cartwright	Wood	Glazier	Easton	Truett	Brett	Stone	Stephenson
1		3	4	5	6		8	10	7		2	9	11											
1		1	1	1	1		1	1	1		1	1	1											
								2																

League Table

	P	W	D	L	F	A	Pts
Portsmouth	46	27	11	8	87	47	65
Grimsby Town	46	28	6	12	80	56	62
Bournemouth	46	21	17	8	69	45	59
Queen's Park Rangers	46	24	11	11	111	73	59
Peterborough United	46	26	6	14	107	82	58
Bristol City	46	23	8	15	94	72	54
Reading	46	22	9	15	77	66	53
Northampton Town	46	20	11	15	85	57	51
Swindon Town	46	17	15	14	78	71	49
Hull City	46	20	8	18	67	54	48
Bradford Park Avenue	46	20	7	19	80	78	47
Port Vale	46	17	11	18	65	58	45
Notts County	46	17	9	20	67	74	43
Coventry City	46	16	11	19	64	71	43
Crystal Palace	46	14	14	18	83	80	42
Southend United	46	13	16	17	57	69	42
Watford	46	14	13	19	63	74	41
Halifax Town	46	15	10	21	62	84	40
Shrewsbury Town	46	13	12	21	73	84	38
Barnsley	46	13	12	21	71	95	38
Torquay United	46	15	6	25	76	100	36
Lincoln City	46	9	17	20	57	87	35
Brentford	46	13	8	25	53	93	34
Newport County	46	7	8	31	46	102	22

1962-63

Division Three

Manager: Arthur Rowe until 30 November 1962, then Dick Graham

Did you know that?

On 18 April Palace memorably took on the mighty Real Madrid in a friendly to mark the switching on of new floodlights at Selhurst Park. A crowd of 25,000 turned up in the rain to see them go down fighting to a 4–3 defeat. Although Johnny Byrne had left Palace the month before, he guested in the Palace side against the likes of Puskas and Di Stefano in the Spaniards line up.

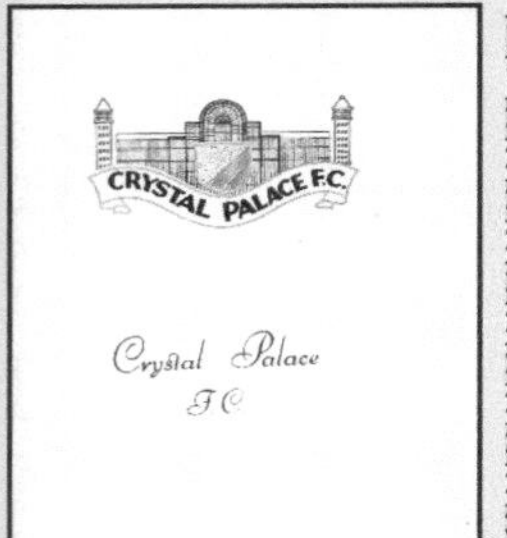

Match No.	Date		Venue	Opponents	Result		Scorers	Attendance
1	Aug	18	H	Halifax Town	D	0-0		17,598
2		22	A	Shrewsbury Town	L	1-3	Cartwright	6,827
3		25	A	Bristol Rovers	L	0-2		10,889
4		29	H	Shrewsbury Town	D	2-2	Burridge, Allen	15,755
5	Sep	1	H	Brighton & Hove Albion	D	2-2	Petchey, Stephenson	18,464
6		3	A	Queen's Park Rangers	L	1-4	Smillie	16,353
7		8	A	Carlisle United	D	2-2	Summersby, Uphill	6,591
8		12	H	Queen's Park Rangers	W	1-0	Summersby	21,958
9		15	H	Swindon Town	D	0-0		16,326
10		20	A	Hull City	D	0-0		9,718
11		22	A	Peterborough United	D	0-0		12,856
12		29	H	Barnsley	L	1-2	Allen	14,062
13	Oct	2	A	Northampton Town	L	1-3	Lewis	14,204
14		6	H	Southend United	L	2-3	Smillie 2	13,186
15		10	H	Northampton Town	L	1-2	Smillie	13,319
16		13	A	Colchester United	W	2-1	Smillie 2	6,282
17		20	H	Notts County	D	1-1	Smillie	13,700
18		27	A	Bournemouth	L	0-3		10,455
19	Nov	10	A	Bradford Park Avenue	L	1-2	Allen	5,811
20		17	H	Watford	L	0-1		10,716
21	Dec	1	H	Reading	W	2-1	Allen, Heckman	12,391
22		8	A	Port Vale	L	1-4	Allen	6,537
23		15	A	Halifax Town	D	2-2	Burridge, Long	20,055
24		26	H	Millwall	W	3-0	Burridge, Allen (pen), Dowsett	20,414
25	Jan	12	A	Brighton & Hove Albion	W	2-1	Burridge, Holton	12,333
26	Feb	2	A	Swindon Town	L	0-1		9,895
27	Mar	9	A	Notts County	W	2-0	Dowsett 2	5,536
28		16	H	Bournemouth	W	1-0	Allen	16,191
29		20	H	Bristol Rovers	W	2-1	Holton 2	15,451
30		23	A	Coventry City	L	0-1		17,860
31		27	H	Colchester United	L	0-1		11,898
32		30	H	Bradford Park Avenue	W	6-0	Burridge 2, Petchey, Allen, Holton, Dowsett	9,146
33	Apr	1	A	Millwall	D	1-1	Dowsett	21,996
34		6	A	Watford	W	4-1	Holton 3, Dowsett	8,471
35		12	A	Wrexham	W	4-3	Dowsett 2, Allen, Werge	10,820
36		13	H	Bristol City	W	3-2	Burridge, Holton, Dowsett	14,645
37		15	H	Wrexham	W	5-0	Burridge 3, Long, own-goal (Metcalfe)	17,332
38		19	A	Reading	W	1-0	Holton	9,839
39		24	H	Peterborough United	L	0-2		21,777
40		27	H	Port Vale	W	2-1	Dowsett, Burridge	13,183
41	May	1	H	Hull City	D	1-1	Dowsett	11,210
42		7	A	Bristol City	D	1-1	Burridge	8,732
43		15	H	Coventry City	D	0-0		12,672
44		18	H	Carlisle United	W	3-0	Burridge, Long, Allen	10,242
45		20	A	Southend United	L	0-1		7,962
46		22	A	Barnsley	W	4-0	Burridge, Allen, Dowsett, Forster	3,807

Final League Position: 11th in Division Three

Appearances

1 own-goal — Goals

FA Cup

	Date		Venue	Opponents	Result		Scorers	Attendance
1	Nov	3	H	Hereford United	W	2-0	Wood, Werge	15,317
2		24	H	Mansfield Town	D	2-2	Burridge, Allen (pen)	13,414
R		26	A	Mansfield Town	L	2-7	own-goal (Phillips), Summersby	17,118

Appearances

1 own-goal — Goals

League Cup

	Date		Venue	Opponents	Result		Scorers	Attendance
2	Sep	26	A	Leeds United	L	1-2	Long	7,274

Appearances

Goals

Glazier	McNichol	Townsend	Long	Wood	Summersby	Lewis	Cartwright	Burridge	Smillie	Imlach	Petchey	Allen	Stephenson	Evans	Werge	Dodge	Heckman	Uphill	Rouse	Howe	Little	Lunnis	Newman	Dowsett	Holton	Forster	Fuller
1	2	3	4	5	6	7	8	9	10	11																	
1	2	3	4	5	6	7	8	9	10								11										
1	2	3	4	5	6	7	8	9	10	11																	
1	2	3	4	5		7		10	8	11	6	9															
1	2	3	4			7		10	8	11	6	9	5														
1		3	2		8				10	11	6	9		5	7	4											
1		3	2	5	8				10	11	6	7				4		9									
		3	2	4	8			10		11	6	7		5				9	1								
		3	2	4	7			10		11	6	9		5				8	1								
		3	2	4	7			10		11	6	9		5				8	1								
	3		2	4	8	7		10						5	6		11	9	1								
		3	2	4		7		10				8		5	6		11	9	1								
			2	4	8	7		11	10					5	6			9	1		3						
	7	3	4	5	8				10						6		11		1	2		9					
	11	3	4	5					10		6				8			9	1	2			7				
	4			5				11	10		6				8			9	1	2	3		7				
	4			5	8			11	10		6							9	1	2	3		7				
				5	8		9	11	10						6	4			1	2	3		7				
1				6	4				10			11		5	8			9		2	3		7				
1				6	4				10			11		5	8			9		2	3		7				
1			4	5	8				10		6	7					11			2	3			9			
1			4	5	8				10		6	7					11			2	3			9			
1		3	4	5		7		8			6	10			11					2				9			
1		3	4	5				8			6	7			11					2				9	10		
1		3	4	5				8			6	7			11					2				9	10		
1		3	4	5				8			6	7			11					2				9	10		
1		3	4	5				8			6	7			11					2				9	10		
1		3	4	5		8					6	7			11					2				9	10		
1		3		5				8			4	11			7					2	6			9	10		
1		3		5		11		8			6	7			4					2				9	10		
1		3	4	5				8			6	7			11					2				9	10		
1		3	4	5				8			6	7			11					2				9	10		
1		3	4	5				8			6	7			11					2				9	10		
1		3	4	5				8			6	7			11					2				9	10		
1		3	4	5				8			6	7			11					2				9	10		
1		3	4	5				8			6	7			11					2				9	10		
1		3	4	5				8			6	7			11					2				9	10		
1		3	4	5				8			6	7			11					2				9	10		
1		3	4	5				8			6	7			11					2				9	10		
1		3	4	5				8			6	7			11					2				9	10		
1		3	4	5		6		8				7			11					2				9	10		
1		4	5	3		7		10				11			8					2				9	6		
1		4	5	3				10			8	11			7					2				9	6		
1		3	4	5				10			8	11			7					2				9	6		
1		4	5	3				10			8	11								2				9	6	7	
1		6	2	5				10				7								4				9	8	11	3
35	10	37	39	44	17	13	4	37	17	9	33	36	1	9	32	3	6	12	11	33	9	1	6	26	23	2	1
		3			2	1	1	14	7		2	11	1		1		1	1						12	9	1	

Glazier	McNichol	Townsend	Long	Wood	Summersby	Lewis	Cartwright	Burridge	Smillie	Imlach	Petchey	Allen	Stephenson	Evans	Werge	Dodge	Heckman	Uphill	Rouse	Howe	Little	Lunnis	Newman
1				6	4				10			11		5	8			9		2	3		7
1			4		6			8	10			11		5	7			9		2	3		
1			4		8			9	10			11		5	6			7		2	3		
3			2	1	3			2	3			3		3	3			3		3	3		1
				1	1			1				1			1								

Glazier	McNichol	Townsend	Long	Wood	Summersby	Lewis	Cartwright	Burridge	Smillie	Imlach	Petchey	Allen	Stephenson	Evans	Werge	Dodge	Heckman	Uphill	Rouse	Howe	Little
			4	5		7		10				8			6		11	9	1	2	3
			1	1		1		1				1			1		1	1	1	1	1
			1																		

League Table

	P	W	D	L	F	A	Pts
Northampton Town	46	26	10	10	109	60	62
Swindon Town	46	22	14	10	87	56	58
Port Vale	46	23	8	15	72	58	54
Coventry City	46	18	17	11	83	69	53
Bournemouth	46	18	16	12	63	46	52
Peterborough United	46	20	11	15	93	75	51
Notts County	46	19	13	14	73	74	51
Southend United	46	19	12	15	75	77	50
Wrexham	46	20	9	17	84	83	49
Hull City	46	19	10	17	74	69	48
Crystal Palace	46	17	13	16	68	58	47
Colchester United	46	18	11	17	73	93	47
Queen's Park Rangers	46	17	11	18	85	76	45
Bristol City	46	16	13	17	100	92	45
Shrewsbury Town	46	16	12	18	83	81	44
Millwall	46	15	13	18	82	87	43
Watford	46	17	8	21	82	85	42
Barnsley	46	15	11	20	63	74	41
Bristol Rovers	46	15	11	20	70	88	41
Reading	46	16	8	22	74	78	40
Bradford Park Avenue	46	14	12	20	79	97	40
Brighton & Hove Albion	46	12	12	22	58	84	36
Carlisle United	46	13	9	24	61	89	35
Halifax Town	46	9	12	25	64	106	30

1963-64

Division Three

Manager: Dick Graham

Did you know that?

Palace's highest-ever win in the FA cup was the 8–2 victory over non-League Harwich and Parkeston in the first round during November. Although they went out tamely to Yeovil Town during the next round, promotion to Division Two at the end of the season more than compensated for that fact.

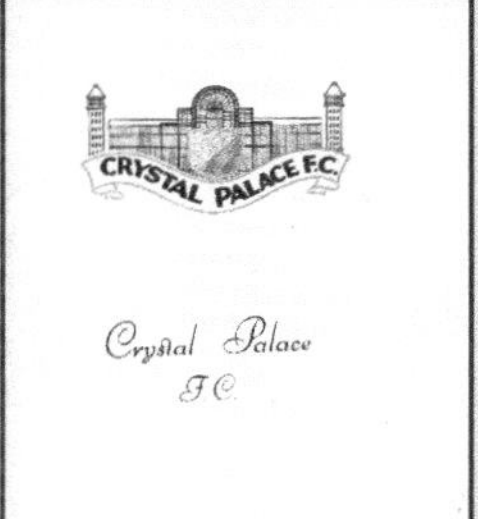

Match No.	Date	Venue	Opponents	Result		Scorers	Attendance
1	Aug 24	A	Coventry City	L	1-5	Burridge	26,037
2	28	A	Reading	D	0-0		10,118
3	31	H	Mansfield Town	W	3-1	Burridge, Petchey, Werge	14,180
4	Sep 7	A	Brentford	L	1-2	Wood	15,883
5	11	H	Reading	W	4-1	Spiers (og), Dowsett, Burridge, Werge	12,059
6	14	H	Shrewsbury Town	W	3-0	Dowsett 2, Allen	14,469
7	18	A	Luton Town	W	4-0	Allen 2, Holton, Dowsett	6,152
8	21	A	Bristol City	D	1-1	Burridge	9,782
9	28	H	Port Vale	W	2-0	Dowsett, Holton	15,044
10	Oct 2	H	Luton Town	D	1-1	Dowsett	16,304
11	5	A	Notts County	D	1-1	Burridge	7,207
12	9	H	Watford	W	2-0	Burridge 2	16,913
13	12	H	Millwall	W	2-1	Holton 2	25,056
14	15	A	Watford	L	1-3	Allen (pen)	9,595
15	19	A	Oldham Athletic	L	1-3	Burridge	17,458
16	23	A	Crewe Alexandra	W	2-0	Allen, Holton	5,883
17	26	H	Bristol Rovers	W	1-0	Burridge	18,389
18	30	H	Crewe Alexandra	W	1-0	Burridge	15,178
19	Nov 2	A	Queen's Park Rangers	W	4-3	Holton 2, Burridge 2	9,826
20	9	H	Wrexham	W	2-1	Holton 2	16,601
21	23	H	Hull City	D	2-2	Allen (pen), Whitehouse	16,929
22	30	A	Barnsley	L	0-2		5,539
23	Dec 14	H	Coventry City	D	1-1	Stephenson	18,942
24	21	A	Mansfield Town	D	1-1	Petchey	5,526
25	26	A	Southend United	L	1-2	Burridge	8,392
26	28	H	Southend United	W	3-0	Holton, Stephenson, Imlach	16,168
27	Jan 4	A	Bournemouth	L	3-4	Burridge 2, Holton	8,491
28	11	H	Brentford	W	1-0	Burridge	16,630
29	18	A	Shrewsbury Town	D	1-1	Werge	4,303
30	25	H	Peterborough United	W	1-0	Holton	15,308
31	Feb 1	H	Bristol City	W	1-0	Kellard	16,539
32	8	A	Port Vale	W	2-1	Holton 2	8,204
33	15	H	Notts County	W	2-0	Holton, Burridge	15,867
34	22	A	Millwall	W	1-0	Burridge	20,264
35	29	H	Colchester United	D	0-0		15,421
36	Mar 7	A	Bristol Rovers	W	3-1	Burridge 2, Kellard	10,598
37	14	H	Queen's Park Rangers	W	1-0	Allen	15,370
38	18	H	Walsall	W	1-0	Whitehouse	12,784
39	28	H	Bournemouth	W	2-1	Holton, Whitehouse	22,175
40	30	A	Walsall	D	2-2	Holton, Whitehouse	5,356
41	Apr 4	A	Hull City	D	1-1	Holton (pen)	6,602
42	11	H	Barnsley	L	1-2	Whitehouse	21,205
43	15	A	Colchester United	D	1-1	Imlach (pen)	5,633
44	18	A	Peterborough United	D	1-1	Whitehouse	11,837
45	22	A	Wrexham	D	2-2	Whitehouse, Holton (pen)	3,492
46	25	H	Oldham Athletic	L	1-3	Holton (pen)	27,967

Final League Position: 2nd in Division Three

Appearances

1 own-goal

Goals

FA Cup

No.	Date	Venue	Opponents	Result		Scorers	Attendance
1	Nov 16	H	Harwich & Parkeston	W	8-2	Burridge, Holton 3, Allen 2, Sewell, Howe	15,759
2	Dec 7	A	Yeovil Town	L	1-3	Wood	10,925

Appearances

Goals

League Cup

No.	Date	Venue	Opponents	Result		Scorers	Attendance
2	Sep 25	A	Bristol Rovers	L	0-2		4,859

Appearances

Goals

Glazier	Howe	Townsend	Long	Wood	Petchey	Allen	Holton	Dowsett	Burridge	Werge	Kellard	Fuller	Stephenson	Birch	Sewell	Lucas	Whitehouse	Imlach	Brooks	Forster	
1	2	3	4	5	6	7	8	9	10	11											
1	2	3	4	5	6	7	8	9	10	11											
1	2	3	4	5	6	7	8	9	10	11											
1	2	3	4	5	6	7	9		10	11	8										
1	2	3	4	5	6	7	8	9	10	11											
1	2	3	4	5	6	7	8	9	10	11											
1	2	3	4	5	6	7	8	9	10	11											
1	2	3	4	5	6	7	8	9	10	11											
1	2	3	4	5	6	7	8	9	10	11											
1	2	3	4	5	6		8	9	10	11	7										
1	2	3	4	5	6	7	8	9	10	11											
1	2	3	4	5	6	7	8	9	10	11											
1	2	3	4	5	6	7	8	9	10	11											
1	2	3	4	5	6	7	8	9	10	11											
1	2	3	4	5	6	7	8	9	10	11											
1	2	3		5		7	8	9	10			4	6	11							
1	4	3		5		7	8	9	10					11	2	6					
1	4	3		5		7	8	9	10					11	2	6					
1	4	3				7	9		10	11	8		5		2	6					
1	4	3		5		7	9		10	11	8				2	6					
1	4	3		5		7	9		10		11				2	6	8				
1	4	3		5		7	9		10		11				2	6	8				
1	4			5	6	7			10		11		3	9	2		8				
1	4			5	6	7	9		10		11		3		2		8				
1	4			5	6	7	9		10		11		3		2		8				
1	4			5	3		9				11		6	8	2	10		7			
1	4			5	3		9		10		11		6		2	8		7			
1	4	3		5			9		10	7			6		2	8		11			
1	4	3		5			9		10	7			6		2	8		11			
1	4	3		5		7	9		10				6		2	8		11			
1	4	3		5			9		10		8		6		2			11	7		
1	4	3		5			9		10		8		6		2			11	7		
1	4	3		5			9		10				6		2		8	11	7		
1	4	3		5			9		10				6		2		8	11	7		
1	4	3	2	5			9		10				6				8	11	7		
1	4	3	2	5		7	9		10		11		6				8				
1	4	3	2	5		7	9		10		11		6				8				
1	4	3	2	5			9	7	10		11		6				8				
1	4	3	2	5			9		10		7		6				8	11			
1	4	3	2	5			9		10		7		6				8	11			
1	4	3	2	5			9		10		11		6				8		7		
1	4	3	2	5			9		10		11		6				8		7		
1	4		2	5	3				10		7		6			8	9	11			
1	4		2	5	3				10		7		6			8	9	11			
1	4		2	5	3		9	10		7	11		6				8				
1	4		2	5	3		9		10	7	11		6				8				
46	46	37	27	45	24	27	43	19	44	21	24	1	26	5	18	13	19	14	7		
				1	2	7	20	6	20	3	2		2				7	2			
1	4	3		5		11	9		10	7	8				2	6					
1	4	3		5		11	9		10	7					2	6	8				
2	2	2		2		2	2		2	2	1				2	2	1				
	1			1		2	3		1						1						
1	6	3			4		8			10	11	2	5	9							7
1	1	1			1		1			1	1	1	1	1							1

League Table

	P	W	D	L	F	A	Pts
Coventry City	46	22	16	8	98	61	60
Crystal Palace	46	23	14	9	73	51	60
Watford	46	23	12	11	79	59	58
Bournemouth	46	24	8	14	79	58	56
Bristol City	46	20	15	11	84	64	55
Reading	46	21	10	15	79	62	52
Mansfield Town	46	20	11	15	76	62	51
Hull City	46	16	17	13	73	68	49
Oldham Athletic	46	20	8	18	73	70	48
Peterborough United	46	18	11	17	75	70	47
Shrewsbury Town	46	18	11	17	73	80	47
Bristol Rovers	46	19	8	19	91	79	46
Port Vale	46	16	14	16	53	49	46
Southend United	46	15	15	16	77	78	45
Queen's Park Rangers	46	18	9	19	76	78	45
Brentford	46	15	14	17	87	80	44
Colchester United	46	12	19	15	70	68	43
Luton Town	46	16	10	20	64	80	42
Walsall	46	13	14	19	59	76	40
Barnsley	46	12	15	19	68	94	39
Millwall	46	14	10	22	53	67	38
Crewe Alexandra	46	11	12	23	50	77	34
Wrexham	46	13	6	27	75	107	32
Notts County	46	9	9	28	45	92	27

1964-65

Division Two

Manager: Dick Graham

Did you know that?

On almost the same site as Palace's original 1905 ground at the Crystal Palace, the National Sports Centre stadium was opened, with the Glaziers playing a pre-season friendly in August, which they won 4–1 against West Ham.

Match No.	Date		Venue	Opponents	Result		Scorers	Attendance
1	Aug	22	H	Derby County	L	2-3	Holton, Burridge	22,935
2		25	A	Swindon Town	L	0-2		17,446
3		29	A	Swansea Town	L	1-2	Whitehouse	13,000
4	Sep	2	H	Swindon Town	W	3-1	Holton, Dowsett 2	18,517
5		5	H	Rotherham United	W	2-1	Burridge 2	18,200
6		12	A	Norwich City	W	2-1	Holton 2 (1 pen)	20,893
7		15	A	Charlton Athletic	W	2-1	Kellard, Dowsett	31,498
8		19	H	Plymouth Argyle	W	2-1	Holton, Dowsett	21,074
9		26	H	Bury	L	0-2		19,299
10		30	H	Charlton Athletic	W	3-1	Allen 3 (1 pen)	29,878
11	Oct	3	A	Leyton Orient	W	1-0	Burridge	17,711
12		7	H	Ipswich Town	D	1-1	Werge	22,690
13		10	A	Bolton Wanderers	L	0-3		13,484
14		17	H	Middlesborough	W	3-1	Whitehouse 2, Kellard	18,055
15		24	A	Newcastle United	L	0-2		28,750
16		31	H	Northampton Town	L	1-2	Holton	21,331
17	Nov	7	A	Southampton	W	1-0	Burridge	20,161
18		14	H	Huddersfield Town	W	3-0	Smith 2, Kellard	14,084
19		21	A	Coventry City	D	0-0		24,145
20		28	H	Cardiff City	D	0-0		18,188
21	Dec	5	A	Preston North End	L	0-1		11,390
22		12	A	Derby County	D	3-3	Burridge 2, Smith	11,828
23		19	H	Swansea Town	D	3-3	Holton 2, Long	13,585
24		26	H	Portsmouth	W	4-2	Burnside 2, Smith, Stephenson	18,758
25		28	A	Portsmouth	D	1-1	Holsgrove	15,450
26	Jan	2	A	Rotherham United	L	0-1		9,385
27		16	H	Norwich City	W	2-0	Holton, Burnside	17,103
28		23	A	Plymouth Argyle	D	1-1	Smith	15,582
29	Feb	6	A	Bury	L	1-3	Smith	5,580
30		13	H	Leyton Orient	W	1-0	Woods	17,776
31		27	A	Middlesborough	D	0-0		12,071
32	Mar	13	A	Northampton Town	D	1-1	Cutler	17,350
33		17	H	Preston North End	W	1-0	Holton	14,976
34		20	H	Southampton	L	0-2		12,737
35		27	A	Huddersfield Town	L	0-2		10,255
36	Apr	3	H	Coventry City	D	2-2	Holsgrove, Woods	15,900
37		7	H	Bolton Wanderers	W	2-0	Smith, Stephenson	14,022
38		10	A	Cardiff City	D	0-0		10,000
39		16	A	Manchester City	W	2-0	Smith 2	15,885
40		17	H	Newcastle United	D	1-1	Stephenson	21,756
41		19	H	Manchester City	D	1-1	Stephenson	12,175
42		24	A	Ipswich Town	L	2-3	Holton, Burnside	14,642

Final League Position: 7th in Division Two

Appearances
Goals

FA Cup

3	Jan	9	H	Bury	W	5-1	Burnside, Wood, Holton 3	18,672
4		30	A	Southampton	W	2-1	Holton, Smith	26,398
5	Feb	20	H	Nottingham Forest	W	3-1	Burnside, Burridge, Holton	*41,667
6	Mar	10	H	Leeds United	L	0-3		*45,384

*Ground attendance record

Appearances
Goals

League Cup

2	Sep	23	A	Tranmere Rovers	W	2-0	Holton, Burridge	11,098
3	Oct	26	H	Southampton	W	2-0	Burridge 2	11,538
4	Nov	4	A	Leicester City	D	0-0		11,141
R		11	H	Leicester City	L	1-2	Burridge	15,808

Appearances
Goals

Glazier	Long	Howe	Wood	Stephenson	Holsgrove	Holton	Whitehouse	Kellard	Burridge	Allen	Jackson	Townsend	Werge	Birch	Lucas	Imlach	Sewell	Dowsett	Millington	Smith	Woods	Payne	Burnside	Horobin	Cutler	Fuller	Petchey
1	2	3	4	5	6	7	8	9	10	11																	
		2		5	4			10		7	1	3	6	8	9	11											
1	4	3		5		7	8	9	10				11		6		2										
1		3	5	6		9	4	10	8							11	2	7									
1		3	5	6		9	4	10	8							11	2	7									
1		3	5	6		9	4	8	10							11	2	7									
1		3	5	6		9	4	10	8							11	2	7									
1		3		5		9	4	10	8						6	11	2	7									
1		3		6		9	4	8	10			5				11	2	7									
1		3	5	6		9	4	10	8	7			11				2										
1		3	5	6		9	4	10	8	7			11				2										
1		3	5	6		9	4	8	10	7			11				2										
1		3	5	6	9		4	8	10				11			7	2										
	4	3	5	6		9	10	8		11			7				2		1								
	4	3	5	6		9	10	8		11			7				2		1								
		6		5		9	4	10	8			3	7				2	11	1								
	2	3	5			8	4	11	10							7	6		1	9							
	2	3	5	6		9	4	11	10							7			1	8							
	2	3	6	5		9	4	11					10			7			1	8							
	2	3	5	4			6	11	10		1					7				8	9						
	2	3	5	4			6	11			1							7		8	10	9					
	3	4	5			9	6	11	7								2		1	10	8						
	6		3	5		9	4	11	8								2		1	10	7						
		3	5	4	6	9	7	11			1						2			10			8				
		3	5	4	6	9	10	11		7							2		1				8				
		3	5	4		9	6	11		7							2		1	10			8				
	2	3		5	6	9	7	11	4										1	10			8				
		3		5	6	9	4	11			1						2			10	7		8				
	2	4		5	6	9	3	11											1	10			8	7			
		2		5	6		3	11			1									10	9	4	8	7			
		2		5	4	9		11			1		3							7	6		10	8			
	2			5	4		7	11	8		1									10	3		6		9		
	2			4	6	5	3	9			1									8	10		7		11		
	3	4		5	6	8	7	10			1									9	2		11				
		2		5	6								11				4		1	10	7	3	8		9		
	4	2		6	11	5	9				1							8			7			10		3	
		3		5	4	9	2	11	6		1									10	7		8				
		3		5	4	9	2	11	6		1									10	7		8				
		3		5		9	2	11	6		1									10	7	4	8				
		3		5		9	2	11	6		1									10	7	4	8				
		3		5		9	2	11	6		1									10	7	4	8				
		3		5	7	9	2	11	6		1									10		4	8				
12	17	39	21	40	18	35	39	40	26	9	17	3	12	1	3	12	22	9	13	24	17	7	18	4	3	1	
	1			4	2	11	3	3	7	3			1					4		9	2		4		1		

Glazier	Long	Howe	Wood	Stephenson	Holsgrove	Holton	Whitehouse	Kellard	Burridge	Allen	Jackson	Townsend	Werge	Birch	Lucas	Imlach	Sewell	Dowsett	Millington	Smith	Woods	Payne	Burnside	Horobin	Cutler	Fuller	Petchey
	2	3	5	4	6	9	7	11											1	10			8				
		2		5	6	9	3	11	4		1									10			8	7			
	3	2		5	4	9	7	11	6		1												10	8			
		2		5	6	9	3	11											1	10			8	7			4
	2	4	1	4	4	4	4	4	2		2								2	3			4	3			1
			1			5			1											1			2				

Glazier	Long	Howe	Wood	Stephenson	Holsgrove	Holton	Whitehouse	Kellard	Burridge	Allen	Jackson	Townsend	Werge	Birch	Lucas	Imlach	Sewell	Dowsett	Millington	Smith	Woods	Payne	Burnside	Horobin	Cutler	Fuller	Petchey
1	2	3		6		9	4	8	10			5				11		7									
		6		5		8	10	11	9		1	3			4		2	7									
	3	4	2	5		9	6	11			1					7						10			8		
	3	6	8	5		9	4	11	10							7	2		1								
1	3	4	2	4		4	4	4	3		2	2			1	3	2	2	1			1			1		
						1			4																		

League Table

	P	W	D	L	F	A	Pts
Newcastle United	42	24	9	9	81	45	57
Northampton Town	42	20	16	6	66	50	56
Bolton Wanderers	42	20	10	12	80	58	50
Southampton	42	17	14	11	83	63	48
Ipswich Town	42	15	17	10	74	67	47
Norwich City	42	20	7	15	61	57	47
Crystal Palace	42	16	13	13	55	51	45
Huddersfield Town	42	17	10	15	53	51	44
Derby County	42	16	11	15	84	79	43
Coventry City	42	17	9	16	72	70	43
Manchester City	42	16	9	17	63	62	41
Preston North End	42	14	13	15	76	81	41
Cardiff City	42	13	14	15	64	57	40
Rotherham United	42	14	12	16	70	69	40
Plymouth Argyle	42	16	8	18	63	79	40
Bury	42	14	10	18	60	66	38
Middlesbrough	42	13	9	20	70	76	35
Charlton Athletic	42	13	9	20	64	75	35
Leyton Orient	42	12	11	19	50	72	35
Portsmouth	42	12	10	20	56	77	34
Swindon Town	42	14	5	23	63	81	33
Swansea Town	42	11	10	21	62	84	32

1965-66

Division Two

Manager: Dick Graham until 3 January 1966; Arthur Rowe caretaker until April 1966, then Bert Head from 18 April 1966

Did you know that?

Palace manager and former goalkeeper Dick Graham, who had been in charge for the previous three and a half seasons before being dismissed, had a system of making his team use the outfield numbers two to 11 shirts out of playing position to disguise his tactics.

Match No.	Date		Venue	Opponents	Result		Scorers	Attendance
1	Aug	21	A	Birmingham City	L	1-2	Lawson	19,205
2		25	H	Bolton Wanderers	D	1-1	Lawson	20,843
3		28	H	Leyton Orient	W	2-1	Whitehouse, Woods	16,543
4	Sep	1	A	Bolton Wanderers	L	0-3		15,431
5		4	A	Middlesborough	D	2-2	Lawson, Stephenson	10,160
6		8	H	Portsmouth	W	4-1	Kevan, Lawson, Burridge, Kellard	15,744
7		11	H	Huddersfield Town	W	2-1	Kevan, Lawson	16,684
8		15	A	Portsmouth	D	1-1	Woods	18,926
9		18	A	Coventry City	W	1-0	Smith	25,203
10		25	A	Preston North End	L	0-2		12,661
11	Oct	2	H	Charlton Athletic	W	2-0	Woods, Whitehouse	23,144
12		9	H	Bristol City	W	2-1	Kevan, Lawson	16,356
13		16	A	Manchester City	L	1-3	own-goal (Oakes)	24,765
14		23	H	Rotherham United	D	2-2	own-goal (Madden), Smith	15,833
15		30	A	Wolverhampton Wanderers	L	0-1		21,623
16	Nov	6	H	Norwich City	D	0-0		15,906
17		13	A	Bury	D	2-2	Burnside, Yard	7,689
18		20	H	Southampton	W	1-0	Kevan	12,697
19		27	A	Derby County	L	0-4		13,865
20	Dec	4	H	Cardiff City	D	0-0		11,527
21		11	A	Carlisle United	L	1-3	Kevan	9,577
22		18	H	Manchester City	L	0-2		12,847
23		27	H	Ipswich Town	W	3-1	Stephenson 2, Smith	16,064
24	Jan	1	A	Bristol City	D	1-1	Long	16,456
25		8	H	Bury	W	1-0	Kember	13,699
26		15	A	Rotherham United	L	0-3		8,410
27		29	H	Birmingham City	W	1-0	Whitehouse	14,190
28	Feb	5	A	Leyton Orient	W	2-0	Whitehouse, Smith	7,508
29		11	A	Ipswich Town	D	2-2	Whitehouse 2	9,151
30		19	H	Middlesborough	D	1-1	Smith	13,902
31		26	A	Huddersfield Town	D	1-1	Whitehouse	17,250
32	Mar	12	H	Coventry City	L	0-1		15,717
33		19	H	Preston North End	D	1-1	Stephenson	11,786
34		26	A	Charlton Athletic	L	0-1		12,856
35	Apr	2	A	Norwich City	L	1-2	Sewell	11,215
36		8	H	Plymouth Argyle	W	3-1	Burnside, Bannister, Kember	12,026
37		9	H	Wolverhampton Wanderers	L	0-1		14,403
38		11	A	Plymouth Argyle	W	2-1	Yard, Bannister	11,289
39		16	A	Southampton	L	0-1		15,780
40		23	H	Derby County	D	1-1	Burnside	11,923
41		30	A	Cardiff City	L	0-1		9,577
42	May	7	H	Carlisle United	W	2-0	Bannister, Yard	9,413

Final League Position: 11th in Division Two

Appearances
Sub Appearances
2 own-goals Goals

FA Cup

3	Jan	22	A	Carlisle United	L	0-3		13,740

Appearances
Goals

League Cup

2	Sep	22	H	Grimsby Town	L	0-1		13,285

Appearances
Goals

Jackson	Howe	Whitehouse	Woods	Stephenson	Long	Smith	Burnside	Lawson	Kevan	Yard	Sewell	Payne	Kellard	Burridge	Stack	Wood	Millington	Bannister	Smout	Cutler	Kember	Imlach
1	2	3	4	5	6	7	8	9	10	11												
1	2	3	4	5				9	10	11	6	8	7									
1	3	8	7	5		12		**9**	10	4		6		2	11							
1	3	**2**	7	5		8		12	10	9		6			11	4						
1	2		7	5	3		12	9	10	8		6	11			**4**						
1	2		7	5	3		8	9	10			6	11	4								
	2		7	5	3		8	9	10	4			11	6			1					
1			7	5	3		8	9	10		2	6	11	4								
1		2	7	5	3	8	10			4			11			9		6				
1		2	7	5	3		12	9	**10**			4	11	8				6				
1	3	4	7	5	2	10			9			8	11					6				
1	3	8	7	5	**2**			9	10	12		4	11					6				
1	3	6	7	5	2		8	9	10			4	11									
	3		7	5		10	8	9		4	2	6	11				1					
1	3	7		5	2		10	8	9	11		4						6				
1	3			5	4	7	9			8	2	6	11	10								
1	3			5	4	7	8		10	9		6	11					2				
1	2	6	11	5	4		9		10	8	3			7								
1		6	11	5	3	8	9		10	7		2						4				
		4	7	5	3	12	10	8	9	11	2							6	1			
1	3	4	**7**		5	10	8	12	9	11	2							6				
	3	7	8	5	6		9		10	11	2						1	4				
1		6	7	5		8		9	10	11	2	4								3		
1		6	3	5	4	8	12			**11**	2	10								9	7	
1	3	6	7	5	4	10	9				2									11	8	
1	3	6	11	5	4	10	8		9		2										7	
1	3	9		5	4	8	10			**7**	2	6								11	12	
1	3	9		5	4	8	10			7	2							6		11		
1	3	9		5	4	8	10			7	2							6		11		
1	3	9		5	4	10	8			7	2	6										11
1	3	9		5	4	8	12			**7**	2	10						6				11
1	3				4	10	9			7	2	5						6			8	11
1	3			5	4	10	8	9		7	2							6				11
1	3		7	5	4	**8**	10			9	2							6			12	11
1	3		7	5	4	9	10				2	6									8	11
1	3		7	5			10			9	2	4						6			8	11
1	3		7	5	6	12	10			9	2	4									8	**11**
1	3		7	5	4	10	8			11	2	12						6		**9**		
1	3		7	5			9			10	2	6						4			8	11
1	3		7	5			10			9	2	6						4			8	11
1	3		7	5			10			9	2	12				4		**6**			8	11
1	3		7	5						9	2	10				4		6			8	11
38	35	24	32	40	32	23	31	15	21	33	28	27	13	7	2	5	3	22	1	7	11	12
						3	4	2		1		2									2	
			3	4	1	5	3	6	5	3	1		1	1				3			2	

Jackson	Howe	Whitehouse	Woods	Stephenson	Long	Smith	Burnside	Lawson	Kevan	Yard	Sewell	Payne	Kellard	Burridge	Stack	Wood	Millington	Bannister	Smout	Cutler	Kember	Imlach
	3	6	7	5	4	10	8			9	2						1				11	
	1	1	1	1	1	1	1			1	1						1				1	

Jackson	Howe	Whitehouse	Woods	Stephenson	Long	Smith	Burnside	Lawson	Kevan	Yard	Sewell	Payne	Kellard	Burridge	Stack	Wood	Millington	Bannister	Smout	Cutler	Kember	Imlach
1			7	5	3	9	8		10	4			11			2		6				
1			1	1	1	1	1		1	1			1			1		1				

League Table

	P	W	D	L	F	A	Pts
Manchester City	42	22	15	5	76	44	59
Southampton	42	22	10	10	85	56	54
Coventry City	42	20	13	9	73	53	53
Huddersfield Town	42	19	13	10	62	36	51
Bristol City	42	17	17	8	63	48	51
Wolverhampton W	42	20	10	12	87	61	50
Rotherham United	42	16	14	12	75	74	46
Derby County	42	16	11	15	71	68	43
Bolton Wanderers	42	16	9	17	62	59	41
Birmingham City	42	16	9	17	70	75	41
Crystal Palace	42	14	13	15	47	52	41
Portsmouth	42	16	8	18	74	78	40
Norwich City	42	12	15	15	52	52	39
Carlisle United	42	17	5	20	60	63	39
Ipswich Town	42	15	9	18	58	66	39
Charlton Athletic	42	12	14	16	61	70	38
Preston North End	42	11	15	16	62	70	37
Plymouth Argyle	42	12	13	17	54	63	37
Bury	42	14	7	21	62	76	35
Cardiff City	42	12	10	20	71	91	34
Middlesbrough	42	10	13	19	58	86	33
Leyton Orient	42	5	13	24	38	80	23

1966-67

Division Two

Manager: Bert Head

Did you know that?

Palace's popular goalkeeper John Jackson shared his name and position with a counterpart from the 1940s who featured as a guest player for the club during 1940–41 in one game. This first John Jackson later became a pro golfer who competed in the British open of 1950.

Match No.	Date		Venue	Opponents	Result		Scorers	Attendance
1	Aug	20	H	Carlisle United	W	4-2	White 2, Woodruff 2	11,374
2		23	A	Bristol City	W	1-0	Burnside	13,365
3		27	A	Blackburn Rovers	L	1-2	Woodruff	15,015
4		31	H	Bristol City	W	2-1	Woodruff, Kember	16,478
5	Sep	3	H	Bolton Wanderers	W	3-2	Woodruff, Kember, Imlach	16,578
6		7	A	Wolverhampton Wanderers	D	1-1	Kember	18,000
7		10	A	Charlton Athletic	D	1-1	Woodruff	16,986
8		17	H	Derby County	W	2-1	Woodruff, Kember	17,617
9		24	A	Plymouth Argyle	L	0-1		12,865
10	Oct	1	A	Huddersfield Town	W	2-0	Kember, Stephenson	12,609
11		8	H	Northampton Town	W	5-1	Dyson 3, Woodruff 2	18,507
12		15	A	Millwall	D	1-1	Dyson	28,664
13		22	H	Rotherham United	D	1-1	Payne	19,846
14		29	A	Preston North End	L	0-1		13,471
15	Nov	5	H	Bury	W	3-1	Dyson, O'Connell, Kember	12,810
16		12	A	Coventry City	W	2-1	C. Jackson, Kember	23,035
17		19	H	Norwich City	D	0-0		17,114
18		26	A	Birmingham City	L	1-3	C. Jackson	16,820
19	Dec	3	H	Portsmouth	L	0-2		15,700
20		10	A	Hull City	L	1-6	White	21,818
21		17	A	Carlisle United	L	0-3		10,324
22		26	A	Cardiff City	W	2-1	White, Long	17,158
23		27	H	Cardiff City	W	3-1	Dyson 2, Woodruff	13,553
24		31	H	Blackburn Rovers	W	2-1	C. Jackson, Kember	17,703
25	Jan	14	H	Charlton Athletic	W	1-0	White	24,399
26		21	A	Derby County	L	0-2		15,996
27	Feb	4	H	Plymouth Argyle	W	2-1	Woodruff, Bannister	17,695
28		11	H	Huddersfield Town	D	1-1	Woodruff	18,927
29		25	A	Northampton Town	L	0-1		13,081
30	Mar	7	H	Preston North End	W	1-0	O'Connell	19,719
31		11	A	Bolton Wanderers	D	0-0		9,617
32		18	A	Rotherham United	W	1-0	White	7,916
33		25	H	Millwall	L	1-2	Byrne	30,845
34		27	H	Ipswich Town	L	0-2		16,029
35		28	A	Ipswich Town	L	0-2		17,176
36	Apr	1	A	Bury	D	1-1	Kember	7,106
37		8	H	Coventry City	D	1-1	Kember	23,247
38		15	A	Norwich City	L	3-4	Payne, Bannister, Woodruff	13,714
39		22	H	Birmingham City	W	2-1	Woodruff, Dyson	13,064
40		29	A	Portsmouth	D	1-1	Woodruff	13,392
41	May	6	H	Hull City	W	4-1	Woodruff 2, Light 2	11,329
42		13	H	Wolverhampton Wanderers	W	4-1	Woodruff, Bannister, Dyson, Light	26,930

Final League Position: 7th in Division Two

Appearances
Sub appearances
Goals

FA Cup

3	Jan	28	A	Leeds United	L	0-3		37,768

Appearances
Sub appearances
Goals

League Cup

2	Sep	13	A	Fulham	L	0-2		9,906

Appearances
Sub appearances
Goals

Jackson J	Sewell	Howe	Payne	Stephenson	Bannister	Kember	Burnside	White	Woodruff	O'Connell	McCormick	Yard	Imlach	Long	Dyson	Jackson C	Wood	Robertson	Presland	Byrne	Parsons	Light	Brophy	Shaw	Smith
1	2	3	4	5	6	7	8	9	10	11															
1	2	3	4	5	6	7	8	9	10	11															
1	2	3	4	5	6	7	8	9	10		**11**	12													
1	2	3	4	5	6	7	8	9	10				11												
1	2	3	4	5	6	7	8	9	10				11												
1	2	3	4	5	6	8		9	10			7	11												
1	2	3	4	5	6	8		9	10			7	11												
1		2	4	5	3	8			10	7				6	9	11									
1		2	4	5	3	8			10	7				6	9	11									
1			4	5	3	8			10	7				2	9	11	6								
1		12	4	5	6	**8**			10	7				2	9	11	3								
1		2		5	6	8			10	7				3	9	11	4								
1		2	4	5	6	8			10	7					9	11	3								
1		2	9	5	6	8			11					4	10	7	3								
1		2	4	5	3	8			10	7				6	9	11									
1		2	4	5	6	8			10						9	11	3	7							
1		2	4	5	6	8			10					12	9	11	**3**	7							
1		2	4	5	3	8			10		6				9	11		7							
1		2	4	5	3	7		8	10						9	11	6								
1			4	5	6	7		8	10					2	9		3	11							
1	2		4	5	6	8		9	**10**					3		11	12	7							
1	2		4	5	6	8		9	10					3	7	11									
1	2		4	5	6	8		9	10					3	7	11									
1	2		4	5	6	8		9	10					3	7	11									
1	2		4	5	6	8		9	10					3	7	11									
1	2		4	5	6	8		9	10					3	7	11									
1	2		8	5	6	10			9					3	7	11			4						
1			4	5	6	8			10	7				3	9	11			2						
1	2			5	6	8			10	11				3	7				4	9					
1			4	5	6	7		9	10	11				3					2	8					
1			4	5	6	7		9	10	11				3					2	8					
1	3		4	5	6	7		9	10	11									2	8					
1	3		4	5	6	7		9	10	11									2	8					
1	3		4	5	6	**8**			10					12	7	11			2	9					
1	2		10	5	6				7	11				4	9				3	8					
1	2		4	5	6	**8**			7	11				12	9				3	10					
1	2		4	5	6	8			7	11				12	**9**				3	10					
1	2		4	5	6	8			7	11					9				3	10					
	2		4	5	6	**8**			7	11				12	9				3	10	1				
	2		4	5	6	8			7						9	11			3	10	1				
	2		4	5	6				8	12					9	11			3	10	1	**7**			
	2		4	5	6				10						9	11			3	**8**	1	7	12		
38	26	17	40	42	42	39	5	19	42	20	2	2	4	20	30	24	9	5	16	14	4	2			
		1								1		1		5			1						1		
			2	1	3	10	1	6	18	2			1	1	9	3				1		3			

Jackson J	Sewell	Howe	Payne	Stephenson	Bannister	Kember	Burnside	White	Woodruff	O'Connell	McCormick	Yard	Imlach	Long	Dyson	Jackson C	Wood	Robertson	Presland	Byrne	Parsons	Light	Brophy	Shaw	Smith
1	**2**		8	5	6	10			9					3	7	11			4					12	
1	1		1	1	1	1			1					1	1	1			1						
																								1	

Jackson J	Sewell	Howe	Payne	Stephenson	Bannister	Kember	Burnside	White	Woodruff	O'Connell	McCormick	Yard	Imlach	Long	Dyson	Jackson C	Wood	Robertson	Presland	Byrne	Parsons	Light	Brophy	Shaw	Smith
1	**2**	3	4	5	6	8			10	11	9	12													7
1	1	1	1	1	1	1			1	1	1														1
												1													

League Table

	P	W	D	L	F	A	Pts
Coventry City	42	23	13	6	74	43	59
Wolverhampton W	42	25	8	9	88	48	58
Carlisle United	42	23	6	13	71	54	52
Blackburn Rovers	42	19	13	10	56	46	51
Ipswich Town	42	17	16	9	70	54	50
Huddersfield Town	42	20	9	13	58	46	49
Crystal Palace	42	19	10	13	61	55	48
Millwall	42	18	9	15	49	58	45
Bolton Wanderers	42	14	14	14	64	58	42
Birmingham City	42	16	8	18	70	66	40
Norwich City	42	13	14	15	49	55	40
Hull City	42	16	7	19	77	72	39
Preston North End	42	16	7	19	65	67	39
Portsmouth	42	13	13	16	59	70	39
Bristol City	42	12	14	16	56	62	38
Plymouth Argyle	42	14	9	19	59	58	37
Derby County	42	12	12	18	68	72	36
Rotherham United	42	13	10	19	61	70	36
Charlton Athletic	42	13	9	20	49	53	35
Cardiff City	42	12	9	21	61	87	33
Northampton Town	42	12	6	24	47	84	30
Bury	42	11	6	25	49	83	28

1967-68

Division Two

Manager: Bert Head

Did you know that?

Steve Kember has held multiple roles at Palace. As well as playing in two spells for the club, he has also been manager, assistant manager, reserve-team manager and chief scout.

Match No.	Date		Venue	Opponents	Result		Scorers	Attendance
1	Aug	19	A	Rotherham United	W	3-0	Woodruff, Payne, White	7,661
2		26	H	Derby County	W	1-0	Woodruff	17,875
3		30	A	Cardiff City	L	2-4	Byrne (pen), C. Jackson	14,780
4	Sep	2	A	Preston North End	D	0-0		13,313
5		6	H	Plymouth Argyle	W	5-0	Woodruff 2, Payne, Byrne, Kember	16,372
6		9	H	Charlton Athletic	W	3-0	Byrne, Woodruff 2	23,181
7		16	A	Hull City	D	1-1	Light	15,993
8		23	A	Aston Villa	W	1-0	Woodruff (pen)	12,484
9		27	H	Cardiff City	W	2-1	Kember, Woodruff	20,424
10		30	H	Queen's Park Rangers	W	1-0	Long	38,006
11	Oct	7	H	Bristol City	W	2-0	Kember, Woodruff	19,938
12		14	A	Blackpool	L	0-2		20,905
13		23	H	Blackburn Rovers	W	1-0	Byrne (pen)	23,771
14		28	A	Carlisle United	L	0-3		11,399
15	Nov	11	A	Huddersfield Town	D	1-1	White	11,055
16		18	H	Millwall	D	2-2	White 2	30,304
17		25	A	Birmingham City	L	0-1		27,538
18	Dec	2	H	Bolton Wanderers	L	0-3		15,780
19		9	A	Middlesbrough	L	0-3		16,651
20		16	H	Rotherham United	W	1-0	White	13,541
21		23	A	Derby County	D	1-1	White	20,224
22		26	H	Portsmouth	D	2-2	Kember, Woodruff	23,122
23		30	A	Portsmouth	D	2-2	Stephenson, Tomkins	28,379
24	Jan	20	H	Hull City	L	0-1		15,431
25	Feb	3	H	Aston Villa	L	0-1		10,214
26		10	A	Queen's Park Rangers	L	1-2	Tomkins	18,954
27		24	A	Bristol City	L	1-2	Woodruff	13,082
28	Mar	2	H	Blackpool	W	3-1	White, Kember, Lazarus	11,860
29		5	A	Charlton Athletic	W	1-0	McCormick	20,201
30		16	A	Blackburn Rovers	L	1-2	C. Jackson	10,204
31		23	H	Carlisle United	D	1-1	Lazarus	9,149
32		30	A	Ipswich Town	D	2-2	Kember, C. Jackson	24,889
33	Apr	6	H	Huddersfield Town	L	0-1		10,929
34		13	A	Millwall	L	1-5	Woodruff	14,782
35		15	A	Norwich City	L	1-2	Woodruff	16,343
36		16	H	Norwich City	W	6-0	Woodruff 2, Light, Lazarus, Vansittart 2	7,745
37		20	H	Birmingham City	D	0-0		14,949
38		27	A	Bolton Wanderers	D	2-2	Woodruff 2	6,600
39	May	1	H	Ipswich Town	L	1-3	Woodruff	19,999
40		4	H	Middlesbrough	L	1-3	Lazarus	9,669
41		11	A	Plymouth Argyle	L	1-2	Lazarus	4,768
42		15	H	Preston North End	W	2-0	Kember, C. Jackson	7,357

Final League Position: 11th in Division Two

Appearances
Sub appearances
Goals

FA Cup

Round	Date		Venue	Opponents	Result		Scorers	Attendance
3	Jan	27	A	Walsall	D	1-1	White	15,333
R		31	H	Walsall	L	1-2	Byrne	27,414

Appearances
Sub appearances
Goals

League Cup

Round	Date		Venue	Opponents	Result		Scorers	Attendance
2	Sep	13	A	Barrow	L	0-1		7,908

Appearances
Sub appearances
Goals

Jackson J	Sewell	Presland	Payne	Stephenson	Bannister	Kember	Byrne	White	Woodruff	Jackson C	Long	Light	McCormick	Dyson	Lazarus	Tomkins	Dawkins	Vansittart	Hoadley	Oliver	Cook
1	**2**	3	4	5	6	7	8	9	10	11	12										
1	2	3	4	5	6	7	9	10	8	11											
1	2	3	4	5	6	7	8	9	10	11											
1	2	3	4	5	6	7	9		10	11	8										
1	2	3	4	**5**	6	8	9		10	11	12	7									
1	2	3	4		6	8	9		10	11		7	5								
1		3	4		6	8	9		10	11	2	7	5								
1		3	4		6	8		12	10	11	2	**7**	5	9							
1		3	4		6	8		12	10	11	2	7	5	**9**							
1	2	3	4		6	8		9	10		11	7	5								
1	2	3	4		6	8		9	10	**11**	12	7	5								
1	2	3	4		6	8	9		10	11	12	**7**	5								
1	2	3	4		6	8	9		10	11		7	5								
1	**2**	3	7	4	6	8	9		10	12	11		5								
1		3	4	5	6	8	9	7	10	11	2										
1		3	4	5	6	8	9	7	10	11	2										
1		3	4	5	6	8		7	10	11	2			9							
1		3	4	5	6	8	9	7	10	**11**	2			12							
1		3	4	5	6	8	9	7	10	11	2										
1	2	3	4	5	6	8	10	9	11						7						
1		2	4	5	6	8	10	9	11				3		7						
1		2	4	5	6	10	8	9	11	12			**3**		7						
1		3	4	5	6	10		9	8		2				7	11					
1	2	3		5	6	8	10	9	11						**7**	12	4				
1	2	3		4	6	8	9		10	7			5			11					
1	2	3		4	6	8	9		10		12		5		**7**	11					
1	2		4	5	3	8		9	10				6		7	11					
1	2	3	4	5	12	8		9	10				**6**		7	11					
1	2	3	4		6	8	11	9	10				5		7						
1	2	3	4		6	8	9		10	7		12	**5**			11					
1	2	3	4		6	8			9	11					7	10		5			
1	2	3	4		6	8			9	12	11				7	**10**		5			
1	2	3	4		6	8			9	12			5		7	**10**		11			
1	2	3	4		6	8			9		11		5		7	10					
1	2	3	4		6	8			9				5		7	11		10			
1	2	3	4		**6**	8			9	12		11	5		7			10			
1	2	3	4		6	8			9			11	5		7	12		**10**			
1	2		4		6	8			9			11	5		7	**10**			12	3	
1	2	3	4		6	8			9			11	5		7			**10**	12		
1	2	6	4			8			9			11	5		7					3	10
1	2	3	4		6				9		11	8	5		7	10					
1	2	3	4		6	8			9	10		11	5		7						
42	31	40	39	20	40	41	22	18	42	22	14	16	27	3	21	13	1	7		2	1
					1			2		5	5	1		1		2			2		
			2	1		7	4	7	18	4	1	2	1		5	2		2			

Jackson J	Sewell	Presland	Payne	Stephenson	Bannister	Kember	Byrne	White	Woodruff	Jackson C	Long	Light	McCormick	Dyson	Lazarus	Tomkins	Dawkins	Vansittart	Hoadley	Oliver	Cook
1		3	4	5	6	8	10	9	**11**		2	7					12				
1		3	**4**	5	6	8	9				2	10			7	11	12				
2		2	2	2	2	2	2	1	1		2	2			1	1					
																	2				
							1	1													

Jackson J	Sewell	Presland	Payne	Stephenson	Bannister	Kember	Byrne	White	Woodruff	Jackson C	Long	Light	McCormick	Dyson	Lazarus	Tomkins	Dawkins	Vansittart	Hoadley	Oliver	Cook
1	2	3	4		6	8	9		10	11	**7**	12	5								
1	1	1	1		1	1	1		1	1	1		1								
												1									

League Table

	P	W	D	L	F	A	Pts
Ipswich Town	42	22	15	5	79	44	59
Queen's Park Rangers	42	25	8	9	67	36	58
Blackpool	42	24	10	8	71	43	58
Birmingham City	42	19	14	9	83	51	52
Portsmouth	42	18	13	11	68	55	49
Middlesbrough	42	17	12	13	60	54	46
Millwall	42	14	17	11	62	50	45
Blackburn Rovers	42	16	11	15	56	49	43
Norwich City	42	16	11	15	60	65	43
Carlisle United	42	14	13	15	58	52	41
Crystal Palace	42	14	11	17	56	56	39
Bolton Wanderers	42	13	13	16	60	63	39
Cardiff City	42	13	12	17	60	66	38
Huddersfield Town	42	13	12	17	46	61	38
Charlton Athletic	42	12	13	17	63	68	37
Aston Villa	42	15	7	20	54	64	37
Hull City	42	12	13	17	58	73	37
Derby County	42	13	10	19	71	78	36
Bristol City	42	13	10	19	48	62	36
Preston North End	42	12	11	19	43	65	35
Rotherham United	42	10	11	21	42	76	31
Plymouth Argyle	42	9	9	24	38	72	27

1968-69

Division Two

Manager: Bert Head

Did you know that?

Finishing second, Palace were promoted to Division One and the top flight for the first time in their history. Between February and the end of the season they went on a 16-game unbeaten run.

Official Programme

Match No.	Date		Venue	Opponents	Result		Scorers	Attendance
1	Aug	10	A	Cardiff City	W	4-0	Payne, C. Jackson 2, Blyth	16,359
2		14	H	Huddersfield Town	W	2-1	Lazarus 2	16,620
3		17	H	Birmingham City	W	3-2	C. Jackson 2, Payne	17,679
4		20	A	Middlesbrough	L	0-4		21,622
5		24	A	Bury	L	1-2	Blyth	7,811
6		28	H	Norwich City	W	2-0	C. Taylor, Woodruff	12,857
7		31	H	Charlton Athletic	D	3-3	C. Taylor, Blyth, C. Jackson	22,991
8	Sep	7	H	Carlisle United	W	5-0	C. Taylor 2, Kember 2, Lazarus	15,170
9		13	A	Fulham	L	0-1		23,132
10		21	H	Preston North End	L	1-2	C. Jackson	13,577
11		28	A	Portsmouth	D	3-3	C. Jackson, Kember, Woodruff	18,998
12	Oct	5	H	Sheffield United	D	1-1	Woodruff	16,978
13		9	A	Norwich City	W	1-0	Lazarus	18,993
14		12	A	Aston Villa	D	1-1	Bannister	15,887
15		19	H	Bristol City	W	2-1	Lazarus, Woodruff	15,033
16		26	A	Blackpool	L	0-3		15,224
17	Nov	2	H	Bolton Wanderers	W	2-1	C. Jackson, Payne	13,027
18		9	A	Oxford United	W	2-0	Kember, Woodruff	10,444
19		16	H	Blackburn Rovers	W	1-0	C. Jackson	13,505
20		23	A	Millwall	W	2-0	Woodruff, Lazarus	27,913
21		30	H	Derby County	L	1-2	McCormick	20,751
22	Dec	7	A	Hull City	L	0-2		13,785
23		14	H	Aston Villa	W	4-2	C. Taylor 2, Hoy, A. Taylor	11,071
24		26	A	Sheffield United	D	1-1	C. Jackson	21,682
25	Jan	11	A	Bolton Wanderers	D	2-2	Lazarus, Dawkins	9,082
26		25	H	Blackpool	L	1-2	Kember	17,003
27	Feb	22	H	Hull City	W	2-0	Lazarus, McCormick	14,172
28		25	A	Bristol City	D	1-1	Woodruff	14,695
29	Mar	1	H	Cardiff City	W	3-1	A. Taylor, Hoy, C. Taylor	19,663
30		5	A	Derby County	W	1-0	Woodruff	31,748
31		8	A	Birmingham City	W	1-0	Kember	25,298
32		15	H	Bury	W	1-0	Woodruff	19,439
33		19	H	Millwall	W	4-2	Woodruff 2, C. Taylor, McCormick	32,516
34		22	A	Charlton Athletic	D	1-1	Hoy	32,768
35		26	H	Oxford United	D	1-1	C. Jackson	20,158
36		29	A	Carlisle United	W	2-1	Lazarus, own-goal (Marsland)	8,172
37	Apr	4	H	Middlesbrough	D	0-0		43,381
38		5	H	Portsmouth	W	3-1	Sewell (pen), Kember, C. Jackson	24,830
39		8	A	Huddersfield Town	D	0-0		12,113
40		12	A	Preston North End	D	0-0		10,245
41		19	H	Fulham	W	3-2	Lazarus, C. Jackson, Kember	36,126
42		28	A	Blackburn Rovers	W	2-1	C. Jackson, Lazarus	4,777

Final League Position: 2nd in Division Two

Appearances
Sub appearances
1 own-goal Goals

FA Cup

3	Jan	4	A	Charlton Athletic	D	0-0		32,334
R		8	H	Charlton Athletic	L	0-2		39,404

Appearances
Sub appearances
Goals

League Cup

2	Sep	4	H	Preston North End	W	3-1	C. Jackson 2, Payne	12,574
3		24	A	Orient	W	1-0	C. Taylor	13,617
4	Oct	16	H	Leeds United	W	2-1	C. Jackson, C. Taylor	26,217
5		30	A	Burnley	L	0-2		17,895

Appearances
Sub appearances
Goals

Jackson J	Sewell	Presland	Payne	McCormick	Bannister	Lazarus	Kember	Jackson C	Blyth	Taylor C	Woodruff	Hoadley	Long	Dawkins	Hoy	Loughlan	Taylor A	Snowdon
1	2	3	4	5	6	7	8	9	10	11								
1	2	3	4	5	6	7	8	9	10	11								
1	2	3	4	5	6	7	8	9	10	11								
1	2	3	4	5	6	7	8	9	10	11								
1	2	3	4	5	6	7	8	9	10		11							
1	2		4	5	3	7	8	9	6	11	10							
1	2		4	5	3	7	8	9	6	11	10							
1	2		4	5	3	7	8	9	6	11	10							
1	2		4	5	3	7	8	9	6		10	11						
1	2		4	5	3	7	8	9	10	11			6					
1			4	5	3		8	9	6	11	10		2	7				
1			4	5	12		**8**	9	6	11	10			7	2	3		
1			**4**	5	12	7	8	9	6	11	10				2	3		
1				5	4	7	8	9	6	11	10				2	3		
1	12			5	4	7	8	9	**6**	11	10				2	3		
1			4	5		7	8	9	6	11	10				2	3		
1	2		4	5		7	8	9		11	10				6	3		
1	2		4	5		7	8	9			10				6	3	11	
1	2		4	5		7	8	9			10				6	3	11	
1	2		**4**	5		7	8	9	12		10				6	3	11	
1	2			5		7	8	9	6		10				4	3	11	
1	2			5		**7**	8	9	6	12	10				4	3	11	
1	2			5			8	9	6	11	10				4	3	7	
1			2	5		7	8	9	6	11	10					3	4	
1	2		4	5		7	8	9	6					10		3	11	
1	2		4	5		7	8	9			10				6	3	11	
1	2		4	5		7	8	9		11					6	3	10	
1	2			5		7	8		6	12	9			**10**	4	3	11	
1	2			5		7	8		6	11	9				4	3	10	
1	2			5		7	8		6	11	9				4	3	10	
1	2			5		7	8		6	11	9				4	3	10	
1	2			5		7	8		6	11	9				4	3	10	
1	2			5		7	8		6	11	9				4	3	10	
1	2			5		7	8		6	11	9				**4**	3	10	12
1	2		3	5		7	8	4	6	11	**9**						10	12
1	2		4	5		7	8	9	6	11							10	3
1	2		4	5		7	8	9		11					6	3	10	
1	2		4	5		7	8	9		11					6	3	**10**	12
1	2		4	5		7	8	9		11					6	3	10	
1	2		4	5		7	8	9		11					6	3	10	
1	2		4	5		7	8	9		11					6	3	10	
1	2		4	5		7	8	9	6	**11**						3	10	12
42	35	5	30	42	13	38	42	34	31	32	30	1	2	4	26	29	25	1
	1				2				1	2								4
	1		3	3	1	11	8	14	3	8	11			1	3		2	

Jackson J	Sewell	Presland	Payne	McCormick	Bannister	Lazarus	Kember	Jackson C	Blyth	Taylor C	Woodruff	Hoadley	Long	Dawkins	Hoy	Loughlan	Taylor A	Snowdon
1	2		4	5		7	8	9		11	10				6	3		
1	2		4	5		**7**	8	9	6	11	10					3	12	
2	2		2	2		2	2	2	1	2	2				1	2		
																	1	

Jackson J	Sewell	Presland	Payne	McCormick	Bannister	Lazarus	Kember	Jackson C	Blyth	Taylor C	Woodruff	Hoadley	Long	Dawkins	Hoy	Loughlan	Taylor A	Snowdon
1	2		4	5	3	7	8	9	6	11	10							
1	2		4	5	3		8	9	6	11	10			7				
1				5	4	7	8	9	6	11	10				2	3		
1	2		4	5		7	8	**9**	6	11	12				10	3		
4	3		3	4	3	3	4	4	4	4	3			1	2	2		
											1							
			1					3		2								

League Table

	P	W	D	L	F	A	Pts
Derby County	42	26	11	5	65	32	63
Crystal Palace	42	22	12	8	70	47	56
Charlton Athletic	42	18	14	10	61	52	50
Middlesbrough	42	19	11	12	58	49	49
Cardiff City	42	20	7	15	67	54	47
Huddersfield Town	42	17	12	13	53	46	46
Birmingham City	42	18	8	16	73	59	44
Blackpool	42	14	15	13	51	41	43
Sheffield United	42	16	11	15	61	50	43
Millwall	42	17	9	16	57	49	43
Hull City	42	13	16	13	59	52	42
Carlisle United	42	16	10	16	46	49	42
Norwich City	42	15	10	17	53	56	40
Preston North End	42	12	15	15	38	44	39
Portsmouth	42	12	14	16	58	58	38
Bristol City	42	11	16	15	46	53	38
Bolton Wanderers	42	12	14	16	55	67	38
Aston Villa	42	12	14	16	37	48	38
Blackburn Rovers	42	13	11	18	52	63	37
Oxford United	42	12	9	21	34	55	33
Bury	42	11	8	23	51	80	30
Fulham	42	7	11	24	40	81	25

1969-70

Division One

Manager: Bert Head

Did you know that?

Featured on *Match of the Day*, Palace's first-ever fixture in the top division, against Manchester United, was played in front of a then record crowd at Selhurst Park, 48,610. Mel Blyth scored the first-ever Palace goal in Division One.

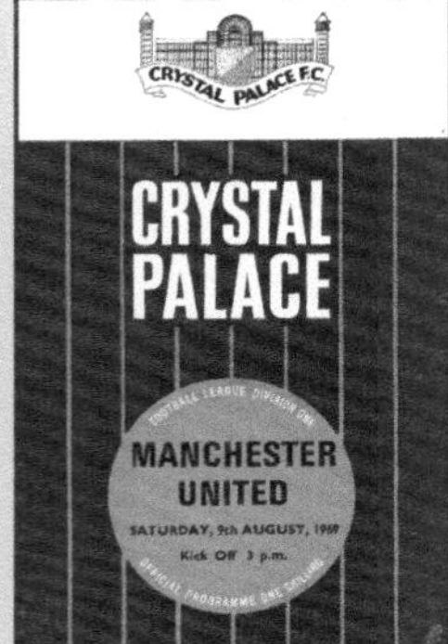

Match No.	Date	Venue	Opponents	Result		Scorers	Attendance
1	Aug 9	H	Manchester United	D	2-2	Blyth, Queen	*48,610
2	13	H	Sunderland	W	2-0	Taylor, C. Jackson	28,897
3	16	A	Everton	L	1-2	Blyth	50,700
4	20	A	Sunderland	D	0-0		16,192
5	23	H	Tottenham Hotspur	L	0-2		39,494
6	27	H	Liverpool	L	1-3	Sewell	36,639
7	30	A	Chelsea	D	1-1	Hoy	41,908
8	Sep 6	H	Stoke City	W	3-1	Bartram, Lazarus, Woodruff	26,745
9	13	A	Coventry City	D	2-2	Queen 2	29,314
10	20	H	West Bromwich Allbion	L	1-3	C. Jackson	27,682
11	27	A	Nottingham Forest	D	0-0		23,250
12	Oct 4	H	Newcastle United	L	0-3		28,407
13	8	H	Everton	D	0-0		33,967
14	11	A	Burnley	L	2-4	Kember, Queen	12,640
15	18	H	Leeds United	D	1-1	Queen	31,910
16	25	A	Sheffield Wednesday	D	0-0		19,162
17	Nov 1	H	Arsenal	L	1-5	Bartram	34,903
18	8	A	West Ham United	L	1-2	own-goal (Bonds)	31,515
19	15	A	Ipswich Town	L	0-2		18,041
20	22	H	Wolverhampton Wanderers	W	2-1	Dawkins 2	23,585
21	29	A	Southampton	D	1-1	Kember	19,876
22	Dec 6	H	Derby County	L	0-1		20,833
23	13	H	Coventry City	L	0-3		16,763
24	20	A	Stoke City	L	0-1		12,426
25	26	A	Tottenham Hotspur	L	0-2		32,845
26	27	H	Chelsea	L	1-5	Queen	*49,498
27	Jan 10	A	West Bromwich Albion	L	2-3	Queen, C. Jackson	20,907
28	17	H	Nottingham Forest	D	1-1	Payne	22,531
29	31	A	Newcastle United	D	0-0		35,440
30	Feb 11	H	Burnley	L	1-2	Queen	20,857
31	14	A	Manchester United	D	1-1	Sewell	55,262
32	21	H	Sheffield Wednesday	L	0-2		25,723
33	28	A	Leeds United	L	0-2		37,138
34	Mar 11	A	Manchester City	W	1-0	Queen	25,381
35	14	H	Southampton	W	2-0	C. Jackson, Hoy	20,867
36	18	A	Wolverhampton Wanderers	D	1-1	Kember	20,594
37	21	A	Derby County	L	1-3	C. Jackson	30,192
38	24	H	West Ham United	D	0-0		34,801
39	28	H	Ipswich Town	D	1-1	McCormick	27,499
40	30	A	Arsenal	L	0-2		34,244
41	Apr 3	A	Liverpool	L	0-3		30,999
42	6	H	Manchester City	W	1-0	Hoy	27,704

Final League Position: 20th in Division One — Appearances

*Ground attendance record (broken twice) — Sub appearances

1 own-goal — Goals

FA Cup

Round	Date	Venue	Opponents	Result		Scorers	Attendance
3	Jan 3	H	Walsall	W	2-0	own-goal (Gregg), Blyth	17,015
4	24	A	Tottenham Hotspur	D	0-0		43,949
R	28	H	Tottenham Hotspur	W	1-0	Queen	45,980
5	Feb 7	H	Chelsea	L	1-4	Hoy	48,479

Appearances

Sub appearances

1 own-goal — Goals

League Cup

Round	Date	Venue	Opponents	Result		Scorers	Attendance
2	Sep 3	H	Cardiff City	W	3-1	Sewell 2 (2 pens), Bartram	18,616
3	24	H	Blackpool	D	2-2	own-goal (James), Queen	17,990
R	Oct 1	A	Blackpool	W	1-0	Hoadley	13,973
4	15	H	Derby County	D	1-1	C. Jackson	30,539
R	29	A	Derby County	L	0-3		33,059

Appearances

Sub appearances

1 own-goal — Goals

Jackson J	Sewell	Loughlan	Hoy	McCormick	Hynd	Lazarus	Kember	Jackson C	Queen	Blyth	Taylor A	Woodruff	Bartram	Hoadley	Payne	Oliver	Dawkins	Tomkins	Vansittart	Pinkney	Thorup	Tambling	Scott
1	2	3	4	5	6	7	8	9	10	11													
1	2	3	4	5	6		8	9	**10**	11	7	12											
1	2	3	4	5	6		8	9	**10**	11	7	12											
1	2	3	4	5	6		8	**9**		11	7	10	12										
1	2	3	4	5	6		8			11	7	**10**	9	12									
1	2	3	4	5	6		8			11	7	10	9										
1	2	**3**	4	5	6		8			11	7	10	9	12									
1	2		4	5		7	8		12	6	11	**10**	9	3									
1	2	3	4	5	6	**7**	8	9	10		11			12									
1	2	3		5	6	7	8	9	10	**4**	11			12									
1	2	3	4	5			7	9	10	6	12		**8**	11									
1	2	3	4	5	6		8	9	10	11				7									
1	**2**	3	4	5	6		7	9	10	12	11		8										
1		3		5	6		7	9	10		11	8		2	4								
1		3		5	6		7	**9**	10		11	8	12	4	2								
1		2	10	5	6		7		9		11				4	3	8						
1		2		5	6		7		10		8	9	11	3	4								
1		2	9	5	6		7		10	3	8				4		11						
1	2			5	3		7	10	9	6		8			4		11						
1	2		8	5	6		7		9					3	4		10	11					
1	2		8	5	6		7		9					3	4		10	11					
1	2	3		5	6		7		9					8	4		10	11					
1	2			5	6		8		10	11			**9**	3	4		7		12				
1	2		**10**	5	6		7		8	12				3	4			11	9				
1	2			5	6		8		10	4				3			7	**9**	11	12			
1	2	3		5	6				10	8				**4**			7		11	9	12		
1	2	3		5	6			9	10	11	7				4							8	
1	2	3	8	5	6			9	10		11				4							7	
1	2	3	8		**9**			12	10	6	7			5	4							11	
1	2	3	8	5	9				10	6	11				4								7
1	2	3		5	12			9	10	6	11			8	4								**7**
1	2	3		5			**8**	9	10	6	11			12	4								7
1	2	3		5	6			9	10	8	11				4								7
1	2		8	5			7		10	6	11			3	4								9
1	2		7	5			8	9	10	6	11			3	4								
1	2		9	5			8		10	6	11			3	4								7
1	2		9	5			8	11	10	6				3	4								7
1	2		9	5			8		10	6	11			3	4								7
1	2		10	5			8		9	6	11			3	4								7
1	2		9	5			8		10	6	11			3	4								7
1	2			5			8		9	6	11			3	4		10						7
1	2		9	5			8	11	10	6	7			3	4								
42	37	26	28	41	29	4	35	20	37	31	30	9	8	24	27	1	10	5	3	1		3	11
					1			1	1	2	2	2	2	5					1	1	1		
	2		3	1		1	3	5	9	2	1	1	2		1		2						

Jackson J	Sewell	Loughlan	Hoy	McCormick	Hynd	Lazarus	Kember	Jackson C	Queen	Blyth	Taylor A	Woodruff	Bartram	Hoadley	Payne	Oliver	Dawkins	Tomkins	Vansittart	Pinkney	Thorup	Tambling	Scott
1	2	3		5	6				10	12				8	4		**9**		11	7			
1	2	3	**8**	5	9			11	10	6	7			12	4								
1	2	3	8	**5**	9			11	10	6	7			12	4								
1	2	3	11	5	9				10	6	7			8	4								
4	4	4	3	4	4			2	4	3	3			2	4		1		1	1			
										1				2									
			1						1	1													

Jackson J	Sewell	Loughlan	Hoy	McCormick	Hynd	Lazarus	Kember	Jackson C	Queen	Blyth	Taylor A	Woodruff	Bartram	Hoadley	Payne	Oliver	Dawkins	Tomkins	Vansittart	Pinkney	Thorup	Tambling	Scott
1	2		4	5	6		8			11	7	10	9	3									
1	2	3		5		11	7	**9**	10	6		8	12	4									
1	2	3	4	5	6		7	9	10	11	12			**8**									
1		3		5	6		7	9	10		11	8		4	2								
1		2		5	6		7	12	10		8	**9**		3	4		11						
5	3	4	2	5	4	1	5	3	4	3	3	4	1	5	2		1						
								1			1		1										
	2							1	1				1	1									

League Table

	P	W	D	L	F	A	Pts
Everton	42	29	8	5	72	34	66
Leeds United	42	21	15	6	84	49	57
Chelsea	42	21	13	8	70	50	55
Derby County	42	22	9	11	64	37	53
Liverpool	42	20	11	11	65	42	51
Coventry City	42	19	11	12	58	48	49
Newcastle United	42	17	13	12	57	35	47
Manchester United	42	14	17	11	66	61	45
Stoke City	42	15	15	12	56	52	45
Manchester City	42	16	11	15	55	48	43
Tottenham Hotspur	42	17	9	16	54	55	43
Arsenal	42	12	18	12	51	49	42
Wolverhampton W	42	12	16	14	55	57	40
Burnley	42	12	15	15	56	61	39
Nottingham Forest	42	10	18	14	50	71	38
West Bromwich Albion	42	14	9	19	58	66	37
West Ham United	42	12	12	18	51	60	36
Ipswich Town	42	10	11	21	40	63	31
Southampton	42	6	17	19	46	67	29
Crystal Palace	42	6	15	21	34	68	27
Sunderland	42	6	14	22	30	68	26
Sheffield Wednesday	42	8	9	25	40	71	25

1970-71

Division One

Manager: Bert Head

Did you know that?

Gerry Queen's son Warren had a stint at Palace in the reserves during the late 1990s. A striker who featured in a Surrey Cup Final for the Eagles, he left after a season to play abroad in America.

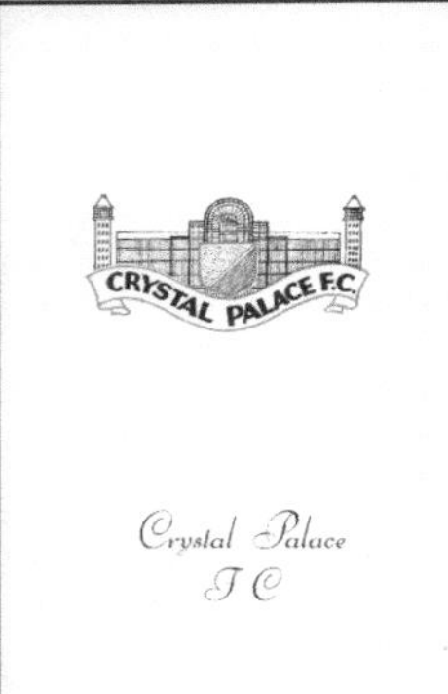

Match No.	Date		Venue	Opponents	Result		Scorers	Attendance
1	Aug	15	A	West Bromwich Albion	D	0-0		24,766
2		19	H	Manchester City	L	0-1		35,118
3		22	H	Newcastle United	W	1-0	Birchenall	27,287
4		25	A	Liverpool	D	1-1	Queen	47,612
5		29	A	Stoke City	D	0-0		13,469
6	Sep	2	H	Blackpool	W	1-0	Queen	26,296
7		5	H	Nottingham Forest	W	2-0	Scott, Queen	26,510
8		12	A	Huddersfield Town	W	2-0	Kember, Queen	18,820
9		19	H	Tottenham Hotspur	L	0-3		41,308
10		26	A	Everton	L	1-3	Scott	43,463
11	Oct	3	H	Southampton	W	3-1	Queen 2, Birchenall	26,663
12		10	A	Manchester United	W	1-0	Tambling	42,979
13		17	H	West Bromwich Albion	W	3-0	Tambling 2, Birchenall	28,330
14		24	H	West Ham United	D	1-1	Taylor	41,486
15		31	A	Burnley	L	1-2	Taylor	12,848
16	Nov	7	H	Leeds United	D	1-1	Sewell	37,963
17		14	A	Arsenal	D	1-1	Birchenall	34,503
18		21	A	Coventry City	L	1-2	Kember	23,054
19		28	H	Wolverhampton Wanderers	D	1-1	Scott	22,605
20	Dec	5	A	Ipswich Town	W	2-1	Sewell (pen), Kember	19,344
21		12	H	Derby County	D	0-0		24,418
22		19	A	Newcastle United	L	0-2		21,740
23	Jan	9	A	Manchester City	L	0-1		27,240
24		13	H	Chelsea	D	0-0		40,489
25		16	H	Liverpool	W	1-0	Queen	28,253
26		30	A	Wolverhampton Wanderers	L	1-2	Birchenall	20,233
27	Feb	6	H	Ipswich Town	W	1-0	Wall	23,482
28		17	A	Derby County	L	0-1		25,521
29		20	H	Coventry City	L	1-2	Birchenall	24,114
30		27	H	Burnley	L	0-2		20,436
31	Mar	6	A	West Ham United	D	0-0		26,157
32		13	H	Arsenal	L	0-2		35,022
33		20	A	Leeds United	L	1-2	Birchenall	31,871
34		24	H	Huddersfield Town	L	0-3		16,646
35		27	A	Nottingham Forest	L	1-3	Birchenall	16,507
36	Apr	3	H	Stoke City	W	3-2	Kember, Birchenall, Wharton	16,693
37		10	A	Chelsea	D	1-1	Scott	38,953
38		17	H	Manchester United	L	3-5	Birchenall, Tambling, Queen	39,145
39		24	A	Tottenham Hotspur	L	0-2		28,619
40		26	A	Blackpool	L	1-3	Queen	8,905
41	May	1	H	Everton	W	2-0	Hoadley, Kember	21,590
42		4	A	Southampton	L	0-6		15,980

Final League Position: 18th in Division One

Appearances
Sub Appearances
Goals

FA Cup

3	Jan	2	H	Chelsea	D	2-2	McCormick, Birchenall	42,123
R		6	A	Chelsea	L	0-2		55,074

Appearances
Sub Appearances
Goals

League Cup

2	Sep	9	H	Rochdale	D	3-3	Birchenall, Jenkins (og), Payne	16,265
R		14	A	Rochdale	W	3-1	Queen, Scott, Taylor	8,911
3	Oct	7	H	Lincoln City	W	4-0	Blyth 2, Tambling, Birchenall	16,988
4		28	H	Arsenal	D	0-0		40,451
R	Nov	9	A	Arsenal	W	2-0	Queen, Tambling (pen)	45,026
5		18	A	Manchester United	L	2-4	Queen, Taylor	43,241

Appearances
Sub Appearances
Goals

Jackson	Sewell	Wall	Payne	McCormick	Blyth	Scott	Kember	Queen	Birchenall	Tambling	Taylor A	Hoadley	Humphries	Proven	Dawkins	Loughlan	Wharton	Pinkney
1	2	3	4	5	6	7	8	9	10	11								
1	2	3	4	5	6	7	8	9	10	11								
1	2	3	4	5	6		8	9	10	11	7							
1	2	3		5	6		8	9	10	11	**7**	4	12					
1	2	3		5	6		**8**	9	10	11	7	4	12					
1	2	3	8	5	6	**11**		9	10		7	4	12					
1	2	3	4	5	6	11	8	**9**	10		7		12					
1	2	3	4	5	6	11	**8**	9			7			10	12			
1	2	3	4	5	6	11	8	9		7	12	**10**						
1	2	3	4	5	6	11	8	9		10	7							
1	2	3	4	5	6		8	9	10	11	7							
1	2	3	4	5	6		8	9	10	11	7							
1	2	3	4	5	6		8		10	11	7	9						
1	2	3	4	5	6		8	**9**	10	11	7	12						
1	2	3	4	5	6		8		10	11	7	9						
1	2	3	4	5	6	8		9	10	11	7							
1		3	4	5	6	11	8	9	10		7	2						
1		3	4	5		11	8	9			7	10			6	2		
1		3	4	5	6	11	8			**9**	7	10	12			2		
1	2	3	4	5	6	11	8	9	10		7							
1	2	3	**4**	5	6	11	8		10		7	9	12					
1	2			5	6	11	8		10		7	3	9		4			
1	2	3			6		8	9	10		7	5	11		4			
1	2	3			6		8	9	10		7	5	11		4			
1	2	3			6		8	9	10		7	5	11		4			
1	2	3			6		8	9	10		7	5			4		11	
1	2	3	8		6		10		9		11	5			4		7	
1	2	3	11		6		8	9	10			5			4		7	
1	2	3	11		6	12	8	**9**	10			5			4		7	
1	2	3	4		6		8	9	10		11	5					7	
1	2		4	3	6	12		**9**	10	8	11	5					7	
1	2	3	11	5	6	**7**	8		9	10		4	12					
1		3	2	5	6	12	8		9	10	11	4					**7**	
1		3	2	5	6		8		9	10	11	4					7	
1		3	2	5	6	7	8		9	10	11	4						
1	12	3	**2**	5		11	8		10	9	6	4					7	
1	2	3		**5**		8	6	12	9	10	11	4					7	
1		3	2	5		11	8	12	10	9	6	4					**7**	
1		3	**2**	5	6	12	8	10	9	7	11	4						
1	2	3			5	7	6	10	9	**8**	11	4					12	
1		3		5	6	12	4	10	**9**	8	11	2					7	
1	12	3			6	9	4	10		8	11	**5**				2	7	
42	31	40	31	32	38	21	39	29	36	26	36	31	4	1	9	3	13	
	2					5		2			1	1	7		1		1	
	2	1				4	5	9	10	4	2	1					1	

Jackson	Sewell	Wall	Payne	McCormick	Blyth	Scott	Kember	Queen	Birchenall	Tambling	Taylor A	Hoadley	Humphries	Proven	Dawkins	Loughlan	Wharton	Pinkney
1	2	3	**4**	5	6	11	8	9	10		7	12						
1	2	3		5	6	11	8	9	10		7	12			**4**			
2	2	2	1	2	2	2	2	2	2		2				1			
												2						
				1					1									

Jackson	Sewell	Wall	Payne	McCormick	Blyth	Scott	Kember	Queen	Birchenall	Tambling	Taylor A	Hoadley	Humphries	Proven	Dawkins	Loughlan	Wharton	Pinkney
1	2	3	4	5	6	11		9	**10**		7		8					12
1	2	3	4	5	6	11		9			7			10	8			
1	2	3	4	5	6		8	9	10	11	7							
1	2	3	4	5	6		8		10	11	7	9						
1	**2**	3	4	5		8		9	10	11	7	6				12		
1		3	4	5	6	11	8	9	**10**		7	2				12		
6	5	6	6	6	5	4	3	5	5	3	6	3	1	1	1			
																2		1
			1		2	1		3	2	2	2							

League Table

	P	W	D	L	F	A	Pts
Arsenal	42	29	7	6	71	29	65
Leeds United	42	27	10	5	72	30	64
Tottenham Hotspur	42	19	14	9	54	33	52
Wolverhampton W	42	22	8	12	64	54	52
Liverpool	42	17	17	8	42	24	51
Chelsea	42	18	15	9	52	42	51
Southampton	42	17	12	13	56	44	46
Manchester United	42	16	11	15	65	66	43
Derby County	42	16	10	16	56	54	42
Coventry City	42	16	10	16	37	38	42
Manchester City	42	12	17	13	47	42	41
Newcastle United	42	14	13	15	44	46	41
Stoke City	42	12	13	17	44	48	37
Everton	42	12	13	17	54	60	37
Huddersfield Town	42	11	14	17	40	49	36
Nottingham Forest	42	14	8	20	42	61	36
West Bromwich Albion	42	10	15	17	58	75	35
Crystal Palace	42	12	11	19	39	57	35
Ipswich Town	42	12	10	20	42	48	34
West Ham United	42	10	14	18	47	60	34
Burnley	42	7	13	22	29	63	27
Blackpool	42	4	15	23	34	66	23

1971-72

Division One

Manager: Bert Head

Did you know that?

Ex-Palace player and then coach George Petchey departed in mid-July to become Leyton Orient manager. George would later turn to Palace to recruit a number of its staff to join him, with coach Terry Long and players David Payne, John Jackson, Gerry Queen, Derek Possee and later Alan Whittle all making the short move to East London.

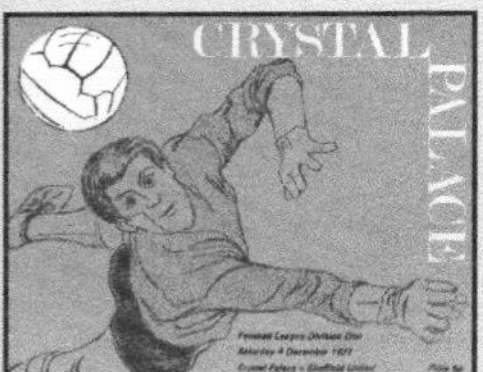

Match No.	Date	Venue	Opponents	Result		Scorers	Attendance
1	Aug 14	H	Newcastle United	W	2-0	Tambling, Taylor	25,281
2	18	A	Manchester City	L	0-4		27,103
3	21	A	Stoke City	L	1-3	Tambling	18,958
4	24	H	Liverpool	L	0-1		28,488
5	28	H	Nottingham Forest	D	1-1	Birchenall	17,699
6	31	A	Wolverhampton Wanderers	L	0-1		24,774
7	Sep 4	A+	Leeds United	L	0-2		18,715
8	11	H	Manchester United	L	1-3	Blyth	44,020
9	18	A	Tottenham Hotspur	L	0-3		37,239
10	25	H	Everton	W	2-1	Jenkins, Scott	25,594
11	Oct 2	A	Leicester City	D	0-0		28,493
12	9	H	West Bromwich Albion	L	0-2		22,399
13	16	A	Newcastle United	W	2-1	Tambling 2	20,510
14	22	A	Coventry City	D	1-1	Tambling	20,801
15	30	H	West Ham United	L	0-3		41,540
16	Nov 6	A	Derby County	L	0-3		30,380
17	13	H	Ipswich Town	D	1-1	Wallace	18,462
18	20	H	Chelsea	L	2-3	Hughes, Queen	34,657
19	27	A	Arsenal	L	1-2	Craven	32,461
20	Dec 4	H	Sheffield United	W	5-1	Taylor, Hughes 2, Queen, McCormick	20,176
21	11	A	Huddersfield Town	W	1-0	Tambling	11,692
22	18	H	Leeds United	D	1-1	Craven	31,456
23	27	A	Southampton	L	0-1		28,310
24	Jan 1	H	Tottenham Hotspur	D	1-1	Queen	35,841
25	8	A	Nottingham Forest	W	1-0	Wallace	19,033
26	22	H	Manchester City	L	1-2	Tambling	31,480
27	29	A	Liverpool	L	1-4	Wall	39,538
28	Feb 12	H	Coventry City	D	2-2	Craven, Queen	19,339
29	19	A	West Ham United	D	1-1	Payne	28,209
30	Mar 4	A	Ipswich Town	W	2-0	Wallace, Tambling	17,222
31	11	A	West Bromwich Albion	D	1-1	Craven	17,217
32	18	H	Wolverhampton Wanderers	L	0-2		24,823
33	21	A	Everton	D	0-0		27,929
34	25	A	Manchester United	L	0-4		41,550
35	28	H	Derby County	L	0-1		21,158
36	Apr 1	H	Southampton	L	2-3	Craven, Kellard (pen)	23,776
37	3	H	Leicester City	D	1-1	Craven	23,736
38	8	A	Chelsea	L	1-2	Blyth	34,105
39	11	H	Arsenal	D	2-2	Kellard (pen). Craven	34,384
40	22	A	Sheffield United	L	0-1		23,250
41	26	H	Stoke City	W	2-0	Kellard (pen), Queen	24,550
42	29	H	Huddersfield Town	D	0-0		18,120

Final League Position: 20th in Division One

+ Played at Leeds Road, Huddersfield.

Appearances
Sub Appearances
Goals

FA Cup

	Date	Venue	Opponents	Result		Scorers	Attendance
3	Jan 15	H	Everton	D	2-2	Wallace 2	32,331
R	18	A	Everton	L	2-3	Tambling 2	45,408

Appearances
Sub Appearances
Goals

League Cup

	Date	Venue	Opponents	Result		Scorers	Attendance
2	Sep 7	H	Luton Town	W	2-0	Queen, Taylor	13,838
3	Oct 5	H	Aston Villa	D	2-2	Craven, Tambling (pen)	21,179
R	13	A	Aston Villa	L	0-2		24,978

Appearances
Sub Appearances
Goals

Jackson	Payne	Wall	Kember	McCormick	Blyth	Wharton	Tambling	Birchenall	Queen	Taylor A	Hoadley	Scott	Loughlan	Jenkins	Bell	Kellard	Craven	Goodwin	Pinkney	Hughes	Wallace	Goldthorpe
1	2	3	4	5	6	7	8	**9**	10	11	12											
1	2	3	4	5	6	**7**	8		10	11	12	9										
1	2	3	4	5	6	12	**8**		10	11	7	9										
1	2	3	4		6		8	9	10	11	5	7										
1	2	3	8	5	6	7	10	9		11	4											
1	2	3	4	5	6	10	8	**9**	12	11	7											
1	2	3	10	4	6	**7**	8		9	11	5	12										
1	4	3	8	**5**	6		10			11	2	7	12	9								
1	4	3	8	5	6		**10**	11	7		2		12	9								
1	4	3		5	6				10	11		12		**9**	2	7	8					
1	2	3		5	8				9	11					6	10	7	4				
1	2	3		5	8				9	11					6	10	4	7				
1	2	3			5		**8**			11				9	6	7	4	10	12			
1	2			5	4		7			3						10	9	8	6	**11**	12	
1	2	3		5	6		7			11						10	8	4		**9**	12	
1	2	5			4		7			11					3		8	6		9	10	
1	2				6		7		8	3					5	10	4			9	11	
1	2	3		5	6				8	10						**4**	7	12		11	9	
1	2	3		5	6				8	10						4	7			11	9	
1	2	3		5	6				8	10						4	7			11	9	
1	2	3		5	6		**11**		8	10						4	7	12			9	
1	2			5	6		11		8	10						4	7	3			9	
1	2	3		5	6				8	10						4	7	12		**11**	9	
1		3		5	6		11		8	10						4	7	2			9	
1	2	3		5	6		11		8	10						4	7				9	
1	2	3		5	6		8			10						4	**7**	12		11	9	
1	2	3		5	6		10		8	11						4	7				9	
1	2	3		**5**	6		11		8	10						4	7	12			9	
1	2			5	6		11		8	10						4	7	3			9	
1	2			5	6		11		8	10						4	7	3			9	
1	2	12		**5**	6		11		8	10						4	7	3			9	
1	2				6		11		8	10						4	7	3			9	5
1	2	12			6		11		8	10					5	4	**7**	3			9	
1	2	12			**6**		11		8	10					5	4	7	3			9	
1	2	12		5			**11**		8	10					6	4	7	3			9	
1	2	11		5	6				8	10					3	4	7				9	
1	2	3		5	6				8	10						4	7	12		**11**	9	
1	2	3		5	6		11			10						4	7	8			9	
1	2	3		5	6		11			10						8	7	4			9	
1	2	3		5	6		11		12	10						4	7	**8**			9	
1	2	3		5	6		11		8	10						4	7				9	
1	2	3		5	6		11		8	10						**4**	7	12			9	
42	41	32	9	35	41	5	33	5	31	41	7	4		4	10	32	33	18	1	10	27	1
		4				1			2		2	2	2					7	1		2	
	1	1		1	2		8	1	5	2		1		1		3	7			3	3	

Jackson	Payne	Wall	Kember	McCormick	Blyth	Wharton	Tambling	Birchenall	Queen	Taylor A	Hoadley	Scott	Loughlan	Jenkins	Bell	Kellard	Craven	Goodwin	Pinkney	Hughes	Wallace	Goldthorpe
1	2	3		5	6				8	10						4	7			11	9	
1	2	3		5	6		11			10						4	7			8	9	
2	2	2		2	2		1		1	2						2	2			2	2	
							2														2	

Jackson	Payne	Wall	Kember	McCormick	Blyth	Wharton	Tambling	Birchenall	Queen	Taylor A	Hoadley	Scott	Loughlan	Jenkins	Bell	Kellard	Craven	Goodwin	Pinkney	Hughes	Wallace	Goldthorpe
1	4	3	8	5	6		10		9	11	2	7										
1	2	3		5	6		9		10	11							8	4	7			
1	2	3		5	6		9			11				10			8	4	7			
3	3	3	1	3	3		3		2	3	1	1		1			2	2	2			
							1		1	1							1					

League Table

	P	W	D	L	F	A	Pts
Derby County	42	24	10	8	69	33	58
Leeds United	42	24	9	9	73	31	57
Liverpool	42	24	9	9	64	30	57
Manchester City	42	23	11	8	77	45	57
Arsenal	42	22	8	12	58	40	52
Tottenham Hotspur	42	19	13	10	63	42	51
Chelsea	42	18	12	12	58	49	48
Manchester United	42	19	10	13	69	61	48
Wolverhampton W	42	18	11	13	65	57	47
Sheffield United	42	17	12	13	61	60	46
Newcastle United	42	15	11	16	49	52	41
Leicester City	42	13	13	16	41	46	39
Ipswich Town	42	11	16	15	39	53	38
West Ham United	42	12	12	18	47	51	36
Everton	42	9	18	15	37	48	36
West Bromwich Albion	42	12	11	19	42	54	35
Stoke City	42	10	15	17	39	56	35
Coventry City	42	9	15	18	44	67	33
Southampton	42	12	7	23	52	80	31
Crystal Palace	**42**	**8**	**13**	**21**	**39**	**65**	**29**
Nottingham Forest	42	8	9	25	47	81	25
Huddersfield Town	42	6	13	23	27	59	25

1972-73

Division One

Manager: Bert Head until 30 March 1973, then Malcolm Allison

Did you know that?

When John Jackson missed the away game at Wolves on 14 October, it was the first game he had not featured in since 19 August 1967 – 254 consecutive matches, including five seasons without missing a League or Cup fixture.

Match No.	Date		Venue	Opponents	Result		Scorers	Attendance
1	Aug	12	A	Stoke City	L	0-2		22,564
2		15	H	Derby County	D	0-0		25,105
3		19	H	Liverpool	D	1-1	Taylor	30,054
4		22	A	Everton	D	1-1	Jenkins	38,429
5		26	A	Birmingham City	D	1-1	Queen	31,066
6		29	H	Manchester City	W	1-0	own-goal (Barrett)	24,731
7	Sep	2	H	Newcastle United	W	2-1	Kellard (pen), Wallace	21,749
8		9	A	Tottenham Hotspur	L	1-2	own-goal (Knowles)	28,545
9		16	H	West Bromwich Albion	L	0-2		17,858
10		23	A	Southampton	L	0-2		15,469
11		30	H	Norwich City	L	0-2		21,255
12	Oct	7	H	Coventry City	L	0-1		22,229
13		14	A	Wolverhampton Wanderers	D	1-1	Hinshelwood	20,630
14		21	H	Arsenal	L	2-3	Craven 2	35,865
15		28	A	West Ham United	L	0-4		28,894
16	Nov	4	H	Everton	W	1-0	Rogers	28,614
17		11	A	Derby County	D	2-2	Rogers, Craven (pen)	26,716
18		18	H	Leeds United	D	2-2	Craven 2	38,167
19		25	A	Chelsea	D	0-0		36,608
20	Dec	9	A	Ipswich Town	L	1-2	Hughes	18,077
21		16	H	Manchester United	W	5-0	Mulligan 2, Rogers 2, Whittle	39,484
22		23	A	Leicester City	L	1-2	Rogers	16,962
23		26	H	Southampton	W	3-0	Craven, Rogers 2	30,935
24		30	A	Liverpool	L	0-1		50,862
25	Jan	20	A	Newcastle United	L	0-2		24,660
26		27	H	Tottenham Hotspur	D	0-0		44,531
27	Feb	10	A	West Bromwich Albion	W	4-0	Whittle 2, Possee 2	14,829
28		17	H	Stoke City	W	3-2	Possee, Whittle, Rogers	32,099
29	Mar	2	A	Coventry City	L	0-2		24,902
30		6	H	Birmingham City	D	0-0		26,014
31		10	H	Wolverhampton Wanderers	D	1-1	Rogers	30,967
32		13	H	Sheffield United	L	0-1		23,976
33		24	H	West Ham United	L	1-3	Possee	36,915
34		26	A	Arsenal	L	0-1		41,879
35		31	H	Chelsea	W	2-0	Philip, Cannon	39,325
36	Apr	7	A	Sheffield United	L	0-2		21,398
37		11	A	Manchester United	L	0-2		46,895
38		14	H	Ipswich Town	D	1-1	Rogers	14,829
39		20	H	Leicester City	L	0-1		36,817
40		21	A	Leeds United	L	0-4		31,173
41		24	A	Norwich City	L	1-2	Rogers (pen)	36,922
42		28	A	Manchester City	W	3-2	Rogers 2 (1 pen), Craven	34,784

Final League Position: 21st in Division One

Appearances
Sub Appearances
2 own-goals Goals

FA Cup

Round	Date		Venue	Opponents	Result		Scorers	Attendance
3	Jan	13	H	Southampton	W	2-0	Rogers, Cooke	31,604
4	Feb	3	A	Sheffield Wednesday	D	1-1	Craven	35,156
R		6	H	Sheffield Wednesday	D	1-1*	Phillip	44,071
2R		19	N+	Sheffield Wednesday	L	2-3*	Payne, Rogers	19,150

* After extra-time. + Played at Villa Park, Birmingham.

Appearances
Sub Appearances
Goals

League Cup

Round	Date		Venue	Opponents	Result		Scorers	Attendance
2	Sep	5	H	Stockport County	L	0-1		11,463

Appearances
Sub Appearances
Goals

Jackson	Payne	Wall	Pinkney	McCormick	Blyth	Craven	Wallace	Jenkins	Kellard	Taylor A	Queen	Roffey	Tambling	Hinshelwood M	Philip	Hughes	Mulligan	Cooke	Hammond	Bell	Rogers	Whittle	Possee	Cannon
1	2	3	4	5	6	**7**	8	9	10	11														
1	2	3	8	5	6	7	10	9	4	11														
1	2	**3**	8	5	6	7	10	9	4	11	12													
1	2		7	5	6	**8**	9	10	4	11	12	3												
1	2		7	5	6		9	10	4	11	8	3												
1	2		8	5	6		10	9	4	11	**7**	3												
1	2		7	5	6	12	8	9	4	11	**10**	3												
1	2		7	5	6	12	9	10	4	11		3	**8**											
1	2		7	5	6		8	9	4	11	10	3												
1	2		7	5		8	12	**9**	10	6		3	11	4										
1	2		7	6		8		9	4			3		10	5	11								
1	8		12	5	6	9			10	11				**3**	4		2	7						
	8		7	5	6	9				3			12	10	4		**2**	11	1					
	2		7	5	6	9				3			8	10	4			11	1					
	2		7	5	6	9				3			11	10	4			8	1					
1	8				6	9				3					4	7	2	10		5	11			
1	8				6	9			12	3					**4**	7	2	10		5	11			
1	8				6	9				3					4	7	2	10		5	11			
1	8				6	9				3					4	7	2	10		5	11			
1	8				6	**9**			12	3					4	11	2	10		5	7			
1	8				6					3					4	7	2	10		5	11	9		
1	8				6	12				3					4	7	**2**	10		5	11	9		
1	2		12		6	**8**				3					4	7		10		5	11	9		
1	2		7		6					3		8			4			10		5	11	9		
1	2				6	9				3					4	7		10		5	11	**8**	12	
1	2				6	9				3					4			10		5	11	8	7	
1	6											3		7	4		2	10		5	11	8	9	
1					6					3				8	4		2	10		5	11	9	7	
	2				6	12				3				8	4			10	1	5	**11**	9	7	
1	2				6	12				3				**8**	4			10		5	11	9	7	
1	2				6	8				7		3			4			10		5	11	9		
1	2				6	**9**				10		3			4			8		5	11	7	12	
1					6					3		2		8	4			10		5	11	9	7	
1	5				6	12				3		2		10	4			8			11	7	**9**	
1	8				5					3				10	4		2				11	9	7	6
1	8				5					3				10	4		2				11	9	7	6
1	11				5	12				3				**8**	4		2	10				9	7	6
1	8	6			5					3		4					2	10			11	9	7	
1	8				5	6				3		4					2	10			11	9	7	
1	12				5					2		3		**6**	10		4	8			11	9	7	
1	8				5	9				3		4			6		2	10			11		7	
1	8				5	9				3		2			4		6	10			11		7	
38	39	4	15	15	39	23	9	11	12	40	4	19	4	16	30	10	19	29	4	18	26	20	15	3
	1		2			7	1		2		2		1										2	
						7	1	1	1	1	1			1	1	1	2				13	4	4	1

Jackson	Payne	Wall	Pinkney	McCormick	Blyth	Craven	Wallace	Jenkins	Kellard	Taylor A	Queen	Roffey	Tambling	Hinshelwood M	Philip	Hughes	Mulligan	Cooke	Hammond	Bell	Rogers	Whittle	Possee	Cannon
1	2				6	9				3					4	7		10		5	11	8		
1	7				6	9				3					4		2	10		5	11	8		
1	7				6	**9**				3					4		2	10		5	11	8	12	
	7				6	12				3				**10**	4		2		1	5	11	8	9	
3	4				4	3				4				1	4	1	3	3	1	4	4	4	1	
						1																	1	
	1					1									1			1			2			

Jackson	Payne	Wall	Pinkney	McCormick	Blyth	Craven	Wallace	Jenkins	Kellard	Taylor A	Queen	Roffey	Tambling	Hinshelwood M	Philip	Hughes	Mulligan	Cooke	Hammond	Bell	Rogers	Whittle	Possee	Cannon
1	2		7	5	6	**10**	9	8	4	11	12	3												
1	1		1	1	1	1	1	1	1	1		1												
											1													

League Table

	P	W	D	L	F	A	Pts
Liverpool	42	25	10	7	72	42	60
Arsenal	42	23	11	8	57	43	57
Leeds United	42	21	11	10	71	45	53
Ipswich Town	42	17	14	11	55	45	48
Wolverhampton W	42	18	11	13	66	54	47
West Ham United	42	17	12	13	67	53	46
Derby County	42	19	8	15	56	54	46
Tottenham Hotspur	42	16	13	13	58	48	45
Newcastle United	42	16	13	13	60	51	45
Birmingham City	42	15	12	15	53	54	42
Manchester City	42	15	11	16	57	60	41
Chelsea	42	13	14	15	49	51	40
Southampton	42	11	18	13	47	52	40
Sheffield United	42	15	10	17	51	59	40
Stoke City	42	14	10	18	61	56	38
Leicester City	42	10	17	15	40	46	37
Everton	42	13	11	18	41	49	37
Manchester United	42	12	13	17	44	60	37
Coventry City	42	13	9	20	40	55	35
Norwich City	42	11	10	21	36	63	32
Crystal Palace	42	9	12	21	41	58	30
West Bromwich Albion	42	9	10	23	38	62	28

1973-74

Division Two

Manager: Malcolm Allison

Did you know that?

Malcolm Allison's first full season in charge of Palace saw a number of sweeping changes. The club nickname was changed from Glaziers to Eagles, and club colours of claret and sky blue became the red-and-blue stripes still used today.

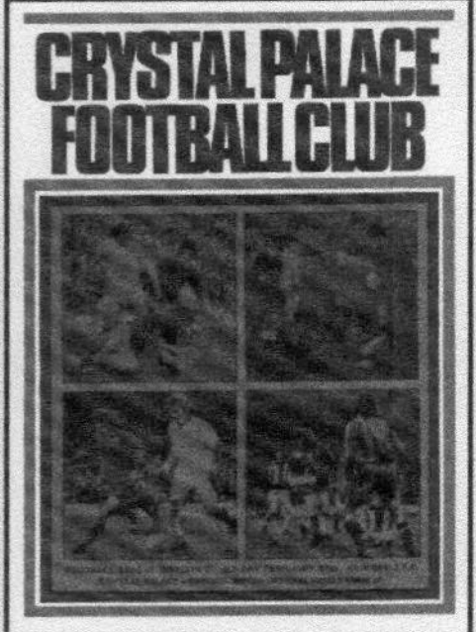

Match No.	Date		Venue	Opponents	Result		Scorers	Attendance
1	Aug	25	H	Notts County	L	1-4	Rogers	20,841
2	Sep	1	A	West Bromwich Albion	L	0-1		18,037
3		8	H	Middlesbrough	L	2-3	Blyth, Cannon	17,554
4		11	H	Aston Villa	D	0-0		20,858
5		15	A	Bolton Wanderers	L	0-2		18,392
6		17	A	Blackpool	L	0-1		9,323
7		22	H	Cardiff City	D	3-3	P. Hinshelwood, Rogers 2	17,789
8		29	A	Sheffield Wednesday	L	0-4		12,861
9	Oct	2	H	Blackpool	L	1-2	Rogers	18,080
10		6	H	Luton Town	L	1-2	Rogers	19,790
11		13	A	Oxford United	D	1-1	Rogers	10,161
12		20	H	Carlisle United	L	0-1		19,678
13		23	A	Aston Villa	L	1-2	Jeffries	26,670
14		27	A	Sunderland	D	0-0		31,935
15	Nov	3	H	Notts F	L	0-1		21,881
16		10	A	Bristol City	W	1-0	Whittle	15,488
17		17	H	Millwall	D	1-1	Whalley	30,054
18		24	A	Portsmouth	D	2-2	Rogers 2 (1 pen)	14,211
19	Dec	1	H	Swindon Town	W	4-2	Rogers, Possee, Anderson, P. Taylor	17,881
20		8	A	Hull City	L	0-3		7,996
21		15	A	Preston North End	D	1-1	Whittle	9,121
22		22	H	Sheffield Wednesday	D	0-0		16,240
23		26	A	Orient	L	0-3		20,611
24		29	A	Middlesbrough	L	0-2		26,115
25	Jan	1	H	West Bromwich Albion	W	1-0	Rogers	23,338
26		12	H	Bolton Wanderers	D	0-0		15,804
27		20	A	Notts County	W	3-1	Barry, Possee 2	14,478
28	Feb	3	H	Preston North End	W	2-0	Possee, P. Taylor	24,575
29		17	H	Oxford United	W	2-0	P. Taylor 2 (1 pen)	23,169
30		23	A	Luton Town	L	1-2	Possee	14,287
31	Mar	3	H	Orient	D	0-0		29,056
32		9	H	Sunderland	W	3-0	Rogers 2, own-goal (Belfitt)	16,529
33		16	A	Carlisle United	L	0-1		6,964
34		23	H	Bristol City	W	3-1	Possee 2, Rogers (pen)	16,690
35		30	A	Notts F	W	2-1	Possee, Rogers	16,340
36	Apr	6	H	Portsmouth	D	0-0		23,662
37		12	A	Fulham	W	3-1	Possee, Johnson 2	22,877
38		13	A	Millwall	L	2-3	P. Taylor, Rogers (pen)	19,770
39		16	H	Fulham	L	0-2		32,124
40		20	H	Hull City	L	0-2		21,408
41		27	A	Swindon Town	W	1-0	P.Taylor	11,964
42		30	A	Cardiff City	D	1-1	Jump	26,781

Final League Position: 20th in Division Two

Appearances
Sub Appearances
1 own-goal — Goals

FA Cup

3	Jan	5	H	Wrexham	L	0-2		16,119
R								

Appearances
Sub Appearances
Goals

League Cup

2	Oct	9	A	Stockport County	L	0-1		8,501

Appearances
Sub Appearances
Goals

Hammond	Roffey	Taylor A	Chatterton	Bell	Blyth	Possee	Cooke	Whittle	Swindlehurst	Rogers	Cannon	Jackson	Whalley	Phillip	Hinshelwood M	Hinshelwood P	Pinkney	McBride	Mulligan	Jefferies	Barry	Wall	Tambling	Taylor P	Anderson	Lindsey	Johnson	Jump	Hill
1	2	3	4	5	6	7	8	9	**10**	11	12																		
1	2	3	9	5	6	7	10	8		11	4																		
	2	3	10	5	6	7		9		11	4	1	8																
	2	3	10		6	7	12	9		11	4	1		5	**8**														
	2	3	10		5	7	12	9		11	4	1		6	8														
		3			6	7	8			11		1		4	2	9	10	5											
		3			6	7	**8**	9		11		1		5	4	10	12		2										
1		**6**				7	9		12	11					8	10			4	2	5	3							
1		3				7	8			11	4					9	10		2	6	5								
1		3				7	**8**	9	12	11	4								2	6	5		10						
1		3				9	8			7	4			10					2	6	5			11					
1		3			6	9	8			10	7									4	5	2		11					
1		3			6	9	8			10	11								2	4	5			7					
1		3			**4**	9	8			10	11								2	6	5	12		7					
1						9	8		10	11	**6**		12						2	4	5	3		7					
1						8	7	12	9	11			4						2	**6**	5	3		10					
1						7		12	9	11			8						2	4	5	**3**		10	6				
1		3				7		9		11	6		8						2	4				10	5				
1		3				7		9		11			8							2	5			10	4	6			
1		3				7		9	12	11	5		8							**2**				10	4	6			
1			2			8		9		11											5			10	6	4	7	3	
1		3			6			10		11									2		5			7			8	4	9
1		3			6			10	12	9									2		5			7		**11**	8	4	
1										11									2	4	5			**7**	6	10	8	3	9
1										10									2	7	5			11	4	8	6	3	9
1		3			4					10										7	5			11		8	6	2	9
1					4	8				10										7	5	3		11	9		6	2	
1					6	8				**10**									12	7	5	3		11			4	2	9
1					6	8		10												7	5	3		11			4	2	9
1					6	8				10										7		3		11	5		4	2	9
1					6				8	10										7		3		11	5		4	2	9
1					6	7				10									2	8	5			11			4	3	9
1					4	7				10									2	8	5			11			6	3	9
1					6	7		9		10									2	8	5			11			4	3	
1					4	7		9		10										8	5	2		11			6	3	
1					4	7		9		10									2	8	5			11			6	3	
1					6	8		9		10									2	7	5			11			4	3	
1			12		6	8		9		**10**										7	5			11	2		4	3	
1					6	8		9		10									2	7	5			11			4	3	
1					6	8		12		10									2	**7**	5			11			4	3	9
1					4	7		9		10									2		5			11			6	3	8
1					6	8		9		10									2	7	5			11			4	3	
37	5	20	6	3	29	36	13	22	5	41	13	5	6	5	5	4	2	1	24	31	31	11	1	32	11	7	22	22	12
			1				2	3	4		1		1				1		1			1							
					1	9		2		15	1		1			1				1	1			6	1		2	1	

Hammond	Roffey	Taylor A	Chatterton	Bell	Blyth	Possee	Cooke	Whittle	Swindlehurst	Rogers	Cannon	Jackson	Whalley	Phillip	Hinshelwood M	Hinshelwood P	Pinkney	McBride	Mulligan	Jefferies	Barry	Wall	Tambling	Taylor P	Anderson	Lindsey	Johnson	Jump	Hill
1							12			10									2	**7**	5			11	4	8	6	3	9
1										1									1	1	1			1	1	1	1	1	1
							1																						

Hammond	Roffey	Taylor A	Chatterton	Bell	Blyth	Possee	Cooke	Whittle	Swindlehurst	Rogers	Cannon	Jackson	Whalley	Phillip	Hinshelwood M	Hinshelwood P	Pinkney	McBride	Mulligan	Jefferies	Barry	Wall	Tambling	Taylor P	Anderson	Lindsey	Johnson	Jump	Hill
1		3		5		7	12			11	4			10	**2**					6			8			9			
1		1		1		1				1	1			1	1					1			1			1			
							1																						

League Table

	P	W	D	L	F	A	Pts
Middlesbrough	42	27	11	4	77	30	65
Luton Town	42	19	12	11	64	51	50
Carlisle United	42	20	9	13	61	48	49
Orient	42	15	18	9	55	42	48
Blackpool	42	17	13	12	57	40	47
Sunderland	42	19	9	14	58	44	47
Nottingham Forest	42	15	15	12	57	43	45
West Bromwich Albion	42	14	16	12	48	45	44
Hull City	42	13	17	12	46	47	43
Notts County	42	15	13	14	55	60	43
Bolton Wanderers	42	15	12	15	44	40	42
Millwall	42	14	14	14	51	51	42
Fulham	42	16	10	16	39	43	42
Aston Villa	42	13	15	14	48	45	41
Portsmouth	42	14	12	16	45	62	40
Bristol City	42	14	10	18	47	54	38
Cardiff City	42	10	16	16	49	62	36
Oxford United	42	10	16	16	35	46	36
Sheffield Wednesday	42	12	11	19	51	63	35
Crystal Palace	42	11	12	19	43	56	34
Preston North End	42	9	14	19	40	62	31
Swindon Town	42	7	11	24	36	72	25

1974-75

Division Three

Manager: Malcolm Allison

Did you know that?

Peter Taylor, who had signed for Palace from Southend United the previous season, made his England debut for the Under-23s at Selhurst Park on 29 October against Czechoslovakia, scoring after three minutes as England won 3–1.

Match No.	Date	Venue	Opponents	Result		Scorers	Attendance
1	Aug 17	A	Brighton & Hove Albion	L	0-1		26,235
2	24	H	Tranmere Rovers	W	2-1	Blyth, Swindlehurst	14,816
3	31	A	Halifax Town	L	1-3	Whittle	3,295
4	Sep 7	H	Swindon Town	W	6-2	Jump, Swindlehurst 2, Whittle 2 (1 pen), Chatterton	13,964
5	13	A	Southend United	W	1-0	Chatterton	17,394
6	18	A	Hereford United	L	0-2		8,488
7	21	H	Wrexham	W	2-0	Taylor, Chatterton	13,226
8	24	H	Preston North End	W	1-0	Hill	19,680
9	28	A	Huddersfield Town	W	1-0	Chatterton	6,524
10	Oct 1	H	Grimsby Town	W	3-0	Whittle, Evans, Taylor	19,105
11	5	H	Chesterfield	L	1-4	Taylor	19,310
12	12	A	Bournemouth	L	0-4		10,407
13	19	H	Walsall	W	1-0	Whittle	15,029
14	22	H	Blackburn Rovers	W	1-0	Taylor	17,754
15	26	A	Port Vale	L	1-2	Taylor	5,148
16	Nov 2	H	Peterborough United	D	1-1	Taylor	18,226
17	6	A	Blackburn Rovers	D	1-1	P.Hinshelwood	13,612
18	9	A	Bury	D	2-2	Whittle, Swindlehurst	6,727
19	16	H	Plymouth Argyle	D	3-3	Whittle, Swindlehurst, P. Hinshelwood	19,308
20	30	H	Charlton Athletic	W	2-1	Cannon, Chatterton	24,274
21	Dec 7	A	Watford	W	2-1	Whittle, Taylor	11,065
22	20	A	Colchester United	D	1-1	Evans	6,914
23	26	H	Southend United	D	1-1	Swindlehurst	21,652
24	28	A	Gillingham	L	1-3	own-goal (Wiltshire)	14,555
25	Jan 4	H	Hereford United	D	2-2	Taylor, Chatterton	16,893
26	11	H	Watford	W	1-0	Hill	17,055
27	17	A	Charlton Athletic	L	0-1		25,535
28	25	A	Aldershot	L	1-2	Hill	8,790
29	Feb 1	H	Bury	D	2-2	Swindlehurst 2	15,046
30	8	A	Peterborough United	D	1-1	Whittle	7,698
31	15	H	Aldershot	W	3-0	Swindlehurst, Taylor, Whittle	15,394
32	22	A	Plymouth Argyle	W	1-0	Swindlehurst	21,022
33	28	H	Halifax Town	D	1-1	Swindlehurst	18,024
34	Mar 8	A	Preston North End	D	1-1	Swindlehurst	12,119
35	15	H	Huddersfield Town	D	1-1	Taylor	15,043
36	18	H	Brighton & Hove Albion	W	3-0	Taylor (pen), J. Johnson, Swindlehurst	18,799
37	22	A	Swindon Town	D	1-1	Swindlehurst	11,545
38	25	H	Colchester United	W	2-1	Evans, Cannon	16,851
39	31	A	Wrexham	D	0-0		5,833
40	Apr 5	H	Port Vale	D	1-1	Taylor (pen)	14,930
41	8	A	Grimsby Town	L	1-2	Wall	8,381
42	12	A	Chesterfield	L	1-2	Hill	6,020
43	19	H	Bournemouth	W	4-1	Hill 2, Cannon, M. Hinshelwood	12,591
44	25	A	Walsall	L	0-3		6,001
45	29	H	Gillingham	W	4-0	Whittle 2, Taylor 2	13,442
46	May 7	A	Tranmere Rovers	L	0-2		2,025

Final League Position: 5th in Division Three

Appearances
Sub Appearances
1 own-goal — Goals

FA Cup

1	Nov 27	A	Tooting & Mitcham United	W	2-1	P. Hinshelwood, Whittle	10,000
2	Dec 14	A	Plymouth Argyle	L	1-2	Swindlehurst	17,473

Appearances
Sub Appearances
Goals

League Cup

1	Aug 21	A	Watford	D	1-1	Lindsay	10,643
R	27	H	Watford	W	5-1	Taylor, Whittle 2, Chatterton, own-goal (Butler)	12,801
2	Sep 10	H	Bristol City	L	1-4	Whittle (pen)	16,263

Appearances
Sub Appearances
1 own-goal — Goals

Hammond	Mulligan	Jump	Jeffries	Blyth	Johnson J	Whittle	Lindsay	Hill	Rogers	Taylor P	Swindlehurst	Barry	Davies	Chatterton	Burns	Cannon	Venables	Evans	Ayres	Hinshelwood P	Hinshelwood M	Johnson P	Love	Wall	Holder	Sansom	Kemp
1	2	3	4	5	6	7	8	**9**	10	11	12																
1		3	4	5	6	7	8		**10**	11	12	2	9														
1		3	4	5	6	7	8			11	12	2	**9**	10													
1		3	5	6	4	7	8		12	11	9	**2**		10													
		3	5		4	8	7			11		2	9	10	1	6											
		3	**5**		12	8	7			11	9	2		10	1		4	6									
		2			3	7	8			11	9	5		10	1		4	6									
		3			5	**8**	7	9		11		2		10	1		4	6	12								
		3			8	7	6	**9**				2		10	1	12	4	5	11								
		3			5	8	7			11	9	**2**		10	1	12	4	6									
		3			7	**8**	6	9		11		2		10	1		4	5		12							
		12	7		2	8	6	**9**		11				10	1	3	4	5									
		3	5		2	8	7			11	12				1	10	**4**	6	9								
		3	10		5	8	7			11	9				1	2		6		4							
		2	5		4	10	8			11	9				**1**	3		6	12	7							
1		2	**6**		4	8	7			11	9					3		5	12	10							
1		2	10		5	8	7			11	9			12		3		6		**4**							
1		2	6		4	8	7			11	9					**3**		5		10	12						
1		2	5		7	8	12			**11**	9					3	4	6		10							
		2	5			8				11	9			7	1	3	4	6		10							
		2	5			**8**	12			11	9			7	1	3	4	6		10							
	2		5			8				11	9			7	1	3	4	6		10							
	2		6			10		12		11	9			7	1	3	4	5		**8**							
	2		5			8	9	10		11				7	1	3	4	6									
	2		5		4			10		11	9	12		8	1	3		6				7					
	2		5		4			10		11	9			8	1	3		6				7					
	2		5		12	10	4	9						7	1	3		6	11			**8**					
	2		5		4	8		9						7	1	3		6			10		**11**	12			
	7		5		4	8		9		11	10				1	3		6						2			
	7		5		4	8		10		11	9				1	3		6						2			
	2		5		4	7		9		11	10				1			6						3	8		
	2		5		4	7		9		11	10				1			6						3	8		
	2		5		4	8		9		11	10			12	1	3		6							7		
			5		4			9		11	**10**			7	1	3		6				12		2	8		
			5		4			9		11	10			7	1	3		6			12			2	**8**		
			5		4			9		11	10			7	1	3		6			8			2			
			5		4	7		9		11	10				1	3		6			8			2			
			5		4	7		9		11	10				1	3		6			8			2			
			5		4	7		9		11	10				1	3		6			8			2			
	3		5		4	7	12	9		11	10				1	6					8			2			
			5		3	7		**9**		11	10			12	1	6					8			2	4		
			5			7		9		11	10				1	3		6			8			2	4		
			5			7		9		11	10				1	3		6			8			2	4		
			5			7		10		11	9				1	3		6			8			2	4		
			5			7		9		11	10				1	3		6			8			2	4		
			5			**7**		12		11	9				1	6					8			2	4	3	10
8	14	20	41	4	34	41	20	27	2	43	34	10	3	22	38	34	14	38	3	10	12	3	1	17	11	1	1
		1			2		3	2	1		4	1		3		2			3	1	2	1		1			
		1		1	1	12		6		14	14			6		3		3		2	1			1			

Hammond	Mulligan	Jump	Jeffries	Blyth	Johnson J	Whittle	Lindsay	Hill	Rogers	Taylor P	Swindlehurst	Barry	Davies	Chatterton	Burns	Cannon	Venables	Evans	Ayres	Hinshelwood P
1		2	5			8				11	9			7		3	4	6		10
	2		5			8	12			11	9			7	1	3	4	6		**10**
1	1	1	2			2				2	2			2	1	2	2	2		2
							1													
						1					1									1

Hammond	Mulligan	Jump	Jeffries	Blyth	Johnson J	Whittle	Lindsay	Hill	Rogers	Taylor P	Swindlehurst	Barry	Davies	Chatterton	Burns	Cannon
1	**2**	3	5	6	4	8	7		10	11	9					12
1		3	5	6	4	8	7			11	9	2		10		
1		3	5	6	4	8	7		12	11	**9**	2		10		
3	1	3	3	3	3	3	3		1	3	3	2		2		
																1
						3	1			1				1		

League Table

	P	W	D	L	F	A	Pts
Blackburn Rovers	46	22	16	8	68	45	60
Plymouth Argyle	46	24	11	11	79	58	59
Charlton Athletic	46	22	11	13	76	61	55
Swindon Town	46	21	11	14	64	58	53
Crystal Palace	46	18	15	13	66	57	51
Port Vale	46	18	15	13	61	54	51
Peterborough United	46	19	12	15	47	53	50
Walsall	46	18	13	15	67	52	49
Preston North End	46	19	11	16	63	56	49
Gillingham	46	17	14	15	65	60	48
Colchester United	46	17	13	16	70	63	47
Hereford United	46	16	14	16	64	66	46
Wrexham	46	15	15	16	65	55	45
Bury	46	16	12	18	53	50	44
Chesterfield	46	16	12	18	62	66	44
Grimsby Town	46	15	13	18	55	64	43
Halifax Town	46	13	17	16	49	65	43
Southend United	46	13	16	17	46	51	42
Brighton & Hove Albion	46	16	10	20	56	64	42
Aldershot	46	14	11	21	53	63	38
Bournemouth	46	13	12	21	44	58	38
Tranmere Rovers	46	14	9	23	55	57	37
Watford	46	10	17	19	52	75	37
Huddersfield Town	46	11	10	25	47	76	32

1975-76

Division Three

Manager: Malcolm Allison

Did you know that?

After just over three seasons, Malcolm Allison's popular but ultimately unrewarding run as manager came to an end when he resigned in May. He departed, though, leaving Palace fans with fond memories of an FA Cup run this season that took the club all the way to the semi-finals, with memorable wins over Leeds, Chelsea and Sunderland.

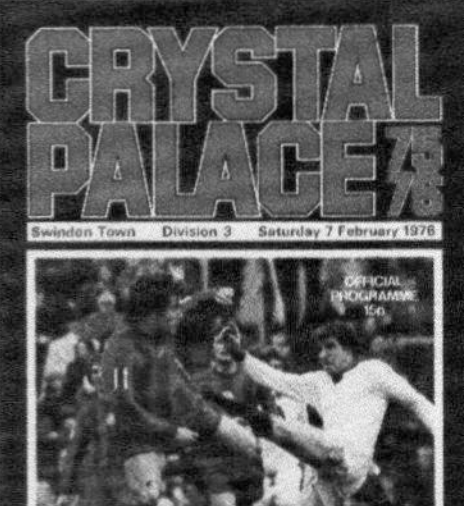

Match No.	Date	Venue	Opponents	Result		Scorers	Attendance
1	Aug 16	H	Chester	W	2-0	Chatterton, Kemp	13,009
2	23	A	Chesterfield	W	2-1	Kemp, Holder	5,386
3	30	H	Colchester United	W	3-2	Evans 3	13,713
4	Sep 6	A	Cardiff City	W	1-0	Kemp	10,479
5	13	H	Rotherham United	W	2-0	Evans, Kemp	16,421
6	16	A	Walsall	D	1-1	Evans	5,496
7	20	A	Shrewsbury Town	W	4-2	Swindlehurst, Kemp, Taylor, own-goal (Durban)	7,480
8	23	H	Brighton & Hove Albion	L	0-1		25,606
9	27	H	Sheffield Wednesday	D	1-1	Kemp	14,840
10	Oct 4	A	Port Vale	D	0-0		6,121
11	11	H	Grimsby Town	W	3-0	Evans, Kemp, Swindlehurst	15,552
12	18	A	Preston North End	D	0-0		10,971
13	21	H	Hereford United	D	2-2	Swindlehurst, Taylor (pen)	20,232
14	25	H	Southend United	D	1-1	Taylor	18,438
15	Nov 1	A	Halifax Town	W	3-1	Cannon, Swindlehurst, Taylor	3,282
16	4	A	Swindon Town	W	2-1	Swindlehurst 2	10,599
17	8	H	Peterborough United	D	1-1	Chatterton	19,000
18	15	A	Wrexham	W	3-1	Swindlehurst 2, Kemp	5,878
19	29	H	Mansfield Town	W	4-1	Swindlehurst 2, M. Hinshelwood, Evans	15,701
20	Dec 6	A	Bury	W	1-0	Kemp	10,035
21	20	A	Millwall	L	1-2	Swindlehurst	9,841
22	27	A	Aldershot	L	0-1		13,997
23	30	H	Gillingham	L	0-1		20,919
24	Jan 6	H	Walsall	L	0-1		16,181
25	10	A	Colchester United	W	3-0	Taylor (pen), Swindlehurst, Whittle	6,240
26	17	H	Shrewsbury Town	D	1-1	J. Johnson	16,531
27	31	A	Hereford United	D	1-1	Swindlehurst	12,970
28	Feb 3	A	Rotherham United	L	1-4	Swindlehurst	7,633
29	7	H	Swindon Town	D	3-3	Taylor (pen), Chatterton 2	15,844
30	18	A	Peterborough United	L	0-2		13,308
31	21	H	Wrexham	D	1-1	Chatterton	16,944
32	24	A	Brighton & Hove Albion	L	0-2		33,300
33	27	A	Southend United	W	2-1	Wall, Taylor (pen)	13,500
34	Mar 9	H	Port Vale	D	2-2	Chatterton, Swindlehurst	23,014
35	13	A	Grimsby Town	W	2-1	Taylor 2	8,412
36	16	H	Preston North End	W	2-0	Taylor, Swindlehurst	22,213
37	20	A	Mansfield Town	D	1-1	Taylor	12,990
38	27	H	Bury	W	1-0	Chatterton	21,328
39	30	H	Millwall	D	0-0		34,893
40	Apr 7	A	Sheffield Wednesday	L	0-1		11,909
41	10	H	Cardiff City	L	0-1		25,603
42	13	H	Halifax Town	D	1-1	Martin	19,175
43	17	A	Gillingham	W	2-1	Cannon, own-goal (Ley)	12,880
44	20	H	Aldershot	D	0-0		25,549
45	28	H	Chesterfield	D	0-0		27,961
46	May 4	A	Chester	L	1-2	Taylor (pen)	6,702

Final League Position: 5th in Division Three

							Appearances
							Sub Appearances
						2 own-goals	Goals

FA Cup

1	Nov 22	H	Walton & Hersham	W	1-0	Kemp	16,241
2	Dec 13	A	Millwall	D	1-1	Swindlehurst	14,920
R	16	H	Millwall	W	2-1	Kemp, Taylor (pen)	18,284
3	Jan 3	A	Scarborough	W	2-1	Taylor, Evans	8,001
4	24	A	Leeds United	W	1-0	Swindlehurst	43,116
5	Feb 14	A	Chelsea	W	3-2	Taylor 2, Chatterton	54,407
6	Mar 6	A	Sunderland	W	1-0	Whittle	50,850
SF	Apr 3	N+	Southampton	L	0-2		52,810

+ Played at Stamford Bridge, Chelsea

Appearances
Sub Appearances
Goals

League Cup

1	Aug 19	H	Colchester United	W	3-0	Swindlehurst, Kemp 2	10,006
	25	A	Colchester United	L	1-3	Chatterton	3,912
2	Sep 9	A	Doncaster Rovers	L	1-2	J. Johnson	6,268

Appearances
Sub Appearances
Goals

Burns	Wall	Johnson J	Holder	Jeffries	Hinshelwood M	Hill	Chatterton	Kemp	Swindlehurst	Taylor	Evans	Cannon	Hammond	Hinshelwood P	Jump	Whittle	Johnson P	Sansom	Martin
1	2	3	4	5	6	7	8	9	10	11									
1	2	3	11	5	4	7	8	9	10		6								
1	2		8	5	4	7		9	10	11	6	3							
	2		4	5	8	7		10	9	11	6	3	1						
	2		8	5	4		7	9	10	11	6	3	1						
	2		8	5	4		7	9	10	11	6	3	1						
	2		8	5	4		7	10	9	11	6	3	1						
	2	12	8	5	4		**7**	9	10	11	6	3	1						
	2	8	7	5	**4**			10	9	11	6	3	1	12					
	2	10	7	5	4			9		11	6	3	1	8					
	2	8	7	5	4			9	**10**	11	6		1	12	3				
		8	7	5	4			9	10	11	6	3	1		2				
		4	8	5			12	9	10	11	6	**3**	1		2	7			
	2	8	4	5				9	10	**11**	6		1	12	3	7			
	2	8	4				7	9	10	11	6	5	1		3				
	2	4	8	5			7	9	10	11	6	3	1						
	2	8	4	5			7	9	10		6	3	1			11			
	2	8	4	5			7	9	10	11	6	3	1						
	2	4		5	**8**		7	9	10	11	6	3	1			12			
	2	8			4		7	9	10	11	6	3	1		5				
	2	8		5	4		7	9	10	11	6	3	1						
	2	4	12	5	8		7	**9**	10	11	6	3	1						
	2	12	4	5	8		7		**10**	11	6	3	1	9					
	2				8		7	9	10	11	6	3	1		5	4			
	2	4			8		7		10	11	6	3	1		5	9			
	2	4			8		7		10	11	6	3	1		5	9			
	2			4	8		7		10	11	6	3	1		5	9			
	2			4	8		7		10	11	6	3	1		5	9			
	2			4	8		7		10	11	6	3	1		5	9			
	2		11	4	8		7	9	10		6	3	1		5				
	2		11	**4**	8		7	9	10		6	3	1		5		12		
	2		11	4	8		7		10	9	6	3	1		5				
	2		5	4	8		7		10	11	6	3	1			9			
	2		4	5	**8**		7	12	10	11	6		1		3	9			
		8	6	4			7		10	11	5		1		3	9		2	
	2	8	**4**				7		10	11	6	3	1		5	9			12
	2	8		4			7		10	11	6	3	1		**5**	12			9
	2	12	4	5			7		10	11	6	3	1			9			8
		8	4	5			7		10	11	6	3	1		2	9			
	2	8	4	5			7		10		6	3	1			9			11
	2	8	4	5			7		10	11	6	3	1			9			
	2	7						12	**10**	11	6	3	1		5	9		4	8
	2	7							10	11	6	3	1		5	9		4	8
	2						8	12	**10**	11	6	3	1		5	9		4	7
	2						7	9		11	6	3	1		5		10	4	8
	2						7	9		11	6	3	1		5		10	4	8
3	42	26	30	35	28	4	36	27	43	41	45	40	43	2	25	20	2	6	8
		3	1				1	3						3		2	1		1
	1	1	1		1		7	9	16	12	7	2				1			1

Burns	Wall	Johnson J	Holder	Jeffries	Hinshelwood M	Hill	Chatterton	Kemp	Swindlehurst	Taylor	Evans	Cannon	Hammond	Hinshelwood P	Jump	Whittle	Johnson P	Sansom	Martin
	2	4	8	5			7	9	10	11	6	3	1						
	2	4			8		7	9	10	11	6	3	1		5				
	2	4		5	8		7	9	10	11	6	3	1						
	2		**4**		8		7	9	10	11	6	3	1		5	12			
	2			4	8		7		10	11	6	3	1		5	9			
	2			4	8		7		10	11	6	3	1		5	9			
	2		4	5	8		7		10	11	6	3	1			9			
	2	8	4	5			7		10	11	6	3	1			9			
	8	4	4	6	6		8	4	8	8	8	8	8		4	4			
																1			
							1	2	2	4	1					1			

Burns	Wall	Johnson J	Holder	Jeffries	Hinshelwood M	Hill	Chatterton	Kemp	Swindlehurst	Taylor	Evans	Cannon	Hammond	Hinshelwood P	Jump	Whittle	Johnson P	Sansom	Martin
1	2	3	12	5	**4**	7	8	9	10	11	6								
1	2	3	12		4	7	**8**	9	10	11	6	5							
	2	12	8	5	4	**7**		9	10	11	6	3	1						
2	3	2	1	2	3	3	2	3	3	3	3	2	1						
		1	2																
		1					1	2	1										

League Table

	P	W	D	L	F	A	Pts
Hereford United	46	26	11	9	86	55	63
Cardiff City	46	22	13	11	69	48	57
Millwall	46	20	16	10	54	43	56
Brighton & Hove Albion	46	22	9	15	78	53	53
Crystal Palace	46	18	17	11	61	46	53
Wrexham	46	20	12	14	66	55	52
Walsall	46	18	14	14	74	61	50
Preston North End	46	19	10	17	62	57	48
Shrewsbury Town	46	19	10	17	61	59	48
Peterborough United	46	15	18	13	63	63	48
Mansfield Town	46	16	15	15	58	52	47
Port Vale	46	15	16	15	55	54	46
Bury	46	14	16	16	51	46	44
Chesterfield	46	17	9	20	69	69	43
Gillingham	46	12	19	15	58	68	43
Rotherham United	46	15	12	19	54	65	42
Chester	46	15	12	19	43	62	42
Grimsby Town	46	15	10	21	62	74	40
Swindon Town	46	16	8	22	62	75	40
Sheffield Wednesday	46	12	16	18	48	59	40
Aldershot	46	13	13	20	59	75	39
Colchester United	46	12	14	20	41	65	38
Southend United	46	12	13	21	65	75	37
Halifax Town	46	11	13	22	41	61	35

1976-77

Division Three

Manager: Terry Venables

Did you know that?

Palace adopted a more free-flowing style of play as Terry Venables stepped up from coach to manager for his first appointment in that role. In his first season as boss, the Eagles sealed promotion to Division Two with four straight wins at the end of the season, and key contributions from Jim Cannon, Kenny Samson and Ian Evans, all of whom played every single League game.

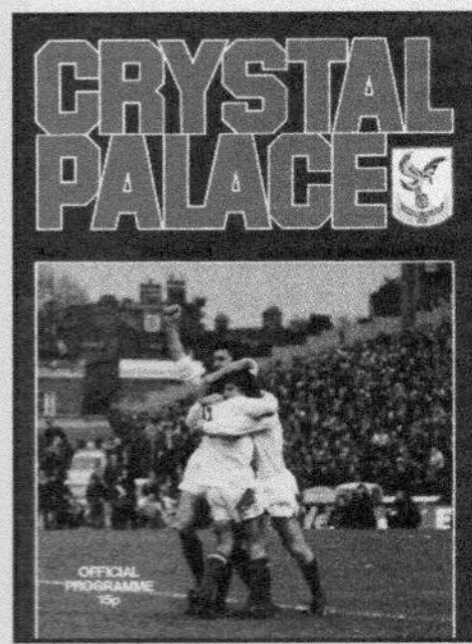

Match No.	Date		Venue	Opponents	Result		Scorers	Attendance
1	Aug	21	H	York City	W	1-0	Taylor	14,426
2		24	A	Grimsby Town	W	1-0	Kemp	5,841
3		27	A	Tranmere Rovers	L	0-1		4,940
4	Sep	4	H	Chester	L	1-2	Swindlehurst	12,746
5		11	H	Bury	W	2-1	Evans, Silkman	12,390
6		18	A	Peterborough United	D	0-0		8,489
7		25	H	Mansfield Town	W	2-0	Perrin, Swindlehurst	14,268
8	Oct	2	A	Brighton & Hove Albion	D	1-1	Cannon	27,059
9		9	H	Oxford United	D	2-2	P. Hinshelwood, Swindlehurst	17,339
10		16	A	Preston North End	L	1-2	Chatterton	10,524
11		23	H	Rotherham United	W	2-1	Swindlehurst, Evans	13,819
12		26	H	Shrewsbury Town	W	2-1	Chatterton, Perrin	15,809
13		30	A	Walsall	D	0-0		6,033
14	Nov	2	A	Swindon Town	D	1-1	Perrin	11,317
15		6	H	Reading	D	1-1	Swindlehurst	15,322
16		9	A	Sheffield Wednesday	L	0-1		14,899
17		27	H	Chesterfield	D	0-0		13,618
18	Dec	18	H	Northampton Town	D	1-1	Silkman	10,642
19		27	A	Gillingham	W	3-0	Swindlehurst, Silkman, Perrin	11,237
20	Jan	1	A	Reading	D	0-0		11,851
21		3	H	Walsall	W	3-0	Chatterton, Harkouk, Holder (pen)	17,614
22		15	H	Grimsby Town	W	2-1	Chatterton, Silkman	13,638
23		22	A	York City	L	1-2	Harkouk	3,427
24	Feb	1	H	Port Vale	W	2-0	Chatterton, Perrin	10,691
25		5	H	Tranmere Rovers	W	1-0	Holder (pen)	14,288
26		12	A	Chester	L	1-2	Harkouk	5,442
27		19	A	Bury	W	1-0	Perrin	5,120
28		22	H	Portsmouth	W	2-1	Cannon, Harkouk	16,483
29		26	H	Peterborough United	D	0-0		16,623
30	Mar	2	A	Lincoln City	L	2-3	Swindlehurst, Brennan	8,280
31		5	A	Mansfield Town	L	0-1		10,944
32		12	H	Brighton & Hove Albion	W	3-1	Harkouk 2, Swindlehurst	28,677
33		15	A	Northampton Town	L	0-3		6,253
34		19	A	Oxford United	W	1-0	Perrin	6,872
35		22	H	Preston North End	W	1-0	Bourne	14,993
36	Apr	2	A	Rotherham United	D	1-1	Harkouk	8,353
37		5	H	Gillingham	W	3-1	Bourne 2, Holder (pen)	17,477
38		9	A	Portsmouth	D	0-0		14,108
39		12	H	Swindon Town	W	5-0	Bourne 2, Holder (pen), Graham, Harkouk	18,501
40		16	A	Shrewsbury Town	D	1-1	Graham	4,240
41		23	H	Sheffield Wednesday	W	4-0	Evans, Bourne, own-goal (Henson), Harkouk	20,018
42		26	A	Port Vale	L	1-4	Bourne	3,990
43		30	A	Chesterfield	W	2-0	Harkouk, Chatterton	5,122
44	May	3	H	Wrexham	W	2-1	P. Hinshelwood (pen), Swindlehurst	18,583
45		7	H	Lincoln City	W	4-1	P. Hinshelwood 2 (2 pens), Bourne, Perrin	18,305
46		11	A	Wrexham	W	4-2	Swindlehurst, Perrin, Harkouk, Bourne	18,451

Final League Position: 3rd in Division Three

Appearances
Sub Appearances
1 own-goal Goals

FA Cup

1	Nov	20	A	Brighton & Hove Albion	D	2-2	Evans, Harkouk	29,510
R		23	H	Brighton & Hove Albion	D	1-1*	Harkouk	29,174
2R	Dec	6	N+	Brighton & Hove Albion	W	1-0	Holder	14,118
2		11	H	Enfield	W	4-0	Swindlehurst 2, Silkman, P. Hinshelwood	13,570
3	Jan	8	A	Liverpool	D	0-0		44,730
R		11	H	Liverpool	L	2-3	P. Hinshelwood, Graham	42,664

* After extra-time. + Played at Stamford Bridge, Chelsea

Appearances
Sub Appearances
Goals

League Cup

1	Aug	14	H	Portsmouth	D	2-2	Kemp 2	12,936
		17	A	Portsmouth	W	1-0	Taylor	9,774
2		31	H	Watford	L	1-3	Swindlehurst	14,105

Appearances
Sub Appearances
Goals

Hammond	Wall	Sansom	Holder	Cannon	Evans	Chatterton	Hinshelwood M	Kemp	Swindlehurst	Taylor	Harkouk	Hinshelwood P	Walsh	Silkman	Burns	Jump	Perrin	Smillie	Heppolette	Graham	Brennan	Hilaire	Bourne	Murphy	Caswell
1	2	3	**4**	5	6	7	8	9	10	11	12														
1	2	3	4	5	6	7	8	9		11	10														
1	2	3	4	5	6	7	**8**	9	10	11		12													
1	2	3	4	5	6	7			9	11			8	10											
	2	3		5	6	7		9	**10**		12	8		11	1	4									
1	2	3		5	6	7			9	11		8		10		4									
1	2	3		5	6	7			9	11		8				4	10								
1	2	3	12	4	6	7			9			8		**11**		5	10								
1	2	3		4	6	7			10			8				5	9	11							
1	12	3	4	2	6	7			**9**			8				5	10		11						
1		3	4	2	6	7			9			8				5	10		11						
1		3	11	2	6	7			10			8				5	9		4						
1		3	11	2	6	7			10			8				5	9		4						
1		3	11	2	6	7			10			8				5	9		4						
1	12	3	11	2	6	7			10			**8**				5	9		4						
1		3	11	2	6	7			10			8				5	9		4						
1		3	7	5	6				10		11	2					9		4	8					
1		3	**4**	5	6	12			10			2		11			9		7	8					
1		3	4	5	6				10			2		11			9		7	8					
1		3	4	5	6				10			2		11			9		7	8					
1		3	4	5	6	8					10	2		11			9		7						
1		3	4	5	6	7			12		10	2		**11**			9			8					
1		3	4	5	6	7					10	2		11			9			8					
1		3	4	5	6	7			**10**		8	2		11			9		12						
1		3	4	5	6	7					8	2		12			9		**11**	10					
1		3	4	5	6	**7**			10		8	2					9		12	11					
	2	3	4	5	6	7			10		11	8			1		9								
	2	3	4	5	6	7			10		11	8		9	1										
		3	4	5	6	7			10		11	2		12	1		9			**8**					
	2	3		5	6				10		11	8		**7**	1		9				4	12			
	2	3	4	5	6				10		**11**	7		12	1		9			8					
	2	3	4	5	6				10		11	7			1					8		12	**9**		
	2	3		5	6				10		11	7			1		4			8			9		
		3	4	6	5	12			10		**11**	2			1		7			8			9		
		3	4	5	6	12			**10**		11	2			1		7			8			9		
		3	4	5	6	7			12		**11**	2			1		8			10			9		
		3	4	5	6	10			12		11	2			1		**7**			8			9		
		3	4	5	6	7			10		**11**	2		12	1					8			9		
		3	4	5	6	10			7		11	2			1					8			9		
		3	4	5	6	7			10		11	2			1					8			9		
		3	4	5	6				10		11	2		7	1					**8**			9	12	
		3	4	5	6				7		**11**	2		10	1					8		12	9		
		3		5	6	4			**10**		11	2		7	1		8				12		9		
		3		5	6	4			10			2		8	1		7			11			9		
		3	4	5	6	12			10			2		11	**1**		7			8			9		
		3	4	5	6	7			8		12	2		**11**			10						9		1
25	15	46	37	46	46	33	3	4	39	6	25	42	1	19	20	12	33	1	13	23	1		15		1
	2		1			4			3		3	1		4					2		1	3		1	
			4	2	3	6		1	10	1	11	4		4			9			2	1		9		

Hammond	Wall	Sansom	Holder	Cannon	Evans	Chatterton	Hinshelwood M	Kemp	Swindlehurst	Taylor	Harkouk	Hinshelwood P	Walsh	Silkman	Burns	Jump	Perrin	Smillie	Heppolette	Graham	Brennan	Hilaire	Bourne	Murphy	Caswell
1	5	3	11	2	6	7			10		12	8					9		**4**						
1	5	3	4	2	6	7			10		**11**	8				12	9								
1	2	3	4	5	6				**10**		12	8		11			9		7						
1		3	4	5	6				10			2		11			9		7	8					
1		3	4	5	6	7			10			2		11			9			8					
1		3	4	5	6	7			10		12	2		**11**			9			8					
6	3	6	6	6	6	4			6		1	6		4			6		3	3					
											3					1									
			1		1				2		2	2		1						1					

Hammond	Wall	Sansom	Holder	Cannon	Evans	Chatterton	Hinshelwood M	Kemp	Swindlehurst	Taylor	Harkouk	Hinshelwood P	Walsh	Silkman	Burns	Jump	Perrin	Smillie	Heppolette	Graham	Brennan	Hilaire	Bourne	Murphy	Caswell
1	2	3	4	5	6	7	8	9	**10**	11	12														
1	2	3	4	5	6	7	8	9	10	11															
1	2	3	4	5	6	7			10	**11**			9	8							12				
3	3	3	3	3	3	3	2	2	3	3			1	1											
											1										1				
								2	1	1															

League Table

	P	W	D	L	F	A	Pts
Mansfield Town	46	28	8	10	78	42	64
Brighton & Hove Albion	46	25	11	10	83	40	61
Crystal Palace	46	23	13	10	68	40	59
Rotherham United	46	22	15	9	69	44	59
Wrexham	46	24	10	12	80	54	58
Preston North End	46	21	12	13	64	43	54
Bury	46	23	8	15	64	59	54
Sheffield Wednesday	46	22	9	15	65	55	53
Lincoln City	46	19	14	13	77	70	52
Shrewsbury Town	46	18	11	17	65	59	47
Swindon Town	46	15	15	16	68	75	45
Gillingham	46	16	12	18	55	64	44
Chester	46	18	8	20	48	58	44
Tranmere Rovers	46	13	17	16	51	53	43
Walsall	46	13	15	18	57	65	41
Peterborough United	46	13	15	18	55	65	41
Oxford United	46	12	15	19	55	65	39
Chesterfield	46	14	10	22	56	64	38
Port Vale	46	11	16	19	47	71	38
Portsmouth	46	11	14	21	53	70	36
Reading	46	13	9	24	49	73	35
Northampton Town	46	13	8	25	60	75	34
Grimsby Town	46	12	9	25	45	69	33
York City	46	10	12	24	50	89	32

1977-78

Division Two

Manager: Terry Venables

Did you know that?

Goalkeeper John 'Budgie' Burridge who signed for Palace in March from Aston Villa, became well known for his pre-match warm ups (including hand stands) that were often captured by ITV's *The Big Match* cameras. John went on to play for 15 League clubs in total, still a record for a player, and last featured aged 46 for Queen of the South. He most recently has worked in Dubai as a TV pundit.

Match No.	Date		Venue	Opponents	Result		Scorers	Attendance
1	Aug	20	A	Millwall	W	3-0	Evans, Hilaire, Chatterton	14,856
2		23	H	Mansfield Town	W	3-1	Harkouk 2, M. Hinshelwood	19,001
3		27	H	Hull City	L	0-1		14,382
4	Sep	3	A	Burnley	D	1-1	Chatterton	10,441
5		10	H	Sunderland	D	2-2	Bourne, Swindlehurst	21,305
6		17	A	Sheffield United	W	2-0	Swindlehurst, Harkouk	14,451
7		24	H	Bolton Wanderers	W	2-1	Harkouk, Chatterton	23,604
8	Oct	1	H	Fulham	L	2-3	Harkouk 2	28,343
9		4	A	Blackpool	L	1-3	Chatterton	9,369
10		8	A	Stoke City	W	2-0	Chatterton, Perrin	17,749
11		15	H	Southampton	L	1-2	Perrin	22,652
12		22	A	Brighton & Hove Albion	D	1-1	P. Hinshelwood	28,208
13		29	H	Charlton Athletic	D	1-1	Chatterton	25,994
14	Nov	5	A	Oldham Athletic	D	1-1	Perrin	7,775
15		12	H	Tottenham Hotspur	L	1-2	Harkouk	40,277
16		19	A	Orient	D	0-0		10,037
17		26	H	Cardiff City	W	2-0	Chatterton (pen), Perrin	16,139
18	Dec	3	A	Blackburn Rovers	L	0-3		12,119
19		10	H	Notts County	W	2-0	Cannon, Walsh	14,608
20		17	A	Tottenham Hotspur	D	2-2	Swindlehurst 2	33,211
21		26	H	Luton Town	D	3-3	Silkman 2, Sansom	22,027
22		27	A	Bristol Rovers	L	0-3		11,688
23		31	A	Mansfield Town	W	3-1	Sansom, Swindlehurst 2	9,291
24	Jan	2	H	Millwall	W	1-0	P. Hinshelwood	27,010
25		14	A	Hull City	L	0-1		5,617
26		21	H	Burnley	D	1-1	Hilaire	15,159
27	Feb	11	H	Sheffield United	W	1-0	Swindlehurst	13,391
28		25	A	Fulham	D	1-1	Nicholas	14,160
29	Mar	4	H	Stoke City	L	0-1		14,702
30		11	A	Southampton	L	0-2		22,480
31		14	A	Sunderland	D	0-0		15,962
32		18	H	Brighton & Hove Albion	D	0-0		26,305
33		24	A	Charlton Athletic	L	0-1		14,971
34		25	H	Bristol Rovers	W	1-0	Cannon	13,428
35		27	A	Luton Town	L	0-1		9,816
36	Apr	1	H	Oldham Athletic	D	0-0		11,272
37		8	A	Cardiff City	D	2-2	Chatterton (pen), Harkouk	9,328
38		15	H	Orient	W	1-0	Swindlehurst	15,414
39		18	A	Bolton Wanderers	L	0-2		23,980
40		22	A	Notts County	L	0-2		7,710
41		25	H	Blackpool	D	2-2	Swindlehurst, Chatterton (pen)	11,115
42		29	H	Blackburn Rovers	W	5-0	Harkouk, Walsh, Swindlehurst 3	12,664

Final League Position: 9th in Division Two

Appearances
Sub Appearances
Goals

FA Cup

Round	Date		Venue	Opponents	Result		Scorers	Attendance
3	Jan	7	A	Hartlepool United	L	1-2	Chatterton	9,502

Appearances
Sub Appearances
Goals

League Cup

Round	Date		Venue	Opponents	Result		Scorers	Attendance
1	Aug	13	A	Brentford	L	1-2	Harkouk	8,930
		16	H	Brentford	W	5-1	Cannon, Graham, own-goal (Salman), Harkouk 2	10,684
2		30	H	Southampton	D	0-0		19,565
	Sep	13	A	Southampton	L	1-2*	Perrin	19,836

* After extra-time

Appearances
Sub Appearances
1 own-goal — Goals

Caswell	Nicholas	Sansom	Cannon	Evans	Chatterton	Graham	Hilaire	Perrin	Bourne	Harkouk	Wall	Hinshelwood P	Hinshelwood M	Silkman	Burns	Swindlehurst	Brennan	Gilbert	Jump	Blyth	Holder	Walsh	Fenwick	Murphy	Smillie	Burridge	Boyle	Fry
1	2	3	4	5	6	7	8	9	10	**11**	12																	
1		3	5	6	8		7	10	9	11		2	**4**	12														
		3	5	6	8	4	**7**	9	10	11		2			1	12												
	5	3		6	8	4		9	10	**11**	12	2			1	7												
		3	5	6	8	4		9	10	11		2			1	7												
		3	5	6	8	4	9		10	11		2			1	7												
		3	5	6	8	4	7		9	11		2			1	10												
		3	5	6	7		8	12	9	10		2			1	**11**	4											
		3	4		8	5	9		10	11		2			1	7		6										
		3	5		**7**	4	8	9	10		6	2			1	11												
		3	5		4		8	9	10	11	6	2			1	7												
		3	5		8	4	9	12	10	11	6	2			1	**7**												
		3	5		8	4	9	12	**10**	11	6	2			1	7												
		3	5		8	4	9	10		**11**	6	2			1	7			12									
		3	5		8	4	9	10		11		2			1	7				6								
		3	5		8	4	9	10		11		2			1	7				6								
		3	5		8	4	9	10				2		11	1	7				6								
		3	5		8	4	9	10				2		11	1	7				6								
	6	3	5		8		9					2		11	1	7					4	10						
	6	5	4		8					10		2		11	1	7					3		9	12				
	6	3	5		**7**					10		2		11	1	9					**4**	12	8					
	2		5		8		7				3			11	1	9		6				10		4				
	7	3	5		8				10			2	12	**11**	1	9		6			4							
	7	3	5		8				10			2		11	1	9		6			4							
	7	3							10			2	8	11	1	9		6		5	4							
	7	3					8		**10**			2		11	1	9		6		5	4				12			
	7	3	5				8			10		2		**11**	1	9		6			4	12						
	7	3	5			12	8			10		2		11	1	**9**		6			4							
	5	3	6			8	7			**10**		2		11	1	9					4	12						
	6	3	5			4	9					**2**		11	1	7						10	8	12				
	6	3	5			8						2		12	1	9					7	10	4	**11**				
	7	3	5			8						2				9		6				10	4	11		1		
	7	3	5			8	12					2				9		6				10	4	**11**		1		
	10	3	5				12					2		11		8		6			4	9	**7**			1		
		3	5		4		**7**					2		**11**		9					8	10		12		1	6	
	7	3	5		8					11		2		12		10		6				9	**4**			1		
	7	3	5		8					11		2				9		6			**4**	10		12		1		
		3	5		8		12			11		2		7		9		6			4	**10**				1		
	11	3	5		8		10					2		7		9		6					4			1		
		3	5		**7**		9			10		2		11		8		6					4			1		
	4	3	5		8		12			**11**		2		7		9		6				10				1		
	4	3	5		8					11		2		7		9		6				10						1
2	23	41	39	8	32	20	26	12	17	26	6	40	2	21	29	39	1	18		6	15	13	10	4		10	1	1
						1	4	3			2		1	3		1			1			3		4	1			
	1	2	2	1	9		2	4	1	9		2	1	2		12						2						

Caswell	Nicholas	Sansom	Cannon	Evans	Chatterton	Graham	Hilaire	Perrin	Bourne	Harkouk	Wall	Hinshelwood P	Hinshelwood M	Silkman	Burns	Swindlehurst	Brennan	Gilbert	Jump	Blyth	Holder	Walsh	Fenwick	Murphy	Smillie	Burridge	Boyle	Fry
	7	3	5		8				10			2		11	1	9		6			4							
	1	1	1		1				1			1		1	1	1		1			1							
					1																							

Caswell	Nicholas	Sansom	Cannon	Evans	Chatterton	Graham	Hilaire	Perrin	Bourne	Harkouk	Wall	Hinshelwood P	Hinshelwood M	Silkman	Burns	Swindlehurst	Brennan	Gilbert	Jump	Blyth	Holder	Walsh	Fenwick	Murphy	Smillie	Burridge	Boyle	Fry
		3	5	6	8	4	7	10	9	11		2			1													
		3	5	6	8	7	4	9	10	11		2			1													
		3	5	6	8	4		9	10	11		2			1	7												
		3	5	6	8	4		9	10	**11**	12	2			1	7												
		4	4	4	4	4	2	4	4	4		4			4	2												
											1																	
			1			1		1		3																		

League Table

	P	W	D	L	F	A	Pts
Bolton Wanderers	42	24	10	8	63	33	58
Southampton	42	22	13	7	70	39	57
Tottenham Hotspur	42	20	16	6	83	49	56
Brighton & Hove Albion	42	22	12	8	63	38	56
Blackburn Rovers	42	16	13	13	56	60	45
Sunderland	42	14	16	12	67	59	44
Stoke City	42	16	10	16	53	49	42
Oldham Athletic	42	13	16	13	54	58	42
Crystal Palace	42	13	15	14	50	47	41
Fulham	42	14	13	15	49	49	41
Burnley	42	15	10	17	56	64	40
Sheffield United	42	16	8	18	62	73	40
Luton Town	42	14	10	18	54	52	38
Orient	42	10	18	14	43	49	38
Notts County	42	11	16	15	54	62	38
Millwall	42	12	14	16	49	57	38
Charlton Athletic	42	13	12	17	55	68	38
Bristol Rovers	42	13	12	17	61	77	38
Cardiff City	42	13	12	17	51	71	38
Blackpool	42	12	13	17	59	60	37
Mansfield Town	42	10	11	21	49	69	31
Hull City	42	8	12	22	34	52	28

1978-79

Division Two

Manager: Terry Venables

Did you know that?

The 51,482 attendance against Burnley that saw Palace promoted in the last game of the season is still a home record attendance.

Match No.	Date		Venue	Opponents	Result		Scorers	Attendance
1	Aug	19	A	Blackburn Rovers	D	1-1	Swindlehurst	9,463
2		22	H	Luton Town	W	3-1	Swindlehurst, Hilaire, Murphy	17,639
3		26	H	West Ham United	D	1-1	Gilbert	32,611
4	Sep	2	A	Sheffield United	W	2-0	Hilaire, Elwiss	17,388
5		9	H	Sunderland	D	1-1	Chatterton (pen)	21,112
6		16	A	Millwall	W	3-0	Murphy, Chatterton, Nicholas	11,693
7		23	H	Oldham Athletic	W	1-0	Swindlehurst	18,318
8		30	A	Stoke City	D	1-1	Murphy	19,070
9	Oct	7	H	Brighton & Hove Albion	W	3-1	Hilaire 2, Swindlehurst	33,685
10		14	A	Preston North End	W	3-2	Walsh 2, Elwiss	10,795
11		21	A	Wrexham	D	0-0		15,132
12		28	H	Fulham	L	0-1		28,733
13	Nov	4	A	Burnley	L	1-2	Chatterton (pen)	11,067
14		11	H	Blackburn Rovers	W	3-0	Walsh, Swindlehurst 2 (1 pen)	17,006
15		18	A	West Ham United	D	1-1	Elwiss	31,245
16		21	H	Sheffield United	W	3-1	Elwiss, Nicholas, Swindlehurst	19,504
17		25	A	Cardiff City	D	2-2	Elwiss, Swindlehurst	8,739
18	Dec	2	H	Newcastle United	W	1-0	Elwiss	19,287
19		9	A	Notts County	D	0-0		11,011
20		16	H	Leicester City	W	3-1	Cannon, Swindlehurst, Elwiss	17,330
21		23	A	Cambridge United	D	0-0		8,081
22		26	H	Bristol Rovers	L	0-1		21,605
23		30	H	Orient	D	1-1	Hilaire	20,100
24	Jan	20	H	Millwall	D	0-0		21,142
25	Feb	10	H	Stoke City	D	1-1	Walsh	23,313
26		17	A	Brighton & Hove Albion	D	0-0		23,795
27		24	H	Preston North End	D	0-0		17,592
28	Mar	3	H	Wrexham	W	1-0	Walsh	15,154
29		10	A	Fulham	D	0-0		16,654
30		14	A	Sunderland	W	2-1	Hilaire, Cannon	34,986
31		24	A	Luton Town	W	1-0	Nicholas	11,008
32		27	A	Charlton Athletic	D	1-1	Swindlehurst	15,065
33		31	H	Cardiff City	W	2-0	Smillie, Walsh	18,672
34	Apr	3	A	Oldham Athletic	D	0-0		5,620
35		7	A	Newcastle United	L	0-1		18,860
36		10	H	Cambridge United	D	1-1	Swindlehurst	21,795
37		14	A	Bristol Rovers	W	1-0	Walsh	10,986
38		17	H	Charlton Athletic	W	1-0	Murphy	30,006
39		20	A	Leicester City	D	1-1	Hinshelwood	16,767
40		28	H	Notts County	W	2-0	Swindlehurst, Murphy	23,880
41	May	5	A	Orient	W	1-0	Swindlehurst	19,945
42		11	H	Burnley	W	2-0	Walsh, Swindlehurst	+51,482

Final League Position: 1st in Division Two.

+ Ground attendance record

Appearances
Sub Appearances
Goals

FA Cup

	Date		Venue	Opponents	Result		Scorers	Attendance
3	Jan	9	A	Middlesbrough	D	1-1	Walsh	21,441
R		15	H	Middlesbrough	W	1-0	Sansom	23,119
4		29	H	Bristol City	W	3-0	Nicholas, Fenwick, Kember	21,463
5	Feb	26	H	Wolverhampton Wanderers	L	0-1		26,790

Appearances
Sub Appearances
Goals

League Cup

	Date		Venue	Opponents	Result		Scorers	Attendance
2	Aug	29	A	Bristol City	W	2-1	Murphy, Swindlehurst	10,433
3	Oct	4	A	Aston Villa	D	1-1	Chatterton (pen)	30,690
R		10	H	Aston Villa	D	0-0*		33,155
2R		16	N+	Aston Villa	L	0-3		25,445

* After extra-time. + Played at Highfield Road, Coventry

Appearances
Sub Appearances
Goals

Burridge	Hinshelwood	Sansom	Nicholas	Cannon	Gilbert	Chatterton	Murphy	Swindlehurst	Elwiss	Hilaire	Fenwick	Silkman	Walsh	Kember	Smillie	Hazell	Sealy
1	2	3	4	5	6	7	**8**	9	10	11	12						
1	2	3	4	5	6	7	8	9	10	11							
1	2	3	4	5	6	7	8	9	10	11							
1	2	3	4	5	6	7	8	9	10	11							
1	2	3	4	5	6	7	**8**	9	10	11		12					
1	2	3	4	5	6	7	8	9	10	11							
1	2	3	4	5	6	7	8	9	10	11							
1	2	3	4	5	6	7	8	9	10	11							
1	2	3	4	5	6	7	8	**9**	10	11			12				
1	2	3	4	5	6	7	8		10	11			9				
1	**2**	3	7		6	4	8	9	10	11	5		12				
1		3	7	**5**	6	4	8	9	10	11	2		12				
1		3	7	5	6	4	12	9	**10**	11	2			8			
1		3	7	5	6		8	9		11	2		10	4			
1		3	7	5	6		8	9	12	**11**	2		10	4			
1		3	7	5	6		8	9	**10**		2		11	4	12		
1		3		5	6		8	9	11	12	4		10	**7**		2	
1		3		5	6		8	9	10		7		11	4		2	
1		3		5	6		8	9	10		2		11	7		4	
1		3	7	5	6		8	9	10		2		11	4			
1	2	3	7	5	6			9	**10**	12	8		11	4			
1		3	7	5	6		8	9		12	2		11	**4**	10		
1		3	7	5	6		**8**	9		10			11	4	12	2	
1	2	3	7	5	6		**8**	9		12	10		11	4			
1	2	3	7	5	6		8	9			10		11	4			
1	2	3	7	5	6		10	9			8		11	4			
1	2	3	7	5	6		8	9			**10**		11	4	12		
1	2	3	7	5	6		**8**	9		11			10	4	12		
1	2	3	7	5	6		8	9		11			10	4			
1	**2**	3	7	5			8	9		10	12		11	4		6	
1	2	3	7	5	6		8	9		11			10	4			
1	2	3	7	5	6		8	9		10			11	4			
1	2	3	7	5	6		8	9					**11**	4	10		12
1	2	3	7	5	6		8				12		10	4	**11**		9
1	2	3	7	5	6		8	9		12	**10**		11	4			
1	2	3	**7**	5	6		8	9		10			11	4	12		
1	2	3	7	5	6		8	**9**			12		11	4			10
1	2	3		5	6		8	9			7		11	4			10
1	2	3		5	6		8	9		12	7		11	**4**			10
1	2	3	7	5	6		8	9		11			10	4			
1	2	3	7	5	6		8	9		11	4		10				
1	2	3	7	5	6		8	9		11			10	4			
42	31	42	37	41	41	13	40	40	19	25	20		30	29	3	5	4
							1		1	6	4	1	3		5		1
	1		3	2	1	3	5	14	7	6			8		1		

Burridge	Hinshelwood	Sansom	Nicholas	Cannon	Gilbert	Chatterton	Murphy	Swindlehurst	Elwiss	Hilaire	Fenwick	Silkman	Walsh	Kember	Smillie	Hazell	Sealy
1	2	3	7	5	6		8	9			10		11	4			
1	2	3	7	5	6		8			10	9		11	4			
1	2	3	7	5	6		8	10			9		11	4			
1	**2**	3	7	5	6		8	9		12	10		11	4			
4	4	4	4	4	4		4	3		1	4		4	4			
										1							
		1	1								1		1	1			

Burridge	Hinshelwood	Sansom	Nicholas	Cannon	Gilbert	Chatterton	Murphy	Swindlehurst	Elwiss	Hilaire	Fenwick	Silkman	Walsh	Kember	Smillie	Hazell	Sealy
1	2	3	8	5	6	4	**7**	9	10	11							
1	2	3	7	5	6	4	8	9	10	11							
1	2	3	7	5	6	4	8	**9**	10	11			12				
1	2	3	7	**5**	6	4	8		10	11	12		9				
4	4	4	4	4	4	4	4	3	4	4			1				
											1		1				
						1	1	1									

League Table

	P	W	D	L	F	A	Pts
Crystal Palace	42	19	19	4	51	24	57
Brighton & Hove Albion	42	23	10	9	72	39	56
Stoke City	42	20	16	6	58	31	56
Sunderland	42	22	11	9	70	44	55
West Ham United	42	18	14	10	70	39	50
Notts County	42	14	16	12	48	60	44
Preston North End	42	12	18	12	59	57	42
Newcastle United	42	17	8	17	51	55	42
Cardiff City	42	16	10	16	56	70	42
Fulham	42	13	15	14	50	47	41
Orient	42	15	10	17	51	51	40
Cambridge United	42	12	16	14	44	52	40
Burnley	42	14	12	16	51	62	40
Oldham Athletic	42	13	13	16	52	61	39
Wrexham	42	12	14	16	45	42	38
Bristol Rovers	42	14	10	18	48	60	38
Leicester City	42	10	17	15	43	52	37
Luton Town	42	13	10	19	60	57	36
Charlton Athletic	42	11	13	18	60	69	35
Sheffield United	42	11	12	19	52	69	34
Millwall	42	11	10	21	42	61	32
Blackburn Rovers	42	10	10	22	41	72	30

1979-80

Division One

Manager: Terry Venables

Did you know that?

Palace twice smashed their record transfer fee at the start of the season. Firstly, with the £465,000 signing of Gerry Francis from Queen's Park Rangers in July, which was beaten the following month when Mike Flanagan signed from Charlton for £650,000.

Match No.	Date		Venue	Opponents	Result		Scorers	Attendance
1	Aug	18	A	Manchester City	D	0-0		40,681
2		21	H	Southampton	D	0-0		31,756
3		25	A	Middlesbrough	D	1-1	Swindlehurst	24,521
4	Sep	1	H	Derby County	W	4-0	Flanagan 2, Nicholas, Swindlehurst	25,127
5		8	A	Wolverhampton Wanderers	D	1-1	Swindlehurst	24,580
6		15	H	Aston Villa	W	2-0	Murphy 2	28,156
7		22	A	Stoke City	W	2-1	Hilaire, Cannon	19,255
8		29	H	Ipswich Town	W	4-1	Swindlehurst, Hinshelwood, Francis (pen), Cannon	29,885
9	Oct	6	H	Tottenham Hotspur	D	1-1	Walsh	45,296
10		9	A	Southampton	L	1-4	Hinshelwood	23,174
11		13	A	Everton	L	1-3	Flanagan	30,645
12		20	H	Bristol City	D	1-1	Cannon (pen)	27,333
13		27	A	Bolton Wanderers	D	1-1	Smillie	15,132
14	Nov	3	H	Manchester City	W	2-0	Walsh, Swindlehurst	29,443
15		10	H	Arsenal	W	1-0	Swindlehurst	42,887
16		17	A	Manchester United	D	1-1	Swindlehurst	52,800
17		24	H	Coventry City	D	0-0		26,209
18	Dec	1	A	Leeds United	L	0-1		21,330
19		8	H	Nottingham Forest	W	1-0	Walsh	34,782
20		15	A	Liverpool	L	0-3		42,898
21		26	A	Brighton & Hove Albion	L	0-3		28,358
22		29	H	Middlesbrough	L	1-2	Francis (pen)	24,880
23	Jan	1	H	Norwich City	D	0-0		30,254
24		12	A	Derby County	W	2-1	Walsh 2	16,872
25		19	H	Wolverhampton Wanderers	W	1-0	Flanagan	22,577
26		26	H	West Bromwich Albion	D	2-2	Hilaire, Kember	23,258
27	Feb	2	A	Aston Villa	L	0-2		29,469
28		9	H	Stoke City	L	0-1		21,181
29		19	A	Ipswich Town	L	0-3		23,012
30		23	H	Everton	D	1-1	Walsh	22,857
31	Mar	1	A	Bristol City	W	2-0	Nicholas, Flanagan	15,947
32		8	H	Bolton Wanderers	W	3-1	Gilbert, Hilaire, Murphy	18,728
33		15	A	Tottenham Hotspur	D	0-0		28,419
34		22	A	Arsenal	D	1-1	Sansom	37,606
35		29	H	Manchester United	L	0-2		33,003
36	Apr	1	A	West Bromwich Albion	L	0-3		17,090
37		5	H	Brighton & Hove Albion	D	1-1	Cannon	31,466
38		7	A	Norwich City	L	1-2	Francis	17,562
39		12	H	Leeds United	W	1-0	Hilaire	25,318
40		19	A	Coventry City	L	1-2	Hilaire	14,401
41		26	H	Liverpool	D	0-0		45,583
42	May	3	A	Nottingham Forest	L	0-4		24,529

Final League Position: 13th in Division One

Appearances
Sub Appearances
Goals

FA Cup

3	Jan	5	A	Swansea City	D	2-2	Kember, Walsh	17,970
R		8	H	Swansea City	D	3-3*	Hinshelwood, Fenwick, Hilaire	27,006
2R		14	N+	Swansea City	L	1-2	Boyle	20,012

* After extra-time. + Played at Ninian Park, Cardiff.

Appearances
Sub Appearances
Goals

League Cup

2	Aug	29	A	Stockport County	D	1-1	Flanagan	6,193
	Sep	4	H	Stockport County	W	7-0	Murphy, Francis, Flanagan 2, Walsh 2, Hilaire	18,465
3		25	H	Wolverhampton Wanderers	L	1-2	Flanagan	30,645

Appearances
Sub Appearances
Goals

Burridge	Hinshelwood	Sansom	Nicholas	Cannon	Gilbert	Murphy	Francis	Swindlehurst	Flanagan	Hilaire	Fenwick	Walsh	Kember	Smillie	Boyle	Goodchild	Fry	Brooks
1	2	3	4	5	6	7	8	9	10	11								
1	2	3	4	5	6	7	8	9	10	11								
1	2	3	4	5	6	7	8	9	10	**11**	12							
1	2	**3**	4	5	6	7		9	10	11		12	8					
1	2	3	4	5	6	7	8	9	10	11								
1	2	3	4	5	6	**7**	8	9	10	11		12						
1	2	3	**4**	5	6	7	8	9	10	11			12					
1	2	3	4	5	6	7	8	9	10	11								
1	2	3	4	5	6	7	8	**9**	10	11		12						
1	2	3	4	5	6	7		9	10	11		12	**8**					
1	2	3	4	5	6	**7**	8	12	10	11		9						
1	2	3	4	5	6	7			10	11		9	8					
1	2	3	4	5	**6**	7			10	11		9	8	12				
1	2	3	4	5	6	7		10		**11**		9	8	12				
1	2	3	4	5	6	7	8	10		11		9						
1	2	3	4	5	6	7	**8**	10	9	11		12						
1	2	3	4	5	6	7	8	10	9	**11**		12						
1	2	3	4	5	6	**7**	8	10		11		9	12					
1	2	3	4	5	6	**7**	8	10		11	12	9						
1	2	3	4	5	6	7	8	10		11		9						
1	2	**3**	4	5	6	7	8	10	9	11	12							
1	2		6	4	5	7	8	**10**	9	11	3	12						
1	2		4	5	6	**7**	8		9	11	3	10	12					
1	2			3	6			7		11	8	9	4	**10**	5	12		
1	2			3	6	7		12	10	**11**	8	9	4		5			
1	2	3		5	6	7	**8**	12	10	11		9	4					
1	2	3	7	5			**8**	12	10	11	9		4		6			
1	2	3	4	5	6	12		9	10	11	**8**		7					
1	2	3	4	5	6	7	8		10	11		9						
1	2		4	5	6	7	8		10	11	3	9						
	2	3	4	5	6	7	8		10	11		9					1	
	2	3	4	5	6	7	8		10	11		9					1	
	2	3	4	5	6	7	8		10	11		9					1	
	2	3	4	5	6	7	8		10	11		9					1	
	2	3	4	5	6		8		10	11	7	9					1	
	2	3	4	5	6		**8**		10	11	7	9		12			1	
1	2	3	4	5	6	7	8		10	11				9				
1	2	3	4	5	6	**7**	8		10	11	12			9				
1	**2**	3	4	5	6		8		10	11	7			9				12
1	2	3	4	5		7	8		9	11				10	6			
1	2		4	5	6	**7**	8		9	11	3	10			12			
1	2	3	4	5	6	7	8		10	11		9						
36	42	36	39	42	40	36	34	21	36	42	11	22	10	5	4		6	
						1		4			4	7	3	3	1	1		1
	2	1	2	4	1	3	3	7	5	5		6	1	1				

Burridge	Hinshelwood	Sansom	Nicholas	Cannon	Gilbert	Murphy	Francis	Swindlehurst	Flanagan	Hilaire	Fenwick	Walsh	Kember	Smillie	Boyle	Goodchild	Fry	Brooks
1	2		4	5	6	12	8		**10**	11	3	9	7					
1	2			5	6	**8**		9		11	3	10	4	7		12		
1	2			3	6	7		9		11	8	10	4		5			
3	3		1	3	3	2	1	2	1	3	3	3	3	1	1			
						1										1		
	1									1	1	1	1		1			

Burridge	Hinshelwood	Sansom	Nicholas	Cannon	Gilbert	Murphy	Francis	Swindlehurst	Flanagan	Hilaire	Fenwick	Walsh	Kember	Smillie	Boyle	Goodchild	Fry	Brooks
1	2	3	4	5	6	7		9	10	11			8					
1	2	3	4	5	6	7	**8**	9	10	11		12						
1	2	3	4	5	6	7	8	9	10	11								
3	3	3	3	3	3	3	2	3	3	3			1					
												1						
						1	1		4	1		2						

League Table

	P	W	D	L	F	A	Pts
Liverpool	42	25	10	7	81	30	60
Manchester United	42	24	10	8	65	35	58
Ipswich Town	42	22	9	11	68	39	53
Arsenal	42	18	16	8	52	36	52
Nottingham Forest	42	20	8	14	63	43	48
Wolverhampton W	42	19	9	14	58	47	47
Aston Villa	42	16	14	12	51	50	46
Southampton	42	18	9	15	65	53	45
Middlesbrough	42	16	12	14	50	44	44
West Bromwich Albion	42	11	19	12	54	50	41
Leeds United	42	13	14	15	46	50	40
Norwich City	42	13	14	15	58	66	40
Crystal Palace	42	12	16	14	41	50	40
Tottenham Hotspur	42	15	10	17	52	62	40
Coventry City	42	16	7	19	56	66	39
Brighton & Hove Albion	42	11	15	16	47	57	37
Manchester City	42	12	13	17	43	66	37
Stoke City	42	13	10	19	44	58	36
Everton	42	9	17	16	43	51	35
Bristol City	42	9	13	20	37	66	31
Derby County	42	11	8	23	47	67	30
Bolton Wanderers	42	5	15	22	38	73	25

1980-81

Division One

Manager: Terry Venables until 14 October 1980; Ernie Walley until 1 December 1980; Malcolm Allison until 26 January 1981, then Dario Gradi.

Did you know that?

Ron Noades arrived as chairman and owner in late January 1981, but a seven-game losing streak and four managers within a season, plus a fair amount of transfer activity in and out, saw Palace relegated 13 points from safety.

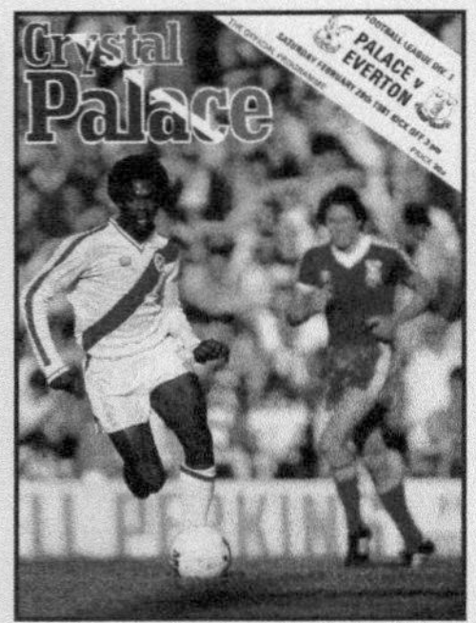

Match No.	Date		Venue	Opponents	Result		Scorers	Attendance
1	Aug	16	A	Liverpool	L	0-3		42,777
2		19	H	Tottenham Hotspur	L	3-4	Hilaire, Smillie, Cannon	27,102
3		23	H	Middlesbrough	W	5-2	Allen 3 (1 pen), Sealy, Francis	16,713
4		30	A	Wolverhampton Wanderers	L	0-2		20,601
5	Sep	6	A	Coventry City	L	1-3	Allen	13,091
6		13	H	Ipswich Town	L	1-2	Lovell	24,282
7		20	A	Everton	L	0-5		26,950
8		27	H	Aston Villa	L	0-1		18,398
9	Oct	4	H	West Bromwich Albion	L	0-1		16,081
10		11	A	Sunderland	L	0-1		25,444
11		18	H	Leicester City	W	2-1	Hilaire, Allen (pen)	16,387
12		21	H	Southampton	W	3-2	Flanagan 3	20,630
13		25	A	Leeds United	L	0-1		19,208
14		29	A	Norwich City	D	1-1	Francis	15,782
15	Nov	1	H	Manchester United	W	1-0	Nicholas	31,181
16		8	A	Birmingham City	L	0-1		16,910
17		12	A	Tottenham Hotspur	L	2-4	Hilaire, Walsh	25,777
18		15	H	Liverpool	D	2-2	Francis (pen), Walsh	31,154
19		22	A	Stoke City	L	0-1		13,422
20		29	H	Manchester City	L	2-3	Walsh, Sealy	16,575
21	Dec	6	A	Nottingham Forest	L	0-3		20,223
22		13	H	Norwich City	W	4-1	Allen 2, Murphy, Francis	15,257
23		20	A	Southampton	L	2-4	Sealy, Allen	19,352
24		26	H	Arsenal	D	2-2	Sealy 2	29,850
25		27	A	Brighton & Hove Albion	L	2-3	Murphy, own-goal (Gregory)	27,367
26	Jan	10	H	Stoke City	D	1-1	Boyle	14,154
27		17	H	Wolverhampton Wanderers	D	0-0		15,080
28		31	A	Middlesbrough	L	0-2		16,099
29	Feb	7	A	Ipswich Town	L	2-3	Walsh, own-goal (Mariner)	25,036
30		17	H	Coventry City	L	0-3		12,268
31		21	A	Aston Villa	L	1-2	Hinshelwood	27,203
32		28	H	Everton	L	2-3	Allen (pen), Hilaire	14,594
33	Mar	7	A	West Bromwich Albion	L	0-1		15,999
34		14	H	Sunderland	L	0-1		16,748
35		21	A	Leicester City	D	1-1	Price	15,176
36		28	H	Leeds United	L	0-1		15,053
37	Apr	4	A	Manchester United	L	0-1		37,974
38		11	H	Birmingham City	W	3-1	Langley 2, Lovell	9,820
39		18	H	Brighton & Hove Albion	L	0-3		18,792
40		20	A	Arsenal	L	2-3	Price, Langley	24,346
41		25	H	Nottingham Forest	L	1-3	Smillie	12,138
42	May	2	A	Manchester City	D	1-1	Walsh	31,017

Final League Position: 22nd in Division One — Appearances / Sub Appearances / 2 own-goals — Goals

FA Cup

3	Jan	3	A	Manchester City	L	0-4		39,347

Appearances
Sub Appearances
Goals

League Cup

2	Aug	26	A	Bolton Wanderers	W	3-0	Murphy 2, Flanagan	9,931
	Sep	2	H	Bolton Wanderers	W	2-1	Francis, Allen	15,536
3		24	A	Tottenham Hotspur	D	0-0		29,654
R		30	H	Tottenham Hotspur	L	1-3*	Allen (pen)	26,885

* After extra-time

Appearances
Sub Appearances
Goals

Barron	Hinshelwood	Fenwick	Nicholas	Cannon	Gilbert	Smillie	Francis	Allen	Flanagan	Hilaire	Murphy	Sealy	Leahy	Lovell	Brooks	Walsh	Boyle	Fry	Gennoe	Carter L	Goodchild	Dare	Banfield	Price	Bason	Langley	Paul
1	**2**	3	4	5	6	7	8	9	10	11	12																
1		3	2	5	6	**7**	8	9	10	11	4	12															
1		3	2	5	6	7	8	9	10		4	12	**11**														
1		3		5	6		8	9	10	11	4	12	**7**	2													
1	2	3		5	6	7	8	9	10	11	4																
1	2	3		5	6	7	8	9	10	**11**		12		4													
1	2	3		5	**6**	7	8	9	10		11			4	12												
1	2	3	4	5	6	7		9	10		11	8															
1	2	3	4	5	6	**7**	8	9	10	11						12											
1	2	3	4	5	6		8	9	7	11						10											
1	2	3	4	5	6	12	8	9	7	**11**						10											
1	2	3	4	5	6		8	9	7	11						10											
1	2	3	4	5	6		**8**	9	7	11				12		10											
1	2	3	4	5	6	**11**	8		10			12		7		9											
1	2	3	4	5	6	11	8		10					7		9											
1	2	3	4	5	6	11			**10**		8			**7**		9	12										
1	2	3	4	5	6		8		10	11				7		9											
1	2	3	4	5	6		8		**10**	11		12		7		9											
1		3	4	5	6		8		10	11				7		9	2										
1	4	3		2	6		**8**		10	11		12		7		9	5										
1	2	3	4	5	6		8	10		11		7				9											
1	2		4	5	6		8	9		11	**7**	10				12	3										
	2		4	5	6		8	9		11	7	10					3	1									
	2		4	5	6	12	8	9		**11**	7	10					3	1									
	2		4	5		11	8	9			7	10		**6**	12		3	1									
	2		4	5	6	12	8			**11**		9		7			3		1	10							
	2		4	5	6	11	8	10			7	9					3		1								
	2		4	5	6	11		10				9		7	**8**		3		1		12						
1	3		8		4	7		9			10			2	6	11	5										
	2		4			8		9		10	**7**				6	11	5	1				3	12				
	2		4			7		9		11		10			8		5	1				3	6				
1	2		4		6	**7**		9		11		10		3	8		5			12							
1	2		4		6					11		9		7	8	10	5						3				
1	2			**5**	7	6				11				3	8	9								4	12	10	
1	2				6					11				3	8	9	5							4	7	10	
1	3				6					11	12			**2**	8	9	5							4	7	10	
1	3				6					11				2	8	9	5							4	7	10	
	3				6					11				2	8	9	5	1						**4**	7	10	12
1	3			6	12					11				2	8	**9**	5							4	7	10	
1	3			5	6			**9**		11	12			2	8									4	7	10	
1	3			5	6	11					4			2	8	9									7	10	
1	3			5	6	7				**11**	12				8	9								4	2	10	
33	38	21	28	33	38	21	25	25	20	31	15	12	2	24	15	23	19	6	3	1		2	2	8	8	9	
					1	3					4	7		1	2	2	1			1	1		1		1		1
	1		1	1		2	4	9	3	4	2	5		2		5	1							2		3	

Barron	Hinshelwood	Fenwick	Nicholas	Cannon	Gilbert	Smillie	Francis	Allen	Flanagan	Hilaire	Murphy	Sealy	Leahy	Lovell	Brooks	Walsh	Boyle	Fry	Gennoe	Carter L	Goodchild	Dare	Banfield	Price	Bason	Langley	Paul
	2		**4**	5	6	11					7	9		8		10	3	1			12						
	1		1	1	1	1					1	1		1		1	1	1									
																					1						

Barron	Hinshelwood	Fenwick	Nicholas	Cannon	Gilbert	Smillie	Francis	Allen	Flanagan	Hilaire	Murphy	Sealy	Leahy	Lovell	Brooks	Walsh	Boyle	Fry	Gennoe	Carter L	Goodchild	Dare	Banfield	Price	Bason	Langley	Paul
1		3	2	5	6		8	9	10	11	**4**	12	7														
1		3		5	6	7	8	9	10	11	**4**			2	12												
1	2	3	4	5	6	7	8	9	10		11																
1	2	3	4	5	6	**7**	8	9	10		11	12															
4	2	4	3	4	4	3	4	4	4	2	4		1	1													
												2			1												
							1	2	1		2																

League Table

	P	W	D	L	F	A	Pts
Aston Villa	42	26	8	8	72	40	60
Ipswich Town	42	23	10	9	77	43	56
Arsenal	42	19	15	8	61	45	53
West Bromwich Albion	42	20	12	10	60	42	52
Liverpool	42	17	17	8	62	42	51
Southampton	42	20	10	12	76	56	50
Nottingham Forest	42	19	12	11	62	44	50
Manchester United	42	15	18	9	51	36	48
Leeds United	42	17	10	15	39	47	44
Tottenham Hotspur	42	14	15	13	70	68	43
Stoke City	42	12	18	12	51	60	42
Manchester City	42	14	11	17	56	59	39
Birmingham City	42	13	12	17	50	61	38
Middlesbrough	42	16	5	21	53	61	37
Everton	42	13	10	19	55	58	36
Coventry City	42	13	10	19	48	68	36
Sunderland	42	14	7	21	52	53	35
Wolverhampton W	42	13	9	20	43	55	35
Brighton & Hove Albion	42	14	7	21	54	67	35
Norwich City	42	13	7	22	49	73	33
Leicester City	42	13	6	23	40	67	32
Crystal Palace	42	6	7	29	47	83	19

1981-82

Division Two

Manager: Dario Gradi until 10 November 1981, then Steve Kember.

Did you know that?

November saw Steve Kember take the manager's hot seat for the first time. This was one of four spells in charge for the popular ex-player that has included two caretaker stints.

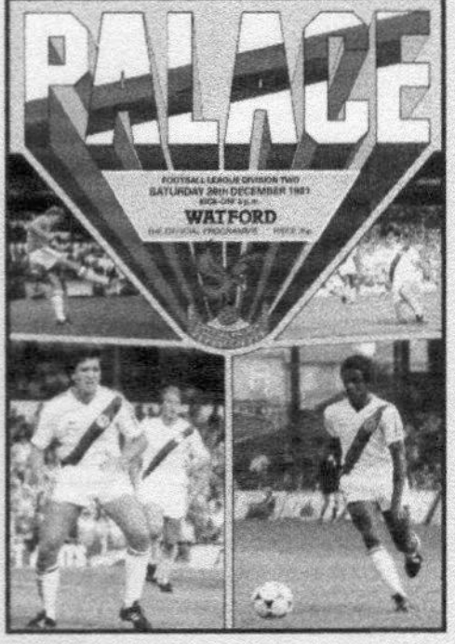

Match No.	Date		Venue	Opponents	Result		Scorers	Attendance
1	Aug	29	H	Cambridge United	W	2-1	Hinshelwood 2 (2 pens)	11,201
2	Sep	2	A	Norwich City	L	0-1		14,434
3		5	A	Sheffield Wednesday	L	0-1		18,476
4		12	H	Charlton Athletic	W	2-0	Walsh 2	14,227
5		19	A	Queen's Park Rangers	L	0-1		17,039
6		22	H	Orient	W	1-0	Hilaire	11,061
7		26	H	Shrewsbury Town	L	0-1		9,037
8	Oct	3	A	Leicester City	D	1-1	Hilaire	12,558
9		10	H	Rotherham United	W	3-1	Smillie, Brooks, Langley	8,021
10		17	A	Wrexham	W	1-0	Lovell	4,795
11		24	H	Derby County	L	0-1		11,127
12		31	A	Luton Town	L	0-1		11,712
13	Nov	7	H	Blackburn Rovers	L	1-2	Cannon (pen)	9,452
14		21	A	Oldham Athletic	D	0-0		5,581
15		24	H	Norwich City	W	2-1	Mabbutt 2	9,010
16		28	H	Bolton Wanderers	W	1-0	own-goal (Jones)	8,889
17	Dec	5	A	Barnsley	L	0-2		14,877
18	Jan	19	H	Sheffield Wednesday	L	1-2	Wicks	8,289
19		26	A	Cambridge United	D	0-0		3,505
20		30	H	Queen's Park Rangers	D	0-0		15,267
21	Feb	6	A	Charlton Athletic	L	1-2	Brooks	9,072
22		21	A	Orient	D	0-0		5,132
23		27	A	Rotherham United	L	0-2		10,007
24	Mar	9	H	Cardiff City	W	1-0	Langley	6,526
25		13	A	Derby County	L	1-4	own-goal (McAlle)	10,248
26		17	A	Chelsea	W	2-1	Mabbutt, Murphy	13,894
27		20	H	Luton Town	D	3-3	Smillie 2, Mabbutt	12,001
28		23	H	Leicester City	L	0-2		9,506
29		27	A	Blackburn Rovers	L	0-1		8,362
30		31	A	Newcastle United	D	0-0		21,610
31	Apr	3	H	Grimsby Town	L	0-3		7,541
32		9	A	Watford	D	1-1	Giles	18,224
33		12	H	Chelsea	L	0-1		17,189
34		17	H	Oldham Athletic	W	4-0	Hilaire 2, Mabbutt 2	6,720
35		20	A	Grimsby Town	W	1-0	Hilaire	7,646
36		24	A	Bolton Wanderers	D	0-0		6,280
37		27	H	Watford	L	0-3		12,355
38	May	1	H	Barnsley	L	1-2	Mabbutt	7,500
39		4	A	Shrewsbury Town	L	0-1		3,159
40		8	A	Cardiff City	W	1-0	Mabbutt	5,762
41		11	H	Wrexham	W	2-1	Wilkins 2	7,272
42		15	H	Newcastle United	L	1-2	Murphy (pen)	8,453

Final League Position: 15th in Division Two

								Appearances
								Sub Appearances
							2 own-goals	Goals

FA Cup

3	Jan	2	A	Enfield	W	3-2	Price, Hilaire 2	3,467
4		23	H	Bolton Wanderers	W	1-0	Cannon (pen)	9,719
5	Feb	13	H	Orient	D	0-0		14,501
R		16	A	Orient	W	1-0	Smillie	10,067
6	Mar	6	A	Queen's Park Rangers	L	0-1		24,653
								Appearances
								Sub Appearances
								Goals

League Cup

2	Oct	6	A	Doncaster Rovers	L	0-1		7,783
		27	H	Doncaster Rovers	W	2-0	Cannon (pen), Murphy	7,819
3	Nov	11	A	Sunderland	W	1-0	Cannon	11,139
4	Dec	15	H	West Bromwich Albion	L	1-3	Langley	10,311
								Appearances
								Sub Appearances
								Goals

Barron	Hinshelwood	Dare	Price	Cannon	Gilbert	Smillie	Murphy	Walsh	Langley	Hilaire	Hughes	Bason	Brooks	Lovell	Wicks	Leahy	Galliers	Mabbutt	Boulter	Giles	Fry	Wilkins	Baxter	Nebbeling
1	2	3	4	5	**6**	7	8	9	10	11	12													
1	2	3	4	5	6	7		9	10			8	**11**	12										
1	2	3	4	5	6	7		9	10		12	11		**8**										
1	2		4	3	6	8		9	10	11		7			5									
1	2		6	3	5	8		9	10	**11**	12	7			4									
1			4	3	6	8		9	10	11		7		2	5									
1			4	3	6	8		9	10	11		7		**2**	5	12								
1		3	4	5	6	8			10	11	9	2	**7**	12										
1				5	6	8	4	12	10		9	2	7	3		**11**								
1				5	6	8	4	**9**	10	11	12	2	7	3										
1				5	6	8	4		10	11	**9**	2	7	3			12							
1			12	5	6	8	4		10			2	**11**	3			7	9						
1			11	5	6	8	**4**		10	12		2		3			7	9						
1			**7**	5		8	4		**10**	11		2		6			12	9	3					
1			**7**	5		8	4		9	11		2		6			12	10	3					
1				5		8	4		9	11			7	6			2	10	3					
1				5		8	4		9	11			7	6			2	10	3					
1	2			6		8	4	9		11			12	**7**	5			10	3					
1	2			6		8	4	**9**		11			7		5		12	10	3					
1	2			6		8	4	9		11			7		5			10	3					
1	2			6		8	4	9		11			12		5			**10**	3	7				
1	2		12	6		8			9	11			7		5			10	3	**4**				
1	**2**			4	6	8			9	11			7		5			10	3	12				
				9	6	**8**	4		12	11				2	5			10	3	7	1			
1	2			5	6	8	4			11			9	3				10		7				
1	2			9	6	8	4		11						5			10	3	7				
1	2			11	6	8	4		**9**	12					5			10	3	7				
1	2			11	6	8	4		9	7			12		5			10	**3**					
1	2		4	11					9	8		12	5	**6**				10	3	7				
1	3		4	5	6	8			9			2	11					10		7				
1	3			5	6	8			9	12		**2**	11	4				10		7				
1	3		4	5	6	8				11			9	2				10		7				
1	3		4	5	6	8				11			9	2				10		7				
1	3			5	6	8				11			9	2			4	10		7				
1	3			5	6	8				11			9	2			4	10		7				
1	3			5	6	8				11			9	2			4	10		7				
1	3			5	6	8	12			11			9	2			**4**	10		7				
1	3			5	6	8	4			11				9				10	2	**7**		12		
1	3		4	5	6	8	9			**11**				2				10		7		12		
1	2		**9**	5	6	8	4			11				3				10		7		12		
1				5	**6**	8	4			11		2		3			12	10		7		9		
				5		8	4			11				2				10		7	1	9	3	6
40	27	4	17	42	31	41	24	12	25	33	3	17	22	28	14	1	8	31	16	20	2	2	1	1
			2				1	1	1	3	4	1	3	2		1	5			1		3		
	2			1		3	2	2	2	5			2	1	1			8		1		2		

Barron	Hinshelwood	Dare	Price	Cannon	Gilbert	Smillie	Murphy	Walsh	Langley	Hilaire	Hughes	Bason	Brooks	Lovell	Wicks	Leahy	Galliers	Mabbutt	Boulter	Giles	Fry	Wilkins	Baxter	Nebbeling
1	2		7	6		8	4	**9**		11				12	5			10	3					
1	2			6		8	4	9		11			**7**		5			10	3					
1	2			6		8	4	9	12	**10**			7		5			11	3					
1	2		12	6		8	**4**		9	11			7		5			10	3					
1	2			9	6	8	4			11					5			10	3	7				
5	5		1	5	1	5	5	3	1	5			3		5			5	5	1				
			1						1					1										
			1	1		1				2														

Barron	Hinshelwood	Dare	Price	Cannon	Gilbert	Smillie	Murphy	Walsh	Langley	Hilaire	Hughes	Bason	Brooks	Lovell	Wicks	Leahy	Galliers	Mabbutt	Boulter	Giles	Fry	Wilkins	Baxter	Nebbeling
1		**3**	4	5	6	8			10		9	2	7	12		11								
1			7	5	6	8	4		10	11		2	12	3		**9**								
1			7	5	6	8	4		10	11	9	2		3										
1			**10**	5		8	4	12	9	11		2	7	6					3					
4		1	4	4	3	4	3		4	3	2	4	2	3		2			1					
								1					1	1										
				2			1		1															

League Table

	P	W	D	L	F	A	Pts
Luton Town	42	25	13	4	86	46	88
Watford	42	23	11	8	76	42	80
Norwich City	42	22	5	15	64	50	71
Sheffield Wednesday	42	20	10	12	55	51	70
Queen's Park Rangers	42	21	6	15	65	43	69
Barnsley	42	19	10	13	59	41	67
Rotherham United	42	20	7	15	66	54	67
Leicester City	42	18	12	12	56	48	66
Newcastle United	42	18	8	16	52	50	62
Blackburn Rovers	42	16	11	15	47	43	59
Oldham Athletic	42	15	14	13	50	51	59
Chelsea	42	15	12	15	60	60	57
Charlton Athletic	42	13	12	17	50	65	51
Cambridge United	42	13	9	20	48	53	48
Crystal Palace	42	13	9	20	34	45	48
Derby County	42	12	12	18	53	68	48
Grimsby Town	42	11	13	18	53	65	46
Shrewsbury Town	42	11	13	18	37	57	46
Bolton Wanderers	42	13	7	22	39	61	46
Cardiff City	42	12	8	22	45	61	44
Wrexham	42	11	11	20	40	56	44
Orient	42	10	9	23	36	61	39

1982-83

Division Two

Manager: Alan Mullery

Did you know that?

Alan Mullery proved to be an unpopular choice among Palace fans as manager after an incident remonstrating with them after a FA Cup second-round replay when he was in charge of Brighton back in December 1976. As a result, attendances at Selhurst Park dropped this and the next season as some fans stayed away.

Match No.	Date		Venue	Opponents	Result		Scorers	Attendance
1	Aug	28	H	Barnsley	D	1-1	Hilaire	7,549
2	Sep	4	A	Rotherham United	D	2-2	Hinshelwood, Mabbutt	6,989
3		7	H	Shrewsbury Town	W	2-1	Mabbutt, Hilaire	6,578
4		11	H	Blackburn Rovers	W	2-0	Mabbutt, Hilaire	7,529
5		18	A	Carlisle United	L	1-4	Hinshelwood	4,390
6		25	H	Middlesbrough	W	3-0	Mabbutt 2, Edwards	7,689
7		28	A	Queen's Park Rangers	D	0-0		12,194
8	Oct	2	A	Bolton Wanderers	L	0-1		5,804
9		9	A	Burnley	L	1-2	Hinshelwood	6,429
10		16	H	Oldham Athletic	W	1-0	Mabbutt	6,843
11		23	A	Newcastle United	L	0-1		22,554
12		30	H	Fulham	D	1-1	Hilaire	14,912
13	Nov	6	A	Chelsea	D	0-0		15,169
14		13	H	Leeds United	D	1-1	Mabbutt	11,673
15		20	A	Leicester City	W	1-0	Mabbutt	8,616
16		27	H	Wolverhampton Wanderers	L	3-4	Cannon, Jones, Hinshelwood	10,225
17	Dec	4	A	Grimsby Town	L	1-4	own-goal (Cooper)	5,295
18		11	H	Sheffield Wednesday	W	2-0	Hinshelwood, Langley	8,498
19		18	A	Derby County	D	1-1	Langley	13,207
20		27	H	Charlton Athletic	D	1-1	Jones	17,996
21		28	A	Cambridge United	L	0-1		4,822
22	Jan	1	H	Leicester City	W	1-0	Langley	8,801
23		3	H	Rotherham United	D	1-1	Hinshelwood (pen)	7,704
24		15	A	Barnsley	L	1-3	Jones	10,120
25		22	H	Queen's Park Rangers	L	0-3		14,621
26	Feb	5	A	Shrewsbury Town	D	1-1	Hinshelwood (pen)	3,716
27		22	H	Bolton Wanderers	W	3-0	Edwards 2, Brooks	4,456
28		26	A	Oldham Athletic	L	0-2		9,780
29	Mar	5	H	Newcastle United	L	0-2		10,239
30		12	A	Fulham	L	0-1		11,234
31		19	H	Chelsea	D	0-0		13,437
32		26	A	Leeds United	L	1-2	Murphy (pen)	13,973
33	Apr	2	H	Cambridge United	D	0-0		5,495
34		4	A	Charlton Athletic	L	1-2	Brown	7,836
35		9	H	Carlisle United	W	2-1	own-goal (Rushbury), Brown	5,696
36		16	A	Blackburn Rovers	L	0-3		4,635
37		23	H	Grimsby Town	W	2-0	Hilaire, Brooks	5,909
38		30	A	Wolverhampton Wanderers	L	0-1		12,523
39	May	7	H	Derby County	W	4-1	Nebbeling, Mabbutt 2, Hughton	8,464
40		10	A	Middlesbrough	L	0-2		10,014
41		14	A	Sheffield Wednesday	L	1-2	Murphy	11,154
42		17	H	Burnley	W	1-0	Edwards	22,714

Final League Position: 15th in Division Two

Appearances
Sub Appearances
2 own-goals — Goals

FA Cup

3	Jan	8	H	York City	W	2-1	Lovell, Langley	7,831
4		29	H	Birmingham City	W	1-0	Edwards	12,327
5	Feb	19	H	Burnley	D	0-0		14,949
R		28	A	Burnley	L	0-1		16,150

Appearances
Sub Appearances
Goals

League Cup

1	Aug	31	H	Portsmouth	W	2-0	Hinshelwood 2	6,631
	Sep	14	A	Portsmouth	D	1-1	Lovell	10,698
2	Oct	6	A	Peterborough United	W	2-0	Edwards 2	3,798
		26	H	Peterborough United	W	2-1	Mabbutt, Hilaire	4,502
3	Nov	9	H	Sheffield Wednesday	L	1-2	Mabbutt	8,146

Appearances
Sub Appearances
Goals

Barron	Hinshelwood	Williams	Hughton	Cannon	Gilbert	Giles	Murphy	Langley	Mabbutt	Hilaire	Lovell	Edwards	Nebbeling	Brooks	Jones	Fry	Locke	Brown	Wilkins	Price
1	2	3	4	5	6	7	**8**	9	10	11	12									
1	2	3	4	5	6	**7**	8		10	11	12	9								
1	2	3	4	5	6	7	8		10	11		9								
1	2	3	4	5	6	7			10	11	8	9								
1	2	3	4	5	6	7			10	11	8	9								
1	2	3	4	5	6	7			10	11	8	9								
1	2	3	4	5	6	7		9	10	11	8									
1	2	3	4	5	6	7			10	11	8	9								
1	2	3		5	6	7	**4**	9	10	11	8		12							
1	2	3	4	5	6	7			10	11	8	9								
1			8	5	6	7			10	11	4	9	2	3						
1			8	5	6	7	3		10	11	4	9	2							
1	6		8	5		7	3		10	11	4	9	2							
1	6		8	5		7	3	12	10	11	4	**9**	2							
1	6		8	**5**	2	7	3	9	10	11	4		12							
1	6		8	5	2	7	3		10	11	4				9					
1	6		8	5	2	7	3	10		11	4				9					
	6		8	5	2	7	3	10		11			4		9	1				
	6		8	5	2	7	3	10		11			4		9	1				
	6		8	5	2	7	3	10		11			4		9	1				
	6		8	5	2	7	3	10		11			4		9	1				
	6		8	5	2	**7**	3	10		11	12		4		9	1				
	6		8	5	2	7		10		11	3		4		9	1				
	6		8	5		7		**10**		11	3	12	4		9	1	2			
	6		8	5		7		10		11		12	4	**3**	9	1	2			
	6		8	5	2		3	10		11		7			9	1	4			
	6			5	2		3	10		11		7		8	9	1	4			
	6		4		2	12	3	10		11		**7**	5	8	9	1				
			6	5		7	3	10		11			4	8	9	1	2			
	6		8	5			3	10		11			4		9	1	2	7		
	6		8	5		10	3			11			4		9	1	2	7		
			8	5	6	10	3			11			4		9	1	2	7		
			8	5	6	10	3	12		11			**4**		9	1	2	7		
			8	5	6	10	3	**9**	12	11			4			1	2	7		
	2		4	5	6	7	10		8	11						1	3	9		
	3		8	5	6	10			9	11			**4**			1	2	7	12	
	2		8	5	6	10			9	11			4	3		1		7		
	2		8	5		10	6		9	11			4	3		1		7		
	2		4	5	6	7	10		8	11			3			1		9		
	2		4	5	6		10	7	8	11			3			1		9		
	2		4	5	6	7	10	12	8	11		9	3			1				
			4	5	6	7	**10**	12	8	11		9	3			1	2			
17	35	10	40	41	34	37	30	20	24	42	16	16	26	7	18	25	13	11		
						1		4	1		3	2	2						1	
	7		1	1			2	3	10	5		4	1	2	3			2		

Barron	Hinshelwood	Williams	Hughton	Cannon	Gilbert	Giles	Murphy	Langley	Mabbutt	Hilaire	Lovell	Edwards	Nebbeling	Brooks	Jones	Fry	Locke	Brown	Wilkins	Price
	6		8	5	2	7		10		11	3		4		9	1				
	6		8	5	2		3	10		11		7			9	1	4			
	6			5	2	12	3	10		11		7		8	**9**	1	4			
	6			5	2		3	10		11		7		8	9	1	4			
	4		2	4	4	1	3	4		4	1	3	1	2	4	4	3			
						1														
								1			1	1								

Barron	Hinshelwood	Williams	Hughton	Cannon	Gilbert	Giles	Murphy	Langley	Mabbutt	Hilaire	Lovell	Edwards	Nebbeling	Brooks	Jones	Fry	Locke	Brown	Wilkins	Price
1	2	3	4	5		7		9	**10**	11	8		6							12
1	2	3	4	5	6		8		10	11	7	9								
1	2	3		5	6	7	4		10	11	8	9								
1			4	5	2	7			10	11	3	9	6	8						
1	2		4	5		7	8	12	10	11	**3**	9	6							
5	4	3	4	5	3	4	3	1	5	5	5	4	3	1						
								1												1
	2								2	1	1	2								

League Table

	P	W	D	L	F	A	Pts
Queen's Park Rangers	42	26	7	9	77	36	85
Wolverhampton W	42	20	15	7	68	44	75
Leicester City	42	20	10	12	72	44	70
Fulham	42	20	9	13	64	47	69
Newcastle United	42	18	13	11	75	53	67
Sheffield Wednesday	42	16	15	11	60	47	63
Oldham Athletic	42	14	19	9	64	47	61
Leeds United	42	13	21	8	51	46	60
Shrewsbury Town	42	15	14	13	48	48	59
Barnsley	42	14	15	13	57	55	57
Blackburn Rovers	42	15	12	15	58	58	57
Cambridge United	42	13	12	17	42	60	51
Derby County	42	10	19	13	49	58	49
Carlisle United	42	12	12	18	68	70	48
Crystal Palace	42	12	12	18	43	52	48
Middlesbrough	42	11	15	16	46	67	48
Charlton Athletic	42	13	9	20	63	86	48
Chelsea	42	11	14	17	51	61	47
Grimsby Town	42	12	11	19	45	70	47
Rotherham United	42	10	15	17	45	68	45
Burnley	42	12	8	22	56	66	44
Bolton Wanderers	42	11	11	20	42	61	44

1983-84

Division Two

Manager: Alan Mullery

Did you know that?

Shirt sponsorship arrived in football. Palace's very first sponsor was Red Rose, a local supermarket whose name adorned the Adidas red-and-blue Eagles strip for exactly one season. Palace's longest sponsor to date (for seven seasons from 2000) is Churchill insurance, the company once run by current club co-chairman Martin Long.

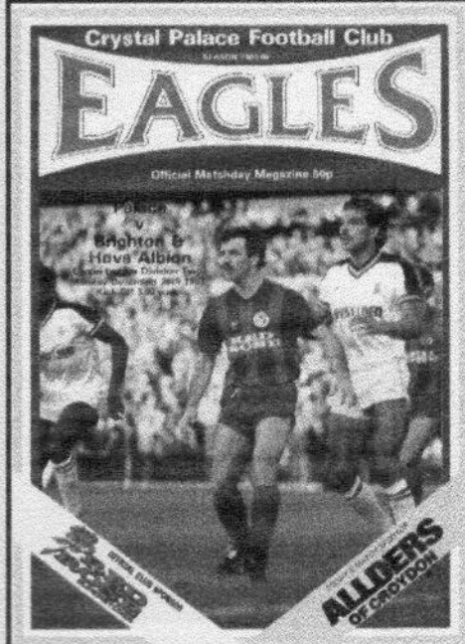

Match No.	Date		Venue	Opponents	Result		Scorers	Attendance
1	Aug	27	H	Manchester City	L	0-2		13,362
2	Sep	3	A	Shrewsbury Town	D	1-1	Cummins	3,849
3		6	A	Huddersfield Town	L	1-2	Cummins	7,814
4		11	H	Fulham	D	1-1	own-goal (Wilson)	11,327
5		17	A	Newcastle United	L	1-3	Evans	22,774
6		27	H	Portsmouth	W	2-1	Wilkins, own-goal (Hateley)	8,486
7	Oct	1	A	Middlesbrough	W	3-1	Hilaire, Evans 2	8,927
8		8	A	Cambridge United	W	3-1	Hilaire, Giles, Evans	4,323
9		15	H	Derby County	L	0-1		7,081
10		22	A	Grimsby Town	L	0-2		6,500
11		29	H	Barnsley	L	0-1		6,377
12	Nov	5	A	Leeds United	D	1-1	Giles	14,847
13		8	H	Cardiff City	W	1-0	Murphy	5,299
14		12	H	Oldham Athletic	W	2-1	McCulloch, Murphy	5,481
15		19	A	Chelsea	D	2-2	Locke, Evans	19,060
16		26	H	Sheffield Wednesday	W	1-0	Giles	11,263
17	Dec	3	A	Swansea City	L	0-1		7,000
18		11	H	Carlisle United	L	1-2	Stebbing	6,460
19		17	A	Blackburn Rovers	L	1-2	Evans	4,794
20		26	H	Brighton & Hove Albion	L	0-2		13,781
21		27	A	Charlton Athletic	L	0-1		10,224
22		31	H	Shrewsbury Town	D	1-1	Stebbing	5,275
23	Jan	14	A	Manchester City	L	1-3	Giles	20,144
24		21	H	Newcastle United	W	3-1	McCulloch, Mabbutt, Gilbert	9,464
25	Feb	4	H	Middlesbrough	W	1-0	Nicholas (pen)	4,819
26		11	A	Fulham	D	1-1	McCulloch	9,119
27		18	A	Barnsley	D	1-1	Nicholas	6,233
28		25	H	Grimsby Town	L	0-1		5,956
29	Mar	3	H	Leeds United	D	0-0		8,077
30		10	A	Oldham Athletic	L	2-3	Barber, Cummins	4,138
31		17	H	Huddersfield Town	D	0-0		5,003
32		24	A	Portsmouth	W	1-0	Evans	10,237
33	Apr	1	H	Cambridge United	D	1-1	Murphy	5,276
34		7	A	Derby County	L	0-3		10,903
35		14	H	Chelsea	L	0-1		20,540
36		17	A	Cardiff City	W	2-0	own-goal (Smith), Cummins	4,091
37		21	A	Brighton & Hove Albion	L	1-3	Nicholas	15,214
38		23	H	Charlton Athletic	W	2-0	Cannon, Mabbutt	7,818
39		28	A	Sheffield Wednesday	L	0-1		27,287
40	May	5	H	Swansea City	W	2-0	Cannon, Mabbutt	5,318
41		7	A	Carlisle United	D	2-2	Giles, Barber	3,013
42		12	H	Blackburn Rovers	L	0-2		5,078

Final League Position: 18th in Division Two

Appearances
Sub Appearances
3 own-goals — Goals

FA Cup

	Date		Venue	Opponents	Result		Scorers	Attendance
3	Jan	7	H	Leicester City	W	1-0	Gilbert	11,497
4		28	H	West Ham United	D	1-1	McCulloch	27,590
R		31	A	West Ham United	L	0-2		27,127

Appearances
Sub Appearances
Goals

League Cup

	Date		Venue	Opponents	Result		Scorers	Attendance
1	Aug	30	H	Peterborough United	W	3-0	Hilaire 2, Brooks	3,975
	Sep	14	A	Peterborough United	L	0-3*		3,504

* Aggregate 3–3, Peterborough United won 4–2 on penalties.

Appearances
Sub Appearances
Goals

Wood	Locke	Gilbert	Hughton	Lacy	Cannon	Evans	Murphy	Cummins	McCulloch	Hilaire	Brooks	Giles	Nebbeling	Stebbing	Fashanu	Strong	Wilkins	Nicholas	Lindsay	Martin	Mabbutt	Barber
1	2	3	4	5	6	7	**8**	9	10	11	12											
1	2	3	4	5	6			9	10	11	8	7										
1	2	3	4	5	6			9	10	11	8	7										
1	**2**	3			5		10	8		11	7	12	4	6	9							
1		2	4	5		11	8	10	9			7	6			3						
1		2	4	5		8	10			11		7	6			3	9					
1			4	5		8		10		11		7	6	2		3	9					
1	10		4	5		8				11		7	6	2		3	9					
1	**2**	12	4	5	9	10	8			11		7	6			3						
1		2	3	5	6	8	4			11		7					9	10				
1			3	12	6	8				11		7	5	2		**4**	9	10				
1	4	5	3		6	8				11		7		2			9	10				
1	2	6	3		5	8	12		9	11		7		**4**				10				
1	2	6	3		**5**	8	4		9	11		7		12				10				
1	2	6	3	10	5	8	7		9	11				4								
1	2	6	3	8	5		4		9	11		7		10								
1	2	6	3	12	**5**	8	4		10	11		7		9								
1	2	6	3	5			4		**9**	11			12	10					7	8		
1	2	6	3	5		10	8		9	11			12	4		**7**						
1	2	6	3	5		8	7		10	11			12	**4**				9				
1	2	6	3	5			4		9	**11**		7	8	10							12	
1	2	6	3	5			4					7	9	8				11			10	
1	2		3				6		9	11		7	5	4				10			8	
1	2	6	3		5		12		**9**	11		7		4				10			8	
1	2	6	3		5				9	11		7		4				10			8	
1	**2**	6			5	12	3		9	11		7		4				10			8	
1	2				5	8	3		9	11		7	6	4				10				
1	2			12	**5**		3	8		11		7	6	4				10				9
1	2	6			5	12	3	8	**9**	11		7		4				10				
1	2	6		9	5		3	8		11				4				10				7
1	2	6		10	5		3	8		11				4			9					7
1	2	6	9		5	8	3			11				4				10				7
1	2	6	9		5	8	3	12		11				**4**				10				7
1	2	6	9		5	**8**	3	4	7	11								10				12
1	2	6	3	7	5				9	11				4				10				8
1	2	6	3	10	5			7	9	11				8				4				
1	2	6	3	8	5			7	9	11		12		**4**				10				
1	2	6	3		5		4	8	9	11		**7**						10			12	
1	2	6	3		5		4	8	9	11								10			7	
1			3	6	5		4	**7**		11		12		2				10			8	9
1	2	6	3	5			4			11		8						10			7	9
1	2		3	5			10	9		11		7	6	4							8	
42	36	33	35	24	30	19	30	17	25	40	3	26	13	30	1	7	7	25	1	1	9	8
		1		3		2	2	1			1	3	3	1							2	1
	1	1			2	7	3	4	3	2		5		2			1	3			3	2

Wood	Locke	Gilbert	Hughton	Lacy	Cannon	Evans	Murphy	Cummins	McCulloch	Hilaire	Brooks	Giles	Nebbeling	Stebbing	Fashanu	Strong	Wilkins	Nicholas	Lindsay	Martin	Mabbutt	Barber
1	2	6	3	5					9	11		7		4				10			8	
1	2	6	3		5				9	11		7		4				10			8	
1	2	6	**3**		5	12			9	11		7		4				10			8	
3	3	3	3	1	2				3	3		3		3				3			3	
						1																
		1							1													

Wood	Locke	Gilbert	Hughton	Lacy	Cannon	Evans	Murphy	Cummins	McCulloch	Hilaire	Brooks	Giles	Nebbeling	Stebbing	Fashanu	Strong	Wilkins	Nicholas	Lindsay	Martin	Mabbutt	Barber
1	2	3	4	5	6	**7**		9	10	11	8	12										
1	2	3		6	**5**		10	8		11	4	7	12		9							
2	2	2	1	2	2	1	1	2	1	2	2	1			1							
												1	1									
										2	1											

League Table

	P	W	D	L	F	A	Pts
Chelsea	42	25	13	4	90	40	88
Sheffield Wednesday	42	26	10	6	72	34	88
Newcastle United	42	24	8	10	85	53	80
Manchester City	42	20	10	12	66	48	70
Grimsby Town	42	19	13	10	60	47	70
Blackburn Rovers	42	17	16	9	57	46	67
Carlisle United	42	16	16	10	48	41	64
Shrewsbury Town	42	17	10	15	49	53	61
Brighton & Hove Albion	42	17	9	16	69	60	60
Leeds United	42	16	12	14	55	56	60
Fulham	42	15	12	15	60	53	57
Huddersfield Town	42	14	15	13	56	49	57
Charlton Athletic	42	16	9	17	53	64	57
Barnsley	42	15	7	20	57	53	52
Cardiff City	42	15	6	21	53	66	51
Portsmouth	42	14	7	21	73	64	49
Middlesbrough	42	12	13	17	41	47	49
Crystal Palace	42	12	11	19	42	52	47
Oldham Athletic	42	13	8	21	47	73	47
Derby County	42	11	9	22	36	72	42
Swansea City	42	7	8	27	36	85	29
Cambridge United	42	4	12	26	28	77	24

1984-85

Division Two

Manager: Steve Coppell

Did you know that?

June saw Steve Coppell appointed manager of Palace for the first time. Aged 28 he had been forced to retire from playing due to a serious knee injury. Steve was later a figurehead when the Supporters' Trust was formed after the club went into administration, and has been manager now on four occasions, as well as holding the post of director of football.

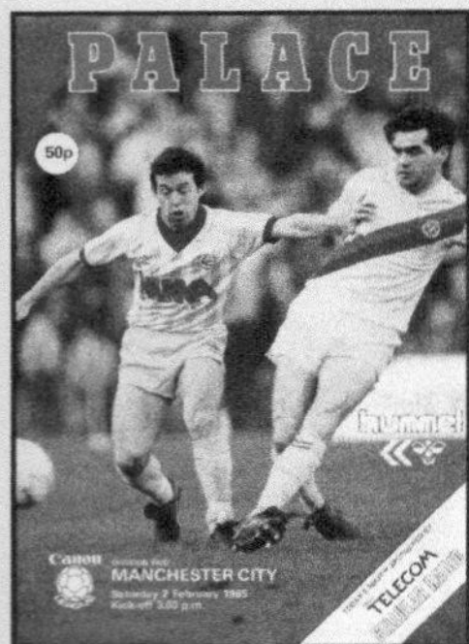

Match No.	Date		Venue	Opponents	Result		Scorers	Attendance
1	Aug	25	H	Blackburn Rovers	D	1-1	Cummins	6,764
2	Sep	1	A	Shrewsbury Town	L	1-4	Sparrow	3,414
3		8	H	Birmingham City	L	0-2		6,519
4		15	A	Brighton & Hove Albion	L	0-1		15,044
5		18	A	Sheffield United	W	2-1	Mahoney, Murphy	12,701
6		22	H	Leeds United	W	3-1	Cummins (pen), Irvine, Murphy	9,460
7		29	A	Manchester City	L	1-2	Irvine	20,252
8	Oct	7	H	Barnsley	L	0-1		6,252
9		13	A	Carlisle United	L	0-1		3,156
10		20	A	Wolverhampton Wanderers	L	1-2	Cummins (pen)	6,665
11		27	H	Fulham	D	2-2	Irvine, Nicholas (pen)	8,035
12	Nov	4	A	Wimbledon	L	2-3	Nicholas (pen), Mahoney	7,674
13		6	H	Shrewsbury Town	D	2-2	Mahoney, Murphy	4,002
14		10	H	Huddersfield Town	D	1-1	Aylott	4,906
15		17	A	Portsmouth	D	1-1	Barber	12,656
16		25	H	Oldham Athletic	W	3-0	Aylott, Mahoney, Sparrow	4,502
17	Dec	1	A	Middlesbrough	D	1-1	Aylott	4,688
18		9	H	Cardiff City	D	1-1	Aylott	6,004
19		15	A	Grimsby Town	W	3-1	Barber, Gray, Nicholas	5,814
20		26	H	Charlton Athletic	W	2-1	Mabbutt, Nicholas	9,540
21		29	A	Oxford United	L	0-5		11,522
22	Jan	1	A	Notts County	D	0-0		5,715
23	Feb	2	H	Manchester City	L	1-2	Gray	7,668
24		5	H	Oxford United	W	1-0	Aylott	6,489
25		16	A	Huddersfield Town	L	0-2		5,678
26		24	H	Wimbledon	L	0-5		8,005
27	Mar	2	A	Fulham	D	2-2	Gray, Stebbing	7,654
28		9	H	Wolverhampton Wanderers	D	0-0		5,413
29		17	H	Carlisle United	W	2-1	Barber 2	4,330
30		23	A	Barnsley	L	1-3	Gray (pen)	4,174
31		30	H	Sheffield United	L	1-3	Droy	4,552
32	Apr	2	H	Brighton & Hove Albion	D	1-1	Aylott	8,025
33		6	A	Charlton Athletic	D	1-1	Aylott	6,131
34		8	H	Notts County	W	1-0	Cannon	4,744
35		13	A	Leeds United	L	1-4	Finnigan	12,286
36		16	A	Birmingham City	L	0-3		10,271
37		20	H	Portsmouth	W	2-1	Droy, Gray	10,215
38		23	A	Blackburn Rovers	W	1-0	Irvine	9,725
39		27	A	Oldham Athletic	L	0-1		2,628
40	May	4	H	Middlesbrough	W	1-0	Cannon	4,900
41		6	A	Cardiff City	W	3-0	Aylott, Galloway, Irvine	5,207
42		11	H	Grimsby Town	L	0-2		4,923

Final League Position: 15th in Division Two

Appearances
Sub Appearances
Goals

FA Cup

3	Jan	5	A	Millwall	D	1-1	Mahoney	11,015
R		23	H	Millwall	L	1-2	Aylott	10,735

Appearances
Sub Appearances
Goals

League Cup

1	Aug	27	H	Northampton Town	W	1-0	Nicholas	3,752
	Sep	4	A	Northampton Town	D	0-0		2,979
2		25	A	Sunderland	L	1-2	Cummins	11,696
	Oct	10	H	Sunderland	D	0-0		6,871

Appearances
Sub Appearances
Goals

Wood	Locke	Sparrow	Stebbing	Whyte	Hughton	Irvine	Murphy	Aylott	Nicholas	Cummins	Cannon	Mahoney	Barber	Lindsay	Nebbeling	Mabbutt	Galloway	Gray	Finnigan	Taylor	Droy
1	2	3	4	5	6	7	8	9	10	11											
1	2	3	4	5	6	**7**	8	9	10	11		12									
1	2	3		5	12	7	8	9	10	11	6	**4**									
1	2	3	4	5		7	8		10	11	6	**9**	12								
1	2	3	4	5		7	8		10	11	6	9									
1	2	3	4	5		7	8		10	11	6	9									
1	2	3	4	5		7	8		10	11	6	9									
1	2	3	4	5		7	8	9	10	11	6										
1	2	3	**4**	5	12	7	8	9	10	11	6										
1	2	3	**4**	5	12	7	8	9	10	11	6										
1		3	12	5	2	7	8	**9**	10		6	11	4								
1			12	5	2	**7**	8	9	10		6	11	4	3							
1			7	5	2		8	9	10		6	11	4	3			12				
1		3			2	7	8	9	10		6	11	4		5						
1		3			2	7	8	9	10		6	11	4		5						
1		3			2	7	8	9	10		6	11	4		5						
1		3			2	7	8	9	10		6	11	4		5						
1		3			2	7	8	9	10		6	**11**	4		5			12			
1		3			2	7		9	10		5	11	4		6			8			
1		3			**2**	7		9	10		6	11	4		5	12		8			
1	2	3				7		9	10		6	**11**	4		5	12		8			
1	2	3				7		9	**10**		6	11	4		5	12		8			
1	**2**	3			11	7	8	9			6		4		5	12		10			
1	2	3			11	7	8	9			6		4		5			10			
1	**2**	3			11	7	8	9			6		4		5			10	12		
1	2	3			11	**7**	8	9			6		4		5	12		10			
1	2	3	5		11	7	8				6		4					10	9		
1	2	3	5		11	7	8				6		4					10	**9**	12	
1	2	3	5		11		8				6		4			7		10	9		
1	2		5		3		8	12			6		4		11	7		**10**	9		
1	2		11		3		8	9			6					7		10	**4**	12	5
1		3	8		2			9			6			11				10	4	7	5
1		3	**8**		2		12	9			6			11				10	4	7	5
1		3			2		8	9			6			11				10	4	7	5
1		3			2	12	8	9			6			11				**10**	4	7	5
1	2	3				7	8	9			6			**11**				12	4	10	5
1	2	3	11			7	8	9			6							10		4	5
1	2	3	**11**			7	8	9			6			12				10		4	5
1	2	3			12	7	8	9			6		10	**11**	5					4	
1		3	11		2	7	**8**	9			6		10		5		12			4	
1		3	11		2	7		9			6			8			10			4	5
1		3	**11**		2	7	8	9			6			12			10			4	5
42	25	38	22	13	28	34	35	34	22	10	40	17	22	9	16	3	2	19	10	11	10
			2		4	1	1	1				1	1	2		5	2	2	1	2	
		2	1			5	3	8	4	3	2	4	4			1	1	5	1		2

Wood	Locke	Sparrow	Stebbing	Whyte	Hughton	Irvine	Murphy	Aylott	Nicholas	Cummins	Cannon	Mahoney	Barber	Lindsay	Nebbeling	Mabbutt	Galloway	Gray	Finnigan	Taylor	Droy
1	2	3				7	8	9			6	11	4	10	5						
1	2	3				7	8	9	10		6	11	4		5						
2	2	2				2	2	2	1		2	2	2	1	2						
								1				1									

Wood	Locke	Sparrow	Stebbing	Whyte	Hughton	Irvine	Murphy	Aylott	Nicholas	Cummins	Cannon	Mahoney	Barber	Lindsay	Nebbeling	Mabbutt	Galloway	Gray	Finnigan	Taylor	Droy
1	2	3	**4**	5	6	7	8	9	10	11		12									
1	2	3		5	6	7	8	9	10	11		4									
1	2	3	4	5	12	7	**8**		10	11	6	9									
1		3	**4**	5	2	7	8	9	10	11	6	12									
4	3	4	3	4	3	4	4	3	4	4	2	2									
					1							2									
									1	1											

League Table

	P	W	D	L	F	A	Pts
Oxford United	42	25	9	8	84	36	84
Birmingham City	42	25	7	10	59	33	82
Manchester City	42	21	11	10	66	40	74
Portsmouth	42	20	14	8	69	50	74
Blackburn Rovers	42	21	10	11	66	41	73
Brighton & Hove Albion	42	20	12	10	54	34	72
Leeds United	42	19	12	11	66	43	69
Shrewsbury Town	42	18	11	13	66	53	65
Fulham	42	19	8	15	68	64	65
Grimsby Town	42	18	8	16	72	64	62
Barnsley	42	14	16	12	42	42	58
Wimbledon	42	16	10	16	71	75	58
Huddersfield Town	42	15	10	17	52	64	55
Oldham Athletic	42	15	8	19	49	67	53
Crystal Palace	42	12	12	18	46	65	48
Carlisle United	42	13	8	21	50	67	47
Charlton Athletic	42	11	12	19	51	63	45
Sheffield United	42	10	14	18	54	66	44
Middlesbrough	42	10	10	22	41	57	40
Notts County	42	10	7	25	45	73	37
Cardiff City	42	9	8	25	47	79	35
Wolverhampton W	42	8	9	25	37	79	33

1985-86

Division Two

Manager: Steve Coppell

Did you know that?

31 August saw the debut of Palace's prolific striker Ian Wright. A late bloomer to professional football, Steve Coppell had signed him aged 21 from non-League Greenwich Borough but showed he had a keen eye for talent as Wright went on to score 117 goals in his seven-year stay at Selhurst Park.

Match No.	Date		Venue	Opponents	Result		Scorers	Attendance
1	Aug	18	A	Shrewsbury Town	W	2-0	Barber, Gray	4,293
2		24	H	Sunderland	W	1-0	Droy	7,040
3		27	A	Carlisle United	D	2-2	Aylott, Barber	3,080
4		31	H	Huddersfield Town	L	2-3	Barber 2	6,026
5	Sep	7	A	Charlton Athletic	L	1-3	Gray (pen)	6,637
6		14	H	Fulham	D	0-0		6,381
7		18	A	Norwich City	L	3-4	Gray 2 (1 pen), Droy	13,475
8		21	H	Millwall	W	2-1	Barber, Gray	8,713
9		28	A	Stoke City	D	0-0		7,130
10	Oct	1	H	Hull City	L	0-2		5,003
11		5	A	Middlesbrough	W	2-0	Barber, Ketteridge	4,991
12		12	H	Oldham Athletic	W	3-2	Irvine, Taylor, Wright	5,243
13		19	A	Portsmouth	L	0-1		16,538
14		26	H	Blackburn Rovers	W	2-0	Barber, Wright	5,408
15	Nov	2	A	Bradford City	L	0-1		5,604
16		9	H	Grimsby Town	W	2-1	Droy, Taylor	4,620
17		16	A	Leeds United	W	3-1	Cannon, Finnigan 2	10,378
18		23	H	Barnsley	W	1-0	Taylor	5,625
19		30	A	Sheffield United	D	0-0		13,765
20	Dec	7	A	Hull City	W	2-1	Aylott 2	6,058
21		15	H	Shrewsbury Town	L	0-1		8,253
22		22	A	Sunderland	D	1-1	Barber	16,710
23		26	H	Wimbledon	L	1-3	Droy	7,929
24	Jan	1	A	Brighton & Hove Albion	L	0-2		15,469
25		11	H	Charlton Athletic	W	2-1	Finnigan, Taylor	11,523
26		18	A	Huddersfield Town	D	0-0		5,729
27		25	H	Norwich City	L	1-2	Barber	8,369
28	Feb	1	H	Carlisle United	D	1-1	Gray	3,744
29		15	A	Blackburn Rovers	W	2-1	Gray, Wright	4,825
30	Mar	8	H	Middlesbrough	W	2-1	Taylor, Wright	4,863
31		15	A	Oldham Athletic	L	0-2		3,726
32		18	H	Stoke City	L	0-1		4,501
33		22	A	Fulham	W	3-2	Taylor (pen), Ketteridge, Wright	4,951
34		29	H	Brighton & Hove Albion	W	1-0	Brush	9,124
35	Apr	1	A	Wimbledon	D	1-1	Wright	8,429
36		5	H	Bradford City	W	2-1	Gray, Brush	5,079
37		8	H	Portsmouth	W	2-1	Gray 2	11,731
38		12	A	Grimsby Town	L	0-3		4,222
39		19	H	Leeds United	W	3-0	Wright, Irvine 2	6,285
40		22	A	Millwall	L	2-3	Higginbottom, Ketteridge	5,618
41		26	A	Barnsley	W	4-2	Wright 2, Aylott, Ketteridge	3,862
42	May	3	H	Sheffield United	D	1-1	Higginbottom	6,375

Final League Position: 5th in Division Two

Appearances
Sub Appearances
Goals

FA Cup

3	Jan	6	H	Luton Town	L	1-2	Taylor	9,886

Appearances
Sub Appearances
Goals

League Cup

1	Aug	20	A	Charlton Athletic	W	2-1	Barber 2	4,930
	Sep	3	H	Charlton Athletic	D	1-1	Gray	6,051
2		24	H	Manchester United	L	0-1		21,506
	Oct	9	A	Manchester United	L	0-1		26,118

Appearances
Sub Appearances
Goals

Full Members Cup

Gp	Oct	16	H	Brighton & Hove Albion	L	1-3	Aylott	2,207
Gp		23	H	West Bromwich Albion	L	1-3	Cannon	3,764

Appearances
Sub Appearances
Goals

Wood	Hughton	Lindsay	Ketteridge	Droy	Cannon	Irvine	Stebbing	Barber	Gray	Sparrow	Finnigan	Aylott	Wright	Higginbottom	Galloway	Locke	Taylor	Brush	Nebbeling	O'Doherty	Howard	Hardwick	Hughes
1	2	3	4	5	6	7	8	9	10	11													
1	2	3	8	5	6	7		11	10		4	9											
1	2	3	8	5	6	7		11	10		4	9											
1	2	**3**	8	5	6	7		11	10		4	9	12										
1	2	3	8	5	6	**7**		11	10		4			12	9								
1		**3**	8	5	6	7		9	10		4		12	11		2							
1			8	5	6	7		9	10	3	4		12	**11**		2							
1			8	5	6	7		9	10	3	4					2	11						
1			8	5	6	7	11	9	10	3	4		12			**2**							
1			8	5	6	7	11	9	10	**4**	12					2		3					
1			8		6	7		9	10	**11**	12					2	4	3	5				
1				5	6	7		9			8	**10**	12	11		2	4	3					
1				5	6	7		11			8	10	9			2	4	3					
1		3			6	7		9			8	10	12	11		**5**	4			2			
1		3		5	6	7		10			8	9	12	**11**			4			2			
1			11	5	6	7		10	12		8	**9**					4	3		2			
1			11	5	6	7		10			8	9					4	3		2			
1			11	5	6	7		**10**			8	9	12				4	3		2			
1			11	5	6	7		10			8	9					4	3		2			
1			11	5	6	7		**10**			8	9	12				4	3		2			
1			11	5	6	7		10			**8**	9	12				4	3		2			
1			11	5	6	7		10				9	8				4	3		2			
1	12		11	5	6	7		10				9	8				4	**3**		2			
1	3		11	5	6	7		10			**8**	9	12			2	4						
1	3			5	6	7		10	9		11		8				4				2		
1	3			5	6	**7**		10	9		11		8	12			4				2		
1	3				6			10	9	11	7		8				4		5		2		
1					6	7		10	9	3	8		12	**11**			4		5		2		
1				5	6	7		10	9	11	**8**		12				4	3		2			
			8	5	6	7		10	9	**11**			12				4	3		2		1	
			8	5	6	7		10	9	11			12				4	3		**2**		1	
	2		8		6	7		10	9	11			12				4	3	5			1	
1			8		6	7		10	9		2		11				4	3	5				
1			8		6	7		**10**	9		2		11	12			4	3	5				
1			8		6	7		10	9		2		11				4	3	5				
1			8		6	7		**10**	9		2		11	12			4	3	5				
1			8		6	7			9		2		11	10			4	3	5				
1		12	8		6	7			9		2		**11**	10			4	3	5				
1			8		6	7			9		2		11	10			4	3	5				
1			8		6	**7**		12	9		2		11	10			4	3	5				
1			8		6	7		4	**9**		2	12	11	10				3	5				
1			8		6	7		4	9		**2**	12	11	10				3	5				
39	10	8	33	27	42	41	3	38	29	12	34	16	16	12	1	10	31	26	14	13	4	3	
	1	1						1	1		2	2	16	4									
			4	4	1	3		9	10		3	4	9	2			6	2					

Wood	Hughton	Lindsay	Ketteridge	Droy	Cannon	Irvine	Stebbing	Barber	Gray	Sparrow	Finnigan	Aylott	Wright	Higginbottom	Galloway	Locke	Taylor	Brush	Nebbeling	O'Doherty	Howard	Hardwick	Hughes
1	3		11	5	6	7		**10**	9				8	12		2	4						
1	1		1	1	1	1		1	1				1			1	1						
														1									
																	1						

Wood	Hughton	Lindsay	Ketteridge	Droy	Cannon	Irvine	Stebbing	Barber	Gray	Sparrow	Finnigan	Aylott	Wright	Higginbottom	Galloway	Locke	Taylor	Brush	Nebbeling	O'Doherty	Howard	Hardwick	Hughes
1	2	3	8	5	6	7		9	10	11	4												
1	2	3	4	5	6	7		11	10		8		**9**		12								
1			8	5	6	7	11	9	10	3	4					2							
1	3		8		6	7		9	**10**		11	12				2	4		5				
4	3	2	4	3	4	4	1	4	4	2	4		1			2	1		1				
												1			1								
								2	1														

Wood	Hughton	Lindsay	Ketteridge	Droy	Cannon	Irvine	Stebbing	Barber	Gray	Sparrow	Finnigan	Aylott	Wright	Higginbottom	Galloway	Locke	Taylor	Brush	Nebbeling	O'Doherty	Howard	Hardwick	Hughes
	8			5		7	12	9				10	14	11		2	4	3	6				1
1		12		5	6	7		10			8	9	14	11			4	**3**		2			
1	1			2	1	2		2			1	2		2		1	2	2	1	1			1
		1					1						2										
					1							1											

League Table

	P	W	D	L	F	A	Pts
Norwich City	42	25	9	8	84	37	84
Charlton Athletic	42	22	11	9	78	45	77
Wimbledon	42	21	13	8	58	37	76
Portsmouth	42	22	7	13	69	41	73
Crystal Palace	**42**	**19**	**9**	**14**	**57**	**52**	**66**
Hull City	42	17	13	12	65	55	64
Sheffield United	42	17	11	14	64	63	62
Oldham Athletic	42	17	9	16	62	61	60
Millwall	42	17	8	17	64	65	59
Stoke City	42	14	15	13	48	50	57
Brighton & Hove Albion	42	16	8	18	64	64	56
Barnsley	42	14	14	14	47	50	56
Bradford City	42	16	6	20	51	63	54
Leeds United	42	15	8	19	56	72	53
Grimsby Town	42	14	10	18	58	62	52
Huddersfield Town	42	14	10	18	51	67	52
Shrewsbury Town	42	14	9	19	52	64	51
Sunderland	42	13	11	18	47	61	50
Blackburn Rovers	42	12	13	17	53	62	49
Carlisle United	42	13	7	22	47	71	46
Middlesbrough	42	12	9	21	44	53	45
Fulham	42	10	6	26	45	69	36

1986-87

Division Two

Manager: Steve Coppell

Did you know that?

Jim Cannon heads the list of 12 Palace players who have played over 300 times for the club. The three-times Player of the Year still holds the club record for the number of appearances made (660).

Match No.	Date		Venue	Opponents	Result		Scorers	Attendance
1	Aug	23	A	Barnsley	W	3-2	Barber, Brush, Wright	4,629
2		30	H	Stoke City	W	1-0	Barber	6,864
3	Sep	3	A	Bradford City	W	2-1	Irvine, Ketteridge	3,856
4		6	A	Derby County	L	0-1		12,058
5		9	H	Huddersfield Town	W	1-0	Droy	6,601
6		13	H	Sheffield United	L	1-2	Irvine	7,003
7		20	A	Blackburn Rovers	W	2-0	Taylor, Gray	5,921
8		27	H	Reading	L	1-3	Taylor (pen)	7,926
9	Oct	4	H	Millwall	W	2-1	Otulakowski, Finnigan	8,150
10		11	A	Leeds United	L	0-3		14,316
11		18	A	Birmingham City	L	1-4	Taylor	5,987
12		25	H	Shrewsbury Town	L	2-3	Wright, Finnigan	4,865
13	Nov	1	A	Plymouth Argyle	L	1-3	Taylor	11,708
14		8	H	Grimsby Town	L	0-3		5,052
15		15	H	Ipswich Town	D	3-3	Bright, Taylor, Wright	7,138
16		22	A	Oldham Athletic	L	0-1		6,708
17		29	H	Sunderland	W	2-0	Finnigan, Bright	6,930
18	Dec	6	A	Portsmouth	L	0-2		10,907
19		13	H	Hull City	W	5-1	Taylor (pen), Barber, Gray, Finnigan 2	4,839
20		20	A	Huddersfield Town	W	2-1	Bright 2	4,181
21		26	H	Brighton & Hove Albion	W	2-0	Irvine, Barber	10,365
22		27	A	Ipswich Town	L	0-3		15,007
23	Jan	1	A	West Bromwich Albion	W	2-1	Barber, Bright	8,420
24		3	H	Derby County	W	1-0	Gray	9,526
25		24	H	Barnsley	L	0-1		6,011
26	Feb	7	A	Stoke City	L	1-3	Ketteridge	13,156
27		14	H	Bradford City	D	1-1	Gray	5,129
28		21	A	Reading	L	0-1		7,209
29		28	H	Blackburn Rovers	W	2-0	Wright, Irvine	5,891
30	Mar	14	H	Birmingham City	W	6-0	Wright 2, Gray, Taylor, Cannon, Finnigan	6,201
31		17	A	Sheffield United	L	0-1		6,647
32		21	H	Leeds United	W	1-0	Gray (pen)	8,781
33		24	A	Shrewsbury Town	D	0-0		2,555
34		28	A	Millwall	W	1-0	Bright	6,285
35	Apr	4	A	Grimsby Town	W	1-0	Bright	3,071
36		11	H	Plymouth Argyle	D	0-0		10,589
37		18	H	West Bromwich Albion	D	1-1	Taylor	7,127
38		20	A	Brighton & Hove Albion	L	0-2		10,062
39		25	H	Oldham Athletic	W	2-1	Wright, Bright	6,097
40	May	2	A	Sunderland	L	0-1		11,461
41		4	H	Portsmouth	W	1-0	Wright	18,029
42		9	A	Hull City	L	0-3		7,656

Final League Position: 6th in Division Two

Appearances
Sub Appearances
Goals

FA Cup

Round	Date		Venue	Opponents	Result		Scorers	Attendance
3	Jan	11	H	Nottingham Forest	W	1-0	Irvine	11,618
4		31	A	Tottenham Hotspur	L	0-4		29,603

Appearances
Sub Appearances
Goals

League Cup

Round	Date		Venue	Opponents	Result		Scorers	Attendance
2	Sep	24	H	Bury	D	0-0		4,017
	Oct	7	A	Bury	W	1-0	Wright	3,347
3		29	H	Nottingham Forest	D	2-2	Irvine, Gray	12,020
R	Nov	5	A	Nottingham Forest	L	0-1		13,029

Appearances
Sub Appearances
Goals

Full |Members Cup

Round	Date		Venue	Opponents	Result		Scorers	Attendance
1	Sep	16	A	Portsmouth	L	0-4		2,515

Wood	Finnigan	Stebbing	Taylor	Brush	Cannon	Irvine	Ketteridge	Barber	Wright	Otulakowski	Droy	Gray	Higginbottom	Sparrow	O'Doherty	Nebbeling	Bright	O'Reilly	Salako
1	2	3	4	5	6	7	8	9	10	11									
1	2		4	3	6	7	8	9	10	11	5								
1	2		4	3	6	7	8	9	10	11	5								
1	2		4	3	6	**7**	8	9	10	11	5	12							
1	2		4	3	6		8	9	10	11	5	7							
1	2		4	3	6	7	8	9	10		5	12	**11**						
1	**2**		4	3	6	7	8	9	10		5	12	11						
1	2		4	3	6	7	8	12	10		5	9	**11**						
1	2	7	4	3	6		8		10	**11**	5	9	12						
1	11	2	4	3	6	**7**	8	9	10		5		12						
1	7	2	4	**3**	6		8	9	10	11	5		12						
1	12	2	4		6	7	8		10	11	5	**9**		3					
1	12	2	4		6	7			10	11	5	**9**	8	3					
1	9	2	4		6	7	8		10	**11**		12			3	5			
1	3	2	4		6	**7**	8		10	11				12		5	9		
1	12	2	4		6	**7**	8		10	11				3		5	9		
1	11	2	4		6		8		10			7		3		5	9		
1	11	2	4		6		8	10				7		3		5	9		
1	11	2	4		6		8	10				7		3		5	9		
1	8	2	4		6	7		11				10		3		5	9		
1	8	2	4		6	7		11	12			10		**3**		5	9		
1	3	2	4		6	7	12	**11**	8			10				5	9		
1	3	2	4		6	7	8	11	10							5	9		
1	3	2			6	7	8	11	10			4				5	9		
1	7	2	4	3	6		**8**	11				10					9	5	12
1	12	2	**4**	3	6		8	11	10			7					9	5	
1	12	2	4	3	6	7	8		10			11				5	**9**		
1			4	3	6	7	8	11	10						2	5	9		
1	2		4		6	7	8	11	10					3		5	9		
1	2	12	4		6	7		11	**10**			8		3		5	9		
1	2		4		6	7		11	10			8		3		5	9		
1	2		4		6	7		11	10			8		**3**		5	9	12	
1	2		4		6	7		11	10			8			3		9	5	
1	2	7	4		6			11	**10**			8			3		9	5	12
1	2	12	4		6	7		11	**10**			8			3		9	5	
1	2		4		6	7		11	10			8			3		9	5	
1	8		4		6	7		11	10						3	2	9	5	
1	8		4		6	7		11	10						3	2	9	5	
1	11		4		6	7			10			8			3	2	9	5	
1	**11**		4		6	7		12	10			8			3	2	9	5	
1	**11**		4		6	7			10			8			3	2	9	5	12
1	11		4		6	7			10			8			**3**	2	9	5	12
42	36	21	41	15	42	33	25	29	37	12	12	26	4	12	12	23	28	12	
	5	2					1	2	1			4	3	1				1	4
	6		8	1	1	4	2	5	8	1	1	6					8		

Wood	Finnigan	Stebbing	Taylor	Brush	Cannon	Irvine	Ketteridge	Barber	Wright	Otulakowski	Droy	Gray	Higginbottom	Sparrow	O'Doherty	Nebbeling	Bright	O'Reilly	Salako
1	3	2			6	7	8	11	10			4					9	5	
1	7	2	4	**3**	6		8	11				10	12				9	5	
2	2	2	1	1	2	1	2	2	1			2					2	2	
													1						
						1													

Wood	Finnigan	Stebbing	Taylor	Brush	Cannon	Irvine	Ketteridge	Barber	Wright	Otulakowski	Droy	Gray	Higginbottom	Sparrow	O'Doherty	Nebbeling	Bright	O'Reilly	Salako
1	**2**		4	3	6	7	8	9	10		5	14	11		12				
1	11	2	4	3	6	**7**	8	12	10		5	**9**							
1	12	2	4		6	7	**8**		10	11	5	9		3					
1	9	2	4		6	7	12	14	10	11			**8**		3	5			
4	3	3	4	2	4	4	3	1	4	2	3	2	2	1	1	1			
	1						1	2				1			1				
						1			1			1							

Wood	Finnigan	Stebbing	Taylor	Brush	Cannon	Irvine	Ketteridge	Barber	Wright	Otulakowski	Droy	Gray	Higginbottom	Sparrow	O'Doherty	Nebbeling	Bright	O'Reilly	Salako
1	**7**		4	3	6		8	9	10	11		12		14	2	5			
1	1		1	1	1		1	1	1	1					1	1			
												1		1					

League Table

	P	W	D	L	F	A	Pts
Derby County	42	25	9	8	64	38	84
Portsmouth	42	23	9	10	53	28	78
Oldham Athletic	42	22	9	11	65	44	75
Leeds United	42	19	11	12	58	44	68
Ipswich Town	42	17	13	12	59	43	64
Crystal Palace	42	19	5	18	51	53	62
Plymouth Argyle	42	16	13	13	62	57	61
Stoke City	42	16	10	16	63	53	58
Sheffield United	42	15	13	14	50	49	58
Bradford City	42	15	10	17	62	62	55
Barnsley	42	14	13	15	49	52	55
Blackburn Rovers	42	15	10	17	45	55	55
Reading	42	14	11	17	52	59	53
Hull City	42	13	14	15	41	55	53
West Bromwich Albion	42	13	12	17	51	49	51
Millwall	42	14	9	19	39	45	51
Huddersfield Town	42	13	12	17	54	61	51
Shrewsbury Town	42	15	6	21	41	53	51
Birmingham City	42	11	17	14	47	59	50
Sunderland	42	12	12	18	49	59	48
Grimsby Town	42	10	14	18	39	59	44
Brighton & Hove Albion	42	9	12	21	37	54	39

1987-88

Division Two

Manager: Steve Coppell

Did you know that?

Palace favourite Geoff Thomas arrived in May 1987 at Selhurst for a fee of £50,000 from Crewe, quickly proving to be a bargain. Winning the Player of the Year award in his first year at Palace, Geoff went on to be capped nine times for England between 1991 and 1992 and was never once in a losing team.

Match No.	Date		Venue	Opponents	Result		Scorers	Attendance
1	Aug	15	A	Huddersfield Town	D	2-2	Bright 2	6,132
2		22	H	Hull City	D	2-2	Gray 2 (2 pens)	6,688
3		29	A	Barnsley	L	1-2	Bright	4,853
4	Sep	1	H	Middlesbrough	W	3-1	Thomas, Bright 2	6,866
5		5	A	Birmingham City	W	6-0	Bright, Redfearn, Thomas, Gray 2 (1 pen), Cannon	7,011
6		8	H	West Bromwich Albion	W	4-1	Bright 2, Redfearn, Wright	8,554
7		12	H	Leicester City	W	2-1	Thomas, Wright	8,925
8		15	A	Sheffield United	D	1-1	Wright	7,767
9		19	A	Reading	W	3-2	Wright, Nebbeling, Bright	6,819
10		26	H	Ipswich Town	L	1-2	Nebbeling	10,828
11	Oct	3	A	Shrewsbury Town	L	0-2		3,999
12		10	H	Millwall	W	1-0	Bright	10,678
13		21	A	Aston Villa	L	1-4	Wright	12,755
14		24	H	Swindon Town	W	2-1	Bright, Gray, (pen)	9,077
15		31	A	Bradford City	L	0-2		13,012
16	Nov	3	H	Plymouth Argyle	W	5-1	Wright 3, Gray, Nebbeling	7,424
17		7	A	Bournemouth	W	3-2	Thomas, Bright 2	9,083
18		14	H	Stoke City	W	2-0	Bright, Wright	8,309
19		21	A	Blackburn Rovers	L	0-2		6,372
20		28	H	Leeds United	W	3-0	Bright, own-goal (Ashurst), Wright	8,749
21	Dec	5	A	Manchester City	W	3-1	Redfearn (pen), Bright 2	23,161
22		13	H	Sheffield United	W	2-1	Redfearn (pen), Barber	8,174
23		19	A	Hull City	L	1-2	Barber	6,780
24		26	A	Ipswich Town	W	3-2	Redfearn (pen), Wright 2	17,200
25		28	H	Reading	L	2-3	Wright, Cannon	12,449
26	Jan	1	H	Barnsley	W	3-2	own-goal (McGugan), Wright, Bailey	8,563
27		2	A	Leicester City	D	4-4	Barber, Pennyfather, Wright 2	10,104
28		16	H	Huddersfield Town	W	2-1	Barber, Cannon	9,013
29		23	A	Middlesbrough	L	1-2	Wright	12,597
30		29	A	Oldham Athletic	L	0-1		6,169
31	Feb	6	H	Birmingham City	W	3-0	Bright, Barber, Salako	8,809
32		13	A	West Bromwich Albion	L	0-1		8,944
33		27	H	Shrewsbury Town	L	1-2	Redfearn (pen)	8,210
34	Mar	5	H	Oldham Athletic	W	3-1	Wright, Nebbeling 2	7,032
35		12	A	Millwall	D	1-1	Cannon	12,815
36		19	H	Bradford City	D	1-1	Barber	9,801
37		27	A	Swindon Town	D	2-2	Bright, Wright	12,915
38	Apr	2	H	Bournemouth	W	3-0	Redfearn 2 (2 pens), Bright	9,557
39		4	A	Stoke City	D	1-1	Bright	9,613
40		9	H	Aston Villa	D	1-1	Wright (pen)	16,476
41		23	A	Plymouth Argyle	W	3-1	Barber, Bright 2	8,370
42		30	H	Blackburn Rovers	W	2-0	Bright, Thomas	13,059
43	May	2	A	Leeds United	L	0-1		13,217
44		7	H	Manchester City	W	2-0	Nebbeling, Thomas	17,555

Final League Position: 6th in Division Two

Appearances
Sub Appearances
2 own-goals Goals

FA Cup

3	Jan	9	A	Newcastle United	L	0-1		20,203

Appearances
Sub Appearances
Goals

League Cup

2	Sep	22	H	Newport County	W	4-0	Wright 2, Salako, Barber	6,085
	Oct	6	A	Newport County	W	2-0	Wright, Bright	1,303
3		28	A	Manchester United	L	1-2	O'Doherty	27,285

Appearances
Sub Appearances
Goals

Simod Cup

1	Nov	11	A	Oxford United	L	0-1		1,478

Appearances
Sub Appearances
Goals

Wood	Stebbing	Brush	Gray	Nebbeling	Cannon	Redfearn	Thomas	Bright	Wright	Salako	Barber	Finnigan	O'Reilly	O'Doherty	Shaw	Taylor	Burke	Hone	Pardew	Pennyfather	Bailey	Suckling	Pemberton	Powell
1	2	3	4	5	6	7	8	9	10	**11**	12													
1	2	3	4	5	6	7	8	9	10	11														
1	2	3	4	5	6	7	8	9	10	**11**		12												
1	2	3	4	5	6	7	8	9	10	11														
1	2	3	4	5	6	7	8	**9**	10	11	12		14											
1	**2**	3	4	5	6	7	8	9	10	11			12											
1		3	4	5	6	7	8	9	10	**11**	12		2											
1		3	4	5	6	7	8	9	10	11			**2**	12										
1		3	4	5	**6**	7	8	9	10	11	12			2	14									
1			4	5		7	8	9	10	11				2	3	6								
1			4	5		7	3	9	10	11	12			6	**2**	8								
1			4		6	7	8	9	**10**	11	12			2			3	5						
1			4	5	6	7	8	9	10	11				2				3						
1			4	5	6	7	8	9	10	**11**	12			2				3						
1			4	5	6	7	8	9	10	**11**	12			2			3							
1	14		4	5	6	7	8	9	10	**11**	12			2			3							
1	12		4	5	6	7	8	9	10		11			**2**			3							
1	2			5		7	8	9	10		11			6			3		4					
1	2			5		7	8	9	10	12	**11**			6			3		4					
1	2			5	6	7	8	9	10		11						3		4					
1	2			5	6	7	**8**	9	10		11						3		4	12				
1	2			5	6	7	8		10	**11**	9	12					3		4					
1	2			5	6	7	8		10		9						3		**4**	11	12			
1	2			5	6	**7**	8		10	11	9						3		12	4				
1	2			5	6	7	8		10	11	**9**						3			4	12			
1	2			5	6	7	8		10	**11**	9						3			4	12			
1	2			5	6	11	8		10		**9**						3		7	4	12			
	2			5	6	7		9	10		11						3		4	8		1		
	2				6	7		9	10		11			5			3		4	8		1		
	2				6	7		9	10		**11**	14		5			3		4	8	12	1		
					6	11	8	9		12	10	5		2			3		**7**	4		1		
					6	11	8	9		7	10	5		2			3		12	**4**		1		
				12	6	7	8	9	10	14	**11**	5		2			3		4			1		
				5	6	7	8	9	10		11	2					3		4			1		
				5	6	7	8	9	10	12	**11**	2					3		4			1		
				5	6	7	8	**9**	10	12	11	2					3		4			1		
				5	6		8	9	10		11	2					3		4	7		1		
				5	6	7	8	9	10		11	2					3			4		1		
				5	6	**7**	8	9	10	12	11	2					3		14	4		1		
				5	6		8	9	10	**7**	11	2					3		14	4		1	12	
				5	6	**7**	8	9		11	10	2					3			4		1	12	
				5	6	**7**	8	9	10	12	11	2					3			4		1		
				5	6	**7**	8	9	10	12	11	2					3			4		1		
				5	6	7	8	9	10		11	2					3			4		1		
27	19	9	17	38	40	42	41	38	41	23	28	14	2	16	2	2	31	3	16	18		17		
	2			1						8	9	3	2	1	1				4	1	5		2	
			6	6	4	8	6	24	20	1	7									1	1			

Wood	Stebbing	Brush	Gray	Nebbeling	Cannon	Redfearn	Thomas	Bright	Wright	Salako	Barber	Finnigan	O'Reilly	O'Doherty	Shaw	Taylor	Burke	Hone	Pardew	Pennyfather	Bailey	Suckling	Pemberton	Powell
1	2			5	6	11	8	12	10		9	14		**7**			3		4					
1	1			1	1	1	1		1		1			1			1		1					
								1				1												

Wood	Stebbing	Brush	Gray	Nebbeling	Cannon	Redfearn	Thomas	Bright	Wright	Salako	Barber	Finnigan	O'Reilly	O'Doherty	Shaw	Taylor	Burke	Hone	Pardew	Pennyfather	Bailey	Suckling	Pemberton	Powell
1			**4**	5		7	8		10	11	9			2	3	6			12					14
1			4	5		7	6	9	10	11	3			2		**8**		14	12					
1	14		4	5	6	7	8	9	10	**11**	12			2				3						
3			3	3	1	3	3	2	3	3	2			3	1	2		1						
	1										1							1	2					1
								1	3	1	1			1										

Wood	Stebbing	Brush	Gray	Nebbeling	Cannon	Redfearn	Thomas	Bright	Wright	Salako	Barber	Finnigan	O'Reilly	O'Doherty	Shaw	Taylor	Burke	Hone	Pardew	Pennyfather	Bailey	Suckling	Pemberton	Powell
1	2			5	**6**	7	8	9	10		11			12			3		4					
1	1			1	1	1	1	1	1		1						1		1					
														1										

League Table

	P	W	D	L	F	A	Pts
Millwall	44	25	7	12	72	52	82
Aston Villa	44	22	12	10	68	41	78
Middlesbrough	44	22	12	10	63	36	78
Bradford City	44	22	11	11	74	54	77
Blackburn Rovers	44	21	14	9	68	52	77
Crystal Palace	44	22	9	13	86	59	75
Leeds United	44	19	12	13	61	51	69
Ipswich Town	44	19	9	16	61	52	66
Manchester City	44	19	8	17	80	60	65
Oldham Athletic	44	18	11	15	72	64	65
Stoke City	44	17	11	16	50	57	62
Swindon Town	44	16	11	17	73	60	59
Leicester City	44	16	11	17	62	61	59
Barnsley	44	15	12	17	61	62	57
Hull City	44	14	15	15	54	60	57
Plymouth Argyle	44	16	8	20	65	67	56
Bournemouth	44	13	10	21	56	68	49
Shrewsbury Town	44	11	16	17	42	54	49
Birmingham City	44	11	15	18	41	66	48
West Bromwich Albion	44	12	11	21	50	69	47
Sheffield United	44	13	7	24	45	74	46
Reading	44	10	12	22	44	70	42
Huddersfield Town	44	6	10	28	41	100	28

1988-89

Division Two

Manager: Steve Coppell

Did you know that?

Introduced by the Football League in 1986, Palace have flirted regularly with the Play-offs ever since then in their quest for the top flight. This season saw the Eagles' first participation, though, as they beat Swindon Town and then Blackburn Rovers over two-legged affairs to secure promotion to Division One.

Match No.	Date		Venue	Opponents	Result		Scorers	Attendance
1	Aug	30	H	Chelsea	D	1-1	Redfearn	17,490
2	Sep	3	H	Watford	L	0-2		10,474
3		10	A	Walsall	D	0-0		6,525
4		17	H	Shrewsbury Town	D	1-1	Wright	7,006
5		20	A	Sunderland	D	1-1	O'Reilly	13,150
6		24	A	Portsmouth	D	1-1	Wright	11,249
7	Oct	1	H	Plymouth Argyle	W	4-1	Wright, Thomas, Bright, Pardew	8,047
8		4	H	Ipswich Town	W	2-0	Bright, Wright	10,325
9		8	A	Blackburn Rovers	L	4-5	Thomas, Wright, Bright, O'Reilly	8,022
10		15	A	Bradford City	W	1-0	Wright	11,098
11		22	H	Hull City	W	3-1	Wright, Barber 2	8,464
12		25	H	Oxford United	W	1-0	Redfearn (pen)	10,114
13		29	A	Stoke City	L	1-2	Bright	9,118
14	Nov	5	H	Barnsley	D	1-1	Bright	7,768
15		12	A	Bournemouth	L	0-2		7,500
16		19	H	Leicester City	W	4-2	Thomas, Barber 2, Bright	8,843
17		26	A	West Bromwich Albion	L	3-5	Dyer, Nebbeling, Thomas	11,099
18	Dec	3	H	Manchester City	D	0-0		12,444
19		10	A	Birmingham City	W	1-0	Dyer	6,523
20		17	H	Leeds United	D	0-0		9,847
21		26	A	Brighton & Hove Albion	L	1-3	Wright	13,515
22		30	A	Oldham Athletic	W	3-2	Thomas, Wright 2 (1 pen)	6,562
23	Jan	2	H	Walsall	W	4-0	Wright, Bright 3	9,352
24		14	A	Chelsea	L	0-1		24,184
25		21	H	Swindon Town	W	2-1	Bright 2	8,109
26	Feb	4	A	Ipswich Town	W	2-1	Wright 2 (1 pen)	14,569
27		11	H	Blackburn Rovers	D	2-2	Wright, Bright	11,270
28		25	H	Bradford City	W	2-0	Bright 2	7,455
29	Mar	1	A	Oxford United	L	0-1		6,020
30		4	H	Bournemouth	L	2-3	Pemberton, Wright	10,022
31		11	A	Barnsley	D	1-1	own-goal (Futcher)	7,055
32		18	H	Sunderland	W	1-0	Bright (pen)	9,108
33		24	A	Watford	W	1-0	Barber	15,095
34		27	H	Brighton & Hove Albion	W	2-1	Wright, Bright (pen)	14,384
35	Apr	1	A	Shrewsbury Town	L	1-2	Madden	4,160
36		5	A	Leeds United	W	2-1	Wright, Madden (pen)	25,604
37		8	H	Oldham Athletic	W	2-0	Barber, Bright	9,089
38		11	A	Hull City	W	1-0	Wright	5,050
39		15	H	Portsmouth	W	2-0	Wright, Bright	12,358
40		22	A	Plymouth Argyle	W	2-0	Bright 2	8,492
41		25	A	Swindon Town	L	0-1		11,045
42		29	H	West Bromwich Albion	W	1-0	Wright	13,728
43	May	1	A	Manchester City	D	1-1	Wright	33,456
44		6	A	Leicester City	D	2-2	Madden 2 (2 pens)	9,917
45		9	H	Stoke City	W	1-0	Madden (pen)	12,159
46		13	H	Birmingham City	W	4-1	Wright 3, own-goal (Clarkson)	17,581
Final League Position: 3rd in Division Two								Appearances
								Sub Appearances
							2 own-goals	Goals

Play-offs

	Date		Venue	Opponents	Result		Scorers	Attendance
SF	May	21	A	Swindon Town	L	0-1		16,656
		24	H	Swindon Town	W	2-0	Bright, Wright	23,677
F		31	A	Blackburn Rovers	L	1-3	McGoldrick	16,421
	June	3	H	Blackburn Rovers	W	3-0*	Wright 2, Madden (pen)	30,000
* After extra-time								Appearances
								Sub Appearances
								Goals

FA Cup

	Date		Venue	Opponents	Result		Scorers	Attendance
3	Jan	7	A	Stoke City	L	0-1		12,294
								Appearances
								Sub Appearances
								Goals

League Cup

	Date		Venue	Opponents	Result		Scorers	Attendance
2	Sep	27	A	Swindon Town	W	2-1	Bright, Wright	7,084
	Oct	12	H	Swindon Town	W	2-0	own-goal (Henry), Thomas	6,015
3	Nov	1	A	Bristol City	L	1-4	Pardew	12,167
								Appearances
								Sub Appearances
							1 own-goal	Goals

Simod Cup

	Date		Venue	Opponents	Result		Scorers	Attendance
1	Nov	22	H	Walsall	W	4-2	Barber, Dyer 2, Wright	2,893
2	Dec	13	A	Southampton	W	2-1	Wright, Dyer	4,914
3	Jan	10	H	Luton Town	W	4-1	Bright 3, Wright	5,842
4		28	A	Middlesbrough	W	3-2	Pardew, Barber, Wright	16,314
SF	Feb	22	A	Nottingham Forest	L	1-3	Wright	20,374
								Appearances
								Sub Appearances
								Goals

Suckling	Pemberton	Burke	Pennyfather	Nebbeling	O'Reilly	Redfearn	Thomas	Bright	Wright	Salako	Pardew	Barber	Madden	Parkin	Hopkins	Hone	Shaw	Powell	Dyer	Hedman	McGoldrick	Harris
1	2	3	**4**	5	6	7	8	9	10	11	12	14										
1	2	3	4		6	7	8	9	10	11	**5**	14	12									
	2	3			6	7	8	9	10		4	11		1	5							
	2	3			6	**7**	8	9	10	12	4	11		1	5							
	2	3			6	**7**	8	9	10	12	4	11		1	5							
	2	3			6	7	8	9	10		4	11		1	5							
	2	3			6	7	8	9	10		4	11		1	5							
		3			6	7	8	9	**10**	12	4	11		1	5	2						
	2	3			6	7	8	9	10	12	4	**11**		1	5							
	2	3			6	7	8	9	10		4	11		1	5		12					
	2	3			6	7	8	9	**10**	12	4	11		1	5							
	2	3			6	7	8	9		10	4	11		1	5							
	2	**3**			6	7	8	9		10	4	11		1	5		12					
	2				6	7	8	9	12	10	4	11		1	5			3				
	2				6	**7**	8	9	10		4	11		1	5			3	12			
			3	6			8	9	**10**	12	4	11		1	5		2	14	7			
	2		**3**	6			8	9	10	12	4	11		1	5		14		7			
	2	3		6			8	9	10	12	4	**11**		1	5				7			
	2	3		6			8	9	10		4	11		1	5				7			
	2	3		6			8	9	10		4	11		1	5				7			
	2	3	12	6			8	9	10		4	**11**		1	5				7	14		
1	2	3	4	6			**8**	9	10	7	12	11			5							
1	2	3	4	6				9	**10**	7	8	11			5					12		
1	2	3	4	6				9	10	12	8	**11**			5						7	
1	2	3	4	6				9	10		8	11			5						7	
1	2	3	4		6			9	10		8	11			5						7	
1	2	3	4		6			9	10	12	**8**	11			5						7	
1	2	3	4		6			9		10	8	11					5				7	
1	2	3	**4**		6			9		10	8	11	12		5						7	
1	2	3			6			9	10		8	11	4		5						7	
1	**3**		12		6			9	10		8	11	4		5		2				7	
1	2				6			9	10		8	11	4		5		3				7	
1	2				6			9	10	12	8	11	4		5		3				**7**	
1	2	12			6			9	10		8	11	4		5		**3**				7	
1	2	3			6			9	10	12	8	11	**4**		5						7	
1	2	3			6			9	10		8	11	4		5						7	
1	2	3			6			9	10		**8**	11	4		5		12				7	
1	2	3			6			9	10	12	8	11	4		5						**7**	
1	2	3			6			9	10	12	8	11	4		5						**7**	
1	2	3			6			9	**10**	7	8	11	4		5		12					
1	2	3			6			9	10	7	8	**11**	4		5							12
1	2	3			6			9	10	**7**	8	11	4		5		14				12	
1	2	3						9	10		8	11	**4**		5		6				7	12
1		3		6				9	10	12	8	11	4		5		2			14	**7**	
1		3		6				9	10		8	11	4		5					2	7	
1	2	3	**8**	6				9	10	12		11	4		5					14	7	
27	42	38	13	14	32	15	22	46	41	12	43	44	17	19	43	1	8	2	6	1	20	
		1	2						1	16	2	2	2				6	1	1	4	1	2
	1			1	2	2	5	20	24		1	6	5						2			

Suckling	Pemberton	Burke	Pennyfather	Nebbeling	O'Reilly	Redfearn	Thomas	Bright	Wright	Salako	Pardew	Barber	Madden	Parkin	Hopkins	Hone	Shaw	Powell	Dyer	Hedman	McGoldrick	Harris
1	2	3	12					9	10		8	**11**	4		5					6	7	
1	2	3						9	10		8	11	4		5					6	7	
1	2	3	12					9	10		8	11	**4**		5					6	7	
1	2	3			6			9	10		8	11	4		5						7	
4	4	4			1			4	4		4	4	4		4					3	4	
			2																			
								1	3				1								1	

Suckling	Pemberton	Burke	Pennyfather	Nebbeling	O'Reilly	Redfearn	Thomas	Bright	Wright	Salako	Pardew	Barber	Madden	Parkin	Hopkins	Hone	Shaw	Powell	Dyer	Hedman	McGoldrick	Harris
1	2	3	4	6			8	9	10	7		11			5							
1	1	1	1	1			1	1	1	1		1			1							

Suckling	Pemberton	Burke	Pennyfather	Nebbeling	O'Reilly	Redfearn	Thomas	Bright	Wright	Salako	Pardew	Barber	Madden	Parkin	Hopkins	Hone	Shaw	Powell	Dyer	Hedman	McGoldrick	Harris
	2	3				7	8	9	10		4	11		1	6	5						
	2	3			6	7	8	9	10	12	4	**11**		1	5		14					
	2				6	7	8	9		10	4	11		1	5	3						
	3	2			2	3	3	3	2	1	3	3		3	3	2						
										1							1					
							1	1	1		1											

Suckling	Pemberton	Burke	Pennyfather	Nebbeling	O'Reilly	Redfearn	Thomas	Bright	Wright	Salako	Pardew	Barber	Madden	Parkin	Hopkins	Hone	Shaw	Powell	Dyer	Hedman	McGoldrick	Harris
			3	6			8	9	12	**10**	4	11		1	5		2	14	7			
	2	3		6			8	9	10		4	11		1	5				7			
1	2	3	4	6				9	10	**7**	8	11			5						12	
1	2	3	4	6				9	10		8	11			5						7	
1	2	3	4	**5**	6			9	10	14	8	11					12				7	

League Table

	P	W	D	L	F	A	Pts
Chelsea	46	29	12	5	96	50	99
Manchester City	46	23	13	10	77	53	82
Crystal Palace	46	23	12	11	71	49	81
Watford	46	22	12	12	74	48	78
Blackburn Rovers	46	22	11	13	74	59	77
Swindon Town	46	20	16	10	68	53	76
Barnsley	46	20	14	12	66	58	74
Ipswich Town	46	22	7	17	71	61	73
West Bromwich Albion	46	18	18	10	65	41	72
Leeds United	46	17	16	13	59	50	67
Sunderland	46	16	15	15	60	60	63
Bournemouth	46	18	8	20	53	62	62
Stoke City	46	15	14	17	57	72	59
Bradford City	46	13	17	16	52	59	56
Leicester City	46	13	16	17	56	63	55
Oldham Athletic	46	11	21	14	75	72	54
Oxford United	46	14	12	20	62	70	54
Plymouth Argyle	46	14	12	20	55	66	54
Brighton & Hove Albion	46	14	9	23	57	66	51
Portsmouth	46	13	12	21	53	62	51
Hull City	46	11	14	21	52	68	47
Shrewsbury Town	46	8	18	20	40	67	42
Birmingham City	46	8	11	27	31	76	35
Walsall	46	5	16	25	41	80	31

1989-90

Division One

Manager: Steve Coppell

Did you know that?

The ZDS Cup Southern area first leg Final against Chelsea in February became the first Palace game ever to be shown live on TV when it was broadcast on satellite channel Sky One. The second leg was also shown live three weeks later on Sky, but Palace lost both games to an identical 2–0 scoreline.

Match No.	Date		Venue	Opponents	Result		Scorers	Attendance
1	Aug	19	A	Queen's Park Rangers	L	0-2		16,161
2		22	H	Manchester United	D	1-1	Wright	22,423
3		26	H	Coventry City	L	0-1		11,122
4	Sep	9	H	Wimbledon	W	2-0	Thomas, Wright	12,116
5		12	A	Liverpool	L	0-9		35,779
6		16	A	Southampton	D	1-1	Hopkins	15,368
7		23	H	Nottingham Forest	W	1-0	Wright	12,899
8		30	H	Everton	W	2-1	Wright, Pardew	15,943
9	Oct	14	A	Derby County	L	1-3	Pardew	14,585
10		21	H	Millwall	W	4-3	Bright 2, Wright 2	18,920
11		28	A	Aston Villa	L	1-2	Pardew	15,724
12	Nov	4	A	Manchester City	L	0-3		23,768
13		11	H	Luton Town	D	1-1	Bright	11,346
14		18	H	Tottenham Hotspur	L	2-3	Bright 2	26,366
15		25	A	Sheffield Wednesday	D	2-2	Gray, Hopkins	17,277
16	Dec	2	H	Queen's Park Rangers	L	0-3		12,784
17		9	A	Manchester United	W	2-1	Bright 2	33,514
18		16	A	Charlton Athletic	W	2-1	Thorn, Bright	15,929
19		26	H	Chelsea	D	2-2	Pemberton, Wright	24,680
20		30	H	Norwich City	W	1-0	Wright	14,250
21	Jan	1	A	Arsenal	L	1-4	Pardew	38,711
22		13	A	Coventry City	L	0-1		10,839
23		20	H	Liverpool	L	0-2		29,870
24	Feb	3	A	Nottingham Forest	L	1-3	Salako	19,739
25		10	H	Southampton	W	3-1	Gray, Barber, Salako	13,363
26		24	H	Sheffield Wednesday	D	1-1	Bright	11,857
27	Mar	3	A	Tottenham Hotspur	W	1-0	Pardew	26,181
28		17	A	Everton	L	0-4		19,290
29		20	H	Derby County	D	1-1	Gray	10,051
30		24	H	Aston Villa	W	1-0	Thompson	18,586
31		31	A	Millwall	W	2-1	Gray, Bright	13,421
32	Apr	4	A	Norwich City	L	0-2		12,640
33		14	H	Arsenal	D	1-1	Gray	28,094
34		16	A	Chelsea	L	0-3		16,553
35		21	H	Charlton Athletic	W	2-0	Bright, Thompson	15,276
36		28	A	Luton Town	L	0-1		10,369
37	May	2	A	Wimbledon	W	1-0	Bright	8,266
38		5	H	Manchester City	D	2-2	Gray, Pardew	20,056

Final League Position: 15th in Division One

Appearances
Sub appearances
Goals

FA Cup

3	Jan	6	H	Portsmouth	W	2-1	Gray (pen), Thomas	12,644
4		27	H	Huddersfield Town	W	4-0	Hopkins, own-goal (Lewis), Bright, Salako	12,920
5	Feb	17	H	Rochdale	W	1-0	Barber	17,044
6	Mar	10	A	Cambridge United	W	1-0	Thomas	10,084
SF	Apr	8	N+	Liverpool	W	4-3*	Bright, O'Reilly, Gray, Pardew	38,389
F	May	12	N+	Manchester United	D	3-3*	O'Reilly, Wright 2	80,000
rep		17	N+	Manchester United	L	0-1		80,000

* After extra-time
+ SF at Villa Park, Final and Final replay at Wembley Stadium

Appearances
Sub appearances
1 own-goal — Goals

League Cup

2	Sep	19	H	Leicester City	L	1-2	Wright	7,382
	Oct	4	A	Leicester City	W	3-2*	Hopkins, Thomas, Bright	10,283
3		24	H	Nottingham Forest	D	0-0		14,250
R	Nov	1	A	Nottingham Forest	L	0-5		18,625

* After extra-time

Appearances
Sub appearances
Goals

Zenith Data Systems Cup

2	Nov	27	H	Luton Town	W	4-1	Bright 2, Wright, Pardew	3,747
3	Dec	19	H	Charlton Athletic	W	2-0	Gray, Wright	6,621
SFs	Feb	13	H	Swindon Town	W	1-0	Gray	6,027
Fs1		21	H	Chelsea	L	0-2		14,839
Fs2	Mar	12	A	Chelsea	L	0-2		15,061

Appearances
Sub appearances
Goals

Suckling	Pemberton	Burkel	Gray	Hopkins	O'Reilly	McGoldrick	Thomas	Bright	Wright	Barber	Pardew	Dyer	Shaw	Madden	Hedman	Salako	Parkin	Dennis	Martyn	Thorn	Thompson	Whyte
1	2	3	4	5	6	7	8	9	10	11	12											
1	2	3	4	5	6	7	8	9	10			11										
1	2	3	4	5	6	7	8	9	10			11										
1	2	3	4	5	6	7	8	9	10		11											
1	2	3	4	5	6	7	8	9	10		11											
1	2	3	4	5	6	7	8	9	10		11											
1		3	4	5		7	8	9	10		11	6	2									
1		3	4	5		7	8	9	10	12	11	6	2									
1	2		4	5		7	8	9	10	12	11	6	3	14								
1	2		4	5		7	8	9	10	12	11	6	3									
1	2		4	5			8	9	10	7	11	6	3									
1	2		4	5		7	8	9	10	12	11	6	3		14							
	2		4	5		7	8	9	10		11	6					1	3				
	2		4	5		7	8	9	10		11	6				12		3	1			
	2		4	5	12	7	8	9	10	6	11							3	1			
	2		4	5	12	7	8	9	10	6	11					14		3	1			
	2		4	5	6		8	9	10	12	11							3	1	7		
	2		4	5	3	7		9	10	8	11								1	6		
	2		4	5		7	12	9	10	8	11							3	1	6		
	2		4	5		7		9	10	8	11							3	1	6		
	2		4	5		7	12	9	10	8	11							3	1	6		
	2	3		5	4	12	8	9	10	7	11								1	6		
	2	3		5		7	8	9	10	4	11		14			12			1	6		
	2	3	4	5			8	9		10	11		7			12			1	6		
	2		4	5			8	9		7	11		3			10			1	6		
	2		4	5			8	9		7	11		3			10			1	6		
	2		4	5			8	9	12	7	11		3			10			1	6		
	2		4		5		8		10	7	11		3	12	14	9			1	6		
			4		5		8		10	7	11		3	12	2	9			1	6		
			4		5		8	9		7	11		3		2				1	6	10	
	2		4		5		8	9		7	11		3		6	12			1		10	
	2		4		5		8	9		7	11		3		6	12			1		10	
	2		4		5		8	9		7	11		3		14	12			1	6	10	
	2		4		6		8	9		7	11		3	12	5	14			1		10	
	2		4		5		8	9		7	11		3	14	6	12			1		10	
	2		4		5		8	9		7	11		3	14	6	12			1		10	
	2						8	9		7	12		3	4	5	11			1	6	10	
	2		4		5	12		9		3	11			8	14	7			1	6	10	
12	34	11	35	27	19	20	33	36	25	25	34	10	20	2	8	7	1	8	25	17	9	
					2	2	2		1	5	2		1	6	4	10						
	1		6	2			1	12	8	1	6					2				1	2	

Suckling	Pemberton	Burkel	Gray	Hopkins	O'Reilly	McGoldrick	Thomas	Bright	Wright	Barber	Pardew	Dyer	Shaw	Madden	Hedman	Salako	Parkin	Dennis	Martyn	Thorn	Thompson	Whyte
	2		4	5	3		12	9	10	8	11					7			1	6		
	2	3	4	5			8	9		11		7				10			1	6		
	2		4	5			8	9		7	11	12	3			10			1	6		
	2		4		5		8		10	7	11		3			9			1	6		
	2		4		5		8	9		7	11		3			10			1	6		
	2		4		5		8	9	14	7	11		3	12		10			1	6		
	2		4		5		8	9	12	7	11		3	14		10			1	6		
	7	1	7	3	5		6	6	2	7	6	1	5			7			7	7		
							1		2			1		2								
			2	1	2		2	2	2	1	1					1						

Suckling	Pemberton	Burkel	Gray	Hopkins	O'Reilly	McGoldrick	Thomas	Bright	Wright	Barber	Pardew	Dyer	Shaw	Madden	Hedman	Salako	Parkin	Dennis	Martyn	Thorn	Thompson	Whyte
1	2	3	4	5	6	7	8	9	10		11	12	14									
1	12	3	4	5		7	8	9	10	14	11	6	2									
1	2		4	5		7	8	9	10	12	11	6	3									
1	2		4	5			8	9	10	7	11	6	3		12	14						
4	3	2	4	4	1	3	4	4	4	1	4	3	3									
	1									2		1	1		1	1						
				1			1	1	1													

Suckling	Pemberton	Burkel	Gray	Hopkins	O'Reilly	McGoldrick	Thomas	Bright	Wright	Barber	Pardew	Dyer	Shaw	Madden	Hedman	Salako	Parkin	Dennis	Martyn	Thorn	Thompson	Whyte
	2		4	5	12	7	8	9	10	6	11					14		3	1			
	2		4	5	3	7	14	9	10	8	11					12			1	6		
	2		4	5			8	9		7	11		3			10			1	6		
	2		4	5			8	9		7	11	12	3			10			1	6		
			4		12		8		10	7	11	5	3		2	9			1	6		14
	4		5	4	1	2	4	4	3	5	5	1	3		1	3		1	5	4		
					2		1					1				2						1
			2					2	2		1											

League Table

	P	W	D	L	F	A	Pts
Liverpool	38	23	10	5	78	37	79
Aston Villa	38	21	7	10	57	38	70
Tottenham Hotspur	38	19	6	13	59	47	63
Arsenal	38	18	8	12	54	38	62
Chelsea	38	16	12	10	58	50	60
Everton	38	17	8	13	57	46	59
Southampton	38	15	10	13	71	63	55
Wimbledon	38	13	16	9	47	40	55
Nottingham Forest	38	15	9	14	55	47	54
Norwich City	38	13	14	11	44	42	53
Queen's Park Rangers	38	13	11	14	45	44	50
Coventry City	38	14	7	17	39	59	49
Manchester United	38	13	9	16	46	47	48
Manchester City	38	12	12	14	43	52	48
Crystal Palace	38	13	9	16	42	66	48
Derby County	38	13	7	18	43	40	46
Luton Town	38	10	13	15	43	57	43
Sheffield Wednesday	38	11	10	17	35	51	43
Charlton Athletic	38	7	9	22	31	57	30
Millwall	38	5	11	22	39	65	26

1990-91

Division One

Manager: Steve Coppell

Did you know that?

Palace claimed their 1,000th Football League victory on 29 September. A 2–0 away victory over Derby.

The end of season saw the Eagles record their highest-ever League finish, third in Division One (now the Premier League).

Match No.	Date		Venue	Opponents	Result		Scorers	Attendance
1	Aug	25	A	Luton Town	D	1-1	Young	9,583
2		28	H	Chelsea	W	2-1	Gray (pen), Wright	27,101
3	Sep	1	H	Sheffield United	W	1-0	Thompson	16,831
4		8	A	Norwich City	W	3-0	Barber, Salako, Wright	15,271
5		15	H	Nottingham Forest	D	2-2	Shaw, Thomas	20,545
6		22	A	Tottenham Hotspur	D	1-1	Thomas	34,859
7		29	A	Derby County	W	2-0	Wright, Bright	15,202
8	Oct	6	H	Leeds United	D	1-1	Thomas	22,445
9		20	A	Everton	D	0-0		24,505
10		27	H	Wimbledon	W	4-3	Humphrey, Gray, Thomas, Bright	17,220
11	Nov	3	A	Manchester United	L	0-2		45,724
12		10	H	Arsenal	D	0-0		28,181
13		17	A	Queen's Park Rangers	W	2-1	Wright 2	14,360
14		24	A	Southampton	W	3-2	Wright 2, Bright	14,426
15	Dec	1	H	Coventry City	W	2-1	Gray, Bright	17,052
16		8	A	Chelsea	L	1-2	Thorn	21,558
17		16	H	Luton Town	W	1-0	Bright	15,579
18		22	A	Manchester City	W	2-0	own-goal (Pointon), Wright	25,321
19		26	H	Sunderland	W	2-1	Salako, Bright	15,560
20		30	H	Liverpool	W	1-0	Bright	26,280
21	Jan	1	A	Aston Villa	L	0-2		25,523
22		12	A	Sheffield United	W	1-0	Bright	17,139
23		19	H	Norwich City	L	1-3	Bright	17,201
24	Feb	2	A	Nottingham Forest	W	1-0	Young	17,045
25		16	H	Queen's Park Rangers	D	0-0		16,006
26		23	A	Arsenal	L	0-4		42,162
27	Mar	2	A	Coventry City	L	1-3	Wright	10,225
28		9	H	Southampton	W	2-1	Thomas 2	14,439
29		16	H	Derby County	W	2-1	Gray (pen), Wright	14,752
30		23	A	Leeds United	W	2-1	Salako, Wright	28,683
31		30	A	Sunderland	L	1-2	Pardew	20,147
32	Apr	1	H	Manchester City	L	1-3	Salako	18,001
33		13	H	Aston Villa	D	0-0		18,331
34		17	H	Tottenham Hotspur	W	1-0	Young	26,285
35		20	H	Everton	D	0-0		16,439
36		23	A	Liverpool	L	0-3		36,767
37	May	4	A	Wimbledon	W	3-0	Wright 3	10,060
38		11	H	Manchester United	W	3-0	Salako 2, Wright	25,301

Final League Position: 3rd in Division One

Appearances
Sub appearances
1 own-goal Goals

FA Cup

Round	Date		Venue	Opponents	Result		Scorers	Attendance
3	Jan	6	H	Nottingham Forest	D	0-0		15,396
R		21	A	Nottingham Forest	D	2-2*	Salako, Wright	23,301
R2		28	A	Nottingham Forest	L	0-3		22,164

* After extra-time

Appearances
Goals

League Cup

Round	Date		Venue	Opponents	Result		Scorers	Attendance
2	Sep	25	H	Southend United	W	8-0	Wright 3, Hodges, Thompson, Bright 3	9,653
	Oct	9	A	Southend United	W	2-1	Young, Salako	5,199
3		30	H	Leyton Orient	D	0-0		12,958
R	Nov	7	A	Leyton Orient	W	1-0	Bright	10,158
4		27	A	Southampton	L	0-2		13,765

Appearances
Sub appearances
Goals

Zenith Data Systems Cup

Round	Date		Venue	Opponents	Result		Scorers	Attendance
2	Dec	18	H	Bristol Rovers	W	2-1	Gray, Salako	5,209
3	Feb	18	A	Brighton & Hove Albion	W	2-0*	Wright, Bright	9,633
SFs		26	H	Luton Town	W	3-1	Wright 2, McGoldrick	7,170
Fs1	Mar	5	A	Norwich City	D	1-1	Thomas	7,554
Fs2		19	H	Norwich City	W	2-0	Wright, Bright	13,857
F	Apr	7	N+	Everton	W	4-1	Thomas, Salako, Wright 2	52,460

* After extra-time
+ Played at Wembley Stadium

Appearances
Sub appearances
Goals

Martyn	Humphrey	Shaw	Gray	Young	Thorn	Barber	Thomas	Salako	Wright	Hodges	Dennis	Thompson	Bright	Hedman	Pardew	McGoldrick	Southgate	Collymore	Bodin	Osborn
1	2	3	4	5	6	7	8	9	10	**11**	12									
1	2	3	4	5	6	12	8	7	10	**11**		9								
1	2	3	4	5	6	12	8	7	10	**11**		9	14							
1	2	3	4	5	6	11	8	7	10			9								
1	2	3		5	6	**11**	8	7	10	12		9	14	4						
1	2	3		5	6	11	8		10			**9**	12		4	7				
1	2	3		5	**6**	11	8		10	12			9		4	7				
1	2	3	12	5	6	11	8		10				9		**4**	7				
1	2	3	12	5	6	**11**	8	7	10				9		4					
1	2	3	4	5	6	12	8	7	10	**11**			9							
1	2	3	4	5	6	11	8	7	10				9							
1	2	3	4	5	6	**11**	8	7	10				9			12				
1	2	3	4	5	6	**11**	8	7	10				9			12				
1	2	3	4	5	6		8	7	**10**				9		12	11				
1	2	3	4	5			8	7	10	**6**			9		12	11				
1	2	3	4	5	6		8	7	10			12	9			**11**				
1	2	3	4	5	6		8	7	10				9			11				
1	2	3	4	5	6		8	7	10				9			11				
1	2	3	4	5	6		8	7	10				9			11				
1	2	3	4	5	6		8	7	10				9			11				
1	2	3	4	**5**	6		8	7	10			12	9			11				
1	2	3	4	5	6		8	7	10				9			11				
1	2	3	4	5	6	12	8	7	10				9			**11**				
1	2	3	4	5		11	8	7	10				9		6					
1	2	3	**4**	5	6	11	8	7	10				9		12			14		
1	2	3	4	5		**11**	8	7	10				9		6	12				
1	2	3	4	5	6	12	8	7	10				9			**11**				
1	2	3	4		6	12	8	7	10			**5**	9		11					
1	2	3	4	5	6		8	7	10				9		12	**11**				
1	2	3	4	5	6		8	7	10				9		11					
1	2	3	4	5	6		8	7	10				9		**11**	12				
1	2	3	4	5	6		8	7	10				9		**11**	12				
1	2	3		5	6		8	7	10				9		4	**11**		12		
1	2			5	6		8	**7**	10				9		4	11		12	3	14
1	2			5	6		8	7	10			9			4	**11**		12	3	14
1	2	6					8	7	10			14			4	11	5	12	**3**	9
1	2	5			6		8	7	10			**9**			4	11		12	3	
1	2	5	12		6		8	7	10				9			**11**			3	4
38	38	36	27	34	34	13	38	35	38	5		8	29	1	15	21	1		5	2
			3			6				2	1	3	3		4	5		6		2
	1	1	4	3	1	1	6	6	15			1	9		1					

Martyn	Humphrey	Shaw	Gray	Young	Thorn	Barber	Thomas	Salako	Wright	Hodges	Dennis	Thompson	Bright	Hedman	Pardew	McGoldrick	Southgate	Collymore	Bodin	Osborn
1	**2**	3	4	5	6		8	7	10				9			11				
1	2	3	4	5	6		8	7	10				9			11				
1	2	3	4	5			8	7	10				9		6	11				
3	3	3	3	3	2		3	3	3				3		1	3				
								1	1											

Martyn	Humphrey	Shaw	Gray	Young	Thorn	Barber	Thomas	Salako	Wright	Hodges	Dennis	Thompson	Bright	Hedman	Pardew	McGoldrick	Southgate	Collymore	Bodin	Osborn
1	**2**	3		5	6	11	8		10	14		12	9		4	7				
1	2	3	4	**5**	6		8	7	10	11			9		14		12			
1	2	3	4	5	6	12	8	7	10	**11**			9							
1	2	3	4	5	6	**11**	8	7	10				9			12				
1	2	3	4	5	**6**		8	7	10	12			9			11				
5	5	5	4	5	5	2	5	4	5	2			5		1	2				
						1				2		1			1	1	1			
				1				1	3	1		1	4							

Martyn	Humphrey	Shaw	Gray	Young	Thorn	Barber	Thomas	Salako	Wright	Hodges	Dennis	Thompson	Bright	Hedman	Pardew	McGoldrick	Southgate	Collymore	Bodin	Osborn
1	2	3	4	5	6		8	7	10				9			11				
1	2	3	4	5		11	8	**7**	10				9		6					12
1	2	3	4	5		12	8	7	10				9		6	**11**				
1	2	3	4		6	12	8	7	10				9		**11**		5			
1	2	3	4	5	6		8	7	10				9		11					
1	2	3	**4**	5	6		8	7	10			14	9		11	12				
6	6	6	6	5	4	1	6	6	6				6		5	2	1			
						2						1				1				1
			1				2	2	6				2			1				

League Table

	P	W	D	L	F	A	Pts
Arsenal	38	24	13	1	74	18	83
Liverpool	38	23	7	8	77	40	76
Crystal Palace	38	20	9	9	50	41	69
Leeds United	38	19	7	12	65	47	64
Manchester City	38	17	11	10	64	53	62
Manchester United	38	16	12	10	58	45	59
Wimbledon	38	14	14	10	53	46	56
Nottingham Forest	38	14	12	12	65	50	54
Everton	38	13	12	13	50	46	51
Tottenham Hotspur	38	11	16	11	51	50	49
Chelsea	38	13	10	15	58	69	49
Queen's Park Rangers	38	12	10	16	44	53	46
Sheffield United	38	13	7	18	36	55	46
Southampton	38	12	9	17	58	69	45
Norwich City	38	13	6	19	41	64	45
Coventry City	38	11	11	16	42	49	44
Aston Villa	38	9	14	15	46	58	41
Luton Town	38	10	7	21	42	61	37
Sunderland	38	8	10	20	38	60	34
Derby County	38	5	9	24	37	75	24

1991-92

Division One

Manager: Steve Coppell

Did you know that?

Sixty different players have scored hat-tricks for Palace during the club's 105-year existence.

Match No.	Date		Venue	Opponents	Result		Scorers	Attendance
1	Aug	24	A	Manchester City	L	2-3	Thomas, Bright	28,053
2		27	H	Wimbledon	W	3-2	Gray (pen), Bright, Wright	16,736
3		31	H	Sheffield United	W	2-1	Thomas, Wright	15,507
4	Sep	4	A	Aston Villa	W	1-0	Wright	20,740
5		7	A	Everton	D	2-2	Gray (pen), Bright	21,217
6		14	H	Arsenal	L	1-4	Bright	24,228
7		17	H	West Ham United	L	2-3	Salako, Wright	21,363
8		21	A	Oldham Athletic	W	3-2	Salako, Bright, Wright	13,391
9		28	H	Queen's Park Rangers	D	2-2	Bright, Collymore	15,372
10	Oct	1	H	Leeds United	W	1-0	Bright	18,520
11		5	A	Sheffield Wednesday	L	1-4	Bright	26,230
12		19	A	Coventry City	W	2-1	Bright, Gabbiadini	10,540
13		26	H	Chelsea	D	0-0		21,841
14	Nov	2	A	Liverpool	W	2-1	Thomas, Gabbiadini	34,231
15		16	H	Southampton	W	1-0	Thomas	15,861
16		23	A	Nottingham Forest	L	1-5	Thomas	22,387
17		30	H	Manchester United	L	1-3	Mortimer	29,017
18	Dec	7	A	Norwich City	D	3-3	own-goal (Newman), McGoldrick, Osborn	12,667
19		22	H	Tottenham Hotspur	L	1-2	own-goal (Fenwick)	22,491
20		26	A	Wimbledon	D	1-1	Gabbiadini	15,009
21		28	A	Sheffield United	D	1-1	Gabbiadini	17,969
22	Jan	1	H	Notts County	W	1-0	Gabbiadini	14,202
23		11	H	Manchester City	D	1-1	Bright	14,766
24		18	A	Leeds United	D	1-1	Thomas	27,717
25	Feb	1	H	Coventry City	L	0-1		14,118
26		8	A	Chelsea	D	1-1	Whyte	17,810
27		16	A	Tottenham Hotspur	W	1-0	McGoldrick	19,834
28		22	A	Manchester United	L	0-2		46,347
29		25	H	Luton Town	D	1-1	Bright	12,109
30		29	H	Norwich City	L	3-4	Bright 2, Osborn	14,021
31	Mar	3	H	Nottingham Forest	D	0-0		12,608
32		7	A	Luton Town	D	1-1	McGoldrick	8,591
33		11	A	Southampton	L	0-1		11,110
34		14	H	Liverpool	W	1-0	Young	23,680
35		21	H	Aston Villa	D	0-0		15,368
36		28	A	Notts County	W	3-2	Bright, Mortimer, Coleman	7,675
37	Apr	4	H	Everton	W	2-0	Bright (pen), Coleman	14,338
38		11	A	Arsenal	L	1-4	Coleman	36,016
39		18	H	Oldham Athletic	D	0-0		12,267
40		20	A	West Ham United	W	2-0	Bright, Coleman	17,710
41		25	H	Sheffield Wednesday	D	1-1	Bright	21,573
42	May	2	A	Queen's Park Rangers	L	0-1		14,903

Final League Position: 10th in Division One

Appearances
Sub appearances
2 own-goals — Goals

FA Cup

3	Jan	4	A	Leicester City	L	0-1		19,613

Appearances
Sub appearances

League Cup

2	Sep	25	A	Hartlepool United	D	1-1	Bright	6,697
	Oct	8	H	Hartlepool United	W	6-1	Gray (pen), Bright 2, Thorn, Collymore, Gabbiadini	9,153
3		29	A	Birmingham City	D	1-1	Gray	17,270
R	Nov	19	H	Birmingham City	D	1-1*	Thomas	10,698
R2	Dec	3	H	Birmingham City	W	2-1	Gray (pen), Thorn	11,384
R4		17	A	Swindon Town	D	1-0	Gray	10,044
R5	Jan	8	H	Nottingham Forest	D	1-1	own-goal (Walker)	14,941
rep	Feb	5	A	Nottingham Forest	L	2-4	Bright, Whyte	18,918

* After extra-time

Appearances
Sub appearances
1 own-goal — Goals

Zenith Data Systems Cup

2	Oct	22	H	Southend United	W	4-2*	Gray, Thomas, Bright, McGoldrick	7,185
3	Nov	26	A	Queen's Park Rangers	W	3-2	Thomas, Young, Gabbiadini	4,492
SFs	Dec	10	H	Chelsea	L	0-1		8,416

* After extra-time

Appearances
Sub appearances
Goals

Martyn	Humphrey	Bodin	Gray	Shaw	Sinnott	Salako	Thomas	Bright	Wright	McGoldrick	Pardew	Thorn	Suckling	Southgate	Young	Collymore	Osborn	Gabbiadini	Rodger	Gordon	Mortimer	Coleman	Whyte	Moralee	Hedman	Sullivan	Barnes
1	2	**3**	4	5	6	7	8	9	10	11	12																
1	2	12	4	**3**	5	7	8	9	10	11		6															
1	2		4	3	5	7	8	9	10	11		6															
1	2		4	3	5	7	8	9	10	11		6															
1	2		4	3	5	7	8	9	**10**	11	12	6															
	2		4	3	5	7	**8**	9	10	11	12	6	1	14													
	2		4		3	7		9	10	**11**	8	6	1		5	12											
	2	3	4		6	7		9	10	11	8		1		5												
1	2	3	4		6	10		9		11	7			14	5	12	**8**										
1			4		3	**11**	8	9				6		2	5	12	7	10									
1			4		3		8	9			14	6		2	5	12	**7**	10	11								
1			4	12	3		8	9		11		6		2	5			10			**7**						
1			4		3		8	9		11		6		2	5			**10**			7	12					
1	6		4		3		8	9		11	14			2	5			10	12		**7**						
1	6		4		3		8	9		11				2	5	12		10			**7**	14					
1	3		4				8	9		11		6		2	5			10			7						
1	14		4				8	9		11		6		2	5	12		10			**7**	3					
1			4					9		11		6		2	5		8	**10**	12		7	3					
1	6		4					9		11				2			7	10	8	12	5	**3**					
1	6		4		3			9		11				2			8	10	7		**5**		12				
1	2		4		3			9		11					5		8	10	7		6						
1	2		4		3		8	9		11					5			10	7		6						
1	2		4		3		8	9		**11**		6			5			10	7				12				
1	2		4		3		8	9		11		6		5				**10**	7				12				
1	2		4		3		8	9		11		6		5			12				7		**10**	14			
1	2				3		8	9		11		6		5			4		7				10				
1	2				3		8	9		11		6			5		4		7				10				
1	2				3		8	9		11		6			5		4		7				10				
1	2				3		8	9		11		6		12	5		4		7			14	**10**				
1	2			3			**8**	9		11		6		12	5		4		7			14	10				
1	2			3				9		11		6		8	5		**4**		7		12	10					
1	2			3	14			9		11		6		8	5				7		**4**	10	12				
1	2				3			9		11		6		8	5	14			7		12		**10**	4			
1	2				3			9		11		6		8	5				7		4	10					
1	2				3			9				6		8	5	11			7		4	10					
1	2				3		8	9				6		4	5	**11**			7		12	10					
1	2				3		8	9				6		4	5	**11**			7		12	10		14			
1	2				3		8	9				6		4	5	**11**					7	10			12		
1	2				3		8	9		11		6		**4**	5	14					7	10			12		
1	2				3		8	9		11		6		4	5					**7**		10		12			
1	2				3		8	9		11		6		4	5					7		**10**		12	14		
	2				3		8	9		11		6		4					**7**	14		5		10		1	12
38	36	3	25	9	35	10	30	42	8	36	3	33	3	26	30	4	13	15	20	2	17	14	7	2		1	
	1	1		1	1						5			4		8	1		2	2	4	4	4	4	3		1
			2			2	6	17	5	3					1	1	2	5			2	4	1				

Martyn	Humphrey	Bodin	Gray	Shaw	Sinnott	Salako	Thomas	Bright	Wright	McGoldrick	Pardew	Thorn	Suckling	Southgate	Young	Collymore	Osborn	Gabbiadini	Rodger	Gordon	Mortimer	Coleman	Whyte	Moralee	Hedman	Sullivan	Barnes
1	2		4		3		8	9		11		6			5			**10**	12		7						
1	1		1		1		1	1		1		1			1			1			1						
																			1								

Martyn	Humphrey	Bodin	Gray	Shaw	Sinnott	Salako	Thomas	Bright	Wright	McGoldrick	Pardew	Thorn	Suckling	Southgate	Young	Collymore	Osborn	Gabbiadini	Rodger	Gordon	Mortimer	Coleman	Whyte	Moralee	Hedman	Sullivan	Barnes
1	2	3	4		6	10		9		11	8				5		7										
1			4		3		8	9		11		6		**2**	5	7		10		12							
1	12		4		3		8	9		11		**6**		2	5			10	7								
1	3		4				8	9		11		**6**		2	5	14		10	7			12					
1			4					9		11		6		2	5	12	8	**10**	7			3					
1	12		4					9		11		**6**		2	5		8	10	7			3	14				
1	2		4		3		8	9		11		6			5			10	**7**				12				
1	2				3		**8**	9		11		6		5			4		7			12	10				
8	4	1	7		5	1	5	8		8	1	7		6	7	1	4	6	6			2	1				
	2															2				1		2	2				
			4				1	4				2				1		1					1				

Martyn	Humphrey	Bodin	Gray	Shaw	Sinnott	Salako	Thomas	Bright	Wright	McGoldrick	Pardew	Thorn	Suckling	Southgate	Young	Collymore	Osborn	Gabbiadini	Rodger	Gordon	Mortimer	Coleman	Whyte	Moralee	Hedman	Sullivan	Barnes
1			4		3		8	**9**		11		6		2	5		14	10		12	7						
1	12		4				8	9		11		6		**2**	5		14	10			7	3					
1			4					9		11		6		**2**	5		8	10	12		7	3	14				
3			3		1		2	3		3		3		3	3		1	3			3	2					
	1																2		1	1			1				
			1				2	1		1					1			1									

League Table

	P	W	D	L	F	A	Pts
Leeds United	42	22	16	4	74	37	82
Manchester United	42	21	15	6	63	33	78
Sheffield Wednesday	42	21	12	9	62	49	75
Arsenal	42	19	15	8	81	46	72
Manchester City	42	20	10	12	61	48	70
Liverpool	42	16	16	10	47	40	64
Aston Villa	42	17	9	16	48	44	60
Nottingham Forest	42	16	11	15	60	58	59
Sheffield United	42	16	9	17	65	63	57
Crystal Palace	42	14	15	13	53	61	57
Queen's Park Rangers	42	12	18	12	48	47	54
Everton	42	13	14	15	52	51	53
Wimbledon	42	13	14	15	53	53	53
Chelsea	42	13	14	15	50	60	53
Tottenham Hotspur	42	15	7	20	58	63	52
Southampton	42	14	10	18	39	55	52
Oldham Athletic	42	14	9	19	63	67	51
Norwich City	42	11	12	19	47	63	45
Coventry City	42	11	11	20	35	44	44
Luton Town	42	10	12	20	38	71	42
Notts County	42	10	10	22	40	62	40
West Ham United	42	9	11	22	37	59	38

1992-93

Premiership

Manager: Steve Coppell

Did you know that?

Palace participated this season in the first year of the newly formed Premier League, but were relegated after a last-day defeat at Arsenal, with Steve Coppell deciding to step down as manager shortly after the end of the season.

Match No.	Date		Venue	Opponents	Result		Scorers	Attendance
1	Aug	15	H	Blackburn Rovers	D	3-3	Southgate, Bright, Osborn	17,086
2		19	A	Oldham Athletic	D	1-1	McGoldrick	11,063
3		22	A	Tottenham Hotspur	D	2-2	Young, McGoldrick	22,328
4		25	H	Sheffield Wednesday	D	1-1	Young	14,005
5		29	H	Norwich City	L	1-2	McGoldrick	12,033
6	Sep	2	A	Manchester United	L	0-1		29,736
7		5	A	Aston Villa	L	0-3		17,120
8		12	H	Oldham Athletic	D	2-2	Armstrong 2	11,224
9		19	A	Everton	W	2-0	Armstrong 2	18,083
10		26	H	Southampton	L	1-2	Young	13,829
11	Oct	3	A	Coventry City	D	2-2	Coleman, McGoldrick	11,833
12		17	H	Manchester City	D	0-0		14,005
13		24	A	Ipswich Town	D	2-2	Coleman, Armstrong	17,302
14	Nov	2	H	Arsenal	L	1-2	McGoldrick	20,734
15		7	A	Chelsea	L	1-3	Young	17,141
16		21	H	Nottingham Forest	D	1-1	Armstrong	15,330
17		28	A	Liverpool	L	0-5		36,380
18	Dec	5	H	Sheffield United	W	2-0	Southgate, Armstrong	12,361
19		12	A	Queen's Park Rangers	W	3-1	McGoldrick 2, Armstrong	14,571
20		20	H	Leeds United	W	1-0	Thorn	14,462
21		26	H	Wimbledon	W	2-0	Coleman, Thomas	16,825
22		28	A	Middlesbrough	W	1-0	Osborn	21,123
23	Jan	9	H	Everton	L	0-2		13,227
24		16	A	Southampton	L	0-1		13,397
25		27	A	Norwich City	L	2-4	Thomas, Armstrong	13,543
26		30	H	Tottenham Hotspur	L	1-3	own-goal (Ruddock)	20,937
27	Feb	2	A	Blackburn Rovers	W	2-1	Rodger, Armstrong	14,163
28		10	H	Aston Villa	W	1-0	Bowry	12,270
29		20	A	Sheffield Wednesday	L	1-2	Armstrong	26,459
30		27	H	Coventry City	D	0-0		12,248
31	Mar	3	A	Nottingham Forest	D	1-1	Southgate	20,603
32		15	H	Chelsea	D	1-1	Armstrong	12,610
33		20	A	Sheffield United	W	1-0	Coleman	18,857
34		23	H	Liverpool	D	1-1	Armstrong	18,688
35	Apr	3	H	Queen's Park Rangers	D	1-1	own-goal (Bardsley)	14,705
36		9	A	Wimbledon	L	0-4		12,275
37		12	H	Middlesbrough	W	4-1	Young, Coleman, Rodger, Armstrong	15,123
38		17	A	Leeds United	D	0-0		27,545
39		21	H	Manchester United	L	0-2		30,115
40	May	1	H	Ipswich Town	W	3-1	Young, McGoldrick, Armstrong	18,881
41		5	A	Manchester City	D	0-0		21,167
42		8	A	Arsenal	L	0-3		25,225

Final League Position: 20th in Premiership

Appearances

Sub appearances

2 own-goals — Goals

FA Cup

3	Jan	2	A	Hartlepool United	L	0-1		6,721

Appearances

League Cup

2	Sep	22	H	Lincoln City	W	3-1	Southgate, Salako, McGoldrick	6,947
	Oct	6	A	Lincoln City	D	1-1	Southgate	6,255
3		28	A	Southampton	W	2-0	Salako, McGoldrick	9,060
4	Dec	1	A	Liverpool	D	1-1	Coleman	18,525
R		16	H	Liverpool	W	2-1*	Thorn, Watts	19,622
5	Jan	6	H	Chelsea	W	3-1	Coleman, Ndah, Watts	28,510
SF	Feb	7	H	Arsenal	L	1-3	Osborn (pen)	26,508
SF	Mar	10	A	Arsenal	L	0-2		28,584

* After extra-time

Appearances

Sub appearances

Goals

Martyn	Humphrey	Shaw	Southgate	Young	Thorn	Coleman	Thomas	Bright	Salako	McGoldrick	Rodger	Osborn	Sinnott	Gordon	Armstrong	Massey	Williams	Collymore	Ndah	Mortimer	Bowry	Watts	Newman
1	2	3	4	5	6	7	8	9	**10**	11	12	14											
1	2	3	4	5	6	7	8		**10**	11			9	12									
1	2	3	4	5	6	7	8			11			9	10									
1	2	3	4	5	6	7	8	9		11				10									
1	2		4	5	6	**7**	8	9	12	11		14	3	10									
1	12		4	5	6		8	9	**10**	11		2	3		7								
1	**2**		4	5		12	8	9	10	11		6	3		7	14							
1	2		4	5		12	**8**		10	11		6	3		9		7						
1	2		4	5		8			10	11		6	3		9		7						
1	**2**		4	5		8			10	11		6	3		9		7	12					
1		2	4	5		8			10	11		6	3		9		7						
1		2	4	5		8			10	**11**		6	3		9		7	12					
1		2	4	5		8			10	11		6	3		9		7						
1		2	4	5	6	14	12		10	11		7	3		**9**		8						
1		2	4	5	6	12			10	11		7	3		9		**8**						
1	2	3	4	5	6	12				11		7			9		8			**10**			
1	2	3	4	5	6	12				11		7	8		9		**10**		14				
1	2	3	4	5	6	10				11		**7**			9				8		12		
1	2	3	4	5	6	**10**				11		7			9				8		12	14	
1	2	3	**4**	5	6		8			11	10	7			9						12		
1	2	3	**4**	5	6	7	8			11	10	12			9								
1	2	3		5	**6**	4	8			11	10	7			9						12		
1	2			5	**6**	4	8			11	10				9				14		3	7	12
1	2				6	4	8			11	10		3	14	9				7		12	**5**	
1	**2**	3			6	4	8			11	10	7	5		9				12				
1		3		5	6	4	**8**			11	10	7	2		9				12				
1		2		5	6	4				11	10	7	3		9						8		
1	12	**3**		5	6	4	8			11	10	7			9		14				2		
1	2	3		5	6	12				11	10	7			9		**8**				4		
1	2	**3**		5	6	4	8			11	10				9				12		7		
1	12		2	5	6	4	8			11	10			**3**	9				14		7		
1	**2**	12	3	5		4	8			11	10	7		6	9				14				
1		2	3	5	6	4	8			11	10	7			9								
1		**2**	3	5	6	4	8			11	10	7			9				12				
1		2	3		6	4	8			11	10	7		12			9		**5**				
1	12	2	3		6	4	8			11	10	**7**		5			9					14	
1	7	2	3	5	6	4	8			11	10		12		**9**		14						
1	7	2	3	5	6	4	8			11	**10**	12			9								
1	7	2	3	5	6	4				11		**10**			9				12				8
1	7	2	3	5	6	**4**	8			11	10				9		12						
1	7	2	3	5	6		8			11	10				9		4						
1	7	**2**	3	5	6		8			11	10			12	9		4						
42	28	32	33	38	34	31	28	5	12	42	22	27	18	6	35		15		4	1	6	2	1
	4	1				7	1		1		1	4	1	4		1	3	2	9		5	2	1
			3	6	1	5	2	1		8	2	2			15						1		

Martyn	Humphrey	Shaw	Southgate	Young	Thorn	Coleman	Thomas	Bright	Salako	McGoldrick	Rodger	Osborn	Sinnott	Gordon	Armstrong	Massey	Williams	Collymore	Ndah	Mortimer	Bowry	Watts	Newman
1	2	3		5		4	8			11	10	7			9						6		
1	1	1		1		1	1			1	1	1			1						1		

Martyn	Humphrey	Shaw	Southgate	Young	Thorn	Coleman	Thomas	Bright	Salako	McGoldrick	Rodger	Osborn	Sinnott	Gordon	Armstrong	Massey	Williams	Collymore	Ndah	Mortimer	Bowry	Watts	Newman
1	2		4	5		8			10	11		6	3				7	**9**	12				
1	2		4	5		8	**9**		10	11		6	3				7	12					
1		2	4	5	6	9			10	11		7	3				8						
1	2	3	4	5	6	9				11		7							8		10		
1	2	3	4	5	6					11	9	7	14						12		8	**10**	
1	2			5	6	4	8			11	10			12					7		3	**9**	
1		3		5	6	4	8			11	10	7	**2**								9	12	
1	2		3	5		4	8			11	10	7		6					12			**9**	
8	6	4	6	8	5	7	4		3	8	4	7	4	1			3	1	2		4	3	
													1	1				1	3			1	
			2		1	2			2	2		1							1			2	

League Table

	P	W	D	L	F	A	Pts
Manchester United	42	24	12	6	67	31	84
Aston Villa	42	21	11	10	57	40	74
Norwich City	42	21	9	12	61	65	72
Blackburn Rovers	42	20	11	11	68	46	71
Queen's Park Rangers	42	17	12	13	63	55	63
Liverpool	42	16	11	15	62	55	59
Sheffield Wednesday	42	15	14	13	55	51	59
Tottenham Hotspur	42	16	11	15	60	66	59
Manchester City	42	15	12	15	56	51	57
Arsenal	42	15	11	16	40	38	56
Chelsea	42	14	14	14	51	54	56
Wimbledon	42	14	12	16	56	55	54
Everton	42	15	8	19	53	55	53
Sheffield United	42	14	10	18	54	53	52
Coventry City	42	13	13	16	52	57	52
Ipswich Town	42	12	16	14	50	55	52
Leeds United	42	12	15	15	57	62	51
Southampton	42	13	11	18	54	61	50
Oldham Athletic	42	13	10	19	63	74	49
Crystal Palace	42	11	16	15	48	61	49
Middlesbrough	42	11	11	20	54	75	44
Nottingham Forest	42	10	10	22	41	62	40

1993-94

Division One

Manager: Alan Smith

Did you know that?

Promoting from within, Alan Smith became the new manager and Palace returned to the top flight at the first time of asking, finishing top of what became Division One.

The Holmesdale Road terrace was demolished after the last game of the season, to make way for the massive new Holmesdale stand that would appear in 1995.

Match No.	Date		Venue	Opponents	Result		Scorers	Attendance
1	Aug	14	H	Tranmere Rovers	D	0-0		14,785
2		21	A	Bristol City	L	0-2		12,068
3		24	H	Nottingham Forest	W	2-0	Young, Gordon	15,048
4		28	H	Portsmouth	W	5-1	Southgate, Armstrong 3, Gordon	14,428
5		31	A	Birmingham City	W	4-2	Armstrong 2, Williams, Shaw	13,856
6	Sep	12	H	Sunderland	W	1-0	Armstrong	11,318
7		18	A	West Bromwich Albion	W	4-1	Coleman, Southgate, Armstrong, Whyte	17,873
8		26	A	Charlton Athletic	D	0-0		7,903
9	Oct	2	H	Stoke City	W	4-1	Southgate, Salako 3	13,339
10		17	H	Wolverhampton Wanderers	D	1-1	Humphrey	13,056
11		23	A	Derby County	L	1-3	Armstrong	16,586
12		30	H	Grimsby Town	W	1-0	Southgate	12,202
13	Nov	2	H	Luton Town	W	3-2	Young, Whyte, Shaw	10,925
14		6	A	Notts County	L	2-3	Armstrong 2	6,904
15		20	A	Barnsley	W	3-1	Armstrong, Williams 2	5,384
16		24	A	Bolton Wanderers	L	0-1		7,486
17		28	A	Watford	W	3-1	Southgate, Williams, Salako	7,485
18	Dec	5	H	Notts County	L	1-2	Armstrong	13,704
19		8	A	Leicester City	D	1-1	Williams	16,706
20		11	H	Birmingham City	W	2-1	Southgate, Salako	11,935
21		19	A	Tranmere Rovers	W	1-0	Williams	7,011
22		27	A	Oxford United	W	3-1	Armstrong 2, Salako	10,354
23		29	H	Southend United	W	1-0	Rodger	18,255
24	Jan	1	A	Millwall	L	0-3		16,731
25		15	A	Wolverhampton Wanderers	L	0-2		23,851
26		22	H	Leicester City	W	2-1	Coleman, Armstrong	17,644
27	Feb	1	H	Peterborough United	W	3-2	Armstrong, Rodger, Salako	13,083
28		5	H	Derby County	D	1-1	Gordon	16,027
29		12	A	Grimsby Town	D	1-1	Southgate	6,302
30		19	A	Nottingham Forest	D	1-1	Matthew	24,232
31		22	H	Bristol City	W	4-1	Armstrong 2, Gordon (pen), Salako	12,417
32		26	H	Bolton Wanderers	D	1-1	Southgate	18,093
33	Mar	5	A	Portsmouth	W	1-0	Young	13,508
34		12	H	West Bromwich Albion	W	1-0	Stewart	17,106
35		16	A	Sunderland	L	0-1		15,716
36		20	H	Charlton Athletic	W	2-0	Armstrong, Stewart	14,743
37		23	H	Middlesbrough	L	0-1		13,278
38		26	A	Stoke City	W	2-0	Williams, Gordon (pen)	18,037
39		29	A	Peterborough United	D	1-1	Rodger	8,412
40	Apr	2	H	Oxford United	W	2-1	Armstrong, Stewart	15,928
41		6	A	Southend United	W	2-1	Young, Armstrong	9,793
42		9	H	Millwall	W	1-0	Armstrong	23,562
43		16	A	Luton Town	W	1-0	Coleman	9,880
44		23	H	Barnsley	W	1-0	Young	20,522
45	May	1	A	Middlesbrough	W	3-2	Southgate, Armstrong, Whyte	8,638
46		8	H	Watford	L	0-2		28,694

Final League Position: 1st in Division One

Appearances
Sub appearances
Goals

FA Cup

3	Jan	8	A	Wolverhampton Wand.	L	0-1		25,047

Appearances
Sub appearances

League Cup

2	Sep	21	H	Charlton Athletic	W	3-1	Southgate, Gordon, Whyte	9,615
	Oct	5	A	Charlton Athletic	W	1-0	Armstrong	5,224
3		26	A	Everton	D	2-2	Southgate, Thorn	11,547
R	Nov	10	H	Everton	L	1-4	Southgate	14,662

Appearances
Sub appearances
Goals

Anglo-Italian Cup

Gp	Sep	7	A	Charlton Athletic	L	1-4	Williams	3,868
Gp		14	H	Millwall	W	3-0	Armstrong (pen), Williams, Whyte	2,712

Appearances
Sub appearances
Goals

Martyn	Humphrey	Coleman	Southgate	Young	Thorn	Osborn	Bowry	Armstrong	Williams	Gordon	Whyte	Rodger	Shaw	Massey	Salako	Mortimer	O'Connor	Newman	Stewart	Ndah	Matthew	Dyer	Simott
1	2	3	4	5	6	**7**	8	9	10	11	12												
1	2	3	4	5	6		8	9	10	12	7	**11**	14										
1	2	3	4	5	**6**		8	9	10	12		11	7										
1	2	6	4	5			8	9	10	3		11	7										
1	2	6	4	5			8	9	10	3		11	7										
1	2	6	4	5				9	10	3		11	7	8									
1	2	3	4	5	6		8	9	**10**	14	12	11	7										
1	2	3	4	5	6		8		10	12	9	**11**	7		14								
1	2	3	4	5	6		8		12		9	11	7		**10**								
1	2	3	4	5	6		**8**	9		12	10	14	7		11								
1	2	3	**4**	5	6			9		12	10	8	7		11								
1	2	3	4	5	6			9		11	10	8	7										
1	2	3	4	5	**6**			9		11	10	8	7		12								
1	2	6	4	5			14	9	12	3	**10**	8	7		11								
1		6	4	5		**7**		9	10	3		8	12		11		2						
1		6	4	5		**7**		9	10	3	14	8	12		11		2						
1		6	4	5		7		9	10	3		8	2		11								
1		6	4	5		7	12	9	10	3	14	**8**	2		11								
1		6	4	5			7	9	10	3			2		11			8					
1		6	4	5			7	9	10	3			2		11			8					
1		6	4	5			7	9	10	3		12	2		**11**			8					
1		6	4	5			7	9	**10**	3		12	2		11			8					
1		6	4	5			7	9	**10**	3		12	2		11			8					
1		6	4	5		14	7	9	**10**	3		12	2		11			8					
1		6	4	5				9	**10**	3	12	7	2		11			8					
1		6	4	5				9		3		7	2		11			8	10				
1		6	4	5			12	9		3		7	2		**11**			8	10				
1		6	4	5			12	**9**		3		7	2		11			8	10	14			
1	2	6	4	5				9		3		7			11				10		8		
1	2	6	4	5				9		3		7			11				10		8		
1	2	6	4	5				9		3	12		7		11				**10**		8		
1	2	6	4	5				9		3		7			11				10		8		
1	2	6	4	5				9		3		7			11				10		8		
1	2	6	4	5				9		**3**		7			11				10		8	12	
1	2	6	4	5				9		3		7			11				10		**8**	12	
1	2	6	4	5			8	9		3		7			11				**10**			12	
1	2	6	4	5			8	9		**3**		7	14		11				10			12	
1	2	6	4	**5**				9	14	3		7	8		12				10			11	
1	2	6	4	5					9	**3**		7	8		12				10			11	
1	2	6	4	5				**9**		3		7	8		11				10			12	
1	2	6	4	5				9	**10**	3		7	8		11							12	
1	2	6	4	5				9		3		7	**8**		11				10		12		
1	2	6	4	5				9		3		7			11				10		8		
1	2	6	4	5				9		3		7			11				10		**8**	12	
1	2	6	4	5				9		3	**10**	7			11			14			8	12	
1	2	6	4	5				9		3	10	7			11						**8**	12	
46	32	46	46	46	10	5	17	43	21	39	10	37	30	1	34		2	10	18		11	2	
						1	4		3	6	6	5	4		4			1		1	1	9	
	1	3	9	5				23	7	5	3	3	2		8				3		1		

Martyn	Humphrey	Coleman	Southgate	Young	Thorn	Osborn	Bowry	Armstrong	Williams	Gordon	Whyte	Rodger	Shaw	Massey	Salako	Mortimer	O'Connor	Newman	Stewart	Ndah	Matthew	Dyer	Simott
1		6	4	5		**10**		9		3	12	7	2		11			8					
1		1	1	1		1		1		1		1	1		1			1					
											1												

Martyn	Humphrey	Coleman	Southgate	Young	Thorn	Osborn	Bowry	Armstrong	Williams	Gordon	Whyte	Rodger	Shaw	Massey	Salako	Mortimer	O'Connor	Newman	Stewart	Ndah	Matthew	Dyer	Simott
1	2	6	4	5			8		**10**	3	9	11	7		12								
1	**2**	3	4	5	6		8	9		12	10	11	7		14								
1	2	3	4	5	6			9		11	**10**	8	**7**		12								
1	2	6	4	5			**11**	9	12		10	8	7			3							
4	4	4	4	4	2		3	3	1	2	4	4	4			1							
									1	1					3								
			3		1			1		1	1												

Martyn	Humphrey	Coleman	Southgate	Young	Thorn	Osborn	Bowry	Armstrong	Williams	Gordon	Whyte	Rodger	Shaw	Massey	Salako	Mortimer	O'Connor	Newman	Stewart	Ndah	Matthew	Dyer	Simott
1	2		4					9	10	3	14	11	7				8	**5**		12			6
1	2		4					**9**	10	3	12	11	7	8			14	5		6			
2	2		2					2	2	2		2	2	1			1	2		1			1
											2						1			1			
								1	2		1												

League Table

	P	W	D	L	F	A	Pts
Crystal Palace	46	27	9	10	73	46	90
Nottingham Forest	46	23	14	9	74	49	83
Millwall	46	19	17	10	58	49	74
Leicester City	46	19	16	11	72	59	73
Tranmere Rovers	46	21	9	16	69	53	72
Derby County	46	20	11	15	73	68	71
Notts County	46	20	8	18	65	69	68
Wolverhampton W	46	17	17	12	60	47	68
Middlesbrough	46	18	13	15	66	54	67
Stoke City	46	18	13	15	57	59	67
Charlton Athletic	46	19	8	19	61	58	65
Sunderland	46	19	8	19	54	57	65
Bristol City	46	16	16	14	47	50	64
Bolton Wanderers	46	15	14	17	63	64	59
Southend United	46	17	8	21	63	67	59
Grimsby Town	46	13	20	13	52	47	59
Portsmouth	46	15	13	18	52	58	58
Barnsley	46	16	7	23	55	67	55
Watford	46	15	9	22	66	80	54
Luton Town	46	14	11	21	56	60	53
West Bromwich Albion	46	13	12	21	60	69	51
Birmingham City	46	13	12	21	52	69	51
Oxford United	46	13	10	23	54	75	49
Peterborough United	46	8	13	25	48	76	37

1994-95

Premiership

Manager: Alan Smith

Did you know that?

With the Premier League reducing itself from 22 to 20 teams the next season, Palace under Alan Smith were cruelly relegated as the extra side of the four that went down this campaign, missing out on safety by three points.

Match No.	Date		Venue	Opponents	Result		Scorers	Attendance
1	Aug	20	H	Liverpool	L	1-6	Armstrong	18,084
2		24	A	Norwich City	D	0-0		19,015
3		27	A	Aston Villa	D	1-1	Southgate	23,305
4		30	H	Leeds United	L	1-2	Gordon	14,453
5	Sep	10	A	Manchester City	D	1-1	Dyer	19,971
6		17	H	Wimbledon	D	0-0		12,366
7		24	H	Chelsea	L	0-1		16,064
8	Oct	1	A	Arsenal	W	2-1	Salako 2	34,136
9		8	A	West Ham United	L	0-1		16,959
10		15	H	Newcastle United	L	0-1		17,739
11		22	H	Everton	W	1-0	Preece	15,026
12		29	A	Leicester City	W	1-0	Preece	20,022
13	Nov	2	A	Coventry City	W	4-1	Preece 2, Salako, Newman	10,729
14		5	H	Ipswich Town	W	3-0	Armstrong, Salako, Newman	13,450
15		19	A	Manchester United	L	0-3		43,788
16		26	H	Southampton	D	0-0		14,186
17	Dec	3	A	Sheffield Wednesday	L	0-1		21,930
18		11	A	Liverpool	D	0-0		30,972
19		17	H	Norwich City	L	0-1		12,473
20		26	H	Queen's Park Rangers	D	0-0		16,699
21		27	A	Tottenham Hotspur	D	0-0		27,730
22		31	H	Blackburn Rovers	L	0-1		14,232
23	Jan	2	A	Nottingham Forest	L	0-1		21,326
24		14	H	Leicester City	W	2-0	Newman, Ndah	12,707
25		21	A	Everton	L	1-3	Coleman	23,734
26		25	H	Manchester United	D	1-1	Southgate	18,224
27	Feb	4	A	Ipswich Town	W	2-0	Gordon (pen), Dowie	15,361
28		11	H	Coventry City	L	0-2		12,076
29		25	H	Arsenal	L	0-3		17,063
30	Mar	5	A	Chelsea	D	0-0		14,130
31		14	H	Sheffield Wednesday	W	2-1	Armstrong, Dowie	10,964
32		18	A	Wimbledon	L	0-2		8,835
33	Apr	1	H	Manchester City	W	2-1	Armstrong, Patterson	13,451
34		4	H	Aston Villa	D	0-0		12,949
35		14	H	Tottenham Hotspur	D	1-1	Armstrong	18,068
36		17	A	Queen's Park Rangers	W	1-0	Dowie	14,227
37		20	A	Blackburn Rovers	L	1-2	Houghton	28,005
38		29	H	Nottingham Forest	L	1-2	Dowie	16,335
39	May	3	A	Southampton	L	1-3	Southgate	15,151
40		6	H	West Ham United	W	1-0	Armstrong	18,224
41		9	A	Leeds United	L	1-3	Armstrong	30,963
42		14	A	Newcastle United	L	2-3	Armstrong, Houghton	35,626

Final League Position: 19th in Premiership

Appearances
Sub appearances
Goals

FA Cup

3	Jan	8	H	Lincoln City	W	5-1	Gordon (pen), Coleman, Armstrong, Salako 2	6,541
4		28	A	Nottingham Forest	W	2-1	Armstrong, Dowie	16,790
5	Feb	18	A	Watford	D	0-0		13,814
R	Mar	1	H	Watford	W	1-0*	Ndah	10,321
6		11	H	Wolverhampton Wand.	D	1-1	Dowie	14,604
R		22	A	Wolverhampton Wand.	W	4-1	Pitcher, Armstrong 2, Dowie	27,548
SF	Apr	9	N+	Manchester United	D	2-2*	Armstrong, Dowie	38,256
R		12	N+	Manchester United	L	0-2		17,987

* After extra-time
+ Played at Villa Park

Appearances
Sub appearances
Goals

League Cup

2	Sep	20	A	Lincoln City	L	0-1		4,310
	Oct	4	H	Lincoln City	W	3-0*	Gordon, Armstrong, Dyer	6,870
3		25	A	Wimbledon	W	1-0	Armstrong	9,394
4	Nov	30	H	Aston Villa	W	4-1	Southgate 2, Armstrong 2	12,653
5	Jan	11	H	Manchester City	W	4-0	Pitcher, Armstrong, Preece, Salako	16,668
SF1	Feb	15	A	Liverpool	L	0-1		25,480
SF2	Mar	8	H	Liverpool	L	0-1		18,224

* After extra-time

Appearances
Sub appearances
Goals

Martyn	Pitcher	Gordon	Southgate	Young	Coleman	Rodger	Wilkins	Armstrong	Preece	Salako	Bowry	Dyer	Patterson	Shaw	Newman	Cox	Matthew	Ndah	Launders	Humphrey	Williams	Wilmot	Dowie	Houghton
1	2	3	4	5	6	7	**8**	9	10	11	12	14												
1		3	4		**6**	7		9		11	8	10	2	5	12	14								
1	12	3	4		6	7		9		11		**10**	5	2	8	14								
1		3	4		6	**7**		9	10	11		8	2	5	12									
1		3	4		6			9		11		7	2	5	8		10							
1	2	3	4		6			9		11		7		5	8		**10**	12						
1		3	4		6			9		11		12	2	5	8			7	**10**					
1		3	4		6			9		10	7		2	5	8			11						
1		3	4		6			9		10	7	12	2	5	8			**11**	14					
1		3	4		6			9	10	11	7			5	8					2				
1	12	3	4		6			9	10	11	**7**			5	8					2				
1	12	3	4		6			9	10	11	**7**			5	8					2				
1		3	4		6			9	10	11			2	5	8					7				
1		3	4		6			9	10	11	7			5	8					2				
1		3	4		6			9	10	11	12		**2**	5	8					7				
1		3	4		6			9	**10**	11	7	12		5	8					2				
1		3	4		6			9	10	11	**7**			5	8			12		2				
1	4	3	6					9	10	11	7			5	8					2				
1	14	3	4		6			9	10	11	**7**	12		5	8					2				
1		3	4		6			9	10	11				5	8	**7**				2	12			
1	7	3	4		6			9		**10**	11		2	5	8						12			
1		3	4		6			9	11				**2**	5	8			12		7	10			
1	**11**	3	4		6			9					2	5	8			12		7	10	14		
1	7	3	4		6			9	12	10				5	8			**11**		2				
1	7	3	4		6			9		11				5	8			12		2			**10**	
1	7	3	4		6			9	12	11			2	5	8								**10**	
1	7	3	4		6			**9**		11	12		2	5	8								10	
1	7	3	4		6				12	10	**8**		2	5				11					9	
1	11	3	4		6			9		10		12	**2**	5	8		14			7				
1	7	3	4	5					**10**	11			2	6	8		14	12					9	
1	4	12	2	5	3			9	**11**	7				6	8								10	
1	4	12	2	5	3			9	**11**	7				6	8					14			10	
1	8		4	5	3			9		11		**10**	2	6		14		12						7
1	8	12	4	**5**	3			9		11		10	2	6		14								7
	8	3	4	5				9		11			2	6	12	14						1	10	7
		3	4	5	6			9		**11**	14			2	8	12						1	10	7
		11	4	**5**	3			9					2	6	8	14				12		1	10	7
		3	4		6			9		11	14			5	**8**	12				2		1	10	7
	8	3	4	5				9		11		12		6						**2**		1	10	7
1	8	3	4	5				9		11				6						2			10	7
1	8	3	4	5				9		**11**		12	2	6		14							10	7
1	4	3	2	5				9		**11**		12		6	8	14							10	7
37	21	38	42	13	35	4	1	40	17	39	13	7	22	41	32	1	2	5	1	19	2	5	15	10
	4	3							3		5	9			3	10	2	7	1	2	2	1		
		2	3		1			8	4	4		1	1		3			1					4	2

Martyn	Pitcher	Gordon	Southgate	Young	Coleman	Rodger	Wilkins	Armstrong	Preece	Salako	Bowry	Dyer	Patterson	Shaw	Newman	Cox	Matthew	Ndah	Launders	Humphrey	Williams	Wilmot	Dowie	Houghton
1	7	3	4		6			9	12	10				5	8			**11**		2				
1	7	3	4		6			**9**	12	11			2	5	8								10	
1	8	3	4		6			9	10	11			2	5						7				
1	7	3	4						12	11		10	6	5	8			14		**2**			9	
1	7		2	5	3				11	10		14		6	8		**4**			12			9	
1	8		4	5	3			9		11		14	2	6	12	**7**							10	
1	8	12	4	5	**3**			9		11			2	6									10	7
	8	3	4	5				9		11			2	6	12	14						1	10	7
7	8	5	8	4	6			6	2	8		1	6	8	4	1	1	1		3		1	6	2
		1							3			2			2	1		1		1				
	1	1			1			5		2								1					4	

Martyn	Pitcher	Gordon	Southgate	Young	Coleman	Rodger	Wilkins	Armstrong	Preece	Salako	Bowry	Dyer	Patterson	Shaw	Newman	Cox	Matthew	Ndah	Launders	Humphrey	Williams	Wilmot	Dowie	Houghton
1		3	4		6			9	12	11		**10**	2	5	7			8						
1		3	4		6			9		10	8	12	**2**	5	7			11	14					
1		3	4		6			9	10	11	8			5	7					2				
1		3	4		6			9	10	11	7			5	8					2				
1	7	3	4		6			9	12	10				5	8			**11**		2				
1	11	3	4		6				9	10			2	5			8			7				
1	7	3	4	5	9				10	11		12	2	6				**8**						
7	3	7	7	1	7			5	4	7	3	1	4	7	5		1	4		4				
									2			2							1					
	1	1	2					5	1	1		1												

League Table

	P	W	D	L	F	A	Pts
Blackburn Rovers	42	27	8	7	80	39	89
Manchester United	42	26	10	6	77	28	88
Nottingham Forest	42	22	11	9	72	43	77
Liverpool	42	21	11	10	65	37	74
Leeds United	42	20	13	9	59	38	73
Newcastle United	42	20	12	10	67	47	72
Tottenham Hotspur	42	16	14	12	66	58	62
Queen's Park Rangers	42	17	9	16	61	59	60
Wimbledon	42	15	11	16	48	65	56
Southampton	42	12	18	12	61	63	54
Chelsea	42	13	15	14	50	55	54
Arsenal	42	13	12	17	52	49	51
Sheffield Wednesday	42	13	12	17	49	57	51
West Ham United	42	13	11	18	44	48	50
Everton	42	11	17	14	44	51	50
Coventry City	42	12	14	16	44	62	50
Manchester City	42	12	13	17	53	64	49
Aston Villa	42	11	15	16	51	56	48
Crystal Palace	42	11	12	19	34	49	45
Norwich City	42	10	13	19	37	54	43
Leicester City	42	6	11	25	45	80	29
Ipswich Town	42	7	6	29	36	93	27

1995-96

Division One

Manager: Steve Coppell (as technical director) with Ray Lewington and Peter Nicholas as caretaker managers, Dave Bassett manager from 8 February 1996

Did you know that?

Dougie Freedman scored the fastest-ever League hat-trick for Palace when he stuck three goals past Grimsby Town in 11 minutes on 5 March. Palace won 5–0, with all the goals coming in the first half.

Match No.	Date	Venue	Opponents	Result		Scorers	Attendance
1	Aug 12	H	Barnsley	W	4-3	Gordon (pen), Houghton, Dowie 2	12,166
2	19	A	Ipswich Town	L	0-1		12,326
3	26	H	Charlton Athletic	D	1-1	Dyer	14,092
4	29	A	Sheffield United	W	3-2	Gordon, Dyer 2	10,378
5	Sep 9	A	Birmingham City	D	0-0		19,403
6	12	A	Watford	D	0-0		8,780
7	16	H	Huddersfield Town	D	0-0		15,980
8	23	A	Oldham Athletic	L	1-3	Hopkin	6,586
9	30	H	Stoke City	D	1-1	Freedman	15,010
10	Oct 7	H	Sunderland	L	0-1		14,329
11	15	A	Port Vale	W	2-1	Gordon, Freedman	6,935
12	22	H	Millwall	L	1-2	Gordon	15,136
13	28	A	Leicester City	W	3-2	Hopkin, Dyer 2	18,376
14	Nov 4	H	Reading	L	0-2		16,687
15	11	A	Norwich City	L	0-1		14,156
16	19	A	Southend United	D	1-1	own-goal (Lapper)	5,089
17	22	H	Wolverhampton Wanderers	W	3-2	Freedman 3	13,340
18	25	H	Derby County	D	0-0		14,109
19	Dec 3	A	Sunderland	L	0-1		12,740
20	9	H	Oldham Athletic	D	2-2	Freedman, Davies	14,108
21	16	A	Stoke City	W	2-1	Freedman, Taylor	12,076
22	23	A	West Bromwich Albion	W	3-2	Gordon 3 (2 pens)	13,098
23	Jan 1	A	Portsmouth	W	3-2	Hopkin 2, Freedman	12,926
24	13	H	Ipswich Town	D	1-1	Davies	14,401
25	20	A	Barnsley	D	1-1	Gordon	6,637
26	Feb 4	A	Charlton Athletic	D	0-0		13,535
27	10	H	Sheffield United	D	0-0		16,451
28	17	H	Watford	W	4-0	Dyer 2, Freedman 2	13,930
29	20	H	Tranmere Rovers	W	3-2	Houghton, Freedman, Boere	5,253
30	24	A	Huddersfield Town	L	0-3		13,041
31	27	H	Birmingham City	W	3-2	Dyer 3	13,415
32	Mar 2	A	Luton Town	D	0-0		8,478
33	5	H	Grimsby Town	W	5-0	Hopkin, Houghton, Freedman 3	12,623
34	9	H	West Bromwich Albion	W	1-0	Freedman	19,254
35	12	H	Tranmere Rovers	W	2-1	Hopkin, Ndah	14,552
36	16	A	Grimsby Town	W	2-0	Ndah, Tuttle	5,059
37	19	H	Luton Town	W	2-0	Dyer 2	14,703
38	23	H	Portsmouth	D	0-0		17,465
39	30	A	Millwall	W	4-1	Hopkin, Ndah 2, Brown	13,214
40	Apr 2	H	Port Vale	D	2-2	Freedman 2	14,717
41	6	H	Leicester City	L	0-1		17,750
42	8	A	Reading	W	2-0	Houghton, Freedman	12,576
43	13	H	Southend United	W	2-0	Freedman 2	15,819
44	20	A	Wolverhampton Wanderers	W	2-0	Hopkin, Dyer	24,350
45	28	A	Derby County	L	1-2	Brown	17,041
46	May 5	H	Norwich City	L	0-1		20,664

Final League Position: 3rd in Division One

Appearances
Sub appearances
1 own-goal Goals

Play-offs

	Date	Venue	Opponents	Result		Scorers	Attendance
SF1	May 12	A	Charlton Athletic	W	2-1	Brown, Veart	14,618
SF2	15	H	Charlton Athletic	W	1-0	Houghton	22,880
F	27	N+	Leicester City	L	1-2*	Roberts	73,573

+ Played at Wembley Stadium. * After extra-time

Appearances
Sub appearances
Goals

FA Cup

	Date	Venue	Opponents	Result		Scorers	Attendance
3	Jan 6	H	Port Vale	D	0-0		10,456
R	16	A	Port Vale	L	3-4*	Dyer, Cox, Taylor	6,754

* After extra-time

Appearances
Sub appearances
Goals

League Cup

	Date	Venue	Opponents	Result		Scorers	Attendance
2	Sep 19	A	Southend United	D	2-2	Hopkin 2	4,031
	Oct 3	H	Southend United	W	2-0	Vincent, McKenzie	6,588
3	25	H	Middlesbrough	D	2-2	Hopkin 2	11,873
R	Nov 8	A	Middlesbrough	L	0-2		16,150

Appearances
Sub appearances
Goals

Martyn	Edworthy	Gordon	Hopkin	Coleman	Shaw	Houghton	Pitcher	Dowie	Dyer	Ndah	Cox	Matthew	Scully	Vincent	Rodger	Freedman	Roberts	Taylor	Launders	McKenzie	Sparrow	Davies	Boere	Cundy	Gale	Andersen	Tuttle	Veart	Brown	Boxall	Quinn
1	2	3	4	5	6	7	8	9	10	11	12																				
1	2	3	4	5	6	7	8	9	10	11	12	13																			
1	2	3	4	5	6	7	8	9	10	11		12	13																		
1	2	3	4	5	6	7	8	9	10			11		12	13																
1	2		4	5	6	7	8		10	12		11		3	13	9															
1	2	11	4	5	6	7	8		10	12				3	13	9															
1	2	3	4	5	6	8			10	12		11	13	14	7	9															
1	2	3	4	5	6	8	7		10			11		13	12	9	14														
1	2	11	4	5	6	8	7							3		9	12	10	13												
1	2	11	7	5	6	8			12					3		9	4	10		13											
1		3	7	5	6	8			11			12			2	9	4	10													
1	2	3	7	5	6	8			12			13			11	9	4	10													
1	2	3	7	5	6	8	11		9							12	4	10													
1	2	3	7	5	6	8	11		9							12	4	10													
1	2		7	5	6		8		11					3		9	4	10		12											
1	2	3	11	5		8	7		10							9	4	12		13	6										
1	2	3	6			8	7							11		9	4	10		12		5	13								
1	2	3	6			8	7							11		9	4	10		12		5									
1	2	3	6			8	7							11		9	4	10		12		5	13								
1	2	3	6	5			7		12							9	4	10		11		8	13								
1	2	3				8	7		12					6		9	4	10		11			13	5							
1	2	3	12			8	7							6		9	4	10		11			13	5							
1	2	3	6			8	7							11		9	4	10		12		13		5							
1	2	3	6			8	7		12						13	9	4	10		14		11		5							
1	2	3				8	7		12		11				6	9	4	10				5									
1	2	3				8	7		12						6	9	4	10		11		5									
1	2	3				8	7		11	12				13	6	9	4	10				5									
1	2	3	6			8	7		10	12				13	11	9	4						14			5					
1	2	3	6			8	7			10	12			11		9	4						13		5	14					
1	2	3	6			8				10					11	9	4					13	12		5	7					
1	2	3	6			8			11	10					12	9	4					5				7					
1	2	3	6			8			11	10				7		9	4	12				5				13					
1	2	3	6			8	7			10					12	9	4		13			5				11					
1	2	3	6			8	7		12	10						9	4					5				11	13				
1	2	3	6			8	7		12	10					13	9	4									11	5	14			
1	2	3	6				7			10					8	9	4									11	5	12			
1	2		6			8	7		12	10				3		9	4									11	5	13			
1	2		6			8	7		12	10				3		9	4					13				11	5	14			
1	2		6			8	7			10				3			4					5						9	11		
1	2		6			8	7		13	10					12	9	4					5						11	3		
1	2		6			8	7		9	10				3	12		4									11	5	13			
1	2		6			8			12						7	9	4					5				13	11	10	3		
1	2		6			8			12						7	9	4					5				13	11	10	3		
1	2		6				8		10					3	7	9	4									5	11	12			
1	2		6			8	7		10	12				13	11	9	4									5		14	3		
1			6						9	10				3	7							5					4	11	12	2	8
46	44	34	41	17	15	41	36	4	21	17	1	4		19	14	37	36	18		4	1	17		4	2	12	9	5	5	1	1
			1						14	6	3	4	2	6	10	2	2	2	2	8		3	8			4	1	7	1		
		8	8			4		2	13	4						20		1				2	1				1		2		

Martyn	Edworthy	Gordon	Hopkin	Coleman	Shaw	Houghton	Pitcher	Dowie	Dyer	Ndah	Cox	Matthew	Scully	Vincent	Rodger	Freedman	Roberts	Taylor	Launders	McKenzie	Sparrow	Davies	Boere	Cundy	Gale	Andersen	Tuttle	Veart	Brown	Boxall	Quinn
1	2					8	7			10						9	4									5	11	6	3		12
1	2					8	7		12	10						9	4										11	6	3		5
1	2		6			8	7		13	10					14	9	4										11	12	3		5
3	3		1			3	3			3						3	3									1	3	2	3		2
									2						1													1			1
						1											1											1	1		

Martyn	Edworthy	Gordon	Hopkin	Coleman	Shaw	Houghton	Pitcher	Dowie	Dyer	Ndah	Cox	Matthew	Scully	Vincent	Rodger	Freedman	Roberts	Taylor	Launders	McKenzie	Sparrow	Davies	Boere	Cundy	Gale
1	2	3	6			8	7							11	12	9	4	10		13		5			
1	2	3				8	7		12		14				13	9	4	10		11		5			6
2	2	2	1			2	2							1		2	2	2		1		2			1
									1		1				2					1					
									1		1							1							

Martyn	Edworthy	Gordon	Hopkin	Coleman	Shaw	Houghton	Pitcher	Dowie	Dyer	Ndah	Cox	Matthew	Scully	Vincent	Rodger	Freedman	Roberts	Taylor	Launders	McKenzie	Sparrow
1	2	11	4	5	6	8	14		10	12		9		3	7		13				
1	2	11	7	5	6	8			10					3			4		12	9	
1	2	3	7	5	6	8	11		10								4			9	
1	2	3	7	5	6	8	11		9			14		12			4			10	13
4	4	4	4	4	4	4	2		4			1		2	1		3			3	
							1			1		1		1			1		1		1
			4											1						1	

League Table

	P	W	D	L	F	A	Pts
Sunderland	46	22	17	7	59	33	83
Derby County	46	21	16	9	71	51	79
Crystal Palace	46	20	15	11	67	48	75
Stoke City	46	20	13	13	60	49	73
Leicester City	46	19	14	13	66	60	71
Charlton Athletic	46	17	20	9	57	45	71
Ipswich Town	46	19	12	15	79	69	69
Huddersfield Town	46	17	12	17	61	58	63
Sheffield United	46	16	14	16	57	54	62
Barnsley	46	14	18	14	60	66	60
West Bromwich Albion	46	16	12	18	60	68	60
Port Vale	46	15	15	16	59	66	60
Tranmere Rovers	46	14	17	15	64	60	59
Southend United	46	15	14	17	52	61	59
Birmingham City	46	15	13	18	61	64	58
Norwich City	46	14	15	17	59	55	57
Grimsby Town	46	14	14	18	55	69	56
Oldham Athletic	46	14	14	18	54	50	56
Reading	46	13	17	16	54	63	56
Wolverhampton W	46	13	16	17	56	62	55
Portsmouth	46	13	13	20	61	69	52
Millwall	46	13	13	20	43	63	52
Watford	46	10	18	18	62	70	48
Luton Town	46	11	12	23	40	64	45

1996-97

Division One

Manager: Dave Bassett until 27 February 1997, Steve Coppell from 28 February

Did you know that?

After last-minute Play-off Final heartache the previous season, the tables were turned at Wembley as David Hopkin curled in a top corner last minute shot to fire Palace back into the Premier League as they beat Sheffield United 1–0 on a hot day at Wembley on 26 May. Thanks to TV commentary, the phrase 'Hopkin looking to curl one' has been etched in every fan's brain since.

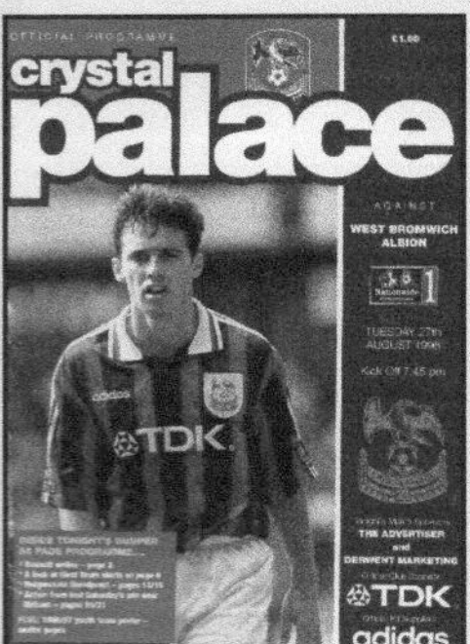

Match No.	Date	Venue	Opponents	Result		Scorers	Attendance
1	Aug 18	A	Birmingham City	L	0-1		18,765
2	24	H	Oldham Athletic	W	3-1	Dyer, Hopkin 2	13,675
3	27	H	West Bromwich Albion	D	0-0		14,328
4	31	A	Huddersfield Town	D	1-1	Freedman	11,166
5	Sep 7	A	Stoke City	D	2-2	Freedman, Hopkin	13,523
6	10	H	Ipswich Town	D	0-0		12,978
7	14	H	Manchester City	W	3-1	Andersen, Hopkin 2	18,205
8	21	A	Reading	W	6-1	Muscat, Tuttle, Freedman, Dyer (pen), Veart, Ndah	9,675
9	28	H	Southend United	W	6-1	Muscat, Houghton, Hopkin, Freedman, Dyer, Veart	15,222
10	Oct 1	A	Portsmouth	D	2-2	Freedman, Veart	7,212
11	12	A	Barnsley	D	0-0		9,169
12	16	A	Port Vale	W	2-0	Roberts, Dyer	4,522
13	19	H	Swindon Town	L	1-2	Dyer (pen)	15,544
14	26	H	Grimsby Town	W	3-0	Freedman, Dyer, Veart	13,941
15	29	A	Bradford City	W	4-0	Freedman, Hopkin, Shipperley 2	10,091
16	Nov 2	A	Tranmere Rovers	W	3-1	Freedman, Dyer, Hopkin	8,613
17	10	H	Queen's Park Rangers	W	3-0	Dyer, Hopkin, Shipperley	16,136
18	16	A	Bolton Wanderers	D	2-2	Freedman, Hopkin	16,892
19	23	H	Wolverhampton Wanderers	L	2-3	Dyer, Veart	21,410
20	30	A	Grimsby Town	L	1-2	Shipperley	5,288
21	Dec 7	H	Oxford United	D	2-2	Dyer 2	18,592
22	14	A	Norwich City	D	1-1	Shipperley	16,395
23	17	H	Sheffield United	L	0-1		13,623
24	21	H	Charlton Athletic	W	1-0	Shipperley	17,401
25	26	A	Ipswich Town	L	1-3	Gordon (pen)	15,605
26	Jan 11	A	Manchester City	D	1-1	Ndah	27,395
27	18	H	Portsmouth	L	1-2	Quinn	15,771
28	28	A	Southend United	L	1-2	Freedman	4,930
29	Feb 1	A	Queen's Park Rangers	W	1-0	Hopkin	16,467
30	8	H	Bradford City	W	3-1	Freedman, Ndah, Shipperley	15,459
31	15	A	Wolverhampton Wanderers	W	3-0	Tuttle, Dyer, Veart	25,919
32	22	H	Tranmere Rovers	L	0-1		16,169
33	Mar 1	A	Oxford United	W	4-1	Dyer 2, Hopkin, Gordon	8,576
34	4	H	Bolton Wanderers	D	1-1	Linighan	16,572
35	8	A	Charlton Athletic	L	1-2	Dyer	14,816
36	15	H	Norwich City	W	2-0	McKenzie, Gordon (pen)	18,706
37	23	A	Oldham Athletic	W	1-0	McKenzie	5,282
38	29	H	Birmingham City	L	0-1		17,114
39	Apr 5	H	Huddersfield Town	D	1-1	Shipperley	14,900
40	9	A	West Bromwich Albion	L	0-1		12,906
41	12	A	Sheffield United	L	0-3		20,051
42	15	H	Stoke City	W	2-0	Dyer 2	12,633
43	19	H	Barnsley	D	1-1	Shipperley	20,205
44	23	H	Reading	W	3-2	Hopkin, Shipperley, Linighan	13,747
45	26	A	Swindon Town	W	2-0	Shipperley 2	11,621
46	May 4	H	Port Vale	D	1-1	Roberts	17,616

Final League Position: 6th in Division One

Appearances
Sub appearances
Goals

Play-offs

	Date	Venue	Opponents	Result		Scorers	Attendance
SF1	May 10	H	Wolverhampton Wanderers	W	3-1	Shipperley, Freedman 2	21,053
SF2	14	A	Wolverhampton Wanderers	L	1-2	Hopkin	26,403
F	26	N+	Sheffield United	W	1-0	Hopkin	64,383

+ Played at Wembley Stadium

Appearances
Sub appearances
Goals

FA Cup

	Date	Venue	Opponents	Result		Scorers	Attendance
3	Jan 14	H	Leeds United	D	2-2	Dyer (pen), Veart	21,052
R	25	A	Leeds United	L	0-1		21,903

Appearances
Sub appearances
Goals

League Cup

	Date	Venue	Opponents	Result		Scorers	Attendance
2	Sep 17	A	Bury	W	3-1	Edworthy, Hopkin 2	3,472
	24	H	Bury	W	4-0	Muscat, Quinn, Freedman, Veart	5,195
3	Oct 22	A	Ipswich Town	L	1-4	Veart	8,390

Appearances
Sub appearances
Goals

Day	Boxall	Muscat	Roberts	Tuttle	Edworthy	Quinn	Houghton	Freedman	Dyer	Veart	Andersen	Hopkin	Ndah	Pitcher	McKenzie	Mimms	Nash	Harris	Rodger	Trollope	Scully	Shipperley	Gordon	Davies	Cyrus	Linighan
1	**2**	3	4	5	6	7	8	9	10	*11*	12	13	14													
1	8	3	4	5	2	14	13	9	10	**11**		6	12	7												
1		3	4	5	2	8		9	10	13		6	**11**	7	12											
	12	3	4	5	2	8		9		11		6	13	**7**	10	1										
1	**7**	3	4	5	2		8	9	10	11	12	6	13													
1	**7**	3	4	5	2		8	9	*10*	11	12	6	13		14											
1	13	3	4	5	2		8	9	**10**	11	7	6	12													
		3	4	5	2	14	**8**	9	*10*	11	7	6	13				1	12								
		3	4	**5**	2	6	8	9	*10*	11	7	12	13				1	14								
		3	4	**5**	2	8		9	10	11	7	6	13				1		12							
1		3		5	2	4		*9*		11	**7**	6	10		13				8	12	14					
1		3	4	5	2	7		9	**10**	11		6			12				8	13						
1		3	4	5	2	**7**		9	10	*11*	12	6			13				8	14						
1		3	4	5	2	**7**		9	*10*	11	12	6			13					14		8				
1		3	4	5	2	7		9	**10**	11	14	*6*			12					13		8				
1		3	4	5	2	7		9	**10**	11		6			12					13		8				
1		3	4	5	2	7		*9*	**10**	11		6			12					14		8	13			
1		3	4	5	2	**7**		9	10	11		6								13		8	12			
1		3	4	5	2			9	10	11	**7**	6	13									8	12			
1		3	4	5	2			**9**	10	11		6	13							12		8	7			
1		3	4	5	2		12	9	10	11		6	13									**8**	7			
1		7	4	5	2	**6**	8	13	10	11												9	3	12		
1		7	4	5	2		8	6	10	11			12		13							9	**3**			
1		3	4	5	2	6	**8**	14	*10*	11	7		13									9	12			
1		7	4	5	**2**	*6*		13	10	11		12	8		14							9	3			
1			4	5	2				10	11	12	6	8		13							9	3		**7**	
1		7	4	5	2	6		12	10	11			**8**		13							9	3			
1		7	4	5	2			10	12	**11**		8	13									9	3			6
		7	4	5	2			9	**10**	11		8	13				1					12	3			6
		7	4	**5**	2			9	13	11		8	12				1					10	3			6
		7	4	5	2			**9**	12	11		8	13				1					10	3			6
		7	4	5	2			10	13	11		8	12				1					9	3			6
		7	4	**5**	2	12		10	11			8					1					9	3			6
		7	4	5	2			10	11			8	12				1					**9**	3			6
		7	4	**5**	2	12		*10*	11	14		8	13				1					9	3			6
		7	4		2		12	**10**	11	5		8			9		1						3			6
		7	4		2		8	13	10	11					**9**		1		5			12	3			6
		7	4		2		8	13	10	**5**		11			9		1		14			12	3			6
		12	4	5	**2**		8	11	10			7			13		1					9	3			6
		2	4	**5**	12		8	13	10			7					1		11			9	3			6
		2	4		12		8	13	10			7					1		11			9	3	5		6
		12	4		2		8	13	10			**7**			14		1		11			*9*	3	5		6
			4		2		**8**	12	10			7					1		11			9	3	5		6
		2	4	5			8		10	12		7			13		1		**11**			9	3			6
		2	4	5	13			12	**10**	11		7					1					9	3	8		6
		2	4		11		8	10		12		**7**			13		1					9	3	5		6
24	4	42	45	39	42	17	18	33	39	35	7	38	5	3	4	1	21		9			29	26	5	1	19
	2	2			3	4	3	11	4	4	7	3	21		17			2	2	9	1	3	4	1		
		2	2	2		1	1	11	17	6	1	13	3		2							12	3			2

Day	Boxall	Muscat	Roberts	Tuttle	Edworthy	Quinn	Houghton	Freedman	Dyer	Veart	Andersen	Hopkin	Ndah	Pitcher	McKenzie	Mimms	Nash	Harris	Rodger	Trollope	Scully	Shipperley	Gordon	Davies	Cyrus	Linighan
			4		2		**8**	13	10	12		7					1		11			9	3	5		6
		7	4	5	2			12	**10**			8					1		11			9	3			6
		7	4	5	2				10			8					1		11			9	3			6
		2	3	2	3		1		3			3					3		3			3	3	1		3
								2		1																
								2				2										1				

Day	Boxall	Muscat	Roberts	Tuttle	Edworthy	Quinn	Houghton	Freedman	Dyer	Veart	Andersen	Hopkin	Ndah	Pitcher	McKenzie	Mimms	Nash	Harris	Rodger	Trollope	Scully	Shipperley	Gordon	Davies	Cyrus	Linighan
1		7	4		2				10	11	5	6	**8**		12							9	3			
1		7	4	5	2			12	10	**11**		6	8		13							9	3			
2		2	2	1	2				2	2	1	2	2									2	2			
								1							2											
									1	1																

Day	Boxall	Muscat	Roberts	Tuttle	Edworthy	Quinn	Houghton	Freedman	Dyer	Veart	Andersen	Hopkin	Ndah	Pitcher	McKenzie	Mimms	Nash	Harris	Rodger	Trollope	Scully	Shipperley	Gordon	Davies	Cyrus	Linighan
1		3	4	5	2	9	8	13	**10**	11	7	6	12													
	13	3	4	5	2	6	**8**	9	14	*11*	7		10				1	12								
1		3	4	5	2	12		9	10	11	**7**	6			8			13								
2		3	3	3	3	2	2	2	2	3	3	2	1		1		1									
	1					1		1	1				1					2								
		1			1	1		1		2		2														

League Table

	P	W	D	L	F	A	Pts
Bolton Wanderers	46	28	14	4	100	53	98
Barnsley	46	22	14	10	76	55	80
Wolverhampton W	46	22	10	14	68	51	76
Ipswich Town	46	20	14	12	68	50	74
Sheffield United	46	20	13	13	75	52	73
Crystal Palace	46	19	14	13	78	48	71
Portsmouth	46	20	8	18	59	53	68
Port Vale	46	17	16	13	58	55	67
Queen's Park Rangers	46	18	12	16	64	60	66
Birmingham City	46	17	15	14	52	48	66
Tranmere Rovers	46	17	14	15	63	56	65
Stoke City	46	18	10	18	51	57	64
Norwich City	46	17	12	17	63	68	63
Manchester City	46	17	10	19	59	60	61
Charlton Athletic	46	16	11	19	52	66	59
West Bromwich Albion	46	14	15	17	68	72	57
Oxford United	46	16	9	21	64	68	57
Reading	46	15	12	19	58	67	57
Swindon Town	46	15	9	22	52	71	54
Huddersfield Town	46	13	15	18	48	61	54
Bradford City	46	12	12	22	47	72	48
Grimsby Town	46	11	13	22	60	81	46
Oldham Athletic	46	10	13	23	51	66	43
Southend United	46	8	15	23	42	86	39

1997-98

Premiership

Manager: Steve Coppell until 13 March 1998, Attilio Lombardo until 29 April 1998, then Ron Noades, Ray Lewington and Brian Sparrow for the last three matches

Did you know that?

Valerian Ismael who signed in January 1998 from RC Strasbourg for £2.75 million, remains the club's most expensive signing. Another future Palace player, Michael Hughes, also played for the French League outfit back in the early 1990s.

Match No.	Date		Venue	Opponents	Result		Scorers	Attendance
1	Aug	9	A	Everton	W	2-1	Lombardo, Dyer (pen)	35,716
2		12	H	Barnsley	L	0-1		21,547
3		23	A	Leeds United	W	2-0	Warhurst, Lombardo	29,108
4		27	A	Southampton	L	0-1		15,032
5		30	H	Blackburn Rovers	L	1-2	Dyer	20,849
6	Sep	13	H	Chelsea	L	0-3		26,186
7		20	A	Wimbledon	W	1-0	Lombardo	16,747
8		24	A	Coventry City	D	1-1	Fullarton	15,910
9		27	H	Bolton Wanderers	D	2-2	Warhurst, Gordon	17,134
10	Oct	4	A	Manchester United	L	0-2		55,143
11		18	H	Arsenal	D	0-0		26,180
12		25	A	Sheffield Wednesday	W	3-1	Hreidarsson, Rodger, Shipperley	22,072
13	Nov	8	H	Aston Villa	D	1-1	Shipperley	21,097
14		24	A	Tottenham Hotspur	W	1-0	Shipperley	25,634
15		29	H	Newcastle United	L	1-2	Shipperley	26,085
16	Dec	3	A	West Ham United	L	1-4	Shipperley	23,335
17		6	A	Leicester City	D	1-1	Padovano	19,191
18		13	H	Liverpool	L	0-3		25,790
19		20	A	Derby County	D	0-0		26,590
20		26	H	Southampton	D	1-1	Shipperley	22,853
21		28	A	Blackburn Rovers	D	2-2	Dyer, Warhurst	23,872
22	Jan	10	H	Everton	L	1-3	Dyer (pen)	23,311
23		17	A	Barnsley	L	0-1		17,831
24		31	H	Leeds United	L	0-2		25,248
25	Feb	9	H	Wimbledon	L	0-3		14,410
26		21	A	Arsenal	L	0-1		38,094
27		28	H	Coventry City	L	0-3		21,810
28	Mar	11	A	Chelsea	L	2-6	Hreidarsson, Bent	31,844
29		14	A	Aston Villa	L	1-3	Jansen	33,781
30		18	A	Newcastle United	W	2-1	Lombardo, Jansen	36,565
31		28	H	Tottenham Hotspur	L	1-3	Shipperley	26,116
32	Apr	11	H	Leicester City	L	0-3		18,771
33		13	A	Liverpool	L	1-2	Bent	43,007
34		18	H	Derby County	W	3-1	Jansen, Curcic, Bent	18,101
35		27	H	Manchester United	L	0-3		26,180
36	May	2	A	Bolton Wanderers	L	2-5	Gordon, Bent	24,449
37		5	H	West Ham United	D	3-3	Bent, Rodger, Lombardo	19,129
38		10	H	Sheffield Wednesday	W	1-0	Morrison	16,878

Final League Position: 20th in Premiership

Appearances
Sub appearances
Goals

FA Cup

Round	Date		Venue	Opponents	Result		Scorers	Attendance
3	Jan	3	H	Scunthorpe United	W	2-0	Emblen 2	11,624
4		24	H	Leicester City	W	3-0	Dyer 3	15,489
5	Feb	15	A	Arsenal	D	0-0		37,164
R		25	H	Arsenal	L	1-2	Dyer	15,674

Appearances
Sub appearances
Goals

League Cup

Round	Date		Venue	Opponents	Result		Scorers	Attendance
2	Sep	16	A	Hull City	L	0-1		9,323
		30	H	Hull City	W	2-1*	Veart, Ndah	6,407

* After extra-time., lost on away Goalsrule

Appearances
Sub appearances
Goals

Miller	Edworthy	Gordon	Roberts	Tuttle	Linighan	Lombardo	Rodger	Warhurst	Dyer	Muscat	Veart	Fullarton	Shipperley	Freedman	Hreidarsson	Emblen	Zohar	McKenzie	Quinn	Boxall	Ndah	Bonetti	Smith	Padovano	Davies	Ginty	Burton-Godwin	Brolin	Bent	Ismael	Jansen	Billio	Curcic	Folan	Morrison
1	2	3	4	5	6	7	8	9	10	11	13	12	14																						
1	2	3	4	5	6	7	8	9	10	11		12	13																						
1	2	3	4	5	6	7	8	9	10	11		14	13	12																					
1	2	3	4	5	6	7	8	9	10	11			13	12																					
1	2	3	4	5	6	7	8	9	10	11			14		13	12																			
1		3	4	5	6	7			10	2	14	11	9	12		8	13																		
1	13	3	4	5	6	7		9	10	2		11	14	12	8																				
1	2	3	4		6	7				8	12	11	9	10	5			13																	
1	2	3	4		6	7		9		8	14	11	13	10	5				12																
1	2	3	4		6	7	8	9				11		12	5		13				10														
1	2	3	4		6	7	8	10				11	9		5						12	13													
1	5	3	4		6		7		10				9		8	13					11	12	2												
1	5	3	4		6	7	11		10				9		8	12							2												
1	2	3	4		6		11	7	10		12		9		5									8											
1	2	3	4		6		11	7	10				9		5	14	13						12	8											
1	5	3			6		11	7					9		4	8	10						2	12											
1	2	3			6		11	10			7	12	9		5	4								8	13										
1	2	3	4		6	7		10				11	9		5	12								8		13									
1		3	4		6		7	9	12			11			5	8	10										2								
1		3	2		6		8	4	10			11	9		5		13									7	12								
1		3	4		6		11	9	10						5	8		12					2			7									
1	2	3	4		6		7		10			11			5	8				12								9	13						
1	4	3	7		6				10			11			5								2			12		9	8						
1	8	3	7		6				10						5								2					9	11	4					
1	8	3	7		6		12		10						5								2			13		9	11	4					
1	6	3	7	13			8		10			11			5								2					9	12	4					
1	6	3	7				8		10			11			5			14					2					9	13	4	12				
1	6			5		13	7		10			11			3	8							2					9	14	4	12				
1	5	3				14	12		10			11	9			6							2					7	8	4	13				
1	5	3				7	6					11			14								2	12				9	8	4	10	13			
1	5	3				7	6						13		12								2	8				9		4	10	14	11		
1	5	3				7	6	9	13			11											2	8					14	4		10	12		
1	2	12				4	3	6				11	9		5													7	8		10		13		
1	5	3				12	6						9										2	8				7	13	4	10		11		
1	5	3				6			13			12	9		14								2	8				7	10	4			11		
1	2	3				7		6				11	12		5														9	4	10		8		
1	2	3				7	11	6				13	9		5								12						10	4			8		
1	2	3			6	7	11	4					9		5														10				8	12	13
38	33	36	25	8	26	21	27	22	21	9	1	19	17	2	26	8	2				2		16	8		2	1	13	10	13	5	1	6		
	1	1		1		3	2		3		5	6	9	5	4	5	4	3	1	1	1	2	2	2	1	3	1		6		3	2	2	1	1
		2				5	2	3	4			1	7		2									1					5		3		1		1

Miller	Edworthy	Gordon	Roberts	Tuttle	Linighan	Lombardo	Rodger	Warhurst	Dyer	Muscat	Veart	Fullarton	Shipperley	Freedman	Hreidarsson	Emblen	Zohar	McKenzie	Quinn	Boxall	Ndah	Bonetti	Smith	Padovano	Davies	Ginty	Burton-Godwin	Brolin	Bent	Ismael	Jansen	Billio	Curcic	Folan	Morrison
1	4	3	7		6		11	9	10						5	8							2			12	13								
1	8	3	7		6				10			11			5								2					9		4					
1	6	3	7				8		10			11			5								2					9		4					
1	6	3	7		13		8		10			11			5	14		12					2					9		4					
4	4	4	4		2		3	1	4			3			4	1							4					3		3					
					1											1		1								1	1								
									4							2																			

Miller	Edworthy	Gordon	Roberts	Tuttle	Linighan	Lombardo	Rodger	Warhurst	Dyer	Muscat	Veart	Fullarton	Shipperley	Freedman	Hreidarsson	Emblen	Zohar	McKenzie	Quinn	Boxall	Ndah	Bonetti	Smith	Padovano	Davies	Ginty	Burton-Godwin	Brolin	Bent	Ismael	Jansen	Billio	Curcic	Folan	Morrison
1		3	4	5	6				13	2	12	11	9	10	8		7																		
1	2	3			6		14	10			8	11	9	13	5		7			4	12														
2	1	2	1	1	2			1		1	1	2	2	1	2		2			1															
							1		1		1			1							1														
											1										1														

League Table

	P	W	D	L	F	A	Pts
Arsenal	38	23	9	6	68	33	78
Manchester United	38	23	8	7	73	26	77
Liverpool	38	18	11	9	68	42	65
Chelsea	38	20	3	15	71	43	63
Leeds United	38	17	8	13	57	46	59
Blackburn Rovers	38	16	10	12	57	52	58
Aston Villa	38	17	6	15	49	48	57
West Ham United	38	16	8	14	56	57	56
Derby County	38	16	7	15	52	49	55
Leicester City	38	13	14	11	51	41	53
Coventry City	38	12	16	10	46	44	52
Southampton	38	14	6	18	50	55	48
Newcastle United	38	11	11	16	35	44	44
Tottenham Hotspur	38	11	11	16	44	56	44
Wimbledon	38	10	14	14	34	46	44
Sheffield Wednesday	38	12	8	18	52	67	44
Everton	38	9	13	16	41	56	40
Bolton Wanderers	38	9	13	16	41	61	40
Barnsley	38	10	5	23	37	82	35
Crystal Palace	**38**	**8**	**9**	**21**	**37**	**71**	**33**

1998-99

Division One

Manager: Terry Venables until 15 January 1999 then Steve Coppell

Did you know that?

Fan Zhiyi and Sun Jihai became the first Chinese players in English football when they signed in August 1998, ensuring Palace had a following of hundreds of millions watching in China whenever games were live on TV, the first being a late September victory against Sheffield United. As a result, the club for a while ran a Chinese language version of its website.

Match No.	Date		Venue	Opponents	Result		Scorers	Attendance
1	Aug	8	H	Bolton Wanderers	D	2-2	Jansen, Curcic	19,029
2		16	A	Birmingham City	L	1-3	Mullins	16,699
3		22	H	Oxford United	W	2-0	Lombardo, Dyer	14,827
4		29	A	Stockport County	D	1-1	Shipperley	7,739
5	Sep	8	A	Crewe Alexandra	W	1-0	Jansen	4,977
6		12	H	Port Vale	L	0-1		15,983
7		19	A	Barnsley	L	0-4		15,597
8		27	H	Sheffield United	W	1-0	Curcic	20,370
9		30	H	Bury	W	4-2	Lombardo (pen), Warhurst, Dyer, Morrison	13,219
10	Oct	3	A	Ipswich Town	L	0-3		16,837
11		17	H	Norwich City	W	5-1	Lombardo, Jansen 2, Rizzo, Svensson	18,100
12		20	H	Wolverhampton Wanderers	W	3-2	Curcic, Burton-Godwin, Moore	16,417
13		31	A	Grimsby Town	L	0-2		6,948
14	Nov	3	A	West Bromwich Albion	L	2-3	Jansen, Moore	11,606
15		7	H	Portsmouth	W	4-1	Moore, own-goal (Thomson), Mullins, Foster	20,188
16		14	H	Bristol City	W	2-1	Jansen, Bradbury	17,821
17		21	A	Swindon Town	L	0-2		11,718
18		28	H	Watford	D	2-2	Curcic (pen), Tuttle	19,521
19	Dec	5	A	Huddersfield Town	L	0-4		10,453
20		8	H	Tranmere Rovers	D	1-1	Jansen	12,919
21		12	A	Bristol City	D	1-1	own-goal (Bell)	13,014
22		15	A	Sunderland	L	0-2		33,870
23		19	H	Queen's Park Rangers	D	1-1	Rodger	17,684
24		26	A	Oxford United	W	3-1	Morrison, Foster, Bradbury (pen)	8,375
25		28	H	West Bromwich Albion	D	1-1	Morrison	19,137
26	Jan	10	A	Bolton Wanderers	L	0-3		15,410
27		16	H	Stockport County	D	2-2	Morrison, Zhiyi	15,517
28		19	A	Bradford City	L	1-2	Tuttle	14,368
29		30	A	Tranmere Rovers	L	1-3	Bradbury	6,017
30	Feb	6	H	Birmingham City	D	1-1	own-goal (Rowett)	15,996
31		13	H	Crewe Alexandra	D	1-1	Morrison	14,823
32		20	A	Port Vale	L	0-1		6,051
33		28	H	Barnsley	W	1-0	Mullins	17,021
34	Mar	2	A	Sheffield United	D	1-1	Petric	12,896
35		6	A	Bury	D	0-0		4,334
36		9	H	Ipswich Town	W	3-2	Mullins, Morrison 2	16,360
37		13	A	Portsmouth	D	1-1	Bradbury	15,520
38		20	H	Grimsby Town	W	3-1	Mullins, Morrison 2	15,228
39		28	H	Bradford City	W	1-0	Zhiyi	15,626
40	Apr	3	A	Norwich City	W	1-0	Austin	16,754
41		5	H	Sunderland	D	1-1	Morrison	22,096
42		10	A	Wolverhampton Wanderers	D	0-0		23,643
43		17	H	Swindon Town	L	0-1		18,660
44		24	A	Watford	L	1-2	McKenzie	15,590
45	May	1	H	Huddersfield Town	D	2-2	Morrison 2	17,282
46		9	A	Queen's Park Rangers	L	0-6		18,498

Final League Position: 14th in Division One

Appearances
Sub appearances
3 own-goals — Goals

FA Cup

3	Jan	2	A	Newcastle United	L	1-2	Bradbury	36,5364

Appearances
Sub appearances
Goals

League Cup

1	Aug	11	A	Torquay United	D	1-1	Lombardo	3,042
		25	H	Torquay United	W	2-1*	Hreidarsson, Lombardo	6,872
2	Sep	15	A	Bury	L	0-3		2,780
		23	H	Bury	W	2-1	Morrison, Zhiyi	3,546

* After extra-time

Appearances
Sub appearances
Goals

InterToto Cup

3	Jul	19	H	Samsunspor	L	0-2		11,758
3		25	A	Samsunspor	L	0-2		

Appearances
Sub appearances

Miller	Austin	Smith	Curcic	Tuttle	Hreidarsson	Lombardo	Warhurst	Dyer	Jansen	Mullins	Edworthy	Linighan	Bent	Digby	Rodger	Padovano	Amsalem	Shipperley	Morrison	Folan	Thomson	Rizzo	Jihai	Zhiyi	Del Rio	Burton-Godwin	Svensson	Foster	Moore	Bradbury	Petric	Crowe	Turner	McKenzie	Fullarton	Carlisle	Evans	Woozley	Frampton	Martin	Graham	Harris	Hibburt
1	2	**3**	4	5	6	7	8	9	10	11	12																																
1	13	3	4		5	7	8	**9**	10	11	2	6	12																														
	2	3	4		12	7	**8**	9	*10*	11	13	6		1	5	14																											
	2	3			8	7			10	11		6	13	1	**5**		4	9	12																								
	2	3			8	7			10	11		6	12	1	5		4	**9**	13																								
	2	3			8	7			10	11		6	13	1	5		**4**	9				12																					
	12	**3**			8	7			10	11		6	9	1	*5*				13			14		2	4																		
			12	5		7		10		11		6		1		13	**3**		9			*4*		8	14	2																	
			12	5		7	8	10				6		1					9		**3**	4		11		2	13																
			4	5		7	8	12		11				1							13	10		3		2	9	6															
		3	13			7			10	11				1							12	8	2	4		14	*9*	**6**	5														
		3	14			7			10	11				1					13			*8*	2	4		12	9	6	5														
	2					7			10	11			14	1					**9**			8	3	4		12		6	5	13													
	2					7			10	11			**9**	1			13						3	4		6		8	5	12													
	2					7			**10**	11			12	1					13			8	3	4		14		*6*	5	9													
	2		13	12		7			10	11				1					14			8	3			5		6		*9*	4												
			13	12		7				11			14	1					10			*8*				**2**		6	5	9	4	3											
		2	12	11		7							13	1					10			**8**						6	5	9	4	3											
		2	12	11					10	6				1			13		14			8					*7*		5	9	4	**3**											
		2		11					10	5				1	**7**		12		13							4	9	6		8		3											
1				11					10	8					7		2				13					5	9	6		12	**4**	3											
1		11								8		5			7		**2**		10							4		6		9		3	12										
1		11	12						10	8		5			7				13			**3**				4		6		9		2											
1		3							**10**			5			11				12			13	2	8		7		6	4	9													
1		3		7						12		5	9		*11*				10			13	2	8				**6**	4				14										
1				7						5			12		*11*		13		**10**			14	2	8		4		6		9		3											
1	14		12	3		**7**									11				10			*2*		8		6			5	9				13	4								
1				6											11				10				3	**8**		2		7	5	9				12	4								
1		12		**6**						14					11				10				3	8		2		7	5	9				13	4								
1		2								8		6									12							**7**	5	9	3			10	4	11	13						
1		2								8		6			11				10			13						12	5	9	3			7	**4**								
1		2		14						*11*		6							10				13	**8**				7	5		3			9	4		12						
1		2								11		6							10		**9**		4	8				7	5		3			13			12						
1		2		6						9					11				10		12		4	8				**7**	5		3			13									
1		2		6								12			11				10		7		**4**	13					5	9	3			8									
1		2		12						11		6							10		7		**4**	8					5	9	3			13									
1		2		4						11		6							10		7			8					5	9	**3**						12						
1		2	13	3						11		6							10				**7**	8				12	5	9					4								
1	4									11									10				3	8		2		7	5					9				6					
1	4									11									**10**		6		3	8				7								12		5	2	9			13
1	4									11									10		6		2	8				7			3			9				5					
1	4									11									10		6		**2**	8				7			3			9				5	12				
1	4									11									10		6		2			**5**	12	7			3			9		13			8				
1	4									11									10		*6*		2	8				7			**3**			9		13		5	12		14		
1	4									11									10					8		6		7						**9**		*3*		5	2	12		14	13
1	4			14						11									10		6			8		13		7			*3*					12		5	2	**9**			
28	17	25	4	17	6	19	5	5	18	38	1	19	3	18	18		6	3	27		11	13	22	28	1	18	6	30	23	19	18	8		10	7	2		7	4	2			
	3	1	11	5	1			1		2	2	1	9			2	4		10		5	6	1	1	1	5	2	2		3			2	6		4	4		2	1	1	1	2
	1		4	2		3	1	2	7	5					1			1	12			1		2		1	1	2	3	4	1			1									

Miller	Austin	Smith	Curcic	Tuttle	Hreidarsson	Lombardo	Warhurst	Dyer	Jansen	Mullins	Edworthy	Linighan	Bent	Digby	Rodger	Padovano	Amsalem	Shipperley	Morrison	Folan	Thomson	Rizzo	Jihai	Zhiyi	Del Rio	Burton-Godwin	Svensson	Foster	Moore	Bradbury	Petric	Crowe	Turner	McKenzie	Fullarton	Carlisle	Evans	Woozley	Frampton	Martin	Graham	Harris	Hibburt
1		3		7					12	5		14	13		11				10				2	*8*				**6**	4	9													
1		1		1						1					1				1				1	1				1	1	1													
									1			1	1																														
																														1													

Miller	Austin	Smith	Curcic	Tuttle	Hreidarsson	Lombardo	Warhurst	Dyer	Jansen	Mullins	Edworthy	Linighan	Bent	Digby	Rodger	Padovano	Amsalem	Shipperley	Morrison	Folan	Thomson	Rizzo	Jihai	Zhiyi	Del Rio	Burton-Godwin	Svensson	Foster	Moore	Bradbury	Petric	Crowe	Turner	McKenzie	Fullarton	Carlisle	Evans	Woozley	Frampton	Martin	Graham	Harris	Hibburt
1	2	3	*4*	**5**	6	7	8	9	10	11	14	12							13																								
	2	3	4		8	7		9	*10*	11		6	12	1	**5**		14		13																								
	2	3			8	7			10	11			12	1	5			9					**4**	6																			
	2			5		7		13	10	11		12		1			3		9			8		4	14	*6*																	
1	4	3	2	2	3	4	1	2	4	4		1		3	2		1	1	1			1	1	2		1																	
								1			1	2	2				1		2						1																		
					1	2													1					1																			

Miller	Austin	Smith	Curcic	Tuttle	Hreidarsson	Lombardo	Warhurst	Dyer	Jansen	Mullins	Edworthy	Linighan	Bent	Digby	Rodger	Padovano	Amsalem	Shipperley	Morrison	Folan	Thomson	Rizzo	Jihai	Zhiyi	Del Rio	Burton-Godwin	Svensson	Foster	Moore	Bradbury	Petric	Crowe	Turner	McKenzie	Fullarton	Carlisle	Evans	Woozley	Frampton	Martin	Graham	Harris	Hibburt
1	3	12	**11**		5	7			9	4	*2*				13			10		6	14														8								
1	3	**2**		5	6				9	11	8	4						10	13		7					12																	14
2	2	1	1	1	2	1			2	2	2	1						2		1	1														1								
		1													1				1		1					1																	1

League Table

	P	W	D	L	F	A	Pts
Sunderland	46	31	12	3	91	28	105
Bradford City	46	26	9	11	82	47	87
Ipswich Town	46	26	8	12	69	32	86
Birmingham City	46	23	12	11	66	37	81
Watford	46	21	14	11	65	56	77
Bolton Wanderers	46	20	16	10	78	59	76
Wolverhampton W	46	19	16	11	64	43	73
Sheffield United	46	18	13	15	71	66	67
Norwich City	46	15	17	14	62	61	62
Huddersfield Town	46	15	16	15	62	71	61
Grimsby Town	46	17	10	19	40	52	61
West Bromwich Albion	46	16	11	19	69	76	59
Barnsley	46	14	17	15	59	56	59
Crystal Palace	46	14	16	16	58	71	58
Tranmere Rovers	46	12	20	14	63	61	56
Stockport County	46	12	17	17	49	60	53
Swindon Town	46	13	11	22	59	81	50
Crewe Alexandra	46	12	12	22	54	78	48
Portsmouth	46	11	14	21	57	73	47
Queen's Park Rangers	46	12	11	23	52	61	47
Port Vale	46	13	8	25	45	75	47
Bury	46	10	17	19	35	60	47
Oxford United	46	10	14	22	48	71	44
Bristol City	46	9	15	22	57	80	42

1999-2000

Division One

Manager: Steve Coppell

Did you know that?

After 47 memorable appearances and 10 goals, the Eagles Italian international Attilio Lombardo departed for Lazio in January. The highly popular Italian had opted to stay at Palace following relegation, but with the club heading into financial trouble his final appearance came at home to Stockport County on 16 January.

Match No.	Date		Venue	Opponents	Result		Scorers	Attendance
1	Aug	7	H	Crewe Alexandra	D	1-1	Rodger	13,664
2		14	A	Barnsley	W	3-2	Austin, Bradbury, Rodger	14,461
3		21	H	Swindon Town	L	1-2	Morrison	12,726
4		28	A	Huddersfield Town	L	1-7	Morrison	10,656
5	Sep	4	A	Sheffield United	L	1-3	Morrison	11,886
6		11	A	Manchester City	L	1-2	Morrison	31,541
7		18	H	Grimsby Town	W	3-0	Mullins, Morrison, Svensson	13,294
8		25	A	West Bromwich Albion	D	0-0		13,161
9		28	H	Wolverhampton Wanderers	D	1-1	Bradbury	12,720
10	Oct	2	H	Portsmouth	W	4-0	Mullins, Carlisle, Svensson, Zhiyi	15,221
11		16	A	Birmingham City	L	0-2		21,582
12		20	A	Blackburn Rovers	D	1-1	Mullins	15,819
13		23	H	Tranmere Rovers	D	2-2	Austin, Svensson	18,645
14		26	H	West Bromwich Albion	L	0-2		12,203
15		30	A	Portsmouth	L	1-3	Linighan	13,018
16	Nov	6	A	Bolton Wanderers	L	0-2		12,744
17		14	H	Queen's Park Rangers	W	3-0	Svensson, McKenzie, Mullins (pen)	15,861
18		20	A	Port Vale	D	2-2	Svensson, McKenzie	5,170
19		23	H	Norwich City	W	1-0	Svensson	12,110
20		27	H	Nottingham Forest	W	2-0	Svensson, McKenzie	15,920
21	Dec	4	A	Crewe Alexandra	L	0-2		4,925
22		7	H	Ipswich Town	D	2-2	Svensson, own-goal (Mowbray)	13,176
23		18	H	Fulham	D	0-0		17,480
24		26	A	Charlton Athletic	L	1-2	Martin	20,047
25		28	H	Walsall	W	3-2	Svensson (pen), Mullins, Carlisle	13,943
26	Jan	3	A	Stockport County	W	2-1	Mullins, Carlisle	8,570
27		15	H	Barnsley	L	0-2		14,225
28		21	A	Swindon Town	W	4-2	Morrison 2, Foster, Mullins (pen)	5,214
29		29	H	Huddersfield Town	D	2-2	Linighan, Mullins	14,290
30	Feb	5	A	Wolverhampton Wanderers	L	1-2	Martin	20,756
31		12	H	Sheffield United	D	1-1	Morrison	14,877
32		19	A	Nottingham Forest	L	0-2		16,421
33		26	A	Grimsby Town	L	0-1		5,421
34	Mar	4	H	Manchester City	D	1-1	Morrison	21,052
35		7	H	Bolton Wanderers	D	0-0		15,236
36		11	A	Norwich City	W	1-0	Morrison	15,064
37		18	H	Port Vale	D	1-1	own-goal (Rougier)	18,954
38		22	A	Queen's Park Rangers	W	1-0	Morrison	12,842
39		25	H	Charlton Athletic	L	0-1		22,577
40	Apr	1	A	Fulham	L	0-1		16,358
41		8	H	Stockport County	D	3-3	McKenzie, Forssell 2	16,646
42		15	A	Walsall	D	2-2	Mullins, Forssell	6,323
43		22	H	Birmingham City	L	0-2		17,144
44		25	A	Ipswich Town	L	0-1		18,788
45		29	H	Blackburn Rovers	W	2-1	Morrison, Cole	18,272
46	May	7	A	Tranmere Rovers	W	2-1	Mullins, Morrison	8,891

Final League Position: 15th in Division One

Appearances
Sub appearances
2 own-goals Goals

FA Cup

3	Dec	10	A	Cambridge United	L	0-2		5,631

Appearances
Sub appearances

League Cup

1	Aug	10	A	Colchester United	D	2-2	Smith, Rizzo	4,242
		24	H	Colchester United	W	3-1	Smith, Rizzo, Morrison	5,471
R2	Sep	14	H	Leicester City	D	3-3	Mullins, Morrison, Zhiyi	5,006
		22	A	Leicester City	L	2-4	Bradbury, Thomson	12,762

Appearances
Sub appearances
Goals

Digby	Austin	Smith	Rizzo	Linighan	Mullins	Frampton	Carlisle	Bradbury	Morrison	Rodger	Evans	Tuttle	Thomson	Woozley	Harris	Hibburt	Svensson	Zhiyi	Sharpling	Antunes Fumaca	Fullarton	De Ornelas	Phelan	Martin	Launders	McKenzie	Foster	Kabba	Mautone	Cole	Forssell	Hankin	Gregg	Hunt
1	2	3	4	5	6	7	8	9	10	11	12	13
1	2	3		5	8	7		9	10	11			4	6	14	12	13
1	2	3	13	5	8	7		9	10	11			4	6	14		12
1	2	3		12	8	7		9	10	11			4	13	6		14	5
1	2	3	13	5	8			9	10	11			4	6	14			7	12
1	2	3	14	5	8			9	10	11			4	6			13	7		12
1	2	3		5	8	12		13	10	11			14				9	4	6	7
1	2	3		5	6			9	10	11			12				8	4	13	7
1	2	3	12	5	6			9	10	11			7	13			8	4
1	2	3		5	6	12	8	9					7	14			10	4			11	13
1	2	3		5	6		8			7				12			9	4			11	10
1	2	3		5	6					7			8	4			9		12		11	10
1	2			5	6					7			8	4			9		12		11	10	3
1	2			5	6					7			8	4			9				11	10	3	12
1	2			5	6					7				4			9				11	10	3	12	8
1	2			5	6					7				4		8	9				11		3	10	12
1	2		14	5	6					7							9	4			11	13	3	10		8	12
1	2		12	5	6					7							9	4				13	3	10		8	11
1	2			5	6		13			7				12			9	4				14	3	10		8	11
1	2		13	5	6		12			7							9	4					3	10		8	11
1	2		13	5	6	3				7					12		9	4						10			11	8
1	2		13	5	6	3				7				12			9	4						10		8	11
1	4	2		5	6		12			7							9	10					3			8	11
1	4	2	13	5			8			9				14		12		6			11		3	10			7
	4	2		5	6		8			7							9				11		3	12		10			1
1	4	2		5	6		8			7							9				11		3			10
1		2		5	6		8		12	7				4			9				11		3	13		10	14
1	4	2		5	6		8		9	7													3	12		10	11
1	3	2		5	6		8		9	7				4										12		10	11
1	3	2	12	5	6		8		9	7								4						10			11
1	3	2	12	5	11		8		9	7				6				4	13					10
	3	2	13	5	10		8		9	7				6				4			11			12					1
1	2		11	5	6		8		9	7								4								12				3	10
1	2			5	6		8		9	7								4								11				3	10
1	2		13	5	6		8		9	7								4								11				3	10	12
1	2			5	6		8		9				7					4								11				3	10
1	2		12	5	6		8		9				7					4								11				3	10
1	2			5	6		8		9				7					4						12		11				3	10
1	2			5	6		8		9				7					4						13		11	12			3	10
	2			5	6		8		9									4								11	7			3	10		1	12
1	2			5	6		8		9									4								11	7			3	10
	2	7		5	6				9				14	12				4								11	8			3	10		1	13
	4	2		5	6		8		9				12													11	7			3	10		1	13
	4	2		5	6		8		9				7													10	11			3			1
	4	2		5	6				9				7	12												11	8			3	10		1
	4	2			6	12			9				7	5	13	14										11	8			3	10		1
38	45	27	2	44	45	6	23	9	28	34			17	14	1	1	20	29	1	2	13	5	14	10	1	24	17	1	2	14	13		6	
			15	1		3	3	1	1		1	1	4	9	5	3	4		5	1		4		9	1	1	3					1		3
	2			2	10		3	2	13	2							9	1						2		4	1			1	3			

Digby	Austin	Smith	Rizzo	Linighan	Mullins	Frampton	Carlisle	Bradbury	Morrison	Rodger	Evans	Tuttle	Thomson	Woozley	Harris	Hibburt	Svensson	Zhiyi	Sharpling	Antunes Fumaca	Fullarton	De Ornelas	Phelan	Martin	Launders	McKenzie	Foster	Kabba	Mautone	Cole	Forssell	Hankin	Gregg	Hunt
1	2	12	10	5	6	3				7				13			9	4								8	11
1	1		1	1	1	1				1							1	1								1	1
		1												1

Digby	Austin	Smith	Rizzo	Linighan	Mullins	Frampton	Carlisle	Bradbury	Morrison	Rodger	Evans	Tuttle	Thomson	Woozley	Harris	Hibburt	Svensson	Zhiyi	Sharpling	Antunes Fumaca	Fullarton	De Ornelas	Phelan	Martin	Launders	McKenzie	Foster	Kabba	Mautone	Cole	Forssell	Hankin	Gregg	Hunt
1	2	3	12		8	7		9	10	11	14	5	4	6	13
1	2	3	13			7	12	9	10	11			4	5	6		8
1	2	3	12	5	8			9	10	11				6				4		7
1	2	3		5	8	6		14	10	11			13	12			9	4		7
4	4	4		2	3	3		3	4	4		1	2	3	1		2	2		2
			3				1	1			1		1	1	1
		2	2		1			1	2				1					1

League Table

	P	W	D	L	F	A	Pts
Charlton Athletic	46	27	10	9	79	45	91
Manchester City	46	26	11	9	78	40	89
Ipswich Town	46	25	12	9	71	42	87
Barnsley	46	24	10	12	88	67	82
Birmingham City	46	22	11	13	65	44	77
Bolton Wanderers	46	21	13	12	69	50	76
Wolverhampton W	46	21	11	14	64	48	74
Huddersfield Town	46	21	11	14	62	49	74
Fulham	46	17	16	13	49	41	67
Queen's Park Rangers	46	16	18	12	62	53	66
Blackburn Rovers	46	15	17	14	55	51	62
Norwich City	46	14	15	17	45	50	57
Tranmere Rovers	46	15	12	19	57	68	57
Nottingham Forest	46	14	14	18	53	55	56
Crystal Palace	46	13	15	18	57	67	54
Sheffield United	46	13	15	18	59	71	54
Stockport County	46	13	15	18	55	67	54
Portsmouth	46	13	12	21	55	66	51
Crewe Alexandra	46	14	9	23	46	67	51
Grimsby Town	46	13	12	21	41	67	51
West Bromwich Albion	46	10	19	17	43	60	49
Walsall	46	11	13	22	52	77	46
Port Vale	46	7	15	24	48	69	36
Swindon Town	46	8	12	26	38	77	36

2000-01

Division One

Manager: Alan Smith until 29 April 2001 then Steve Kember (caretaker)

Did you know that?

With a few thousand Eagles fans making the trip to the North West, Palace needed a win at Stockport County to ensure survival in Division One, in the final game of the season for caretaker managers Steve Kember and Terry Bullivant. Dougie Freedman went on a fine run and scored with only three minutes remaining to send Eagles fans onto the pitch in celebration and ensure Palace stayed up with a 1–0 victory.

Match No.	Date		Venue	Opponents	Result		Scorers	Attendance
1	Aug	12	A	Blackburn Rovers	L	0-2		18,733
2		20	H	Queen's Park Rangers	D	1-1	Forssell	19,020
3		26	A	Huddersfield Town	W	2-1	Ruddock, Gray	10,670
4		28	H	Nottingham Forest	L	2-3	Zhiyi, Black	18,865
5	Sep	3	A	West Bromwich Albion	L	0-1		13,980
6		9	H	Burnley	L	0-1		18,531
7		12	H	Barnsley	W	1-0	C. Morrison	16,287
8		16	A	Norwich City	D	0-0		16,828
9		23	H	Sheffield United	L	0-1		17,521
10		30	A	Preston North End	L	0-2		13,028
11	Oct	14	A	Birmingham City	L	1-2	C. Morrison	17,191
12		18	A	Fulham	L	1-3	Ruddock	16,040
13		21	H	Portsmouth	L	2-3	Black 2	15,693
14		24	H	Grimsby Town	L	0-1		16,685
15		28	A	Bolton Wanderers	D	3-3	C. Morrison, Freedman 2	12,879
16	Nov	4	H	Sheffield Wednesday	W	4-1	Pollock 2, C. Morrison, Freedman	15,333
17		11	A	Wolverhampton Wanderers	W	3-1	C. Morrison 2, Freedman	17,658
18		18	H	Tranmere Rovers	W	3-2	Pollock, C. Morrison, Staunton	14,221
19		25	H	Stockport County	D	2-2	Forssell 2	18,819
20	Dec	2	A	Grimsby Town	D	2-2	C. Morrison, Forssell	5,802
21		5	H	Wimbledon	W	3-1	C. Morrison 2, Forssell	16,699
22		9	H	Watford	W	1-0	C. Morrison	16,049
23		16	A	Crewe Alexandra	D	1-1	Freedman	5,752
24		22	H	Blackburn Rovers	L	2-3	Mullins, Forssell	15,010
25		26	A	Gillingham	L	1-4	Freedman (pen)	10,334
26		30	A	Queen's Park Rangers	D	1-1	C. Morrison	14,154
27	Jan	14	A	Nottingham Forest	W	3-0	Forssell 2, Freedman	21,198
28		20	H	Gillingham	D	2-2	Forssell, Freedman	18,823
29	Feb	3	H	West Bromwich Albion	D	2-2	Pollock, Forssell	16,692
30		10	A	Burnley	W	2-1	C. Morrison, Forssell	14,973
31		17	H	Norwich City	D	1-1	Forssell	16,417
32		20	A	Barnsley	L	0-1		12,895
33		24	A	Sheffield United	L	0-1		18,924
34	Mar	3	H	Preston North End	L	0-2		15,160
35		6	H	Birmingham City	L	1-2	Austin	13,987
36		10	A	Wimbledon	L	0-1		13,167
37		17	H	Fulham	L	0-2		21,133
38		31	H	Crewe Alexandra	W	1-0	Austin	20,872
39	Apr	3	H	Huddersfield Town	D	0-0		15,324
40		7	A	Watford	D	2-2	Austin (pen), Black	15,599
41		14	A	Sheffield Wednesday	L	1-4	C. Morrison	19,877
42		16	H	Bolton Wanderers	L	0-2		16,268
43		21	A	Tranmere Rovers	D	1-1	Hopkin	8,119
44		28	H	Wolverhampton Wanderers	L	0-2		18,993
45	May	2	A	Portsmouth	W	4-2	Forssell, Riihilahti, Freedman 2	19,013
46		6	A	Stockport County	W	1-0	Freedman	9,782

Final League Position: 21st in Division One

Appearances
Sub appearances
Goals

FA Cup

3	Jan	6	A	Sunderland	D	0-0		30,908
R		17	H	Sunderland	L	2-4*	C. Morrison, Thomson	15,454

* After extra-time

Appearances
Sub appearances
Goals

League Cup

1	Aug	23	H	Cardiff City	W	2-1	Ruddock, C. Morrison	5,983
	Sep	5	A	Cardiff City	D	0-0		4,904
2		19	A	Burnley	D	2-2	Forssell, Black	5,889
		26	H	Burnley	D	1-1*	Linighan	5,720
3	Nov	1	A	Leicester City	W	3-0	C. Morrison, Thomson, Rubins	12,965
4		28	H	Tranmere Rovers	D	0-0#		10,271
5	Dec	19	H	Sunderland	W	2-1	C. Morrison, Forssell	15,945
SF1	Jan	10	H	Liverpool	W	2-1	C. Morrison, Rubins	25,933
SF2		24	A	Liverpool	L	0-5		41,854

* After extra-time. # After extra-time, won 6–5 on penalties

Appearances
Sub appearances
Goals

Taylor	Smith	Harrison	Austin	Zhiyi	Ruddock	Pollock	Mullins	Morrison C	Fossell	Fullarton	Black	Gray	Carlisle	Rodger	McKenzie	Gregg	Harris	Kitson	Kolinko	Linighan	Morrison A	Thomson	Rubins	Staunton	Freedman	Martin	Kabba	Frampton	Berhalter	Fuller	Karic	Upson	Hopkin	Riihilahti	Verhoene	Evans
1	*2*	3	4	5	6	7	8	**9**	10	11	14	13	12																							
1		3		5	6	**4**	8	*9*	10	12	7	13	2	11	14																					
1		3		5	6	4	2	9	**10**		7	8		11	12																					
1		3	12	5	**6**	4	2	*9*	10		7	8	14	11	13																					
1	13	3		5	6	4	2	9			7	8		11	**10**		12																			
1		3	2	5	6	4	11	9	13		7	8			12		**10**																			
1		3	2	5	6	4	11	9	12		7	8			**10**																					
1		3	2	5	6	4	11	9			7	**8**			12			10																		
1		3	2	5	6	4	11	9	13		7	8		14	12			**10**																		
1		3	2	*5*	6	4	8	12	10		**7**	14		11				9		13																	
	2	3	6			**4**		9	12			8		11				10	1		5	7															
	2	3			**6**	4	8	9	*10*		7	13	14	11					1		5		12															
	2	3				4	8	9	**10**		7		12	13					1		5		11	6													
	2	*3*				4	8	12	**10**		7	14		13					1		5		11	6	9												
			2			4	6	10	12		7	13		11					1		5		**8**	3	9												
			2	5		4	6	10			7		13	11					1			12	**8**	3	9												
			2	5		4	6	10			7			11					1			12	**8**	3	9												
	12		2	5		4	6	10			7	**8**	13	11					1					3	9												
	14	*3*	2	5		4	6	9	10		7	8	13	**11**						1			12															
	2	3	4	5	6	**8**	11	9	10		7										1			12															
	2	13	4	5	6	8	11	9	10		7										1			12						3								
	2		4	5	6	8	11	9	**10**		7			13					1						12			3								
	2	3	4	5	6	8	11	9	**10**		7			13					1						12											
	12	13	2	5	*6*	8	4	9	10		7			3					1				**11**		14											
	3		**2**	5	12	4	6	9	10		7		13							1				11		8											
	2	3		5			6	9	**10**		7			4					1			8	11		12											
	2	3	5		6	12	4	9	10					7					1			**8**	*11*		13			14								
	2		5		6	12		9	10		7	14		4					1			**8**	*11*		13			3								
	2	3	5		6	4		9	10		12			7					1			**8**	11		13											
	4	3	5			*8*	6	9	10		12	13		7		1						14	11					**2**								
	2	3	5			4	6		10			8		7					1				11		**9**		12									
	2	3	5			4	11	9	10		12	*8*		7					1				14					**6**	13						
	2		5				*11*	9	10		7		14	4					1			8	13		12			**3**	6							
	2		3	**5**			13	9	10		7	14		*11*					1			8	12								4	6				
	2		3	**5**			11	14	*10*		7	12							1			8			9					13	4	6				
	2		3				4	*9*	10		13									1			8	11		7			12		14	**5**	6				
			2				6	12	10		7			4					1				11		**9**			3		13		5	8			
		3	2	5				9	10		12			11					1						**7**							6	8	4	13	
		3	2	5				9	10		**7**			11					1				12									6	8	4		
		3	2	5			8	*9*	13		12			**11**					1						14					10		6	7	4		
	2	3	4	5			6	*9*	14		12			11					1						13					10			7	8		
	2	3	4	5			6	9	13		12									1				11		10								7	8		
		3	5				6	9					12	**11**					1			8			10			2		13			7	4		
		3	5				6	9				12	8							1				**11**		10			2	14	13			7	4		
	2		4				6	9	10				**3**							1			11			7				5					8		12
	2		4				6	9	10		13		**3**							1			11			7				5				12	8		
10	25	30	38	28	19	29	40	41	31	1	30	12	4	28	2	1	1	4	35		5	12	17	6	16			8	4	2	3	7	8	9		
	4	2	1		1	2	1	4	8	1	10	11	10	5	6		1			1		6	5		10		1	2	1	6			1		1	1
			3	1	2	4	1	14	13		4	1													1	11								1	1		

Taylor	Smith	Harrison	Austin	Zhiyi	Ruddock	Pollock	Mullins	Morrison C	Fossell	Fullarton	Black	Gray	Carlisle	Rodger	McKenzie	Gregg	Harris	Kitson	Kolinko	Linighan	Morrison A	Thomson	Rubins	Staunton	Freedman	Martin	Kabba	Frampton	Berhalter	Fuller	Karic	Upson	Hopkin	Riihilahti	Verhoene	Evans
		3	5				6	**10**	12				4	7					1			8	11		9			2								
	2	3	4	**5**	12		6	9	10		14			7					1			8	11		13											
	1	2	2	1			2	2	1				1	2					2			2	2		1			1								
					1				1		1															1											
								1															1															

Taylor	Smith	Harrison	Austin	Zhiyi	Ruddock	Pollock	Mullins	Morrison C	Fossell	Fullarton	Black	Gray	Carlisle	Rodger	McKenzie	Gregg	Harris	Kitson	Kolinko	Linighan	Morrison A	Thomson	Rubins	Staunton	Freedman	Martin	Kabba	Frampton	Berhalter	Fuller	Karic	Upson	Hopkin	Riihilahti	Verhoene	Evans
		3		5	6	*4*	8	9	10	14	7	12	**2**	11	13	1																					
	2	3	14	5	6	4	11	**9**	10		7	8			12	1	13																				
		3	2	5		4	11	9	**8**		7	12			10				1	6																
		3	2	5	6	4	8	12	10		7	13		11			**9**		1	14																
	2	3	5				6	9			7		4	11					1			10	8														
	2	3	4	*5*	6		11	9	10		7		12						1			**8**				14	13									
	2		4	5	6	8	11	9	10		**7**		13	3					1			12															
	2	3	4	5			6	9	10					7					1			8	11													
	6	3	5			12		9	*10*		7	13	**2**	4		14			1			8	11													
	6	8	7	7	5	5	8	8	8		8	1	3	6	1	2	1		7	1		4	3													
			1			1		1		1		4	2		2	1	1			1		1				1	1									
					1			4	2		1									1		1	2													

League Table

	P	W	D	L	F	A	Pts
Fulham	46	30	11	5	90	32	101
Blackburn Rovers	46	26	13	7	76	39	91
Bolton Wanderers	46	24	15	7	76	45	87
Preston North End	46	23	9	14	64	52	78
Birmingham City	46	23	9	14	59	48	78
West Bromwich Albion	46	21	11	14	60	52	74
Burnley	46	21	9	16	50	54	72
Wimbledon	46	17	18	11	71	50	69
Watford	46	20	9	17	76	67	69
Sheffield United	46	19	11	16	52	49	68
Nottingham Forest	46	20	8	18	55	53	68
Wolverhampton W	46	14	13	19	45	48	55
Gillingham	46	13	16	17	61	66	55
Crewe Alexandra	46	15	10	21	47	62	55
Norwich City	46	14	12	20	46	58	54
Barnsley	46	15	9	22	49	62	54
Sheffield Wednesday	46	15	8	23	52	71	53
Grimsby Town	46	14	10	22	43	62	52
Stockport County	46	11	18	17	58	65	51
Portsmouth	46	10	19	17	47	59	49
Crystal Palace	46	12	13	21	57	70	49
Huddersfield Town	46	11	15	20	48	57	48
Queen's Park Rangers	46	7	19	20	45	75	40
Tranmere Rovers	46	9	11	26	46	77	38

2001-02

Division One

Manager: Steve Bruce until 31 October 2001, Steve Kember (caretaker) until 30 November 2001 then Trevor Francis

Did you know that?

Palace's US international defender Gregg Berhalter become the first Eagles player to appear in a World Cup when he featured for the USA in the South Korea/Japan tournament of May and June 2002.

Match No.	Date		Venue	Opponents	Result		Scorers	Attendance
1	Aug	11	A	Rotherham United	W	3-2	Smith, Riihilahti, Freedman (pen)	6,994
2		18	H	Stockport County	W	4-1	Riihilahti, Freedman, Morrison 2	15,760
3		25	A	Nottingham Forest	L	2-4	Freedman 2	18,239
4	Sep	8	H	Millwall	L	1-3	Morrison	21,641
5		15	A	Portsmouth	L	2-4	Freedman, Rodger	18,149
6		18	H	Grimsby Town	W	5-0	Freedman, Morrison, Kirovski, Popovic 2	13,970
7		22	H	Barnsley	W	1-0	Riihilahti	15,433
8		25	A	Sheffield United	W	3-1	Smith, Hopkin, Freedman (pen)	14,180
9		29	H	Sheffield Wednesday	W	4-1	Freedman 2, Morrison 2	17,066
10	Oct	13	H	Wimbledon	W	4-0	Riihilahti, Morrison, Kirovski, own-goal (Brown)	20,009
11		16	H	Bradford City	W	2-0	Morrison 2	15,271
12		20	A	Wolverhampton Wanderers	W	1-0	Kirovski	26,471
13		23	A	Burnley	L	0-1		14,713
14		28	H	Norwich City	W	3-2	Freedman, Morrison 2	19,553
15		31	H	West Bromwich Albion	L	0-1		17,273
16	Nov	3	A	Walsall	D	2-2	Hopkin, Freedman	6,795
17		17	H	Crewe Alexandra	W	4-1	own-goal (Walton), Freedman, Morrison, Kirovski	21,802
18		21	A	Gillingham	L	0-3		9,396
19		24	A	Preston North End	L	1-2	Freedman	15,264
20		28	A	Coventry City	L	0-2		13,695
21	Dec	1	H	Burnley	L	1-2	Morrison	18,457
22		8	H	Manchester City	W	2-1	Freedman, Kirovski	22,080
23		11	A	Birmingham City	L	0-1		20,119
24		15	A	Watford	L	0-1		16,499
25		20	H	Nottingham Forest	D	1-1	Morrison	15,645
26		26	A	Millwall	L	0-3		16,630
27		29	A	Bradford City	W	2-1	Berhalter, Benjamin	14,233
28	Jan	13	A	Stockport County	W	1-0	Freedman	5,541
29		16	H	Gillingham	W	3-1	Freedman, Morrison 2	17,646
30		19	H	Rotherham United	W	2-0	Smith, Morrison	17,311
31		29	H	Coventry City	L	1-3	Freedman	16,197
32	Feb	2	A	Sheffield Wednesday	W	3-1	Smith, Freedman, Morrison	20,099
33		7	H	Wolverhampton Wanderers	L	0-2		18,475
34		16	A	Wimbledon	D	1-1	Morrison	13,564
35		23	H	Sheffield United	L	0-1		18,009
36		26	A	Barnsley	W	4-1	Gray, Riihilahti, Freedman, Akinbiyi	11,207
37	Mar	2	A	Grimsby Town	L	2-5	Gray, Morrison	5,924
38		5	H	Portsmouth	D	0-0		15,915
39		9	H	Watford	L	0-2		16,817
40		16	A	Manchester City	L	0-1		33,637
41		23	H	Walsall	W	2-0	Freedman (pen), Morrison	21,038
42		30	A	Norwich City	L	1-2	Morrison	21,251
43	Apr	1	H	Birmingham City	D	0-0		19,598
44		7	A	Crewe Alexandra	D	0-0		6,724
45		13	H	Preston North End	W	2-0	Hopkin, Akinbiyi	21,361
46		21	A	West Bromwich Albion	L	0-2		26,712

Final League Position: 10th in Division One

Appearances
Sub appearances
2 own-goals — Goals

FA Cup

3	Jan	5	A	Newcastle United	L	0-2		38,089

Appearances
Sub appearances

League Cup

1	Aug	21	A	Leyton Orient	W	4-2	Morrison 2, Black 2	4,290
2	Sep	12	A	Everton	D	1-1*	Freedman (pen)	21,128
3	Oct	10	A	Sheffield Wednesday	D	2-2#	Riihilahti, Rodger	8,796

* After extra-time, won 5–4 on penalties
# After extra-time, lost 1–3 on penalties

Appearances
Sub appearances
Goals

Kolinko	Smith	Gray	Austin	Zhiyi	Mullins	Hopkin	Riihilahti	Freedman	Morrison	Kirovski	Rodger	Berhalter	Thomson	Rubins	Black	Carlisle	Popovic	Clarke	Harrison	Kabba	Vickers	Routledge	Edwards	Symons	Benjamin	Gooding	Granville	Fleming	Murphy	Akinbiyi	Carasso	Frampton
1	2	3	4	5	6	**7**	8	9	10	11	12	13																				
1	2	3	**4**	5	6		8	9	*10*		11	12	7	13	14																	
1	2	3			5		8	9	10	14	12	4	11	13	**7**		*6*															
	2	6	4		5		**8**	9	10	13	7				12		11	1	3													
	2		4		5		8	9	10	11	7			12	13		6	1	3	14												
	2	3	4		5		8	9	10	*11*	**7**		12	14	13		6	1														
	2	3			5		8	*9*	10	11	**7**		13	14	12		6	1			4											
	2	3	13		5	12	8	**9**	10	11	7						6	1			4											
	2	3	13		5	12	*8*	9	10	**11**	7		14				6	1			4											
	2	3	12		5	14	8	*9*	10	11	7		13				6	1			**4**											
	2	3	4		5	12	8	9	10	**11**	7	13					6	1														
	2	3	13		5	12	8	9	10	**11**	7						6	1			4											
	2	3			5	11	8		10	9	7		13		12		6	1			4											
	2	3	4		5	12	8	9	10	11	**7**						6	1														
	2	3	4		5		8	9	10	*11*	7	12			13		**6**	1				14										
		3	4		5	2	8	9	10	11	7	6						1														
12		3	4		5	2	8	9	10	11	7		13					**1**					6									
		3	4		5	2	8	9	10	11	**7**	13			12			1					6									
		3	4		5		8	9	10	11	7				2			1					6									
		3	4		5	2	8	9	**10**	11	7				13			1		12			6									
		3	4		5		8	9	10	11	7	6			2			1														
1	**2**	3	12		6		8	9	*10*	11	7		13							14			4	5								
1	*2*	3	14		6		8	9		11	7		12		13					**10**			4	5								
1	2				6	*11*	8	9	10	13	**7**		12		14				3				4	5								
1	2	13				7	8	*9*	10	14		12	6						3				**4**	5	11							
1	*2*	3				7	8		10	**11**		6	12						13				4	5	9	14						
1		**3**			5	2	8		10	11		6	7				4		12						9							
1	14	13			6		8	9	10	*12*	**7**						4							5	11		3	2				
1	12	11			6		8	9	10		13						4							5	**7**		3	2				
1	13	12			6		8	*9*	10	11	**7**						4							5	14		3	2				
1	7	11	12		6		8	9	10		13				14		**4**							5			3	2				
1	**7**	11	4				8	9	10	12	6	13															3	2	5			
1		12			4	**7**	8	11	10		6																3	2	5	9		
	2	13	4		6		8	11	10		7	14			12			1										*3*	5	**9**		
	2	13	4		6	8			10	*11*	7	5	14		12			1										3		9		
	2	*11*	4		6		8	**9**	10	14	13		7					1										3	5	12		
	2	*11*	14		6		8	9	10				7		12			1									3	4	5	13		
	12	11	4		6		8	9	10						7			1									3	**2**	5	13		
	2	*11*	4		6		8	9	10	14			13		**7**			1									3		5	12		
	2	**11**	4		6		8	9	10	12	14		7					1									3		5	13		
		11	4		6		8	13	10	**7**			12		14			1									3	*2*	5	9		
		12	4		6		8	11	10	13			7		14			1									**3**	2	*5*	9		
		13	4		6		8	*11*	10				7		14			**1**									3	2	5	9	12	
1		6	4		5		8	11	10		12		**7**		*13*												3	2		9		14
1		**11**	4		6	13	8		10					*12*			5					14					3	2		9		7
1			4		6	11	*8*		10	14	7			13	12		5										3	2		**9**		
18	28	35	27	2	43	13	45	39	45	25	29	6	10		5		20	28	4	1	6		9	9	5		16	17	11	9		1
1	4	8	8			7		1		11	7	8	13	7	20				2	3		2			1	1				5	1	1
	4	2				3	5	20	22	5	1	1					2								1					2		

Kolinko	Smith	Gray	Austin	Zhiyi	Mullins	Hopkin	Riihilahti	Freedman	Morrison	Kirovski	Rodger	Berhalter	Thomson	Rubins	Black	Carlisle	Popovic	Clarke	Harrison	Kabba	Vickers	Routledge	Edwards	Symons	Benjamin	Gooding	Granville	Fleming	Murphy	Akinbiyi	Carasso	Frampton
1		2			6	**11**	8		10	9	12		7				4							5			3					
1		1			1	1	1		1	1			1				1							1			1					
											1																					

Kolinko	Smith	Gray	Austin	Zhiyi	Mullins	Hopkin	Riihilahti	Freedman	Morrison	Kirovski	Rodger	Berhalter	Thomson	Rubins	Black	Carlisle	Popovic	Clarke	Harrison	Kabba	Vickers	Routledge	Edwards	Symons	Benjamin	Gooding	Granville	Fleming	Murphy	Akinbiyi	Carasso	Frampton
1		3	4		5		8		10		**11**	12	6	13	7	2	9															
	2	3	4		5		12	9	10	11	7	**6**	13				8	1														
	2	6	13		5	14	8	**9**	10	11	7				12		3	1			4											
1	2	3	2		3		2	2	3	2	3	1	1		1	1	3	2			1											
			1			1	1					1	1	1	1																	
							1	1	2		1				2																	

League Table

	P	W	D	L	F	A	Pts
Manchester City	46	31	6	9	108	52	99
West Bromwich Albion	46	27	8	11	61	29	89
Wolverhampton W	46	25	11	10	76	43	86
Millwall	46	22	11	13	69	48	77
Birmingham City	46	21	13	12	70	49	76
Norwich City	46	22	9	15	60	51	75
Burnley	46	21	12	13	70	62	75
Preston North End	46	20	12	14	71	59	72
Wimbledon	46	18	13	15	63	57	67
Crystal Palace	46	20	6	20	70	62	66
Coventry City	46	20	6	20	59	53	66
Gillingham	46	18	10	18	64	67	64
Sheffield United	46	15	15	16	53	54	60
Watford	46	16	11	19	62	56	59
Bradford City	46	15	10	21	69	76	55
Nottingham Forest	46	12	18	16	50	51	54
Portsmouth	46	13	14	19	60	72	53
Walsall	46	13	12	21	51	71	51
Grimsby Town	46	12	14	20	50	72	50
Sheffield Wednesday	46	12	14	20	49	71	50
Rotherham United	46	10	19	17	52	66	49
Crewe Alexandra	46	12	13	21	47	76	49
Barnsley	46	11	15	20	59	86	48
Stockport County	46	6	8	32	42	102	26

2002-03

Division One

Manager: Trevor Francis until 18 April 2003 then Steve Kember

Did you know that?

Palace fielded four different 'keepers and four different nationalities in goal this season. It had been over 50 years since they had last been forced to use such a high number of custodians (1950–51).

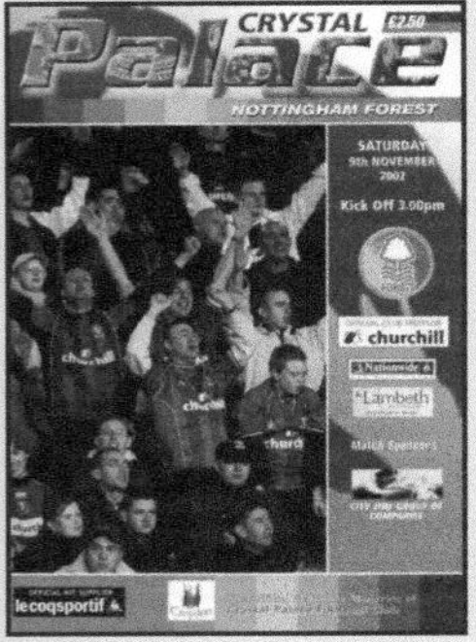

Match No.	Date		Venue	Opponents	Result		Scorers	Attendance
1	Aug	10	A	Preston North End	W	2-1	Powell, Kabba	14,663
2		13	H	Bradford City	D	1-1	Popovic	15,205
3		17	H	Portsmouth	L	2-3	Popovic, Freedman	18,315
4		24	A	Coventry City	L	0-1		15,526
5		27	H	Leicester City	D	0-0		15,440
6		31	A	Burnley	D	0-0		12,407
7	Sep	14	H	Wolverhampton Wanderers	W	4-2	Freedman 2 (1 pen), Thomson, Routledge	16,961
8		17	H	Derby County	L	0-1		14,948
9		21	A	Watford	D	3-3	Granville, Mullins 2	12,153
10		25	A	Sheffield Wednesday	D	0-0		16,112
11		29	H	Gillingham	D	2-2	Granville, Routledge	15,699
12	Oct	5	A	Stoke City	D	1-1	Adebola	14,214
13		19	A	Wimbledon	D	2-2	Johnson, Gray	6,538
14		26	H	Brighton & Hove Alb.	W	5-0	Freedman (pen), Johnson 3 (1 pen), Gray	21,796
15		29	A	Walsall	W	4-3	Freedman, Johnson 3	6,368
16	Nov	3	A	Ipswich Town	W	2-1	Butterfield, Johnson	24,941
17		9	H	Nottingham Forest	D	0-0		18,971
18		16	A	Norwich City	L	0-2		20,907
19		23	H	Grimsby Town	W	2-0	Derry, Adebola	20,093
20		26	H	Reading	L	0-1		15,712
21		30	A	Sheffield United	L	1-2	Riihilahti	16,686
22	Dec	7	H	Millwall	W	1-0	Granville	19,301
23		14	H	Norwich City	W	2-0	Black, Adebola	16,791
24		22	A	Rotherham United	W	3-1	Black 2, Gray	6,829
25		26	A	Portsmouth	D	1-1	Gray	19,217
26		28	H	Preston North End	W	2-0	Black 2	18,484
27	Jan	1	H	Coventry City	D	1-1	Akinbiyi	17,362
28		18	H	Burnley	D	1-1	Popovic (pen)	16,344
29	Feb	1	A	Leicester City	L	0-1		27,005
30		8	A	Nottingham Forest	L	1-2	Johnson (pen)	26,012
31		22	H	Sheffield Wednesday	D	0-0		16,707
32	Mar	1	A	Wolverhampton Wanderers	L	0-4		26,010
33		5	A	Derby County	W	1-0	Black	22,682
34		8	A	Bradford City	L	1-2	Whelan	11,016
35		11	H	Ipswich Town	D	1-1	Johnson	15,990
36		15	A	Reading	L	1-2	Johnson	18,063
37		18	H	Wimbledon	L	0-1		13,713
38		22	H	Walsall	W	2-0	Freedman (pen), Routledge	19,102
39		25	A	Brighton & Hove Alb.	D	0-0		6,786
40	Apr	5	H	Sheffield United	D	2-2	Adebola, Whelan	15,377
41		8	H	Watford	L	0-1		14,051
42		12	A	Grimsby Town	W	4-1	Freedman, Routledge, Gray, Whelan	4,707
43		19	H	Rotherham United	D	0-0		15,508
44		21	A	Millwall	L	2-3	own-goal (Ryan), Freedman	10,670
45		26	H	Stoke City	W	1-0	Adebola	16,064
46	May	4	A	Gillingham	L	1-2	Freedman (pen)	9,315

Final League Position: 14th in Division One

Appearances
Sub appearances
1 own-goal — Goals

FA Cup

Round	Date		Venue	Opponents	Result		Scorers	Attendance
3	Jan	4	A	Blackpool	W	2-1	Black 2	9,062
4		26	H	Liverpool	D	0-0		26,054
R	Feb	5	A	Liverpool	W	2-0	Gray, own-goal (Henchoz)	35,109
5		16	H	Leeds United	L	1-2	Gray	24,512

Appearances
Sub appearances
1 own-goal — Goals

League Cup

Round	Date		Venue	Opponents	Result		Scorers	Attendance
1	Sep	10	H	Plymouth Argyle	W	2-1*	Powell, Johnson	6,385
2	Oct	2	H	Cheltenham Town	W	7-0	own-goal (Walker), Popovic, Mullins, Freedman 2, Adebola 2	4,901
3	Nov	6	H	Coventry City	W	3-0	Johnson 2, Gray	8,102
4	Dec	3	H	Oldham Athletic	W	2-0	Black 2	7,431
5		17	A	Sheffield United	L	1-3	own-goal (Page)	22,211

* After extra-time

Appearances
Sub appearances
2 own-goals — Goals

Clarke	Fleming	Granville	Popovic	Powell	Mullins	Butterfield	Riihilahti	Freedman	Johnson	Derry	Kabba	Thomson	Black	Austin	Adebola	Routledge	Kolinko	Frampton	Rubins	Gray	Michopoulos	Antwi	Symons	Williams	Borrowdale	Hunt	Togwell	Akinbiyi	Berthelin	Whelan	Smith	Watson
1	2	3	4	5	6	7	8	*9*	**10**	11	13	14	12																			
1	**2**	3	4	5	6	7	13	9	*10*	11	14		8	12																		
1	13	3	4	**5**	6	2	8	9		11	14	*7*		12	10																	
1	*2*	3	4	5	6	7	8	9	12	**11**		14	13		10																	
1	2	3	4	5	6	**7**	14	9	10	*11*		8			12	13																
1	2	3	4	5	6	**7**	8	*9*	11			12			10	14	13															
	2	3	4	5	6	7		*9*	10			8	14		13	**11**	1		12													
	2	3	4	5	**6**	7		9	*10*			8	12		13	11	1	14														
	2	3	4	5	6	7		9	*10*			8		13	14	11	1			12												
		3	4	5	6	2	12	13	10			**7**			9	11	1			8												
		3	4	5	6	2	7	9		13			12		10	11				**8**	1											
	2	3	4	5	6	*7*	13	9	**11**	8			14		10					12	1											
		3	4		5	2	7	12	10	8					9	**11**				6	1											
		3	4	5	6	2		9	*10*	8			14		12	**11**	1		13	7												
		3	4	**5**	6	2	12	*9*	11	8			13		10		1			7		14										
		3	4	5	6	2	*7*	9	11	8			13		10		1			12			14									
		3	4	5	6	2	14		10	8	13	**7**			9					*11*	1		12									
		3		5		2	13		10	6		8	**7**		9					11	1	14	*4*	12								
				5	6	2	12		10	11		8	**7**		9		1			*3*			4	13	14							
		3		5	6	2			10	8		**7**	13		9	12	1			11			4									
		3	2	5	6	7	12		10	8			13		9	**11**	1						4									
		3	2	5	6	7	8			13			10		9	12	1			**11**			4									
		3	**2**	5	6	7	8		10	12			*11*		9		1			13			4	14								
				5	6	**2**	8			10			7		9		1			11			4		3		12					
			3	5	6	2	8			10			**7**		9		1			11			4					12				
		3	2	**5**	6	7	12			8			*10*		9	13	1			11			4					14				
		3	5		6	2	8			10			7		**9**	13	1			11			4					12				
		14	5		6	2	8		10	11			7		**9**	13				*3*			4					12	1			
	12	3	2	5	6	*8*			**10**	11			7		9					13			4					14	1			
			2	5	6	7		**9**	11	8		13	12		10					3			4					14	1			
		3		5	6	2	8		10			**4**	7		13	12				*11*					14			9	1			
			2	5	6	7	8		**10**	11			14		*9*	13				3			4					12	1			
		14	4	5	6	2				10		8	*7*		**9**					11			13		3			12	1			
		12	5		6	2		13		7		8	14							**11**			*4*		3			9	1	10		
		3	4	5	6	2		13	10	8		12	**7**							*11*					14				1	9		
			4	5	6	2		14	10	8		7				11	12						13		3				**1**	9		
		13		5	6	2		9	**10**	8			7			12	1			11			4		14						*3*	
		3				8		9		6		12	*7*		10	13	1			11		14	4		5						**2**	
		3		5		2				6		8	*7*		9		1			**11**		14	4	13	12					10		
			5		6	2		12		7		13	14		*9*		1			11			4		3	**8**				10		
			5		6	2		9		**7**		14			10	12	1			3			4			8				13		*11*
			4	5	6	2		12				8			9	7	1			11					3					**10**		13
		13		5	6	2		9		7			12		*10*	14	1			11			4		**3**							8
		3		5	6	2		9		4		8	10			7	1			**11**				13								12
			4	**5**	6	2		9		3		12	7		13	11	1													10		8
			4	5	6	2		9		3		8	7		10	**11**	1			12												
6	9	30	36	39	43	46	15	22	27	36		18	20		32	13	26			29	5		21		8	2		2	9	7	2	3
	2	5					10	7	1	3	4	9	16	3	7	13	2	1	2	6		4	4	5	5		1	8		1		2
		3	3	1	2	1	1	9	11	1	1	1	6		5	4				5								1		3		

Clarke	Fleming	Granville	Popovic	Powell	Mullins	Butterfield	Riihilahti	Freedman	Johnson	Derry	Kabba	Thomson	Black	Austin	Adebola	Routledge	Kolinko	Frampton	Rubins	Gray	Michopoulos	Antwi	Symons	Williams	Borrowdale	Hunt	Togwell	Akinbiyi	Berthelin	Whelan	Smith	Watson
		3	5		6	2	8			10			7		*9*		1			11			4		14			12	13			
	2	14	5		6	8			10	11			**7**		9	12	1			*3*			4					13				
		3	2	5	6	7		12	10	8		13			*9*					11			4					14	1			
		12		*5*	6	2	8	13	10	11			7		9					3			**4**					14	1			
	1	2	3	2	4	4	2		3	4			3		4		2			4			4						2			
		2						2				1				1									1			4	1			
													2							2												

Clarke	Fleming	Granville	Popovic	Powell	Mullins	Butterfield	Riihilahti	Freedman	Johnson	Derry	Kabba	Thomson	Black	Austin	Adebola	Routledge	Kolinko	Frampton	Rubins	Gray	Michopoulos	Antwi	Symons	Williams	Borrowdale	Hunt	Togwell	Akinbiyi	Berthelin	Whelan	Smith	Watson
	2	3		5	6	12		9	*10*			7	13	**4**	8	11	1	14														
		3	*4*	**5**	6	2		9		8			7	12	10	11				13	1	14										
		3	4	5	6	2	*7*	**9**	11	8		14			10		1			12	13											
		3	2	5	6	7	8						*11*		9		1					13	4	**10**	12	14						
				5	6	2	8		10				7		9		1			11		**3**	4	13	12							
	1	4	3	5	5	4	3	3	3	2		1	3	1	5	2	4			1	1	1	2	1								
						1						1	1	1				1		2	1	2		1	2	1						
			1	1	1			2	3				2		2					1												

League Table

	P	W	D	L	F	A	Pts
Portsmouth	46	29	11	6	97	45	98
Leicester City	46	26	14	6	73	40	92
Sheffield United	46	23	11	12	72	52	80
Reading	46	25	4	17	61	46	79
Wolverhampton W	46	20	16	10	81	44	76
Nottingham Forest	46	20	14	12	82	50	74
Ipswich Town	46	19	13	14	80	64	70
Norwich City	46	19	12	15	60	49	69
Millwall	46	19	9	18	59	69	66
Wimbledon	46	18	11	17	76	73	65
Gillingham	46	16	14	16	56	65	62
Preston North End	46	16	13	17	68	70	61
Watford	46	17	9	20	54	70	60
Crystal Palace	46	14	17	15	59	52	59
Rotherham United	46	15	14	17	62	62	59
Burnley	46	15	10	21	65	89	55
Walsall	46	15	9	22	57	69	54
Derby County	46	15	7	24	55	74	52
Bradford City	46	14	10	22	51	73	52
Coventry City	46	12	14	20	46	62	50
Stoke City	46	12	14	20	45	69	50
Sheffield Wednesday	46	10	16	20	56	73	46
Brighton & Hove Albion	46	11	12	23	49	67	45
Grimsby Town	46	9	12	25	48	85	39

2003-04

Division One

Manager: Steve Kember until 3 November 2003, Kit Symons (caretaker) until 22 December 2003 then Iain Dowie

Did you know that?

Palace finished runners-up in a Cup competition, albeit the Philips Cup, awarded to the winners of the pre-season friendly at Selhurst Park against Philips-sponsored PSV Eindhoven, who won the match 1–0.

Match No.	Date		Venue	Opponents	Result		Scorers	Attendance
1	Aug	9	A	Burnley	W	3-2	Freedman 3 (1 pen)	12,976
2		16	H	Watford	W	1-0	Shipperley	15,333
3		23	A	Wimbledon	W	3-1	Butterfield, Freedman (pen), Hughes	6,113
4		26	H	Sheffield United	L	1-2	Johnson (pen)	15,466
5		30	A	Millwall	D	1-1	Watson	14,425
6	Sep	13	A	Sunderland	L	1-2	Johnson	27,324
7		16	H	Bradford City	L	0-1		13,514
8		20	H	West Bromwich Albion	D	2-2	Johnson, Freedman	17,477
9		27	A	Norwich City	L	1-2	Derry	16,425
10	Oct	1	A	West Ham United	L	0-3		31,861
11		4	H	Cardiff City	W	2-1	Shipperley, Routledge	16,160
12		14	H	Derby County	D	1-1	Butterfield	14,344
13		18	H	Rotherham United	D	1-1	Freedman	18,715
14		21	H	Ipswich Town	L	3-4	Johnson, Freedman 2 (1 pen)	15,483
15		25	A	Gillingham	L	0-1		8,889
16	Nov	1	A	Wigan Athletic	L	0-5		6,796
17		8	H	Preston North End	D	1-1	Johnson	14,608
18		22	A	Walsall	D	0-0		6,910
19		25	A	Stoke City	W	1-0	Johnson	10,277
20		29	H	Coventry City	D	1-1	Edwards	14,622
21	Dec	6	A	Preston North End	L	1-4	Derry	12,836
22		9	H	Crewe Alexandra	L	1-3	Butterfield	12,259
23		13	H	Nottingham Forest	W	1-0	Johnson	16,935
24		20	A	Reading	W	3-0	Johnson 2, Routledge	12,743
25		26	H	Millwall	L	0-1		19,737
26		28	A	Ipswich Town	W	3-1	Johnson 2, Gray	27,629
27	Jan	10	H	Burnley	D	0-0		15,276
28		17	A	Watford	W	5-1	Johnson 2 (1 pen), Freedman, Routledge, Gray	15,017
29		24	A	Bradford City	W	2-1	Johnson, Shipperley	10,310
30		31	H	Wimbledon	W	3-1	Johnson 2, Granville	20,552
31	Feb	7	A	Sheffield United	W	3-0	Popovic, Johnson, Shipperley	23,816
32		14	H	Stoke City	W	6-3	Johnson 3 (2 pen), Shipperley, Routledge, Hughes	16,715
33		21	A	Derby County	L	1-2	Hughes	21,856
34		28	H	Gillingham	W	1-0	Butterfield	17,485
35	Mar	6	H	Reading	D	2-2	Johnson, Freedman	17,853
36		13	A	Nottingham Forest	L	2-3	Shipperley, Granville	28,306
37		20	H	Norwich City	W	1-0	Routledge	23,798
38		27	A	West Bromwich Albion	L	0-2		24,990
39	Apr	6	A	Rotherham United	W	2-1	Shipperley 2	6,001
40		10	A	Cardiff City	W	2-0	Johnson, Routledge	16,656
41		12	H	West Ham United	W	1-0	Freedman	23,977
42		17	H	Wigan Athletic	D	1-1	Granville	18,799
43		21	H	Sunderland	W	3-0	Johnson (pen), Freedman, Shipperley	18,291
44		24	A	Crewe Alexandra	W	3-2	Johnson 3 (1 pen)	8,136
45	May	1	H	Walsall	W	1-0	Johnson	21,518
46		9	A	Coventry City	L	1-2	Freedman	22,195

Final League Position: 6th in Division One

Appearances
Sub appearances
Goals

Play-offs

	Date		Venue	Opponents	Result		Scorers	Attendance
SF1	May	14	H	Sunderland	W	3-2	Shipperley, Butterfield, Johnson	25,287
SF2		17	A	Sunderland	L	1-2*	Powell	34,536
F		29	N+	West Ham United	W	1-0	Shipperley	72,523

* After extra-time, won 5–4 on penalties. + Played at the Millennium Stadium, Cardiff

Appearances
Sub appearances
Goals

FA Cup

	Date		Venue	Opponents	Result		Scorers	Attendance
3	Jan	3	A	Tottenham Hotspur	L	0-3		32,340

Appearances
Sub appearances

League Cup

	Date		Venue	Opponents	Result		Scorers	Attendance
1	Aug	12	A	Torquay United	D	1-1*	Freedman	3,366
2	Sep	23	H	Doncaster Rovers	W	2-1	Johnson 2 (2 pens)	4,904
3	Oct	28	A	Blackpool	W	3-1	Johnson 2, Freedman (pen)	6,010
4	Dec	3	A	Aston Villa	L	0-3		24,258

* After extra-time, won 3–1 on penalties

Appearances
Sub appearances
Goals

Clarke	Butterfield	Watson	Symons	Powell	Popovic	Johnson	Derry	Freedman	Shipperley	Routledge	Borrowdale	Riihilahti	Smith	Berthelin	Black	Hughes	Mullins	Fleming	Williams	Myhre	Granville	Heeroo	Edwards	Gray	Hudson	Leigertwood	Soares	Vaesen	Nabil
1	2	3	**4**	5	6	7	8	9	10	11	*12*	13	14																
1	2	8		5	6	**7**	4	9	10	12		13	3			11													
1	2	8	4	**5**		13		9	10		12	14	3		7	11	*6*												
1	2	13	4			12	8	**9**	10	14	*5*		3		7	11	6												
	2	10		5		9	8			11		4	3	1	7		6												
	2	12	**4**			9	8		10	*7*	13	14	3	1		11	6	5											
	2	14			4	9	*8*		10	12	13		3	1	7	11	6	**5**											
	2		12		**4**	7	8	*9*	10	14	5		3	1		11	6	13											
	2			5		7	8	9	10		**3**	12		1		11	6	4											
	2			*5*		7	8	9	10	13	12	4	**3**	1		11	6	14											
	2			5			8	9	10	11	12			1	**7**	3	6	4											
	2	12	6	5			8	9	10	11				1	7	**3**		4											
	2			5		11	**8**	9	10	3		12		1	7		6	4											
	2			**5**	6	11	8	9	10	3		12	13	1	7			4											
			5		6	11	2	9	10	12	13	8	3		**7**			4		1									
	7	12			6	11	8	9	10	13	14	**4**	2					5		1	*3*								
	2	*11*	4		6	7	8	9	10	12			3		13			5		1		14							
	2	**8**	4		6	7		*9*	10	14	3				12	11		5		1			13						
	2	14	13		6	*10*	8	9		12	4				**7**	11		5		1			3						
	2	13			6	**10**	8	9		12	4				7	11		5		1			3						
	2		4		6		8		10	12	5	9			**7**	11				1			3						
	2		4				8	9	10	11	6	7			12			**5**		1			3						
	7		13		5	**9**		12		10	4	8	2			11				1			6	3					
	2				5	9	12		10	7	4	8				**11**				1			6	3					
	2		4		5	9		13	10	7	6	**8**			12	11				1				3					
	2		4		5	9	12		10	7	6	8				**11**				1				3					
	6	8			*5*	9		13	10	7	12		2		14			**4**		1	3			11					
	2	**6**				9	12	13	10	*7*	4	8			14					1	3			11	5				
	2					*9*	13	14	10	**7**	4	8			12	6				1	3			11	5				
	2				4	9			10	7		8		1		6					3			11	5				
	2				4	9	12		10	7		8		1		**6**					3			11	5				
	2				4	*9*	12	14	10	7		8		1		**6**					3			11	5	13			
	2				4	**9**	13	12	10	7		8		1	14	6					3			11	5				
	2				4	9	8		10	**7**				1		6					3			11	5	12	13		
	2				4	10	**8**	9		7				1		6					3			11	5		12		
	2				4	9	**8**	12	10	7				1		6					3			11		5			
	2				4	9		12	**10**	7						8					3			11	5	6		1	
	2				4	9			10	7					12	8					3			11	5	**6**		1	
	2				4	9			10	7		**8**				6					3			11	5	12		1	
	2				4	9	14	12	**10**	7		8				*6*					3			11	5	13		1	
	2				4	*10*	12	9		7		**8**				6					3			11	5	13	14	1	
	2				4	9	12	13	10	7		**8**				6					3			11	5			1	
	2				4	9	13	12	**10**	7		8			14	6					3			11		5		1	
	2				4	9	6	12	**10**	7		8			13						3			11		5		1	
	2	13			4	9	**6**	12	10	7		8			14						3			11		5		1	
	2				4	9	13	12	*10*	7		8			14	6					3			11		**5**		1	
4	45	8	12	10	34	40	25	20	40	32	14	24	13	17	12	34	10	15		15	21		6	24	14	7		10	
		8	3			2	12	15		12	9	7	2		13			2				1	1			5	3		
	4	1			1	27	2	13	9	6						3					3		1	2					

Clarke	Butterfield	Watson	Symons	Powell	Popovic	Johnson	Derry	Freedman	Shipperley	Routledge	Borrowdale	Riihilahti	Smith	Berthelin	Black	Hughes	Mullins	Fleming	Williams	Myhre	Granville	Heeroo	Edwards	Gray	Hudson	Leigertwood	Soares	Vaesen	Nabil
	2			13	4	9	12		10	7		8				**6**					3			11		5		1	
	2			14	4	9	12	13	10	7		**8**				6					*3*			11		5		1	
	2			12	4	9	6		10	7		8				11					3					5		1	
	3				3	3	1		3	3		3				3					3			2		3		3	
				3			2	1																					
	1			1		1			2																				

Clarke	Butterfield	Watson	Symons	Powell	Popovic	Johnson	Derry	Freedman	Shipperley	Routledge	Borrowdale	Riihilahti	Smith	Berthelin	Black	Hughes	Mullins	Fleming	Williams	Myhre	Granville	Heeroo	Edwards	Gray	Hudson	Leigertwood	Soares	Vaesen	Nabil
	2	8	4		5	**9**		12	10	7	*6*		13	1		11					14			3					
	1	1	1		1	1			1	1	1			1		1								1					
								1					1								1								

Clarke	Butterfield	Watson	Symons	Powell	Popovic	Johnson	Derry	Freedman	Shipperley	Routledge	Borrowdale	Riihilahti	Smith	Berthelin	Black	Hughes	Mullins	Fleming	Williams	Myhre	Granville	Heeroo	Edwards	Gray	Hudson	Leigertwood	Soares	Vaesen	Nabil
	2	13	*4*	5	6	7	3	9	10	**11**		8	12	1	14														
	2	4		5		**9**	8		10	12	3	13		1		11	*6*	14	7										
	2	13	5			8	6	9	*10*	7	12	4	**3**			11				1									14
	2	14	4		6		*8*	9	10	12	3	13		1	**7**	11		5											
	4	1	3	2	2	3	4	3	4	2	2	2	1	3	1	3	1	1	1	1									
		3								2	1	2	1		1			1											1
						4		2																					

League Table

	P	W	D	L	F	A	Pts
Norwich City	46	28	10	8	79	39	94
West Bromwich Albion	46	25	11	10	64	42	86
Sunderland	46	22	13	11	62	45	79
West Ham United	46	19	17	10	67	45	74
Ipswich Town	46	21	10	15	84	72	73
Crystal Palace	46	21	10	15	72	61	73
Wigan Athletic	46	18	17	11	60	45	71
Sheffield United	46	20	11	15	65	56	71
Reading	46	20	10	16	55	57	70
Millwall	46	18	15	13	55	48	69
Stoke City	46	18	12	16	58	55	66
Coventry City	46	17	14	15	67	54	65
Cardiff City	46	17	14	15	68	58	65
Nottingham Forest	46	15	15	16	61	58	60
Preston North End	46	15	14	17	69	71	59
Watford	46	15	12	19	54	68	57
Rotherham United	46	13	15	18	53	61	54
Crewe Alexandra	46	14	11	21	57	66	53
Burnley	46	13	14	19	60	77	53
Derby County	46	13	13	20	53	67	52
Gillingham	46	14	9	23	48	67	51
Walsall	46	13	12	21	45	65	51
Bradford City	46	10	6	30	38	69	36
Wimbledon	46	8	5	33	41	89	29

2004-05

Premiership

Manager: Iain Dowie

Did you know that?

2005 saw Palace celebrate its 100th year of existence. A fans-voted 'Centenary Team' was revealed as: Nigel Martyn, Kenny Samson, Chris Coleman, Jim Cannon, Paul Hinshelwood, Geoff Thomas, Andy Gray, John Salako, Atillio Lombardo, Andy Johnson, Ian Wright.

Match No.	Date		Venue	Opponents	Result		Scorers	Attendance
1	Aug	14	A	Norwich City	D	1-1	Johnson	23,717
2		21	H	Everton	L	1-3	Hudson	23,666
3		24	H	Chelsea	L	0-2		24,953
4		28	A	Middlesbrough	L	1-2	Johnson (pen)	31,560
5	Sep	11	A	Portsmouth	L	1-3	Granville	20,019
6		18	H	Manchester City	L	1-2	Johnson (pen)	25,052
7		25	A	Aston Villa	D	1-1	Johnson	34,843
8	Oct	4	H	Fulham	W	2-0	Johnson, Riihilahti	21,825
9		16	A	Bolton Wanderers	L	0-1		25,501
10		23	H	West Bromwich Albion	W	3-0	Hall, Johnson 2 (1 pen)	22,922
11		30	A	Birmingham City	W	1-0	Johnson	28,916
12	Nov	6	H	Arsenal	D	1-1	Riihilahti	26,193
13		13	A	Liverpool	L	2-3	Hughes, Kolkka	42,862
14		20	H	Newcastle United	L	0-2		22,937
15		27	A	Southampton	D	2-2	own-goal (Jakobsson), Johnson	31,833
16	Dec	5	H	Charlton Athletic	L	0-1		20,705
17		11	H	Blackburn Rovers	D	0-0		22,010
18		18	A	Manchester United	L	2-5	Granville, Kolkka	67,814
19		26	H	Portsmouth	L	0-1		25,238
20		28	A	Tottenham Hotspur	D	1-1	Johnson	36,100
21	Jan	1	A	Fulham	L	1-3	Johnson (pen)	18,680
22		3	H	Aston Villa	W	2-0	Johnson 2 (1 pen)	24,140
23		15	A	Manchester City	L	1-3	Powell	44,010
24		22	H	Tottenham Hotspur	W	3-0	Granville, Johnson (pen), Leigertwood	23,723
25	Feb	1	A	West Bromwich Albion	D	2-2	Johnson, Riihilahti	25,092
26		5	H	Bolton Wanderers	L	0-1		23,163
27		14	A	Arsenal	L	1-5	Johnson (pen)	38,056
28		26	H	Birmingham City	W	2-0	Johnson 2 (2 pens)	23,376
29	Mar	5	H	Manchester United	D	0-0		26,021
30		19	A	Chelsea	L	1-4	Riihilahti	41,667
31	Apr	2	H	Middlesbrough	L	0-1		24,274
32		10	A	Everton	L	0-4		36,519
33		16	H	Norwich City	D	3-3	Hughes, Johnson (pen), Kolkka	25,754
34		20	A	Blackburn Rovers	L	0-1		18,006
35		23	H	Liverpool	W	1-0	Johnson	26,043
36		30	A	Newcastle United	D	0-0		52,123
37	May	7	H	Southampton	D	2-2	Hall, Ventola	26,066
38		15	A	Charlton Athletic	D	2-2	Johnson (pen), Freedman	26,870

Final League Position: 18th in the Premiership

Appearances
Sub appearances
1 own-goal — Goals

FA Cup

3	Jan	8	A	Sunderland	L	1-2	own-goal (Collins)	17,536

Appearances
1 own-goal — Sub appearances

League Cup

2	Sep	21	H	Hartlepool United	W	2-1*	Freedman, Soares	4,233
3	Oct	27	A	Charlton Athletic	W	2-1	Freedman, Torghelle	19,030
4	Nov	10	A	Manchester United	L	0-2		48,891

* After extra-time

Appearances
Sub appearances
Goals

Speroni	Boyce	Granville	Popovic	Hudson	Hall	Routledge	Hughes	Torghelle	Johnson	Kolkka	Riihilahti	Freedman	Derry	Kaviedes	Ventola	Watson	Kiraly	Sorondo	Powell	Borrowdale	Soares	Lakis	Butterfield	Leigertwood	Danze	Shipperley	Andrews
1	2	3	4	5	**6**	7	*8*	9	10	<u>11</u>	12	14	13														
1	<u>2</u>	3	4	5	6	7			10	11	**8**	9	12	13													
1	2	3	4	5	6	7	12		10	11	8			**9**													
1	2	3	4	5	6	<u>7</u>	10		9	11	**8**		12	13													
1	2	3	4	5	6	*7*	13	9	10	**11**	<u>8</u>		14		12												
1	2	3		5	4	7	11	*9*	10	14	**8**		<u>6</u>		13	12											
	2	3	4		**5**	7	10		9	<u>11</u>	8					6	1	12			13						
	2	3	4		**5**	<u>7</u>	10		9	11	*8*			14		6	1	12				13					
	2	3	4		5	7	10		9	**11**	*8*	13	14			<u>6</u>	1					12					
	2	3	4		5	7	**10**		9	<u>11</u>	8	13				*6*	1	14				12					
	2	3	**4**		5	7	*10*		9	<u>11</u>	8	13	14			6	1	12									
	2	3	4			<u>7</u>	10		9	*11*	8	14				6	1	**5**				13		12			
	5	3	4			**7**	10			11	<u>8</u>	9				6	1				13	12		2			
	2	3	4		5	7	10		9	**11**	<u>8</u>	13				6	1					12					
	2	3	4		5	7	10		9	11	8					6	1										
	2	3	4		5	7	10		9	**11**	<u>8</u>	13				6	1					12					
	2	3	4		5	7	10	14	9	<u>11</u>	**8**					6	1					13					12
	2	3			5	7	**10**		9	11	<u>8</u>					6	1	4			13	12					14
		3			5	<u>7</u>	10		9	11	*8*	13				**6**	1	4			12		2				14
		3			5	**7**	10	12	9		8						1	4			6	11	2				
		3	4		5	7	<u>10</u>	14	9		*8*						1				6	**11**	2	13			12
	13	3			5	7	10		9		8					**6**	1		4			11	<u>2</u>	12			
	2				5	7			9							**8**	1	3	4	13	10	<u>11</u>		6		14	12
	2	3			5	7	11		<u>9</u>			10					1	4		12	**8**			6			13
	2				5	7	*11*		9		13	**10**					1	4	<u>12</u>	3	8			6			14
	2	3			5	**7**	11		9	12	13	10					1		4		*8*			<u>6</u>			14
	2	3			5	<u>7</u>	11		9	14	**8**	*10*					1	4			6	13		12			
	2	3			5	7	11	12	9			**10**					1	4		13	<u>8</u>	14		6			
	2	3			5	**7**	10		9								1	4		12	8	11		6			
	2	3			5	**7**	11	12	9		*8*	13				14	1	<u>4</u>			10			6			
		3		4	5	7	11		9		*8*	10					1			12	<u>6</u>	13		2			14
		3			5	7	10	13	9		**8**					12	1		4		6	<u>11</u>		2			
		3	14		5	7	8	13	9	*11*		10					1	4			12		<u>2</u>	**6**			
			14		5	7	8	13	9	**11**		<u>10</u>					1	4		3	12		*2*	6			
		3	4		5	7	11		9		8					12	1	2			10			**6**			
		3	4		5	**7**	11	12	9		8						1	2			10			6			
		3	**4**		5	7	11		9		<u>8</u>				12	13	1	2			10			6			
		3	4		5	7	11		9		14	12				*8*	1		13		<u>10</u>		**2**	6			
6	26	35	21	7	36	38	34	3	37	20	28	10	1	1		16	32	16	4	2	16	6	7	16			
	1		2				2	9		3	4	10	6	3	3	5		4	2	5	6	12		4		1	9
		3		1	2		2		21	3	4	1			1				1					1			

Speroni	Boyce	Granville	Popovic	Hudson	Hall	Routledge	Hughes	Torghelle	Johnson	Kolkka	Riihilahti	Freedman	Derry	Kaviedes	Ventola	Watson	Kiraly	Sorondo	Powell	Borrowdale	Soares	Lakis	Butterfield	Leigertwood	Danze	Shipperley	Andrews
		3			5	7	10		9							<u>8</u>	1		4		12	**11**	2	6		13	
		1			1	1	1		1							1	1		1		0	1	1	1			
																					1					1	

Speroni	Boyce	Granville	Popovic	Hudson	Hall	Routledge	Hughes	Torghelle	Johnson	Kolkka	Riihilahti	Freedman	Derry	Kaviedes	Ventola	Watson	Kiraly	Sorondo	Powell	Borrowdale	Soares	Lakis	Butterfield	Leigertwood	Danze	Shipperley	Andrews
	2	3				7		**9**		11		10	<u>6</u>	12		8	1	*4*	5	14	13						
1				5				9				10	11			**8**		4	12	3	7		2	6			
1				5				<u>9</u>				10	11	13					4	3	7	12	*2*	6	**8**	14	
2	1	1		2		1		3		1		3	3			2	1	2	2	2	2		2	2	1		
														2					1	1	1	1				1	
								1				2									1						

League Table

	P	W	D	L	F	A	Pts
Chelsea	38	29	8	1	72	15	95
Arsenal	38	25	8	5	87	36	83
Manchester United	38	22	11	5	58	26	77
Everton	38	18	7	13	45	46	61
Liverpool	38	17	7	14	52	41	58
Bolton Wanderers	38	16	10	12	49	44	58
Middlesbrough	38	14	13	11	53	46	55
Manchester City	38	13	13	12	47	39	52
Tottenham Hotspur	38	14	10	14	47	41	52
Aston Villa	38	12	11	15	45	52	47
Charlton Athletic	38	12	10	16	42	58	46
Birmingham City	38	11	12	15	40	46	45
Fulham	38	12	8	18	52	60	44
Newcastle United	38	10	14	14	47	57	44
Blackburn Rovers	38	9	15	14	32	43	42
Portsmouth	38	10	9	19	43	59	39
West Bromwich Albion	38	6	16	16	36	61	34
Crystal Palace	38	7	12	19	41	62	33
Norwich City	38	7	12	19	42	77	33
Southampton	38	6	14	18	45	66	32

2005-06

Championship

Manager: Iain Dowie

Did you know that?

Fittingly, Dougie Freedman's 100th goal for Palace came in November 2005, a 3–2 win away at Brighton in front of the live TV cameras on a Sunday afternoon.

Match No.	Date	Venue	Opponents	Result		Scorers	Attendance
1	Aug 6	H	Luton Town	L	1-2	Johnson	21,166
2	9	A	Wolverhampton Wanderers	L	1-2	McAnuff	24,745
3	13	A	Norwich City	D	1-1	Johnson	25,102
4	20	H	Plymouth Argyle	W	1-0	Ward	18,781
5	27	H	Stoke City	W	2-0	Johnson 2	17,637
6	Sep 10	H	Hull City	W	2-0	Johnson, Morrison	18,630
7	13	A	Reading	L	2-3	Johnson, Morrison	17,562
8	17	A	Cardiff City	L	0-1		11,647
9	24	H	Preston North End	D	1-1	Morrison	17,291
10	27	H	Sheffield Wednesday	W	2-0	Boyce, Morrison	17,413
11	Oct 3	A	Queen's Park Rangers	W	3-1	Soares, Reich 2	13,433
12	15	A	Coventry City	W	4-1	Watson, Macken, Ward, Morrison	24,438
13	18	H	Brighton & Hove Alb.	L	0-1		22,400
14	22	H	Burnley	W	2-0	Freedman, Morrison	20,127
15	29	A	Crewe Alexandra	D	2-2	Freedman, Morrison	6,766
16	Nov 5	H	Sheffield United	L	2-3	Hughes, Freedman (pen)	20,344
17	20	A	Brighton & Hove Alb.	W	3-2	McAnuff, Freedman 2	7,273
18	22	H	Coventry City	W	2-0	Boyce, Andrews	17,343
19	26	A	Luton Town	L	0-2		10,248
20	Dec 3	H	Millwall	D	1-1	Watson	19,571
21	10	H	Wolverhampton Wanderers	D	1-1	Johnson	19,385
22	17	A	Plymouth Argyle	L	0-2		14,582
23	26	A	Ipswich Town	W	2-0	Macken, Hughes	27,392
24	28	H	Derby County	W	2-0	Ward, Morrison	18,978
25	31	A	Watford	W	2-1	Johnson (pen), Ward	15,856
26	Jan 2	H	Leicester City	W	2-0	McAnuff, Johnson	20,089
27	14	A	Hull City	W	2-1	Ward, own-goal (Cort)	18,886
28	20	H	Reading	D	1-1	Johnson (pen)	19,888
29	25	A	Southampton	D	0-0		24,651
30	31	A	Preston North End	L	0-2		13,867
31	Feb 4	H	Cardiff City	W	1-0	Riihilahti	17,962
32	11	A	Sheffield Wednesday	D	0-0		24,784
33	14	H	Queen's Park Rangers	W	2-1	McAnuff, Morrison	17,550
34	18	A	Millwall	D	1-1	Watson	12,296
35	25	H	Norwich City	W	4-1	Hall, Watson, Johnson, Morrison	19,066
36	Mar 4	H	Leeds United	L	1-2	McAnuff	23,843
37	13	A	Stoke City	W	3-1	own-goal (Sidibe), McAnuff, Johnson	10,121
38	18	H	Ipswich Town	D	2-2	Riihilahti, Morrison	22,076
39	21	A	Leeds United	W	1-0	McAnuff	24,507
40	25	A	Derby County	L	1-2	Morrison	24,857
41	31	H	Watford	W	3-1	Freedman, own-goals (Stewart and Demerit)	18,619
42	Apr 7	A	Leicester City	L	0-2		23,211
43	15	H	Crewe Alexandra	D	2-2	Johnson 2	18,358
44	17	A	Burnley	D	0-0		11,449
45	22	H	Southampton	W	2-1	Johnson, Morrison	20,995
46	30	A	Sheffield United	L	0-1		27,120

Final League Position: 6th in the Championship

Appearances
Sub appearances
4 own-goals — Goals

Play-offs

	Date	Venue	Opponents	Result		Scorers	Attendance
SF1	May 6	H	Watford	L	0-3		22,880
SF2	9	A	Watford	D	0-0		19,041

Appearances
Sub appearances

FA Cup

	Date	Venue	Opponents	Result		Scorers	Attendance
3	Jan 7	H	Northampton Town	W	4-1	McAnuff, Johnson (pen), Hughes, Freedman (pen)	10,391
4	28	A	Preston North End	D	1-1	Johnson	9,489
R	Feb 7	H	Preston North End	L	1-2	Ward	7,356

Appearances
Sub appearances
Goals

League Cup

	Date	Venue	Opponents	Result		Scorers	Attendance
1	Aug 23	H	Walsall	W	3-0	Popovic (pen), Granville, Hughes	5,508
2	Sep 20	H	Coventry City	W	1-0	Reich	5,341
3	Oct 25	H	Liverpool	W	2-1	Freedman, Reich	19,673
4	Nov 30	A	Middlesbrough	L	1-2	own-goal (Queudrue)	10,791

Appearances
Sub appearances
1 own-goal — Goals

Kiraly	Boyce	Borrowdale	Hudson	Hall	Watson	McAnuff	Soares	Johnson	Macken	Hughes	Ward	Kolkka	Andrews	Leigertwood	Butterfield	Riihilahti	Freedman	Speroni	Fray	Granville	Popovic	Black	Togwell	Grabban	Berry	Morrison	Danze	Reich
1	2	3	4	5	6	7	8	9	10	11	13	12	14															
1	2	3	14	5	8	7	11	9	10		4	12	13	6														
1	2	3		5	8		7	9	10		4	11	12	6	13													
1	2	3		5	8	7	11	9			4		10	6	14	13	12											
1	2	3		5	8	7	11	9	10	12	4			6		13										14		
1	2	3		5	6		8	9	10	11	4		14		13	12										7		
1	2	3		5	6		7	9	12	11	4		13			8										10		
1		3	14	5	6	12	7		10	11	4		13		2	8										9		
1	5	3	14		6	7	10			11	4				2	8	12									9		13
1	3	14		5	6	7	8			12	4		13		2		9									10		11
1	3	14		5	6	7	8			12	4		13		2		9									10		11
1	3			5	6	7	8	13	14	12	4				2		9									10		11
1	3			5	13	7	8		12	6	4		14		2		9									10		11
1	3			5	6	7	8		10	14	4		13		2		12									9		11
1	3	12		5	6	14	7			8	4				2		9	13								10		11
1	2	3		5	6	12	7			8	4		13				9									10		11
1	2	3	14	5	6	12	7			8	4		13				9									10		11
1	2	3		5	6	7	8		12		4		11	13			9					14				10		
1	2	3		5	6	7	8	13	14	11	4		12				9									10		
	2	3		5	8	7	14	9		12			11	6			10	1			4					13		
	2				6	13	8	9	12	11	4			3			10	1			5					7		
	2			5	6	13	8	9	14	11				3			10	1			4					7		12
1			12	2	6	7	8	9	10	11	4			3							5					13		
1	2			3		7	8	9		12	4		13	6			10				5					11		
1	2		14	3		7	8	9		11	4		12	6			13				5					10		
1	2			3	8	7	11	9		14	4		13	6			12				5					10		
1	2	3	5		6	7		9	10	11	4		8			14	12									13		
1	2		5	3	6	7	8	9	10	11	4																	
1	2		5	3	6	7	8	9	10	11	4		12				13									14		
1	2		5	3		7	8	9	13	11	4			6			14									10		12
1	2	12		5	13	7		9		6	4			3		8	10									14		11
1	2		5			7	12	9	14	6	4			3		8	10									13		11
1	2	3			6	7	8		9	13	4		11	5			12									10		
1	2	3		5	6	7	8			11	4		13	12			9									10		
1	2	3		5	6	7	8	9		11	4		12	13			14									10		
1	2	3		5	6	7	8	9		11	4			13		12										10		
1	2	3		5	6	7	13	9		11	4			12		8										10		
1	2	3		5	6	7	11	9			4			14		8	12									10		13
1	2			5	6	7	12	9		11	4			3		8										10		13
1	2			5	6	7	13	9		11	4			3		8	14									10		12
1	2			3	6	7	8	9		11	4			14		13	12				5					10		
1	2	3		5	6	7	8	9	14	11	4						12									10		13
1	2	3	5		6		7	9		8	4			12			10											11
1	2	3	5		8		7	13	9	12	4			6			14									10		11
1		3		5	6	7	14	9		8				12	2		10				4					13		11
1		3	14	2	6	7	8		13		4				12		9				5					10		11
43	42	26	8	39	40	35	38	30	13	30	42	1	5	18	9	9	19	3			10					32		14
		4	7		2	6	6	3	11	10	1	2	19	9	4	6	15	1				1				8		7
	2			1	4	7	1	15	2	2	5		1			2	6									13		2

Kiraly	Boyce	Borrowdale	Hudson	Hall	Watson	McAnuff	Soares	Johnson	Macken	Hughes	Ward	Kolkka	Andrews	Leigertwood	Butterfield	Riihilahti	Freedman	Speroni	Fray	Granville	Popovic	Black	Togwell	Grabban	Berry	Morrison	Danze	Reich
1	2			3	6	7	8	9		11	4				13		12				5					10		
1	2	3		5	12	7	8	9	13	11				6			10				4							14
2	2	1		2	1	2	2	2		2	1			1			1				2					1		0
					1				1						1		1											1

Kiraly	Boyce	Borrowdale	Hudson	Hall	Watson	McAnuff	Soares	Johnson	Macken	Hughes	Ward	Kolkka	Andrews	Leigertwood	Butterfield	Riihilahti	Freedman	Speroni	Fray	Granville	Popovic	Black	Togwell	Grabban	Berry	Morrison	Danze	Reich
1	2	3	5		6	7		9		11	4		8			13	10					12			14			
1	2		5	3			8	9	13				11	6		12	10				4					7		14
1	2	3	5		6	7	13	9	12		4		14			8	10											11
3	3	2	3	1	2	2	1	3		1	2		2	1		1	3				1					1		1
							1		2				1			2						1			1			1
						1		2		1	1						1											

Kiraly	Boyce	Borrowdale	Hudson	Hall	Watson	McAnuff	Soares	Johnson	Macken	Hughes	Ward	Kolkka	Andrews	Leigertwood	Butterfield	Riihilahti	Freedman	Speroni	Fray	Granville	Popovic	Black	Togwell	Grabban	Berry	Morrison	Danze	Reich
			5							10		11	9		6	8		1	2	3	4	7	12	14	13			
			4	5		7							9		2	8		1	3			10	6	13	14		11	12
	2	3	4	5	6		7			8			12				9	1				13	14			10		11
	2	3	5		8	7		9	10				11	6			14	1			4	13				12		
	2	2	4	2	2	2	1	1	1	2		1	3	1	2	2	1	4	2	1	2	2	1			1	1	1
													1				1					2	2	2	2	1		1
										1							1			1	1							2

League Table

	P	W	D	L	F	A	Pts
Reading	46	31	13	2	99	32	106
Sheffield United	46	26	12	8	76	46	90
Watford	46	22	15	9	77	53	81
Preston North End	46	20	20	6	59	30	80
Leeds United	46	21	15	10	57	38	78
Crystal Palace	46	21	12	13	67	48	75
Wolverhampton W	46	16	19	11	50	42	67
Coventry City	46	16	15	15	62	65	63
Norwich City	46	18	8	20	56	65	62
Luton Town	46	17	10	19	66	67	61
Cardiff City	46	16	12	18	58	59	60
Southampton	46	13	19	14	49	50	58
Stoke City	46	17	7	22	54	63	58
Plymouth Argyle	46	13	17	16	39	46	56
Ipswich Town	46	14	14	18	53	66	56
Leicester City	46	13	15	18	51	59	54
Burnley	46	14	12	20	46	54	54
Hull City	46	12	16	18	49	55	52
Sheffield Wednesday	46	13	13	20	39	52	52
Derby County	46	10	20	16	53	67	50
Queen's Park Rangers	46	12	14	20	50	65	50
Crewe Alexandra	46	9	15	22	57	86	42
Millwall	46	8	16	22	35	62	40
Brighton & Hove Albion	46	7	17	22	39	71	38

2006-07

Championship

Manager: Peter Taylor

Did you know that?

In May 2006, Simon Jordan claimed a first by establishing an English club in America. Crystal Palace FC USA, based in Baltimore and playing in the USL Second Division, was intended to act as a potential feeder club but only ever finished as high as fourth in their League. The project was eventually canned by Palace, with the club renaming in 2011 and going a separate direction from its English parent.

Match No.	Date		Venue	Opponents	Result		Scorers	Attendance
1	Aug	5	A	Ipswich Town	W	2-1	McAnuff, Scowcroft	25,413
2		8	H	Southend United	W	3-1	Hudson, Cort, Freedman	18,072
3		13	H	Leeds United	W	1-0	Morrison	17,218
4		19	A	Birmingham City	L	1-2	McAnuff	20,223
5		26	H	Burnley	D	2-2	Cort, Scowcroft	16,396
6	Sep	9	A	Luton Town	L	1-2	Scowcroft	9,187
7		12	H	Southampton	L	0-2		17,084
8		16	A	Norwich City	W	1-0	Kuqi	24,618
9		23	H	Coventry City	W	1-0	Morrison	16,093
10		30	A	Hull City	D	1-1	Cort	18,099
11	Oct	14	H	Cardiff City	L	1-2	Green	18,876
12		17	H	West Bromwich Albion	L	0-2		16,105
13		21	A	Leicester City	D	1-1	Soares	28,762
14		28	H	Plymouth Argyle	L	0-1		17,084
15		31	A	Sheffield Wednesday	L	2-3	Soares, Kuqi	19,034
16	Nov	4	A	Queen's Park Rangers	L	2-4	Soares, Morrison	13,989
17		11	H	Stoke City	L	0-1		18,868
18		18	H	Barnsley	W	2-0	Morrison, Scowcroft	20,159
19		25	A	Preston North End	D	0-0		14,202
20		28	A	Wolverhampton Wanderers	D	1-1	Freedman	17,806
21	Dec	2	H	Queen's Park Rangers	W	3-0	Morrison, Freedman, Kuqi	17,017
22		9	H	Colchester United	L	1-3	Morrison	16,762
23		16	A	Derby County	L	0-1		23,875
24		22	H	Sunderland	W	1-0	Hudson	17,439
25		26	A	Southampton	D	1-1	McAnuff	30,548
26		30	A	Cardiff City	D	0-0		13,704
27	Jan	1	H	Norwich City	W	3-1	Hudson, Kuqi, Green	16,765
28		13	A	Coventry City	W	4-2	Cort, Fletcher, McAnuff, Kuqi	16,582
29		20	H	Hull City	D	1-1	Fletcher	17,012
30		30	A	Sunderland	D	0-0		26,958
31	Feb	3	H	Ipswich Town	W	2-0	Cort, Ifill	17,090
32		10	A	Leeds United	L	1-2	Cort	19,228
33		17	H	Birmingham City	L	0-1		17,233
34		20	A	Southend United	W	1-0	Ifill	10,419
35		24	H	Luton Town	W	2-1	Morrison 2	16,177
36	Mar	3	A	Burnley	D	1-1	Morrison	10,659
37		10	H	Leicester City	W	2-0	Fletcher, Watson (pen)	16,969
38		14	A	West Bromwich Albion	W	3-2	Morrison, Watson (pen), Grabban	17,960
39		17	A	Plymouth Argyle	L	0-1		11,239
40		31	H	Sheffield Wednesday	L	1-2	Morrison	21,523
41	Apr	7	H	Preston North End	W	3-0	Cort, Kuqi 2	15,985
42		9	A	Stoke City	L	1-2	own-goal (Zakuani)	13,616
43		14	H	Wolverhampton Wanderers	D	2-2	Hudson, McAnuff	17,981
44		21	A	Barnsley	L	0-2		10,277
45		29	H	Derby County	W	2-0	Morrison, Kennedy	19,545
46	May	6	A	Colchester United	W	2-0	Scowcroft, Watson	5,857

Final League Position: 12th in the Championship

Appearances
Sub appearances
1 own-goal Goals

FA Cup

3	Jan	6	H	Swindon Town	W	2-1	McAnuff, Kuqi	10,238
4		27	H	Preston North End	L	0-2		8,422

Appearances
Sub appearances
Goals

League Cup

1	Aug	22	H	Notts County	L	1-2	Hughes	4,481

Appearances
Sub appearances
Goals

Kiraly	Butterfield	Granville	Hudson	Cort	Fletcher	McAnuff	Soares	Morrison	Scowcroft	Kennedy	Freedman	Watson	Macken	Lawrence	Rinders	Borrowdale	Ward	Hughes	Reich	Black	Spence	Kuqi	Green	Turner	Speroni	Hill	Martin	Grabban
1	2	3	4	5	6	7	8	**9**	10	11	12	13																
1	2	3	4	5	6	7	8		10	11	12	13	**9**															
1	2	3	4	5	6	7	9	13	10	11	12	**8**																
1	2	3	4	5	6	7	9	14	*10*	11	12	**8**		13														
1	2	3	4	5	**6**	7	8	13	10	11	9							12										
1	2	3	4	5	**6**	7	8	14	10	11	13							12				*9*						
1			4	5		7	**8**	14	10	11	13			2		3		6				*9*	12					
1	2			5		7		9	10	11				8		3	4	**6**				13	12					
1	**2**			5		7		*9*	10	11	14	12		8		3	4	6				13						
1				5		7		**10**	8	11	13	6		2		3	4					9	12					
1			12	5		7	14		10	11	13	6		**2**		3	4					9	*8*					
1			**4**	5	6		7	14	10	11	12	8				3	2					*9*	13					
1				5	6		*8*	10		11	13	14		2		3	4		**7**			9	12					
1	12			5	**6**		8	10		11	9			2		3	*4*		7			13	14					
	2			5	6	13	7	10		12	14	8		4	1	3			**11**			*9*						
	2	3		5		7	8	10		11	12			6	1		4	13				9						
1	2	3	4	5		7	**8**	9	10	11	12							6				13						
	2	3	5		14	7	8	9	**10**	*11*	13						4	6				12		1				
	2	3	5		14	7	8	9	**10**	*11*	13						4	6				12		1				
	2	3	5		12	7	8	9	*10*	11	13						4	**6**				14		1				
	2	3	5			7	8	13			9	6		12			4	*11*				10	14	1				
		3	5			7	8	10	14			6		2	12		4	11				*9*	13	**1**				
		3	5		12	7	8	10	14	11		**6**		2			4					9	13		1			
	2		5		6	7	8	10	12	*11*	13			14		3	4					**9**			1			
	2	3	5		**6**	7	8	10		11	13				1		4		12			9						
	3		5		6	7		9	10	11		**8**		2	1		4		12			13						
			5	3	6	12		13			9			2	1		4	8	**11**			10	7					
			5	3	6	7	13			11	**9**			2	1		4					10	8			12		
			5	3	6	7	13	14		*11*	9			2	1		4					10	**8**			12		
1	3		4	5	6	7	12			11	13			2								9	8			**10**		
1	3		4	5	6		8		14	**11**	9	12		2		13						*10*				7		
1	*2*		4	5	6			9	**10**	11	13			8		3					14	12				7		
1	2		4	5	6	12		13	14	**11**	*9*			8		3						10				7		
1	**2**		4	5	6			9	10	11	12			8		3										7	14	13
1	12		4	5	6		7	10	8	**11**	9			2		3											13	
1	3		4	5	6		7	10	8		**9**	13		2							11							12
1			4	5	6		7	10	8		**9**	11		2		3		12										13
1	12		4	5	6		7	9	10			8		2		**3**		*11*									13	14
1	2		4	5	6		7	9	10		12	8				3		**11**				14						13
1			4	5	6	7	11	9	*10*	14		**8**		2		3						13				12		
1			4	5	6	**7**	11	9		13		*8*		2		3						10				12		14
1			4	5	6		8	9	14	*11*				2		3						10				**7**	13	12
1			4	5	6	7	**11**	9	13	14		8		2		3						10				12		
			4	5	6	7	11	*9*	13			**8**		2		3						10			1		12	14
			4	5	6	7		9	12	11		8		2		3						**10**			1	13		
			4	5	**6**	7	12	9	10	11		8		2		3									1	13		
29	25	15	38	37	33	31	32	31	26	34	11	19	1	31	7	24	20	12	4		1	24	5	5	5	6		
	3		1		4	3	5	10	9	4	23	6		3	1	1		4	2		1	11	9			7	5	8
			4	8	3	5	3	12	5	1	3	3										7	2			2		1

Kiraly	Butterfield	Granville	Hudson	Cort	Fletcher	McAnuff	Soares	Morrison	Scowcroft	Kennedy	Freedman	Watson	Macken	Lawrence	Rinders	Borrowdale	Ward	Hughes	Reich	Black	Spence	Kuqi	Green	Turner	Speroni	Hill	Martin	Grabban
	13		5	3	6	7		14		12	*9*			2	1		4	**11**				10	8					
	3		5		6	7		9	10	11	14			2	1		4					13	**8**			12		
	1		2	1	2	2		1	1	1	1			2	2		2	1				1	2					
	1							1		1	1											1				1		
						1																1						

Kiraly	Butterfield	Granville	Hudson	Cort	Fletcher	McAnuff	Soares	Morrison	Scowcroft	Kennedy	Freedman	Watson	Macken	Lawrence	Rinders	Borrowdale	Ward	Hughes	Reich	Black	Spence	Kuqi	Green	Turner	Speroni	Hill	Martin	Grabban
			5					10			7	6	**9**	2	1	3	4	8	11	12	13							
			1					1			1	1	1	1	1	1	1	1	1									
																				1	1							
																		1										

League Table

	P	W	D	L	F	A	Pts
Sunderland	46	27	7	12	76	47	88
Birmingham City	46	26	8	12	67	42	86
Derby County	46	25	9	12	62	46	84
West Bromwich Albion	46	22	10	14	81	55	76
Wolverhampton	46	22	10	14	59	56	76
Southampton	46	21	12	13	77	53	75
Preston North End	46	22	8	16	64	53	74
Stoke City	46	19	16	11	62	41	73
Sheffield Wednesday	46	20	11	15	70	66	71
Colchester United	46	20	9	17	70	56	69
Plymouth Argyle	46	17	16	13	63	62	67
Crystal Palace	46	18	11	17	59	51	65
Cardiff City	46	17	13	16	57	53	64
Ipswich Town	46	18	8	20	64	59	62
Burnley	46	15	12	19	52	49	57
Norwich City	46	16	9	21	56	71	57
Coventry City	46	16	8	22	47	62	56
Queen's Park Rangers	46	14	11	21	54	68	53
Leicester City	46	13	14	19	49	64	53
Barnsley	46	15	5	26	53	85	50
Hull City	46	13	10	23	51	67	49
Southend United	46	10	12	24	47	80	42
Luton Town	46	10	10	26	53	81	40
Leeds United	46	13	7	26	46	72	36

2007-08

Championship

Manager: Peter Taylor until 8 October 2007 then Neil Warnock from 11 October 2007

Did you know that?

John Bostock became the youngest-ever player to start for the Palace first team when he made his debut at home to Watford in the League on 29 October 2007, aged 15 and 287 days. His last appearance in January the following year was also against Watford, this time in an away League Cup fixture.

Match No.	Date	Venue	Opponents	Result		Scorers	Attendance
1	Aug 11	A	Southampton	W	4-1	Morrison, Scowcroft 3	25,054
2	18	H	Leicester City	D	2-2	Green, Morrison	15,607
3	26	A	Ipswich Town	L	0-1		19,382
4	Sep 1	H	Charlton Athletic	L	0-1		18,556
5	15	A	Norwich City	L	0-1		24,228
6	18	H	Coventry City	D	1-1	Green	14,455
7	22	H	Sheffield United	W	3-2	Watson (pen), Soares, Fletcher	14,131
8	29	A	Burnley	D	1-1	Hudson	10,711
9	Oct 2	A	Plymouth Argyle	L	0-1		10,451
10	6	H	Hull City	D	1-1	Scowcroft	15,769
11	20	A	Blackpool	D	1-1	Soares	9,037
12	23	H	Stoke City	L	1-3	Freedman	14,237
13	29	H	Watford	L	0-2		13,986
14	Nov 3	A	Scunthorpe United	D	0-0		6,778
15	6	A	Cardiff City	D	1-1	Watson (pen)	11,781
16	10	H	Queen's Park Rangers	D	1-1	Morrison	17,010
17	24	A	Colchester United	W	2-1	Morrison 2	5,856
18	27	H	Preston North End	W	2-1	Morrison, Hill	13,048
19	Dec 1	H	West Bromwich Albion	D	1-1	Morrison	15,247
20	4	A	Queen's Park Rangers	W	2-1	Morrison, Hill	13,300
21	8	A	Barnsley	D	0-0		10,298
22	15	H	Sheffield Wednesday	W	2-1	Morrison, Scannell	14,865
23	22	H	Plymouth Argyle	W	2-1	Scowcroft, Hill	15,097
24	26	A	Coventry City	W	2-0	Morrison, Ifill	22,134
25	29	A	Sheffield United	W	1-0	Scowcroft	23,982
26	Jan 1	H	Norwich City	D	1-1	Morrison	17,199
27	12	A	Wolverhampton Wanderers	W	3-0	Morrison, Scowcroft, Scannell	22,650
28	19	H	Bristol City	W	2-0	Hudson, Morrison	19,010
29	28	A	Leicester City	L	0-1		21,764
30	Feb 2	H	Southampton	D	1-1	Scowcroft	17,967
31	8	A	Charlton Athletic	L	0-2		26,202
32	12	H	Ipswich Town	L	0-1		16,090
33	18	A	Bristol City	D	1-1	Hills	16,446
34	23	H	Wolverhampton Wanderers	L	0-2		15,679
35	Mar 1	A	Preston North End	W	1-0	Morrison	12,347
36	4	H	Cardiff City	D	0-0		13,446
37	8	H	Colchester United	W	2-1	own-goal (Ifil), Watson	13,895
38	12	A	West Bromwich Albion	D	1-1	Moses	20,378
39	15	H	Barnsley	W	2-0	Soares, Scowcroft	17,459
40	22	A	Sheffield Wednesday	D	2-2	Lawrence, Watson	19,875
41	29	H	Blackpool	D	0-0		16,028
42	Apr 7	A	Stoke City	W	2-1	Soares, Fonte	15,756
43	12	H	Scunthorpe United	W	2-0	Soares, Morrison	15,975
44	19	A	Watford	W	2-0	Ifill, Moses	17,694
45	26	A	Hull City	L	1-2	Sinclair	24,350
46	May 4	H	Burnley	W	5-0	Watson (pen), Moses, Soares, Sinclair, Morrison	23,950

Final League Position: 5th in the Championship

Appearances
Sub appearances
1 own-goal — Goals

Play-offs

Match No.	Date	Venue	Opponents	Result		Scorers	Attendance
SF1	May 10	H	Bristol City	L	1-2	Watson (pen)	22,869
SF2	13	A	Bristol City	L	1-2*	Watson	18,842

* After extra-time

Appearances
Sub appearances
Goals

FA Cup

Match No.	Date	Venue	Opponents	Result		Scorers	Attendance
3	Jan 5	A	Watford	L	0-2		10,480

Appearances
Sub appearances

League Cup

Match No.	Date	Venue	Opponents	Result		Scorers	Attendance
1	Aug 14	A	Bristol Rovers	D	1-1*	Freedman	5,566

* After extra-time, lost 1-4 on penalties

Appearances
Sub appearances
Goals

Speroni	Lawrence	Craig	Hudson	Cort	Watson	Soares	Green	Morrison	Scowcroft	Kennedy	Kuqi	Freedman	Butterfield	Flinders	Fonte	Martin	Grabban	Fletcher	Hughes	Ifill	Idrizaj	Dickov	Hills	Songo'o	Bostock	Hill	Moses	Hall	Derry	Scannell	Halls	Danns	Robinson	Kudjodji	Ashton	Sinclair	Reid
1	2	3	4	5	6	7	8	**9**	*10*	11	12	14	13																								
1	2	3	4	5		7	8	9	10	*11*	13	14	12		**6**																					
1	2	3	4	5		7	**8**	*9*	10	11	12	13						6	14																			
1	2	3	4	5		7		9	10	11						14		*6*	**8**	12	13																	
1		3	4	5		7	*8*	13	11			12	2					6	14		**9**	10																
1		3	4	5	8	7	11		10			9	2					6																				
1		3	4	5	8	7	**11**		*10*			12	2					6	13		14	9																
1		3	4	5	8	7	11	14	*10*				2					6	13		12	**9**																
1	8	3	4	5	13	7	14	12					*2*					6	11		**9**	10																
1		3	4	5	*8*	7	14	13	10				2			12		6	**11**			9																
1	12	3	4	5	*8*	7		14	10			**9**	2			11		6				13																
1	2	3	4	5	8		14	9	7			12			13	*11*		6				**10**																
1	2		4		8			14	10			**9**			5			6	*7*		12		3	11	13													
1	2	3	4		8			12	10	11		14			5			*6*			**9**			7	13													
1	2		4		6	7		13	10	11					5					12				**9**	*8*	3	14											
1	2		4		6	*7*		9		11		14			5					10				**8**	13	3		12										
1	2		4		8	13		*9*	10	11			14		5	12				**7**						3			6								
1	2		4		8	7		10	11			**9**	14		5	12						13				3			6								
1	2		4		8	7		**9**	10						5	13						12		11		3			6								
1			4		8	*7*		9	10				2		**5**			14				12	11		3			6	13							
1	5		4		8	7		9	*10*				2					13					14	**11**		3			6	12							
1	5		4		8	7		*9*	10				2			13		14					**11**		3			6	12							
1	5		4		8	7		*9*	10			14	2											**11**		3			6	12							
1	5		4		8	7		**9**	10				2					13		14			12			3			6	*11*							
1	5		4		8	7		**9**	10				2					12		14			13			3			6	11							
1	5		4		8	7		9	10			14	**2**		12			13							3			6	*11*							
1	5		4		8	7		9	10								13					12			**3**	14		*6*	11	2						
1	5		4		8	7		**9**	10								13					12			3			6	11	2						
1	5		4		8	7		9	10		12															3	13		6	**11**	2						
1	5		4		8	**7**		9	10			13														3	14		6	*11*	2	12					
1	5		4		8			*9*	10		13	14	2							**7**									6	12	3	11					
1	5		4		**8**			9	10		13	14	2					12				3						*6*	11		7					
1	5		4		8	**7**			13		9		2		14			10				11			3			*6*	12							
1	5		4		8	7		12	14		*9*		2					10		13			**11**			3			6								
1	5		4		8			9				12	2					10		**7**			3				11		6				13				
1	5		4		8			9	12			14	2					*10*		**7**						3	11		6	13							
1	5				8	7		9	10				2		13							3			4	*11*		**6**	14			12				
1	2		4		**8**	**7**		12	9						5			10	14							3	11		6	13							
1	2		4		8	7		9	10						5											3			6	**11**			12	13			
1	2		4		8	**7**		9	10						5				14							3			6	*11*		12	13				
1	5		4		8	7		9	10				2		13														6				14		**3**	11	12
1	2		4		8	7		9							5			14							3	**10**		6	13						*11*	12
1			4		8	7		*9*				2		5			13							3	**10**		6	12			14			11	
1	**2**		4		8	7		*9*				12		5			14		13						3	10		6							11	
1			4		8	7		9				2		5					12						3	10		6	13						**11**	
1			4		8	7		*9*				2		5			13		12						3	**10**		6	14						11	
46	36	13	45	12	41	38	7	33	35	8	2	4	25		17	2		17	4	5	3	6	6	9	1	28	9		30	10	5	2			1	6	
	1				1	1	3	10	3		6	15	5		5	7	2	11	6	8	4	3	6		3		4	1		13		2	6	1			2
	1		2		5	6	2	16	9			1			1			1		2			1			3	3			2						2	

Speroni	Lawrence	Craig	Hudson	Cort	Watson	Soares	Green	Morrison	Scowcroft	Kennedy	Kuqi	Freedman	Butterfield	Flinders	Fonte	Martin	Grabban	Fletcher	Hughes	Ifill	Idrizaj	Dickov	Hills	Songo'o	Bostock	Hill	Moses	Hall	Derry	Scannell	Halls	Danns	Robinson	Kudjodji	Ashton	Sinclair	Reid
1	14		4		8	7		9	12				2		5					13						3	**10**		*6*							11	
1	**5**		4		8	7		9					2		12					14						3	13		6	10						*11*	
2	1		2		2	2		2					2		1											2	1		2	1						2	
	1								1						1					2							1											
					2																																	

Speroni	Lawrence	Craig	Hudson	Cort	Watson	Soares	Green	Morrison	Scowcroft	Kennedy	Kuqi	Freedman	Butterfield	Flinders	Fonte	Martin	Grabban	Fletcher	Hughes	Ifill	Idrizaj	Dickov	Hills	Songo'o	Bostock	Hill	Moses	Hall	Derry	Scannell	Halls	Danns	Robinson	Kudjodji	Ashton	Sinclair	Reid
	2		4		8			9	10					1	*5*			6					3		**7**	14	12	13		11							
	1		1		1			1	1					1	1			1					1		1					1							
																										1	1	1										

Speroni	Lawrence	Craig	Hudson	Cort	Watson	Soares	Green	Morrison	Scowcroft	Kennedy	Kuqi	Freedman	Butterfield	Flinders	Fonte	Martin	Grabban	Fletcher	Hughes	Ifill	Idrizaj	Dickov	Hills	Songo'o	Bostock	Hill	Moses	Hall	Derry	Scannell	Halls	Danns	Robinson	Kudjodji	Ashton	Sinclair	Reid
	12	3	4		**6**	7	8	14			10	9	2	1	5	*11*	13																				
	0	1	1		1	1	1				1	1	1	1	1	1																						
	1							1									1																				
												1																								

League Table

	P	W	D	L	F	A	Pts
West Bromwich Albion	46	23	12	11	88	55	81
Stoke City	46	21	16	9	69	55	79
Hull City	46	21	12	13	65	47	75
Bristol City	46	20	14	12	54	53	74
Crystal Palace	46	18	17	11	58	42	71
Watford	46	18	16	12	62	56	70
Wolverhampton	46	18	16	12	53	48	70
Ipswich Town	46	18	15	13	65	56	69
Sheffield United	46	17	15	14	56	51	66
Plymouth Argyle	46	17	13	16	60	50	64
Charlton Athletic	46	17	13	16	63	58	64
Cardiff City	46	16	16	14	59	55	64
Burnley	46	16	14	16	60	67	62
Queen's Park Rangers	46	14	16	16	60	66	58
Preston North End	46	15	11	20	50	56	56
Sheffield Wednesday	46	14	13	19	54	55	55
Norwich City	46	15	10	21	49	59	55
Barnsley	46	14	13	19	52	65	55
Blackpool	46	12	18	16	59	64	54
Southampton	46	13	15	18	56	72	54
Coventry City	46	14	11	21	52	64	53
Leicester City	46	12	16	18	42	45	52
Scunthorpe United	46	11	13	22	46	69	46
Colchester United	46	7	17	22	62	86	38

2008-09

Championship

Manager: Neil Warnock

Did you know that?

Palace were deducted one point by the FA at the end of the season for fielding an ineligible player. Young striker Rui Fonte, brother of Palace's Jose Fonte and on loan from Arsenal, was the reason. The Portuguese forward was a used substitute for the last game of the season against Sheffield United but his loan had already expired.

Match No.	Date	Venue	Opponents	Result		Scorers	Attendance
1	Aug 9	H	Watford	D	0-0		15,614
2	16	A	Preston North End	L	0-2		14,225
3	23	H	Burnley	D	0-0		14,071
4	30	A	Reading	L	2-4	Carle (pen), Soares	20,441
5	Sep 13	H	Swansea City	W	2-0	Carle, Watson	14,621
6	16	A	Wolverhampton Wanderers	L	1-2	Ifill	22,200
7	20	H	Plymouth Argyle	L	1-2	McCarthy	14,209
8	27	A	Ipswich Town	D	1-1	Moses	19,032
9	30	H	Charlton Athletic	W	1-0	Beattie	16,358
10	Oct 4	A	Nottingham Forest	W	2-0	Ifill, Kuqi	22,811
11	18	H	Barnsley	W	3-0	Watson 2 (1 pen), Kuqi	16,494
12	21	A	Birmingham City	L	0-1		17,706
13	25	A	Blackpool	D	2-2	Ifill, Beattie	7,597
14	28	H	Nottingham Forest	L	1-2	Kuqi	15,162
15	Nov 1	H	Sheffield Wednesday	D	1-1	Watson (pen)	14,650
16	8	A	Coventry City	W	2-0	Hill, Watson	16,883
17	15	A	Cardiff City	L	1-2	Scannell	17,478
18	22	H	Bristol City	W	4-2	Scannell, J. Fonte, Oster, Beattie	14,599
19	25	A	Norwich City	W	2-1	Oster, Beattie	24,034
20	29	H	Queen's Park Rangers	D	0-0		16,411
21	Dec 6	A	Derby County	W	2-1	McCarthy, Kuqi	27,203
22	8	H	Southampton	W	3-0	Ifill, Beattie, Kuqi	13,799
23	13	H	Doncaster Rovers	W	2-1	Lee, Kuqi (pen)	13,811
24	20	A	Sheffield United	D	2-2	McCarthy, Carle	23,045
25	26	H	Norwich City	W	3-1	Butterfield, J. Fonte 2	17,180
26	28	A	Bristol City	L	0-1		18,265
27	Jan 17	H	Ipswich Town	L	1-4	Lee	15,348
28	27	A	Charlton Athletic	L	0-1		20,627
29	31	H	Blackpool	L	0-1		13,810
30	Feb 17	A	Plymouth Argyle	W	3-1	Oster, Lee, Danns	10,710
31	21	A	Sheffield Wednesday	L	0-2		22,687
32	24	H	Birmingham City	D	0-0		12,847
33	28	A	Watford	L	0-2		15,529
34	Mar 3	H	Wolverhampton Wanderers	L	0-1		14,907
35	7	H	Preston North End	W	2-1	Danns, Stokes	16,340
36	11	A	Burnley	L	2-4	Kuqi, own-goal (Carlisle)	10,312
37	14	A	Swansea City	W	3-1	Moses, J. Fonte, Kuqi	13,663
38	17	A	Barnsley	L	1-3	Kuqi	10,885
39	21	H	Reading	D	0-0		14,567
40	Apr 4	A	Queen's Park Rangers	D	0-0		15,234
41	7	H	Coventry City	D	1-1	Cadogan	12,898
42	11	H	Cardiff City	L	0-2		14,814
43	13	A	Southampton	L	0-1		23,220
44	18	H	Derby County	W	1-0	Kuqi	14,736
45	25	A	Doncaster Rovers	L	0-2		12,031
46	May 3	H	Sheffield United	D	0-0		22,824

Final League Position: 15th in the Championship

Appearances
Sub appearances
1 own-goal — Goals

FA Cup

Round	Date	Venue	Opponents	Result	Scorers	Attendance
3	Jan 3	A	Leicester City	0-0		15,976
R	14	H	Leicester City	2-1	Scannell, Ifill	6,023
4	24	A	Watford	3-4	Hill, Ifill, Danns	10,006

Appearances
Sub appearances
Goals

League Cup

Round	Date	Venue	Opponents	Result	Scorers	Attendance
1	Aug 12	H	Hereford United	2-1	Carle, Oster	3,094
2	26	A	Leeds United	0-4		10,765

Appearances
Sub appearances
Goals

Speroni	Butterfield	Hill	Lawrence	McCarthy	Derry	Soares	Scowcroft	Scannell	Carle	Moses	Ifill	Andrew	Flahavan	Fonte J	Oster	Fletcher	Djilali	Hills	Griffit	Ertl	Watson	Lee	Thomas	Beattie	Kuqi	Danns	Clyne	Wiggins	Fonte R	Davis	Stokes	Comley	Cadogan	Pinney
1	2	3	4	5	6	7	8	**9**	10	11	12	13																						
1	2	3	4	5	6	8	9		10	12	14	13			*7*			**11**																
1	2	3	4	5	6	8	10		*11*			12		13	**7**		14		9															
1	2	3	4	**5**	*6*	8		13	10			9			7	14		11				12												
1	2	3	4		6		9	14	10		*7*	13		5	**11**		12				8													
1	2	3	4	14	6			**9**	*10*		7			5			11		12		8		13											
1	2	3	4	13	6				10	12	7			5			*11*		14		8	**9**												
1	2	3		5	6			13	*10*	11	**7**			4		14					8			9	12									
1	2	3		5	6			14	10	*11*	7			4		13					8			**9**	12									
1	2	3	12	**5**	6				10	*11*	7			4							8			9	14	13								
1		3	4		6				10	11	**7**			5	13					14	8			*9*	12		2							
1	2	3	4		6				10	**11**	7			5						14	8			9	12	13								
1	2	3	4	5	*6*				10	13	**7**				11						8			9	12	14								
1	*2*		4	5	6				10	11	7						13			14	8			**9**	12			3						
1		3	2	5	6			12			7	13		4	11						8			**10**	9									
1		3	2	5	6			**10**	12		7			4	11					13	8			9										
		3	2	5	6			10		13	7		1	4	11						8			**9**	12									
1		3		5				*10*	8	14	**7**			4	11					13	6			9	12		2							
1		3	14	5	12			11	**8**			13		4	7						6			*10*	9		2							
1		3		5	13			*10*	8		**7**			4	11				14		6			9	12		2							
1	14	3		5	12			*11*	**8**					4	7						6	13		10	9		2							
1	13	3		5	12			*11*	8		14			4	7						**6**			10	9		2							
1	14	3		*5*	6			13	8		7			4	11				10			12			**9**		2							
1	14	3		5	6			10	8	13	7			4	*11*							12			**9**		2							
1	12	3	14	**5**	6			10	8		7			4	11							*9*			13		2							
1	8		4		6			14	10		7			5	11			**3**				*9*			12	13	2							
1	12	3	**4**		6			10	8		7			5	*11*		14					9			13		2							
1	2	3	4		6			10	*8*	13	**7**			5	11							12			9	14								
1	2	4			6		13		**8**	11				5	7			3				9			*10*	14			12					
1	14	3			6			10			7			5	*11*			13				**9**			12	8	2			4				
1	14	3	12		*6*			10		11				5	7							9			13	8	2			**4**				
1	13	3	4						8	**11**				5	7			12		14		9				6	2		10					
1	6	3	4				**10**	12			7			5	*11*			14				9				8	2		13					
1		3	4		6		14	**10**			7			5	13			11				*9*				8	2				12			
1		3	**2**		6			13			7			5	11					14					9	8	12			4	*10*			
1		3			6				12	14	7			5	**11**							13			*9*	8	2			4	10			
1		4			6				7	*11*	14			5	12			3		13					9	8	2				**10**			
1		4			6				*7*	11				**5**	13			3		12					9	8	2				10	14		
1		3	4		6					11	12			5	7										9	8	2		13		**10**			
1		**3**	4		6		14		7	11	13			12											*9*	8	2			5	10			
1			2		6					11	**7**			5				3							9	8			13	4	10		12	
1		3		5	**6**				8	11															9		2		*7*	4	10	12	13	14
1		3	6	5					8	**11**				*4*				14							9		2		10		13	7	12	
1		3	4	5					8	11										6					9		2		**7**		10	12		
1		3	4	5			13		**7**									14		6					9	8	2		*11*		10		12	
1		3	2	5			14		7	**11**				4				13		6					9	*8*			12		10			
45	17	43	28	25	35	4	5	16	35	19	27	1	1	36	27		2	8	2	3	18	10		15	20	14	25	1	5	7	11	1		
	9		4	2	4		5	9	2	8	6	6		2	4	3	4	6	3	9		6	1		15	6	1		5		2	3	4	1
	1	1		3		1		2	3	2	4			4	3						5	3		5	10	2					1		1	

Speroni	Butterfield	Hill	Lawrence	McCarthy	Derry	Soares	Scowcroft	Scannell	Carle	Moses	Ifill	Andrew	Flahavan	Fonte J	Oster	Fletcher	Djilali	Hills	Griffit	Ertl	Watson	Lee	Thomas	Beattie	Kuqi	Danns	Clyne
1	8	3	4						10	12	7			5					**11**			9				6	2
1	2	5	4		6			12	10	**11**	*7*	14										9			13	8	3
1	13	3	4		**6**					10	7			5	11	12						*9*			14	8	2
3	2	3	3		2				2	2	3			2	1				1			3				3	3
	1							1		1		1				1									2		
		1						1			2															1	

Speroni	Butterfield	Hill	Lawrence	McCarthy	Derry	Soares	Scowcroft	Scannell	Carle	Moses	Ifill	Andrew	Flahavan	Fonte J	Oster	Fletcher	Djilali	Hills	Griffit	Ertl	Watson
	2	3		5	6			14	8	10	**7**	9	1	4	*11*	12	13				
		3	4	5		7			8	**10**	13	9	1			14	11	12		2	*6*
	1	2	1	2	1	1			2	2	1	2	2	1	1		1			1	1
								1			1					2	1	1			
									1						1						

League Table

	P	W	D	L	F	A	Pts
Wolverhampton	46	27	9	10	80	52	90
Birmingham City	46	23	14	9	54	37	83
Sheffield United	46	22	14	10	64	39	80
Reading	46	21	14	11	72	40	77
Burnley	46	21	13	12	72	60	76
Preston North End	46	21	11	14	66	54	74
Cardiff City	46	19	17	10	65	53	74
Swansea	46	16	20	10	63	50	68
Ipswich Town	46	17	15	14	62	53	66
Bristol City	46	15	16	15	54	54	61
Queen's Park Rangers	46	15	16	15	42	44	61
Sheffield Wednesday	46	16	13	17	51	58	61
Watford	46	16	10	20	68	72	58
Doncaster Rovers	46	17	7	22	42	53	58
Crystal Palace*	46	15	12	19	52	55	56
Blackpool	46	13	17	16	47	58	56
Coventry City	46	13	15	18	47	58	54
Derby County	46	14	12	20	55	67	54
Nottingham Forest	46	13	14	19	50	65	53
Barnsley	46	13	13	20	45	58	52
Plymouth Argyle	46	13	12	21	44	57	51
Norwich City	46	12	10	24	57	70	46
Southampton	46	10	15	21	46	69	45
Charlton Athletic	46	8	15	23	52	74	39

* Palace were deducted one point for fielding an ineligible player.

2009-10

Championship

Manager: Neil Warnock until 2 March 2010 then Paul Hart

Did you know that?

Danny Butterfield became the scorer of the fastest hat-trick in Palace history when he scored one in six minutes and 48 seconds against Wolves in the fourth round of the FA Cup at Selhurst Park on 2 February.

Match No.	Date		Venue	Opponents	Result		Scorers	Attendance
1	Aug	8	H	Plymouth Argyle	D	1-1	Lee	14,358
2		15	A	Bristol City	L	0-1		14,603
3		18	A	Ipswich Town	W	3-1	Danns, Ambrose 2	20,348
4		22	H	Newcastle United	L	0-2		20,643
5		31	A	Peterborough Utd.	D	1-1	Lee	8,473
6	Sep	12	H	Scunthorpe United	L	0-4		12,912
7		19	H	Derby County	W	1-0	Ambrose	12,760
8		26	A	West Bromwich Albion	W	1-0	N'Diaye	21,007
9		29	H	Sheffield Wednesday	D	0-0		12,476
10	Oct	3	H	Blackpool	W	4-1	N'Diaye, Danns, Ambrose, Lee	15,749
11		17	A	Cardiff City	D	1-1	Lee	21,457
12		20	A	Leicester City	L	0-2		22,220
13		24	H	Nottingham Forest	D	1-1	Ambrose	15,692
14		31	A	Preston North End	D	1-1	Ambrose	12,558
15	Nov	3	A	Queen's Park Rangers	D	1-1	Ambrose (pen)	14,377
16		7	H	Middlesbrough	W	1-0	Ambrose	15,321
17		21	A	Coventry City	D	1-1	Ambrose	18,400
18		28	H	Watford	W	3-0	Moses, Ambrose, Lee	14,085
19	Dec	5	H	Doncaster Rovers	L	0-3		13,985
20		8	A	Reading	W	4-2	Clyne, Moses 2, Ambrose	16,629
21		12	A	Sheffield United	L	0-2		25,510
22		19	H	Barnsley	D	1-1	Moses	14,279
23		26	H	Ipswich Town	W	3-1	Danns, Moses, Fonte	16,496
24		28	A	Swansea City	D	0-0		18,794
25	Jan	16	A	Plymouth Argyle	W	1-0	Moses	9,318
26		27	A	Newcastle United	L	0-2		37,886
27		30	H	Peterborough Utd.	W	2-0	Danns 2	14,699
28	Feb	6	A	Scunthorpe United	W	2-1	Danns, Ambrose	7,543
29		9	H	Swansea City	L	0-1		12,328
30		17	H	Reading	L	1-3	Scannell	13,259
31		20	H	Coventry City	L	0-1		13,333
32		27	A	Doncaster Rovers	D	1-1	Djilali	9,779
33	Mar	6	H	Sheffield United	W	1-0	Lee	13,455
34		9	H	Bristol City	L	0-1		12,844
35		13	A	Barnsley	D	0-0		11,416
36		16	H	Leicester City	L	0-1		12,721
37		20	A	Blackpool	D	2-2	Ambrose, Carle	9,702
38		23	A	Nottingham Forest	L	0-2		20,025
39		27	H	Cardiff City	L	1-2	Hill	13,464
40		30	A	Watford	W	3-1	Danns, John, Scannell	15,134
41	Apr	3	A	Middlesbrough	D	1-1	N'Diaye	18,428
42		5	H	Preston North End	W	3-1	Danns, Ambrose, Andrew	16,642
43		10	H	Queen's Park Rangers	L	0-2		20,430
44		17	A	Derby County	D	1-1	John	30,255
45		26	H	West Bromwich Albion	D	1-1	own-goal (S. Reid)	17,798
46	May	2	A	Sheffield Wednesday	D	2-2	Ambrose, Lee	37,121

Final League Position: 21st in the Championship

Appearances

Sub appearances

1 own-goals — Goals

FA Cup

3	Jan	2	A	Sheffield Wednesday	W	2-1	Danns, Andrew	8,690
4		23	A	Wolverhampton Wanderers	D	2-2	Ambrose, Lee	14,449
R	Feb	2	H	Wolverhampton Wanderers	W	3-1	Butterfield 3	10,282
5		14	H	Aston Villa	D	2-2	Ambrose, Ertl	20,486
R		24	A	Aston Villa	L	1-3	Ambrose (pen)	31,874

Appearances

Sub appearances

Goals

League Cup

R1	Aug	11	H	Torquay United	W	2-1	Ambrose 2 (1 pen)	3,140
R2		27	H	Manchester City	L	0-2		14,725

Appearances

Sub appearances

Goals

Speroni	Clyne	Hill	Lawrence	McCarthy	Derry	N'Diaye	Danns	John	Sears	Moses	Ambrose	Lee	Scannell	Butterfield	Fonte J	Ertl	Djilali	Rahavan	Smith	Carle	Hills	Davis	Andrew	Wynter	Comley	Zaha
1	2	3	4	5	6	7	8	9	10	11	13	12	14													
1		3	12	5	6	11	8		10	13	7	9	14	2	4											
1		3		5	6	11	8		10		7	9		2	4											
		3		5	6	11	8		10	12	7	9	13	2	4			1								
1		3	14	5	6	11	8		10	13	7	9		2	4				12							
1		3	5		6	10	8		13	11	7	9	12	2	4				14							
1		3		5	6		8				7	9	10	2	4	11				12						
1		3		5	6	9	8			11	7	12	10	2	4					13						
1		3		5	6	10	8			11	7	9	12	2	4				14	13						
1	2	4		5	6	13	8				7	9	10	3		11				12	14					
1		3		5	6	10	8	14	12	11	7	9	13	2	4											
1		3		5	6	11	8	12	10		13	9		2	4					7		14				
1		3		5	6		8	13	10	12	7	9		2	4	11					14					
1	2				6		8	13		10	7	9		3	4	11			12		14	5				
1		3			6	10	8	9	12		7	13		2	4	11					14	5				
1		3			6	13	8		10		7	9		2	4	11				12		5				
1		3			6	14	8	12	10		7	9		2	4	11						5	13			
1		3			6	14	8			10	7	9		2	4	11			13			5	12			
1		3			6		8		12	10	7	9		2	4	11				14		5	13			
1	2	5			6	13	8		14	10	7	12		3	4	11							9			
1	13	3			6		8		14	10	7	9	12	2	4	11						5				
1	2	3			6		8		10	11	7	9			4						13	5	12			
1	2	3			6		8		10	11	7	9			4	12						5	13			
1	2	5			6		8		13	10	7	12	14		4	11					3		9			
1	2	4			6	13	8			10	7	9		14		11					3	5	12			
1	2	5	12		6		8				7	14		3		4	13			10	11		9			
1	2	4			6		8				7	9	14	3			12			10	11	5	13			
1	2	3	4		6		8				7	9		11			12			10	14	5	13			
1	2	5			6		8				7	9	14	11		4	13			10	3		12			
1	2	4			6	14	8				7	13	12	3		11				10		5	9			
1	2	3	4		6						7	9	10			11	12			8		5	13			
1	2	3	4		6						7	9		11		13	10			8	12	5	14			
1	2	4			6	12					7	9	13	3		11				8	14	5	10			
1	2	5	4		6		12	13			7	9		3		11				8			10			
1	2	5	4		6	14	8				7	9		3		12	11			10			13			
1	2	4	12		6		8				7	9	14	3		11					13	5	10			
1		5	4		6	12	8				7	9		2		11				10	3					
1		5	4		6		8	10			7	9	12	2		11	14				3		13			
1		4		5	6		8	9			7		11			2					3		10			12
1			12	4	6	14	8	9			7		11			2				13	3	5	10			
1			2	4	6	11	8				7	9	12			3				10		5	13			
1		3	4	5	6		8	9			7		11			2				12			10			
1	12	3	4	5	6		8	9			7	13	11	2		14							10			
1	12	4		5	6	14	8	13			7		9	2		11				10	3					
1		3	4	5	6	14	8	13			7	12	9	2		11							10			
1		3	4	5	6	12		13			7	9	8	2		11						14	10			
45	19	43	14	20	46	12	41	7	11	14	44	33	11	36	22	29	2	1		14	10	19	13			
	3		5			14	1	9	7	4	2	9	15	1		4	6		5	8	9	2	14			1
	1	1				3	8	2		6	15	7	2		1		1			1			1			

Speroni	Clyne	Hill	Lawrence	McCarthy	Derry	N'Diaye	Danns	John	Sears	Moses	Ambrose	Lee	Scannell	Butterfield	Fonte J	Ertl	Djilali	Rahavan	Smith	Carle	Hills	Davis	Andrew	Wynter	Comley	Zaha
1	2	3			6		8				7	9	10		4	11						5	12	13		
1	2		12		6	10	8			11	7	9		3		4						5	13			
1	2	3	4		6		8				7	9		11			14			10		5	12		13	
1	2	4			6		8				7	9		3		11				10		5	12			
1	2		4		6		8				7	9		3		11	14			10		5	13		12	
5	5	3	2		5	1	5			1	5	5	1	4	1	4				3		5				
			1														2						5	1	2	
							1				3	1		3		1							1			

Speroni	Clyne	Hill	Lawrence	McCarthy	Derry	N'Diaye	Danns	John	Sears	Moses	Ambrose	Lee	Scannell	Butterfield	Fonte J	Ertl	Djilali	Rahavan	Smith	Carle	Hills	Davis	Andrew	Wynter	Comley	Zaha
1		3		5	6	10	8			11	7	9	14	2	4	13	12									
1	2	3		5	6	10	8		9	11	7		13		4				12	14						
2	1	2		2	2	2	2		1	2	2	1		1	2											
													2			1	1		1	1						
											2															

League Table

	P	W	D	L	F	A	Pts
Newcastle United	46	30	12	4	90	35	102
West Bromwich Albion	46	26	13	7	89	48	91
Nottingham Forest	46	22	13	11	65	40	79
Cardiff City	46	22	10	14	73	54	76
Leicester City	46	21	13	12	61	45	76
Blackpool	46	19	13	14	74	58	70
Swansea	46	17	18	11	40	37	69
Sheffield United	46	17	14	15	62	55	65
Reading	46	17	12	17	68	63	63
Bristol City	46	15	18	13	56	65	63
Middlesbrough	46	16	14	16	58	50	62
Doncaster Rovers	46	15	15	16	59	58	60
Queen's Park Rangers	46	14	15	17	58	65	57
Derby County	46	15	11	20	53	63	56
Ipswich Town	46	12	20	14	50	61	56
Watford	46	14	12	20	61	68	54
Preston North End	46	13	15	18	58	73	54
Barnsley	46	14	12	20	53	69	54
Coventry City	46	13	15	18	47	64	54
Scunthorpe United	46	14	10	22	62	84	52
Crystal Palace *	46	14	17	15	50	53	49
Sheffield Wednesday	46	11	14	21	49	69	47
Plymouth Argyle	46	11	8	27	43	68	41
Peterborough United	46	8	10	28	46	80	34

* 10 points deducted for Administration

2010-11

Championship

Manager: George Burley until 1 January 2011, Dougie Freedman from 11 January 2011

Did you know that?

Dougie Freedman became the 13th ex-Palace player to take up the managerial reigns when he took charge in January 2011.

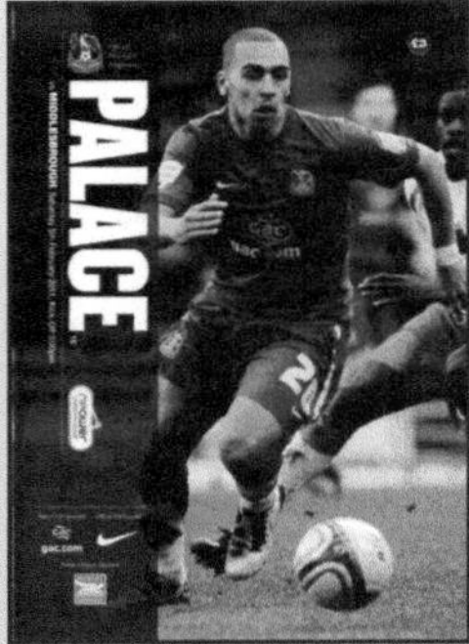

Match No.	Date		Venue	Opponents	Result		Scorers	Attendance
1	Aug	7	H	Leicester City	W	3-2	Zaha, Ambrose, Lee	17,486
2		14	A	Barnsley	L	0-1		11,353
3		21	H	Ipswich Town	L	1-2	Danns	15,781
4		28	A	Scunthorpe United	L	0-3		5,292
5	Sep	11	A	Reading	L	0-3		17,921
6		14	H	Portsmouth	W	4-1	Vaughan 3, Danns (pen)	14,219
7		18	H	Burnley	D	0-0		14,451
8		25	A	Derby County	L	0-5		28,258
9		28	A	Cardiff City	D	0-0		22,007
10	Oct	2	H	Queen's Park Rangers	L	1-2	Cadogan	17,171
11		16	H	Millwall	L	0-1		19,131
12		19	A	Norwich City	W	2-1	Bennett, Gardner	24,975
13		23	A	Preston North End	L	3-4	Garvan, Dorman, Vaughan (pen)	10,116
14		30	H	Swansea City	L	0-3		16,223
15	Nov	6	A	Middlesbrough	L	1-2	Counago	15,400
16		9	H	Watford	W	3-2	Ambrose, Garvan 2	12,353
17		13	H	Coventry City	W	2-0	Ambrose 2 (1 pen)	13,278
18		20	A	Sheffield United	L	2-3	Danns (pen), Vaughan	20,420
19		27	H	Doncaster Rovers	W	1-0	Counago	12,470
20	Dec	4	A	Leeds United	L	1-2	Danns	25,476
21		11	H	Hull City	D	0-0		13,341
22		18	A	Nottingham Forest	L	0-3		22,359
23		28	A	Bristol City	D	1-1	Danns	15,760
24	Jan	1	A	Millwall	L	0-3		16,170
25		3	H	Preston North End	W	1-0	Iversen	14,061
26		15	A	Swansea City	L	0-3		13,369
27		22	H	Bristol City	D	0-0		14,128
28		29	H	Norwich City	D	0-0		16,327
29	Feb	1	A	Watford	D	1-1	Vaughan	12,664
30		5	H	Middlesbrough	W	1-0	Vaughan	14,060
31		12	A	Coventry City	L	1-2	Iversen	16,454
32		19	H	Sheffield United	W	1-0	Ambrose	14,214
33		22	A	Portsmouth	L	0-1		15,641
34		26	H	Reading	D	3-3	Ambrose, Danns, Easter	13,845
35	Mar	5	A	Burnley	L	0-1		14,848
36		8	H	Cardiff City	W	1-0	Dikgacoi	12,549
37		12	A	Queen's Park Rangers	L	1-2	Vaughan	18,116
38		19	H	Derby County	D	2-2	Moxey, Ambrose (pen)	14,686
39	Apr	2	H	Barnsley	W	2-1	Danns, Vaughan (pen)	19,344
40		9	A	Ipswich Town	L	1-2	McCarthy	24,378
41		12	A	Leicester City	D	1-1	Scannell	22,303
42		16	H	Scunthorpe United	L	1-2	Scannell	17,810
43		22	A	Doncaster Rovers	D	0-0		14,312
44		25	H	Leeds United	W	1-0	Easter	20,142
45		30	A	Hull City	D	1-1	Sekajja	20,407
46	May	7	H	Nottingham Forest	L	0-3		18,443

Final League Position: 20th in the Championship

Appearances
Sub Appearances
Goals

FA Cup

3	Jan	8	A	Coventry City	L	1-2	Danns	8,162

Appearances
Sub Appearances
Goals

League Cup

1	Aug	10	A	Yeovil Town	W	1-0	Lee	3,720
2		24	A	Portsmouth	D	1-1*	own-goal (Sonko)	8,412

* After extra-time, lost 3–4 on penalties

Appearances
Sub Appearances
1 own-goal Goals

Speroni	Clyne	Bennett	Dorman	McCarthy	Davis	Ambrose	Garvan	Lee	Zaha	Cadogan	N'Diaye	Andrew	Djilali	Barrett	Pinney	Wright	Danns	Obika	Marrow	Counago	Davids	Parsons	Gardner	Vaughan	O'Keefe	Scannell	Iversen	Easter	Moxey	Dikgacoi	Price	Agustien	Sekajja
1	2	3	4	5	6	7	8	9	*10*	**11**	12	14	13																				
1	3		4	5	6	7	8	9	10	**11**			14			2	12																
1	2	3	4	5	6		8	*9*	10	**11**				12			7	14	13														
1	2		14	**5**	6		8			11		13	10				7	12	4	*9*	3												
1	2	3	**7**	5			8			14		13	10				11		4	12			6	*9*									
1	3		4	5			8			7		12	11				10		2	14			6	**9**									
1	3	14	4	5	6		8		12	**7**		13	*11*				10		2					9									
1	3	12	13	5	6		8		7			14	**11**				10		2		*4*			9									
1	3	12	14	5	**6**		8		7	13			*11*				10		2	9	4												
1	2	3	*10*	5			8		7	12		13	11						6	**9**	4		14										
1	2	3	10	5	6		8		7	**11**			12					14	4	9													
1	2	3	10	5			8		7				12						4	14	**11**		6	9									
1	2	3	10	5			8		7	12	13		**11**						*4*	14			6	9									
1	2		10	5		14	**8**		7		13		11	6		3		12			*4*			9									
1	2		14	5		7	8		12		13			6		*3*	11		4	**10**				9									
1	2			5	14	*7*	8		12		13			6		3	11		4	**10**				9									
1	2			5	**6**	*7*	8		10		13					3	11		4	14			12	9									
1	2			**5**	6		8		10		7					3	11		4	14				9	12								
1	2		12		6	7			10		14					3	11	13	**4**	8			5	*9*									
1	2				6	7			14		4		**10**			3	11			8			5	9	12								
1	2			5	6		10		11		4					3	7	14		8				**9**		12							
1	2		**9**	5	6	*11*	10		12		4	14				3	7			8						13							
1	2	3		5	**6**				10		14	9		12		4	7	13		8						*11*							
1	2	3		5		*7*	8		12	14		13		6			11		**4**	9						10							
1	2	3	7	5			8		*10*	12		14				13	11						6		**4**		9						
1	2		**7**	5			4		10			12				3	11			*8*			6		13		9	14					
1	3			5		7			10			13				4	11		2	**8**			6			14	12	9					
1	2			5		7			12							4	11		8			3	6	9		**10**							
1	2			5	13	**7**			*10*					6		4	11		8			3		9		12		14					
1	2			5		**7**			11							4			8	14			6	*9*		12	13	10	3				
1	2			5		7	8		11							4				12			6	*9*		14	13	**10**	3				
1	2			5	14	7			**11**							4	10			13			6	*9*		12			3	8			
1	2			5		7			14							4	10						6	*9*		**11**	13	12	3	8			
1	2			5		7			13							4	*11*						6	**9**		14	10	12	3	8			
	2			5		7										*4*	11			12			6	9		14	**10**	13	3	8	1		
1	2			5	14	7			13							4	11			12			6	*9*		13	**10**	14	3	8			
1	2			5	12	7			13							*4*	11						6	9			**10**	14	3	8			
1	2				5	7			13							*4*	11			14			6	**9**			10	12	3	8			
1	2			5		**7**			12								11						6	*9*		14	10	12	3	4		8	
1	2			5		7			14	13							11						6	**9**		12	10		3	4		*8*	
1	2			5			**8**		7								10			*9*			6	14		11	13		3	4		12	
1	2			5		7			12								11			13			6	9		14	*10*		3	**4**		8	
1	2			5		7			10	14							11			**9**			6				12		3	4		8	
1	2			5	13				7							4	11						6	12			*9*	**10**	3	8		14	
1	2		14	5	6	7	**8**		10	12						4												*9*	3			11	13
1	2			5	12	7			13							*4*	11			**9**			6			14		10	3			8	
45	46	10	14	43	17	27	26	3	26	7	4	1	10	5		27	36		20	17	6	2	26	28	1	5	11	6	17	13	1	6	
		3	6		7	1			15	9	8	12	4	2		1	1	7	1	13			2	2	3	14	6	8				2	1
		1	1	1		7	3	1	1	1							7			2			1	9		2	2	2	1	1			1

Speroni	Clyne	Bennett	Dorman	McCarthy	Davis	Ambrose	Garvan	Lee	Zaha	Cadogan	N'Diaye	Andrew	Djilali	Barrett	Pinney	Wright	Danns	Obika	Marrow	Counago	Davids	Parsons	Gardner	Vaughan	O'Keefe	Scannell	Iversen
1	2		*11*	5			4		13	7	**10**	14				3	8			12			6				9
1	1		1	1			1			1	1					1	1						1				1
									1			1								1							
																	1										

Speroni	Clyne	Bennett	Dorman	McCarthy	Davis	Ambrose	Garvan	Lee	Zaha	Cadogan	N'Diaye	Andrew	Djilali	Barrett	Pinney	Wright	Danns	Obika	Marrow	Counago	Davids	Parsons
1	2	3	4	5		7		9	12	11		10	13	6	**8**							
1	2		**4**	5			8		10	13			11	6				12	7	9	*3*	14
2	2	1	2	2		1	1	1	1	1		1	1	2	1				1	1	1	
									1	1			1					1				1
								1														

League Table

	P	W	D	L	F	A	Pts
Queen's Park Rangers	46	24	16	6	71	32	88
Norwich City	46	23	15	8	83	58	84
Swansea	46	24	8	14	69	42	80
Cardiff City	46	23	11	12	76	54	80
Reading	46	20	17	9	77	51	77
Nottingham Forest	46	20	15	11	69	50	75
Leeds United	46	19	15	12	81	70	72
Burnley	46	18	14	14	65	61	68
Millwall	46	18	13	15	62	48	67
Leicester City	46	19	10	17	76	71	67
Hull City	46	16	17	13	52	51	65
Middlesbrough	46	17	11	18	68	68	62
Ipswich Town	46	18	8	20	62	68	62
Watford	46	16	13	17	77	71	61
Bristol City	46	17	9	20	62	65	60
Portsmouth	46	15	13	18	53	60	58
Barnsley	46	14	14	18	55	66	56
Coventry City	46	14	13	19	54	58	55
Derby County	46	13	10	23	58	71	49
Crystal Palace	46	12	12	22	44	69	48
Doncaster Rovers	46	11	15	20	55	81	48
Preston North End	46	10	12	24	54	79	42
Sheffield United	46	11	9	26	44	79	42
Scunthorpe United	46	12	6	28	43	87	42

Club Honours and Records

Club Honours

Division Two/One/Championship
Champions 1978–79, 1993–94
Runners-up 1968–69
Play-off Winners 1988–89, 1996–97, 2003–04

Division Three/Three South
Champions 1920–21
Runners-up 1928–29, 1930–31, 1938–39, 1963–64

Division Four
Runners-up 1960–61

FA Cup
Final 1990
Semi-final 1976, 1995

League Cup
Semi-final 1993, 1995, 2001

Zenith Data Systems Cup
Winners 1991

Southern League Division Two
Champions 1905–06

Southern League Division One
Runners-up 1913–14

Football League South 'D' Division
Champions 1939–40

Football League South Regional League
Champions 1940–41

Football League Division Three South (South Region)
Champions 1945-46

FA Youth Cup
Winners 1977, 1978
Final 1992, 1997

PLAYERS RECORDS

Appearances

Most Senior Appearances – 660 Jim Cannon
Most League Appearances – 571 Jim Cannon
Most Consecutive Appearances – 254 John Jackson
Youngest First Team player – John Bostock 15 years 287 days
Most Full International Caps won as a Palace player

England 9	Kenny Sansom, Geoff Thomas
Scotland 2	David Hopkin, Dougie Freedman
Wales 19	Eric Young
Northern Ireland 8	Darren Patterson
Republic of Ireland 14	Paddy Mulligan
Other 36	Aki Riihilahti (Finland)

Goalscoring

Most goals scored (all senior competitions) – 165 Peter Simpson (1929–35)
Most League goals scored – 153 Peter Simpson (1929–35)
Most League goals scored in a season – 46 Peter Simpson (1930–31)
Most goals scored in a season – 54 Peter Simpson (1930–31)
Most League goals scored in a Division One/Premiership season – 21 Andy Johnson (2004–05)
Most goals scored in the FA Cup – 12 Peter Simpson
Most goals scored in the League Cup – 11 Mark Bright
Most hat-tricks scored (all competitions) – 20 Peter Simpson (includes double hat-trick v Exeter City)
Most goals scored in a League game – 6 Peter Simpson v Exeter City (home) 4 October 1930
Most goals scored in an FA Cup game – 4 Peter Simpson v Newark Town (home) 13 December 1930
Most goals scored in a League Cup game – 3 Mark Bright v Southend United (home) 25 September 1990
Ian Wright v Southend United (home) 25 September 1990
Fastest recorded goal =– 6 seconds Keith Smith v Derby County (away) 12 December 1964

Club Records

Most League Points
64 (2 for a win) 1960–61 Division Four
90 (3 for a win) 1993–94 Division One

Most League Goals
110 1960–61 Division Four

Biggest Home League Win
9–0 10 October 1959 v Barrow Division Four

Biggest Away League Win
6–0 26 January 1935 v Exeter City Division Three South
6–0 5 September 1987 v Birmingham City Division Two

Heaviest Home League Defeat
1–6 7 May 1927 v Millwall, Division Three South
1–6 27 January 1951 v Nottingham Forest, Division Three South
1–6 20 August 1994 v Liverpool, Premiership

Heaviest Away League Defeat
0–9 11 September 1989 v Liverpool, Division One

Consecutive Victories
17 14 October 1905 – 7 April 1906

Consecutive League Victories
8 9 February – 26 March 1921

Consecutive League Draws
5 28 March – 16 April 1921, 30 December 1978 – 24 February 1979, 21 September – 19 October 2002

Consecutive League Defeats
8 18 April – 19 September 1925, 1 January – 14 March 1998

Consecutive League games undefeated
18 22 February – 13 August 1969

Consecutive League games undefeated, single season
17 17 November 1928 – 23 March 1929

Consecutive League home games undefeated
32 28 February 1931 – 17 September 1932

Consecutive League away games undefeated
10 18 November 1978 – 3 April 1979

Consecutive League games without a win
20 3 March – 8 September 1962

Consecutive League home games without a win
16 4 May 1997 – 11 April 1998

Consecutive League away games without a win
31 15 March 1980 – 3 October 1982

Consecutive League games scoring
24 27 April – 28 December 1929

Consecutive League games without scoring
9 19 November 1994 – 2 January 1995

Biggest Home FA Cup win
7–0 7 October 1905 v Clapham
7–0 16 January 1929 v Luton Town

Biggest Away FA Cup win
6–0 7 January 1922 v Everton

Heaviest Home FA Cup defeat
0–6 24 January 1931 v Everton

Heaviest Away FA Cup defeat
0–9 10 February 1909 v Burnley

Biggest Home League Cup win
8–0 25 September 1990 v Southend United

Biggest Away League Cup win
3–0 26 August 1980 v Bolton Wanderers
3–0 1 November 2000 v Leicester City

Heaviest Home League Cup defeat
1–4 10 September 1974 v Bristol City
1–4 10 November 1993 v Everton

Heaviest Away League Cup defeat
0–5 1 November 1989 v Nottingham Forest
0–5 24 January 2001 v Liverpool

Highest transfer fee paid
£2.75 million Valerian Ismael January 1998 from RC Strasbourg

Highest transfer fee received
£8.6 million Andy Johnson June 2006 to Everton

Record attendance at Selhurst Park
51,482 versus Burnley, 11 May 1979, Division Two

Lowest attendance at Selhurst Park
2,165 versus Newport County 18 December 1935, Division Three South

Longest serving manager
Edmund Goodman, 18 years, 1907–25

Palace's League Records 1920-2011

BIGGEST VICTORY

Home

Division One/Premier	5–0 v Manchester Utd 16 December 1972
Division Two/One/Champ.	6–0 v Norwich City 16 April 1968, 6–0 v Birmingham City 14 March 1987
Division Three/Three South	8–0 v Exeter City 6 February 1937
Division Four	9–0 v Barrow 10 October 1959

Away

Division One/Premier	4–0 v WBA 10 February 1973
Division Two/One/Champ.	6–0 v Birmingham City 5 September 1987
Division Three/Three South	6–0 v Exeter City 26 January 1935
Division Four	5–1 v Doncaster Rovers 27 August 1960

BIGGEST DEFEAT

Home

Division One/Premier	1–6 v Liverpool 20 August 1994
Division Two/One/Champ.	0–5 v Wimbledon 24 February 1985
Division Three/Three South	1–6 v Millwall 7 May 1927, 1–6 v Nottingham Forest 27 January 1951
Division Four	1–3 v Walsall 29 April 1959, 0–2 v Carlisle Utd 21 March 1959, 0–2 v Peterborough Utd 7 September 1960, 0–2 v Millwall 31 March 1961

Away

Division One/Premier	0–9 v Liverpool 12 September 1989
Division Two/One/Champ.	0–6 v Derby County 25 December 1922, 0–6 v Sheffield Wed 22 December 1923, 0–6 v QPR 19 May 1999
Division Three/Three South	2–10 v Reading 4 September 1946, 0–8 v Coventry City 6 February 1932, 0–8 v Leyton Orient 12 November 1955
Division Four	1–7 v Notts County 2 January 1960

HIGHEST ATTENDANCE

Home

Division One/Premier	49,498 v Chelsea 27 December 1969
Division Two/One/Champ.	51,482 v Burnley 11 May 1979
Division Three/Three South	33,160 v QPR 29 March 1929
Division Four	37,774 v Millwall 31 March 1961

Away

Division One/Premier	67,814 v Manchester Utd 18 December 2004
Division Two/One/Champ.	37,886 v Newcastle Utd 27 January 2010
Division Three/Three South	33,300 v Brighton & HA 24 February 1976
Division Four	21,171 v Peterborough Utd 12 September 1960

LOWEST ATTENDANCE

Home

Division One/Premier	9,820 v Birmingham City 11 April 1981
Division Two/One/Champ.	3,744 v Carlisle Utd 1 February 1986
Division Three/Three South	2,165 v Newport C. 18 December 1935
Division Four	8,848 v Walsall 29 April 1959

Away

Division One/Premier	8,209 v Wimbledon 2 May 1990
Division Two/One/Champ.	2,555 v Shrewsbury Town. 24 March 1987
Division Three/Three South	842 v Merthyr Town 19 April 1930
Division Four	2,280 v Southport 1 January 1959

VICTORIES

Most Home Wins

Division One/Premier	11	1990–91
Division Two/One/Champ.	16	1987–88
Division Three/Three South	17	1930–31, 1963–64, 1976–77
Division Four	16	1960–61

Most Away Wins

Division One/Premier	9	1990–91
Division Two/One/Champ.	11	1993–94, 1995–96, 2003–04
Division Three/Three South	11	1975–76, 1995–96, 2003–04
Division Four	13	1960–61

Most Wins

Division One/Premier	20	1990–91
Division Two/One/Champ.	27	1993–94
Division Three/Three South	24	1920–21
Division Four	29	1960–61

Fewest Home Wins

Division One/Premier	2	1997–98
Division Two/One/Champ.	6	1973–74, 2000–01
Division Three/Three South	6	1950–51
Division Four	12	1958–59, 1959–60

Fewest Away Wins

Division One/Premier	0	1980–81
Division Two/One/Champ.	1	1982–83, 2010–11
Division Three/Three South	1	1947–48, 1948–49
Division Four	7	1959–60

Fewest Wins

Division One/Premier	6	1969–70, 1980–81
Division Two/One/Champ.	11	1973–74
Division Three/Three South	8	1948–49, 1950–51
Division Four	19	1959–60

DEFEATS

Most Home Defeats

Division One/Premier	12	1997–98
Division Two/One/Champ.	11	2000–01
Division Three/Three South	13	1955–56
Division Four	5	1959–60

Most Away Defeats

Division One/Premier	18	1980–81
Division Two/One/Champ.	16	2010–11
Division Three/Three South	17	1948–49
Division Four	11	1958–59

Most Defeats

Division One/Premier	21	1980–81, 1997–98
Division Two/One/Champ.	21	2000–01
Division Three/Three South	27	1950–51
Division Four	15	1959–60

Fewest Home Defeats

Division One/Premier	2	1990–91
Division Two/One/Champ.	2	1978–79, 1988–89
Division Three/Three South	0	1931–32
Division Four	3	1958–59, 1960–61

Fewest Away Defeats

Division One/Premier	7	1990–91, 1991–92
Division Two/One/Champ.	2	1978–79
Division Three/Three South	5	1920–21
Division Four	8	1960–61

Fewest Defeats

Division One/Premier	9	1990–91
Division Two/One/Champ.	4	1978–79
Division Three/Three South	7	1920–21
Division Four	11	1960–61

DRAWS

Most Home Draws

Division One/Premier	9	1979–80, 1992–93
Division Two/One/Champ.	11	1999–2000
Division Three/Three South	12	1975–76
Division Four	8	1958–59

Most Away Draws

Division One/Premier	9	1969–70
Division Two/One/Champ.	12	1978–79, 2009–10
Division Three/Three South	10	1963–64
Division Four	6	1959–60

Most Draws

Division One/Premier	16	1979–80, 1992–93
Division Two/One/Champ.	19	1978–79
Division Three/Three South	18	1956–57
Division Four	12	1958–59, 1959–60

Fewest Home Draws

Division One/Premier	4	1980–81
Division Two/One/Champ.	2	1981–82
Division Three/Three South	1	1925–26
Division Four	4	1960–61

Fewest Away Draws

Division One/Premier	2	1989–90
Division Two/One/Champ.	1	1986–87
Division Three/Three South	1	1935–36
Division Four	2	1960–61

Fewest Draws

Division One/Premier	7	1980–81
Division Two/One/Champ.	5	1986–87
Division Three/Three South	3	1925–26
Division Four	6	1960–61

GOALS SCORED

Most Home Goals

Division One/Premier	32	1980–81
Division Two/One/Champ.	50	1987–88
Division Three/Three South	71	1930–31
Division Four	64	1960–61

Most Away Goals

Division One/Premier	29	1991–92
Division Two/One/Champ.	39	1996–97
Division Three/Three South	36	1930–31
Division Four	46	1960–61

Most Goals

Division One/Premier	53	1991–92
Division Two/One/Champ.	86	1987–88
Division Three/Three South	107	1930–31
Division Four	110	1960–61

Fewest Home Goals

Division One/Premier	15	1997–98
Division Two/One/Champ.	18	1983–84
Division Three/Three South	18	1950–51
Division Four	54	1958–59

Fewest Away Goals

Division One/Premier	13	1971–72
Division Two/One/Champ.	9	1981–82
Division Three/Three South	11	1948–49
Division Four	23	1959–60

Fewest Goals

Division One/Premier	34	1969–70
Division Two/One/Champ.	34	1981–82
Division Three/Three South	33	1950–51
Division Four	84	1959–60

GOALS CONCEDED

Most Home Goals

Division One/Premier	39	1997–98
Division Two/One/Champ.	34	2000–01
Division Three/Three South	39	1950–51
Division Four	28	1960–61

Most Away Goals

Division One/Premier	46	1980–81
Division Two/One/Champ.	46	1922–23, 1923–24
Division Three/Three South	58	1925–26
Division Four	44	1958–59

Most Goals

Division One/Premier	83	1980–81
Division Two/One/Champ.	72	1998–99
Division Three/Three South	86	1953–54
Division Four	71	1958–59

Fewest Home Goals

Division One/Premier	13	1979–80
Division Two/One/Champ.	11	1978–79
Division Three/Three South	12	1931–32
Division Four	27	1958–59, 1959–60

Fewest Away Goals

Division One/Premier	24	1990–91
Division Two/One/Champ.	13	1978–79
Division Three/Three South	17	1920–21
Division Four	37	1959–60

Fewest Goals

Division One/Premier	41	1990–91
Division Two/One/Champ.	24	1978–79
Division Three/Three South	34	1920–21
Division Four	64	1959–60

CUP COMPETITIONS (1905–2011)

Rounds Eliminated

FA Cup		**League Cup**	
Final	1	Final	
Semi-final	2	Semi-final	3
6	3	5	4
5	11	4	7
4	14	3	13
3	44	2	19
2	9	1	5
1	11		

Prior to the 1925–26 season the present third round of the FA Cup was called the first round, and the table reflects this current situation.

Summary of Palace's League Seasons

SEASON	DIV.		HOME					AWAY					Pts.	Pos.
		P	W	D	L	F	A	W	D	L	F	A		
SOUTHERN LEAGUE														
Division Two														
1905-06		24	10	1	1	42	7	9	3	0	24	7	42	1
Division One														
1906-07		38	7	4	8	29	28	1	5	13	17	38	25	19
1907-08		38	10	4	5	35	28	7	6	6	19	23	44	4
1908-09		40	10	4	6	42	23	2	8	10	20	39	36	16
1909-10		42	13	3	5	48	20	7	3	11	21	30	46	7
1910-11		38	11	5	3	35	23	6	8	5	20	25	47	4
1911-12		38	11	5	3	43	14	4	5	10	27	32	40	7
1912-13		38	13	3	3	38	13	4	8	7	17	23	45	5
1913-14		38	12	5	2	41	13	5	11	3	19	19	50	2
1914-15		38	8	4	7	24	25	5	4	10	23	36	34	15
Competition suspended due to World War One														
1919-20		42	15	5	1	44	15	7	7	7	25	28	56	3
FOOTBALL LEAGUE														
Division Three														
1920-21		42	15	4	2	45	17	9	7	5	25	17	59	1
Division Two														
1921-22		42	9	6	6	28	20	4	7	10	17	31	39	14
1922-23		42	10	7	4	33	16	3	4	14	21	46	37	16
1923-24		42	11	7	3	37	19	2	6	13	16	46	39	15
1924-25		42	8	4	9	23	19	4	6	11	15	35	34	21
Division Three South														
1925-26		42	16	1	4	50	21	3	2	16	25	58	41	13
1926-27		42	12	6	3	57	33	6	3	12	27	48	45	6
1927-28		42	15	3	3	46	23	3	9	9	33	49	48	5
1928-29		42	14	2	5	40	25	9	6	6	41	42	54	2
1929-30		42	14	5	2	56	26	3	7	11	25	48	46	9
1930-31		42	17	2	2	71	20	5	5	11	36	51	51	2
1931-32		42	14	7	0	48	12	6	4	11	26	51	51	4
1932-33		42	14	4	3	51	21	5	4	12	27	43	46	5
1933-34		42	11	6	4	40	25	5	3	13	31	42	41	12

SEASON	DIV.		HOME					AWAY					Pts.	Pos.
		P	W	D	L	F	A	W	D	L	F	A		
1934-35		42	15	3	3	51	14	4	7	10	35	50	48	5
1935-36		42	15	4	2	64	20	7	1	13	32	54	49	6
1936-37		42	11	7	3	45	20	2	5	14	17	41	38	14
1937-38		42	14	4	3	45	17	4	8	9	22	30	48	7
1938-39		42	15	4	2	49	18	5	8	8	22	34	52	2
Competition suspended due to World War Two														
1946-47		42	9	7	5	29	19	4	4	13	20	43	37	18
1947-48		42	12	5	4	32	14	1	8	12	17	35	39	13
1948-49		42	7	8	6	27	27	1	3	17	11	49	27	22
1949-50		42	12	5	4	35	21	3	9	9	20	33	44	7
1950-51		46	6	5	12	18	39	2	6	15	15	45	27	24
1951-52		46	9	7	7	32	28	6	2	15	29	52	39	19
1952-53		46	12	7	4	40	26	3	6	14	26	56	43	13
1953-54		46	11	7	5	41	30	3	5	15	19	56	40	22
1954-55		46	9	11	3	32	24	2	5	16	20	56	38	20
1955-56		46	7	3	13	27	32	5	7	11	27	51	34	23
1956-57		46	7	10	6	31	28	4	8	11	31	47	40	20
1957-58		46	12	5	6	46	30	3	8	12	24	42	43	14
Division Four														
1958-59		46	12	8	3	54	27	8	4	11	36	44	52	7
1959-60		46	12	6	5	61	27	7	6	10	23	37	50	8
1960-61		46	16	4	3	64	28	13	2	8	46	41	64	2
Division Three														
1961-62		46	8	8	7	50	41	6	6	11	33	39	42	15
1962-63		46	10	7	6	38	22	7	6	10	30	36	47	11
1963-64		46	17	4	2	38	14	6	10	7	35	37	60	2
Division Two														
1964-65		42	11	6	4	37	24	5	7	9	18	27	45	7
1965-66		42	11	7	3	29	16	3	6	12	18	36	41	11
1966-67		42	14	4	3	42	23	5	6	10	19	32	48	7
1967-68		42	11	4	6	34	19	3	7	11	22	37	39	11
1968-69		42	14	4	3	45	24	8	8	5	25	23	56	2
Division One														
1969-70		42	5	6	10	20	36	1	9	11	14	32	27	20
1970-71		42	9	5	7	24	24	3	6	12	15	33	35	18
1971-72		42	4	8	9	26	31	4	5	12	13	34	29	20
1972-73		42	7	7	7	25	21	2	5	14	16	37	30	21
Division Two														
1973-74		42	6	7	8	24	24	5	5	11	19	32	34	20
Division Three														
1974-75		46	14	8	1	48	22	4	7	12	18	35	51	5

SEASON	DIV.		HOME					AWAY					Pts.	Pos.
		P	W	D	L	F	A	W	D	L	F	A		
1975-76		46	7	12	4	30	20	11	5	7	31	26	53	5
1976-77		46	17	5	1	46	15	6	8	9	22	25	59	3
Division Two														
1977-78		42	9	7	5	31	20	4	8	9	19	27	41	9
1978-79		42	12	7	2	30	11	7	12	2	21	13	57	1
Division One														
1979-80		42	9	9	3	26	13	3	7	11	15	37	40	13
1980-81		42	6	4	11	32	37	0	3	18	15	46	19	22
Division Two														
1981-82*		42	9	2	10	25	26	4	7	10	9	19	48	15
1982-83		42	11	7	3	31	17	1	5	15	12	35	48	15
1983-84		42	8	5	8	18	18	4	6	11	24	34	47	18
1984-85		42	8	7	6	25	27	4	5	12	21	38	48	15
1985-86		42	12	3	6	29	22	7	6	8	28	30	66	5
1986-87		42	12	4	5	35	20	7	1	13	16	33	62	6
1987-88		44	16	3	3	50	21	6	6	10	36	38	75	6
1988-89		46	15	6	2	42	17	8	6	9	29	32	81	3
Division One														
1989-90		38	8	7	4	27	23	5	2	12	15	43	48	15
1990-91		38	11	6	2	26	17	9	3	7	24	24	69	3
1991-92		42	7	8	6	24	25	7	7	7	29	36	57	10
Premiership														
1992-93		42	6	9	6	27	25	5	7	9	21	36	49	20
Division One														
1993-94		46	16	4	3	39	18	11	5	7	34	28	90	1
Premiership														
1994-95		42	6	6	9	16	23	5	6	10	18	26	45	19+
Division One														
1995-96		46	9	9	5	34	22	11	6	6	33	26	75	3
1996-97		46	10	7	6	39	22	9	7	7	39	26	71	6
Premiership														
1997-98		38	2	5	12	15	39	6	4	9	22	32	33	20
Division One														
1998-99		46	11	10	2	43	27	3	6	14	15	45	58	14
1999-2000		46	7	11	5	33	26	6	4	13	24	41	54	15
2000-01		46	6	6	11	28	34	6	7	10	29	36	49	21
2001-02		46	13	3	7	42	22	7	3	13	28	40	66	10
2002-03		46	8	10	5	29	17	6	7	10	30	35	59	14
2003-04		46	10	8	5	34	25	11	2	10	38	36	73	6
Premiership														
2004-05		38	6	5	8	21	19	1	7	11	20	43	33	18

SEASON	DIV.	HOME						AWAY					Pts.	Pos.
		P	W	D	L	F	A	W	D	L	F	A		
Championship														
2005-06		46	13	6	4	39	20	8	6	9	28	28	75	6
2006-07		46	12	3	8	33	22	6	8	9	26	29	65	12
2007-08		46	9	9	5	31	23	9	8	6	27	19	71	5
2008-09		46	9	8	6	26	19	6	4	13	26	36	56#	15
2009-10		46	8	5	10	24	27	6	12	5	26	26	49##	21
2010-11		46	11	6	6	28	24	1	6	16	16	45	48	20

NOTES

When the Premiership was introduced the former Division Two became known as Division One and subsequently The Championship. *First season of three points for win. +Relegated fourth from bottom (only season) to reduce number of clubs to 20. #One point deducted for fielding an ineligible player. ##Ten points deducted for entering Administration.

Summary For League Records

	Seasons	P	W	D	L	F	A
Premiership	4	160	37	49	74	160	243
Division One	9	370	100	107	163	386	547
Division Two/One/Championship	35	1536	569	427	540	1974	1891
Division Three/Three South	33	1442	551	378	513	2250	2185
Division Four	3	138	68	30	40	284	204
Total	**84**	**3646**	**1325**	**991**	**1330**	**5054**	**5070**
Southern League							
Division One	10	390	158	107	125	587	495
Division Two	1	24	19	4	1	66	14
Total	**11**	**414**	**177**	**111**	**126**	**653**	**509**
FA Cup		260	96	68	96	370	367
League Cup *		173	75	42	56	267	218
Full Members/Simod/Zenith Data Cup		23	14	1	8	44	33
Play-offs		17	8	1	8	22	21
Inter-Toto Cup (1998–99)	2	0	0	2	0	4	
Anglo-Italian (1993–94)	2	1	0	1	4	4	

* League Cup ties decided by the 'away goals' rule or a penalty shoot out are not included. Crystal Palace have won one tie and lost one tie on 'away goals'. Crystal Palace have won three ties and lost three ties on penalty shoot-outs.

Against Other Clubs

CLUB	P	HOME W	HOME D	HOME L	HOME F	HOME A	AWAY W	AWAY D	AWAY L	AWAY F	AWAY A
Aberdare Athletic	4	0	1	1	0	1	1	0	1	3	4
Accrington Stanley	2	1	0	0	9	2	1	0	0	3	2
Aldershot	48	16	6	2	44	16	6	4	14	25	40
Arsenal	26	1	6	6	12	25	1	2	10	10	32
Aston Villa	26	5	6	2	12	6	2	3	8	10	23
Barnsley	56	13	4	11	34	28	8	6	14	36	46
Barrow	6	2	1	0	15	4	2	0	1	4	1
Birmingham City	40	10	5	5	31	17	5	2	13	20	29
Blackburn Rovers	40	11	4	5	33	18	5	4	11	22	33
Blackpool	12	5	3	4	18	13	2	3	7	11	24
Bolton Wanderers	34	7	7	3	23	18	0	7	10	12	33
Bournemouth	64	19	7	6	60	29	3	8	21	31	75
Bradford City	24	8	3	1	22	7	6	2	4	15	11
Bradford Park Avenue	12	4	2	0	14	2	0	1	5	3	15
Brentford	30	10	2	3	27	18	3	2	10	21	36
Brighton & Hove Albion	84	23	9	10	73	40	7	11	25	43	74
Bristol City	70	22	7	6	73	37	5	13	17	27	56
Bristol Rovers	52	19	2	5	52	23	7	5	14	30	50
Burnley	28	4	6	4	16	11	2	5	7	15	22
Bury	22	8	2	1	20	10	3	5	3	13	14
Cambridge United	8	1	3	0	4	3	1	2	1	3	2
Cardiff City	56	17	6	5	51	25	9	12	7	34	30
Carlisle United	26	7	3	3	24	13	1	5	7	15	29
Charlton Athletic	54	18	4	5	45	19	6	9	12	30	35
Chelsea	32	3	6	7	12	21	1	8	7	15	29
Chester City	10	2	1	2	14	10	1	0	4	5	10
Chesterfield	6	0	2	1	1	4	2	0	1	5	3
Colchester United	28	4	5	5	18	21	6	4	4	22	21
Coventry City	96	15	19	14	56	57	13	13	22	126	154
Crewe Alexandra	20	5	4	1	21	10	4	4	2	13	13
Darlington	6	3	0	0	9	3	2	1	0	6	2
Derby County	60	13	9	8	39	24	5	6	19	23	64
Doncaster Rovers	10	4	0	1	12	5	2	2	1	8	5
Everton	26	6	3	4	15	14	2	4	7	11	28
Exeter City	60	15	11	4	54	26	9	6	15	44	65
Fulham	38	7	7	5	28	23	3	6	10	19	31

CLUB		HOME					AWAY				
	P	W	D	L	F	A	W	D	L	F	A
Gateshead	12	2	3	1	8	6	2	2	2	7	7
Gillingham	64	17	8	7	71	38	8	8	16	39	55
Grimsby Town	38	14	0	5	40	14	7	3	9	22	28
Halifax Town	8	1	3	0	6	5	1	2	1	7	7
Hartlepool United	6	1	1	1	8	6	2	0	1	6	6
Hereford United	4	0	2	0	4	4	0	1	1	1	3
Huddersfield Town	36	5	10	3	20	18	6	6	6	17	27
Hull City	40	6	8	6	26	21	4	7	9	19	36
Ipswich Town	76	14	14	10	62	51	10	9	19	52	70
Leeds United	48	10	9	5	27	18	5	4	15	19	41
Leicester City	44	12	3	7	31	25	3	10	9	20	32
Leyton Orient	60	18	9	3	48	26	7	8	15	25	48
Lincoln City	4	1	0	1	5	4	0	0	2	4	6
Liverpool	26	4	4	5	10	19	1	2	10	7	38
Luton Town	50	14	8	3	56	32	4	7	14	28	50
Manchester City	42	7	6	8	24	25	5	6	10	22	32
Manchester United	32	4	5	7	23	27	2	2	12	9	33
Mansfield Town	18	8	1	0	29	8	2	4	3	9	11
Merthyr Town	12	5	1	0	17	2	1	2	3	9	16
Middlesbrough	36	10	3	5	31	19	4	6	8	17	27
Millwall	82	15	13	13	56	53	10	10	21	47	71
Nelson	2	0	1	0	1	1	0	0	1	2	4
Newcastle United	26	5	1	7	12	17	2	3	8	7	18
Newport County	52	18	7	1	65	18	11	6	9	41	37
Northampton Town	70	14	10	11	64	49	3	11	21	30	81
Norwich City	102	31	9	11	95	48	12	8	31	56	90
Nottingham Forest	46	7	9	7	27	29	5	3	15	20	43
Notts County	38	9	5	5	30	22	7	6	6	21	25
Oldham Athletic	40	13	4	3	40	20	3	6	11	18	31
Oxford United	16	5	3	0	13	6	4	2	2	14	10
Peterborough United	18	4	3	2	13	10	0	6	3	6	14
Plymouth Argyle	46	11	6	6	44	28	8	2	13	23	49
Portsmouth	50	14	4	7	51	28	4	14	7	30	36
Port Vale	46	8	10	5	26	19	6	4	13	24	48
Preston North End	40	14	4	2	29	10	3	7	10	15	28
Queen's Park Rangers	88	15	17	12	55	47	14	9	21	54	75
Reading	72	12	13	11	54	51	10	7	19	48	78
Rochdale	4	2	0	0	8	1	0	1	1	2	6
Rotherham United	26	8	5	0	23	8	5	3	5	18	22
Scunthorpe United	6	1	0	2	3	6	1	1	1	2	4

CLUB		HOME					AWAY				
	P	W	D	L	F	A	W	D	L	F	A
Sheffield United	50	11	6	8	32	25	9	6	10	28	29
Sheffield Wednesday	48	11	9	4	36	18	3	6	15	20	44
Shrewsbury Town	42	7	7	7	33	29	3	10	8	24	29
Southampton	58	13	7	9	43	36	4	7	18	25	52
Southend United	72	22	8	6	77	43	11	7	18	52	74
Southport	6	2	1	0	8	2	1	1	1	6	6
Stockport County	18	5	4	0	23	11	4	3	2	12	12
Stoke City	46	13	3	7	39	23	7	8	8	26	30
Sunderland	28	9	3	2	20	7	1	6	7	6	13
Swansea City	16	3	2	3	12	9	1	2	5	4	12
Swindon Town	78	23	10	6	87	35	8	12	19	49	74
Thames	4	2	0	0	4	2	2	0	0	5	1
Torquay United	54	16	8	3	70	30	6	7	14	35	52
Tottenham Hotspur	28	2	4	8	16	24	3	6	5	12	19
Tranmere Rovers	16	4	3	1	11	8	4	1	3	11	11
Walsall	60	23	2	5	72	27	5	14	11	35	49
Watford	94	25	10	12	84	46	15	10	22	70	81
West Bromwich Albion	44	7	8	7	25	24	6	5	11	28	34
West Ham United	22	2	4	5	12	21	1	4	6	7	19
Wigan Athletic	2	0	1	0	1	1	0	0	1	0	5
Wimbledon	24	7	1	4	22	19	4	4	4	15	16
Wolverhampton Wand.	50	8	9	8	37	34	6	6	13	24	31
Workington	6	1	1	1	5	4	1	1	1	5	2
Wrexham	16	7	1	0	18	6	5	3	0	16	9
York City	6	2	1	0	2	0	1	1	1	4	3

Southern League Record Against Other Clubs

CLUB		HOME					AWAY				
	P	W	D	L	F	A	W	D	L	F	A
Bradford Park Avenue	2	0	1	0	1	1	1	0	0	1	0
Brentford	16	5	2	1	13	8	1	2	5	6	10
Brighton & Hove Albion	20	3	6	1	15	8	4	1	5	10	16
Bristol Rovers	20	8	2	0	30	11	1	7	2	12	13
Cardiff City	6	1	1	1	5	3	1	0	2	3	8
Coventry City	12	4	0	2	12	4	2	2	2	8	8
Croydon Common	4	1	0	1	3	5	1	1	0	2	1
Exeter City	16	4	3	1	10	1	1	5	2	10	12
Fulham	2	0	0	1	0	3	0	0	1	1	2
Fulham Reserves	2	1	0	0	5	0	0	1	0	2	2
Grays United	2	1	0	0	9	1	1	0	0	3	0
Leyton	14	4	2	1	16	8	5	1	1	11	4
Luton Town	16	5	0	3	19	12	4	1	3	14	15
Merthyr Town	6	2	1	0	6	3	2	1	0	3	1
Millwall	20	9	0	1	21	3	3	3	4	7	8
New Brompton/Gillingham	20	5	2	3	21	15	2	3	5	14	21
Newport County	2	1	0	0	3	0	0	0	1	0	1
Northampton Town	20	3	4	3	15	12	1	3	6	7	16
Norwich City	20	8	0	2	25	7	2	3	5	8	14
Plymouth Argyle	20	5	1	4	15	12	1	6	3	7	12
Portsmouth	18	7	1	1	18	9	1	4	4	3	13
Portsmouth Reserves	2	1	0	0	1	0	0	1	0	1	1
Queen's Park Rangers	20	6	1	3	21	11	3	2	5	12	17
Reading	18	6	3	0	23	8	0	4	5	6	15
Reading Reserves	2	1	0	0	3	0	1	0	0	1	0
Southampton	20	5	3	2	23	9	5	3	2	24	19
Southampton Reserves	2	0	0	1	3	4	1	0	0	2	0
Southend United	12	1	4	1	8	4	1	3	2	7	10
Southern United	2	1	0	0	4	0	1	0	0	1	0
St Leonard's United	2	1	0	0	3	1	1	0	0	3	0

CLUB		HOME					AWAY				
	P	W	D	L	F	A	W	D	L	F	A
Stoke City	4	1	0	1	2	2	0	1	1	1	2
Swansea Town	2	1	0	0	2	1	1	0	0	1	0
Swindon Town	20	5	2	3	19	15	1	3	6	9	18
Swindon Town Reserves	2	1	0	0	3	0	1	0	0	2	1
Tottenham Hotspur	4	0	0	2	0	3	1	0	1	2	4
Watford	20	7	1	2	18	9	0	3	7	6	24
Watford Reserves	2	1	0	0	4	0	1	0	0	3	1
West Ham United	18	3	3	3	15	15	4	3	2	15	10
West Ham United Reserves	2	1	0	0	3	1	0	1	0	0	0
Wycombe Wanderers	2	1	0	0	4	0	1	0	0	4	1

First XI Friendlies

This section contains friendly matches played by a First XI of the football club. We acknowledge that this may not be considered complete but is as comprehensive as we have researched and gives a flavour of the variety of fixtures undertaken. This section also contains pre-season matches that took place between the club's own players, usually known as Trial or Practice Games. In recent years friendlies have become more difficult to differentiate between first team and reserves (or Club XI) as successive managers have chosen to involve as many players as possible, sometimes changing the whole XI between start and finish.

DATE	OPPONENTS	VENUE	RESULT
SOUTHERN LEAGUE			
1905–06			
9 September 1905	Eltham	H	4–0
21 September 1905	Fulham	H	1–1
30 September 1905	Second Grenadier Guards	H	1–0
30 November 1905	Norwich City	A	2–0
16 December 1905	Newcastle United Reserves	A	2–2
3 February 1906	Croydon Common	A	4–0
24 February 1906	West Beckenham	H	17–2
31 March 1906	Woolwich Arsenal Reserves	A	2–2
28 April 1906	Luton Town	A	1–0
1906–07			
12 September 1906	Chelsea	H	4–0
25 December 1906	West Norwood	A	3–1
1907–08			
26 December 1907	Plymouth Argyle	H	1–1
17 April 1908	Norwich City	A	0–3
29 April 1908	Croydon Common	A	3–2
16 May 1908	Slavia (Prague)	A	5–4
17 May 1908	Slavia (Prague)	A	4–1
20 May 1908	Smichov (Prague)	A	7–1
21 May 1908	Slavia (Prague)	A	2–0
23 May 1908	Koniggratz	A	10–1
24 May 1908	Kladno	A	6–1
1908–09			
9 April 1909	Nunhead	A	4–2
1909–10			
4 October 1909	Ton Pentre	A	1–3

DATE	OPPONENTS	VENUE	RESULT
5 October 1909	Cardiff City (at Cardiff Arms Park)	A	3–3
5 February 1910	Clapton Orient	A	3–2
1910–11			
14 December 1910	Reading	A	2–1
4 April 1911	Aberdare	A	0–1
14 April 1911	Nunhead	A	6–2
22 April 1911	East Anglian League XI (at Colchester)	A	4–2
24 April 1911	East Anglian League XI (at Yarmouth)	A	4–0
29 April 1911	Croydon Common	A	1–1
1911–12			
2 December 1911	Portsmouth	A	1–0
1913–14			
8 May 1914	Copenhagen Select XI (Denmark)	A	1–2
10 May 1914	Copenhagen Select XI (Denmark)	A	2–4
15 May 1914	Gothenburg	A	4–1
17 May 1914	Gothenburg	A	3–1
22 May 1914	Christians (Norway)	A	6–1
24 May 1914	Christians (Norway)	A	4–1
1914–15			
27 August 1914	Millwall (Prince of Wales War Relief)	A	1–5
World War One			
29 January 1916	Croydon Common (War Comforts Fund)	A	2–0
5 May 1917	Millwall (J. Williams Benefit)	A	4–1
13 April 1918	Queen's Park Rangers	A	1–2
20 April 1918	Queen's Park Rangers	H	3–1
27 April 1918	Clapton Orient (National War Fund)	H	2–0
4 May 1918	Clapton Orient (National War Fund)	A	2–0
11 May 1918	Millwall	A	0–0
31 August 1918	Millwall (first game at The Nest)	H	4–1
26 April 1919	Tottenham Hotspur	H	2–1
3 May 1919	Millwall	A	2–0
10 May 1919	Millwall	H	0–4
1919–20			
21 February 1920	Corinthians	H	4–3

DATE	OPPONENTS	VENUE	RESULT
FOOTBALL LEAGUE			
1920–21			
20 August 1920	Public Trial (Colours v Stripes)	H	0–1
1921–22			
20 August 1921	Public Trial (Stripes v Reds)	H	4–2
26 April 1922	Metropolitan Police A.A, Team (Beckenham)		
1922–23			
19 August 1922	Public Practice Match (Reds v Blues)	H	5–0
2 October 1922	Northampton Town	A	2–0
3 February 1923	Corinthians (at The Crystal Palace)	A	3–3
25 April 1923	Croydon & District XI (Phil Bates Benefit)	H	3–0
1923–24			
18 August 1923	Public Practice Match (Reds v Blues)	H	1–2
1924–25			
August 1924	Private Practice Match (Reds v Blues) (Played behind closed doors at The Nest)	H	3–0
19 November 1924	Folkestone (Albert Feebery Benefit)	H	2–2
21 February 1925	Corinthians	H	4–0
29 April 1925	Corinthians (at The Crystal Palace)	A	2–4
1925–26			
22 August 1925	Public Trial Game (Reds v Blues)	H	2–1
28 April 1926	Sutton United	A	9–1
1926–27			
21 August 1926	Public Trial Game (Cardinals v Blues)	H	6–3
11 December 1926	Corinthians	H	2–4
8 January 1927	Bristol City	H	7–3
27 April 1927	Jack Little's XI (Jack Little Benefit)	H	2–0
1927–28			
20 August 1927	Public Trial Game (Reds v Blues)	H	2–1
1928–29			
18 August 1928	Public Trial Game (Reds v Blues)	H	2–2
2 January 1929	Corinthians (at The Crystal Palace)	A	1–4
13 March 1929	Corinthians (Harry, Hamilton & Greener Benefit)	H	3–3
1929–30			
24 August 1929	Public Trial Game (Reds v Blues)	H	4–3
25 January 1930	West Bromwich Albion	H	1–2
1 May 1930	Kettering Town (Kettering Hospital Cup)	A	1–0

DATE	OPPONENTS	VENUE	RESULT
1930–31			
23 August 1930	Public Trial Game (Reds v Blues)	H	3–4
15 April 1931	Oxford & Cambridge Universities (Billy Callender Benefit)	H	4–0
1931–32			
15 August 1931	Public Trial Game (Reds v Blues)	H	6–1
22 August 1931	Public Trial Game (Reds v Blues)	H	1–1
13 February 1932	Charlton Athletic	A	5–4
20 February 1932	Corinthians	H	2–3
27 April 1932	British Army (George Clarke & Billy Turner Benefit)	H	3–1
1932–33			
13 August 1932	Public Trial Game (Cardinal & Blues v Blues)	H	2–2
20 August 1932	Public Trial Game (Cardinal & Blues v Blues)	H	3–3
24 April 1933	Guildford City	A	1–7
26 April 1933	Fulham (Albert Harry Second Benefit)	H	2–2
3 May 1933	Beckenham (Phil Bates Second Benefit)	A	4–2
1933–34			
12 August 1933	First Practice Match (Reds v Blues)	H	4–4
19 August 1933	Final Practice Match (Reds v Blues)	H	4–1
1934–35			
11 August 1934	Public Trial Game (Reds v Blues)	H	3–1
18 August 1934	Public Trial Game (Reds v Blues)	H	0–1
31 October 1934	Corinthians (Peter Simpson Benefit)	H	3–2
8 December 1934	Millwall	H	6–2
30 April 1935	Aberdeen	H	1–1
1935–36			
17 August 1935	Public Trial Game (Reds v Blues)	H	5–2
24 August 1935	Public Trial Game (Reds v Blues)	H	3–3
20 November 1935	Corinthians	H	3–1
25 January 1936	Millwall	H	3–2
1936–37			
15 August 1936	Public Trial Game (Blues v Reds)	H	0–0
22 August 1936	Public Trial Game (Blues v Reds)	H	3–2
28 October 1936	Corinthians	H	4–0
12 December 1936	Aldershot	H	4–1
24 February 1937	Dutch National XI (Rotterdam)	A	2–2
10 April 1937	Grimsby Town	H	6–3
1937–38			
14 August 1937	Public Trial Game (Red & Blue Stripes v Whites)	H	1–0
21 August 1937	Public Trial Game (Red & Blue Stripes v Whites)	H	0–5
16 February 1938	The Army (Central Command Ground, Aldershot)	A	5–4

DATE	OPPONENTS	VENUE	RESULT
23 March 1938	Royal Netherlands Voetbalbond (Sparta Rotterdam FC)	A	2–3
24 March 1938	Colchester United (Ronnie Dunn Benefit)	A	1–2
28 March 1938	Tunbridge Wells Rangers (Charles Goddard Benefit)	A	1–3
1938–39			
13 August 1938	Public Trial Game (Colours v Whites)	H	1–1
4 January 1939	Belgium National XI (Brussels)	A	4–5
1939–40			
12 August 1939	Public Trial Game (Blues v Whites)	H	4–3
World War Two			
23 September 1939	Guildford City	A	0–5
30 September 1939	Brentford	A	0–3
7 October 1939	Brighton & Hove Albion	H	2–2
14 October 1939	Brentford	H	1–1
26 April 1941	Royal Air Force	H	3–2
3 May 1941	Short's Sports	A	3–2
25 April 1942	Leicester City	H	1–3
2 May 1942	Charlton Athletic	H	1–3
16 May 1942	Reading	A	2–1
25 May 1942	Tottenham Hotspur	H	3–5
17 April 1943	Brentford	A	4–3
24 April 1943	Brentford	H	2–2
26 April 1943	Millwall	H	4–2
1 May 1943	Short's Sports	A	6–0
1 April 1944	Millwall	H	7–0
15 April 1944	West Ham United	H	4–1
7 April 1945	Tottenham Hotspur	H	3–1
5 May 1945	Portsmouth	A	5–4
19 May 1945	Leicester City	A	1–0
26 May 1945	Leicester City	H	1–4
20 October 1945	Gillingham	H	5–2
27 October 1945	Gillingham	A	4–6
17 November 1945	Norwich City	A	5–2
24 November 1945	Norwich City	H	4–0
8 December 1945	Clapton Orient	H	5–1
26 January 1946	Plymouth Argyle	A	7–4
27 April 1946	Bristol City	H	4–4
6 May 1946	Ipswich Town (Ipswich Hospital Cup)	A	4–0
1946–47			
24 August 1946	Public Trial Match (Possibles v Probables)	H	3–1

DATE	OPPONENTS	VENUE	RESULT
1947–48			
2 July 1947	Combined Services (Wuppertal, Germany)	A	2–2
5 July 1947	British Army (Bad Geynhausen, Germany)	A	0–1
9 August 1947	Public Trial Match (Blues v Reds)	H	1–1
16 August 1947	Public Trial Match (Probables v Possibles)(Nick Collins Benefit)	H	3–0
7 February 1948	Nottingham Forest	H	1–0
1 May 1948	Aberdeen	H	3–0
1948–49			
14 August 1948	Public Trial Match (Colours v Whites)	H	5–1
11 December 1948	Doncaster Rovers	A	1–0
18 December 1948	Stockport County	H	2–0
2 May 1949	Sunderland (Jack Lewis Benefit)	H	2–0
1949–50			
13 August 1949	Public Trial Match (Colours v Whites)	H	7–1
10 December 1949	Leyton Orient	H	2–0
24 April 1950	Bath City (Ted Owens Benefit)	A	2–1
26 April 1950	King's Lynn (Culey Victory Cup)	A	6–2
3 May 1950	Hastings United (Freeman Thomas Charity Shield)	A	2–1
8 May 1950	March Town United	A	5–1
1950–51			
12 August 1950	Trial Match (Colours v Whites)	H	3–4
16 May 1951	Nancy (Festival of Britain)	H	1–2
1951–52			
11 August 1951	Public Trial Match (Colours v Whites)	H	2–2
15 December 1951	Plymouth Argyle	A	0–4
12 May 1952	Dundee United	A	1–1
13 May 1952	Inverness Select XI (Inverness Caledonian FC)	A	1–3
15 May 1952	Morayshire Select XI (Elgin City FC)	A	4–1
1952–53			
16 August 1952	Public Trial Match (Colours v Whites)	H	4–1
5 November 1952	Gloucester City	A	2–2
6 May 1953	Hastings United (Freeman Thomas Charity Shield)	A	1–2
1953–54			
15 August 1953	Public Trial Match (Colours v Whites)	H	5–1
28 September 1953	Chelsea (Inaugural Floodlight game)	H	1–1
6 October 1953	Cardiff City	H	2–2
13 October 1953	Derby County	H	1–1
20 October 1953	Leeds United	H	0–3
27 October 1953	Stade Francais	H	4–2
12 December 1953	Colchester United	H	2–1
23 February 1954	FC Vienna	H	4–3

DATE	OPPONENTS	VENUE	RESULT
2 March 1954	Brentford	H	0–0
9 March 1954	Charlton Athletic	H	2–2
16 March 1954	Queen of the South	H	2–2
23 March 1954	Chelsea	H	0–2
30 March 1954	Fulham	H	0–5
30 April 1954	London XI (Wally Hanlon Benefit)	H	6–5
1954–55			
14 August 1954	Public Trial Match (Colours v Whites)	H	4–0
4 October 1954	Queen of the South	H	2–1
13 October 1954	Clyde	H	1–1
18 October 1954	Third Lanark	H	0–1
26 October 1954	WAS Vienna	H	2–2
1 November 1954	St Mirren	H	0–1
6 December 1954	EFB Esbjerg	H	5–2
21 February 1955	Plymouth Argyle	H	0–0
10 March 1955	Bromsgrove Rovers	A	3–0
21 March 1955	Rotherham United	H	1–2
30 March 1955	Headington United	A	2–0
4 April 1955	Hamilton Academicals	H	4–1
1955–56			
13 August 1955	Public Trial Match (Whites v Colours)	H	9–1
5 October 1955	Wycombe Wanderers	A	5–0
17 October 1955	Leyton Orient (Jack Edwards & Roy Bailey Benefit)	H	2–2
7 November 1955	England Amateur XI	H	3–0
21 November 1955	West Ham United	H	2–1
10 December 1955	Gillingham	A	1–2
8 February 1956	Army XI	H	1–2
20 February 1956	Croydon Professional XI	H	7–2
9 April 1956	Walthamstow Avenue	H	3–2
16 April 1956	Fulham	H	3–3
5 May 1956	International Managers XI	H	5–6
1956–57			
4 August 1956	Public Trial Match (Whites v Colours)	H	2–1
11 August 1956	Public Trial Match (Whites v Colours)	H	5–1
8 October 1956	Army XI	H	3–3
15 October 1956	Leyton Orient	H	2–0
29 October 1956	International Manager's XI	H	2–7
18 March 1957	Walthamstow Avenue	H	2–1
8 April 1957	Clyde	H	3–4
15 April 1957	Fulham	H	1–2
2 May 1957	Kingstonian	A	1–3
4 May 1957	International Manager's XI	H	2–

DATE	OPPONENTS	VENUE	RESULT
1957–58			
10 August 1957	Public Trial Game (Whites v Colours)	H	3–2
17 August 1957	Public Trial Game (Whites v Colours)	H	6–2
14 October 1957	Wycombe Wanderers	H	3–3
7 March 1958	England Amateur XI	H	1–0
28 April 1958	Walthamstow Avenue	H	4–0
29 April 1958	Beckenham Town	A	4–0
1958–59			
16 August 1958	Public Trial Game (Whites v Colours)	H	1–2
27 October 1958	Sutton United	H	6–1
6 April 1959	Everton	H	2–2
22 April 1959	Chelmsford City	A	1–1
2 May 1959	Queen's Park Rangers (Charlie Catlett Testimonial)	H	2–1
1959–60			
15 August 1959	Public Trial Game (Whites v Colours)	H	5–2
14 October 1959	Caribbean XI	H	11–1
9 November 1959	Margate	A	6–1
23 November 1959	Sutton United	H	4–2
2 May 1960	Tottenham Hotspur	H	2–2
1960–61			
17 August 1960	Public Trial Game (Whites v Colours)	H	6–3
16 November 1960	Margate	A	6–2
15 March 1961	Ex-Palace XI (Roy Greenwood Benefit)	H	2–3
20 March 1961	Eastbourne United	A	3–1
14 April 1961	Bangu (Brazil)	H	0–2
1961–62			
9 August 1961	Reading	A	2–7
15 August 1961	Public Trial Game (Whites v Colours)	H	2–1
31 January 1962	Bratislava	H	3–2
18 April 1962	Real Madrid	H	3–4
30 April 1962	Bexleyheath & Welling	A	0–2
6 May 1962	Bermuda Football League XI (Somerset, Bermuda)	A	6–0
8 May 1962	Bermuda FA XI (Devonshire Recreation Field)	A	7–2
10 May 1962	Bermuda FA XI (National Field)	A	7–3
13 May 1962	Toronto City (Hamilton, Bermuda)	N	5–0
15 May 1962	West End Rovers (Bermuda)	A	11–2
1962–63			
8 August 1962	Reading	A	2–2
11 August 1962	Charlton Athletic	A	2–3
13 August 1962	Redhill	A	7–3
15 August 1962	Public Trial Game (Whites v Colours)	H	2–1
24 October 1962	Corinthian Casuals	H	5–2

DATE	OPPONENTS	VENUE	RESULT
2 March 1963	Gillingham	A	0–1
1963–64			
14 August 1963	Charlton Athletic (Ron Brett Testimonial Fund)	H	3–0
20 August 1963	Tottenham Hotspur (Played behind closed doors)	A	6–2
24 February 1964	Poole Town	A	2–2
9 May 1964	Croydon Amateurs	A	4–0
15 May 1964	Italia Montreal (Canada)	A	1–0
17 May 1964	Hamilton Steelers (Canada)	A	7–0
19 May 1964	Bermuda FA XI	A	3–0
c22 May 1964	Bermuda XI	A	8–1
c24 May 1964	Bermuda XI	A	6–1
c27 May 1964	Bermuda XI	A	4–0
1964–65			
8 August 1964	Dover	A	2–0
19 August 1964	West Ham United (at Crystal Palace National Recreation Centre)	N	4–1
1965–66			
14 August 1965	West Ham United (at Crystal Palace National Recreation Centre)	N	1–2
4 March 1966	Nottingham Forest	H	4–1
30 March 1966	Alkmaar (Holland)	H	1–0
12 May 1966	Stoke City	H	4–0
17 May 1966	Aberdeen	H	1–0
1966–67			
6 August 1966	DOS Utrecht (Holland)	A	1–0
7 August 1966	Alkmaar (Holland)	A	2–0
9 August 1966	Feyenoord (Holland)	A	1–3
11 October 1966	International XI (Terry Long Testimonial)	H	5–7
16 February 1967	Leicester City	H	1–1
21 February 1967	Slovan Bratislava	H	1–0
5 April 1967	Metz (France)	A	3–1
17 April 1967	Dundee United	H	1–1
1967–68			
1 August 1967	MVV Maastricht (Holland)	A	0–2
3 August 1967	Go Ahead Deventer (Holland)	A	0–3
6 August 1967	Feyenoord (Holland)	A	1–1
11 August 1967	Burnley	H	2–3
15 November 1967	International XI (George Petchey Testimonial)	H	6–3
8 March 1968	Millwall	H	1–3
22 April 1968	Oxford United (Oxfordshire Benevolent Cup)	A	1–1
24 May 1968	Horley	A	9–3

DATE	OPPONENTS	VENUE	RESULT
1968–69			
29 July 1968	West Ham United (at Crystal Palace National Recreation Centre)	N	2–4
31 July 1968	Chelsea	H	1–1
2 May 1969	Morton	H	0–0
6 May 1969	Swindon Town	A	5–3
8 May 1969	Swindon Town	H	2–1
14 May 1969	Benidorm (Spain)	A	4–2
21 May 1969	Aruella (Spain)	A	3–2
22 May 1969	Hercules (Alicante, Spain)	A	0–0
1969–70			
28 July 1969	Chelsea (at Crystal Palace National Recreation Centre)	N	0–2
30 July 1969	Asante Kotoko (Ghana)	H	3–1
2 August 1969	Morton	H	1–1
26 November 1969	International XI (Arthur Rowe Testimonial)	H	3–5
20 April 1970	Oxford United (Oxfordshire Benevolent Cup)	A	1–0
7 May 1970	San Paulo (Spain)(Fisherman's Cup)	A	3–2
14 May 1970	Athletico Madrid XI (Spain)	A	1–1
21 May 1970	Mahon (Minorca, Spain)	A	2–1
1970–71			
1 August 1970	St Mirren	H	4–0
3 August 1970	Wrexham	A	1–1
5 August 1970	Paykaan (Iran)	H	8–1
7 August 1970	Arsenal (at Crystal Palace National Recreation Centre)	N	0–2
23 September 1970	Croydon Amateurs	A	5–1
19 January 1971	Israel National XI	A	0–0
12 February 1971	PSV Eindhoven (Holland)	H	2–4
3 March 1971	ADO Den Haag (Holland)	H	0–0
8 March 1971	First Tower United (Jersey)	A	2–1
10 May 1971	Gillingham	A	4–1
13 May 1971	Bruges (Belgium)(John Sewell Testimonial)	H	1–3
21 May 1971	Clyde	H	1–1
1971–72			
28 July 1971	Feyenoord (Holland)	A	0–1
1 August 1971	ADO Den Haag (Holland)	A	0–0
4 August 1971	PSV Eindhoven (Holland)	A	3–2
6 August 1971	Maccabi Nathanya (Israel)	H	4–1
26 February 1972	Partick Thistle	H	2–0
2 May 1972	Oxford United (Oxfordshire Benevolent Cup)	A	0–2
1972–73			
29 July 1972	Dundee United	H	3–1
30 July 1972	MVV Maastricht (Holland)	A	0–1
5 August 1972	Dundee	A	4–1
24 October 1972	MVV Maastricht (Holland)	H	2–1

DATE	OPPONENTS	VENUE	RESULT
8 November 1972	Persepolis (Iran)	A	5–1
14 November 1972	Leningrad Zenit (Russia)	H	1–1
5 December 1972	Lincoln City All Stars	A	1–3
9 January 1973	Aberdeen	A	0–2
1973–74			
22 July 1973	IK Sirius (Sweden)(Juli Cup)	A	1–1
24 July 1973	Sandvikens IF (Sweden)(Juli Cup)	A	1–1
29 July 1973	Västerhaninge (Sweden)(Juli Cup Final)	A	3–2
30 July 1973	A Swedish Second Division Club	A	1–0
11 August 1973	Brighton & Hove Albion	A	1–2
15 August 1973	Charlton Athletic	A	1–0
18 August 1973	Southampton	A	1–2
11 December 1973	Chelsea (John Jackson Testimonial)	H	1–3
26 January 1974	Gillingham	A	1–0
3 May 1974	Queen's Park Rangers	A	1–2
1974–75			
21 July 1974	IF Helsingborg (Sweden)	A	1–1
23 July 1974	IF Saab (Sweden)	A	2–1
25 July 1974	IFK Norrköping (Sweden)	A	2–2
6 August 1974	Maidstone United	A	0–1
10 August 1974	Wimbledon	A	0–1
12 August 1974	Millwall	A	1–1
3 September 1974	Queen's Park Rangers (John McCormick Testimonial)	H	1–1
14 October 1974	Camberley Town	A	1–1
1975–76			
6 August 1975	East Ham United	A	3–0
11 August 1975	Epsom and Ewell	H	3–0
7 May 1976	Chelsea	A	2–2
1976–77			
24 July 1976	Alemania Aachen (Holland)	A	2–3
28 July 1976	SC Heracles Almelo (Holland)	A	2–0
30 July 1976	Rijnsburge Boys (Holland)	A	6–0
1 August 1976	Wageningen (Holland)	A	2–1
7 August 1976	AFC Bournemouth	A	2–1
9 August 1976	Orient	H	3–1
29 January 1977	Millwall	A	1–1
1977–78			
18 July 1977	Jersey Under-23 XI	A	2–0
21 July 1977	Jersey XI	A	9–3
30 July 1977	Derby County	H	0–2
6 August 1977	Gillingham	A	1–1
10 August 1977	Wolverhampton Wanderers	H	1–2

DATE	OPPONENTS	VENUE	RESULT
6 September 1977	Wimbledon	A	1–2
20 September 1977	Surrey County FA XI	H	1–0
18 February 1978	Hibernian	H	0–1
c20 May 1978	Corfu Select XI (Greece)	A	3–1
c22 May 1978	Corfu Select XI (Greece)	A	2–0
1978–79			
25 July 1978	Sandvikens IF(Sweden)	A	3–0
27 July 1978	IK Brage Borlange (Sweden)	A	3–1
31 July 1978	Brommapofkarna (Sweden)	A	4–0
3 August 1978	IK Sirius (Sweden)	A	1–0
8 August 1978	Wimbledon	A	5–0
12 August 1978	Arsenal	A	1–1
13 November 1978	Wycombe Wanderers	A	2–0
12 December 1978	Chelsea (Charlie Cooke Testimonial)	A	0–2
22 May 1979	Memphis Rogues (USA)	A	3–1
23 May 1979	Fort Lauderdale Strikers (USA)	A	2–0
1979–80			
24 July 1979	Storm FK (Norway)	A	1–0
26 July 1979	FK Ørn (Norway)	A	1–1
28 July 1979	FK Jerv (Norway)	A	3–0
31 July 1979	Viking FA (Norway)	A	1–0
2 August 1979	Lillestrom (Norway)	A	2–1
7 August 1979	Wimbledon	A	1–0
11 August 1979	Chelsea	H	5–0
16 February 1980	Notts County	H	2–2
15 April 1980	Tottenham Hotspur (Martin Hinshelwood Testimonial)	H	2–3
29 April 1980	Tottenham Hotspur	A	2–0
5 May 1980	Chelsea (George Graham Testimonial)	A	3–1
7 May 1980	Charlton Athletic	A	0–2
15 May 1980	Wimbledon (Played at Mitcham Training Ground)	H	2–6
25 May 1980	Malaga (Spain)	A	0–2
1980–81			
23 July 1980	Ornskoldsvik (Sweden)	A	5–0
25 July 1980	IKK Stromsund (Sweden)	A	3–0
27 July 1980	Kramfors (Sweden)	A	4–0
30 July 1980	Edsbyns (Sweden)	A	8–0
2 August 1980	Oxford United	A	4–1
5 August 1980	Wimbledon	A	3–0
9 August 1980	Luton Town	A	1–2
14 October 1980	Portsmouth	A	3–2
25 November 1980	Vince Hilaire's XI (Jim Cannon Testimonial)	H	5–3
23 March 1981	Minnesota Kicks (USA)	H	1–1
10 May 1981	East Grinstead (Richards Hospital Rose Bowl)	A	5–1

DATE	OPPONENTS	VENUE	RESULT
1981–82			
3 August 1981	Milton Keynes	A	1–0
7 August 1981	Maidstone United	A	2–1
13 August 1981	Fulham (Played at Mitcham Training Ground)	H	1–0
18 August 1981	Bristol City	A	0–1
21 August 1981	Birmingham City	H	1–0
	(Match abandoned after 66 minutes – floodlight failure)		
14 November 1981	Brighton & Hove Albion	H	1–1
30 December 1981	Folkestone Town	A	5–0
24 February 1982	I.F.K. Gothenburg (Denmark)	H	1–3
16 May 1982	East Grinstead	A	7–1
1982–83			
30 July 1982	VFR Neumunster (Germany)	A	4–3
31 July 1982	SV Lurup (Hamburg, Germany)	A	1–3
1 August 1982	SV Bornson (Germany)	A	4–2
7 August 1982	Brighton & Hove Albion	H	1–0
1983–84			
4 August 1983	Gravelines (France)	A	5–1
6 August 1983	Calais (France)	A	2–0
	(Match abandoned after 88 minutes – crowd disturbances)		
9 August 1983	Japan National XI	H	1–2
13 August 1983	Southampton	H	1–1
16 August 1983	Queen's Park Rangers	H	1–2
20 August 1983	Wimbledon	A	2–0
30 April 1984	Queen's Park Rangers (Paul Hinshelwood Testimonial)	H	4–1
14 May 1984	Brighton & Hove Albion (Gary Williams Testimonial)	A	3–3
1984–85			
31 July 1984	Aylesbury	A	0–0
7 August 1984	Wealdstone	A	0–2
10 August 1984	Southend United	A	0–2
14 August 1984	Torquay United	A	2–1
15 August 1984	Plymouth Argyle	A	0–0
17 August 1984	Exeter City	A	1–1
20 August 1984	Hapoel (Tel Aviv, Israel)	H	3–0
26 January 1985	West Ham United	H	1–2
1985–86			
23 July 1985	Aldershot	A	1–1
27 July 1985	Luton Town	A	0–0
	(Restricted admission and match played in three half-hour sessions)		
31 July 1985	Coventry City	H	1–1
3 August 1985	Chelsea	H	0–1
6 August 1985	West Ham United	H	2–1
9 August 1985	Torquay United	A	1–1

DATE	OPPONENTS	VENUE	RESULT
12 August 1985	Southend United	A	1–1
3 February 1986	Qatar Under-21 XI	A	0–0
14 May 1986	Sutton United	H	3–2
16 May 1986	Villerupt (France)	A	1–0
17 May 1986	Selection Maritime (France)	A	3–4
18 May 1986	Gravelines (France)	A	7–1
1986–87			
28 July 1986	Northampton Town (Played behind closed doors)	A	2–5
30 July 1986	Newcastle Town	A	1–0
2 August 1986	Southend United	A	0–1
6 August 1986	Aldershot	A	2–2
9 August 1986	AFC Bournemouth	H	3–0
16 August 1986	Chelsea	H	2–1
18 August 1986	Fulham	A	4–1
21 January 1987	Swansea City	A	3–1
24 February 1987	Worthing	A	2–2
5 June 1987	SV Sparkasse (Austria) (at Gravelines, France)	N	2–0
6 June 1987	Grand Synthe (France)	A	6–4
7 June 1987	Gravelines (France)	A	1–0
1987–88			
18 July 1987	Northampton Town (Played at Mitcham Training Ground in three half-hour sessions)	H	2–0
26 July 1987	ISK Grangesberg (Sweden)	A	5–0
28 July 1987	Smedjebackens (Sweden)	A	3–0
29 July 1987	Frovi IK (Sweden)	A	8–0
*c.*1 August 1987	Rossons IF (Sweden)	A	6–1
*c.*2 August 1987	Lyksele IF (Sweden)	A	8–0
*c.*4 August 1987	Sodertalje (Sweden)	A	1–0
9 August 1987	Watford (Len Chatterton Testimonial)	H	1–2
3 February 1988	Gillingham	A	1–1
2 March 1988	Tottenham Hotspur (Played behind closed doors)	H	1–0
8 March 1988	Aldershot (Played behind closed doors)	A	2–0
23 March 1988	Gillingham (Played behind closed doors)	A	3–2
19 April 1988	Egham Town	A	6–1
26 April 1988	Tottenham Hotspur (Jim Cannon Second Testimonial)	H	3–3
1988–89			
25 July 1988	FK Mjolner (Norway)	A	1–3
27 July 1988	Kemin Pallaseura (Finland)	A	5–1
28 July 1988	Hemingsmarks IF(Sweden)	A	2–1
30 July 1988	Gallivare SK (Sweden)	A	4–1

DATE	OPPONENTS	VENUE	RESULT
2 August 1988	Lulea FF-IFK (Sweden)	A	4–0
3 August 1988	Vasterhaninge (Sweden)	A	9–0
9 August 1988	Carshalton Athletic	A	4–0
13 August 1988	Millwall	A	1–0
16 August 1988	Crewe Alexandra	A	2–1
20 August 1988	Fulham	A	2–0
23 August 1988	Tel Aviv (Israel)	H	1–0
	(Played behind closed doors)		
26 August 1988	Tottenham Hotspur	H	2–0
	(Played at Mitcham Training Ground)		
17 February 1989	Southend United	A	2–2
1989–90			
23 July 1989	IF Norvalla (Sweden)	A	3–1
25 July 1989	Billeshalms GIF (Sweden)	A	7–2
27 July 1989	Verderslov Danninglanda (Sweden)	A	5–1
29 July 1989	Virserums SGF (Sweden)	A	7–1
31 July 1989	Skera IF(Sweden)	A	7–1
1 August 1989	Sodra Vings IF(Sweden)	A	2–0
5 August 1989	Farnborough Town	A	2–1
8 August 1989	Aldershot	A	2–0
11 August 1989	Swansea City	A	4–1
13 August 1989	West Ham United	A	1–3
30 August 1989	Derry City	A	4–2
7 May 1990	Carshalton Athletic	A	6–3
20 May 1990	Trinidad & Tobago XI (Trinidad)	A	2–2
23 May 1990	Caribbean XI (Port of Spain, Trinidad)	A	0–4
*c.*27 May 1990	Jamaican XI (Kingston, Jamaica)	A	2–0
*c.*30 May 1990	Cayman Islands XI	A	4–0
1990–91			
23 July 1990	Hamrange GIF (Sweden)	A	6–0
24 July 1990	Vasby IK (Sweden)	A	5–0
26 July 1990	IF Sylvia (Sweden)	A	5–0
28 July 1990	Hallstahammar SK (Sweden)	A	8–1
30 July 1990	Nykvarn SK (Sweden)	A	6–0
31 July 1990	Alno IF (Sweden)	A	6–1
4 August 1990	Brentford	H	0–3
	(Played behind closed doors at Mitcham)		
11 August 1990	Colchester United	A	1–0
14 August 1990	Hull City	A	2–2
17 August 1990	Bristol City	A	1–1
20 August 1990	Fiorentina (at St Vincent, Italy)(Baretti Tournament)	N	1–2
22 August 1990	Sampdoria (at St Vincent, Italy)(Baretti Tournament)	N	1–1
		(won 5–4 on penalties)	
14 October 1990	Lee Richardson Guest XI (Whyteleafe FC)	A	4–2
10 March 1991	Redhill	A	8–1

DATE	OPPONENTS	VENUE	RESULT
25 April 1991	Gibraltar FA XI	A	2–2
8 May 1991	Britannia XI (at Ramsgate)	A	6–2
13 May 1991	West Ham United	A	2–3
1991–92			
15 July 1991	Crawley Town	A	6–0
22 July 1991	Smogens (Sweden)	A	8–1
24 July 1991	Landskrona (Sweden)	A	3–1
25 July 1991	Bankeryd (Sweden)	A	8–0
27 July 1991	Molnlycke (Sweden)	A	6–0
29 July 1991	Sandesjord (Norway)	A	1–1
30 July 1991	Fredrikstad (Norway)	A	2–2
1 August 1991	Carshalton Athletic	A	6–1
3 August 1991	Fulham	A	2–3
5 August 1991	AEK Athens (Greece)(at Gijon, Spain)(Costa Verde Tournament)	N	2–2
13 August 1991	Levski Spartak (Bulgaria)(at Gijon, Spain)(Costa Verde Tournament)	N	3–1
14 August 1991	Sporting Gijon (Spain)(Costa Verde Tournament)	A	2–2
20 August 1991	Millwall	A	5–3
28 April 1992	Glenn Hoddle All Star XI (at Maidstone)(Dave Madden Testimonial)	A	4–2
1992–93			
18 July 1992	Kaiser Chiefs (Johannesburg, South Africa)	A	3–2
19 July 1992	Orlando Pirates (Durban, South Africa)	A	1–2
26 July 1992	Horred (Sweden)	A	1–0
28 July 1992	Karlskrona (Sweden)	A	1–0
29 July 1992	Oskarshan (Sweden)	A	7–2
30 July 1992	Bankeryd (Sweden)	A	11–2
1 August 1992	Malilla (Sweden)	A	5–0
7 August 1992	Brighton & Hove Albion	A	1–0
10 August 1992	Leyton Orient	A	3–1
28 March 1993	Tottenham Hotspur (Malcolm Allison Testimonial)	H	3–3
1993–94			
20 July 1993	Ayamonte (Portugal)	A	4–0
23 July 1993	Loule Tano (Portugal)	A	0–0
27 July 1993	Crawley Town	A	7–1
31 July 1993	Brentford	A	3–1
3 August 1993	Brighton & Hove Albion	A	3–0
7 August 1993	Fulham	A	5–0
13 November 1993	Guernsey XI	A	8–0
26 January 1994	Derry City	A	2–1
17 May 1994	Gibraltar Select XI	A	1–0
19 May 1994	Marbella (Spain)	A	0–2
21 May 1994	Malaga (Spain)	A	1–0

DATE	OPPONENTS	VENUE	RESULT
1994–95			
25 July 1994	Portuguese XI (Portugal)	A	3–1
30 July 1994	Carshalton Athletic	A	5–0
2 August 1994	Charlton Athletic	A	1–0
2 August 1994	Crawley Town	A	2–0
6 August 1994	Fulham	A	3–0
13 August 1994	Arsenal	A	3–1
8 November 1994	Sutton United	A	1–2
23 April 1995	Happy Valley (Hong Kong)	A	1–1 (lost on penalties)
1995–96			
12 July 1995	Muglaspor (Turkey)	A	4–0
14 July 1995	Altayspur (Turkey)	A	1–1
22 July 1995	AFC Bournemouth	A	1–2
25 July 1995	Brighton & Hove Albion	A	1–0
28 July 1995	Swansea City	A	1–1
1 August 1995	Kingstonian	A	2–0
5 August 1995	Queen's Park Rangers	A	1–3
1996–97			
26 July 1996	Arjang IF (Sweden)	A	8–0
27 July 1996	Forde IL (Norway)	A	7–2
29 July 1996	Rade IL (Norway)	A	2–0
30 July 1996	Skjetten KF (Norway)	A	4–3
3 August 1996	AL Combination (Norway)	A	8–0
7 August 1996	Barnet	A	3–0
10 August 1996	Notts County	A	1–2
12 August 1996	Leyton Orient	A	2–0
3 September 1996	Carshalton Athletic	A	5–2
3 December 1996	Walton & Hersham	A	5–2
7 January 1997	Dorchester Town	A	3–1
1997–98			
9 July 1997	JJK (Jyvaskyla, Finland)	A	4–0
11 July 1997	King's (Kuopio, Finland)	A	0–0
13 July 1997	Oulu (Finland)	A	1–0
15 July 1997	Santa Claus (Rovaniemi, Finland)	A	5–0
19 July 1997	Gillingham	A	2–2
23 July 1997	Barnet	A	1–1
26 July 1997	Millwall	A	4–0
29 July 1997	Fulham	A	1–0
2 August 1997	Brighton & Hove Albion (at Gillingham)	A	1–1
14 August 1997	Crawley Town	A	7–0
13 November 1997	IFK Gothenburg (Denmark)	A	1–2
30 March 1998	Tonbridge Angels (Freda King Memorial Game)	A	1–0

DATE	OPPONENTS	VENUE	RESULT
1998–99			
11 July 1998	Crawley Town	A	5–1
15 July 1998	Wycombe Wanderers	A	3–1
17 July 1998	Southend United	A	1–0
20 July 1998	AFC Bournemouth	A	2–1
29 July 1998	Gillingham	A	2–1
1 August 1998	Millwall	A	1–1
4 May 1999	Dover Athletic (John Budden Testimonial)	A	4–2
1999–2000			
7 July 1999	Beijing Guoan (China)	A	2–1
*c.*9 July 1999	Shanghai Shensua (China)	A	3–2
13 July 1999	Yunnan Hongta (China)	A	2–2
		(lost 7–8 on penalties)	
15 July 1999	Dalian Wanda (China)	A	0–0
		(won 4–2 on penalties)	
20 July 1999	Reading	A	2–0
	(Played behind closed doors)		
24 July 1999	Millwall	A	2–1
26 July 1999	Luton Town	A	2–2
28 July 1999	Leicester City	H	1–1
31 July 1999	Southend United	A	0–4
2000–01			
11 July 2000	Shan'xi Guoli (Xian, China)	A	2–0
13 July 2000	China XI (Xian, China)	A	1–3
17 July 2000	Guangzohou Shangri (Nanchang, China)	A	2–1
22 July 2000	Crawley Town	A	1–5
25 July 2000	Reading	H	0–4
	(Played behind closed doors)		
29 July 2000	Millwall	A	0–6
5 August 2000	Wycombe Wanderers	A	1–3
23 March 2001	FC Bastia (Corsica, France)	A	3–4
2001–02			
11 July 2001	San Pedro (Spain)	A	4–0
15 July 2001	Cakovec (Croatia)(in Spain)	N	2–0
19 July 2001	Tiverton Town	A	2–1
21 July 2001	Torquay United	A	4–0
24 July 2001	Exeter City	A	5–0
28 July 2001	Cardiff City	A	0–4
31 July 2001	Sutton United	A	5–1
1 August 2001	Fulham	H	0–1
4 August 2001	Oxford United (Bill Halsey Memorial Cup)	A	1–1
19 May 2002	Malmo (Sweden)(in Seville, Spain)(Seville Tournament)	N	2–1
21 May 2002	Real Betis (Seville, Spain)(Seville Tournament)	A	0–2

DATE	OPPONENTS	VENUE	RESULT
2002–03			
12 July 2002	Barnet	A	3–0
17 July 2002	AFC Bournemouth	A	0–2
20 July 2002	Carshalton Athletic	A	2–1
23 July 2002	Cheltenham Town	A	3–1
26 July 2002	Swansea City	A	2–0
31 July 2002	Tottenham Hotspur (Simon Rodger Testimonial)	H	0–4
5 August 2002	Charlton Athletic	H	1–1
2003–04			
18 July 2003	Torremolinos (Spain)	A	3–0
23 July 2003	Whyteleafe	A	6–1
26 July 2003	Luton Town	A	1–1
30 July 2003	PSV Eindhoven (Holland)	H	0–1
2 August 2003	Chelsea	H	1–2
6 September 2003	Brescia (Italy)	H	3–4
2004–05			
13 July 2004	Crusaders (Northern Ireland)	A	2–0
17 July 2004	Glentoran (Northern Ireland)	A	5–0
24 July 2004	Ipswich Town	A	1–2
28 July 2004	Sporting Lisbon (Portugal)	H	1–0
31 July 2004	Queen's Park Rangers	A	0–3
7 August 2004	Sampdoria (Italy)	H	0–1
2005–06			
20 July 2005	FK Teplice (Czech Republic)(at Meisbach, Germany)	N	1–2
23 July 2005	Eintracht Frankfurt (Fussen, Germany)	N	1–1
27 July 2005	Inter Milan (Italy)	H	0–2
30 July 2005	West Ham United	H	0–1
2006–07			
11 July 2006	Stevenage Borough	A	3–0
15 July 2006	Crystal Palace USA	A	3–1
19 July 2006	Los Angeles Galaxy (USA)	A	1–1
	(Abandoned at half-time – electrical storm with heavy rain)		
23 July 2006	Swindon Town	A	2–2
26 July 2006	Boavista (Portugal)	H	2–1
29 July 2006	Millwall	A	0–0
2007–08			
13 July 2007	Chelmsford City	A	2–0
14 July 2007	Bromley	A	2–2
17 July 2007	Aldershot Town	A	2–0
20 July 2007	Dartford	A	3–0
21 July 2007	Barnet	A	3–2
24 July 2007	IFK Gothenburg (Denmark)(at Grebbestad, Sweden)	A	2–1

DATE	OPPONENTS	VENUE	RESULT
27 July 2007	Oddevold (Sweden)	A	4–1
31 July 2007	Anderlecht (Belgium)	H	1–1
4 August 2007	Everton	H	0–0
7 September 2007	Crystal Palace USA	H	1–0
2008–09			
12 July 2008	Bromley	A	1–1
14 July 2008	Crawley Town	A	1–1
17 July 2008	Aldershot Town	A	4–3
21 July 2008	Tavistock Town	A	4–0
23 July 2008	Bodmin Town	A	4–1
25 July 2008	Truro City	A	1–0
29 July 2008	Fulham (Dougie Freedman Testimonial)	H	0–0
2 August 2008	Leicester City	H	1–1
2009–10			
14 July 2009	Crystal Palace (USA)	A	5–2
16 July 2009	Harrisburg City Islanders (USA)	A	3–1
21 July 2009	Brentford	A	2–2
24 July 2009	Bristol Rovers	A	3–0
28 July 2009	Norwich City	H	0–1
30 July 2009	Bromley	A	1–0
2 August 2009	Gillingham	H	0–1
2010–11			
13 July 2010	Crawley Town	A	0–1
17 July 2010	Chelsea	H	0–1
21 July 2010	Dorchester Town	A	3–3
23 July 2010	Exeter City (at Tiverton Town FC)	N	2–0
27 July 2010	Bromley	A	0–0
30 July 2010	Brentford	A	1–1

Reserve Competitions

It should be noted that the first team competed in the United and Western Leagues.

United League	P	W	D	L	F	A	Pts.	Pos.
1905–06	18	13	4	1	51	21	27	1st
1906–07	14	8	5	1	39	20	21	1st
London League								
1906–07	18	5	3	10	27	33	13	6th
1907–08	16	4	4	8	20	33	12	7th
1908–09 **Did not compete**								
1909–10 **Did not compete**								
1910–11	14	5	5	4	22	22	15	4th
1911–12	12	11	0	1	37	12	22	1st
1912–13	10	6	2	2	26	15	14	2nd
1913–14	16	8	1	7	43	28	17	4th
1914–15	16	5	1	10	17	43	11	7th
Western League								
1907–08	12	3	4	5	16	17	10	6th
1908–09	12	5	2	5	23	22	12	3rd
1909–10	12	5	2	5	23	22	12	4th
South Eastern League								
1907–08 (Div. 2)	18	14	3	1	56	13	31	2nd
1908–09 (Div. 1)	38	13	4	21	54	75	30	13th
1909–10	38	8	10	16	43	67	26	16th
Kent League								
1910–11	26	20	2	4	83	36	42	2nd
1911–12	28	15	6	7	75	48	36	3rd
1912–13	28	19	4	5	91	35	42	2nd
1913–14	30	25	1	4	110	25	51	1st
London Professional Midweek League								
1932–33	14	4	2	8	33	38	10	7th
Capital League								
1991–92	22	9	3	10	33	30	30	6th
1992–93	20	8	5	7	33	33	29	7th
Football Combination								
1919–20	36	13	6	17	56	70	32	8th
1920–21	36	12	7	17	41	80	31	8th
1921–22	40	20	4	16	63	80	44	4th
1922–23	40	18	9	13	68	63	45	5th
1923–24	44	20	6	18	81	85	46	5th

	P	W	D	L	F	A	Pts.	Pos.
1924–25	44	12	17	15	62	76	41	8th
1925–26	44	15	9	20	57	71	39	8th
1926–27	42	16	8	18	81	94	40	13th
1927–28	42	7	11	24	63	123	25	22nd
1928–29	42	16	6	20	67	86	38	15th
1929–30	42	17	6	19	88	101	40	13th
1930–31	42	20	3	19	78	73	43	10th
1931–32	42	22	8	12	90	49	52	3rd
1932–33	46	22	8	16	104	84	52	7th
1933–34	46	20	5	21	110	104	45	13th
1934–35	46	22	6	18	101	91	50	6th
1935–36	46	21	10	15	102	98	52	7th
1936–37	46	17	12	17	74	82	46	12th
1937–38	46	18	8	20	89	101	44	14th
1938–39	46	19	7	20	92	89	45	13th
1939–1945 **No Competition**								
1946–47	30	8	6	16	38	73	22	15th
1947–48	30	5	10	15	25	57	20	15th
1947–48 (Cup)	14	4	2	8	18	28	10	6th
1948–49	30	10	8	12	38	53	28	10th
1948–49 (Cup)	14	4	3	7	9	20	11	7th
1949–50	30	14	6	10	41	38	34	4th
1949–50 (Cup)	14	3	4	7	19	25	10	6th
1950–51	30	8	9	13	29	43	25	15th
1950–51 (Cup)	14	3	3	8	12	27	9	8th
1951–52	30	7	5	18	29	56	19	15th
1951–52 (Cup)	14	4	2	8	26	35	10	4th
1952–53	30	10	7	13	38	50	27	11th
1952–53 (Cup)	14	4	0	10	10	29	8	8th
1953–54	30	7	3	20	30	76	17	16th
1953–54 (Cup)	14	2	2	10	12	35	6	8th
1954–55	30	9	4	17	46	65	22	13th
1954–55 (Cup)	14	2	3	9	16	32	7	8th
1955–56	42	18	5	19	78	74	41	16th
1956–57	42	17	10	15	72	84	44	14th
1957–58	42	15	7	20	71	103	37	19th
1958–59	32	11	5	16	37	52	27	14th
1959–60	38	15	5	18	73	76	35	12th
1960–61	38	12	7	19	71	79	31	17th
1961–62	34	15	4	15	67	68	34	8th
1962–63	34	19	6	9	72	48	44	3rd
1963–64	34	11	12	11	59	54	34	9th

	P	W	D	L	F	A	Pts.	Pos.
1964–65	34	14	3	17	57	57	31	10th
1965–66	32	11	4	19	48	80	26	14th
1966–67	32	11	4	17	51	71	26	15th
1967–68	40	16	8	16	67	71	40	6th
1968–69	25	16	3	6	47	31	35	5th
1969–70	25	11	7	7	43	30	29	9th
1970–71	42	11	14	17	54	58	36	14th
1971–72	40	19	10	11	65	52	48	3rd
1972–73	40	15	10	15	50	52	40	9th
1973–74	42	12	11	19	51	70	35	18th
1974–75	40	18	5	17	64	62	41	9th
1975–76	42	12	12	18	49	64	36	18th
1976–77	42	9	12	21	48	70	30	21st
1977–78	42	16	10	16	50	53	42	12th
1978–79	42	11	16	15	60	59	38	12th
1979–80	42	12	13	17	63	71	37	15th
1980–81	42	18	9	15	74	64	45	11th
1981–82	38	12	2	24	46	78	26	17th
1982–83	42	10	11	21	55	86	31	21st
1983–84	42	5	12	25	32	101	22	20th
1984–85	42	12	6	24	57	86	30	17th
1985–86	42	13	10	19	67	104	36	14th
1986–87	38	8	11	19	52	73	27	16th
Sunday Mirror Combination								
1987–88	38	8	7	23	38	78	23	19th
Ovenden Papers Combination								
1988–89	38	16	9	13	55	44	41	10th
1989–90	38	11	10	17	56	50	43	14th
1990–91	38	21	10	7	90	44	73	3rd
Neville Ovenden Combination								
1991–92	38	15	9	14	63	61	54	9th
1992–93	38	18	12	8	66	44	66	4th
1993–94	38	17	11	10	65	42	62	4th
Avon Insurance Combination								
1994–95	38	15	10	13	50	40	55	7th
1995–96	38	16	12	10	50	41	60	6th
1996–97	22	10	6	6	37	33	36	5th
1997–98	33	16	2	15	45	39	50	6th
1998–99	28	9	6	13	43	51	33	19th
FA Premier Reserve League								
1999–2000	24	3	5	16	14	53	14	13th

	P	W	D	L	F	A	Pts.	Pos.
Avon Insurance Combination								
2000–01	24	11	6	7	42	35	39	7th
2001–02	24	14	5	5	50	26	47	2nd
2002–03	25	16	5	4	60	23	53	1st
Pontin's Holidays Combination (Central & East Division)								
2003–04	14	6	3	5	25	18	21	6th
Barclaycard. Premier Reserve League South								
2004–05	28	16	5	7	47	22	53	4th
FA Premier Reserve League South								
2005–06	26	10	5	11	43	42	35	8th
Pontins Combination (Central & East Division)								
2006–07	14	7	1	6	29	25	22	3rd
2007–08	18	5	8	5	23	25	23	4th
Totesport.com Combination (Central Division)								
2008–09	18	10	2	6	50	40	32	3rd
2009–10	18	13	4	1	48	23	43	2nd

London Challenge Cup

The London Challenge Cup was inaugurated in 1908 by the London Football Association and competed for in each season, save for suspension during wartime, until 1974 when it was disbanded. It was revived in 1990 for mainly non-League clubs but lasted only 10 years.

Rd	Date	Opponents	Venue	Score	Scorers
1908–09					
1	9 September 1908	Croydon Common	H	1–0	Swann
2	9 November 1908	Woolwich Arsenal	A	1–2	Bauchop
1909–10					
1	20 September 1909	Leyton	A	1–3	Williams
1910–11					
1	19 September 1910	Bromley	H	1–1	Spottiswood
R	26 September 1910	Bromley	A	0–1	
1911–12					
1	19 September 1911	Chelsea	A	1–2	Hewitt
1912–13					
1	23 September 1912	Croydon Common	H	1–0	Smith
(2	21 October 1912	Tottenham Hotspur	A	0–2	
	(Game to be replayed due to ineligible Tottenham player)				
2	28 October 1912	Tottenham Hotspur	A	3–3 aet	York, Williams Davies
R	11 November 1912	Tottenham Hotspur	H	4–1	York, Williams, Hewitt, Hughes
SF	18 November 1912	Fulham (Played at Stamford Bridge)	N	5–2	Williams 3, York, Hughes
F	9 December 1912	West Ham United (Played at The Den)	N	0–0	
R	16 December 1912	West Ham United (Played at White Hart Lane)	N	1–0	Williams
1913–14					
1	22 September 1913	Croydon Common	H	1–0	Smith
2	20 October 1913	London Caledonians	H	2–0	Smith 2
SF	10 November 1913	Millwall (Played at Upton Park)	N	4–3	Hewitt 2, Hughes, Smith
F	8 December 1913	Tottenham Hotspur (Played at Highbury)	N	2–1	Hewitt, Davies
1914–15					
1	21 September 1914	Dulwich Hamlet	A	1–0	Bateman

Rd	Date	Opponents	Venue	Score	Scorers
2	19 October 1914	Tottenham Hotspur	H	3–1	Smith, Hewitt 2
SF	9 November 1914	Arsenal	N	0–2	
		(Played at White Hart Lane)			
1919–20					
1	24 September 1919	Leytonstone	H	5–0	E. Smith 2, C. Smith 2, Bateman
2	6 October 1919	Tottenham Hotspur	H	3–2	Middleton, E. Smith 2
SF	10 November 1919	Fulham	N	3–1	Whibley, E. Smith, Hughes
		(Played at Stamford Bridge)			
F	8 May 1920	Chelsea	A	0–1	
1920–21					
1	13 October 1920	Fulham	H	1–0	E. Smith
2	15 November 1920	Charlton Athletic	A	2–1	Swift, McCracken
SF	21 February 1921	Queen's Park Rangers	N	4–2	Wood, Conner 3
		(Played at The Den)			
F	9 May 1921	Clapton Orient	N	1–0	Conner
		(Played at White Hart Lane)			
1921–22					
1	17 October 1921	Nunhead	A	4–1	Menlove 2, Hand, Rhodes (pen)
2	31 October 1921	Charlton Athletic	H	2–1	Conner, Jones
SF	14 November 1921	Fulham	N	0–0	
		(Played at The Den)			
R	21 November 1921	Fulham	N	3–1	Menlove, Conner, Rhodes (pen)
		(Played at Stamford Bridge)			
F	8 May 1922	Arsenal	N	0–1	
		(Played at The Den)			
1922–23					
1	18 October 1922	Bromley	H	2–0	Conner, Johnson
2	1 November 1922	Arsenal	H	1–0	Harry
SF	20 November 1922	West Ham United	N	2–1	Johnson, Harry
		(Played at White Hart Lane)			
F	4 December 1922	Charlton Athletic	N	1–2	Whitworth (pen)
		(Played at The Den)			
1923–24					
1	22 October 1923	Tottenham Hotspur	H	1–1	Whitworth
R	29 October 1923	Tottenham Hotspur	A	1–2	Johnson
1924–25					
1	27 October 1924	Brentford	H	2–2	Whitworth, Blakemore
R	3 November 1924	Brentford	A	0–2	
1925–26					
1	14 September 1925	Chelsea	A	0–4	

Rd	Date	Opponents	Venue	Score	Scorers
1926–27					
1	27 September 1926	Ilford	A	2–1	Blakemore, Cherrett
2	18 October 1926	Queen's Park Rangers	A	1–0	Clarke
SF	1 November 1926	Chelsea (Played at The Den)	N	2–3	Turner, Clarke
1927–28					
1	12 October 1927	Leyton	H	0–1	
1928–29					
1	15 October 1928	Clapton Orient	A	1–1	Havelock
R	22 October 1928	Clapton Orient	H	1–2	James
1929–30					
1	14 October 1929	West Ham United	H	2–2	Fishlock, Charlton (pen)
R	21 October 1929	West Ham United	A	0–2	
1930–31					
1	13 October 1930	Walthamstow Avenue	H	2–2	Watson, Swan
R	20 October 1930	Walthamstow Avenue	A	4–0	Charlesworth, Wilcockson, Turner
2	27 October 1930	Arsenal	H	2–2	Butler, Crilly (pen)
R	19 November 1930	Arsenal	A	0–5	
1931–32					
1	7 October 1931	Wimbledon	A	1–0	Charlesworth
2	26 October 1931	Arsenal	H	2–1	Wilcockson, Jewett
SF	16 November 1931	Tottenham Hotspur (Played at Upton Park)	N	2–0	Wilcockson (pen), own-goal
F	9 May 1932	Fulham	H	1–2	Barrie
1932–33					
1	12 October 1932	Wimbledon	A	3–1	Barrie, Manders 2
2	24 October 1932	Tottenham Hotspur	A	3–2	Manders, Walters 2
SF	16 November 1932	West Ham United	H	1–1	Walters
R	3 April 1933	West Ham United	A	0–4	
1933–34					
1	9 October 1933	Barnet	A	4–2	Thompson 3, Manders
2	25 October 1933	Brentford	H	2–2	Rooke 2
R	30 October 1933	Brentford	A	3–4 aet	Rooke 3
1934–35					
1	8 October 1934	Fulham	A	1–7	Rooke
1935–36					
1	7 October 1935	Queen's Park Rangers	A	0–6	

Rd	Date	Opponents	Venue	Score	Scorers
1936–37					
1	5 October 1936	Walthamstow Avenue	H	1–2	Rooke
1937–38					
1	4 October 1937	Queen's Park Rangers	H	4–1	Palethorpe (pen), Robson 3
2	18 October 1937	Charlton Athletic	H	3–2	Jordan 2, Quayle
SF	8 November 1937	West Ham United	H	4–3	Blackman 3, Davis
F	9 May 1938	Millwall	A	0–4	
1938–39					
1	3 October 1938	Arsenal	H	2–2	Waldron 2 (2 pens)
R	10 October 1938	Arsenal	A	1–5	Robson
1946–47					
1	14 October 1946	Millwall	H	1–0	Kurz
2	28 October 1946	Barnet	A	7–0	Reece 3, Robson 2, J. Lewis, G. Lewis
SF	11 November 1946	Brentford	A	2–0	Naylor, Reece
F	2 December 1946	West Ham United (Played at Highbury)	N	2–3	Kurz (pen), Robson
1947–48					
1	13 October 1947	Dulwich Hamlet	A	1–3	Robson
1948–49					
1	11 October 1948	Chelsea	A	2–3	Kurz, Broughton
1949–50					
1	10 October 1949	West Ham United	H	0–1	
1950–51					
1	9 October 1950	Arsenal	H	1–0	Kurz
2	23 October 1950	Tottenham Hotspur	A	1–2	Saward
1951–52					
1	8 October 1951	Brentford	A	0–5	
1952–53					
1	6 October 1952	Wealdstone	H	1–3	Yore
1953–54					
1	5 October 1953	Chelsea	A	0–1	
1954–55					
1	4 October 1954	Chelsea	H	1–2	Randall
1955–56					
1	3 October 1955	Dagenham	H	3–0	Cooper, Tilston, Andrews

Rd	Date	Opponents	Venue	Score	Scorers
2	17 October 1955	Chelsea	A	0–8	
1956–57					
1	1 October 1956	Leyton Orient	H	0–3	
1957–58					
1	7 October 1957	Brentford	H	1–1	Murray
R	15 October 1957	Brentford	A	1–2	Deakin
1958–59					
1	6 October 1958	Chelsea	H	3–1	Pierce 2, Brett
2	20 October 1958	Arsenal	A	2–3	Pierce, Sanders
1959–60					
1	5 October 1959	Fulham	H	2–3	Easton 2 (1 pen)
1960–61					
1–	5 October 1960	West Ham United	H	3–3	Barnett, Easton, Kerrins
R	17 October 1960	West Ham United	A	2–6	Barnett, Colfar
1961–62					
1	2 October 1961	Tottenham Hotspur	A	2–8	Allen, Cartwright
1962–63					
1	1 October 1962	Wimbledon	A	2–2	Griffiths, Allen
R	8 October 1962	Wimbledon	A	0–2	
1963–64					
1	7 October 1963	Hounslow	H	5–3	Birch 2, Foster 3
2	22 October 1963	Fulham	A	1–1	Little
(Extra-time had been erroneously played, at the end of which Fulham had won 3–1 so there was a replay)					
R	28 October 1963	Fulham	H	0–1	
1964–65					
1	5 October 1964	Leyton Orient	A	1–4	Cutler
1965–66					
1	28 September 1965	Carshalton Athletic	H	3–1	Whitehouse 2, Yard
2	18 October 1965	Arsenal	H	3–3	Yard 2, Smith
R	25 October 1965	Arsenal	A	0–0 aet	
2R	1 November 1965	Arsenal	H	3–4 aet	Yard 2, Burnside (pen)
1966–67					
1	3 October 1966	Millwall	A	1–3	Smith
1967–68					
1	4 October 1967	Tottenham Hotspur	H	0–2	

Rd	Date	Opponents	Venue	Score	Scorers
1968–69					
1	30 September 1968	Charlton Athletic	A	3–0	L. Tomkins, Vansittart, own-goal
2	23 October 1968	Queen's Park Rangers	H	0–3	
1969–70					
1	29 September 1969	Barking	A	0–1	
1970–71					
1	30 September 1970	Bexley United	H	7–1	Bartram 3, L. Tomkins 2, Jenkins 2
2	13 October 1970	Wimbledon	A	1–2	L. Tomkins
1971–72					
1	16 September 1971	Tottenham Hotspur	A	0–0	
R	29 September 1971	Tottenham Hotspur	H	3–2	Pinkney, M. Hinshelwood, Mann
2	12. October 1971	Dagenham	H	1–2	Thomas
1972–73					
1	27 September 1972	Queen's Park Rangers	H	0–1	
1973–74					
1	25 September 1973	Hayes (Middx.)	A	1–3	Lindsay

Surrey Senior Cup

The Surrey Senior Cup was inaugurated by the Surrey Football Association in 1882 and has been competed for in every season since, apart from suspension due to wartime conditions. On most occasions between 1947 and 1959 the Final was held at Selhurst Park, attracting crowds of up to 15,000 spectators. Since 1993 Crystal Palace FC has taken part in the competition with reserve or junior teams, winning the Cup three times in 1997, 2001 and 2002. All of the ties have been played on opponent's grounds.

Rd	Date	Opponents	Venue	Score	Scorers
1993–94					
1	15 December 1993	Chertsey Town	A	1–1	Thompson
R	22 December 1993	Chertsey Town	A	4–3	Scully 2, Barnes, Thompson
2	18 January 1994	Metropolitan Police	A	2–2	Little, Launders
R	2 February 1994	Metropolitan Police	A	3–1	Thompson 2, Ndah
SF	16 March 1994	Sutton United	A	0–4	
1994–95					
1	14 December 1994	Molesley	A	1–3	
1995–96					
2	14 December 1995	Walton & Hersham	A	3–0	Rodger (pen), Taylor, J. Harris
3	29 January 1996	Metropolitan Police	A	3–1	J. Harris, Enqvist, own-goal
SF	8 February 1996	Woking	A	0–0	
R	16 March 1996	Woking	A	1–4	Stevens
1996–97					
1	30 October 1996	Epsom & Ewell	A	3–2	Scully, McKenzie, Wales
2	9 December 1996	Croydon	A	2–1	Ndah 2
3	14 January 1997	Corinthian Casuals	A	3–0	Enqvist, Wales, own-goal
SF	4 March 1997	Sutton United	A	3–1	J. Harris, Wordsworth, Burton (pen)
F	5 May 1997	Carshalton Athletic	A	1–0	J. Harris
1997–98					
1	22 December 1997	Cobham	A	2–1	Morrison, Martin
2	22 January 1998	Whyteleafe	A	0–1	
1998–99					
1	8 December 1998	Ashford Town (Middx.)	A	1–2	Wright
1999–2000					
4	18 January 2000	Tooting & Mitcham United	A	2–0	Sharpling, Hunt
5	22 February 2000	Woking	A	0–2	
2000–01					
4	15 February 2001	Egham	A	4–3	D'sane, Fowler 2, Hunt

Rd	Date	Opponents	Venue	Score	Scorers
5	24 February 2001	Croydon	A	3–2	Evans, Hunt, Fowler
SF	31 March 2001	Woking	A	3–0	Hankin 2, Martin
F	11 May 2001	Tooting & Mitcham United	N	3–0	Kember, Evans, Hunt
		(Played at Sutton United)			

2001–02

4	30 January 2002	Leatherhead	A	3–1	Martin, G. Williams 2
5	12 March 2002	Epsom & Ewell	A	3–1	Routledge, G. Williams, Howell
SF	25 March 2002	Croydon	A	3–1	G. Williams, Dobson 2
F	30 April 2002	Woking	N	3–0	G. Williams 2, Kabba
		(Played at Metropolitan Police, Imber Court)			

2002–03

4	13 January 2003	Metropolitan Police	A	4–1	Smith, Watson, Hunt, Williams (pen)
5	3 March 2003	Leatherhead	A	0–0	
		(Lost 4–5 on penalties)			

2003–04

2	25 November 2003	Kingstonian	A	0–3	

2004–05

2	8 December 2004	Westfield	A	7–0	Kaviedes 2, Watanabe, Dolan, Grabban 3
3	1 February 2005	Chipstead	A	6–2	A. Smith 3 (1 pen), R. Hall 2, Brotherton
4	2 March 2005	AFC Wimbledon	A	0–2	

2005–06

2	1 November 2005	Beckenham Town	A	1–5	Berry

2006–07

2	5 December 2006	Frimley Green	A	5–2	Sheringham 2, Robinson, Hall, Sweeney
3	23 January 2007	Tooting & Mitcham United	A	1–2	Spence

2007–08

2	4 December 2007	Chipstead	A	1–4 aet	Comley

2008–09

2	25 November 2008	Whyteleafe	A	2–3	Edwards, Adelakun

2009–10

2	30 November 2009	Kingstonian	A	3–2	Roberts, Sekajja, Williamson-Murrell
3	11 March 2010	Croydon Athletic	A	2–6 aet	Roberts, Williamson-Murrell

2010–11

2	11 January 2011	Ash United	A	1–2	Dennis

FA Youth Cup

The FA Youth Cup was introduced in the 1952–53 season, and the club has competed in every season since, winning the trophy twice and reaching the Final on two other occasions. Unfortunately, it has proved difficult to find all the main details for some of the early games.

Rd	Date	Opponents	Venue	Score	Scorers
1952–53					
1	18 October 1952	Gillingham	H	4–1	
2	26 October 1952	Brighton & Hove Albion	A	0–1	
1953–54					
1	17 October 1953	Bexleyheath & Welling	A	3–5	Law, Hobbis, Harris
1954–55					
2	27 October 1954	Southampton	A	5–2	
3	29 November 1954	Chelsea	H	0–8	
1955–56					
1	29 September 1955	Halling Minors	A	3–1	
2	29 October 1955	Gillingham	H	1–1	Byrne
R	5 November 1955	Gillingham	A	2–1	Dicks, Taylor
3	28 November 1955	Bexleyheath & Welling	H	1–1	
R	17 December 1955	Bexleyheath & Welling	A	3–5	
1956–57					
1	3 October 1956	Lion Works	H	9–1	Byrne 4, Easton 4, Spriggs
2	22 October 1956	Bexleyheath & Welling	H	3–0	Byrne 3 (1 pen)
3	3 December 1956	West Ham United	A	2–6	Pollington (pen), Byrne
1957–58					
2	21 October 1957	Eastbourne	H	1–0	Shone
3	1957	Bexleyheath & Welling	A	0–4	
1958–59					
1	4 October 1958	Fulham	H	5–4	
2	10 November 1958	Eastbourne	H	1–4	
1959–60					
2	16 November 1959	Gillingham	H	11–0	Mitchell 4, Cook 3, Roberts 2, Lewis, Rythorne
3	6 January 1960	West Ham United	A	0–5	

Rd	Date	Opponents	Venue	Score	Scorers
1960–61					
2	16 November 1960	Worthing	H	6–1	Mitchell 2, Bowant, Lewis (pen), Watts, Kelsey
3	7 January 1961	Charlton Athletic	A	0–3	
1961–62					
2	6 November 1961	Southampton	A	3–3	Burrows, Finch, Griffiths
R	24 November 1961	Southampton	H	3–0	Griffiths, Burrows, Finch
3	15 January 1962	Brighton & Hove Albion	H	0–1	
1962–63					
1	17 November 1962	Millwall	A	6–0	Barrett 2, Buckley, Griffths, Stephenson, Cutler
2	10 December 1962	Bexleyheath	H	2–3	Griffiths, Buckley
1963–64					
1	20 November 1963	Charlton Athletic	A	0–2	
1964–65					
1	9 November 1964	Charlton Athletic	A	0–1	
1965–66					
1	10 November 1965	Tooting & Mitcham United	H	7–1	Light 2, Stack 2, Kay 2, Atkins
2	8 December 1965	Chelsea	A	0–4	
1966–67					
1	9 November 1966	Millwall	H	1–2	Kember
1967–68					
1	8 November 1967	Hayes (Middlesex)	A	8–1	Smith 4, S. Tomkins 2, Mosedale, Lewis
2	5 December 1967	West Ham United	H	2–0	Cook, Harland
3	18 January 1968	Watford	A	1–0	Cook
4	13 February 1968	Charlton Athletic	H	2–1	Cook, Harland
5	26 February 1968	Chelsea	A	5–3	Vansittart 2, Lewis, Cook, Morton
SF L1	3 April 1968	Coventry City	H	1–1	Vansittart
SF L2	9 April 1968	Coventry City	A	0–2	
1968–69					
2	27 November 1968	Queen's Park Rangers	H	1–3	Own-goal
1969–70					
2	1 December 1969	Millwall	A	1–2	M. Brown

Rd	Date	Opponents	Venue	Score	Scorers
1970–71					
1	7 November 1970	Brentford	A	5–2	Crane 2, Pain, Wiltshire, M. Hinshelwood
2	14 December 1970	Luton Town	H	4–0	M. Hinshelwood, Pain, Crane, Thomas
3	11 January 1971	Fulham	A	1–2	Phil Hammond
1971–72					
1	26 October 1971	Brentford	A	4–2	McBride, Chatterton, Norris, Austin
2	29 November 1971	Fulham	A	1–0	McBride (pen)
3	15 December 1971	Tottenham Hotspur	H	1–0	Cannon
4	31 January 1972	Chelsea	A	0–3	
1972–73					
2	29 November 1972	Cambridge United	H	3–0	P. Hinshelwood, Bascombe, own-goal
3	20 December 1972	West Ham United	H	2–2	Walley, P. Hinshelwood
R	10 January 1973	West Ham United	A	2–4 aet	McCarthy, P. Hinshelwood
1973–74					
2	27 November 1973	Arsenal	A	0–3	
1974–75					
2	1974	Southampton	A	1–0	
3	19 December 1974	Fulham	A	0–3	
1975–76					
2	25 November 1975	Croydon	H	6–1	Leahy 3, Hilaire 2, Brennan
3	22 December 1975	Aston Villa	H	1–0	Murphy
4	7 January 1976	Arsenal	A	2–0	Leahy, Smillie
5	28 February 1976	Oldham Athletic	H	2–1	Leahy, Hilaire
SF L1	29 March 1976	West Bromwich Albion	A	2–3	Smillie, Walsh
SF L2	6 April 1976	West Bromwich Albion	H	0–2	
1976–77					
2	20 December 1976	Fulham	H	0–0	
R	6 January 1977	Fulham	A	4–1	Walsh 3, Hilaire
3	1 February 1977	Arsenal	H	2–2	Leahy 2
R	12 February 1977	Arsenal	A	0–0	
2R	5 February 1977	Arsenal	H	4–0	Sansom, Walsh, Hilaire 2
4	4 March 1977	Chelsea	A	3–2	Walsh, Hilaire, Leahy
5	26 March 1977	West Bromwich Albion	H	3–0	Sansom, Hilaire 2
SF L1	6 April 1977	Tottenham Hotspur	H	2–0	Gilbert, Sansom
SF L2	13 April 1977	Tottenham Hotspur	A	6–0	Walsh 2, Leahy 2, Hilaire 2
F L1	5 May 1977	Everton	A	0–0	
F L2	13 May 1977	Everton	H	1–0	Fenwick
1977–78					
2	6 December 1977	Fulham	H	1–0	Carter
3	1 February 1978	Chelsea	A	3–0	Murphy 2, Fenwick
4	21 February 1978	Leeds United	H	0–0	

Rd	Date	Opponents	Venue	Score	Scorers
R	7 March 1978	Leeds United	A	1–0	Lovell
5	22 March 1978	Port Vale	H	3–0	Dare, Mackenzie, Leahy
SF L1	3 April 1978	West Bromwich Albion	H	1–1	Lovell
SF L2	10 April 1978	West Bromwich Albion	A	0–0	
R	13 April 1978	West Bromwich Albion	A	2–2	Murphy, Hilaire
2R	20 April 1978	West Bromwich Albion	H	3–0	Murphy 2, Hilaire
F	27 April 1978	Aston Villa	N	1–0	Fenwick
	(Played at Highbury Stadium)				
1978–79					
2	20 December 1978	Fulham	A	2–0	Carter, Grabban
3	22 January 1979	Tottenham Hotspur	A	2–0	Carter 2
4	20 February 1979	Manchester City	H	1–2	Paul
1979–80					
2	27 November 1979	Orient	H	2–1	Finnigan, Brooks
3	8 January 1980	Southampton	A	1–2	Grabban
1980–81					
2	24 November 1980	Watford	A	0–3	
1981–82					
2	2 December 1981	Chelsea	H	0–1	
1982–83					
1	4 November 1982	Brentford	H	2–1	Leader, Martin
2	29 November 1982	Maidstone United	H	4–2	Leader 2, Howe, Jay
3	13 December 1982	West Ham United	A	1–7	Leader
1983–84					
1	14 November 1983	Faversham	A	2–1	Dodman, Barry
2	5 December 1983	AP Leamington	A	0–2	
1984–85					
1	5 November 1984	Brentford	A	1–4	Boyce
1985–86					
1	5 November 1985	Brentford	H	4–2	Sutcliffe 2, Salako, Boys
2	3 December 1985	Southampton	H	3–7	Sutcliffe, Hone, Boys
1986–87					
1	28 October 1986	Enfield	A	8–2	Davenport, Ansah 2, Salako 2, Porter, Rains, Cann
2	8 December 1986	Croydon	A	2–0	Ansah, Hotston
3	2 February 1987	Fulham	H	2–0	Rains 2
4	17 February 1987	Charlton Athletic	H	0–1	

Rd	Date	Opponents	Venue	Score	Scorers
1987–88					
2	30 November 1987	Wimbledon	A	0–1	
1988–89					
2	6 December 1988	Southampton	H	2–1	Ellis, Butler
3	18 January 1989	Brentford	A	0–1	
1989–90					
2	21 November 1989	Southampton	A	2–0	Osborn, Roberts
3	8 January 1990	Brentford	H	1–1	Osborn
R	17 January 1990	Brentford	A	1–0	Moralee
4	6 February 1990	Manchester City	A	0–3	
1990–91					
2	19 November 1990	Queen's Park Rangers	H	3–3	Chester, Thomas, Brazier
R	29 November 1990	Queen's Park Rangers	A	1–0	Gordon
3	17 January 1991	Chelsea	A	0–3	
1991–92					
2	4 December 1991	Charlton Athletic	A	2–0	McPherson, Ndah
3	13 January 1992	Chelsea	A	2–0	Cutler, Thompson
4	5 February 1992	Crewe Alexandra	H	2–0	Rollison, own-goal
5	4 March 1992	West Ham United	H	2–0	Holman, McCall
SF L1	17 March 1992	Wimbledon	A	2–1	Thompson, Watts (pen)
SF L2	24 March 1992	Wimbledon	H	3–3	Thompson, Holman, Watts
F L1	14 April 1992	Manchester United	H	1–3	McCall
F L2	15 May 1992	Manchester United	A	2–3	McPherson, McCall
1992–93					
2	7 December 1992	Cardiff City	H	2–0	Ndah 2
3	12 January 1993	Millwall	H	0–2	
1993–94					
2	1 December 1993	Dulwich Hamlet	A	5–0	E. Smith 3, Harris, Dixon
3	11 January 1994	Portsmouth	A	0–2	
1994–95					
2	5 December 1994	Southend United	A	1–2	J. Harris
1995–96					
2	15 November 1995	Swindon Town	A	2–0	Morrison, McKenzie
3	8 January 1996	Bristol City	H	7–0	Morrison 2, McKenzie 2, Burton (pen), Garland, Wales
4	12 February 1996	Plymouth Argyle	A	2–0	McKenzie, Thomson
5	18 March 1996	Watford	H	2–0	Mullins, Wales
SF L1	27 March 1996	Liverpool	A	2–4	McKenzie, Thomson
SF L2	15 April 1996	Liverpool	H	3–3	Wales, Enqvist, Morrison

Rd	Date	Opponents	Venue	Score	Scorers
1996–97					
2	3 December 1996	Chelsea	H	3–2	Morrison, R. Harris, Martin
3	22 January 1997	West Ham United	H	2–1	Morrison, Martin
4	17 February 1997	Peterborough United	A	3–1	Stevens, Graham, Morrison
5	12 March 1997	Tottenham Hotspur	H	1–0	Morrison
SF L1	10 April 1997	Blackburn Rovers	H	2–1	Mullins, Folan
SF L2	17 April 1997	Blackburn Rovers	A	2–2	Stevens, Martin
F L1	24 April 1997	Leeds United	A	1–2	R. Harris
F L2	5 May 1997	Leeds United	H	0–1	
1997–98					
2	25 November 1997	Norwich City	A	0–0	
R	9 December 1997	Norwich City	H	2–1	Martin, Sharpling
3	10 January 1998	Leeds United	A	1–3	Sharpling
1998–99					
3	15 December 1998	Tranmere Rovers	H	1–0	Fowler
4	19 January 1999	Charlton Athletic	A	2–0	Kabba, Evans
5	9 February 1999	Arsenal	A	0–0	
R	17 March 1999	Arsenal	H	0–1 aet	
1999–2000					
3	1 December 1999	Barnet	H	3–2	Williams, Dimond 2
4	19 January 2000	Middlesbrough	A	0–6	
2000–01					
3	30 November 2000	Newcastle United	A	2–2	Williams, Amoako
R	16 December 2000	Newcastle United	H	4–1	Gwillim, Williams 3
4	22 January 2001	Ipswich Town	A	1–3	Antwi
2001–02					
3	5 December 2001	Wolverhampton Wanderers (Won 4–2 on penalties)	H	1–1 aet	Winnothai
4	22 January 2002	Hartlepool United	H	1–2	Watson
2002–03					
3	27 November 2002	Burnley	A	2–0	Winnothai, Watson
4	6 February 2003	Notts County	H	3–1	Nabil 2, Watson (pen)
5	20 February 2003	Tottenham Hotspur	H	0–1	
2003–04					
3	2 December 2003	Tranmere Rovers	H	1–2	Grabban
2004–05					
3	16 December 2004	Arsenal	A	0–3	

Rd	Date	Opponents	Venue	Score	Scorers
2005–06					
3	15 December 2005	Colchester United	H	3–2 aet	Hall, Moses, Grabban
4	16 January 2006	Tranmere Rovers	H	3–1	Grabban, Hall, Dayton
5	30 January 2006	Watford	H	3–2 aet	Hall, Watanabe, Grabban
6	9 February 2006	Southampton	H	0–4	
2006–07					
3	11 December 2006	Stoke City	H	4–1	Moses 2, Hughes 2
4	15 January 2007	Plymouth Argyle	H	4–2	Kudjodi 2, Fish (pen), Hughes
5	30 January 2007	Manchester United	A	0–2	
2007–08					
3	11 December 2007	Hull City	H	1–0	Scannell
4	8 January 2008	Leicester City	A	2–3 aet	Robinson 2 (1 pen)
2008–09					
3	2 December 2008	Swindon Town	A	5–1	Comley, Moses, Pinney 3
4	20 January 2009	Ipswich Town	A	2–4 aet	Abnett, Roberts
2009–10					
3	9 December 2009	Bristol City	H	3–2 aet	Sekajja, Wynter, Holness
4	25 January 2010	Derby County	H	2–0	Zaha, Goldsmith
5	11 February 2010	Hull City	A	4–1	Goldsmith 2, Kenlock, Randall
6	25 February 2010	Newcastle United	A	2–4	Goldsmith, Sekajja
2010–11					
3	14 December 2010	Cardiff City	A	3–0	De Silva, Sekajja, Wynter
4	8 January 2011	Liverpool	A	1–3 aet	Sekajja

OTHER FIRST XI COMPETITIONS

This section includes a number of secondary competitions that the club's first team was involved in since its inception in 1905, and as such players appearances are not counted in their full club total. It was decided not to include the London Challenge Cup as this competition was, in the main, for the reserve teams of League clubs while non-League clubs could field their first XIs.

With regard to the Anglo-Italian competitions, that from the 1970s was by invitation while the 1993–94 competition involved all League clubs from the then Division One (former League Division Two) and therefore the players' appearances in the latter do count in their full club total. It is genuinely thought that the club's victory against Inter Milan in the San Siro Stadium in June 1971 is the first there by an English club.

LONDON PROFESSIONAL CHARITY CUP (1908–09 to 1930–31)

1908–09

28 April 1909
Leyton (Away) 0–0
Johnson, Collyer, Needham, Innerd, Ryan, Thorpe, Garratt, Swann, Bauchop, Woodger, Brearley

Replay
30 April 1909
Leytin (Home) 1–1 aet
Innerd
Johnson, Collyer, Needham, Innerd, Ryan, Thorpe, Garratt, Swann, Bauchop, Woodger, Brearley
Leyton players declined to play second period of extra-time, and the medals were withheld

1909–10

5 January 1910
Croydon Common (Home) 1–1
Woodger
Johnson, Collyer, Bulcock, Spottiswood, Clark, Hughes, Garratt, Woodger, Williams, Payne, Griffin
Match abandoned in extra-time

13 January 1910
Croydon Common (Home) 1–0
Garratt
Johnson, Collyer, Bulcock, Spottiswood, Hughes, Hanger, Garratt, Woodger, Williams, Payne, Griffin

1910–11

31 October 1910
Millwall (Away) 3–0
Woodhouse, Davies, Williams
Johnson, Collyer, Bulcock, Hatton, Hughes, Collins, Garratt, Hewitt, Williams, Woodhouse, Davies

1911–12

30 October 1911
Millwall (Away) 1–2
Woodhouse
Johnson, Collyer, Bulcock, Collins, Hughes, Hanger, Garratt, Hewitt, Woodhouse, Williams, Davies

1912–13

30 October 1912
Millwall (Home) 1–2
Smith
Johnson, Collyer, O'Conor, Williams, Hughes, Hanger, Garratt, Hewitt, Smith, York, Davies

1913–14

27 October 1913
Tottenham Hotspur (Away) 2–1
Smith, Hewitt
Johnson, Collyer, Colclough, Spottiswood, York, Hanger, Bateman, Hewitt, Smith, Williams, Whibley

1914–15

28 October 1914
Tottenham Hotspur (Home) 2–2
Whibley, Hewitt
Johnson, Collyer, Colclough, Spottiswood, Feebery, Hanger, Whibley, Hewitt, Smith, York, Davies

1915–16 to 1918–19 No Competition

1919–20

29 October 1919
Clapton Orient (Home) 3–1
Conner, Smith, Page
Alderson, Little, Rhodes, Cracknell, Hughes, Feebery, Storey, Conner, Smith, E. Page, Wood

1920–21

28 October 1920
Clapton Orient (Away) 1–2
Wood
Alderson, Little, Rhodes, McCracken, Bates, Feebery, Storey, Conner, Wood, Menlove, Whibley

1921–22

12 October 1921
Clapton Orient (Home) 1–1
Roberts
Alderson, Little, Rhodes, McCracken, Jones, Dreyer, Hand, Storey, Conner, Menlove, Whibley

Replay
22 March 1922
Clapton Orient (Home) 0–1
Irwin, Little, Rhodes, McCracken, Jones, Feebery, Storey, Dreyer, Wood, Cartwright, Whibley

1922–23

13 November 1922
Clapton Orient (Away) 2–0
Whitworth 2 (1 pen)
Irwin, Little, Cross, Dreyer, Nixon, Greener, Bateman, Whitworth, Harry, Johnson, Morgan

1923–24

28 November 1923
Charlton Athletic (Home) 4–1
Hoddinott 2, Whitworth 2 (2 pens)
Alderson, Little, Nixon, Allen, Hamilton, Greener, Harry, Whitworth, Hoddinott, Morgan, Osborne

1924–25

9 February 1925
Charlton Athletic (Away) 1–0
Whitworth
Harper, Blake, Cross, Middlemiss, Hamilton, Pettit, Hand, Groves, Whitworth, Johnson, Osborne

SOUTHERN CHARITY CUP (1909–10 to 1912–13)

1909–10

Round 1
27 September 1909
Queen's Park Rangers (Away) 1–3
Williams
Johnson, Collyer, Collins, Spottiswood, Clarke, Hughes, Garratt, Payne, Williams, Woodger, Griffin

1910–11

Round 1
28 September 1910
Southend United (Away) 1–1
Woodhouse
Johnson, Collyer, Thompson, Spottiswood, Hatton, Hanger, Davies, Williams, Woodhouse, Lawrence, Myers

Replay
12 October 1910
Southend United (Home) 1–2 aet
Woodhouse
Johnson, Thompson, Bulcock, Spottiswood, Hughes, Hanger, Garratt, Payne, Woodhouse, Lawrence, Myers

1911–12

Round 1
11 October 1911
Queen's Park Rangers (Away) 0–3
Johnson, Collyer, Bulcock, Spottiswood, Williams, Tyler, Garratt, Hewitt, Woodhouse, Lawrence, Davies

1912–13

Round 1
22 January 1913
Southend United (Away) 2–0
Williams, Bourne
Wood, Colclough, O'Conor, Spottiswood, York, Collins, Garratt, Williams, Smith, Bourne, Keene

Round 2
13 February 1913
Queen's Park Rangers (Away) 1–7
Bateman
Wood, O'Conor, Jupp, Collins, York, Page, Bateman, Briant, E. Rogers, J. Rogers

KENT SENIOR SHIELD (1911–12 to 1913–14)

1911–12

Round 1
4 October 1911
Bromley (Away) 5–2
Myers, Davies 2, Williams, Harker
Johnson, Collyer, O'Conor, Spottiswood, Collins, Hanger, Davies, Harker, Williams, Hewitt, Myers

Semi-final
25 October 1911
Millwall (Away) 0–0
Johnson, Collyer, Bulcock, Spottiswood, Hughes, Hanger, Garratt, Hewitt, Woodhouse, Williams, Davies

Replay
15 November 1911
Millwall (Home) 5–0
Hughes, Woodhouse 3 (1 pen), Harker
Johnson, Collyer, Bulcock, Collins, Hughes, Hanger, Garratt, Harker, Woodhouse, Williams, Davies

Final
27 November 1911
New Brompton (The Den) 3–1
Harker, Woodhouse 2 (1 pen)
Johnson, Collyer, Bulcock, Spottiswood, Hughes, Hanger, Garratt, Harker, Woodhouse, Williams, Davies
Att: 1,000

1912–13

Round 1
16 October 1912
Woolwich Arsenal (Home) 1–0
Davies
Johnson, Collyer, Bulcock, Spottiswood, Hanger, York, Garratt, Hewitt, Williams, Lloyd, Davies
Att: 3,000

Semi-final
6 November 1912
Bromley (Home) 6–0
Williams 4, Bourne 2
Johnson, Collyer, Colclough, Spottiswood, Hughes, Hanger, Garratt, Hewitt, Williams, Bourne, Keene

Final
27 November 1912
Millwall (Home) 1–2
Hughes
Johnson, Colclough, Bulcock, Spottiswood, Hughes, Hanger, Garratt, Hewitt, Mortimer, York, Davies

1913–14

Round 1
8 October 1913
Tunbridge Wells Rangers (Home) 6–0
Williams, Hewitt, Smith 4
Johnson, Collyer, Colclough, Spottiswood, Hughes, York, Bateman, Hewitt, Smith, Williams, Whibley

Semi-final
5 November 1913
Millwall (Home) 1–1
Whibley
Johnson, Colclough, O'Conor, Spottiswood, Hughes, Hanger, Bateman, Hewitt, Smith, Williams, Whibley
Att: 5,000

Replay
29 November 1913
Millwall (Away) 0–1
Johnson, Collyer, Colclough, Spottiswood, Hughes, Hanger, Bateman, Hewitt, Smith, Williams, Davies

FOOTBALL LEAGUE DIVISION THREE SOUTH SECTION CUP (1933–34 to 1938–39)

1933–34

Round 1
24 January 1934
Exeter City (Away) 6–11
Fyfe, A. Dawes 2, Thompson 2
Beby, Tyler, T. Brown, C. Brown, Nicholas, Finn, Fyfe, Goddard, A. Dawes, Thompson, Bigg
Att: 3,000

1934–35

Round 2
17 October 1934
Cardiff City (Home) 3–1
A. Dawes 3
Dunn, Owens, Parry, Haynes, Wilde, Heinemann, Carson, Manders, Rooke, A. Dawes, Crompton
Att: 3,000

Round 3
7 February 1935
Coventry City (Away) 1–5
Bigg
Dunn, Purdon, Rumbold, Turner, Wilde, Heinemann, Carson, Manders, Simpson, A. Dawes, Bigg
Att: 2,000

1935–36

Round 1
30 September 1935
Cardiff City (Home) 2–1
Manders, Waldron
Dunn, Haynes, Rumbold, Turner, Wilde, W.S. Smith, Carson, Manders, A. Dawes, Waldron, Bigg
Att: 1,681

Round 2
28 October 1935
Exeter City (Home) 4–2
Bigg, A. Dawes 2, Birtley
Dunn, Owens, Parry, Turner, Purdon, W.S. Smith, Birtley, Waldron Hanson, A. Dawes, Bigg
Att: 1,449

Round 3
11 November 1935
Southend United (Home) 3–2
Rooke 2 (1 pen), Hanson
Stanbury, Thorpe, Waterfield, Wilde, Purdon, W.S. Smith, Turner, Birtley, Rooke, Waldron, Hanson
Att: 1,500

Semi–final
11 January 1936
Coventry City (Home) 1–2
Birtley
Dunn, Thorpe, Booth, Turner, Levene, Collins, Wood, Birtley, Blackman, A. Dawes, Bigg
Att: 10,500

1936–37

Round 1
30 September 1936
Brighton & Hove Albion (Home) 3–2
Levene, Waldron 2
Dunn, Owens, F. Dawes, McMenemy, Walker, Levene, Liddle, Birtley, Rooke, Waldron, Coulston
Att: 2,822

Round 2
21 October 1936
Torquay United (Away) 0–1
Dunn, Owens, Rumbold, McMenemy, Walker, Collins, Liddle, Birtley, Blackman, A. Dawes, Bigg
Att: Not known

1937–38

Round 1
27 September 1937
Mansfield Town (Away) 1–0
Robson
Chesters, Owens, F. Dawes, Lievesley, Shanks, Collins, Pritchard, Fielding, Blackman, Robson, Horton
Att: 1,500

Round 2
17 November 1937
Bristol Rovers (Away) 0–5
Chesters, Owens, F. Dawes, Lievesley, Walker, Birtley, Davis, Waldron, Palethorpe, Robson, Fielding

1938–39

Round 2
10 December 1938
Brighton & Hove Albion (Away) 3–2
Steele 2, Robson
Chesters, Gregory, F. Dawes, Lievesley, Walker, Reece, Robson, T. Smith, Steele, Bott, Bigg
Att: 6,000

Round 3
8 March 1939
Reading (Away) 0–0
Chesters, Owens, F. Dawes, A. Dawes, Shanks, Reece, Birtley, Gillespie, Blackman, Robson, Bigg
Att: 1,218

Replay
22 March 1939
Reading (Home) 6–4
Steele, Waldron 2 (1 pen), Robson 3
Chesters, Gregory, F. Dawes, Reece, J. Lewis, Hudgell, Birtley, Waldron, Robson, Bark, Steele
Att: 2,071

Semi-final
29 March 1939
Torquay United (Away) 2–4
Own-goal, Waldron
Tootill, Owens, F. Dawes, Reece, J. Lewis, Hudgell, Birtley, T. Smith, Robson, Waldron, Steele

FOOTBALL LEAGUE JUBILEE

1938–39

20 August
Brighton & Hove Albion (Home) 5–0
A. Dawes 3, Horton
Chesters, Owens, F. Dawes, Lievesley, Walker, Collins, Davis, T. Smith, Jordan, A. Dawes, Horton
Att: 8,298

1939–40

19 August 1939
Brighton & Hove Albion (Away) 3–3
Robson, Waldron 2 (1 pen)
Chesters, Owens, F. Dawes, Lievesley, Shanks, Collins, Wilson, T. Smith, Robson, Waldron, James
Att: 4,500

SOUTHERN PROFESSIONAL FLOODLIGHT CUP (1955–56 to 1959–60)

1955–56

Round 1
10 October 1955
West Ham United (Away) 0–3
Bailey, Noakes, Greenwood, Moss, Choules, Sanders, Berry, Belcher, Brett, Murray, Gunning
Att: 6,000

1956–57

Round 1
2 October 1956
Arsenal (Away) 0–4
Potter, Edwards, Greenwood, Belcher, Choules, Long, Harrison, Berry, Deakin, Cooper, Morris
Att: 4,685

1957–58

Round 1
22 October 1957
Watford (Away) 1–4
Cooper
Rouse, Edwards, Brown, Long, Truett, Sanders, Berry, Brett, Deakin, Cooper, Harrison
Att: 2,376

1958–59

Round 1
13 October 1958
Reading (Home) 4–2
Byrne, Brett 2, Long
Hopgood, Skingley, Noakes, McNichol, Choules, Long, Nastri, Byrne, Brett, Pierce, Colfar
Att: 2,807

Round 2
19 January 1959
Millwall (Away) 1–1
Byrne
Rouse, Noakes, Sanders, McNichol, Choules, Long, Priestley, Summersby, Brett, Byrne, Colfar
Att: 5,559

Replay
28 January 1959
Millwall (Home) 3–2
Byrne 2, Summersby
Rouse, Howe, Noakes, McNichol, Choules, Long, Priestley, Summersby, Brett, Byrne, Collins
Att: 8,831

Semi-final
1 April 1959
Luton Town (Home) 1–0
Barnett
Rouse, Howe, Noakes, McNichol, Choules, Long, Brett, Summersby, Barnett, Byrne, Colfar
Att: 15, 731

Final
27 April 1959
Arsenal (Home) 1–2
Byrne
Rouse, Choules, Noakes, McNichol, Evans, Long, Brett, Summersby, Deakin, Byrne, Collins
Att: 32,384

1959–60
Round 1
21 October 1959
Brentford (Home) 5–2
Easton 4, Sexton
Rouse, Long, Noakes, Summersby, Choules, McNichol, Roche, Priestley, Sexton, Easton, Rees
Att: 6,600

Round 2
14 December 1959
Southampton (Home) 2–2
Barnett, Byrne
Rouse, Long, Howe, Summersby, Choules, McNichol, Roche, Woan, Barnett, Byrne, Colfar
Att: 6,136

Replay
18 January 1960
Southampton (Away) 1–2
Roche
Rouse, Long, Howe, Summersby, Evans, Pyke, Roche, Woan, Sexton, Easton, Rees
Att: 6,151

SURREY INVITATION CUP (1958–59 to 1959–60)

1958–59
24 November 1958
Dulwich Hamlet (Home) 6–0
Byrne 3, Barnett 3
Rouse, Skingley, Noakes, McNichol, Choules, Long, Harrison, Byrne, Barnett, Pierce, Colfar
Att: 2,350

20 April 1959
Woking (Home) 4–1
Pierce, Deakin, Nastri, Truett
Arnold, Howe, B. Collins, Truett, Evans, Lennon, Nastri, Priestley, Deakin, Pierce, Colfar
Att: 2,367

1959–60
30 November 1959
Dulwich Hamlet (Home) 8–1
Robinson 3, Summersby 2, Barnett 2, Easton
Patterson, Long, Noakes, Summersby, Evans, McNichol, Roche, Easton, Barnett, Robinson, Colfar
Att: 1,910

9 February 1960
Guildford City (Away) 3–0
Noakes, Kerrins 2
Rouse, Lunnis, Noakes, Long, Evans, Petchey, Barnett, Byrne, Uphill, Heckman, Kerrins
Att: 2,659

ANGLO-ITALIAN CUP (1970–71 to 1972–73)

1970–71
Group
26 May 1971
Cagliari (Home) 1–0
Tambling
Jackson, Loughlan, Payne, Kember, McCormick, Blyth, Wharton, Tambling (Scott), Birchenall, Queen, Taylor
Att: 19,326

29 May 1971
Inter Milan (Home) 1–1
Birchenall
Jackson, Loughlan, Payne, Taylor, McCormick, Blyth, Tambling (Scott), Kember, Birchenall, Queen, Wharton
Att: 25,152

1 June 1971
Cagliari (Away) 0–2
Jackson, Payne, Loughlan, Kember, McCormick, Blyth, Tambling, Birchenall, Queen, Taylor, Wharton
Att: 30,000

4 June 1971
Inter Milan (Away) 2–1
Tambling 2
Jackson, Payne, Taylor, Kember, McCormick, Blyth, Tambling, Wharton, Birchenall (Pinkney), Queen, Scott
At: 28,000

1972–73

Group
14 February 1973
Hellas Verona (Home) 4–1
M. Hinshelwood, Bell, Whittle 2
Jackson, Mulligan, Roffey, M. Hinshelwood (Chatterton), Bell, Cannon, Possee, Whittle, Craven (Swindlehurst), Taylor, Rogers
Att: 7,436

21 March 1973
Bari (Away) 1–0
Possee
Towse, Roffey, Taylor, Phillip, Bell, Blyth, Possee, Payne (M. Hinshelwood), Whittle, Cooke, Rogers
Att: 10,862

4 April 1973
Lazio (Home) 3–1
Craven 3
Towse, Roffey, Prince, Chatterton, Parker, Brown, Pain, Mann, Craven, M. Hinshelwood, Thomas
Att: 6,014

2 May 1973
Fiorentina (Away) 2–2
Possee 2
Hammond, Mulligan, Taylor, Roffey, Blyth, Phillip, Possee, Payne, Craven, Cooke, Rogers
Att: Not known

Semi-final First Leg
11 May 1973
Newcastle United (Home) 0–0
Hammond, Roffey, Taylor, Phillip, Blyth, Cannon, Possee, Payne, Whittle (P. Hinshelwood), Cooke, Rogers
Att: 12,001

Semi-final Second Leg
21 May 1973
Newcastle United (Away) 1–5
Cannon
Hammond, Roffey, Taylor, Phillip, Blyth, Cannon, Possee, Payne (P. Hinshelwood), Whittle, Cooke (Swindlehurst), Rogers
Att: 12,510

TEXACO CUP

1972–73

Round 1 First Leg
Hearts (Away) 0–1
Jackson, Prince, Roffey (Jenkins), Payne, Bell, Blyth, Pinkney, Kellard, Queen, Craven, A. Taylor
Att: 9,105

Round 1 Second Leg
Hearts (Home) 0–1
Jackson, Payne, Roffey, Kellard, McCormick, Blyth (Pinkney), M. Hinshelwood, Jenkins, Craven, A. Taylor, Tambling
Att: 9,855

KENT CUP

1975–76

Group
2 August 1975
Charlton Athletic (Home) 0–1
Chatterton, Wall, Sansom (P. Johnson), Holder, Mulligan, Evans, M. Hinshelwood, Hill (Whittle), Swindlehurst, Kemp, P. Taylor
Att: 5,938

5 August 1975
Gillingham (Away) 1–1
Evans
Caswell, Wall, Sansom, Holder, Cannon, Evans, Whittle, M. Hinshelwood, Swindlehurst, Kemp, P. Taylor
Att: 3,262

9 August 1975
Millwall (Away) 1–1
P. Taylor
Caswell, Wall, J. Johnson, Holder, Jeffries, M. Hinshelwood, Hill, Chatterton, Swindlehurst, Kemp, P. Taylor
Att: 3,891

FOOTBALL LEAGUE TROPHY

1982–83

Group
14 August 1982
Brentford (Away) 2–2
Edwards, Brooks
Barron, P. Hinshelwood, Hughton, Cannon, Nebbeling, Gilbert, Langley (Brooks), Wilkins, Edwards, Murphy, Giles
Att: 3,397

17 August 1982
Wimbledon (Home) 1–0
Edwards
Fry, P. Hinshelwood, Hughton, Cannon, Nebbeling, Lovell, Langley (Annon), Wilkins, Edwards, Brooks, Giles
Att: 2,852

21 August 1982
Millwall (Home) 0–3
Barron, P. Hinshelwood, Hughton, Cannon, Nebbeling, Gilbert, Langley, Brooks (Annon), Edwards, Wilkins (Lovell), Giles
Att: 4,844

Southern Junior Floodlit Cup

The Southern Junior Floodlit Cup was introduced in the 1955–56 season and the club competed until the 1997–98 season when it was discontinued, winning the trophy in 1997 and reaching the Final on one other occasion. Some of the latter home games were played at Plough Lane (Wimbledon) or Champion Hill (Dulwich Hamlet) as well as at Selhurst Park.

Rd	Date	Opponents	Venue	Score	Scorers
1955–56					
1	10 October 1955	Brighton & Hove Albion	H	7–0	Byrne 4, Dicks, Spurdens, Denman
2	16 November 1955	Chelsea	H	0–6	
1956–57					
1	31 October 1956	West Ham United	H	0–4	
1957–58					
1	11 November 1957	Chelsea	H	0–10	
1958–59					
1	23 September 1958	Bexleyheath & Welling	H	0–3	
1959–60					
1	12 October 1959	Arsenal	H	1–2 aet	J. Payne
1960–61					
1	31 October 1960	Brentford	H	2–1	C. Lewis 2
2	30 January 1961	Portsmouth	H	0–4	
1961–62					
1	18 October 1961	Bexleyheath & Welling	H	1–2	Chainey
1962–63					
1	26 September 1962	Arsenal	H	1–6	Cutler
1963–64					
1	25 September 1963	Charlton Athletic	H	0–1	
1964–65					
1	16 September 1964	West Ham United	H	0–0 aet	
R	28 September 1964	West Ham United	A	1–2	Nix
1965–66					
1	6 October 1965	Southampton	A	2–4	
1966–67					
1	14 September 1966	Brighton & Hove Albion	H	2–0	Brophy, Mosedale

Rd	Date	Opponents	Venue	Score	Scorers
2	29 September 1966	Brentford	A	2–1	Morris, L. Tomkins
3	8 March 1967	West Ham United	H	2–3	Smith, Cook
1967–68					
P	19 September 1967	Brighton & Hove Albion	H	5–0	Vansittart, Groves, Cook 2, Mills
1	20 November 1967	Coventry City	A	0–4	
1968–69					
1	14 October 1968	Colchester United	A	0–2	
1969–70					
P	15 September 1969	Southampton	A	1–1	Hoadley
R	29 September 1969	Southampton	H	9–1	Norman, Newman, Wiltshire 2, Thomas 2, Crane 2, own-goal
1	29 October 1969	Bournemouth	A	2–1	Jenkins, Wiltshire
2	25 November 1969	Millwall	A	0–3	
1970–71					
1	14 October 1970	Aston Villa	A	3–3	Thomas, Pain 2
R	4 November 1970	Aston Villa	H	2–3 aet	Thomas, Dillon
1971–72					
P	20 October 1971	Brighton & Hove Albion	H	4–1	Chatterton, Norris, Austin, own-goal
1	20 December 1971	Orient	H	1–0	Austin
2	1 March 1972	Swansea City	A	2–1	Austin, Parker
SF	28 March 1972	Coventry City	A	0–2	
1972–73					
	3 October 1972	Swindon Town	A	1–2	P. Hinshelwood
1973–74					
It is believed the club did not take part					
1974–75					
	24 October 1974	Gillingham	H	0–1	
1975–76					
P	16 September 1975	Chelsea	H	2–1	Smillie, Murphy
1	21 October 1975	Arsenal	A	0–1	
1976–77					
1	25 October 1976	Coventry City	A	3–1	Hilaire, Walsh, Leahy (pen)
2	16 November 1976	Oxford United	H	2–2	Hilaire 2
R	1 December 1976	Oxford United	A	3–2	Walsh, Hilaire 2
3	11 March 1977	Gillingham	A	3–0	Leahy 2, Murphy (pen)
SF	29 March 1977	West Ham United	A	2–0	Walsh, Hilaire

Rd	Date	Opponents	Venue	Score	Scorers
F L1	20 April 1977	Queen's Park Rangers	H	2–3	Murphy, Leahy
F L2	9 May 1977	Queen's Park Rangers	A	1–1	Walsh

1977–78

1	27 September 1977	Arsenal	H	1–2	Leahy

1978–79

1	26 September 1978	Wimbledon	A	1–0	Grabban
2	20 November 1978	Reading	A	3–3	Grabban, Mackenzie, Mercer
R	22 November 1978	Reading	H	3–2 aet	Carter, Grabban, Mercer
3	20 March 1979	Aston Villa	H	0–4	

1979–80

1	1 October 1979	Gillingham	A	5–1	Brooks, Grabban, Page 2, Martin
2	19 November 1979	Arsenal	A	1–2	Page

1980–81

1	29 September 1980	Colchester United	A	0–0	
R	8 October 1980	Colchester United	H	2–3	Boulter 2

1981–82

1	30 September 1981	Queen's Park Rangers	A	3–5	Oakley, Leader, Howe (pen)

1982-83

1	7 September 1982	Arsenal	A	0–3	

1983–84

The club did not take part.

1984–85

1	1 October 1984	Arsenal	H	0–4	

1985–86

1	1 October 1985	Portsmouth	A	2–2	Salako 2
R	8 October 1985	Portsmouth	H	0–1	

1986–87

1	18 September 1986	Southend United	A	0–0	
R	29 September 1986	Southend United	H	3–2	Ansah 2, Cann
2	11 November 1986	Watford	A	3–2	Salako, Ansah, Porter
3	5 January 1987	Chelsea	H	0–3	

1987–88

1	14 September 1987	Oxford United	H	0–0	
R	24 September 1987	Oxford United	A	1–3	Green

Rd	Date	Opponents	Venue	Score	Scorers
1988–89					
1	13 September 1988	Wimbledon	A	1–1	Moralee
R	20 September 1988	Wimbledon	H	1–0	Southgate
2	14 November 1988	Charlton Athletic	A	1–1	Moralee

Rd	Date	Opponents	Venue	Score	Scorers
R	16 November 1988	Charlton Athletic	H	1–3	Roberts
1989–90					
P	4 September 1989	Brentford	H	3–1	Brazier 2, Myatt
1	14 September 1989	Arsenal	A	1–1	Line
R	21 September 1989	Arsenal	H	1–2	Roberts
1990–91					
P	5 September 1990	Norwich City	H	1–1	McCall
R	11 September 1990	Norwich City	A	4–0	Thomas 2, Gordon, Brazier
1	19 September 1990	Southend United	H	2–2	Edwards 2
R	24 September 1990	Southend United	A	1–1 aet	Watts
			(Lost 4–5 on penalties)		
1991–92					
1	4 September 1991	Southampton	A	3–1	Ndah, Rollison, Watts
2	28 October 1991	Coventry City	H	2–0	Hawthorne, Watts
3	23 December 1991	Tottenham Hotspur	H	0–4	
1992–93					
1	15 September 1992	Wimbledon	A	2–1	Hall, Smith
2	26 October 1992	Millwall	H	0–2	
1993–94					
1	7 September 1993	Tottenham Hotspur	A	1–6	J. Harris
1994–95					
1	21 September 1994	Coventry City	H	4–0	Quinn (pen), McCluskie 2, J. Harris
2	16 November 1994	Charlton Athletic	A	0–1	
1995–96					
1	19 September 1995	Gillingham	H	1–1	Morrison
R	9 October 1995	Gillingham	A	1–0	McKenzie
2	1 November 1995	Wimbledon	H	0–2	
1996–97					
1	17 September 1996	Coventry City	H	3–3	Morrison 2, Martin
R	30 September 1996	Coventry City	A	3–1	D'Sane, Morrison 2
2	5 November 1996	Leyton Orient	A	4–3	Small-King, Mullins, Martin, own-goal
3	10 December 1996	Charlton Athletic	H	2–2	Martin, R. Harris
R	3 February 1997	Charlton Athletic	A	3–0	Martin, Morrison 2

Rd	Date	Opponents	Venue	Score	Scorers
SF	25 March 1997	Wycombe Wanderers	A	1–1	Morrison
R	2 April 1997	Wycombe Wanderers	H	1–0	Folan
F L1	29 April 1997	Arsenal	H	2–1	Graham, Carlisle
F L2	7 May 1997	Arsenal	A	1–0	Stevens

1997-98

Rd	Date	Opponents	Venue	Score	Scorers
1	9 September 1997	Luton Town	A	1–0	Martin
2	28 October 1997	Watford	A	1–1	Woozley
R	12 November 1997	Watford	H	3–3 aet	Boardman, Carlisle (pen), Martin
			(Won 5–3 on penalties)		
3	22 December 1997	Southend United	H	1–1	Hibburt
R	20 January 1998	Southend United	A	3–0	Sharpling, Carlisle, Hunt
SF	24 March 1998	Queen's Park Rangers	A	0–2	

Abandoned Games

Below are details of fixtures played by Crystal Palace in the United League, Southern League, Football League, FA Cup and League Cup that have been abandoned for whatever reason.

11 November 1905
United League
Luton Town (Away) 1–0
Watkins
Hewitson, Walker, Grant, Innerd, Birnie, Astley, Wallace, Harker, Watkins, Needham, Roberts.
Att: 3,000
85 mins – Bad Light
Rearranged Fixture:
19 February 1906
Luton Town 1 Crystal Palace 2

18 November 1911
Southern League Division One
Plymouth Argyle (Home) 3–1
Harker, Woodhouse, Hughes
Johnson, Collyer, Bulcock, Spottiswood, Hughes, Hanger, Garratt, Harker, Woodhouse, Williams, Davies
Att: 5,500
78 mins – Bad Light
Rearranged Fixture:
28 February 1912
Crystal Palace 0 Plymouth Argyle 1

29 November 1919
Southern League Division One
Exeter City (Home) 0–0
Alderson, Little, Rhodes, Cracknell, Bates, Feebery, Bateman, Conner, Smith, Barber, Whibley
Att: 14,000
85 mins – Bad Light
Rearranged Fixture:
17 March 1920
Crystal Palace 1 Exeter City 0

21 December 1935
Football League Division Three South
Bristol City (Away) 1–1
Carson
Dunn, Booth, Parry, Turner, Wilde, W.S. Smith, Carson, Birtley, Blackman, A. Dawes, Bigg
Att: 3,000
80 mins – Fog
Rearranged Fixture:
29 April 1936
Bristol City 2 Crystal Palace 0

4 December 1937
Football League Division Three South
Northampton Town (Away) 1–1
Blackman
Chesters, Owens, F. Dawes, Lievesley, Walker, T. Smith, Davis, Gillespie, Blackman, Robson, Pritchard
Att: 4,000
55 mins – Snow
Rearranged Fixture:
16 April 1938
Northampton Town 1 Crystal Palace 0

25 November 1950
FA Cup First Round
Millwall (Home) 0–0
Graham, Harding, McDonald, Whittaker, Watson, Buckley, Broughton, Kelly, Rundle, Jones, Stevens
Att: 24,196
34 mins – Fog
Rearranged Fixture:
29 November 1950
Crystal Palace 1 Millwall 4

9 April 1951
Football League Division Three South
Port Vale (Away) 1–5
Thomas
Hughes, Harding, Edwards, Whittaker, Cushlow, Chilvers, Broughton, Kelly, Thomas, Randall, Hanlon
Att: 6,000
60 mins – Mud
Rearranged Fixture:
26 April 1951
Port Vale 2 Crystal Palace 2

6 December 1952
FA Cup Second Round
Finchley (Away) 1–3
Burgess
D. MacDonald, Scott, H. McDonald, Grimshaw, Briggs, Chilvers, Fell, Rainford, Bishop, Burgess, Hanlon
Att: 7,144
63 mins – Fog
Rearranged Fixture:
10 December 1952
Finchley 3 Crystal Palace 1

22 December 1956
Football League Division Three South
Coventry City (Away) 0–0
Potter, Edwards, McDonald, Long, Choules, Noakes, Harrison, Belcher, Berry, Pierce, Deakin
Att: 8,226
55 mins – Floodlight Failure
Rearranged Fixture:
1 April 1957
Coventry City 3 Crystal Palace 3

21 March 1964
Football League Division Three
Colchester United (Away) 1–1
Stephenson
Glazier, Long, Townsend, Stephenson, Wood, Howe, Whitehouse, Holton, Dowsett, Burridge, Kellard
Att: 5,333
57 mins – Rain/Waterlogged Pitch
Rearranged Fixture:
15 April 1964
Colchester United 1 Crystal Palace 1

28 December 1968
Football League Division Two
Blackpool (Home) 1–1
Woodruff
J. Jackson, Payne, Loughlan, A. Taylor, McCormick, Blyth, Lazarus, Kember, C. Jackson, Woodruff, C. Taylor.
Sub (not used): Long
Att: 18,887
43 mins – Icy/Frozen pitch
Rearranged Fixture:
25 January 1969
Crystal Palace 1 Blackpool 2

1 February 1969
Football League Division Two
Blackburn Rovers (Away) 0–0
J. Jackson, Sewell, Loughlan, Payne, McCormick, Blyth, A. Taylor, Kember, Hoy, Dawkins, C. Taylor.
Sub (not used): L. Tomkins
Att: 10,000
18 mins – Rain/Mud
Rearranged Fixture:
28 April 1969
Blackburn Rovers 1 Crystal Palace 2

20 October 1969
League Cup Fourth Round Replay
Derby County (Away) 1–1
Woodruff
J. Jackson, Hoadley, Oliver, Payne, McCormick, Hynd, Kember, Dawkins, Woodruff, Queen, A. Taylor
Sub (not used): C. Jackson
Att: 29,080
85 mins – Fog
Rearranged Fixture:
29 October 1969
Derby County 3 Crystal Palace 0

3 December 1976
Football League Division Three
Lincoln City (Away) 1–0
Heppolette
Hammond, P. Hinshelwood, Sansom, Holder, Cannon, Evans, Graham, Heppolette, Perrin, Silkman, Harkouk.
Sub (not used): Chatterton
Att: 7,582
61 mins – Ice
Rearranged Fixture:
2 March 1977
Lincoln City 3 Crystal Palace 2

3 November 1997
FA Premier League
West Ham United (Away) 2–2
Shipperley 2
Miller, Edworthy, Gordon, Roberts, Hreidarsson, Tuttle, Lombardo, Dyer (Ndah), Shipperley, Rodger, J. Smith.
Subs (not used): Emblen, Nash, Veart, Zohar
Att: 23,728
66 mins – Floodlight Failure
Rearranged Fixture
3 December 1997
West Ham United 4 Crystal Palace 1

24 October 1998
League One
Bradford City (Away) 1–1
Morrison
Digby, Jihai, Austin, Foster, Zhiyi, Moore, Lombardo, Rizzo, Morrison, Jansen, Mullins
Subs (not used): Amsalem, Burton, Bent
Att: 15,157
45 mins – Waterlogged pitch
Rearranged Fixture:
19 January 1999
Bradford City 2 Crystal Palace 1

Crystal Palace Attendances

It was not until 1925 that official attendance figures were recorded by the Football League, a couple of years after the Football Association, and attendances were not reported on a regular basis by the press until 1938.

Prior to this, the number of spectators at a game as reported by the press was usually an estimate which naturally led to some wildly differentiating figures.

It has, therefore, been decided to produce figures only from Crystal Palace's time in the Football League and these in turn make for some interesting comparisons and show the club at its highest and lowest ebbs. The first four seasons shown (1920–24) are for when the club was at its previous ground of The Nest, Selhurst which had a capacity around the 20,000 mark.

The figures can also show the social tendencies of an earlier age when midweek fixtures were played in the afternoon and although there was a half-day closing of shops on a Wednesday many of the lowest figures occurred for these games. The weather also had an influence as quite a number of fixtures were started and completed in appalling conditions which also deterred all but the most hardy supporter to venture forth and pay cash at a turnstile.

At Selhurst Park average League attendances remained in five figures from its opening in 1924 and for almost 60 years continuously thereon until the nadir was reached in the 1980s but since then it recovered although the seasons from 2005–06 witnessed a steady loss until the 2010–11 season showed a slight but encouraging increase. The somewhat lower figures for the Premiership season of 1994–95 was due to the closure of the Holmesdale end for the building of the stand. The official capacity of Selhurst Park now stands at 26,427.

The highest attendance figure at Selhurst Park was on that magical evening of Friday 11 May 1979 when the team under manager Terry Venables defeated Burnley 2–0 to win the Division Two Championship. The number originally reported was 51,801, but this was later amended to 51,482, although many of those present were aware of a large number of spectators gaining 'unofficial' entrance to swell this figure even more.

The lowest League attendance at Selhurst Park occurred on the afternoon of Wednesday 18th December 1935 when there were only 2,165 spectators in attendance for a Division Three South encounter with Newport County. As mentioned earlier, midweek games back then were notorious for smaller crowds and, coupled with dull freezing conditions, together with Palace's exit from the FA Cup against Margate four days earlier, it all added to a sparse attendance. Those present were warmed somewhat by a 6–0 victory for Palace, although it has to be said that the Newport goalkeeper was carried off and taken to hospital suffering from concussion midway through the first half with an outfield player going in goal – no substitutes at all then!

Season by Season Attendances since 1920–21

Season	Division	Highest	Average	Lowest
1920–21	Three	22,000	14,762	6,000
1921–22	Two	20,000	12,333	7,000
1922–23	Two	18,000	10,333	6,000
1923–24	Two	15,000	10,277	6,000
1924–25	Two	25,000	14,383	8,000
1925–26	Three South	23,617	12,767	4,228
1926–27	Three South	20,497	11,645	4,101
1927–28	Three South	18,930	10,716	4,299
1928–29	Three South	33,160	15,555	6,041
1929–30	Three South	20,268	13,455	2,862
1930–31	Three South	21,110	13,183	5,127
1931–32	Three South	29,335	15,132	8,905
1932–33	Three South	20,261	10,868	5,805
1933–34	Three South	22,126	11,161	3,683
1934–35	Three South	27,110	13,338	8,029
1935–36	Three South	23,025	12,423	2,165
1936–37	Three South	18,348	10,867	3,769
1937–38	Three South	25,522	12,829	5,242
1938–39	Three South	29,155	14,791	4,403
1946–47	Three South	27,517	13,605	2,906
1947–48	Three South	22,086	14,936	9,994
1948–49	Three South	30,925	14,870	7,869
1949–50	Three South	30,432	16,878	7,416
1950–51	Three South	24,968	13,827	5,258
1951–52	Three South	21,220	14,846	7,214
1952–53	Three South	24,830	12,415	4,916
1953–54	Three South	18,856	12,427	7,154
1954–55	Three South	17,238	10,731	6,165
1955–56	Three South	20,284	11,061	5,739
1956–57	Three South	22,627	12,082	8,371
1957–58	Three South	22,680	13,229	6,498
1958–59	Four	20,977	14,943	8,848
1959–60	Four	28,929	15,630	9,045
1960–61	Four	37,774	19,092	11,161
1961–62	Three	28,886	17,481	7,041
1962–63	Three	21,777	14,853	9,146
1963–64	Three	27,967	17,195	12,059
1964–65	Two	29,878	18,239	12,175
1965–66	Two	23,144	14,821	9,413
1966–67	Two	30,845	18,052	11,329
1967–68	Two	38,006	17,124	7,357
1968–69	Two	43,381	19,835	11,071
1969–70	One	49,498	29,900	16,763
1970–71	One	41,486	28,768	16,646

Season	Division	Highest	Average	Lowest
1971–72	One	44,020	26,999	17,699
1972–73	One	44,531	29,596	14,829
1973–74	Two	32,124	21,285	15,804
1974–75	Three	24,274	16,974	12,591
1975–76	Three	34,893	19,942	13,009
1976–77	Three	28,677	15,925	10,642
1977–78	Two	40,277	19,466	11,115
1978–79	Two	51,482	23,327	15,154
1979–80	One	45,583	29,523	18,728
1980–81	One	31,181	18,678	9,820
1981–82	Two	17,189	10,030	6,526
1982–83	Two	22,714	9,858	4,456
1983–84	Two	20,540	8,119	4,819
1984–85	Two	10,215	6,440	4,002
1985–86	Two	11,731	6,754	3,744
1986–87	Two	18,029	7,583	4,839
1987–88	Two	17,555	9,763	6,688
1988–89	Two	17,581	10,671	7,006
1989–90	One	29,870	17,368	10,051
1990–91	One	28,181	19,660	14,439
1991–92	One	29,017	17,619	12,109
1992–93	Premiership	30,115	15,748	11,224
1993–94	One	28,694	15,656	10,925
1994–95	Premiership	18,224	14,990	10,964
1995–96	One	20,664	15,248	12,166
1996–97	One	21,410	16,085	12,633
1997–98	Premiership	26,186	21,983	14,410
1998–99	One	22,096	17,123	12,919
1999–2000	One	22,577	15,662	12,110
2000–01	One	21,133	17,061	13,987
2001–02	One	22,080	18,120	13,970
2002–03	One	21,796	16,867	13,713
2003-04	One	23,977	17,344	12,259
2004–05	Premiership	26,193	24,161	20,705
2005–06	Championship	23,843	19,457	17,291
2006–07	Championship	21,523	17,541	15,985
2007–08	Championship	23,950	16,030	13,048
2008–09	Championship	22,824	15,220	12,847
2009–10	Championship	20,643	14,770	12,328
2010–11	Championship	20,142	15,457	12,353

NOTE: The regional Third Divisions ceased at the end of 1957–58 and were replaced by the national Third and Fourth Divisions. The League was restructured again in 1992–93 with the formation of the Premier League. After this date Football League Division Two became Football League Division One, Three became Two and Four became Three. In 2004–05 the Football League renamed its Division One as 'The Championship', with Division Two becoming known as League One and Division Three as League Two. The attendances at Play-off fixtures are excluded from the above analysis.

Attendance Records

The Crystal Palace

League

20,000	Estimated on three different occasions.	

FA Cup

35,000	14 January 1911	Everton

West Norwood FC, Herne Hill

Between March 1915 and April 1918 the estimated attendances here varied between 500 and 10,000.

The Nest

League

22,000	27 December 1920	Brighton & Hove Albion

FA Cup

25,000	28 January 1922	Millwall

Selhurst Park

League

25,000*	30 August 1924	The Wednesday
24,229	26 December 1924	Portsmouth
25,072	9 March 1929	Northampton Town
33,160	29 March 1929	Queen's Park Rangers
36,478	7 September 1960	Peterborough United
37,774	31 March 1961	Millwall
38,006	30 September 1967	Queen's Park Rangers
43,381	4 April 1969	Middlesbrough
48,610	9 August 1969	Manchester United
49,498	27 December 1969	Chelsea
51,482	11 May 1979	Burnley

* An estimated figure given by the press.

FA Cup

41,586	30 January 1926	Chelsea
41,667	20 February 1965	Nottingham Forest
45,384	10 March 1965	Leeds United

Palace in World War Two

Crystal Palace 1939–40

Appearances and Goalscorers in the three Wartime Competitions, comprising 40 matches.

	Apps	Goals		Apps	Goals		Apps	Goals
Bark, W.	28	14	Gregory, F.	38	13	Owens, E.	32	1
Bigg, R.	1		Gregory, M.	4		Robson, A.	37	28
Blackman, J.	28	13	Hudgell, A.	39		Shanks, R.	1	
Chesters, A.	5		James, A.	3		Smith, T.	37	17
Collins, N.	38		Joy, B.	1		Taylor, H.	2	
Dawes, A.	12	8	Lewis, J.	2		Tootill, A.	35	
Dawes, F.	9		Millbank, J.	34		Wilson, A.	33	11
Gillespie, I.	20	3	Milligan, G.	1		Own-goal		1

Crystal Palace 1940–41

Appearances and Goalscorers in three Wartime competitions, comprising 40 matches.

	Apps	Goals		Apps	Goals		Apps	Goals
Bark, W.	8	3	Gregory, M.	40	2	Robson, A.	40	36
Blackman, J.	37	16	Halliday, W.	5		Smith, T.	26	7
Collins, N.	39	1	Hudgell, A.	32	5	Taylor, H.	7	
Dawes, A.	23	27	Jackson, J.	1		Tootill, A.	39	
Dawes, F.	38		Lievesley, L.	4		Waite, E.	13	2
Eastman, D.	2		Millbank, J.	28		Wilson, A.	21	9
Gillespie, I.	26	5	Revill, J.	4		Wilson, R.	2	
Gregory, F.	2	1	Ridley, T.	3				

Crystal Palace 1941–42

Appearances and Goalscorers in two Wartime competitions, comprising 36 games.

	Apps	Goals		Apps	Goals		Apps	Goals
Bark, W.	19	10	Gregory, M.	24	1	Mulligen, G.	1	
Bartram, S.	2		Halford, D.	1		Muttitt, E.	2	
Blackman, J.	17	4	Hawkes, D.	2	1	Oakes, J.	1	
Boulton, F.	1		Henley, L.	3	1	Raynor, G.	1	
Catlin	1		Hitchins, A.	1		Reece, T.	2	
Chilvers, G.	1		Hobbins, S.	3		Robson, A.	32	22
Collins, N.	36	3	Hooper, P.	1		Scaife, G.	2	
Dawes, A.	24	13	Hudgell, A.	35	1	Sibley, A.	1	
Dawes, F.	29		Lester, F.	1		Smith, J.	1	1

	Apps	Goals		Apps	Goals		Apps	Goals
Duncan, A.	1		Lewis, G.	1	1	Smith, T.	22	6
Forder, J.	2		Lewis, J.	1		Tootill, A.	28	
Fuller, C.	1		McPhee, M.	1	2	Tweedy, G.	1	
Geldard, A.	1	1	Mather, H.	1		Weale, J.	1	
Gillespie, I.	26	7	Millbank, J.	11		Wilson, A.	29	3
Gregory, F.	1		Morris, J.	23		Young, A.	1	
Own-goal		1						

Crystal Palace 1942–43

Appearances and Goalscorers in two Wartime competitions, comprising 34 matches.

	Apps	Goals		Apps	Goals		Apps	Goals
Allen, J.	2		Ford, W.	4		Forritt, W.	1	
Bark, W.	12	7	Gillespie, I.	16	2	Potts, H.	1	1
Barnes, S.	1		Girling, H.	1		Reece, T.	11	
Bassett, W.	14		Gregory, F.	2		Robson, A.	24	9
Bastin, F.	5	2	Gregory, M.	6	1	Scaife, G.	2	
Batey, R.	1		Harding, E.	6		Smith, C.	3	
Blackman, J.	21	1	Hawkes, D.	1		Smith, J.	1	
Bratley, G.	2		Henley, L.	3		Smith, T.	29	10
Briscoe, J.	2		Hobbins, S.	1		Spencer, H.	7	
Brown, H.	4		Hudgell, A.	7		Tootill, A.	12	
Buckley, A.	1		Johnson, I.	4		Turner, M.	1	
Callend, R.	1		Joslin, P.	3		Walker, C.	1	
Collins, N.	1		Kirk, J.	1		Walker	1	
Davie, J.	1		Lewis, G.	6		Waller, H.	5	
Dawes, A.	28	10	Lewis, J.	9		Ward, T.	4	2
Dawes, F.	24		Lowe, H.	1		Ware, H.	3	1
Delaney, L.	1		Lowes, A.	7	2	Williams, C.	1	
Driver, A.	1		Mennie, R.	1		Williams, C.E.	3	
Farmer, A.	1		Millbank, J.	3		Wilson, A.	26	5
Fenton, B.	1		Milton, G.	1		Winter, D.	1	
Finch, J.	3		Morris, R.	6		Wright, E.	5	2
Fletcher, H.	1		Poland, G.	9		Young, A.	6	
Own-goal	1							

Crystal Palace 1943–44

Appearances and Goalscorers in two Wartime competitions, comprising 36 games.

	Apps	Goals		Apps	Goals		Apps	Goals
Allen, K.	2	2	Franko, J.	1		Pond, H.	1	
Bassett, W.	6		Gallagher, P	3		Redfern, R.	5	1
Biggs, A.	1	1	Gilbert, A.	1		Robinson, J.	1	1
Blackman, J.	9		Girling, H.	8	4	Robinson, P.	4	
Bray, G.	1		Gregory, M.	1		Robson, A.	30	10
Briscoe, J.	1	1	Grogan, J.	1		Russell, R.	1	
Brophy, H.	2		Henley, L.	1		Smith, T.	30	11
Brown, A.	1		Humphreys, J.	8		Somerfield, A.	1	1

Name	Apps	Goals
Brown, J.	1	
Bryant, B.	4	2
Cabrelli, P.	19	
Collins, L.	1	
Compton, L.	1	
Cuthbertson, J.	2	1
Dawes, A.	32	15
Dawes, F.	11	
Embleton, E.	1	
Ferrier, R.	25	21
Flavell, R.	3	
Lambert, E.	1	
Lewis, G.	11	1
Lewis, J.	3	1
Malpass, S.	1	
McAra, A.	2	
Millbank, J.	2	
Mountford, R.	30	
Muttitt, E.	1	
Nunn, A.	2	
Page, A.	3	
Spencer, H.	28	2
Tennant, A.	3	
Thompson, D.	1	
Tootill, A.	29	
Tunney, E.	4	
Ward, T.	2	1
Williams, E.	6	
Wilson, A.	29	15
Wilson, C.	1	
Young, A.	17	

Crystal Palace 1944–45

Appearances and Goalscorers in two Wartime competitions, comprising 36 games.

	Apps	Goals
Barrett, J.	1	
Betts, E.	4	2
Blackman, J.	10	5
Blair, J.	2	
Bradshaw, R.	1	
Briscoe, J.	5	
Brown, H.	2	
Buchanan, P.	1	
Burke, C.	2	
Burley, B.	1	
Challis, S.	4	
Cheddingham	1	
Cheetham, T.	7	3
Clarkson, H.	1	
Conner, J.	1	1
Cruickshanks, J.	1	
Dawes, A.	19	6
Dawes, F.	8	1
Driver, A.	2	3
Ferrier, H.	22	
Ferrier, R.	1	3
Foreman, G.	1	
Gillespie, I.	2	
Gregory, E.	1	
Harding, E.	5	
Horn, E.	1	
Hudgell, A.	29	
Hurrell, W.	1	
Jackman, D.	1	
Jones, E.	13	3
Kurz, F.	20	15
Lewis, G.	9	1
Lewis, J.	9	
Lievesley, L.	4	
Lowes, A.	4	
McCormick, J.	1	
McFarlane, D.	17	
Millbank	3	
Moore, N.	3	
Morrad, F.	2	
Mountford, R.	31	2
Muir, M.	1	
Parlane, J.	5	1
Paton, J.	1	
Phillips, W.	14	
Ramplin, D.	1	
Redfern, R.	1	
Reece, T.	3	
Robson, A.	12	4
Scarr, R.	1	
Somerfield, A.	22	14
Spencer, H.	23	1
Stanley, E.	1	
Stephens, R.	3	
Stevens, L.	4	2
Stewart, J.	1	
Stock, A.	1	1
Storey, W.	1	
Taylor, G.	1	
Tickeridge, S.	1	
Tootill, A.	14	
Townsend, H.	3	
Wales, H.	1	
Ward, I.	1	
Wilson, A.	26	9
Young, G.	1	
Own-goals		2

Crystal Palace 1945–46

Appearances and Goalscorers in three Wartime competitions (inc FA Cup), comprising 39 games.

	Apps	Goals
Addinall, A.	2	4
Allen, K.	1	
Bark, W.	8	3
Bassett, W.	17	
Gillespie, I.	1	
Girling, H.	6	1
Graham, D.	26	
Gregory, F.	25	
Matthewson, G.	2	
McFarlane, D.	1	
Millbank, J.	3	
Morris, R.	3	

Blackman, J.	14	6
Burrell, L.	4	
Chilvers, G.	1	
Collins, N.	1	
Corbett, J.	1	
Dawes, A.	8	3
Dawes, F.	34	1
Eastman, D.	3	
Fagan, W.	3	1
Ferrier, R.	1	1
Ford, W.	11	
Forder, J.	2	

Harding, E.	3	
Henley, L.	1	
Hindle, F.	1	
Hudgell, A.	36	1
Hughes, W.	1	
Humphreys, J.	15	
Jackman, D.	1	
Kurz, F.	33	32
Lewis, G.	17	7
Lewis, J.	37	1
Lievesley, J.	9	5
Male, G.	5	

Reece, T.	23	8
Robson, A.	10	5
Smith, T.	17	2
Stamps, J.	5	3
Stevens, L.	2	2
Stewart, J.	1	
Surtees, J.	1	1
Waldron, E.	2	1
Wilson, A.	29	4
Winter, D.	1	
Woodward, V.	1	

PLAYER OF THE YEAR

Since 1972, the club has awarded a Player of the Year Award which for many years has been presented at the Annual Dinner in May. Paul Hinshelwood was the first player to received this award in successive years, Jim Cannon the first to win the trophy three times and Julian Speroni the first to receive this accolade for three successive seasons.

1972	John McCormick
1973	Tony Taylor
1974	Peter Taylor
1975	Derek Jeffries
1976	Peter Taylor
1977	Kenny Sansom
1978	Jim Cannon
1979	Kenny Sansom
1980	Paul Hinshelwood
1981	Paul Hinshelwood
1982	Paul Barron
1983	Jerry Murphy
1984	Billy Gilbert
1985	Jim Cannon
1986	George Wood
1987	Jim Cannon
1988	Geoff Thomas
1989	Ian Wright
1990	Mark Bright
1991	Geoff Thomas
1992	Eddie McGoldrick
1993	Andy Thorn
1994	Chris Coleman
1995	Richard Shaw
1996	Andy Roberts
1997	David Hopkin
1998	Marc Edworthy
1999	Hayden Mullins
2000	Andy Linighan
2001	Fan Zhiyi
2002	Dougie Freedman
2003	Hayden Mullins
2004	Andrew Johnson
2005	Andrew Johnson
2006	Emmerson Boyce
2007	Leon Cort
2008	Julian Speroni
2009	Julian Speroni
2010	Julian Speroni
2011	Nathaniel Clyne

APPEARANCES AND GOALSCORERS

(Southern League, Football League, FA Cup & League Cup)

League Records

(Southern and Football Leagues combined)

Total League Appearances

Jim Cannon	571
Terry Long	442
Albert Harry	410
John Jackson	346
Dougie Freedman	327
Bobby Greener	293
David Payne	284
Clinton Morrison	281
Billy Turner	281
Paul Hinshelwood	276
Simon Rodger	276
Josh Johnson	276
George Clarke	274
Nigel Martyn	272
Jimmy Wilde	270
Danny Butterfield	269
Harry Collyer	263
Steve Kember	260
Len Choules	258
Vince Hilaire	255

League Goals

Player	Goals
Peter Simpson	153
Ted Smith	120
Clinton Morrison	103
George Clarke	99
Dougie Freedman	95
Mark Bright	91
Albert Dawes	91
Johnny Byrne	90
Ian Wright	89
Andy Johnson	74
David Swindlehurst	73
Roy Summersby	59
Percy Cherrett	58
Jimmy Williams	57
Mike Deakin	56
John Conner	55
Cecil Blakemore	54
Albert Harry	53
Jack Blackman	52

FA Cup Appearances

Jim Cannon	42
Albert Harry	30
Terry Long	30
Paul Hinshelwood	26
George Clarke	25
Bobby Greener	24
Jimmy Wilde	23
Wilf Innerd	22
Nigel Martyn	22
Billy Callender	22
David Swindlehurst	22
Len Choules	21
Billy Turner	21
John Salako	20

FA Cup Goals

Player	Goals
Peter Simpson	12
Johnny Byrne	11
Dick Harker	8
Cliff Holton	8
Percy Cherrett	7
George Clarke	7
Mike Deakin	7
Bruce Dyer	6
Walter Watkins	6
Chris Armstrong	5

League Cup Appearances

Jim Cannon	44
Nigel Martyn	36
Simon Rodger	31
Richard Shaw	30
Chris Coleman	26
Andy Gray	25
John Humphrey	25
Eric Young	25
John Jackson	24
Hayden Mullins	24
John Salako	24
Gareth Southgate	24
Geoff Thomas	24
Clinton Morrison	23
Mark Bright	22
Eddie McGoldrick	22
Jerry Murphy	22
Dean Austin	21
Tommy Black	21
Vince Hilaire	21
John McCormick	21
Dougie Freedman	20

League Cup Goals

Mark Bright	11
Dougie Freedman	10
Clinton Morrison	9
Ian Wright	9
Andy Johnson	7
Gareth Southgate	7
Chris Armstrong	6
Andy Gray	6
David Hopkin	6
Tommy Black	5
Mike Flanagan	5
Jerry Murphy	5
Gerry Queen	5
John Salako	5

Total Appearances

Jim Cannon	660
Terry Long	480
Albert Harry	440
John Jackson	388
Dougie Freedman	368
Nigel Martyn	349
Simon Rodger	328
Paul Hinshelwood	319
David Payne	318
Bobby Greener	317
Clinton Morrison	316
Billy Turner	302
George Clarke	299
Josh Johnson	295
Jimmy Wilde	293
Vince Hilaire	293
Steve Kember	291
Phil Barber	288
Mark Bright	286
Harry Collyer	281
Len Choules	280
Ian Wright	277
David Swindlehurst	276

Total Goals

Peter Simpson	165
Ted Smith	124
Ian Wright	117
Mark Bright	113
Clinton Morrison	113
Dougie Freedman	108
George Clarke	106
Johnny Byrne	101
Albert Dawes	92
Andy Johnson	84
David Swindlehurst	81
Percy Cherrett	65
Mike Deakin	63
Roy Summersby	60
Chris Armstrong	58
Jimmy 'Ginger' Williams	58
John Conner	57
Cecil Blakemore	56
Albert Harry	55
Jack Blackman	55
Andy Gray	51
George Whitworth	50

Palace's International Players

Details of International (Full, Under-23 and Under-21) and major representative honours gained by players while they were associated with the club. In respect of players on loan, only those loaned by Crystal Palace FC are included.

Bill Davies was the first Crystal Palace FC player to gain International recognition when selected to play for Wales against Scotland (in Dundee) on 7 March 1908. Horace Colclough was the first Palace player to gain a cap for England when he appeared against Wales (in Cardiff) on 16 March 1914. This was also the first time that the club had two of its players facing each other in an international as Bill Davies was in the Welsh team.

Aki Riihilahti (Finland) has gained the most number of caps (36) while with the club and Carl Fletcher (Wales – 21) has the most of the four 'home countries'.

Craig Foster (Australia), Riihilahti (Finland) and Ian Walsh (Wales) have all scored seven goals for their countries at Full International level whil with the club.

Full International Appearances

Australia
Nick Carle (5), Craig Foster (9), Kevin Muscat (5), Tony Popovic (18), Carl Veart (2)
Goals: Foster 7, Muscat 1, Popovic 1

Barbados
Paul Ifill (2)

Canada
Niall Thompson (1)

China
Fan Zhiyi (23), 5 goals

Ecuador
Ivan Kaviedes (3), 1 goal

England
Jack Alderson (1), Johnny Byrne (1), Horace Colclough (1), Andy Gray (1), Andy Johnson (1), Nigel Martyn (3), John Salako (5), Kenny Sansom (9), Peter Taylor (4), Geoff Thomas (9), Ian Wright (4).
Goals: Taylor 2

Finland
Joonas Kolkka (9), Shefki Kuqi (11), Aki Riihilahti (36)
Goals: Riihilahti 7, Kuqi 2

Greece
Vassilis Lakis (2)

Hungary
Gabor Kiraly (22), Sandor Torghelle (13)
Goals: Torghelle 3

Iceland
Hermann Hreidarsson (10)

Israel
David Amsalem (1)

Italy
Attilio Lombardo (1)

Jamaica
Ricardo Fuller (3)

Latvia
Alexandrs Kolinko (20), Andrejs Rubins (15)
Goals: Rubins 3

Mauritius
Gavin Heeroo (1)

Northern Ireland
Iain Dowie (6), Michael Hughes (6), Robert McCracken (4), Darren Patterson (8)
Goals: Dowie 4

Norway
Steffen Iverson (1)

Republic of Ireland
Ray Houghton (6), Eddie McGoldrick (8), Clinton Morrison (12), Paddy Mulligan (14), Jerry Murphy (3)
Goals: Morrison 2, Houghton 1

Scotland
Dougie Freedman (2), David Hopkin (2)
Goals: Freedman 1

United States of America
Gregg Behalter (11), Jovan Kirovski (5)

Wales
Paul Bodin (7), Terry Boyle (2), Chris Coleman (11), Bill Davies (2), Andy Dorman (2), Jermaine Easter (2), Ian Evans (13), Carl Fletcher (21), David Giles (3), Jeff Hopkins (2), J. 'Tom' Jones (5), Steve Lovell (1), Tony Millington (2), Peter Nicholas (17), Vic Rouse (1), Kit Symons (1), Gareth Taylor (2), Ian Walsh (14), James Williams (2), Eric Young (19)
Goals: Walsh 7, Coleman 3, Bodin 2, Boyle 1, Evans 1, Fletcher 1, Nicholas 1

Yugoslavia
Sasa Curcic (1)

B International Appearances

England
Chris Armstrong (1), Mike Flanagan (1), Vince Hilaire (1), Nigel Martyn (4), Kenny Sansom (2*), Geoff Thomas (2), Ian Wright (2)
Goals: Flanagan 1, Hilaire 1
* Fixture at Klagenfurt (Austria) abandoned after 60 minutes due to lightning.

Other International Appearances

England
Joe Bulcock (2), Jimmy Hamilton (4),

England Triallists Appearances

Albert Dawes (1)

Under-23 International Appearances

England
Johnny Byrne (6), Steve Kember (1), David Payne (1), Alan Stephenson (3), Peter Taylor (4)
Goals: Byrne 4, Taylor 4

Scotland
Iain Philip (1)

Wales
Ian Evans (1), Jeff Johnson (2), Vic Rouse (1)

UNDER-21 INTERNATIONAL APPEARANCES

England
Clive Allen (2), Marcus Bent (2), Chris Day (3), Bruce Dyer (11), Terry Fenwick (4), Billy Gilbert (11), Dean Gordon (13), Vince Hilaire (9), Paul Hinshelwood (2), Matt Jansen (3), Hayden Mullins (3), Andy Roberts (2), Wayne Routledge (3), Kenny Sansom (8), Tom Soares (4), Perry Suckling (5), David Swindlehurst (1), Ben Watson (1)
Goals: Dyer 4, Hilaire 1

Northern Ireland
Wayne Carlisle (9), Gareth Graham (5), Darren Patterson (1)
Goals: Carlisle 1

Republic of Ireland
Danny Boxall (3), Tony Folan (3), Owen Garvan (1), Stephen Hunt (1), Brian Launders (9), Clinton Morrison (1), Ken O'Doherty (1), Robert Quinn (6), Sean Scannell (9), Tony Scully (8)

Scotland
Dougie Freedman (1)

Wales
Terry Boyle (1), Gareth Davies (1), Stephen Evans (2), David Giles (1), Lee Kendall (2), Andrew Martin (1) Peter Nicholas (2), Ian Walsh (1), Rhoys Wiggins (9), Gareth Williams (5), Jonathan Williams (4)

INTER LEAGUE REPRESENTATIVE APPEARANCES

Football League
John Jackson (1)

Football League Division Three South
Jimmy Belcher (1), Bernard Harrison (1)

Southern League
Joe Bulcock (1), Horace Colclough (3), Harry Collyer, (5), Harry Hanger (1), Jimmy Hughes (1), Josh Johnson (3), Robert Spottiswood (1)

AMATEUR APPEARANCES

England
Ben Bateman (1)

CRYSTAL PALACE

PLAYER RECORDS

SURNAME	NAME	BIRTHPLACE	DATE OF BIRTH	DIED	SEASONS	FROM
ADDINALL	Bert	Paddington	30 January 1921	2005	1954–55	Brighton & Hove Albion
ADEBOLA	Bamberdele 'Dele'	Lagos (Nigeria)	23 June 1975		2002–03	Birmingham City
AGUSTIEN	Kemy	Tilburg (Holland)	20 Augst 1986		2010–11	Swansea City (Loan)
AKINBIYI	Adeola 'Ade'	Hackney	10 October 1974		2001–03	Leicester City
ALDERSON	Jack	Crook	28 November 1891	1972	1919–24	Newcastle United
ALLEN	Clive	Stepney	20 May 1961		1980–81	Arsenal
ALLEN	James	Newcastle	1899		1921–24	Walker Celtic
ALLEN	Ronnie	Fenton (Staffs.)	15 January 1929	2001	1961–65	West Bromwich Albion
AMBROSE	Darren	Harlow	29 February 1984		2009–	Charlton Athletic
AMSALEM	David	Israel	4 September 1971		1998–99	Beitar Jerusalem (Israel)
ANDERSEN	Lief	Fredrickstad (Norway)	19 April 1971		1995–97	Moss F.K. (Norway)
ANDERSON	Ben	Aberdeen	18 February 1946		1973–74	Cape Town City (S. Africa)
ANDERSON	Bob	Prestwick	9 November 1924	1994	1951–53	Blackhall Colliery
ANDREW	Calvin	Luton	19 December 1986		2008–	Luton Town
ANDREWS	Cecil 'Archie'	Alton	1 November 1930	1986	1952–56	Portsmouth
ANDREWS	Wayne	Paddington	25 November 1977		2004–06	Colchester United
ANTUNES	Jose 'Fumaca'	Bahia (Brazil)	15 July 1976		1999–2000	Barnsley
ANTWI	Will	London	19 October 1982		2002–03	Junior
ARMSTRONG	Chris	Newcastle	19 June 1971		1992–95	Millwall
ASHTON	Nathan	Beckton	30 January 1987		2007–08	Fulham (Loan)
ASTLEY	Horace	Bolton	1882		1905–07	Middlesbrough
AUSTIN	Dean	Hemel Hempstead	26 April 1970		1998–2003	Tottenham Hotspur
AYLOTT	Trevor	Bermondsey	26 November 1957		1984–86	Luton Town
AYRES	Ken	Oxford	15 May 1956		1974–75	Manchester United
BAILEY	Dennis	Lambeth	13 November 1965		1987–88	Farnborough Town
BAILEY	Roy	Epsom	26 May 1932	1993	1949–56	Junior
BAKER	Robert	Morpeth	1884	1968	1907–08	Redhill
BALDING	Henry	Tottenham	1884		1907–09	Bromley
BANFIELD	Neil	Poplar	20 January 1962		1980–81	Apprentice
BANNISTER	Jack	Chesterfield	26 January 1942		1965–69	Scunthorpe United
BARBER	Tom	West Stanley	22 July 1886	1925	1919–20	Stalybridge Celtic
BARBER	Phil	Tring	10 June 1965		1983–91	Aylesbury United
BARK/NAYLOR	Bill	Sheffield	23 November 1919	1989	1946–47	Hampton Sports
BARKER	H				1908–09	Wimbledon
BARNES	Andy	Croydon	31 March 1967		1991–92	Sutton United
BARNES	Howard	Wandsworth	1910		1934–35	Wimbledon
BARNES	Victor	Twickenham	12 September 1905	1971	1926–28	Kingstonian
BARNETT	Tom	Muswell Hill	12 October 1936		1958–61	Chatham Town
BARRETT	Adam	Dagenham	29 November 1979		2010–	Southend United
BARRIE	George	Balgonie	17 July 1904		1929–34	Kettering Town
BARRON	Paul	Woolwich	16 September 1953		1980–83	Arsenal
BARRY	Roy	Edinburgh	19 September 1942		1973–75	Coventry City
BARTRAM	Per	Denmark	8 January 1944		1969–70	Morton
BASON	Brian	Epsom	3 September 1955		1980–82	Plymouth Argyle
BASSETT	Bill	Brithdir	8 June 1912	1977	1945–49	Cardiff City
BATEMAN	Ben	Chelsea	20 November 1892	1961	1913–24	Sutton Court
BATES	Phil	Beckenham	1897		1919–21	Beckenham Wanderers
BAUCHOP	James	Sauchie	22 May 1886	1968	1907–09	Norwich City
BAXTER	Paul	Hackney	22 April 1964		1981–82	Tottenham Hotspur
BEACH	Daniel	Mexborough	1890		1911–13	Mexborough
BEATTIE	Craig	Glasgow	16 January 1984		2008–09	West Bromwich Albion (Loan)
BELCHER	Jimmy	Stepney	31 October 1932		1954–58	West Ham United
BELL	Bobby	Cambridge	26 October 1950		1971–74	Blackburn Rovers
BENJAMIN	Trevor	Kettering	8 February 1979		2001–02	Leicester City (Loan)
BENNETT	Julian	Nottingham	17 December 1984		2010–11	Nottingham Forest (Loan)
BENNETT	Ken	Wood Green	2 October 1921	1994	1953–54	Brighton & Hove Albion
BENNETT	Ron	Hinckley	8 May 1927	1997	1951–53	Portsmouth
BENT	Marcus	Hammersmith	19 May 1978		1997–99	Brentford
BERESFORD	Frank	Chesterfield	8 October 1910	1974	1936–37	Luton Town
BERESFORD	Reg	Walsall	3 June 1921		1948–49	Birmingham City
BERHALTER	Gregg	Englewood (USA)	1 August 1973		2000–02	Cambuur Leeuwarden (Holland)
BERRY	Peter	Aldershot	20 September 1933		1953–58	Junior
BERRY	Tyrone	Brixton	20 February 1987		2005–06	Junior
BERRY	William	Hackney	10 August 1904	1972	1932–33	Brentford
BERTHELIN	Cedric	Courrieres (France)	25 December 1976		2002–04	Luton Town
BESAGNI	Remo	Clerkenwell	22 April 1935		1952–53	Junior
BETTERIDGE	Walter	Romsey	24 December 1896	1979	1928–29	Peterborough City
BIGG	Bob	Cairo (Egypt)	11 March 1911	1991	1934–39	Redhill
BILLIO	Patrizio	Treviso (Italy)	19 April 1974		1997–98	Monza (Italy)
BIRCH	Billy	Southport	20 October 1944		1963–65	West Bromwich Albion

TO	APPEARANCES S.LEAGUE	F. LEAGUE	FA CUP	FL CUP	OTHER	APPS	GOALS S.LEAGUE	F.LEAGUE	FA CUP	FL CUP	OTHER	GOALS
Snowdown Colliery		12				12		2				2
Coventry City		32+7	4	5		41+7		5		2		7
		6+2				6+2						
Stoke City		11+13	0+4			11+17		3				3
Pontypridd	42	150	13			205						
Queen's Park Rangers		25		4		29		9		2		11
Hartlepools United		16				16						
Wolverhampton Wand. (coach)		100	7	2		109		34	3			37
		71+3	5	3		79+3		22	3	2		27
Hapoel Haifa (Israel)		6+4		1+1		7+5						
Moss F.K. (Norway)		19+11	1	3	1	24+11			1			1
Cape Town City (S. Africa)		11	1			12		1				1
Bristol Rovers		38				38						
		15+32	0+7	3		18+39		1	1			2
Queen's Park Rangers		104	1			105		12				12
Coventry City		5+28	2+1	3+1		10+30		1				1
Newcastle United		2+1		2		4+1						
Ljungskile SK (Sweden)		0+4		1+2		1+6						
Tottenham Hotspur		118	8	8	2	136		46	5	6	1	58
		1				1						
Heywood United	32		14			46	12		4			16
Woking		127+15	3	18+3	2	150+18		6				6
AFC Bournemouth		50+3	2	3+1	2	57+4		12	1		1	14
Charlton Athletic		3+3				3+3						
Birmingham City		0+5				0+5		1				1
Ipswich Town		118	1			119						
Norwich City	4					4						
Northfleet	7					7						
Adelaide City (Australia)		2+1				2+1						
Luton Town		117+3	3	6		126+3		7				7
Merthyr Town	19		1			20	7					7
Millwall		207+27	14	13+6	19+2	253+35		35	1	3	2	41
Brentford		18	1			19		9	2			11
	6					6	1					1
Retired through injury		0+1				0+1						
Wimbledon		1				1						
		4	2			6		1				1
Margate		14		1		15		2				2
		5+2		2		7+2						
Gillingham		77	3			80						
West Bromwich Albion		90	5	13		108						
Hibernian		41+1	1	2		44+1		1				1
Morton		8+2		1+1		9+3		2		1		3
Reading		25+2		4		29+2						
Portmadoc		70	4			74						
Dartford	75	97	8			180	4	5	1			10
Scunthorpe United	25	40	3			68	1	2				3
Derby County	43		4			47	23		3			26
Leytonstone & Ilford		1				1						
	4					4						
		15				15		5				5
Ipswich Town		127	10			137		22				22
Hellenic (S. Africa)		31	4	1		36						
		5+1				5+1		1				1
		10+3		1		11+3		1				1
Tonbridge		17				17		2				2
Brighton & Hove Albion		27				27		5				5
Port Vale		13+15	0+1	0+2		13+18		5				5
Carlisle United		3				3						
		7				7		1				1
Energie Cottbus (Ger.)		10+9		1+1		11+10		1				1
Ipswich Town		151	10			161		27	1			28
Rushden & Diamonds			0+1	0+2		0+3						
Bournemouth & Boscombe		17				17		4				4
R.A.E.C. Mons (Belgium)		26	3+1	3		32+1						
		2				2						
Loughborough Corinthians		1				1						
Aldershot		109	5			114		41				41
Ancona (Italy)		1+2				1+2						
Wellington Town		6		1		7						

SURNAME	NAME	BIRTHPLACE	DATE OF BIRTH	DIED	SEASONS	FROM
BIRCHENALL	Alan	East Ham	22 August 1945		1970–72	Chelsea
BIRNIE	Ted	Sunderland	25 August 1878	1935	1905–06	Newcastle United
BIRTLEY	Bob	Easington	15 July 1908	1961	1935–39	Coventry City
BLACK	Tommy	Chigwell	26 November 1979		2000–07	Arsenal
BLACKMAN	Jack	Bermondsey	25 November 1912	1987	1935–46	Queen's Park Rangers
BLACKSHAW	Bill	Ashton-under-Lyne	6 September 1920	1994	1949–51	Oldham Athletic
BLAKE	William	Worcester	1902		1924–26	Kidderminster Harriers
BLAKEMORE	Cecil	Stourbridge	8 December 1897	1963	1922–27	Redditch Town
BLORE	Vincent	Uttoxeter	25 February 1907	1997	1936–38	West Ham United
BLYTH	Mel	Norwich	28 July 1944		1968–75	Scunthorpe United
2 spells					1977–78	Southampton (Loan)
BODIN	Paul	Cardiff	13 September 1964		1990–92	Swindon Town
BOERE	Jeroen	Arnhem (Holland)	18 November 1967	2007	1995–96	West Ham United
BONETTI	Ivano	Brescia (Italy)	1 August 1964		1997–98	Bologna (Italy)
BOOTH	Samuel	Northwich	30 January 1910	1956	1935–38	Margate
BORROWDALE	Gary	Sutton	16 July 1985		2002–07	Junior
BOSTOCK	Benjamin 'Roy'	Mansfield	19 April 1929	1993	1948–49	Epsom
BOSTOCK	John	Camberwell	15 January 1992		2007–08	Crystal Palace FC Academy
BOULTER	David	Stepney	5 October 1962		1981–82	Junior
BOURNE	Jeff	Repton	19 June 1948		1976–78	Derby County
BOURNE	W	Milton Regis	1890		1911–13	Sittingbourne
BOWLER	James	Hanley, Stoke-on-Trent	1895		1914–15	Newcastle Town
BOWRY	Bobby	Hampstead	19 May 1971		1992–95	Queen's Park Rangers
BOXALL	Danny	Croydon	24 August 1977		1995–98	Junior
BOYCE	Emmerson	Aylesbury	24 September 1979		2004–06	Luton Town
BOYD	A				1911–12	Redhill
BOYLE	Terry	Ammanford	29 October 1958		1977–81	Tottenham Hotspur
BRADBURY	Lee	Cowes	3 July 1975		1998–2000	Manchester City
BRADLEY	Charles				1909–11	Leytonstone
BREARLEY	John	West Derby	1875	1944	1907–09	Tottenham Hotspur
BRENNAN	Steve	Mile End	3 September 1958		1976–78	Junior
BRENNAN	Tom	Calderbank	7 February 1911		1930–31	Gillingham
BRETT	Ron	Tilbury	4 September 1937	1962	1955–59	Junior
2 spells					1961–62	West Ham United
BRIGGS	George 'Harry'	Easington	27 February 1923		1948–55	Shotton Colliery
BRIGHT	John				1913–14	Sittingbourne
BRIGHT	Mark	Stoke-on-Trent	6 June 1962		1986–93	Leicester City
BROLIN	Tomas	Hudiksvall (Sweden)	29 November 1969		1997–98	Leeds United
BROOKS	Johnny	Reading	23 December 1931		1963–64	Brentford
BROOKS	Shaun	Reading	9 October 1962		1979–84	Junior
BROPHY	Hugh	Dublin	2 September 1948		1966–67	Shamrock Rovers (Eire)
BROUGHTON	Ted	Bradford	9 February 1925		1948–53	New Brighton
BROWN	Ally	Musselburgh	12 April 1951		1982–83	West Bromwich Albion
BROWN	Bert	Bristol	4 March 1934		1957–58	Exeter University
BROWN	Charles	Wandsworth	7 December 1909		1932–34	Hayes (Middlesex)
BROWN	John	Belfast	1895		1927–28	Merthyr Town
BROWN	Kenny	Upminster	11 July 1967		1995–96	West Ham United (Loan)
BROWN	Tom	Troed-y-Rhiw	July 1912		1934–35	Folkestone
BRUSH	Paul	Plaistow	22 February 1958		1985–88	West Ham United
BRYDEN	W	Tyneside	1884		1905–06	
BUCKLEY	Frank	Lichfield	11 May 1922	1973	1947–51	Notts County
BULCOCK	Joe	Burnley	1884	1918	1909–14	Exeter City
BUMSTEAD	Charlie	Croydon	8 January 1922	1974	1948–52	Millwall
BURGESS	Albert 'Cam'	Bebington	21 September 1919	1978	1951–53	Chester City
BURKE	David	Liverpool	6 August 1960		1987–90	Huddersfield Town
BURNS	Tony	Edenbridge	27 March 1944		1974–78	Maritzburg (South Africa)
BURNSIDE	David	Kingswood (Bristol)	10 December 1939	2009	1964–67	Southampton
BURRELL	Les	Brighton	8 August 1917	2008	1946–48	Margate
BURRIDGE	John	Workington	3 December 1951		1977–80	Aston Villa
BURRIDGE	Peter	Harlow	30 December 1933		1962–66	Millwall
BURTON	Osagyefo 'Sagi'	Birmingham	25 November 1977		1997–99	Junior
BUTLER	Hubert	Atherton	11 July 1905		1928–32	Chorley
BUTTERFIELD	Danny	Boston (Lincs.)	21 November 1979		2002–10	Grimsby Town
BYRNE	Johnny	West Horsley	13 May 1939	1999	1956–62	Junior
2 spells					1966–68	West Ham United
CADOGAN	Kieron	Tooting	3 August1990		2008–	Junior
CALLENDER	Billy	Prudhoe	5 January 1903	1932	1923–32	Prudhoe Castle
CANNON	Jim	Glasgow	2 October 1953		1972–88	Junior
CARASSO	Cedric	Avignon (France)	30 December 1981		2001–02	Olympique Marseilles (Fr.) (Loan)
CARLE	Nick	Sydney (Australia)	23 November 1981		2008–10	Bristol City
CARLISLE	Wayne	Lisburn (N.I.)	9 September 1979		1998–2002	Junior
CARSON	James	Clydebank	1912		1934–36	Bradford Park Avenue
CARTER	Les	Farnborough (Kent)	24 October 1960		1980–81	Junior
CARTWRIGHT	Joe	Lower Walton (Lancs.)	11 December 1888		1921–23	Manchester City
CARTWRIGHT	John	Brixworth	5 November 1940		1961–63	West Ham United
CASWELL	Peter	Leatherhead	16 January 1957		1976–78	Junior

	APPEARANCES						GOALS					
TO	S.LEAGUE	F. LEAGUE	FA CUP	FL. CUP	OTHER	APPS	S.LEAGUE	F.LEAGUE	FA CUP	FL CUP	OTHER	GOALS
Leicester City		41	2	5		48		11	1	2		14
Chelsea	22		7			29	2		1			3
Gateshead		65	4			69		15	1			16
Southend United		67+60	3+2	15+6		85+68		10	2	5		17
Guildford City		99	7			106		52	3			55
Rochdale		32				32		5				5
Kidderminster Harriers		34				34						
Bristol City		133	8			141		54	2			56
Exeter City		33	2			35						
Southampton		219+3	12+1	19		250+4		9	1	2		12
Swindon Town		8+1		1		9+1						
Southend United		0+8				0+8		1				1
Genoa (Italy)		0+2				0+2						
Southport		25	4			29						
Coventry City		74+24	3+1	7+4	1	85+29						
Canterbury City		4				4						
Tottenham Hotspur		1+3	1			2+3						
Crawley Town		16	5	1		22						
Dallas Tornado (USA)		32	1	4		37		10				10
	9					9	4					4
	1		1			2						
Millwall		36+14	1	10		47+14		1				1
Brentford		5+3		1+1		6+4						
Wigan Athletic		68+1	3	3	2	76+1		2				2
Redhill	1					1						
Bristol City		24+2	2			26+2		1	1			2
Portsmouth		28+4	1	3+1		32+5		6	1	1		8
Barking	4					4						
Millwall	70		7			77	3					3
Plymouth Argyle		2+1		0+1		2+2		1				1
Tunbridge Wells Rangers		2				2						
West Ham United		44	5			49		13				13
Killed in car crash												
Retired		150	7			157		4				4
	18		2			20	9					9
Sheffield Wednesday		224+3	13+1	22	23	282+4		91	2	11	9	113
Hudiksvalls ABK (Sweden)		13	3			16						
Toronto (Canada)		7				7						
Leyton Orient		47+7	5	5+2		57+9		4		1		5
Shamrock Rovers (Eire)		0+1				0+1						
Retired		96	4			100		6				6
Walsall		11				11		2				2
Queen's Park Rangers		3				3						
Watford		29				29						
Aberdare		8				8		2				2
		5+1			3	8+1					1	1
Clapton Orient		4				4						
Southend United		50	1	2	3	56		3				3
	1					1						
Guildford City		69	4			73						
Swansea Town	137		9			146	2					2
Dover Town		53	2			55						
York City		47	3			50		40				40
Bolton Wanderers		80+1	3	4	9	96+1						
Plymouth Argyle		90	2	6		98						
Wolverhampton Wand.		54+4	5	1		60+4		8	2			10
Ipswich Town		19				19		5				5
Queen's Park Rangers		88	7	7		102						
Charlton Athletic		114	6	4		124		42	3	4		49
Colchester United		19+6	0+1	1	0+1	20+8		1				1
Chester City		108	16			124		31	8			39
Southampton		210+22	13+2	15+1	5+1	243+26		6	3		1	10
West Ham United		239	18	2		259		90	11			101
Fulham												
		7+13	1	1+1		9+14		2				2
Died at Selhurst Park		203	22			225						
Croydon		568+3	42	43+1	3	656+4		30	1	3	1	35
		0+1				0+1						
Sydney FC (Australia)		49+10	5	2+1		56+11		4		1		5
Bristol Rovers		29+17	1	4+3		34+20		3				3
Burnley		52	2			54		17				17
Bristol City		1+1				1+1						
Llanelly		19	2			21		4				4
Bath City		11	1			12		1				1
Crewe Alexandra		3				3						

SURNAME	NAME	BIRTHPLACE	DATE OF BIRTH	DIED	SEASONS	FROM
CHARLESWORTH	George	Bristol	29 November 1901	1965	1928–32	Kettering Town
CHARLTON	Stan	Little Holton	16 November 1900	1971	1928–32	Exeter City
CHASE	Charlie	Steyning	31 January 1924		1948–50	Watford
CHATTERTON	Nick	Norwood	18 May 1954		1973–79	Junior
CHERRETT	Percy	Christchurch	12 September 1899	1984	1925–27	Plymouth Argyle
CHESTERS	Arthur	Salford	14 February 1910		1937–39	Exeter City
CHILVERS	Geoff	Epsom	31 January 1925	1971	1948–54	Sutton United
CHOULES	Len	Orpington	29 January 1932		1952–62	Sutton United
CLARK	Charles	Allanton	1878	1930	1909–10	Plymouth Argyle
CLARKE	George	Bolsover	24 July 1900	1977	1925–33	Aston Villa
CLARKE	Matt	Sheffield	3 November 1973		2001–04	Bradford City
CLARKE	Wally	Anerley			1933–34	Wimbledon
CLELLAND	David	Larkhall	18 March 1924		1949–50	Brighton & Hove Albion
CLIFFORD	John	Newport (Monmouth)	24 September 1906	1961	1931–33	Newport County
CLOUGH	Jimmy	Newcastle	30 August 1918	1998	1947–49	Southport
CLYNE	Nathaniel	Stockwell	5 April 1991		2008–	Junior
COATES	John	Limehouse	13 May 1920		1946–47	ex-Amateur
COLCLOUGH	Horace	Meir (Staffs.)	1891	1941	1912–15	Crewe Alexandra
COLE	Ashley	Stepney	20 December 1980		1999–2000	Arsenal (Loan)
COLEMAN	Chris	Swansea	10 June 1970		1991–96	Swansea City
COLFAR	Ray	Liverpool	4 December 1935		1958–61	Sutton United
COLLIER	James	Seaton Delaval			1920–21	Blyth Spartans
COLLINS	Edward	Manchester	1886		1908–10	Carlisle United
COLLINS	James	South Shields	1889		1910–15	Sunderland
COLLINS	Nick	Chopwell	7 September 1911	1990	1934–39	Canterbury Waverley
COLLINS	Tony	Kensington	19 March 1926		1957–59	Watford
COLLYER	Harry	Bromley	1885		1906–15	Catford Southend
COLLYMORE	Stan	Stone (Staffs.)	22 January 1971		1990–93	Stafford Rangers
COMLEY	James	Holloway	24 January 1991		2008–10	Junior
COMRIE	Malcolm	Denny	26 August 1908		1935–36	Burnley
CONATY	Thomas	North Shields	1906	1964	1928–29	South Shields
CONNER	John 'Jack'	Glasgow	27 December 1896		1919–23	Belfast Distillery
COOK	Micky	Sutton (Surrey)	25 January 1950		1967–68	Junior
COOKE	Charlie	St Monance (Fife)	14 October 1942		1972–74	Chelsea
COOPER	George	Kingwinsford	1 October 1932	1994	1954–59	Brierley Hill Alliance
CORBETT	John	Bow	9 January 1920		1946–47	Swansea Town
CORT	Leon	Bermondsey	11 September 1979		2006–08	Hull City
COTTON	Fred	Halesowen	12 March 1932	1994	1956–57	Halesowen
COULSTON	Wally	Wombwell (Yorkshire)	31 January 1912	1990	1936–37	Manchester City
COUNAGO	Pablo	Pontevedra (Spain)	9 August 1979		2010–11	Ipswich Town (Loan)
COYLE	Terrence	Broxburn (Scotland)	16 July 1887		1925–27	East Fife
COX	Ian	Croydon	25 March 1971		1994–96	Carshalton Athletic
CRACKNELL 2 spells	Dick	Newcastle			1919–20 1923–26	Newcastle United Maidstone United
CRAIG	Tony	Greenwich	20 April 1985		2007–08	Millwall
CRAVEN	John	St Anne's (Lancs.)	15 May 1947	1996	1971–73	Blackpool
CRILLY	Tom	Stockton	20 July 1895	1960	1928–33	Derby County
CROMPTON	Arthur	Birmingham	9 January 1903	1987	1933–35	Brentford
CROPPER	Reg	Staveley	21 January 1902	1942	1931–32	Guildford City
CROSS	Charlie	Coventry	15 May 1900		1922–28	Coventry City
CROWE	Jason	Sidcup	30 September 1978		1998–99	Arsenal (Loan)
CUBBERLEY	Stan	Edmonton (Middlesex)	18 July 1882	1933	1905–06	Asplin Rovers
CUMMINS	Stan	Ferryhill	6 December 1958		1983–85	Sunderland
CUNDY	Jason	Wimbledon	12 November 1969		1995–96	Tottenham Hotspur (Loan)
CURCIC	Sasa	Belgrade (Yugoslavia)	14 February 1972		1997–99	Aston Villa
CUSHLOW	Dick	Shotton (Co. Durham)	15 June 1920	2002	1950–52	Derby County
CUTLER	Paul	Welwyn Garden City	18 June 1946		1964–66	Junior
CYRUS	Andy	Lambeth	30 September 1976		1996–97	Youth Trainee
DANIELS	George	Winsford	1913		1937–39	Torquay United
DANNS	Neil	Liverpool	23 November 1982		2007–	Birmingham City
DANZE	Anthony	Perth (Australia)	15 March 1984		2004–06	Perth Glory (Australia)
DARE	Kevin	Finchley	15 November 1959		1980–82	Junior
DAVIDS	Edgar	Paramarito (Surinam)	13 March 1973		2010–11	Unattached
DAVIDSON	Alex	Langholm	6 June 1920		1948–49	Chelsea
DAVIES 2 spells	Bill	Forden	1883	1960	1907–08 1910–15	Stoke City West Bromwich Albion
DAVIES	Wyn	Caernavon	20 March 1942		1974–75	Blackpool (Loan)
DAVIS	Arthur	Birmingham	1900	1955	1928–29	Notts County
DAVIS 2 spells	Claude	Kingston (Jamaica)	6 March 1979		2008–09 2009–11	Derby County (Loan) Derby County
DAVIS	Harold	Bradford	11 August 1906	1961	1937–39	Leicester City
DAWES 2 spells	Albert	Frimley Green	23 April 1907	1973	1933–37 1937–39	Northampton Town Luton Town
DAWES	Fred	Frimley Green	2 May 1911	1989	1935–50	Northampton Town
DAWKINS	Trevor	Southend	7 October 1945		1967–71	West Ham United
DAY	Chris	Walthamstow	28 July 1975		1996–97	Tottenham Hotspur

	APPEARANCES						GOALS					
TO	S.LEAGUE	F. LEAGUE	FA CUP	F. L. CUP	OTHER	APPS	S.LEAGUE	F.LEAGUE	FA CUP	FL CUP	OTHER	GOALS
Kettering Town		21				21		8				8
Newport County		121	14			135		7	2			9
Beckenham (Manager)		55	2			57		2				2
Millwall		142+9	15	15		172+9		31	2	3		36
Bristol City		75	6			81		58	7			65
Rochdale		78	7			85						
Gravesend		118	5			123		1				1
Romford		258	21	1		280		2	1			3
	31		1			32						
Queen's Park Rangers		274	25			299		99	7			106
Retired through injury		38		2		40						
Folkestone		16	4			20						
Weymouth		2				2						
Newport County		12				12						
Southend United		67	4			71		12	1			13
		90+4	9	3		102+4		1				1
Kingstonian		4				4						
Retired through injury	81		4			85						
		14				14		1				1
Blackburn Rovers		143+11	8	24+2	2	177+13		13	1	2		16
Cambridge United		41	3			44		6				6
Ashington (Co. Durham)		1				1						
Fulham	25		3			28						
Maidstone	49		1			50		2				2
Yeovil Town		143	9			152		7				7
Rochdale		55	6			61		14	2			16
Ramsgate	263		18			281	1					1
Southend United		4+16		2+3		6+19		1		1		2
Released		1+3	0+2			1+5						
York City		2				2						
Barrow		3				3						
Newport County	37	61	6			104	18	37	2			57
Brentford		1				1						
Chelsea		42+2	3+1	0+1		45+4			1			1
Rochdale		69	5			74		27	1			28
		1				1		1				1
Stoke City		49	1			50		8				8
Headington United		4				4						
Exeter City		12				12		1				1
		17+13	0+1	1		18+14		2				
		29	4			33		2				2
AFC Bournemouth		2+13	1+2			3+15			1			1
Maidstone United Dartford	33	47	8			88	1					1
Millwall		13		1		14						
Coventry City		56+7	5+1	3		64+8		14	1	1		16
Northampton Town		116	10			126		1				1
Tranmere Rovers		26	1			27		6				6
Mansfield Town		3				3		1				1
Wolverhampton Wand.		221	16			237						
		8				8						
Leeds City	1					1						
Sunderland		27+1		6		33+1		7		1		8
		4				4						
New York Metro Stars (USA)		10+13		2	1	13+13		5				5
Retired		28				28						
Nuneaton Borough		10		1		11		1				1
Exeter City		1				1						
Hartlepools United		7				7						
		93+10	9	2		104+10		17	3			20
Inglewood (Australia)				2		2						
Enfield		6		1		7						
		6		1		7						
Clacton Town		11				11		2				2
West Bromwich Albion	193		14			207	21		3			24
		3				3						
Kidderminster Harriers		5				5		2				2
		43+9	5			48+9						
Bradford Park Avenue		26	3			29		4	1			5
Luton Town Aldershot		149	7			156		91	1			92
Retired through injury		222	15			237		2				2
Durban United (South Africa)		24+1	2+2	3		29+3		3				3
Watford		24	2	2		28						

SURNAME	NAME	BIRTHPLACE	DATE OF BIRTH	DIED	SEASONS	FROM
DEAKIN	Fred	Birmingham	5 February 1920	2000	1946–48	Birmingham City
DEAKIN	Mike	Birmingham	25 October 1933		1954–60	Bromsgrove Rovers
DELANEY	Louis	Bothwell	28 February 1921	1968	1949–50	Arsenal
DEL RIO	Walter	Buenos Aires (Argentina)	16 June 1976		1998–99	Boca Juniors (Argentina) (Loan)
DENNIS	Mark	Streatham	2 May 1961		1989–91	Queen's Park Rangers
DE ORNELAS	Fernando	Caracas (Venezuela)	29 July 1976		1999–2000	South China (Hong Kong)
DERRY	Shaun	Nottingham	6 December 1977		2002–05	Portsmouth
2 spells					2007–10	Leeds United
DEVONSHIRE	Les	West Ham	13 June 1926		1951–55	Chester City
DICK	John	Eaglesham	1876		1905–06	Woolwich Arsenal
DICKOV	Paul	Livingston	1 November 1972		2007–08	Manchester City (Loan)
DIGBY	Fraser	Sheffield	23 April 1967		1998–2000	Swindon Town
DIKGACOI	Kagisho	Brandfort (South Africa)	24 November 1984		2010–11	Fulham (Loan)
DJILALI	Kieran	Lambeth	22 January 1991		2008–	Junior
DODGE	Bill	Hackney	10 March 1937		1962–63	Tottenham Hotspur
DONCASTER	Richard	Barry Dock	13 May 1908		1932–33	Exeter City
DORMAN	Andy	Chester	1 May 1982		2010–	St. Mirren
DOUGLAS	Edward	Hebburn	26 March 1899		1922–23	Crook Town
DOWIE	Iain	Hatfield	9 January 1965		1994–96	Southampton
DOWNS	Ronnie	Southwark	27 August 1932	1994	1952–54	Grove United
DOWSETT	Gilbert 'Dickie'	Chelmsford	3 July 1931		1962–65	Bournemouth & Boscombe
DREYER	Henry	Sunderland	9 March 1892	1953	1921–23	South Shields
DROY	Micky	Highbury	7 May 1951		1984–87	Chelsea
DUNN	Ronnie	Southall	24 November 1908		1931–37	Army
DUNSIRE	Andrew	Buckhaven (Fife)	11 October 1902	1980	1928–30	Kettering Town
DUTHIE	John	Fraserburgh	7 January 1903	1969	1929–30	York City
DYER	Alex	West Ham	14 November 1965		1988–90	Hull City
DYER	Bruce	Ilford	13 April 1975		1993–99	Watford
DYSON	Barry	Oldham	6 September 1942	1995	1966–68	Tranmere Rovers
EARLE	Edwin	Newbiggin	17 June 1905	1987	1933–34	Boston Town
EASTER	Jermaine	Cardiff	15 January 1982		2010–	MK Dons
EASTMAN	Don	Eastry	9 August 1923		1946–47	ex-Amateur
EASTON	Harry	Shoreham-by-Sea	12 September 1938		1959–62	Junior
EDWARDS	Christian	Caerphilly	23 November 1975		2001–02	Nottingham Forest (Loan)
EDWARDS	Frank	Merstham	23 May 1885	1970	1906–07	Croydon Wanderers
EDWARDS	Ian	Wrexham	30 January 1955		1982–83	Wrexham
EDWARDS	Jack	Risca	6 July 1929		1949–59	Lovells Athletic
EDWARDS	Leslie	Nuneaton	1912		1933–36	Folkestone
EDWARDS	Matthew	South Shields	1882	1944	1905–08	Barnsley
EDWARDS	Rob	Telford	25 December 1982		2003–04	Aston Villa (Loan)
EDWORTHY	Marc	Barnstaple	24 December 1972		1995–99	Plymouth Argyle
ELWISS	Mike	Doncaster	2 May 1954		1978–79	Preston North End
EMBLEN	Neil	Bromley (Kent)	19 June 1971		1997–98	Wolverhampton Wand.
ERTL	Johannes	Graz (Austria)	12 November 1982		2008–10	Austria Wien
EVANS	Fred	Petersfield	20 May 1923		1950–53	Notts County
EVANS	Gwyn	Ton Pentre	24 February 1935	2000	1958–63	Cwm Parc
EVANS	Ian	Egham	30 January 1952		1974–78	Queen's Park Rangers
EVANS	Stephen	Caerphilly	25 September 1980		1998–2001	Junior
EVANS	Tony	Liverpool	11 January 1954		1983–84	Birmingham City
FARRELL	Ray	Cardiff	31 May 1933	1999	1957–59	Treharris
FARRINGTON	Roy	Tonbridge	6 June 1925	2006	1947–49	Junior
FASHANU	John	Kensington	18 September 1962		1983–84	Norwich City (Loan)
FEEBERY	Albert	Hucknall	9 April 1889	1964	1914–24	Coventry City
FELL	Les	Leyton	16 December 1920	2010	1952–54	Charlton Athletic
FELTON	Robert	Gateshead	12 August 1918	1982	1946–47	Port Vale
FELTON	Vivien	Southgate	13 August 1929	2005	1954–56	Barnet
FENWICK	Terry	Seaham	17 November 1959		1977–81	Junior
FIELDING	Horace	Heywood	14 October 1906	1969	1936–38	Reading
FINN	Arthur	Folkestone	24 March 1911		1933–34	Folkestone
FINNIGAN	Tony	Wimbledon	17 October 1962		1984–88	Corinthian Casuals
FISHLOCK	Laurie	Battersea	2 January 1907	1986	1929–32	Dulwich Hamlet
FLAHAVAN	Darryl	Southampton	28 November 1978		2008–10	Southend United
FLANAGAN	Mike	Ilford	9 November 1952		1979–81	Charlton Athletic
FLEMING	Curtis	Manchester	8 October 1968		2001–04	Middlesbrough
FLETCHER	Carl	Camberley	7 April 1980		2006–09	West Ham United
FLETCHER	Charlie	Homerton	28 October 1905	1980	1928–29	Clapton Orient
FLINDERS	Scott	Rotherham	12 June 1986		2006–08	Barnsley
FLOOD	Joe	Dublin	1901		1926–28	Shamrock Rovers (Ireland)
FOLAN	Tony	Lewisham	18 September 1978		1997–99	Junior
FONTE	Jose	Penafiel (Portugal)	22 December 1983		2007–08	Benfica (Loan)
2 spells					2008–10	Benfica
FONTE	Rui	Lisbon (Portugal)	23 April 1990		2008–09	Arsenal (Loan)
FORGAN	Thomas		1887		1909–10	Gainsborough
FORSSELL	Mikael	Steinfurt (Germany)	15 March 1981		1999–2000	Chelsea (Loan)
2 spells					2000–01	Chelsea (Loan)
FORSTER	Bill		1882		1906–08	Sheffield United

	APPEARANCES						GOALS					
TO	S.LEAGUE	F. LEAGUE	FA CUP	F. L. CUP	OTHER	APPS	S.LEAGUE	F.LEAGUE	FA CUP	FL CUP	OTHER	GOALS
Kidderminster Harriers		6				6						
Northampton Town		143	9			152		56	7			63
Bedford Town		3				3						
		1+1		0+1		1+2						
Southampton (coach)		8+1			1	9+1						
Celtic		5+4				5+4						
Leeds United		173+25	11	12	3+2	199+27		3				3
Queen's Park Rangers												
Margate		83	4			87		12				12
	1					1						
		6+3				6+3						
Barry Town		56	1	7		64						
		13				13		1				1
		14+14	0+2	2+3		16+19		1				1
Kettering		3				3						
Reading		15				15		4				4
		14+6	2	1		17+6		1				1
Crook Town		2				2		1				1
West Ham United		19	6			25		6	4			10
Power Semas		23				23		2				2
Weymouth		54		2		56		22				22
Southend United		55	3			58		2				2
Brentford		49	1	6	2	58		7				7
Colchester United		167	8			175						
Dartford		5				5		1				1
York City		13				13		3				3
Charlton Athletic		16+1	1+1	3+1	3+1	23+4		2			3	5
Barnsley		95+40	7+3	9+5	3+2	114+50		37	6	1		44
Watford		33+1	1			34+1		9				9
Gresley Rovers		10	1			11		3				3
		6+8				6+8		2				2
Kingstonian		1				1						
Gravesend & Northfleet		8	1			9		1				1
		9				9						
	1					1						
Chorley		16+2	3	4		23+2		4	1	2		7
Rochdale		223	16			239						
Newport County		23	1			24		2				2
Doncaster Rovers	57		14			71	5					5
		6+1				6+1		1				1
Coventry City		120+6	8	8+1	8	144+7				1		1
Retired through injury		19+1		4		23+1		7				7
Wolverhampton Wand.		8+5	1+1			9+6			2			2
Sheffield United		32+13	4	1+1		37+14			1			1
Rochdale		52	1			53		11				11
Christchurch Utd (New Zealand)		80	8	1		89						
Barnsley		137	16	10		163		14	2			16
Brentford		0+6		0+1		0+7						
Wolverhampton Wand.		19+2	0+1	1		20+3		7				7
		5				5						
Tunbridge Wells		3	1			4			1			1
		1		1		2						
Folkestone	66	92	6			164	1	7				8
Margate		65	4			69		6	2			8
South Liverpool		1				1						
Tonbridge		2				2						
Queen's Park Rangers		62+8	7	4+1		73+9			2			2
Peterborough United		22				22		1				1
Cannes (France)		9				9						
Blackburn Rovers		94+11	2+1	7+1	2	105+13		10				10
Aldershot		18	1			19		2				2
Portsmouth		2		2		4						
Queen's Park Rangers		56	1	7		64		8		5		13
Darlington		41+4	1	2+1		44+5						
Plymouth Argyle		50+18	3+1	0+2		53+21		4				4
Merthyr Town		7				7						
		7+1	3	2		12+1						
Shamrock Rovers (Ireland)		34	5			39		5				5
Brentford		0+1			1	1+1						
		75+7	4	4	1+1	84+8		6				6
Southampton												
		5+5				5+5						
Aberdare	1					1						
		44+8	1+1	8		53+9		16		2		18
Grimsby Town	50		11			61						

SURNAME	NAME	BIRTHPLACE	DATE OF BIRTH	DIED	SEASONS	FROM
FORSTER	Stan	Aylesham	1 November 1943		1962–64	Margate
FORWARD	Fred	Croydon	8 September 1999	1977	1921–24	Brighton Railways
FOSTER	Craig	Melbourne (Australia)	15 April 1969		1998–2000	Portsmouth
FOULDS	Albert	Salford	8 August 1919		1953–54	Rochdale
FRAMPTON	Andrew	Wimbledon	3 September 1979		1998–2003	Junior
FRANCIS	Gerry	Chiswick	6 December 1951		1979–81	Queen's Park Rangers
FRAY	Arron	Beckenham	1 May 1987		2005–06	Junior
FREEDMAN	Dougie	Glasgow	21 January 1974		1995–98	Barnet
2 spells					2000–08	Nottingham Forest
FREEMAN	Alf	Bethnal Green	2 January 1920		1948–49	Southampton
FROST	James 'Jack'	Oakenshaw	1909		1930–31	Arsenal
FRY	Bob	Pontypridd	29 June 1935		1955–56	Southall
FRY	David	Bournemouth	5 January 1960		1977–83	Weymouth
FULLARTON	Jamie	Bellshill (Glasgow)	20 July 1974		1997–2001	FC Bastia (France)
FULLER	Bill	Brixton	6 April 1944		1962–65	Junior
FULLER	Ricardo	Kingston (Jamaica)	31 October 1979		2000–01	Tivoli Gardens (Jamaica)
GABBIADINI	Marco	Nottingham	20 January 1968		1991–92	Sunderland
GAILLARD	Marcel	Charlerois (Belgium)	15 January 1927	1976	1947–50	Tonbridge
GALE	Tony	Westminster	19 November 1959		1995–96	Blackburn Rovers
GALLAGHER	Hugh	Clydebank			1926–28	Clyde
GALLIERS	Steve	Preston	21 August 1957		1981–82	Wimbledon
GALLOWAY	Steve	Hannover (Germany)	13 February 1963		1984–86	Sutton United
GARDNER	Anthony	Stone	19 September 1980		2010–11	Hull City (Loan)
GARRATT	George	Byker	April 1884	1960	1908–13	West Bromwich Albion
GARVAN	Owen	Dublin (Eire)	29 January 1988		2010–	Ipswich Town
GAVIN	Johnny	Limerick (Ireland)	20 April 1928	2007	1959–61	Watford
GENNOE	Terry	Shrewsbury	16 March 1953		1980–81	Southampton (Loan)
GEORGE	Ron	Bristol	14 August 1922	1989	1948–54	Bristol Aeroplane Co.
GIBSON	Robert	Brownieside	1887		1909–10	Bury
GILBERT	Billy	Lewisham	10 November 1959		1977–84	Junior
GILES	David	Cardiff	21 September 1956		1981–84	Swansea City
GILL	James	Sheffield	9 November 1954		1928–29	Derby County
GILLESPIE	Ian	Plymouth	6 May 1913	1988	1936–46	Harwich & Parkestone
GINTY	Rory	Galway (Eire)	23 January 1977		1997–98	Junior
GIRLING	Howard 'Dickie'	Birmingham	24 May 1922	1992	1946–47	
GLAZIER	Bill	Nottingham	2 August 1943		1961–65	Junior
GLOVER	F				1910–11	Army
GODDARD	Charles	Ranceby	6 April 1910		1932–34	Northfleet
2 spells					1935–36	After trial
GOLDTHORPE	Bobby	Osterley	6 December 1950		1971–72	Junior
GOODCHILD	Gary	Chelmsford	27 January 1958		1979–81	Kramfors (Sweden)
GOODCLIFFE	William	London			1932–36	Dulwich Hamlet
GOODHIND	George				1910–11	Dartford
GOODING	Scott	Reading	21 August 1982		2001–02	Junior
GOODWIN	Sam	Tarbolton	14 March 1943	2005	1971–72	Airdrieonians
GORDON	Dean	Thornton Heath	10 February 1973		1991–98	Junior
GRABBAN	Lewis	Croydon	12 January 1988		2005–08	Junior
GRAHAM	Dick	Corby	6 May 1922		1945–51	Leicester City
GRAHAM	Gareth	Belfast	6 December 1978		1998–99	Junior
GRAHAM	George	Bargeddie	30 November 1944		1976–78	Portsmouth
GRAINGER	John	Cannock	1896		1919–20	
GRANT	Archie				1905–06	East Fife
GRANT	Walter	Aberdeen	1890	1940	1926–28	Raith Rovers
GRANVILLE	Danny	Islington	19 January 1975		2001–07	Manchester City
GRAY	Andy	Lambeth	22 February 1964		1984–88	Dulwich Hamlet
2 spells					1989–92	Queen's Park Rangers
GRAY	Julian	Lewisham	21 September 1979		2000–04	Arsenal
GREEN	Albert	Rickmansworth	7 October 1892		1919–20	Watford
GREEN	Stuart	Whitehaven	15 June 1981		2006–08	Hull City
GREENER	Bobby	Birtley	17 July 1899	1970	1921–32	Birtley Colliery
GREENWOOD	Alex	Fulham	17 June 1933		1954–55	Chelsea
GREENWOOD	Roy	Croydon	22 May 1931		1954–59	Beckenham Town
GREGG	Matt	Cheltenham	30 November 1978		1999–2001	Torquay United
GREGORY	Fred	Doncaster	24 October 1911	1985	1937–46	Reading
GRIEVE	David	Selkirk	15 February 1929		1954–55	Reading
GRIFFIN	Michael	Middlesbrough	1887		1909–10	Liverpool
GRIFFIT	Leandre	Maubeuge (France)	21 May 1984		2008–09	IF Elfsborg (Sweden)
GRIFFITHS	Lewis	Tonypandy	7 September 1903	1985	1928–30	Torquay United
GRIMSHAW	Colin	Betchworth	16 September 1925	1995	1952–53	Arsenal
GROVES	Fred	Lincoln	6 May 1892	1980	1924–26	Stoke City
GUNNING	Harry	Leigh-on-Sea	8 February 1932	2005	1954–57	West Ham United
GUTHRIE	Jimmy	Luncarty	6 August 1912	1981	1946–47	Guildford City
HALL	Fitz	Leytonstone	20 December 1980		2004–06	Southampton
HALL	Ryan	Dulwich	4 January 1988		2007–08	Junior
HALL	William	Bolton	1884		1907–08	Manchester City
HALLAM	Charles	Longton	17 January 1902	1970	1927–28	Stoke City

			APPEARANCES						GOALS			
TO	S.LEAGUE	F. LEAGUE	FA CUP	F. L. CUP	OTHER	APPS	S.LEAGUE	F.LEAGUE	FA CUP	FL CUP	OTHER	GOALS
Dover		2		1		3		1				1
Newport County		6				6						
Northern Spirit (Australia)		47+5	2			49+5		3				3
Crewe Alexandra		17	1			18		4				4
Brentford		19+9	2	3+1		24+10						
Queen's Park Rangers		59	1	6		66		7		2		9
Bromley				2		2						
Wolverhampton Wand. Southend United		213+114	7+6	17+3	4+4	241+127		95	1	10	2	108
Reading		2				2						
Retired through injury		4				4		2				2
Bath City		6				6						
Gillingham		40	5			45						
Dundee United		40+7	3	2+1	1	46+8		1				1
Wellington Town		3		1		4						
Heart of Midlothian		2+6				2+6						
Derby County		15	1	6	3	25		5		1	1	7
Portsmouth		21				21		3				3
Maidenhead United		2	1			3						
		35	2			37						
Wimbledon		8+5				8+5						
Maidstone United		3+2		0+1		3+3		1				1
		26+2	1			27+2		1				1
Millwall	173		12			185	7		1			8
		26	1	1		28		3				3
Cambridge City		66	2			68		15	2			17
		3				3						
Colchester United		123	3			126		2				2
Middlesbrough	2					2	1					1
Portsmouth		235+2	17	19		271+2		3	1			4
Birmingham City		83+5	5+1	5+1		93+7		6				6
		10				10		3				3
Ipswich Town		21	6			27		4	1			5
Shelbourne (Eire)		2+3	0+1			2+4						
Brentford		26	1			27		6				6
Coventry City		106	5	2		113						
Army	1					1						
Returned to family business		24				24		8				8
Charlton Athletic		1				1						
Viking Stavanger (Norway)		0+2	0+2			0+4						
Dulwich Hamlet		2				2		1				1
	1					1						
Whyteleafe		0+1				0+1						
Motherwell		18+7		2		20+7						
Middlesbrough		181+20	14+1	16+3	5+1	216+25		20	1	2		23
Millwall		0+10		0+3		0+13		1				1
Retired through injury		155	9			164						
Brentford		0+1				0+1						
Retired through injury		43+1	3	4		50+1		2	1	1		4
Tranmere Rovers	1					1						
Chelsea	15		2			17						
		21				21		5				5
Colchester United		117+5	4+3	6	3	130+8		9		1		10
Aston Villa Tottenham Hotspur		178+10	14	24+1	14+1	230+12		39	2	6	4	51
Birmingham City		100+25	6	5+6	2	113+31		10	2	1		13
Sheppey United	9					9	3					3
Blackpool		12+12	2	1		15+12		2				2
York City		293	24			317		5	1			6
Darlington		2				2						
Bedford Town		111	5			116						
Bray Wanderers (Eire)		7		2+1		9+1						
Hartlepools United		43	3			46		9				9
Worcester City		22				22		3				3
Hartlepools United	34		1			35	2					2
URS Du Centre (Belgium)		2+3	1			3+3						
Fulham		36	6			42		20	3			23
Guildford City		32	3			35		3				3
Rhyl Athletic		14	1			15		2	1			3
Reading		62	2			64		4				4
To Club Coach		5				5						
Wigan Athletic		75	2	2	2	81		3				3
Bromley		0+1	0+1			0+2						
	10					10						
Sandbach Ramblers		2				2		2				2

SURNAME	NAME	BIRTHPLACE	DATE OF BIRTH	DIED	SEASONS	FROM
HALLS	John	Islington	14 February 1982		2007–08	Reading (Loan)
HAMILTON	Jimmy	Hetton-le-Hole	1904		1923–31	Coldstream Guards
HAMMOND	Paul	Nottingham	26 July 1953		1972–77	Thorneywood
HAMPTON	Colin	Brechin	1 September 1888		1925–26	Brechin City
HANCOX	Ray	Mansfield	1 May 1929		1950–53	Sutton United
HAND	Bill	Codnor	5 July 1898		1920–26	Sutton Town
HANDLEY	George	Wednesbury	1913	1943	1934–35	West Bromwich Albion
HANGER	Harry	Kettering	1886	1918	1909–15	Bradford City
HANKIN	Sean	Camberley	28 February 1981		1999–2000	Junior
HANLON	Wally	Glasgow	23 September 1919	1999	1949–55	Bournemouth & Boscombe
HANN	Ralph	Whitburn (Co. Durham)	4 July 1911	1990	1946–47	Derby County (trainer)
HANSON	Fred	Sheffield	23 May 1915	1967	1935–36	Wolverhampton Wand.
HARDING	Ted	Croydon	5 April 1925		1946–53	Coalville (Croydon)
HARDWICK	Steve	Mansfield	6 September 1956		1985–86	Oxford United (Loan)
HARKER	Dick	Wardley (Northumberland)	1885		1905–07	Newcastle United
2 spells					1911–12	Hearts Darlington
HARKOUK	Rachid	Chelsea	19 May 1956		1976–78	Feltham
HARPER	Bill	Wishaw	15 November 1900		1924–26	Manchester City
HARRIS	Jason	Sutton	24 November 1976		1996–97	Junior
HARRIS	Mark	Reading	15 July 1963		1988–89	Wokingham Town
HARRIS	Richard	Croydon	23 October 1980		1998–2001	Junior
HARRISON	Bernard	Worcester	28 September 1934	2006	1955–59	Portsmouth
HARRISON	Craig	Gateshead	10 November 1977		2000–02	Middlesbrough
HARRY	Albert	Surbiton	8 March 1897	1966	1921–34	Kingstonians
HATTON	Albert	Nottingham	1879	1963	1910–12	Grimsby Town
HAVELOCK	Harry	Hull	20 January 1901	1973	1927–31	Portsmouth
HAWKINS	Alf	Malden	October 1904		1925–27	Southall
HAYNES	Alfred	Oxford	4 April 1907	1953	1933–36	Arsenal
HAYWARD	John 'Jack'	Warsop Vale	October 1903	1974	1933–34	Bournemouth & Boscombe
HAYWOOD	Adam	Horninglow	1875	1932	1908–09	Blackpool
HAZELL	Tony	High Wycombe	19 September 1947		1978–79	Millwall
HEARN	Frank	Camden	5 November 1929		1954–55	Northampton Town
HECKMAN	Ron	Peckham	23 November 1929	1990	1960–63	Millwall
HEDLEY	Ralph	Byker	1897	1969	1924–26	Hull City
HEDMAN	Rudi	Lambeth	16 November 1964		1988–92	Colchester United
HEEROO	Gavin	Harringay	2 September 1984		2003–04	Junior
HEINEMANN	Geoffrey 'George'	Stafford	17 December 1905	1970	1934–35	Coventry City
HENWOOD	A.E. 'Curly'				1905–06	Catford Southend
HEPPOLETTE	Ricky	Bhusawal (India)	8 April 1949		1976–77	Orient
HERBERT	Trevor	Reading	3 June 1929		1950–51	Leyton Orient
HEWITSON	Bob	Blyth	26 February 1884	1957	1905–07	Barnsley
HEWITT	Charles	West Hartlepool	10 April 1884	1966	1910–15	West Bromwich Albion
HIBBURT	James	Ashford (Middlesex)	30 October 1979		1998–2000	Junior
HIGGINBOTTOM	Andy	Chesterfield	22 October 1964		1985–87	Cambridge United
HIGGINS	Fred	Hackney	21 January 1930		1952–54	Wood Green
HIGGINS	H	New Southgate	1883		1907–09	Streatham
HILAIRE	Vince	Forest Hill	10 October 1959		1976–84	Junior
HILL	Clint	Huyton	19 October 1978		2007–10	Stoke City
HILL	Mick	Hereford	3 December 1947	2008	1973–76	Ipswich Town
HILLS	Lee	Croydon	13 April 1990		2007–	Junior
HILLEY	Cornelius	Glasgow	29 September 1902	1959	1926–28	Third Lanark
HINSHELWOOD	Martin	Reading	16 June 1953		1972–78	Junior
HINSHELWOOD	Paul	Bristol	14 August 1956		1973–83	Junior
HOADLEY	Phil	Battersea	6 January 1952		1967–72	Junior
HODDINOTT	Tom	Brecon	27 November 1894	1980	1923–26	Chelsea
HODGES	Glyn	Streatham	30 April 1963		1990–91	Watford
HODGKINSON	Joe	Bolton	1882		1906–07	Bury
HOLDER	Phil	Kilburn	19 January 1952		1974–78	Tottenham Hotspur
HOLMES	Eddie	Manchester	15 November 1900	1975	1927–28	Altrincham
HOLSGROVE	John	Southwark	27 September 1945		1964–65	Junior
HOLTON	Cliff	Oxford	29 April 1929	1996	1962–65	Northampton Town
HONE	Mark	Croydon	31 March 1968		1987–89	Junior
HOOPER	Arthur	Brierley Hill	1889	1916	1914–15	Manchester United
HOPGOOD	Ron	Balham	24 November 1934	1990	1957–60	Spicers Athletic
HOPKIN	David	Greenock	21 August 1970		1995–97	Chelsea
2 spells					2000–02	Bradford City
HOPKINS	Henry	Pontypridd			1926–28	Barry Town
HOPKINS	Idris	Merthyr Tydfil	11 October 1910	1994	1932–33	Dartford
HOPKINS	Jeff	Swansea	14 April 1964		1988–90	Fulham
HOROBIN	Roy	Brownhills	10 March 1935		1964–65	Peterborough United
HORTON	John 'Jack'	Fairburn (near Castleford)	14 July 1905		1937–39	Chelsea
HOUGHTON	Ray	Glasgow	9 January 1962		1994–97	Aston Villa
HOWARD	Terry	Stepney	26 February 1966		1985–86	Chelsea (Loan)
HOWE	Bert	Greenwich	16 November 1938		1958–67	Faversham Town
HOWE	Harold	Hemel Hempstead	9 April 1906	1976	1933–34	Queen's Park Rangers
HOWELLS	Ray	Rhondda	27 June 1926		1946–50	Mid Rhondda United

TO	APPEARANCES						GOALS					
	S.LEAGUE	F. LEAGUE	FA CUP	F. L. CUP	OTHER	APPS	S.LEAGUE	F.LEAGUE	FA CUP	FL CUP	OTHER	GOALS
		5				5						
Hartlepools United		180	16			196		4	1			5
Tampa Bay Rowdies (USA)		117	17	8		142						
		3				3						
Southend United		20				20		3				3
Contract cancelled		101	9			110		15	1			16
		5				5						
	168		10			178	7		1			8
Torquay United		0+1				0+1						
Sudbury Town		126	4			130		8	1			9
Luton Town (trainer)		1				1						
Rotherham United		1				1						
Whitstable		151	5			156						
		3				3						
Hibernian	66		17			83	19		8			27
Queen's Park Rangers		51+3	1+3	4+1		56+7		20	2	3		25
Luton Town		57	2			59						
Leyton Orient		0+2		0+2		0+4						
Swansea City		0+2				0+2						
Wycombe Wanderers		2+7		2+2		4+9						
Southampton		92	8			100		12				12
Retired through injury		34+4	2	8		44+4						
Dartford		410	30			440		53	2			55
Aberdare Athletic	43		2			45						
Hull City		67	9			76		39	4			43
		20	2			22		8	1			9
		48	3			51		1				1
		19	1			20		1				1
Retired	9					9	2					2
Charlton Athletic		5				5						
Gladesville-Ryde (Australia)		8				8		1				1
Bedford Town		84	6	3		93		25	4			29
Durham City		4				4						
Dulwich Hamlet		10+11		0+1	3+1	13+13						
Billericay Town		0+1				0+1						
Clapton Orient		25	1			26						
Charlton Athletic	1					1						
Chesterfield		13+2	3			16+2						
		8				8		2				2
Oldham Athletic	60		15			75						
Hartlepools United	151		11			162	39		2			41
Woking		1+5			0+1	1+6						
Maidstone United		16+7	0+2	2	3	21+9		2				2
Retired		11				11						
Watford	2					2						
Luton Town		239+16	16+1	21		276+17		29	3	4		36
Queen's Park Rangers		114	6+1	4	2	126+1		5	1			6
Cape Town (South Africa)		43+2	1	3		47+2		6				6
		24+21	1	0+1		25+22		1				1
Thames		43	2			45		4				4
Retired through injury		66+3	7	6		79+3		4				4
Oxford United		271+5	26	17		314+5		22	4	2		28
Orient		63+10	2+4	9		74+14		1		1		2
Rhyl Athletic		79	10			89		20	2			22
Sheffield United		5+2		2+2		7+4				1		1
Stockport County	5					5	1					1
Memphis Rogues (USA)		93+2	11	4+2		108+4		5	1			6
Reading		17	3			20						
Wolverhampton Wand.		18	4			22		2				2
Watford		101	6	5		112		40	8	1		49
Welling United		4		3+1		7+1						
	18					18	2					2
Folkestone		14	2			16						
Leeds United Greenock Morton		100+12	4	6+1	3	113+13		25		6	2	33
		40	3			43		13	3			16
Brentford		4				4						
Bristol Rovers		70	4	7	12	93		2	1	1		4
Weymouth		4	3			7						
		38	3			41		7				7
Reading		69+3	4	6	4	83+3		7			1	8
		4				4						
Orient		192+1	12	7		211+1			1			1
Rochdale		2				2						
Exeter City		25	1			26		5				5

SURNAME	NAME	BIRTHPLACE	DATE OF BIRTH	DIED	SEASONS	FROM
HOY	Roger	Poplar	6 December 1946		1968–70	Tottenham Hotspur
HREIDARSSON	Hermann	Reykjavik (Iceland)	11 July 1974		1997–99	I.B.V. Knattspyrnurad (Iceland)
HUDGELL	Arthur	Hackney	28 December 1920	2000	1945–47	Eton Manor
HUDSON	Mark	Guildford	30 March 1982		2003–04	Fulham (Loan)
2 spells					2004–08	Fulham
HUGHES	Jeff	Larne (N.I.)	29 May 1985		2007–08	Lincoln City
HUGHES	Jimmy	Bootle	December 1885		1909–20	Liverpool
HUGHES	John	Coatbridge	3 April 1943		1971–73	Glasgow Celtic
HUGHES	Ken	Barmouth	9 January 1966		1985–86	Junior
HUGHES	Michael	Larne (N.I.)	2 August 1971		2003–07	Unattached
HUGHES	Stephen 'Billy'	Folkestone	29 July 1960		1981–82	Gillingham
HUGHES	William 'Archie'	Holyhead	2 February 1919	1992	1950–52	Rochdale
HUGHTON	Henry	Stratford	18 November 1959		1982–86	Orient
HULLOCK	James	Newcastle			1908–10	
HUMPHREY	John	Paddington	31 January 1961		1990–95	Charlton Athletic
HUMPHREYS	C		1890		1910–11	
HUMPHREYS	Gerry	Llandudno	14 January 1946		1970–71	Everton
HUNT	David	Dulwich	10 September 1982		2002–03	Junior
HUNT	Revd. Kenneth	Oxford	24 February 1884	1949	1912–20	Wolverhampton Wand.
(As an amateur, he had three different spells with Crystal Palace spread over eight years.)						
HUNT	Michael	Croydon			1925–28	North Croydon
HUNT	Stephen	Port Laoise (Eire)	1 August 1980		1999–2000	Junior
HUNTER	Herbert	Trimdon Colliery			1906–07	Middlesbrough
HYATT	John	Feltham	20 December 1932		1954–55	Feltham
HYND	Roger	Falkirk	2 February 1942		1969–70	Glasgow Rangers
IDRIZAJ	Besian	Baden bei Wien (Austria)	12 October 1987	2010	2007–08	Liverpool (Loan)
IFILL	Paul	Brighton	20 October 1979		2006–09	Sheffield United
IMLACH	Stuart	Lossiemouth	6 January 1932	2001	1962–65	Coventry City
2 spells					1965–67	Chelmsford City
IMRIE	James	Markinch			1928–31	Kettering Town
INNERD	Wilf	Newcastle	1878		1905–09	Newcastle United
IRVINE	Alan	Glasgow	12 July 1958		1984–87	Everton
IRWIN	George	Smethwick	7 January 1891		1921–23	West Bromwich Albion
ISLEY	Arthur	Battersea			1919–20	
ISMAEL	Valerien	Strasbourg (France)	28 September 1975		1997–98	RC Strasbourg (France)
IVERSEN	Steffen	Oslo (Norway)	10 November 1976		2010–	Rosenborg (Norway)
IVEY	Lawrence	Abingdon	5 October 1900	1969	1927–28	Sutton United
JACKSON	Cliff	Swindon	3 September 1941		1966–70	Plymouth Argyle
JACKSON	J. Richard	Middlesbrough	1877		1906–07	Portsmouth
JACKSON	John	Hammersmith	5 September 1942		1964–74	St Clement Danes School
JAMES	Wilfred	Stratford	1905		1927–29	Newport County
JAMIESON	Harold	Wallsend	9 December 1908		1929–30	Crawcrook Albion
JANSEN	Matt	Carlisle	20 October 1977		1997–99	Carlisle United
JEFFRIES	Derek	Manchester	22 March 1951		1973–76	Manchester City
JENKINS	Ross	Kensington	4 November 1951		1971–73	Junior
JEWETT	George	Southampton	2 April 1906	1998	1931–32	Southampton
JIHAI	Sun	Dalian (China)	30 September 1977		1998–99	Dalian Wanda (China)
JOHN	Stern	Tunapuna (Trinidad)	30 October 1976		2009–10	Southampton
JOHNSON	Andy	Bedford	10 February 1981		2002–06	Birmingham City
JOHNSON	Jeff	Cardiff	26 November 1953		1973–76	Manchester City
JOHNSON	Joseph	Wednesbury			1922–25	Cannock Town
JOHNSON	Joshua 'Josh'	Tibshelf	1884		1907–15	Plymouth Argyle
JOHNSON	Peter	Hackney	18 February 1954		1974–76	AEK Athens (Greece)
JONES	Chris	Jersey (Channel Islands)	18 April 1956		1982–83	Manchester City
JONES	J.W. 'Eddie'	Whitwell (Derbyshire)	1896	1968	1924–25	Brighton & Hove Albion
JONES	Ivor	Rhondda	1 April 1925	1999	1946–47	Amateur
JONES	Joseph T. 'Tom'	Rhos-y-medre	1887	1941	1920–22	Stoke City
JONES	Ken	Wrexham	11 May 1937		1960–61	Wrexham
JONES	Morris	Liverpool	30 November 1919	1993	1950–51	Swindon Town
JORDAN	David	Belfast			1937–39	Wolverhampton Wand.
JUMP	Stewart	Crumpsall	27 January 1952		1973–78	Stoke City
KABBA	Steve	Lambeth	7 March 1981		1999–2003	Junior
KARIC	Amir	Oramovica Ponja (Yugoslavia)	31 December 1973		2000–01	Ipswich Town (Loan)
KAVIEDES	Ivan	Santo Domingo (Ecuador)	24 October 1977		2004–05	Barcelona Sporting Club (Ecu.)
KEENAN	Arnold	Belfast			1925–26	Glentoran (NI)
KEENE	Percy	Ashford (Kent)			1912–15	Ashford Railway Works
KELLARD	Bobby	Edmonton	1 March 1943		1963–66	Southend United
2 spells					1971–73	Leicester City
KELLY	John	Mossend	4 May 1902		1927–28	Gillingham
KELLY	Noel	Dublin	28 December 1921	1991	1949–51	Arsenal
KEMBER	Steve	Croydon	8 December 1948		1965–72	Junior
2 spells					1978–80	Leicester City
KEMP	David	Harrow	20 February 1953		1974–77	Slough Town
KENNEDY	Andrew	Belfast	1 September 1895	1963	1920–22	Glentoran (N.I.)
KENNEDY	Mark	Dublin (Eire)	15 May 1976		2006–08	Wolverhampton Wand.
KERRINS	Pat	Fulham	13 September 1936		1960–61	Queen's Park Rangers

TO	APPEARANCES						GOALS					
	S.LEAGUE	F. LEAGUE	FA CUP	F. L. CUP	OTHER	APPS	S.LEAGUE	F.LEAGUE	FA CUP	FL CUP	OTHER	GOALS
Luton Town		54	4	4		62		6	1			7
Brentford		32+5	4	5	2	43+5		2		1		3
Sunderland		25	4			29		1				1
		126+8	6	8	2	142+8		7				7
Charlton Athletic												
Bristol Rovers		4+6				4+6						
Chatham	200		9			209	15					15
Sunderland		20	3			23		4				4
Shrewsbury Town					1	1						
Coventry City		110+16	4	6	5	125+16		7	1	2		10
Wimbledon		3+4		2		5+4						
Canterbury City		18				18						
Brentford		113+5	6	11+1	1	131+6		1				1
Third Lanark	7					7						
Charlton Athletic		153+7	8+1	23+2	8+1	192+11		2				2
	1					1						
Crewe Alexandra		4+7		1		5+7						
Leyton Orient		2		0+1		2+1						
Wolverhampton Wand.	16					16						
North Croydon		3	1			4						
Brentford		0+3				0+3						
Wingate Albion	2					2						
Folkestone		1				1						
Birmingham City		29+1	4	4		37+1						
		3+4				3+4						
Wellington Phoenix (N. Zealand)		38+21	3+1	1+1	0+2	42+25		8	2			10
Dover		51		3		54		3				3
Notts County (coach)												
Luton Town		35	1			36						
Shildon Athletic	111		22			133	4		3			7
Dundee United		108+1	4	12	2	126+1		12	1	1		14
Reading		17				17						
	8					8						
Lens (France)		13	3			16						
		11+6	1			12+6		2				2
Sutton United		1				1						
Torquay United		100+6	5	8+1		113+7		26		4		30
Darlington	7					7						
Orient		346	18	24		388						
Notts County		4				4		1				1
Gillingham		4				4						
Blackburn Rovers		23+3	0+1	4	2	29+4		10				10
Chester		107	9	6		122		1				1
Watford		15		2		17		2				2
Basingstoke		1				1						
Dalian Wanda (China)		22+1	1	1		24+1						
		7+9				7+9		2				2
Everton		134+6	8	7	5	154+6		74	2	7	1	84
Sheffield Wednesday		82+5	5	5+1		92+6		4		1		5
Barnsley		29	2			31		6				6
Nottingham Forest	276		19			295						
Bournemouth		5+2				5+2						
Charlton Athletic		18	4			22		3				3
Frickley Colliery		4				4						
Arsenal		1				1		1				1
Coventry City		61	5			66		6				6
Swindon Town		4	1			5						
Watford		17	1			18		3				3
		7				7						
Houston Hurricane (USA)		79+2	6+1	3		88+3		2				2
Sheffield United		2+8		0+1		2+9		1				1
		3				3						
Barcelona Sporting Club (Ecu.)		1+3		0+2		1+5						
Philadelphia Celtic (USA)		4				4						
Maidstone United	15		2			17	3					3
Ipswich Town		121+2	7	7		135+2		10				10
Portsmouth												
Thames		22	1			23						
Nottingham Forest		42	1			43		5	1			6
Chelsea		255+5	15	16		286+5		36	2			38
Vancouver Whitecaps (Canada)												
Portsmouth		32+3	4	5		41+3		10	2	4		16
Arsenal		4	1			5						
Cardiff City		42+4	1+1			43+5		1				1
Southend United		5		1		6						

SURNAME	NAME	BIRTHPLACE	DATE OF BIRTH	DIED	SEASONS	FROM
KETTERIDGE	Steve	Stevenage	7 November 1959		1985–87	Wimbledon
KEVAN	Derek	Ripon	6 March 1935		1965–66	Manchester City
KIRALY	Gabor	Szombathely (Hungary)	1 April 1976		2004–07	Hertha Berlin (Germany)
KIROVSKI	Jovan	Escandido (USA)	18 March 1976		2001–02	Sporting Lisbon (Portugal)
KITSON	Paul	Murton (Co. Durham)	9 January 1971		2000–01	West Ham United (Loan)
KNOX	Thomas	Ushaw Moor (Co. Durham)	11 November 1905		1936–37	Notts County
KOLINKO	Aleksandrs	Latvia	18 June 1975		2000–03	Skonto Riga (Latvia)
KOLKKA	Joonas	Lahti (Finland)	28 September 1974		2004–06	Borussia Moenchgladbach (Ger.)
KUDJODI	Ebenezer 'Ben'	Dunstable	23 April 1989		2007–08	Junior
KUQI	Shefki	Vuqitern (Albania)	10 November 1976		2006–09	Blackburn Rovers
KURZ	Fred	Grimsby	3 September 1918	1978	1945–51	Grimsby Town
KYLE	Jack				1908–09	Woking
LACY	John	Liverpool	14 August 1951		1983–84	Tottenham Hotspur
LAKIS	Vassilios	Thessaloniki (Greece)	10 September 1976		2004–05	AEK Athens (Greece)
LANE	Harry	Marbourne (W. Midlands)			1914–15	Walsall
LANE	John 'Jack'	Birmingham	29 May 1898	1984	1930–32	Brentford
LANGLEY	Tommy	Lambeth	8 February 1958		1980–83	Queen's Park Rangers
LAUNDERS	Brian	Dublin (Eire)	8 January 1976		1994–96	Cherry Orchard (Eire)
2 spells					1999–2000	Colchester United
LAWRENCE	Bill				1906–14	Summerstown
Spread over three separate spells also played for Woolwich Arsenal						
LAWRENCE	Matt	Northampton	19 June 1974		2006–10	Millwall
LAWSON	Ian	Ouston (Co. Durham)	24 March 1939		1965–66	Leeds United
LAZARUS	Mark	Stepney	5 December 1938		1967–70	Queen's Park Rangers
LEAHY	Steve	Battersea	23 September 1959		1980–82	Junior
LEDGER	Bill				1906–07	Pryhope Villa
LEE	Alan	Galway (Eire)	21 August 1978		2008–11	Ipswich Town
LEE	Frank		1889		1908–09	Northfleet United
LEGG	Harry	Swindon	July 1910		1930–31	Swindon Town
LEIGERTWOOD	Mikele	Enfield	12 November 1982		2003–06	Wimbledon
LEVENE	David	Bethnal Green	25 February 1908	1970	1935–37	Tottenham Hotspur
LEWIS	Brian	Woking	26 January 1943	1998	1960–63	Junior
LEWIS	Fred	Birmingham	1886		1907–09	Tottenham Hotspur
LEWIS	Glyn	Abertillery	3 July 1921	1992	1945–48	RAF
LEWIS	John 'Jack'	Walsall	26 August 1919	2002	1938–50	West Bromwich Albion
LIDDLE	James	Felling	July 1912	1994	1936–37	Reading
LIEVESLEY	Les	Staveley	July 1911	1949	1936–39	Torquay United
LIGHT	Danny	Chiswick	10 July 1948		1966–68	Junior
LINDSAY	David	Havering	17 May 1966		1983–86	Junior
LINDSAY	Mark	Lambeth	6 March 1955		1973–75	Junior
LINIGHAN	Andy	Hartlepool	18 June 1962		1996–2001	Arsenal
LITTLE	Joseph 'Jack'	Seaton Delaval	25 January 1885	1965	1919–26	Croydon Common
LITTLE	Roy	Manchester	1 June 1931		1961–63	Brighton & Hove Albion
LITTLEWORT	Henry	Cosford	7 July 1882	1934	1906–07	West Norwood
LLOYD	Herbert	Cannock Chase	13 March 1888	1960	1912–13	Rotherham County
LLOYD	James	Bristol	1909		1930–32	Southend United
LOCKE	Gary	Willesden	12 July 1954		1982–86	Chelsea
LOMBARDO	Attilio	St Maria La Fossa (Italy)	6 January 1966		1997–99	Juventus (Italy)
LONG	Terry	Tylers Green (Bucks.)	17 November 1934		1955–69	Wycombe Wanderers
LOUGHLAN	John	Coatbridge	12 June 1943		1968–72	Morton
LOVE	John	Hillingdon	22 April 1951		1974–75	Staines Town
LOVELL	Steve	Swansea	16 July 1960		1980–83	Junior
LUCAS	Fred	Erith	29 September 1933		1963–65	Charlton Athletic
LUCAS	Robert	Bethnal Green	6 January 1925	2010	1946–47	Hendon
LUNNIS	Roy	Islington	4 November 1939	2010	1959–63	Carshalton Athletic
MABBUTT	Kevin	Bristol	5 December 1958		1981–85	Bristol City
McANUFF	Jobi	Edmonton	9 November 1981		2005–07	Cardiff City
McBRIDE	Andy	Nakura (Kenya)	15 March 1954		1973–74	Junior
McCARTHY	Patrick	Dublin	31 May 1983		2008–	Charlton Athletic
McCORMICK	James	Rotherham	26 September 1912	1968	1948–49	Lincoln City
McCORMICK	John	Glasgow	18 July 1936		1966–73	Aberdeen
McCRACKEN	Robert	Dromore (NI)	25 June 1900		1920–26	Belfast Distillery
McCULLOCH	Andy	Northampton	3 January 1950		1983–84	Sheffield Wednesday
MacDONALD	David	Dundee	9 May 1931		1952–55	Dundee Violett
McDONALD	Gordon	Hampstead	7 February 1932	1995	1954–57	Eastbourne
McDONALD	Harry	Salford	11 September 1926	2004	1950–55	Ashton United
McGEACHIE	George	Glasgow	26 October 1916	1972	1951–52	Rochdale
McGIBBON	Charles	Portsmouth	21 April 1880	1954	1908–09	New Brompton
McGOLDRICK	Eddie	Islington	30 April 1965		1988–93	Northampton Town
McGREGOR	John	Darlington	2 August 1900		1932–33	Gillingham
McKENNA	John	Newcastle	28 October 1901	1974	1923–25	Wallsend
McKENZIE	Leon	Croydon	17 May 1978		1995–2001	Junior
McMENEMY	Frank	Rutherglen	5 December 1906		1936–37	Northampton Town
McNICHOL	Johnny	Kilmarnock	20 August 1925	2007	1957–63	Chelsea
MACKEN	Jon	Manchester	7 September 1977		2005–07	Manchester City
MADDEN	Dave	Stepney	6 January 1963		1988–90	Reading

TO	APPEARANCES S.LEAGUE	F. LEAGUE	FA CUP	F. L. CUP	OTHER	APPS	GOALS S.LEAGUE	F.LEAGUE	FA CUP	FL CUP	OTHER	GOALS
Leyton Orient		58+1	3	7+1	1	69+2		6				6
Peterborough United		21		1		22		5				5
Burnley		104	4	1	2	111						
Birmingham City		25+11	1	2		28+11		5				5
		4				4						
Norwich City		3				3						
Rostov–na–Donu (Russia)		79+3	5	12		96+3						
A.D.O. Den Haag (Holland)		21+5		2		23+5		3				3
Croydon Athletic		0+1				0+1						
TuS Koblenz (Germany)		46+32	1+3	1		48+35		17	1			18
Boston United		148	6			154		48				48
Woking	3					3						
Stavangstadt (Norway)		24+3	1	2		27+3						
A.E.K. Athens (Greece)		6+12	1	0+1		7+13						
	16					16	5					5
Aldershot		34				34		10				10
A.E.K. Athens (Greece)		54+5	5+1	5+1		64+7		8	1	1		10
Crewe Alexandra Sheffield United		2+4		0+2		2+6						
Merthyr Town	25		5			30	5		1			6
Gillingham		109+13	8+1	2+1	1+1	120+16		1				1
Port Vale		15+2				15+2		6				6
Orient		63	3	4		70		17				17
Dartford		3+1		3		6+1						
Sunderland	11		2			13						
Huddersfield Town		46+15	8	2		56+15		11	1	1		13
Dartford	6					6	2					2
Dartford		1				1						
Sheffield United		41+18	2	3	4	50+18		1				1
France		22	1			23						
Portsmouth		32		1		33		4				4
West Bromwich Albion	16		1			17						
Bristol City		60	6			66		4				4
Bournemouth & Boscombe		124	6			130		5				5
		13	1			14		1				1
Coach in Spain		75	7			82		3				3
Colchester United		18+1	2	0+1		20+2		5				5
Welling United		18+3	1	2	0+1	21+4						
Tampa Bay Rowdies		27+3	1+1	4		32+4				1		1
Oxford United		108+3	3+2	6+3	4	121+8		4		1		5
Sittingbourne	42	200	19			261						
Dover Town		38	3	2		43		1				1
West Norwood	1					1						
Wolverhampton Wand.	3					3						
Bath City		14	2			16						
Halmstads B.K. (Sweden)		84	9	7	1	101		1				1
Lazio (Italy)		40+3		4	1	45+3		8		2		10
To club coach		432+10	30	8		470+10		16	1	1		18
Wimbledon		58+2	6	6+2		70+4						
Staines Town		1				1						
Millwall		68+6	2+1	9+1		79+8		3	1	1		5
Retired		16	2	1		19						
Weymouth		4				4						
Portsmouth		25		2		27		1				1
Vancouver (Canada)		67+8	8	5		80+8		22		2		24
Watford		66+9	4	2	2	74+9		12	2			14
Hellenic (S. Africa)		1				1						
		88+2	1	6		95+2		4				4
Sliema Wanderers (Malta)		12				12		2				2
Wealdstone		194	10	21		225		6	1			7
Portadown (NI)		175	15			190		1	1			2
Aldershot		25	3	1		29		3	1			4
Bath City		30	5			35						
Swindon Town		13	4			17						
Kettering Town		140	6			146		1				1
Wigan Athletic		46	1			47		5				5
Southampton	17					17	13					13
Arsenal		139+8	5	21+1	13+2	178+11		11		2	3	16
		4				4						
Walker Celtic		3				3						
Peterborough United		44+41	2+4	5+2		51+47		7		1		8
Guildford City		25	2			27		3				3
Tunbridge Wells Rangers		189	15	1		205		15				15
Derby County		14+11	0+2	2	0+1	16+14		2				2
Maidstone United		19+8	0+2		4	23+10		5			1	6

SURNAME	NAME	BIRTHPLACE	DATE OF BIRTH	DIED	SEASONS	FROM
MAHONEY	Tony	Barking	29 September 1959		1984–85	Brentford
MANDERS	Frank	Camberley	13 June 1914	1942	1931–36	Aldershot
MARROW	Alex	Tyldesley	21 January 1990		2010–	Blackburn Rovers
MARSDEN	Eric	Bolsover	3 January 1930		1950–53	Winchester City
MARTIN	Andrew	Cardiff	28 February 1980		1998–2001	Junior
MARTIN	David	Erith	3 June 1985		2006–08	Dartford
MARTIN	Neil	Alloa	20 October 1940		1975–76	Brighton & Hove Albion
MARTIN	Wayne	Basildon	16 December 1965		1983–84	Junior
MARTYN	Nigel	St Austell	11 August 1966		1989–96	Bristol Rovers
MASSEY	Stuart	Crawley	17 November 1964		1992–94	Sutton United
MATTHEW	Damien	Islington	23 September 1970		1993–96	Chelsea
MAUTONE	Steve	Myrtleford (Australia)	10 August 1970		1999–2000	Wolverhampton Wand.
MAY	Harold	Abingdon	1909		1931–34	Woking
MENLOVE	Bert	Barnes	8 December 1892	1970	1919–22	Aston Villa
MENZIES	Harry		1882		1906–07	Arthurlie
MICHAEL	Arthur	Worcester	1891	1959	1914–15	Worcester City
MICHOPOULOS	Nikolaus	Khardie (Greece)	20 February 1970		2002–03	Burnley (Loan)
MIDDLEMISS	James	Benwell	October 1904		1924–25	Scotswood
MIDDLETON	William	Birmingham	1895		1913–20	Aston Villa
MILLARD	Bert	West Bromwich	1 October 1898		1922–24	Coventry City
MILLBANK	Joe	Edmonton	30 September 1919	1999	1946–48	Wolverhampton Wand.
MILLER	Kevin	Falmouth	15 March 1969		1997–99	Watford
MILLIGAN	George	Glasgow			1920–21	Clyde
MILLINGTON	Tony	Hawarden	5 June 1943		1964–66	West Bromwich Albion
MILLS	W.				1905–06	Beckenham
MIMMS	Bobby	York	12 October 1963		1996–97	Blackburn Rovers
MITCHELL	Harry		1887		1910–11	Bury
MOODY	F.				1905–06	Beckenham
MOORE	Craig	Canterbury (Australia)	12 December 1975		1998–99	Glasgow Rangers
MOORE	John	Inkerman (Co. Durham)			1925–26	Aberdeen
MORALEE	Jamie	Streatham	2 December 1971		1991–92	Junior
MORGAN	Billy	Old Hill	3 November 1891		1922–25	Coventry City
MORGAN	Ken	Swansea	28 July 1932		1955–56	Northampton Town
MORGAN	Reginald				1926–27	Tooting Town
MORRIS	Frank	Penge	28 March 1932		1956–57	Twinlocks
MORRISON	Andy	Inverness	30 July 1970		2000–01	Manchester City (Loan)
MORRISON	Clinton	Tooting	14 May 1979		1997–2002	Junior
2 spells					2005–08	Birmingham City
MORTIMER	Francis 'Fred'	Draycott			1912–13	Grenadier Guards
MORTIMER	Paul	Kensington	8 May 1968		1991–93	Aston Villa
MORTON	Keith	Consett	11 August 1934		1953–54	Sutton United
MOSES	Victor	Lagos (Nigeria)	12 December 1990		2007–10	Junior
MOSS	Don	Tamworth	27 June 1925		1953–57	Cardiff City
MOULT	Joseph 'Jack'	Birmingham			1909–10	Coventry City
MOXEY	Dean	Exeter	14 October 1986		2010–	Derby County
MOYLE	Walter	New Tredegar	October 1902		1928–29	Manchester United
MOYSE	Alex	Mitcham	5 August 1935	1994	1955–57	Chatham Town
MULCAHY	Pat	Tanlobie	1904		1927–29	Annfield Plain
MULHERON	Peter	Glasgow	21 June 1921		1948–50	Tonbridge
MULLEN	Jimmy	Larne (N.I.)	10 January 1921	2002	1948–49	Barrow
MULLIGAN	Paddy	Dublin	17 March 1945		1972–75	Chelsea
MULLINS	Hayden	Reading	27 March 1979		1998–2004	Junior
MURPHY	Jerry	Stepney	23 September 1959		1976–85	Junior
MURPHY	Joe	Waterford (Eire)	30 March 1924		1948–51	Shelbourne (Eire)
MURPHY	John	Dowlais	16 March 1907	1993	1931–32	Fulham
MURPHY	Shaun	Sydney (Australia)	5 November 1970		2001–02	Sheffield United (Loan)
MURRAY	Jimmy	Lambeth	16 March 1935	2002	1955–58	Junior
MUSCAT	Kevin	Crawley	7 August 1973		1996–98	South Melbourne (Australia)
MUXWORTHY	Graham	Bristol	11 October 1938		1957–58	Exeter University
MYCOCK	Albert	Manchester	31 January 1923	2003	1946–48	Manchester United
MYERS	Ernest	Chapeltown	1894	1984	1909–12	Northfleet
MYHRE	Thomas	Sarpsborg (Norway)	16 October 1973		2003–04	Sunderland (Loan)
NABIL	Tariq	Ashford (Middlesex)	29 March 1985		2003–04	Junior
NASH	Carlo	Bolton	13 September 1973		1996–97	Clitheroe
NASH	Edward	Swindon	12 April 1902	1985	1932–33	Brentford
NASTRI	Carlo	Finsbury	22 October 1935		1958–59	Kingstonian
NDAH	George	Camberwell	23 December 1974		1992–98	Junior
N'DIAYE	Alassane	Audincourt (France)	25 February 1990		2009–	Toulouse (France)
NEBBELING	Gavin	Johannesburg (S. Africa)	15 May 1963		1981–89	Arcadia Shepherds (S. Africa)
NEEDHAM	Archie	Sheffield	2 August 1881	1950	1905–09	Sheffield United
NELSON	David	Douglas Water	3 February 1918	1988	1951–53	Queen's Park Rangers
NEWMAN	Ricky	Guildford	5 August 1970		1992–95	Camberley Town
NEWMAN	Ron	Fareham	19 January 1934		1962–63	Leyton Orient
NICHOLAS	George	Barnsley	26 February 1908		1930–34	Treharris
NICHOLAS	Peter	Newport (Monmouth)	10 November 1959		1977–81	Junior
2 spells					1983–85	Arsenal

TO	APPEARANCES S.LEAGUE	F. LEAGUE	FA CUP	F. L. CUP	OTHER	APPS	GOALS S.LEAGUE	F.LEAGUE	FA CUP	FL CUP	OTHER	GOALS
Grays Athletic		17+1	2	2+2		21+3		4	1			5
Norwich City		97	5			102		31	3			34
		20+1		1		21+1						
Southend United		34				34		11				11
Torquay United		12+10		0+1		12+11		2				2
Millwall		2+12		1		3+12						
St Patrick's Athletic (Eire)		8+1				8+1		1				1
Arcadia Shepherds (S. Africa)		1				1						
Leeds United		272	22	36	19	349						
Oxford United		1+1			1	2+1						
Burnley		17+7	1	2+1		20+8		1				1
Gillingham		2				2						
Dartford		31	1			32		11				11
Sheffield United	12	48	5			65	5	12	3			20
	4					4						
Worcester City	1					1						
		5		1+1		6+1						
		1				1						
	32		2			34	7		1			8
Charlton Athletic		34	1			35		4				4
Queen's Park Rangers		38	3			41		1				1
Barnsley		66	5	3	2	76						
Armadale (Scotland)		2				2		1				1
Peterborough United		16	3	1		20						
Croydon	1					1						
Preston North End		1				1						
Barnet Alston	1					1						
Croydon Common	1					1	1					1
Glasgow Rangers		23	1			24		3				3
Hamilton Academicals		1				1						
Millwall		2+4				2+4						
Cradley Heath		76	8			84		14	2			16
Guildford City		1				1						
Sutton United		1				1						
Tunbridge Wells Rangers		8				8						
		5				5						
Birmingham City		237+44	7+1	18+5	3+1	265+51		103	1	9		113
Coventry City												
Mansfield Town	1					1						
Charlton Athletic		18+4	1	1	3	23+4		2				2
Sunderland		5				5		3				3
Wigan Athletic		42+16	3+2	4	1+1	50+19		11				11
Retired through injury		56	2			58		2				2
Walsall	1		1			2						
		17				17		1				1
Merthyr Town		5				5		1				1
Swindon Town		4				4		1				1
Eden Colliery Welfare		23				23		5				5
Tonbridge		38	2			40		2				2
Bristol City		11	1			12						
West Bromwich Albion		57+1	5	1		63+1		2				2
West Ham United		219+3	9	24	2	254+3		18		2		20
Chelsea		214+15	17+1	22		253+16		20		5		25
Bedford Town		37				37						
Merthyr Town		8	2			10		2				2
		11				11						
Walsall		37	1			38		13	1			14
Wolverhampton Wand.		51+2	2	4	2	59+2		2		1		3
Chippenham Town		2				2						
Barrow		59	3			62		9				9
Hickleton Main Colliery	22		1			23	1					1
		15		1		16						
Dagenham & Redbridge				0+1		0+1						
Stockport County		21		1		3		25				
Scout with Arsenal		1				1						
Bedford Town		2				2						
Swindon Town		33+45	3+1	7+6	4+1	47+53		8	1	2		11
		16+22	2	2		20+22		3				3
Fulham		145+6	5	8+1	8	166+7		8				8
Glossop	103		19			122	24		2			26
Ashford Town (Kent)		12				12						
Millwall		43+5	5+2	5	2	55+7		3				3
Gillingham		6	1			7						
Dartford		39				39						
Arsenal		174	11	14		199		14	1	1		16
Luton Town												

SURNAME	NAME	BIRTHPLACE	DATE OF BIRTH	DIED	SEASONS	FROM
NICHOLSON	George	West Ham			1923–24	West Stanley
NIXON	Joe	Prudhoe			1921–27	Prudhoe Castle
NOAKES	Alf	West Ham	14 August 1933	2005	1955–62	Sittingbourne
NORRIS	Fred	Aston	14 August 1903		1933–34	West Ham United
O'CONNELL	Brian 'Pat'	Fulham	13 September 1937		1966–67	Fulham
O'CONNOR	Martyn	Walsall	10 December 1967		1993–94	Bromsgrove Rovers
O'CONOR	Eric	Catford			1911–13	Catford Southend
O'DOHERTY	Ken	Dublin (Eire)	30 March 1963		1985–88	University College Dublin (Eire)
OBIKA	Jonathan	Enfield	12 September 1990		2010–11	Tottenham Hotspur (Loan)
O'KEEFE	Stuart	Eye	4 March 1991		2010–	Southend United
OLIVER	Jimmy	Uxbridge	28 August 1949		1967–70	Junior
O'REILLY	Gary	Isleworth	21 March 1961		1986–90	Brighton & Hove Albion
ORR	Robert	Hardgate (Clydebank)	1888		1926–28	Morton
OSBORN	Simon	New Addington	19 January 1972		1990–94	Junior
OSBORNE	Ernest	Wolverhampton	12 May 1899	1958	1923–26	Evesham Town
OSTER	John	Boston (Lincs.)	8 December 1978		2008–09	Reading
OTULAKOWSKI	Anton	Dewsbury	29 January 1956		1986–87	Millwall
OWENS	Isaac	Darlington	1881		1907–08	Bristol Rovers
OWENS	Ted	Trimdon Grange	1913		1934–39	Preston North End
PADOVANO	Michele	Turin (Italy)	28 August 1966		1997–99	Juventus (Italy)
PAGE	David	Thornton Heath	1891		1911–12	Old Kingstonians
PALETHORPE	Jack	Leicester	23 November 1909	1984	1936–38	Aston Villa
PALMER	Charles		c.1880		1905–06	Crown United
PARDEW	Alan	Wimbledon	18 July 1961		1987–92	Yeovil Town
PARKER	Edward	Anerley	8 December 1913	1983	1933–34	Croydon
PARKIN	Brian	Birkenhead	12 October 1965		1988–90	Crewe Alexandra
PARRY	Oswald 'Ossie'	Merthyr Tydfil	16 August 1908	1991	1931–36	Wimbledon
PARSONS	Frank	Amersham	29 October 1947		1966–67	Junior
PARSONS	Matthew	Lewisham	25 December 1991		2010–	Junior
PATTERSON	Darren	Belfast (N.I.)	15 October 1969		1994–95	Wigan Athletic
PAUL	Tony	Islington	6 April 1961		1980–81	Junior
PAYNE	David	Thornton Heath	25 April 1947		1964–73	Junior
PAYNE	George	Hitchin	17 February 1887	1932	1909–11	Tottenham Hotspur
PEMBERTON	John	Oldham	18 November 1964		1987–90	Crewe Alexandra
PENN	Frank	Edmonton	15 April 1927		1949–50	Fulham (amateur)
PENNYFATHER	Glenn	Billericay	11 February 1963		1987–89	Southend United
PERRIN	Steve	Paddington	13 February 1952		1976–78	Wycombe Wanderers
PETCHEY	George	Whitechapel	24 June 1931		1960–65	Queen's Park Rangers
PETRIC	Gordan	Belgrade (Yugoslavia)	30 July 1969		1998–99	Glasgow Rangers
PETTIT	Harold	Sydenham			1924–26	Kingstonian
PHELAN	Terry	Manchester	16 March 1967		1999–2000	Everton (Loan)
PHILIP	Iain	Broughty Ferry	14 February 1951		1972–74	Dundee
PIERCE	Barry	Liverpool	13 August 1934		1955–59	Truro City
PINKNEY	Alan	Battersea	1 January 1947		1969–74	Exeter City
PINNEY	Nathaniel	South Norwood	28 December 1990		2008–	Junior
PITCHER	Darren	Stepney	12 October 1969		1994–97	Charlton Athletic
POLLOCK	Jamie	Stockton-on-Tees	16 February 1974		2000–01	Manchester City
POPOVIC	Tony	Sydney (Australia)	4 July 1973		2001–06	Sanfrecce Hiroshima (Japan)
POSSEE	Derek	Southwark	14 February 1946		1972–74	Millwall
POTTER	Ray	Beckenham	7 May 1936	2005	1953–58	Beckenham Town
POWELL	Chris	Lambeth	8 September 1969		1987–89	Junior
POWELL	Darren	Hammersmith	10 March 1976		2002–05	Brentford
PREECE	Andy	Evesham	27 March 1967		1994–95	Stockport County
PRESLAND	Eddie	Loughton	27 March 1943		1966–69	West Ham United
PRICE	David	Caterham	23 June 1955		1980–83	Arsenal
PRICE	Ernest	Easington	12 May 1926		1951–53	Darlington
PRICE	Lewis	Bournemouth	19 July 1984		2010–	Derby County
PRIESTLEY	Gerry	Halifax	2 March 1931		1958–60	Grimsby Town
PRITCHARD	Harvey	Meriden (Warwickshire)	30 January 1918	2000	1937–38	Coventry City
PROUDLER	Arthur	Kingswinford	3 October 1929	2000	1956–59	Aston Villa
PROVAN	David	Falkirk	11 March 1941		1970–71	Glasgow Rangers
PURDON	James	Springburn	14 March 1906	1985	1934–36	Bradford Park Avenue
PYKE	Malcolm	Eltham	6 March 1938		1959–60	West Ham United
QUAYLE	Charles	Kirkdale	1907		1936–38	Drumcondra (Eire)
QUEEN	Gerry	Glasgow	15 January 1945		1969–73	Kilmarnock
QUINN	Robert	Sidcup	8 November 1976		1995–98	Junior
RAINFORD	Johnny	Camden	11 December 1930	2001	1948–53	Junior
RANDALL	Ernie	Bognor Regis	13 January 1926		1953–55	Chelsea
RANSOM	Frank	Ireland			1906–07	Southern United (Ireland)
READ	Tom	West Bromwich	2 April 1900		1935–36	Grimsby Town
REDFEARN	Neil	Dewsbury	20 June 1965		1987–89	Doncaster Rovers
REDMOND	Harold	Manchester	24 March 1933	1985	1957–58	Tavistock
REECE	Tom	Wolverhampton	17 May 1919	1990	1938–48	Wolverhampton Wand.
REED	George	Altofts	7 February 1904		1934–35	Plymouth Argyle
REES	William	Swansea	30 September 1937		1959–60	Peterborough United
REEVE	Fred	Clapton	1 May 1918	1994	1936–37	Ashford Town

TO	APPEARANCES						GOALS					
	S.LEAGUE	F. LEAGUE	FA CUP	F. L. CUP	OTHER	APPS	S.LEAGUE	F.LEAGUE	FA CUP	FL CUP	OTHER	GOALS
Dundee United		2				2						
Prudhoe Castle		29	2			31		1				1
Portsmouth		195	14			209		14				14
Olympique Lillois (France)		11	1			12		4				4
Vancouver Royals (Canada)		20+1		1		21+1		2				2
Walsall		2			1+1	3+1						
Maidstone United	10					10						
Huddersfield Town		41+1	1	4+1	2+1	48+3				1		1
		0+7		0+1		0+8						
		1+3				1+3						
Germiston Callies (S. Africa)		3				3						
Brighton & Hove Albion		65+5	7	3	3+2	78+7		2	2			4
Dumbarton		70	1			71		2				2
Reading		47+8	2	11	1+3	61+11		4		1		5
Lincoln City		30				30		3				3
Doncaster Rovers		27+4	1	1		29+4		3		1		4
Hastings United		12		2		14		1				1
Grimsby Town	22					22	8					8
Bath City		164	8			172			1			1
Metz (France)		8+4				8+4		1				1
Sittingbourne	1					1						
Newport County		39	5			44		11				11
Fulham	1					1						
Charlton Athletic		111+17	8	9+3	20	148+20		8	1	1	2	12
Mansfield Town		2				2						
Bristol Rovers		20		3	2	25						
Ipswich Town		142	8			150						
Cardiff City		4				4						
		2		0+1		2+1						
Luton Town		22	6	4		32		1				1
Croydon		0+1				0+1						
Orient		281+3	16	18		315+3		9	1	2		12
Sunderland	45		1			46	30		1			31
Sheffield United		76+2	8	6+1	12	102+3		2				2
Bromley		1				1						
Ipswich Town		31+3	1		4+2	36+5		1				1
Plymouth Argyle		45+3	6	4		55+3		13		1		14
To club coach		143	7	3		153		12				12
A.E.K. Athens (Greece)		18				18		1				1
		2				2						
		14				14						
Dundee		35	4	1		40		1	1			2
Millwall		85	8			93		23	4			27
Cape Town City (S. Africa)		19+5	1	3+1		23+6						
		0+1		1		1+1						
Retired through injury		60+4	10	5+1	3	78+5			1	1		2
Grimsby Town		29+2		5+1		34+3		4				4
A-Arabi (Qatar)		121+2	6	10	5	142+2		6		2		8
Orient		51+2	1+1	1		53+3		13				13
West Bromwich Albion		44	5			49						
Southend United		2+1		0+1	0+1	2+3						
Southampton		53+2	3	9+1	0+3	65+6		2		1	1	4
Blackpool		17+3	2+3	4+2		23+8		4		1		5
Wealdstone		61	3	1		65						
Orient		25+2	1+1	4+1		30+4		2	1			3
Weymouth		34	1			35		5				5
		1				1						
Halifax Town		28	7			35		2				2
Manchester City		30	5			35		6	2			8
Dorchester Town		26				26		2				2
Plymouth Argyle		1		1		2						
Southport		14				14		2				2
Dartford		2				2						
Bradford City		10				10		3				3
Orient		101+7	7	11+1		119+8		24	1	5		30
Brentford		18+5		2+1	2+1	22+7		1		1		2
Cardiff City		64	3			67		8	2			10
Bognor Regis Town		22	2			24		11	1			12
Leicester Fosse	1					1						
Shirley Town		16				16						
Watford		57	1	6	1	65		10				10
Millwall		2	1			3						
Kidderminster Harriers		76	5			81		5				5
Clapton Orient		2				2						
Hastings United		17	1			18		1				1
Tottenham Hotspur		1				1						

SURNAME	NAME	BIRTHPLACE	DATE OF BIRTH	DIED	SEASONS	FROM
REICH	Marco	Meisenheim (Germany)	30 December 1977		2005–07	Derby County
REID	Kyel	Deptford	26 November 1987		2007–08	West Ham United (Loan)
RHODES	Ernie	South Bank (Yorks.)	1882	1960	1913–23	Gravesend
RIIHILAHTI	Aki	Helsinki (Finland)	9 September 1976		2000–06	Valerenga (Norway)
RIVERS	Walter	Walbottle-on-Tyne	8 January 1909		1929–33	Gillingham
RIZZO	Nicky	Sydney (Australia)	9 June 1979		1998–2000	Liverpool
ROBERTS	Andy	Dartford	20 March 1974		1995–98	Millwall
ROBERTS	Charles	Halesowen	28 February 1901	1980	1932–34	Exeter City
ROBERTS	Richard 'Dickie'	Redditch	January 1878	1931	1905–09	Middlesbrough
ROBERTSON	Peter	Dundee	7 February 1908	1964	1933–34	Charlton Athletic
ROBERTSON	Tom	Coventry	28 September 1944		1966–67	St Mirren
ROBINSON	Ashley-Paul	Croydon	5 December 1989		2007–08	Junior
ROBSON	Albert	Crook	14 November 1916	1990	1936–48	Godalming
ROCHE	Johnny	Poplar	18 May 1932	1988	1959–60	Millwall
RODGER	Simon	Shoreham-by-Sea	3 October 1971		1991–2002	Bognor Regis Town
ROFFEY	Bill	Stepney	6 February 1954		1972–74	Junior
ROGERS	Don	Paulton	25 October 1945		1972–75	Swindon Town
ROOKE	Ronnie	Guildford	7 December 1911	1985	1933–37	Guildford City
2 spells					1949–51	Arsenal
ROSS	Alex	Pollockshields	17 December 1923		1948–51	West Bromwich Albion
ROSS	Robert				1905–06	Arthurlie
ROSSITER	Abbott 'Bud'	Ashford (Kent)	24 November 1907		1933–35	Folkestone Town
ROUSE	Vic	Swansea	16 March 1936		1956–63	Millwall
ROUTLEDGE	Wayne	Sidcup	7 January 1985		2001–05	Junior
RUBINS	Andrejs	Riga (Latvia)	26 November 1978		2000–03	Skonto Riga (Latvia)
RUDDOCK	Neil	Wandsworth	9 May 1968		2000–01	West Ham United
RUMBOLD	George	Alton	10 July 1911	1995	1935–36	Farringdon (Hants)
RUNDLE	Charles	Fowey	17 January 1923	1997	1950–52	Tottenham Hotspur
RUSSELL	James	Edinburgh	14 September 1916	1994	1946–48	Norwich City
RUTTER	Brian	Poplar	11 May 1933		1954–55	Cardiff City
RYAN	Charles	Camberwell			1906–09	Nunhead
SALAKO	John	Lagos (Nigeria)	11 February 1969		1986–95	Junior
SALT	Harold 'Henry'	Sheffield	20 November 1899	1971	1927–29	Grays Thurrock
SANDERS	James	Marlborough	15 October 1932		1955–59	Bristol City
SANDERS	Sidney				1914–15	Nunhead
SANS	Arthur	Edmonton (Middlesex)	1886	1954	1906–07	Watford (amateur)
SANSOM	Kenny	Camberwell	26 September 1958		1974–80	Junior
SAUNDERS	John	Middlesbrough	24 August 1924		1954–56	Chelsea
SAWARD	Len	Aldershot	6 July 1927		1948–51	Beddington
SCANNELL	Sean	Croydon	19 September 1990		2007–	Junior
SCOTT	Jimmy	Falkirk	21 August 1940		1969–72	Newcastle United
SCOTT	Laurie	Sheffield	23 April 1917	1999	1951–53	Arsenal
SCOWCROFT	James	Bury St Edmunds	15 November 1975		2006–09	Coventry City
SCULLY	Tony	Dublin	12 June 1976		1995–97	Junior
SEALY	Tony	Hackney	7 May 1959		1978–81	Southampton
SEARS	Freddie	Hornchurch	27 November 1989		2009–10	West Ham United (Loan)
SEKAJJA	Ibra	Kampala (Uganda)	31 October 1992		2010–	Junior
SEWELL	John	Brockley	7 July 1936		1963–71	Charlton Athletic
SEXTON	Dave	Islington	6 April 1930		1959–60	Brighton & Hove Albion
SHANKS	Robert	Sunniside (Co. Durham)	14 December 1911	1989	1937–39	Swindon Town
SHARPLING	Chris	Bromley	21 April 1981		1999–2000	Junior
SHAW	Harry	South Kirkby (Yorkshire)	1890		1914–15	Metrogas
SHAW	Richard	Brentford	11 September 1968		1987–96	Junior
SHAW	Stuart	Saltney	9 October 1944		1966–67	Everton
SHERWOOD	Henry 'Jack'	Reading	3 September 1913	1985	1949–50	Aldershot
SHIPPERLEY	Neil	Chatham	30 October 1974		1996–99	Southampton
2 spells					2003–05	Wimbledon
SILKMAN	Barry	Stepney	29 September 1952		1976–79	Hereford United
SILLE	Les	Liverpool	12 April 1928		1948–49	Ipswich Town
SIMPSON	Peter	Leith	13 November 1904	1974	1929–35	Kettering Town
SIMPSON	William	Glasgow	22 May 1928	2002	1952–55	Aston Villa
SINCLAIR	Scott	Bath	26 March 1989		2007–08	Chelsea (Loan)
SINNOTT	Lee	Pelsall	12 July 1965		1991–94	Bradford City
SKINGLEY	Brian	Ilford	28 August 1937	1999	1958–59	Bristol Rovers
SMILLIE	Andy	Minster, Isle of Sheppey	15 March 1941		1961–63	West Ham United
SMILLIE	Neil	Barnsley	19 July 1958		1976–82	Junior
SMITH	Cyril	Knighton	1893		1919–20	Croydon Common
SMITH	Edwin 'Ted'	Birmingham	1884		1911–22	Hull City
SMITH	George				1907–08	Bristol City
SMITH	George	Portsmouth	24 March 1919	2001	1950–51	Southampton
SMITH	James 'Jamie'	Birmingham	17 September 1974		1997–04	Wolverhampton Wand.
SMITH	Keith	Woodville (Derbyshire)	15 September 1940		1964–67	Peterborough United
SMITH	Lewis	Blisworth			1925–29	Hampstead Town
SMITH	Ryan	Islington	10 November 1986		2009–10	Southampton
SMITH	Thomas				1932–33	Sunderland
SMITH	Trevor	Stanley (Co. Durham)	8 September 1910	1997	1937–46	Fulham

			APPEARANCES						GOALS			
TO	S.LEAGUE	F. LEAGUE	FA CUP	F. L. CUP	OTHER	APPS	S.LEAGUE	F.LEAGUE	FA CUP	FL CUP	OTHER	GOALS
Kickers Offenbach (Germany)		18+9	1+1	2+1	0+1	21+12		2		2		4
		0+2				0+2						
Sheppey United	47	89	6			142		1				1
Kaiserslautern (Germany)		130+27	4+2	9+3	3	146+32		13		1		14
Queen's Park Rangers		81	8			89		2				2
Ternana (Italy)		15+21	1	1+3		17+24		1		2		3
Wimbledon		106+2	8	7+1	6	127+3		2			1	3
Chester City		47	3			50		18	1			19
Worcester City	82		17			99	20		6			26
Dundee United		4				4						
Southern Suburbs (S. Africa)		5				5						
Bromley		0+6				0+6						
Tunbridge Wells		85	4			89		22	1			23
Margate		36	4			40		11	2			13
Brighton & Hove Albion		242+34	9+4	30+1	5+3	286+42		11		1		12
Orient		24		1		25						
Queen's Park Rangers		69+1	5	2+1		76+2		28	2			30
Fulham Bedford Town		63	1			64		32				32
Tonbridge		33				33						
	4		1			5	3					3
Gillingham		24	3			27						
Northampton Town		238	17	2		257						
Tottenham Hotspur		83+27	2+1	5+2	3	93+30		10				10
Shinnik Yaroslavi (Russia)		17+14	2	3+1		22+15				2		2
Swindon Town		19+1	0+1	5		24+2		2		1		3
Clapton Orient		5				5						
Tonbridge		38	2			40		2				2
New Brighton		43				43		6				6
Leytonstone		3				3		1				1
Croydon Common	82		12			94	2					2
Coventry City		172+43	20	19+5	11+3	222+51		23	4	5	2	34
Brentford		42	2			44		1				1
Rochdale		46	4			50						
	1					1						
Tottenham Hotspur	2					2						
Arsenal		172	11	14		197		3	1			4
Chester		59	2			61						
Cambridge United		9				9		1				1
		42+51	2+1	0+3	1	45+55		8	1			9
Falkirk		36+7	2	5		43+7		5		1		6
Retired as a player		28	2			30						
Leyton Orient		66+17	2		0+1	68+18		14				14
Manchester City		0+3				0+3						
Queen's Park Rangers		16+8	1	0+2		17+10		5				5
		11+7		1		12+7						
		0+1				0+1		1				1
Orient		228+3	12	15		255+3		6	1	2		9
Retired through injury		27	1			28		11	1			12
Swindon Town		18				18						
Woking		1+5				1+5						
	6					6						
Coventry City		193+14	18	28+2	12+1	251+17		3				3
Southport			0+1			0+1						
		2				2						
Nottingham Forest Sheffield United		89+13	3+1	7+1	8	107+15		29			3	32
Plymouth Argyle		40+8	5	1		46+8		6	1			7
Tranmere Rovers		3				3						
West Ham United		180	15			195		153	12			165
South Africa		38				38		13				13
		6			2	8		2				2
Bradford City		53+2	1	9+1	2	65+3						
Queen's Park Rangers		11	1			12						
Scunthorpe United		53	5	1		59		23	1	2		26
Brighton & Hove Albion		71+12	7	7		85+12		7	1			8
Charlton Athletic	7					7						
	155	25	12			192	109	11	4			124
	9		2			11	2		1			3
Kings Lynn		7				7						
Bristol City		136+13	6+2	16+1	1+1	159+17		4		2		6
Darlington		47+3	4	2		53+3		14	1			15
		45	3			48		1	1			2
Kansas City Wizards (USA)		0+5		0+1		0+6						
		9				9						
Yeovil Town		57	4			61		14				14

SURNAME	NAME	BIRTHPLACE	DATE OF BIRTH	DIED	SEASONS	FROM
SMITH	Wilf	Sheffield	28 March 1910		1935–36	Burnley
SMITH	William	South Shields	22 October 1903		1933–36	Brentford
SMOUT	John	Newtown	30 October 1941		1965–66	Newtown
SNOWDON	Brian	Bishop Auckland	1 January 1935	1995	1968–69	Detroit Cougars (USA)
SOARES	Tom	Reading	10 July 1986		2003–09	Junior
SOMERFIELD	Alf	South Kirkby	22 March 1918	1985	1947–48	Wrexham
SONGO'O	Franck	Yaounde (Cameroon)	14 May 1987		2007–08	Portsmouth (Loan)
SORONDO	Gonzalo	Montevideo (Uruguay)	9 October 1979		2004–05	Inter Milan (Loan)
SOUTHGATE	Gareth	Watford	3 September 1970		1990–95	Junior
SPARROW	Brian	Bethnal Green	24 June 1962		1984–87	Arsenal
SPARROW	Paul	Wandsworth	24 March 1975		1995–96	Junior
SPENCE	Lewwis	Kennington	29 October 1987		2006–07	Junior
SPERONI	Julian	Buenos Aires (Argentina)	18 May 1979		2004–	Dundee
SPOTTISWOOD	Bob	Carlisle	20 January 1884		1909–15	Croydon Common
STACK	Bill	Liverpool	17 January 1948		1965–66	Junior
STANBURY	George	Plymouth	24 October 1905		1936–37	Gillingham (coach)
STAUNTON	Steve	Drogheda (Eire)	19 January 1969		2000–01	Liverpool (Loan)
STEBBING	Gary	Croydon	11 August 1965		1983–88	Junior
STEELE	Ernest	Middleton (Lancs.)	18 June 1908	1972	1938–39	Millwall
STEPHENSON	Alan	Cheshunt	26 September 1944		1961–68	Junior
STEVENS	Les	Croydon	15 August 1920	1991	1950–51	Bradford Park Avenue
STEWART	Paul	Manchester	7 October 1964		1993–94	Liverpool (Loan)
STOKES	Anthony	Dublin	25 July 1988		2008–09	Sunderland (Loan)
STONE	Edward	Aberdeen	5 January 1942		1961–62	Charlton Athletic
STOREY	Tom	Crook	23 November 1892		1920–22	Middlesbrough
STRANG	Dick	Rutherglen	19 March 1900		1924–26	Birmingham City
STRONG	Les	Streatham	3 July 1953		1983–84	Fulham
STUBBS	Alf	West Ham	18 April 1922	1986	1947–49	Junior
SUCKLING	Perry	Leyton	12 October 1965		1987–92	Manchester City
SULLIVAN	Neil	Sutton (Surrey)	24 February 1970		1991–92	Wimbledon (Loan)
SUMMERSBY	Roy	Lambeth	19 March 1935		1958–63	Millwall
SURTEES	Hubert	Durham	16 July 1921	1979	1949–50	Watford
SVENSSON	Mathias 'Matt'	Boros (Sweden)	24 September 1974		1998–2000	FC Tirol Innsbruck (Austria)
SWAN	Chris	Byker	4 December 1900	1979	1929–30	Hull City
SWANN	Herbert	Lytham	28 March 1882	1954	1906–09	Plymouth Argyle
SWANNELL	John	Walton-on-Thames	26 January 1939		1960–61	Corinthian Casuals (amateur)
SWIFT	Arthur	West Hartlepool	27 November 1889	1954	1920–21	West Bromwich Albion
SWINDLEHURST	David	Edgware	6 January 1956		1973–80	Junior
SYMONS	Kit	Basingstoke	8 March 1971		2001–04	Fulham
TAMBLING	Bobby	Storrington	18 September 1941		1969–70	Chelsea (Loan)
2 spells					1970–74	Chelsea
TAYLOR	Colin	Stourbridge	24 August 1940	2005	1968–69	Walsall
TAYLOR	Gareth	Weston-super-Mare	25 February 1973		1995–96	Bristol Rovers
TAYLOR	John	Durham	10 July 1926	1981	1948–49	Leytonstone
TAYLOR	Kevin	Wakefield	22 January 1961		1984–88	Derby County
TAYLOR	Peter	Rochford	3 January 1953		1973–77	Southend United
TAYLOR	Robert	Croydon	16 March 1936		1954–55	Fulham
TAYLOR	Stuart	Romford	28 November 1980		2000–01	Arsenal (Loan)
TAYLOR	Tony	Glasgow	6 September 1946		1968–74	Morton
TELLING	Hubert	Swindon	28 March 1913		1936–37	Reading
THOMAS	Bob	Stepney	2 August 1919	1990	1952–55	Fulham
THOMAS	Geoff	Manchester	5 August 1964		1987–93	Crewe Alexandra
THOMAS	John	Walsall	15 July 1922	1999	1948–52	West Bromwich Albion
THOMAS	Simon	Stratford (London)	21 July 1984		2008–09	Borehamwood
THOMPSON	Garry	Birmingham	7 October 1959		1989–91	Watford
THOMPSON	George	Wolverhampton	1878	1943	1905–06	Newcastle United
THOMPSON	Henry	North Shields	1886		1910–11	Newcastle United
THOMPSON	Len	Sheffield	18 February 1901		1933–34	Arsenal
THOMS	Harry	Greatham	19 November 1896	1970	1928–29	Derby County
THOMSON	Steven	Glasgow	23 January 1978		1998–2003	Junior
THORN	Andy	Carshalton	12 November 1966		1989–94	Newcastle United
THORPE	Albert	Pilsley	14 July 1910	1971	1935–36	Norwich City
THORPE	James 'Joe'		1885		1908–09	Leeds City
THORUP	Borge	Copenhagen (Denmark)	4 October 1943		1969–70	Morton
TILSTON	Tommy	Chester	19 February 1926		1953–56	Wrexham
TIZARD	Charles	Blandford	10 January 1914		1934–35	Winchester City
TOGWELL	Sam	Beaconsfield	14 October 1984		2002–06	Junior
TOMKINS	Len	Isleworth	16 January 1949		1967–70	Junior
TONNER	John 'Jack'	Holytown	20 February 1898	1978	1927–28	Fulham
TONNER	Sam	Dunfermline	10 August 1894	1976	1926–27	Bristol City
TORGHELLE	Sandor	Budapest (Hungary)	5 May 1982		2004–05	M.T.K. Hungaria (Hungary)
TOOTILL	Alf	Ramsbottom	12 November 1908	1975	1938–39	Fulham
TOWNSEND	Don	Swindon	17 September 1930		1962–65	Charlton Athletic
TROLLOPE	Paul	Swindon	3 June 1972		1996–97	Derby County (Loan)
TRUETT	Geoff	West Ham	23 May 1935		1957–62	Wycombe Wanderers

TO	APPEARANCES						GOALS					
	S.LEAGUE	F. LEAGUE	FA CUP	F. L. CUP	OTHER	APPS	S.LEAGUE	F.LEAGUE	FA CUP	FL CUP	OTHER	GOALS
		2				2						
Burnley		38	3			41		1				1
Exeter City		1				1						
Brentwood		1+4				1+4						
Stoke City		128+21	1+2	5+1	4	138+24		11		1		12
Worcester City		10	2			12		3				3
		9				9						
		16+4		2		18+4						
Aston Villa		148+4	9	23+1	6	186+5		15		7		22
Enfield		62+1	2	7	0+1	71+2		2				2
Preston North End		1		0+1		1+1						
Wycombe Wanderers		1+1		0+1		1+2						
		195+1	9	10	2	216+1						
Clapton Orient	178		11			189	2					2
Chelmsford City		2				2						
Club Assistant Trainer		1				1						
		6				6		1				1
K.V. Oostende (Belgium)		95+7	6	7+1	1+1	109+9		3				3
Rochdale		30	2			32		8				8
West Ham United		170	8	7		185		13				13
Tonbridge		20	1			21		3				3
		18				18		3				3
		11+2				11+2		1				1
Hastings United		1				1						
Coventry City		52				52		5				5
Poole Town		24				24						
Rochdale		7				7						
		3				3						
Watford		59	1	4	7	71						
		1				1						
Portsmouth		176	13	1		190		59	1			60
Snowdown Colliery		5				5						
Charlton Athletic		26+6	1	2		29+6		10				10
Scarborough		6				6						
Queen's Park Rangers	69		3			72	15		1			16
Corinthian Casuals				1		1						
Retired through injury		1				1						
Derby County		221+16	22	17		260+16		73	5	3		81
To club coaching staff		42+7	6	5		53+7						
Cork Celtic (Eire)		67+1	1	7		75+1		12	2	3		17
Walsall		32+2	2	4		38+2		8		2		10
Sheffield United		18+2	2			20+2		1	1			2
Dartford		1				1						
Scunthorpe United		85+2	2	7	3	97+2		14	1			15
Tottenham Hotspur		122	11	9		142		33	4	2		39
Gillingham		2				2						
		10				10						
Southend United		192+3	11+1	14+1		217+5		8		3		11
Hartlepools United		3				3						
Tunbridge Wells		96	6			102		31	2			33
Wolverhampton Wand.		192+3	13+1	24	15+1	244+5		26	2	3	4	35
Cambridge Unted		53	1			54		17				17
Billericay Town		0+1				0+1						
Queen's Park Rangers		17+3		0+1	0+1	17+5		3		1		4
Carlisle United	10		1			11	4					4
	4					4						
Islington Corinthians		2				2						
Glentoran		6	1			7		1				1
Peterborough United		68+37	3+1	8+4	1+1	80+43		1	1	2		4
Wimbledon		128	10	19	11	168		3		4		7
Scunthorpe United		4				4						
Darwen	17					17						
Morton		0+1				0+1						
Chelmsford City		58	1			59		13				13
Mansfield Town		4				4						
Barnsley		0+1		1+2		1+3						
Toronto Metros (Canada)		18+2	1			19+2		2				2
Thames		24				24		9				9
Armadale		2	1			3						
P.A.O.K. Thessaloniki (Greece)		3+9		3		6+9				1		1
Retired		1				1						
Retired		77	2	3		82						
		0+9				0+9						
Tonbridge		38	1			39		5				5

SURNAME	NAME	BIRTHPLACE	DATE OF BIRTH	DIED	SEASONS	FROM
TURNBULL	Robert	Dumbarton	22 June 1894	1946	1932–33	Coaching staff
TURNER	Andy	Woolwich	23 March 1975		1998–99	Portsmouth
TURNER	Billy	Tipton	16 November 1901	1989	1925–36	Bromsgrove Rovers
TURTON	Geoff	Wortley	21 April 1912	1981	1935–38	Gillingham
TURNER	Iain	Stirling	26 January 1984		2006–07	Everton (Loan)
TUTTLE	David	Reading	6 February 1972		1995–2000	Sheffield United
UPHILL	Dennis	Bath	11 August 1931	2007	1960–63	Watford
UPSON	Matthew	Stowmarket	18 April 1979		2000–01	Arsenal (Loan)
VAESEN	Nico	Ghent (Belgium)	28 September 1969		2003–04	Birmingham City (Loan)
VANSITTART	Tommy	Merton	23 January 1950		1967–70	Junior
VAUGHAN	James	Birmingham	14 July 1988		2010–	Everton (Loan)
VEART	Carl	Whyalla (Australia)	21 May 1970		1995–98	Sheffield United
VENABLES	Terry	Dagenham	6 January 1943		1974–75	Queen's Park Rangers
VENTOLA	Nicola	Bari (Italy)	24 May 1978		2004–05	Inter Milan (Loan)
VERHOENE	Kenny	Ghent (Belgium)	15 April 1973		2000–01	K.R.C. Harelbeke (Belgium)
VICKERS	Steve	Bishop Auckland	13 October 1967		2001–02	Middlesbrough (Loan)
VINCENT	Jamie	Wimbledon	18 June 1975		1995–96	Junior
WAITE	Norman	South Shields			1921–23	Preston Colliery
WALDRON	Ernie	Birmingham	3 June 1913	1994	1934–47	Bromsgrove Rovers
WALKER	George	Wednesbury	1877	1930	1905–06	Wolverhampton Wand.
2 spells					1907–09	New Brompton
WALKER	George	Musselburgh	24 May 1909		1936–39	Notts County
WALL	Peter	Brockton	13 September 1944		1970–78	Liverpool
WALLACE	Charles	Sunderland	20 January 1885	1970	1905–07	Southwick (Co. Durham)
WALLACE	Willie	Kirkintilloch	23 June 1941		1971–73	Glasgow Celtic
WALLEY	Keith	Weymouth	19 October 1954		1973–74	Junior
WALSH	Ian	St David's	4 September 1958		1976–82	Junior
WALSH	Tom	Bolton	12 February 1900	1950	1928–29	Bristol City
WALTERS	Thomas	Trealaw	15 June 1909	1968	1932–33	Bolton Wanderers
WARD	Darren	Harrow	13 September 1978		2005–07	Millwall
WARD	Edward	Cowpen	16 June 1896		1922–23	Newcastle United
WARD	Tom	Chatham	28 April 1913	1997	1933–34	Chatham
WARHURST	Paul	Stockport	26 September 1969		1997–99	Blackburn Rovers
WATERFIELD	George	Swinton	2 June 1901	1988	1935–36	Burnley
WATKINS	Walter	Caersws	1880	1942	1905–06	Sunderland
WATSON	Ben	Camberwell	9 July 1985		2002–09	Junior
WATSON	George	Milton Regis	10 April 1907	1974	1930–31	Maidstone United
WATSON	John	Wolsingham (Co. Durham)	1912		1936–37	Coventry City
WATSON	John 'Jock'	Hamilton	31 December 1917	1976	1949–51	Real Madrid (Spain)
WATTS	Grant	Croydon	5 November 1973		1992–93	Junior
WEBB	Ron	Brentford	13 March 1925	1999	1946–47	Queen's Park Rangers
WELLS	Albert	Watford	1898		1921–23	Ramsgate Athletic
WERGE	Eddie	Sidcup	9 September 1936	2007	1961–65	Charlton Athletic
WESTON	William	Wearside	1885		1906–07	Sunderland
WETHERBY	Thomas	Worcester			1928–31	Newport County
WHARTON	Terry	Bolton	1 July 1942		1970–72	Bolton Wanderers
WHELAN	Noel	Leeds	30 December 1974		2002–03	Middlesbrough (Loan)
WHIBLEY	John	Sittingbourne	1892		1912–23	Sittingbourne
WHITE	Tom	Musselburgh	12 August 1939		1966–68	Aberdeen
WHITEAR	John	Isleworth	31 May 1935		1956–57	Aston Villa
WHITEHOUSE	Brian	West Bromwich	8 September 1935		1963–66	Wrexham
WHITTAKER	Bill	Charlton	20 December 1922	1977	1950–51	Huddersfield Town
WHITTLE	Alan	Liverpool	10 March 1950		1972–76	Everton
WHITWORTH	George	Wellingborough	14 July 1896		1921–25	Northampton Town
WHYTE	Chris	Hornsey	2 September 1961		1984–85	Arsenal (Loan)
WHYTE	David	Greenwich	20 April 1971		1989–94	Greenwich Borough
WICKS	Steve	Reading	3 October 1956		1981–82	Queen's Park Rangers
WIGGINS	Ralph	Penarth			1919–20	Penarth
WIGGINS	Rhoys	Hillingdon	4 November 1987		2008–09	Junior
WILCOCKSON	Ernest	Poplar	11 May 1905	1965	1930–32	Crittalls Athletic
WILDE	William 'Jimmy'	Lyndhurst	24 September 1904	1976	1928–37	Army
WILKINS	Paul	Hackney	20 March 1964		1981–84	Tottenham Hotspur
WILKINS	Ray	Hillingdon	14 September 1956		1994–95	Queen's Park Rangers
WILLARD	Cecil 'Jess'	Chichester	16 January 1924	2005	1953–55	Brighton & Hove Albion
WILLIAMS	Gareth	Germiston (S. Africa)	10 September 1982		2002–04	Junior
WILLIAMS	Gary	Liverpool	8 March 1954		1982–83	Brighton & Hove Albion
WILLIAMS	Jimmy 'Ginger'	Buckley (N. Wales)	1884	1916	1909–14	Accrington Stanley
WILLIAMS	Paul	Stratford (London)	16 August 1965		1992–95	Sheffield Wednesday
WILLIAMSON	Bill	Pollockshaws	7 April 1900	1976	1927–28	Dunfermline Athletic
WILLIAMSON	Percy				1911–13	Catford Southend
WILLS	Thomas	Kilmarnock	1878	1912	1906–07	Newcastle United
WILMOT	Rhys	Newport (Monmouth)	21 February 1962		1994–95	Grimsby Town
WILSON	Arthur 'Art'				1905–09	Crown United
WILSON	Albert	Rotherham	28 January 1915	1998	1938–46	Mansfield Town
WOAN	Alan	Liverpool	8 February 1931		1959–61	Northampton Town
WOOD	Alan	Walsall			1919–22	Talbot Stead Tube Works

TO	APPEARANCES						GOALS					
	S.LEAGUE	F. LEAGUE	FA CUP	F. L. CUP	OTHER	APPS	S.LEAGUE	F.LEAGUE	FA CUP	FL CUP	OTHER	GOALS
Coaching staff		2				2						
Wolverhampton Wanderers		0+2				0+2						
Worcester City		281	21			302		36	1			37
Folkestone		12	2			14						
		5				5						
Barnsley		73+8	2	7	6	88+8		5				5
Rugby Town		63	9	2		74		17	3			20
		7				7						
		10			3	13						
Wrexham		10+1	1			11+1		2				2
		28+2				28+2		9				9
Millwall		41+16	2	4+1	2+2	49+19		6	1	3	1	11
To club coach		14	2			16						
		0+3				0+3		1				1
K.V. Kortrijk (Belgium)		0+1				0+1						
		6		1		7						
AFC Bournemouth		19+6	1	2+1		22+7				1		1
		16				16		3				3
Aberdeen		80	6			86		30	2			32
New Brompton	66		10			76	2					2
Watford		102	9			111		1				1
St Louis All Stars (USA)		167+10	15	15+1		197+11		4				4
Aston Villa	54		14			68	14		1			15
Dumbarton		36+3	2	1		39+3		4	2			6
Weymouth		6+1				6+1		1				1
Swansea City		101+16	11	2+3		114+19		23	2	2		27
Hurst		8	1			9		1				1
Exeter City		14				14		4				4
Wolverhampton Wand.		62+1	4	1	1	68+1		5	1			6
Nelson		4				4						
Grimsby Town		7	2			9						
Bolton Wanderers		27	1	2		30		4				4
Nelson		2				2						
Northampton Town	15		6			21	7		6			13
Wigan Athletic		145+24	5	8+3	3+1	161+28		18			2	20
Clapton Orient		2				2						
Ashington (Co. Durham)		12				12		3				3
Canterbury City		61	2			63		1				1
Sheffield United		2+2		3+1		5+3				2		2
Gresley Rovers		3				3						
		5				5						
Arcadia Shepherds (S. Africa)		82	6	2		90		6	1			7
Blackpool	6					6	1					1
		65	6			71						
Durban City (S. Africa)		18+2				18+2		1				1
		7+1				7+1		3				3
Sittingbourne	55	91	4			150	11	15	1			27
Blackpool		37+2	1			38+2		13	1			14
Dartford		5				5		1				1
Charlton Athletic		82	6	4		92		17				17
Cambridge United		35	1			36		1				1
Orient		103+5	10+1	3		116+6		19	2	3		24
The Wednesday (Sheffield)		111	7			118		48	2			50
		13		4		17						
Charlton Athletic		17+10	0+1	5+2	0+4	22+17		4		2	1	7
Queen's Park Rangers		14	5			19		1				1
	1					1						
Norwich City		1				1						
Dartford		5	1			6		1				1
Retired		270	23			293		5	1			6
Preston North End		9+4				9+4		3				3
Queen's Park Rangers		1				1						
To club coach		46	1			47		5				5
Colchester United		0+5		2+1		2+6						
Retired through injury		10		3		13						
Millwall	142		7			149	57		1			58
Charlton Athletic		38+8		4+1	2	44+9		7			2	9
Dunfermline Athletic		6				6		1				1
Maidstone United	2					2						
Carlisle United	17		1			18						
Torquay United		5+1	1			6+1						
	11					11						
Rotherham United		20	3			23		6				6
Aldershot		41	4	1		46		21	2			23
Coventry City	13	34	4			51	2	9	1			12

SURNAME	NAME	BIRTHPLACE	DATE OF BIRTH	DIED	SEASONS	FROM
WOOD	Brian	Hamworthy	8 December 1940		1961–67	West Bromwich Albion
WOOD	Fred	Bromley			1913–14	Clapton Orient
WOOD	George	Douglas (South Lanarkshire)	26 September 1952		1983–88	Arsenal
WOOD	James	Royton (Lancs.)			1935–36	West Ham United
WOOD	Norman	Streatham	1890	1916	1909–10	Tottenham Hotspur
WOODGER	George 'Lady'	Croydon	3 September 1883	1961	1905–11	Croydon Wanderers
WOODHOUSE	Charles	Birmingham	1885	1911	1910–12	Halesowen Town
WOODRUFF	Bobby	Highworth	9 November 1940		1966–70	Wolverhampton Wand.
WOODS	Charlie	Whitehaven	18 March 1941		1964–66	Bournemouth & Boscombe
WOODS	Ray	Peterborough	27 April 1930		1953–55	Southend United
WOOZLEY	David	Ascot	6 December 1979		1998–2000	Junior
WRIGHT	David	Warrington	1 May 1980		2010–	Ipswich Town
WRIGHT	Ian	Woolwich	3 November 1963		1985–92	Greenwich Borough
WYATT	George	Whitechapel	28 March 1924	1957	1948–49	Junior
WYNTER	Alex	Lambeth	15 September 1993		2009–	Junior
YARD	Ernie	Stranraer	3 May 1941	2004	1965–67	Bury
YORK	Ernest	Kettering	1889		1912–15	Kettering
YOUNG	Eric	Singapore	25 March 1960		1990–95	Wimbledon
YOUNG	John 'Jock'	Kilmarnock			1909–10	Hurlford
ZAHA	Wilfred	Ivory Coast	10 November 1992		2009–	Junior
ZHIYI	Fan	Shanghai (China)	22 January 1970		1998–2002	Shanghai Shenhai (China)
ZOHAR	Itzik	Tel Aviv (Israel)	31 October 1970		1997–98	Antwerp (Belgium)

TO	APPEARANCES S.LEAGUE	F. LEAGUE	FA CUP	F. L. CUP	OTHER	APPS	GOALS S.LEAGUE	F.LEAGUE	FA CUP	FL CUP	OTHER	GOALS
Orient		142+1	5	4		151+1		1	3			4
Millwall	3					3						
Cardiff City		192	9	17	3	221						
		10				10		4				4
Plymouth Argyle	1					1						
Oldham Athletic	161		16			177	44		3			47
	44		1			45	21					21
Cardiff City		123+2	4	9+1		136+3		48				48
Ipswich Town		49	1	1		51		5				5
Folkestone		18				18						
Torquay United		21+9	0+1	3+1		24+11						
		27+1	1			28+1						
Arsenal		206+19	9+2	19	19+3	253+24		89	3	9	16	117
Retired		7				7						
			0+1			0+1						
Reading		35+2	1	1+1		37+3		3				3
	55		3			58	6					6
Wolverhampton Wand.		161	10	25	8	204		15		1	1	17
Hurlford	15					15	7					7
		26+16	0+1	1+1		27+18		1				1
Dundee		87+1	3	11		101+1		4		2		6
Maccabi Haifa (Israel)		2+4		2		4+4						

ND - #0161 - 090625 - C0 - 234/156/36 - PB - 9781780912219 - Gloss Lamination